D0074579

Human Evolution and Culture

Highlights of Anthropology

EIGHTH EDITION

Carol R. Ember
Human Relations Area Files

Melvin Ember

Peter N. Peregrine
Lawrence University and the Santa Fe Institute

PEARSON

Boston   Columbus   Indianapolis   New York   San Francisco   Upper Saddle River
Amsterdam   Cape Town   Dubai   London   Madrid   Milan   Munich   Paris   Montréal   Toronto
Delhi   Mexico City   São Paulo   Sydney   Hong Kong   Seoul   Singapore   Taipei   Tokyo

Editorial Director: Dickson Musslewhite

Publisher: Charlyce Jones-Owen

Editorial Assistant: Maureen Diana

Program Manager: Emily Tamburri

Project Manager: Nicole Conforti

Marketing Coordinator: Jessica Warren

Procurement Manager: MaryAnn Gloriande

Art Director: Kathryn Foot

Cover Art: Jean-Marc Charles/age fotostock/Robert Harding

Director, Digital Studio: Sacha Laustein

Media Product Manager: David Alick

Media Project Manager: Amanda Smith

Full-Service Project Management: Jenna Vittorioso

Composition: Lumina Datamatics, Inc.

Printer/Binder and Cover Printer: RR Donnelley; Phoenix Color

 DK Maps designed and productioned by DK Education, a division of Dorling Kindersley Limited, 80 Strand, London WC2R ORL. DK and the DK logo are registered trademarks of Dorling Kindersley Limited.

This book was set in 10/12, ITC Galliard Std.

Credits and acknowledgments borrowed from other sources and reproduced, with permission, in this textbook appear on the appropriate page within the text (or on pages 525–526).

Copyright © 2015, 2011, 2007, 2005, 2002, 1999 Pearson Education, Inc., 330 Hudson Avenue, Hoboken, NJ. All rights reserved. Manufactured in the United States of America. This publication is protected by Copyright, and permission should be obtained from the publisher prior to any prohibited reproduction, storage in a retrieval system, or transmission in any form or by any means, electronic, mechanical, photocopying, recording, or likewise. To obtain permission(s) to use material from this work, please submit a written request to Pearson Education, Inc., Permissions Department, 330 Hudson Ave., Hoboken, NJ.

Library of Congress Cataloging-in-Publication Data

Ember, Carol R.

  Human evolution and culture / Carol R. Ember, Melvin Ember, Peter N. Peregrine, Lawrence University and the Santa Fe Institute. — Eighth edition.

       pages cm

  Includes bibliographical references and index.

  ISBN 978-0-205-99932-3 (alk. paper) — ISBN 0-205-99932-8 (alk. paper)

  1. Anthropology.   I. Ember, Melvin.   II. Peregrine, Peter N. (Peter Neal), 1963-   III. Title.

  GN25.E46 2015

  301—dc23

                                                                      2014028406

3 16

Student Edition

ISBN-10: 0-205-99932-8

ISBN-13: 978-0-205-99932-3

A la Carte Edition

ISBN-10: 0-13-394774-2

ISBN-13: 978-0-13-394774-8

For Mel–

Always the optimist, who believed that there were laws governing human behavior that could be found if you thought hard enough, worked hard enough, and tested ideas against the anthropological record.

1933–2009

Brief Contents

Contents

Part I   Introduction

Chapter 1   What Is Anthropology?   1

Chapter 2   Research Methods in Anthropology   17

Part II   Human Evolution: Biological and Cultural

Chapter 3   Genetics and Evolution   44

Chapter 4   Human Variation and Adaptation   64

Boxes

Migrants and Immigrants

Perspectives on Gender

Preface

This eighth edition of *Human Evolution and Culture* has a major redesign. Its purpose is the same—it is designed for those who want a shorter version of the four-field *Anthropology* book, now in its fourteenth edition. We have 19 chapters rather than 27. We have shortened the text by eliminating a few chapters and by combining some related chapters into one by reducing discussion, examples, and illustrations. However, in contrast to the last edition, where almost all of the chapters were shortened, we have only shortened and combined about a third of the chapters. Perhaps most noticeable is the full-color format. The changes go far beyond style. To add interest, we have added 23 new boxes. As always, we spend considerable time updating the research.

We have always tried to go beyond descriptions to explain not only *what* humans are and were like but also *why* they got to be that way, in all their variety. This edition is no different. An important part of updating the text is finding new explanations, and we try to communicate the necessity to evaluate these new explanations logically as well as on the basis of the available evidence. Throughout the book, we try to communicate that no idea, including ideas put forward in textbooks, should be accepted even tentatively without supporting tests that could have gone the other way.

What's New to This Edition

Engaging Pedagogically-Driven Design

NEW! Learning Objectives have been added to each chapter helping readers to focus on the material ahead. Chapter-ending summary materials have been completely revised to link back to the Learning Objectives presenting a more clear overview of the important material covered in the chapter.

A Clear Understanding of Humans

NEW! Application of major topics. *Applied Anthropology* Boxes provide students a better understanding of the vast range of issues to which anthropological knowledge can be usefully applied. These boxes offer an additional way to show how anthropology helps people lead better lives.

Focus on Contemporary issues

NEW! Environmental issues. An expanded focus on environmental issues is presented.

Chapter-by-Chapter Changes
Part I: Introduction

Chapter 1: What Is Anthropology? Three new boxes on individual anthropologists–an ethnographer, an archaeologist, and a physical anthropologist–and their work.

Chapter 2: Research Methods in Anthropology In a new section we provide a brief introduction to some of the major ideas that have guided this history of anthropology in the United States. A new box explains how alternative theories are evaluated.

Part II: Human Evolution: Biological and Cultural

Chapter 3: Genetics and Evolution We incorporate a brief history of evolutionary thought to give context to the extensive review of genetics and the processes of evolution, including natural selection and what it means, that follows. There are two new box features—one on ownership of DNA and the second on the emerging field of molecular anthropology.

Chapter 5: Primates: Past and Present There are two new boxes in this chapter. The first is on endangered primates and the second is on studying biodiversity.

Chapter 6: The First Hominins and the Emergence of *Homo* This chapter has been revised to include discussions of new species and information on early hominin diets. One box feature, discusses what we know about the first hominins to leave Africa. A new box feature discusses ideas about how environmental change contributed to hominin evolution.

Chapter 7: The Emergence of *Homo sapiens* and the Upper Paleolithic World In this edition, we discuss the new hominin species from Denesovia Cave in southern Siberia, and update the discussion of modern human origins based on new DNA evidence. We revised the section on human colonization of North and South America, based on new archaeological sites and genetic research. The first of two new boxes is on depictions of women in Upper Paleolithic art and the second is on the controversy over whether fossil remains of the earliest humans to reach North America are related to contemporary Native populations.

Chapter 8: Food Production and the Rise of States A new box feature discusses the question of whether Cahokia, a pre-Columbian city located near present-day St. Louis, Missouri, was a state.

Part III: Cultural Variation

Chapter 9: Culture and Culture Change This chapter has been revised considerably to make it more engaging. New examples on food preferences and taboos are used to illustrate that culture is learned. The section on controversies about the concept of culture has been rewritten. A new section and figure on baby names in the United States illustrates random copying of neutral traits. A broader and more historical view of globalization is introduced. The revolution section now contains a discussion of the Arab Spring and the difficulties of bringing about change by revolution. Both boxes in the chapter are new. The first is on culture change and persistence in China and the second is a case study of Bedouin development programs.

Chapter 10: Communication and Language In an extensively rewritten section on nonverbal human communication, we include new research on handshaking, pheromones, and other communication such as whistle communication. There are two new boxes. The first is on whether languages can be kept from extinction and the second is on why "mother tongues" are retained longer for some immigrant groups.

Chapter 11: Economics We have introduced a body of experimental and observational research providing evidence that sharing and cooperation may be universally associated with pleasure. Three boxes are new. The first is on the global movement of food. The second is on working abroad to send money home and the third is on the impact of the world system on the deforestation of the Amazon.

Chapter 12: Social Stratification: Class, Ethnicity, and Racism
We have expanded our section on caste, adding a discussion of occupational caste in Africa. The section on "race" is extensively expanded with a new section on the concept of race in biology. We have introduced a new box on global inequality and the rising gap between countries. The second box updates the discussion of why there are disparities in death by disease between African Americans and European Americans.

Chapter 13: Sex and Gender
This chapter has been extensively rewritten to be more engaging and easier to read with more subheadings for clarity. Two new boxes have been added. The first is on why some societies have allowed women in combat. The second is on women's electoral success on the U.S. Northwest Coast.

Chapter 14: Marriage, Family, and Kinship
Two of the boxes are new. The first is on arranging marriages in the diaspora and the second is on love, intimacy, and sexual jealousy in marriage.

Chapter 15: Political Life: Social Order and Disorder
We have added a new section that discusses the concepts of nation-states, nationalism and political identity, pointing out that people living in states may not identify with the state they live in nor have their notion of nationhood correspond to political boundaries. In the warfare section we also discuss the controversy about whether violence has increased or decreased in human history. Two of the three boxes are new. The first is on the growth of cities; the second is on how new courts in Papua New Guinea allow women to address grievances.

Chapter 16: Religion and Magic
We have added a new theoretical discussion on the need for human cooperation and the recent research that supports that theory. Also added is new research on the relationships between religiosity and stress and anxiety as well as a new discussion on how most religions began as minority sects or cults. The first box, which is updated, raises the question of whether and to what degree religion promotes moral behavior, cooperation, and harmony. The second box is new and is on the impact of colonialism on religious affiliation.

Chapter 17: The Arts
In a new section we discuss the problematic and fuzzy distinctions made in labeling some art negatively as "tourist" art versus more positively as "fine" art. We have added two new boxes—one is the importance of preserving rock art and the second is on the spread of popular music.

Part IV: Using Anthropology

Chapter 18: Global Problems
We have extensively updated the research in this chapter. In revising the section on natural disasters and the famines that frequently result from them, we give increasing attention to the inequalities that contribute to them. New research on relationships to gender equality is included in the family violence section. In the section on war, we discuss changes over the long course of history, the complex relationship between disasters and war, and the increasing attention to how the vulnerability of populations to disasters can be reduced. Two new boxes have been added. One is on climate

change and what anthropologists might be able to contribute. The second is on ethnic conflicts.

Chapter 19: Practicing and Applying Anthropology
This chapter is considerably expanded with new sections. We have updated the ethics section with an extended discussion of displacement projects, their risks, and whose lives are actually improved. The sections on environmental anthropology and business and organizational anthropology, business and organizational anthropology, and museum anthropology are new to this chapter. The first box is new to this chapter and is about how to get development programs to include more women. The second box is new and is about anthropological work to help a car company improve its business culture.

Organization of the Text

Part I: Introduction
We see anthropology as a unified discipline that combines the insights of ethnographers, linguists, archaeologists, and physical anthropologists to create a holistic understanding of humans. In this section, we introduce the discipline of anthropology, outline its history and its major theoretical perspectives, and give an overview of the methods employed by anthropologists.

Chapter 1: What Is Anthropology?
Chapter 1 introduces the student to anthropology. We discuss what we think is distinctive about anthropology in general, and about each of its subfields in particular. We outline how each of the subfields is related to other disciplines such as biology, psychology, and sociology. We direct attention to the increasing importance of applied anthropology and the importance of understanding others in today's more globalized world. To emphasize the excitement of research we include three boxes on individual researchers (an ethnographer, an archaeologist, and a physical anthropologist).

Chapter 2: Research Methods in Anthropology
In this chapter, we begin by discussing what it means to explain and what kinds of evidence are needed to evaluate an explanation. We provide a brief introduction to some of the major ideas that have guided the history of anthropology in the United States. We then turn to the major types of study in anthropology—ethnography, within-culture comparisons, regional comparisons, worldwide cross-cultural comparisons, and historical research. We follow this with a brief introduction to the unique methods that archaeologists and biological anthropologists use and end with a discussion of ethics in anthropological research. There are two boxes: the first box evaluates alternative theories and the second explores changes in gender roles during the Shell Mound Archaic period in the southeastern United States.

Part II: Human Evolution: Biological and Cultural
This section of the book focuses on the evolution of humans from early primates to the present. We emphasize evolution as both a foundational and potentially unifying perspective within anthropology. We also emphasize the fact that humans continue to adapt to their environments both physically and culturally. Thus, anthropology must combine biological understanding and cultural understanding if we wish to develop an accurate understanding of humans.

Chapter 3: Genetics and Evolution
This chapter discusses evolutionary theory as it applies to all forms of life, including

humans. We have incorporated a brief history of evolutionary thought to give context to the extensive review of genetics and the processes of evolution, including natural selection and what it means, that follows. We also discuss how natural selection may operate on behavioral traits and how cultural evolution differs from biological evolution. We provide a thorough discussion of creationism and intelligent design. The first box features the emerging issue of who owns DNA samples. The second box feature introduces the emerging field of molecular anthropology.

Chapter 4: Human Variation and Adaptation
We bring the discussion of human genetics and evolution into the present, dealing with physical variation in living human populations and how physical anthropologists study and explain such variation. We examine how both the physical environment and the cultural environment play important roles in human physical variation. In a section on "race" and racism, we discuss why many anthropologists think the concept of "race" as applied to humans is not scientifically useful. We discuss the myths of racism and how "race" is largely a social category in humans. One box feature explores the use of "race" in forensic anthropology, and another box examines physical differences between native and immigrant populations.

Chapter 5: Primates Past and Present
In this chapter, we describe the living nonhuman primates and their variable adaptations as background for understanding the evolution of primates in general and humans in particular. After describing the various kinds of primates, we discuss the distinctive features of humans in comparison with the other primates. We then go on to discuss the evolution of the primates. One box feature deals with how and why many primates are endangered and how they might be protected. Another box feature discusses the importance of studying the diversity of primates, both ancient and modern, for understanding our planet's biodiversity.

Chapter 6: The First Hominins and the Emergence of *Homo*
This chapter discusses the evolution of bipedal locomotion—the most distinctive feature of the group that includes our genus and those of our direct ancestors. We discuss the various types of early hominins and how they might have evolved. One box feature discusses ideas about how environmental change contributed to hominin evolution. A second box discusses what we know about the first hominins to leave Africa.

Chapter 7: The Emergence of *Homo sapiens* and the Upper Paleolithic World
This chapter examines the transition between *Homo erectus* and *Homo sapiens* and the emergence of modern-looking humans. We give special consideration to the Neandertals and the question of their relationship to modern humans. We also discuss the new hominin species from Denisova Cave in southern Siberia. This chapter then considers the cultures of modern humans in the period before agriculture developed—roughly 40,000 years to 10,000 years ago. We examine their tools, their economies, and their art—the first art made by humans. We discuss the human colonization of North and South America, based on new archaeological sites and genetic research. The first box considers how women are depicted in Upper Paleolithic art. The second box discusses the evidence that the first colonists of the Americas may have died out and may be only distantly related to modern Native Americans.

Chapter 8: Food Production and the Rise of States
This chapter deals with the emergence of broad-spectrum collecting and settled life, the domestication of plants and animals, the rise and fall of cities and states, and what may explain those developments. One box describes the work of archaeologists who are re-creating ancient agricultural systems in the Andes and elsewhere to help local populations produce more food. A second box explores the question of whether Cahokia, an ancient city located near St. Louis, Missouri, was the capital of a state.

Part III: Cultural Variation
In the chapters that follow, we try to convey the range of cultural variation with ethnographic examples from all over the world. Wherever we can, we discuss possible explanations of why societies may be similar or different in regard to some aspect of culture. If anthropologists have no explanation as yet for the variation, we say so. If we are to train students to go beyond what we know now, we have to tell them what we do not know, as well as what we think we know.

Chapter 9: Culture and Culture Change
After introducing the concept of culture and some of the controversies surrounding the concept, we emphasize that culture is always changing. Throughout the chapter we discuss individual variation and how such variation may be the beginning of new cultural patterns. We also discuss attitudes that hinder the study of culture, cultural relativism and the issue of human rights, patterning of culture, culture and adaptation, and mechanisms of culture change, before getting to the emergence of new cultures and the impact of globalization. The first box is on culture change and persistence in China. The second box discusses an applied anthropologist's attempts to accommodate Bedouin needs in designed change programs with the Oman government. The third box discusses the increasing cultural diversity within countries of the world as a result of immigration and migration.

Chapter 10: Communication and Language
To place language in perspective, the chapter begins with a discussion of communication more broadly, including nonverbal human communication and communication in other animals. We discuss how language differs from other forms of communication and ideas about the origins of language. We then turn to some fundamentals of descriptive linguistics, the processes of linguistic divergence, and postulated relationships between language and other aspects of culture. Toward the end of the chapter we discuss the ethnography of speaking, and writing and literacy. The first box, an applied box, discusses language extinction and what some anthropologists are doing about it. The second box discusses the varying retention of "mother tongues" amongst immigrant groups in North America. And to stimulate thinking about the possible impact of language on thought, we ask in the last box whether the English language promotes sexist thinking.

Chapter 11: Economics
This chapter begins with a discussion of how societies vary in getting their food, how they have changed over time, and how that variation seems to affect other kinds of cultural variation. We then discuss how societies vary in the ways they allocate resources, convert or transform resources through labor into usable goods, and distribute and perhaps exchange goods and services. The first box discusses the global movement of food around the world. The second box discusses the impact of working abroad and sending money home. The third illustrates the impact of the world system on local economies, with special reference to the deforestation of the Amazon.

Chapter 12: Social Stratification: Class, Ethnicity, and Racism
This chapter explores the variation in degree of social stratification and how the various forms of social inequality may develop. We point out concepts of how "race," racism,

and ethnicity often relate to the inequitable distribution of resources. The first box discusses the degree of global inequality and why the gap between rich and poor countries may have widened. The second box discusses why there are disparities in death by disease between African Americans and European Americans.

Chapter 13: Sex and Gender
This chapter opens with a section on culturally varying gender concepts, including diversity in what genders are recognized. After discussing universals and differences in gender roles in subsistence and leadership, we turn to theories about why men dominate political leadership and what may explain variation in relative status of women and men. In the second part of the chapter we discuss variation in attitudes and practices regarding heterosexual and homosexual sexuality. In the first box, we examine cross-cultural research about why some societies allow women to participate in combat. A second box discusses research on why women's political participation may be increasing in some Coast Salish communities of western Washington State and British Columbia now that they have elected councils. The last is a box that examines the impact of economic development on women's status.

Chapter 14: Marriage, Family and Kinship
After discussing various theories and evidence about why marriage might be universal, we move on to discuss variation in how one marries, restrictions on marriage, whom one should marry, and how many one should marry. We explain variation in family form, including the phenomenon of couples choosing to live together, and to better prepare students for understanding kinship charts in the chapter that follows, we have a diagram explaining different types of family structures. In discussing variation in marital residence and kinship structure, we emphasize how understanding residence is important for understanding social life in all societies. Our first box discusses arranged marriage and how it has changed among South Asian immigrants in England and the United States. The second box discusses variation in love, intimacy, and sexual jealousy. The third box discusses the impact of different residence and kinship structures on the lives of women.

Chapter 15: Political Life: Social Order and Disorder
We look at how societies have varied in their levels of political organization, the various ways people become leaders, the degree to which they participate in the political process, and the peaceful and violent methods of resolving conflict. We emphasize change, including what may explain shifts from one type of organization to another, such as colonialization and other outside forces have transformed legal systems and ways of making decisions. We then discuss the concepts of nation-states, nationalism, and political identity. The first box is on the role of migrants in the growth of cities. The second box deals with the cross-national and cross-cultural relationship between economic development and democracy. The third box deals with how new local courts among the Abelam of New Guinea are allowing women to address sexual grievances.

Chapter 16: Religion and Magic
The chapter opens with a discussion of how the concepts of the supernatural and natural have varied over time and space and then turn to theories about why religion is universal. We go on to discuss variation in the types, nature, and structure of gods, spirits, and forces; human/god interactions, concepts of life after death; ways to interact with the supernatural; and the number and types of

religious practitioners. A major portion of the chapter deals with religious change, religious conversion and revitalization, and fundamentalist movements. The first box, raises the question of whether and to what degree religion promotes moral behavior, cooperation, and harmony. The second discusses the role of colonialism in religious change.

Chapter 17: The Arts
After discussing how art might be defined and the appearance of the earliest art, we discuss variation in the visual arts, music, and folklore, and review how some of those variations might be explained. In regard to how the arts change over time, we discuss the myth that the art of "simpler" peoples is timeless, as well as how arts have changed as a result of European contact. We address the role of ethnocentrism in studies of art in a section on how Western museums and art critics look at the visual art of less complex cultures. Similarly we discuss the problematic and fuzzy distinctions made in labeling some art negatively as "tourist" art versus more positively as "fine" art. The first box explores ancient and more recent rock art and the methods that can be used to help preserve it. The second box discusses the global spread of popular music. The last box deals with universal symbolism in art, particularly research on the emotions displayed in masks.

Part IV: Using Anthropology
Anthropology is not a discipline that focuses on pure research; rather, most anthropologists believe their work is truly valuable only if it can be used to improve the lives of others. In this section we examine how anthropological knowledge is used in a variety of settings and towards a variety of ends.

Chapter 18: Global Problems
We begin this chapter with a discussion of the relationship between basic and applied research, and how research may suggest possible solutions to various global social problems, including natural disasters and famines, homelessness, crime, family violence, war, and terrorism. There are three boxes. The first now emphasizes climate change and ways anthropologists can contribute to understanding solutions. The second box is on how the problem of refugees has become a global problem. The last box describes ethnic conflicts and whether or not they are inevitable.

Chapter 19: Practicing and Applying Anthropology
This chapter explores some of the many subfields of practicing and applied anthropology. It begins with a discussion of the increasing importance of applied anthropology, some of the ethical issues. We move on to an expanded section on ethics, evaluating the effects of planned change, and difficulties in bringing about change. Since most of the examples in the first part of the chapter have to do with development, the remainder of the chapter gives an introduction to a number of other specialties; environmental anthropology, business and organizational anthropology, museum anthropology, cultural resource management, and forensic anthropology. The second half of the chapter is devoted to medical anthropology, including cultural understandings of health and illness, political and economic influences on health, and we discuss approaches to a few selected diseases and illnesses. The first box examines what anthropologists can do to help inform policy on climate change. The second box is a case study of an applied project to create a better business culture at General Motors. And the third box is on eating disorders and the cultural construction of beauty.

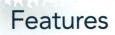

Features

Applied Anthropology Boxes.   Anthropology is not a discipline focused on pure research. Most anthropologists want their work to be actively used to help others. And in our increasingly interconnected world, it would seem that anthropological knowledge would become increasingly valuable for understanding others. For these reasons, in the last few editions we have emphasized applied anthropology. Fourteen of the 19 chapters have an applied anthropology box in each chapter. We hope this will provide students a better understanding of the vast range of issues to which anthropological knowledge can be usefully applied.

Current Research and Issues Boxes.   These boxes deal with current research, topics students may have heard about in the news, and research controversies in anthropology. Examples include molecular anthropology, variation in love, intimacy, and sexual jealousy in the husband-wife relationship; increasing global inequality; and whether ethnic conflicts are ancient hatreds.

Migrants and Immigrants Boxes.   These boxes deal with humans on the move, and how migration and immigration have impacted recent and contemporary social life. Examples include why some immigrant groups retained their "mother tongues" longer than others, the spread of foods in recent times, arranging marriages in the diaspora, and the problem of refugees.

Perspectives on Gender Boxes.   These boxes involve issues pertaining to sex and gender, both in anthropology and everyday life. Examples are sexism in language, women in Upper Paleolithic art and why some societies allow women in combat.

Student-Friendly Pedagogy

Readability.   We derive a lot of pleasure from trying to describe research findings, especially complicated ones, in ways that introductory students can understand. Thus, we try to minimize technical jargon, using only those terms students must know to appreciate the achievements of anthropology and to take advanced courses. We think readability is important not only because it may enhance the reader's understanding of what we write but also because it should make learning about anthropology more enjoyable! When new terms are introduced, which of course must happen sometimes, they are set off in boldface type and defined in the text, set off in the margins for emphasis, and of course also appear in the glossary at the end of the book.

Learning Objectives.   Learning objectives are new to this edition. Each chapter begins with learning objectives that indicate what students should know after reading the material. The learning objectives are reinforced with specific questions at the end of each chapter that unite the topics, help students gauge their comprehension, and signal what topics they might have to reread.

Key Terms and Glossary.   Important terms and concepts appearing in boldface type within the text are defined in the margins where they first appear. All key terms and their definitions are repeated in the Glossary at the end of the book.

Summaries.   In addition to the learning objectives provided at the beginning of each chapter, each chapter has a detailed summary organized in terms of the learning objectives that will help students review the major concepts and findings discussed, along with review questions to reinforce and to complement the summary.

End of Book Notes.   Because we believe in the importance of documentation, we think it essential to tell our readers, both professionals and students, what our conclusions are based on. Usually the basis is published research. The abbreviated notes in this edition provide information to find the complete citation in the bibliography at the end of the book.

Supplements

This textbook is part of a complete teaching and learning package that has been carefully created to enhance the topics discussed in the text.

Instructor's Resource Manual with Tests: For each chapter in the text, this valuable resource provides a detailed outline, list of objectives, discussion questions, and classroom activities. In addition, test questions in multiple-choice and short-answer formats are available for each chapter; the answers to all questions are page-referenced to the text.

MyTest: This computerized software allows instructors to create their own personalized exams, to edit any or all of the existing test questions and to add new questions. Other special features of this program include random generation of test questions, creation of alternate versions of the same test, scrambling question sequence, and test preview before printing.

PowerPoint™ Presentation Slides: These PowerPoint slides combine text and graphics for each chapter to help instructors convey anthropological principles in a clear and engaging way.

Strategies in Teaching Anthropology, Sixth Edition (0-205-71123-5):   Unique in focus and content, this book focuses on the "how" of teaching anthropology across all four fields and provides a wide array of associated learning outcomes and student activities. It is a valuable single-source compendium of strategies and teaching "tricks of the trade" from a group of seasoned teaching anthropologists, working in a variety of teaching settings, who share their pedagogical techniques, knowledge, and observations.

The Dorling Kindersley/Prentice Hall Atlas of Anthropology (0-13-191879-6):   Beautifully illustrated by Dorling Kindersley, with narrative by leading archaeological author Brian M. Fagan, this striking atlas features 30 full-color maps, timelines, and illustrations to offer a highly visual but explanatory geographical overview of topics from all four fields of anthropology. Please contact your Prentice Hall representative for ordering information.

Acknowledgments

Over the years we have had many editors, but we especially want to thank Nancy Roberts for her long and steadfast stewardship over many editions, her insightful suggestions, and especially her passionate interest in the educational enterprise. We also want to thank Nicole Conforti and Jenna Vittorioso for seeing the manuscript through the production process. Carol Ember thanks Kathy Ember Levy for her suggestions on combining and shortening three of the cultural chapters. She especially wants to thank Tulin Duda for her extensive research help and her thoughtful and inquisitive editing to make the book more accessible to students.

We want to thank the following people for reviewing our chapters and offering suggestions for the fourteenth edition: Richard Blanton, *Purdue University*; Kristrina Shuler, *Auburn University*; Wanda Clark, *South Plains College*; Jim Mielke, *University of Kansas*; Heidi Luchsinger, *East Carolina University*; and Andrew Buckser, *Purdue University*.

We continue to appreciate reviewers from previous editions: Alice Baldwin-Jones, *City College of New York*; Richard E. Blanton, *Purdue University*; James L. Boone, *University of New Mexico*; Beau Bowers, *Central Piedmont Community College*; Gregory Campbell, *University of Montana*; Garrett Cook, *Baylor University*; Daniel R. Maher, *University of Arkansas-Fort Smith*; Sheperd Jenks, *Albuquerque TVI Community College*; Max E. White, *Piedmont College*; Jean M. Wynn, *Manchester Community College*

Thank you all, named and unnamed, who gave us advice.
Carol R. Ember, Melvin Ember,
and Peter N. Peregrine

About the Authors

CAROL R. EMBER started at Antioch College as a chemistry major. She began taking social science courses because some were required, but she soon found herself intrigued. There were lots of questions without answers, and she became excited about the possibility of a research career in social science. She spent a year in graduate school at Cornell studying sociology before continuing on to Harvard, where she studied anthropology, primarily with John and Beatrice Whiting.

For her PhD dissertation, she worked among the Luo of Kenya. While there, she noticed that many boys were assigned "girls' work," such as babysitting and household chores, because their mothers (who did most of the agriculture) did not have enough girls to help out. She decided to study the possible effects of task assignment on the social behavior of boys. Using systematic behavior observations, she compared girls, boys who did a great deal of girls' work, and boys who did little such work. She found that boys assigned girls' work were intermediate in many social behaviors compared with the other boys and girls. Later, she did cross-cultural research on variation in marriage, family, descent groups, and war and peace, mainly in collaboration with Melvin Ember, whom she married in 1970. All of these cross-cultural studies tested theories on data for worldwide samples of societies.

From 1970 to 1996, she taught at Hunter College of the City University of New York. She has served as president of the Society of Cross-Cultural Research and was one of the directors of the Summer Institutes in Comparative Anthropological Research, which were funded by the National Science Foundation. She has recently served as President of the Society for Anthropological Sciences and is currently the Past President. Since 1996, she has been at the Human Relations Area Files, Inc., a nonprofit research agency at Yale University, first serving as Executive Director, then as Acting President, and is currently President of that organization.

MELVIN EMBER majored in anthropology at Columbia College and went to Yale University for his PhD. His mentor at Yale was George Peter Murdock, an anthropologist who was instrumental in promoting cross-cultural research and building a full-text database on the cultures of the world to facilitate cross-cultural hypothesis testing. This database came to be known as the Human Relations Area Files (HRAF) because it was originally sponsored by the Institute of Human Relations at Yale. Growing in annual installments and now distributed in electronic format, the HRAF database currently covers more than 385 cultures, past and present, all over the world.

Melvin Ember did fieldwork for his dissertation in American Samoa, where he conducted a comparison of three villages to study the effects of commercialization on political life. In addition, he did research on descent groups and how they changed with the increase of buying and selling. His cross-cultural studies focused originally on variation in marital residence and descent groups. He has also done cross-cultural research on the relationship between economic and political development, the origin and extension of the incest taboo, the causes of polygyny, and how archaeological correlates of social customs can help us draw inferences about the past.

After four years of research at the National Institute of Mental Health, he taught at Antioch College and then Hunter College of the City University of New York. He served as president of the Society for Cross-Cultural Research. From 1987 until his death in September, 2009, he was president of the Human Relations Area Files, Inc., a nonprofit research agency at Yale University.

PETER N. PEREGRINE came to anthropology after completing an undergraduate degree in English. He found anthropology's social scientific approach to understanding humans more appealing than the humanistic approach he had learned as an English major. He undertook an ethnohistorical study of the relationship between Jesuit missionaries and Native American peoples for his master's degree and realized that he needed to study archaeology to understand the cultural interactions experienced by Native Americans before their contact with the Jesuits.

While working on his PhD at Purdue University, Peter Peregrine did research on the prehistoric Mississippian cultures of the eastern United States. He found that interactions between groups were common and had been shaping Native American cultures for centuries. Native Americans approached contact with the Jesuits simply as another in a long string of intercultural exchanges. He also found that relatively little research had been done on Native American interactions and decided that comparative research was a good place to begin examining the topic. In 1990, he participated in the Summer Institute in Comparative Anthropological Research, where he met Carol R. Ember and Melvin Ember.

Peter Peregrine is professor of anthropology at Lawrence University in Appleton, Wisconsin and external professor at the Santa Fe Institute in Santa Fe, New Mexico. He also serves as research associate for the Human Relations Area Files. He continues to do archaeological research, and to teach anthropology and archaeology to undergraduate students.

Human Evolution and Culture

What Is Anthropology?

LEARNING OBJECTIVES

Explain the general definition and purpose of anthropology.	1.1
Describe the scope of anthropology.	1.2
Explain the holistic approach.	1.3
Explain anthropology's distinctive curiosity.	1.4
Differentiate among the five major fields of anthropology.	1.5
Explain the ways in which anthropologists specialize within their fields of study.	1.6
Communicate the relevance of anthropology.	1.7

1.1 Explain the general definition and purpose of anthropology.

Anthropology A discipline that studies humans, focusing on the study of differences and similarities, both biological and cultural, in human populations. Anthropology is concerned with typical biological and cultural characteristics of human populations in all periods and in all parts of the world.

What Is Anthropology?

Anthropology, by definition, is a discipline of infinite curiosity about human beings. The term comes from the Greek *anthropos* for "man, human" and *logos* for "study." Anthropologists seek answers to an enormous variety of questions about humans. They are interested in both universals and differences in human populations. They want to discover when, where, and why humans appeared on the earth, how and why they have changed, and how and why the biological and cultural features of modern human populations vary. Anthropology has a practical side too. Applied and practicing anthropologists put anthropological methods, information, and results to use in efforts to solve practical problems.

The study of human beings is not an adequate definition of anthropology, however, since it would appear to incorporate a whole catalog of disciplines: sociology, psychology, political science, economics, history, human biology, and perhaps even the humanistic disciplines of philosophy and literature. Most of the disciplines concerned with human beings have existed longer than anthropology, and each has its distinctive focus. There must, then, be something unique about anthropology—a reason for its having developed and grown as a separate discipline for over a century.

• • •

1.2 Describe the scope of anthropology.

The Scope of Anthropology

Anthropologists are generally thought of as individuals who travel to little-known corners of the world to study exotic peoples or dig deep into the earth to uncover the fossil remains, tools, and pots of people who lived long ago. Though stereotypical, this view does suggest how anthropology differs from other disciplines concerned with humans. Anthropology is broader in scope, both geographically and historically. Anthropology is concerned explicitly and directly with all varieties of people throughout the world, not just those close at hand or within a limited area. Anthropologists are also interested in people of all periods. Beginning with the immediate ancestors of humans, who lived a few million years ago, anthropology traces the development of humans until the present. Every part of the world that has ever contained a human population is of interest to anthropologists.

Anthropologists have not always been as global and comprehensive in their concerns as they are today. Traditionally, they concentrated on non-Western cultures and left the study of Western civilization and similarly complex societies, with their recorded histories, to other disciplines. In recent years, however, this division of labor among the disciplines has begun to disappear. Now anthropologists work in their own and other complex societies.

What induces anthropologists to choose so broad a subject for study? In part, they are motivated by the belief that any suggested generalization about human beings, any possible explanation of some characteristic of human culture or biology, should be shown to apply to many times and places of human existence. If a generalization or explanation does not prove to apply widely, anthropologists are entitled or even obliged to be skeptical about it. The skeptical attitude, in the absence of persuasive evidence, is our best protection against accepting invalid ideas about humans.

Because anthropologists are acquainted with human life in an enormous variety of geographic and historical settings, they are also often able to correct mistaken beliefs about different groups of people.

For example, when American educators discovered in the 1960s that African American schoolchildren rarely drank milk, they assumed that lack of money or education was the cause. But evidence from anthropology suggested a different explanation. Anthropologists had known for years that people do not drink fresh milk in many parts of the world where milking animals are kept; rather, they sour it before they drink it, or they make it into cheese. Why they do so is now clear. Many people lack the enzyme lactase that is necessary for breaking down lactose, the sugar in milk. When such people drink regular milk, it actually interferes with digestion. Not only is the lactose in milk not digested, but other nutrients are less likely to be digested as well. In many cases, drinking milk will cause cramps, stomach gas, diarrhea, and nausea. Studies indicate that milk intolerance is found in many parts of the world.[1] The condition is common in adulthood among Asians, southern Europeans, Arabs and Jews, West Africans, Inuit (Eskimos), and North and South American native peoples, as well as African Americans.

The Holistic Approach

1.3 Explain the holistic approach.

In addition to its worldwide and historical scope, anthropology has the distinguishing feature of having a **holistic** approach to the study of human beings. Anthropologists study the many aspects of human experience as an integrated whole. For example, an anthropologist's description of a group of people is likely to encompass their physical environment, a history of the area, how their family life is organized, general features of their language, their settlement patterns, their political and economic systems, their religion, and their styles of art and dress. The goal is not only to understand these aspects of physical and social life separately but to glean connections among them. Throughout this book, you will see that these seemingly separate factors in a culture regularly co-occur; that is, they form patterns of traits. Anthropologists want not only to identify those patterns but to explain them.

Holistic Refers to an approach that studies many aspects of a multifaceted system.

Anthropological Curiosity

1.4 Explain anthropology's distinctive curiosity.

Thus far, we have described anthropology as being broader in scope, both historically and geographically, and more holistic in approach than other disciplines concerned with human beings. But this statement again implies that anthropology is the all-inclusive human science. How, then, is anthropology really different from the other disciplines? We suggest that anthropology's distinctiveness lies principally in the kind of curiosity it arouses.

Anthropologists tend to focus on the *typical* characteristics of the human populations they study rather than on individual variation or variation in small groups. Why do some populations have lighter skin than others? Why do some societies practice polygamy whereas others prohibit it? Where and when did people first start to farm rather than collecting and hunting wild resources? Anthropologists want to know why the characteristics that others might take for granted exist. Whereas economists take a monetary system for granted and study how it operates, anthropologists ask how frequently monetary systems occur, why they vary, and why only some societies have had them during the last few thousand years. It is not that anthropologists do not concern themselves with individuals. For instance, in studying political systems, anthropologists might want to know why certain people tend to be leaders. But when they study individual traits of leaders in order to answer the question, it may be because they want to better understand the political process in a larger social group, such as a society. Or, anthropologists might ask an even broader question, such as whether certain qualities of leaders are universally preferred.

Because anthropologists view human groups holistically, their curiosity may lead them to find patterns of relationships between seemingly unrelated characteristics. So, for example, the presence of the ability to digest lactose (a physical trait) in a population seems to be found in societies that depend heavily on dairying. In recent times, as more anthropologists work in larger and more complex societies, the focus of inquiry has shifted from looking at a whole society to smaller entities such as neighborhoods, communities, organizations, or social networks. But the focus on the whole entity is still strong.

Fields of Anthropology

1.5 Differentiate among the five major fields of anthropology.

In the past, an anthropologist covered as many subjects as possible. Today, as in many other disciplines, so much information has accumulated that anthropologists tend to specialize in one topic or area (see Figure 1.1). Some are concerned primarily with the *biological* or *physical characteristics* of human populations; others are interested principally in what we call *cultural characteristics*. Hence, there are two broad classifications of subject

Biological (physical) anthropology The study of humans as biological organisms, dealing with the emergence and evolution of humans and with contemporary biological variations among human populations.

Cultural anthropology The study of cultural variation and universals in the past and present.

Applied (practicing) anthropology The branch of anthropology that concerns itself with applying anthropological knowledge to achieve practical goals.

Human paleontology The study of the emergence of humans and their later physical evolution. Also called **paleoanthropology**.

Human variation The study of how and why contemporary human populations vary biologically.

Fossils The hardened remains or impressions of plants and animals that lived in the past.

Primate A member of the mammalian order Primates, divided into the two suborders of prosimians and anthropoids.

Primatologists People who study primates.

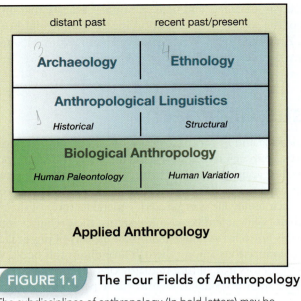

FIGURE 1.1   **The Four Fields of Anthropology**

The subdisciplines of anthropology (In bold letters) may be classified according to the period with which each is concerned (distant past or recent past and present) or by subject matter. Traditionally, the three fields shown in Blue are classified as Cultural Anthropology, as distinct from Biological (or Physical) Anthropology, shown in green. Found in all four fields is a fifth subfield Applied Anthropology.

matter in anthropology: **biological (physical) anthropology** and **cultural anthropology**. While biological anthropology is one major field of anthropology, cultural anthropology is divided into three subfields—archaeology, linguistics, and ethnology. Ethnology, the study of recent cultures, is now usually referred to by the parent name cultural anthropology. Crosscutting these four fields is a fifth, **applied** or **practicing anthropology**.

Biological Anthropology

Biological (physical) anthropology seeks to answer two distinct sets of questions. **Human paleontology** or paleoanthropology poses questions about the emergence of humans and their later evolution. A focus on **human variation** includes questions about how and why contemporary human populations vary biologically.

To reconstruct evolution, human paleontologists search for and study the buried, hardened remains or impressions—known as **fossils**—of humans, prehumans, and related animals. Paleontologists working in East Africa, for instance, have excavated the fossil remains of humanlike beings that lived more than 4 million years ago. These findings have suggested the approximate dates when our ancestors began to develop two-legged walking, very flexible hands, and a larger brain.

In attempting to clarify evolutionary relationships, human paleontologists may use not only the fossil record but also geological information on the succession of climates, environments, and plant and animal populations. Moreover, when reconstructing the past of humans, paleontologists are interested in the behavior and evolution of our closest relatives among the mammals—the prosimians, monkeys, and apes—which, like ourselves, are members of the order of **Primates**. Anthropologists, psychologists, and biologists who specialize in the study of primates are called **primatologists**. The various species of primates are observed in the wild and in the laboratory. One especially popular subject of study is the chimpanzee, which bears a close resemblance to humans in behavior and physical appearance, has a similar blood chemistry, and is susceptible to many of the same diseases. It now appears that chimpanzees share 99 percent of their genes with humans.[2]

From primate studies, biological anthropologists try to discover characteristics that are distinctly human, as opposed to those that might be part of the primate heritage. With this information, they may be able to infer what our prehistoric ancestors were like.

Birute Galdikas works with two orangutans in Borneo.

The inferences from primate studies are checked against the fossil record. The evidence from the earth, collected in bits and pieces, is correlated with scientific observations of our closest living relatives. In short, biological anthropologists piece together bits of information obtained from different sources. They construct theories that explain the changes observed in the fossil record and then attempt to evaluate their theories by checking one kind of evidence against another. Human paleontology thus overlaps such disciplines as geology, general vertebrate (particularly primate) paleontology, comparative anatomy, and the study of comparative primate behavior.

The second major focus of biological anthropology, the study of human variation, investigates how and why contemporary human populations differ in biological or physical characteristics. All living people belong to one species, ***Homo sapiens***. Yet much varies among human populations. Investigators of human variation ask such questions as: Why are some peoples generally taller than others? How have human populations adapted physically to their environmental conditions? Are some peoples, such as Inuit (Eskimos), better equipped than other peoples to endure cold? Does darker skin pigmentation offer special protection against the tropical sun?

To understand better the biological variations among contemporary human populations, biological anthropologists use the principles, concepts, and techniques of at least three other disciplines: human genetics (the study of inherited human traits); population biology (the study of environmental effects on, and interaction with, population characteristics); and epidemiology (the study of how and why diseases affect different populations in different ways). Although research on human variation overlaps research in other fields, biological anthropologists remain primarily concerned with human populations and how they vary biologically.

> **Homo sapiens** All living people belong to one biological species, *Homo sapiens*, which means that all human populations on earth can successfully interbreed. The first *Homo sapiens* may have emerged about 200,000 years ago.

Cultural Anthropology

Cultural anthropology is the study of how and why cultures in the past and present vary or are similar. But what is *culture*? The concept of culture is so central to anthropology that we will devote an entire chapter it. Briefly, the term *culture* refers to the customary ways that a particular population or society thinks and behaves. The culture of a social group includes many things—from the language that people speak, childrearing, and the roles assigned to males and females to religious beliefs and practices and preferences in music. Anthropologists are interested in all of these and other learned behaviors and ideas that have come to be widely shared or customary in the group.

Current Research and Issues

Researcher at Work: Alyssa Crittenden

When an anthropologist's best-laid plans meet the "facts on the ground," the results can be unexpected. For Alyssa Crittenden, an anthropology professor at the University of Nevada, fieldwork also brought some delightful revelations.

In 2004, Crittenden began working with the Hadza, a hunter-gatherer people in Tanzania. (Because hunter-gatherers subsist by foraging for their food, they represent the basic economy and way of life that has characterized most of human history. Therefore, such few remaining peoples are valued subjects for anthropological study.) As a biological anthropologist, Crittenden was especially interested in what Hadza culture might reveal about the evolution of the human diet. She chose the diets of women for study and measured the relationship between their reproductive capacity and the amount and nutritional value of the food they foraged. Yet that data told only part of the previously untold story of Hadza women.

"I quickly realized," Crittenden says, "that I could not study the women's diet in isolation. These women belonged to a community of people, a support system of kin and neighbors. To understand women's contributions to the Hadza economy, I had to be an ethnographer, as well as a biological anthropologist." Thus, after 10 years of fieldwork among the Hadza, Crittenden characterizes herself as a biocultural anthropologist.

One surprising discovery Crittenden made was that Hadza children were hunters and gatherers in their own right. They were helping their mothers indirectly by providing their own food and thus contributing to their economy. This evidence contradicted what was known about the

Alyssa Crittenden interacting with Hadza children.

children of other hunter-gatherer groups, such as the San of the Kalahari Desert, whose children were observed to help process mongongo nuts but otherwise do little else but play. The difference may partly be due to the environment. The Kalahari has less variable terrain, less water, and more predators than southwestern Tanzania.

For Hadza children, foraging for their own food becomes an extension of play. Children who are 5 years old and younger can contribute up to 50 percent of their caloric needs by foraging for their own food. By the time they turn 6, children can contribute up to 75 percent of their own food. While girls collect water and plant foods, boys also hunt, using a bow and arrow like their elders. Indeed, at age 3, Hadza boys receive their own child-sized bow and arrow and begin

to hunt for the birds, rodents, bush babies, and lizards that make up their meat diet. Moreover, children learn to process and cook their own food. Crittenden observed children as young as 4 years old building their own miniature fires with embers from camp to cook their foraged meals.

Hadza children spend their days together in groups, seemingly unsupervised, though there is usually an older child nearby keeping an eye on them. Toddlers join a group of children as soon as they are weaned—that is, when their mothers can no longer carry them, usually between 1 1/2 and 3 years of age.

"Observing Hadza children, you can't help but wonder how the long, dependent childhood most of us experience evolved," says Crittenden.

Source: Crittenden 2013.

Archaeology **Archaeology** is the study of past cultures, primarily through their material remains. Archaeologists seek not only to reconstruct the daily life and customs of peoples who lived in the past but also to trace cultural changes and to offer possible explanations for those changes. While their subject matter is similar to that of historians, archaeologists reach much farther back in time. Historians deal only with societies that left written records, which limits their scope to the last 5,000 years of human history and to the small proportion of societies that developed writing. Human societies have existed for more than a million years, however, and archaeologists serve as historians for all those past societies that lacked a written record. With scant or no written records to study, archaeologists must try to reconstruct history from the remains of human cultures. Some of these remains are as grand as the Mayan temples discovered at Chichén Itzá in Yucatán, Mexico. More often, what remains is as ordinary as bits of broken pottery, stone tools, and garbage heaps.

Most archaeologists deal with **prehistory**, the time before written records. But a specialty within archaeology, called **historical archaeology**, studies the remains of recent peoples who left written records. This specialty, as its name implies, employs the methods of both archaeologists and historians to study recent societies.

To understand how and why ways of life have changed through time in different parts of the world, archaeologists collect materials from sites of human occupation. Usually, these sites must be unearthed. On the basis of materials they have excavated and otherwise collected, they then ask a variety of questions: Where, when, and why did the distinctive human characteristic of toolmaking first emerge? Where, when, and why did agriculture first develop? Where, when, and why did people first begin to live in cities?

To collect the data they need to suggest answers to these and other questions, archaeologists use techniques and findings borrowed from other disciplines, as well as what they can infer from anthropological studies of recent and contemporary cultures. For example, to guess where to dig for evidence of early toolmaking, archaeologists rely on geology to tell them where sites of early human occupation are likely to be found, because of erosion and uplifting, near the surface of the earth. More recently, archaeologists have employed aerial photography and even radar imaging via satellite (a technique developed

Archaeology The branch of anthropology that seeks to reconstruct the daily life and customs of peoples who lived in the past and to trace and explain cultural changes. Often lacking written records for study, archaeologists must try to reconstruct history from the material remains of human cultures. See also **Historical archaeology**.

Prehistory The time before written records.

Historical archaeology A specialty within archaeology that studies the material remains of recent peoples who left written records.

Archaeologists try to reconstruct the cultures of past societies like those who created this "Cliff Palace" in what is today Mesa Verde National Park.

Perspectives on Gender

Researcher at Work: Elizabeth M. Brumfiel

Elizabeth M. Brumfiel (1945–2012) became interested in the origins of social inequality when she was an undergraduate. Archaeologists had known for some time that substantial wealth differences between families developed only recently—that is, only since about 6,000 years ago. Some archaeological indicators of inequality are clear: elaborate burials with valuable goods for some families and large differences in houses and possessions. When Brumfiel was in graduate school at the University of Michigan, she did not accept the then-current explanation that inequality provided benefits to the society—for example, that the standard of living of most people improved as the leaders got richer. Consequently, when Brumfiel undertook her PhD research in central Mexico, she began to test the "benefit" explanation in an area that had been independent politically and then became part of the Aztec Empire. She studied the surface material remains in the area and historical documents written by Europeans and Aztec nobility. Her findings contradicted the benefit explanation of social inequality; she found little improvement in the standard of living of the local people after the Aztec Empire had absorbed them.

Brumfiel also focused on how everyday women lived and how the expansion of the Aztec Empire had affected them. She found that women's workload increased under the Aztecs. Brumfiel studied Aztec artwork for evidence of differences in status based on gender. In art from the Aztec capital of Tenochtitlán, images of militarism and masculinity became increasingly important with the growth of the empire, thus elevating the position of men. Sculptures of women, on the other hand, showed them in positions of work (kneeling). Yet the images of women in the area of Brumfiel's fieldwork did not change. Unlike their rulers, these commoners usually depicted women as standing, not kneeling.

Aztec artwork showing daily activities of women.

Just as Brumfiel challenged conventional wisdom, she recognized that others too will challenge her work. As she said, she was quite comfortable with knowing that someone will think that she has "gotten it wrong, and will set out on a lifetime of archaeological research to find her own answers."

Sources: Brumfiel 2008, 2009.

by NASA) to pinpoint sites. To infer when agriculture first developed, archaeologists date the relevant excavated materials by a process originally developed by chemical scientists. Information from the present and recent past can also help illuminate the distant past. For example, to try to understand why cities first emerged, archaeologists may use information from historians, geographers, and political scientists about how recent and contemporary cities are related economically and politically to their hinterlands. By discovering what recent and contemporary cities have in common, archaeologists can speculate about why cities developed originally.

Anthropological Linguistics

Anthropological linguistics is the anthropological study of language. Linguistics, or the study of languages, is an older discipline than anthropology, but the early linguists concentrated on the study of languages that had been written for a long time—languages such as English, which existed in written form for nearly a thousand years. Anthropological linguists began to do fieldwork in places where the language was not yet written. This meant that anthropologists could not consult a dictionary or grammar to help them learn the language. Instead, they first had to construct a dictionary and grammar. Then they could study the structure and history of the language.

Like biological anthropologists, linguists study changes that have taken place over time as well as contemporary variation. **Historical linguistics** is the study of how languages change over time and how they may be related. **Descriptive** or **structural linguistics** is the study of how contemporary languages differ, especially in their construction. **Sociolinguistics** examines how language is used in social contexts.

In contrast with human paleontologists and archaeologists, who have physical remains to help them reconstruct change over time, historical linguists deal only with languages—and usually unwritten ones at that. (Remember that writing is only about 5,000 years old, and only a few languages have been written.) Because unwritten languages are transmitted orally, the historical evidence dies with the speakers. Linguists interested in reconstructing the history of unwritten languages must begin in the present, with comparisons of contemporary languages. On the basis of these comparisons, they draw inferences about the kinds of change in language that may have occurred in the past and that may account for similarities and differences observed in the present. Historical linguists might typically ask, for example, whether two or more contemporary languages diverged from a common ancestral language. And if so, how far back in time they began to differ?

Unlike historical linguists, descriptive (structural) linguists are concerned with discovering and recording the principles that determine how sounds and words are put together in speech. For example, a structural description of a particular language might tell us that the sounds *t* and *k* are interchangeable in a word without causing a difference in meaning. In American Samoa, one could say *Tutuila* or *Kukuila* to name the largest island, and everyone, except perhaps newly arrived anthropologists who knew little about the Samoan language, would understand that the same island was meant.

Sociolinguists are interested in the social aspects of language, including what people speak about, how they interact conversationally, their attitudes toward speakers of other dialects or languages, and how they speak differently in different contexts. In English, for example, we do not address everyone we meet in the same way. "Hi, Sandy" may be the customary way a person greets a friend. But we would probably feel uncomfortable addressing a doctor by her or his first name; instead, we would probably say, "Good morning, Dr. Brown." Such variations in language use, which are determined by the social status of the people being addressed, are significant for sociolinguists.

Ethnology (Cultural Anthropology)

The subfield of **ethnology**, now commonly called *cultural anthropology*, seeks to understand how and why peoples today and in the recent past differ or are similar in their customary ways of thinking and acting. They ask how and why cultures develop and change and how one aspect of culture affects others. Cultural anthropologists seek answers to a variety of questions, such as: Why is the custom of marriage nearly universal in all cultures? Why do families live with or near their kin in some societies but not in others? What changes result from the introduction of money to a previously nonmonetary economy? How are relationships impacted when family members move far away to work? What happens to a society that suffers severe stress because

Anthropological linguistics The anthropological study of languages.

Historical linguistics The study of how languages change over time.

Descriptive (structural) linguistics The study of how languages are constructed.

Sociolinguistics The study of cultural and subcultural patterns of speaking in different social contexts.

Ethnology The study of how and why recent cultures differ and are similar.

Current Research and Issues

Researcher at Work: Timothy G. Bromage

When Timothy Bromage was young, his parents took him to hear a lecture by the legendary paleoanthropologist Louis Leakey. He was not sure why they had driven so far and paid so much to hear the lecture nor why they had dragged him along, but he knows that visit started him on the way to becoming a paleoanthropologist himself. Decades later, Bromage's lectures have undoubtedly inspired other young people to study the life histories of our ancient ancestors. He hopes future paleoanthropologists will also think outside the box of their discipline when they begin their research. That approach has led Bromage to major breakthroughs in his study of ancient teeth and facial bones.

In graduate school, Bromage was struck by the fact that fossils were treated as static, as if age did not make a difference. Yet humans—ancient and modern—change physically during their lives. Working with new methods and a scanning electron microscope at the University College London, Bromage found that it is possible to determine how ancient faces change as an organism matures. Different individuals die at different ages, but, in examining fossils, Bromage and his colleagues saw distinctive patterns of bone tissue forming and dissolving across the period of development. Working with specimens that were about 2 million years old, Bromage found that the hominins commonly referred to as australopithecines grew to adulthood in an apelike manner. The front parts of the skull built up tissue that grew into forward-jutting faces and jaws.

Bromage found that a later group ahominin, the paranthropoids, had a pattern of facial growth that resulted in a flatter face, more like the face of a modern human than that of the australopithecines.

Bromage has also looked at patterns of enamel deposition in ancient fossil teeth using similar techniques. Early hominin teeth are important specimens in paleoanthropology because they tend to survive well-preserved, which means they can be analyzed in much the same way as the teeth of recent humans. It has been known for some time that when children grow, tooth enamel is put down daily, but every 8 or 9 days there are substantial changes in tooth enamel formation. Why this happens was not well understood. But Bromage and his colleagues have

discovered that these rhythmic cycles may be a kind of systemic growth spurt. Bone and tissue (muscle and organs) grow at the same time, and heart and respiration rates increase, suggesting that our bodies have a metabolic clock that makes sure that cells divide and bones grow in time to accommodate growing organs. Smaller animals have shorter cycles. Comparisons with other primates have enabled Bromage to infer some life history differences in fossil forms. Such research shows the promise of the integrative approach Bromage favors. Working across disciplines and collaboratively adds to our knowledge of human evolution as well as to health research today.

Sources: Bromage 2009; Lacruz, Rossi, and Bromage 2005, 2006.

Ethnographer A person who spends some time living with, interviewing, and observing a group of people to describe their customs.

Ethnography A description of a society's customary behaviors and ideas.

of natural disasters or violent conflicts? Although the aim of ethnologists is largely the same as that of archaeologists, ethnologists generally use data collected through observation and interviews of living peoples.

One type of ethnologist, the **ethnographer**, usually spends a year or so living with, interviewing, and observing the people whose customs are being studied. This fieldwork provides the data for a detailed description (**ethnography**) of customary behavior and thought. Earlier ethnographers tended to strive for holistic coverage of a people's way of life. In part because those earlier ethnographies already exist for many cultures, recent ethnographers have tended to specialize or focus on narrower realms such as ritual healing or curing, interaction with the environment, effects of modernization or globalization, or gender issues. Ethnographies often go beyond description; they may address current anthropological issues or try to explain some aspect of culture.

Because many cultures have undergone extensive change in the recent past, an accurate view of them may depend on understanding what their life was like before the changes came about. **Ethnohistorians** study how the way of life of a culture has changed over time. They examine such written documents as missionary accounts, reports by traders and explorers, and government records to identify the cultural changes that have occurred. Unlike ethnographers, who rely mostly on their own observations and interviewing, ethnohistorians rely on the reports of others. They often must piece together and make sense of widely scattered, and even apparently contradictory, information.

Ethnographic and ethnohistorical research are both very time-consuming, and it is rare for one person to study more than a few cultures. It is the role of the **cross-cultural researcher** (who may be a cultural anthropologist or some other kind of social scientist) to discover general patterns across cultures—that is, what characteristics are universal, which traits vary and why, and what the consequences of the variability might be. They may ask such questions as: Why is there more gender inequality in some societies than in others? Is family violence related to aggression in other areas of life? What are the effects of living in a very unpredictable environment? In testing possible answers to such questions, cross-cultural researchers use data from samples of cultures (usually described initially by ethnographers) to try to arrive at explanations or relationships that hold across cultures. Archaeologists may find the results of cross-cultural research useful for making inferences about the past, particularly if they can discover material indicators of cultural variation.

Because ethnologists may be interested in many aspects of customary behavior and thought—from economic behavior to political behavior to styles of art, music, and religion—ethnology overlaps with disciplines that concentrate on some particular aspect of human existence, such as sociology, psychology, economics, political science, art, music, and comparative religion. But the distinctive feature of cultural anthropology is its interest in how all these aspects of human existence vary from society to society, in all historical periods, and in all parts of the world.

Ethnohistorian An ethnologist who uses historical documents to study how a particular culture has changed over time.

Cross-cultural researcher An ethnologist who uses ethnographic data about many societies to test possible explanations of cultural variation to discover general patterns about cultural traits—what is universal, what is variable, why traits vary, and what the consequences of the variability might be.

Applied (Practicing) Anthropology

All knowledge may turn out to be useful. In the physical and biological sciences, it is well understood that technological breakthroughs like DNA splicing, spacecraft docking in outer space, and the development of miniscule computer chips could not have taken place without an enormous amount of basic research to uncover the laws of nature in the physical and biological worlds. If we did not understand fundamental principles, the technological achievements we are so proud of would not be possible. Researchers are often driven simply by curiosity, with no thought to where the research might lead, which is why such research is sometimes called *basic research*. The same is true of the social sciences. If a researcher finds out that societies with combative sports tend to have more wars, it may lead to other inquiries about the relationships between one kind of aggression and another. The knowledge acquired may ultimately lead to discovering ways to correct social problems, such as family violence and war.

For most of anthropology's history as a profession, anthropologists generally worked in academic institutions. But more and more, anthropologists are increasingly working outside academia—today there are probably more anthropologists who work outside academia than in it.[3] Applied or practicing anthropology is explicitly intended to making anthropological knowledge useful.[4] Practicing anthropologists, as practitioners of the subdiscipline increasingly call themselves, may be trained in any or all of the fields of anthropology. In contrast to basic researchers, who are almost always employed in colleges, universities, and museums, applied anthropologists are commonly employed in settings outside traditional academia, including government agencies, international development agencies, private consulting firms, businesses, public health organizations, medical schools, law offices, community development agencies, and charitable foundations.

A large number of emigrants from the former Soviet Union, particularly from Black Sea cities and towns such as Odessa, live in the Brighton Beach neighborhood of Brooklyn. Migrant and immigrant communities, such as "Little Odessa," are an increasing focus of anthropological study.

Biological anthropologists may be called upon to give forensic evidence in court, or they may work in public health or design clothes and equipment to fit human anatomy. Archaeologists may be involved in preserving and exhibiting artifacts for museums and in doing contract work to find and preserve cultural sites that might be damaged by construction or excavation. Linguists may work in bilingual educational training programs or may work on ways to improve communication. Ethnologists may work in a wide variety of applied projects ranging from community development, urban planning, health care, and agricultural improvement to personnel and organizational management and assessment of the impact of change programs on people's lives.[5]

In the past two decades, the speed of globalization has created great changes in applied or practicing anthropology. Whereas the field used largely to be the province of Western—and often colonizing—nations, it has since grown into a vital localized discipline all over the world. In a number of countries, among them Russia, China, Mexico, Egypt, Ecuador, and Brazil, applied or practicing anthropology focused on solving practical social problems dominates over the research-driven four fields.[6]

Specialization

1.6 Explain the ways in which anthropologists specialize within their fields of study.

As disciplines grow, they tend to develop more and more specialties. This trend is probably inevitable since, as knowledge accumulates and methods become more advanced, there is a limit to what any one person can reasonably master. Thus, in addition to the general divisions we have outlined already, particular anthropologists tend to identify themselves with a variety of specializations. Anthropologists commonly have a geographic specialty, which may be as broad as Old World or New World or as narrow as the southwestern United States. Those who study the past (archaeologists or human paleontologists) may specialize in specific time periods. Ethnologists often specialize in specific subject matters in addition to one or two cultural areas. Just as most of the chapters in this book refer to broad subject specialties, so do some ethnologists identify themselves as *economic anthropologists, political anthropologists,* or *psychological anthropologists.* Others may identify themselves by theoretical orientations, such as *cultural ecologists,* anthropologists who are concerned with the relationship between culture and the physical and social environments. These specialties are not mutually exclusive, however. A cultural ecologist, for example, might be interested in the effects of the environment on economic behavior, political behavior, or childrearing.

Does specialization isolate an anthropologist from other kinds of research? Not necessarily. Some specialties have to draw on information from several fields, inside and outside anthropology. For example, *medical anthropologists* study the cultural and biological contexts of human health and illness. Therefore, they need to understand the economy, diet, and patterns of social interaction as well as attitudes and beliefs regarding illness and health. They may also need to draw on research in human genetics, public health, and medicine.

The Relevance of Anthropology

1.7 Communicate the relevance of anthropology.

Anthropology is a comparatively young discipline. Anthropologists only began to go to live with people in faraway places in the late 1800s. Compared to our knowledge of the physical laws of nature, we know much less about people, about how and why they behave as they do. That anthropology and other sciences dealing with humans began to develop only relatively recently is not in itself a sufficient reason for our knowing less than in the physical sciences. Why, in our quest for knowledge of all kinds, did we wait so long to study ourselves? Leslie White has suggested that those phenomena most remote from us and least significant as determinants of human behavior were the first to be studied. The reason, he surmises, is that humans like to think of themselves as citadels of free will, subject to no laws of nature. Hence, White concludes, there is no need to see ourselves as objects to be explained.[7]

The idea that it is impossible to account for human behavior scientifically, either because our actions and beliefs are too individualistic and complex or because human beings are understandable only in otherworldly terms, is a self-fulfilling notion. We cannot discover principles explaining human behavior if we neither believe such principles exist nor bother to look for them. The result is ensured from the beginning; disbelief in principles of human behavior will be reinforced by the failure to find them. If we are to increase our understanding of human beings, we first have to believe it is possible to do so.

If we aim to understand humans, it is essential that we study humans in all times and places. We must study ancient humans and modern humans. We must study their cultures and their biology. How else can we understand what is true of humans generally or how they are capable of varying? If we study just our own society, we may come up only with explanations that are culture-bound, not general or applicable to most or all humans. Anthropology is useful, then, to the degree that it contributes to our understanding of human beings everywhere.

In addition, anthropology is relevant because it helps us avoid misunderstandings between peoples. If we can understand why other groups are different from ourselves, we might have less reason to condemn them for behavior that appears strange to us. We may then come to realize that many differences between peoples are products of physical and cultural adaptations to different environments. For example, someone who first finds out about the !Kung as they lived in the Kalahari Desert of southern Africa in the 1950s might assume that the !Kung were "backward." (The exclamation point in the name !Kung signifies one of the clicking sounds made with the tongue by speakers of the !Kung language.) The !Kung wore little clothing, had few possessions, lived in meager shelters, and enjoyed none of our technological niceties, such as radio and computers.

But let us reflect on how a typical North American community might react if it awoke to find itself in an environment similar to that in which the !Kung lived. People would find that the arid land makes both agriculture and animal husbandry impossible, and they might have to think about adopting a nomadic existence. They might then discard many of their material possessions so that they could travel easily to take advantage of changing water and food supplies. Because of the extreme heat and the lack of extra water for laundry, they might find it more practical to be almost naked than to wear clothes. They would undoubtedly find it impossible to build elaborate homes. For social security, they might start to share the food brought into the group. Thus, if they survived at all, they might end up looking and acting far more like the !Kung than like typical North Americans.

Physical differences, too, may be seen as results of adaptations to the environment. For example, in our society, we admire people who are tall and slim. If these same individuals were forced to live above the Arctic Circle, however, they might wish they could trade their tall, slim bodies for short, compact ones because stocky physiques conserve body heat more effectively and may therefore be more adaptive in cold climates.

Exposure to anthropology might also help to alleviate misunderstandings that arise between people of different cultural groups from subtle causes operating below the level of consciousness. For example, different cultures have different conceptions of the gestures and interpersonal distances that are appropriate under various circumstances. For example, different cultures have different conceptions of eye contact during conversation. Whereas some people—North Americans, most Europeans, and Arabs, among them—expect to maintain eye contact during conversation, in Japanese culture the gaze is averted when interacting with a superior or venerated older person. North Americans may feel suspicious when someone does not look them in the eye when speaking. But in another culture that same direct gaze may be experienced as brazen. If our intolerance for others results in part from a lack of understanding of why peoples vary, then the knowledge that anthropologists accumulate may lessen that intolerance.[8]

As the world becomes increasingly interconnected or globalized, the importance of understanding and trying to respect cultural and physical differences becomes more and more important. Minor misunderstandings can escalate quickly into more serious problems. Even when powerful countries think they are being helpful, they may convey that other countries are inferior. They may also unknowingly promote behaviors that are not in the best interest of the people they are trying to help. At the extreme, misunderstandings can lead to violent confrontations. In today's world, going to war with modern weapons of mass destruction can kill more people than ever before.

Is understanding and respecting cultural and biological differences enough? Although education is undoubtedly useful, many anthropologists believe that more direct action is needed to solve real-world problems at both the global and local levels. At the global level, we have to deal with many types of violent conflict, the degradation of the environment, the growing inequality between rich and poor countries, and major threats to health. At the local level, we have to grapple with whether particular development plans are advantageous and how to improve nutrition and health of particular societies. One solution does not necessarily fit all—what is good for some may not be good for others in different circumstances. To find out if some change will be advantageous requires careful study. Many ethical issues arise. Is it ethical to try to interfere with other people's lives? Is it ethical not to, if they are suffering or ask for help?

Knowledge of our past may bring both a feeling of humility and a sense of accomplishment. If we are to attempt to deal with the problems of our world, we must be aware of our vulnerability so that we do not think that problems will solve themselves. But we also have to think enough of our accomplishments to believe that we can find solutions to problems. Much of the trouble we get into may be a result of feelings of self-importance and invulnerability—in short, our lack of humility. Knowing something about our evolutionary past may help us to understand and accept our place in the biological world. Just as for any other form of life, there is no guarantee that any particular human population, or even the entire human species, will perpetuate itself indefinitely. The earth changes, the environment changes, and humanity itself changes. What survives and flourishes in the present might not do so in the future.

Yet our vulnerability should not make us feel powerless. We have many reasons to feel confident about the future. Consider what we have accomplished so far. By means of tools and weapons fashioned from sticks and stones, we were able to hunt animals larger and more powerful than ourselves. We discovered how to make fire, and we learned to use it to keep ourselves warm and to cook our food. As we domesticated plants and animals, we gained greater control over our food supply and were able to establish more permanent settlements. We mined and smelted ores to fashion more durable tools. We built cities and irrigation systems, monuments and ships. We made it possible to travel from one continent to another in a single day. We conquered some illnesses and prolonged human life.

In short, human beings and their cultures have changed considerably over the course of history. Human populations have often been able to adapt to changing circumstances. Let us hope that humans continue to adapt to the challenges of the present and future.

Summary and Review

What Is Anthropology?

1.1 Explain the general definition and purpose of anthropology.

- Anthropology is a discipline of curiosity about human beings that seeks to understand both universals and differences in human populations.
- Anthropology seeks answers to biological and cultural questions about humans for both academic and practical purposes.
- Anthropology is distinct from other disciplines concerned with human beings in its scope, its holistic approach, and its distinctive curiosity.

? What are the academic and practical purposes of anthropology?

The Scope of Anthropology

1.2 Describe the scope of anthropology.

- The field of anthropology has a broad scope, both geographically and historically.
- Anthropologists are interested in all varieties of people in every part of the world.
- Anthropologists are interested in people of all periods, from millions of years ago to the present.
- The broad scope of anthropology is required to confirm that any suggested generalization about human beings, any explanation of some characteristic of human culture or biology, is applicable to many times and places of human existence, not just a limited group.

 ? What are the global goals of anthropological study?

The Holistic Approach

1.3 Explain the holistic approach.

- Anthropologists study the many aspects of human experience as an integrated whole.

- Anthropologists look for patterns of traits and attempt to explain them.

? What elements of the human experience might be considered in a holistic approach in anthropology?

Anthropological Curiosity

1.4 Explain anthropology's distinctive curiosity.

- Anthropology's distinctiveness lies principally in the kind of curiosity it arouses.
- Anthropologists tend to focus on *typic*al characteristics of the human populations they study rather than on individual variation or variation in small groups.
- Because anthropologists view human groups holistically, their curiosity may lead them to find patterns of relationships between seemingly unrelated characteristics.

? What typifies anthropological curiosity?

Fields of Anthropology

1.5 Differentiate among the five major fields of anthropology.

- Anthropology comprises two broad classifications of subject matter: biological (physical) anthropology and cultural anthropology.
- Biological anthropology poses questions about the emergence of humans and their later evolution (paleontology) and about how and why contemporary human populations vary biologically (human variation).
- Cultural anthropology is the study of how and why cultures in the past and present vary or are similar in terms of the ways that a particular population or society thinks and behaves.

- Cultural anthropology includes three subfields: archaeology, linguistics, and ethnology (often called *cultural anthropology*).

- A fifth subfield, applied or practicing anthropology, cuts across all four subfields.

- The purpose of applied (or practicing) anthropology is explicitly to make anthropological knowledge useful. Practicing anthropologists may be trained in any or all of the fields of anthropology.

 How are the five major fields of anthropology different? What are some examples of applied anthropology?

Specialization

1.6 Explain the ways in which anthropologists specialize within their fields of study.

- Anthropologists specialize by focusing on a geographic area; a period of time; particular subject matter such as economics, politics, or psychology; or particular theoretical orientations.

- Anthropologists might have more than one specialization.

 What are some examples of anthropological specializations and their purposes?

The Relevance of Anthropology

1.7 Communicate the relevance of anthropology.

- Anthropology is a young discipline, beginning in the late 1800s. Initially, especially among Westerners, there was resistance to the idea of accounting for human behavior scientifically.

- Anthropology considers both culture and biology of humans in all times and places. Anthropology is useful to the degree that it contributes to our understanding of human beings everywhere.

- In addition, anthropology is relevant because it helps to avoid misunderstandings between peoples. If those in one culture can understand why other groups are different from them, they might have less reason to condemn others for behavior that appears strange.

- As the world becomes increasingly interconnected or globalized, the importance of understanding and trying to respect cultural and physical differences becomes more and more important.

How is anthropology relevant to society?

Think on it

1. Why study **anthropology**? What are its goals, and how is it useful?

2. How does anthropology differ from other **fields** you have encountered that deal with humans? (Compare with psychology, sociology, political science, history, or biology, among others.)

3. Compare the three anthropologists featured in this chapter. What do their **stories** have in common?

4. How might the **knowledge** gained from anthropology be both humbling and empowering?

Research Methods in Anthropology

LEARNING OBJECTIVES

Define "explanation" and discuss its role in anthropology.	2.1
Describe some of the main theoretical approaches in anthropology.	2.2
Explain the process of operationalization, the importance of measurement, and the value of statistical evaluation in testing explanations.	2.3
Differentiate the types of research in anthropology.	2.4
Describe the four kinds of evidence that archaeologists and paleoanthropologists find and how they analyze it.	2.5
Describe the ethical requirements of anthropological research.	2.6

The intellectuals who developed science in the mid-17th century understood very well that human knowledge of the world could be biased and incomplete. Rather than rejecting the possibility of objective understanding, the founders of science created a way of generating understanding based on the rigorous testing of ideas. As anthropologist Philip Salzman explains:

> The scientific method, the heart of science, was invented because it was understood that human error, wish-fulfillment, duplicity, dishonesty, and weakness would commonly distort research findings. The scientific requirements that the procedures of all studies must be specified in detail so that others could repeat them, and the actual replication of findings by other scientists in other venues, were established to minimize the distorting effects of human subjectivity and moral weakness in the quest for knowledge.[1]

Although one goal of anthropology is to understand what it means to be a human in a different cultural context, a goal for which science and its pursuit of explanations may not be appropriate, most anthropologists believe that objective knowledge about other cultures is possible through science.

Explanations

2.1 ▶ Define "explanation" and discuss its role in anthropology.

Explanation An answer to a *why* question. In science, there are two kinds of explanation that researchers try to achieve: associations and theories.

Variable A thing or quantity that varies.

Laws (scientific) Associations or relationships that almost all scientists accept.

An **explanation** is an answer to a *why* question. There are many types of explanations, some more satisfying than others. For example, suppose we ask why a society has a long postpartum sex taboo. We could guess that the people in that society want to abstain from sex for a year or so after the birth of a baby. Is this an explanation? Yes, because it does suggest that people have a purpose in practicing the custom; it therefore partly answers the *why* question. But such an explanation would not be very satisfying because it does not specify what the purpose of the custom might be. How about the idea that people have a long postpartum sex taboo because it is their tradition? That too is an explanation, but it is not satisfactory for a different reason. It is a *tautology;* that is, the thing to be explained (the taboo) is being explained by itself, by its prior existence. To explain something in terms of tradition is to say that people do it because they already do it, which is not informative. What kinds of explanations are more satisfactory, then? In science, investigators try to achieve two kinds of explanations: *associations* and *theories.*

Associations or Relationships

One way of explaining something (an observation, an action, a custom) is to say how it conforms to a general principle or relationship. So to explain why the water left outside in the basin froze, we say that it was cold last night and that water freezes at 32°F (0°C). The statement that water solidifies (becomes ice) at 32°F is a statement of a relationship or association between two **variables**—things or quantities that vary. In this case, variation in the state of water (liquid vs. solid) is related to variation in the temperature of the air (above vs. below 32°F). The truth of the relationship is suggested by repeated observations. In the physical sciences, such relationships are called **laws** when almost all scientists accept them. We find such explanations satisfactory because they allow us to predict what will happen in the future or understand something that has happened regularly in the past.

In the social sciences, associations are usually stated *probabilistically;* that is, we say that two or more variables

The statement that water becomes ice at 32°F (0°C) defines an association between two variables: water and temperature. A theory explains why an association exists.

tend to be related in a predictable way, which means that there are usually some exceptions. For example, to explain why a society has a long postpartum sex taboo, we can point to the association (or correlation) that John Whiting found in a worldwide sample of societies: Societies with apparently low-protein diets tend to have long postpartum sex taboos.[2] We call the relationship between low-protein diets and the sex taboo a **statistical association**, which means that the observed relationship is unlikely to be due to chance.

Theories

Even though laws and statistical associations explain by relating what is to be explained to other things, we want to know more: why those laws or associations exist. Why does water freeze at 32°F? Why do societies with low-protein diets tend to have long postpartum sex taboos? Therefore, scientists try to formulate theories that will explain the observed relationships (laws and statistical associations).[3]

Theories—explanations of laws and statistical associations—are more complicated than the observed relationships they are intended to explain. It is difficult to be precise about what a theory is. By way of example, let us return to the question of why some societies have long postpartum sex taboos. We have already seen that a known statistical association can be used to help explain it. If a society has a low-protein diet, it will generally have a long postpartum sex taboo. But most people would ask additional questions: Why does a low-protein diet explain the taboo? What is the mechanism by which a society with such a diet develops the custom of a long postpartum sex taboo? A theory is intended to answer such questions.

John Whiting theorized that a long postpartum sex taboo may be an adaptation to certain conditions. Particularly in tropical areas, where the major food staples are low in protein, babies are vulnerable to the protein-deficiency disease called *kwashiorkor.* But if a baby could continue to nurse for a long time, it might have more of a chance to survive. The postpartum sex taboo might be adaptive, Whiting's theory suggests, because it increases the likelihood of a baby's survival. That is, if a mother puts off having another baby for a while, the first baby might have a better chance to survive because it can be fed mother's milk for a longer time. Whiting suggests that parents may be aware, whether unconsciously or consciously, that having another baby too soon might jeopardize the survival of the first baby, and so they might decide that abstaining from intercourse for more than a year after the birth of the first baby would be a good idea.

As this example of a theory illustrates, there are differences between a theory and an association. A theory is usually more complicated, containing a series of statements. An association usually states quite simply that there is a relationship between two or more measured variables. Another difference is that although a theory may mention some things that are observable, such as the presence of a long postpartum sex taboo, it contains other concepts or statements that could not be observed. For example, with regard to Whiting's theory, it would be difficult to find out if the people who adopted the custom of a long postpartum sex taboo had some awareness that babies would thereby have a better chance to survive. Then, too, the concept of adaptation—that some characteristic promotes greater reproductive success—is difficult to verify because of the challenge of finding out whether different individuals or groups have different rates of reproduction because they do or do not practice the supposedly adaptive custom. Thus, some concepts or implications in a theory are unobservable (at least at the present time), and only some aspects may be observable. In contrast, statistical associations or laws are based entirely on observations.[4]

Why Theories Cannot Be Proved

Many people think that the theories they learned in physics or chemistry courses have been proved. Unfortunately, many students get that impression because their teachers present lessons in an authoritative manner. Scientists and philosophers of science now generally agree that no theory can be said to be proved or unquestionably true, although some theories may have considerable evidence supporting them. This is because many of the concepts and ideas in theories are not directly observable and therefore not directly verifiable. For example, scientists may try to explain how light behaves by postulating

Statistical association A relationship or correlation between two or more variables that is unlikely to be due to chance.

Theories Explanations of associations or laws.

Theoretical construct
Something that cannot be observed or verified directly.

that it consists of particles called photons, but photons cannot be observed, even with the most powerful microscope. So, exactly what a photon looks like and exactly how it works remain in the realm of the unprovable. The photon is a **theoretical construct**, something that cannot be observed or verified directly. Because all theories contain such constructs, theories cannot be proved entirely or with absolute certainty.[5]

Why should we bother with theories, then, if we cannot prove that they are true? Perhaps the main advantage of a theory as a kind of explanation is that it may lead to new understanding or knowledge. A theory can suggest new relationships or imply new predictions that might be supported or confirmed by new research. For example, Whiting's theory about long postpartum sex taboos has implications that researchers could investigate. Because the theory discusses how a long postpartum sex taboo might be adaptive, we would expect that certain changes would result in the taboo's disappearance. For example, suppose people adopted either mechanical birth-control devices or began to give supplementary high-protein foods to babies. With birth control, a family could space births without abstaining from sex, so we would expect the custom of postpartum abstinence to disappear. Additionally, we would expect it to disappear with protein supplements for babies because *kwashiorkor* would then be less likely to afflict the babies. Whiting's ideas might also prompt investigators to try to find out whether parents are consciously or unconsciously aware of the problem of close birth spacing in areas with low supplies of protein.

Falsification Showing that a theory seems to be wrong by finding that implications or predictions derivable from it are not consistent with objectively collected data.

Although theories cannot be proved, they are rejectable. The method of **falsification**, which shows that a theory seems to be wrong, is the main way that theories are judged.[6] Scientists derive implications or predictions that should be true if the theory is correct. So, for example, Whiting predicted that societies with long postpartum sex taboos would be found more often in the tropics than in temperate regions and that they would be likely to have low-protein food supplies. Such predictions of what might be found are called **hypotheses**. If the predictions turn out not to be correct, the researcher is obliged to conclude that something may be wrong with the theory or something wrong with the test of the theory. Theories that are not falsified are accepted for the time being because the available evidence seems to be consistent with them. But remember that no matter how much the available evidence seems to support a theory, we can never be certain it is true. There is always the possibility that some implication of it, some hypothesis derivable from it, will not be confirmed in the future.

Hypotheses Predictions, which may be derived from theories, about how variables are related.

2.2 Describe some of the main theoretical approaches in anthropology.

A Brief History of Anthropological Theory

John Whiting's theory explaining why a long postpartum sex taboo might be adaptive is only one of many theories that anthropologists employ in their research. The history of anthropology reflects broad themes the types of theories anthropologists have used. Whiting's theory, for example, can be placed within the body of ecological theories. Let's take a look at some of the variety of **theoretical orientations** that have been important to anthropologists.

Theoretical orientation
A general attitude about how phenomena are to be explained.

Early Evolutionism

The theory of evolution had a strong impact on anthropology in the 19th century. The prevailing view was that culture generally develops (or evolves) in a uniform and progressive manner, just as Darwin argued species did. It was thought that most societies pass through the same series of stages, to arrive ultimately at a common end. Two 19th-century anthropologists whose writings exemplified the theory that culture generally evolves uniformly and progressively were Edward B. Tylor (1832–1917) and Lewis Henry Morgan (1818–1881). Both maintained that culture evolved from the simple to the complex and that all societies passed through three basic stages of development: from savagery through barbarism to civilization.[7] "Progress" was therefore possible for all. To account for cultural variation, Tylor and Morgan postulated that different contemporary societies were at different stages of evolution. According to this view, the "simpler" peoples of the day had not yet reached "higher" stages. Though important at the beginning of anthropology, the evolutionism of Tylor and Morgan is largely rejected today.

"Race" Theory

Evolutionism also influenced another branch of early anthropological theory, one that posited that the reason human cultures differed in their behaviors was because they represented separate subspecies of humans, or "races." This idea was also influenced by the fact that, by the 19th century at least, it became clear that few cultures were being "civilized" in the way Europeans expected. Rather than attribute this to the strength of cultural tradition, some attributed it to the innate capabilities of the people—in other words, to their "race." Members of "uncivilized races" were, by their very nature, incapable of being "civilized." Such ideas were widely held during the late 19th and early 20th centuries, and American anthropology played a large role in showing that "race" theory was unsupported in a variety of contexts. Unfortunately, "race" theory persists in some disciplines.[8]

Boasian Anthropology

The beginning of the 20th century brought the end of evolutionism's reign in American anthropology. Its leading opponent was Franz Boas (1858–1942), whose main disagreement with the evolutionists involved their assumption that universal laws governed all human culture. Boas pointed out that these 19th-century "armchair anthropologists" lacked sufficient data to formulate many useful generalizations. Boas also strongly opposed "race" theory, and made significant contributions to the study of human variation that demonstrated how supposedly "racial" characteristics actually varied depending on where a person grew up.[9]

Boas stressed the idea that single cultural traits had to be studied in the context of the society in which they appeared. According to the method he advocated, the essence of science is to mistrust all expectations and to rely only on facts. But, as we argue in this chapter, collecting data without some preliminary theorizing, without ideas about what to expect, is problematic, for the facts that are most important may be ignored whereas irrelevant ones may be recorded. Boas's concern with innumerable local details did not encourage a belief that it might be possible to explain the major variations in culture, and by the 1950s many anthropologists felt that the Boasian focus on describing cultures rather than explaining how and why cultures varied limited the scope of anthropology. Two major approaches to anthropology emerged from this movement away from description: ecological and interpretive.

Ecological Approaches

Julian Steward (1902–1972) was one of the first to advocate the study of **cultural ecology**—the analysis of the relationship between a culture and its environment. Steward felt that the explanation for some aspects of cultural variation could be found in the adaptation of societies to their particular environments.[10] Cultural ecologists assume that cultural adaptation involves the mechanism of *natural selection*—the more frequent survival and reproduction of the better adapted. Environment, including the physical and social environments, affects the development of culture traits in that "individuals or populations behaving in certain different ways have different degrees of success in survival and reproduction and, consequently, in the transmission of their ways of behaving from generation to generation."[11]

Today anthropologists who refer to themselves as evolutionary or behavioral ecologists (as opposed to cultural ecologists) explore how particular characteristics may be adaptive for an individual in a given environment (cultural ecologists tend to focus on the group or culture more than the individual).[12] *Adaptive* means the ability of individuals to get their genes into future generations. This viewpoint implies that behavior is transmitted in some way (by genes or learning) to people who share your genes (usually offspring).[13] If a certain behavior is adaptive for individuals in a particular environment (or a particular historical context in which these individuals are able to reproduce more than others), it should become more widespread in future generations as the individuals with those traits increase in number. One important contemporary idea, dual-inheritance theory, gives much more weight to culture as part of the evolutionary process. Dual inheritance refers to both genes and culture playing different but nonetheless important and interactive roles in transmitting traits to future generations.[14]

Cultural ecology The analysis of the relationship between a culture and its environment.

Current Research and Issues

Evaluating Alternative Theories

In working among the Abelam of New Guinea, Richard Scaglion was puzzled why they invest so much energy in growing giant ceremonial yams, sometimes more than 10 feet long. Also, why do they abstain from sex for six months while they grow them? Of course, to try to understand, we need to know much more about the Abelam way of life. Scaglion had read about them, lived among them, and talked to them, but, as many ethnographers have discovered, answers to why questions don't just leap out at you. Answers, at least tentative ones, often come from theoretical orientations that suggest how or where to look for answers. Scaglion considers several possibilities. As Donald Tuzin had suggested for a nearby group, the Plains Arapesh, yams may be symbols of, or stand for, shared cultural understandings. (Looking for the meanings of symbols is a kind of interpretative approach to ethnographic data.) The Abelam think of yams as having souls that appreciate tranquility. Yams also have family lines; at marriage, the joining of family lines is symbolized by planting different yam lines in the same garden. During the yam-growing cycle (remember that yams appreciate tranquility), lethal warfare and conflict become channeled mostly into competitive but nonlethal yam-growing contests. So yam growing may be functional in the sense that it helps to foster harmony.

Then again, ceremonial yam growing may have adaptive ecological consequences. Just as the Tsembaga pig feasts seemed to keep human population in line with resources, Scaglion thinks that ceremonial yam growing did too. Growing pig populations damage gardens and create conflicts, but pigs are also given away during competitive yam ceremonies, so the pig population declines. Wild animals that are hunted also have a chance to replenish themselves because hunting is frowned upon during the yam-growing cycle.

As Scaglion's discussion illustrates, theoretical orientations help researchers derive explanations. They do not have to be "rival" explanations, in the sense that one has to be right and others wrong; more than one theory may help explain some phenomenon. But we can't assume that a theory is correct and helps us to understand just because it sounds good. The important point is that we need something more to evaluate theory.

The Abelam create elaborate ceremonial masks to adorn their largest yams during the harvest festival.

We have to find ways to test a theory against evidence. Until we do that, we really don't know how many, or if indeed any, of the theories available are helpful.

Source: Scaglion 2009a.

The ecological approaches have led to an active program of research in anthropology. However, these approaches have aroused considerable controversy, particularly from those cultural anthropologists who do not believe that biological considerations or cultural adaptations have much to do with understanding culture.

Interpretive Approaches

Since the 1960s, writers in the field of literary criticism have influenced the development of a variety of "interpretive" approaches in cultural anthropology, particularly with respect to ethnography.[15] Clifford Geertz (1926–2006) popularized the idea that a culture is like a literary text that can be analyzed for meaning. According to Geertz, ethnographers choose to interpret the meaning of things in the cultures they study that are of interest to themselves. Then they try to convey their interpretations of cultural meaning to people of their own culture. Thus, according to Geertz, ethnographers are a kind of selective intercultural translator.[16]

For many interpretive anthropologists, the goal of anthropology is to understand what it means to be a person living in a particular culture, rather than to explain why cultures vary. The task of understanding meaning, these scholars claim, cannot be achieved scientifically, but can only be approached through forms of literary analysis.

Many of these anthropologists think that interpretation is the only achievable goal in cultural anthropology because they do not believe it is possible to describe or measure cultural phenomena in objective or unbiased ways. Scientific anthropologists do not agree. To be sure, interpretive ethnographies provide insights into other cultures. But we do not have to believe what an interpretation suggests, no matter how eloquently it is stated. (We are rarely given objective evidence to support the interpretation.) As we discuss below, scientific researchers have developed many techniques for minimizing bias and increasing the objectivity of measurement. Thus, interpretative anthropologists who deny the possibility of scientific understanding of human behavior and thinking may not know how much has been achieved so far by scientific studies of cultural phenomena. Let's take a look at how scientific anthropologists test explanations of cultural phenomenon.

Evidence: Testing Explanations

In any field of investigation, theories are generally the most plentiful commodity, apparently because of the human predisposition to try to make sense of the world. It is necessary, then, for us to have procedures that enable us to select from among the many available theories those that are more likely to be correct. As Peter Caws pointed out, "Just as mutations arise naturally but are not all beneficial, so hypotheses [theories] emerge naturally but are not all correct. If progress is to occur, therefore, we require a superfluity of hypotheses and also a mechanism of selection."[17] In other words, generating a theory or interpretation is not enough. We need some reliable method of testing whether or not that theory is likely to be correct. If a theory is not correct, it may detract from our efforts to achieve understanding by misleading us into thinking the problem is already solved.

The strategy in all kinds of testing in science is to predict what one would expect to find if a particular theory were correct, and then to conduct an investigation to see if the prediction is generally consistent with the data. If the prediction is not supported, the investigator is obliged to accept the possibility that the theory is wrong. If, however, the prediction holds true, then the investigator is entitled to say that evidence supports the theory. Thus, conducting research designed to test expectations derived from theory allows researchers to eliminate some theories and to accept others, at least tentatively.

Operationalization and Measurement

We test predictions derived from a theory to see if the theory may be correct—to see if it is consistent with observable events or conditions in the real world. A theory and the predictions derived from it are not useful if there is no way to measure the events or conditions mentioned in the predictions. If there is no way of relating the theory to observable events, it does not matter how good the theory sounds; it is still not a useful scientific theory.[18] To transform theoretical predictions into statements that might be verified, a researcher provides an **operational definition** of each of the concepts or variables mentioned in the prediction. An operational definition is a description of the procedure that is followed to measure the variable.[19]

Whiting predicted that societies with a low-protein diet would have a long postpartum sex taboo. Amount of protein in the diet is a variable; some societies have more, others have less. Length of the postpartum sex taboo is a variable; a society may have a short taboo or a long taboo. Whiting operationally defined the first variable, *amount of protein*, in terms of staple foods.[20] For example, if a society depended mostly on root and tree crops (such as cassava and bananas), Whiting rated the society as having low protein. If the society depended mostly on cereal crops (such as wheat, barley, corn, oats), he rated it as having moderate protein because cereal crops have more protein by weight than root and tree crops. If the society depended mostly on hunting, fishing, or herding for food, he rated it as having high protein. The other variable in Whiting's prediction, *length of postpartum sex taboo*, was operationalized as follows: A society was rated as having a long taboo if couples customarily abstained from sex for more than a year after the birth of a baby; abstention for a year or less was considered a short taboo.

Specifying an operational definition for each variable is extremely important because it allows other investigators to check a researcher's results.[21] Science depends on *replication*, the repetition of results. Only when many researchers observe a particular association can we call that association or relationship a law. Providing operational definitions is also

2.3 Explain the process of operationalization, the importance of measurement, and the value of statistical evaluation in testing explanations.

Operational definition A description of the procedure that is followed in measuring a variable.

Yanomamö Indians of Brazil depend on plantains (shown here) and cassava root crops and have a relatively low-protein diet.

extremely important because it allows others to evaluate whether a measure is appropriate. Only when we are told exactly how something was measured can we judge whether the measure reflects what it is supposed to reflect. Specifying measures publicly is so important in science that we are obliged to be skeptical of any conclusions offered by a researcher who fails to say how variables were measured.

Measure To describe how something compares with other things on some scale of variation.

To **measure** something is to say how it compares with other things on some scale of variation. People often assume that a measuring device is always a physical instrument, such as a scale or a ruler, but physical devices are not the only way to measure something. *Classification* is also a form of measurement. When we classify people as male or female or employed versus unemployed, we are dividing them into *types*. Deciding which type they belong to is a kind of measurement because doing so allows us to compare them. We can also measure things by deciding which cases or examples have more or less of something (e.g., more or less protein in the diet). The measures employed in physical science are usually based on scales that allow us to assign numbers to each case; we measure height in meters and weight in grams, for example. However we measure our variables, the fact that we can measure them means that we can test our hypotheses to see if the predicted relationships actually exist, at least most of the time.

Sampling

After deciding how to measure the variables in some predicted relationship, investigators must decide how to select which cases to study to see if the predicted relationship holds. If the prediction is about the behavior of people, the sampling decision involves which people to observe. If the prediction is about an association between societal customs, the sampling decision involves which societies to study. Investigators must decide not only which cases to choose but also how many to choose. No researcher can investigate all the possible cases, and so choices must be made. Some choices are better than others. The best sample is almost always some kind of random sample. A **random sample** is one in which all cases selected have an equal chance of being included in the sample. Almost all statistical tests used to evaluate the results of research require random sampling because only results based on a random sample can be assumed to be probably true for some larger set or universe of cases.

Random sample A sample in which all cases selected have had an equal chance to be included.

Sampling universe The list of cases to be sampled from.

Before researchers can sample randomly, they must specify the **sampling universe**, that is, the list of cases to be sampled from. Suppose an anthropologist is doing fieldwork in a society. Unless the society is very small, it is usually not practical to use the whole society as the sampling universe. Because most fieldworkers want to remain in a community for a considerable

The Inuit of Nunavut depend largely on sea mammals and fish and have a relatively high-protein diet.

length of time, the community usually becomes the sampling universe. If a cross-cultural researcher wants to test an explanation, it is necessary to sample the world's societies. But we do not have descriptions of all the societies—past and present—that have existed in the world. Thus, samples are usually drawn from published lists of described societies that have been classified or coded according to standard cultural variables,[22] or they are drawn from the Human Relations Area Files *eHRAF World Cultures,* a finely-indexed, online, and annually growing collection of ethnographies on more than 285 societies—past and present—around the world.[23] There is also a collection of archaeological traditions—*eHRAF Archaeology.*

Random sampling is not often employed in anthropology, but a nonrandom sample might still be fairly representative if the investigator has not personally chosen the cases for study. We should be particularly suspicious of any sample that may reflect the investigator's own biases or interests. For example, if investigators pick only the people with whom they are friendly, the sample is suspicious. If researchers select sample cases (i.e., societies and traditions) because books on them happen to be on their own bookshelves, such samples are also suspicious. A sampling procedure should be designed to get a fair, unbiased representation of the sampling universe. If we want to increase our chances of getting a representative sample, we have to use a random sampling procedure. To do so, we conventionally number the cases in the statistical universe and then use a table of random numbers to draw our sample cases.

Statistical Evaluation

When researchers have measured the variables of interest for all the sample cases, they are ready to see if the predicted relationship actually exists in the data. Remember, the results may not turn out to be what the theory predicts. Sometimes researchers construct a *contingency table,* like that shown in Table 2.1, to see if the variables are associated as predicted. In Whiting's sample of 172 societies, each case is assigned to a box, or cell, in the table, depending on how the society is measured on the two variables of interest. For example, a society that has a long postpartum sex taboo and a low-protein diet is placed in the third row of the Long Duration column. (In Whiting's sample [see Table 2.1], there are 27 such societies.) A society that has a short postpartum sex taboo and a low-protein diet is placed in the third row in the Short Duration column. (There are 20 such societies in the sample.) The statistical question is: Does the way the cases are distributed in the six central cells of the table generally support Whiting's prediction? If we looked just at the table, we might not know what to answer. Many cases appear to be in the expected places. For example, most of the high-protein cases

| | TABLE 2.1 | Association Between Availability of Protein and Duration of Postpartum Sex Taboo |

AVAILABILITY OF PROTEIN	DURATION OF POSTPARTUM SEX TABOO		
	Short (0–1 Year)	Long (More Than One Year)	Total
High	47	15	62
Medium	38	25	63
Low	20	27	47
Total	105	67	172

Source: Based on Whiting 1964, 520.

(47 of 62) have short taboos, and most of the low-protein cases (27 of 47) have long taboos. But there are also many exceptions (e.g., 20 cases have low protein and a short taboo). So, although many cases appear to be in the expected places, there are also many exceptions. Do the exceptions invalidate the prediction? How many exceptions would compel us to reject the hypothesis? Here is where we resort to *statistical tests of significance.*

Statisticians have devised various tests that tell us how "perfect" a result must be to convince us to believe that there is probably an association between the variables of interest, and that one variable generally predicts the other. Essentially, every statistical result is evaluated in the same objective way. We ask: What is the chance that this result is purely accidental, that there is no association at all between the two variables? Although some of the mathematical ways of answering this question are complicated, the answer always involves a **probability value** (or *p-value*)—the likelihood that the observed result or a stronger one could have occurred by chance. The statistical test used by Whiting gives a *p*-value of less than .01 ($p < .01$) for the observed result. In other words, there is less than 1 chance out of 100 that the relationship observed is purely accidental. A *p*-value of less than .01 is a fairly low probability; most social scientists conventionally agree to call any result with a *p*-value of .05 or less (5 or fewer chances out of 100) a **statistically significant**, or probably true, result. When we describe relationships or associations in the rest of this book, we are almost always referring to results that have been found to be statistically significant.

But why should a probably true relationship have any exceptions? If a theory is really correct, shouldn't *all* the cases fit? There are many reasons why we can never expect a perfect result. First, even if a theory is correct (e.g., if a low-protein diet really does favor the adoption of a long postpartum sex taboo), there may still be other causes that we have not investigated. Some of the societies could have a long taboo even though they have high protein. For example, societies that depend mostly on hunting for their food, and would therefore be classified as having a high-protein diet, may have a problem carrying infants from one campsite to another and may practice a long postpartum sex taboo so that two infants will not have to be carried at the same time.

Exceptions to the predicted relationship might also occur because of *cultural lag.*[24] Cultural lag occurs when change in one aspect of culture takes time to produce change in another aspect. Suppose that a society recently changed crops and is now no longer a low-protein society but still practices the taboo. This society would be an exception to the predicted relationship, but it might fit the theory if it stopped practicing the taboo in a few years. Measurement inaccuracy is another source of exception. Whiting's measure of protein, which is based on the major sources of food, is not a very precise measure of protein in the diet. It does not take into account the possibility that a "tree crop" society might get a lot of protein from fishing or raising pigs. Some supposedly low-protein societies might therefore have been misclassified, which could be one reason why there are 20 cases in the lowest cell in the left-hand column of Table 2.1. Measurement error usually produces exceptions.

Significant statistical associations that are predictable from a theory offer tentative support for the theory. But much more is needed before we can be fairly confident about the theory. Replication is needed to confirm whether other researchers can reproduce the predictions using other samples. Other predictions should be derived from the theory to see if they too are supported. The theory should be pitted against alternative explanations to see which

Probability value (*p-value*) The likelihood that an observed result could have occurred by chance.

Statistically significant Refers to a result that would occur very rarely by chance. The result (and stronger ones) would occur fewer than 5 times out of 100 by chance.

theory works better. We may have to combine theories if the alternative explanations also predict the relationship in question. The research process in science thus requires time and patience. Perhaps most important, it requires that researchers be humble. No matter how wonderful one's own theory seems, it is important to acknowledge that it may be wrong. If we do not acknowledge that possibility, we cannot be motivated to test our theories. If we don't test our theories, we can never tell the difference between a better or worse theory, and we will be saddled forever with our present ignorance. In science, knowledge or understanding is explained variation. Thus, if we want to understand more, we have to keep testing our beliefs against sets of objective evidence that could contradict our beliefs.

Types of Research in Anthropology

2.4 Differentiate the types of research in anthropology.

Anthropologists use several methods to conduct research. Each has certain advantages and disadvantages in generating and testing explanations. The types of research in anthropology can be classified according to two criteria. One is the spatial scope of the study (e.g., the analysis of a single society, analysis of societies in a region, or analysis of a worldwide sample of societies). The other criterion is the temporal scope of the study—historical versus nonhistorical. Combinations of these criteria are shown in Table 2.2.

In this section, we mostly discuss research strategies in cultural anthropology. However, most of these have parallels in archaeology and biological anthropology, as Table 2.2 makes clear. Archaeology and biological anthropology have special methods, and we devote the last section of the chapter to some of those methods.

Ethnography

Around the beginning of the 20th century, anthropologists realized that, if they were to produce anything of scientific value, they would have to study their subject in depth. To describe cultures more accurately, they started to live among the people they were studying. They observed, and even took part in, the important events of those societies and carefully questioned the people about their native customs. This method is known as **participant-observation**. Participant-observation always involves **fieldwork**, which is firsthand experience with the people being studied, but fieldwork may also involve other methods, such as conducting a census or a survey.[25]

Fieldwork, the cornerstone of modern anthropology, is the means by which most anthropological information is obtained. Regardless of other methods that anthropologists may use, participant-observation conducted usually for a year or more is regarded as

Participant-observation Living among the people being studied—observing, questioning, and (when possible) taking part in the important events of the group. Writing or otherwise recording notes on observations, questions asked and answered, and things to check out later are parts of participant-observation.

Fieldwork Firsthand experience with the people being studied and the usual means by which anthropological information is obtained. Regardless of other methods that anthropologists may use (e.g., censuses, surveys), fieldwork usually involves participant-observation for an extended period of time, often a year or more. See **Participant-observation**.

TABLE 2.2	Types of Research in Anthropology	
Scope	**Nonhistorical**	**Historical**
Single case	Ethnography/fieldwork*	Ethnohistory*
	Archaeological site excavation*	Culture history*
	Single species study/fieldwork*	Evolutionary history of a species*
	Language study/fieldwork*	Language history
Region	Controlled comparison	Controlled comparison
	Regional comparison of archaeological or other sites	Regional comparison of archaeological or other sites
	Cross-species comparison	Cross-species comparison
	Language family comparison	Language family comparison
Worldwide sample	Cross-cultural research	Cross-historical research
	Cross-archaeological research	Cross-archaeological research
	Cross-species comparison	Cross-species comparison
	Cross-linguistic comparison	Comparative historical linguistics

*All of these can also involve comparisons within the research setting—of different individuals, social groups, populations, or sites.

fundamental. In contrast to the casual descriptions of travelers and adventurers, anthropologists' descriptions record, describe, analyze, and eventually formulate a picture of the culture, or at least part of it.[26] After doing fieldwork, an anthropologist may prepare an *ethnography*, a description and analysis of a single society.

How an anthropologist goes about doing long-term participant-observation in another culture—and, more important, doing it well—is not so straightforward. Much of it depends on the person, the culture, and the interaction between the two. Without a doubt, the experience is physically and psychologically demanding, comparable often to a rite of passage. Although it helps enormously to learn the local language before going, often it is not possible to do so, and so most anthropologists find themselves struggling to communicate in addition to trying to figure out how to behave properly. Participant-observation carries its own dilemma. Participation implies living like the people who are being studied, trying to understand subjectively what they think and feel by doing what they do, whereas observation implies a certain amount of objectivity and detachment.[27] Because participant-observation is such a personal experience, it is not surprising that anthropologists have begun to realize that *reflecting* on their experiences and their personal interaction with the people they live with is an important part of understanding the enterprise.

An essential part of the participant-observation process is finding some knowledgeable people who are willing to work with you (anthropologists call them *informants*) to help you interpret what you observe and tell you about aspects of the culture that you may not have a chance to see or may not be entitled to see. For example, it is not likely that you will see many weddings in a village of 200 people in a year or two of fieldwork. So how can you know who will be a good informant? It is obviously important to find people who are easy to talk to and who understand what information you need. But how do you know who is knowledgeable? You can't just assume that the people you get along with have the most knowledge. (Besides, knowledge is often specialized; one person may know much more about some subjects than others.) At a minimum, you have to try out a few different people to compare what they tell you about a subject. What if they disagree? How do you know who is more trustworthy or accurate? Fortunately, formal methods have been developed to help anthropologists select the most knowledgeable informants. One method, called the cultural consensus model, relies on the principle that those things that most informants

Anthropologist Nadine Peacock doing fieldwork among the Efe in the Ituri Forest, Zaire.

agree on are probably cultural. After you establish which things appear to be cultural by asking a sample of informants the same questions about a particular cultural domain, it will be easy to discover which informants are very likely to give answers that closely match the cultural consensus. These individuals are your best bets to be the most knowledgeable in that domain.[28] It may seem paradoxical, but the most knowledgeable and helpful individuals are not necessarily "typical" individuals. Many anthropologists have pointed out that key informants are likely to feel somewhat marginal in their culture. After all, why would they want to spend so much time with the visiting anthropologist?[29]

Participant-observation is valuable for understanding some aspects of culture, particularly the things that are the most public, readily talked about, and most widely agreed upon. But more systematic methods are important too: mapping, house-to-house censuses, behavior observations (e.g., to determine how people spend their time), as well as focused interviews with a sample of informants.

Ethnographies and ethnographic articles on particular topics provide much of the essential data for all kinds of studies in cultural anthropology. To make a comparison of societies in a given region or worldwide, anthropologists would require ethnographic data on many societies. With regard to the goal of generating theory, ethnography—with its in-depth, firsthand, long-term observation—provides investigators with a wealth of descriptive material covering a wide range of phenomena. Thus, it may stimulate interpretations about the way different aspects of the culture are related to each other and to features of the environment. Ethnographers in the field have the opportunity to get to know the context of a society's customs by directly asking the people about those customs and by observing the phenomena that appear to be associated with those practices. In addition, ethnographers who develop a possible explanation for some custom can test that hunch by collecting new information related to it. In this sense, ethnographers are similar to physicians who are trying to understand why a patient has certain symptoms of illness.

Although ethnography is extremely useful for generating explanations, a field study of a single site does not generally provide sufficient data to test a hypothesis. For example, an ethnographer may think that a particular society practices *polygyny* (one man married to two or more women simultaneously) because it has more women than men. But the ethnographer could not be reasonably sure that this explanation was correct unless the results of a comparative study of a sample of societies showed that most polygynous societies have more women than men. After all, the fact that one society has both these conditions could be a historical accident rather than a result of some necessary connection between the two conditions.

Ethnography as Source Material

Ethnography is a valuable source of information for anthropologists in all the subfields of the discipline. Data from ethnographies is particularly useful in cross-cultural research and remains the single best source of information on the many aspects of culture that anthropologists seek to understand. Because undertaking ethnographic research is time-consuming and challenging, however, the available data on a particular culture may be several decades old. How, then, do we know whether the data are still valid? The answer lies in how the concept of time is treated by anthropologists. Changes in fundamental cultural beliefs, customs, and traits have occurred slowly in most cultures—a fact that explains why anthropologists use the present tense, or the so-called ethnographic present, in their written observations. It can safely be assumed that general observations will probably hold true whether the ethnography was written 20 years or 10 years ago. However, anthropologists are also aware that dramatic cultural change occurs. When using ethnographic data from several cultures, anthropologists make sure that all of the information was gathered in the same time period. That way, the data are considered valid for each of the cultures at the same point in time and a comparison can be made reliably.

Within-Culture Comparisons

Ethnographers could test a theory within one society if they decide to compare individuals, families, households, communities, or districts. The natural variability that exists can be used to create a comparison. Suppose we want to verify Whiting's assumption that longer postpartum taboos enhance the survival of babies in a society with a low-protein diet. Although almost all couples might practice a long postpartum sex taboo because it is customary, some couples might not adhere to the taboo consistently, and some couples might not conceive quickly after the taboo is lifted. So we would expect some variation in spacing between births. If we collected information on the births of each mother and the survival outcome of each birth, we would be able to compare the survival rates of children born a short time after the mother's last pregnancy with those of children born after longer intervals. A significantly higher survival rate for the births after longer intervals would support Whiting's theory. What if some communities within the society had access to more protein than others? If Whiting's theory is correct, those communities with more protein should also have a higher survival rate for babies. If there were variation in the length of the postpartum sex taboo, the communities with more protein should have shorter taboos.

Whether or not we can design intracultural tests of hypotheses depends on whether we have sufficient variability in the variables of the hypotheses. We do more often than not, and we can make use of that variation to test hypotheses within a culture.

Regional Controlled Comparisons

In a regional controlled comparison, anthropologists compare ethnographic information obtained from societies found in a particular region—societies that presumably have similar histories and occupy similar environments. Anthropologists who conduct a regional comparison are apt to be familiar with the complex of cultural features associated with that region. These features may provide a good understanding of the context of the phenomenon that is to be explained. An anthropologist's knowledge of the region under study, however, is probably not as great as the ethnographer's knowledge of a single society. Still, the anthropologist's understanding of local details is greater in a regional comparison than in a worldwide comparison. The worldwide comparison is necessarily so broad that the investigator is unlikely to know a great deal about any of the societies being compared.

The regional controlled comparison is useful not only for generating explanations but also for testing them. Because some of the societies being compared will have the characteristic that is to be explained and some will not, anthropologists can determine whether the conditions hypothesized to be related are in fact related, at least in that region. We must remember, however, that two or more conditions may be related in one region for reasons peculiar to that region. Therefore, an explanation supported in one region may not fit others.

Cross-Cultural Research

Anthropologists can generate interpretations on the basis of worldwide comparisons by looking for differences between those societies having and those lacking a particular characteristic. But the most common use of worldwide comparisons has been to test explanations. An example is Whiting's test of his theory about the adaptive functions of a long postpartum sex taboo. Recall that Whiting hypothesized that, if his theory were correct, variation in protein supplies in the adult diet should predict variation in the duration of the postpartum sex taboo. Cross-cultural researchers first identify conditions that should generally be associated if a particular theory is correct. Then they look at a worldwide sample of societies to see if the expected association generally holds true. Although it is possible for cross-cultural researchers to choose any set of societies upon which to test theories and hypotheses, it is preferable to avoid personal bias in the selection of the sample societies. One of the worst possible samples would be to choose the ethnographies from your own bookshelf (you are unlikely to have collected them in a random way). As we indicated in the sampling section, most cross-culturalists choose a published sample of societies that was not constructed for any specific hypothesis test. Two of the most widely used samples are the Standard Cross-Cultural Sample (SCCS) of 186 societies and the annually growing *eHRAF World Cultures*. Because HRAF actually contains ethnographies that are subject-indexed by paragraph, researchers can quickly find information to code a new variable across a large number of societies. In contrast, the SCCS sample contains pointers to ethnography, not ethnographies themselves. However, thousands of variables have now been coded by other researchers for this sample, so researchers who want to use data coded by others tend to use this sample[30] or the overlap between the SCCS sample and eHRAF.[31]

The advantage of cross-cultural research is that the conclusion drawn from it is probably applicable to most societies, if the sample used for testing has been more or less randomly selected and therefore is representative of the world. In other words, the results of a cross-cultural study are probably applicable to most societies and most regions, in contrast with the results of a regional comparison, which may or may not be applicable to other regions.

As we have noted, the greater the number of societies examined in a study, the less likely investigators will have detailed knowledge of the societies involved. So, if a cross-cultural test does not support a particular explanation, the investigators may not know enough about the sample societies to know how to modify the interpretation or come up with a new one. In this situation, the anthropologists may reexamine the details of one or more particular societies to stimulate fresh thinking on the subject. Another limitation of cross-cultural research, as a means of both generating and testing explanations, is that only those explanations for which the required information is generally available in ethnographies can be tested. Investigators interested in explaining something that has not been generally described must resort to some other research strategy to collect data.

Historical Research

Ethnohistory consists of studies based on descriptive materials about a single society at more than one point in time. It provides the essential data for historical studies of all types, just as ethnography provides the essential data for all nonhistorical types of research. Ethnohistorical data may consist of sources other than the ethnographic reports prepared by anthropologists—accounts by explorers, missionaries, traders, and government officials. Ethnohistorians, like historians, cannot simply assume that all the documents they find are simply descriptions of fact; they were written by very different kinds of people with very different goals and purposes. So they need to separate carefully what may be fact from what may be speculative interpretation. To reconstruct how a culture changed over hundreds of years, where the natives left few or no written accounts, anthropologists have to seek out travelers' accounts and other historical documents that were written by non-natives. Mary Helms had to do this when she decided to do fieldwork among the Miskito of Nicaragua, to reconstruct how their life had changed under the conditions of European colonialism. She was particularly interested in discovering why the Miskito were able to preserve a lot of political independence.[32]

In terms of generating and testing hypotheses, studies of single societies over time tend to be subject to the same limitations as studies of single societies confined to a single period. Like their nonhistorical counterparts, studies that concentrate on a single society observed through time are likely to generate more than one hypothesis, but they do not generally provide the opportunity to establish with reasonable certainty which of those hypotheses is correct. Cross-cultural historical studies (of which we have only a few examples thus far) suffer from the opposite limitation. They provide ample means of testing hypotheses through comparison, but, because of the necessity of working with secondhand data, they are severely constrained in their ability to generate hypotheses derived from the available data.

There is, however, one advantage to historical studies of any type. The goal of theory in cultural anthropology is to explain variation in cultural patterns, that is, to specify what conditions will favor one cultural pattern rather than another. Such specification

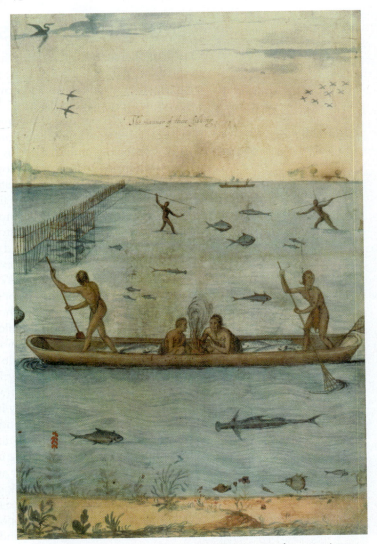

Ethnohistorians need to analyze pieces of information from a variety of sources such as the accounts of European explorers. Pictured here is a group of Roanoke Native Americans fishing in the late 1500s. It provides ethnohistorians with good information on how these people harvested fish.

Source: John White/Copyright The British Museum.

requires us to assume that the supposed causal, or favoring, conditions antedated the pattern to be explained. Theories or explanations, then, imply a sequence of changes over time, which are the stuff of history. Therefore, if we want to come closer to an understanding of the reasons for the cultural variations we are investigating, we should examine historical sequences. They will help us determine whether the conditions we think caused various phenomena truly antedated those phenomena and thus might more reliably be said to have caused them. If we can examine historical sequences, we may be able to make sure that we do not put the cart before the horse.

The major impediment to historical research is that collecting and analyzing historical data—particularly when they come from the scattered accounts of explorers, missionaries, and traders—tends to be very time consuming. It may be more efficient to test explanations nonhistorically first to eliminate some interpretations. Only when an interpretation survives a nonhistorical test should we look to historical data to test the presumed sequence. Archaeological evidence is one answer to this problem; many archaeological sites contain evidence from several cultures that lived in that location over time. Even when sites contain evidence for only one period of time, sites dating from different times can be compared to examine historical trends.

Studying the Distant Past

2.5 Describe the four kinds of evidence that archaeologists and paleoanthropologists find and how they analyze it.

One goal of archaeological research is the description or reconstruction of what happened in the past. Archaeologists attempt to determine how people lived in a particular place at a particular time, and when and how their lifestyles changed. Also of interest, of course, is whether new populations carrying new cultures arrived, or whether people with a particular culture moved out of a given area. Creating histories of cultures and their changes over time is called, simply enough, culture history. Doing culture history was the primary goal of archaeology until the 1950s.[33]

Culture history A history of the cultures that lived in a given area over time. Until the 1950s, building such culture histories was a primary goal of archaeological research.

A second major goal of archaeological research, and one that has become the primary goal since the 1950s, is testing specific explanations about human evolution and behavior. In part, this change in focus results from our increased knowledge about the past—the culture history of many areas is well known today. But this change is also due to changes going on in anthropology as a whole. Historical particularism was dominant in American anthropology until the 1950s. It suggested that variation in human cultures was best explained by considering the specific historical developments of particular cultures. Like the purpose of historical particularism, the purpose of culture history was to trace historical developments. After the 1950s, a variety of new approaches arose in anthropology, most of them sharing the idea that the environment and how humans use it actively shapes cultures and mostly explains cultural variability. Archaeology became a key tool for anthropologists attempting to understand how changes in the ways humans used the environment explained variation in human cultures. One of the results of this focus on hypothesis testing and human use of the environment was research on agricultural origins. Another was a concern with the rise of cities and states, which radically transformed human use of the environment. In addition to testing explanations, archaeology has a primary role within anthropology in its attempt to identify and understand general trends and patterns in human biological and cultural evolution. As we discussed earlier, cross-cultural research (comparative ethnography) has this goal as well. But only archaeology is able to look through long stretches of time and directly examine evolutionary trends. A major emphasis in paleoanthropology is demonstrating long-term trends and patterns in the biological evolution of humans. These trends and patterns help us understand how and why we have come to be the way we are.

Archaeologists and paleoanthropologists rely on four kinds of evidence to learn about the past: *artifacts, ecofacts, fossils,* and *features*.

Artifacts

Artifact Any object made by a human.

Anything made or modified by humans is an **artifact**. The book you are reading now, the chair you are sitting in, the pen you are taking notes with are all artifacts. In fact, we are surrounded by artifacts, most of which we will lose or throw away. That is exactly how things enter what we call the "archaeological record." Think about it: How much garbage do you produce in a day? What kinds of things do you throw away? Mostly paper, probably, but also wood (from the ice cream bar you ate at lunch), plastic (like the pen that ran out of ink last night), and even metal (the dull blade on your razor). Into the garbage they go and out to the dump or landfill. Under the right conditions, many of those items will survive for future archaeologists to find. Most of the artifacts that make up the archaeological record are just this kind of mundane waste—the accumulated garbage of daily life that archaeologists may recover and examine to reconstruct what daily life was like long ago. By far the most common artifacts from the past are stone tools, which archaeologists call **lithics**. Indeed, lithics are the only kind of artifact available for 99 percent of human history.

Lithics The technical name for tools made from stone.

2 Ecofacts

Ecofacts are natural objects that humans have used or affected. A good example is the bone from animals that people have eaten. These bones are somewhat like artifacts, but they haven't been made or modified by humans, just used and discarded by them. Another example is pollen found at archaeological sites. Because humans bring plants back to their houses to use, pollens from many plants are commonly found. These pollens may not have come from the same location. The only reason they are together is that they have been brought together by human use. Other examples are the remains of insect and animal pests that associate with humans, such as cockroaches and mice. Their remains are found in sites because they associate with humans and survive by taking advantage of the conditions that humans create. Their presence is in part caused by human presence, and thus they are also considered ecofacts.

Ecofacts Natural items that humans have used; things such as the remains of animals eaten by humans or plant pollens found on archaeological sites are examples of ecofacts.

3 Fossils

Fossils, although rare, are particularly informative about human biological evolution. **Fossils** may be impressions of an insect or leaf on a muddy surface that now is stone. A fossil may also consist of the actual hardened remains of an animal's skeletal structure. When an animal dies, the organic matter that made up its body begins to deteriorate. The teeth and skeletal structure are composed largely of inorganic mineral salts, and soon they are all that remains. Under most conditions, these parts eventually deteriorate too. But once in a great while, conditions are favorable for preservation—for instance, when volcanic ash, limestone, or highly mineralized groundwater is present to form a high-mineral environment. If the remains are buried under such circumstances, the minerals in the ground may become bound into the structure of the teeth or bone, hardening the remains and thus making them less likely to deteriorate.

Fossils The hardened remains or impressions of plants and animals that lived in the past.

But we don't have fossil remains of everything that lived in the past, and sometimes we only have fragments from one or a few individuals. So the fossil record is very incomplete. For example, Robert Martin estimates that the earth has probably seen 6,000 primate species; remains of only 3 percent of those species have been found. It is hardly surprising that primate paleontologists cannot identify most of the evolutionary connections between early and later forms. The task is particularly difficult with small mammals, such as the early primates, which are less likely than large animals to be preserved in the fossil record.[34]

4 Features

Features are kinds of artifacts, but archaeologists distinguish them from other artifacts because they cannot be easily removed from an archaeological site. Hearths are good examples. When humans build a fire on bare ground, the soil becomes heated and is changed—all the water is driven out of it and its crystalline structure is broken down and reformed. When archaeologists find a hearth, what exactly is found? An area of hard, reddish, even slightly magnetic soil, often surrounded by charcoal and ash. Here, then, is an artifact—an object of human manufacture. But it would be very hard, if not impossible, for archaeologists to take the hearth back to the lab for study like a lithic or ceramic. A hearth is really an intrinsic feature of a site—hence the name *feature*.

Features Artifacts of human manufacture that cannot be removed from an archaeological site. Hearths, storage pits, and buildings are examples of features.

Hearths are common features, but the most common features by far are called *pits*. Pits are simply holes dug by humans that are later filled with garbage or eroded soil. They are usually fairly easy to distinguish because the garbage or soil they are filled with is often different in color and texture from the soil the pit was dug into. *Living floors* are another

Vietnamese archaeologists expose the remains of the ancient citadel of Hanoi, preserved below the modern city.

common type of feature. These are the places where humans lived and worked. The soils in these locations are often compacted through human activity and are full of minute pieces of garbage—seeds, small stone flakes, beads, and the like—that became embedded in the floor. A large or very deep area of such debris is called a *midden*. Middens are often the remains of garbage dumps or areas repeatedly used over long periods of time, such as caves. Finally, *buildings* are common features on archaeological sites. These can range from the remains of stone rings that once held down the sides of tents to palaces built of stones that had been shaped and fitted together. Even the remains of wooden houses (or parts of them) have been preserved under some conditions. Features can be a diverse array of things that provide lots of information about the past.

Finding the Evidence of the Past

Evidence of the past is all around us, but finding it is not always easy or productive. Archaeologists and paleoanthropologists usually restrict their searches to what are called *sites*. **Sites** are known or suspected locations of past human activity that contain a record of that activity. Sites can be small, such as places where humans camped for perhaps only one night, or as large as ancient cities.

Sites are created when the remnants of human activity are covered or buried by some natural process. The most dramatic process is volcanic activity. The most impressive example of this must be Pompeii, an entire city that was buried in the eruption of Mount Vesuvius in A.D. 79. Today, archaeologists are digging out the city and finding the remains of ancient life just as it was left in the moments before the eruption.[35] Less dramatic processes are the natural processes of dirt accumulation and erosion. Wind- or water-borne soil and debris can cover a site either quickly (as in a flood) or over a long period of time, preserving intact the artifacts, ecofacts, fossils, and features left by humans. Finally, the processes through which soils are built up can also bury artifacts, ecofacts, fossils, and features in a way that allows archaeologists to uncover them later. In forests, for example, falling leaves cover the locations where humans camped. Over time, the leaves decay and build up soil, covering the remains of the human encampment slowly but completely over many years.

Sites Locations where the material remains of human activity have been preserved in a way that archaeologists or paleoanthropologists can recover them.

Because humans often reuse good locations to live and work in, many sites contain the remains of numerous human occupations. The most valuable sites to archaeologists and paleoanthropologists are those in which the burial processes worked quickly enough that each use of the site is clearly separated from the previous one. Such sites are called **stratified**; each layer, or *stratum,* of human occupation is separate, like a layer in a layer cake. Not only do stratified sites allow archaeologists or paleoanthropologists to distinguish the sequence of site occupations, but the strata themselves provide a way to know the relative ages of the occupations—earlier occupations will always be below later ones.

There is no single method of finding sites, and indeed many sites are found by happenstance. But when archaeologists and paleoanthropologists want to go out and find sites, they typically employ one of two basic methods: pedestrian survey and remote sensing. *Pedestrian survey* is what the name suggests—walking around and looking for sites. But archaeologists and paleoanthropologists can use sampling and systematic surveying methods to reduce the area to be covered on foot. *Remote sensing* techniques allow archaeologists and paleoanthropologists to find archaeological deposits from a remote location, usually the current surface of the ground beneath which the archaeological deposits are buried. Most remote sensing techniques are borrowed from exploration geology and are the same ones geologists use to find mineral or oil deposits. They typically involve the measurement of minute variations in phenomena like the earth's magnetic or gravitational field, or changes in an electric current or pulse of energy directed into the ground. When these subtle changes, called *anomalies,* are located, more detailed exploration can be done to map the extent and depth of the buried archaeological deposits.

Whether they are identified by pedestrian survey or remote sensing, there is only one way to recover archaeological deposits once they are found them—by *excavation.* **Excavation** itself is a complex process with two goals: (1) to find every scrap of evidence (or a statistically representative sample) about the past that a given site holds and (2) to record the horizontal and vertical location of that evidence with precision. Archaeologists and paleoanthropologists have developed many excavation strategies and techniques to accomplish these goals, but all of them involve the careful removal of the archaeological deposits; the recovery of artifacts, ecofacts, fossils, and features from the soil in which those deposits have been buried; and the detailed recording of where each artifact, ecofact, fossil, and feature was located on the site.

To date, no one has figured out a way to recover artifacts, ecofacts, fossils, and features from a site without destroying the site in the process, and this is one of the strange ironies of archaeological research. As we discuss shortly, the relationships between and among artifacts, ecofacts, fossils, and features are of most interest to archaeologists, and precisely these relationships are destroyed when archaeologists remove them from a site. For this reason, most excavation by professional archaeologists today is done only when a site is threatened with destruction, and then only by highly trained personnel using rigorous techniques. Archaeologists and paleoanthropologists collect data in basically the same ways, with one important difference. Archaeologists are most concerned with recovering intact features, whereas paleoanthropologists are most concerned with recovering intact fossils. This leads to some differences in approaches to collecting data, particularly where to look. So archaeologists tend to seek out undisturbed sites where intact features can be found. In contrast, disturbances are a plus for paleoanthropologists, because disturbed sites may make finding fossils easier—they may be eroding out of the surface of the ground and be easily visible without digging. This doesn't mean archaeologists never excavate disturbed sites, because they do. And paleoanthropologists have sometimes made important discoveries by excavating undisturbed sites.[36]

Putting It All in Context

You might have gained the impression from our discussion that archaeologists and paleoanthropologists analyze artifacts, ecofacts, fossils, and features as individual objects,

Stratified An archaeological deposit that contains successive layers or strata.

Excavation The careful removal of the archaeological deposits; the recovery of artifacts, ecofacts, fossils, and features from the soil in which those deposits have been buried.

Perspectives on Gender

Women in the Shell Mound Archaic

How we can learn about and understand gender roles in prehistoric cultures? How is gender preserved in the archaeological record? Information about gender roles can be recovered if one is aware of how particular kinds of material culture are associated ethnographically with particular gender roles and with changes in them over time. Archaeologists argue that such an awareness leads not only to a better understanding of gender in prehistory but can also lead to a fuller understanding of prehistoric cultures overall.

An example is Cheryl Claassen's work on the Shell Mound Archaic culture of the Tennessee River Valley. The Shell Mound Archaic peoples were hunter and gatherers who lived between about 5,500 and 3,000 years ago. The most distinctive feature of the Shell Mound Archaic is the large mounds of mollusk shells they constructed for burying their dead. Tens of thousands of shells were piled together to create these mounds. Yet, around 3,000 years ago, shellfishing and thus the creation of shell burial mounds stopped abruptly. Claassen wondered why.

Suggested explanations include climate change, overexploitation of shellfish, and the migration of shellfishing peoples from the area. None has proven wholly satisfactory. In contemporary cultures, women and children typically do the shellfishing, and Claassen decided to approach the problem through the perspective of women's workloads. The end of shellfishing would have meant that women would have had a lot of free time—free time that could have been put to use in some other way. Did some other activities become more important, so that women's labor was needed more for those other tasks?

Artist's interpretation of a Shell Mound Archaic camp.

Women's labor might have been redirected toward domesticated crops. There is archaeological evidence that about 3,000 years ago several productive crops that required intensive labor came into wide use. Women were likely the ones burdened with such work. They not only would have harvested these crops but also would have been the ones to process and prepare meals from them. Thus, the emergence of agricultural economies would have required women to undertake new labor in food production and processing that may well have forced them to stop engaging in other tasks, like shellfishing, especially if the new tasks produced a larger food supply.

The development of agricultural activities might also have brought about changes in ritual and ceremonialism. The shell burial mounds were clearly central to Shell Mound Archaic death ceremonies. Later societies in the region buried their dead in earthen mounds. Could this be a reflection of the new importance dirt had in an emerging agricultural economy? If so, what role did women play in ceremonies of death and burial? If they were no longer the providers of the raw materials needed for burial, does that mean their status in society as a whole changed?

We may never know exactly why the Shell Mound Archaic disappeared or how women's work and women's roles in society changed. But as Claassen points out, taking a gender perspective provides new avenues along which to pursue answers to these questions as well as interesting new questions to pursue.

Sources: Claassen 1991, 2009.

Context The relationships between and among artifacts, ecofacts, fossils, and features.

separate from one another. Nothing could be farther from the truth. In fact, putting these materials in context with one another is really what archaeology and paleoanthropology are all about. **Context** is how and why the artifacts and other materials are related. Artifacts, ecofacts, fossils, and features in isolation may be beautiful or interesting by themselves, but only when they are placed in context with the other materials found on a site are we able to "read" and tell the story of the past.

To illustrate this point, let's consider a set of letters that were found separately: A E G I M N N. They are arranged here in alphabetical order, the way a set of beautiful artifacts might be arranged in a museum display in order of size. Do these arrangements tell us anything? No. What if we knew something about the relationships between and among these letters—their context? What if, for example, we knew that the *M* was the first letter found, and that the *A* and *E* were found next to the *M,* but in reverse order, that one *N* was found between the *E* and *I,* and that the other *N* was found between the *I* and the *G?* Knowing in what context the letters were found would tell us that the letters should be arranged like this: *M E A N I N G.* And meaning is exactly what context gives to artifacts, ecofacts, fossils, and features.

Dating the Evidence from the Past

An important, indeed vital, part of putting artifacts and other materials into context is putting them in chronological order. To reconstruct the evolutionary history of the primates, for example, one must know how old primate fossils are. For some time, relative dating methods were the only methods available. The last half century has seen important advances in absolute dating, including techniques that allow the dating of the earliest phases of primate evolution. **Relative dating** is used to determine the age of a specimen or deposit relative to another specimen or deposit. **Absolute dating,** or **chronometric dating,** is used to measure how old a specimen or deposit is in years.

Relative Dating Methods   The earliest, and still the most commonly used, method of relative dating is based on **stratigraphy,** the study of how different rock or soil formations are laid down in successive layers or strata (see Figure 2.1). Older layers are generally deeper or lower than more recent layers. Indicator artifacts or ecofacts are used to establish a stratigraphic sequence for the relative dating of new finds. These **indicator artifacts or ecofacts** are items of human manufacture or remains from animals and plants that spread widely over short periods of time, or that disappeared or changed fairly rapidly. Different artifacts and ecofacts are used as indicators of relative age in different areas of the world. In Africa, elephants, pigs, and horses have been particularly important in establishing stratigraphic sequences. Figure 2.1 shows the stratigraphy of Olduvai Gorge, an important site where early human fossils have been found. The stratigraphy here was established in part on the basis of fossil pigs.[37] The various species of pig in the successive strata are different, allowing archaeologists or paleoanthropologists to differentiate the strata based on the species found within them. Once the stratigraphy of an area is established, the relative ages of two different fossils, or features, in the same or different sites are indicated by the associated indicator artifacts or ecofacts. Major transitions in indicator artifacts or ecofacts define the epochs and larger units of geologic time. The dates of the boundaries between such units are estimated by absolute dating, described in the next section.

If a site has been disturbed, stratigraphy will not be a satisfactory way to determine relative age. As noted earlier, remains from different periods may be washed or blown together by water or wind. Or a landslide may superimpose an earlier layer on a later layer. Still, it may be possible using absolute, or chronometric, dating methods to estimate the relative age of the different fossils found together in a disturbed site.

Absolute, or Chronometric, Dating Methods   Many of the absolute dating methods are based on the decay of a radioactive isotope. Because the rate of decay is known, the age of the specimen can be estimated, within a range of possible error. **Radiocarbon,** or **carbon-14 (^{14}C), dating** is perhaps the most popularly known method of determining the absolute age of a specimen. It is based on the principle that all living matter possesses a certain amount of a radioactive form of carbon (carbon-14, or ^{14}C). Radioactive carbon, produced when nitrogen-14 is bombarded by cosmic rays, is absorbed from the air by plants and then ingested by animals that

Relative dating A method of dating fossils that determines the age of a specimen or deposit relative to a known specimen or deposit.

Absolute dating A method of dating fossils in which the actual age of a deposit or specimen is measured. Also known as **chronometric dating**.

Chronometric dating See **Absolute dating**.

Stratigraphy The study of how different rock formations and fossils are laid down in successive layers or strata. Older layers are generally deeper or lower than more recent layers.

Indicator artifacts and ecofacts Items that changed relatively rapidly and which, thus, can be used to indicate the relative age of associated items.

Radiocarbon (or carbon-14, ^{14}C) dating A dating method uses the decay of carbon-14 to date organic remains. It is reliable for dating once-living matter up to 50,000 years old.

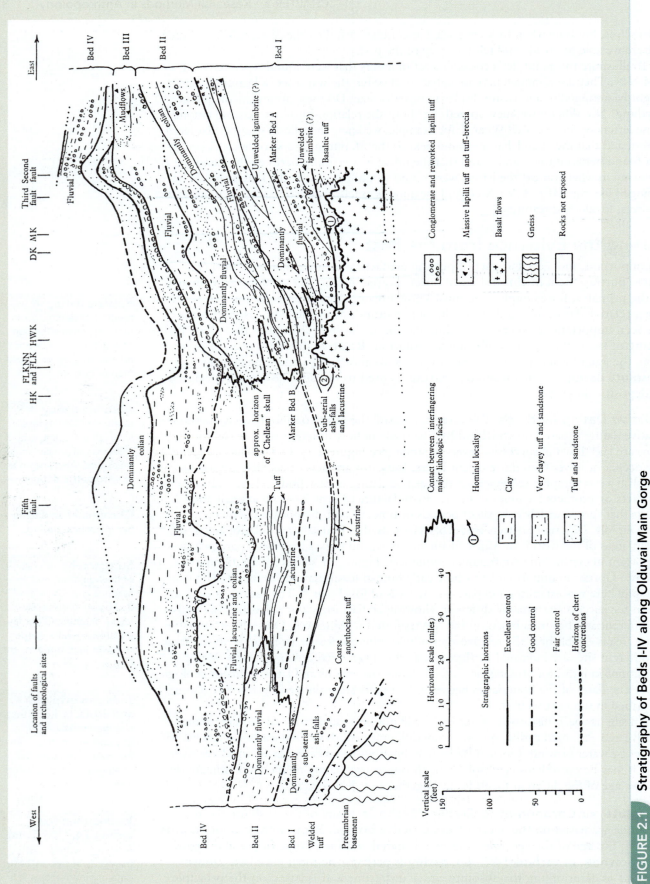

FIGURE 2.1 Stratigraphy of Beds I–IV along Olduvai Main Gorge

Notice how complex the four stratigraphic layers are—each has numerous layers of soil and rock within them. Index fossils, particularly pigs, along with a series of potassium-argon dates, allowed the researchers to identify the four major strata of the site, which correspond to four major periods of human occupation. Reprinted by permission of Cambridge University Press. Copyright © 1965.

Source: Leakey 1965.

eat the plants (see Figure 2.2). After an organism dies, it no longer takes in any of the radioactive carbon. Carbon-14 decays at a slow but steady pace and reverts to nitrogen-14. (By *decays*, we mean that the ^{14}C gives off a certain number of beta radiations per minute.) The rate at which the carbon decays—its **half-life**—is known: ^{14}C has a half-life of 5,730 years. In other words, half of the original amount of ^{14}C in organic matter will have disintegrated 5,730 years after the organism's death; half of the remaining ^{14}C will have disintegrated after another 5,730 years; and so on. After about 50,000 years, the amount of ^{14}C remaining in the organic matter is too small to permit reliable dating.

To discover how long an organism has been dead—that is, to determine how much ^{14}C is left in the organism and therefore how old it is—we either count the number of beta radiations given off per minute per gram of material or use a particle accelerator to measure the actual amount of ^{14}C in a sample. Modern ^{14}C emits about 15 beta radiations per minute per gram of material, but ^{14}C that is 5,730 years old emits only half that amount (the half-life of ^{14}C) per minute per gram. So, if a sample of some organism gives off 7.5 radiations a minute per gram, which is only half the amount given off by modern ^{14}C, the organism must be 5,730 years old. Similarly, because the amount of ^{14}C in a sample slowly declines over time, the atoms in a sample can be sent through a particle accelerator to separate them by weight (the lighter ^{12}C accelerates faster than the heavier ^{14}C) and measure the actual amount of each. This method, called accelerator mass spectrometry (AMS), is more accurate than the beta radiation method, requires only a very small sample of material, and provides a way to date specimens that are up to 80,000 years old.[38]

Another very common absolute dating technique based on radioactive decay uses potassium-40 (^{40}K), a radioactive form of potassium that decays at an established rate and forms argon-40 (^{40}Ar). The half-life of ^{40}K is a known quantity, so the age of a material containing potassium can be measured by the amount of ^{40}K compared with the amount of ^{40}Ar it contains.[39] Radioactive potassium's (^{40}K's) half-life is very long—1,330 million years. This means that **potassium-argon (K-Ar) dating** may be used to date samples from 5,000 years up to 3 billion years old.

The K-Ar method is used to date potassium-rich minerals in rock, not the fossils that may be found in the rock. A very high temperature, such as occurs in a volcanic event, drives off any original argon in the material. The amount of argon that accumulates afterward from the decay of radioactive potassium is directly related to the amount of time since the volcanic event. This type of dating has been extremely useful in East Africa, where volcanic events have occurred frequently since the Miocene, which began 24 million years ago. If the material to be dated is not rich in potassium, or the area did not experience any high-temperature events, other methods of absolute dating are required.

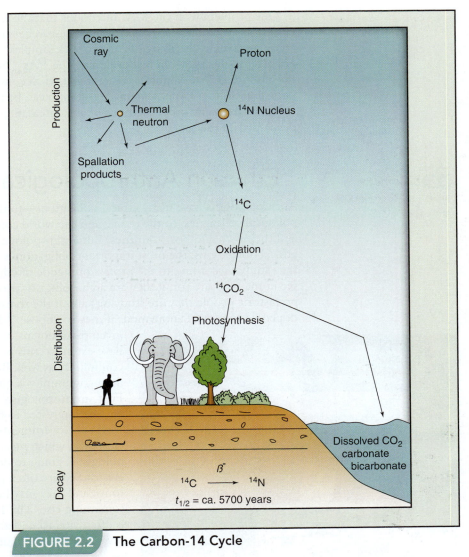

FIGURE 2.2   **The Carbon-14 Cycle**

Source: Taylor and Aitken 1997.

Half-life The time it takes for half of the atoms of a radioactive substance to decay into atoms of a different substance.

Potassium-argon (K-Ar) dating A chronometric dating method that uses the rate of decay of a radioactive form of potassium (^{40}K) into argon (^{40}Ar) to date samples from 5,000 years to 3 billion years old. The K-Ar method dates the minerals and rocks in a deposit, not the fossils themselves.

One problem with the K-Ar method is that the amounts of potassium and argon must be measured on different rock samples; researchers must assume that the potassium and argon are evenly distributed in all the rock samples from a particular stratum. Researchers got around this problem by developing the **^{40}Ar-^{39}Ar dating** method. After measuring the amount of ^{40}Ar, a nuclear reactor is used to convert another kind of argon, ^{39}Ar, to potassium so that the potassium-argon ratio can be measured from the same sample.[40]

There are many other methods of absolute dating; indeed, new methods are being developed all the time.

Ethics in Anthropological Research

2.6 Describe the ethical requirements of anthropological research.

Anthropologists have many ethical obligations—to the people they study, to their anthropological colleagues, to the public and the world community, and even to their employers and their own and host countries. But anthropologists agree that, should a conflict arise in ethical obligations, the most important obligation is to protect the interests of the people they study. According to the profession's code of ethics, anthropologists should tell people in the field site (or, if they are archaeologists, people who are direct descendants of the prehistoric people they are studying) about the research, and they should respect the right of people to remain anonymous if they so choose.[41] For this reason, informants are often given pseudonyms, or fake names; many anthropologists have extended this principle to using a fake name for the community as well. But the decision to create a fake name for a community is questionable in many circumstances.[42] First, anthropologists "stick out," and it is not hard for anyone interested to figure out where they lived and worked. Governments may have to be asked for research clearance, which means that they know where the anthropologist is going to do the fieldwork. Second, people who are studied are often proud of their place and their customs, and they may be insulted if their community is called something else. Third, important geographic information is often vital to understanding the community. You have to reveal if it is located at the confluence of two major rivers or if it is the trading center of the region. Lastly, it may be difficult for future anthropologists to conduct follow-up studies if the community is disguised. Of course, if a community were truly in danger, there would be no question that an anthropologist has an obligation to try to protect it.

Honest, objective reporting is also an obligation to the anthropological profession, to the public at large, and to the observed community. But suppose a custom or trait that the community views as reasonable is considered objectionable by outsiders? Such customs could range from acts that outsiders consider criminal, such as infanticide, to those that are considered repugnant, such as eating dogs. Archaeologists have caused outrage by presenting evidence of cannibalism in ancient populations.[43] An anthropologist may believe that publication of the information could bring harm to the population. Kim Hill and Magdalena Hurtado faced this situation when they realized that infanticide rates were high in the group they studied in South America. They did not want to play up their findings, nor did they want to dissimulate. After they met with community leaders to discuss the situation, they agreed not to publish their findings in Spanish to

Archaeologists must be aware of the effects of their work on descendant communities. Many people, for example, find the excavation of ancestor's remains to be offensive.

minimize the possibility that the local media or neighboring groups might learn of their findings.[44]

Everyday decisions like how to compensate people for their time are not easy either. Nowadays, many if not most informants expect to be paid or receive gifts. But in the early days of anthropology, in places where money was not an important part of the native economy, the decision to pay people was not a clear ethical choice. If money is rare, paying people increases the importance of money in that economy. Even nonmonetary gifts can increase inequalities or create jealousies. On the other hand, doing nothing by way of compensation doesn't seem right either. As an alternative, some anthropologists try to find some community project that they can help with—that way, everyone benefits. This is not to say that the anthropologists are necessarily a burden on the community. People often like to talk about their customs, and they may want others to appreciate their way of life. And anthropologists are often amusing. They may ask "funny" questions, and when they try to say or do customary things, they often do them all wrong. Probably every anthropologist has been laughed at sometimes in the field.

Archaeologists must always be concerned with the ethics of their work when undertaking or reporting the results of their research. Archaeology does not simply describe past cultures; it can also have a profound effect on living peoples. For example, many people find the idea of archaeologists excavating, cleaning, and preserving the remains of ancestors to be offensive. Therefore, archaeologists must be sensitive to the desires and beliefs of the populations that descend from the ones they are researching. In addition, artifacts from some ancient cultures are in great demand by art and antiquities collectors, and archaeological finds can lead to uncontrolled looting if archaeologists are not careful about how and to whom they report their discoveries. Wholesale ransacking of ancient cemeteries in some parts of China, for example, started because new archaeological discoveries led Chinese antiquities to become increasingly popular among collectors and hence increasingly valuable to those able to discover them.[45]

Although it is the ethical responsibility of archaeologists to consult with descendant populations and to be careful about how archaeological finds are reported, it is also an ethical responsibility of archaeologists to present the results of their work to the general public. Publishing archaeological results increases public awareness about the past and the importance of historic preservation. If people know how much can be learned from the archaeological record, they may be less likely to destroy it or to support those who destroy it for personal gain. Of course, when archaeologists excavate sites, they also destroy some of the context of the artifacts, ecofacts, fossils, and features found in the sites. But if they leave some of the sites unexcavated, they are preserving them (at least partially) for future investigation. To offset their partial destruction, archaeologists are ethically obligated to publish the results of their work. Reporting the results of archaeological research, therefore, plays a central role in both archaeological research and archaeological ethics.

^{40}Ar-^{39}Ar dating Used in conjunction with potassium-argon dating, this method gets around the problem of needing different rock samples to estimate potassium and argon. A nuclear reactor is used to convert the ^{39}Ar to ^{39}K, on the basis of which the amount of ^{40}K can be estimated. In this way, both argon and potassium can be estimated from the same rock sample.

Summary and Review

Explanations

2.1 Define "explanation" and discuss its role in anthropology.

- Scientists try to achieve two kinds of explanations—associations (observed relationships between two or more variables) and theories (explanations of associations).

- A theory is more complicated than an association. Some concepts or implications in a theory are unobservable; an association is based entirely on observations.

- Theories can never be proved with absolute certainty. There is always the possibility that some implication, some derivable hypothesis, will not be confirmed by future research.

- A theory may be rejectable through the method of falsification. Scientists derive predictions that should be true if the theory is correct. If the predictions turn out to be incorrect, scientists are obliged to conclude that something may be wrong with the theory.

 How do associations and theory differ as explanations?

Brief History of Theoretical Approaches

2.2 Describe some of the main theoretical approaches in anthropology.

- The prevailing evolutionary theory during the 19th century was based on a belief that culture generally evolves in a uniform and progressive manner.

- During the early 20th century, the leading opponent of early evolutionism was Franz Boas, whose historical particularism rejected the idea that universal laws governed all human culture. Boas championed collecting as much data as possible, from which laws would supposedly emerge.

- Later in the 20th century, the idea of cultural ecology, the analysis of interactions between a culture and its environment, began a debate about whether biological ecology should be separated from cultural ecology. Cultural ecologists ask how a particular culture trait may be adaptive in its environment.

- Today anthropologists who refer to themselves as evolutionary or behavioral ecologists explore how particular characteristics may be adaptive for an individual in a given environment (cultural ecologists tend to focus on the group or culture more than the individual). However, dual-inheritance theory, gives much more weight to culture as part of the evolutionary process. Dual inheritance refers to both genes and culture playing different but nonetheless important and interactive roles in transmitting traits to future generations.

- Influenced by literary criticism, a variety of "interpretive" approaches developed beginning in the 1960s. For many interpretive anthropologists, the goal of anthropology is to understand what it means to be a person living in a particular culture, rather than to explain why cultures vary. The task of understanding meaning, these scholars claim, cannot be achieved scientifically.

- Scientific anthropologists do not agree that explanation is not achievable and have developed many techniques for minimizing bias and increasing the objectivity of measurement.

 What are some examples of different theoretical approaches in anthropology?

Evidence: Testing Explanations

2.3 Explain the process of operationalization, the importance of measurement, and the value of statistical evaluation in testing explanations.

- A theory needs to be tested to determine whether it is likely to be correct. A general strategy is to predict what one would expect to find if a particular theory were correct and then to conduct an investigation to see whether the prediction is generally consistent with the data.

- A satisfactory test specifies operationally how to measure the variables involved in the relationships that are expected to exist so other researchers can try to replicate, or repeat, the results.

- Tests of predictions should use samples that are unbiased and representative of the whole. The most objective way to obtain a representative sample is to select the sample cases randomly, but sometimes anthropologists must depend on a sample that is not random.

- The results of tests are evaluated by statistical methods that assign probability values to the results. These values make it possible to distinguish between probably true and probably accidental results.

What are the main steps in testing explanations?

Types of Research in Anthropology

2.4 Differentiate the types of research in anthropology.

- The types of research in anthropology can be classified according to two criteria: (1) the spatial scope of the study and (2) the temporal scope of the study.

- In cultural anthropology, the basic research methods within the two main criteria are (a) ethnographic fieldwork and ethnohistory, (b) historical and nonhistorical regional controlled comparisons, and (c) historical and nonhistorical cross-cultural research.

What are the main types of research in anthropology?

Studying the Distant Past

2.5 Describe the four kinds of evidence that archaeologists and paleoanthropologists find and how they analyze it.

- Three goals of archaeology are (1) to understand a culture's history, (2) to test specific explanations about human evolution and behavior, and (3) to identify and understand general trends and patterns in human biological and cultural evolution.

- Archaeologists and paleoanthropologists collect four basic types of evidence about the past: artifacts, ecofacts, fossils, and features. Artifacts are any objects made by humans. Ecofacts are natural objects that humans use or modify. Fossils are the preserved remains of ancient plants and animals. Features are artifacts that cannot be removed from archaeological sites.

- Archaeological sites are locations where the evidence of the past has been preserved. Sites are found through pedestrian survey or remote sensing, and artifacts, ecofacts, fossils, and features are recovered from sites through excavation.

- A key part of any archaeological survey or excavation is the preservation of context—the relationships between and among artifacts, ecofacts, fossils, and features.

- Accurate techniques for dating archaeological material contribute significantly to determining context. Relative dating techniques determine the age of archaeological materials relative to other materials of known ages. Absolute dating techniques determine the age of the archaeological deposits or materials themselves.

 What are examples of each kind of evidence that might be found at an archaeological site?

Ethics in Anthropological Research

2.6 Describe the ethical requirements of anthropological research.

- Anthropologists must inform the people they are studying (or the descendants of those people) about their work and its purpose.

- Anthropologists must ensure that their work does no harm and that the confidentiality of people they study is protected. They must be particularly careful to identify appropriate and nondisruptive ways to compensate groups who participate in studies.

- Archaeologists must present the results of their work to the general public. Publishing archaeological results increases public awareness about the past and the importance of historic preservation.

 Give an example of unethical behavior for an anthropologist and then a different example of ethical behavior. Explain why each is either unethical or ethical.

Think on it

1. Why are **theories** important?

2. Can a **unique event** be explained?

3. How does measurement go beyond **observation**?

4. Why is **scientific understanding** always uncertain?

3 Genetics and Evolution

LEARNING OBJECTIVES

3.1 Trace the history of thinking leading to the concept of evolution.

3.2 Describe the process of natural selection.

3.3 Specify the principles of genetics.

3.4 Identify the sources of genetic variability and discuss how each leads to new variations, becomes shuffled through populations, or becomes hybridized.

3.5 Explain what may lead to the origin of species.

3.6 Explore the concept of natural selection of behavioral traits.

Astronomers estimate that the universe has been in existence for some 15 billion years, plus or minus a few billion. To make this awesome history more understandable, Carl Sagan devised a calendar that condenses this span into a single year.[1] Using 24 days for every billion years and 1 second for every 475 years as a scale, Sagan moves from the "big bang" or beginning of the universe on January 1 to the origin of the Milky Way on May 1. In this system, September 9 marks the beginning of our solar system, and September 25 the origin of life on earth. At 10:30 in the evening of December 31, the first humanlike primates appear. Sagan's compression of history provides us with a manageable way to compare the short span of human existence with the total time span of the universe. Humanlike beings have been around for only about 90 minutes out of a 12-month period. In this book, we are concerned with what has happened in the last few hours of that year.

Some 55 million to 65 million years ago, the first primates appeared. They were ancestral to all living primates, including monkeys, apes, and humans. The early primates may or may not have lived in trees, but they had flexible digits and could grasp things. Later, about 35 million years ago, the first monkeys and apes appeared. About 15 million years ago, some 20 million years after the appearance of monkeys and apes, the immediate apelike ancestors of humans probably emerged. About 4 million years ago, the first humanlike beings appeared. Modern-looking humans evolved only about 100,000 years ago.

In this chapter, we focus on how the modern theory of evolution developed and how it accounts for change over time.

The Evolution of Evolution

Older Western ideas about nature's creatures were very different from Charles Darwin's theory of *evolution*, which suggested that different species developed, one from another, over long periods of time. In the 4th century B.C., the Greek philosophers Plato and Aristotle believed that animals and plants form a single, graded continuum going from more perfection to less perfection. Humans, of course, were at the top of this scale. Later Greek philosophers added the idea that the creator gave life or "radiance" first to humans, but some of that essence was lost at each subsequent creation.[2] Macrobius, summarizing the thinking of Plotinus, used an image that was to persist for centuries, the image of what came to be called the "chain of being": "The attentive observer will discover a connection of parts, from the Supreme God down to the last dregs of things, mutually linked together and without a break. And this is Homer's golden chain, which God, he says, bade hand down from heaven to earth."[3]

Belief in the chain of being was accompanied by the conviction that an animal or plant species could not become extinct. In fact, all things were linked to one another in a chain, and all links were necessary. Moreover, the notion of extinction threatened people's trust in God; it was unthinkable that a whole group of God's creations could simply disappear.

The idea of the chain of being persisted through the years, but philosophers, scientists, poets, and theologians did not discuss it extensively until the 18th century. Those discussions prepared the way for evolutionary theory. Ironically, although the chain of being did not allow for evolution, its idea that nature had an order of things encouraged studies of natural history and comparative anatomical studies, which stimulated the development of the idea of evolution. People were also now motivated to look for previously unknown creatures. Moreover, humans were not shocked when naturalists suggested that humans were close to apes. This notion was perfectly consistent with the idea of a chain of being; apes were simply thought to have been created with less perfection.

Early in the 18th century, an influential scientist, Carolus Linnaeus (1707–1778), classified plants and animals in a *systema naturae*, which placed humans in the same order (Primates) as apes and monkeys. Linnaeus did not suggest an evolutionary relationship between humans and apes; he mostly accepted the notion that all species were created by God and fixed in their form. Not surprisingly, then, Linnaeus is often viewed as an

3.1 ▶ Trace the history of thinking leading to the concept of evolution.

Genus A group of related species; pl., genera.

anti-evolutionist. But Linnaeus's hierarchical classification scheme, in descending order from kingdom to class, order, **genus** (a group of related species), and species, provided a framework for the idea that humans, apes, and monkeys had a common ancestor.

Others did not believe that species were fixed in their form. According to Jean-Baptiste Lamarck (1744–1829), acquired characteristics could be inherited, and therefore species could evolve; individuals who in their lifetime developed characteristics helpful to survival would pass those characteristics on to future generations, thereby changing the physical makeup of the species. For example, Lamarck explained the long neck of the giraffe as the result of successive generations of giraffes stretching their necks to reach the high leaves of trees. The stretched muscles and bones of the necks were somehow transmitted to the offspring of the neck-stretching giraffes, and eventually all giraffes came to have long necks. But because Lamarck and later biologists failed to produce evidence to support the hypothesis that acquired characteristics can be inherited, this explanation of evolution is now generally dismissed.[4]

By the 19th century, some thinkers were beginning to accept evolution whereas others were trying to refute it. For example, Georges Cuvier (1769–1832) was a leading opponent of evolution. Cuvier's theory of catastrophism proposed that a quick series of catastrophes accounted for changes in the earth and the fossil record. Cataclysms and upheavals such as Noah's flood had killed off previous sets of living creatures, which each time were replaced by new creations.

Major changes in geological thinking occurred in the 19th century. Earlier, geologist James Hutton (1726–1797) had questioned catastrophism, but his work was largely ignored. In contrast, Sir Charles Lyell's (1797–1875) volumes of the *Principles of Geology* (1830–1833), which built on Hutton's earlier work, received immediate acclaim. Their concept of *uniformitarianism* suggested that the earth is constantly being shaped and reshaped by natural forces that have operated over a vast stretch of time. Lyell also discussed the formation of geological strata and paleontology. He used fossilized fauna to define different geological epochs. Lyell's works were read avidly by Charles Darwin before and during Darwin's now-famous voyage on the *Beagle*. The two corresponded and subsequently became friends.

After studying changes in plants, fossil animals, and varieties of domestic and wild pigeons, Charles Darwin (1809–1882) rejected the notion that each species was created at one time in a fixed form. The results of his investigations pointed clearly, he thought, to the evolution of species through the mechanism of natural selection. While Darwin was completing his book on the subject, naturalist Alfred Russel Wallace (1823–1913) sent him a manuscript that came to conclusions about the evolution of species that matched Darwin's own.[5] In 1858, the two men presented the astonishing theory of natural selection to their colleagues at a meeting of the Linnaean Society of London.[6]

In 1859, when Darwin published *The Origin of Species by Means of Natural Selection*,[7] he wrote, "I am fully convinced that species are not immutable; but that those belonging to what are called the same genera are lineal descendants of some other and generally extinct species, in the same manner as the acknowledged varieties of any one species."[8] His conclusions outraged those who believed in the biblical account of creation, and the result was bitter controversy that continues to this day.[9]

Until 1871, when his *The Descent of Man* was published, Darwin avoided stating categorically that humans were descended from nonhuman forms, but the implications of his theory were clear. People immediately began to take sides. In June 1860, at the annual meeting of the British Association for the Advancement of Science,

Although Darwin's idea of evolution by natural selection was strongly challenged when first published (particularly, as illustrated here, the idea that humans and primates shared a common ancestor), it has withstood rigorous testing and is the foundation of many anthropological theories.

Bishop Wilberforce saw an opportunity to attack the Darwinists. Concluding his speech, he faced Thomas Huxley, one of the Darwinists' chief advocates, and inquired, "Was it through his grandfather or his grandmother that he claimed descent from a monkey?" Huxley responded,

> *If . . . the question is put to me would I rather have a miserable ape for a grandfather than a man highly endowed by nature and possessing great means and influence and yet who employs those faculties and that influence for the mere purpose of introducing ridicule into a grave scientific discussion—I unhesitatingly affirm my preference for the ape.*[10]

Although Huxley's retort to Bishop Wilberforce displays both humor and quick wit, it does not answer the bishop's question very well. A better answer is that Darwinists would claim that we descended from monkeys neither through our grandmother or our grandfather, but that both we and monkeys are descended from a common ancestor who lived long ago. Darwinists would further argue that natural selection was the process through which the physical and genetic form of that common ancestor diverged to become both monkey and human.

The Principles of Natural Selection

Natural selection is the main process that increases the frequency of adaptive traits through time. The operation of natural selection involves three conditions or principles. The first is *variation*: Every species is composed of a great variety of individuals, some of which are better adapted to their environment than others. The existence of variety is important. Without it, natural selection has nothing on which to operate; without variation, one kind of characteristic could not be favored over another. The second principle of natural selection is *heritability*: Offspring inherit traits from their parents, at least to some degree and in some way. The third principle of natural selection is *differential reproductive success*: Because better-adapted individuals generally produce more offspring over the generations than poorer-adapted individuals, the frequency of adaptive traits gradually increases in subsequent generations. A new species emerges when changes in traits or geographic barriers result in the reproductive isolation of the population.[11]

When we say that certain traits are **adaptive** or advantageous, we mean that they result in greater reproductive success in a particular environment. The phrase "particular environment" is very important. Even though a species may become more adapted to a particular environment over time, we cannot say that one species adapted to its environment is "better" than another species adapted to a different environment. For example, we may like to think of ourselves as "better" than other animals, but humans are clearly less adapted than fish for living underwater, than bats for catching flying insects, or than raccoons for living on suburban garbage.

Although the theory of natural selection suggests that disadvantageous or **maladaptive traits** will generally decline in frequency or even disappear eventually, it does not necessarily follow that all such traits will do so. After all, species derive from prior forms that have certain structures. This means that not all changes are possible; it also means that some traits are linked to others that might have advantages that outweigh the disadvantages. Choking may be very maladaptive for any animal, yet all vertebrates are capable of choking because their digestive and respiratory systems cross in the throat. This trait is a genetic legacy, probably from the time when the respiratory system developed from tissue in the digestive system of some ancestral organism. Apparently, the propensity to choke has not been correctable evolutionarily.[12]

Changes in a species can be expected to occur as the environment changes or as some members of the species move into a new environment. With environmental change, different traits become adaptive. The forms of the species that possess the more adaptive traits will become more frequent, whereas those forms whose characteristics make continued existence more difficult or impossible in the modified environment will eventually become extinct.

3.2 Describe the process of natural selection.

Natural selection The outcome of processes that affect the frequencies of traits in a particular environment. Traits that enhance survival and reproductive success increase in frequency over time.

Adaptive traits Cultural traits that enhance survival and reproductive success in a particular environment.

Maladaptive traits Cultural traits that diminish the chances of survival and reproduction in a particular environment.

Consider how the theory of natural selection would explain why giraffes became long-necked. Originally, the necks of giraffes varied in length, as happens with virtually any physical characteristic in a population. During a period when food was scarce, those giraffes with longer necks, who could reach higher tree leaves, might be better able to survive and suckle their offspring, and thus they would leave more offspring than shorter-necked giraffes. Because of heredity, the offspring of long-necked giraffes are more likely to have long necks. Eventually, the shorter-necked giraffes would diminish in number and the longer-necked giraffes would increase. The resultant population of giraffes would still have variation in neck length but on the average would be longer-necked than earlier forms.

Natural selection does not account for all variation in the frequencies of traits. In particular, it does not account for variation in the frequencies of neutral traits—that is, those traits that do not seem to confer any advantages or disadvantages on their carriers. Changes in the frequencies of neutral traits may result rather from random processes that affect gene frequencies in isolated populations—*genetic drift*—or from matings between populations—*gene flow*. We discuss these other processes later in the chapter.

Observed Examples of Natural Selection

Natural selection is a process we can see at work in the world today. It is a process that has been studied in both the laboratory and nature, and it is a process that most scientists would argue is very well understood. However, as in all scientific endeavors, understanding grows and changes as new information is obtained. The understanding of natural selection we have today is quite different from that originally put forward by Darwin. A century and a half of research has added tremendously to the information Darwin had to work with, and entirely new fields, like population genetics, have emerged. With this new information, we know that Darwin was unaware of some things. For example, it seems clear that natural selection is not always a uniform process but can act in jumps and starts. The fact that the ideas put forward by Darwin have changed, and are changing as new research is done, does not mean they were wrong. Darwin's ideas were simply incomplete. As we add to our knowledge base each day, we move closer to an even more complete understanding of natural selection. Because the process of natural selection may involve nearly imperceptible gradations over generations, it is often difficult to observe directly. Nevertheless, because some life forms reproduce rapidly, some examples of natural selection have been observed over relatively short periods in changing environments.

For example, scientists think they have observed natural selection in action in British moths. In 1850, an almost black moth was spotted for the first time in Manchester. That was quite unusual, for most of the moths were speckled gray. A century later, 95 percent of the moths in industrial parts of Britain were black; only in the rural areas were the moths mostly gray. How is this to be explained? It seems that, in the rural areas, the gray-speckled moth is hard to spot by bird predators against the lichen growing on the bark of trees. But in industrial areas, lichen is killed by pollution. The gray-speckled moths, formerly well adapted to blend into their environment, became clearly visible against the darker background of the lichen-free trees and were easier prey for birds. In contrast, the black moths, which previously would have had a disadvantage against the lighter bark, were now better adapted for survival. Their dark color was an advantage, and subsequently the darker moths became the predominant variety in industrial regions.

How can we be sure that natural selection was the mechanism accounting for the change? Consistent evidence comes from a series of experiments performed by H. B. D. Kettlewell. He deliberately released specially marked moths, black and gray, into two areas of England—one urban industrial and one rural—and then set light traps to recapture them subsequently. The proportions of the two kinds of moths recovered tell us about differential survival. Kettlewell found that proportionately more black moths compared with gray moths were recovered in the urban industrial area. Just the reverse happened in the rural area; proportionately more gray-speckled moths were recovered.[13] Questions have been raised recently about whether the Kettlewell experiments were properly conducted.[14] However, the basic conclusion has been replicated by subsequent research.[15] The same transformation—the switch to darker color—has occurred in 70 other species of moth, as well as in a beetle and a millipede. And the transformation did not just occur in Britain; it also happened in other highly polluted areas, including the Ruhr area of Germany and the Pittsburgh area of the United States. Moreover, in the Pittsburgh area, antipollution measures in the last 50 years have apparently caused the black moth to dwindle in number once again.[16]

The type of natural selection in the moth example is called **directional selection** because a particular trait seems to be positively favored and the average value shifts over time toward the adaptive trait. But there can also be **normalizing selection**. In this type of selection, the average value does not change, but natural selection removes the extremes. An example is the birth weight of babies. Both very low birth weights and very high birth weights are disadvantageous and would be selected against. Directional and normalizing selection both assume that natural selection will either favor or disfavor genes, but there is a third possibility—balancing selection. **Balancing selection** occurs when a *heterozygous* (varied) combination of *alleles* (genes) is positively favored, even though a *homozygous* (genes in the pairs are the same) combination is disfavored.

Another well-known example of observed natural selection is the acquired resistance of houseflies to the insecticide DDT. When DDT was first used to kill insects, beginning in the 1940s, several new, DDT-resistant strains of housefly evolved. In the early DDT environment, many houseflies were killed, but the few that survived were the ones that reproduced, and their resistant characteristics became common to the housefly populations. To the chagrin of medical practitioners, similar resistances develop in bacteria. A particular antibiotic may lose its effectiveness after it comes into wide use because new, resistant bacterial strains emerge. These new strains will become more frequent than the original ones because of natural selection. In the United States now, a few strains are resistant to all antibiotics on the market, a fact that worries medical practitioners. One possible way to deal with the problem is to stop using antibiotics for a few years, so resistance to those antibiotics might not develop or develop only slowly.

The theory of natural selection answered many questions, but it also raised at least one whose answer eluded Darwin and others. The appearance of a beneficial trait may assist the survival of an organism, but what happens when the organism reproduces by mating with members that do not possess this new variation? Will not the new adaptive trait eventually disappear if subsequent generations mate with individuals that lack this trait? Darwin knew variations were transmitted through heredity, but he did not have a clear model of the mode of inheritance. Gregor Mendel's pioneering studies in the science of genetics provided the foundation for such a model, but his discoveries did not become widely known until 1900.

Directional selection A type of natural selection that increases the frequency of a trait (the trait is said to be positively favored, or adaptive).

Normalizing selection The type of natural selection that removes harmful genes that arose by mutation.

Balancing selection A type of selection that occurs when a heterozygous combination of alleles is positively favored even though a homozygous combination is disfavored.

Heredity

Gregor Mendel's Experiments

3.3 Specify the principles of genetics.

Mendel (1822–1884), a monk and amateur botanist who lived in what is now the Czech Republic, bred several varieties of pea plants and made detailed observations of their offspring. He chose as breeding partners plants that differed by only one observable trait. Tall plants were crossed with short ones, and yellow ones with green, for example.

When the pollen from a yellow pea plant was transferred to a green pea plant, Mendel observed a curious phenomenon: All of the first-generation offspring bore yellow peas. It seemed that the green trait had disappeared. But when seeds from this first generation were crossed, they produced both yellow and green pea plants in a ratio of three yellow to one green pea plant (see Figure 3.1). Apparently, Mendel reasoned, the green trait had not been lost or altered; the yellow trait was simply **dominant** and the green trait was **recessive**. Mendel observed similar results with other traits. Tallness dominated shortness, and the factor for smooth-skinned peas dominated the factor for wrinkled ones. In each cross, the three-to-one ratio appeared in the second generation. Self-fertilization, however, produced different results. Green pea plants always yielded green pea plants, and short plants always produced short plants.

Dominant The allele of a gene pair that is always phenotypically expressed in the heterozygous form.

recessive An allele phenotypically suppressed in the heterozygous form and expressed only in the homozygous form.

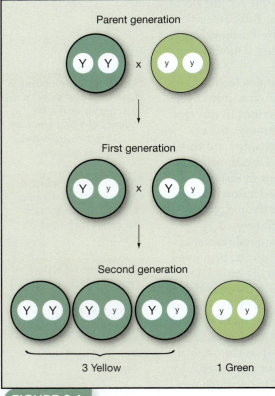

Parent generation

First generation

Second generation

3 Yellow   1 Green

FIGURE 3.1

When Mendel crossed a plant having two genes for yellow peas (YY) with a plant having two genes for green peas (yy), each offspring pea was yellow but carried one gene for yellow and one gene for green (Yy). The peas were yellow because the gene for yellow is dominant over the recessive gene for green. Crossing the first generation yielded three yellow pea plants for each green pea plant.

Genotype The total complement of inherited traits or genes of an organism.

From his numerical results, Mendel concluded that some yellow pea plants were pure (*homozygous*) for that trait, whereas others also possessed a green factor (the plants were *heterozygous*). That is, although two plants might both have yellow peas, one of them might produce offspring with green peas. In such cases, the genetic makeup, the **genotype**, differed from the observable appearance, or **phenotype**.

Genes: The Conveyors of Inherited Traits

Mendel's units of heredity were what we now call **genes**. He concluded that these units occurred in pairs for each trait and that offspring inherited one unit of the pair from each parent. Each member of a gene pair or group is called an **allele**. If the two genes, or alleles, for a trait are the same, the organism is **homozygous** for that trait; if the two genes for a characteristic differ, the organism is **heterozygous** for that trait. A pea plant that contains a pair of genes for yellow is homozygous for the trait. A yellow pea plant with a dominant gene for yellow and a recessive gene for green, although phenotypically yellow, has a heterozygous genotype. As Mendel demonstrated, the recessive green gene can reappear in subsequent generations. But Mendel knew nothing of the composition of genes or the processes that transmit them from parent to offspring. Many years of scientific research have yielded much of the missing information.

The genes of higher organisms (not including bacteria and primitive plants such as blue-green algae) are located on ropelike bodies called **chromosomes** within the nucleus of every one of the organism's cells. Chromosomes, like genes, usually occur in pairs. Each allele for a given trait is carried in the identical position on corresponding chromosomes. The two genes that determined the color of Mendel's peas, for example, were opposite each other on a pair of chromosomes.

Mitosis and Meiosis The body cells of every plant or animal carry chromosome pairs in a number appropriate for its species. Humans have 23 pairs, or a total of 46 chromosomes, each carrying many times that number of genes. Each new body cell receives this number of chromosomes during cellular reproduction, or **mitosis**, as each pair of chromosomes duplicates itself.

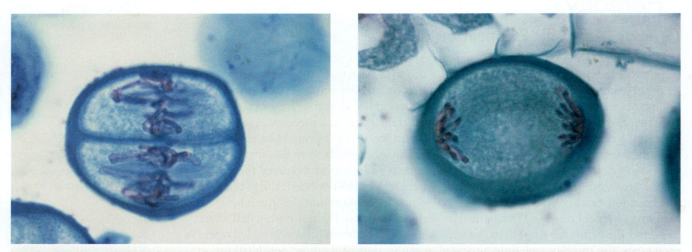

Meiosis in a plant cell. The left image shows the metaphase stage. Note how the chromosomes (stained dark red) lie against and even on top of one another. The right image shows the anaphase stage, when the chromosomes separate and the cell is ready to divide.

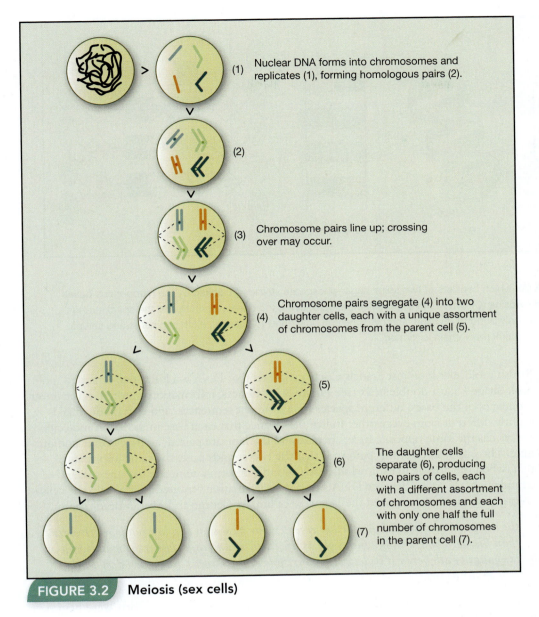

(1) Nuclear DNA forms into chromosomes and replicates (1), forming homologous pairs (2).

(2)

(3) Chromosome pairs line up; crossing over may occur.

(4) Chromosome pairs segregate (4) into two daughter cells, each with a unique assortment of chromosomes from the parent cell (5).

(5)

(6) The daughter cells separate (6), producing two pairs of cells, each with a different assortment of chromosomes and each with only one half the full number of chromosomes in the parent cell (7).

(7)

FIGURE 3.2   **Meiosis (sex cells)**

Gene Chemical unit of heredity.

Phenotype The observable physical appearance of an organism, which may or may not reflect its genotype or total genetic constitution.

Allele One member of a pair of genes.

Homozygous Possessing two identical genes or alleles in corresponding locations on a pair of chromosomes.

Heterozygous Possessing differing genes or alleles in corresponding locations on a pair of chromosomes.

Chromosomes Paired rod-shaped structures within a cell nucleus containing the genes that transmit traits from one generation to the next.

Mitosis Cellular reproduction or growth involving the duplication of chromosome pairs.

Meiosis The process by which reproductive cells are formed. In this process of division, the number of chromosomes in the newly formed cells is reduced by half, so that when fertilization occurs the resulting organism has the normal number of chromosomes appropriate to its species, rather than double that number.

DNA Deoxyribonucleic acid; a long, two-stranded molecule in the genes that directs the makeup of an organism according to the instructions in its genetic code.

But what happens when a sperm cell and an egg cell unite to form a new organism? What prevents the human baby from receiving twice the number of chromosomes characteristic of its species—23 pairs from the sperm and 23 pairs from the egg? The process by which the reproductive cells are formed, **meiosis**, ensures that this will not happen (see Figure 3.2). Each reproductive cell contains half the number of chromosomes appropriate for the species. Only one member of each chromosome pair is carried in every egg or sperm. At fertilization, the human embryo normally receives 23 separate chromosomes from its mother and the same number from its father, which add up to the 23 pairs.

DNA As we have said, genes are located on chromosomes. Each gene carries a set of instructions encoded in its chemical structure. It is from this coded information carried in genes that a cell makes all the rest of its structural parts and chemical machinery. It appears that, in most living organisms, heredity is controlled by the same chemical substance, **DNA**—deoxyribonucleic acid. An enormous amount of research has been directed toward understanding DNA—what its structure is, how it duplicates itself in reproduction, and how it conveys instructions for the formation of a complete organism.

One of the most important keys to understanding human development and genetics is the structure and function of DNA. In 1953, American biologist James Watson, with

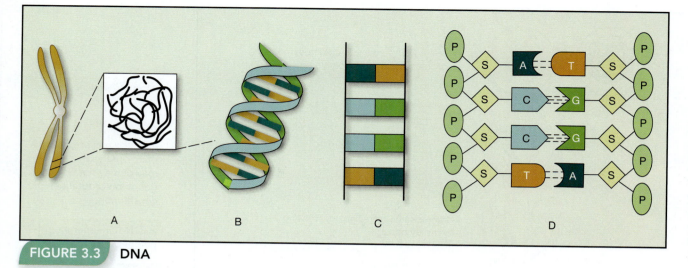

FIGURE 3.3   **DNA**

Chromosomes are built of DNA (A), which consists of two spiral sugar-phosphate strands (B) linked by the nitrogenous bases adenine, guanine, thymine, and cytosine (C). When the DNA molecule reproduces, the bases separate and the spiral strands unwind (D). Because adenine can only bond to thymine, and cytosine can only bond to guanine, each original strand serves as a mold along which a new complementary chain is formed.

British molecular biologist Francis Crick, proposed that DNA is a long, two-stranded molecule shaped like a double helix (see Figure 3.3). Genetic information is stored in the linear sequences of the bases; different species have different sequences, and every individual is slightly different from every other individual. Notice that each base in the DNA molecule always has the same opposite base; adenine and thymine are paired, as are cytosine and guanine. The importance of this pattern is that the two strands carry the same information, so that, when the double helix unwinds, each strand can form a template for a new strand of complementary bases. Because DNA stores the information required to make up the cells of an organism, it has been called the language of life. As George and Muriel Beadle put it,

> *the deciphering of the DNA code has revealed our possession of a language much older than hieroglyphics, a language as old as life itself, a language that is the most living language of all—even if its letters are invisible and its words are buried deep in the cells of our bodies.*[17]

Once it was understood that genes are made of DNA, concerted efforts were begun to map DNA sequences and their locations on the chromosomes of different organisms. A project known as the Human Genome Project set out to assemble a complete genetic map for humans. In 2000, the initial mapping of the human genome was completed.[18] This was a significant achievement and has already led to several breakthroughs in our understanding of how the genetic code functions (but see the box feature "Who Owns Your DNA?").[19] For example, researchers recently reported finding two genes that appear to provide partial resistance to malaria. These newly found genes appear to have evolved recently, perhaps only a few thousand years ago. If researchers can discover how these genes help to defend their carriers against malaria, that may help medical science discover how to prevent or treat this devastating disease.[20]

Messenger RNA   DNA stores the information to make cells, but it does not directly affect the formation of cells. One type of ribonucleic acid (RNA), **messenger RNA (mRNA)**, is copied from a portion of DNA and moves outside the cell nucleus to direct the formation of proteins. Proteins have so many functions that they are considered to be responsible for most of the characteristics of an organism. They act as catalysts for synthesizing DNA and RNA and for the activities of cells; they also contribute many structural elements that determine the shape and movement of cells. Messenger RNA is like DNA in that it has a linear sequence of bases attached to a sugar-phosphate backbone, but it is slightly different chemically. One difference is that messenger RNA has the base uracil instead of the base thymine. Messenger RNA also has a different sugar-phosphate backbone

Messenger RNA (mRNA) A type of ribonucleic acid that is used in the cell to copy the DNA code for use in protein synthesis.

Applied Anthropology

Who Owns Your DNA?

Your DNA is a blueprint for you. What happens to your DNA when you give blood or have a biopsy? Have you given away a part of you, or do you always retain control of your DNA because it is the essence of you? These questions have become increasingly important as DNA is now more easily extracted and sequenced from blood and body cells, and because medical research has found some DNA sources valuable for the design of new drugs.

Consider the case of Henrietta Lacks, who died of cervical cancer in 1951. Mrs. Lacks's cancer was particularly virulent; indeed, the cells grew more quickly than any human cells doctors had previously seen. Samples of her cancer were cultured and, because of their ability to reproduce so rapidly, became the targets of decades of medical research. More than half a century after her death, the cells Henrietta Lacks provided are still alive, growing in labs on every continent and interacting daily with thousands of scientists. Are these cells Henrietta Lacks? Has she gained a type of immortality? Or are they simply samples of highly virulent cancer tissue? It is important to note that Mrs. Lacks did not give permission for her cells to be used in this way, nor did she need to. In 1951, as today, cells obtained through surgery or medical treatment are considered the property of the doctor or facility that obtained them.

For anthropologist Margaret Everett, the question of who controls an individual's DNA came to the forefront of her research when her infant son Jack was diagnosed with, and later died from, a genetic disorder. Samples of Jack's DNA were taken as part of

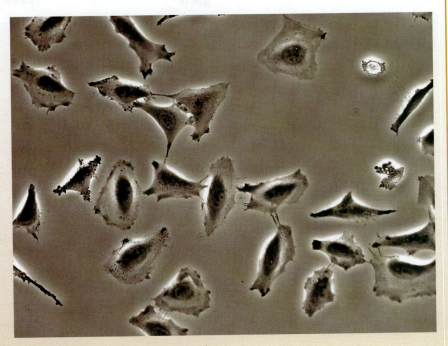

Cervical cancer cells from Henrietta Lacks.

his autopsy. Dr. Everett later learned these samples were being used in labs in England and Italy and that several research papers had been published on them. As she relates about one of these publications, "I soon found myself combing through the article, looking for Jack in a handful of samples described in a series of tables." But was Jack there? From research conducted to explore the impact of an Oregon law that makes genetic information the property of the individuals from which it is derived, Dr. Everett learned that her questions and concerns were widely held. Oregonians, she discovered, wanted to control access to their own DNA and felt that privacy and consent needed to be ensured when samples were taken.

In non-Western cultures, the situation may become even more complex. In the United States, we view the individual as autonomous and self-defining. We create ourselves through our work and contributions to our communities. But in many cultures, who you are may be mostly defined by others, not by you. In such situations, ensuring privacy and consent may mean keeping private the location or identity of whole communities or gaining consent from kin group leaders in addition to individuals. As Dr. Everett puts it, "Property is never a thing—it is a bundle of rights, embedded in social relations." This is nowhere more true than when dealing with genetic property.

Sources: Everett 2007; Landecker 2000.

and is single- rather than double-stranded. Messenger RNA is formed when a double-stranded DNA molecule unwinds and forms a template for the mRNA. After a section of DNA is copied, the mRNA releases from the DNA and leaves the nucleus, and the double helix of the DNA is reformed.

Protein Synthesis   Once the mRNA is released from the DNA, it travels out of the cell nucleus and into the body of the cell. There it attaches to a structure in the cell called a **ribosome**, which uses the information on the mRNA to make proteins. The ribosome essentially "reads" the chemical bases on the mRNA in commands that tell the ribosome the specific amino acids to join together to form a protein (see Figure 3.4). For example,

Ribosome A structure in the cell used in making proteins.

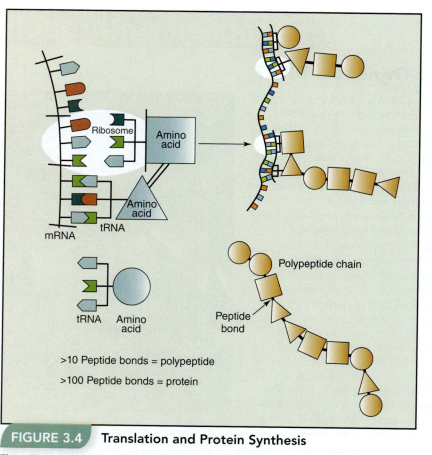

FIGURE 3.4   **Translation and Protein Synthesis**

The mRNA copy of the cellular DNA is "read" by a ribosome that attaches the amino acid with the corresponding transfer RNA (tRNA) to a growing chain of amino acids (called a polypeptide chain because the amino acids are linked together by peptide bonds). A chain more than 100 amino acids long is called a protein.

the mRNA sequence adenine, adenine, guanine (AAG) tells the ribosome to place the amino acid lysine in that location, whereas the sequence adenine, adenine, cytosine (AAC) calls for the amino acid histidine. There are also mRNA commands that tell the ribosome when to begin and when to stop constructing a protein. Thus, the DNA code copied onto mRNA provides all the information necessary for ribosomes to build the proteins that make up the structures of organisms and drive the processes of life.

3.4 Identify the sources of genetic variability and discuss how each leads to new variations, becomes shuffled through populations, or becomes hybridized.

Sources of Variability

Natural selection proceeds only when individuals within a population vary. There are two genetic sources of new variation: genetic recombination and mutation. There are also two processes through which variations are shuffled through populations: gene flow and genetic drift. Scholars have recently begun to consider one other potential source of variability: hybridization.

Genetic Recombination

The distribution of traits from parents to children varies from one offspring to another. Brothers and sisters, after all, do not look exactly alike, nor does each child resemble 50 percent of the mother and 50 percent of the father. This variation occurs because, when a sperm cell or an egg is formed, the single member of each chromosome pair it receives is a matter of chance. Each reproductive cell, then, carries a random assortment of chromosomes and their respective genes. At fertilization, the egg and sperm that unite are different from every other egg carried by the mother and every other sperm carried by the father. A unique offspring is thus produced by a shuffling of the parents' genes. One cause of this shuffling is the random **segregation**, or sorting, of chromosomes in meiosis. Conceivably, an individual could get any of the possible assortments of the paternal and maternal chromosomes. Another cause of the shuffling of parental genes is **crossing-over**, the exchange of sections of chromosomes between one chromosome and another (see Figure 3.5). Thus, after meiosis, the egg and sperm do not receive just a random mixture of complete paternal and maternal chromosomes; because of crossing-over, they also receive chromosomes in which some of the sections may have been replaced.

The traits displayed by each organism are not simply the result of combinations of dominant and recessive genes, as Mendel had hypothesized. In humans, most traits are influenced by the activity of many genes. Skin color, for example, is the result of several inherited characteristics. A brownish shade results from the presence of a pigment known as *melanin*; the degree of darkness in the hue depends largely on the amount of melanin present and how it is distributed in the layers of the skin. Another factor contributing to the color of all human skin is the blood that flows in blood vessels located in the outer layers of the skin. Humans carry at least five different genes for the manufacture of melanin and many other genes for the other components of skin hue. In fact, almost all physical characteristics in humans are the result of the concerted action of many genes. Some traits are sex-linked. The X chromosome, which together with the presence or absence of a Y chromosome determines sex, may also carry the gene for hemophilia or the gene for color blindness. The expression of these two characteristics depends on the sex of the organism.

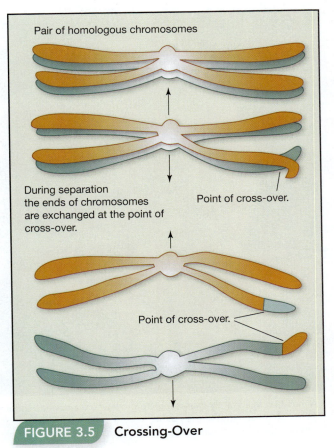

FIGURE 3.5   **Crossing-Over**

Source: From Boaz and Almquist 1997.

Genetic recombination produces variety, which is essential for the operation of natural selection. Ultimately, however, the major source of variability is mutation. This is because mutation replenishes the supply of variability, which is constantly being reduced by the selective elimination of less fit variants. Mutation also produces variety in organisms that reproduce asexually.

Mutation

A **mutation** is a change in the DNA sequence. Such a change produces an altered gene. The majority of mutations are thought to occur because of occasional mismating of the chemical bases that make up DNA. Just as a typist will make errors in copying a manuscript, so will DNA, in duplicating itself, occasionally change its code. A mutation will result from such an error. Some mutations have more drastic consequences than others. Suppose the error is in one base on a DNA strand. The effect depends on what that portion of the DNA controls. The effect may be minimal if the product hardly affects the organism. On the other hand, if the change occurs at a place where the DNA regulates the production of many proteins, the effect on the organism can be serious.

Although it is very difficult to estimate the proportions of mutations that are harmful, neutral, or beneficial, there is no doubt that some mutations have lethal consequences. We can discuss the relative merits or disadvantages of a mutant gene only in terms of the physical, cultural, and genetic environment of that gene. Galactosemia, for example, is caused by a recessive mutant gene and usually results in mental retardation and blindness. But it can be prevented by dietary restrictions begun at an early age. In this instance, the intervention of human culture counteracts the mutant gene and allows the afflicted individual to lead a normal life. Thus, some cultural factors can modify the effects of natural selection by helping to perpetuate a harmful mutant gene. People with the galactosemia trait who are enabled to function normally can reproduce and pass on one of the recessive genes to their children. Without cultural interference, natural selection would prevent such reproduction. Usually, natural selection acts to retain only those mutations that aid survival.

Segregation The random sorting of chromosomes in meiosis.

Crossing-over Exchanges of sections of chromosomes from one chromosome to another.

Mutation A change in the DNA sequence, producing an altered gene.

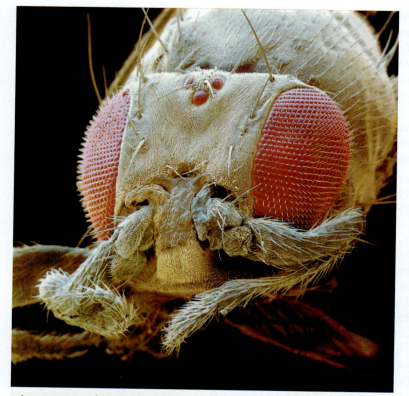

A mutation in a fruit fly causes legs to grow where antennae should be. Although most mutations are either neutral or harmful (like this one), some can be adaptive and spread rapidly through a population.

Even though most mutations may not be adaptive, those that are will multiply in a population relatively quickly by natural selection. As Theodosius Dobzhansky has suggested:

Consistently useful mutants are like needles in a haystack of harmful ones. A needle in a haystack is hard to find, even though one may be sure it is there. But if the needle is valuable, the task of finding it is facilitated by setting the haystack on fire and looking for the needle among the ashes. The role of the fire in this parable is played in biological evolution by natural selection.[21]

The black moth that was spotted in Manchester in 1850 probably resulted from a mutation. If the tree trunks had been light-colored, that moth or its offspring probably would have died out. But as industrialization increased and the tree trunks became darker, a trait that was once maladaptive became adaptive.

Genetic recombination and mutation are the sources of new variations, but evolutionary biologists have identified two other processes that are important in distributing those variations through populations: genetic drift and gene flow.

Genetic Drift

Genetic drift The various random processes that affect gene frequencies in small, relatively isolated populations.

The term **genetic drift** refers to various random processes that affect gene frequencies in small, relatively isolated populations. Genetic drift is also known as the *Wright effect,* after geneticist Sewall Wright, who first directed attention to this process. Over time in a small population, genetic drift may result in a neutral or nearly neutral gene becoming more or less frequent just by chance.

One variety of genetic drift, called the *founder effect,* occurs when a small group of organisms recently derived from a larger population migrates to a relatively isolated location. If a particular gene is absent just by chance in the migrant group, the descendants are also likely to lack that gene, assuming that the group remains isolated. Similarly, if all members of the original migrant group just by chance carried a particular gene, their descendants would also be likely to share that gene. Isolation can occur for physical reasons, such as when a group moves to a previously uninhabited place and does not return. The populations that traveled over land when the Bering land bridge connected Asia to North America could not readily return when the sea level rose. This may explain why Native Americans have a higher proportion of individuals with type O blood than other populations—the first migrants may have had, by chance, a predominance of individuals with type O blood.

Isolation can also occur for social reasons. A religious sect of Anabaptists called "Dunkers" emigrated from Germany to the United States in the early 1700s. The fact that the 50 original families kept to themselves probably explains why some of their gene frequencies differ from what is found in both the German and general U.S. populations.[22]

Gene Flow

Gene flow The process by which genes pass from the gene pool of one population to that of another through mating and reproduction.

Gene flow is the process whereby genes pass from one population to another through mating and reproduction. Unlike the other processes of natural selection and genetic drift, which generally increase the differences between populations in different environments, gene flow tends to work in the opposite direction—it *decreases* differences between populations. Two populations at opposite ends of a region may have different frequencies of a particular gene, but the populations located between them have an intermediate gene frequency because of gene flow between them. The variation in gene frequency from one end of the region to the other is called a **cline**. In Europe, for example, there is a cline in the distribution of type B blood, which gradually diminishes in frequency from east to west.[23]

Most genetically determined characteristics in humans have gradually or clinally varying frequencies as one moves from one area to another. Neighboring regions have more similar gene frequencies than regions widely separated. But these clines do not always coincide, which makes the concept of "race" as applied to humans not very useful for understanding human biological variation.[24] Gene flow may occur between distant as well as close populations. Long-range movements of people, to trade or raid or settle, may result in gene flow. But they do not always do so.

Hybridization

A **species** is a population that consists of organisms able to interbreed and produce fertile and viable offspring. In general, individuals from one species do not successfully mate with members of a different species because of genetic and behavioral differences. If members of different species do mate, fertilization usually does not occur and, if it does, the embryo does not survive. In the cases where offspring are born, they are usually infertile. However, recent studies have suggested that **hybridization**, the creation of a viable offspring from two different species, may be more possible than once thought. Hybridization may be an important source of new variation in some populations.

The finches of the Galápagos Islands provide an example of hybridization in action. Many female cactus finches (*Geospiza scandens*) died during a period of severe drought, leaving an abundance of males. High competition for mates led some female ground finches (*Geospiza fortis*) to mate with the abundant male cactus finches, something that would not normally occur. The result was hybrid offspring with unique characteristics. These hybrids, both male and female, went on to mate only with cactus finches, because they imprinted on the male cactus finch song as infants. The end result was a one-time influx of ground finch genes into the cactus finch population, adding new variations upon which natural selection could work.[25]

Cline The gradually increasing (or decreasing) frequency of a gene from one end of a region to another.

Species A population that consists of organisms able to interbreed and produce viable and fertile offspring.

Hybridization The creation of a viable offspring from the mating of two different species.

A wolf-dog hybrid. Hybridization is sometimes a source of new variation.

3.5 Explain what may lead to the origin of species.

Speciation The development of a new species.

The Origin of Species

One of the most controversial aspects of Darwin's theory was the suggestion that one species could, over time, evolve into another. How could one species evolve into another? What is the explanation for this differentiation? How does one group of organisms become so unlike another group with the same ancestry that it forms a totally new species? **Speciation**, or the development of a new species, may occur if one subgroup of a species finds itself in a radically different environment. In adapting to their separate environments, the two populations may undergo enough genetic changes to prevent them from interbreeding, should they renew contact. Numerous factors can prevent the exchange of genes. Two species living in the same area may breed at different times of the year, or their behavior during breeding—their courtship rituals—may be distinct. The difference in body structure of closely related forms may in itself bar interbreeding. Geographic barriers may be the most common barriers to interbreeding.

Do new species diverge quickly or slowly from their ancestors? Paleontologists disagree about the pace of speciation. The traditional view is that evolution occurs very slowly over time; new species emerge gradually. Others who espouse what's called "punctuated equilibrium" believe that species are very stable over long periods of time, but when divergence occurs it is quick.

Speciation Versus Creation

But some people, particularly those who call themselves "scientific creationists," argue that although natural selection can produce variation within species (often referred to as *microevolution*), it cannot produce new species (often referred to as *macroevolution*). Creationists argue that God created all living things and that evolution has only changed those living things in minor ways and has not created new kinds of living things. The major problem with the creationist view is that there is solid empirical evidence for speciation. For example, William Rice and George Salt demonstrated that, if they sorted fruit flies by their environmental preferences (such as light intensity and temperature) and then bred the sorted groups separately, they could produce flies incapable of interbreeding—separate species—in as little as 35 generations.[26] The fossil record contains numerous examples of speciation and even the development of entirely new kinds of creatures. For example, the evolution of birds from terrestrial creatures is clearly evidenced in the fossil record.[27] Although many creationists downplay the evidence for speciation, the evidence is plentiful and can be seen by the public in museums all over the world.

With the abundant evidence for speciation found in both the fossil record and experimental observations, creationists have recently developed a new argument to discount the role of natural selection in the process of speciation. The new argument is that life in general, and species in particular, are so complex that a random, undirected process like natural selection could never have created them. The complexity of life, these creationists argue, must stem from "intelligent design." This new appeal to intelligent design in the origin of species is actually an old, and widely discredited, one. In his 1802 book *Natural Theology*, William Paley wrote, "Suppose I had found a watch upon the ground, and it should be enquired how the watch happened to be in that place…the inference, we think, is inevitable; that the watch must have had a maker…."[28] By this, Paley implied that if we find a complex mechanism at work in the world, like a watch, we must conclude that a maker exists. Paley extended the argument to the complexity of life, and concluded that life must stem from an intelligent designer—God.

Darwin wrote *On the Origin of Species* in part as a response to Paley, and Darwinists have been responding ever since. But in recent years, the "intelligent design" movement, or as proponents call it, the "wedge," has brought Paley's ideas back with force. Indeed, the force is an active political one, with the explicit purpose "to reverse the stifling dominance of the materialist world view, and to replace it with a science consonant with Christian and theistic convictions."[29] Intelligent design is, at the core, a political movement. The problem, however, is that intelligent design cannot explain speciation in a scientific way. The central argument made by proponents of intelligent design is simply that what we see in the world is too complex to be accounted for by natural selection, but they offer no alternative natural mechanism. They argue that, if natural selection may not account for all cases of speciation, then the only alternative is divine intervention. Clearly, this reasoning is flawed. Just because we do not understand something today does not mean we should toss out all we do know. Rather, the scientific approach is to continue to examine unexplained phenomena to learn more about them.

Intelligent design proponents also fail to answer critics who point out that natural selection can and has accounted for even the most complex of features—such as wings and eyes—and hence that intelligent design arguments lack a basis in fact. The key facts that intelligent design and other creationist scholars appeal to are biblical ones. But it is important to point out that most biblical scholars do not agree with creationist arguments. As theologian Ernan McMullin suggests, the Bible "ought to be understood as conveying fundamental theological truths about dependence of the natural and human worlds on their Creator, rather than explaining how exactly these worlds first took shape."[30] On the other hand, there is nothing in science that can absolutely rule out supernatural intervention in the natural world because supernatural activities are beyond the realm of scientific explanation. For example, although we now know that people with a condition called hypertrichosis grow hair all over their faces because of a single mutation on the X chromosome, science cannot rule out the possibility that the mutation was caused by the "curse of the werewolf" or a divine punishment for sin.[31] Science cannot rule out such possibilities because they cannot be observed, measured, or experimentally tested. Science and religion should be regarded as different ways of understanding the world, the former relying on evidence, the latter relying on faith.

Natural Selection of Behavioral Traits

3.6 Explore the concept of natural selection of behavioral traits.

Until now, we have discussed how natural selection might operate to change a population's physical traits, such as the color of moths or the neck length of giraffes. But natural selection can also operate on the behavioral characteristics of populations. Although this idea is not new, it is now receiving more attention. The approaches called **sociobiology**,[32] **behavioral ecology**,[33] **evolutionary psychology**,[34] and **dual-inheritance theory**[35] involve the application of evolutionary principles to the behavior of animals and humans (also see the box feature on "Molecular Anthropology"). Behavioral ecology looks at how all kinds of behavior related to the environment; sociobiology looks at social organization and social behavior; evolutionary psychology looks at how evolution may have produced lasting variation in the way humans behave, interact, and perceive the world; and dual-inheritance theory looks at how beneficial cultural traits might be selected for and transmitted. The typical behaviors of a species are assumed to be adaptive and to have evolved by natural selection. For example, why do related species exhibit different social behaviors even though they derive from a common ancestral species?

Consider the lion, as compared with other cats. Although members of the cat family are normally solitary creatures, lions live in social groups called *prides*. Why? George Schaller has suggested that lion social groups may have evolved primarily because group hunting is a more successful way to catch large mammals in open terrain. He has observed that not only are several lions more successful in catching prey than are solitary lions, but several lions are more likely to catch and kill large and dangerous prey such as giraffes. Then, too, cubs are generally safer from predators when in a social group than when alone with their mothers. Thus, the social behavior of lions may have evolved primarily because it provided selective advantages in the lions' open-country environment.[36]

It is important to remember that natural selection operates on expressed characteristics, or the phenotype, of an individual. In the moth example, the color of the moth is part of its *phenotype*, subject to natural selection. Behavior is also an expressed characteristic. If hunting in groups, a behavioral trait, gets you more food, then individuals who hunt in groups will do better. But we must also remember that natural selection requires traits to be heritable. Can the concept of heritability be applied to learned behavior, not

Sociobiology Systematic study of the biological causes of human behavior. Compare with **behavioral ecology, evolutionary psychology,** and **dual-inheritance theory**.

Current Research and Issues

Molecular Anthropology

Physical anthropologists and archaeologists are increasingly relying on genetic data to help them understand the relationships between modern humans and other species, to explore the ancestry of modern human populations, and to examine human variation. This study of modern and ancient DNA to explore the human variation and the human past is typically referred to as molecular anthropology, and many see it as the most exciting area of current research in anthropology. But how does molecular anthropology work?

Genetic mutations are the focus of molecular anthropology. As DNA replicates during meiosis, the process that creates sperm and egg cells, there are frequently errors, or mutations. Since these mutations occur in the process of creating sperm and eggs, they can be passed on to descendants. A single mutation, particularly one that confers an adaptive advantage to carriers, can be transferred through many generations and provide a way to identify related populations and trace their common ancestry back through time.

Two basic types of mutations are commonly studied by molecular anthropologists. One is called a single nucleotide polymorphism or SNP. These occur when a single base in a string of DNA changes. The other is called a short tandem repeat or STR. For reasons that are not fully understood, multiple copies of short segments of DNA are sometimes created, and STRs refer to these repeated segments.

Until recently, molecular anthropologists typically restricted their work to either mitochondrial DNA or the Y chromosome. There are two reasons

Researcher preparing DNA samples for PCR.

for this. First, there is no mixing of DNA from an individual's mother and father, as mitochondrial DNA is inherited directly from one's mother and the Y chromosome directly from a man's father. Second, both sets of DNA are relatively small and thus can be more easily searched for SNPs and STRs. Recent developments in computing and statistical analysis now allow molecular anthropologists to work with cellular DNA as well.

Three technical advances have led to the recent burgeoning of molecular anthropology. The first was the development in the late 1980s of the polymerase chain reaction or PCR, a process that uses a chemical chain reaction to make thousands of copies of a given specimen of DNA—copies required to provide enough DNA to analyze for SNPs and STRs. The second was the development since the 1990s

of various "high throughput" methods of DNA sequencing that allow for rapid "reading" of large DNA samples. Finally, because DNA breaks apart into shorter and shorter strands very quickly after death, it was almost impossible to piece these strands back together until very recently. In the past decade molecular anthropologists have developed several very successful ways to do so.

All the discussions of genetic relationships between populations, the movement of ancient populations, the genetic differences between humans and other species, the genetic fallacy of race, genes that cause or prevent illness, and the like that you may read in this and other books are based on the fascinating work of molecular anthropologists.

Sources: Harris 2008; Jobling, Hurles, and Tylor-Smith 2004; Stone and Lurquin 2007.

just genetically transmitted behavior? And, even more controversially, if the concept of heritability can include learning, can it also include cultural learning? Recent research on domesticated dogs suggests it may. Domesticated dogs appear to inherently understand social cues used by humans, such as pointing, whereas wolves do not. These findings suggest that some aspects of cultural learning in animals may be heritable.[37]

Early theorizing in sociobiology and behavioral ecology appeared to emphasize the genetic component of behavior. For example, Edward O. Wilson, in his book *Sociobiology*, defined sociobiology as "the systematic study of the biological causes of behavior."[38] But

Bobbi Low points out that although the term *biological* may have been interpreted to mean "genetic," most biologists understand that expressed or observable characteristics are the results of genes, environment, and life history all interacting. Behavior is a product of all three. If we say that some behavior is heritable, we mean that the child's behavior is more likely to resemble the parents' behavior than the behavior of others.[39] Learning from a parent could be an important part of why the offspring is like the parent. If the child is more like the parent than like others, then the likeness is heritable, even if it is entirely learned from the parent.

The sociobiological approach has aroused considerable controversy in anthropology, probably because of its apparent emphasis on genes, rather than experience and learning, as determinants of human behavior. Anthropologists have argued that the customs of a society may be more or less adaptive because cultural behaviors also have reproductive consequences. It is not just an individual's behavior that may have reproductive consequences. So, does natural selection also operate in the evolution of culture? Many biologists think not. They say there are substantial differences between biological and cultural evolution. How do cultural evolution and biological evolution compare? To answer this question, we must remember that the operation of natural selection requires three conditions, as we already noted: variation, heritability or mechanisms that duplicate traits in offspring, and differential reproduction because of heritable differences. Do these three requirements apply to cultural behavior?

Domesticated dogs have evolved the ability to understand human social cues far better than wolves.

In biological evolution, variability comes from genetic recombination and mutation. In cultural evolution, it comes from recombination of learned behaviors and from invention.[40] Cultures are not closed or reproductively isolated, as species are. A species cannot borrow genetic traits from another species, but a culture can borrow new things and behaviors from other cultures. The custom of growing corn, which has spread from the New World to many other areas, is an example of this phenomenon. As for the requirement of heritability, although learned traits obviously are not passed to offspring through purely genetic inheritance, parents who exhibit adaptive behavioral traits are more likely to "reproduce" those traits in their children, who may learn them by imitation or by parental instruction. Children and adults may also copy adaptive traits they see in people outside the family. Finally, as for the requirement of differential reproduction, it does not matter whether the trait in question is genetic or learned or both. As Henry Nissen emphasized, "behavioral incompetence leads to extinction as surely as does morphological disproportion or deficiency in any vital organ. Behavior is subject to selection as much as bodily size or resistance to disease."[41]

Many theorists are comfortable with the idea of applying the theory of natural selection to cultural evolution, but others prefer to use different terminology when dealing with traits that do not depend on purely genetic transmission from one generation to the next. For example, Robert Boyd and Peter Richerson discuss human behavior as involving "dual inheritance." They distinguish cultural transmission, by learning and imitation, from genetic transmission, but they emphasize the importance of understanding both and the interaction between them.[42] William Durham also deals separately with cultural transmission, using the term *meme* (analogous to the term *gene*) for the unit of cultural transmission. He directs our attention to the interaction between genes and culture, calling that interaction "coevolution," and provides examples of how genetic evolution and cultural evolution may lead to changes in each other, how they may enhance each other, and how they may even oppose each other.[43]

So biological and cultural evolution in humans may not be completely separate processes. Some of the most important biological features of humans—such as our relatively large brains—may have been favored by natural selection because our ancestors made tools, a cultural trait. Conversely, the cultural trait of informal and formal education may have been favored by natural selection because humans have a long period of immaturity, a biological trait.

As long as the human species continues to exist and the social and physical environment continues to change, there is reason to think that natural selection of biological and cultural traits will also continue. However, as humans learn more about genetic structure, they will become more capable of curing genetically caused disorders and even altering the way evolution proceeds. Today, genetic researchers are capable of diagnosing genetic defects in developing fetuses, and parents can and do decide often whether to terminate a pregnancy. Soon, genetic engineering will probably allow humans to fix defects and even try to "improve" the genetic code of a growing fetus. Whether and to what extent humans should alter genes will undoubtedly be the subject of continuing debate. Whatever the decisions we eventually make about genetic engineering, they will affect the course of human biological and cultural evolution.

Summary and Review

The Evolution of Evolution

3.1 ▸ Trace the history of thinking leading to the concept of evolution.

- Ideas about evolution took a long time to take hold because they contradicted biblical thinking that species were fixed in their form by the creator. But in the 18th and early 19th centuries, increasing evidence suggested that evolution was a viable theory.

- In geology, the concept of uniformitarianism suggested that the earth is constantly subject to shaping and reshaping by natural forces working over vast stretches of time.

- Charles Darwin and Alfred Wallace proposed the mechanism of natural selection to account for the evolution of species.

? How did geological ideas and evidence influence the concept of evolution?

The Principles of Natural Selection

3.2 ▸ Describe the process of natural selection.

- The process of natural selection increases proportions of individuals within a species with advantageous traits.

- Adaptive traits result in greater reproductive success *within a particular environment*. Maladaptive traits eventually decline in frequency or even disappear, but not all maladaptive traits do so. With environmental change, different traits become adaptive.

- Natural selection does not account for all variation in the frequencies of traits. In particular, it does not account for variation in the frequencies of neutral traits—that is, those traits that do not seem to confer any advantages or disadvantages on their carriers.

- Types of natural selection include directional selection, normalizing selection, and balancing selection.

? What are the basic processes of natural selection?

Heredity

3.3 ▸ Specify the principles of genetics.

- Gregor Mendel's research on pea plants helped scientists to understand the biological mechanisms by which traits may be passed from one generation to the next.

- The basic units of heredity are genes. Genes occur in pairs, and each member of a pair is called an allele. Genes are inherited through sperm and egg cells, which are created through the process of meiosis.

- Genes, made up of DNA, provide instructions for cells to make proteins. Proteins are long chains of amino acids that make up the structures of organisms and drive life processes. Segments of DNA are transferred from the cell nucleus by mRNA. The mRNA is then "read" by a ribosome in the cell to construct proteins.

 What is DNA, and why it is important to understanding evolution?

Sources of Variability

3.4 Identify the sources of genetic variability and discuss how each leads to new variations, becomes shuffled through populations, or becomes hybridized.

- Natural selection depends on genetic variation within a population. New variation can occur through genetic recombination or mutation. Recent studies have suggested that hybridization, the creation of viable offspring from two different species, may be possible and may become another source of variation.

- Variations of particular genes are mixed in a population through the processes of genetic drift and gene flow. Genetic drift describes various random processes that affect gene frequencies in small, relatively isolated populations. Gene flow is the process whereby genes pass from one population to another through mating and reproduction.

 What are three sources of genetic variability? How does each work?

The Origin of Species

3.5 Explain what may lead to the origin of species.

- Speciation, the development of a new species, may occur if one subgroup becomes separated from other subgroups. In adapting to different environments, these subpopulations may undergo enough genetic changes to prevent interbreeding, even if they reestablish contact.

- So-called creation scientists and proponents of intelligent design theory argue that the origin of species cannot be accounted for through natural selection. This argument ignores the enormous body of evidence—experimental, fossil, and field data—that demonstrates how natural selection works to create new species.

 Under what conditions might a new species evolve? What is an example of a situation in which that process might happen?

Natural Selection of Behavioral Traits

3.6 Explore the concept of natural selection of behavioral traits.

- Natural selection can also operate on the behavioral characteristics of populations. Approaches such as sociobiology and behavioral ecology involve the application of evolutionary principles to the behavior of animals.

- Much controversy surrounds the degree to which the theory of natural selection can be applied to human behavior, particularly cultural behavior. There is more agreement that biological and cultural evolution in humans may influence each other.

 How might natural selection lead to new behaviors?

Think on it

1. Do you think the theory of **natural selection** is compatible with religious beliefs?

2. How might the discovery of genetic cures and the use of **genetic engineering** affect the future of evolution?

3. Why do you think humans have remained one **species** for at least the last 50,000 years?

CHAPTER 4

Human Variation and Adaptation

LEARNING OBJECTIVES

4.1 Differentiate between adaptation and acclimatization.

4.2 Explain specific variations in human populations in terms of adaptation.

4.3 Contrast the contemporary views on "race" held by most anthropologists and common racist explanations of differences in behavior, intelligence, and cultural complexity.

4.4 Discuss the impact of modern technology on the future of human variation.

In any given human population, individuals vary in external features such as skin color or height and in internal features such as blood type or susceptibility to a disease. If you measure the frequencies of such features in different populations, you will typically find differences on average from one population to another. So, for example, some populations are typically darker in skin color than other populations.

Why do these physical differences exist? They may be largely the product of differences in genes. They may be largely due to growing up in a particular environment, physical and cultural. They are perhaps the result of an interaction between environmental factors and genes.

We turn first to the processes that may singly or jointly produce the varying frequencies of physical traits in different human populations. Then we discuss specific differences in external and internal characteristics and how they might be explained. Finally, we close with a critical examination of racial classification and whether it helps or hinders the study of human variation.

· · ·

Processes in Human Variation and Adaptation

Mutations—changes in the structure of a gene—are the ultimate source of all genetic variation. Because different genes make for greater or lesser chances of survival and reproduction, natural selection results in more favorable genes becoming more frequent in a population over time. We call this process **adaptation**. Adaptations are genetic changes that give their carriers a better chance to survive and reproduce than individuals without the genetic change who live in the same environment. It is the environment, of course, that favors the reproductive success of some traits rather than others.

How adaptive a gene or trait is depends on the specific environment; what is adaptive in one environment may not be adaptive in another. For example, dark-colored moths might have an advantage over light-colored moths where trees are darkened by pollution. Predators could not easily see the darker moths against the dark trees, and these moths might soon outnumber the lighter variety. Indeed, this is precisely what happened in certain areas of Europe and the United States as these countries became industrialized and industrial pollution increased.[1] Similarly, human populations live in a great variety of environments, so we would expect natural selection to favor different genes and traits in those different environments. As we shall see, variations in skin color and body build are among the many features that may be at least partly explainable by how natural selection works in different environments.

Adaptation through natural selection does not account for variation in frequencies of neutral traits—that is, traits that do not confer any advantages or disadvantages on their carriers. The sometimes different and sometimes similar frequencies of neutral traits in human populations may result, then, from genetic drift or gene flow. Genetic drift refers to variations in a population that appear because of random processes such as isolation (the "founder effect"), mating patterns, and the random segregation of chromosomes during meiosis. Gene flow involves the exchange of genes between populations. Neither genetic drift nor gene flow is an adaptive process. Genetic drift may increase the differences between populations. Gene flow tends to work in the opposite direction—it tends to decrease differences between populations.

Acclimatization

Natural selection may favor certain genes because of certain physical environmental conditions, as in the case of the moths in England. But the physical environment can sometimes produce variation even in the absence of genetic change. As we shall see, climate may influence the way the human body grows and develops, and therefore some kinds of human variation may be explainable largely as a function of

4.1 Differentiate between adaptation and acclimatization.

adaptation Refers to genetic changes that allow an organism to survive and reproduce in a specific environment.

Acclimatization Impermanent physiological changes that people make when they encounter a new environment.

environmental variation. We call this process *acclimatization*. **Acclimatization** involves physiological adjustments to environmental conditions in individuals. Acclimatizations may have underlying genetic factors, but they are not themselves genetic. Individuals develop them during their lifetimes rather than being born with them.

Many acclimatizations are simple physiological changes in the body that appear and disappear as the environment changes. For example, when we are chilled, our bodies attempt to create heat by making our muscles work, a physiological response to the environment that we experience as shivering. Longer exposure to cold weather leads our bodies to increase our metabolic rates so that we generate more internal heat. Both these physiological changes are acclimatizations, one short-term (shivering) and one longer-term (increased metabolic rate).

As we discuss later in this chapter, some long-term acclimatizations are difficult to distinguish from adaptations because they become established as normal operating processes, and they may persist even after the individual moves into an environment that is different from the one that originally fostered the acclimatization. It also appears that some acclimatizations are closely related to genetic adaptations. For example, tanning, an acclimatization among light-skinned people when exposed to high levels of solar radiation, is likely in people where light skin color is adapted to environments with typically low solar radiation.

Influence of the Cultural Environment

Not only are humans influenced by their environments through adaptations and acclimatizations, but humans can also dramatically affect their environments. Culture allows humans to modify their environments, and such modifications may lessen the likelihood of genetic adaptations and physiological acclimatizations. For example, the effects of cold may be modified by the culture traits of living in houses, harnessing energy to create heat, and clothing the body to insulate it. In these cultural ways, we alter our "microenvironments." Iron deficiency may be overcome by the culture trait of cooking in iron pots. If a physical environment lacks certain nutrients, people may get them by the culture trait of trading for them; trading for salt has been common in world history. Culture can also influence the direction of natural selection. As we shall see, the culture of dairying seems to have increased the frequency of genes that allow adults to digest milk.[2]

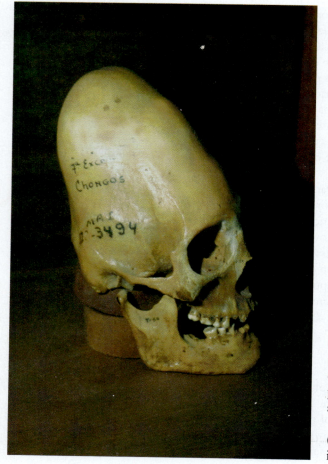

A cranium from the prehistoric Paracas culture of Peru, showing the effects of head binding.

In addition, individual cultures sometimes practice behaviors that lead to physical variations between their members and between members of one culture and another. For example, elites in many highland Andean societies (e.g., the Inca) practiced head binding. The heads of elite children were tightly bound with cloth. As the children grew, the binding forced the skull to take on an elongated, almost conical shape. This cultural practice, then, created physical variations among individuals that were intended to identify members of elite groups.[3] Many cultures have practices that are intended to create physical variations that distinguish members of their culture from members of other cultures. The Hebrew Bible, for example, tells the story of how Abraham was instructed by God to circumcise himself and all his male descendants as a sign of the covenant between them.[4] Thus, male descendants of Abraham traditionally share a culturally induced physical variation (lack of a foreskin) to identify themselves as a group.

In the next section, we discuss some aspects of human (physical) variation for which we have explanations that involve one or more of the processes just described.

Physical Variation in Human Populations

4.2 Explain specific variations in human populations in terms of adaptation.

The most noticeable physical variations among populations are those that are external, on the surface—body build, facial features, skin color, and height. No less important are those variations that are internal, such as variation in susceptibility to different diseases and differences in the ability to produce certain enzymes.

We begin our survey with some physical features that appear to be strongly linked to variation in climate, particularly variation in temperature, sunlight, and altitude.

Body Build and Facial Construction

Scientists have suggested that the body build of many birds and mammals may vary according to the temperature of the environment in which they live. Bergmann and Allen, two 19th-century naturalists, suggested some general rules for animals, but researchers did not begin to examine whether these rules applied to human populations until the 1950s.[5] **Bergmann's rule** describes what seems to be a general relationship between body size and temperature: The slenderer populations of a species inhabit the warmer parts of its geographic range, and the more robust populations inhabit the cooler areas.

D. F. Roberts's studies of variation in mean body weight of human populations in regions with widely differing temperatures have provided support for Bergmann's rule.[6] Roberts discovered that the lowest body weights were found among residents of areas with the highest mean annual temperatures, and vice versa. Figure 4.1 shows the relationship between body weight of males and average annual temperature for four different geographic populations. Although the slope of the relationship is slightly different for each group, the trend is the same—with colder temperatures, weight is greater. Looking at the general trend across populations (see the "Total" line), we see that where the mean annual temperatures are about freezing (32°F; 0°C), the average weight for males is about 143 pounds (65 kilograms); where the mean annual temperatures are about 77°F (25°C), men weigh, on average, about 110 pounds (50 kilograms).

Allen's rule refers to another kind of variation in body build among birds and mammals: Protruding body parts (e.g., limbs) are relatively shorter in the cooler areas of a species' range than in the warmer areas. Research comparing human populations tends to support Allen's rule.[7]

The rationale behind these theories is that the long-limbed, lean body type often found in equatorial regions provides more surface area in relation to body mass and thus facilitates the dissipation of body heat. In contrast, the chunkier, shorter-limbed body type found among residents of cold regions promotes retention of body heat because the amount of surface area relative to body mass is lessened. The build of the Inuit (Eskimo) appears to exemplify Bergmann's and Allen's rules. The relatively large bodies and short legs of the Inuit may be adapted to the cold temperatures in which they live.

It is not clear whether differences in body build among populations are due solely to natural selection of different genes under different conditions of cold or heat. Some of the variations may be acclimatizations induced during the life span of individuals.[8] Alphonse Riesenfeld provided experimental evidence that extreme cold can affect body proportions during growth and development. Rats raised under conditions of extreme cold generally showed changes that resemble characteristics of humans in cold environments. These cold-related changes included shortening of the long bones, consistent with Allen's rule.[9]

maybe not so true

Bergmann's rule The rule that smaller-sized subpopulations of a species inhabit the warmer parts of its geographic range and larger-sized subpopulations the cooler areas.

Might be true

Allen's rule The rule that protruding body parts (particularly arms and legs) are relatively shorter in the cooler areas of a species' range than in the warmer areas.

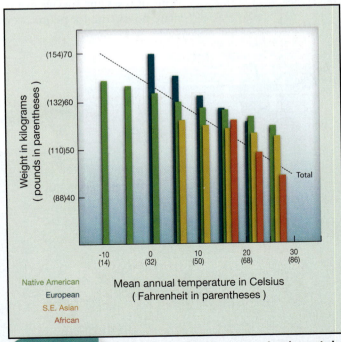

FIGURE 4.1   **The relationship between body weight in males and average annual temperature for four major population groups.**

In colder temperatures weight is greater.

Source: From Roberts 1953.

Like body build, facial structure may also be affected by environment. Riesenfeld found experimentally that the facial width of rats increased in cold temperatures and their nasal openings grew smaller.[10] Because the rats raised in cold environments were genetically similar to those raised in warmer environments, we can confidently conclude that the environment, not genes, brought about these changes in the rats. How much the environment directly affects variation in the human face is not clear. We know that variation in climate is associated with facial variation. For example, people living in the humid tropics tend to have broad, short, flat noses, whereas people living in climates with low humidity (with cold or hot temperatures) tend to have long, thin noses. A narrow nose may be a more efficient humidifier of drier air than a broad nose.[11]

Skin Color

Human populations obviously differ in average skin color. Many people consider skin color the most important indicator of "race," and they sometimes treat others differently solely on this basis. But anthropologists, in addition to being critical of prejudice, also note that skin color is not a good indicator of ancestry. For example, dark skin is commonly found in sub-Saharan Africa. However, natives of southern India have skin as dark or darker than that of many Africans. Yet these people are not closely related to Africans, either genetically or historically.

How can we explain the wide range of skin colors among the peoples of the world? The color of a person's skin depends on both the amount of dark pigment, or melanin, in the skin and the amount of blood in the small blood vessels of the skin.[12] Despite the fact that there is still much to understand about the genetics of skin color, we can explain much of the variation.

The amount of melanin in the skin seems to be related to the climate in which a person lives. **Gloger's rule** states that populations of birds and mammals living in warmer climates have more melanin, and therefore darker skin, fur, or feathers, than do populations of the same species living in cooler areas. On the whole, this association with climate holds true for people as well as for other mammals and birds.

This Inuit father and son illustrate Allen's rule. Both have relatively large bodies and short limbs, which help them maintain body heat in the cold climate they inhabit.

These East African young men live in a warm climate and have long limbs and torsos, which is thought to help them dissipate body heat.

The populations of darker-skinned humans do live mostly in warm climates, particularly sunny climates (see Figure 4.2). Dark pigmentation seems to have at least one specific advantage in sunny climates. Melanin protects the sensitive inner layers of the skin from the sun's damaging ultraviolet rays; therefore, dark-skinned people living in sunny areas are safer from sunburn and skin cancers than are light-skinned people. Dark skin may also confer other important biological advantages in tropical environments, such as greater resistance to tropical diseases.[13]

What, then, might be the advantages of light-colored skin? Presumably, there must be some benefits in some environments; otherwise, all human populations would tend to have relatively dark skin. Although light-skinned people are more susceptible to sunburn and skin cancers, the ultraviolet radiation that light skin absorbs also facilitates the body's production of vitamin D. Vitamin D helps the body incorporate calcium and thus is necessary for the proper growth and maintenance of bones. Too much vitamin D, however, can cause illness. Thus, the light-colored skin of people in temperate latitudes maximizes ultraviolet penetration, perhaps ensuring production of sufficient amounts of vitamin D for good health, whereas the darker skin of people in tropical latitudes minimizes ultraviolet penetration, perhaps preventing illness from too much vitamin D.[14] Light skin may also confer another advantage in colder environments: It is less likely to be damaged by frostbite.[15]

We now have direct evidence that confirms the connection between solar radiation and skin pigmentation. Anthropologists Nina Jablonski and George Chaplin used data from NASA satellites to determine the average amount of ultraviolet radiation people were exposed to in different parts of the world. They compared these average radiation amounts to data on skin reflectance (the lighter one's skin, the more light it reflects) and found that dark skin is more prevalent where ultraviolet radiation is more intense. Interestingly, there seems to be one notable exception—Native Americans tend to be lighter-skinned than expected. Jablonski and Chaplin suggest that this is because they are recent migrants to the New World, and their skin colors have not adapted to the varying levels of ultraviolet radiation they encountered in the Americas, just as the skin colors of European colonizers have not.[16]

Gloger's rule The rule that populations of birds and mammals living in warm, humid climates have more melanin (and therefore darker skin, fur, or feathers) than populations of the same species living in cooler, drier areas.

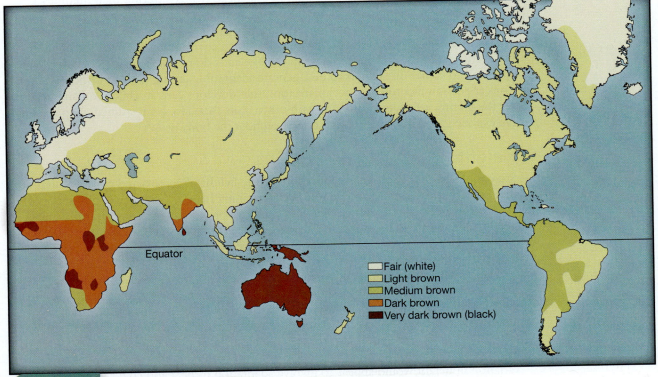

FIGURE 4.2   **Variation in Skin Color**

Source: From Robins 1991.

Human skin color varies dramatically, and Gloger's rule explains this variation as an adaptation to climate. In humans, the intensity of sunlight is a key factor in skin color variation.

hypoxia A condition of oxygen deficiency that often occurs at high altitudes. The percentage of oxygen in the air is the same as at lower altitudes, but because the barometric pressure is lower, less oxygen is taken in with each breath. Often, breathing becomes more rapid, the heart beats faster, and activity is more difficult.

Adaptation to High Altitude

Oxygen constitutes 21 percent of the air we breathe at sea level. At high altitudes, the percentage of oxygen in the air is the same, but because the barometric pressure is lower, we take in less oxygen with each breath.[17] We breathe more rapidly, our hearts beat faster, and all activity is more difficult. The net effects are discomfort and a condition known as **hypoxia**, or oxygen deficiency.

If high altitude presents such difficulties for many human beings, how is it that populations numbering in the millions can live out their lives, healthy and productive, at altitudes of 6,000, 12,000, or even 17,000 feet? Populations in the Himalayas and the Andes have adapted to their environments and do not display the symptoms that low-altitude dwellers suffer when they are exposed to high altitudes. Moreover, high-altitude dwellers have come to terms physiologically with extreme cold, deficient nutrition, strong winds, rough countryside, and intense solar radiation.[18]

Early studies of Andean high-altitude dwellers found that they differed in certain physical ways from low-altitude dwellers. Compared with low-altitude dwellers, high-altitude Andean Indians had larger chests and greater lung capacity, as well as more surface area in the capillaries of the lungs (which was believed to facilitate the transfer of oxygen to the blood).[19] Early researchers thought that genetic changes had allowed the Andeans to maximize their ability to take in oxygen at the lower barometric pressure of their high-altitude environment. Recent research, however, has cast some doubt on this conclusion. It appears now that other populations living at high altitudes do not show the Andean pattern of physical differences. In the Himalayas, for example, low-altitude dwellers and high-altitude dwellers do not differ in chest size or lung size, even though both groups show adequate lung functioning.[20]

Thus, current research does not suggest that high-altitude living requires biological adaptations that are purely genetic. In fact, some evidence suggests that humans who grow up in a high-altitude environment may adapt to hypoxia during their lifetimes as they mature. For example, Peruvians who were born at sea level but who grew up at high altitudes developed the same amount of lung capacity as people who spent their entire lives at high altitudes.[21] Consistent with a presumed environmental effect, the children of high-altitude Peruvians who grow up in the lowlands do not develop larger chests. What appeared to earlier researchers to be a genetic adaptation among highland Andean populations appears in fact to be an acclimatization that develops early in childhood and persists for the lifetime of an individual. As with other traits that have been studied, it appears that life experiences can have profound effects on how the body grows.

Height

Studies of identical twins and comparisons of the height of parents and children suggest that heredity plays a considerable role in determining height,[22] so genetic differences must at least partly explain differences between populations in average height. But if average height can increase dramatically in a few decades, as in Japan between 1950 and 1980, and in many other countries in recent times,[23] then environmental influences are also likely to be important.

The considerable variation in average height among human populations may be partly explained by temperature differences. The Dutch, in Europe, are among the tallest populations in the world on average, and the Mbuti of Zaire, in central Africa, are among the shortest.[24] We already know that weight is related to mean annual temperature (Bergmann's rule). Weight is also related to height (taller people are likely to be heavier). So, because the taller (heavier) Dutch live in a cooler climate, some of the population variation in height would appear to involve adaptation to heat and cold.[25] Other factors besides heat and cold must also be operating, however, because tall and short peoples can be found in most areas of the world.

Many researchers think that poor nutrition and disease lead to reduced height and weight. In many parts of the world, children in higher social classes are taller on the average than children in lower social classes,[26] and this difference is more marked in economically poorer countries,[27] where the wealth and health differences between the classes are particularly large. During times of war and poor nutrition, children's stature often decreases. For example, in Germany during World War II, the stature of children 7 to 17 years of age declined as compared with previous time periods despite the fact that stature had generally increased over time.[28]

More persuasive evidence for the effects of poor nutrition and disease comes out of longitudinal studies of the same individuals over time. For example, Reynaldo Martorell found that children in Guatemala who had frequent bouts of diarrhea were on the average over an inch shorter at age 7 than children without frequent diarrhea.[29] Although malnourished or diseased children can catch up in their growth, follow-up research on Guatemalan children suggests that, if stunting occurs before 3 years of age, stature at age 18 will still be reduced.[30]

A controversial set of studies links a very different environmental factor to variation in height in human populations. The factor at issue is stress, physical and emotional, in infancy.[31] Contrary to the view that any kind of stress is harmful, it appears that some presumably stressful experiences in infancy are associated with greater height and weight. Experimental studies with rats provided the original stimulus for the studies investigating the possible effect of stress on height. The experiments showed that rats that were physically handled ("petted") by the experimenters grew to be longer and heavier than rats not petted. Researchers originally thought that this was because the petted rats had received "tender loving care." But someone noticed that the petted rats seemed terrified (they urinated and defecated) when petted by humans, which suggested that the petting might have been stressful. It turned out in subsequent studies that even more obviously stressful experiences such as electric shock, vibration, and temperature extremes also produced rats with longer skeletons as compared with unstressed rats.

Thomas Landauer and John Whiting thought that stress in human infants might similarly produce greater adult height. Many cultures have customs for treating infants that could be physically stressful, including circumcision; branding of the skin with sharp objects; piercing the nose, ears, or lips for the insertion of ornaments; molding and stretching the head and limbs for cosmetic purposes; and vaccination. In addition, Shulamith Gunders and John Whiting suggested that separating the baby from its mother right after birth is another kind of stress. In cross-cultural comparisons by Whiting and his colleagues,[32] it seems that *both* physical stress and mother–infant separation, *if practiced before 2 years of age,* predict greater adult height; males are on the average 2 inches taller in such societies. (It is important to note that the stresses being discussed are short in duration, often a one-time occurrence, and do not constitute prolonged stress or abuse, which can have opposite effects.)

Because the cross-cultural evidence is associational, not experimental, it is possible that the results are due to some factor confounded with infant stress. Perhaps societies with infant stress have better nutrition or have climates that favor tallness. Recently, using new cross-cultural comparisons, J. Patrick Gray and Linda Wolfe attempted to assess different possible predictors of height variation between populations. The predictors compared were nutrition, climate, geography, physical stress, and mother–infant separation. Gray and Wolfe's analysis indicated which of those factors predicted adult height independently of the others. It turned out that geographic region, climatic zone, and customs of infant stress were all significant independent predictors of height,[33] so the results now available clearly show that the effect of infant stress cannot be discounted.

Persuasive evidence for the stress hypothesis also comes from an experimental study conducted in Kenya.[34] Landauer and Whiting arranged for a randomly selected sample of children to be vaccinated before they were 2 years old. Other children were vaccinated soon after they were 2. A few years later, the two groups were compared with respect to height. Consistent with the cross-cultural evidence on the possible effect of stress on height, the children vaccinated before the age of 2 were significantly taller than the children vaccinated later. The children vaccinated before the age of 2 were selected randomly for early vaccination, so it is unlikely that nutritional or other differences between the two groups account for their difference in height.

As we noted earlier, people have been getting taller in several areas of the world. What accounts for this recent trend toward greater height? Several factors may be involved. Some researchers think that it may be the result of improved nutrition and lower incidence of infectious diseases.[35] But it might also be that infant stress has increased as a result of giving birth in hospitals, which usually separate babies from mothers and also subject the newborns to medical tests, including taking blood. Various kinds of vaccinations have also become more common in infancy.[36]

In short, differences in human size seem to be the result of both adaptations and acclimatizations, with both of these, in turn, affected by cultural factors such as nutrition and stress.

Susceptibility to Infectious Diseases

Certain populations seem to have developed inherited resistances to particular infectious diseases. That is, populations repeatedly decimated by certain diseases in the past now have a high frequency of genetic characteristics that ameliorate the effects of these diseases. As Arno Motulsky pointed out, if there are genes that protect people from dying when they are infected by one of the diseases prevalent in their area, these genes will tend to become more common in succeeding generations.[37]

A field study of the infectious disease myxomatosis in rabbits supports this theory. When the virus responsible for the disease was first introduced into the Australian rabbit population, more than 95 percent of the infected animals died. But among the offspring of animals exposed to successive epidemics of myxomatosis, the percentage of animals that died from the disease decreased from year to year. The more epidemics the animals' ancestors had lived through, the smaller the percentage of current animals that died of the disease. Thus, the data suggested that the rabbits had developed a genetic resistance to myxomatosis.[38]

Infectious diseases seem to follow a similar pattern among human populations. When tuberculosis first strikes a population that has had no previous contact with it, the disease is usually fatal. But some populations seem to have inherited a resistance to death from tuberculosis. For example, the Ashkenazi Jews in America (those whose ancestors came from central and eastern Europe) are one of several populations whose ancestors survived many years of exposure to tuberculosis in the crowded European ghettos where they had previously lived. Although the rate of tuberculosis infection is identical among American Jews and non-Jews, the rate of tuberculosis mortality is significantly lower among Jews than among non-Jews in the United States.[39] After reviewing other data on this subject, Motulsky thought it likely "that the present relatively high resistance of Western populations to tuberculosis is genetically conditioned through natural selection during long contact with the disease."[40]

We tend to think of measles as a childhood disease that kills virtually no one, and we now have a vaccine against it. But when first introduced into populations, the measles virus can kill large numbers of people. In 1949, the Tupari Indians of Brazil numbered about 200 people. By 1955, two-thirds of the Tupari had died of measles introduced into the tribe by rubber gatherers in the area.[41] Large numbers of people died of measles in epidemics in the Faeroe Islands in 1846, in Hawaii in 1848, in the Fiji Islands in 1874, and among

Permanent settlements and high population densities allow diseases to spread rapidly and produce epidemics. Shown here is Banda Aceh's Peunayong Market in Indonesia. Close contact between chickens and humans in markets like this one provided the opportunity for the deadly H5N1 strain of bird flu to evolve.

the Canadian Inuit very recently. It is possible that where mortality rates from measles are low, populations have acquired a genetic resistance to death from this disease.[42]

Why is a population susceptible to a disease in the first place? Epidemiologist Francis Black suggests that lack of genes for resistance is not the whole answer. A high degree of genetic homogeneity in the population may also increase susceptibility.[43] A virus grown in one host is preadapted to a genetically similar new host and is therefore likely to be more virulent in the new host. For example, the measles virus adapts to a host individual; when it replicates, the viral forms that the host cannot kill are those most likely to survive and continue replicating. When the virus passes to a new host with similar genes, the preadapted virus is likely to kill the new host. On the other hand, if the next host is very different genetically, the adaptation process starts over again; the virus is not so virulent at first because the host can kill it.

Populations that recently came to an area, and that had a small group of founders (as was probably true for the first Native Americans and the Polynesian seafarers who first settled many islands in the Pacific), tended to have a high degree of genetic homogeneity. Therefore, epidemic diseases introduced by Europeans (such as measles) would be likely to kill many of the natives within the first few years after contact. Up to an estimated 56 million people died in the New World after contact with Europeans, mostly because of introduced diseases such as smallpox and measles. Similarly caused depopulation occurred widely in the Pacific.[44]

Some researchers suggest that nongenetic factors may also partly explain differential resistance to infectious disease. For example, cultural practices may partly explain the epidemics of measles among the Yanomamö Indians of Venezuela and Brazil. The Yanomamö frequently visit other villages, and that, together with the non-isolation of sick individuals, promoted a very rapid spread of the disease. Because many individuals were sick at the same time, there were not enough healthy people to feed and care for the sick; mothers down with measles could not even nurse their babies. Thus, cultural factors may increase exposure to a disease and worsen its effect on a population.[45]

Epidemics of infectious disease may occur only if many people live near each other. Hunter-gatherers, who usually live in small dispersed bands, do not have enough people in and near the community to keep an epidemic going. Without enough people to infect, short-lived microorganisms that cause or carry diseases die out. In contrast, among agriculturalists, there are larger numbers of people in and around the community to whom a disease can spread. Permanent settlements, particularly urban settlements, also are likely to have poor sanitation and contaminated water. Tuberculosis is an example of an infectious disease that, although very old, began to kill large numbers of people only after the emergence of sedentary, larger communities.[46]

Sickle-Cell Anemia

Another biological variation is an abnormality of the red blood cells known as **sickle-cell anemia**, or sicklemia. This is a condition in which normal, disk-shaped red blood cells assume a crescent (sickle) shape when deprived of oxygen. The sickle-shaped red blood cells do not move through the body as readily as normal cells and thus cause more oxygen deficiency and damage to the heart, lungs, brain, and other vital organs. In addition, the red blood cells tend to die more rapidly, worsening the anemia still more.[47]

Sickle-cell anemia is caused by a variant form of the genetic instructions for hemoglobin, the protein that carries oxygen in the red blood cells. Individuals who have sickle-cell anemia have inherited the same allele (Hb^S) from both parents and are therefore homozygous for that gene. Individuals who receive this allele from only one parent are heterozygous; they have one Hb^S allele and one allele for normal hemoglobin (Hb^A). Heterozygotes generally will not show the full-blown symptoms of sickle-cell disease, although a heterozygous individual may have a mild case of anemia in some cases. A heterozygous person has a 50 percent chance of passing on the sickle-cell allele to a child, and if the child later mates with another person who is also a carrier of the sickle-cell allele, the statistical probability is that 25 percent of their children will develop sickle-cell anemia. Without advanced medical care, most individuals with two Hb^S alleles are unlikely to live more than a few years.[48]

sickle-cell anemia (sicklemia) A condition in which red blood cells assume a crescent (sickle) shape when deprived of oxygen, instead of the normal (disk) shape. The sickle-shaped red blood cells do not move through the body as readily as normal cells, and thus cause damage to the heart, lungs, brain, and other vital organs.

Why has the allele for sickle-cell persisted in various populations? If people with sickle-cell anemia do not usually live to reproduce, we would expect a reduction in the frequency of Hb^S to near zero through the process of *normalizing selection*. But the sickle-cell allele occurs fairly often in some parts of the world, particularly in the wet tropical belt of Africa, where frequencies may be between 20 percent and 30 percent, and in Greece, Sicily, and southern India.[49]

Because the sickle-cell gene occurs in these places much more often than expected, researchers in the 1940s and the 1950s began to suspect that heterozygous individuals (who carry one Hb^S allele) might have a reproductive advantage in a malarial environment.[50] If the heterozygotes were more resistant to attacks of malaria than the homozygotes for normal hemoglobin (who get the Hb^A allele from both parents), the heterozygotes would be more likely to survive and reproduce, and therefore the recessive Hb^S allele would persist at a higher-than-expected frequency in the population. This kind of outcome is an example of *balancing selection*.[51]

A number of pieces of evidence support the "malaria theory." First, geographic comparisons show that the sickle-cell allele tends to be found where the incidence of malaria is high (see Figure 4.3). Second, as land in the tropics is opened to yam and rice agriculture, the incidence of the sickle-cell allele also increases. Indeed, recent studies suggest malaria may have evolved alongside agriculture in these regions.[52] The reason seems to be that malaria, carried principally by the *Anopheles gambiae* mosquito, becomes more prevalent as tropical forest gives way to more open land where mosquitoes can thrive in warm, sunlit ponds. Indeed, even among peoples of similar cultural backgrounds, the incidence of the sickle-cell allele increases with greater rainfall and surpluses of water. Third, children who are heterozygous for the sickle-cell trait tend to have fewer malarial parasites in their bodies than do homozygous normal individuals, and they are more likely to survive.[53] The sickling trait does not necessarily keep people from contracting malaria, but it greatly decreases the rate of mortality from malaria—and in evolutionary terms, the overall effect is the same.[54] Fourth, if there is no balancing selection because malaria is no longer present, we should find a rapid decline in the incidence of the sickle-cell allele. Indeed, we find such a decline in populations with African ancestry. Those who live in malaria-free

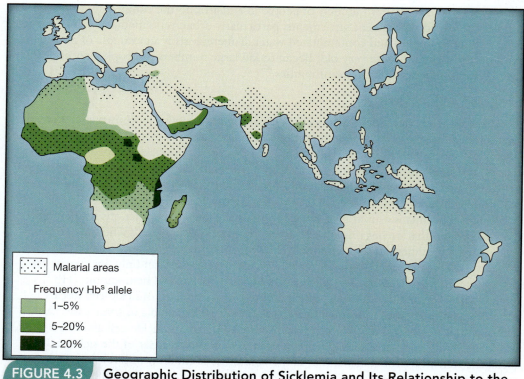

Malarial areas

Frequency Hb^S allele
1–5%
5–20%
≥ 20%

FIGURE 4.3 Geographic Distribution of Sicklemia and Its Relationship to the Distribution of Malaria

zones of the New World have a much lower incidence of sicklemia than do those who live in malarial regions of the New World.[55]

HbS is not the only abnormal hemoglobin to have a distribution related to malaria. It seems that a number of abnormal hemoglobins may be widespread because of the advantage that heterozygotes have against the disease. For example, another abnormal hemoglobin, HbE, occurs in populations from India through Southeast Asia and New Guinea where malaria occurs, but HbS is not that common. Why should HbE heterozygotes have resistance to malaria? One possibility is that malarial parasites are less able to survive in an individual's blood with some normal and some abnormal hemoglobin. Abnormal hemoglobin cells are more delicate and live less long, so they may not readily support malarial parasites.[56]

Lactase Deficiency

When American educators discovered that African American schoolchildren very often did not drink milk, they assumed that lack of money or education was the reason. These assumptions provided the impetus for establishing the school milk programs prevalent around the country. However, it now appears that, after infancy, many people lack the enzyme lactase, which is necessary for breaking down the sugar in milk—lactose—into simpler sugars that can be absorbed into the bloodstream.[57] Thus, a person without lactase cannot digest milk properly, and drinking it may cause bloating, cramps, stomach gas, and diarrhea. A study conducted in Baltimore among 312 African American and 221 European American children in grades 1 through 6 in two elementary schools indicated that 85 percent of the African American children and 17 percent of the European American children were milk-intolerant.[58]

More recent studies indicate that lactose intolerance occurs frequently in adults in many parts of the world. The condition is common in Southeast and East Asia, India, the Mediterranean and the Near East, sub-Saharan Africa, and among Native North and South Americans. The widespread incidence of lactose intolerance should not be surprising. After infancy, mammals normally stop producing lactase.[59]

If lactose intolerance in adulthood in mammals is normal, we need to understand why only some human populations have the ability to make lactase in adulthood and digest lactose. Why would selection favor this genetic ability in some populations but not in others? In the late 1960s, F. J. Simoons and Robert McCracken noted a relationship between lactose absorption and dairying (raising cows for milk). They suggested that, with the advent of dairying, individuals with the genetic ability to produce lactase in adulthood would have greater reproductive success; hence, dairying populations would come to have a high proportion of individuals with the ability to break down lactose.[60]

But people in some dairying societies do not produce lactase in adulthood. Rather, they seem to have developed a cultural solution to the problem of lactase deficiency; they transform their milk into cheese, yogurt, sour cream, and other milk products that are low in lactose. To make these low-lactose products, people separate the lactose-rich whey from the curds or treat the milk with a bacterium (*Lactobacillus*) that breaks down the lactose, thus making the milk product digestible by a lactase-deficient person.[61]

So why did natural selection favor a biological solution (the production of the enzyme lactase in adulthood) in some dairying societies rather than the cultural solution? William Durham has collected evidence that natural selection may favor the biological solution in dairying societies farther from the equator. The theory is that lactose behaves biochemically like vitamin D, facilitating the absorption of calcium—but only in people who produce lactase so that they can absorb the lactose. Because people in more temperate latitudes are not exposed to that much sunlight, particularly in the winter, and therefore make less vitamin D in their skin, natural selection may have favored the lactase way of absorbing dietary calcium.[62] In other words, natural selection may favor lactase production in adulthood, as well as lighter skin, at higher latitudes (where there is less sunlight).

This is an example of how culture may influence the way natural selection favors some genes over others. Without dairying, natural selection may not have favored the genetic propensity to produce lactase. This propensity is yet another example of the complex ways in which genes, environment, and culture interact to create human variation.

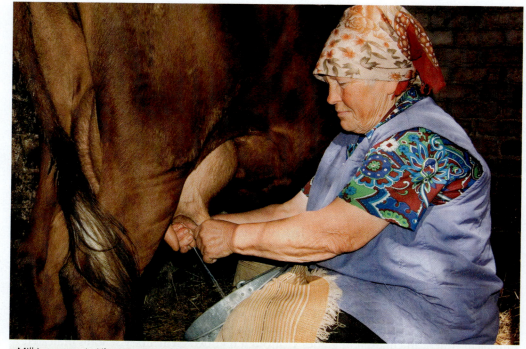

Milking a cow in Ukraine. Natural selection may favor production of the enzyme lactase, a genetic way of making milk digestible in dairying populations far from the equator.

4.3 ▶ Contrast the contemporary views on "race" held by most anthropologists and common racist explanations of differences in behavior, intelligence, and cultural complexity.

Race In biology, race refers to a subpopulation or variety of a species that differs somewhat in gene frequencies from other varieties of the species. All members of a species can interbreed and produce viable offspring. Many anthropologists do not think that the concept of race is usefully applied to humans because humans do not fall into geographic populations that can be easily distinguished in terms of different sets of biological or physical traits. Thus, race in humans is largely a culturally assigned category.

"Race" and Racism

Fortunately, internal variations such as lactase deficiency have never been associated with intergroup tensions—perhaps because such differences are not immediately obvious. Unfortunately, the same cannot be said for some of the more obvious external human differences such as skin color.

For as long as any of us can remember, countless aggressive actions—from fistfights to large-scale riots and civil wars—have stemmed from tensions and misunderstandings between various groups commonly referred to by many as "races." *Race* has become such a common term that most of us take the concept for granted, not bothering to consider what it does and does not mean. We may talk about the "human race," which means that all humans belong to the same breeding population. Yet we are often asked to check a box to identify our particular "race." We discuss first how biologists sometimes use the term *race;* then we turn to why most biological anthropologists now conclude that the concept of race does not apply usefully to humans. We discuss how racial classifications are largely social constructions that have been used to justify discrimination, exploitation, and even the extermination of certain categories of people.

Race as a Construct in Biology

Biological variation is not uniformly distributed in any species. Although all members of a species can potentially interbreed with others, most matings take place within smaller groups or breeding populations. Through the processes of natural selection and genetic drift, populations inhabiting different geographic regions will come to exhibit some differences in biological traits. When differences within a species become sufficiently noticeable, biologists may classify different populations into different *varieties,* or *races.* If the term **race** is understood to be just a shorthand or classificatory way that biologists describe slight population variants within a species, the concept of race would probably not be controversial. Unfortunately, as applied to humans, racial classifications have often

A Masai woman milking a cow in Kenya. Natural selection may favor the souring of milk, a cultural way of making it digestible in dairying populations close to the equator.

been confounded with **racism**, the belief that some "races" are innately inferior to others. The misuse and misunderstanding of the term *race* and its association with racist thinking is one reason why many biological anthropologists and others have suggested that the term should not be applied to human biological differences (but see the box feature on "Use of Race in Forensic Anthropology").

A second reason for not applying racial classification to humans is that humans have exhibited so much interbreeding that different populations are not clearly classifiable into discrete groups that can be defined in terms of the presence or absence of particular biological traits.[63] Therefore, many argue that "race" is not scientifically useful for describing human biological variation. The difficulty in employing racial classification is evident by comparing the number of "races" that classifiers come up with. The number of "racial" categories in humans has varied from as few as 3 to more than 37.[64]

How can human groups be clearly divided into "races" if most adaptive biological traits show clines or gradual differences from one region to another?[65] Skin color is a good example of clinal variation. In the area around Egypt, there is a gradient of skin color as one moves from north to south in the Nile Valley. Skin generally becomes darker closer to the equator (south) and lighter closer to the Mediterranean. But other adaptive traits may not have north-south clines because the environmental predictors may be distributed differently. Nose shape varies with humidity, but clines in humidity do not particularly correspond to variation in latitude. So the gradient for skin color would not be the same as the gradient for nose shape. Because adaptive traits tend to be clinally distributed, there is no line you could draw on a world map that would separate "white" from "black" people or "whites" from "Asians."[66] Only traits that are neutral in terms of natural selection will tend (because of genetic drift) to cluster in regions.[67]

Racial classification is problematic also because there is sometimes more physical, physiological, and genetic diversity *within* a single geographic group that might be called a "race" (e.g., Africans) than there is *between* supposed "racial" groups. Africans vary more among themselves than they do in comparison with people elsewhere.[68] Analyses of all human populations have demonstrated that between 93 percent and 95 percent of genetic variation is due to individual differences within populations, whereas only 3 percent to 5 percent of genetic variation is due to differences between major human population groups.[69] "Race," when applied to humans, is a social category, not a scientific one.

Racism The belief, without scientific basis, that some "races" are inferior to others.

Applied Anthropology

The Use of "Race" in Forensic Anthropology

In this chapter, we have made the point that human "races" are not valid biological entities. There is more genetic variation within alleged "races" than between them, and the characteristics used to define "races" are primarily visual—skin color, hair form, eye form, and the like. Most anthropologists (over 70 percent according to a recent survey) disagree with the statement, "There are biological races in the species *Homo sapiens*." Given this fact, it seems odd that many forensic anthropologists still employ "race" as one of the categories for identifying skeletal remains.

Diana Smay and George Armelagos suggest three reasons why forensic anthropologists still employ the concept of "race." First, some forensic anthropologists genuinely believe that "race" is a useful analytical tool. For these anthropologists, the fact that it is easy for anyone to categorize others into "races" must mean something is genuine about the concept. Indeed, some forensic anthropologists suggest that they can determine "race" with 80 percent accuracy from skeletal remains (although others argue that without clear information about the specific geographical location where the remains were found, accuracy drops to less than 20 percent). Second, in some circumstances the "race" concept seems to work. Within local areas, at least, a well-trained forensic anthropologist can determine whether a skeleton comes from one of the major "race" groups. But as forensic anthropologist Madeleine Hinkes explains, "sometimes it is only the anthropologist's experience that tells him there is an undefinable 'something' about the skeleton that

Forensic anthropologists are often asked to determine the race of a skeletal corpse.

suggests one race over another"—not a very convincing argument for the analytical utility of "race."

A third reason Smay and Armelagos give for why many forensic anthropologists continue to employ the concept of "race" is that they are asked to do so. As Stanley Rhine points out, "The forensic anthropologist who can tell officials that an unknown skull is, for instance, Hispanic, provides a datum useful in narrowing search parameters. By contrast, the forensic anthropologist who delivers a philosophical lecture to the sheriff on the non-existence of human races is unlikely to be consulted again." But is this a good reason to employ the concept of "race"? Might there be a better way to provide information to police and other officials to help them identify a set of human remains?

Alice Brues thinks so. She argues that forensic anthropologists should focus on local, geographic variations among populations that we know do exist and avoid the large "race" categories that we know do not. In Alaska, for example, forensic anthropologists might be able to distinguish between Inuit and Aleut remains, or between Chinese, Japanese, and Polynesian in California. Brues argues that by lumping the real variation that is present in these local populations into predefined "racial" categories, forensic anthropologists limit their ability to use the full range of variation to identify unique, local variations that might be useful in identifying human remains.

Sources: Brues 1992; Hinkes 1993, 51; Lieberman et al. 2003; Rhine 1993, 55; Smay and Armelagos 2000.

"Race" and Civilization

Many people hold the racist viewpoint that the biological inferiority of certain groups, which they call "races," is reflected in the supposedly "primitive" quality of their cultures. They will argue that the "developed" nations are "white" and the "underdeveloped" nations are not. (We put terms like "white," which are used as racial categories, in quotes to indicate the problematic nature of the categories.) But to make such an argument ignores much of history. Many of today's so-called underdeveloped nations—primarily in Asia,

Africa, and South America—had developed complex and sophisticated civilizations long before European nations expanded and acquired considerable power. The advanced societies of the Shang dynasty in China, the Mayans in Mesoamerica, and the African empire of Ghana were all founded and developed by "nonwhites."

Between 1523 and 1028 B.C., China had a complex form of government, armies, metal tools and weapons, and production and storage facilities for large quantities of grain. The early Chinese civilization also had writing and elaborate religious rituals.[70] From A.D. 300 to 900, the Mayans were a large population with a thriving economy. They built many large and beautiful cities in which were centered great pyramids and luxurious palaces.[71] According to legend, the West African civilization of Ghana was founded during the 2nd century A.D. By A.D. 770, the time of the Sonniki rulers, Ghana had developed two capital cities—one Muslim and the other non-Muslim—each with its own ruler and both supported largely by Ghana's lucrative gold market.[72]

Considering how recently northern Europeans developed cities and central governments, it seems odd that some "whites" should label Africans, Native Americans, and others backward in terms of historical achievement or biologically inferior in terms of capacity for civilization. But racists, both "white" and "nonwhite," choose to ignore the fact that many populations have achieved remarkable advances in civilization. Most significant, racists refuse to believe that they can acknowledge the achievements of another group without in any way downgrading the achievements of their own.

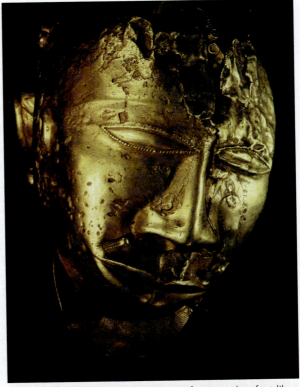

African metal workers created magnificent works of art like this golden head from Ghana long before Europeans arrived.

"Race", Conquest, and the Role of Infectious Disease

There are those who would argue that Europeans' superiority accounted for their ability to colonize much of the world during the last few hundred years. But it now appears that Europeans were able to dominate at least partly because many native peoples were susceptible to diseases they introduced.[73] Earlier, we discussed how continued exposure to epidemics of infectious diseases, such as tuberculosis and measles, can cause succeeding generations to acquire a genetic resistance to death from such diseases. Smallpox had a long history in Europe and Africa; genetic resistance eventually made it mostly a survivable childhood disease. But in the New World, it was quite another story. Cortez and the conquistadores were inadvertently aided by smallpox in their attempt to defeat the Aztecs of Mexico. In 1520, a member of Cortez's army unwittingly transmitted smallpox to the natives. The disease spread rapidly, killing at least 50 percent of the population, and so the Aztecs were at a considerable disadvantage in their battling with the Spanish.[74]

Outbreaks of smallpox repeatedly decimated many Native American populations in North America a century or two later. In the early 19th

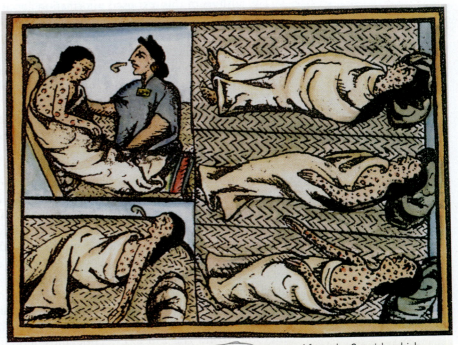

The conquest of the Aztecs was aided by smallpox contracted from the Spanish, which killed at least half the population.

century, the Massachusett and Narragansett Indians, with populations of 30,000 and 9,000, respectively, were reduced by smallpox to a few hundred members. Extremely high mortality rates were also noted among the Crow, the Blackfoot, and other Native American groups during the 19th century. The germ theory alone may not completely explain these epidemics; Europeans may have deliberately encouraged the spread of one new disease, smallpox, by purposely distributing infected blankets to the natives. Motulsky calls the spread of smallpox "one of the first examples of biological warfare."[75]

"Race" and Behavior

As an outgrowth of earlier attempts to show that inferior "races" have "primitive" cultures, some scholars have attempted to demonstrate behavioral differences between "races." One of the most active has been psychologist J. Philippe Rushton, whose 1995 book *Race, Evolution, and Behavior* purports to demonstrate behavioral differences between the "Negroid," "Caucasoid," and "Mongoloid" "races" in terms of sexual practices, parenting, social deviance, and family structure, among others.

Rushton argues that these behaviors have a genetic basis rooted in adaptations to particular environments. He suggests that "Negroids" are adapted to the warm environments of East Africa, where humans first evolved, through a reproductive strategy in which individuals have many offspring but put little energy into their children's upbringing and care. This strategy is known in evolutionary theory as *r-selected*, and is well documented among creatures such as fish, reptiles, and even some mammals (e.g., rabbits).[76] Rushton further suggests that as humans left Africa, they adapted to the "colder" climates of Asia by adopting a more *K-selected* reproductive strategy, which involves having few offspring but putting lots of energy into their upbringing and care. K-selected strategies are also well documented in the animal world, and it is interesting to note that apes (and humans) are often presented as examples of highly K-selected species.[77]

The data Rushton uses to support his argument come almost entirely from modern nations, many with a history of racial discrimination (such as South Africa, Japan, and the United States). But if genetic differences in behavior do exist among these three "races," differences that have their origins in the exodus of modern humans from Africa more than 100,000 years ago, then those differences should be apparent both between and among all the cultures of the world. That is, "Negroid" cultures should all share behaviors that are clearly different from those of "Caucasoid" cultures; "Caucasoid" cultures should all share behaviors that are different from those of "Mongoloid" cultures; and so on. Do such differences exist?

The authors of this text used information about the 186 cultures composing the Standard Cross-Cultural Sample to test whether Rushton's ideas hold up.[78] We examined 26 separate behaviors that Rushton predicted would differ among the "races." Contrary to Rushton's predictions, most of the behaviors showed no differences between the supposed "racial" groups. Only one of them showed the differences that Rushton predicted, and five of them demonstrated a pattern that was the *opposite* of what Rushton predicted. So Rushton's gross division of humans into three "races" does not generally predict variation in human behavior. His ideas appear plainly wrong and do not support the belief that it is scientifically useful to distinguish human "races."[79]

"Race" and Intelligence

Attempts to document differences in intelligence among the so-called races have a fairly long history. In the 19th century, European white supremacists tried to find scientific justification for what they felt was the genetically inherited mental inferiority of "blacks." They did this by measuring skulls (see the box "Physical Differences Between Migrants and Immigrants" for an example). It was believed that the larger the skull, the greater the cranial capacity and the bigger (hence, also better) the brain. Although the skull-measuring mania quickly disappeared and is no longer considered seriously as a way to measure intelligence, other "facts" may be used to demonstrate the presumed intellectual superiority of "white" people—namely, statistics from intelligence tests.

The first large-scale intelligence testing in the United States began with the nation's entry into World War I in 1917. Thousands of draftees were given the so-called alpha and beta IQ tests to determine military assignments. Later, psychologists arranged the test

Migrants and Immigrants

Physical Differences Between Natives and Immigrants

Physical anthropologists in the late 19th century were fascinated with the concept of "race." There was no debate about the biological reality of human "races," as there is today; rather, the idea that "races" existed seemed obviously true to anyone with eyes. People differed, and those differences could be identified, measured, and compared to show that specific variations were more common among one group of people than another. Some of the greatest scientists of the 19th century—Louis Agassiz, Paul Broca, Francis Galton, Karl Pearson—actively contributed to the identification and description of human "races."

Franz Boas, the founder of anthropology in the United States, saw an opportunity to test the stability of "racial" characteristics using data on the massive influx of immigrants into the United States at the close of the 19th century. Boas convinced the U.S. Immigration Commission that a large-scale study of immigrants and their children would help the federal government better serve these new citizens. He received funding to conduct a thorough physical study of several thousand immigrant families, and, over the course of several years, collected data on nearly 18,000 individuals.

Boas's results were surprising. He found that immigrants and their children differed in small but statistically significant ways. In particular, he found that cranial shape was not immutable, as physical anthropologists had assumed at the time, but rather could change in a single generation. And the direction of change was not always the same. The heads of first-generation offspring born in the United States of relatively long-headed Italians and relatively round-headed Eastern European Jews were more like one another than either was like their parents. What was going on?

Boas provided no clear answer, although he suggested that the similar environment of New York where all these children grew up might have played a role. Boas's study of immigrants proved to be very controversial. At the time, it questioned the assumption that "racial" characteristics were stable and unchanging and, in doing so, questioned the entire notion of "race" that had guided physical anthropology for a half century. Interestingly, Boas's study still remains somewhat controversial. In 2003, two groups of scholars published contradictory reanalyses of Boas's original data. One group claimed Boas got it wrong—that Boas overstated his findings and that, in reality, "racial" features were remarkably stable; the other group claimed that Boas basically got it right, despite the comparatively limited statistical analyses available to him. Both agree, however, with Boas that supposedly stable "racial" characteristics can change within a generation.

Sources: Brace 2005; Gravlee, Bernard, and Leonard 2003; Sparks and Jantz 2003

---

results according to the "racial" categories of "white" and "black" and found what they had expected—"blacks" scored consistently lower than "whites." This result was viewed as scientific proof of the innate intellectual inferiority of "blacks" and was used to justify further discrimination against them, both in and out of the army.[80]   *4-Bias*

Otto Klineberg's subsequent statistical analyses of IQ test results demonstrated that "blacks" from northern states scored higher than "blacks" from the South. Although dedicated racists explained that this difference was due to the northward migration of innately intelligent "blacks," most academics attributed the result to the influence of superior education and more stimulating environments in the North. When further studies showed that northern "blacks" scored higher than southern "whites," the better-education-in-the-North theory gained support, but again racists insisted such results were due to northward migration by more intelligent "whites."

As a further test of his conclusions, Klineberg gave IQ tests to "black" schoolgirls born and partly raised in the South who had spent varying lengths of time in New York City. He found that the longer the girls had been in the North, the higher their average IQ. In addition to providing support for the belief that "blacks" are not inherently inferior to "whites," these findings suggested that cultural factors can and do influence IQ scores, and that IQ is not a fixed quantity.

The controversy about race and intelligence was fueled again in 1969 by Arthur Jensen.[81] He suggested that although the IQ scores of American "blacks" overlapped considerably with the IQ scores of "whites," the average score for "blacks" was 15 points lower than the average for "whites." IQ scores presumably have a large genetic component, so the lower average score for "blacks" implied to Jensen that "blacks" were genetically inferior to "whites." Jensen's arguments were further developed by Richard Herrnstein and Charles Murray in their 1994 book, *The Bell Curve*. Herrnstein and Murray purported to show that the intelligence of an individual was largely inherited and unchangeable throughout the life span, that an individual's success was largely based on intelligence, and that African Americans were likely to remain at the bottom of society because they had less intelligence than European Americans.[82] Herrnstein and Murray appealed to a lot of studies to buttress their argument. But their argument was still faulty.

If you look at the average scores on many standard intelligence tests, you might conclude, as racists have, that African Americans are less intelligent than European Americans. The averages are different between the two groups; African Americans typically have lower scores. But what does this average difference mean? Herrnstein and Murray, like Jensen and others before them, fail to distinguish between a measure, such as a particular IQ test, and what is supposedly being measured, intelligence. If a test only imperfectly measures what it purports to measure, lower average IQ scores merely mean lower scores on that particular IQ test; they do not necessarily reflect lower intelligence.[83] There are many reasons why some smart people might not do well on particular kinds of IQ tests. For example, the way the tests are administered may affect performance, as may lack of familiarity with the format or the experiences and objects referred to. The test might also not measure particular kinds of intelligence such as social "smarts" and creativity.

If African Americans were really less intelligent, more than their average IQ scores would be lower. The whole frequency distribution of their individual scores should also be lower—they should have fewer geniuses and more retarded individuals. That is, the bell-shaped curve showing how their scores are distributed should range lower than the curve for other Americans, and African Americans should also have proportionately fewer scores at the very high end of the scale. But neither expectation is confirmed.[84] Critics have pointed to many other problems with the evidence presented in *The Bell Curve*. But the fundamental problem is the same as with all attempts to use differences in average IQ scores to make judgments about the capability of different groups. IQ tests may not adequately measure what they purport to measure.

First, there is widespread recognition now that IQ tests are probably not accurate measures of "intelligence" because they are probably biased in favor of the subculture of those who construct the tests. That is, many of the questions on the test refer to things that "white," middle-class children are familiar with, thus giving such children an advantage.[85] So far, no one has come up with a "culture-fair," or bias-free, test. There is more agreement that, although the IQ test may not measure "intelligence" well, it may predict scholastic success or how well a child will do in the primarily "white"-oriented school system.[86]

A second major problem with a purely genetic interpretation of the IQ difference is that many studies show that IQ scores can be influenced by the social environment. Economically deprived children, whether "black" or "white," will generally score lower than affluent "white" or "black" children, and training of children with low IQ scores clearly improves their test scores.[87] More dramatic evidence is provided by Sandra Scarr and her colleagues. "Black" children adopted by well-off "white" families have IQ scores above the average for "whites," and those "blacks" with more European ancestry do not have higher IQ scores.[88] So the average difference between "blacks" and "whites" in IQ cannot be attributed to a presumed genetic difference. For all we know, the 15-point average difference may be due completely to differences in environment or to test bias. New studies show very subtle effects of the social environment on test and school performance. Simply reminding "blacks" of their "race" before a test causes them to do worse. The difference on the Graduate Record Exam between "blacks" and "whites" disappeared

Until all people have an equal education and opportunities to achieve, there is no way we can be sure that some people are smarter than others.

after President Obama's election. These and other results strongly suggest that the pervasive stereotype of "blacks" not performing as well as "whites" (particularly potent prior to Obama's election) caused worse performance among "blacks."[89]

Geneticist Theodosius Dobzhansky reminded us that conclusions about the causes of different levels of achievement on IQ tests cannot be drawn until all people have equal opportunities to develop their potentials. He stressed the need for an open society operating under the democratic ideal, where all people are given an equal opportunity to develop whatever gifts or aptitudes they possess and choose to develop.[90]

The Future of Human Variation

4.4 Discuss the impact of modern technology on the future of human variation.

Laboratory fertilization, subsequent transplantation of the embryo, and successful birth have been accomplished with humans and nonhumans. *Cloning*—the exact reproduction of an individual from cellular tissue—has been achieved with frogs, sheep, and other animals. *Genetic engineering*—the substitution of some genes for others—is increasingly practiced in nonhuman organisms. And *stem cells,* which can be induced to grow into any tissue type, are in clinical use. What are the implications of such practices for the genetic future of humans? Will it really be possible someday to control the genetic makeup of our species? If so, will the effects be positive or negative?

It is interesting to speculate on the development of a "perfect human." Aside from the serious ethical question of who would decide what the perfect human should be like, there is the serious biological question of whether such a development might in the long run be detrimental to the human species, for what is perfectly suited to one physical or social environment may be totally unsuited to another. The collection of physical, emotional, and intellectual attributes that might be "perfect" in the early 21st century might be inappropriate in the 22nd century.[91] Even defects such as the sickle-cell trait may confer advantages under certain conditions, as we have seen.

In the long run, the perpetuation of genetic variability is probably more advantageous than the creation of a "perfect" and invariable human being. In the event of dramatic changes in the world environment, absolute uniformity in the human species might be an evolutionary dead end. Such uniformity might lead to the extinction of the human species if new conditions favored genetic or cultural variations that were no longer present in the species. Perhaps our best hope for maximizing our chances of survival is to tolerate, and even encourage, the persistence of many aspects of human variation, both biological and cultural.[92]

Summary and Review

Processes in Human Variation and Adaptation

4.1 Differentiate between adaptation and acclimatization.

- Human populations vary widely in the frequencies of physical traits, and anthropologists are able to explain this variation as a product of one or more of the following factors: adaptation, acclimatization, and the influence of the social or cultural environment.

- Adaptation involves permanent, genetic physical changes such as skin color or body build that help individuals survive in a particular environment.

- Acclimatization involves temporary, nongenetic physiological changes that help individuals survive in a particular environment.

- Culture is perhaps the most important factor in allowing people to live in diverse environments. Culture allows humans to modify their environments, and such modifications may lessen the likelihood of genetic adaptations and physiological acclimatizations.

 Using examples, how do they represent an adaptation, an acclimatization, and a cultural modification?

Physical Variation in Human Populations

 4.2 Explain specific variations in human populations in terms of adaptation.

- Physical variations in human populations include differences in body build and weight (Bergmann's rule), size of body parts (Allen's rule), skin color (Gloger's rule), and facial features such as nose shape, eye form, and hair form.

- Most physical variations are thought to be adapted to variation in climate, although some research suggests that factors such as infant stress may also produce variations.

- Some physical variations, such as the ability to resist certain diseases or make lactase, may be adapted partially to variation in cultural environment.

> **?** What are Bergmann's, Allen's, and Gloger's rules?

Race and Racism

 4.3 Contrast the contemporary views on "race" held by most anthropologists and common racist explanations of differences in behavior, intelligence, and cultural complexity.

- Physical traits that are adaptive vary clinally, which makes it meaningless to divide humans into discrete "racial" entities.

- "Racial" classifications are mostly social categories that are presumed to have a biological basis. Most biological anthropologists today agree that "race" is not a useful way of referring to human biological variation because human populations do not unambiguously fall into discrete groups defined by a particular set of biological traits.

- Civilizations have developed among all "races," so no "race" has a greater propensity for social, political, or economic development than others.

- Perhaps the most controversial aspect of racial discrimination is the relationship supposed between "racial" categories and intelligence. Attempts have been made to show the innate intellectual superiority of one "racial" category over another.

- Because evidence indicates that IQ scores are influenced by both genes and environment, conclusions about the causes of differences in IQ scores cannot be drawn until all the people being compared have equal opportunities to develop their potentials.

> **?** What problems are there with common racist explanations of differences in behavior, intelligence, and cultural complexity?

The Future of Human Variation

4.4 Discuss the impact of modern technology on the future of human variation.

- New advances in genetic engineering and gene therapy might provide ways to improve the lives of some, but maintaining variation in human populations is important, as populations with low genetic variation can rapidly go extinct.

> **?** What impacts might modern technology have on the future of human variation?

Think on it

1. Why is skin color used more often than hair or eye color or body proportions in "racial" **classifications**?

2. If Europeans had been more susceptible to New World and Pacific **diseases**, would the world be different today?

3. How might studies of **natural selection** help increase tolerance of other populations?

Primates: Past and Present

LEARNING OBJECTIVES

Identify common primate traits.	5.1
Describe the major types of living primates and their geographical distribution.	5.2
Describe the traits that distinguish hominins from other anthropoids.	5.3
Discuss the emergence of primates in relation to environment and adaptation.	5.4
Describe the emergence of anthropoids.	5.5
Differentiate between the various early anthropoids and hominoids.	5.6
Discuss the challenges to identifying any clear emergence of hominins.	5.7

Humans belong to the order Primates. All living primates, including humans, evolved from earlier primates that are now extinct. How do primates differ from other mammals? And what distinguishes humans from the other primates? After discussing these questions, we turn to the evolution of the primates: When, where, and why did the early primates emerge, and how and why did they diverge? Our overview covers the period from about 65 million years ago to the end of the Miocene, a little over 5 million years ago.

Common Primate Traits

5.1 Identify common primate traits.

All primates belong to the class Mammalia, and they share all the common features of mammals. Except for humans, the bodies of primates are covered with dense hair or fur, which provides insulation. Even humans have hair in various places, though perhaps not always for insulation. Mammals are *warm-blooded*; that is, their body temperature is more or less constantly warm and usually higher than that of the air around them. Almost all mammals give birth to live young that develop to a considerable size within the mother and are nourished by suckling from the mother's mammary glands. The young have a relatively long period of dependence on adults after birth. This period is also a time of learning, for a great deal of adult mammal behavior is learned rather than instinctive. Play is a learning technique common to mammal young and is especially important to primates.

The primates have a number of physical and social traits that set them apart from other mammals. No one of the primates' physical features is unique to primates; animals from other orders share one or more of the following described characteristics. But the complex of all these physical traits is unique to primates.[1]

Arboreal Adapted to living in trees.

Many skeletal features of the primates reflect an **arboreal** (tree-living) existence. All primate hind limbs are structured principally to provide support, but the "feet" in most primates can also grasp things (see Figure 5.1). Some primates—orangutans, for

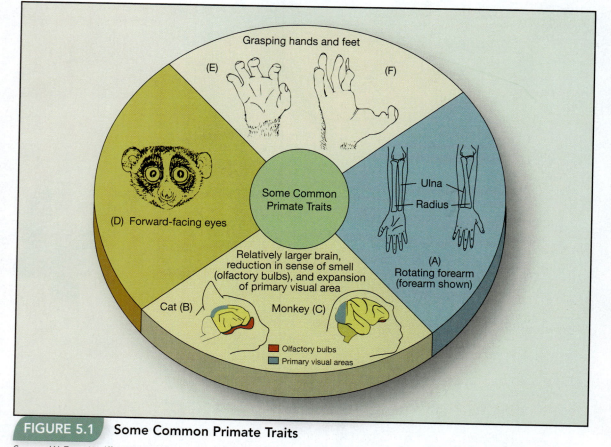

| **FIGURE 5.1** | **Some Common Primate Traits** |

Source: (A) From Wolff 1991, 255. Reprinted with permission of D.C. Heath; (B, C) from Deacon 1992, 110; (D) from Cartmill 1992b, 25; and (E, F) from Cartmill 1992b, 24.

instance—can suspend themselves from their hind limbs. The forelimbs are especially flexible, built to withstand both pushing and pulling forces. Each of the hind limbs and forelimbs has one bone in the upper portion and two bones in the lower portion (with the exception of the tarsier). This feature has changed little since the time of the earliest primate ancestors. It has remained in modern primates (although many other mammals have lost it) because the double bones give great mobility for rotating arms and legs.

Another characteristic structure of primates is the clavicle, or collarbone. The clavicle also gives primates great freedom of movement, allowing them to move the shoulders both up and down and back and forth. Although humans obviously do not use this flexibility for arboreal activity, we do use it for other activities. Without a clavicle, we could not throw a spear or a ball; we could not make any fine tools or turn doorknobs if we did not have rotatable forearms.

Primates generally are **omnivorous**; that is, they eat all kinds of food, including insects and small animals, as well as fruits, seeds, leaves, and roots. The teeth of primates reflect this omnivorous diet. The chewing teeth—the *molars* and *premolars*—are unspecialized, particularly in comparison with those of other groups of animals, such as the grazers. The front teeth—the *incisors* and *canines*—are often very specialized, principally in the lower primates. For example, the slender, tightly packed lower incisors and canines in many prosimians form a "dental comb" that the animals use in grooming or for scraping hardened tree gum (which is a food for them) from tree trunks.[2]

Primate hands are extremely flexible. All primates have prehensile—grasping—hands, which can be wrapped around an object. Primates have five digits on both hands and feet (in some cases, one digit may be reduced to a stub), and their nails, with few exceptions, are broad and flat, not clawlike. This structure allows them to grip objects; the hairless, sensitive pads on their fingers, toes, heels, and palms also help them grip. Most primates have **opposable thumbs**, a feature that allows an even more precise and powerful grip.

Vision is very important to primate life. Compared with other mammals, primates have a relatively larger portion of the brain devoted to vision rather than smell. Primates are characterized by stereoscopic, or depth, vision. Their eyes are directed forward rather than sideways, as in other animals—a trait that allows them to focus on an object (insects or other food or a distant branch) with both eyes at once. Most primates also have color vision, perhaps to recognize when plant foods are ready to eat.

Another important primate feature is a large brain relative to body size. That is, primates generally have larger brains than animals of similar size, perhaps because their survival depends on an enormous amount of learning, as we discuss later. In general, animals with large brains seem to mature more slowly and to live longer than animals with small brains.[3] The more slowly an animal matures and the longer it lives, the more it can learn.

For the most part, primates are social animals. For most primates, particularly those that are **diurnal**—that is, active during the day—group life may be crucial to survival. Social relationships begin with the mother and other adults during the fairly long dependency period of primates. The prolonged dependency of infant monkeys and apes probably offers an evolutionary advantage in that it allows infants more time to observe and learn the complex behaviors essential to survival while enjoying the care and protection of mature adults.

Omnivorous Eating both meat and vegetation.

Opposable thumbs A thumb that can touch the tips of all the other fingers.

Diurnal Active during the day.

Prosimians Literally "pre-monkeys," one of the two suborders of primates; includes lemurs, lorises, and tarsiers.

Anthropoids One of the two suborders of primates; includes monkeys, apes, and humans.

The Various Living Primates

5.2 Describe the major types of living primates and their geographical distribution.

The order Primates is traditionally divided into two suborders: the *prosimians*—literally, premonkeys—and the *anthropoids*. (A newer classification divides the primates into those with wet noses, the *strepsirrhines*, and those with dry noses, the *haplorhines*. We use the traditional classification because we think it is easier to understand.) The **prosimians** include lemurs, lorises, and tarsiers. The **anthropoid** suborder includes New World monkeys, Old World monkeys, the lesser apes (gibbons, siamangs), the great apes (orangutans, gorillas, and chimpanzees), and humans.

Applied Anthropology

Endangered Primates

In contrast to many human populations that are too numerous for their resources, many populations of nonhuman primates face extinction because they are not numerous enough. The two trends—human overpopulation and nonhuman primate extinctions—are related. Were it not for human expansion in many parts of the world, the nonhuman primates living in those habitats would not be endangered. Various lemur and other prosimian species of Madagascar, gorillas and red colobus monkeys of Africa, langurs, gibbons, orangutans of Asia, and the tamarin monkeys of Brazil are among the species most at risk.

Many factors are responsible for the difficulties that nonhuman primates face, but most of them are directly or indirectly the result of human activity. Perhaps the biggest problem is the destruction of tropical rain forest, the habitat of most nonhuman primates, because of encroaching agriculture and cattle ranching and the felling of trees for wood products. The people who live in these areas are partly responsible for the threats to nonhuman primates—population pressure in the human populations increases the likelihood that more forest will be cleared and burned for agriculture, and

A cotton-top tamarin.

nonhuman primates are an important source of hunted food in some areas. But world market forces are probably more important. The increasing need for "American" hamburger in fast-food restaurants has accelerated the search for places to raise beef inexpensively. There is also enormous demand for wood products from tropical forests;

Japan imports half of all the timber from rain forests to use for plywood, cardboard, paper, and furniture.

Some would argue that it is important to preserve all species. Primatologists remind us that it is especially important to preserve primate diversity. One reason is the scientific one of needing those populations to study and understand how humans are similar and different and how they came to be that way. Another reason is the usefulness of nonhuman primates in biomedical research on human diseases; we share many of our diseases, and many of our genes, with our primate relatives (chimpanzees share more than 98 percent of their genes with humans). The film *The Planet of the Apes*, in which the humans are subordinate to the apes, tells us that the primates in zoos could have been us.

So how can nonhuman primates be protected from us? There really are only two major ways: Either human population growth in many places has to be curtailed, or we have to preserve substantial populations of nonhuman primates in protected parks and zoos. Both are difficult but humanly possible.

Sources: Nishida 1992, 303–304; Mittermeier et al. 2009.

Prosimians

The prosimians resemble other mammals more than the anthropoid primates do. For example, the prosimians depend much more on smell for information than do anthropoids. Also in contrast with the anthropoids, they typically have more mobile ears, whiskers, longer snouts, and relatively fixed facial expressions. The prosimians also exhibit many traits shared by all primates, including grasping hands, stereoscopic vision, and enlarged visual centers in the brain.

Quadrupeds Animals that walk on all fours.

Vertical clinging and leaping A locomotor pattern characteristic of several primates, including tarsiers and galagos. The animal normally rests by clinging to a branch in a vertical position and uses its hind limbs alone to push off from one vertical position to another.

Nocturnal Active during the night.

Lemurlike Forms Lemurs and their relatives, the indris and the aye-ayes, are found only on two island areas off the southeastern coast of Africa: Madagascar and the Comoro Islands. These primates range in size from the mouse lemur to the 4-foot-long indri. Members of the lemur group usually produce single offspring, although twins and even triplets are common in some species. Many of the species in this group are **quadrupeds**—animals that move on all fours; they walk on all fours in the trees as well as on the ground. Some species, such as the indris, use their hind limbs alone to push off from one vertical position to another in a mode of locomotion called **vertical clinging and leaping**. Lemurs are mostly vegetarians, eating fruit, leaves, bark, and flowers. Lemur species vary greatly in their group size. Many lemur species, particularly those that are **nocturnal** (active during the night), are solitary during their active hours. Others are much more social, living in groups ranging in size from a small family to as many as 60 members.[4] An unusual feature of the lemurlike primates is that females often dominate males, particularly over access to food. In most primates, and in most other mammals, female dominance is rarely observed.[5]

Lorislike Forms Members of the loris group, found in both Southeast Asia and sub-Saharan Africa, are all nocturnal and arboreal. They eat fruit, tree gum, and insects and usually give birth to single infants.[6] There are two major subfamilies, the lorises and the bush babies (galagos), and they show wide behavioral differences. Bush babies are quick, active animals that hop between branches and tree trunks in the vertical-clinging-and-leaping pattern. On the ground, they often resort to a kangaroolike hop. Lorises are much slower, walking sedately along branches hand over hand in the quadrupedal fashion.

Tarsiers The nocturnal, tree-living tarsiers, found now only on the islands of the Philippines and Indonesia, are the only primates that depend completely on animal foods. They are usually insect eaters, but they sometimes capture and eat other small animals. They are well equipped for night vision, possessing enormous eyes, extraordinary eyesight, and enlarged visual centers in the brain. The tarsiers get their name from their elongated tarsal bones (the bones of the ankle), which give them tremendous leverage for their long jumps. Tarsiers are very skilled at vertical clinging and leaping. They live in family groups composed of a mated pair and their offspring. Like some higher primates, male and female tarsiers sing together each evening to advertise their territories.[7] The classification of tarsiers is somewhat controversial. Some classifiers group tarsiers with anthropoids rather than with prosimians. In this classification scheme, the suborders of primates are labeled *strepsirrhines* (which includes lemurs and lorises) and *haplorhines* (which includes tarsiers and anthropoids). Tarsiers have chromosomes similar to those of other prosimians; they also have claws for grooming on some of their toes, more than two nipples, and a uterus shaped like that of other prosimians (two-horned). Tarsiers are more like anthropoids in having a reduced dependence on smell. And, in common with the anthropoids, their eyes are closer together and are protected by bony orbits.[8]

Anthropoids

The anthropoid suborder includes humans, apes, and monkeys. Most anthropoids share several traits in varying degrees. They have rounded braincases; reduced, nonmobile outer ears; and relatively small, flat faces instead of muzzles. They have highly efficient reproductive systems. They also have highly dexterous hands.[9] The anthropoid order is divided into two main groups: **platyrrhines** and **catarrhines** (see Figure 5.2). Platyrrhines have broad, flat-bridged noses, with nostrils facing outward; these monkeys are found only in the New World, in Central and South America. Catarrhines have narrow noses with nostrils facing downward. Catarrhines include monkeys of the Old World (Africa, Asia, and Europe) as well as apes and humans.

New World Monkeys Besides the shape of the nose and the position of the nostrils, other anatomical features distinguish the New World monkeys (platyrrhines) from the catarrhine anthropoids. The New World species have three premolars, whereas the Old World species have two. Some New World monkeys have a **prehensile** (grasping) tail; no Old World monkeys do. All the New World monkeys are completely arboreal; they vary a lot in the size of their groups; and their food ranges from insects to nectar and sap to fruits and leaves.[10]

A ring-tailed lemur mother and its baby holding on. Prosimians such as ring-tailed lemurs depend much more on smell than do anthropoids. Prosimians also have more mobile ears, whiskers, longer snouts, and relatively fixed facial expressions.

Platyrrhines The group of anthropoids that have broad, flat-bridged noses, with nostrils facing outward; these monkeys are currently found only in the New World (Central and South America).

Catarrhines The group of anthropoids with narrow noses and nostrils that face downward. Catarrhines include monkeys of the Old World (Africa, Asia, and Europe), as well as apes and humans.

Prehensile Adapted for grasping objects.

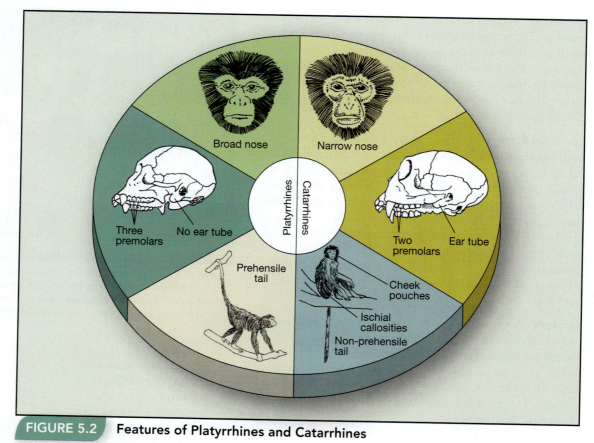

FIGURE 5.2   **Features of Platyrrhines and Catarrhines**

Source: Boaz and Almquist 1999.

Cercopithecoids Old World monkeys.

Terrestrial Adapted to living on the ground.

Two main families of New World monkeys have traditionally been defined. One family, the *callitrichids*, contains marmosets and tamarins; the other family, the *cebids*, contains all the other New World monkeys. The callitrichids are very small, have claws instead of fingernails, and give birth to twins who mature in about 2 years. Perhaps because twinning is so common and the infants have to be carried, callitrichid mothers cannot take care of them alone. Fathers and older siblings have often been observed carrying infants. Indeed, males may do more carrying than females. Callitrichid groups may contain a mated pair (monogamy) or a female mated to more than one male (polyandry). The callitrichids eat a lot of fruit and tree sap, but like other very small primates, they obtain a large portion of their protein requirements from insects.[11]

Cebids are generally larger than callitrichids, take about twice as long to mature, and tend to bear only one offspring at a time.[12] The cebids vary widely in size, group composition, and diet. For example, squirrel monkeys weigh about 2 pounds, whereas woolly spider monkeys weigh more than 16 pounds. Some cebids have small groups with one male–female pair; others have groups of up to 50 individuals. Some of the smallest cebids have a diet of leaves, insects, flowers, and fruits, whereas others are mostly fruit eaters with lesser dependence on seeds, leaves, or insects.[13]

Old World Monkeys The Old World monkeys, or **cercopithecoids**, are related more closely to humans than to New World monkeys. They have the same number of teeth as apes and humans. The Old World monkey species are not as diverse as their New World cousins, but they live in a greater variety of habitats. Some live both in trees and on the ground; others, such as the gelada baboon, are completely **terrestrial**, or ground-living.

The squirrel monkey, like all platyrrhines, almost never leaves the trees. It is well suited to an arboreal lifestyle; note how it uses both hands and feet to grasp branches.

Macaques are found both in tropical jungles and on snow-covered mountains, and they range from the Rock of Gibraltar to Africa to northern India, Pakistan, and Japan. There are two major subfamilies of Old World monkeys: the *colobines* and the *cercopithecines*.

The colobines live mostly in trees, and their diet consists principally of leaves and seeds. Their digestive tracts are equipped to obtain maximum nutrition from a high-cellulose diet; they have pouched stomachs, which provide a large surface area for breaking down plant food, and very large intestinal tracts. One of the most noticeable features of colobines is the flamboyant color typical of newborns. For example, in one species, dusky gray mothers give birth to brilliant orange babies.[14]

The cercopithecine subfamily of monkeys includes more terrestrial species than any other subfamily of Old World monkeys. Many of these species are characterized by a great deal of **sexual dimorphism** (the sexes look very different); the males are larger, have longer canines, and are more aggressive than the females. Cercopithecines depend more on fruit than do colobines. They are also more capable of surviving in arid and seasonal environments.[15] Pouches inside the cheeks allow cercopithecines to store food for later eating and digestion. An unusual physical feature of these monkeys is the ischial callosities, or callouses, on their bottoms—an adaptation that enables them to sit comfortably in trees or on the ground for long periods of time.[16]

This infant dusky leaf monkey has bright orange fur, but the fur will turn dull gray as the infant grows into an adult.

sexual dimorphism Refers to a marked difference in size and appearance between males and females of a species.

Hominoids The group of hominoids consisting of humans and their direct ancestors. It contains at least two genera: *Homo* and *Australopithecus*.

Hylobates The family of hominoids that includes gibbons and siamangs; often referred to as the lesser apes (as compared with the great apes such as gorillas and chimpanzees).

Pongids Hominoids whose members include both the living and extinct apes.

The Hominoids: Apes and Humans

The **hominoids** group includes three separate families: the lesser apes, or **hylobatids** (gibbons and siamangs); the great apes, or **pongids** (orangutans, gorillas, and chimpanzees); and humans, or **hominins** (actually a subfamily of the hominid family, one of several classificatory technicalities that we try to avoid here in order to simplify the discussion). Their brains are relatively large, especially the areas of the cerebral cortex associated with the ability to integrate data. All hominoids have fairly long arms; short, broad trunks; and no tails. The wrist, elbow, and shoulder joints of hominoids allow a greater range of movement than in other primates. Hominoid hands are longer and stronger than those of other primates. These skeletal features probably evolved along with the hominoids' unique abilities in suspensory locomotion. Unlike other anthropoids, who move quadrupedally along the ground or along the tops of tree branches, hominoids often suspend themselves from below the branches and swing or climb hand over hand from branch to branch.[17] This suspensory posture also translates to locomotion on the ground; all hominoids, at least occasionally, move bipedally, as we discuss in more detail later in this chapter.

The dentition of hominoids demonstrates some unique features as well (see Figure 5.3). Hominoid molars are flat and rounded compared to those of other anthropoids and have what is called a "Y-5" pattern on the lower molars—that is, the lower molars have five cusps with a Y-shaped groove opening toward the cheek running between them.

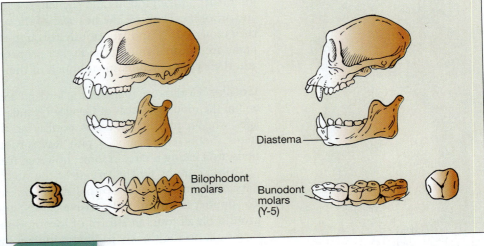

Bilophodont molars

Diastema

Bunodont molars (Y-5)

FIGURE 5.3

Difference in dentition between an Old World monkey (left) and an ape (right). In Old World monkeys, the cusps of the lower molars form two parallel ridges; in apes, the five cusps form a Y-shaped pattern. Apes also have a space between the lower canine and first premolar, called a diastema.

Source: Adapted from Boaz and Almquist 1999, 164.

A white-handed gibbon demonstrates its ability as a brachiator.

hominins The group of hominoids consisting of humans and their direct ancestors.

Bilophodont Having four cusps on the molars that form two parallel ridges. This is the common molar pattern of Old World monkeys.

A young gorilla shows how it knuckle-walks. The back feet are flat on the ground, and only the knuckles of the "hands" touch the ground.

Other anthropoids have what is called a **bilophodont** pattern—their molars have two ridges or "loafs" running perpendicular to the cheeks. All hominoids, except for humans, also have long canine teeth that project beyond the tops of the other teeth and a corresponding space on the opposite jaw, called a **diastema**, where the canine sits when the jaws are closed. The contact of the upper canine and the lower third premolar creates a sharp cutting edge, in part due to the premolar being elongated to accommodate the canine.[18] These dental features are related to the hominoids' diets, which often include both fibrous plant materials, which can be efficiently cut with sharp canines against elongated premolars, and soft fruits, which can be efficiently chewed with wide, flat molars.

The skeletal and dental features that the hominoids share point toward their common ancestry. Their proteins and DNA show many similarities, too. This genetic likeness is particularly strong among chimpanzees, gorillas, and humans.[19] For this reason, primatologists think chimpanzees and gorillas are evolutionarily closer to humans than are the lesser apes and orangutans, which probably branched off at some earlier point. We discuss the fossil evidence that supports an early split for the orangutans later in the chapter.

Gibbons and Siamangs   The agile gibbons and their close relatives, the siamangs, are found in the jungles of Southeast Asia. The gibbons are small, weighing only between 11 and 15 pounds. The siamangs are somewhat larger, but no more than 25 pounds. Both are mostly fruit eaters, although they also eat leaves and insects. They are spectacular **brachiators**; their long arms and fingers let them swing hand over hand through the trees.[20] A gibbon can move more than 30 feet in a single forward swing.

Gibbons and siamangs live in small family groups consisting of an adult pair, who appear to mate for life, and one or two immature offspring. When the young reach adulthood, they are driven from home by the adults. There is little sexual dimorphism—males and females do not differ in size or appearance—nor is there any clear pattern of dominance by either sex. These lesser apes are also highly territorial; an adult pair advertises their territory by singing and defends it by chasing others away.[21]

Orangutans   Orangutans survive only on the islands of Borneo and Sumatra. Unlike gibbons and siamangs, they are clearly recognizable as males or females. Males not only weigh almost twice as much as females (up to 200 pounds) but they also have large cheek pads, throat pouches, beards, and long hair.[22] Like gibbons and siamangs, orangutans are primarily fruit eaters and arboreal. They are the heaviest of the arboreal primates, and perhaps they move slowly and laboriously through the trees for this reason. Orangutans are unusual among the higher primates in that, except for mothers and their young, adults spend much of their time alone.

Gorillas   Gorillas are found in the lowland areas of western equatorial Africa and in the mountain areas of Congo, Uganda, and Rwanda.[23] Unlike the other apes, who are mostly fruit eaters, gorillas mostly eat other parts of plants—stems, shoots (e.g., bamboo), pith, leaves, roots, and flowers. In many populations, fruit eating is rare; in some, however, fruit is a common part of the diet.[24]

Gorillas are by far the largest of the surviving apes. In their natural habitats, adult males weigh up to 450 pounds and females up to 250 pounds. To support the weight of massive chests, gorillas travel mostly on the ground on all fours in a form of locomotion known as **knuckle walking**: they walk on the thickly padded middle joints of their fingers. Gorillas' arms and legs, especially those of the young, are well suited for climbing. As adults, their heavier bodies make climbing more precarious.[25] They sleep on the ground or in tub-shaped nests they make from nonfood plants each time they bed down.[26]

Gorillas tend to live in groups consisting of a dominant male, called a silverback, other adult males, adult females, and immature offspring. Both males and females, when mature, seem to leave the groups into which they were born to join other groups. The dominant male is very much the center of attention; he acts as the main protector of the group and the leader in deciding where the group will go next.[27]

Chimpanzees Chimpanzees live in the forested areas of Africa, from Guinea Bissau in the west to Tanzania in the east. There are two distinct species of chimpanzee—the common chimpanzee (*Pan troglodytes*) and the bonobo, or pygmy, chimpanzee (*Pan paniscus*). Bonobos tend to be more slender than common chimpanzees, with longer limbs and digits, smaller heads, darker faces, and a distinct part in their hair. Unlike common chimpanzees, bonobos show almost no sexual dimorphism in dentition or skeletal structure. More significant seem to be differences in social behavior. Bonobos are more gregarious than common chimpanzees, and groups tend to be more stable. Groups also tend to be centered around females rather than males.[28]

Although they are primarily fruit eaters, chimpanzees show many similarities to their close relatives, the gorillas. Both are arboreal and terrestrial. Like gorillas, chimpanzees move best on the ground, and when they want to cover long distances, they come down from the trees and move by knuckle walking. Occasionally, they stand and walk upright, usually when they are traveling through tall grass or are trying to see long distances. Chimpanzees sleep in tree nests that they carefully prepare anew, complete with a bunch of leaves as a pillow, each time they bed down.[29]

Chimpanzees (including bonobos) are less sexually dimorphic than the other great apes. Males weigh a little more than 100 pounds on the average, females somewhat less. Males also have longer canines.

After five decades of studies at Gombe National Park in Tanzania and elsewhere, researchers have found that common chimpanzees not only eat insects, small lizards, and birds, but they also actively hunt and kill larger animals.[30] At Gombe, the red colobus monkey is by far the most often hunted animal. Hunting appears to be undertaken more

Diastema A gap between the canine and first premolar found in apes.

Brachiators Animals that move through the trees by swinging hand over hand from branch to branch. They usually have long arms and fingers.

Knuckle walking A locomotor pattern of primates such as the chimpanzee and gorilla in which the weight of the upper part of the body is supported on the thickly padded knuckles of the hands.

Chimpanzees, though they spend much time in the trees, can also move very quickly on the ground.

often during the dry season when food is scarce.[31] Prey is caught mostly by the males, which hunt either alone or in small groups. It is then shared with—or, perhaps more accurately, begged by—as many as 15 other chimpanzees in friendly social gatherings that may last up to 9 hours.[32]

Hominins   According to the classification we use here, the hominoids we call hominins include only one living species—modern humans. Humans have many distinctive characteristics that set them apart from other anthropoids and other hominoids, which lead many to place humans in a category separate from the pongids. However, others believe that the differences are not so great as to justify a separate hominin category for humans. For example, humans, chimpanzees, and gorillas are very similar in their proteins and DNA. Whether we stress the similarities or differences between humans and apes does not matter that much; what does matter is that we try to understand the reasons for those similarities and differences.

Distinctive Hominin Traits

5.3 Describe the traits that distinguish hominins from other anthropoids.

We turn now to some of the features that distinguish us—the hominins—from the other primates. Although we like to think of ourselves as unique, many of the traits we discuss here are at the extreme of a continuum that can be traced from the prosimians through the apes.

Physical Traits

Of all the primates, only hominins consistently walk erect on two feet. All other primates require thick, heavy musculature to hold their heads erect; this structure is missing in hominins, for our heads are more or less balanced on top of our spinal columns. A dish-shaped pelvis (peculiar to hominins), a lumbar curve in the spine, straight lower limbs, and arched, nonprehensile feet are all related to **bipedalism**. Because hominins are fully bipedal, we can carry objects without impairing our locomotor efficiency.

Bipedalism Locomotion in which an animal walks on its two hind legs.

Although many primates have an opposable thumb, which enables them to grasp and examine objects, the greater length and flexibility of the hominin thumb allow us to handle objects with greater dexterity. We are capable of both a power grip, to hold large or heavy objects firmly, and a precision grip, to hold small or delicate objects without dropping or breaking them. We also have remarkable hand–eye coordination, as well as a remarkably sophisticated brain.

Cerebral cortex The "gray matter" of the brain; the center of speech and other higher mental activities.

The hominin brain is large and complex, particularly the **cerebral cortex**, the center of speech and other higher mental activities. The brain of the average adult modern human measures more than 79 cubic inches (1,300 cubic centimeters), compared with 32 cubic inches (525 cubic centimeters) for the gorilla, the primate with the next largest brain. The frontal areas of the hominin brain are also larger than those of other primates, so that hominins have more prominent foreheads than monkeys or gorillas. Hominins have special areas of the brain that are dedicated to speech and language. The large hominin brain requires an enormous amount of blood, and the way blood is carried to and from the brain is also unique.[33] We'll say more about the hominin brain and its evolution in the next chapter.

Hominin teeth reflect our completely omnivorous diet, and they are not very specialized, which may reflect the fact that we use tools and cooking to prepare our food. As discussed earlier, other hominoids have long canines and a diastema, whereas hominin canines do not usually project beyond the tops of the other teeth. This allows hominins to move their jaws both vertically and horizontally when chewing; horizontal movement would be prevented by the long upper canines of the other hominoids. Hominin molars have thicker enamel than the molars of other hominoids, and both horizontal movement and thickened molars may be related to a dietary emphasis on coarse grains and seeds. The hominin jaw is shaped like a parabolic arch, rather than a U-shape, as in the apes, and is composed of relatively thin bones and light muscles. Modern humans have chins; other primates do not.

One other important hominin trait is the sexuality of hominin females, who may engage in intercourse at any time throughout the year; most other primate females engage in sex only periodically, just around the time they can conceive.[34] Hominins are also unusual among the primates in having female–male bonding.[35]

Why, then, does hominin female sexuality differ from that of most other primates? One suggestion is that more or less continuous female sexuality became selectively advantageous in hominins after female–male bonding developed in conjunction with local groups consisting of at least several adult males and adult females.[36] More specifically, the combination of group living and male–female bonding—a combination unique to hominins among the primates—may have favored a switch from the common higher-primate pattern of periodic female sexuality to the pattern of more or less continuous female sexuality. Such a switch may have been favored in hominins because periodic, rather than continuous, female sexuality would undermine female–male bonding in multi-male–multi-female groups.

Field research on nonhuman primates strongly suggests that males usually attempt to mate with any females ready to mate. If the female (or females) a male was bonded to was not interested in sex at certain times, but other females in the group were, it seems likely that the male would try to mate with those other females. Frequent "extramarital affairs" might jeopardize the male–female bond and thereby presumably reduce the reproductive success of both males and females. Hence, natural selection may have favored more or less continuous sexuality in hominin females if hominins already had the combination of group living (and the possibility of "extramarital affairs") and marriage. If bonded adults lived alone, as do gibbons, noncontinuous female sexuality would not threaten bonding, because "extramarital" sex would not be likely to occur. Similarly, seasonal breeding would also pose little threat to male–female bonds, because all females would be sexually active at more or less the same time.[37] So the fact that the combination of group living and male–female bonding occurs only in hominins may explain why continuous female sexuality developed in hominins. The bonobo, or pygmy chimpanzee, female does engage in intercourse throughout the year, but bonobos do not have male–female bonding, and the females are not interested in sex quite as often as hominin females.[38]

Behavioral Abilities

In comparison with other primates, a much greater proportion of hominin behavior is learned and culturally patterned. As with many physical traits, we can trace a continuum in the learning abilities of all primates. The great apes, including orangutans, gorillas, and chimpanzees, are probably about equal in learning ability.[39] Old and New World monkeys do much less well in learning tests, and, surprisingly, gibbons perform more poorly than most monkeys.

Toolmaking The same kind of continuum is evident in inventiveness and toolmaking. There is scant evidence of nonhuman primates except great apes using tools, although several species of monkeys use "weapons"—branches, stones, or fruit dropped onto predators below them on the ground. Chimpanzees both fashion and use tools in the wild. They strip leaves from sticks and then use the sticks to "fish" termites from their mound-shaped nests. They use leaves to mop up termites, to sponge up water, or to wipe themselves clean. Indeed, tool use varies enough in chimpanzees that primatologist Christophe Boesch has suggested that local chimpanzee groups have cultural differences in terms of the tools they employ.[40]

One example of chimpanzee tool use suggests planning. In Guinea, West Africa, observers watched a number of chimpanzees crack oil palm nuts with two stones. The "platform" stone had a hollow depression; the other stone was used for pounding. The observers assumed that the stones had been brought by the chimpanzees to the palm trees because no stones like them were nearby and the chimps were observed to leave the pounding stone on top of or near the platform stone when

Chimps in the wild use tools—in this case, a stone to crack palm nuts. As far as we know, though, they don't use tools to make other tools, as humans do.

they were finished.[41] Observers in other areas of West Africa have also reported that chimpanzees use stones to crack nuts. In one location in Liberia, an innovative female appeared to have started the practice; it seems to have been imitated within a few months by 13 others who previously showed no interest in the practice.[42]

Hominins have usually been considered the only toolmaking animal, but observations such as these call for modification of the definition of toolmaking. If we define toolmaking as adapting a natural object for a specific purpose, then at least some of the great apes are toolmakers too. Perhaps it would be more accurate to say hominins are the only habitual toolmaking animal, just as we say hominins are the only habitual bipedal hominoid, even though the other hominoids all can and do walk bipedally sometimes. As far as we know, though, hominins are unique in their ability to use one tool to make another.

Language Only modern humans have spoken, symbolic language. But, as with toolmaking abilities, the line between modern human language and the communications of other primates is not as sharp as we once thought. In the wild, vervet monkeys make different alarm calls to warn of different predators. Observers playing tape recordings of these calls found that monkeys responded to them differently depending on the call. If the monkeys heard an "eagle" call, they looked up; if they heard a "leopard" call, they ran high into the trees.[43]

Common chimpanzees are also communicative, using gestures and many vocalizations in the wild. Researchers have used this "natural talent" to teach chimpanzees symbolic language in experimental settings. In their pioneering work, Beatrice T. Gardner and R. Allen Gardner raised a female chimpanzee named Washoe and trained her to communicate with startling effectiveness by means of American Sign Language hand gestures.[44] After a year of training, she was able to associate gestures with specific activities. For example, if thirsty, Washoe would make the signal for "give me" followed by the one for "drink." As she learned, the instructions grew more detailed. If all she wanted was water, she would merely signal for "drink." But if she craved soda pop, as she did more and more, she prefaced the drink signal with the sweet signal—a quick touching of the tongue with her fingers. Later, the Gardners had even more success in training four other common chimpanzees, who were taught by fluent deaf users of American Sign Language.[45]

Bonobos have provided strong evidence that they understand simple grammatical "rules," very much like 2-year-old humans. Pointing to graphic symbols for different particular meanings, a bonobo named Kanzi regularly communicated sequences of types of symbols; for example, he would point to a symbol for a verb ("bite") and then point to a symbol for an object ("ball," "cherry," or "food").[46]

Other Hominin Traits Although many primates are omnivores, eating insects and small reptiles in addition to plants—some even hunt small mammals—only hominins hunt very large animals. Also, hominins are one of the few primates that are completely terrestrial. We do not even sleep in trees, as many other ground-living primates do. Perhaps our ancestors lost their perches when the forests receded, or cultural advances such as weapons or fire may have eliminated the need to seek nightly shelter in the trees. In addition, as we have noted, we have the longest dependency period of any of the primates, requiring extensive parental care and support for up to 20 years or so.

Finally, hominins are unlike almost all other primates in having a division of labor by gender in food-getting and food-sharing in adulthood. Among nonhuman primates, both females and males forage for themselves after infancy. Hominins have more gender-role specialization, perhaps because men, unencumbered by infants and small children, were freer to hunt and chase large animals.

Having examined our distinctive traits, those traits we share with other primates, now we turn to the fossil evidence about primate evolution, from the earliest forms to apes.

Paleocene The geological epoch 65 million to 55 million years ago.

5.4 Discuss the emergence of primates in relation to environment and adaptation.

The Emergence of Primates

When did the primates first emerge? This question turns out to be hard to answer with the current fossil record. Some paleoanthropologists have suggested that fossil finds from the **Paleocene** epoch, which began about 65 million years ago, are from archaic primates.

These are the *plesiadapiforms*. They have been found in both Europe and North America, which were one connected landmass in the Paleocene. The best-known plesiadapiform is **Plesiadapis**. This squirrellike animal had a large snout and large incisors. It also had a large nasal cavity and eye orbits located on the sides of the skull, suggesting a well-developed sense of smell and little or no stereoscopic vision (depth perception). The fingers of *Plesiadapis* had claws, and its hands and feet did not appear to allow for grasping. These features suggest that *Plesiadapis* was not a primate. However, the elbow and ankle joints suggest great mobility, and the teeth suggest a primatelike omnivorous diet despite the large incisors. The structure of their inner ears also resembled that of modern primates. Because it had these primatelike features, some scholars believe that the plesiadapiforms were archaic primates.[47]

Other paleoanthropologists find so few similarities between the plesiadapiforms and later obvious primates that they do not include the plesiadapiforms in the order Primates.[48] There is no dispute, however, about fossils dating from the early **Eocene**, about 55 million years ago. These oldest definite primates appear in two major groups of prosimians—*adapids* and *omomyids*. Because these two kinds of primates are different from each other in major ways, and because they both appeared rather abruptly at the border of the Paleocene and Eocene, there presumably was an earlier common primate ancestor. One strong candidate for the common primate ancestor is *Carpolestes simpsoni*, a mouse-size arboreal creature from Wyoming dating to about 56 million years ago. **Carpolestes** has an interesting mix of primate and nonprimate characteristics. Although it lacks stereoscopic vision, *Carpolestes* has nails instead of claws on its big toes, and it has grasping hands and feet.[49] Not all scholars are convinced that *Carpolestes* is the common ancestor of all primates, and in Figure 5.4, the circled P represents where paleontologist Robert D. Martin placed the common ancestor of primates, in the late Cretaceous.

Plesiadipis The most well known of the plesia-dipiforms, possibly an archaic primate.

Eocene A geological epoch 55 million to 34 million years ago during which the first definite primates appeared.

Carpolestes A mouse-sized arboreal creature living about 56 million years ago; a strong candidate for the common primate ancestor.

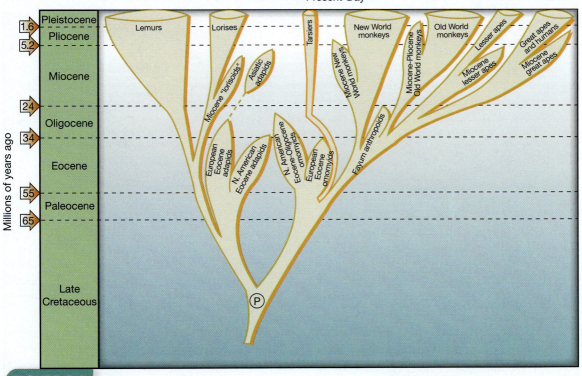

FIGURE 5.4

A view of the evolutionary relationships between early primates and living primates, adapted from one suggested by R. D. Martin. The primate lineages that do not extend to the present day indicate presumed extinctions. Branching from a common "stalk" suggests divergence from a common ancestor. P represents the unknown common ancestor of all primates.

Source: From Martin 1990. The dates for the Paleocene, Eocene, Oligocene, and the beginning of the Miocene are from Berggren et al. 1992, 29–45. The dates for the end of the Miocene, Pliocene, and Pleistocene are from Jones et al. 1992.

The Environment

Cretaceous Geological epoch 135 million to 65 million years ago, during which dinosaurs and other reptiles ceased to be the dominant land vertebrates, and mammals and birds began to become important.

It is generally agreed that the earliest primate may have emerged by the Paleocene, 65 million to 55 million years ago, and perhaps earlier, in the late **Cretaceous**. The beginning of the Paleocene marked a major geological transition, what geologists call the transition from the Mesozoic to the Cenozoic era. About 75 percent of all animal and plant life that lived in the last part of the Cenozoic (the late Cretaceous) vanished by the early Paleocene. The extinction of the dinosaurs is the most famous of these disappearances.[50]

The climate of the Cretaceous period was almost uniformly damp and mild, but temperatures began falling at the end of the Cretaceous. Around the beginning of the Paleocene epoch, both seasonal and geographic fluctuations in temperature began to develop. The climate became much drier in many areas, and vast swamplands disappeared. The climate of the Paleocene was generally somewhat cooler than in the late Cretaceous, but by no means cold. Forests and savannas thrived in fairly high latitudes. Subtropical climates existed as far north as latitude 62 in Alaska.[51]

Continental drift The movement of the continents over the past 135 million years.

One important reason for the very different climates of the past is **continental drift** (Figure 5.5). In the early Cretaceous (circa 135 million years ago), the continents were actually clumped into two large landmasses or "supercontinents"—*Laurasia*, which included North America and Eurasia, and *Gondwanaland*, which included Africa, South America, India, Australia, and Antarctica. By the beginning of the Paleocene (circa 65 million years ago), Gondwanaland had broken apart, with South America drifting west away from Africa, India drifting east, and Australia and Antarctica drifting south. As the continents changed position, they moved into locations with different climatic conditions. More importantly, however, the very movement of the continents affected the climate, sometimes on a global scale.[52]

With changes in climate come changes in vegetation. Although the first deciduous trees (that lose their leaves in winter) and flowering plants (called *angiosperms*) arose during the Cretaceous, large trees with large fruits and seeds also became common during the late

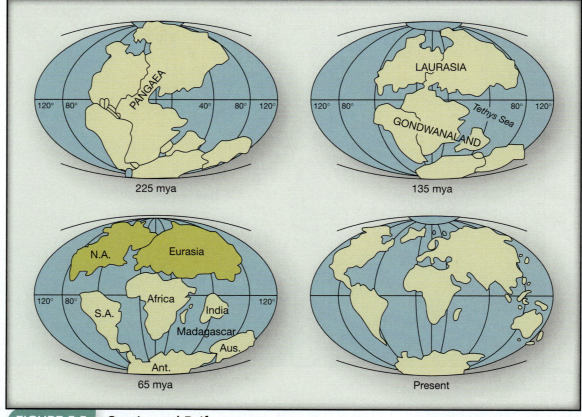

FIGURE 5.5 ▸ **Continental Drift**

The supercontinent Pangea split into Laurasia and Gondwanaland 135 million years ago (mya). These further divided into the continents as we know them today.

Source: Boaz and Almquist 1999.

Applied Anthropology

Studying Biodiversity

The late Miocene is known as the age of the apes. Literally dozens of ape species were in the forests of Europe and Asia. What happened to all the diversity of apes, and why is there such a relative paucity of ape species today? We might ask the same question about humans. Two million years ago, there were at least four hominin species in Africa, and perhaps more, but today, there is only one. What leads to a great diversity of species, and what causes that diversity to diminish? These are central questions for applied anthropologists who study biodiversity.

Biodiversity refers to the richness of genes, species, and ecosystems within a given region. Regions with greater biodiversity are generally considered healthier and more stable than those with less biodiversity. However, there are also broad geographic differences in biodiversity, with tropical areas generally having greater biodiversity, and polar areas having lower biodiversity. Biodiversity has also changed over time, with periods of mass extinction dramatically lowering global biodiversity. Although it is clear from the primate fossil record (and

the fossil record of many other species) that biodiversity changes over time through natural processes, many scholars now believe that humans are impacting biodiversity in far more dramatic and rapid ways than ever before. And most scholars think this is a significant problem that needs to be addressed.

Biodiversity benefits humans in at least three ways. First, the maintenance of genetic variation in plant and animal species provides for innovations in agriculture such as increased yield and resistance to disease. Second, the maintenance of species diversity provides sources for new resources or technologies in things such as building materials and medicines. Finally, and perhaps most importantly, biodiversity appears to be a measure of environmental health and stability, and working to maintain biodiversity may, therefore, also serve to maintain a stable and healthy environment.

Applied anthropologists who conduct research on biodiversity tend to focus on two related aspects of biodiversity. First, they document local knowledge of biodiversity. Second, they document local practices that

help maintain biodiversity. For example, Terence Hays has spent much of his career documenting knowledge of plants among the Ndumba people of Papua New Guinea. Hays's research and that of other anthropologists has helped scholars to more fully understand the biodiversity of the New Guinea highlands. Similarly, Terence Turner has documented the political struggles of the Kayapo peoples of Brazil, who have fought logging companies and miners to protect the rain forest environment in which they live. Turner hopes that the Kayapo example can be a model for other indigenous groups struggling to protect the biodiversity of their homelands.

Even though the study of our ancient primate roots may appear to have little impact on the world today, applied anthropologists have recognized that an understanding of evolutionary patterns of biodiversity is essential to identifying trends in the modern world that point to human-imposed damage to the earth's living systems.

Sources: Hays 2009; Orlove and Brush 1996; Turner 1993; 1995; Abel and Stepp 2003.

Paleocene and early Eocene.[53] Although some mammals date from the Cretaceous, the Paleocene saw the evolution and diversification of many different types of mammals, and the expansion and diversification of deciduous trees and flowering plants probably played a large role in mammalian expansion and diversification. Indeed, primate paleontologists think primates evolved from one of these mammalian *radiations*, or extensive diversifications, probably from the **insectivore** order of mammals, including modern shrews and moles, that is adapted to eating insects—insects that would have lived off the new deciduous trees and flowering plants.

The insectivores were very adaptable and were able to take advantage of many different habitats—under the ground, in water, on the ground, and above the ground, including the woody habitat of bushes, shrubs, vines, and trees. It was the last kind of adaptation, above the ground, that may have been the most important for primate evolution. The woody habitat had been exploited only partially in earlier periods. But then several different kinds, or taxa, of small animals, one of which may have been the archaic primate, began to take advantage of the woody habitat.

Insectivore The order or major grouping of mammals, including modern shrews and moles, that is adapted to feeding on insects.

What in Particular May Have Favored the Emergence of Primates?

The traditional explanation of primate origins (the *arboreal theory*) suggests that the primates evolved from insectivores that took to the trees. Different paleoanthropologists emphasized different possible adaptations to life in the trees. In 1912, G. Elliot Smith suggested that taking to the trees favored vision over smell. Vision would be more useful in an animal that searched for food in the maze of tree branches. With smaller snouts and the declining importance of the sense of smell, the eyes of the early primates would have come to face forward. In 1916, Frederic Wood Jones emphasized changes in the hand and foot. He thought that tree climbing would favor grasping hands and feet, with the hind limbs becoming more specialized for support and propulsion. In 1921, Treacher Collins suggested that the eyes of the early primates came to face forward not just because the snout got smaller. Rather, he thought that three-dimensional binocular vision would be favored because an animal jumping from branch to branch would be more likely to survive if it could accurately judge distances across open space.[54] In 1968, Frederick Szalay suggested that a shift in diet—from insects to seeds, fruits, and leaves—might have been important in the differentiation of primates from insectivores.[55]

Arboreal theory still has some proponents, but Matt Cartmill highlighted some crucial weaknesses in the theory.[56] He argued that tree living is not a good explanation for many of the primate features because there are living mammals that dwell in trees but seem to do very well without primatelike characteristics. One of the best examples, Cartmill says, is the tree squirrel. Its eyes are not front-facing, its sense of smell is not reduced in comparison with other rodents, it has claws rather than nails, and it lacks an opposable thumb. Yet these squirrels are very successful in trees. They can leap accurately from tree to tree, they can walk over or under small branches, they can go up and down vertical surfaces, and they can even hang from their hind legs to get food below them. Furthermore, other animals have some primate traits but do not live in trees or do not move around in trees as primates do. For example, carnivores, such as cats, hawks, and owls, have forward-facing eyes, and the chameleon, a reptile, and some Australian marsupial mammals that prey on insects in bushes and shrubs have grasping hands and feet.

Cartmill thinks, then, that some factor other than moving about in trees may account for the emergence of the primates. He proposes that the early primates may have been basically insect eaters and that three-dimensional vision, grasping hands and feet, and reduced claws may have been selectively advantageous for hunting insects on the slender vines and branches that filled the undergrowth of tropical forests. Three-dimensional vision would allow insect hunters to gauge the prey's distance accurately. Grasping feet would allow predators to move quietly up narrow supports to reach the prey, which could then be grabbed with the hands. Claws, Cartmill argues, would make it difficult to grasp very slender branches. And the sense of smell would have become reduced, not so much because it was no longer useful, but because the location of the eyes at the front of the face would leave less room for a snout.

Robert Sussman's theory builds on Cartmill's *visual predation theory* and on Szalay's idea about a dietary shift.[57] Sussman accepts Cartmill's point that the early primates were likely to eat and move about mostly on small branches, not on large trunks and branches (as do squirrels). If they did, grasping hands and feet, and nails rather than claws (as squirrels have), would have been advantageous. Sussman also accepts Szalay's point that the early primates probably ate the new types of plant foods (flowers, seeds, and fruits) that were beginning to become abundant as flowering trees and plants spread throughout the world. But Sussman asks an important question: If the early primates ate mostly plant foods rather than quick-moving insects, why did they become more reliant on vision than on smell? Sussman suggests it was because the early primates were probably nocturnal (as many prosimians still are): If they were to locate and manipulate small food items at the ends of slender branches in dim light, they would need improved vision.

We still have very little fossil evidence of the earliest primates. *Carpolestes* suggests that grasping hands and feet evolved first, sometime in the late Paleocene, and stereoscopic vision evolved somewhat later. When more fossils become available, we may be better able to evaluate the various explanations that have been suggested for the emergence of primates.

Early Eocene Primates: Omomyids and Adapids

Two groups of prosimians appear in the early Eocene. One group, called **omomyids**, had many tarsierlike features; the other group, **adapids**, had many lemurlike features. The omomyids were very small, no bigger than squirrels; the adapids were kitten- and cat-sized.

Omomyids A type of prosimian with many tarsierlike features that appeared in the early Eocene.

adapids A type of prosimian with many lemurlike features; appeared in the early Eocene.

Omomyids are considered tarsierlike because of their large eyes, long tarsal bones, and very small size. The large eyes suggest that they were active at night; the smaller-sized omomyids may have been insect eaters and the larger ones may have relied more on fruit.[58] Most of the omomyids had dental formulas characteristic of modern prosimians: two incisors and three premolars on each side of the lower jaw rather than the three incisors and four premolars of early mammals.[59] The importance of vision is apparent in a fossilized skull of the Eocene omomyid *Tetonius*. Imprints in the skull show that the brain had large occipital and temporal lobes, the regions associated with perception and the integration of visual memory.[60]

The lemurlike adapids were more active during the day and relied more on leaf and fruit vegetation. In contrast to the omomyids, adapid remains show considerable sexual dimorphism in the canines. They also retain the four premolars characteristic of earlier mammals (although with fewer incisors).[61] One adapid known from its abundant fossil finds is *Notharctus*. It had a small, broad face with full stereoscopic vision and a reduced muzzle. It appears to have lived in the forest and had long, powerful hind legs for leaping from tree to tree.[62]

There was a great deal of diversity among all mammals during the Eocene epoch, and the primates were no exception. Evolution seems to have proceeded rapidly during those years. Both the omomyids and adapids had a few features that suggest links between them and the anthropoids that appear later, in the Oligocene, but there is no agreement that either group gave rise to the anthropoids.[63] Although the omomyids had some resemblances to modern tarsiers and the adapids had some resemblances to lemurs and lorises, paleoanthropologists are not sure that either group was ancestral to modern prosimians. But it is generally thought that the populations ancestral to lemurs and lorises as well as tarsiers did emerge in the Eocene or even earlier, in the late Paleocene.[64]

An artist's reconstruction of Notharctus, a lemurlike primate from the Eocene.

The Emergence of Anthropoids

The anthropoids of today—monkeys, apes, and humans—are the most successful living primates and include well over 150 species. Unfortunately, the fossil record documenting the emergence of the anthropoids is extremely spotty, and there is no clear fossil record of the Old World forms (the catarrhines) in the two areas where they are most abundant today—the rain forests of sub-Saharan Africa and Southeast Asia.[65] Some paleoanthropologists think that recent Eocene primate finds from China, Southeast Asia, and Algeria have anthropoid affinities, but there is no clear agreement on their evolutionary status.[66]

Undisputed remains of early anthropoids date from a somewhat later period, the late Eocene and early Oligocene, about 34 million years ago, in the **Fayum** area, southwest of Cairo, Egypt. One of the earliest fossil primates at Fayum is *Catopithecus*, dating to around 35 million years ago. *Catopithecus* was about the size of a modern marmoset or squirrel monkey. Its dentition suggests a mixed diet of fruit and insects. Its eyes were small, suggesting it was active during the day (diurnal). The few skeletal remains of *Catopithecus* suggest it was an agile arboreal quadruped.[67]

Oligocene Anthropoids

The Fayum is an uninviting area of desert badlands, but it has yielded a remarkable array of early anthropoid fossils. During the **Oligocene** epoch, 34 million to 24 million years ago, the Fayum was a tropical rain forest very close to the shores of the Mediterranean Sea. The area had a warm climate, and it contained many rivers and lakes. The Fayum, in fact, was far more inviting than the northern continents then, for the climates of both North America and Eurasia were beginning to cool during the Oligocene. The general cooling seems to have resulted in the virtual disappearance of primates from the northern areas, at least for a time.

Oligocene anthropoids from the Fayum are grouped into two main types: the monkeylike **parapithecids** and the apelike **propliopithecids**. Dating from 35 million to 31 million years ago, the parapithecids and the propliopithecids had enough features to be unquestionably classified as anthropoids.

5.5 Describe the emergence of anthropoids.

Fayum A site southwest of Cairo, Egypt, where the world's best record of Oligocene primate fossils has been found.

Oligocene The geological epoch 34 million to 24 million years ago during which definite anthropoids emerged.

Parapithecids Small monkeylike Oligocene primates found in the Fayum area of Egypt.

Propliopithecids Apelike anthropoids dating from the early Oligocene, found in the Fayum area of Egypt.

Parapithecids The monkeylike parapithecids had three premolars (in each quarter), as do most prosimians and the New World monkeys. They were similar to modern anthropoids, with a bony partition behind the eye sockets, broad incisors, projecting canines, and low, rounded cusps on their molars. But they had prosimianlike premolars and relatively small brains. The parapithecids were small, generally weighing less than 3 pounds, and resembled the squirrel monkeys living now in South and Central America.[68] Their relatively small eye sockets suggest that they were not nocturnal. Their teeth suggest that they ate mostly fruits and seeds. Locomotion is best known from one of the parapithecids, *Apidium*, an arboreal quadruped that also did a considerable amount of leaping.[69] The parapithecids are the earliest definite anthropoid group, and although there is still disagreement among paleoanthropologists, most believe that the emergence of the anthropoids preceded the split between the New World monkeys (platyrrhines) and the Old World monkeys (catarrhines).[70]

That parapithecids may be ancestral to New World monkeys (platyrrhines) raises an interesting puzzle in primate evolution: the origin of the New World monkeys. Anthropoidal primates such as *Dolichocebus*, a small fruit-eating monkey similar to the modern squirrel monkey,[71] appear suddenly and without any apparent ancestors in South America around 25 million years ago. Because the parapithecids predate the appearance of anthropoids in South America, and resemble them in many ways, it seems reasonable to view them as part of the population ancestral to the New World monkeys.[72]

But how did anthropoidal primates get from Africa to South America? Although the continents were closer together in the late Oligocene, when primates first appeared in South America, at least 1,864 miles (3,000 kilometers) separated South America and Africa. An extended continental shelf and islands created by lower sea levels in the late Oligocene may have made it possible to "island-hop" from Africa to South America over ocean stretches as short as 125 miles (200 kilometers), but that is still a long distance for an arboreal primate.

Going from Africa to Europe and North America, which were still joined in the late Oligocene, is not a likely route either. North America and South America were not joined until some 5 million years ago, so even if the ancestors of the New World monkeys made it to North America, they would still have needed to make a long ocean crossing to reach South America. One suggestion is that the ancestors of the New World monkeys "rafted" across the Atlantic on large mats of vegetation. Such rafts of matted plants, roots, and soil break away from the mouths of major rivers today, and they can be quite large. It seems an unlikely scenario, but many scholars believe such drifting vegetation must have been the means of bringing anthropoids to South America.[73]

Propliopithecids The other type of anthropoid found in the Fayum, the propliopithecids, had the dental formula of modern catarrhines. This trait clearly places the propliopithecids with the catarrhines.[74] In contrast with the parapithecids, which had three premolars (in each quarter of the jaw), the propliopithecids had only two premolars, as do modern apes, humans, and Old World monkeys. Propliopithecids shared with the parapithecids the anthropoid dental characteristics of broad lower incisors, projecting canines, and lower molars with low, rounded cusps. And, like parapithecids, propliopithecids had a bony partition behind the eye socket.

Aegyptopithecus, the best-known propliopithecid, probably moved around quadrupedally in the trees and weighed about 13 pounds. Its molars were low with large cusps, and it had relatively large incisors, suggesting that *Aegyptopithecus* ate mostly fruit. Its eyes were relatively small, and thus it was probably active during the day. It had a long muzzle and a relatively small brain. Endocasts of the brain cavity suggest *Aegyptopithecus* had a relatively large area of the brain dedicated to vision and a relatively small area dedicated to smell.

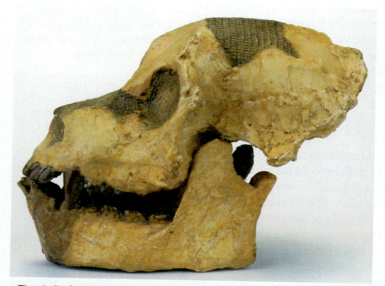

Aegyptopithecus An Oligocene anthropoid and probably the best-known propliopithecid.

The skull of an Aegyptopithecus from the Fayum. Its dentition, small bony eye sockets, and relatively large brain make it an unambiguous ancestor of Old World monkeys and apes.

The skulls of *Aegyptopithecus* show considerable sexual dimorphism, and individuals also changed dramatically as they aged, developing bony ridges along the top and across the back of the skull, much like modern great apes. Although its teeth, jaws, and some aspects of the skull were apelike, the rest of *Aegyptopithecus*'s skeleton was monkeylike,[75] and most scholars classify them as primitive catarrhines. Because the propliopithecids lack the specialized characteristics of living Old World monkeys and apes (catarrhines) but share the dental formula of the catarrhines, some paleoanthropologists think that the propliopithecids included the ancestor of both the Old World monkeys and the hominoids (apes and humans).[76]

The Emergence of Hominoids

During the **Miocene** epoch, 24 million to 5.2 million years ago, monkeys and apes clearly diverged in appearance, and numerous kinds of apes appeared in Europe, Asia, and Africa. In the early Miocene, the temperatures were considerably warmer than in the Oligocene. From early to late Miocene, conditions became drier, particularly in East Africa. The reasons for this relate again to continental drift. By about 18 million years ago, Africa came into contact with Eurasia, ending the moderating effect that the Tethys Sea, which separated Africa from Eurasia, had on the climates of both continents. The contact of Africa and, more significantly, India with the Eurasian continent also initiated mountain building, changing established weather patterns. The overall effect was that southern Eurasia and eastern Africa became considerably drier than they had been. Once again, these changes appear to have significantly influenced primate evolution.

Early Miocene Proto-Apes

Most of the fossils from the early Miocene are described as proto-apes. They have been found mostly in Africa. The best-known genus is **Proconsul**, found in sites in Kenya and Uganda that are about 20 million years old.[77]

All of the various *Proconsul* species that have been found were much bigger than any of the anthropoids of the Oligocene, ranging from about the size of a gibbon to that of a female gorilla.[78] They lacked a tail. That lack is one of the most definitive features of hominoids, and most paleoanthropologists now agree that *Proconsul* was definitely hominoid but quite unlike any ape living today. Modern hominoids have many anatomical features of the shoulder, elbow, wrists, and fingers that are adapted for locomotion by suspension (brachiation). Suspension was apparently not *Proconsul*'s method of getting around. Its elbows, wrists, and fingers may have permitted brachiation,[79] but, like the Oligocene anthropoids, *Proconsul* was primarily an arboreal quadruped. Some of the larger forms may have sometimes moved on the ground. Judging by teeth, most *Proconsul* species appear to have been fruit eaters, but larger species may have also consumed leaves.[80]

Middle Miocene Apes

The first definitely apelike finds come from the middle Miocene, 16 million to 10 million years ago. The oldest, dating to about 13 million years ago, is **Pierolapithecus**, and was recently found near Barcelona, Spain.[81] Another hominoid, **Kenyapithecus**, was found on Maboko Island and nearby locations in Kenya.[82]

Both *Pierolapithecus* and *Kenyapithecus* have many of *Proconsul*'s features but have teeth and faces that resemble those of more modern hominoids. And, in contrast to *Proconsul*, *Kenyapithecus* was probably more terrestrial. It also had very thickly enameled teeth and robust jaws, suggesting a diet of hard, tough foods, or possibly a great deal of grit in the food because *Kenyapithecus* lived mostly on the ground. Whether *Kenyapithecus* is ancestral to the later apes and humans is something of a puzzle because its limbs do not show the capacity for brachiation that is characteristic of all the later apes.[83] *Pierolapithecus*, however, has wrists and vertebrae that would have made it capable of brachiation, but also has relatively short fingers like modern monkeys. *Pierolapithecus* probably spent most of its time in trees, walking along larger branches as monkeys do, and also brachiating among smaller branches, as apes do.[84] Thus, *Pierolapithecus* is a good candidate for the ancestor of later forest-dwelling apes.

Miocene The geological epoch from 24 million to 5.2 million years ago.

Proconsul The best-known genus of proto-apes from the early Miocene.

5.6 Differentiate between the various early anthropoids and hominoids.

Pierolapithecus A middle Miocene ape that has wrists and vertebrae that would have made it capable of brachiation, but also has relatively short fingers like modern monkeys.

Kenyapithecus An apelike primate from the middle Miocene found in East Africa. It had very thickly enameled teeth and robust jaws, suggesting a diet of hard, tough foods. Probably somewhat terrestrial.

The skull of a *Proconsul* specimen from Kenya. *Proconsul* is considered an early hominoid because it lacked a tail, but it was unlike modern hominoids in being a quadruped.

Late Miocene Apes

From the end of the middle Miocene into the late Miocene, the apes diversified and moved into many areas. Fossils are abundant in Europe and Asia, less so in Africa. This does not mean that apes were more numerous than monkeys. In fact, the fossil record suggests that monkeys in the Old World became more and more numerous than apes toward the end of the Miocene, and this trend continues to the present day.

One well-known late Miocene ape from Europe is *Oreopithecus*, which dates from about 8 million years ago. It is particularly interesting because, despite being well represented by fossils, including nearly complete ones preserved in beds of hard coal, its classification is enigmatic. *Oreopithecus* was clearly adapted to life in thickly forested marshlands. It had extremely long arms and hands and mobile joints, and was likely an agile brachiator. Its dentition suggests it had a diet that consisted mostly of leaves. However, the dentition and skull of *Oreopithecus* also had a number of unique features that suggest affinity to some Old World monkeys. In short, *Oreopithecus* had an apelike body and a monkeylike head. Because of its suspensory locomotion and other apelike features, most scholars today consider it an early, albeit specialized, ape.[85]

Most paleoanthropologists divide the later Miocene apes into at least two main groups: the sivapithecids, represented primarily by the genus *Sivapithecus* and found primarily in western and southern Asia, and the dryopithecids, represented primarily by the genus *Dryopithecus* and found primarily in Europe.

Sivapithecids At one time, **Sivapithecus**, which dates from roughly 13 million to 8 million years ago, was thought to be ancestral to hominins. It had flat and thickly enameled molars, smaller canines, and less sexual dimorphism than other Miocene apes, and had a parabolic dental arcade in some reconstructions (now considered faulty)—all hominin features. It also lived in a mixed woodland–grassland environment. However, as more fossil material was uncovered, scholars recognized that *Sivapithecus* was remarkably similar to the modern orangutan in the face, and it is now thought to be ancestral to the orangutan.[86]

Dryopithecids **Dryopithecus**, which appears about 15 million years ago, was a chimpanzee-sized ape that lived in the forests of Eurasia. It was mainly arboreal and apparently omnivorous. *Dryopithecus* had thinner tooth enamel than *Sivapithecus*, lighter jaws, and pointed molar cusps. In the palate, jaw, and midface, *Dryopithecus* looked like the African apes and humans. In contrast to later hominoids, however, *Dryopithecus* had a very short face and a relatively small brow ridge.[87]

The fingers and elbows of *Dryopithecus* and *Sivapithecus* suggest that they were much more capable of suspending themselves than were earlier hominoids. *Sivapithecus* may have moved about more on the ground than *Dryopithecus*, but both were probably mostly arboreal.[88] Indeed, recent finds of *Dryopithecus* hand, arm, shoulder, and leg bones strongly suggest that *Dryopithecus* was highly efficient at suspensory locomotion and probably moved through the trees like modern orangutans do.

It is still very difficult to identify the particular evolutionary lines leading from the Miocene apes to modern apes and humans. Only the orangutans have been linked to a late Miocene ape genus, *Sivapithecus*, so presumably that lineage continued into modern times.[89] *Dryopithecus* disappears from the fossil record after about 10 million years ago, leaving no descendants, perhaps because less rainfall and more seasonality reduced the forests where they lived.[90]

Sivapithecus A genus of ape from the later Miocene known for its thickly enameled teeth, suggesting a diet of hard, tough, or gritty items. Found primarily in western and southern Asia and now thought to be ancestral to orangutans.

Dryopithecus Genus of ape from the later Miocene found primarily in Europe. It had thin tooth enamel and pointed molar cusps very similar to those of the fruit-eating chimpanzees of today.

5.7 Discuss the challenges to identifying any clear emergence of hominins.

The Divergence of Hominins from the Other Hominoids

The later Miocene apes are best known from Europe and Asia. Until recently, there has been an almost complete lack of African fossil hominoids dating between 13.5 million and 5 million years ago.[91] Recently, two species, *Orrorin tugenensis*, from Kenya and dated to about 6 million years ago, and *Sahelanthropus tchadensis*, from Chad and dated to perhaps 7 million years ago, have provided a glimpse of hominoid evolution during this time period. Still, this scarcity of fossils from 13.5 to 5 million years ago is unfortunate for our understanding of human evolution because the earliest unambiguous bipedal primates (hominins) appear in Africa near the beginning of the Pliocene, after 5 million years ago. To understand the evolutionary links between the apes of the Miocene and the hominins of Africa, we need more fossil evidence from late Miocene times in Africa.

Summary and Review

Common Primate Traits

5.1 ▶ Identify common primate traits.

- No one trait is unique to primates. However, primates do share a distinct complex of features that include skeletal, dietary, sensory, brain, and developmental elements.

- Specific shared features include two bones in the lower part of the leg and in the forearm, a collarbone, omnivorous eating patterns, flexible prehensile hands, forward-facing eyes and stereoscopic vision, a large brain relative to body size, long maturation of the young, and a high degree of dependence on social life and learning.

 What traits are common to all primates?

The Various Living Primates

5.2 ▶ Describe the major types of living primates and their geographical distribution.

- The order Primates is divided into two suborders: the prosimians, including lemur forms (Madagascar and the Comoro Islands, off the southeastern coast of Africa), loris forms (in Southeast Asia and sub-Saharan Africa), and tarsiers (the islands of the Philippines and Indonesia), and the anthropoids.

- Prosimians more resemble other mammals and typically have mobile ears, whiskers, longer snouts, relatively fixed facial expressions, and more dependence on smell for information than other primates. But they share with anthropoids grasping hands, stereoscopic vision, and enlarged visual centers in the brain.

- Anthropoids (humans, apes, and monkeys) have rounded braincases; reduced, nonmobile outer ears; and relatively small, flat faces instead of muzzles. They also have highly efficient reproductive systems and highly dexterous hands.

- The Anthropoid order is divided into two main groups: platyrrhines and catarrhines. Platyrrhines

have broad, flat-bridged noses, with nostrils facing outward. The catarrhines are subdivided into cercopithecoids and hominoids.

- The Hominoids have distinct locomotor patterns, including brachiation, knuckle walking, and bipedalism; high conceptual abilities; and relatively large brains.

- The Hominoids include three groups: (1) the hylobates, or lesser apes; (2) the pongids, or great apes that include orangutans, gorillas, and chimpanzees; and (3) the hominins (humans).

 What are the differences between prosimians, anthropoids, and hominoids?

Distinctive Hominin Traits

5.3 ▶ Describe the traits that distinguish hominins from other anthropoids.

- The differences between hominins and the other anthropoids show us what makes humans distinctive as a species.

- Hominins are totally bipedal; they walk on two legs and do not need the arms for locomotion. The hominin brain, particularly the cerebral cortex, is the largest and most complex of all anthropoids. Hominins can move their jaws both vertically and horizontally when chewing.

- Hominin females are not limited as to when they may engage in intercourse. Hominin offspring have a proportionately longer dependency stage. And in comparison with other primates, more hominin behavior is learned and culturally patterned.

- The use of tools to make other tools and spoken, symbolic language are uniquely modern human behavioral traits. Hominins also generally have a division of labor in food-getting and food-sharing in adulthood.

 Explain three differences between hominins and anthropoids and how those differences may have influenced hominin ability to thrive.

The Emergence of Primates

5.4 ▶ Discuss the emergence of primates in relation to environment and adaptation.

- The surviving primates—prosimians, New World monkeys, Old World monkeys, apes, and humans—are thought to be descendants of small, originally terrestrial insectivores. However, exactly who the common ancestor was and when it emerged are not yet known.

- The traditional view of primate evolution was that arboreal (tree) life would have favored many of the common primate features, including distinctive dentition, greater reliance on vision over smell, three-dimensional binocular vision, and grasping hands and feet.

- The earliest definite primates, dating from the early Eocene, about 55 million years ago, are clearly primates. They are classified into two major groups of prosimians—adapids (lemurlike features) and omomyids (tarsierlike features).

 What are two of the environmental factors that may have led to the emergence of primates?

The Emergence of Anthropoids

5.5 ▶ Describe the emergence of anthropoids.

- Undisputed remains of early anthropoids unearthed in Egypt date from the early Oligocene (after 34 million years ago).

- Early anthropoids included the monkeylike parapithecids and the apelike propliopithecids. The parapithecids are the earliest definite anthropoid group and may be the ancestors of the New World monkeys.

 Discuss how the parapithecids may be ancestral to New World monkeys (platyrrhines).

The Emergence of Hominoids

5.6 ▶ Differentiate between the various early anthropoids and hominoids.

- During the Miocene epoch (24 million to 5.2 million years ago), monkeys and apes clearly diverged in appearance, and numerous kinds of apes appeared in Europe, Asia, and Africa.

- From the end of the middle Miocene into the late Miocene, the apes diversified and spread geographically. They were much bigger than earlier anthropoids, and they lacked a tail.

- Most paleoanthropologists divide the later Miocene apes into at least two main groups: dryopithecids, found primarily in Europe, and sivapithecids, found primarily in western and southern Asia.

 Explain what paleoanthropologists considered when trying to classify *Oreopithecus* and *Sivapithecus*.

The Divergence of Hominins from the Other Hominoids

5.7 ▶ Discuss the challenges to identifying any clear emergence of hominins.

- Hominins probably diverged from the hominoids between about 8 million years ago and 6 million years ago, although the timing is difficult to determine because of a paucity of fossils from between 13.5 million years ago and about 5 million years ago.

 Which regions would likely be the best sources for evidence of hominin emergence and why?

Think on it

1. How could you infer that a **fossil primate** lived in the trees?

2. We like to think of the human lineage as **biologically unique**, which of course it is (like all evolutionary lineages). But some paleoanthropologists say that humans, chimpanzees, and gorillas are so similar that all three should be grouped as hominins. What do you think, and why do you think so?

3. Why are humans **immature** for so long?

The First Hominins and the Emergence of *Homo*

LEARNING OBJECTIVES

Evaluate theories for the evolution of bipedal locomotion.	6.1
Identify species involved in the transition from hominoids to hominins.	6.2
Describe the distinctive traits of hominins.	6.3
Describe early *Homo* species.	6.4
Identify the main trends in hominin evolution.	6.5
Explain the evolution of *Homo erectus*.	6.6
Identify features of Lower Paleolithic cultures.	6.7

Bipedal locomotion is a defining feature of the hominins. Undisputed bipedal hominins lived in East Africa about 4 million years ago. These hominins, and some others who may have lived later in eastern and southern Africa, are generally classified in the genus *Australopithecus*. In this chapter, we discuss what we know or suspect about the transition from hominoids to hominins, the emergence of australopithecines, and their relationship to later hominins, including ourselves.

6.1 Evaluate theories for the evolution of bipedal locomotion.

The Evolution of Bipedal Locomotion

Perhaps the most crucial change in early hominin evolution was the development of *bipedal locomotion,* or walking on two legs. We know from the fossil record that other important physical changes—including the expansion of the brain, modification of the female pelvis to allow bigger-brained babies to be born, and reduction of the face, teeth, and jaws—did not occur until about 2 million years after the emergence of bipedalism. Other human characteristics, such as an extended period of infant and child dependency and increased meat-eating, may also have developed after that time.

We do not know whether bipedalism developed quickly or gradually, because the fossil record for the period between 8 million and 4 million years ago is very slim. We do know, on the basis of their skeletal anatomy, that many of the Miocene anthropoids were capable of assuming an upright posture. For example, *brachiation*, swinging by the arms through the trees, puts an animal in an upright position; so does climbing up and down trees with the use of grasping hands and feet.[1] It is also likely that the protohominins were capable of occasional bipedalism, just as many modern monkeys and apes are.[2]

Definitely bipedal hominins emerged in Africa, judging by the available fossil record. The emergence of bipedal hominins coincides with a change from extensive tropical forest cover to more discontinuous patches of forest and open country.[3] About 16 million to 11 million years ago, a drying trend set in that continued into the Pliocene. Gradually, the African rain forests, deprived of intense humidity and rainfall, dwindled in extent; areas of **savanna** (grasslands) and scattered deciduous woodlands became more common. The tree-dwelling primates did not completely lose their customary habitats, because some tropical forests remained in wetter regions, and natural selection continued to favor the better-adapted tree dwellers in those forested areas. But the new, more open country probably favored characteristics adapted to ground living in some primates as well as other animals. In the evolutionary line leading to humans, these adaptations included bipedalism (see the box on "Environmental Changes and Evolutionary Consequences in Hominins").

Savanna Tropical grassland.

Theories for the Evolution of Bipedalism

What in particular may have favored the emergence of bipedal hominins? There are several possible explanations for this development. One idea is that bipedalism was adaptive for life amid the tall grasses of the savannas because an erect posture may have made it easier to spot ground predators as well as potential prey.[4] This theory does not adequately account for the development of bipedalism, however. Baboons and some other Old World monkeys also live in savanna environments, yet, although they can stand erect and occasionally do so, they have not evolved fully bipedal locomotion. And recent evidence suggests that the area where early hominins lived in East Africa was not predominantly savanna; rather, it seems to have been a mix of woodland and open country.[5]

Other theories stress the importance of freeing the hands to perform other activities at the same time. Gordon Hewes emphasized the importance of carrying food from one locale to another.[6] C. Owen Lovejoy has suggested that food carrying might have been important because males provisioning females and their babies by carrying food back to a

Current Research and Issues

Environmental Changes and Evolutionary Consequences in Hominins

Jonathan Wells and Jay Stock argue that environmental change led humans to become "colonizing apes," able to live in diverse environments because of developmental plasticity and learned behaviors. It makes sense that early hominins would have changed, both physically and behaviorally, to adapt to the changing environment at the end of the Pliocene. Indeed bipedalism seems obviously linked to the emergence of mixed woodland-savannah environments in eastern Africa. But what other adaptations accompanied the changing environment? Paleoanthropologists have proposed many hypotheses.

Elizabeth Vrba suggested that the long cooling period at the end of the Pliocene would have resulted in hominin bodies becoming larger, and limbs relatively shorter following Bergmann's and Allen's rules. But what was the mechanism for bringing about this change? Vrba suggests

that hominin maturation slowed and therefore hominins retained more juvenile body forms and limb proportions (juveniles have bigger bodies proportional to their legs and arms). And since the hominin brain grows most rapidly during maturation, the longer period of childhood or maturation allowed hominin brains to grow proportionally larger.

Barry Bogin suggested that there were additional adaptive consequences of a long period of childhood. Brain growth requires a lot of calories that mothers cannot provide solely from breast milk; those mothers who worked with others to provision their children with high calorie foods might produce children with more brain power. In addition, if mothers provide high calorie foods and stop nursing somewhat earlier, they can have more offspring. Also Bogin suggests that a long childhood has other advantages.

Particularly important is a great degree of developmental plasticity; that is, the ability to acclimatize to an environment or to learn new behaviors necessary to survival in a changing environment.

As Vrba and Bogin have suggested, developmental plasticity and a brain that is capable of social learning may have emerged among hominins ultimately because of late Pliocene cooling. The greater reproductive rate in early hominins would have led to population increases that Wells and Stock suggest may have forced hominins to expand their ranges, ultimately leading them to colonize new areas.

Thus these scholars consider much of what constitutes the core of hominin behavior to have resulted directly from environmental change.

Sources: Vrba 1996; Bogin 1997; Wells and Stock 2007.

---

home base would have allowed females to conserve energy by not traveling and therefore be able to produce and care for more babies.[7]

But carrying food or provisioning families might not have been the only benefit of freeing the hands; feeding itself may have been more efficient. Clifford Jolly has argued that bipedalism would have allowed early hominins to efficiently harvest small seeds and nuts because both hands could be used to pick up food and move it directly to the mouth.[8] In the changing environments of East Africa, where forests were giving way to more open woodlands and savannas, an advantage in foraging for small seeds and nuts might well have proven important for survival and thus have been favored by natural selection.

Bipedalism might also have been favored by natural selection because the freeing of the hands would allow protohominins to use, and perhaps even make, tools that they could carry with them. Sherwood Washburn noted that some contemporary ground-living primates dig for roots to eat, "and if they could use a stone or a stick they might easily double their food supply."[9] David Pilbeam suggested that tool use by the more open-country primates may have appreciably increased the number and amount of plant foods they could eat: In order to be eaten, many of the plant foods in the grassy areas probably had to be chopped, crushed, or otherwise prepared with the aid of tools.[10] Tools may also have been used to kill and butcher animals for food. Without tools, primates in general are not well equipped physically for regular hunting or even scavenging. Their teeth and jaws are not sharp and strong enough, and their speed afoot is not fast enough.

Finally, tools may have been used as weapons against predators, which would have been a great threat to the relatively defenseless ground-dwelling protohominins. In Milford

Wolpoff's opinion, it was the advantage of carrying weapons *continuously* that was responsible for transforming occasional bipedalism to completely bipedal locomotion.[11] In particular, the ability to abduct or snap the wrist would have permitted early humans to develop effective throwing skills.[12]

But some anthropologists question the idea that tool use and toolmaking favored bipedalism. They point out that the first clear evidence of stone tools appears more than 2 million years *after* the emergence of bipedalism. So how could toolmaking be responsible for bipedalism? Wolpoff suggests an answer. Even though bipedalism appears to be at least 2 million years older than stone tools, protohominins might have used tools made of wood and bone, neither of which would be as likely as stone to survive in the archaeological record. Moreover, unmodified stone tools present in the archaeological record might not be recognizable as tools.[13]

Some researchers have taken a closer look at the mechanics of bipedal locomotion to see if it might be a more efficient form of locomotion in the savanna-woodland environment, where resources are likely to be scattered. Compared with the quadrupedal locomotion of primates such as chimpanzees, bipedalism appears to be more efficient for long-distance travel.[14] But why travel long distances? If the ancestors of humans had the manipulative ability and tool-using capability of modern chimpanzees (e.g., using stones to crack nuts), and those ancestors had to move around in a more open environment, then those individuals who could efficiently travel longer distances to exploit those resources might do better.[15]

Finally, bipedalism might have been favored by natural selection as a way of regulating body temperature, particularly in the increasingly hot and dry environments of East Africa at the end of the Miocene and the beginning of the Pliocene. Peter Wheeler has argued that a bipedal posture limits the area of the body directly exposed to the sun, especially when the sun is at its hottest, at midday.[16] Bipedal posture would also facilitate convective heat loss by allowing heat to rise up and away from the body rather than being trapped underneath it. Cooling through the evaporation of sweat would also be facilitated by a bipedal posture, as more skin area would be exposed to cooling winds. Thus, natural selection may have favored bipedalism because it reduced heat stress in the warming environments of East Africa.

All theories about the origin of bipedalism are speculative. We do not yet have direct evidence that any of the factors we have discussed were actually responsible for bipedalism. Any or all of the factors may explain the transformation of an occasionally bipedal protohominin to a completely bipedal hominin.

The "Costs" of Bipedalism

We must remember that there are also "costs" to bipedal walking. Bipedalism makes it harder to overcome gravity to supply the brain with sufficient blood,[17] and the weight of the body above the pelvis and lower limbs puts greater stress on the hips, lower back, knees, and feet. As Adrienne Zihlman points out, the stresses on the lower body are even greater for pregnant and nursing females who carry their infants.[18]

We must also remember that the evolution of bipedalism required some dramatic changes in the ancestral ape skeleton. Although apes today can and do walk bipedally, they cannot do so efficiently or for long periods of time. To be habitually bipedal, the ancestral ape skeleton had to be modified, and the major changes that allowed the early hominins to become fully bipedal occurred primarily in the skull, pelvis, knees, and feet.[19] Let's take a look at each of these changes.

In both ancient and modern apes, the spinal column enters the skull toward the back, which makes sense because apes generally walk on all fours, with the spine roughly parallel to the ground. In bipedal hominins, the spinal column enters the skull at the bottom, through a hole called the **foramen magnum.** Thus, when hominins became bipedal, the skull ended up on top of the spinal column.

The shape of ancient and modern ape pelvises is considerably different from that of a bipedal hominin. Ape pelvises are long and flat, forming a bony plate in the lower back

Foramen magnum
Opening in the base of the skull through which the spinal cord passes en route to the brain.

to which the leg muscles attach. In bipedal hominins, the pelvis is bowl-shaped, which supports the internal organs and also lowers the body's center of gravity, allowing better balance on the legs. The hominin pelvis also provides a different set of muscle attachments and shifts the orientation of the femurs (the upper leg bones) from the side of the pelvis to the front. These changes allow hominins to move their legs forward in a bipedal stride (and do things like kick a soccer ball). Apes, in comparison, move their legs forward (when they walk bipedally) by shifting their pelvis from side to side, not by kicking each leg forward alternately as we do.[20]

Another change associated with the hominin ability to kick the leg forward is our "knock-kneed" posture. Ape legs hang straight down from the pelvis. Bipedal hominin legs, on the other hand, angle inward toward one another. This configuration not only helps us move our legs forward but also helps us maintain a center of gravity in the midline of our bodies, so that our center of gravity does not shift from side to side when we walk or run.

Finally, the feet of bipedal hominins have two major changes compared to those of apes. First, hominin feet have an enlarged group of ankle bones forming a robust heel that can withstand the substantial forces placed on them as a result of habitual bipedalism. Second, hominin feet have an arch, which also aids in absorbing the forces endured by the feet during bipedal locomotion. We know this arch is vital to our ability to be habitually bipedal because "flat-footed" people who lack it have chronic problems in their feet, ankles, knees, and back.[21]

When did these changes take place? We don't know for sure, but fossils from East Africa—Ethiopia, Tanzania, and Kenya—clearly show that bipedal hominins lived there between 4 million and 5 million years ago, perhaps even earlier.

The Transition from Hominoids to Hominins

Western Chad, in north-central Africa, and its windswept deserts do not seem a likely place to find fossil apes or hominins, but paleoanthropologist Michel Brunet thinks it might be.[22] Western Chad was covered by an ancient lake and for several million years was a location where forest-dwelling mammals, including primates, congregated. Around 7 million years ago, a primate called **Sahelanthropus tchadensis** lived on the shores of the lake, where Brunet and his colleagues recovered its fossilized bones in 2001. *Sahelanthropus,* represented by an almost complete skull, has a unique mix of hominin and hominoid traits. Although the skull itself is hominoid, with a small brain, large brow ridges, and wide face, the teeth seem more homininlike, especially the canines, which do not project below the tooth row.[23] Unfortunately, there is no evidence that *Sahelanthropus* was bipedal. For now, we have to wait for additional evidence to know whether *Sahelanthropus* was the first bipedal ape.

There is, however, tantalizing evidence that another possible early hominin, **Orrorin tugenensis,** was bipedal. Discovered in western Kenya by Brigitte Senut and colleagues in 1998, *Orrorin tugenensis* consists of 19 specimens of jaw, teeth, finger, arm, and leg bones, including the top of a femur.[24] The femur in *Orrorin,* according to Brian Richmond and William Jungers, shows adaptations to bipedalism, including a long, angled "head" (or top).[25] *Orrorin* dates between 5.8 million and 6 million years, so it may turn out to be the earliest hominin if further research supports *Orrorin* bipedalism.

Sahelanthropus tchadensis A hominoid found in Chad dating to around 7 million years ago.

Orrorin tugenensis An apparently bipedal primate dating to between 5.8 and 6 million years, making it possibly the earliest known hominin.

6.2 Identify species involved in the transition from hominoids to hominins.

Reconstructed skull of *Sahelanthropus tchadensis*, possibly the earliest hominin, dating to almost 7 million years ago.

In 1992, a team of researchers led by anthropologist Tim White began surveying a 4.4-million-year-old fossil deposit at Aramis, in the Middle Awash region of Ethiopia. There, they discovered 17 fossils of what may be the earliest hominin (more have been found since, including some fragments dating perhaps as early as 5.8 million years ago). Although initially suggested to be a new australopithecine species, White and his colleagues decided that *ramidus*, the species name given to the new fossils, was distinct enough from the australopithecines to warrant a new genus: *Ardipithecus*.[26]

What makes ***Ardipithecus ramidus*** unique is the combination of apelike dentition along with evidence of bipedal locomotion and an overall homininlike skeleton. Like apes, *Ardipithecus* has relatively small cheek teeth with thin enamel and relatively large canines. But its arm bones seem homininlike, and the base of its skull shows the foramen magnum positioned underneath the skull, just as in definitely bipedal hominins.[27] The feet of *Ardipithecus* also seem adapted to bipedalism.[28] Although more evidence is needed to be sure, *Ardipithecus* may be the earliest hominin yet found.

Ardipithecus ramidus
Perhaps the first hominin, dating to about 4.5 million years ago. Its dentition combines apelike and australopithecine-like features, and its skeleton suggests it was bipedal.

6.3 Describe the distinctive traits of hominins.

Australopithecus
Genus of Pliocene and Pleistocene hominins.

Australopithecines
Members of the genus *Australopithecus*.

The First Definite Hominins

Although some doubt remains about the status of *Ardipithecus* as a hominin genus, there is no doubt that the australopithecines (members of the genus ***Australopithecus***) dating from about 4 million years ago in eastern Africa were hominins. Their teeth share the basic hominin characteristics of small canines, flat and thickly enameled molars, and a parabolic dental arch, and there is unambiguous evidence that even the earliest australopithecines were fully bipedal. Not only do their skeletons reflect bipedal locomotion, but at Laetoli, Tanzania, more than 50 hardened humanlike footprints about 3.6 million years old give striking confirmation that the hominins there were fully bipedal. The bipedalism of the australopithecines does not mean that these earliest definite hominins were terrestrial all of the time. All of the australopithecines, including the later ones, seem to have been capable of climbing and moving in trees, judging by arm versus leg length and other skeletal features.[29] The **australopithecines** include *A. anamensis, A. afarensis,* and *A. africanus*.

Australopithecus anamensis

The earliest australopithecine species is *Australopithecus anamensis,* which has been found in several locations in northern Kenya and is dated between 3.9 million and 4.2 million years ago.[30] Although there is controversy about some of the specimens included in *A. anamensis,* the general picture is that it was a small bipedal hominin with teeth similar to those of the later *A. afarensis*.[31] The more controversial specimens have long bones, suggesting well-developed bipedalism, but their elbow and knee joints look more like those of the later *Homo* genus than like those of any other species of *Australopithecus*. It has been said that *A. anamensis* is "*afarensis*-like from the neck up and *Homo*-like from the neck down."[32]

Australopithecus afarensis

A. afarensis dates from about 4 million to 3 million years ago. Remains from at least two dozen individuals were unearthed at Laetoli, Tanzania.[33] There is no question that the Laetoli hominins were bipedal, because the now-famous trail of footprints was found at the Laetoli site. Two hominins walking erect and side by side left their tracks in the ground 3.6 million years ago. The remains of at least 35 individuals have been found at another site, Hadar, in Ethiopia. The Hadar finds are remarkable for their completeness. Whereas paleoanthropologists often find just parts of the cranium and jaws, many parts of the skeleton were also found at Hadar. For example, paleoanthropologist Donald Johanson found 40 percent of the skeleton of a female hominin he named Lucy, after the Beatles's song "Lucy in the Sky with Diamonds."[34]

Dating of the hominin remains at Laetoli suggests that the hominins there lived between 3.8 million and 3.6 million years ago.[35] Although Lucy and the other hominins at Hadar were once thought to be about as old as those at Laetoli, recent dating suggests that they are somewhat younger—less than 3.2 million years old. Lucy probably lived 2.9 million years ago.[36] The environment Lucy lived in was semiarid, upland savanna with rainy and dry seasons.[37]

A. afarensis was a small hominin, but, like most of the living great apes, was sexually dimorphic. Females weighed perhaps 65 pounds and stood a little more than 3 feet tall; males weighed more than 90 pounds and stood about 5 feet tall.[38] *A. afarensis* teeth were large compared to their body size, and they had thick molar enamel. They also had large, apelike canines, which, on some specimens, projected beyond the adjacent teeth. But even the longer canines did not rub against the lower teeth or fit into a diastema (a space between the teeth), and thus did not prevent side-to-side movement of the lower jaw.[39] This is important, because side-to-side movement of the lower jaw allowed *A. afarensis* to efficiently chew small seeds and grasses. The thick enamel on the molars and wear patterns on the molar crowns suggest that such small tough materials made up a significant part of the diet of *A. afarensis*.[40] The cranium of *A. afarensis* reflects

Mary Leakey's expedition discovered a trail about 70 yards long of 3.8-million-year-old fossilized footprints at Laetoli, Tanzania. Shown here is one part of the trail left by two adults who were clearly upright walkers. The footprints shows a well-developed arch and forward-facing big toe.

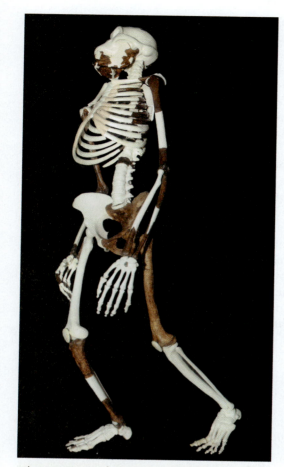

A reconstruction of a female *Australopithecus afarensis* skeleton. Note how long the arms are relative to the legs, and the long fingers. Both suggest *A. afarensis* was at least partially arboreal.

Australopithecus bahrelghazali An early australopithecine, dating to about 3 million years ago, and currently represented by only a single jaw. It is an interesting species because it is found in western Chad, distant from the East African Rift Valley where all other early australopithecines have been found.

Australopithecus garhi An australopithecine, dating to about 2.5 million years ago.

Australopithecus sediba An australopithecine from South Africa that dates to around 2 million years ago and has some *Homo*-like features.

its dentition. The face juts forward because of the large teeth and jaws, and the base of the skull flares out to provide attachment areas for large neck muscles to support the heavy face. The brain is small, about 400 cubic centimeters (cc), but relatively large for an animal this size.[41]

The arms and legs of *A. afarensis* were about the same length, and the fingers and toe bones were curved, suggesting they were heavily muscled. Most scholars believe these limb proportions and strong hands and feet point to a partially arboreal lifestyle.[42] In other words, it appears that *A. afarensis* spent a lot of time in the trees, probably feeding, sleeping, and avoiding terrestrial predators. The pelvis and leg bones of *A. afarensis*, however, demonstrate that it moved bipedally when on the ground. The pelvis is wide and flaring, but has the bowl-like shape of all later hominins. The legs angle inward, and the feet have an arch and an ankle much like later hominins.[43] Detailed analyses of the Laetoli footprints suggest that *A. afarensis* may have had a shorter and less efficient stride than modern humans.[44]

Although *A. afarensis* is the most well-represented australopithecine species, it was not the first one discovered. That distinction rests with *Australopithecus africanus*.

Australopithecus africanus

In 1925, Raymond Dart, professor of anatomy at the University of Witwatersrand in Johannesburg, South Africa, presented the first evidence that an erect bipedal hominin existed in the Pliocene epoch—the skull of an infant bipedal hominin, which has come to be known as the Taung Child. Since the Taung child's discovery 80 years ago, the remains of hundreds of other similar australopithecines have been unearthed from caves at Sterkfontein and Makapansgat in South Africa. Dating of the australopithecine finds from the South African limestone caves is somewhat difficult because none of the absolute dating techniques can be applied. But relative dating is possible. Comparisons of the fauna found in the strata with fauna found elsewhere suggest that the South African *A. africanus* lived between 3 million and 2 million years ago. The climate was probably semiarid, not too different from the climate of today.[45] *A. africanus* had a rounded braincase, a fairly large forehead, moderate brow ridges, and a projecting face.[46] The estimated cranial capacity for the various finds from Taung and Sterkfontein is between 428 and 485 cc.[47]

Like *A. afarensis*, *A. africanus* was very small; the adults were 3 ½ to 4 ½ feet tall, weighed 60 to 90 pounds, and were sexually dimorphic.[48] The large, chinless jaw of *A. africanus* resembles that of *A. afarensis*, but some of the dental features of *A. africanus* are similar to those of modern humans—broad incisors and small, short canines. And, although the premolars and molars were larger than in modern humans, their form was very similar. Presumably, function and use were also similar.

Other Australopithecines

New fossils from eastern Africa found in the last three decades suggest there may have been other species of australopithecine as well. Most scholars consider three groups of fossils in particular to represent new australopithecine species, named *Australopithecus bahrelghazali*, *Australopithecus garhi*, and *Australopithecus sediba*. *A. bahrelghazali* is currently represented by a single, fragmentary jaw, a handful of skull and limb fragments represent *A. garhi*, and two partial skeletons represent

A. sediba. Although the finds are intriguing, we will not know how important either species is, or how they may change our understanding of early hominin evolution, until more fossils from them are found.

Australopithecus garhi, found in rock dating to approximately 2.5 million years ago, is particularly interesting, as it is similar to, but is not clearly a member of, any of the other australopithecine species. *A. garhi* has larger molars than *A. afarensis* but lacks the enlarged brain of early *Homo.* Several limb bones were found in the same rock layers, and these do resemble *A. afarensis. A. garhi,* then, looks to be an *afarensis*-like creature but with greatly enlarged molars.[49] It may represent one end of the range of variation in *afarensis,* or it may represent an adaptation to eating tough foods.

It is interesting, however, that the remains of butchered animals were found in the same rock layer as the *A. garhi* remains. Several bones found near the *A. garhi* fossils show unambiguous cut marks and signs of having been broken with a stone tool. Unfortunately, no stone tools have been found, but the evidence for butchery suggests they must have been used. And since no other species of hominin have been found in the area, it is reasonable to think that *A. garhi* was the toolmaker and butcher. The fossil's discoverer, Berhane Asfaw, suggests that *A. garhi* is in the right place, at the right time, and has the right physical and behavioral traits to be the direct ancestor of early *Homo.*[50]

Equally intriguing is *Australopithecus sediba.* Found by Lee Burger in Malapa cave in South Africa, the two skeletons representing *A. sediba* and dated to around 2 million years ago present a strange mix of australopithecine and early *Homo* features. While the legs and feet of *A. sediba* seem australopithecine-like, the pelvis is more like early *Homo,* as are the hands.[51] The brain is smaller than other australopithecines, but appears to have some features found in early *Homo,* and the teeth seem more *Homo*-like as well.[52] Indeed, some have suggested that *A. sediba* may be better categorized as *Homo,* though this idea is controversial and certainly will not be resolved until more specimens are found.

Finally, *Australopithecus bahrelghazali,* is interesting not so much because of its physical features, but because it was found further west than any other australopithecine, in what is now central Chad. Indeed, *A. bahrelghazali* is the first early hominin to be found outside of the Rift Valley (a long valley in East Africa where the earth is pulling apart, exposing fossils from millions of years ago), and until *A. bahrelghazali* surfaced, few thought early hominins were present anywhere else. *A. bahrelghazali* dates to about 3 million years ago, and is very similar to contemporary *A. afarensi*'s fossils from the Rift Valley. It differs from *A. afarensis* in some distinct ways (its premolars, for example, have thinner enamel and more well-defined roots), but the important difference is where *A. bahrelghazali* lived. Most scholars assume the early hominins represent a specific adaptation to the Rift Valley. The discovery of an early australopithecine some 2,500 kilometers (1,550 or so miles) west of the Rift Valley calls this assumption into question.[53]

A related hominin genus, **Kenyanthropus platyops,** is thought by some scholars to be yet another australopithecine (and hence should not be regarded as a separate genus). The nearly complete 3.5-million-year-old skull of *Kenyanthropus platyops* from western Kenya shows traits that Meave Leakey and her colleagues suggest separate it from the australopithecines that lived at the same time. Its face is smaller and flatter, and its molars are smaller than those of the australopithecines. Leakey believes *Kenyanthropus* may be a direct link to *Homo,* but others are not so sure. The skull is distorted, and scholars are not convinced that its features lie outside the range of the australopithecines.[54] The debate over the relation of *Kenyanthropus* to *Australopithecus* will continue until more fossils are found.

Fossil skull of an *Australopithecus africanus* (STS 5) nicknamed "Mrs. Ples" found by Robert Broom at Sterkfontein cave in 1947.

Kenyanthropus platyops A nearly complete 3.5-million-year-old skull found in western Kenya. It is thought by some scholars to be a species of australopithecine (and hence should not be regarded as a separate genus).

Pliocene The geological epoch 5.2 million to 1.6 million years ago during which the earliest definite hominids appeared.

The picture that emerges from this brief overview of the first hominins is one of diversity. There seem to have been many different species of hominins, and even within species there seems to be a relatively high level of variation.[55] All shared similar environments in eastern and southern Africa, but those environments were diverse and changing. Forests were giving way to open woodlands and grasslands. Large lakes were formed and then broken apart through uplifting and volcanic activity in the Rift Valley of eastern Africa. And the climate continued to warm until the end of the **Pliocene,** some 1.6 million years ago.

At this point, you may well be wondering how all these species fit together. Figure 6.1 shows one model about how the known fossils may be related. The main disagreement among paleontologists concerns which species of *Australopithecus* were ancestral to the line leading to modern humans. For example, the model shown in Figure 6.1 suggests that *A. africanus* is not ancestral to *Homo* but rather that *A. afarensis* was the last common ancestor of all the hominin lines.[56] Despite the uncertainty and disagreements about what species was ancestral to the *Homo* line, paleoanthropologists widely agree about other aspects of early hominin evolution: (1) There were at least two separate hominin lines between 3 million and 1 million years ago; (2) the group in the figure labeled paranthropoids were not ancestral to modern humans (which is why we do not discuss them here) and became extinct about 1 million years ago; and (3) *Homo habilis* (and successive *Homo* species) were in the direct ancestral line to modern humans.

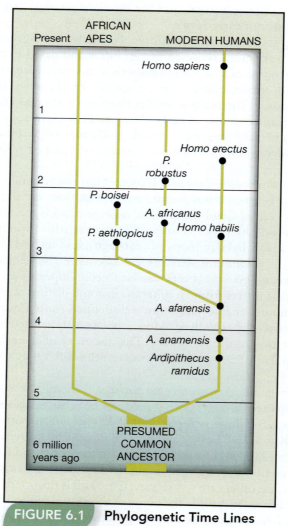

FIGURE 6.1   **Phylogenetic Time Lines**

Source: Adapted from The New York Times, September 5, 1995, p. C9. Dates changed slightly to reflect recent redating.

Early *Homo* Species

Early hominins classified in our own genus, *Homo,* are generally divided into two species: **Homo habilis** and **Homo rudolfensis**. Both are known primarily from the western parts of Kenya and Tanzania, but remains have been found elsewhere in eastern and southern Africa, including the Omo Basin of Ethiopia and Sterkfontein cave in South Africa. *Homo habilis* appears to be the earlier of these two species, appearing around 2.3 million years ago. Compared with the australopithecines, *H. habilis* had a significantly larger brain, averaging 630–640 cc,[57] and reduced molars and premolars.[58] The rest of the skeleton is reminiscent of the australopithecines, including the presence of powerful hands and relatively long arms, suggesting that *H. habilis* was at least partially arboreal. *H. habilis* may also have been sexually dimorphic like the australopithecines, as individuals seem to have greatly differed in size.

Homo rudolfensis is roughly contemporary with *Homo habilis* and shares many of its features. Indeed, many paleoanthropologists make no distinction between the two species, putting *H. rudolfensis* into *H. habilis*. Those who do see them as distinct species point to the larger and more thickly enameled cheek teeth of *H. rudolfensis,* its flatter and broader face, and its more modernlike limb proportions. Even with its larger teeth and broader face, the dentition of *H. rudolfensis* is considerably reduced over the australopithecines and, as in *H. habilis,* its brain is at least a third larger. We have little postcranial skeletal material for either early *Homo* species, so it is impossible to tell whether the female pelvis had changed. But with brains averaging a third larger than that of the australopithecines, it seems likely that some modifications must have developed to allow bigger-brained babies to be born.

The expansion of the brain is only one of a number of trends in hominid evolution. Another is the routine use of patterned or nearly standardized stone tools, which is considered one sign of the emergence of culture. It is assumed, but not known for sure, that patterned stone tools were made by the first members of our own genus, *Homo,* because it is in our genus that we first see a number of trends that may have started because of habitual stone toolmaking and use: expansion of the brain, modification of the female pelvis to accommodate bigger-brained babies, and reduction in the teeth, face, and jaws.

Even though stone tools are found at various sites in East Africa before the time early *Homo* appeared, most anthropologists surmise that members of early *Homo* species, rather than the australopithecines, made those tools. After all, early *Homo* had a brain capacity almost one-third larger than that of the australopithecines. But the fact is that none of the earliest stone tools are clearly associated with early *Homo,* so it is impossible as yet to know who made them.[59] We turn now to a discussion of those earliest stone tools and what archaeologists and paleoanthropologists infer about the lifestyles of their makers, the hominins (whoever they were) who lived between about 2.5 million and 1.5 million years ago.

The earliest identifiable stone tools found so far come from various sites in East Africa and date from about 2.5 million years ago,[60] and maybe earlier. They range from very small flakes (thumb-size) to cobble or core tools that are fist-size.[61] These early tools were apparently made by striking a stone with another stone, a technique called **percussion flaking.** Both the sharp-edged flakes and the sharp-edged cores (the pieces of stone left after flakes are removed) were probably used as tools. Unfortunately, little can be inferred about lifestyles from the earliest tool sites because little else was found

6.4 Describe early *Homo* species.

Homo habilis Dating from about 2 million years ago, an early species belonging to our genus, *Homo,* with cranial capacities averaging about 630–640 cc, about 50 percent of the brain capacity of modern humans.

Homo rudolfensis Early species belonging to our genus, *Homo.* Similar enough to *Homo habilis* that some paleoanthropologists make no distinction between the two.

Percussion flaking A toolmaking technique in which one stone is struck with another to remove a flake.

The skull of a *Homo habilis/rudolfensis* (ER-1470) found by Richard Leakey in 1972. Note its high forehead and large braincase.

with the tools. In contrast, finds of later tool assemblages at Olduvai Gorge in Tanzania have yielded a rich harvest of cultural information. The Olduvai site was uncovered accidentally in 1911, when a German entomologist followed a butterfly into the gorge and found fossil remains. Well-known paleoanthropologists Louis and Mary Leakey searched the gorge for clues to the evolution of early humans beginning in the 1930s. Of the Olduvai site, Louis Leakey wrote,

Unifacial tool A tool worked or flaked on one side only.

Bifacial tool A tool worked or flaked on two sides.

> *[It] is a fossil hunter's dream, for it shears 300 feet through stratum after stratum of earth's history as through a gigantic layer cake. Here, within reach, lie countless fossils and artifacts which but for the faulting and erosion would have remained sealed under thick layers of consolidated rock.*[62]

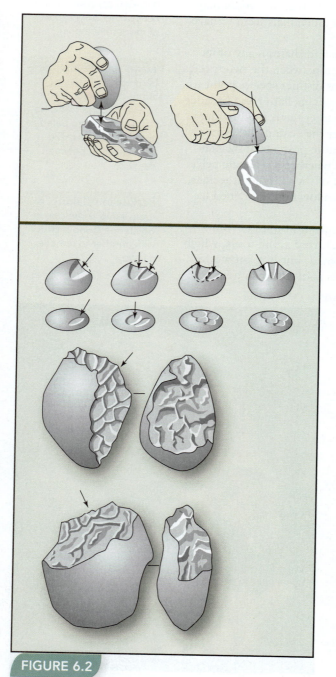

FIGURE 6.2

The Production of a Simple Oldowan Chopper Core and the Resultant Flakes

The oldest cultural materials from Olduvai (Bed I) date from Lower Pleistocene times (about 1.6 million years ago). The stone artifacts include core tools and sharp-edged flakes. Flake tools predominate. Among the coare tools, so-called choppers are common. Choppers are cores that have been partially flaked and have a side that might have been used for chopping. Other core tools, with flaking along one side and a flat edge, are called scrapers. Whenever a stone has facets removed from only one side of the cutting edge, we call it a **unifacial tool.** If the stone has facets removed from both sides, we call it a **bifacial tool.** Although there are some bifacial tools in the early stone tool assemblages, they are not as plentiful or as elaborated as in later tool traditions. The kind of tool assemblage found in Bed I and to some extent in later (higher) layers is referred to as **Oldowan** (see Figure 6.2).[63]

Archaeologists have experimented with what can be done with Oldowan tools. The flakes appear to be very versatile; they can be used for slitting the hides of animals, dismembering animals, and whittling wood into sharp-pointed sticks (wooden spears or digging sticks). The larger stone tools (choppers and scrapers) can be used to hack off branches or cut and chop tough animal joints.[64] Those who have made and tried to use stone tools for various purposes are so impressed by the sharpness and versatility of flakes that they wonder whether most of the core tools were really used as tools. The cores could mainly be what remained after wanted flakes were struck off.[65] Archaeologists surmise that many early tools were also made of wood and bone, but these do not survive in the archaeological record. Present-day populations use sharp-pointed digging sticks for extracting roots and tubers from the ground; stone flakes are very effective for sharpening wood to a very fine point.[66] None of the early flaked stone tools can plausibly be thought of as weapons. So, if the toolmaking hominins were hunting or defending themselves with weapons, they had to have used wooden spears, clubs, or unmodified stones as missiles. Later, Oldowan tool assemblages also include stones that were flaked and battered into a rounded shape. The unmodified stones and the shaped stones might have been lethal projectiles.[67]

Experiments may indicate what can be done with tools, but they cannot tell us what was *actually* done with them. Other techniques, such as microscopic analysis of the wear on tools, are more informative. Lawrence Keeley used high-powered microscopes in his experimental investigations of tools and found that different kinds of "polish" develop on tools when they are used on different materials. The polish on tools used for cutting meat is different from the polish on tools used for woodworking. On the basis of microscopic investigation of the 1.5-million-year-old tools from the eastern side of Lake Turkana, Keeley and his colleagues concluded that at least some of the early tools were probably used for cutting meat, others for cutting or whittling wood, and still others for cutting plant stems.[68]

For many years, it seemed plausible to assume that hominins were the hunters and the animals their prey. But, archaeologists had to reexamine this assumption with the emergence of the field of *taphonomy,* which studies the processes that can alter and distort an assemblage of bones. So, for example, flowing water can bring bones and artifacts together, which may have happened at Olduvai Gorge about 1.8 million years ago. (The area of what is now the gorge bordered the shores of a shallow lake at that time.) Other animals such as hyenas could have also brought carcasses to some of the same places that hominins spent time.[69]

But there is little doubt that hominins were cutting up animal carcasses for meat shortly after 2 million years ago. Pat Shipman suggested that scavenging, not hunting, was the major meat-getting activity of the hominins living there between 2 million and 1.7 million years ago. For example, the cut marks made by the stone tools usually (but not always) overlie teeth marks made by carnivores. This suggests that the hominins were often scavenging the meat of animals killed and partially eaten by nonhominin predators. The fact that the cut marks were sometimes made first, however, suggested to Shipman that the hominins were also sometimes the hunters.[70] There is also no consensus about how to characterize the Olduvai sites that contain concentrations of stone tools and animal bones. In the 1970s, there was a tendency to think of them as home bases to which hominins (presumably male) brought meat to share with others (presumably nursing mothers and young children). Indeed, Mary Leakey identified two locations where she thought early hominins had built simple structures. One was a stone circle that she suggested formed the base of a small brush windbreak. The other was a circular area of dense debris surrounded by an area virtually without debris. Leakey suggested that the area lacking debris may represent the location of a ring of thorny brush with which early hominins surrounded their campsite in order to keep out predators—much like pastoralists living in the region do today.[71] But archaeologists today are not so sure that these sites were home bases. For one thing, carnivores also frequented the sites. Places with meaty bones lying around may not have been so safe for hominins to use as home bases. Second, the animal remains at the sites had not been completely dismembered and butchered. If the sites had been hominin home bases, we would expect more complete processing of carcasses.[72] Third, natural processes as simple as trees growing through a site can create circular areas of debris such as the ones Leakey identified as structures, and without better evidence that early hominins made them, one cannot be sure that the circles of debris were indeed structures.[73]

Alternatively, some archaeologists are beginning to think that these early sites with many animal bones and tools may just have been places where hominins processed food but did not live. Why would the hominins return repeatedly to a particular site? Richard Potts suggests one possible reason—that hominins left caches of stone tools and stones for toolmaking at various locations to facilitate recurrent food-collecting and processing activities.[74]

Stone Tools and Culture

The presence of patterned stone tools means that these early hominins had probably developed *culture.* Archaeologists consider a pattern of behavior, such as a particular way to make a tool that is shared and learned by a group of individuals, to be a sign of cultural behavior. To be sure, toolmaking does not imply that early humans had anything like the

Oldowan The earliest stone toolmaking tradition, named after the tools found in Bed I at Olduvai Gorge, Tanzania, from about 2.5 million years ago. The stone artifacts include core tools and sharp-edged flakes made by striking one stone against another. Flake tools predominate. Among the core tools, so-called choppers are common.

complex cultures of humans today. Chimpanzees have patterns of tool use and toolmaking that appear to be shared and learned, but they do not have that much in the way of cultural behavior.

It seems clear from the archaeological record that early hominins were making and using stone tools on a regular basis. Tools are frequently found in discrete concentrations, and often in association with animal bones and other debris from human activity suggesting, as we have already noted, campsites or even small shelters used by groups of individuals over periods of time. In such a situation, sharing of food among closely related individuals is very likely. Even when food sharing takes place among chimpanzees, it is usually among closely related individuals.[75] Thus, the ancient locations of early hominin social activity may be evidence of family groups. How would such a system of social behavior—the creation of a common meeting, resting, and living place for a group of related individuals to share food—have evolved? Let's consider one model.

One Model for the Evolution of Culture

Early *Homo* had a brain almost one-third larger than that of the australopithecines. As we discuss later in the section on trends in hominin evolution, one of the possible consequences of brain expansion was the lessening of maturity at birth. The fact that babies were born more immature may at least partly explain the lengthening of the period of infant and child dependency in hominins. Compared with other animals, we spend not only a longer proportion of our life span, but also the longest absolute period, in a dependent state. Prolonged infant dependency has probably been of great significance in human cultural evolution. According to Theodosius Dobzhansky,

> *it is this helplessness and prolonged dependence on the ministrations of the parents and other persons that favors . . . the socialization and learning process on which the transmission of culture wholly depends. This may have been an overwhelming advantage of the human growth pattern in the process of evolution.*[76]

It used to be thought that the australopithecines had a long period of infant dependency, just as modern humans do, but the way their teeth apparently developed suggests that the early australopithecines followed an apelike pattern of development. Thus, prolonged maturation may be relatively recent, but just how recent is not yet known.[77]

Although some use of tools for digging, defense, or scavenging may have influenced the development of bipedalism, full bipedalism may have made possible more efficient toolmaking and consequently more efficient foraging and scavenging. As we have seen, there are archaeological signs that early hominins may have been scavenging (and perhaps even hunting) animals as far back as the late Pliocene. Indeed, we have fairly good evidence that early hominins were butchering and presumably eating big game some 2 million years ago.

Whenever it was that hominins began to scavenge for game and perhaps hunt regularly, the development of scavenging would have required individuals to travel long distances frequently in search of suitable carcasses. Among groups of early *Homo,* longer infant and child dependency may have fostered the creation of home bases or at least established meeting places. The demands of childbirth and caring for a newborn might have made it difficult for early *Homo* mothers to travel for some time after the birth. Certainly, it would have been awkward for a mother carrying a nursing child to travel long distances to hunt. Although carrying an infant might be possible with a sling, successful hunting might not be so likely with a needy and potentially noisy child along. Because early *Homo* males (and perhaps females without young children) would have been freer to roam farther from home, they probably became the scavengers or hunters. Women with young children may have gathered wild plants within a small area that could be covered without traveling far from the home base or meeting place.

The creation of home bases or meeting places among early *Homo* groups may have increased the likelihood of food sharing. If mothers with young children were limited to gathering plant foods in a relatively small area, the only way to ensure that they and their children could obtain a complete diet would have been to share the other foods obtained elsewhere. With whom would such sharing take place? Most likely with close relatives. Sharing with them would have made it more likely that their offspring would survive to have offspring. Thus, if early *Homo* had home bases and families, those characteristics could have encouraged the development of the learned and shared behaviors we call culture.[78] Obviously this is a "just-so" story—a tale that we may never be able to prove really happened. But it is a tale that is consistent with the archaeological record.[79]

Trends in Hominin Evolution

Expansion of the Brain

The australopithecines had relatively small cranial capacities, about 380–530 cc—not much larger than that of chimpanzees. But around 2.3 million years ago, close to the time that patterned stone tools first appeared, some hominins show evidence of enlarged brain capacity. These hominins, early *Homo*, had cranial capacities averaging about 630–640 cc, which is about 50 percent of the brain capacity of modern humans (which averages slightly more than 1,300 cc). (See Figure 6.3.) The australopithecines were small, and the earliest *Homo* finds were hardly bigger, so much of the increase in brain size over time might have been a result of later hominins' bigger bodies. When we correct for body size, however, it turns out that brain size increased not only absolutely but also relatively after 2 million years ago. Between about 4 million and 2 million years ago, relative brain size remained just about the same.

> **6.5** ▶ Identify the main trends in hominin evolution.

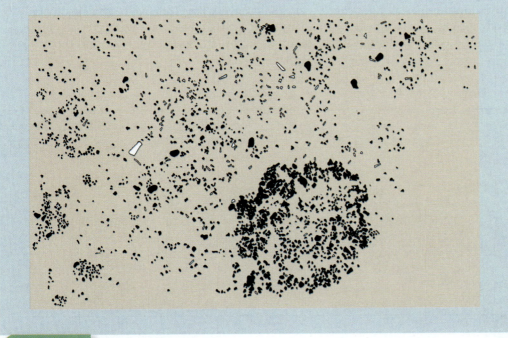

FIGURE 6.3   **Olduvai "Hut"**

A ring of stones and bones found in Bed I of Olduvai Gorge that Mary Leakey interpreted as the remains of an ancient hut.

Only in the last 2 million years has the hominin brain doubled in relative size and tripled in absolute size.[80]

What may have favored the increase in brain size? Many anthropologists think that the increase is linked to the emergence of stone toolmaking about 2.5 million years ago. The reasoning is that stone toolmaking was important for the survival of our ancestors, and therefore natural selection would have favored bigger-brained individuals because they had motor and conceptual skills that enabled them to be better toolmakers. According to this view, the expansion of the brain and more sophisticated toolmaking would have developed together. Other anthropologists think that the expansion of the brain may have been favored by other factors, such as warfare, hunting, longer life, and language.[81] One intriguing theory is that life in complex social groups requires increased intelligence and memory, and that the creation of home bases and family groups may have fostered the expansion of the hominin brain.[82] Whatever the factors favoring bigger brains, they also provided humans with an expanded capacity for culture. Thus, along with bipedalism, the expansion of the brain marks a watershed in human evolution.

As the hominin brain expanded, natural selection also favored the widening of the female pelvis to allow larger-brained babies to be born.[83] But there was probably a limit to how far the pelvis could widen and still be adapted to bipedalism. Something had to give, and that something was the degree of physical development of the human infant at birth—for instance, the human infant is born with cranial bones so plastic that they can overlap. Because birth takes place before the cranial bones have hardened, the human infant with its relatively large brain can pass through the opening in the mother's pelvis. Human infants are born at a relatively early stage of development, and are wholly dependent on their parents for many years. As we have noted, this lengthy period of infant dependency may have been an important factor in the evolution of culture.

Reduction of the Face, Teeth, and Jaws

As in the case of the brain, substantial changes in the face, teeth, and jaws do not appear in hominin evolution until after about 2 million years ago. The australopithecines all have cheek teeth that are very large relative to their estimated body weight, perhaps because the diet of the australopithecines was especially high in plant foods,[84] including small, tough objects such as seeds, grasses, and tubers.

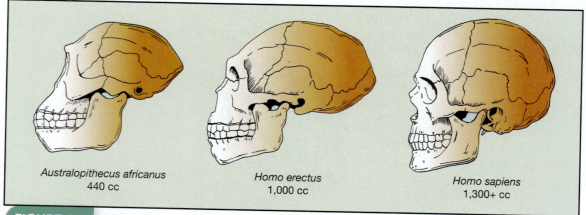

Australopithecus africanus
440 cc

Homo erectus
1,000 cc

Homo sapiens
1,300+ cc

FIGURE 6.4

Comparison of the estimated cranial capacities of *Australopithecus africanus*, *Homo erectus*, and *Homo sapiens*, demonstrating the expansion of the brain in hominin evolution.

Source: Estimated cranial capacities from Tattersall et al. 2000. Reproduced by permission of Routledge, Inc., part of The Taylor & Francis Group.

Migrants and Immigrants

The First Migrants

Hominins evolved in Africa, yet today hominins are found on every continent. Who were the first hominins to leave Africa, and when did they first leave? For many years, the clear answer was that *Homo erectus* were the first to leave Africa, and they did so perhaps 700,000 to 1 million years ago. In recent years, new findings and sources of evidence have led scholars to question this established answer.

The first new information came from geochemist Carl Swisher, who in the mid-1990s redated the Java sites where *Homo erectus* fossils had been found and determined they dated to perhaps 1.8 million years ago. Because the earliest *H. erectus* fossils in Africa share a similar date, this created a problem—how did *H. erectus* appear in Java at about the same time they appeared in Africa? As this question was being pondered, a remarkable set of new *H. erectus* fossils were being uncovered in Dmanisi, Georgia. Dated at 1.7 million years ago, these fossils made it clear that *H. erectus* left Africa

almost as soon as they had evolved. The discovery of a *Homo habilis*-like fossil at Dmanisi, and of Oldowan-like tools at Riwat, Pakistan and Longgupo, China, suggested that *H. habilis* may have been the first to leave Africa, and *H. erectus* followed a path their predecessors blazed. If they were following an earlier migration, it could explain how *H. erectus* were able to move so quickly across Asia.

A more unusual source of information on when hominins first left Africa comes from the parasites that accompanied them. All hominoids are plagued by lice, but humans host a distinct species, *Pediculus humanus*. Geneticist David Reed and his colleagues found that *P. humanus* diverged from other lice about 5.6 million years ago—about the time the first hominins appeared. More interesting, however, Reed and colleagues discovered that there are two subspecies of *P. humanus* that appear to have diverged about 1.2 million years ago. One subspecies is found worldwide today; the other is restricted to the New World. Reed

and colleagues suggest this is evidence that at least some hominin migrants (probably *H. erectus*) became isolated in Asia by at least 1.2 million years ago, where their lice diverged from that of other hominin populations, only to be picked up much later by modern human migrants who ended up colonizing the New World.

So, who were the first hominin migrants? They may have been *H. habilis*, or they may have been very early *H. erectus*. When did the first hominin migrations out of Africa take place? Probably slightly less than 2 million years ago, but once these hominins left, they moved quickly, and they moved long distances. By 1.6 million years ago, *H. erectus* was in both western and southern Asia, and by 1.2 million years ago, their populations had moved far enough to have become isolated from one another. Whether or not they were the first migrants out of Africa, *H. erectus* migrated fast and far.

Sources: Reed et al. 2004; Tattersall 1997.

The australopithecines have thick jawbones, probably also related to their chewing needs. The australopithecines have relatively large faces that project forward below the eyes. But when we get to the *Homo* forms, we see reduction in the size of the face, cheek teeth, and jaws (see Figure 6.4). It would seem that natural selection in favor of a bigger and stronger chewing apparatus was relaxed. One reason might be that members of the *Homo* genus started to eat foods that were easier to chew. Such foods might have included roots, fruits, and meat. As we discuss later, it may have been the development of habitual tool use and the control of fire that allowed members of the *Homo* genus to change their diet to include foods that are easier to chew, including meat. If food is cooked and easy to chew, individual humans with smaller jaws and teeth would not be disadvantaged, and therefore the face, cheek teeth, and jaw would get smaller on average over time.[85]

The expansion of the brain and reduction of the face occurred at about the same time, and were probably related. A recent discovery in human genetics appears to provide direct evidence of a connection. Researchers studying muscle diseases in modern humans discovered that humans have a unique myosin gene called MYH16 (myosin is a protein in muscle tissue) that is only present in jaw muscles. Comparing MYH16 to related genes in primates, the researchers determined that MYH16 evolved about 2.4 million years ago—around the time the brain began to enlarge and the face and jaw began to shrink. So, the expansion of the brain may have been aided by a mutation in myosin that caused jaw muscles to shrink.[86]

6.6 Explain the evolution of *Homo erectus*.

Homo erectus

Homo erectus was the first hominin species to be widely distributed in the Old World (see the box feature on "The First Migrants"). Examples of *H. erectus* were found first in Java, later in China, and still later in Africa. Most paleoanthropologists agree that some human ancestor moved from Africa to Asia at some point. Until recently, it was assumed that it was *H. erectus* who moved, because *H. erectus* lived in East Africa about 1.6 million years ago but not until after about 1 million years ago in Asia.[87] But *H. erectus* was in Java perhaps 1.8 million years ago,[88] and *H. erectus* fossils from Dmanisi, in the southeastern European nation of Georgia, are dated to at least 1.7 million years ago.[89] So early hominins may have moved out of Africa earlier. Indeed, one well-preserved skull found at Dmanisi in 2001 has some features that are reminiscent of *H. habilis*—a brain only about 600 cc, relatively large canines, and a relatively thin browridge.[90] Although the excavators initially classified the skull as *H. erectus,* they now think it may be *H. habilis,* and it does make one wonder whether *H. habilis* or transitional *habilis-erectus* individuals were the first to leave Africa.

Some scholars see enough differences between Asian and African populations of *H. erectus* to argue that they should be separated into two distinct species, *Homo erectus* for the Asian populations and **Homo ergaster** for the African ones. Furthermore, *Homo erectus* (or *Homo ergaster*) fossils are also found in Europe. But some paleoanthropologists think that the finds in Europe typically classified as *H. erectus* are actually early examples of *H. sapiens.*[91] Others think that the European fossils and similar ones found in southern Africa and the Near East should be grouped into a distinct species, *Homo heidelbergensis.* There is also *Homo floresiensis,* a diminutive hominin that appears to be a miniature form of *Homo erectus* that evolved only on the isolated island of Flores, Indonesia. It is all a bit confusing. Later we will try to sort it all out.

Physical Characteristics of *Homo erectus*

The *Homo erectus* skull generally was long, low, and thickly walled, with a flat frontal area and prominent browridges. It had a unique pentagonal shape when looked at from the back, formed in part by a rounded ridge, called a **sagittal keel,** running along the crest of the skull. There was also a ridge of bone running horizontally along the back of the skull, called an **occipital torus,** which added to the skull's overall long shape (see Figure 6.5).[92]

Compared with early *Homo, H. erectus* had relatively small teeth. *H. erectus* was the first hominin to have third molars that were smaller than the second or first molars, as in modern humans. The molars also had an enlarged pulp cavity, called **taurodontism,** which may have allowed the teeth to withstand harder use and wear than the teeth of modern humans. But the *H. erectus* jaw was lighter and thinner than in either early *Homo* or the australopithecines, and the face was less **prognathic,** or forward thrusting, in the upper and lower jaw. The brain, averaging 895–1,040 cc, was larger than that found in any of the australopithecines or early *Homo* species, but smaller than the average brain of a modern human.[93] Endocasts, which provide a picture of the surface of the brain, suggest that it was organized more like the brain of modern humans than like that of australopithecines.

Homo erectus had a prominent, projecting nose, in contrast to the australopithecines' flat, nonprojecting nose.[94] From the neck down, *H. erectus* was practically indistinguishable from *H. sapiens.* In contrast to the smaller australopithecines and early *Homo* species who lived in East Africa around the same time, *H. erectus* was comparable to modern humans in size. The almost complete skeleton of the boy at Nariokotome suggests that he was about 5 ½ feet tall and about 8 years of age when he died; researchers estimate that he would have been over 6 feet tall had he lived to maturity. About 1.6 million years ago, the Nariokotome region was probably open grassland, with trees mostly along rivers.[95] *Homo erectus* in East Africa was similar in size to Africans today who live in a similarly open, dry environment.[96] *H. erectus* was also less sexually dimorphic than either the

---

Homo erectus The first hominin species to be widely distributed in the Old World. The earliest finds are possibly 1.8 million years old. The brain (averaging 895–1,040 cc) was larger than that found in any of the australopithecines or *H. habilis* but smaller than the average brain of a modern human.

Homo ergaster A species closely related to *Homo erectus* but found only in East Africa. Some scholars do not see enough difference between *Homo erectus* and *Homo ergaster* to count them as different species.

Sagittal keel An inverted V-shaped ridge running along the top of the skull in *Homo erectus.*

Occipital torus A ridge of bone running horizontally across the back of the skull in apes and some hominids.

Taurodontism Having teeth with an enlarged pulp cavity.

Prognathic A physical feature that is sticking out or pushed forward, such as the faces in apes and some hominid species.

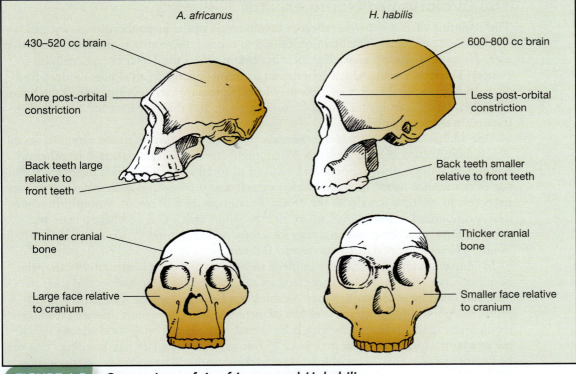

A. africanus | H. habilis

430–520 cc brain | 600–800 cc brain

More post-orbital constriction | Less post-orbital constriction

Back teeth large relative to front teeth | Back teeth smaller relative to front teeth

Thinner cranial bone | Thicker cranial bone

Large face relative to cranium | Smaller face relative to cranium

FIGURE 6.5   Comparison of *A. africanus* and *H. habilis*

australopithecines or early *Homo*. The degree of sexual dimorphism in *H. erectus* was comparable to that in modern humans.

Homo floresiensis

Whether or not there are distinct African and Asian species of *Homo erectus*, most scholars agree that **Homo floresiensis** is a distinct species that is closely related to *Homo erectus*. *H. floresiensis* has only been found on the Indonesian island of Flores, and only a handful of individuals have been located to date. All are tiny (they stood perhaps 3 feet tall), and have very small brains, on the order of 380 cc.[97] The structure of the brain, however, seems closely related to that of *H. erectus*, as do the structures of the skull.[98] In other words, *H. floresiensis* appears to be a tiny version of *H. erectus*. *H. floresiensis* even made tools that look similar to those made by *H. erectus*, and in some cases the tools look even more sophisticated.[99]

The body of *Homo floresiensis* also seems to resemble *Homo erectus*, or perhaps even *Homo habilis*. The wrist of *H. floresiensis* is not like that of modern humans or Neandertals, but resembles that of the great apes and australopithecines (unfortunately, no wrists of *H. erectus* or *H. habilis* have been found, so no comparison can be made to them).[100] Similarly, the foot of *H. floresiensis* resembles that of *H. erectus* and earlier hominins more than that of modern humans.[101] Once again, *H. floresiensis* appears to be a tiny version of *H. erectus*.

How might a miniature version of *H. erectus* have evolved? The answer is that both dwarfism and gigantism are common phenomena in isolated populations. Dwarfism appears to be an adaptation that occurs when there are few predators—a species in isolation can become smaller, and have a large population, if there are no predators threatening them. This may be what happened on Flores.[102] It is interesting that the island also hosted a number of dwarf species in addition to *H. floresiensis*, including a dwarf elephant that appears to have been one of the favorite foods of *H. floresiensis*. Perhaps even more interesting is the fact that *H. floresiensis* may have survived until as recently as 12,000 years ago—well into the time period when modern humans were living in Indonesia.

Homo floresiensis
A dwarf species of hominin that lived on the Indonesian island of Flores until about 12,000 years ago and probably descended from an isolated *Homo erectus* population.

The Evolution of *Homo erectus*

The evolution of *Homo erectus* reflects a continuation of the general evolutionary trends we discussed previously. The brain continued to expand, increasing more than a third over early *Homo* (just as early *Homo* had increased more than a third over the australopithecines). The face, teeth, and jaws continued to shrink, taking on an almost modern form. An increasing use and variety of tools may have led to a further development of the brain. *Homo erectus* was eating and probably cooking meat, and this may have led to further reduction in the teeth and jaws.

One additional change in *Homo erectus* is an apparent reduction in the extent of sexual dimorphism to almost modern levels. What might have caused this change? In other primates, sexual dimorphism appears to be linked to social systems in which males are at the top of dominance hierarchies due to physical size and prowess and such males control sexual access to multiple females in the group. In contrast, lack of sexual dimorphism seems most pronounced in the animals where *pair bonding* exists—that is, where a male and a female form a breeding pair that lasts for a long period of time.[103] Could male-female bonding have developed in *Homo erectus*? It seems possible.

In animal species where females can feed themselves and their babies after birth, pair bonding is rare. But in species where females cannot feed both themselves and their babies, pair bonding is common. Why? We think it is because a strong male-female bond provides a good solution to the problem of incompatibility between a mother's feeding requirements and tending a newborn baby. A male partner can bring food and/or watch the newborn while the mother gets food.[104] But most primates lack pair bonding. This may be because primate infants are able to cling to their mother's fur soon after birth, so that the mother's hands are free to forage. Human infants demonstrate a residual form of this innate ability to cling during their first few weeks of life. This is called the *Moro reflex*.[105]

We have no way of knowing if *Homo erectus* had fur like other primates, but we think probably not, because we think they may have worn clothing, as we discuss later. The brain in *Homo erectus* may also have already expanded enough that *Homo erectus* infants, like modern human infants, could not adequately support their heads even if they could hold onto their mother's fur. In any case, when early hominins began to depend on scavenging and hunting for food (and for skins to be used in clothing), it would have been difficult and hazardous for a parent with a newborn baby to engage in these activities with a baby along. Marriage would have been an effective solution to this problem because each parent could help protect the baby while the other was away getting food. Another important aspect of the evolution of *Homo erectus* was the movement of populations out of eastern and southern Africa. As with the lessening of sexual dimorphism, it seems likely that cultural innovations were the key to allowing *Homo erectus* to move into new environments. Why? Because upon entering new environments, *Homo erectus* would have been faced with new (and generally colder) climatic conditions, new and different sources of raw material for tools, and new plants and animals to rely on for food. All animals adapt to such changes through natural selection, but natural selection typically takes a relatively long time and requires physical changes in the adapting organisms. *Homo erectus* was able to adapt to new environments very quickly and without apparent physical changes. This suggests that the primary mechanisms of adaptation for *Homo erectus* were cultural rather than biological.

What cultural adaptations might *Homo erectus* have made? Fire might have been the crucial cultural adaptation to colder climates. As we discuss later, there is tantalizing evidence that *Homo erectus* used fire. But fire can only warm people when they are stationary; it doesn't help when people are out collecting food. To be mobile in colder climates, *Homo erectus* may have begun to wear animal furs for warmth. Some *Homo erectus* tools look like the hide-processing tools used by more recent human groups,[106] and it seems unlikely that *Homo erectus* could have survived in the colder locations where they have been found, in eastern Europe and Asia, without some form of clothing. And if *Homo erectus* was wearing furs for warmth, they must have been hunting. *Homo erectus* could not have depended on scavenging to acquire skins—the skin is the first thing predators destroy when they dismember a carcass.

Lower Paleolithic Cultures

The stone tool traditions of *Homo erectus* are traditionally called **Lower Paleolithic.** These stone tool traditions involve "core" tool techniques, in which a core of stone, rather than a flake, is used as the basic raw material for finished tools (we will talk more about Lower Paleolithic stone tool technology shortly). Because stone tools are the most common cultural material in the archaeological record of these ancient peoples, the entire culture of *Homo erectus* is often termed *Lower Paleolithic,* a practice we follow here.

The archaeological finds of tools and other cultural artifacts dating from 1.5 million years to about 200,000 years ago are assumed to have been produced by *Homo erectus.* But hominin fossils are not usually associated with these materials. Therefore some of the tools during this period were possibly produced by hominins other than *H. erectus,* such as australopithecines earlier and *H. sapiens* later. But the so-called *Acheulian* tool assemblages dating from 1.5 million years ago to more than a million years later are very similar to each other, and *H. erectus* is the only hominin that spans the entire period. Thus, it is conventionally assumed that *H. erectus* was responsible for most if not all of the Acheulian tool assemblages we describe.[107]

The Acheulian Tool Tradition

The stone toolmaking tradition known as the **Acheulian** was named after the site at St. Acheul, France, where the first examples were found. But the oldest Acheulian tools recovered are from East Africa, on the Peninj River, Tanzania, dating back about 1.5 million years.[108] In contrast to Oldowan, Acheulian assemblages have more large tools created according to standardized designs or shapes. Oldowan tools have sharp edges made by a few blows. Acheulian toolmakers shaped the stone by knocking more flakes off most of the edges. Many of these tools were made from very large flakes that had first been struck from very large cores or boulders.

One of the most characteristic and common tools in the Acheulian tool kit is the so-called **hand axe,** which is a teardrop-shaped, bifacially flaked tool with a thinned sharp tip. Other large tools resemble cleavers and picks. There were also many kinds of flake tools, such as scrapers with a wide edge.

Early Acheulian tools appeared to have been made by blows with a hard stone, but later tools are wider and flatter and may have been made with a **soft hammer** of bone or antler.[109] Tools made by a **hard hammer** technique, rock against rock, have limits in terms of their sharpness and form, because only large and thick flakes can be made with a hard hammer technique. Flakes created by soft hammer flaking are much thinner and longer than hard hammer flakes, and the flintknapper generally has better control over their size and shape. This means that thinner and sharper tools can be made, as well as tools with complex shapes.[110]

Were hand axes made for chopping trees, as their name suggests? We cannot be sure what they were used for, but experiments with them suggest that they are not good for cutting trees; they seem more suited for butchering large animals.[111] Lawrence Keeley microscopically examined some Acheulian hand axes, and the wear on them is more consistent with animal butchery. They may also have been used for woodworking, particularly hollowing and shaping wood, and they are also good for digging.[112] William Calvin has even suggested that a hand axe could be used as a projectile thrown like a discus into a herd of animals in the hope of injuring or killing an animal.[113]

Acheulian tools are found widely in Africa, Europe, and western Asia, but bifacial hand axes, cleavers, and picks are not found as commonly in eastern and southeastern Asia.[114] Because *H. erectus* has been found in all areas of the Old World, it is puzzling that the tool traditions seem to differ from west to east. Some archaeologists have suggested that large bifacial tools may be lacking in eastern and southeastern Asia because *H. erectus* in Asia had a better material to make tools out of—bamboo. Bamboo has been used recently in Southeast Asia for many purposes, including incredibly sharp

---

6.7 Identify features of Lower Paleolithic cultures.

Lower Paleolithic The period of the Oldowan and Acheulian stone tool traditions.

Acheulian A stone toolmaking tradition dating from 1.5 million years ago. Compared with the Oldowan tradition, Acheulian assemblages have more large tools created according to standardized designs or shapes. One of the most characteristic and prevalent tools in the Acheulian tool kit is the so-called hand axe, which is a teardrop-shaped bifacially flaked tool with a thinned sharp tip. Other large tools might have been cleavers and picks.

Hand axe A teardrop-shaped stone tool characteristic of Acheulian assemblages.

Soft hammer A technique of stone tool manufacture in which a bone or wood hammer is used to strike flakes from a stone.

Hard hammer A technique of stone tool manufacture where one stone is used to knock flakes from another stone. Flakes produced through hard hammer percussion are usually large and crude.

arrows and sticks for digging and cutting. Geoffrey Pope has shown that bamboo is found precisely in those areas of Asia where hand axes and other large bifacial tools are largely missing.[115]

Big Game Eating

Some of the Acheulian sites have produced evidence of big game eating. F. Clark Howell, who excavated sites at Torralba and Ambrona, Spain, found a substantial number of elephant remains and unmistakable evidence of human presence in the form of tools. Howell suggests that the humans at those sites used fire to frighten elephants into muddy bogs from which they would be unable to escape.[116] To hunt elephants in this way, the humans would have had to plan and work cooperatively in fairly large groups.

But do these finds of bones of large- and medium-sized animals, in association with tools, tell us that the humans definitely were big game hunters? Some archaeologists who have reanalyzed the evidence from Torralba think that the big game may have been scavenged. Because the Torralba and Ambrona sites are near ancient streams, many of the elephants could have died naturally, their bones accumulating in certain spots because of the flow of water.[117] What seems fairly clear is that the humans did deliberately butcher different kinds of game—different types of tools are found with different types of animals.[118] Thus, whether the humans hunted big game at Torralba and Ambrona is debatable; all we can be sure of, as of now, is that they consumed big game and probably hunted smaller game.

Control of Fire

One way in which *H. erectus* is thought to have hunted is by using *fire drives*—a technique still used by hunting and gathering peoples in recent times. It is highly effective: Animals are driven out of their hiding places and homes by fire and dispatched by hunters positioned downwind of the oncoming flames. Most peoples who use this technique today set fires deliberately, but fires caused by lightning strikes may have also been utilized. Did *H. erectus* set these fires? Because *H. erectus* was the first hominin to be found

Homo erectus ate—and probably hunted—large game animals, and they probably also learned to control fire.

throughout the Old World and in areas with freezing winters, most anthropologists presume that *H. erectus* had learned to control fire, at least for warmth. There is archaeological evidence of fire in some early sites, but fires can be natural events.[119]

Suggestive but not conclusive evidence of the deliberate use of fire comes from Wonderwerk cave in South Africa and dating to over 1.7 million years ago.[120] More persuasive evidence of human control of fire, dating from nearly 800,000 years ago, comes from the site of Gesher Benot Ya'aqov in Israel. Here, researchers found evidence of burned seeds, wood, and stone, as well as concentrations of burned items suggestive of hearths.[121] Evidence of the deliberate use of fire comes from Europe somewhat later. Unfortunately, the evidence of control of fire at Gesher Benot Ya'aqov and European sites is not associated with *H. erectus* fossils, so the link between deliberate use of fire and *H. erectus* cannot definitely be established yet.[122] Even so, the control of fire was a major step in increasing the energy under human control. Cooking would have made all kinds of food (not just meat) more safely digestible and therefore more usable.[123] Fires would also have kept predators away, a not inconsiderable advantage given that there were many.

Campsites

Acheulian sites were usually located close to water sources, lush vegetation, and large stocks of herbivorous animals. Some camps have been found in caves, but most were in open areas surrounded by rudimentary fortifications or windbreaks. Several African sites are marked by stony rubble brought there by *H. erectus,* possibly for the dual purpose of securing the windbreaks and providing ammunition in case of a sudden attack.[124]

The presumed base campsites display a wide variety of tools, indicating that the camp was the center of many group functions. More specialized sites away from camp have also been found. These are marked by the predominance of a particular type of tool. For example, a butchering site in Tanzania contained dismembered hippopotamus's carcasses and rare heavy-duty smashing and cutting tools. Workshops are another kind of

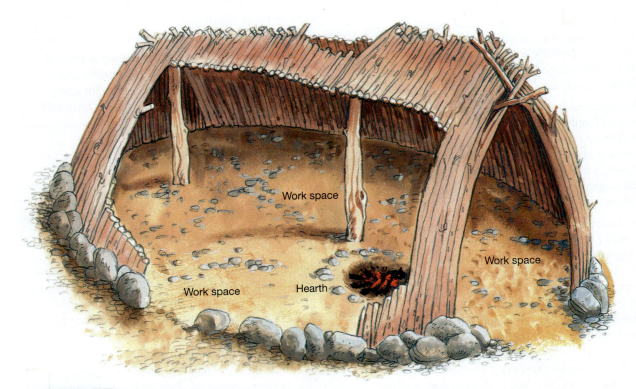

FIGURE 6.6   **A Reconstruction of the Oval Huts Built at Terra Amata.**

These huts were approximately 30 feet by 15 feet.

Source: Copyright © 1969 by Eric Mose.

specialized site encountered with some regularity. They are characterized by tool debris and are located close to a source of natural stone suitable for toolmaking.[125]

A camp has been excavated at the Terra Amata site near Nice, on the French Riviera. The camp appears to have been occupied in the late spring or early summer, judging by the pollen found in fossilized human feces. The excavator describes stake holes driven into the sand, paralleled by lines of stones, presumably marking the spots where the people constructed huts of roughly 30 feet by 15 feet (see Figure 6.6). A basic feature of each hut was a central hearth that seems to have been protected from drafts by a small wall built just outside the northeast corner of the hearth. The evidence suggests that the Terra Amata occupants gathered seafood such as oysters and mussels, did some fishing, and hunted in the surrounding area. The animal remains suggest that they obtained both small and large animals but mostly got the young of larger animals such as stags, elephants, boars, rhinoceroses, and wild oxen. Some of the huts contain recognizable toolmakers' areas, scattered with tool debris; occasionally, the impression of an animal skin shows where the toolmaker actually sat.[126]

Summary and Review

The Evolution of Bipedal Locomotion

6.1 Evaluate theories for the evolution of bipedal locomotion.

- Bipedal locomotion, or walking on two legs, was perhaps the most crucial change in early hominin evolution. The available fossil record confirms that bipedal hominins emerged in Africa, but how quickly it emerged is unclear.

- The drying trend in climate that began about 16 million to 11 million years ago diminished the extent of African rain forests and gave rise to areas of savanna (grasslands) and scattered deciduous woodlands, which probably favored characteristics adapted to ground living in some primates, including bipedalism.

- Several theories try to explain the development of bipedalism: (a) bipedalism may have increased the emerging hominin's ability to see predators and potential prey amid the tall grasses of the savanna; (b) it may have freed up hands, thus facilitating the transfer of food from one place to another; (c) it may have been linked to tool use; (d) it may have made long-distance traveling more efficient; and (e) it might have enabled hominins to regulate body temperature in the increasingly hot and dry environments of East Africa. At this point, no direct evidence proves that any of the theories, alone or in combination, account for the development of bipedalism.

- Any advantages of bipedalism must be greater than the disadvantages. Bipedalism makes it harder to overcome gravity to supply the brain with sufficient blood, and the weight of the body above the pelvis and lower limbs puts greater stress on the lower skeleton. Anatomical changes helped to resolve some of these disadvantages.

 Discuss two theories for the evolution of bipedal locomotion. What specific anatomical changes were required for early hominoids to become habitually bipedal?

The Transition from Hominoids to Hominins

6.2 Identify species involved in the transition from hominoids to hominins.

- The first hominins probably appeared around 6 million years ago. *Sahelanthropus* (7 million years ago), *Orrorin* (5.8–6 million years ago), and *Ardipithecus* (5.8–4.4 million years ago) are likely candidates for the first hominin.

 Among the current possible candidates to be recognized as the first hominin, why is *Ardipithecus* unique?

The First Definite Hominins

6.3 Describe the distinctive traits of hominins.

- Undisputed hominins dating before 4 million years ago have been found in East Africa. These definitely bipedal hominins are now generally classified in the genus *Australopithecus*.

- The large number of other suggested australopithecine species indicates that diversity was prevalent among early hominins. All shared similar but diverse and changing environments in eastern and southern Africa. One idea about the apparent diversity of the first hominins may reflect an adaptive radiation (a dispersal and divergence) of bipedal hominins to these dynamic environmental conditions.

- The most well-known australopithecine species include *A. anamensis, A. afarensis,* and *A. africanus.*

 What are three distinctive traits of hominins?

Early *Homo* Species

6.4 Describe early *Homo* species.

- *Homo habilis* and *Homo rudolfensis,* from about 2.3 million years ago, have larger brains, and smaller faces and teeth than other contemporary (and earlier) hominins.

- Early *Homo* appears to have used tools and scavenged or possibly hunted meat. The evolution of cultural behavior also seems to have played a role in physical changes.

 How do *Homo habilis* and *Homo rudolfensis* differ from each other and from earlier hominins?

Trends in Hominin Evolution

6.5 Identify the main trends in hominin evolution.

- Physical changes in early hominins that led to the evolution of our genus, *Homo,* include the expansion of the brain; the widening of the female pelvis to allow birth of bigger-brained babies; and the reduction of the face, teeth, and jaws.

- Increased brain size may be linked to the emergence of stone toolmaking and possibly to life in complex social groups. Expansion of the brain and reduction of the face occurred at about the same time and were probably related.

 How did reductions in the teeth, face, and jaws of early hominins affect their life styles?

Homo erectus

6.6 Explain the evolution of *Homo erectus.*

- *Homo erectus* emerged about 1.8 million to 1.6 million years ago. It had a larger brain capacity than *Homo habilis* and an essentially modern skeleton. What differentiates *H. erectus* most from modern humans is the long, low, skull with prominent browridges.

- *Homo erectus* was the first hominin species to be widely distributed in the Old World. Some scholars reserve *Homo erectus* for those populations living outside of Africa and call the African populations *Homo ergaster.*

- Another species of hominin lived at this time: *Homo floresiensis,* a miniature form of *Homo erectus* found only on an island in Indonesia.

- As *Homo erectus* evolved, brain size increased, tooth and jaw size decreased, and tool use increased. Sexual dimorphism decreased, perhaps explained by pair bonding patterns.

- *Homo erectus* was able to adapt to new environments very quickly and without apparent physical changes, which suggests that the species' primary mechanisms of adaptation were cultural rather than biological.

 How does *Homo erectus* differ from *Homo habilis?*

Lower Paleolithic Cultures

6.7 Identify features of Lower Paleolithic cultures.

- The stone tool traditions of *Homo erectus* are traditionally called Lower Paleolithic cultures. Lower Paleolithic tools and other cultural artifacts from about 1.6 million to about 200,000 years ago were probably produced by *H. erectus.*

- The most well-known tool tradition of this period is called Acheulian. Acheulian tools include small flake tools, but hand axes and large bifacial tools are characteristic.

- Evidence indicates that *H. erectus* ate big game but may not have hunted those animals. Although *H. erectus* possibly used fire to survive in colder areas, no evidence confirms that *H. erectus* controlled fire. Evidence of ritual behavior among *H. erectus* is scant.

 What are the main differences between Oldowan and Acheulean tools?

Think on it

1. What behavioral changes may have accompanied the evolution of **bipedal locomotion**?

2. How could there have been more than one species of **hominin** living in East Africa at the same time? Given the huge variation within modern humans, how can researchers be sure that the various fossils of earlier hominins they examine are, indeed, distinct species?

3. Why might early hominins have begun to make **stone tools**? How would stone tools have been more useful than wood or bone tools?

4. How do the **physical changes** that occur in early hominins correlate with the apparent changes in their behavior?

The Emergence of *Homo sapiens* and the Upper Paleolithic World

LEARNING OBJECTIVES

7.1 Discuss the anatomical characteristics of the Neandertals and the relationship between Neandertals and *Homo sapiens*.

7.2 Describe the features of Middle Paleolithic cultures.

7.3 Explain the relationship of Denisovans to Neandertals and modern humans.

7.4 Explain theories about the origins of modern humans and how they differed from earlier species.

7.5 Evaluate competing scenarios for the disappearance of Neandertals.

7.6 Describe the environment of the Upper Paleolithic world.

7.7 Describe Upper Paleolithic tools and cultures in Europe.

7.8 Describe Upper Paleolithic migration from Africa to Asia.

7.9 Evaluate scenarios for the migration of humans into the New World.

7.10 Relate the end of the Upper Paleolithic to climate change and the development of Maglemosian culture.

Recent finds in Africa indicate the presence of *Homo sapiens* perhaps 160,000 years ago. Completely modern-looking humans appeared by 50,000 years ago. One paleoanthropologist, Christopher Stringer, characterizes the modern human as having "a domed skull, a chin, small eyebrows, browridges, and a rather puny skeleton."[1] Some of us might not like to be called puny, but except for our larger brain, most modern humans definitely are puny compared with *Homo erectus* and even with earlier forms of our own species, *H. sapiens*. We are relatively puny in several respects, including our thinner and lighter bones, as well as our smaller teeth and jaws.

In this chapter, we discuss the fossil evidence, as well as the controversies, about the transition from *H. erectus* to modern humans, which may have begun 500,000 years ago. We also discuss what we know archaeologically about the Middle Paleolithic (about 300,000 and 40,000 years ago) and Upper Paleolithic (40,000 to 10,000 years ago).

7.1 Discuss the anatomical characteristics of the Neandertals and the relationship between Neandertals and *Homo sapiens*.

The Transition from *Homo erectus* to *Homo sapiens*

Most paleoanthropologists agree that *H. erectus* evolved into *H. sapiens*, but they disagree about how and where the transition occurred. There is also disagreement about how to classify some fossils from about 500,000 years to 200,000 years ago that have a mix of *H. erectus* and *H. sapiens* traits.[2] A particular fossil might be called *H. erectus* by some anthropologists and "archaic" *Homo sapiens* by others. Still other anthropologists see so much continuity between *H. erectus* and *H. sapiens* that they think it is completely arbitrary to call them different species. According to these anthropologists, *H. erectus* and *H. sapiens* may just be earlier and later varieties of the same species and therefore all should be called *H. sapiens*. (*H. erectus* would then be *H. sapiens erectus*.)

Homo heidelbergensis

Homo heidelbergensis
A transitional species between *Homo erectus* and *Homo sapiens*.

Some scholars have suggested that the "transitional" fossils share common traits and may actually represent a separate species—***Homo heidelbergensis***, named after a jaw found in 1907, in the village of Mauer near Heidelberg, Germany.[3] Other specimens that have been suggested as members of this species have been found in many parts of the Old World. To simplify things, we will call all these "transitional" specimens *H. heidelbergensis*.

Homo heidelbergensis differs from *Homo erectus* in having smaller teeth and jaws, a much larger brain (on the order of 1,300 cc), a skull that lacks a sagittal keel and occipital torus, a browridge that divides into separate arches above each eye, and a more robust skeleton (see Figure 7.1). *Homo heidelbergensis* differs from *Homo sapiens* in retaining a large and prognathic face with relatively large teeth and jaws, a browridge, a long, low cranial vault with a sloping forehead, and in its more robust skeleton.[4]

Neandertals: *Homo sapiens* or *Homo neandertalensis*?

Homo neandertalensis
The technical name for the Neandertals, a group of robust and otherwise anatomically distinct hominin that are close relatives of modern humans.

Neandertal The common name for the species *Homo neandertalensis*.

There may be disagreement about how to classify the mixed-trait fossils from 500,000 to 200,000 years ago, but until a decade ago there was an outright battle about many of the fossils that are less than 200,000 years old. Some anthropologists argued that they were definitely *Homo sapiens* and classified them as *Homo sapiens neandertalensis*. Other anthropologists argued that they were part of a distinct species, ***Homo neandertalensis***, more commonly referred to as the **Neandertals**. The Neandertals have been a confusing hominin fossil group since the first specimen was found in 1856. Somehow through the years, the Neandertals have become the victims of their cartoon image, which usually misrepresents them as burly and more ape than human. Actually, they might go unnoticed in a cross-section of the world's population today. Were they part of our species? For a while, the answer seemed to be yes. But recent archaeological and genetic evidence has led most to question the relationship between Neandertals and modern humans. Let's take a look at some of the history of research on the Neandertals.

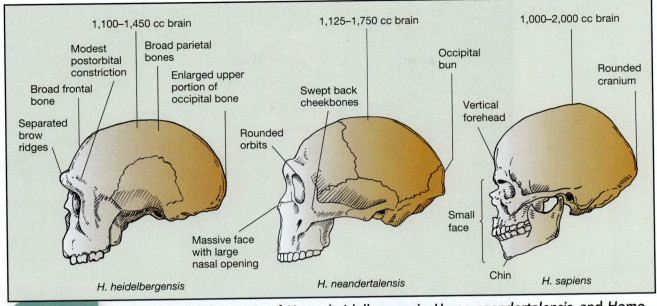

Comparison of the crania of *Homo heidelbergensis*, *Homo neandertalensis*, and *Homo sapiens*, showing important differences.

In 1856, three years before Darwin's publication of *Origin of Species,* a skullcap and other fossilized bones were discovered in a cave in the Neander Valley (*tal* is the German word for "valley"), near Düsseldorf, Germany. The fossils in the Neander Valley were the first that scholars could tentatively consider as an early hominin. (The fossils classified as *Homo erectus* were not found until later in the 19th century, and the fossils belonging to the genus *Australopithecus* were not found until the 20th century.) After Darwin's revolutionary work was published, the Neandertal find aroused considerable controversy. A few evolutionist scholars, such as Thomas Huxley, thought that the Neandertal was not that different from modern humans. Others dismissed the Neandertal as irrelevant to human evolution; they saw it as a pathological freak, a peculiar, disease-ridden individual. But similar fossils turned up later in Belgium, Yugoslavia, France, and elsewhere in Europe, which meant that the original Neandertal find could not be dismissed as an oddity.[5]

The predominant reaction to the original and subsequent Neandertal-like finds was that the Neandertals were too "brutish" and "primitive" to have been ancestral to modern humans prevailed in the scholarly community until well into the 1950s. It is now universally agreed that the skeletal traits of the Neandertals are completely consistent with modern humans. Perhaps more important, when the much more ancient australopithecine and *H. erectus* fossils were accepted as hominins in the 1940s and 1950s, anthropologists realized that the Neandertals did not look that different from modern humans—despite their sloping foreheads, large browridges, flattened braincases, large jaws, and nearly absent chins (see Figure 7.1).[6] And they had brains averaging more about 150 cc greater than modern humans.[7] Some scholars believe that the large brain capacity of Neandertals suggests that they were capable of the full range of behaviors characteristic of modern humans. Their skeletons did, however, attest to one behavioral trait markedly different from behaviors of most modern humans: Neandertals apparently made very strenuous use of their bodies.[8]

It took almost 100 years for scholars to accept the idea that Neandertals were not that different from modern humans and perhaps should be classified as *Homo sapiens neandertalensis.* But in the last 15 years, there has been a growing debate over whether the Neandertals in western Europe were ancestral to modern-looking people who lived later in western Europe, after about 40,000 years ago. In 1997, a group of researchers from the United States and Germany published findings that forced a reconsideration of the Neandertals and their relationship to modern humans. These scholars reported that they

Reconstructions of ancient hominins.

had been able to extract mitochondrial DNA (mtDNA, which is DNA located in cellular structures called mitochondria and is different from the nuclear DNA that is the blueprint for our bodies) from the original Neandertal specimen found in 1856.[9] The only source of change in mtDNA is random mutation. Mitochondrial DNA is inherited only from mothers in animals; it is not carried into an egg cell by sperm but is left with the sperm's tail on the outside of the egg. These unique characteristics make it possible to use mtDNA to measure the degree of relatedness between two species, and even to say how long ago those species diverged. The longer two species have been separated, the more differences there will be in their mtDNA. Among individual modern humans, there are usually five to ten differences in the sequence of mtDNA examined by the United States and German researchers. Between modern humans and the Neandertal specimen, there tend to be about 25 differences—more than three times that among modern humans (see Figure 7.2). This suggested to the researchers that the ancestors of modern humans and the Neandertal must have diverged about 600,000 years ago.[10] If the last common ancestor of ours and the Neandertal lived that long ago, the Neandertal would be a much more distant relative than previously thought. This research has since been replicated with mtDNA from other Neandertal fossils.[11]

But mtDNA is only part of the story. Subsequently, nuclear DNA has been recovered and sequenced from Neandertals.[12] Analysis of the Neandertal DNA has found that Neandertals and modern humans have identical versions of several genes that were thought to only be found in modern humans, and that the two species occasionally interbred.[13] Neandertals also had fair skin, and at least some had red hair.[14] But, some significant differences between Neandertal and modern human nuclear DNA have also been identified. For example, Neandertals apparently lack the modern human version of *microcephalin,* a gene that is associated with brain development.[15] And initial analyses of the nuclear DNA suggest that the ancestral modern human and Neandertal populations split more than a half million years ago.[16]

Archaeological findings from Europe and the Near East also seem to indicate that Neandertals and modern humans were different species. It has been known for decades that both modern human and Neandertal fossils are found in the same locations in parts of the Levant, but recent improvements in dating technology and newly discovered fossils have even more clearly demonstrated that the two kinds of hominin coexisted. In fact, several caves in the Mount Carmel region of Israel contain both modern

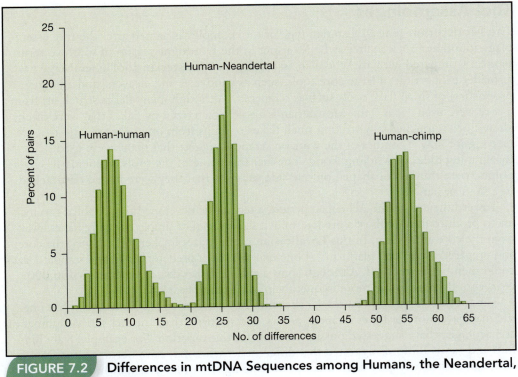

FIGURE 7.2 **Differences in mtDNA Sequences among Humans, the Neandertal, and Chimpanzees**

The x-axis shows the number of sequence differences; the y-axis shows the percent of individuals that share that number of sequence differences.

Source: Krings 1997, 25.

human and Neandertal occupations. The fact that these two groups of hominins cohabited the Near East for perhaps as much as 30,000 years and did not interbreed or share much in the way of tool technology strongly suggests that the two are different species.[17] Finds in Europe seem to corroborate that assessment. As early modern humans began moving into Europe, they appear to have displaced populations of Neandertals already living there. Sites with tools thought to be associated with Neandertals disappear throughout Europe as sites with tools thought to be associated with modern humans expand their range.[18] Significantly, the area of Europe last colonized by modern humans (Iberia) contains the very latest Neandertal fossils yet found, dating to some 30,000 years ago.[19]

With all this evidence pointing to Neandertals not being part of the modern human species, why is there an ongoing debate? In part, this is because none of the evidence is conclusive, and much of it can be interpreted in alternate ways. Perhaps more important, however, Neandertal culture, typically referred to as Middle Paleolithic after the predominant tool technology, has some features that make it seem similar to the culture of early modern humans.

Middle Paleolithic The time period of the Mousterian stone tool tradition.

Middle Paleolithic Cultures

7.2 Describe the features of Middle Paleolithic cultures.

The period of cultural history associated with the Neandertals is traditionally called the **Middle Paleolithic** in Europe and the Near East and dates from about 300,000 years to about 40,000 years ago.[20] For Africa, the term *Middle Stone Age* is used instead of Middle Paleolithic. The tool assemblages from this period are generally referred to as Mousterian in Europe and the Near East and as *post-Acheulian* in Africa.

Tool Assemblages

The Mousterian   The Mousterian type of tool complex is named after the tool assemblage found in a rock shelter at Le Moustier in the Dordogne region of southwestern France. Compared with an Acheulian assemblage, a **Mousterian tool assemblage** has a smaller proportion of large core tools, such as hand axes and cleavers, and a bigger proportion of small flake tools such as scrapers.[21] Although many flakes struck off from a core were used "as is," the Mousterian is also characterized by flakes that were often altered or "retouched" by striking small flakes or chips from one or more edges (see Figure 7.3).[22] Studies of the wear on scrapers suggest that many were used for scraping hides or working wood. The fact that some of the tools, particularly points, were thinned or shaped on one side suggests that they were hafted or attached to a shaft or handle.[23]

Toward the end of the Acheulian period, a technique developed that enabled toolmakers to produce flake tools of a predetermined size instead of simply chipping flakes away from the core at random. In this **Levalloisian method,** toolmakers first shaped the core and prepared a "striking platform" at one end. Flakes of predetermined and standard sizes could then be knocked off. Although some Levallois flakes date as far back as 400,000 years ago, they are found more frequently in Mousterian tool kits.[24]

The tool assemblages in particular sites may be characterized as Mousterian, but one site may have more or fewer scrapers, points, and so forth, than another site. A number of archaeologists have suggested possible reasons for this variation. For example, Sally Binford and Lewis Binford suggested that different activities may have occurred in different sites. Some sites may have been used for butchering and other sites may have been base camps; hence, the kinds of tools found in different sites should vary.[25] And Paul Fish has suggested that some sites may have more tools produced by the Levalloisian technique because larger pieces of flint were available.[26]

> **Mousterian tool assemblage**   Named after the tool assemblage found in a rock shelter at Le Moustier in the Dordogne region of southwestern France. Compared with an Acheulian assemblage, the Middle Paleolithic (300,000–40,000 years ago) Mousterian has a smaller proportion of large core tools such as hand axes and cleavers and a bigger proportion of small flake tools such as scrapers. Flakes were often altered or "retouched" by striking small flakes or chips from one or more edges.

The Post-Acheulian in Africa   Like Mousterian tools, many of the post-Acheulian tools in Africa during the Middle Stone Age were struck off prepared cores in the Levalloisian way. The assemblages consist mostly of various types of flake tools. A well-described sequence of such tools comes from the area around the mouth of the Klasies River on the southern coast of South Africa. This area contains rock shelters and small caves in which early and later *Homo sapiens* lived. The oldest cultural remains in one of the caves may date back 120,000 years.[27] These earliest tools include parallel-sided flake blades (probably used as knives), pointed flakes (possibly spearpoints), burins or gravers (chisel-like tools), and scrapers. Similar tools discovered at Border cave, South Africa, may have been used almost 200,000 years ago.[28]

Homesites

Most of the excavated Middle Paleolithic homesites in Europe and the Near East are located in caves and rock shelters. The same is true for the excavated Middle Stone Age homesites in sub-Saharan Africa. We might conclude, therefore, that Neandertals (as well as many early modern humans) lived mostly in caves or rock shelters. But that conclusion could be incorrect. Caves and rock shelters may be overrepresented in the

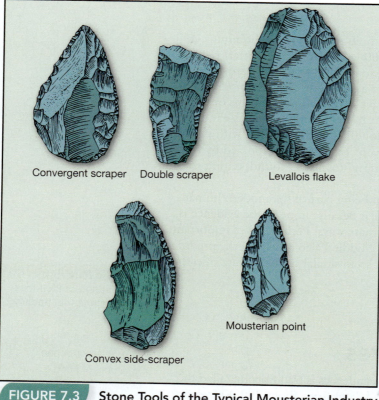

Convergent scraper   Double scraper   Levallois flake

Convex side-scraper   Mousterian point

FIGURE 7.3   Stone Tools of the Typical Mousterian Industry

Flakes were carefully retouched, usually on two sides. Mousterian tools, associated with Neandertals, are part of what archaeologists call the Middle Paleolithic, about 300,000 to 40,000 years before the present.

archaeological record because they are more likely to be found than are sites that originally were in the open but now are hidden by thousands of years, and many feet, of sediment. Sediment is the dust, debris, and decay that accumulate over time; when we dust the furniture and vacuum the floor, we are removing sediment.

Still, we know that many Neandertals lived at least part of the year in caves. This was true, for example, along the Dordogne River in France. The river gouged deep valleys in the limestone of that area. Below the cliffs are rock shelters with overhanging roofs and deep caves, many of which were occupied during the Middle Paleolithic. Even if the inhabitants did not stay all year, the sites do seem to have been occupied year after year.[29] Although there is evidence of some use of fire in earlier cultures, Middle Paleolithic humans seem to have relied more on fire. There are thick layers of ash in many rock shelters and caves and evidence that hearths were used to increase the efficiency of the fires.[30]

Quite a few Neandertal homesites were in the open. In Africa, open-air sites were located on floodplains, at the edges of lakes, and near springs.[31] Many open-air sites have been found in Europe, particularly eastern Europe. The occupants of the well-known site at Moldova in western Russia lived in river-valley houses framed with wood and covered with animal skins. Bones of mammoths, huge elephants now extinct, surround the remains of hearths and were apparently used to help hold the animal skins in place. Even though the winter climate near the edge of the glacier nearby was cold at that time, there still would have been animals to hunt because the plant food for the game was not buried under deep snow.

The hunters probably moved away in the summer to higher land between the river valleys. In all likelihood, the higher ground was grazing land for the large herds of animals the Moldova hunters depended on for meat. In the winter river valley sites, archaeologists have found skeletons of wolf, arctic fox, and hare with their paws missing. These animals probably were skinned for pelts that were made into clothing.[32]

Getting Food

How Neandertals and early modern humans got their food probably varied with their environment. In Africa, they lived in savanna and semiarid desert. In western and eastern Europe, they had to adapt to cold; during periods of increased glaciation, much of the environment was steppe grassland and tundra.

The European environment during this time was much richer in animal resources than the tundra of northern countries is today. Indeed, the European environment inhabited by Neandertals abounded in game, both big and small. The tundra and alpine animals included reindeer, bison, wild oxen, horses, mammoths, rhinoceroses, and deer, as well as bears, wolves, and foxes.[33] Some European sites have also yielded bird and fish remains. For example, people in a summer camp in northern Germany apparently hunted swans and ducks and fished for perch and pike.[34] Little, however, is known about the particular plant foods the European Neandertals may have consumed; the remains of plants are unlikely to survive thousands of years in a nonarid environment.

In Africa, too, early *Homo sapiens* varied in how they got food. For example, we know that the people living at the mouth of the Klasies River in South Africa ate shellfish as well as meat from small grazers, such as antelopes, and large grazers, such as eland and buffalo.[35] But archaeologists disagree about how the Klasies River people got their meat when they began to occupy the caves in the area.

Richard Klein thinks they hunted both large and small game. Klein speculates that, because the remains of eland of all ages have been found in Cave 1 at the Klasies River site, the people there probably hunted the eland by driving them into corrals or other traps, where animals of all ages could be killed. Klein thinks that buffalo were hunted differently. Buffalo tend to charge attackers, which would make it difficult to drive them into traps. Klein believes that, because bones from mostly very young and very old buffalo are found in the cave, the hunters were able to stalk and kill only the most vulnerable animals.[36]

Lewis Binford thinks the Klasies River people hunted only small grazers and scavenged the eland and buffalo meat from the kills of large carnivores. He argues that sites should contain all or almost all of the bones from animals that were hunted.

Levalloisian method A method that allowed flake tools of a predetermined size to be produced from a shaped core. The toolmakers first shaped the core and prepared a "striking platform" at one end. Flakes of predetermined and standard sizes could then be knocked off. Although some Levallois flakes date from as far back as 400,000 years ago, they are found more frequently in Mousterian tool kits.

According to Binford, because more or less complete skeletons are found only from small animals, the Klasies River people were not, at first, hunting all the animals they used for food.[37]

But evidence suggests that people were hunting big game as much as 400,000 years ago. Wooden spears that old were found in Germany in association with stone tools and the butchered remains of more than ten wild horses. The heavy spears resemble modern aerodynamic javelins, which suggests they would have been thrown at large animals such as horses, not at small animals. This new evidence strongly suggests that hunting, not just scavenging, may be older than archaeologists once thought.[38]

Rituals

At Drachenloch cave in the Swiss Alps, for example, a stone-lined pit holding the stacked skulls of seven cave bears was found in association with a Neandertal habitation. Why preserve these skulls? One reason might be for rituals intended to placate or control bears. Cave bears were enormous—some nearly nine feet tall—and competed with Neandertals for prime cave living sites. Perhaps the Neandertals preserved the skulls of bears they killed in the cave as a way of honoring or appeasing either the bears or their spirits. But, as with funeral rituals, the evidence is not completely persuasive. In our own society, some may hang a deer or moose head on the wall without any associated ritual. At this point, we cannot say for certain whether or not Neandertals engaged in ritual behavior.[39]

7.3 Explain the relationship of Denisovans to Neandertals and modern humans.

The Denisovans

While there remain many unanswered questions about the Neandertals and their culture, a recent find in Siberia has created a new mystery, in this case involving a potentially new species of hominin living contemporaneously with the Neandertals and modern humans—the Denisovans. Surprisingly, this new hominin species is known from only one site, Denisova cave in the Altai region of southern Siberia, and through only a single molar and several fragmentary bones. How can a new species be defined through such a tiny amount of evidence? The answer is that the Denisovan finds were subjected to a new DNA recovery process, and the results were spectacular. We now have the most complete genetic picture of any ancient human, and it is different from either ancient modern humans or Neandertals.[40]

Who were the Denisovans? It's a difficult question to answer with so little information, but we do know several things. The Denisovans were neither Neandertals nor modern humans, but a separate species that was more closely related to Neandertals than to modern humans. They appear to have separated from our lineage a little earlier than the Neandertals, and from the Neandertals a bit later.[41] If artifacts associated with the Denisovan remains were made by the Denisovans (both Neandertals and modern humans lived in the cave after Denisovans), then they fashioned Middle Paleolithic-style tools, but the stratigraphy of the cave makes this conclusion uncertain. Far less uncertain is the contribution of Denisovans to the modern human genome—people in Melanesia can count 4 percent to 6 percent of their DNA as coming from the Denisovans.[42]

Cro-Magnons Humans who lived in western Europe about 35,000 years ago, were once thought to be the earliest specimens of modern-looking humans. But it is now known that modern-looking humans appeared earlier outside of Europe; the earliest so far found lived in Africa.

7.4 Explain theories about the origins of modern humans and how they differed from earlier species.

The Emergence of Modern Humans

Cro-Magnon humans, who appear in western Europe about 35,000 years ago, were once thought to be the earliest specimens of modern humans, or *Homo sapiens*. (The Cro-Magnons are named after the rock shelter in France where they were first found, in 1868.[43]) But we now know that modern-looking humans appeared earlier outside of Europe. As of now, the oldest unambiguous fossils classified as *H. sapiens* come from

Ethiopia and date to perhaps 160,000 years ago.[44] Additional fossils, discovered in one of the Klasies River mouth caves in South Africa, are possibly as old as 100,000 years.[45] Other *Homo sapiens* fossils of about the same age have been found in Border cave in South Africa.[46] Remains of anatomically modern humans found at two sites in Israel, at Skhul and Qafzeh, which used to be thought to date back 40,000 years to 50,000 years, may be 90,000 years old.[47] There are also anatomically modern human finds in Borneo, at Niah, from about 40,000 years ago and in Australia, at Lake Mungo, from about 30,000 years ago.[48]

These modern-looking humans differed from the Neandertals in that they had higher, more bulging foreheads, thinner and lighter bones, smaller faces and jaws, chins (the bony protuberances that remain after projecting faces recede), and only slight browridges (or no ridges at all; see Figure 7.1).

This *Homo sapiens* skull from Ethiopia is the oldest member of our species yet found, dating to 160,000 years ago.

Theories about the Origins of Modern Humans

Three theories about the origins of modern humans continue to be debated among anthropologists. One, which can be called the *single-origin theory*, (sometimes called the total replacement theory) suggests that modern humans emerged in just one part of the Old World and then spread to other parts, replacing Neandertals, Denisovans, and perhaps other hominin species. (Africa is generally thought to be the place of modern humans' origin.) The second theory, which has been called the *multiregional theory*, developed in opposition to the single-origin theory, and suggested that modern humans evolved in various parts of the Old World after *Homo erectus* spread out of Africa.[49] The multiregional theory has largely been supplanted with the *assimilation theory*, which suggests that modern humans replaced Neandertals and Denisovans, but that interbreeding during the replacement process led to some assimilation between the various hominins.[50] Let's take a look at each of these theories.

Single-Origin Theory According to the single-origin theory, the Neandertals and Denisovans did not evolve into modern humans. Rather, Neandertals became extinct after 30,000 years ago because they were replaced by modern humans (we do not know yet when Denisovans became extinct). Single-origin theorists think that the originally small population of *H. sapiens* had some biological or cultural advantage, or both, that allowed them to spread and replace Neandertals, Denisovans, and other hominins.

The main evidence for the single-origin theory comes from the genes of living peoples. In 1987, Rebecca Cann and colleagues used mtDNA differences between living peoples to determine how long ago modern humans separated from our closest ancestors. Cann and colleagues argued that these differences pointed to a common ancestral population for all modern humans living about 200,000 years ago. They further claimed that, because the amount of variation among individuals was greatest in African populations, the common ancestor of all lived in Africa.[51] Thus was born what the media called the "mitochondrial Eve" and the "Eve hypothesis" for the origins of modern humans. Of course, there wasn't just one "Eve"; there must have been more than one of her generation with similar mtDNA. More detailed analyses of mtDNA diversity in modern humans have allowed scholars to identify the ancestral roots of contemporary populations around the world, and these analyses also point to modern human origins in East Africa and a subsequent spread out of that region.[52]

Evidence for an East African origin of modern humans and the subsequent expansion also comes from research on variation in the Y chromosome. The Y chromosome is the chromosome that determines whether a person is male. A female inherits an X chromosome from both her mother and father, whereas a male inherits an X chromosome from his mother and a Y chromosome from his father. Only men have a

Y chromosome, and because there is only one copy in any given man, the Y chromosome is the only nuclear chromosome that, like mtDNA, does not undergo recombination. Although the Y chromosome can be affected by selection, it is thought that most variation in the Y chromosome, like variation in mtDNA, is caused by random mutations. Variation in the Y chromosome can therefore be analyzed in much the same way as variation in mtDNA.[53]

The results of research on variation in the Y chromosome mirror those on variation in mtDNA to a remarkable extent. Analysis of Y chromosome variation points to Africa as the source of modern humans, and suggests an exodus from Africa of modern humans. One of the major differences between mtDNA studies and those employing the Y chromosome is in the dating of the most recent common ancestor. As noted previously, studies of mtDNA suggest the most recent common ancestor lived about 200,000 years ago, whereas studies of the Y chromosome suggest the most recent ancestor lived only about 100,000 years ago.[54] Additional research, including new research on variation in nuclear DNA, may help to resolve these differences. For now, however, it seems clear that the modern human gene pool has a single, and fairly recent, origin in Africa.[55]

The mtDNA and nuclear DNA analyses of Neandertals, and the archaeological evidence suggesting that Neandertals and modern humans lived without apparent interaction in Europe and the Near East, also tend to support the single-origin theory. The *Homo sapiens* skeletal material from Ethiopia, Africa, in the 150,000–200,000-year-ago time range, further supports the single-origin theory.[56] But such evidence does not necessarily contradict the validity of the multiregional theory of human origins.

Multiregional Theory According to the multiregional theory, *Homo erectus* populations in various parts of the Old World gradually evolved into anatomically modern-looking humans. The few scholars who continue to support this view believe that the "transitional" or "archaic" *H. sapiens* and the Neandertals represent phases in the gradual development of more "modern" anatomical features. Indeed, as we have noted, some of these scholars see so much continuity between *Homo erectus* and modern humans that they classify *Homo erectus* as *Homo sapiens erectus.*

Continuity is the main evidence multiregional theorists use to support their position. In several parts of the world, there seem to be clear continuities in distinct skeletal features between *Homo erectus* and *Homo sapiens.* For example, *Homo erectus* fossils from China tend to have broader faces with more horizontal cheekbones than specimens from elsewhere in the world, traits that also appear in modern Chinese populations.[57] Southeast Asia provides more compelling evidence, according to multiregional theorists. There, a number of traits—relatively thick cranial bones, a receding forehead, an unbroken browridge, facial prognathism, relatively large cheekbones, and relatively large molars—appear to persist from *Homo erectus* through modern populations .[58] But others suggest that these traits cannot be used to establish a unique continuation from *Homo erectus* in Southeast Asia because these traits are found in modern humans all over the world. Still others argue that the traits are not as similar as the multiregional theorists claim.[59]

Assimilation Theory The assimilation theory, which is perhaps the most widely supported of the three theories of modern human origins today, suggests that while there may have been some replacement of one population by another, interbreeding between early modern humans who spread out of Africa and populations encountered in North Africa, Europe, and Asia also contributed to the emergence of modern humans.[60]

Genetic data provide the strongest support for the assimilation theory. Not only does it appear that modern human nuclear DNA contains from 1 percent to 6 percent of Neandertal and Denisovan nuclear DNA, but some of that DNA provided important benefits to modern humans. For example, it appears that an important part of the modern human immune system, human leukocyte antigens (HLA), were inherited from Neandertals and Denisovans.[61] Presumably, these antigens provided unique benefits to modern humans, and so were transmitted throughout the human population despite their introduction through what appears to be a very low level of interbreeding.

What Happened to the Neandertals?

7.5 Evaluate competing scenarios for the disappearance of Neandertals.

Regardless of which theory (single-origin, multiregional, or assimilation) is correct, it seems clear that Neandertals and modern humans coexisted in Europe and the Near East for at least 20,000 years, and maybe as long as 60,000 years. What happened to the Neandertals? Three answers have generally been considered. The multiregional theorists assume considerable interbreeding and gradual change, so the disappearance of Neandertal traits would not be surprising. The single-origin theorists assume that replacement occurred—either because they were killed off by modern humans, or they were driven to extinction due to competition with modern humans. Let's take a look at each of these scenarios.

Interbreeding

The interbreeding scenario seems the most probable, yet genetic evidence supporting it is ambiguous. If the interbreeding hypothesis were correct, then we would expect to find Neandertal traits in modern humans. According to the nuclear DNA evidence, we do find a small percentage of Neandertal traits. But the mtDNA and Y chromosome analyses we have discussed several times suggest a divergence between Neandertals and modern humans 100,000 to 200,000 years ago with very little interbreeding.

Recent research on Neandertal tools suggests that some Neandertal groups adopted new techniques of tool manufacture that are thought to be uniquely associated with modern humans, and that they produced jewelry.[62] If Neandertals were learning from modern humans, then the idea that they could have interbred and perhaps been absorbed within the modern human population gains credibility.

Genocide

The genocide scenario, that modern humans killed off Neandertals, has appeal as a sensational story, but little evidence. Not a single "murdered" Neandertal has ever been found, and one might wonder, in a fight between the powerful Neandertals and the more gracile modern humans, who might get the better of whom.

Extinction

Finally, the extinction scenario, that Neandertals simply could not compete with modern humans, seems to have the best archaeological support. As we discussed earlier, there appear to be "refugee" populations of Neandertals in Iberia as recently as perhaps 30,000 years ago. The "retreat" of Neandertals from the Near East, eastern Europe, and finally western Europe following the movement of modern humans into the region seems to support the "refugee" interpretation.[63] More importantly, physical anthropologist Erik Trinkaus has argued, based on both physical characteristics of the Neandertal skeleton and their apparent patterns of behavior, that Neandertals were less efficient hunters and gatherers than modern humans.[64] And not only may Neandertals have been less efficient than modern humans in getting food, they may have needed more of it. Steve Churchill has suggested that Neandertals' stocky bodies and great muscle mass might have required 25 percent more calories than modern humans.[65] If this is true, a modern human group would have been able to live and reproduce more easily than a Neandertal group in the same territory, and this would likely drive the Neandertals away. When there were no new territories to run to, the Neandertals would go extinct—precisely what the archaeological record seems to suggest.[66]

But were modern humans and their cultures really that much more efficient than Middle Paleolithic cultures? As we will see, the Upper Paleolithic does seem to mark a watershed in the evolution of human culture, allowing humans to expand their physical horizons throughout the world and their intellectual horizons into the realms of art and ritual.

The Upper Paleolithic World

7.6 Describe the environment of the Upper Paleolithic world.

The period of cultural history in Europe, the Near East, and Asia known as the Upper Paleolithic dates from about 40,000 years ago to the period known as the *Neolithic* (beginning about 10,000 years ago, depending on the area). In Africa, the cultural period comparable to the Upper Paleolithic is known as the *Later Stone Age* and may have begun much earlier. In North and South America, the period begins when humans first entered the New World, some time before 12,000 years ago (these colonizers are typically called *Paleo-Indians*) and continues until what are called *Archaic traditions* emerged some 10,000 years ago. To simplify terminology, we use the term *Upper Paleolithic* to refer to cultural developments in all areas of the Old World during this period.

In many respects, lifestyles during the Upper Paleolithic were similar to lifestyles before. People were still mainly hunters, gatherers, and fishers who probably lived in small mobile bands. They made their camps out in the open in skin-covered huts and in caves and rock shelters. And they continued to produce smaller and smaller stone tools.

But the Upper Paleolithic is also characterized by a variety of new developments. One of the most striking is the emergence of art—painting on cave walls and stone slabs, and carving tools, decorative objects, and personal ornaments out of bone, antler, shell, and stone. (Perhaps for this as well as other purposes, people began to obtain materials from distant sources.) Because more archaeological sites date from the Upper Paleolithic than from any previous period and some Upper Paleolithic sites seem larger than any before, many archaeologists think that the human population increased considerably during the Upper Paleolithic.[67] And new inventions, such as the bow and arrow, the spear thrower, and tiny replaceable blades that could be fitted into handles, appear for the first time.[68]

The Last Ice Age

The Upper Paleolithic world had an environment very different from today's. The earth was gripped by the last ice age, with glaciers covering Europe as far south as Berlin and Warsaw, and North America as far south as Chicago. To the south of these glacial fronts was a tundra zone extending in Europe to the Alps and in North America to the Ozarks, Appalachians, and well out onto the Great Plains. Environmentally, both Europe and North America probably resembled contemporary Siberia and northern Canada. Elsewhere in the world conditions were not as extreme, but were still different from conditions today.[69]

Annual temperatures were as much as 50 degrees Fahrenheit (10 degrees Celsius) below today's, and changes in ocean currents would have made temperature contrasts (i.e., the differences between summer and winter months) more extreme as well. Europe experienced heavy annual snowfall. The presence of huge ice sheets in the north changed the climate throughout the world. North Africa, for example, appears to have been much wetter than today, and South Asia was apparently drier. And everywhere the climate seems to have been highly variable.[70]

The plants and animals of the Upper Paleolithic world were adapted to these extreme conditions. Among the most important, and dramatic, were the large game animals collectively known as *Pleistocene megafauna*.[71] These animals, as their name suggests, were huge compared to their contemporary descendants. In North America, for example, giant ground sloths stood some 8 feet to 10 feet tall and weighed several thousand pounds. Siberian mammoths were the largest elephants ever to live—some standing more than 14 feet tall.

Indirect percussion A toolmaking technique common in the Upper Paleolithic. After shaping a core into a pyramidal or cylindrical form, the toolmaker can put a punch of antler or wood or another hard material into position and strike it with a hammer. Using a hammer-struck punch enabled toolmakers to strike off consistently shaped blades.

7.7 Describe Upper Paleolithic tools and cultures in Europe.

Upper Paleolithic Europe

With the vast supplies of meat available from megafauna, it is not surprising that many Upper Paleolithic cultures relied on hunting, and this was particularly true of the Upper Paleolithic peoples of Europe, on whom we focus here. Their way of life represents a common pattern throughout the Old World. But as people began to use more diverse resources in their environments, the use of local resources allowed Upper Paleolithic groups in much of the Old World to become more sedentary than their predecessors. They also began to trade with neighboring groups to obtain resources not available in their local territories.[72]

As was the case in the known Middle Paleolithic sites, most of the Upper Paleolithic remains that have been excavated were situated in caves and rock shelters. In southwestern France, some groups seem to have paved parts of the shelter floors with stones. Tentlike structures were built in some caves, apparently to keep out the cold.[73] Some open-air sites have also been excavated.

The site at Dolni Vestonice in what is now the Czech Republic, dated to around 25,000 years ago, is one of the first for which there is an entire settlement plan.[74] The settlement seems to have consisted of four tentlike huts, probably made from animal skins, with a great open hearth in the center. Around the outside were mammoth bones, some rammed into the ground, which suggests that the huts were surrounded by a wall. All told, there were bone heaps from about 100 mammoths. Each hut probably housed a group of related families—about 20 to 25 people. (One hut was approximately 27 feet by 45 feet and had five hearths distributed inside it, presumably one for each family.) With 20 to 25 people per hut, and assuming that all four huts were occupied at the same time, the population of the settlement would have been 100 to 125 people.

Up a hill from the settlement was a fifth and different kind of hut. It was dug into the ground and contained a bake oven and more than 2,300 small, fired fragments of animal figurines. There were also some hollow bones that may have been musical instruments. Another interesting feature of the settlement was a burial find, of a woman with a disfigured face. She may have been a particularly important personage; her face was found engraved on an ivory plaque near the central hearth of the settlement.

Upper Paleolithic Tools

Upper Paleolithic toolmaking appears to have had its roots in the Mousterian and post-Acheulian traditions, because flake tools are found in many Upper Paleolithic sites. But the Upper Paleolithic is characterized by a preponderance of blades; there were also burins, bone and antler tools, and microliths. In addition, two new techniques of toolmaking appeared— *indirect percussion* and *pressure flaking*. Blades were found in Middle Paleolithic assemblages, but they were not widely used until the Upper Paleolithic. Although blades can be made in a variety of ways, **indirect percussion** using a hammer-struck punch was common in the Upper Paleolithic. After shaping a core into a pyramidal or cylindrical form, toolmakers put a punch of antler, wood, or other hard material into position and struck it with a hammer. Because the force is readily directed, toolmakers were able to strike off consistently shaped **blades,** which are more than twice as long as they are wide[75].

The Upper Paleolithic is also noted for the production of large numbers of bone, antler, and ivory tools; needles, awls, and harpoons made of bone appear for the first time.[76] The manufacture of these implements may have been made easier by the development of many varieties of burins. **Burins** are chisel-like stone tools used for carving; bone and antler needles, awls, and projectile points could be produced with them.[77] Burins have been found in Middle and Lower Paleolithic sites but are present in great number and variety only in the Upper Paleolithic.

Upper Paleolithic bone needle and spear or harpoon points. Upper Paleolithic peoples made a much wider variety of tools than their predecessors.

Blade A thin flake whose length is usually more than twice its width. In the blade technique of toolmaking, a core is prepared by shaping a piece of flint with hammerstones into a pyramidal or cylindrical form. Blades are then struck off until the core is used up.

Burin A chisel-like stone tool used for carving and for making such artifacts as bone and antler needles, awls, and projectile points.

Pressure flaking Tool-making technique whereby small flakes are struck off by pressing against the core with a bone, antler, or wooden tool.

Microlith A small, razorlike blade fragment that was probably attached in a series to a wooden or bone handle to form a cutting edge.

Pressure flaking also appeared during the Upper Paleolithic. Rather than using percussion to strike off flakes as in previous technologies, pressure flaking works by employing pressure with a bone, wood, or antler tool at the edge of the tool to remove small flakes. Pressure flaking would usually be used in the final stages of retouching a tool.[78]

As time went on, all over the Old World, smaller and smaller blade tools were produced. The very tiny ones, called **microliths,** were often hafted or fitted into handles, one blade at a time or several blades together, to serve as spears, adzes, knives, and sickles. The hafting required inventing a way to trim the blade's back edge so that it would be blunt rather than sharp. In this way, the blades would not split the handles into which they might be inserted; the blunting would also prevent the users of an unhafted blade from cutting themselves.[79]

Some archaeologists think that the blade technique was adopted because it made for more economical use of flint. André Leroi-Gourhan of the Musée de l'Homme in Paris calculated that, with the old Acheulian technique, a 2-pound lump of flint yielded 16 inches of working edge and produced only two hand axes. If the more advanced Mousterian technique were used, a lump of equal size would yield 2 yards of working edge. The indirect percussion method of the Upper Paleolithic would yield as much as 25 yards of working edge.[80] Getting the most out of a valuable resource may have been particularly important in areas lacking large flint deposits.

Jacques Bordaz suggested that the evolution of toolmaking techniques, which continually increased the amount of usable edge that could be gotten out of a lump of flint, was significant because people could then spend more time in regions where flint was unavailable. Another reason for adopting the blade toolmaking technique may have been that it made for easy repair of tools. For example, the cutting edge of a tool might consist of a line of razorlike microliths set into a piece of wood. The tool would not be usable if just one of the cutting edge's microliths broke off or was chipped. But if the user carried a small prepared core of flint from which an identical-sized microlith could be struck off, the tool could be repaired easily by replacing the lost or broken microlith. A spear whose point was lost could be repaired similarly. Thus, the main purpose of the blade toolmaking technique may not have been to make more economical use of flint but rather to allow easy replacement of damaged blades.[81]

How Were the Tools Used? Ideally, the study of tools should reveal not only how the implements were made but also how they were used. One way of suggesting what a particular tool was used for in the past is to observe the manner in which similar tools are used by members of recent or contemporary societies, preferably societies with subsistence activities and environments similar to those of the ancient toolmakers. This method of study is called reasoning from **ethnographic analogy.** The problem with such reasoning, however, is obvious: We cannot be sure that the original use of a tool was the same as the present use. When selecting recent or contemporary cultures that may provide the most informative and accurate comparisons, we should try to choose those that derive from the ancient culture in which we are interested. If the cultures being compared are historically related, there is a greater likelihood that the two groups used a particular kind of tool in similar ways and for similar purposes.[82]

Ethnographic analogy Method of comparative cultural study that extrapolates to the past from recent or current societies.

Another way of suggesting what a particular kind of tool was used for is to compare the visible and microscopic wear marks on the prehistoric tools with the wear marks on similar tools made and experimentally used by contemporary researchers. The idea behind this approach is that different uses leave different wear marks. A pioneer in this research was S. A. Semenov, who recreated prehistoric stone tools and used them in a variety of ways to find out which uses left which kinds of wear marks. For example, by cutting into meat with his recreated stone knives, he produced a polish on the edges that was like the polish found on blades from a prehistoric site in Siberia. This finding led Semenov to infer that the Siberian blades were probably also used to cut meat.[83]

The tools made by Upper Paleolithic peoples suggest that they were much more effective hunters and fishers than their predecessors.[84] During the Upper Paleolithic, and

Here we see the type of mammoth-bone shelters constructed about 15,000 years ago on the East European Plain. Often mammoth skulls formed part of the foundation for the tusk, long bone, and wooden frame, covered with hide. As many as 95 mammoth mandibles were arranged around the outside in a herringbone pattern.

probably for the first time, spears were shot from a spear thrower rather than thrown with the arm. We know this because bone and antler **atlatls** (the Aztec word for "spear thrower") have been found in some sites. A spear propelled off a grooved board could be sent through the air with increased force, causing it to travel farther and hit harder, and with less effort by the thrower. The bow and arrow was also used in various places during the Upper Paleolithic; and harpoons, used for fishing and perhaps for hunting reindeer, were invented at this time.

These new tools and weapons for more effective hunting and fishing do not rule out the possibility that Upper Paleolithic peoples were still scavenging animal remains. Olga Soffer suggests that Upper Paleolithic peoples may have located their settlements near places where many mammoths died naturally in order to make use of the bones for building. For example, in Moravia, the mammoths may have come to lick deposits of calcite and other sources of magnesium and calcium, particularly during the late spring and early summer when resources were short and mortality was high. Consistent with this idea is that there are few human-made cut marks on mammoth bones. For example, at Dolni Vestonice, where bones of 100 mammoths were found, few bones show cut marks from butchering and few bones were found inside the huts. In contrast, the site is littered with bison, horse, and reindeer bones, suggesting that these other animals were deliberately killed and eaten by humans. If the people had been able to kill all the mammoths we find the remains of, why would they have hunted so many other animals?[85]

Upper Paleolithic Art

The earliest discovered traces of art are beads and carvings, and then paintings, from Upper Paleolithic sites. We might expect that early artistic efforts were crude, but the cave paintings of Spain and southern France show a marked degree of skill. So do the naturalistic paintings on slabs of stone excavated in southern Africa. Some of those slabs appear to have been painted as much as 28,000 years ago, which suggests that painting in Africa

Atlatl A spear propelled off a grooved board; named for the Aztec word for "spear-thrower".

is as old as painting in Europe.[86] But painting may be even older than that. The early Australians may have painted on the walls of rock shelters and cliff faces at least 30,000 years ago and maybe as much as 60,000 years ago.[87] And at Blombos cave in South Africa, engraved pieces of red ochre date back to more than 77,000 years ago.[88]

Peter Ucko and Andrée Rosenfeld identified three principal locations of paintings in the caves of western Europe: (1) in obviously inhabited rock shelters and cave entrances—art as decoration or "art for art's sake"; (2) in "galleries" immediately off the inhabited areas of caves; and (3) in the inner reaches of caves, whose difficulty of access has been interpreted by some as a sign that magical-religious activities were performed there.[89]

The subjects of the paintings are mostly animals. The paintings are on bare walls, with no backdrops or environmental trappings. Perhaps, like many contemporary peoples, Upper Paleolithic men and women believed that the drawing of a human image could cause death or injury. If that were indeed their belief, it might explain why human figures are rarely depicted in cave art. Another explanation for the focus on animals might be that these people sought to improve their luck at hunting. This theory is suggested by evidence of chips in the painted figures, perhaps made by spears thrown at the drawings. Perhaps then the paintings were inspired by the need to increase the supply of animals. Cave art seems to have reached a peak toward the end of the Upper Paleolithic period, when the herds of game were decreasing.

The particular symbolic significance of the cave paintings in southwestern France is more explicitly revealed by the results of Patricia Rice and Ann Paterson's statistical study.[90] The data suggest that the animals portrayed in the cave paintings were mostly the ones that the painters preferred for meat and for materials such as hides. For example, wild cattle (bovines) and horses are portrayed more often than we would expect by chance, probably because they were larger and heavier (meatier) than the other animals in the environment. In addition, the paintings mostly portray animals that the

Paintings of wild horses from Chauvet cave in France. Cave paintings like this demonstrate the remarkable skill of Upper Paleolithic artists.

Perspectives on Gender

Depictions of Women in Upper Paleolithic Art

It is a common misperception that depictions of the human form in Upper Paleolithic art are restricted to Venus figurines. To the contrary, there are many other depictions of humans, both female and male, running the whole range of ages from infants to elderly people. For women, figures of obese or pregnant women, like those sometimes depicted in Venus figurines, appear to be only one type in a wide range of images, many of which offer accurate rather than stylized representations.

In a survey of Upper Paleolithic art, Jean-Pierre Duhard found that all shapes and sizes of women as well as all age ranges were present. Indeed, he argued that a range of female body types can be seen. One engraved figure from Gönnersdorf cave on the Rhine River, for example, depicts four women. Three are the same size, but one is smaller and has small breasts—she may be an adolescent. Of the three larger figures, one appears to have a child tied to her back, and she also

has large, rounded breasts, as opposed to the flat and pointed breasts of the other two. Duhard argued that this is an accurate depiction of four women, one with a child she is breast-feeding.

Duhard also argued that, although depictions of women are common in Upper Paleolithic art, similar depictions of men and children are comparatively rare. He suggested this disparity may reflect women's status in Upper Paleolithic societies. Most depictions of women show them in some motherhood role—pregnant, in childbirth, or carrying an infant (and perhaps walking with older children). Duhard suggested that women's roles as mothers may have given them a privileged status in Upper Paleolithic life, which may be why that status is the most frequently depicted subject in Upper Paleolithic art.

In a similar way, Patricia Rice has argued that Venus figurines accurately reflect the social importance of women in Upper Paleolithic society. She demonstrated that a

range of body types and ages are represented in Venus figurines, and argued that, because the Venuses depict real women of all ages, not just pregnant women, they should be seen as symbols of "womanhood" rather than "motherhood." The wide distribution of Venus figurines and their apparent importance to Upper Paleolithic peoples reflect, according to Rice, the recognized importance of women in Upper Paleolithic society.

Arguing along similar lines, Olga Soffer examined the clothing worn by some Venus figures. Soffer and her colleagues show that woven items are the most frequently depicted, and argue that, because these woven items would have been highly valued in Upper Paleolithic society, their presence on some Venus figurines suggests that some women held positions of high status in Upper Paleolithic society.

Sources: Duhard 1993; Rice 1981; Soffer et al. 2000.

---

painters may have feared the most because of their size, speed, natural weapons such as tusks and horns, and unpredictability of behavior (mammoths, bovines, and horses). Thus, the paintings are consistent with the idea that "the art is related to the importance of hunting in the economy of Upper Paleolithic people."[91] Consistent with this idea, according to the investigators, is the fact that the art of the cultural period that followed the Upper Paleolithic, when getting food no longer depended on hunting large game (because they were becoming extinct), the art ceased to focus on portrayals of animals.

Upper Paleolithic Cultures in Africa and Asia

7.8 Describe Upper Paleolithic migration from Africa to Asia.

Europe was not the only region where Upper Paleolithic peoples thrived. In North Africa, for example, Upper Paleolithic peoples hunted large animals on the grasslands that covered the region during that period. They lived in small communities located within easy access to water and other resources, and moved regularly, probably to follow the animal herds. Trade took place between local groups, particularly for high-quality stone used in making tools.[92] In eastern and southern Africa, a way of life known as the Later Stone Age developed that persisted in some areas until very recently. People lived in small, mobile groups, hunting large animals and collecting a wide variety of plant foods. Interaction was common among these bands. Among their ethnographically known descendants, individuals would regularly switch their membership from one band to another.[93]

In South Asia, the Upper Paleolithic saw an increasingly sedentary lifestyle developing along the banks of freshwater streams. The Upper Paleolithic peoples in South Asia combined hunting, fishing, and gathering with seasonal movements to exploit seasonally abundant resources.[94] In East and Southeast Asia, ocean resources became vital to coastal-dwelling peoples, whereas those inland lived primarily in caves, hunting and collecting broadly in the local environment. Many of these sites appear to have been occupied for long periods of time, suggesting some degree of sedentism. During the Upper Paleolithic, peoples from Asia also populated Australia, New Guinea, and some of the islands of western Melanesia, clearly demonstrating the ability of these peoples to navigate on the sea and to use its resources.[95]

7.9 Evaluate scenarios for the migration of humans into the New World.

The Earliest Humans and Their Cultures in the New World

So far in this chapter, we have dealt only with the Old World—Africa, Europe, and Asia. What about the New World—North and South America? How long have humans lived there, and what were their earliest cultures like?

Because only *Homo sapiens* fossils have been found in North and South America, migrations of humans to the New World had to have taken place some time after the emergence of *H. sapiens*. But exactly when these migrations occurred is subject to debate, particularly about when people got to areas south of Alaska (see the box feature on "Who Were the First Americans?"). On the basis of similarities in biological traits such as tooth forms and blood types, and on possible linguistic relationships, anthropologists agree that Native Americans originally came from Asia. The traditional assumption is that they came to North America from Siberia, walking across a land bridge (Beringia) that is now under water (the Bering Strait) between Siberia and Alaska. The ice sheets or glaciers that periodically covered most of the high latitudes of the world contained so much of the world's water (the ice sheets were thousands of feet thick in some places) that Beringia was dry land in various periods (see Figure 7.4).

Until recently, the prevailing view was that humans were not present south of Alaska until after 11,500 years ago. Now it appears that from an archaeological site called Monte Verde in Chile that modern humans were in North America as early as 13,800 years ago.[96] The Monte Verde site contains more than 700 stone tools, the remains of hide-covered huts, and a child's footprint next to a hearth.[97] And there are other possible sites of early occupation.[98] For example, in Meadowcroft Rockshelter in western Pennsylvania, a small fragment of human bone, a spearpoint, and chipped knives and scrapers in a layer dating as early as 19,600 years ago were found.[99] Perhaps the most surprising physical evidence for early people in the Americas comes from the Paisley caves in southern Oregon, where human coprolites (dried feces) have been found and dated to 14,400 years ago.[100]

It was geologically possible for humans to have walked into the New World at various times, and they could also have traveled by boat. Parts of the Beringia land bridge were exposed from about 60,000 years to 25,000 years ago. Not until between 20,000 years and 18,000 years

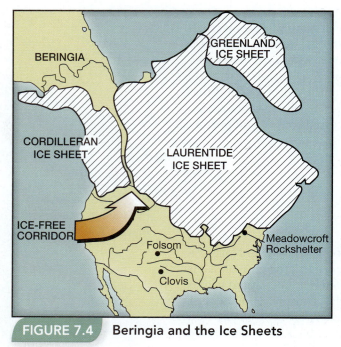

FIGURE 7.4   **Beringia and the Ice Sheets**

Source: Meltzer 1993.

Applied Anthropology

Who Were the First Americans?

A key element of laws protecting archaeological materials in the United States is that descendant groups are given the right to decide how human remains and sacred objects unearthed from archaeological sites should be treated. Many descendant groups have requested such items be repatriated to the group or reburied in a location where they will not be disturbed. But a major problem has arisen surrounding the first Americans and their relationship to contemporary peoples. The most widely accepted model for how humans entered the New World is by walking across Beringia, which joined Asia and North America at the end of the last ice age, when sea levels were lower than today. There is good evidence to support this model, both archaeological and geological. But there are also some problems. There are sites that appear to date before the time when glacial ice had retreated far enough to allow access to North America. There are also South American sites that appear to be older than the oldest North American ones, which seems contradictory to a model based on humans moving into the New World from north to south.

An alternative model for human entry into the New World, which solves some of the problems with the Beringia model, suggests that some people came to the New World from Asia by boat. These people would have moved along the sea edge of the glaciers, subsisting on fish and sea mammals. Once past the glaciers, they either would have moved farther down the coast, perhaps all the way to the tip of South America, or proceeded inland into North America. Small groups of people may have made such voyages on many occasions, and it may be that

Humans may have travelled to North America by boat along the glaciated coastline of the Bering Sea.

none established communities that lasted more than a few generations.

Some scholars posit that the few very early archaeological sites may be the remnants of these early explorers. The small numbers would leave only a small archaeological record, so it is not surprising that more material has not been found. The fact that early occupations at a number of sites are separated from later occupations by soil showing no signs of human presence may also be evidence that these early explorers were present, but died out. Additional support for the coastal migration model has recently come from archaeological explorations of ancient coastlines now lying deep beneath the Bering Sea. Archaeologists have found stone tools in locations that would have been coastal during the last ice age.

Skeletons of very early Americans also suggest there may have been early populations that died out, as many appear more similar to East

Asians than to contemporary Native Americans in their skeletal features. If the colonization of the Americas was not as simple as the Beringia model suggests, how are archaeologists to determine descendant groups? What if no descendants remain? Current historic preservation laws make the situation difficult, and a number of lawsuits have tested the question of whether or not the first Americans were directly ancestral to contemporary Native Americans. The most well known of these legal cases involved a 9,300-year-old skeleton found along the Columbia River near Kennewick, Washington. After a nearly decade-long legal battle, a federal court decided that the skeleton was not "Native American" under current laws. Other cases are pending, and Congress may step in to clarify the legal status of the first Americans.

Sources: Dillehay 2000; Powell 2005; Thomas 2000.

ago was the land bridge at its maximum, but that corridor is not likely to have supported big game, and permitted humans to hunt enough for sustenance, until after about 14,000 years ago.[101] Thus it is likely that humans didn't arrive in the New World over land until after 14,000 years ago, but they could have arrived by a coastal route in boats much earlier, and certainly after 16,000 years ago.[102]

The Paleo-Indians

Archaeological remains of early New World hunters, called *Paleo-Indians,* have been found in the United States, Mexico, and Canada. Just south of the farthest reaches of the last glaciation, the area east of the Rockies known as the High Plains abounded with mammoths, bison, wild camels, and wild horses. The tools found with mammoth kills are known as the *Clovis complex,* which includes the Clovis projectile point as well as stone scrapers and knives and bone tools. The Clovis projectile point is large and leaf-shaped, flaked on both sides. It has a broad groove in the middle, presumably so that the point could be attached to a bone or antler spear fore-shaft.[103] Because one mammoth was found with eight Clovis points in it, there is little dispute that Clovis people hunted large game.[104] Recent dating places most Clovis sites between 11,200 years and 10,900 years ago.[105]

The mammoth disappeared about 10,000 years ago, and the largest game animal became the now-extinct large, straight-horned bison. The hunters of that bison used a projectile point called the *Folsom point,* which was much smaller than the Clovis point. Tools are also found with many other kinds of animal remains, including wolf, turtle, rabbit, horse, fox, deer, and camel, so the bison hunters obviously depended on other animals as well.[106] In the Rio Grande valley, the Folsom toolmakers characteristically established a base camp on low dune ridges overlooking both a large pond and broad, open grazing areas. If we assume that the pond provided water for the grazing herds, the people in the camp would have been in an excellent position to watch the herds.[107]

As the climate of what is now the American Southwest became drier, the animals and the cultural adaptations changed somewhat. About 9,000 years ago, the smaller modern bison replaced the earlier straight-horned variety.[108] Base camps began to be located farther from ponds and grazing areas and closer to streams. If the ponds were no longer reliable sources of water during these drier times, the animals probably no longer frequented them, which would explain why the hunters had to change the sites of their base camps. Not much is known about the plant foods these Paleo-Indian people may have exploited, but plant gathering on the desert fringes may have been vital. In Nevada and Utah, archaeologists have found milling stones and other artifacts for processing plant food.[109]

The Olsen-Chubbuck site, a kill site excavated in Colorado, shows the organization that may have been involved in hunting bison.[110] In a dry gulch dated to 6500 B.C. were the remains of 200 bison. At the bottom were complete skeletons and at the top, completely butchered animals. This find clearly suggests that Paleo-Indian hunters deliberately stampeded the animals into a natural trap—an arroyo, or steep-sided dry gully. The animals in front were probably pushed into the arroyo by the ones behind. Joe Ben Wheat estimated that the hunters may have obtained 55,000 pounds of meat from this one kill. If we judge from 19th-century Plains Indians, who could prepare bison meat to last a month, and estimate that each person would eat a pound a day, the kill at the Olsen-Chubbuck site could have fed more than 1,800 people for a month (they probably did not all live together throughout the year). The hunters must have been highly organized not only for the stampede itself but also for butchering. It seems that the enormous carcasses had to be carried to flat ground for that job. In addition, the 55,000 pounds of meat and hides had to be carried back to camp.[111]

Although big game may have been most important on the High Plains, other areas show different adaptations. For example, Paleo-Indian people in woodland regions of what is now the United States seem to have depended more heavily on plant food and smaller game. In some woodland areas, fish and shellfish may have been a vital part of the diet.[112] On the Pacific coast, some Paleo-Indian people developed food-getting strategies more dependent on fish.[113] And in other areas, the lower Illinois River valley being one example, Paleo-Indian people who depended on game and wild vegetable foods managed to get enough food to live in permanent villages of perhaps between 100 and 150 people.[114]

The End of the Upper Paleolithic

7.10 Relate the end of the Upper Paleolithic to climate change and the development of Maglemosian culture.

After about 10,000 years ago, the glaciers began to disappear, and with their disappearance came other environmental changes. The melting of the glacial ice caused the oceans to rise, and, as the seas moved inland, the waters inundated some of the richest fodder-producing coastal plains, creating islands, inlets, and bays. Other areas were opened up for human occupation as the glaciers retreated and the temperatures rose.[115] The cold, treeless plains, tundras, and grasslands eventually gave way to dense mixed forests, mostly birch, oak, and pine, and the Pleistocene megafauna became extinct. The warming waterways began to be filled with fish and other aquatic resources.[116]

Archaeologists believe that these environmental changes induced some populations to alter their food-getting strategies. When the tundras and grasslands disappeared, hunters could no longer obtain large quantities of meat simply by remaining close to large migratory herds of animals, as they probably did during Upper Paleolithic times. Even though deer and other game were available, the number of animals per square mile (density) had decreased, and it became difficult to stalk and kill animals sheltered in the thick woods. Thus, in many areas, people seemed to have turned from a reliance on big game hunting to the intensive collecting of wild plants, mollusks, fish, and small game to make up for the extinction of the large game animals they had once relied upon.

The Maglemosian Culture of Northern Europe

Some adaptations to the changing environment can be seen in the cultural remains of the settlers in northern Europe who archaeologists call *Maglemosians*. Their name derives from the peat bogs (*magle mose* in Danish means "great bog") where their remains have been found.

To deal with the new, more forested environment, the Maglemosians made stone axes and adzes to chop down trees and form them into various objects. Large timbers appear to have been split for houses; trees were hollowed out for canoes; and smaller pieces of wood were made into paddles. The canoes presumably were built for travel and perhaps for fishing on the lakes and rivers that abounded in the postglacial environment.

We do not know to what extent the Maglemosians relied on wild plant foods, but there were a lot of different kinds available, such as hazelnuts. We do know, however, many other things about the Maglemosians' way of life. Although fishing was fairly important, as suggested by the frequent occurrence of bones from pike and other fish, as well as fishhooks, these people apparently depended mainly on hunting for food. Game included elk, wild ox, deer, and wild pig. In addition to many fishing implements and the adzes and axes, the Maglemosians' tool kit included the bow and arrow. Some of their tools were ornamented with finely engraved designs. Ornamentation independent of tools also appears in amber and stone pendants and small figurines representing, for example, the head of an elk.[117]

Like the Maglemosian finds, many of the European post–Upper Paleolithic sites are along lakes, rivers, and oceanfronts. But these sites probably were not inhabited year-round; there is evidence that at least some groups moved seasonally from one place of settlement to another, perhaps between the coast and inland areas.[118] Finds such as kitchen *middens* (piles of shells) that centuries of post–Upper Paleolithic seafood eaters had discarded, and the remains of fishing equipment, canoes, and boats indicate that these people depended much more heavily on fishing than had their ancestors in Upper Paleolithic times.

The Archaic Cultures of Eastern North America

A related set of adaptations to the changing environment can be seen among the peoples who inhabited eastern North America at the end of the ice age. As the climate became warmer and drier, the flora and fauna of North America changed. Megafauna, as elsewhere in the world, went extinct, and were replaced by smaller mammals, particularly deer. The availability of meat was greatly reduced—hunters could count on coming home with pounds, not tons, of meat. Warmer-adapted plants replaced cold-adapted plants, and

Some examples of Archaic ground stone woodworking tools from eastern North America (wooden handles are reproductions). Archaic peoples apparently used wood more extensively than the Paleo-Indians.

were used for food to replace the meat that was no longer available. Warmer-adapted plants had advantages as food resources for humans over cold-adapted ones because edible seeds, fruits, and nuts were more common, and often more plentiful and accessible, on the warmer-adapted plants. Thus, the Archaic peoples came to use a much greater diversity of plants and animals.[119]

The Archaic peoples of North America, like the Maglemosian peoples in Europe, began to follow a more sedentary lifestyle. Two forms of Archaic settlement appear to have been typical. One was a residential base camp, which would have been inhabited seasonally by several, probably related, families. The other was a special-purpose camp, which would have been a short-term habitation near a particular resource or perhaps used by a group of hunters for a short period of time.[120] On the Atlantic coast, for example, individual groups apparently moved seasonally along major river valleys, establishing summer base camps in the piedmont and winter camps near the coast. Special-purpose camps were created year-round as groups went out from the base camp to hunt and collect particular resources, such as stone for making tools.[121]

One of the innovations of the Archaic peoples was the development of ground stone woodworking tools. Axes, adzes, and tools for grinding seeds and nuts become more and more common in the tool kit.[122] This probably reflects the emergence of greater areas of forest following the retreat of the glaciers from North America, but it also demonstrates a greater reliance on forest products and, most likely, a greater use of wood and wood products. Fish and shellfish also came to be relied upon in some areas, and this too reflects the adjustment made by the Archaic peoples to the changing conditions they faced at the end of the last ice age.

The innovation of most lasting importance in both the New and Old Worlds, however, was the development of domesticated plants and animals. In both parts of the world, peoples at the end of the ice age began to experiment with plants. By around 14,000 years ago in the Old World, and 10,000 years ago in the New World, some species had been domesticated. While hunting and gathering did not disappear, the domestication of plants and animals became more important in the next period of cultural history, the Neolithic.

Summary and Review

The Transition from *Homo erectus* to *Homo sapiens*

7.1 Discuss the anatomical characteristics of the Neandertals and the relationship between Neandertals and *Homo sapiens*.

- Most anthropologists agree that *Homo erectus* began to evolve into *Homo sapiens* after about 500,000 years ago, but do not agree about how and when the transition occurred.

- The mixed traits of the transitional fossils include large cranial capacities (well within the range of modern humans), together with low foreheads and large browridges, which are characteristic of *H. erectus* specimens.

- Some scholars have suggested that the "transitional" fossils share common traits and may actually represent a separate species—*Homo heidelbergensis*.

- The Neandertals, genetically distinct from modern humans, evolved in Europe by about 200,000 years ago. They were robust, with large brains and faces, and had a complex culture that used sophisticated stone tools and practiced possibly complex ritual behavior.

- The earliest definite *H. sapiens,* who did not look completely like modern humans, appeared about 160,000 years ago.

- *Homo sapiens* have been found in many parts of the Old World—in Africa and Asia as well as in Europe.

 What is the likely relationship between Neandertals and modern humans?

Middle Paleolithic Cultures

7.2 Describe the features of Middle Paleolithic cultures.

- The period of cultural history associated with the Neandertals is traditionally called the Middle Paleolithic in Europe and the Near East and dates from about 300,000 years to about 40,000 years ago.

- Assemblages of flake tools from this period are referred to as Mousterian (Europe, Near East) and as post-Acheulian (Africa). A Mousterian assemblage proportionally has fewer large hand axes and cleavers and more small flake tools than an Acheulian assemblage.

- Middle Paleolithic humans lived at least part of the year in caves and seem to have relied more on fire than earlier species. Some Mousterian sites show signs of intentional burial.

 What features are common among Middle Paleolithic cultures?

The Denisovans

7.3 Explain the relationship of Denisovans to Neandertals and modern humans.

- The Denisovans are known from a handful of skeletal fragments found at a single site in southern Siberia.

- DNA recovered from those fragments revealed that they belonged to a unique species of hominin that had interbred with modern humans and contributed some of its DNA to us.

 Who were the Denisovans?

The Emergence of Modern Humans

7.4 Explain theories about the origins of modern humans and how they differed from earlier species.

- Modern-looking humans differed from the Neandertals and other early *H. sapiens* in that they had higher, more bulging foreheads, thinner and lighter bones, smaller faces and jaws, chins, and only slight browridges (or no ridges at all).

- Anthropologists continue to debate three theories about the origins of modern humans: the single-origin theory, the multiregional theory, and the assimilation theory.

 Which of the three theories about the origins of modern humans is most widely supported and why?

What Happened to the Neandertals?

7.5 Evaluate competing scenarios for the disappearance of Neandertals.

- The area inhabited by Neandertals shrunk after about 60,000 years ago, and by about 30,000 years ago, Neandertals had disappeared.

- Neandertals probably became extinct because they could not compete with modern humans, who were more efficient hunters and gatherers.

 What are the competing scenarios for the disappearance of Neandertals?

The Upper Paleolithic World

7.6 Describe the environment of the Upper Paleolithic world.

- The period of cultural history known as the Upper Paleolithic in Europe, the Near East, and Asia or the Later Stone Age in Africa dates from about 40,000 years ago to about 14,000–10,000 years ago.

- An ice age dominated this period. Glaciers covered much of northern Europe and North America, and annual temperatures reached 50 degrees Fahrenheit

(10 degrees Celsius) below today's temperatures. North Africa was much wetter than today and South Asia, drier.

How did Ice-age conditions during the Upper Paleolithic period affect the environment globally?

Upper Paleolithic Europe

7.7 Describe Upper Paleolithic tools and cultures in Europe.

- The Upper Paleolithic tool kit is characterized by the preponderance of blades; there were also burins, bone and antler tools, and (later) microliths.

- In many respects, Upper Paleolithic lifestyles were similar to lifestyles before. People were still mainly hunters, gatherers, and fishers who probably lived in highly mobile bands. They made their camps out in the open and in caves and rock shelters.

- This period is also characterized by a variety of new developments: new tool making techniques, evidence of trade among groups, the emergence of art, population growth, and new inventions such as the bow and arrow, the spear thrower (atlatl), and the harpoon.

How did the emergence of art suggest that language might also have been developing during the Upper Paleolithic?

Upper Paleolithic Cultures in Africa and Asia

7.8 Describe Upper Paleolithic migration from Africa to Asia.

- Upper Paleolithic peoples spread throughout the world. The first Upper Paleolithic cultures are found in Africa about 60,000 years ago, but had spread to South and East Asia by about 50,000 years ago and to New Guinea and Australia by about 40,000 years ago.

- In North Africa Upper Paleolithic peoples hunted large animals on grasslands. They lived in small communities located within easy access to water and other resources and moved regularly, probably to follow the animal herds. Trade took place between local groups.

- In South Asia, peoples developed an increasingly sedentary lifestyle along the banks of freshwater streams.

How did the Upper Paleolithic cultures of Europe, Africa, and Asia differ?

The Earliest Humans and Their Cultures in the New World

7.9 Evaluate scenarios for the migration of humans into the New World.

- The earliest remains of people in North America date to about 14,000 years ago. Migrations of humans to the New World took place some time after the emergence of *H. sapiens*.

- The prevailing opinion is that humans migrated to the New World over a land bridge between Siberia and Alaska in the area of what is now the Bering Strait, or by boat along the Alaskan coast.

- By about 11,000 years ago, there were many people living in both North and South America.

- The Clovis people created unique projectile points that have a single long flake, or "flute" knocked from their base to thin them and make them easy to haft. They lived by hunting big game animals, especially bison and mammoth.

- Paleo-Indians had diverse ways of life, some hunting and following herds, some relying on fish and shellfish, and others developing semi-sedentary riverine communities.

What were the basic features of Paleo-Indian life?

The End of the Upper Paleolithic

7.10 Relate the end of the Upper Paleolithic to climate change and the development of Maglemosian culture.

- At the end of the ice age, around 14,000 years ago, the climate began to become more temperate. Many large animals that Upper Paleolithic peoples relied upon for food went extinct, and at the same time new, warmer-adapted plants provided a rich, new food source.

- Evidence from the Maglemosian culture of northern Europe shows adaptations from big game hunting to reliance on smaller animal food sources.

Maglemosians used stone tools to chop down trees and use the wood for shelter and canoes.

- Around the world, people began to use more plant foods and a broader range of resources overall. In many parts of the world, people began experimenting with domesticating plants and animals as they began to follow a more sedentary lifestyle.

 How did climate change at the end of the Upper Paleolithic period lead to other cultural changes?

Think on it

1. If the single-origin or "out-of-Africa" theory were correct, by what mechanisms could **Homo sapiens** have been able to replace *Homo erectus* and *Homo neandertalensis* populations?

2. If modern human traits emerged in **Homo erectus populations** in different areas more or less at the same time, what mechanisms would account for similar traits emerging in different regions?

3. How do **Middle Paleolithic** cultures differ from **Lower Paleolithic** cultures?

4. What is the significance of differences between Middle Paleolithic and Upper Paleolithic **tools** in terms of human culture?

5. What factors might have led humans to **colonize** the New World?

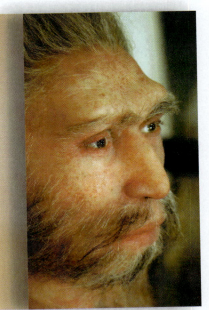

Food Production and the Rise of States

LEARNING OBJECTIVES

8.1 Explain the relationship between broad-spectrum collecting, sedentarism, and population growth in terms of preagricultural developments.

8.2 Discuss the domestication of plants and animals in the Near East, Mesoamerica, and elsewhere in the world.

8.3 Evaluate theories for why food production developed.

8.4 Critically analyze the consequences of food production.

8.5 Explain how archaeologists infer that a particular people in the past had social classes, cities, or a centralized government.

8.6 Describe the emergence of cities and states in southern Iraq.

8.7 Describe the emergence of cities and states in Mesoamerica.

8.8 Describe the first cities and states in other areas of the world.

8.9 Evaluate the major theories about the origin of the state.

8.10 Identify and explain consequences of state formation.

8.11 Discuss explanations for the decline and collapse of states.

eginning about 14,000 years ago, people in some regions began to depend less on big game hunting and more on relatively stationary food resources, such as fish, shellfish, small game, and wild plants (see Figure 8.1). In some areas, particularly Europe and the Near East, the exploitation of local, relatively permanent resources may account for an increasingly settled way of life. The cultural period in which these developments took place is usually now called the **Epipaleolithic** in the Near East and the **Mesolithic** in Europe. Other areas of the world show a similar switch to what is called *broad-spectrum* food-collecting, but they do not always show an increasingly settled lifestyle, as, for example, in Mesoamerica where this period is called the **Archaic**.

We see the first clear evidence of a changeover to **food production**—the cultivation and domestication of plants and animals—in the Near East, about 8000 B.C.[1] This shift, called the *Neolithic revolution* by archaeologist V. Gordon Childe, occurred, probably independently, in other areas of the Old and New Worlds within the next few thousand years. In the Old World, there were independent centers of domestication in China, Southeast Asia (what is now Malaysia, Thailand, Cambodia, Vietnam, and New Guinea), and Africa around 6000 B.C.[2] In the New World, there were centers of cultivation and domestication in the highlands of Mesoamerica (about 7000 B.C.), the central Andes around Peru (about 7000 B.C.), and the Eastern Woodlands of North America (about 2000 B.C., but perhaps earlier).[3] Most of the world's major food plants and animals were domesticated well before 2000 B.C. Also developed by that time were techniques of plowing, fertilizing, fallowing, and irrigation.[4] Figure 8.2 shows the regions of the world that domesticated today's main food crops.

In this chapter, after discussing preagricultural developments, we turn to what is believed about the origins of food production and settled life, called **sedentarism**—how and why people in different places may have come to cultivate and domesticate plants and animals (referred to as **agriculture**) and to live in permanent villages. Then we discuss

Epipaleolithic Time period during which food production first developed in the Near East.

Mesolithic The archaeological period in the Old World beginning about 12,000 B.C. Humans were starting to settle down in semipermanent camps and villages, as people began to depend less on big game (which they used to have to follow over long distances) and more on relatively stationary food resources such as fish, shellfish, small game, and wild plants rich in carbohydrates, proteins, and oils.

Archaic Time period in the New World during which food production first developed.

Food production The form of subsistence technology in which food-getting is dependent on the cultivation and domestication of plants and animals.

Sedentarism Settled life.

Agriculture The practice of raising domesticated crops.

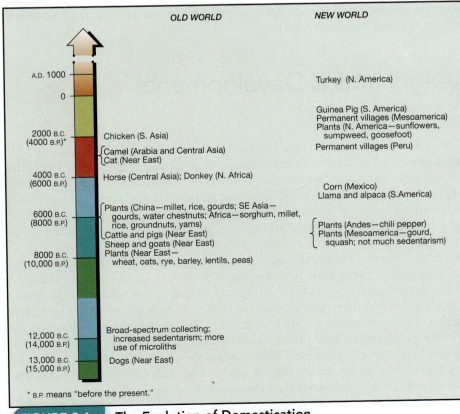

FIGURE 8.1   The Evolution of Domestication

Source: Dates for animal domestication are from Clutton-Brock 1992.

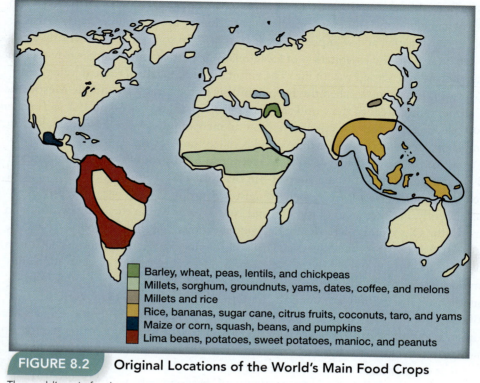

Barley, wheat, peas, lentils, and chickpeas
Millets, sorghum, groundnuts, yams, dates, coffee, and melons
Millets and rice
Rice, bananas, sugar cane, citrus fruits, coconuts, taro, and yams
Maize or corn, squash, beans, and pumpkins
Lima beans, potatoes, sweet potatoes, manioc, and peanuts

FIGURE 8.2   **Original Locations of the World's Main Food Crops**
The world's main food crops were originally domesticated in different regions.
Source: Hole 1992.

the origins of cities and states. Much of our discussion focuses on the Middle East and Mesoamerica, the areas we know best archaeologically for the developments leading to food production and the rise of states.

Preagricultural Developments

8.1 Explain the relationship between broad-spectrum collecting, sedentarism, and population growth in terms of preagricultural developments.

The Middle East

In the Near East, there seems to have been a shift from mobile big game hunting to the utilization of a broad spectrum of natural resources at the end of the Upper Paleolithic.[5] There is evidence that people subsisted on a variety of resources, including fish, mollusks, and other water life; wild deer, sheep, and goats; and wild grains, nuts, and legumes.[6] The increased utilization of stationary food sources such as wild grain may partly explain why some people in the Near East began to lead more sedentary lives during the Epipaleolithic.

Even today, a traveler passing through the Anatolian highlands of Turkey and other mountainous regions in the Near East may see thick stands of wild wheat and barley growing as densely as if they had been cultivated.[7] Wielding flint sickles, Epipaleolithic people could easily have harvested a bountiful crop from such wild stands. Just how productive these resources can be was demonstrated in a field experiment duplicating prehistoric conditions. Using the kind of flint-blade sickle an Epipaleolithic worker would have used, researchers were able to harvest a little over two pounds of wild grain in an hour. A family of four, working only during the few weeks of the harvest season, probably could have reaped more wheat and barley than they needed for the entire year.[8]

The amount of wild wheat harvested in the experiment prompted Kent Flannery to conclude, "Such a harvest would almost necessitate some degree of sedentism—after all, where could they go with an estimated metric ton of clean wheat?"[9] Moreover, the stone

Nahal Mearot Cave on Mount Carmel, Israel, showing Paleolithic life in the cave. Epipaleolithic peoples built small shelters and lived sendentary life here.

equipment used for grinding would have been a clumsy burden to carry. Part of the harvest would probably have been set aside for immediate consumption, ground, and then cooked either by roasting or boiling. The rest of the harvest would have been stored to supply food for the remainder of the year. A grain diet, then, could have been the impetus for the construction of roasters, grinders, and storage pits by some preagricultural people, as well as for the construction of solid, fairly permanent housing. Once a village was built, people may have been reluctant to abandon it. We can visualize the earliest preagricultural settlements clustered around such naturally rich regions, as archaeological evidence indeed suggests they were.

The Natufians of the Middle East Eleven thousand years ago, the Natufians, a people living in the area that is now Israel and Jordan, inhabited caves and rock shelters and built villages on the slopes of Mount Carmel in Israel. At the front of their rock shelters, they hollowed out basin-shaped depressions in the rock, possibly for storage pits. For example, the site of Eynan contains the remains of three villages in sequence, one atop another. Each village consisted of about 50 circular *pit houses*. The floor of each house was sunk a few feet into the ground, so that the walls of the house consisted partly of earth, below ground level, and partly of stone, above ground level. The villages appear to have had stone-paved walks; circular stone pavements ringed with what seem to be permanent hearths; and the dead were interred in village cemeteries.

The tools suggest that the Natufians harvested wild grain intensively. Sickles recovered from their villages have a specific sheen, which experiments have shown to be the effect of flint striking grass stems, as the sickles would have been used in the cutting of grain. The Natufians are the earliest Epipaleolithic people known to have stored surplus crops. Beneath the floors of their stone-walled houses, they constructed plastered storage pits. The remains of many wild animals are found in Natufian sites; Natufians appear to have concentrated on hunting gazelle, which they would take by surrounding whole herds.[10]

The Natufians show many differences as compared with foragers in earlier periods.[11] Not only was Natufian foraging based on a more intensive use of stationary resources such as wild grain, but the archaeological evidence suggests increasing social complexity. Natufian sites on the average were five times larger than those of their predecessors. Communities were occupied for most of the year, if not year-round. Burial patterns suggest more social differences between people. Although the available wild cereal resources appear to have enabled the Natufians to live in relatively permanent villages, their diet seems to have suffered. Their tooth enamel shows signs of nutritional deficiency, and their stature declined over time.[12]

Mesoamerica

A similar shift toward more broad-spectrum hunting and gathering occurred in the New World at the end of the Paleo-Indian period, about 10,000 years ago. The retreat of glacial ice from North America and overall warmer and wetter climate brought dramatic changes to plant and animal communities throughout North America and Mesoamerica. Pleistocene megafauna, such as mammoths, mastodon, rhinoceros, giant ground sloth, and others, as well as a variety of smaller game animals, such as the horse, all went extinct in a relatively short period of time.[13] Hunting strategies shifted toward a broader range of game species, particularly deer, antelope, bison, and small mammals. At the same time, deciduous woodlands and grasslands expanded, providing a range of new plants to exploit. Ground stone woodworking tools such as axes and adzes first appeared, as did nut-processing tools such as mortars and pestles. Shellfish began to be exploited in some areas. Throughout North America and Mesoamerica, people began to expand the range of plants and animals they relied upon.[14]

The Archaic Peoples of Highland Mesoamerica   In Highland Mesoamerica, the mountainous regions of central and southern Mexico, we also see a shift from big game hunting to a broader use of resources, in part due to a change in climate more like today's. Altitude became an important factor in the hunting and collecting regime, as different altitudes have different plant and animal resources. Valleys tend to have scrubby, grassland vegetation, whereas foothills and mountains have "thorn forests" of cactuses and succulents, giving way to oak and pine forests at higher altitudes, where there is more moisture. This vertical zonation means that a wide range of plants and animals were available in relatively close proximity—different environments were close by—and the Archaic peoples took advantage of these varied conditions to hunt and collect a broad range of resources.[15]

About 8,000 years ago, the Archaic peoples in Mesoamerica appear to have moved seasonally between communities of two different sizes: camps with 15 to 30 residents (*macrobands*) and camps with only 2 to 5 residents (*microbands*). Macroband camps were located near seasonally abundant resources, such as acorns or mesquite pods. Several families would have come together when these resources were in season, both to take advantage of them and to work together to harvest them while they were plentiful, perhaps to perform rituals, and simply to socialize. Microband camps were also inhabited seasonally, probably by a single family, when groups were not assembled into macroband camps. Remains of these microband camps are often found in caves or rock shelters from which a variety of environments could be exploited by moving either upslope or downslope from the campsite.[16] Unlike the Natufians of the Near East, there is no evidence of social differences among the Archaic peoples of Highland Mesoamerica.

Other Areas

The still-sparse archaeological record suggests that such a change occurred in Southeast Asia, which may have been one of the important centers of original plant and animal domestication.[17] For example, at inland base camps, we find the remains of animals from high mountain ridges as well as lowland river valleys, birds and primates from nearby forests, bats from caves, and fish from streams. The few coastal sites indicate that many kinds of fish and shellfish were collected and that animals such as deer, wild cattle, and rhinoceros were hunted.[18] The preagricultural developments in Southeast Asia probably were responses to changes in the climate and environment, including a warming trend, more moisture, and a higher sea level.[19]

In Africa, too, the preagricultural period was marked by a warmer, wetter environment. The now-numerous lakes, rivers, and other bodies of water provided fish, shellfish, and other resources that apparently allowed people to settle more permanently than they had before. For example, there were lakes in what is now the southern and central Sahara Desert, where people fished and hunted hippopotamuses and crocodiles. This pattern of broad-spectrum food-collecting seems also to have been characteristic of the areas both south and north of the Sahara.[20] One area showing increased sedentarism is the Dakhleh Oasis in the Western Desert of Egypt. Between 9,000 years and 8,500 years ago, the inhabitants lived in circular stone huts on the shores of rivers and lakes. Bone harpoons and pottery are found there and in other areas from the Nile Valley through the central and southern Sahara westward to what is now Mali. Fishing seems to have allowed people to remain along the rivers and lakes for much of the year.[21]

Why Did Broad-Spectrum Collecting Develop?

It is apparent that the preagricultural switch to broad-spectrum collecting was fairly common throughout the world. Climate change was probably at least partly responsible for the exploitation of new sources of food. For example, the worldwide rise in sea level because of glacial melting may have increased the availability of fish and shellfish. Changes in climate may have also been partly responsible for the decline in the availability of big game, particularly the large herd animals.[22] Another possible cause of that decline was human activity, specifically overkilling of some of these animals.[23] The extinction in the New World of many of the large Pleistocene animals, such as the mammoth, coincided with the movement of humans from the Bering Strait region into the Americas.[24] But an enormous number of bird species also became extinct during the last few thousand years of the North American Pleistocene, and it is difficult to argue that human hunters caused all of those extinctions. Because the bird and mammal extinctions occurred simultaneously, it is likely that most or nearly all the extinctions were due to climatic and other environmental changes.[25] Then again, the example of the New Zealand moas, which went extinct soon after humans colonized the islands, may be instructive. Moas had low reproductive rates; computer simulations suggest their population would have been very sensitive to increases in adult mortality. Because many large animals have low reproductive rates like moas, human overhunting may have been responsible for their extinction.[26]

Population growth may also have led to broad-spectrum collecting. As Mark Cohen has noted, hunter-gatherers were "filling up" the world, and they may have had to seek new, possibly less desirable sources of food.[27] We might think of shellfish as more desirable than mammoths, but only because we don't have to do the work to get such food. A lot of shellfish have to be collected, shelled, and cooked to produce the amount of animal protein obtainable from one large animal.

Broad-spectrum collecting does not necessarily mean that people were eating better. A decline in stature often indicates a poorer diet. During the preagricultural period, height apparently declined by as much as two inches in many parts of the Old World (Greece, Israel, India, and northern and western Europe).[28] In other areas of the world, such as Australia and what is now the midwestern United States, skeletal evidence also suggests a decline in the general level of health with the rise of broad-spectrum collecting.[29]

Broad-Spectrum Collecting and Sedentarism

Does the switch to broad-spectrum collecting explain the increasingly sedentary way of life we see in various parts of the world in preagricultural times? The answer seems to be both yes and no. In some areas of the world—some sites in Europe, the Near East, Africa, and Peru—settlements became more permanent. In other areas, such as the semiarid highlands of Mesoamerica, the switch to broad-spectrum collecting was not associated with increasing sedentarism. Even after the Highland Mesoamericans began to cultivate plants, they still did not live in permanent villages.[30] Why?

It would seem that it is not simply the switch to broad-spectrum collecting that accounts for increasing sedentarism in many areas. Rather, a comparison of settlements on the Peruvian coast suggests that the more permanent settlements were located nearer, within 3½ miles, to most, if not all, of the diverse food resources exploited during the year. The community that did not have a year-round settlement seems to have depended on more widely distributed resources. What accounts for sedentarism may thus be the nearness[31] or the high reliability and yield[32] of the broad-spectrum resources, rather than the broad spectrum itself.

Sedentarism and Population Growth

Although some population growth undoubtedly occurred throughout the hunting and gathering phase of world history, some anthropologists have suggested that populations would have increased dramatically when people began to settle down.

The settling down of a nomadic group may reduce the typical spacing between births.[33] Nomadic San people of Namibia and Botswana have children spaced four years apart on the average; in contrast, recently sedentarized San have children about three years apart. Why might birth spacing change with settling down? If effective contraceptives are not available, prolonged sexual abstinence after the birth of a child (the postpartum sex taboo), common in recent human societies, may be one way of reducing births. Another way is abortion or infanticide.[34] Nomadic groups may be motivated to have children farther apart because of the problem of carrying small children.

Although some nomadic groups may have deliberately spaced births by abstinence or infanticide, there is no evidence that such practices explain why four years separate births among nomadic San. There may be another explanation, involving an unintended effect of how babies are fed. Nancy Howell and Richard Lee have suggested that the presence of baby foods other than mother's milk may be responsible for the decreased birth spacing in sedentary agricultural San groups.[35] It is now well established that the longer a mother nurses her baby without supplementary foods, the longer it is likely to be before she starts ovulating again. Nomadic San women have little to give their babies in the way of soft, digestible food, and the babies depend largely on mother's milk for two to three years. But sedentary San mothers can give their babies soft foods such as cereal (made from

A group of !Kung women heading out to collect plant foods. On some days, women will walk several miles to find the plants they want to harvest. Spacing births an average of four years apart helps to ensure that a woman will not have to carry more than one child at a time.

cultivated grain) and milk from domesticated animals. Such changes in feeding practices may shorten birth spacing by shortening the interval between birth and the resumption of ovulation. In preagricultural sedentary communities, it is possible that baby foods made from wild grains might have had the same effect. For this reason alone, therefore, populations may have grown even before people started to farm or herd.

Some investigators suspect that a critical minimum of fat in the body may be necessary for ovulation. A sedentary San woman may have more fatty tissue than a nomadic San woman, who walks many miles daily to gather wild plant foods, often carrying a child with her. Thus, sedentary San women might resume ovulating sooner after the birth of a baby, and so for that reason alone may be likely to have more closely spaced children. If some critical amount of fat is necessary for ovulation, that would explain why many women who have little body fat in our own society—long-distance runners, gymnasts, and ballet dancers are examples—do not ovulate regularly.[36]

The Domestication of Plants and Animals

Neolithic means "of the new stone age"; the term originally signified the cultural stage in which humans invented pottery and ground-stone tools. We now know, however, that both were present in earlier times, so now archaeologists generally define the **Neolithic** in terms of the presence of domesticated plants and animals. In this type of culture, people began to produce food rather than merely collect it.

The line between food-collecting and food-producing occurs when people begin to plant crops and to keep and breed animals. How do we know when this transition occurred? In fact, archaeologically we do not see the beginning of food production; we can see signs of it only after plants and animals show differences from their wild varieties. When people plant crops, we refer to the process as cultivation. It is only when the crops cultivated and the animals raised are *modified*—different from wild varieties—that we speak of plant and animal **domestication.**

We know, in a particular site, that domestication occurred if plant remains have characteristics different from those of wild plants of the same types. For example, wild grains of barley and wheat have a fragile **rachis**—the seed-bearing part of the stem—which shatters easily, releasing the seeds. Domesticated grains have a tough rachis, which does not shatter easily. In addition, the grain of wild barley and wheat has a tough shell protecting the seed from premature exposure, whereas domesticated grain has a brittle shell that can be easily separated, which facilitates preparing the seed for grinding into flour.

Consider how the rachis of wheat and barley may have changed. When humans arrived with sickles and flails to collect the wild stands of grain, the seeds harvested probably contained a high proportion of tough-rachis mutants, because these could best withstand the rough treatment of harvest processing. If planted, the harvested seeds would be likely to produce tough-rachis plants. If, in each successive harvest, seeds from tough-rachis plants were the least likely to be lost, tough-rachis plants would come to predominate.[37]

Domesticated species of animals also differ from the wild varieties. For example, the horns of wild goats in the Near East are shaped differently from those of domesticated goats.[38]

Domestication in the Near East

For some time, most archaeologists have thought that the Fertile Crescent (see Figure 8.3), the arc of land stretching up from Israel and the Jordan Valley through southern Turkey and then downward to the western slopes of the Zagros Mountains in Iran, was one of the earliest centers of plant and animal domestication. We know that several varieties of domesticated wheat were being grown there after about 8000 B.C., as were oats, rye, barley, lentils, peas, and various fruits and nuts (apricots, pears, pomegranates, dates, figs, olives, almonds, and pistachios).[39] It appears that animals were first domesticated in the Near East. Dogs were first domesticated before the rise of agriculture, around 13,000 B.C.; goats, sheep, cattle, and pigs around 7000 B.C., and perhaps even earlier.[40]

8.2 Discuss the domestication of plants and animals in the Near East, Mesoamerica, and elsewhere in the world.

Neolithic Originally meaning "of the new stone age," now meaning the presence of domesticated plants and animals. The earliest evidence of domestication comes from the Near East about 8000 B.C.

Domestication Modification or adaptation of plants and animals for use by humans. When people plant crops, we refer to the process as cultivation. It is only when the crops cultivated and the animals raised have been modified—are different from wild varieties—that we speak of plant and animal domestication.

Rachis The seed-bearing part of a plant. In the wild variety of grain, the rachis shatters easily, releasing the seeds. Domesticated grains have a tough rachis, which does not shatter easily.

FIGURE 8.3   **Early Agricultural Settlements in the Near East**

Modern cities are represented by a dot, early settlements by a square. The yellow color indicates the area known as the Fertile Crescent.

Ali Kosh   At the stratified site of Ali Kosh in what is now southwestern Iran (see Figure 8.3), we see the remains of a community that started out about 7500 B.C., living mostly on wild plants and animals. Over the next 2,000 years, until about 5500 B.C., agriculture and herding became increasingly important. After 5500 B.C., we see the appearance of two innovations—irrigation and the use of domesticated cattle—that seem to have stimulated a minor population explosion during the following millennium.

From 7500 to 6750 B.C., the people at Ali Kosh cut little slabs of raw clay out of the ground to build small, multiroom structures. There is evidence that the people at Ali Kosh may have moved for the summer (with their goats) to the grassier mountain valleys nearby, which were just a few days' walk away.

We have a lot of evidence about what the people at Ali Kosh ate. They got some of their food from cultivated emmer wheat and a kind of barley and a considerable amount from domesticated goats. We know the goats were domesticated because wild goats do not seem to have lived in the area. Also, the fact that virtually no bones from elderly goats were found in the site suggests that the goats were domesticated and herded rather than hunted. Moreover, it would seem from the horn cores found in the site that mostly young male goats were eaten, so the females probably were kept for breeding and milking. But with all these signs of deliberate food production, there is an enormous amount of evidence—literally tens of thousands of seeds and bone fragments—that the people at the beginning of Ali Kosh depended mostly on wild plants (legumes and grasses) and wild animals (including gazelles, wild oxen, and wild pigs). They also collected fish, such as carp and catfish, and shellfish, such as mussels, as well as waterfowl that visited the area during part of the year.

The flint tools used during this earliest phase at Ali Kosh were varied and abundant. Finds from this period include tens of thousands of tiny flint blades, some only a few millimeters wide. About 1 percent of the chipped stone that archaeologists found was **obsidian,** or volcanic glass, which came from what is now eastern Turkey, several hundred miles away. Thus, the people at Ali Kosh during its earliest phase definitely had some kind of contact with people elsewhere.

From 6750 to 6000 B.C., the people increased their consumption of cultivated food plants; 40 percent of the seed remains in the hearths and refuse areas were now from emmer wheat and barley. The proportion of the diet coming from wild plants was much reduced, probably because the cultivated plants have the same growing season and grow in the same kind of soil as the wild plants. Grazing by the goats and sheep that were kept may also have contributed to the reduction of wild plant foods in the area and in the diet. The village may or may not have grown larger, but the multiroom houses definitely had. The rooms were now larger than 10 feet by 10 feet; the walls were much thicker; and a mud mortar now held the clay-slab bricks together. Also, the walls now often had a coat of smooth mud plaster on both sides. There were courtyards with domed brick ovens and brick-lined roasting pits.

Even though the village probably contained no more than 100 individuals, it participated in an extensive trading network. Seashells were probably obtained from the Persian Gulf, which is some distance to the south; copper may have come from what is now central Iran; obsidian was still coming from eastern Turkey; and turquoise somehow made its way from what is now the border between Iran and Afghanistan. Some of these materials were used as ornaments worn by both sexes—or so it seems from the remains of bodies found buried under the floors of houses.

After about 5500 B.C., the area around Ali Kosh began to show signs of a much larger population, apparently made possible by a more complex agriculture employing irrigation and plows drawn by domesticated cattle. In the next thousand years, by 4500 B.C., the population of the area probably tripled. This population growth was apparently part of the cultural developments that culminated in the rise of urban civilizations in the Near East.[41]

Domestication in Mesoamerica

A very different pattern of domestication is seen in Mesoamerica. Here the seminomadic Archaic hunting and gathering lifestyle persisted long after people first domesticated plants.[42] People sowed a variety of plants, but after doing so, they went on with their seasonal rounds of hunting and gathering, and came back later to harvest what they had sown. Domestication may have been a way for Archaic peoples to make desirable plants more common in their environment. For example, one of the first domesticates was the bottle gourd. These were not eaten but were used to carry water. Joyce Marcus and Kent Flannery hypothesize that people deliberately domesticated the bottle gourd by planting them in areas where they did not grow naturally, so that as groups moved through those areas, they always had access to gourds for carrying water.[43]

Other domesticates include tomatoes, cotton, a variety of beans and squashes, and, perhaps most importantly, maize. The earliest domesticated form of maize (corn), dating from about 5000 B.C., has been found in Tehuacán, Mexico. Genetic studies of maize show that it was domesticated from teosinte, a tall wild grass that still grows widely in Mexico.[44] Indeed, these genetic studies suggest that changes occurred in only two genes, one related to the kernel glumes (outer casing), and one related to the stalk shape.[45] The genes of modern corn were already established 4,000 to 6,000 years ago.

Early maize was quite different from modern maize. The oldest maize cobs—dating to about 7,000 years ago—are tiny, only about an inch long. They have only a half-dozen rows of seeds, and each seed is tiny. Maize is almost completely dependent on humans to reproduce—the shift from seeds with brittle coats to cobs with a tough husk meant that someone had to open the husk without damaging the seeds for them to be dispersed and reproduce.[46]

People who lived in Mesoamerica, Mexico, and Central America are often credited with the invention of planting maize, beans, and squash together in the same field. This planting strategy provides some important advantages. Maize takes nitrogen from the soil; beans, like all legumes, put nitrogen back into the soil. The maize stalk provides a natural pole for

Obsidian A volcanic glass that can be used to make mirrors or sharp-edged tools.

the bean plant to twine around, and the low-growing squash can grow around the base of the tall maize plant. Beans supply people with the amino acid lysine, which is missing in maize. Thus, maize and beans together provide all the essential amino acids that humans need to obtain from their food. Teosinte may have provided the model for this unique combination, as wild runner beans and wild squash occur naturally where teosinte grows.[47]

Domestication Elsewhere in the World

South America and the Eastern United States Outside of Mesoamerica, evidence of independent domestication of plants comes from at least two areas in the New World: South America and the eastern United States. The first plants to be domesticated in the New World were members of the cucurbit family, including the bottle gourd and a variety of squashes, all probably domesticated some time after 7500 B.C.. In addition to these and other plants domesticated in Mesoamerica, we can trace more than 200 domesticated plants to the Andes in South America, including potatoes, lima beans, peanuts, amaranth, and quinoa (see the box feature on "Raised Field Agriculture"). The first clear domesticates were squashes and gourds, which may date back to 8000 B.C., which makes domestication in the Andes as old as in Mesoamerica, and perhaps even older.[48] The origins of the root crops manioc and sweet potato are less certain, but those crops probably originated in lowland tropical forest regions of South America.[49]

Many of the plants grown in North America, such as corn, beans, and squash, were apparently introduced from Mesoamerica. But at least three seed plants were probably domesticated independently in North America at an earlier time—sunflowers, sumpweed, and goosefoot. Sunflowers and sumpweed contain seeds that are highly nutritious in terms of protein and fat; goosefoot is high in starch and similar to corn in food value.[50] Sumpweed is an unusually good source of calcium, rivaled only by greens, mussels, and bones. It is also a very good source of iron (better than beef liver) and thiamine.[51] These plants may have been cultivated in the area of Kentucky, Tennessee, and southern Illinois beginning around 2000 B.C. (Corn was introduced about A.D. 200.)

On the whole, domestic animals were less important economically in the New World than they were in many parts of the Old World. The central Andes was the only part of the New World where animals were a significant part of the economy. Used for meat, transportation, and wool, llamas and alpacas (members of the camel family) were domesticated as early as 5000 B.C. in the Andes.[52] Guinea pigs, misnamed because they are neither pigs nor from Guinea, are rodents that were domesticated in the Andes sometime later. They were an important source of food even before domestication.[53] Since they were domesticated, they have been raised in people's dwellings.

Animal domestication in the New World differed from that in the Old World because different wild species were found in the two hemispheres. The Old World plains and forests were the homes for the wild ancestors of the cattle, sheep, goats, pigs, and horses we know today. In the New World, the Pleistocene herds of horses, mastodons, mammoths, and other large animals were long extinct, allowing few opportunities for domestication of large animals.[54]

East Asia The earliest clear evidence of cereal cultivation outside the Near East is from China. Late in the 6th millennium B.C. in northern China, there were sites where foxtail millet was cultivated. Storage pits, storage pots, and large numbers of grinding stones suggest that millet was an enormously important item in the diet. The wild animal bones and the hunting and fishing tools that have been found suggest that people still depended on hunting and fishing somewhat, even though domesticated pigs (as well as dogs) were present. In southern China, from about the same time, archaeologists have found a village by the edge of a small lake where people cultivated rice, bottle gourds, water chestnuts, and the datelike fruit called jujube. The people in southern China also raised water buffalo, pigs, and dogs. And, as in the northern China sites, some of their food came from hunting and fishing.[55]

Mainland Southeast Asia may have been a place of domestication as early as the Near East was. The dating of domestication in Southeast Asia is not yet clear; the dates of the oldest site with probable domesticates—Spirit cave in northwest Thailand—range from about 9500 B.C. to 5500 B.C. Some of the plants found at Spirit cave are not clearly distinguishable from wild varieties, but others, such as gourds, betel nut, betel leaf, and water chestnut, were probably domesticates.[56] Some early cultivated crops may not have

Applied Anthropology

Raised Field Agriculture

Most agricultural systems in the Americas today rely upon either animal power or large machines to cultivate the soil and harvest food. But in the past, people had no traction animals or machines to help with agricultural production. How did the ancient farmers in the Americas till the soil and harvest crops? The answer is that they used human labor. In most cases, animal or mechanical power is much more efficient than human power, and allows more food to be grown on the same piece of land. Archaeologists, however, have found that some ancient, human-powered agricultural systems are actually better suited to specific local environments and produce more food than modern, mechanized systems. These archaeologists have started to use their knowledge of ancient food production to help modern communities improve their lives.

Archaeologist Clark Erickson calls this work "applied archaeology," and he has been conducting applied archaeological work in South America for decades. One of his most significant projects involved the reconstruction of raised fields in the community of Huatta near Lake Titicaca in highland Peru. The environment there is relatively harsh. Early agricultural development projects tried and failed to make the land surrounding Huatta productive. But Erickson recognized that most of the area surrounding the community had once been highly productive raised fields, and he wondered if rebuilding these ancient agricultural structures might help the community.

Raised-field agriculture in practice.

Raised fields are created by piling soil into a long mound, which becomes surrounded by a ditch as soil is taken from it and piled on the mound. Over time, the ditch fills with water and aquatic plants. The aquatic plants are harvested annually and placed on top of the mound as fertilizer. The water in the ditch both keeps the mound soil moist and helps control the soil temperature. As a system, raised fields form a self-sustaining agricultural microenvironment. The major drawback is that mechanized equipment cannot be used easily on these mounds and ditches, so significant amounts of human labor are often required.

Erickson began working with members of the Huatta community to rebuild several of the ancient raised fields. About five years later it was clear that raised field agriculture was well suited to the area. Raised fields were not as labor-intensive as initially thought and were as productive as nearby agricultural fields built upon better soils. More significantly, the "manure" from aquatic plants maintained the soils in the raised fields and actually improved them over time. So, although more labor-intensive, raised fields were able to bring otherwise marginal land into full agricultural production. Although many problems have arisen, including some failures, parts of the Lake Titicaca basin have been returned to raised-field agriculture.

Sources: Bandy 2005; Erickson 1988; 1989; 1998; Guttman-Bond 2010; Morris 2004.

been used for food at all. In particular, bamboo may have been used to make cutting tools and for a variety of building purposes, and gourds were probably used as containers or bowls. We do not know yet exactly when rice was first domesticated, but there is definite evidence of cultivated rice in Thailand after 4000 B.C.

Bananas and taro may have been first domesticated in New Guinea. Analyses of soils from archaeological deposits at Kuk Swamp have identified phytoliths (small silica crystals formed between plant cells that are unique to particular species of plants) from bananas and taro dating from almost 7,000 years ago.[57] Archaeologists have known that agricultural fields with soil mounds and irrigation features have a long history in New Guinea, dating back as far as 10,000 years. The findings of very early taro and banana cultivation suggest that New Guinea may have been the location where these plants were first domesticated. Other major food plants domesticated in Southeast Asia include yams, breadfruit, and coconuts.[58]

Bananas and taro were domesticated in New Guinea nearly 7,000 years ago. Bananas are now grown in many tropical regions, including Ghana pictured here.

Africa Some plants and animals were domesticated first in Africa. Most of the early domestications probably occurred in the wide, broad belt of woodland-savanna country south of the Sahara and north of the equator. Among the cereal grains, sorghum was probably first domesticated in the central or eastern part of this belt, bulrush millet and a kind of rice (different from Asian rice) in the western part, and finger millet in the east. Groundnuts (peanuts) and yams were first domesticated in West Africa.[59] We do know that farming became widespread in the northern half of Africa after 6000 B.C.; investigators continue to debate whether the earliest crops grown there were indigenous or borrowed from the Near East. There is little doubt, however, that some of the plant foods were first domesticated in sub-Saharan Africa because the wild varieties occur there. Many of the important domestic animals in Africa today, especially sheep and goats, were first domesticated elsewhere in the Old World, but one form of cattle, as well as donkey and guinea fowl, were probably first domesticated in Africa.[60]

8.3 Evaluate theories for why food production developed.

Why Did Food Production Develop?

There are many theories of why food production developed; most have tried to explain the origin of domestication in the area of the Fertile Crescent. Gordon Childe's theory, popular in the 1950s, was that a drastic change in climate caused domestication in the Near East.[61] According to Childe, the postglacial period was marked by a decline in summer rainfall in the Near East and northern Africa. As the rains decreased, people were forced to retreat into shrinking pockets, or oases, of food resources surrounded by desert. But we now know that the climatic changes that occurred in the Near East after the retreat of the last glaciers had probably occurred at earlier interglacial periods too, but there had never been a similar food-producing revolution before. Hence, according to Robert Braidwood, there must be more to the explanation of why people began to produce food than simply changes in climate.[62]

Lewis Binford and Kent Flannery thought that the incentive to domesticate animals and plants may have been a desire to reproduce what was wildly abundant in the most bountiful or optimum hunting and gathering areas. Because of population growth in the optimum areas, people might have moved to surrounding areas containing fewer wild resources. In those marginal areas, people might have first turned to food production to reproduce what they used to have. The Binford-Flannery model seems to fit the archaeological record in the Levant, the southwestern part of the Fertile Crescent, where population increase did precede the first signs of domestication.[63] But, as Flannery admitted, in some regions, such as southwestern Iran, the optimum hunting and gathering areas do not show population increase before the emergence of domestication.[64]

The Binford-Flannery model focuses on population pressure in a small area as the incentive to turn to food production. Mark Cohen theorizes that population pressure on a global scale explains why so many of the world's peoples adopted agriculture within the span of a few thousand years.[65] He argues that hunter-gatherers all over the world gradually increased in population so that the world was more or less filled with foragers by about 10,000 years ago. Thus, people could no longer relieve population pressure by moving to uninhabited areas. To support their increasing populations, they would have had to exploit a broader range of less desirable wild foods; that is, they would have had to switch to broad-spectrum collecting, or they would have had to increase the yields of the most desirable wild plants by weeding, protecting them from animal pests, and perhaps deliberately planting the most productive among them. Cohen thinks that people might have tried a variety of these strategies but would generally have ended up depending on cultivation because that would have been the most efficient way to allow more people to live in one place.

Recently, some archaeologists have returned to the idea that climatic change might have played a role in the emergence of agriculture. It seems clear from the evidence now available that the climate of the Near East about 13,000 years to 12,000 years ago became more seasonal: The summers got hotter and drier than before and the winters became colder. These climatic changes may have favored the emergence of annual species of wild grain, which archaeologically we see proliferating in many areas of the Middle East.[66] People such as the Natufians intensively exploited the seasonal grains, developing an elaborate technology for storing and processing the grains and giving up their previous nomadic existence to do so. The transition to agriculture may have occurred when sedentary foraging no longer provided sufficient resources for the population. This could have happened because sedentarization led to population increase and therefore resource scarcity,[67] or because local wild resources became depleted after people settled down in permanent villages.[68] In the area of Israel and Jordan where the Natufians lived, some of the people apparently turned to agriculture, probably to increase the supply of grain, whereas other people returned to nomadic foraging because of the decreasing availability of wild grain.[69]

Change to a more seasonal climate might also have led to a shortage of certain nutrients for foragers. For example, grazing animals get lean when grasses are not plentiful, so meat from hunting would have been in short supply in the dry seasons. Although it may seem surprising, some recent hunter-gatherers have starved when they had to rely on lean meat. If they could have increased their carbohydrate or fat intake somehow, they might have been more likely to get through the periods of lean game.[70] So it is possible that some foragers in the past thought of planting crops to get them through the dry seasons when hunting, fishing, and gathering did not provide enough carbohydrates and fat for them to avoid starvation.

Mesoamerica presents a very different picture, because the early domesticates were not important to subsistence. Theories about population pressure and nutrient shortage don't seem to fit Mesoamerica well. But there were apparently shortages of desired plants, such as bottle gourds, and domestication may well have occurred as humans actively sowed these desired plants. The difference between this model and the ones described previously is that humans in Mesoamerica were apparently not forced into domestication by climate change or population pressure, but actively turned to domestication to obtain more of the most desired or useful plant species. The most interesting case is maize, which only became a staple food some 2,500 or more years after it was first domesticated. Why did it become a staple? Probably both because it was a suitable staple crop (especially when intercropped with beans and squash, as discussed earlier) and because people liked it, so they grew it in large quantities. Over time, and perhaps because of conflict, population pressure, and other forces similar to those that apparently led to domestication in the Near East, people in Mesoamerica and later North and South America came to rely on maize as their dietary mainstay.

8.4 ▶ Critically analyze the consequences of food production.

Consequences of the Rise of Food Production

We know that intensive agriculture (permanent rather than shifting cultivation) probably developed in response to population pressure, but we do not know for sure that population pressure was even partly responsible for plant and animal domestication in the first place. Still, population growth certainly accelerated after the rise of food production (see Figure 8.4), possibly because the spacing between births was reduced further and therefore fertility (the number of births per mother) increased. Increased fertility may have been advantageous because of the greater value of children in farming and herding economies; there is evidence from recent population studies that fertility rates are higher where children contribute more to the economy.[71] The increased workload of mothers may also (but inadvertently) decrease birth spacing. The busier a mother is, the less frequently she may nurse and the more likely her baby will be given supplementary food by other caretakers such as older siblings.[72] Less frequent nursing[73] and greater reliance on food other than mother's milk may result in an earlier resumption of ovulation after the birth of a baby.

Although the rise of food production may have led to increased fertility, this does not mean that health generally improved. In fact, it appears that health declined at least sometimes with the transition to food production. The two trends may seem paradoxical, but rapid population growth can occur if each mother gives birth to a large number of babies, even if many of them die early because of disease or poor nutrition. Nutritional and disease problems are indicated by such features as incomplete formation of tooth enamel, nonaccidental bone lesions (incompletely filled-in bone), reduction in stature, and decreased life expectancy. Many of the studied prehistoric populations that relied heavily on agriculture seem to show less adequate nutrition and higher infection rates than populations living in the same areas before agriculture.[74] Some of the agricultural populations are shorter and had lower life expectancies.

The reasons for a decline in health in those populations are not yet clear. Greater malnutrition can result from an overdependence on a few dietary staples that lack some necessary nutrients. Overdependence on a few sources of food may also increase the risk of famine because the fewer the staple crops, the greater the danger to the food supply posed by a weather-caused crop failure. But some or most nutritional problems may be the result of social and political factors, particularly the rise of different socioeconomic classes of people and unequal access, between and within communities, to food and other resources.[75]

For the first time, apparel made of woven textiles appeared. This development was not simply the result of the domestication of flax (for linen), cotton, and wool-growing sheep. These sources of fiber alone could not produce cloth. It was the development by Neolithic society of the spindle and loom for spinning and weaving that made textiles possible. True, textiles can be woven by hand without a loom, but to do so is a slow, laborious process, impractical for producing garments.

There is also evidence of long-distance trade in the Neolithic. Obsidian from southern Turkey was being exported to sites in

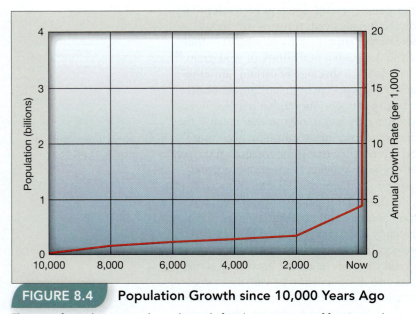

FIGURE 8.4   Population Growth since 10,000 Years Ago

The rate of population growth accelerated after the emergence of farming and herding 10,000 years ago. The rate of growth accelerated even more dramatically in recent times.

Source: Coale 1974.

the Zagros Mountains of Iran and to what are now Israel, Jordan, and Syria in the Levant. Great amounts of obsidian were exported to sites about 190 miles from the source of supply; more than 80 percent of the tools that residents of those areas used were made of this material.[76] Marble was being sent from western to eastern Turkey, and seashells from the coast were traded to distant inland regions.

From the time agriculture first developed until about 6000 B.C., people in the Near East lived in fairly small villages. There were few differences in wealth and status from household to household, and apparently there was no governmental authority beyond the village. There is also no evidence that these villages had any public buildings or craft specialists or that one community was very different in size from its neighbors. In short, these settlements had none of the characteristics we commonly associate with "civilization."

But sometime around 6000 B.C., in parts of the Near East—and at later times in other places—a great transformation in the quality and scale of human life seems to have begun. For the first time, we can see evidence of differences in status among households. For example, some are much bigger than others. Communities begin to differ in size and to specialize in certain crafts. Also, there are signs that some political officials had acquired authority over several communities—that what anthropologists call "chiefdoms" had emerged.

Somewhat later, by about 3500 B.C., we can see many, if not all, of the conventional characteristics of **civilization:** the first inscriptions, or writing; cities; many kinds of full-time craft specialists; monumental architecture; great differences in wealth and status; and the kind of strong, hierarchical, centralized political system we call the **state** (see Figure 8.5).

This type of transformation has occurred many times and in many places in human history. The most ancient civilizations arose in the Near East around 3500 B.C., in northwestern India and in Peru about 2500 B.C., in northern China around 1750 B.C., in Mexico a few hundred years before the time of Christ, and in tropical Africa somewhat later.[77] At least some of these civilizations evolved independently of the others—for example, those in the New World and those in the Old World. Why did they do so? What conditions favored the

Civilization Urban society, from the Latin word for "city-state."

State An autonomous political unit with centralized decision making over many communities with power to govern by force (e.g., to collect taxes, draft people for work and war, and make and enforce laws). Most states have cities with public buildings; full-time craft and religious specialists; an "official" art style; a hierarchical social structure topped by an elite class; and a governmental monopoly on the legitimate use of force to implement policies.

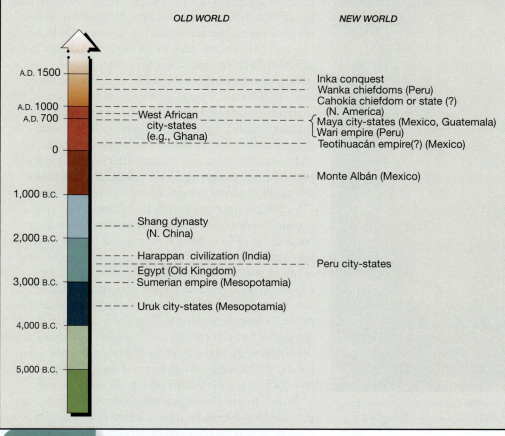

FIGURE 8.5 The Emergence of Civilization

emergence of centralized, statelike political systems? What conditions favored the establishment of cities? We ask this last question separately, because archaeologists are not yet certain that all the ancient state societies had cities when they first developed centralized government. Our discussion focuses primarily on the Near East and Mexico because archaeologists know the most about the sequences of cultural development in those two areas.

Archaeological Inferences About Civilization

8.5 Explain how archaeologists infer that a particular people in the past had social classes, cities, or a centralized government.

Archaeologists rather than historians have studied the most ancient civilizations because those civilizations evolved before the advent of writing. How do archaeologists infer that a particular people in the preliterate past had social classes, cities, or a centralized government? It appears that the earliest Neolithic societies were *egalitarian;* that is, people did not differ much in wealth, prestige, or power. Some later societies show signs of social inequality, indicated by burial finds. Archaeologists generally assume that inequality in death reflects inequality in life, at least in status and perhaps also in wealth and power. Thus, we can be fairly sure that a society had differences in status if only some people were buried with special objects, such as jewelry or pots filled with food.

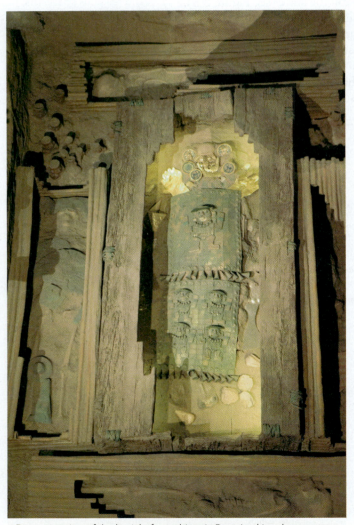

Reconstruction of the burial of a prehistoric Peruvian king, known as the "Lord of Sipan." Note the carefully laid-out wood tomb and the ornate cloth and gold items buried with the individual. Archaeologists assume that such special treatment indicates elite status.

And we can be fairly sure that high status was assigned at birth rather than achieved in later life if we find noticeable differences in children's tombs. For example, some (but not all) child burials from as early as 5500 B.C. to 5000 B.C. at Tell es-Sawwan in Iraq, and from about 800 B.C. at La Venta in Mexico, are filled with statues and ornaments, suggesting that some children had high status from birth.[78] But burials indicating differences in status do not necessarily mean a society had significant differences in wealth. Only when archaeologists find other substantial differences, as in house size and furnishings, can we be sure the society had different socioeconomic classes of people.

Some archaeologists think that states first evolved around 3500 B.C. in greater Mesopotamia, the area now shared by southern Iraq and southwestern Iran. Archaeologists do not always agree on how a state should be defined, but most think that hierarchical and centralized decision making affecting a substantial population is the key criterion. Other characteristics are usually, but not always, found in these first states. They usually have cities with a substantial part of the population not involved directly in the collection or production of food (which means that people in cities are heavily dependent on people elsewhere); full-time religious and craft specialists; public buildings; and often an official art style. There is a hierarchical social structure topped by an elite class from which the leaders are drawn. The government tries to claim a monopoly on the use of force. (Our own state society says that citizens do not have the right "to take the law into their own hands.") The state uses its force or threat of force to tax its population and to draft people for work or war.[79]

How can archaeologists tell, from the information provided by material remains, whether a society was a state or not? This depends in part on what is used as the criterion for a state. For example, Henry Wright and Gregory Johnson defined a state as a centralized political hierarchy with at least three levels of administration.[80] But how might archaeologists infer that such a hierarchy existed in some area? Wright and Johnson suggested that the way settlement sites differ in size is one indication of how many levels of administration there were in an area.

During the early Uruk period (just before 3500 B.C.), in what is now southwestern Iran, there were some 50 settlements that seem to fall into three groups in terms of size.[81] There were about 45 small villages, three or four "towns," and one large center, Susa. These three types of settlements seem to have been part of a three-level administration hierarchy, because many small villages could not trade with Susa without passing through a settlement intermediate in size. Because a three-level hierarchy is Wright and Johnson's criterion of a state, they think a state had emerged in the area by early Uruk times.

Evidence from the next period, middle Uruk, suggests more definitely that a state had emerged. This evidence takes the form of clay seals that were apparently used in trading.[82] *Commodity sealings* were used to keep a shipment of goods tightly closed until it reached its destination, and *message sealings* were used to keep track of goods sent and received. The clay seals found in Susa include many message seals and *bullae,* clay containers that served as bills of lading for goods received. The villages, in contrast, had few message seals and bullae. Again, this finding suggests that Susa administered the regional movement of goods and that Susa was the "capital" of the state.

Let us turn now to the major features of the cultural sequences leading to the first states in southern Iraq.

Cities and States in Southern Iraq

> 8.6 ▶ Describe the emergence of cities and states in southern Iraq.

Farming communities older than the first states have not been found in the arid lowland plains of southern Iraq—the area known as Sumer, where some of the earliest cities and states developed. Perhaps silt from the Tigris and Euphrates rivers has covered them. Or, as has been suggested, Sumer may not have been settled by agriculturalists until people learned how to drain and irrigate river-valley soils otherwise too wet or too dry for cultivation. At any rate, small communities depending partly on agriculture had emerged in the hilly areas north and east of Sumer early in the Neolithic. Later, by about 6000 B.C., a mixed herding and farming economy developed in those areas.

The Formative Era

Elman Service called the period from about 5000 B.C. to 3500 B.C. the *formative era,* for it saw the coming together of many changes that seem to have played a part in the development of cities and states. Service suggested that, with the development of small-scale irrigation, lowland river areas began to attract settlers. The rivers provided not only water for irrigation but also mollusks, fish, and waterbirds for food. They also provided routes by which to import needed raw materials, such as hardwood and stone, that were lacking in Sumer.

Changes during this period suggest an increasingly complex social and political life. Differences in status are reflected in the burial of statues and ornaments with children. Different villages specialized in the production of different goods—pottery in some, copper and stone tools in others.[83] Temples were built in certain places that may have been centers of political as well as religious authority for several communities.[84] Furthermore, some anthropologists think that chiefdoms, each having authority over several villages, had developed by this time.[85]

Sumerian Civilization

By about 3500 B.C., there were quite a few cities in the area of Sumer. Most were enclosed in a fortress wall and surrounded by an agricultural area. About 3000 B.C., all of Sumer was unified under a single government. After that time, Sumer became an empire. It had great urban centers. Imposing temples, commonly set on artificial mounds, dominated the cities. In the city of Warka, the temple mound was about 150 feet high. The empire was very complex and included an elaborate system for the administration of

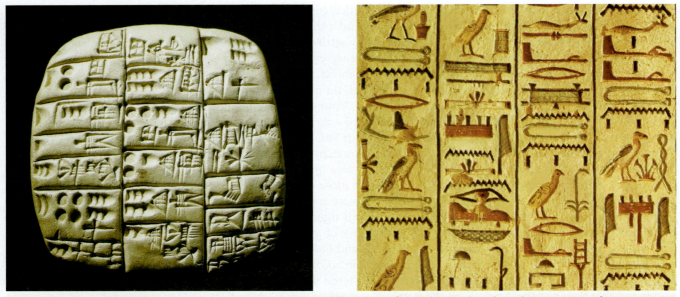

Examples of two of the earliest writing systems on earth. On the left is a cuneiform tablet and on the right is a section of a hieroglyphic panel.

justice, codified laws, specialized government officials, a professional standing army, and even sewer systems in the cities. Among the many specialized crafts were brickmaking, pottery, carpentry, jewelry making, leatherworking, metallurgy, basketmaking, stonecutting, and sculpture. Sumerians learned to construct and use wheeled wagons, sailboats, horse-drawn chariots, and spears, swords, and armor of bronze.[86]

As economic specialization developed, social stratification became more elaborate. Sumerian documents describe a system of social classes: nobles, priests, merchants, craftworkers, metallurgists, bureaucrats, soldiers, farmers, free citizens, and slaves. Slaves were common in Sumer; they often were captives, brought back as the spoils of war.

Cuneiform Wedge-shaped writing invented by the Sumerians around 3000 B.C.

We see the first evidence of writing around 3000 B.C. The earliest Sumerian writings were in the form of ledgers containing inventories of items stored in the temples and records of livestock or other items owned or managed by the temples. Sumerian writing was wedge-shaped, or **cuneiform,** formed by pressing a stylus against a damp clay tablet. For contracts and other important documents, the tablet was fired to create a virtually permanent record. Egyptian writing, or hieroglyphics, appeared about the same time. **Hieroglyphics** were written on rolls woven from papyrus reeds, from which our word *paper* derives.

Hieroglyphics "Picture writing," as in ancient Egypt and in Mayan sites in Mesoamerica (Mexico and Central America).

Cities and States in Mesoamerica

8.7 Describe the emergence of cities and states in Mesoamerica.

Cities and states emerged in Mesoamerica—Mexico and Central America—later than they did in the Near East. The later appearance of civilization in Mesoamerica may be linked to the later emergence of agriculture in the New World and possibly to the near-absence of large animals such as cattle and horses that could be domesticated.[87] We focus primarily on the developments that led to the rise of the city-state of Teotihuacán, which reached its height shortly after the time of Christ. Teotihuacán is located in a valley of the same name, which is the northeastern part of the larger Valley of Mexico.

The Formative Period

The formative period in the area around Teotihuacán (1000 B.C. to 300 B.C.) was characterized initially by small, scattered farming villages on the hilly slopes just south of the Teotihuacán Valley. There were probably a few hundred people in each hamlet, and each of these scattered groups was probably politically autonomous. After about 500 B.C., there seems to have been a population shift to settlements on the valley floor, probably in association with the use of irrigation. Between about 300 B.C. and 200 B.C., small "elite" centers emerged in the valley; each had an earthen or stone raised platform. Residences or small temples of poles and thatch originally stood on these platforms. That some individuals, particularly those in the elite centers, were buried in special tombs supplied with ornaments, headdresses, carved bowls, and a good deal of food indicates some social inequality.[88] The various elite centers may indicate the presence of chiefdoms.

The City and State of Teotihuacán

About 150 years before the time of Christ, no more than a few thousand people lived in scattered villages in the Teotihuacán Valley. In A.D. 100, there was a city of 80,000. By A.D. 500, well over 100,000 people, or approximately 90 percent of the entire valley population, seem to have been drawn or coerced into Teotihuacán.[89]

The city of Teotihuacán, which had its peak in A.D. 500, was a planned city built on a grid pattern. At the center was the Pyramid of the Sun, seen in the background on the left here.

The layout of the city of Teotihuacán, which shows a tremendous amount of planning, suggests that the valley was politically unified under a centralized state from its beginning. Mapping has revealed that the streets and most of the buildings are laid out in a grid pattern following a basic modular unit of over 613 square feet (57 square meters). Residential structures are often squares of this size, and many streets are spaced according to multiples of the basic unit. Even the river that ran through the center of the city was channeled to conform to the grid pattern. Perhaps the most outstanding feature of the city is the colossal scale of its architecture. Two pyramids dominate the metropolis, the so-called Pyramid of the Moon and the Pyramid of the Sun. At its base, the latter is as big as the Great Pyramid of Cheops in Egypt.

The thousands of residential structures built after A.D. 300 follow a standard pattern. Narrow streets separate the one-story buildings, each of which has high, windowless walls. Patios and shafts provide interior light. The layout of rooms suggests that each building consisted of several apartments; more than 100 people may have lived in one of these apartment compounds. There is variation from compound to compound in the size of rooms and the elaborateness of interior decoration, suggesting considerable variation in wealth.[90]

At the height of its power (A.D. 200 to A.D. 500), the metropolis of Teotihuacán encompassed an area larger than imperial Rome.[91] Much of Mesoamerica seems to have been influenced by Teotihuacán. Archaeologically, its influence is suggested by the extensive spread of Teotihuacán-style pottery and architectural elements. Undoubtedly, large numbers of people in Teotihuacán were engaged in production for, and the conduct of, long-distance trade. Perhaps 25 percent of the city's population worked at various specialized crafts, including the manufacture of projectile points and cutting and scraping tools from volcanic obsidian. Teotihuacán was close to major deposits of obsidian, which was apparently in some demand over much of Mesoamerica. Materials found in graves indicate that there was an enormous flow of foreign goods into the city, including precious stones, feathers from colorful birds in the tropical lowlands, and cotton.[92]

Cities and States in Other Areas

8.8 Describe the first cities and states in other areas of the world.

So far, we have discussed the emergence of cities and states in southern Iraq and Mesoamerica, whose development is best, if only imperfectly, known archaeologically. But other state societies probably arose more or less independently in many other areas of the world as well. We say "independently" because such states seem to have emerged without colonization or conquest by other states.

Almost at the same time as the Sumerian empire, the great dynastic age was beginning in the Nile Valley in Egypt. The Old Kingdom, or early dynastic period, began about 3100 B.C., with a capital at Memphis. The archaeological evidence from the early centuries is limited, but most of the population appears to have lived in largely self-sufficient villages. Many of the great pyramids and palaces were built around 2500 B.C.[93]

Elsewhere in Africa, states also arose. In what is present-day Ethiopia, the Axum (or Aksum) state evolved beginning sometime early in the 1st millennium A.D., and ultimately became a center of trade and commerce between Africa and the Arabian Peninsula. Among the unique accomplishments of the Axum state were multistory stone residences built in a singular architectural style. Axum is also notable as being perhaps the first officially Christian state in the world.[94]

In sub-Saharan Africa, by A.D. 800, the savanna and forest zones of western Africa had a succession of city-states. One of them was called Ghana, and it became a major source of gold for the Mediterranean world (as did other states in what came to be known as the "Gold Coast"). In the Congo River basin, a powerful kingdom had evolved by A.D. 1200, with cities described as having tens of thousands of residences and a king that was recognized as an equal by the Portuguese king in the early 1500s.[95] Farther south, states apparently arose in several areas early in the 2nd millennium A.D. One of these was responsible for the large, circular stone structures known today as the Great Zimbabwe.[96]

In the Indus Valley of northwestern India, a large state society had developed by 2300 B.C. This Harappan civilization did not have much in the way of monumental architecture, such as pyramids and palaces, and it was also unusual in other respects. The state apparently controlled an enormous territory—over a million square kilometers. There was not just one major city but many, each built according to a similar pattern and with a municipal water and sewage system.[97]

The Shang dynasty in northern China (1750 B.C.) has long been cited as the earliest state society in the Far East. But recent research suggests that an even earlier one, the Xia dynasty, may have emerged in the same general area by 2200 B.C. In any case, the Shang dynasty had all the earmarks of statehood: a stratified, specialized society; religious, economic, and administrative unification; and a distinctive art style.[98]

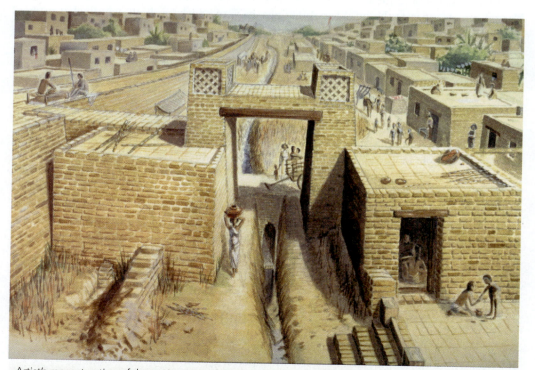

Artist's reconstruction of the ancient city of Harappa. Despite large public works like this water control system, there was little display of grandeur at Harappa. Unlike many other ancient civilizations, all Harappan cities were laid out according to the same basic plan.

Current Research and Issues

Was Cahokia a State?

Cahokia was the largest community to develop in the pre-Columbian Americas north of Mexico, but scholars are not sure if it was a complex chiefdom or a simple state. What factors suggest a state? Factors suggesting that it was a state include its size—the core community covered over 13 square kilometers and included more than 100 earthen mounds. The largest of these mounds was the largest human-made construction in the Americas north of Mexico until the Empire State Building was completed in 1931. The population of Cahokia was at least 10,000 people and may have been more like 40,000. There were also elites—one buried on a blanket decorated with over 20,000 shell beads and surrounded by over 100 other individuals who appear to have been sacrificed at the time of the elite individual's death. Cahokia also engaged in long-distance trade that stretched from the Gulf of Mexico to the Great Lakes, and from the Appalachians to the Black Hills. There were a number of smaller communities in the Cahokia region, and some scholars have suggested a three-level settlement hierarchy was present. Three-level hierarchies are often taken to indicate the presences of states.

So why do most scholars not think Cahokia was a state? Largely because the evidence is lacking on a number of points. There is no evidence of leaders able to control the population by force. There was no standing army, no obvious administrative bureaucracy, and no obvious administrative control over the economy. While there were obvious elites who controlled access to prestige goods (and for whom human sacrifices may have been made upon their deaths), it is not clear that these elites had political power over the entire society or controlled an all-encompassing bureaucracy. The settlement hierarchy, too, may have been informal rather than administrative, and trade may have been carried out by individuals without any government regulation. In short, most scholars think that while Cahokia was clearly a complex social and economic entity, it was not a true state.

Regardless of whether Cahokia was actually a state or not, Cahokia

An embossed copper plate depicting an elite like those who lived at Cahokia.

demonstrates the difficulty of interpreting political and economic organization from the archaeological record.

Sources: Milner 1998; O'Brien 1989; Pauketat 2004.

In South America, a group of distinct state societies may have emerged as early as 2500 B.C. in the Supe and Pativilca valleys north of Lima, Peru. The valley contains a group of large cities that seem to have been interdependent—cities on the coast supplied inland cities with fish, whereas inland cities served as political and economic centers. The cities contain plaza areas and large pyramids, which are thought to be temple structures.[99] After 200 B.C. the major river valleys leading from the Andes to the sea witnessed the development of a complex agricultural system dependent on irrigation. The separate, but similar, states participated in a widespread system of religious symbols and beliefs called Chavín. The various states included the well-known Moche state, creators of some of the most remarkable effigy ceramics ever known, and the Nazca state, the people of which constructed a huge landscape of intaglios (inscribed images and lines) on the hard ground of highland deserts. By A.D. 700, these regional states were integrated into a large, militaristic empire called Wari (or Huari).[100]

In North America, a huge settlement, with over 100 earthen mounds (one of them, Monk's Mound, is the largest pre-Columbian structure north of Mexico) and covering an area of more than 5 square miles (13 square kilometers), developed near present-day St. Louis late in the 1st millennium A.D. The site is called Cahokia, and it was certainly the center of a large and powerful chiefdom. Whether it had achieved a state level of organization is controversial. There is evidence for religious and craft specialists and there is clear social stratification, but whether or not the leaders of Cahokian society were able to govern by force is still unclear.[101]

8.9 Evaluate the major theories about the origin of the state.

Theories About the Origin of the State

We have seen that states developed in many parts of the world. Why did they evolve when and where they did? We consider those that archaeologists have discussed frequently.[102]

Irrigation

Irrigation seems to have been important in many of the areas in which early state societies developed. Irrigation made the land habitable or productive in parts of Mesoamerica, southern Iraq, the Nile Valley, China, and South America. It has been suggested that the labor and management needed for the upkeep of an irrigation system led to the formation of a political elite, the overseers of the system, who eventually became the governors of the society.[103] Proponents of this view believe that both the city and civilization were outgrowths of the administrative requirements of an irrigation system.

Critics note that this theory does not seem to apply to all areas where cities and states may have emerged independently. For example, in southern Iraq, the irrigation systems serving the early cities were generally small and probably did not require extensive labor and management. Large-scale irrigation works were not constructed until after cities had been fully established.[104] Thus, irrigation could not have been the main stimulus for the development of cities and states in Sumer. Even in China, for which the irrigation theory was first formulated, there is no evidence of large-scale irrigation as early as Shang times.[105]

Although large-scale irrigation may not always have preceded the emergence of the first cities and states, even small-scale irrigation systems could have resulted in unequal access to productive land and so may have contributed to the development of a stratified society.[106] In addition, irrigation systems may have given rise to border and other disputes between adjacent groups, thereby prompting people to concentrate in cities for defense and stimulating the development of military and political controls.[107] Finally, as Robert Adams and Elman Service both suggested, the main significance of irrigation, either large or small scale, may have been its intensification of production, a development that in turn may have indirectly stimulated craft specialization, trade, and administrative bureaucracy.[108]

Population Growth, Circumscription, and War

Robert Carneiro has suggested that states may emerge because of population growth in an area that is physically or socially limited. Competition and warfare in such a situation may lead to the subordination of defeated groups, who are obliged to pay tribute and to submit to the control of a more powerful group.[109] Carneiro illustrated his theory by describing how states may have emerged on the northern coast of Peru.

After the people of that area first settled into an agricultural village life, population grew at a slow, steady rate. Initially, new villages were formed as population grew. But in the narrow coastal valleys—blocked by high mountains, fronted by the sea, and surrounded by desert—this splintering-off process could not continue indefinitely. The result, according to Carneiro, was increasing land shortage and warfare between villages as they competed for land. Because the high mountains, the sea, and the desert blocked any escape for losers, the defeated villagers had no choice but to submit to political domination. In this way, chiefdoms may have become kingdoms as the most powerful villages grew to control entire valleys. As chiefs' power expanded over several valleys, states and empires may have been born.

Marvin Harris suggested a somewhat different form of circumscription. He argued that the first states with their coercive authority could emerge only in areas that supported intensive grain agriculture (and the possibility of high food production) and were surrounded by areas that could not support intensive grain agriculture. So people in such areas might put up with the coercive authority of a state because they would suffer a sharp drop in living standards if they moved away.[110]

Carneiro suggested that his theory applies to many areas besides the northern coast of Peru, including southern Iraq and the Indus and Nile valleys. Although there were no geographic barriers in areas such as northern China or the Mayan lowlands on the Yucatán Peninsula, the development of states in those areas may have been the result of social circumscription. Carneiro's theory seems to be supported for southern Iraq, where there is archaeological evidence of population growth, circumscription, and warfare.[111] There is also evidence of population growth before the emergence of the state in the Teotihuacán Valley.[112]

But population growth does not necessarily mean population pressure. For example, the populations in the Teotihuacán and Oaxaca valleys apparently did increase prior to state development, but there is no evidence that they had even begun to approach the limits of their resources. More people could have lived in both places.[113] Nor is population growth definitely associated with state formation in all areas where early states arose. For example, according to Wright and Johnson, there was population growth long before states emerged in southwestern Iran, but the population apparently declined just before the states emerged.[114]

In addition, Carneiro's circumscription theory leaves an important logical question unanswered: Why would the victors in war let the defeated populations remain and pay tribute? If the victors wanted the land so much in the first place, why wouldn't they try to exterminate the defeated and occupy the land themselves, which has happened many times in history?

Local and Long-Distance Trade

It has been suggested that trade was a factor in the emergence of the earliest states.[115] Wright and Johnson theorized that the organizational requirements of producing items for export, redistributing the items imported, and defending trading parties would foster state formation.[116] Does the archaeological evidence support such a theory?

In southern Iraq and the Mayan lowlands, long-distance trade routes may indeed have stimulated bureaucratic growth. In the lowlands of southern Iraq, as we have seen, people needed wood and stone for building, and they traded with highland people for those items. In the Mayan lowlands, the development of civilization seems to have been preceded by long-distance trade. Farmers in the lowland regions traded with faraway places to obtain salt, obsidian for cutting blades, and hard stone for grinding tools.[117] In southwestern Iran, long-distance trade did not become very important until after Susa became the center of a state society, but short-distance trade may have played the same kind of role in the formation of states.

Kwang-chih Chang put forward a similar theory for the origin of states in China. He suggested that Neolithic societies in the Yellow River valley developed a long-distance trade network, which he called an *interaction sphere*, by about 4000 B.C. Trade spread cultural elements among the societies in the interaction sphere, so that they came to share some common elements. Over time, these societies came to depend on each other both as trade partners and as cultural partners, and around 2000 B.C., they unified into a single political unit under the Shang dynasty.[118] Thus, Chang sees political unification in China as an outgrowth of a preexisting system of trade and cultural interaction.

The Various Theories: An Evaluation

Why do states form? As of now, no one theory seems to fit all the known situations. The reason may be that different conditions in different places may have favored the emergence of centralized government. After all, the state, by definition, implies an ability to organize large populations for a collective purpose. In some areas, this purpose may have been the need to organize trade with local or far-off regions. In other cases, the state may have emerged as a way to control defeated populations in circumscribed areas. In still other instances, a combination of factors may have fostered the development of the state type of political system.[119]

The Consequences of State Formation

8.10 Identify and explain consequences of state formation.

We have considered several areas where states arose, as well as a number of theories to explain the origin of states. But what were the consequences for the people living in those societies? The consequences seem to have been dramatic.

One of the ways states change the lifestyles of people is by allowing for larger and denser populations.[120] The presence of agriculture itself gives populations the potential to grow, and the development of a state only furthers that potential. Why? Because a state is able to build infrastructure—irrigation systems, roadways, markets—that allows both the production and distribution of agricultural products to become more efficient. States are able to coordinate information as well, and they can use that information to manage agricultural production cycles and to anticipate or manage droughts, blights, or other natural disasters. States are also able to control access to land (through laws and a military) and thus can both maintain farmers on the land and prevent others (from either within or outside of the state) from removing the farmers or interfering with their ability to produce food.

With increased efficiency of agricultural production and distribution, states also allow many (if not most) people in the society to be relieved of food production. These people are freed to become craftspeople, merchants, and artists, as well as bureaucrats, soldiers, and political leaders. People may also live apart from agricultural fields, and thus cities with dense populations can arise. Cities can also arise in locations that are not suited to agriculture but that perhaps are suited to trade (such as the cities on rivers in southern Mesopotamia) or defense (such as on top of a mountain, as in the case of Monte Albán). Art, music, and literature often flourish in such contexts, and these too are often consequences

Shown is a street in the old city of Jaipur, India. The rise of states allows cities with dense populations to develop and, along with them, the many potentials and problems that cities and their populations create.

of the rise of states. Organized religion also often develops after states appear. Thus, all the hallmarks we associate with civilization can be seen as resulting from the evolution of states.[121]

The development of states can have many negative impacts as well. When states develop, people become governed by force and are no longer able to say "no" to their leaders. Police and military forces can become instruments of oppression and terror.[122] On a less obvious level, the class stratification of states creates differences in access to resources and an underclass of poor, uneducated, and frequently unhealthy people. Health issues are exacerbated by the concentration of people in cities, an environment in which epidemic diseases can flourish.[123] Without direct access to food supplies, people in cities also face the threat of malnutrition or outright starvation if food production and distribution systems fail.[124]

All states appear to be expansionistic, and the emergence of state warfare and conquest seems one of the most striking negative impacts of the evolution of states. In fact, more human suffering can probably be linked to state expansion than to any other single factor. Why do states expand? One basic reason may be that they are able to. States have standing armies ready to fight or be sent to conquer enemies. Another reason for state expansion might be related to the threat of famine and disease, which is more likely with intensive agriculture.[125] A third answer to the question of why states tend to expand might be that belligerence is simply part of the nature of states. States often arise through military means, and it may be vital to the continuation of some states that military power be continually demonstrated.[126] Regardless of the causes, war and conquest are the consequences of state formation. Often, too, defeat in war is the fate of states.

The Decline and Collapse of States

8.11 Discuss explanations for the decline and collapse of states.

When you look over the list of ancient states we have discussed in this chapter, you will notice one element common to them all: Each eventually collapsed; none maintained its power and influence into historic times. Why? It is an important question because, if collapse is the ultimate fate of many if not all states, then we can anticipate that our own state is likely to collapse eventually. Perhaps knowing something about how and why other states have fallen can prevent (or at least hold off) the fall of our own.

One suggested explanation for the decline and collapse of states is environmental degradation. If states originally arose where the environment was conducive to intensive agriculture and harvests big enough to support social stratification, political officials, and a state type of political system, then perhaps environmental degradation—declining soil productivity, persistent drought, and the like—contributed to the collapse of ancient states. Archaeologist Harvey Weiss has suggested that persistent drought helped to bring about the fall of the ancient Akkadian empire, in the Near East. By 2300 B.C., the Akkadians had established an empire stretching over 800 miles (1,300 kilometers) from the Persian Gulf in what is now Iraq to the headwaters of the Euphrates River in what is now Turkey. But a century later, the empire collapsed. Weiss thinks that a long-term drought brought the empire down, as well as other civilizations around at that time too. Many archaeologists doubted there was such a widespread drought, but new evidence indicates that the worst dry spell of the past 10,000 years began just as the Akkadians' northern stronghold was being abandoned.[127] The evidence of the drought, windblown dust in sediment retrieved from the bottom of the Persian Gulf, indicates that the dry spell lasted 300 years. Other geophysical evidence suggests that the drought was worldwide.[128]

Environmental degradation may also have contributed to the collapse of Mayan civilization.[129] Lake sediments show that the region the Maya inhabited experienced an extended period of drought lasting between roughly A.D. 800 and A.D. 1000. The Maya,

The history of Ephesus, a former city lying in ruins in what is now western Turkey, illustrates the waxing and waning of states and empires. From about 1000 B.C to 100 B.C., it was controlled by the Greeks, Lydians, Persians, Macedonians, and Romans, among others.

who depended on rainfall agriculture for subsistence, may not have been able to produce enough food in areas around temple complexes during this long period of drought to feed the resident populations. People would have been forced to move into less populated areas to survive, and the temple complexes would have slowly been abandoned.[130]

The behavior of humans may sometimes be responsible for environmental degradation. Consider the collapse of Cahokia, a city of at least 15,000 people that thrived for a while in the area where the Missouri and Mississippi rivers converge. In the 12th century A.D., Cahokia had large public plazas, a city wall constructed from some 20,000 logs, and massive mounds. But within 300 years, only the mounds were left. Silt from flooding covered former croplands and settled areas. Geographer Bill Woods thinks that overuse of woodlands for fuel, construction, and defense led to deforestation, flooding, and persistent crop failure. The result was the abandonment of Cahokia.[131]

Many other ideas have been put forward to explain collapse, ranging from catastrophes to almost mystical factors such as "social decadence," but, as with theories for the origin of states, no single explanation seems to fit all or even most of the situations. Although it is still not clear what specific conditions led to the emergence, or collapse, of the state in each of the early centers of civilization, the question of why states form and decline is a lively focus of research today. More satisfactory answers may come out of ongoing and future investigations.

Summary and Review

Preagricultural Developments

8.1 Explain the relationship between broad-spectrum collecting, sedentarism, and population growth in terms of preagricultural developments.

- In the period immediately before plants and animals were domesticated, there seems to have been a shift in many areas of the world to less dependence on big game hunting and greater dependence on what is called broad-spectrum collecting.

- The broad spectrum of available resources frequently included aquatic resources such as fish and shellfish and a variety of wild plants, deer, and other game.

- Climatic changes may have been partly responsible for the change to broad-spectrum collecting.

- In Europe, the Near East, Africa, and Peru, the switch to broad-spectrum collecting seems to be associated with more permanent communities. But in areas of Mesoamerica, domestication of plants and animals may have preceded permanent settlements.

 What were some of the preagricultural developments in the Near East and Mesoamerica that might have led to agriculture?

The Domestication of Plants and Animals

8.2 Discuss the domestication of plants and animals in the Near East, Mesoamerica, and elsewhere in the world.

- Domestication refers to changes in plants and animals that make them more useful to humans. Often, without human assistance, domesticated plants and animals cannot reproduce. Neolithic cultures reflect the presence of domestication.

- The earliest evidence of domestication comes from the Near East at about 8000 B.C.

- In the New World, early areas of cultivation and domestication include the highlands of Mesoamerica (about 7000), the Central Andes around Peru (about the same time, but perhaps even earlier), and the Eastern Woodlands of North America (about 2000).

- There were also probably independent centers of domestication in other areas of the Old World—China, Southeast Asia (what is now Malaysia, Thailand, Cambodia, and Vietnam), New Guinea, and Africa—sometime around or after 6000 B.C.

 What of plants and animals were domesticated in the Near East, Mesoamerica, and South America?

Why Did Food Production Develop?

8.3 Evaluate theories for why food production developed.

- Theories about why food production originated remain controversial, but most archaeologists think that conditions must have pushed people to switch from collecting to producing food, rather than food production being a voluntary choice.

- One possible cause of food production may have been population growth in regions of bountiful wild resources, pushing people to move to marginal areas where they tried to reproduce their former abundance.

- Another cause of food production may have been global population growth, filling most of the world's habitable regions and forcing people to use a broader spectrum of wild resources and to domesticate plants and animals.

- Perhaps a third cause of food production was hotter and drier summers and colder winters, favoring sedentarism near seasonal stands of wild grain; resulting population growth may have forced people to plant crops and raise animals to support themselves.

- But climate change or population pressure apparently did not lead to domestication in Mesoamerica; humans in that area seem to have actively turned to domestication to obtain more of the most desired or useful plant species.

 Evaluate the strengths and weaknesses of two theories for the origins of agriculture.

Consequences of the Rise of Food Production

8.4 Critically analyze the consequences of food production.

- Regardless of why food production originated, it seems to have had important consequences for human life.

- Plant and animal domestication led to substantial increases in population.

- A greater reliance on agriculture led to an increase in sedentarism in many areas.

- Populations that relied heavily on agriculture were less healthy compared with earlier foraging populations.

- In more permanent villages, houses and furnishings became more elaborate, people began to make textiles and to paint pottery, long-distance trade seemed to increase, and political assemblies formed.

? What were the consequences of food production?

Archaeological Inferences About Civilization

8.5 Explain how archaeologists infer that a particular people in the past had social classes, cities, or a centralized government.

- Archaeologists rather than historians have studied the most ancient civilizations because those civilizations evolved before the advent of writing.

- Archaeologists generally assume that burial finds reflecting inequality in death reflect inequality in life, at least in status and perhaps also in wealth and power. When archaeologists find other substantial differences, as in house size and furnishings, they can confirm that the society had different socioeconomic classes of people.

- Archaeologists do not always agree on how a state should be defined, but most seem to agree that hierarchical and centralized decision making that affects a substantial population is the key criterion.

- Most states have cities with public buildings, full-time craft and religious specialists, an official art style, and a hierarchical social structure topped by an elite class from which the leaders are drawn.

- Most states maintain power with a monopoly on the use of force. The state uses force or the threat of force to tax its population and to draft people for work or war.

? How do archaeologists infer that a particular people in the past had social classes, cities, or a centralized government?

Cities and States in Southern Iraq

8.6 Describe the emergence of cities and states in southern Iraq.

- Early state societies arose in what is now southern Iraq and southwestern Iran.

- Burial sites from the formative era reflect differences in status. Villages specialized in the production of particular goods. Temples may have been centers of political and religious authority for several communities. Chiefdoms, each having authority over several villages, may have developed.

- The state of Sumer in southern Iraq was unified under a single government just after 3000 B.C. It had writing, large urban centers, imposing temples, codified laws, a standing army, wide trade networks, a complex irrigation system, and a high degree of craft specialization.

> **?** How was Sumer after 3000 B.C. different from earlier societies in southern Iraq?

Cities and States in Mesoamerica

8.7 Describe the emergence of cities and states in Mesoamerica.

- In the formative period, small, autonomous farming villages shifted from the hilly slopes to the floor of the Teotihuacán Valley, probably in association with the use of irrigation. Small "elite" centers emerged, each having a raised platform that supported temples and residences.

- The city and state of Teotihuacán developed somewhat later in the Valley of Mexico and likely influenced much of Mesoamerica. Teotihuacán-style pottery and architectural elements are spread extensively, and graves include significant amounts of foreign goods. Streets and buildings were laid out in a grid pattern that involved much planning.

- The earliest city-state in Mesoamerica developed in the Valley of Oaxaca, with a capital at Monte Albán. It may have originally been founded in the late formative period as a neutral place where different political units in the valley could coordinate activities affecting the whole valley.

- Mayan state societies were densely populated and dependent on intensive agriculture. Their societies may have been more urban and complex than previously thought.

> **?** How did the various Mesoamerican state societies differ from one another?

Cities and States in Other Areas

8.8 Describe the first cities and states in other areas of the world.

- City and states arose early on the African, Asian, South American, and North American continents.

- In Africa, the Nile Valley in Egypt with a capital at Memphis supported a population that lived in self-sufficient villages; later states built the pyramids. The Axum state in Ethiopia was a center of trade with multistory stone residences. Sub-Saharan Africa comprised a succession of city-states.

- In Asia, the Harappan civilization in the Indus Valley of India controlled enormous territory with major cities built on similar patterns that included municipal water and sewage systems. The Shang dynasty in China was a stratified and specialized state society with religious, economic, and administrative unification and a distinctive art style.

- In South America, state societies near present-day Lima, Peru, had independent cities, plazas, large pyramids, and those in the Andes had complex agricultural systems with irrigation, a widespread system of religious symbols and beliefs, and art.

- In North America, Cahokia, near present-day St. Louis, was a huge settlement with a powerful chiefdom, religious and craft specialists, and social stratification.

> **?** What were the first cities and states like in Asia, Africa, South America, and North America?

Theories About the Origin of the State

8.9 Evaluate the major theories about the origin of the state.

- The irrigation theory suggests that the administrative needs of maintaining extensive irrigation systems may have been the impetus for state formation.

- The circumscription theory suggests that states emerge when competition and warfare in circumscribed areas lead to the subordination of defeated groups, which are obliged to submit to the control of the most powerful group.

- Theories involving trade suggest that the organizational requirements of producing exportable items, redistributing imported items, and defending trading parties would foster state formation.

- At this point, no one theory is able to explain the formation of every state. Perhaps different organizational requirements in different areas all favored centralized government.

 Summarize the major theories about the origin of the state and give examples of each.

The Consequences of State Formation

8.10 ▶ Identify and explain consequences of state formation.

- Populations grow and become concentrated in cities.

- More efficient agriculture allows many people to be removed from food production. As a result, art, music, literature, and organized religion can develop and flourish.

- Militaristic expansion and conquest occurs, and leaders wield power over their own populations. An underclass of poor and often unhealthy people emerges.

- Epidemic disease and periodic famine affect the population, often resulting from dense populations and issues with food production.

 Identify a positive and a negative consequence of state formation and explain how each might occur.

The Decline and Collapse of States

8.11 ▶ Discuss explanations for the decline and collapse of states.

- All ancient states collapsed eventually. As with theories for the origin of states, no single explanation seems to fit all or even most of the situations. Research into this question may have implications for prolonging the lives of our modern state systems.

- Four possible reasons may partially explain the collapse of a state: (1) environmental degradation; (2) human behavior that may increase the incidence of disease; (3) overextension that may deplete resources; (4) internal conflict that results from leaders' mismanagement or exploitation.

 Give three explanations for why states collapse and provide an example of each.

Think on it

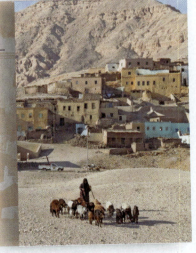

1. What factors might cause people to **work harder** to get food?

2. Do the various theories of the rise of **food production** explain why domestication occurred in many areas of the world within a few thousand years?

3. Like the emergence of food production, the **earliest cities and states** developed within a few thousand years of each other. What might be the reasons?

4. Can you imagine a future **world without states**? What conditions might lead to that "state" of the world?

9 Culture and Culture Change

LEARNING OBJECTIVES

9.1 Discuss the concept of culture as used in anthropology, its salient properties, and controversies surrounding the concept of culture.

9.2 Describe direct and indirect cultural constraints and how they relate to norms.

9.3 Identify attitudes that hinder the study of cultures.

9.4 Critically assess the concept of cultural relativism.

9.5 Describe the methods by which anthropologists describe cultures.

9.6 Explain why culture is integrated or patterned.

9.7 Describe and give examples of how cultures change through discovery and invention, diffusion, and acculturation.

9.8 Relate culture change to the process of adaptation to a changing environment.

9.9 Evaluate the problems and opportunities posed by globalization.

9.10 Describe and give examples of ethnogenesis, or the emergence of new cultures.

9.11 Characterize what anthropologists predict about future cultural diversity.

Perhaps all of us consider ourselves to be unique, with a set of opinions, preferences, habits, and quirks distinct from anyone else's. Indeed, all individuals are unique, and yet most people also share a set of preferences, beliefs, and habits that characterize the society in which they live. People who live in North America, for example, are likely to feel that eating dog meat is wrong, believe that bacteria or viruses cause illness, and habitually sleep on a bed that consists of a mattress supported on some kind of base. Such shared ideas and behaviors are part of what anthropologists mean when they refer to culture. Most people rarely question their shared assumptions and traits until they encounter others who have quite different beliefs and customs. Thus, North Americans may never consider the possibility of eating dog meat until they learn that it is commonly eaten in some societies. (Likewise, people in some other societies may be equally repelled or consider taboo some kinds of meat that North Americans eat). North Americans may realize that their belief in germs is cultural once they see that people in some societies believe that witchcraft or evil spirits cause illness. They may understand that sleeping on a bed is a custom when they learn that people in many societies sleep on the floor or on the ground and, indeed, cook and converse sitting on the floor or ground. When people start to compare and contrast other cultures with their own to learn how they are different, they are beginning to think anthropologically. In fact, anthropology began as a profession when Europeans began to explore and move to faraway places, and they were confronted with the striking facts of cultural variation.

Anthropologists also want to understand how and why cultures change. Most of us are aware that "times have changed," especially when we compare our lives with those of our parents. Some of the most dramatic changes have occurred in women's roles and in attitudes about sex and marriage. Advances in technology have also led to cultural changes that could not have been foreseen. Culture change is not unusual; throughout history, humans have replaced or altered customary behaviors and attitudes as their needs changed. Just as no individual is immortal, no particular cultural pattern is impervious to change. Culture change may be gradual or rapid. Within the last 600 years or so, the pace of change has accelerated, largely because of contact between different societies. Exploration, colonization, trade, and more recently multinational business, the Internet, and social media have led to an economic and cultural interconnectedness among the world's cultures that we call globalization. Anthropologists want to assess not only the impact of these changes on cultures but what they mean for the future of cultural diversity.

Defining Culture

9.1 Discuss the concept of culture as used in anthropology, its salient properties, and controversies surrounding the concept of culture.

In everyday usage, the word *culture* had long referred to a desirable quality we can acquire by attending a sufficient number of plays and concerts and visiting art museums and galleries. But today the anthropological meaning of the term may be more common. People now routinely refer to a particular society's culture, such as American culture, a subgroup's culture, such as Chinese-American, or a transcultural phenomenon, such as "youth culture" and "online culture." In each case, *culture* refers, as Ralph Linton explained, "to the total way of life," from the most mundane activities, such as washing dishes, to the more profound aspects of life. From the point of view of the social scientist, then, "every human being is cultured, in the sense of participating in some culture or other."[1]

Linton emphasized common habits and behaviors in what he considered culture, but the totality of life also includes not just what people do but also how they commonly think and feel. As we define it here, **culture** is the set of learned behaviors and ideas (including beliefs, attitudes, values, and ideals) that are characteristic of a particular society or other social group. Behaviors can also produce products or *material culture*—things such as houses, musical instruments, and tools that are the products of customary behavior. In anthropology, all aspects of culture are important.

Culture The set of learned behaviors and ideas (including beliefs, attitudes, values, and ideals) that are characteristic of a particular society or other social group.

Society A group of people who occupy a particular territory and speak a common language not generally understood by neighboring peoples. By this definition, societies do not necessarily correspond to countries.

Although groups from families to societies share cultural traits, anthropologists have traditionally been concerned with the cultural characteristics of *societies*. Many anthropologists define a **society** as a group of people who occupy a particular territory and speak a common language not generally understood by neighboring peoples. By this definition, societies may or may not correspond to countries. There are many countries—particularly newer ones—that have within their boundaries different peoples speaking mutually unintelligible languages. By our definition of society, such countries are composed of many different societies and therefore many cultures. Also, by our definition of society, some societies may include more than one country. For example, we would have to say that Canada and the United States form a single society because the two groups generally speak English, live next to each other, and share many common ideas and behaviors. That is why we refer to "North American culture." The terms *society* and *culture* are not synonymous. Society refers to a group of people; culture refers to the learned and shared behaviors, ideas, and characteristic of those people. As we will discuss shortly, we also have to be careful to describe culture as of particular time period; what is characteristic of one time may not be characteristic of another.

Culture Is Commonly Shared

If only one person thinks or does a certain thing, that thought or action represents a personal habit, not a pattern of culture. For a thought or action to be considered cultural, some social group must commonly share it. We usually share many behaviors and ideas with our families and friends. We commonly share cultural characteristics with those whose ethnic or regional origins, religious affiliations, and occupations are the same as or similar to our own. We share certain practices and ideas with most people in our society. We also share some cultural traits with people beyond our society who have similar interests (such as rules for international sporting events) or similar roots (as do the various English-speaking nations).

When we talk about the commonly shared customs of *a* society, which constitute the traditional and central concern of cultural anthropology, we are referring to *a* culture. When we talk about the commonly shared customs of a group within a society, which are a central concern of sociologists and increasingly of concern to anthropologists, we are referring to a **subculture**. When we study the commonly shared customs of some group that includes different societies, we usually qualify the term; for example, we may call or refer to the cultural characteristics of societies in or derived from Europe as Western culture, or the presumed cultural characteristics of poor people the world over as the *culture of poverty*.

Subculture The shared customs of a subgroup within a society.

Even when anthropologists refer to something as cultural, there is always individual variation, and not everyone in a society shares a particular cultural characteristic of that society. It is cultural in North American society, for example, for adults to live apart from their parents. But not all adults in the society do so, nor do all adults wish to do so. The custom is considered cultural because most adults practice it. In every society studied by anthropologists—in the simplest as well as the most complex—individuals do not all think and act the same.[2] Indeed, individual variation is a major source of new culture.[3]

Culture Is Learned

Not all things shared generally by a group are cultural. Typical hair color is not cultural, nor is the act of eating. For something to be considered cultural, it must be learned as well as shared. A typical hair color (unless dyed) is not cultural because it is genetically determined. Humans eat because they must; but what and when and how they eat are learned and vary from culture to culture. That food preferences are cultural is especially apparent in which meats a society believes are acceptable to eat. In 2013, the discovery in Europe that ground meat sold as beef also contained horsemeat was greeted with horror. The British, perhaps because they have a high regard for the horse and view horses as pets—that is, with particular familiarity—were especially horrified.[4] Yet horsemeat is considered a delicacy in some parts of Europe and Central Asia. North Americans may be slightly less repelled by the idea of horsemeat, but they generally react with the same horror to eating dog meat.

Guinea pigs, another American household pet, are a common meat in the Andes dating back to the Incas and have recently been introduced in a few Peruvian restaurants in the United States.[5] Is there less aversion to eating guinea pigs than dogs? It appears that there may be, perhaps because dogs have been domesticated for a very long time and are often "part of the family." There is some culture somewhere that avoids every kind of meat North Americans commonly eat. Muslim, Jewish, and Hindu cultures reject pork meat because of religious laws, although why their religions have a pork taboo is still a matter of debate. Many Cushitic-speaking pastoral groups in northeastern Africa reject fish and disapprove of neighboring groups that eat seafood. Meanwhile, some sub-Saharan pastoralists and some cultures in Southeast Asia and the Pacific Islands keep cocks to wake them in the morning and raise chickens for spiritual rites, such as sacrifice and divination, but will not eat the fowl or its eggs. Hindus are generally vegetarian but are especially repelled by the idea of eating beef, for they view the cow as sacred.[6] What accounts for these food preferences and aversions? We know some of the reasons given: religious taboos, age-old superstitions or myths, unfamiliarity, or too much familiarity. And scholars debate their historical and psychological roots. We only know for sure that they are cultural and therefore learned behaviors.

To some extent, all animals exhibit learned behaviors, some of which most individuals in a population may share and may therefore be considered cultural. But different animal species vary in the degree to which their shared behaviors are learned or instinctive. The sociable ants, for instance, despite all their patterned social behavior, do not appear to have much, if any, culture. They divide their labor, construct their nests, form their raiding columns, and carry off their dead—all without having been taught to do so and without imitating the behavior of other ants. Our closest biological relatives, the monkeys and the apes, not only learn a wide variety of behaviors on their own, they also learn from each other. Some of their learned responses are as basic as those involved in maternal care; others are as frivolous as the taste for candy. Frans de Waal reviewed seven long-term studies of chimpanzees and identified at least 39 behaviors that were clearly learned from others.[7] If shared and socially learned, these behaviors could be described as cultural.

The proportion of an animal's life span occupied by childhood roughly reflects the degree to which the animal depends on learned behavior for survival. Monkeys and apes have relatively long childhoods compared to other animals. Humans have by far the longest childhood of any animal, reflecting our great dependence on learned behavior. Although humans may acquire much learned behavior by trial and error and imitation, as do monkeys and apes, most human ideas and behaviors are learned from others. Much of it is probably acquired with the aid of spoken, symbolic language. Using language, a human parent can describe a snake and tell a child that a snake is dangerous and should be avoided. If symbolic language did not exist, the parent would have to wait until the child actually saw a snake and then, through example, show the child that such a creature is to be avoided. Without language, we probably could not transmit or receive information so efficiently and rapidly, and thus would not be heir to so rich and varied a culture.

To sum up, we may say that something is cultural if it is a learned behavior or idea (belief, attitude, value, ideal) that the members of a society or other social group generally share.

Controversies About the Concept of Culture

Not all anthropologists define culture as we do here. We have included learned and shared behaviors as well as ideas. Cognitive anthropologists are most likely to say that culture refers not to behaviors but to the rules and ideas behind them, and that culture therefore resides in people's heads.[8] Although every individual will have slightly different constructs that are based in part on their own unique experiences, many people in a society share many of the same experiences, and therefore they will share many ideas. It is those shared ideas that cognitive anthropologists describe as culture. Whether or not you include behavior as part of culture, both views of culture assume that there will be individual variation, and it is up to the anthropologist to discern the shared nature of culture. Individual variation is the source of new culture.

Another view of culture is that it is an entity, a force, that profoundly affects the individuals who live within its influence. The most extreme version of this view, one that was more acceptable in the past, holds that culture has a "life" of its own that could be studied without much regard for individuals at all.[9] People are born blank slates, it is argued, and culture puts its stamp on in each generation. There are a number of problems with viewing culture as having a life of its own. First, where does it reside exactly? Second, if individuals do not matter, what are the mechanisms of culture change?

People sometimes behave differently when they are in social groups rather than alone. Violent mob behavior is an extreme but telling example. People who would never dream of behaving badly sometimes find themselves doing so to go along with a group. Taking part in a collective ritual that gives a person a feeling of "oneness" is another example of how group behavior can be transformative. If people do or feel things in groups that they would not do alone, we need to look at behavior, as well as the rules or ideas in people's heads, in describing a culture. Therefore, in contrast to many cognitive anthropologists, we define culture as including both behavior and the products of behavior.

| 9.2 | Describe direct and indirect cultural constraints and how they relate to norms. |

Norms Standards or rules about what is acceptable behavior.

Cultural Constraints

The noted French sociologist Émile Durkheim stressed that culture is something *outside* us that exerts a strong coercive power on us and constrains our actions and beliefs. Because we generally conform to our culture, we are not always aware of being constrained by its standards and rules for acceptable behavior.[10] Social scientists refer to these standards or rules as **norms**. Some recent research suggests that people may in fact be biased toward normative information. When a group of undergraduates were asked to read texts about Tikopians, whose culture they knew little about, they were more likely to remember a fact if it was presented as "traditional," "practiced by everyone," or a "custom."[11] The importance of a norm usually can be judged by how members of a society respond when it is violated.

Cultural constraints are of two basic types, *direct* and *indirect*. Naturally, the direct constraints are the more obvious. For example, if you have a loud argument in a restaurant, you are likely to attract disapproval, an indirect constraint, but if the argument turns into a physical fight, you may be arrested for disturbing the peace, which is a direct constraint.

Although indirect forms of cultural constraint are less obvious than direct ones, they are usually no less effective. Durkheim illustrated this point when he wrote, "I am not obliged to speak French with my fellow-countrymen, nor to use the legal currency, but I cannot possibly do otherwise. If I tried to escape this necessity, my attempt would fail miserably."[12] In other words, if Durkheim had decided he would rather speak Icelandic than French, nobody would have tried to stop him. But hardly anyone would have understood him either. And although he would not have been put into prison for trying to buy groceries with Icelandic money, he would have had difficulty convincing the local merchants to sell him food.

In a series of classic experiments on conformity, Solomon Asch revealed how strong social pressure can be. Asch coached the majority of a group of college students to give deliberately incorrect answers to questions involving visual stimuli. A "critical subject," the one student in the room who was not so coached, had no idea that the other participants would purposely misinterpret the evidence presented to them. Asch found that, in one-third of the experiments, the critical subjects consistently gave incorrect answers, seemingly allowing their own correct perceptions to be distorted by the obviously incorrect statements of the others. In another 40 percent of the experiments, the critical subject yielded to the opinion of the group some of the time.[13] These studies have been replicated in the United States and elsewhere. Although the degree of conformity appears to vary in different societies, most studies still show conformity effects.[14] Many individuals still do not give in to the wishes of the majority, but a recent study using MRIs has shown that perceptions can actually be altered if participants consciously alter their answers to conform to others.[15]

Attitudes That Hinder the Study of Cultures

9.3 Identify attitudes that hinder the study of cultures.

Many of the Europeans who first traveled to faraway places were shocked and offended by customs they observed, which is not surprising. People commonly feel that their own behaviors and attitudes are the correct ones and that people who do not share those patterns are immoral or inferior.[16] For example, most North Americans would react negatively to child betrothal, a kind of arranged marriage, but not question their own practice of dating a series of potential partners before selecting one. When we judge other cultures solely in terms of our own culture we are being **ethnocentric**—that is, we hold an attitude called **ethnocentrism**.

Our own customs and ideas may appear bizarre or barbaric to an observer from another society. Hindus in India, for example, would consider our custom of eating beef disgusting. In their culture, the cow is a sacred animal and may not be slaughtered for food. In many societies, a baby is almost constantly carried by someone, in someone's lap, or asleep next to others.[17] People in such societies may think it is cruel of us to leave babies alone for long periods of time, often in devices that resemble cages (cribs and playpens). Even our most ordinary customs—the daily rituals we take for granted—might seem thoroughly absurd when viewed from an outside perspective. An observer of our society might justifiably take notes on certain strange behaviors that seem quite ordinary to us, as the following description shows:

> *The daily body ritual performed by everyone includes a mouth-rite. Despite the fact that these people are so punctilious about the care of the mouth, this rite involves a practice which strikes the uninitiated stranger as revolting. It was reported to me that the ritual consists of inserting a small bundle of hog hairs into the mouth, along with certain magical powders, and then moving the bundle in a highly formalized series of gestures. In addition to the private mouth-rite, the people seek out a holy-mouth man once or twice a year. These practitioners have an impressive set of paraphernalia, consisting of a variety of augers, awls, probes, and prods. The use of these objects in the exorcism of the evils of the mouth involves almost unbelievable ritual torture of the client. The holy-mouth man opens the client's mouth and, using the above-mentioned tools, enlarges any holes which decay may have created in teeth. Magical materials are put into these holes. If there are no naturally occurring holes in the teeth, large sections of one or more teeth are gouged out so that the supernatural substance can be applied. In the client's view, the purpose of these ministrations is to arrest decay and to draw friends. The extremely sacred and traditional character of the rite is evident in the fact that the natives return to the holy-mouth man year after year, despite the fact that their teeth continue to decay.[18]*

Ethnocentric Refers to judgment of other cultures solely in terms of one's own culture.

Ethnocentrism The attitude that other societies' customs and ideas can be judged in the context of one's own culture.

Societies vary in their acceptance of an elderly person living apart from family. In the United States and in the UK it is fairly common for an elderly person to live alone or in a facility with non-family members. But in societies where the elderly, such as this great grandmother in central Poland, regularly live with family, having the elderly live alone may be viewed quite negatively.

We are likely to protest that to understand the behaviors of a particular society—in this case, our own—the observer must try to find out what the people in that society say about why they do things. For example, the observer might find out that periodic visits to the "holy-mouth man" are for medical, not magical, purposes. Indeed, the observer, after some questioning, might discover that the "mouth-rite" has no sacred or religious connotations whatsoever. Actually, Horace Miner, the author of the passage on the "daily rite ritual," was not a foreigner. An American, he described the "ritual" the way he did to show how the behaviors involved might be interpreted by an outside observer.

Ethnocentrism hinders our understanding of the customs of other people and, at the same time, keeps us from understanding our own customs. If we think that everything we do is best, we are not likely to ask why we do what we do or why "they" do what "they" do.

We may not always glorify our own culture. Other ways of life may sometimes seem more appealing. Whenever we are weary of the complexities of civilization, we may long for a way of life that is "closer to nature" or "simpler" than our own. For instance, a young North American whose parent is holding two or three jobs just to provide the family with bare necessities might briefly be attracted to the lifestyle of the !Kung of the Kalahari Desert in the 1950s. The !Kung shared their food and therefore were often free to engage in leisure activities during the greater part of the day. They obtained all their food by men hunting animals and women gathering wild plants. Because they had no facilities for refrigeration, sharing a large freshly killed animal was clearly more sensible than hoarding meat that would soon rot. Moreover, the sharing provided a kind of social security system for the !Kung. If a hunter was unable to catch an animal on a certain day, he could obtain food for himself and his family from someone else in his band. Then, at some later date, the game he caught would provide food for the family of another, unsuccessful hunter. This system of sharing also ensured that people too young or too old to help with collecting food would still be fed.

Could we learn from the !Kung? Perhaps we could in some respects, but we must not glorify their way of life either or think that their way of life might be easily imported into our own society. Other aspects of !Kung life would not appeal to many North Americans. For example, when the nomadic !Kung decided to move their camps, they had to carry all the family possessions, substantial amounts of food and water, and all young children below age 4 or 5. This is a sizable burden to carry for any distance. The nomadic !Kung traveled about 1,500 miles in a single year and, understandably, families had few possessions.[19]

Both ethnocentrism and its opposite, the glorification of other cultures, hinder effective anthropological study.

9.4 Critically assess the concept of cultural relativism.

Cultural Relativism

Early thinkers on human evolution tended to think of Western cultures as being at the highest or most progressive stage of evolution. Not only were these ideas based on poor evidence of the details of world ethnography, they also seemed to be ethnocentric glorifications of Western culture. The influential anthropologist Franz Boas and many of his students—such as Ruth Benedict, Melville Herskovits, and Margaret Mead—rejected the view that cultures progressed through stages of civilization.[20] They stressed that the early evolutionists did not sufficiently understand the details of the cultures they theorized about, nor the context in which these customs appeared. Challenging the attitude that Western cultures were obviously superior, the Boasians insisted that a society's customs and ideas should be described objectively and understood in the context of that society's problems and opportunities. This approach is known as **cultural relativism**. Does cultural relativism mean that the actions of another society, or of our own, should not be judged? Does our insistence on objectivity mean that anthropologists should not make moral judgments about the cultural phenomena they observe and try to explain? Does it mean that anthropologists should not try to bring about change? Not necessarily.

Cultural relativism The attitude that a society's customs and ideas should be viewed within the context of that society's problems and opportunities.

Although the concept of cultural relativism remains an important anthropological tenet, today many anthropologists make a distinction between keeping an open mind when studying other cultures and being morally relativistic—that is, suspending all judgment about behaviors they believe to be wrong. What if, for example, a culture practices slavery, violence against women, torture, or genocide? If the strong doctrine of relativism is adhered to, then these cultural practices are not to be judged, and we should not try to eliminate them. A more measured form of cultural relativism asserts that anthropologists should strive for objectivity in describing a people and should be wary of superficial or quick judgment in their attempts to understand the reasons for cultural behavior. Tolerance should be the basic mode unless there is strong reason to behave otherwise.[21] As Michael Brown concludes, cultural relativism is less a comprehensive theory than a useful rule of thumb that keeps anthropologists alert to perspectives in other cultures that might challenge their own cultural beliefs about what is true.[22]

Human Rights and Relativism

The news increasingly reports behaviors that Western countries consider to be violations of human rights. Examples range from jailing people for expressing certain political ideas to ethnic massacre. But faced with criticism from the West, people in other parts of the world are saying that the West should not dictate its ideas about human rights to other countries. Indeed, many countries say that they have different codes of ethics. Are the Western countries being ethnocentric by taking their own cultural ideas and applying them to the rest of the world? Should we instead rely on the strong version of the concept of cultural relativism, considering each culture on its own terms? If we do that, it may not be possible to create a universal standard of human rights.

What we do know is that all cultures have ethical standards, but they do not emphasize the same things. For example, some cultures emphasize individual political rights; others emphasize political order. Some cultures emphasize protection of individual property; others emphasize the sharing or equitable distribution of resources. People in the United States may have freedom to dissent, but they can be deprived of health insurance or of food if they lack the money to buy them. Cultures also vary markedly in the degree to which they have equal rights for minorities and women. In some societies, women are killed when a husband dies or when they disobey a father or brother.

Some anthropologists argue strongly against cultural relativism. For example, Elizabeth Zechenter says that cultural relativists claim there are no universal principles of morality but insist on tolerance for all cultures. If tolerance is one universal principle, why shouldn't there be others? In addition, she points out that the concept of cultural relativism is often used to justify traditions desired by the dominant and powerful in a society. She points to a case in 1996, in Algeria, where two teenage girls were raped and murdered because they violated the fundamentalist edict against attending school. Are those girls any less a part of the culture than the fundamentalists? Would it make any difference if most Algerian women supported the murders? Would that make it right? Zechenter does not believe that international treaties, such as the Universal Declaration of Human Rights, impose uniformity among diverse cultures. Rather, they seek to create a floor below which no society is supposed to fall.[23]

Can the concept of cultural relativism be reconciled with the concept of an international code of human rights? Probably not completely. Paul Rosenblatt recognizes the dilemma but nonetheless thinks that something has to be done to stop torture and "ethnic cleansing," among other practices. He makes the case that "to the extent that it is easier to persuade people whose viewpoints and values one understands, relativism can be a tool for change . . . a relativist's awareness of the values and understanding of the elite makes it easier to know what arguments would be persuasive. For example, in a society in which the group rather than the individual has great primacy, it might be persuasive to show how respect for individual rights benefits the group."[24]

9.5 ▶ Describe the methods by which anthropologists describe cultures.

Describing a Culture

If all individuals are unique and all cultures have some internal variation, how do anthropologists discover what may be cultural? Understanding what is cultural involves two parts—separating what is shared from what is individually variable, and understanding whether common behaviors and ideas are learned.

To understand better how an anthropologist might make sense of diverse behaviors, let us examine the diversity at a professional football game in the United States. When people attend a football game, various members of the crowd behave differently while "The Star-Spangled Banner" is being played. As they stand and listen, some people remove their hats; a child munches popcorn; a veteran of the armed forces stands at attention; a teenager searches the crowd for a friend; and the coaches take a final opportunity to intone secret chants and spells designed to sap the strength of the opposing team. Yet, despite these individual variations, most of the people at the game respond in a basically similar manner: Nearly everyone stands silently, facing the flag. Moreover, if you go to several football games, you will observe that many aspects of the event are notably similar. Although the plays will vary from game to game, the rules of the game are never different, and although the colors of the uniforms differ by teams, the players never appear on the field dressed in swimsuits.

If an anthropologist observes dancing in mainstream North American culture, she or he will note that most dancing involves a pair, usually a male and female, but sometimes there are group dances such as the rave as shown here. Yet usually individuals or couples will not simply imitate those around them but will create different patterns of movements and steps.

Although the variations in individual reactions to a given stimulus are theoretically limitless, in fact they tend to fall within easily recognizable limits. A child listening to the anthem may continue to eat popcorn but will probably not do a rain dance. Similarly, the coaches are unlikely to react to that same stimulus by running onto the field and embracing the singer. Variations in behavior, then, are confined within socially acceptable limits, and part of the anthropologists' goals is to find out what those limits are. They may note, for example, that some limitations on behavior have a practical purpose: A spectator who disrupts the game by wandering onto the field would be required to leave. Other limitations are purely traditional. In our society, it is considered proper for a man to remove his overcoat if he becomes overheated, but others would undoubtedly frown upon his removing his trousers even if the weather were quite warm. Using observation and interviewing, anthropologists discover the customs and the ranges of acceptable behavior that characterize the society under study.

Similarly, anthropologists interested in describing courtship and marriage in our society would encounter a variety of behaviors. Dating couples vary in where they go (coffee shops, movies, restaurants, bowling alleys), what behaviors they engage in on dates, and how long they date before they split up or move on to more serious relationships. If they decide to marry, ceremonies may be simple or elaborate and involve either religious or secular rituals. Despite this variability, the anthropologists would begin to detect certain regularities in courting practices. Although couples may do many different things on their first and subsequent dates, they nearly always arrange the dates by themselves; they try to avoid their parents when on dates; they often manage to find themselves alone at the end of a date; they put their lips together frequently; and so forth. After a series of more and more closely spaced encounters, a man and woman may decide to declare themselves publicly as a couple, either by announcing that they are engaged or by revealing that they are living together or intend to do so. Finally, if the two of them decide to marry, they must in some way have their union recorded by the civil authorities.

In our society, a person who wishes to marry cannot completely disregard the customary patterns of courtship. If a man saw a woman on the street and decided he wanted to marry her, he could conceivably choose a quicker and more direct form of action than the usual dating procedure. He could get on a horse, ride to the woman's home, snatch her up in his arms, and gallop away with her. In Sicily, until the last few decades, such a couple would have been considered legally married, even if the woman had never met the man before or had no intention of marrying. But in North American society, any man who acted in such a fashion would be arrested and jailed for kidnapping and would probably have his sanity challenged. Although individual behaviors may vary, most social behavior falls within culturally acceptable limits.

In the course of observing and interviewing, anthropologists also try to distinguish actual behavior from the ideas about how people in particular situations ought to feel and behave. In everyday terms, we speak of these ideas as *ideals*; in anthropology, we refer to them as *ideal cultural traits*. Ideal cultural traits may differ from actual behavior because the ideal is based on the way society used to be. (Consider the ideal of "free enterprise," that industry should be totally free of governmental regulation.) Other ideals may never have been actual patterns and may represent merely what people would like to see as correct behavior. Consider the idealized belief, long cherished in North America, that everybody is "equal before the law," that everybody should be treated in the same way by the police and courts. Of course, we know that this is not always true. The rich, for example, may receive less jail time and be sent to nicer prisons. Nevertheless, the ideal is still part of our culture; most of us continue to believe that the law should be applied equally to all.

When dealing with customs that are overt or highly visible within a society—for example, the custom of sending children to school—an investigator can determine the existence of such practices by direct observation and by interviewing a few knowledgeable people. But when dealing with a domain of behavior that may include many individual variations, or when the people studied are unaware of their pattern of behavior and cannot answer questions about it, the anthropologist may need to collect information from

Distance between people conversing varies cross-culturally. The faces of the Rajput Indian men on the left are much closer than the faces of the American women on the right.

a larger sample of individuals to establish what the cultural trait is.

One example of a cultural trait that most people in a society are not aware of is how far apart people stand when they are having a conversation. Yet there is considerable reason to believe that unconscious cultural rules govern such behavior. These rules become obvious when we interact with people who have different rules. We may experience considerable discomfort when another person stands too close (indicating too much intimacy) or too far (indicating unfriendliness). Often we interpret that behavior as individual behavior without realizing that the person is actually following his or her cultural rules. Within Europe, for example, there seems to be a gradient from north to south. Northern Europeans tend to stand further apart, and southern Europeans stand closer.[25]

If we wanted to arrive at the cultural rule for conversational distance between casual acquaintances, we could study a sample of individuals from a society and determine the *modal response,* or *mode.* The mode is a statistical term that refers to the most frequently encountered response in a given series of responses. So, for the North American pattern of casual conversational distance, we would plot the actual distance for many observed pairs of people. Some pairs may be 2 feet apart, some 2.5, and some 4 feet apart. If we count the number of times every particular distance is observed, these counts provide what we call a *frequency distribution.* The distance with the highest frequency is the *modal pattern.* Very often the frequency distribution takes the form of a *bell-shaped curve,* as shown in Figure 9.1. There, the characteristic being measured is plotted on the horizontal axis (in this case, the distance between conversational pairs), and the number of times each distance is observed (its frequency) is plotted on the vertical axis. If we were to plot how a sample of North American casual conversational pairs is distributed, we would probably get a bell-shaped curve that peaks at around 3 feet.[26] Is it any wonder, then, that we sometimes speak of keeping others "at arm's length"?

Although we may be able to discover by interviews and observation that a behavior, thought, or feeling is widely shared within a society, how do we establish that something commonly shared is learned, and therefore cultural? Establishing that something is or is not learned may be difficult. Because children are not reared apart from adult caretakers, the behaviors they exhibit as part of their genetic inheritance are not clearly separated from those they learn from others around them. We suspect that particular behaviors and ideas are largely learned if they vary from society to society. We also suspect genetic influences when particular behaviors or ideas are found in all societies. For example, children the world over seem to acquire language at about the same age and progress through similar stages. These facts suggest that human children have certain genetic capacities for language acquisition. However, the particular languages spoken by people in different societies show considerable variability. This variability suggests that particular

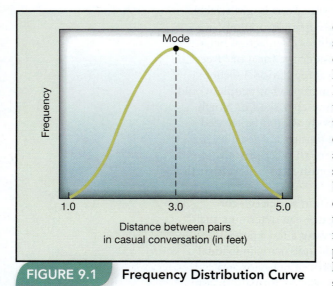

Frequency

1.0   3.0   5.0

Distance between pairs
in casual conversation (in feet)

Mode

FIGURE 9.1   **Frequency Distribution Curve**

languages have to be learned. Similarly, if the courtship patterns of one society differ markedly from those of another, we can be fairly certain that those courtship patterns are learned and therefore cultural.

Culture Is Patterned

9.6 Explain why culture is integrated or patterned.

Anthropologists have always known that culture is not a hodgepodge of unrelated behaviors and ideas—that a culture is mostly integrated. In saying that a culture is mostly *integrated,* we mean that the elements or traits that make up that culture are not just a random assortment of customs but are mostly adjusted to or consistent with one another.

A culture may also tend to be integrated for psychological reasons. The ideas of a culture are stored in the brains of individuals. Research in social psychology has suggested that people tend to modify beliefs or behaviors that are not cognitively or conceptually consistent with other information.[27] We do not expect cultures to be completely integrated, just as we do not expect individuals to be completely consistent. But if a tendency toward cognitive consistency is found in humans, we might expect that at least some aspects of a culture would tend to be integrated for that reason alone. How this pressure for consistency works is not hard to imagine. Children, for example, seem to be very good at remembering *all* the things their parents say. If they ask for something and the parents say no, they may say, "But you said I could yesterday." Such pressure to be consistent may even make parents change their minds! Of course, not everything one wants to do is consistent with the rest of one's desires, but there surely is pressure from within and without to make it so.

Humans are also capable of rational decision making; they can usually figure out that certain things are not easy to do because of other things they do. For example, if a society has a long postpartum sex taboo (a custom in which couples abstain from sex for a year or more after the birth of a baby), we might expect that most people in the society could figure out that it would be easier to observe the taboo if husband and wife did not sleep in the same bed. Or, if people drive on the left side of the road, as in England, it is easier and less dangerous to drive a car with a steering wheel on the right because that placement allows you to judge more accurately how close you are to cars coming at you from the opposite direction.

Consistency or integration of culture traits may also be produced by less conscious psychological processes. People may generalize (transfer) their experiences from one area of life to another. For example, where children are taught that it is wrong to express anger toward family and friends, it turns out that folktales parallel the childrearing; anger and aggression in the folktales tend to be directed only toward strangers, not toward family and friends. It seems as if the expression of anger is too frightening to be expressed close to home, even in folktales.

Adaptation to the environment is another major reason for traits to be patterned. Customs that diminish the survival chances of a society are not likely to persist. Either the people clinging to those customs will become extinct, taking the customs with them, or the customs will be replaced, thereby possibly helping the people to survive. By either process, **maladaptive customs**—those that diminish the chances of survival and reproduction—are likely to disappear. The customs of a society that enhance survival and reproductive success are **adaptive customs** and are likely to persist. Hence, we assume that if a society has survived long enough to be described in the annals of anthropology (the "ethnographic record"), much, if not most, of its cultural repertoire is adaptive, or was at one time.

When we say that a custom is adaptive, however, we mean it is adaptive only with respect to a specific physical and social environment. What may be adaptive in one environment may not be adaptive in another. Therefore, when we ask why a society may have a particular custom, we really are asking if that custom makes sense as an adaptation to that society's particular environmental conditions. If certain customs are more adaptive in

Maladaptive customs Cultural traits that diminish the chances of survival and reproduction in a particular environment.

Adaptive customs Cultural traits that enhance survival and reproductive success in a particular environment.

particular settings, then those "bundles" of traits will generally be found together under similar conditions. For example, the !Kung, as we have mentioned, subsisted by hunting wild animals and gathering wild plants. Because wild game is mobile and different plants mature at different times, a nomadic way of life may be an adaptive strategy. Because this food-getting strategy cannot support that many people in one area, small social groups make more sense than large communities. Since people move frequently, it is also probably more adaptive to have few material possessions. These cultural traits usually occur together when people depend on hunting and gathering for their food.

Culture Is Imperfectly Patterned

Not all aspects of culture are consistent, nor is a society forced to adapt its culture to changing environmental circumstances. Even in the face of changed circumstances, people may choose not to change their customs. The Tapirapé of central Brazil, for example, did not alter their custom of limiting the number of births even though they had suffered severe population losses after contact with Europeans and their diseases. The Tapirapé population fell to fewer than 100 people from over 1,000. They were on the way to extinction, yet they continued to value small families. Not only did they believe that a woman should have no more than three children, but they took specific steps to achieve this limitation. They practiced infanticide if twins were born, if the third child was of the same sex as the first two children, and if the possible fathers broke certain taboos during pregnancy or in the child's infancy.[28]

Of course, it is also possible that a people will behave maladaptively, even if they try to alter their behavior. After all, although people may alter their behavior according to what they perceive will be helpful to them, what they perceive to be helpful may not prove to be adaptive. The tendency for a culture to be integrated or patterned, then, may be cognitively and emotionally, as well as adaptively, induced.

9.7 Describe and give examples of how cultures change through discovery and invention, diffusion, and acculturation.

How and Why Cultures Change

When you examine the history of a society, it is obvious that its culture has changed over time. Some of the shared behaviors and ideas that were common at one time are modified or replaced at another time. That is why, in describing a culture, it is important to understand that a description pertains to a particular time period. (Moreover, in many large societies, the description may only be appropriate for a particular subgroup.) For example, the !Kung of the 1950s were mostly dependent on the collection of wild plants and animals and moved their campsites frequently, but later they became more sedentary to engage in wage labor. Whether we focus on some aspect of past behavior or on contemporary behavior depends on what question we want to answer. If we want to maximize our understanding of cultural variation, such as variation in religious belief and practice, it may be important to focus on the earliest descriptions of a group before they were converted to a major world religion. On the other hand, if we want to understand why a people adopted a new religion or how they altered their religion or resisted change in the face of pressure, we need to examine the changes that occurred over time.

In the remainder of this chapter, we will discuss how and why cultures change and briefly review some of the widespread changes that have occurred in recent times. In general, the impetus for change may come from within the society or from without. From within, the unconscious or conscious pressure for consistency will produce culture change if enough people adjust old behavior and thinking to new. And change can also occur if people try to invent better ways of doing things. Michael Chibnik suggests that people who confront a new problem conduct mental or small "experiments" to decide how to behave. These experiments may give rise to new cultural traits.[29] A good deal of culture change may be stimulated by changes in the external environment. For example, if people move into an arid area, they will either have to give up farming or develop a system of irrigation. In the modern world, changes in the social environment are probably more frequent stimuli for culture change than changes in the physical environment. Many North Americans, for example, started to think seriously about conserving energy and about using sources of energy other than oil only after oil supplies from the Middle East were curtailed in 1973 and 1974. A significant amount of the radical and rapid culture change that has occurred in the last few hundred years has been due to the imperial expansion of Western societies into other areas of the world. Native Americans, for instance, were forced to alter their lifestyles drastically when they were driven off their lands and confined to reservations.

Discovery and Invention Discoveries and inventions, which may originate inside or outside a society, are ultimately the sources of all culture change. But they do not necessarily lead to change. If an invention or discovery is ignored, no change in culture results. Only when society accepts an invention or discovery and uses it regularly can we begin to speak of culture change.

The new thing discovered or invented, the innovation, may be an object—the wheel, the plow, the computer—or it may involve behavior and ideas—buying and selling, democracy, monogamy. According to Ralph Linton, a discovery is any addition to knowledge, and an invention is a new application of knowledge.[30] Thus, a person might discover that children can be persuaded to eat nourishing food if the food is associated with an imaginary character that appeals to them. Someone else might then exploit that discovery by inventing a cartoon character named Popeye who acquires miraculous strength by devouring cans of spinach.

Unconscious Invention Societies have various types of inventions. One type is the consequence of setting a specific goal, such as eliminating tuberculosis or placing a person on the moon. Another type emerges less intentionally. This second process of invention is often referred to as *accidental juxtaposition* or *unconscious invention*. Linton suggested that some inventions, especially those of prehistoric days, were probably the consequences of literally dozens of tiny initiatives by "unconscious" inventors. These inventors made their small contributions, perhaps over many hundreds of years, without being aware of the part they were playing in bringing one invention, such as the wheel or a better form of hand ax, to completion.[31] Consider the example of children playing on a fallen log, which rolls as they walk and balance on it, coupled with the need at a given moment to move a slab of granite from a cave face. The children's play could have suggested the use of logs as rollers and thereby set in motion a series of developments that culminated in the wheel.

In reconstructing the process of invention in prehistoric times, however, we should be careful not to look back on our ancestors with a smugness generated by our more highly developed technology. We have become accustomed to turning to the science sections of our magazines and newspapers and finding, almost daily, reports of miraculous new discoveries and inventions. From our point of view, it is difficult to imagine such a simple invention as the wheel taking so many centuries to come into being. We are tempted to surmise that early humans were less intelligent than we are. But the capacity of the human brain has been the same for perhaps 100,000 years; there is no evidence that the inventors of the wheel were any less intelligent than we are.

Intentional Innovation Some discoveries and inventions arise out of deliberate attempts to produce a new idea or object. It may seem that such innovations are obvious responses to perceived needs. For example, during the Industrial Revolution, there was a great demand for inventions that would increase productivity. James Hargreaves, in 18th-century England, is an example of an inventor who responded to an existing demand. Textile manufacturers were clamoring for such large quantities of spun yarn that cottage laborers, working with foot-operated spinning wheels, could not meet the demand. Hargreaves, realizing that prestige and financial rewards would come to the person who invented a method of spinning large quantities of yarn in a short time, set about the task and developed the spinning jenny.

Current Research and Issues

Culture Change and Persistence in China

Governments can change a culture by force, as communist China has tried to do since its inception in 1949. Among the government's revolutionary policies was the push for intensive agriculture and a one-child-per-family rule. Yet a study by Burton Pasternak, a U.S. anthropologist, and colleagues from Canada and China suggests that, despite strong pressures from the government, what change persists in a culture mainly reflects what is possible ecologically and economically. The researchers studied four communities of Han who had moved outside the Great Wall to colonize the Inner Mongolian frontier (Inner Mongolia is part of China).

Han farmers who crossed the Great Wall were searching for a better life. Though many found the climate and soil conditions too difficult and returned home, others adjusted to the grasslands and remained. Some Han continued to depend on farming on the fringes of the grasslands. Others farther out on the grasslands became herders. The Han who switched to herding are now in many respects more like the native Mongol herders than like Han or Mongol farmers. The gender division of labor among the Han pastoralists became much sharper than among the Han farmers because men are often far away with the herds. Pastoralist children, not that useful in herding because mistakes can be very costly, are more likely than farm children to stay in school for a long time. Perhaps because of the greater usefulness of children on the farm, Han farm families have more children than Han pastoralists. But both groups have more than the prescribed one child per family. Herdsmen are less likely than farmers to need cooperative labor, so Han pastoralists are more likely to live as an independent family apart from kin than as an extended family, which was traditional.

Although an increasing number of Han have become more like Mongols in their pastoral adaptations, many Mongols have adopted an urban way of life and moved away from their pastoral life. The Chinese government was initially responsible for encouraging non-Mongols to move into Inner Mongolia, particularly into its new capital, Hohhot. At the same time, many Mongols moved from the grasslands and into the capital city. Chinese policy was intended to make each non-Han ethnic group a minority in its traditional land, but the government paradoxically also tried to encourage minority ethnic pride in their traditional culture. The city of Hohhot, therefore, is filled with images of the traditional herding culture in its buildings and monuments.

As described by anthropologist William Jankowiak, who studied the Mongols in the capital city of Hohhot, the results were not what the Chinese government intended. In many ways, to be sure, the urban Mongols had abandoned their traditional culture and assimilated to the dominant Han culture. But we see the force of ecology more than the hand of tradition in the outcome. Many Mongols in the city no longer speak the Mongol language. Parents find it difficult to get children to speak Mongol when they live among Han. The scarcity of housing makes it difficult for the Mongols to form an ethnic enclave or even live near kin as they did in the past. In contrast to life in the rural areas, which revolves around kinship, city life requires interacting with strangers as well as relatives. Indeed, nonkin are often more important to you than kin. As one person said to Jankowiak, "We hide from our cousins but not our friends."

Sources: Davis and Harrell 1993; Pasternak 2009; Jankowiak 2004.

But perceived needs and the economic rewards that may be given to the innovator do not explain why only some people innovate. We know relatively little about why some people are more innovative than others. The ability to innovate may depend in part on such individual characteristics as high intelligence and creativity, and creativity may be influenced by social conditions.

A study of innovation among Ashanti artist carvers in Ghana suggests that creativity is more likely in some socioeconomic groups than in others.[32] Some carvers produced only traditional designs; others departed from tradition and produced "new" styles of carving. Two groups were found to innovate the most—the wealthiest and the poorest carvers. These two groups of carvers may tolerate risk more than the middle socioeconomic group. Innovative carving entails some risk because it may take more time and it may not sell. Wealthy carvers can afford the risk, and they may gain some prestige as well as income if their innovation is appreciated. The poor are not doing well anyway, and they have little to lose by trying something new.

Some societies encourage innovativeness more than others, and this can vary substantially over time. Patricia Greenfield and her colleagues describe the changes in weaving in a Mayan community in the Zinacantán region of Chiapas, Mexico.[33] In 1969 and 1970, innovation was not valued. Rather, tradition was; there was the old "true way" to do everything, including how one dressed. There were only four simple weaving patterns, and virtually all males wore ponchos with the same pattern. By 1991, virtually no poncho was the same and the villagers had developed elaborate brocaded and embroidered designs. In a period of 20 years, innovation had increased dramatically. Two other things had also changed. The economy was more commercialized; textiles as well as other items were now bought and sold. Weaving was taught in a less directed way. Whereas mothers used to give their daughters highly structured instruction, often with "four hands" on the loom, they were later allowed to learn more by themselves, by trial and error. The result was more abstract and varied designs.

Who Adopts Innovations? Once someone discovers or invents something, there is still the question of whether others will adopt the innovation. Many researchers have studied the characteristics of "early adopters." Such individuals tend to be educated, high in social status, upwardly mobile, and, if they are property owners, have large farms and businesses. The individuals who most need technological improvements—those who are less well off—are generally the last to adopt innovations. The theory is that only the wealthy can afford to take the substantial risks associated with new ways of doing things. In periods of rapid technological change, therefore, the gap between rich and poor is likely to widen because the rich adopt innovations sooner, and benefit more from them, than the poor.[34]

Does this imply that the likelihood of adopting innovations is a simple function of how much wealth a possible adopter possesses? Not necessarily. Frank Cancian reviewed several studies and found that upper-middle-class individuals show more conservatism than lower-middle-class individuals. Cancian suggested that, when the risks are unknown, lower-middle-class individuals are more receptive to innovation because they have less to lose. Later on, when the risks are better known—that is, as more people adopt the innovation—the upper-middle class catches up to the lower-middle class.[35] In general, people are more likely to adopt a behavior as it becomes more common.[36]

The speed with which an innovation is adopted may depend partly on how new behaviors and ideas are typically transmitted—or taught—in a society. If children learn most of what they know from their parents or from a relatively small number of elders, then innovation will be slow to spread throughout the society, and culture change is likely to be slow. Innovations may catch on more rapidly if individuals are exposed to various teachers and other "leaders" who can influence many in a relatively short time, and the more peers we have, the more we might learn from them.[37] Perhaps this is why the pace of change appears to be so fast today. In societies like North America, and increasingly in the industrializing world, it is likely that people learn in schools from teachers, from leaders in their specialties, and from peers.

Costs and Benefits An innovation that is technologically superior is not necessarily going to be adopted since it comes with costs as well as benefits for both individuals and large-scale industries. Take the computer keyboard. The keyboard used most often on computers today is called the QWERTY keyboard (named after the first letters that appear on the left side of keyboard). This curious ordering of the letters was actually invented to slow typing speed down! Early typewriters had mechanical keys that jammed if the typist went too fast.[38] Since computer keyboards do not have that problem, keys arranged for faster typing would probably be better and have, indeed, been invented. Yet they have not caught on, perhaps because people are reluctant to take the time or make the effort to change.

In large-scale industries, technological innovations may be very costly to implement. A new product or process may require a manufacturing or service facility to be revamped and workers to be retrained. Before a change is made, the costs of doing so are weighed against the potential benefits. If the market is expected to be large for a new product, the product is more likely to be produced. If the market is judged small, the benefits may not be sufficient inducement to change. Companies may also judge the value of an innovation by whether competitors could copy it. If the new innovation can easily be copied, the inventing company may not find the investment worthwhile. Although the market may be large, the inventing company may not be able to hold onto market share if other companies could produce the product quickly without having to invest in research and development.[39]

Diffusion

Diffusion The process by which cultural elements are borrowed from another society and incorporated into the culture of the recipient group.

The source of new cultural elements in a society may also be another society. The process by which cultural elements are borrowed from another society and incorporated into the culture of the recipient group is called **diffusion**. Borrowing sometimes enables a group to bypass stages or mistakes in the development of a process or institution. For example, Germany was able to accelerate its program of industrialization in the 19th century through technological borrowing because it could avoid some of the errors its English and Belgian competitors had made. Japan's industrialization followed the same pattern. Indeed, in recent years, some of the earliest industrialized countries have fallen behind their imitators in certain areas of production, such as automobiles, televisions, cameras, and computers.

Diffusion has far-reaching effects. In a well-known passage, Linton conveyed how integral diffusion is to our lives, even while we are largely ignorant about it. Considering the first few hours in the day of an American man in the 1930s, Linton tells us he

> . . . awakens in a bed built on a pattern which originated in the Near East but which was modified in northern Europe before it was transmitted to America. He throws back covers made from cotton, domesticated in India, or linen, domesticated in the Near East, or silk, the use of which was discovered in China. All of these materials have been spun and woven by processes invented in the Near East. . . . He takes off his pajamas, a garment invented in India, and washes with soap invented by the ancient Gauls. He then shaves, a masochistic rite which seems to have derived from either Sumer or ancient Egypt.
>
> Before going out for breakfast he glances through the window, made of glass invented in Egypt, and if it is raining puts on overshoes made of rubber discovered by the Central American Indians and takes an umbrella, invented in southeastern Asia. . .
>
> On his way to breakfast he stops to buy a paper paying for it with coins, an ancient Lydian invention. . . . His plate is made of a form of pottery invented in China. His knife is of steel, an alloy first made in southern India, his fork a medieval Italian invention, and his spoon a derivative of a Roman original. . . . After his fruit (African watermelon) and first coffee (an Abyssinian plant), . . . he may have the egg of a species of bird domesticated in Indo-China, or thin strips of the flesh of an animal domesticated in eastern Asia which have been salted and smoked by a process developed in northern Europe. . . .
>
> While smoking (an American Indian habit), he reads the news of the day, imprinted in characters invented by the ancient Semites upon a material invented in China by a process invented in Germany. As he absorbs the accounts of foreign troubles he will, if he is a good conservative citizen, thank a Hebrew deity in an Indo-European language that he is 100 percent American.[40]

Patterns of Diffusion The three basic patterns of diffusion are direct contact, intermediate contact, and stimulus diffusion.

1. *Direct contact.* Elements of a society's culture may first be taken up by neighboring societies and then gradually spread farther and farther afield. The spread of the use of paper (a sheet of interlaced fibers) is a good example of extensive diffusion by direct contact. The invention of paper is attributed to the Chinese Ts'ai Lun in A.D. 105. Within 50 years, paper was being made in many places in central China. Although the art of papermaking was kept secret for about 500 years, it was distributed as a commodity to much of the Arab world through the markets at Samarkand. But when Samarkand was attacked by the Chinese in A.D. 751, a Chinese prisoner of war was forced to set up a paper mill. Paper manufacture soon spread to the rest of the Arab world; it was first manufactured in Baghdad in A.D. 793, Egypt about A.D. 900, and Morocco about A.D. 1100. Papermaking was introduced as a commodity in Europe by Arab trade through Italian ports in the 12th century. The Moors built the first European paper mill in Spain about 1150. The technical knowledge then spread throughout Europe, with mills being built in Italy in 1276, France in 1348, Germany in 1390, and England in 1494.[41] In general, the pattern of accepting the borrowed invention was the same in all cases: Paper was first imported as a luxury, then in ever-expanding quantities as a staple product. Finally, and usually within one to three centuries, local manufacture began.

2. *Intermediate contact.* Diffusion by intermediate contact occurs through the agency of third parties. Frequently, traders carry a cultural trait from the society that originated it to another group. For example, Phoenician traders introduced the ancient Greeks to the first alphabet, which the Phoenicians had themselves received from the Ugarit, another Semitic culture. At times, soldiers serve as intermediaries in spreading a culture trait. European crusaders, such as the Knights Templar and the Knights of St. John, acted as intermediaries in two ways: They carried Christian culture to Muslim societies of North Africa and brought Arab culture back to Europe. In the 19th century, Western missionaries in all parts of the world encouraged natives to wear Western clothing. Hence, in Africa, the Pacific Islands, and elsewhere, native peoples can be found wearing shorts, suit jackets, shirts, ties, and other typically Western articles of clothing.

3. *Stimulus diffusion.* In stimulus diffusion, knowledge of a trait belonging to another culture stimulates the invention or development of a local equivalent. A classic example of stimulus diffusion is the Cherokee syllabic writing system created by a Native American named Sequoya so that his people could write down their language. Sequoya got the idea from his contact with Europeans. Yet he did not adopt the English writing system; indeed, he did not even learn to write English. What he did was utilize some English alphabetic symbols, alter others, and invent new ones. All the symbols he used represented Cherokee syllables and in no way echoed English alphabetic usage. In other words, Sequoya took English alphabetic ideas and gave them a new Cherokee form. The stimulus originated with Europeans; the result was singularly Cherokee.

The Selective Nature of Diffusion It is tempting to think that the dynamics of diffusion are like a stone sending concentric ripples over still water, but that would oversimplify the way diffusion actually occurs. Not all cultural traits are borrowed as readily as the ones we have mentioned, nor do they usually expand in neat, ever-widening circles. Rather, diffusion is a selective process. The Japanese, for instance, accepted much from Chinese culture, but they also rejected many traits. Rhymed tonal poetry, civil service examinations, and foot binding, which the Chinese favored, were never adopted in Japan. The poetry form was unsuited to the structure of the Japanese language; the examinations were unnecessary in view of the entrenched power of the Japanese aristocracy; and foot binding was repugnant to a people who abhorred body mutilation of any sort.

A Masai man in Kenya can call home or around the world from the plains of Kenya.

Not only would we expect societies to reject items from other societies that they find repellent, we would also expect them to reject ideas and technology that do not satisfy some psychological, social, or cultural need. After all, people are not sponges; they do not automatically soak up the things around them. If they did, the amount of cultural variation in the world would be extremely small, which is clearly not the case. Diffusion is also selective because the extent to which cultural traits can be communicated differs. Elements of material culture, such as mechanical processes and techniques, and overt practices, such as physical sports, are relatively easy to demonstrate. Consequently, they are accepted or rejected on their merits. When we move beyond the material world, however, we encounter real difficulties, which Linton (again) aptly described:

> *Although it is quite possible to describe such an element of culture as the ideal pattern for marriage . . . it is much less complete than a description of basketmaking. . . . The most thorough verbalization has difficulty in conveying the series of associations and conditioned emotional responses which are attached to this pattern [marriage] and which gave it meaning and vitality within our own society. . . . This is even more true of those concepts which . . . find no direct expression in behavior aside from verbalization. There is a story of an educated Japanese who after a long discussion on the nature of the Trinity with a European friend . . . burst out with: "Oh, I see now, it is a committee."*[42]

Finally, diffusion is selective because the overt form of a particular trait, rather than its function or meaning, frequently seems to determine how the trait will be received. For example, an enthusiasm for women to have bobbed hair (short haircuts) swept through much of North America in the 1920s but never caught on among the Native Americans of northwestern California. To many women of European ancestry, short hair was a symbolic statement of freedom. To Native American women, who traditionally cut their hair short when in mourning, it was a reminder of death.[43]

In the process of diffusion, then, we can identify a number of different patterns. We know that cultural borrowing is selective rather than automatic, and we can describe how a particular borrowed trait has been modified by the recipient culture. But our current knowledge does not allow us to specify when one or another of these outcomes will occur, under what conditions diffusion will occur, and why it occurs the way it does.

Acculturation

On the surface, the process of change called **acculturation** seems to include much of what we have discussed under the label of diffusion because acculturation refers to the changes that occur when different cultural groups come into intensive contact. As in diffusion, the source of new cultural items is the other society. But more often than not, anthropologists use the term *acculturation* to describe a situation in which one of the societies in contact is much more powerful than the other. Thus, acculturation can be seen as a process of extensive cultural borrowing in the context of superordinate-subordinate relations between societies.[44] There is probably always some borrowing both ways, but generally the subordinate or less powerful society borrows the most.

External pressure for culture change can take various forms. In its most direct form—conquest or colonialization—the dominant group uses force or the threat of force to try to bring about culture change in the other group. In the Spanish conquest of Mexico, for example, the conquerors forced many of the native groups to accept Catholicism. Although such direct force is not always exerted in conquest situations, dominated peoples often have little choice but to change. Examples of such indirectly forced change abound in the history of Native Americans in the United States. Although the federal government made few direct attempts to force people to adopt American culture, it did drive many native groups from their lands, thereby obliging them to give up many aspects of their traditional ways of life. To survive, they had no choice but to adopt many of the dominant society's traits. When Native American children were required to go to schools, which taught the dominant society's values, the process was accelerated.

A subordinate society may acculturate to a dominant society even in the absence of direct or indirect force. Perceiving that members of the dominant society enjoy more secure living conditions, the dominated people may identify with the dominant culture in the hope that they will be able to share some of its benefits by doing so. Or they may elect to adopt cultural elements from the dominant society because they perceive that the new element has advantages. For example, in Arctic areas, many Inuit and Saami groups seemed eager to replace dog sleds with snowmobiles without any coercion.[45] There is evidence that the Inuit weighed the advantages and disadvantages of the snowmobile versus the dog sled and that its adoption was gradual. Similarly, rifles were seen as a major technological improvement, increasing the success rate in hunting, but the Inuit did not completely abandon their former ways of hunting. More recently, the Inuit are trying out GPS devices for navigating.[46]

Acculturation processes vary considerably depending upon the wishes of the more powerful society, the attitudes of the less powerful, and whether there is any choice. More powerful societies do not always want individuals from another culture to assimilate or "melt into" the dominant culture completely; instead, they may prefer and even actively promote a *multicultural* society. Multiculturalism can be voluntary or may arise out of deliberate segregation. Then, too, even though the less powerful group may be pressured to acquire some of the dominant group's cultural traits, they may resist or even reject those cultural elements, at least for a considerable length of time.

Many millions of people, however, never had a chance to acculturate after contact with Europeans. They simply died, sometimes directly at the hands of the conquerors, but probably more often as a result of the new diseases the Europeans inadvertently brought with them. Depopulation because of measles, smallpox, and tuberculosis was particularly common in North and South America and on the islands of the Pacific. Those areas had previously been isolated from contact with Europeans and from the diseases of that continuous landmass we call the Old World—Europe, Asia, and Africa.[47] The story of Ishi, the last surviving member of a group of Native Americans in California called the Yahi, is a moving testimonial to the frequently tragic effect of contact with Europeans. In the space of 22 years, the Yahi population was reduced from several hundred to near zero. The historical record on this episode of depopulation suggests that European Americans murdered 30 to 50 Yahi for every European American murdered, but perhaps 60 percent of the Yahi died in the 10 years following their initial exposure to European diseases.[48]

Acculturation The process of extensive borrowing of aspects of culture in the context of superordinate-subordinate relations between societies; usually occurs as the result of external pressure.

Applied Anthropology

Development Programs and Culture Change: A Bedouin Case Study

Most governments of the world today want to "develop" their countries. They want to increase their crop yields and their exports, build major roads and irrigation projects, and industrialize. However, many development schemes have failed in part because they do not adequately consider the cultures of the people whose lives they affect. Governments, as well as international agencies that lend money, increasingly turn for advice to anthropologists to help plan and evaluate projects. While governments may not fully appreciate traditional ways of life, anthropologists understand that people are unlikely to accept a change if it does not integrate well with other aspects of their culture.

In many countries of the Middle East, governments have pressured nomadic Bedouin peoples to settle down. Yet government settlement schemes, by force or with enticements, have also often failed. The Bedouin way of life is essentially at odds with nation states, in which land is increasingly privately owned or converted for industrial uses (such as oil production) and resources are regulated. But Bedouin require vast stretches of grassland and a water source for their herds, resources that were traditionally available to them as members of kinship-based groups that maintained grazing rights over large territories.

Although there are many Bedouin groups in the Middle East and North Africa, they share key cultural traits. They are, as anthropologist Dawn Chatty points out, at once tribal, nomadic, and pastoral. And these three traits are a large part of a Bedouin's identity. When government-built settlements have been created to replace the Bedouin tent, the tribe has often continued its pastoral life near the settlement until overgrazing left a human-made desert or the water supply ran out. The nomadic Bedouin would then abandon such settlements to seek other grazable land and water, and they would again pitch their familiar tents.

Even an enlightened state may find that culture change cannot be imposed on the Bedouin. In the 1980s, Dawn

The Bedouin still often erect tents in fixed housing settlements as in this Israeli Negev settlement.

Chatty was asked by the government of the Middle Eastern country of Oman to help design a project to extend basic social services to the Bedouin without coercing them to alter their way of life. It isn't often that governments fund in-depth studies to try to understand the needs of the people being affected, but Chatty was able to persuade the Oman government that such a study was necessary as a first step. With United Nations funding, she evaluated the needs of the Harasiis pastoralists, a Bedouin group in Oman. Because the government wanted some action right away, the project soon incorporated a mobile health unit that could begin a program of primary care as well as immunization against measles, whooping cough, and polio. After a period of evaluation, the project team also recommended an annual distribution of tents, the establishment of dormitories so that children could live at schools, a new system of water delivery, and veterinary and marketing assistance.

The government was receptive to the recommendations of Chatty's group. Soon a "tribal" complex was built for the Harasiis. It included offices for their government representative, a medical clinic, a school, a mosque, a "reverse osmosis" water plant, a police station, and villas for government employees. But the complex was never occupied. It

appears that the Harasiis would continue to pursue their nomadic way of life.

Yet the Bedouin are not reluctant to change in all respects. As Chatty chronicles, many readily gave up relying on camels for transport in favor of trucks. Trucks are a modern adaptation, yet they still allow mobility. Now the Bedouin are able to get water from wells and transport water to their animals by truck. The adoption of trucks led to other changes. Since small animals can be more readily transported to new pastures by truck, many Bedouin have given up their dependence on camels and shifted to sheep and goat herding. Because money is required to buy trucks and pay for gasoline and repairs, Bedouin spend more time working for wages in temporary jobs. Aside from such adaptations from within, though, they have resisted enforced change. As for Chatty, she views her experience philosophically. She, like other applied anthropologists, has learned a great deal about the environmental and political conditions that impact the world's more marginalized cultures. And she continues to believe that it is her job to push for what Michael Cernea called "putting people first."

Sources: Chatty 1996, 2006; Cernea 1991, 7; Strachan 2011.

Nowadays, many powerful nations—and not just Western ones—may seem to be acting in more humanitarian ways to improve the life of previously subjugated as well as other "developing" peoples. For better or worse, these programs, however, are still forms of external pressure. The tactic used may be persuasion rather than force, but most of the programs are nonetheless designed to bring about acculturation in the direction of the dominant societies' cultures. For example, the introduction of formal schooling cannot help but instill new values that may contradict traditional cultural patterns. Even health care programs may alter traditional ways of life by undermining the authority of shamans and other leaders and by increasing population beyond the number that can be supported in traditional ways. Confinement to reservations or other kinds of direct force are not the only ways a dominant society can bring about acculturation.

The process of acculturation also applies to immigrants, most of whom, at least nowadays, choose to leave one country for another. Immigrants are almost always a minority in the new country and therefore are in a subordinate position. If the immigrant's culture changes, it is almost always in the direction of the dominant culture. Immigrant groups vary considerably in the degree and speed with which they adopt the new culture and the social roles of the new society in which they live. An important area of research is explaining the variation in acculturation and assimilation. (*Assimilation* is a concept very similar to acculturation, but *assimilation* is a term more often used by sociologists to describe the process by which individuals acquire the social roles and culture of the dominant group.)

Revolution

Certainly the most drastic and rapid way a culture can change is as a result of **revolution**—replacement, usually violent, of a country's rulers. Historical records, as well as our daily newspapers, indicate that people frequently rebel against established authority. Rebellions, if they occur, almost always occur in state societies where there is a distinct ruling elite. They take the form of struggles between rulers and ruled, between conquerors and conquered, or between representatives of an external colonial power and segments of the native society. Rebels do not always succeed in overthrowing their rulers, so rebellions do not always result in revolutions. And even successful rebellions do not always result in culture change; the individual rulers may change, but customs or institutions may not. The sources of revolution may be mostly internal, as in the French Revolution, or partly external, as in the Russian-supported 1948 revolution in Czechoslovakia and the United States-supported 1973 revolution against President Allende in Chile.

The American War of Independence was a colonial rebellion against the greatest imperial power of the 18th century, Great Britain. The 13 colonies owed at least a part of their success in the war to aid from France, which had been waging its own "Seven Years' War" against the British, and more indirectly from Spain, which would also declare war on the greater imperial power. Actually, the American war was closely following what we would now call a world war. In the 19th century and continuing into the middle and later years of the 20th century, there would be many other wars of independence against imperial powers in Latin America, Europe, Asia, and Africa. We don't always remember that the American rebellion was the first anti-imperialist wars in modern times and the model for many that followed. Just like many of the most recent liberation movements, the American rebellion was also part of a larger worldwide war involving people from many rival nations. A total of 30,000 German-speaking soldiers fought, for pay, on the British side; an army and navy from France fought on the American side. There were volunteers from other European countries, including Denmark, Holland, Poland, and Russia.

As in many revolutions, those who were urging revolution were considered "radicals." At a now-famous debate in Virginia in 1775, delegates from each colony met at a Continental Congress. Patrick Henry put forward a resolution to prepare for defense against the British armed forces. The motion barely passed, by a vote of 65 to 60. Henry's speech is now a part of American folklore. He rose to declare that it was insane not to oppose the British and that he was not afraid to test the strength of the colonies against Great Britain. Others might hesitate, he said, but he would have "liberty or death." The radicals who supported Henry's resolution included many aristocratic landowners, two of whom,

Revolution A usually violent replacement of a society's rulers.

George Washington and Thomas Jefferson, became the first and third occupants of the highest political office in what became the United States of America.[54]

Not all peoples who are suppressed, conquered, or colonialized eventually rebel against established authority. Why this is so, and why rebellions and revolts are not always successful in bringing about culture change, are still open questions. But some possible answers have been investigated. The historian Crane Brinton examined the classic revolutions of the past, including the American, French, and Russian revolutions, and suggested a set of conditions that may give rise to rebellion and revolution:

1. *Loss of prestige of established authority,* often as a result of the failure of foreign policy, financial difficulties, dismissals of popular ministers, or alteration of popular policies. France in the 18th century lost three major international conflicts, with disastrous results for its diplomatic standing and internal finances. Russian society was close to military and economic collapse in 1917, after 3 years of World War I.

2. *Threat to recent economic improvement.* In France, as in Russia, those sections of the population (professional classes and urban workers) whose economic fortunes had only shortly before taken an upward swing were "radicalized" by unexpected setbacks, such as steeply rising food prices and unemployment. The same may be said for the American colonies on the brink of their rebellion against Great Britain.

3. *Indecisiveness of government,* as exemplified by lack of consistent policy, which gives the impression of being controlled by, rather than in control of, events. The frivolous arrogance of Louis XVI's regime and the bungling of George III's prime minister, Lord North, with respect to the problems of the American colonies are examples.

4. *Loss of support of the intellectual class.* Such a loss deprived the prerevolutionary governments of France and Russia of any avowed philosophical support and led to their unpopularity with the literate public.[55]

The classic revolutions of the past occurred in countries that were industrialized only incipiently at best. For the most part, the same is true of the rebellions and revolutions in recent years; they have occurred mostly in countries we call "developing." The evidence from a worldwide survey of developing countries suggests that rebellions have tended to occur where the ruling classes depended mostly on the produce or income from land and therefore were resistant to demands for reform from the rural classes that worked the land. In such agricultural economies, the rulers are not likely to yield political power or give greater economic returns to the workers because to do so would eliminate the basis (landownership) of the rulers' wealth and power.[56]

Some political scientists have a broader definition of revolution and argue that not all great revolutions occur on the battlefield, nor are they all inspired by public rebellions. Some, like the culture revolution Ataturk brought to Turkey in 1919, for example, are largely the work of charismatic leaders.[57] Ataturk's government was responsible for molding a formerly imperial Muslim nation into a democracy and separating church (or mosque) and state. In retrospect, it was a monumental achievement since the role of clerics in government and the definition of democracy have remained ambiguous in much of the Middle East.

Since the winter of 2010, the world has witnessed a remarkable series of popular uprisings known collectively as the Arab Spring that have affected nearly every Muslim nation. It all began in the winter of 2010, when a street vendor in Tunisia set himself on fire after the police confiscated his fruit and vegetable cart. He had been an educated man, as more and more young Tunisians have been in the last few decades, but was unable to find other work in a country that had a 30 percent unemployment rate. His story was met with widespread and persistent protests, and, with the world watching and listening through social media, Tunisia's president fled to Saudi Arabia less than 2 months later, and the Tunisian people were promised a free and democratic election. Within months, similar public protests toppled the leaders of Egypt, Libya, and Yemen. The leaders of nearly every Muslim nation have been affected by the uprising, and many of those who are still in power have promised reforms, reorganized their governments, or promised to leave when their current terms of office end.[58] But in many of the countries, turmoil and bloodshed is still on-going. It is too soon to know whether these uprisings will lead to the cultural change many Arab citizens want. But we can glean some characteristics these modern revolutions all seem to share. Their success depends on foreign support and intervention, in part because the citizens of authoritarian regimes have not been allowed to organize competing political parties. Social media has played a role in the speed with which change has occurred, in part because many leaders are less likely to use force when the world is watching.[59] The goal in each nation appears to be a democratically elected government and the end of oppressive regimes.

Finally, a particularly interesting question is why revolutions sometimes, perhaps even usually, fail to measure up to the high hopes of those who initiate them. When rebellions succeed in replacing the ruling elite, the result is often the institution of a military dictatorship even more restrictive and repressive than the government that existed before. The new ruling establishment may merely substitute one set of repressions for another rather than bring any real change to the nation. On the other hand, some revolutions have resulted in fairly drastic overhauls of societies.

The idea of revolution has been one of the central myths and inspirations of many groups both in the past and in the present. The colonial empire building of countries, such as England and France, created a worldwide situation in which rebellion became nearly inevitable. In numerous technologically underdeveloped lands, which have been exploited by more powerful countries for their natural resources and cheap labor, a deep resentment has often developed against the foreign ruling classes or their local clients. Where the ruling classes, native or foreign, refuse to be responsive to those feelings, rebellion becomes the only alternative. In many areas, it has become a way of life.

Anti-government protesters during a 2011 rally in Morocco that became part of what is known as the Arab Spring movement.

Culture Change and Adaptation

9.8 Relate culture change to the process of adaptation to a changing environment.

We have discussed the fact that culture is patterned, and that adaptation to the environment is one reason why certain culture traits are clustered, because more than one trait is likely to be *adaptive* in a particular environment. We make the assumption that most of the customary behaviors of a culture are probably *adaptive*, or at least not maladaptive, in that environment. Even though customs are learned and not genetically inherited, cultural adaptation may resemble biological adaptation in one major respect. The frequency of certain genetic alternatives is likely to increase over time if those genetic traits increase their carriers' chances of survival and reproduction. Similarly, the frequency of a new learned behavior will increase over time and become customary in a population if the people with that behavior are most likely to survive and reproduce.

One of the most important differences between cultural evolution and genetic evolution is that individuals often can decide whether or not to accept and follow the way their parents behave or think, whereas they cannot decide whether or not to inherit certain genes. When enough individuals change their behavior and beliefs, we say that the culture has changed. Therefore, it is possible for culture change to occur much more rapidly than genetic change.

A dramatic example of intentional cultural change was the adoption and later elimination of the custom of *sepaade* among the Rendille, a pastoral population that herds camels, goats, and sheep in the desert in northern Kenya. According to the *sepaade* tradition, some women had to wait to marry until all their brothers were married. These women could well have been over 40 by the time they married. The Rendille say that this tradition was a result of intense warfare between the Rendille and the Borana during the mid-19th century. Attacked by Borana on horseback, the male warriors had to leave their camels unattended, and the frightened camels fled. The daughters of one male age-set were appointed to look after the camels, and the *sepaade* tradition developed. In 1998, long after warfare with the Borana ceased, the elders decided to free the *sepaade* from their obligation to postpone their own marriages. Interviews with the Rendille in the 1990s revealed that many individuals were fully aware of the reason for the tradition in the first place. Now, they said, there was peace, so there was no longer any reason for the *sepaade* tradition to continue.[49]

The adoption of the *sepaade* is an example of culture change in a changing environment. But what if the environment is stable? Is culture change more or less likely? Robert Boyd and Peter Richerson have shown mathematically that, when the environment is relatively stable and individual mistakes are costly, staying with customary modes of behavior (usually transmitted by parents) is probably more adaptive than changing.[50] But what happens when the environment, particularly the social environment, is changing? There are plenty of examples in the modern world of circumstances that force a change: People have to migrate to new places for work; medical care leads to increased population so that land is scarcer; people have had land taken away from them and are forced to make do with less land; and so on.

It is particularly when circumstances change that individuals are likely to try ideas or behaviors that are different from those of their parents. Most people would want to adopt behaviors that are more suited to their present circumstances, but how do they know which behaviors are better? There are various ways to find out. One way is by experimenting, trying out various new behaviors. Another way is to evaluate the experiments of others. If a person who tries a new technique seems successful, we would expect that person to be imitated, just as we would expect people to stick with new behaviors they have personally tried and found successful. Finally, one might choose to do what most people in the new situation decide to do.[51]

Why one choice rather than another? In part, the choice may be a function of the cost or risk of the innovation. It is relatively easy, for example, to find out how long it takes to cut down a tree with an introduced steel ax as compared with a stone ax. Not surprisingly, innovations such as a steel ax catch on relatively quickly because comparison is easy and the results clear-cut. But what if the risk is very great? Suppose the innovation involves adopting a whole new way of farming that you have never practiced before. You can try it, but you might not have any food if you fail. As we discussed earlier, risky innovations are likely to be tried only by those individuals who can afford the risk. Other people may then evaluate their success and adopt the new strategy if it looks promising. Similarly, if you migrate to a new area, say, from a high-rainfall area to a drier one, it may pay to look around to see what most people in the new place do; after all, the people in the drier area probably have customs that are adaptive for that environment.

We can expect, then, that the choices individuals make may often be adaptive ones. But it is important to note that adopting an innovation from someone in one's own society or borrowing an innovation from another society is not always or necessarily beneficial, either in the short or the long run. First, people may make mistakes in judgment, especially when some new behavior seems to satisfy a physical need. Why, for example, have smoking and drug use diffused so widely even though they are likely to reduce a person's chances of survival? Second, even if people are correct in their short-term judgment of benefit, they may be wrong in their judgment about long-run benefit. A new crop may yield more than the old crop for five consecutive years, but the new crop may fail miserably in the sixth year because of lower-than-normal rainfall or because the new crop depleted soil nutrients. Third, people may be forced by the more powerful to change with few if any benefits for themselves.

Whatever motivates humans to change their behavior, the theory of natural selection suggests that a new behavior is not likely to become cultural or remain cultural over generations if it has harmful reproductive consequences, just as a genetic mutation with harmful consequences is not likely to become frequent in a population.[52] Still, we know of many examples of culture change that seem maladaptive—the switch to bottle-feeding rather than nursing infants, which may spread infection because contaminated water is used, or the adoption of alcoholic beverages, which may lead to alcoholism and early death.

Baby Girl Names	1970's	1980's	1990's	2000's
Amanda	#17	#3	#6	#63
Amy	#2	#15	#64	#115
Ashley	#140	#4	#2	#10
Emily	#66	#25	#3	#1
Emma			#56	#3
Hannah		#91	#11	#5
Jennifer	#1	#2	#1	#39
Jessica	#11	#1	#16	#23
Kimberly	#5	#17	#36	#56
Madison			#29	#2
Michelle	#4	#12	#32	#72
Olivia		#195	#38	#4
Samantha	#109	#26	#5	#8
Sarah	#19	#5	#4	#12

FIGURE 9.2

The names shown here were in the top 5 baby names for at least one decade from the 1970s to the 2000s. The number shown is the rank for the decade. If a row is blank it means that the name was not in the top 200. Note that although there is some overlap between adjacent decades in popular names, there is, with the exception of Jennifer, no overlap every other decade. Baby names are widely thought to be a type of culture change that results from random copying, but has no adaptive consequences.

Source: http://www.socialsecurity.gov/OACT/babynames/decades/index.htm

Copying others doing something different is an important part of culture change, but sometimes there is no apparent adaptive consequence. Extrapolating from genetic research that shows that biological change can sometimes occur nonselectively—that is, by pure chance—cultural anthropologists have identified coincidences in popular culture change that they explain as examples of neutral or random copying. Random copying appears to occur with enough frequency that it creates patterns and repetitions that are especially apparent in popular culture. For example, random copying may explain why a large proportion of the public chooses the same favorite song or the same names for their babies (see Figure 9.2).[53]

Globalization: Problems and Opportunities

9.9 Evaluate the problems and opportunities posed by globalization.

Investment capital, people, and ideas are moving around the world at an ever faster rate.[60] Transportation now allows people and goods to circle the globe in days; telecommunications and the Internet make it possible to send a message around the world in seconds and minutes. Economic exchange is enormously more global and transnational. The word **globalization** is often used nowadays to refer to "the massive flow of goods, people, information, and capital across huge areas of the earth's surface."[61] The process of globalization has resulted in the worldwide spread of cultural features, particularly in the domain of economics and international trade. We buy from the same companies (that have factories all over the world), and we sell our products and services for prices that are set by world market forces. We can eat pizza, hamburgers, curry, or sushi in most urban centers.

Globalization The ongoing spread of goods, people, information, and capital around the world.

In some ways, cultures are changing in similar directions. They have become more commercial, more urban, and more international. The job has become more important, and kinship less important, as people travel to and work in other countries and return just periodically to their original homes. Ideas about democracy, the rights of the individual, and alternative medical practices and religions have become more widespread; people in many countries of the world watch the same TV shows, wear similar fashions, and listen to the same or similar music. In short, people are increasingly sharing behaviors and beliefs with people in other cultures, and as Paul Durrenberger says, the cultures of the world are less and less things "with edges."[62]

Globalization as we know it began in earnest about A.D. 1500 with exploration by and expansion of Western societies.[63] We tend to think of globalization from a Western perspective. But a form of continental diffusion between Asia, Africa, and Europe had been occurring since at least the beginning of written history, in large part because of the scope and power of empires. The great ancient empires, ruled by Assyrian, Chinese, and Egyptian dynasties, transformed the cultures of the peoples they conquered but were also themselves changed by their encounters. The Roman Empire extended its reach to western Asia in the time of Christ. Arab caliphates ruled parts of medieval Europe and revived long dormant scientific and mathematical traditions. The Mongol Empire swept across Central Asia and into the Baltics in the 13th century. All of these contacts had already transformed parts of the world. Nevertheless, it is safe to say that globalization is occurring today at an unprecedented pace and scale. Very few places in the world have not been affected by globalization.[64] Most of the recent external pressures have come from Western societies, but not all. Far Eastern societies, such as Japan and China, have also stimulated culture change.

But diffusion of a culture trait does not mean that it is incorporated in exactly the same way, and the spread of certain products and activities through globalization does not mean that change happens in the same way everywhere. For example, the spread of multinational fast-food restaurants, such as McDonald's or Kentucky Fried Chicken, has come to symbolize globalization. But the behavior of the Japanese in such restaurants is quite different from that of Americans. Perhaps the most surprising difference is that the Japanese who visit a McDonald's actually engage in more familial intimacy and sharing than they do in their traditional restaurants. We imagine that establishments like McDonald's

Worldwide communication and the spread of ideas is facilitated by technology such as satellite TV and the internet. Balconies are used to dry clothes and to hang satellite dishes in this city in Algeria.

promote fast eating. But Japan has long had fast food—noodle shops at train stations, street vendors, and boxed lunches. Sushi, which is usually ordered in the United States at a sit-down restaurant, is often served in Japan at a bar with a conveyor belt—individuals only need to pluck off the wanted dish as it goes by. Observations at McDonald's in Japan suggest that mothers typically order food for the family while the father spends time with the children at a table, a rare event since fathers often work long hours and cannot get home for dinner often. The French fries are typically shared by the family. Even burgers and drinks are passed around, with many people taking a bite or a sip. Japan has historically borrowed food, such as the Chinese noodle soup now called ramen. Indeed, in a survey, ramen was listed as the most representative Japanese food. The burger was the second most-often listed. McDonald's has become Japanese—the younger generation does not even know that McDonald's is a foreign company—they think it is Japanese.[65]

Enormous amounts of international investment fuel world trade. Shifts in the world marketplace may drastically affect a country's well-being more than ever before. There are many negative effects of colonialism, imperialism, and globalization. For example, 60 percent of Pakistan's industrial employment is in textile and apparel manufacturing, but serious unemployment resulted when that manufacturing was crippled by restrictive American import policies and fears about war between India and Afghanistan.[66] Native peoples in many places have lost their land and been forced to work for inadequate wages in mines, plantations, and factories owned by foreign capitalists. Undernutrition, if not starvation, is a common problem. Also, global travel has hastened the spread of such diseases as HIV and severe acute respiratory syndrome (more widely known by its abbreviation SARS), and increasing deforestation has led to a spread of malaria.[67]

Are there any positive consequences of globalization? The "human development indicators" collected by the United Nations suggest many improvements, including increases in life expectancy and literacy in most countries. The increased life expectancy is undoubtedly largely due to the spread of medicines developed in the advanced economies of the West. There is generally less warfare as colonial powers enforced pacification within the colonies that later became independent states. Most important, perhaps, has been the worldwide growth of middle classes whose livelihoods depend on globalizing commerce. The middle classes in many countries have also become agents of social change; empowered by their strength in numbers, they have pressured governments to reduce social injustice and enact democratic reforms.

World trade is the primary engine of economic development. With it, per capita income is increasing. Forty years ago, the countries of Asia were among the poorest countries in the world in terms of per capita income. Since then, because of their involvement in world trade, their incomes have risen enormously. In 1960, South Korea was as poor as India. Now its per capita income is 20 times higher than India's. Singapore is an even more dramatic example. In the late 1960s, its economy was failing. Today, its per capita income is higher than Britain's.[68] Mexico used to be a place where North Americans built factories to produce garments for the North American market. Now its labor is no longer so cheap. But because Mexico has easy access to the North American market and because its large labor force is acquiring the necessary skills, it is developing high-tech manufacturing with decent salaries.[69]

Not every country has a large labor force, a fact that has promoted a world trade in people. Many countries now export labor to other countries, with their government's blessing. Mexico has done so for a long time. Millions of people from Bangladesh are overseas on government-sponsored work contracts. Virtually every family in a Bangladeshi village depends on someone who works overseas and sends money home. Without those remittances, many would face starvation.[70]

Does the higher per capita income that can come with globalization mean that life has improved generally in a country? Not necessarily. Inequality within countries can increase with technological improvements, since the rich often benefit the most. In addition, economic wealth is increasingly concentrated in a relatively small number of countries. Although most countries may be doing better on average, there is also more income and class inequality, and poverty is more widespread.

Although many of the changes associated with globalization seem to be driven by the economic and political power of the richer countries, the movement of ideas, art, music, and food is more reciprocal, in large part because people who migrate bring their culture with them. Thanks to migration, North Americans regularly eat tortilla chips and salsa, sushi, and curries; listen to reggae music; dance to Latin American rhythms; live with African carvings; and wear beaded necklaces.

In counterreaction to globalization, there has also been increased interest recently in gaining knowledge about the indigenous plants, healing traditions, and shamanistic practices within countries. As indigenous knowledge comes to be viewed as potentially valuable, shamans have been able to speak out on national and international issues. In Brazil, for example, shamans have organized to speak out against "biopiracy"—the perceived unethical appropriation of biological knowledge for commercial purposes. In a more globalized world, such indigenous activists can be heard by more people than ever before: In spite of the fact that indigenous people constitute less than 1 percent of the Brazilian population, some activist groups have been able to keep in touch with international environmentalists, using tape recorders and video cameras to convey information about their local situation.[71]

It is probably not possible to go back to a time when societies were not so dependent on each other, not so interconnected through world trade, and not so dependent on commercial exchange. Even those who are most upset with globalization find it difficult to imagine that it is possible to return to a less connected world. For better or worse, the world is interconnected and will remain so. The question now is whether the average economic improvements in countries will eventually translate into economic improvements for most individuals.

Ethnogenesis Creation of a new culture.

9.10 Describe and give examples of ethnogenesis, or the emergence of new cultures.

Ethnogenesis: The Emergence of New Cultures

Many of the processes that we have discussed—expansion and domination by the West and other powerful nations, peoples' reduced ability to earn their livelihoods by traditional means, the imposition of schools or other methods to force acculturation, attempts to convert people to other religions, and globalization—have led to profound changes in culture. But if culture change in the modern world has made cultures more alike in some ways, it has not eliminated cultural differences. Indeed, many cultures still vary considerably. Moreover, the aftermath of violent events, such as depopulation, relocation, enslavement, and genocide, can lead to **ethnogenesis**, a process whereby a group creates a new culture.[72]

Some of the most dramatic examples of ethnogenesis occur in areas where escaped slaves (called Maroons) have settled. Maroon societies emerged in the past few hundred years in a variety of New World locations, from the United States to the West Indies and northern parts of South America. One such new culture in South America, now known as Aluku, emerged when slaves fled from coastal plantations in Suriname to the swampy interior country along the Cottica River. After a war with the Dutch colonists, this particular group moved to French Guiana. The escaped slaves, originating from widely varying cultures in Africa or born on Suriname plantations, organized themselves into autonomous communities with military headmen.[73] Although Aluku settlements shifted location as a way of evading enemies, co-residence in a community and collective ownership of land became important parts of their emerging identities. Communities took on the names of the specific plantations from which their leaders had escaped. Principles of inheritance through the female line began to develop, and full-fledged

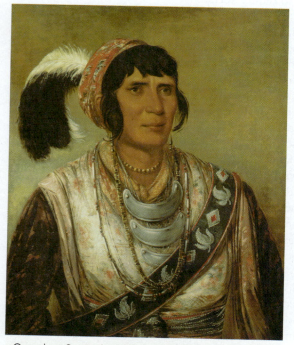

Osceola, a Seminole chief, was born of a British father and a Creek mother. He led his people against the settlers in the Seminole Wars but was captured and died in confinement at Fort Moultrie, South Carolina.

Migrants and Immigrants

Increasing Cultural Diversity Within the Countries of the World

The modern world is culturally diverse in two ways. There are native cultures in every part of the world, and today most countries have people from different cultures who have arrived relatively recently. Recent arrivals may be migrants coming for temporary work, or they may be refugees, forced by persecution or genocide to migrate, or they may be immigrants who voluntarily come into a new country. Parts of populations have moved away from their native places since the dawn of humanity. The first modern-looking humans moved out of Africa only in the last 100,000 years, and people have been moving ever since. The people we call Native Americans were actually the first to come to the New World; most anthropologists think they came from northeast Asia.

In the last 200 years, the United States and Canada have experienced extensive influxes of people. Native Americans are vastly outnumbered by descendants of earlier immigrants and by newcomers from Europe, Africa, Asia, Latin America, and elsewhere. North America not only has native and regional subcultures but also ethnic, religious, and occupational subcultures, each with its own distinctive set of culture traits. Thus, North American culture is partly a "melting pot" and partly a mosaic of cultural diversity. Many of us (aside from anthropologists) like the variety such diversity brings to our lives.

Many of the population movements in the world today, as in the past, are responses to persecution and war. The word *diaspora* is often used nowadays to refer to these major dispersions. Most were and are involuntary; people are fleeing danger and

The large Chinese community in Rome, Italy, celebrates the Chinese New Year in one of the town's main squares.

death. But this is not always the case. Scholars distinguish between different types of diasporas, including "victim," "labor," "trade," and "imperial." The Africans who were sold into slavery; the Armenians who fled genocide in the early 20th century; the Jews who fled persecution and genocide in various places over the centuries; the Palestinians who fled to the West Bank, Gaza, Jordan, and Lebanon in the mid-20th century; and the Rwandans who fled genocide toward the end of the 20th century may have mostly been victims. But the Chinese, Italians, and Poles may have mostly moved to take advantage of job opportunities, the Lebanese to trade, and the British to extend and service their empire.

Often categories of diaspora overlap; population movements can and have occurred for more than one reason. As economics and politics are more globalized, diasporas are becoming more "transnational"; and the ease of global communications allows people to maintain social, economical, and political ties to their homelands. Some diasporic communities play an active role in the politics of their homelands, and some nation-states have begun to recognize their far-flung emigrants as important constituencies.

Cultural anthropologists are increasingly studying migrant, refugee, and immigrant groups and focusing on how the groups have adapted their cultures to new surroundings, what they have retained, how they relate to the homeland, how they have developed an ethnic consciousness, and how they relate to other minority groups and the majority culture.

Sources: M. Ember et al. 2005; Levinson and M. Ember 1997.

matriclans became the core of each village. They practiced slash-and-burn cultivation, with women doing most of the work. Aluku also established spiritual practices. Each village had its own shrine, the *faaka tiki*, where residents invoked the clan ancestors, as well as a special house where the deceased were brought and honored before being taken to the forest for burial. And Aluku clans inherited avenging spirits with whom they could communicate through mediums.

The Aluku are a clear example of ethnogenesis because the culture did not exist 350 years ago. It emerged and was created by people trying to adapt to circumstances not of their own making. In common with other cases of emerging ethnic identity, the Aluku came not only to share new patterns of behavior but also to see themselves as having a common origin (a common ancestor), a shared history, and a common religion.[74]

The emergence of the Seminole in Florida is another example of ethnogenesis. The early settlers who moved to what is now Florida and later became known as Seminole largely derived from the Lower Creek Kawita chiefdom. The Kawita chiefdom, like other southeastern Muskogean chiefdoms, was a large, complex, and multiethnic paramount chiefdom. Its ruler, Kawita, relied on allegiance and tribute from outlying districts on which he imposed ritual and linguistic hegemony.[75]

A combination of internal divisions among the Lower Creek, vacant land in northern Florida, and weak Spanish control over northern Florida apparently prompted dissidents to move away and settle in three different areas in Florida. Three new chiefdoms were established, essentially similar to those the settlers left and still under the supposed control of Kawita.[76] But the three chiefdoms began to act together under the leadership of Tonapi, the Talahassi chief. After 1780, over a period of 40 or so years, the three Seminole chiefdoms formally broke with Kawita. Not only was geographic separation a factor, but the political and economic interests of the Creek Confederacy and of the Seminole had diverged. For example, the Creek supported neutrality in the American Revolution, but the Seminole took the side of the British. During this time, the British encouraged slaves to escape by promising freedom in Florida. These Maroon communities allied themselves with the emerging Seminole. The composition of the Seminole population again changed dramatically after the War of 1812 and the Creek War of 1814.[77] First, a large number of Creek refugees, mostly Upper Creek Talapusa (who spoke a different Muskogean language), became Seminole. Second, the Seminole ranks were also expanded by a large number of escaped slaves and Maroons who fled when the Americans destroyed a British fort in 1816. Larger scale political events continued to influence Seminole history. When the Americans conquered Florida, they insisted on dealing with one unified Seminole council, they removed the Seminole to a reserve in Florida, and later, after the second Seminole war, removed most of them to Oklahoma.[78] It would seem from this and other cases that cultural identities can be shaped and reshaped by political and economic processes.

Cultural Diversity in the Future

9.11 Characterize what anthropologists predict about future cultural diversity.

Measured in terms of travel time, the world today is much smaller than it has ever been. It is possible now to fly halfway around the globe in the time it took people less than a century ago to travel to the next state. In the realm of communication, the world is even smaller. We can talk to someone on the other side of the globe in a matter of minutes, we can send that person a message (by cell phone or the Internet) in seconds, and through television we can see live coverage of events in that person's country. More and more people are drawn into the world market economy, buying and selling similar things and, as a consequence, altering the patterns of their lives in sometimes similar ways. Still, although modern transportation and communication facilitate the rapid spread of some cultural characteristics to all parts of the globe, it is highly unlikely that all parts of the world will end up the same culturally. Cultures are bound to retain some of their original characteristics or develop distinctive new adaptations. Even though television has diffused around the world, local people continue to prefer local programs when they are available. And even when people all over the world watch the same program, they may interpret it in very different ways. People are not just absorbing the messages they get, they often resist or revise them.[79]

Until recently, researchers studying culture change generally assumed that the differences between people of different cultures would become minimal. But in the last 30 years or so, it has become increasingly apparent that, although many differences disappear, many people are affirming ethnic identities in a process that often involves deliberately introducing cultural difference.[80] Eugeen Roosens describes the situation of the Huron of Quebec, who in the late 1960s seemed to have disappeared as a distinct culture. The Huron language had disappeared and the lives of the Huron were not obviously distinguishable from those of the French Canadians around them. The Huron then developed a new identity as they actively worked to promote the rights of indigenous peoples like themselves. That their new defining cultural symbols bore no resemblance to the past Huron culture is beside the point.

One fascinating possibility is that ethnic diversity and ethnogenesis may be a result of broader processes. Elizabeth Cashdan found that the degree of ethnic diversity appears to be related to environmental unpredictability, which is associated with greater distance from the equator.[81] More predictability seems to be associated with greater ethnic diversity. There are many more cultural groups nearer to the equator than in very northern and southern latitudes. Perhaps, Cashdan suggests, environmental unpredictability in the north and south necessitates wider ties between social groups to allow cooperation in case local resources fail. This may minimize the likelihood of cultural divergence, that is, ethnogenesis. Hence, there will be fewer cultures further from the equator.

Future research on culture change should increase our understanding of how and why various types of change are occurring. If we can increase our understanding of culture change in the present, we should be better able to understand similar processes in the past. We may be guided in our efforts to understand culture change by the large number of cross-cultural correlations that have been discovered between a particular cultural variation and its presumed causes.[82] All cultures have changed over time; variation is the product of differential change. Thus, the variations we see are the products of change processes, and the discovered predictors of those variations may suggest how and why the changes occurred.

Summary and Review

Defining Culture

9.1 Discuss the concept of culture as used in anthropology, its salient properties, and controversies surrounding the concept of culture.

- Culture is the set of learned behaviors and ideas (including beliefs, attitudes, values, and ideals) that are characteristic of a particular society or other social group.

- Behaviors can also produce products or material culture, including houses, musical instruments, and tools that are the products of customary behavior.

- Anthropologists have traditionally been concerned with the cultural characteristics of societies. Societies may or may not correspond to countries; many countries, particularly newer ones, contain many societies.

- The terms *society* and *culture* are not synonymous. Society refers to a group of people; culture refers to the learned and shared behaviors, ideas, and characteristic of those people.

- Even when anthropologists refer to something as cultural, there is always individual variation, and not everyone in a society shares a particular cultural characteristic of that society.

- For something to be considered cultural, it must be not only shared but also learned.

- Cognitive anthropologists are most likely to say that culture refers not to behaviors but to the rules and ideas behind them, and that culture therefore resides in people's heads.

- Another view is that culture is an entity, a force, that profoundly affects the individuals who live within its influence.

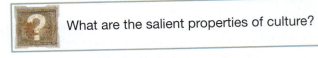 What are the salient properties of culture?

Cultural Constraints

9.2 Describe direct and indirect cultural constraints, and how they relate to norms.

- Because members of a culture generally conform to that culture, they are not always aware of being constrained by its standards and rules for acceptable behavior, which social scientists refer to as norms.

- Cultural constraints can be direct or indirect.

What is an example of a direct cultural constraint and an indirect cultural constraint?

Attitudes That Hinder the Study of Cultures

9.3 Identify attitudes that hinder the study of cultures.

- Ethnocentrism—a view of one's cultural behaviors and attitudes as correct and those of other cultures as immoral or inferior—can bias objectively observing another culture.

- Ethnocentrism also keeps a person from understanding his or her own customs.

- Glorification of one's own culture or that of another also hinders effective anthropological study.

 What are some examples of ethnocentrism?

Cultural Relativism

9.4 Critically assess the concept of cultural relativism.

- The idea of cultural relativism rejects the notion that Western cultures are at the highest or most progressive stage of evolution.

- Cultural relativism attempts to objectively describe and understand a society's customs and ideas in the context of that society's problems and opportunities.

- Following the idea of cultural relativism helps anthropologists be alert to perspectives in other cultures that might challenge their own cultural beliefs about what is true and that might lead them to make moral judgments.

- Approaches using cultural relativism pose conflicts with efforts to create universal standards of human rights. However, universal human rights advocates might increase their persuasiveness if they are aware of the viewpoints and values within a particular culture.

 What are some of the controversies surrounding the concept of cultural relativism?

Describing a Culture

9.5 Describe the methods by which anthropologists describe cultures.

- Understanding what is cultural involves (a) separating what is shared from what is individually variable and (b) understanding whether common behaviors and ideas are learned.

- Variations in behavior are typically confined within socially acceptable limits.

- Anthropologists try to distinguish actual behavior from ideal cultural traits—the ideas about how people in particular situations ought to feel and behave. Ideal cultural traits may differ from actual behavior because the ideal is based on the way society used to be.

- When a domain of behavior includes many individual variations or when the people studied are unaware of their pattern of behavior, the anthropologist may need to collect information from a larger sample of individuals to establish what the cultural trait is.

- Anthropologists suspect that something is largely learned if it varies from society to society and is genetically influenced when it is found in all societies.

 How do anthropologists distinguish between what is cultural or individually variable?

Culture Is Patterned

9.6 Explain why culture is integrated or patterned.

- A culture that is mostly integrated is one in which elements or traits are mostly adjusted to or consistent with one another.

- Integration may be influenced by psychological processes and by people transferring experiences from one area of life to another.

- Cultural traits may become patterned through adaptation. Customs that diminish the survival chances of a society are not likely to persist. However, what may be adaptive in one environment may not be adaptive in another.

What are some examples of cultural patterning or integration?

How and Why Cultures Change

9.7 Describe and give examples of how cultures change through discovery and invention, diffusion, and acculturation.

- Examining the history of a society will reveal that its culture has changed over time. Consequently, in describing a culture, it is important to understand that a description pertains to a particular time period.

- A good deal of culture change may be stimulated by changes in the external environment.

- Inventions and discoveries (including behavior and ideas), when accepted and regularly used by a society, will change the culture. These inventions and discoveries might be unintentional or intentional.

- Relatively little is known about why some people are more innovative than others. The ability to innovate may depend in part on such individual characteristics as high intelligence and creativity. Creativity may be influenced by social conditions.

- In general, people are more likely to adopt a behavior or innovation as it becomes more common. The speed with which an innovation is adopted may depend partly on how new behaviors and ideas are typically transmitted—or taught—in a society.

- New cultural elements in one society may come from another society. Innovation occurring in this way is called diffusion. The three basic patterns of diffusion are direct contact, intermediate contact, and stimulus diffusion.

- Diffusion is a selective process. New traits and elements will be rejected or accepted depending on complex variables.

- Acculturation is another type of change that occurs when different cultural groups come into intensive contact. Acculturation occurs primarily when one of the two societies in contact is more powerful than the other.

- One of the most drastic and rapid way a culture can change is as a result of revolution—replacement, usually violent, of a country's rulers.

- The sources of revolution may be mostly internal, or partly external. Revolutions are not always successful in their goals, nor necessarily in bringing about culture change.

- Not all people who are suppressed, conquered, or colonialized eventually rebel against established authority. Revolutions are more likely in countries that are just becoming industrialized.

 How do cultures change through discovery and invention, diffusion, and acculturation?

Culture Change and Adaptation

9.8 Relate culture change to the process of adaptation to a changing environment.

- The frequency of a new learned behavior will increase over time and become customary in a population if the people exhibiting that behavior are most likely to survive and reproduce. It is possible for culture change to occur much more rapidly than genetic change.

- When circumstances change, individuals are particularly likely to try ideas or behaviors that are different from those of their parents.

? What is an example of how adaptation can lead to culture change?

Globalization: Problems and Opportunities

9.9 Evaluate the problems and opportunities posed by globalization.

- The process of globalization has resulted in the worldwide spread of cultural features, particularly in the domain of economics and international trade.

- In some ways, cultures are changing in similar directions. They have become more commercial, more urban, and more international.

- A form of continental diffusion between Asia, Africa, and Europe had been occurring since at least the beginning of written history, in large part because of the scope and power of empires.

- Worldwide diffusion of a culture trait does not mean that it is incorporated in exactly the same way among societies, and the spread of certain products and activities through globalization does not mean that change happens in the same way everywhere.

- Negative effects of globalization include unemployment, native peoples' loss of land, increasing class inequality, undernutrition and starvation, and spread of disease.

- Positive effects of globalization include increases in life expectancy and literacy, less warfare, and growth of middle classes, which have become agents of social change.

- Movement of ideas, art, music, and food among cultures tends to be reciprocal.

 Using some examples, what are some examples of positive and negative effects of globailization?

Ethnogenesis: The Emergence of New Cultures

9.10 Describe and give examples of ethnogenesis, or the emergence of new cultures.

- Despite the trend of globalization, many cultures still vary considerably, and new cultures have been created—a process called ethnogenesis.
- In particular, cases of violent events such as depopulation, relocation, enslavement, and genocide can lead to ethnogenesis.

 What is ethnogenesis? Under what conditions is it more likely?

Cultural Diversity in the Future

9.11 Characterize what anthropologists predict about future cultural diversity.

- Although modern transportation and communication facilitate the rapid spread of some cultural characteristics to all parts of the globe, it is highly unlikely that all parts of the world will end up the same culturally.
- Many people are affirming ethnic identities in a process that often involves deliberately introducing cultural difference.
- One study suggests that there are many more cultural groups nearer to the equator than in very northern and southern latitudes, possibly associated with levels of greater environmental predictability.

 Why will globalization processes likely not result in the development of a homogenous worldwide culture?

Think on it

1. Would it be adaptive for a **society** to have everyone adhere to the cultural norms? Explain your answer.

2. Not all people faced with **external pressure** to change do so or do so at the same rate. What factors might explain why some societies rapidly change their culture?

3. Does the concept of **cultural relativism** promote international understanding, or does it hinder attempts to have international agreement on acceptable behavior, such as human rights?

Communication and Language

LEARNING OBJECTIVES

Define *communication,* and compare and contrast human and nonhuman communication.	10.1
Explain how the study of creole and pidgin languages and of children's acquisition of language might tell us something about the origins of language.	10.2
Discuss the major components of descriptive linguistics (phonology, morphology, and syntax) and the key findings in each of these areas.	10.3
Describe how historical linguistics establishes historical relationships between languages and language families.	10.4
Identify the processes by which languages diverge.	10.5
Discuss the relationship between language and culture.	10.6
Discuss the relationship between ways of speaking and issues of class, gender, and ethnicity.	10.7
Identify the origins of writing and literacy, and assess the impact of writing and literacy on culture and communication.	10.8

Few of us can remember when we first became aware that words signified something. Yet that moment was a milestone, not only in our acquisition of language but in our process of learning the configuration of attitudes, beliefs, and elaborate behaviors that constitutes our culture. Without language, the transmission of complex traditions would be virtually impossible, and each of us would be left trapped within a world of private sensations.

Helen Keller, whom illness made deaf and blind at the age of 19 months, gives a moving account of the afternoon she first established contact with another human being through words:

> [My teacher] brought me my hat, and I knew I was going out into the warm sunshine. This thought, if a wordless sensation may be called a thought, made me hop and skip with pleasure.
>
> We walked down the path to the well house, attracted by the fragrance of the honeysuckle with which it was covered. Someone was drawing water and my teacher placed my hand under the spout. As the cool stream gushed over one hand she spelled into the other the word water, first slowly, then rapidly. Suddenly I felt a misty consciousness as of something forgotten—a thrill of returning thought; and somehow the mystery of language was revealed to me. I knew then that w-a-t-e-r meant the wonderful cool something that was flowing over my hand. That living word awakened my soul, gave it light, hope, joy, set it free! There were barriers still, it is true, barriers that could in time be swept away.
>
> I left the well house eager to learn. Everything had a name, and each name gave birth to a new thought. As we returned to the house every object which I touched seemed to quiver with life. That was because I saw everything with the strange, new sight that had come to me.[1]

10.1 Define *communication*, and compare and contrast human and nonhuman communication.

Communication

Against all odds, Helen Keller had come to understand the essential function that language plays in all societies—namely, to communicate. The word *communicate* comes from the Latin verb *communicare*, "to impart," "to share," "to make *common*." We communicate verbally by agreeing, consciously or unconsciously, to call an object, a movement, or an abstract concept by a common name. Speakers of English, for example, have agreed to call the color of grass *green*, even though we have no way of comparing precisely how two people actually experience this color. What we share is the agreement to call similar visual sensations *green*. Any system of language consists of publicly accepted symbols by which individuals try to share private experiences and thoughts. Communication is much broader than language. It can involve any means of transmission of information as long as the symbols, signs, or behaviors are shared and commonly understood.

Much research has been devoted to whether the capacity for language makes the human species unique. In the process, scholars have examined human—and nonhuman communication—in all its varieties. While spoken language is considered the major transmitter of human culture, we have also come to understand that we also communicate a great deal nonverbally. And even when we speak, we also tell what we mean through nonverbal signals.[2]

Nonverbal Human Communication

We all know from experience that the spoken word does not communicate everything we perceive about a social situation. As social theorist Anthony Wilden has put it, "every act, every pause, every movement in living and social systems is also a message; silence is communication; short of death it is impossible for an organism or person not to communicate."[3] We can usually tell, for instance, whether people mean it when they say, "Nice to meet you." We often can tell by their demeanor when others are sad, even if they merely say, "I'm fine" in response to the question, "How are you?" We communicate directly not only through spoken language but also indirectly through what we informally call "body language." We also communicate indirectly with nonverbal symbolic systems, such as writing, algebraic equations, chemical formulas, musical scores, code flags, and road signs. And artistically, we communicate with art, music, and dance.

Kinesics is the study of direct communication by nonverbal or nonvocal means, including posture, mannerisms, body movement, facial expressions, and other signs and gestures. Some direct nonverbal communication appears to be universal. Humans the world over, for example, seem to understand common facial expressions in the same way; that is, they are able to recognize a happy, sad, surprised, angry, disgusted, or afraid face.[4] How the face is represented in art also appears to evoke similar feelings in many different cultures. For example, masks intended to be frightening often have sharp, angular features and inward- and downward-facing eyes and eyebrows.[5]

Will everyone the world over interpret a smile or a frown in the same way? Some scholars argue that anger, for example, may be understood differently across cultures, or that the emotion term each culture associates with a facial expression may have different connotations. Paul Ekman, who carried out the experiment with Japanese and American participants, believes that some basic emotions are universal and that his research shows the facial expressions of emotion to be human universals. But he is careful to point out that "universal" does not mean that every person in every culture will interpret an expression the same way. Rather, he uses "universal" in the sense adopted by most anthropologists: to identify a pattern of human behavior that *seems* to hold true in a significantly diverse and random sampling of cultures.[6]

On the other hand, the kinds of facial expressions and other nonverbal gestures that are considered appropriate in a given situation can vary from culture to culture. For example, in a study comparing how the Japanese and Americans express emotions, individuals from both groups were videotaped while they were shown films intended to evoke feelings of fear and disgust. Both groups exhibited expressions of fear and disgust when they watched the films alone. However, when an authority figure was present, the Japanese subjects more often than the Americans tried to mask their negative feelings with a half-smile.[7]

Certainly many body and hand gestures are far from universal. Specific signs and gestures are often culturally variable and the cause of cultural misunderstandings. For example, moving the head up and down signals "yes" in the United States, but "no" in Greece. For governments and their diplomats, learning the fine points of another culture's body language has historically been an essential tool of cross-cultural cooperation. Now that business is conducted on a worldwide scale, kinesics has become an essential part of a business person's training as well.[8]

Nonverbal communication is not always voluntary or conscious. Our words may express one thought while our eyes or body language or tone of voice betray what we truly feel. Moreover, we may rely on unconscious signals when we form opinions of others. In many Western cultures, for example, a limp handshake, especially paired with a shifting gaze, can make us feel uncertain about a new acquaintance. At the very least, we may feel that the person has no interest in interacting with us. Researchers in Alabama performed an experiment with 112 female and male college students to see if such reactions were valid. The students were told that they would be taking a personality test. They did not know that their hand-shaking style would also be assessed by trained "handshake" technicians. The results showed a strong correspondence between particular personality traits and handshaking styles. For example, female participants who tested as "more extroverted and open to experience and less neurotic and shy" also tended to have firmer handshakes.[9] Another study tested a more primal kind of communication: the ability to decode *pheromones*, the molecular compounds that we all secrete through our sweat glands. When female college students were asked to sniff a series of swatches marked with sweat, many were able to identify the samples that came from donors who were experiencing fear or stress.[10] (Perhaps because females are typically taught to be more sensitive to others, they tend to be more skilled at assessing nonverbal behavior.)[11]

Nonverbal symbolic communication systems are yet another way humans interact without speaking. Although no system is used universally, many cultures develop systems that are collectively understood. Among the most interesting of these for anthropologists are so-called gesture calls. These include whistled languages, which, through a system of whistling sounds made by variation in amplitude and frequency, mimic the sounds and syntax of the society's spoken language. Whistled languages appear in low-density societies where communication across considerable distance is needed or where noise in the natural environment may impede hearing normal speech. Some internationally accepted symbolic languages, such as mathematical and musical notation, enable us to communicate across cultural and language boundaries.

Kinesics The study of communication by nonvocal means, including posture, mannerisms, body movement, facial expressions, and signs and gestures.

Apes lack the human capacity for speech, so researchers have explored the capacity of chimpanzees and other apes to communicate with hand gestures. Researcher Joyce Butler teaches Nim, a chimpanzee, a sign for "drink."

Paralanguage Refers to all the optional vocal features or silences apart from the language itself that communicate meaning.

Accents Differences in pronunciation characteristic of a group.

Paralanguage is the study of all the nonverbal vocal sounds, including the silent pauses in speech, with which humans interact.[12] We can tell a lot by the tone and pitch of a voice. A depressed person might speak very quietly and use a flat tone of voice. If a person thought about explaining what was really wrong but thought better of it, a significant pause or silence might come before the words, "I'm fine." **Accents** (differences in pronunciation) can reveal a person's place of origin, education, and, in some cultures, social class. And people communicate a wealth of meaning through their grunts, laughs, giggles, moans, and sighs.

How can silence be a communication? Silence may reflect companionship, as when two people work side by side on a project, or it may be a way to establish personal boundaries, as when strangers share an elevator. Because our silences in social interaction are open to interpretation, they can also be misunderstood. In North America, for example, the pauses in a conversation when one person finishes speaking and another person begins can vary by region. People raised in New York City may signal that they are fully engaged in a conversation by jumping in and responding while the other person is still speaking. In the South and Southwest, where such overlapping speech can be perceived as an interruption—that is, rude—there is typically a slight pause in conversation when one speaker finishes and the other speaker begins.

Nonhuman Communication

Systems of communication are not unique to human beings. Other animal species communicate in a variety of ways. One way is by sound. A bird may communicate by a call that "this is my territory"; a squirrel may utter a cry that leads other squirrels to flee from danger. Another means of animal communication is odor. An ant releases a chemical when it dies, and its fellows then carry it away to the compost heap. Apparently, the communication is highly effective; a healthy ant painted with the death chemical will be dragged to the funeral heap again and again. Bees use another means of communication, body movement, to convey the location of food sources. Karl von Frisch discovered that the black Austrian honeybee—by choosing a round dance, a wagging dance, or a short, straight run—can communicate not only the precise direction of the source of food but also its distance from the hive.[13]

One of the greatest scholarly debates is about the degree to which nonhuman animals, particularly nonhuman primates, differ from humans in their capacity for language. Some scholars see so much discontinuity that they propose that humans must have acquired (presumably through mutation) a specific genetic capability for language. Others see much more continuity between humans and nonhuman primates and point to research that shows much more cognitive

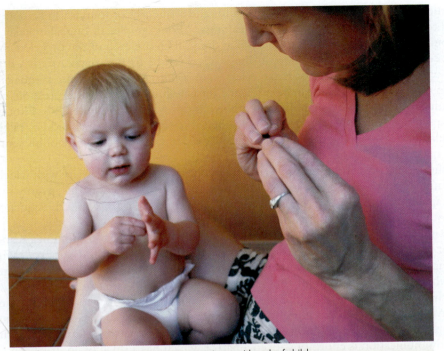

A family employs sign language to communicate with a deaf child.

capacity in nonhuman primates than previously thought possible. They point out that the discontinuity theorists are constantly raising the standards for the capacities thought necessary for language.[14] For example, in the past, only human communication was thought to be symbolic. But recent research suggests that some monkey and ape calls in the wild are also symbolic.

When we say that a call, word, or sentence is **symbolic communication**, we mean at least two things. First, the communication has meaning even when its *referent* (whatever is referred to) is not present. Second, the meaning is arbitrary; the receiver of the message could not guess its meaning just from the sound(s) and does not know the meaning instinctively. In other words, symbols have to be learned. There is no compelling or "natural" reason that the word *dog* in English should refer to a smallish, four-legged omnivore.

Vervet monkeys are not as closely related to humans as are African apes. Nevertheless, scientists who have observed vervet monkeys in their natural environment consider at least three of their alarm calls to be symbolic because each of them *means* (refers to) a different kind of predator—eagles, pythons, or leopards—and monkeys react differently to each call. For example, they look up when they hear the "eagle" call. Experimentally, in the absence of the referent, investigators have been able to evoke the normal reaction to a call by playing it back electronically. Another indication that the vervet's alarm calls are symbolic is that infant vervets appear to need some time to learn the referent for each call. Very young vervets will often make the eagle warning call, for example, when they see any flying bird. They apparently learn the appropriate referent through reinforcement: Adult vervets repeat their "correct" calls. This process is probably not too different from the way a North American infant in an English-speaking family first applies the "word" *dada* to all adult males and gradually learns to restrict it to one person,[15] or from the way the Embers' daughter Kathy named all pictures of four-footed animals, including elephants, "dog" when she was 18 months old.

All of the nonhuman vocalizations we have described so far enable individual animals to convey messages. The sender gives a signal that is received and "decoded" by the receiver, who usually responds with a specific action or reply. How is human vocalization different? Because monkeys and apes appear to use symbols at least some of the time, it is not appropriate to emphasize symbolism as the distinctive feature of human language. However, there is a significant quantitative difference between human language and other primates' systems of vocal communication. All human languages employ a much larger set of symbols.

Another often-cited difference between human and nonhuman vocalizations is that the other primates' vocal systems are *closed*—that is, different calls are not combined to produce new, meaningful utterances. In contrast, human languages are *open* systems,

Symbolic communication An arbitrary (not obviously meaningful) gesture, call, word, or sentence that has meaning even when its *referent* is not present.

governed by complex rules about how sounds and sequences of sounds can be combined to produce an infinite variety of meanings.[16] For example, an English speaker can combine *care* and *full* (*careful*) to mean one thing, then use each of the two elements in other combinations to mean different things. *Care* can be used to make *carefree, careless,* or *caretaker; full* can be used to make *powerful* or *wonderful.* And because language is a system of shared symbols, it can be reformed into an infinite variety of expressions and be understood by all who share these symbols. In this way, for example, T. S. Eliot could form a sentence never before formed—"In the room the women come and go/talking of Michelangelo"[17]—and all speakers of English could understand the sense of his sentence, if not necessarily what he meant.

Although no primatologist disputes the complexity and infinite variety with which human languages can combine sounds, other primates (cotton-top tamarins, pygmy marmosets, capuchin monkeys, and rhesus macaques) also combine calls in orderly sequences[18] but not nearly as much as humans do.

Another trait thought to be unique to humans is the ability to communicate about past or future events. But Sue Savage-Rumbaugh has observed wild bonobos leaving what appear to be messages to other bonobos to follow a trail. They break off vegetation where trails fork and point the broken plants in the direction to follow.

Perhaps most persuasive are the successful attempts to teach apes to communicate with humans and with each other using human-created signs. These successes have led many scholars to question the traditional assumption that the gap between human and other animal communication is enormous. Even a parrot, which has a small brain, has been taught to communicate with a human trainer in ways once thought impossible. Alex (the parrot) could correctly answer questions in English about what objects were made of, how many objects of a particular type there were, and even what made two objects the same or different.[19] When he is not willing to continue a training session, Alex says, "I'm sorry . . . Wanna go back."[20]

Chimpanzees Washoe and Nim and the gorilla Koko were taught hand signs based on American Sign Language (ASL), which is used by the hearing impaired in the United States. The chimpanzee Sarah was trained with plastic symbols. Subsequently, many chimpanzees were trained on symbol keyboards connected to computers. Some of the best examples of linguistic ability come from a chimpanzee named Kanzi. In contrast to other apes, Kanzi initially learned symbols just by watching his mother being taught, and he spontaneously began using the computer symbols to communicate with humans, even indicating his intended actions. Kanzi did not need rewards or to have his hands put in the right position, and he understood a great deal of what was said to him in English. For example, when he was 5 years old, Kanzi heard someone talk about throwing a ball in the river, and he turned around and did so. Kanzi has come close to having a primitive English grammar when he strings symbols together.[21] If chimpanzees and other primates have the capacity to use nonspoken language and even to understand spoken language, then the difference between humans and nonhumans may not be as great as people used to think.

Are these apes really using language in some minimal way? Many investigators do agree about one thing—nonhuman primates have the ability to "symbol," to refer to something (or a class of things) with an arbitrary "label" (gesture or sequence of sounds).[22] For example, Washoe originally learned the sign *dirty* to refer to feces and other soil and then began to use it insultingly, as in "dirty Roger," when her trainer Roger Fouts refused to give her things she wanted.

When we discuss the structure of sounds (phonology) later in this chapter, we will see that every human language has certain ways of combining sounds and ways of not combining those sounds. Apes do not have anything comparable to linguistic rules for allowed and disallowed combinations of sounds. In addition, humans have many kinds of discourse. We make lists and speeches, tell stories, argue, and recite poetry. Apes do none of these things.[23] But apes do have at least some of the capacities for language. Therefore, understanding their capacities may help us better understand the evolution of human language.

The Origins of Language

10.2 ▶ Explain how the study of creole and pidgin languages and of children's acquisition of language might tell us something about the origins of language.

How long humans have had spoken language is not known. There is widespread agreement that human language must have existed at least by about 50,000 years ago because there are archaeological signs of extensive symbolism in both art and ritual in the Upper Paleolithic. But others believe language probably arose earlier. For example, it is now known that Neandertals and modern humans share the same gene called FOXP2. This gene is directly associated with language ability in recent populations. Because Neandertals and modern humans share the same gene, some believe that Neandertals must have had language too.[24] However, genes can have multiple purposes, and the presence of a gene is not unambiguous evidence of language. Because the only unambiguous remains of language are found on written tablets, and the earliest stone tablets date back only about 5,000 years,[25] pinpointing the emergence of earliest languages remains speculative.

Many scholars believe that understanding the emergence of language will be aided by more research on systems of communication in other animals. Certainly this research has led to an understanding that there is much more capacity than previously realized. But there is also an understanding that animal communications systems lack the open-ended power of human language, so it is widely believed that genetic changes must have occurred in human evolution to make language possible after the human line separated from apes.[26] But we do know that the actual development of individual language is not completely biologically determined; if it were, all human beings would speak the same brain-generated language. Instead, over 6,000 mutually unintelligible languages have been identified. More than 2,000 of them were still spoken as of recently, most by peoples who did not traditionally have a system of writing. Can we learn anything about the origins of language by studying the languages of nonliterate (without writing) and technologically simpler societies? The answer is no, because such languages are not simpler or less developed than ours. The sound systems, vocabularies, and grammars of technologically simpler peoples are in no way inferior to those of peoples with more complex technology.[27] Of course, people in other societies, and even some people in our own society, will not be able to name the sophisticated machines used in our society. All languages, however, have the potential for doing so. As we will see later in this chapter, all languages possess the amount of vocabulary their speakers need, and all languages expand in response to cultural changes. A language that lacks terminology for some of our conveniences may have a rich vocabulary for events or natural phenomena that are of particular importance to the people in that society.

If there are no primitive languages, and if the earliest languages have left no traces that would allow us to reconstruct them, does that mean we cannot investigate the origins of language? Some linguists think that understanding the way children acquire language, which we discuss shortly, can help us understand the origins of language. Other linguists have suggested that an understanding of how creole languages develop will also tell us something about the origins of language.

Pidgin and Creole Languages

In many contact situations where one group is much more powerful than the other, people shift to the dominant language, and their native language gradually becomes lost. However, some contact situations led to a different result—the development of a new language, different from the dominant language or the previous native languages.

Some languages developed where European colonial powers established commercial enterprises that relied on imported labor, generally slaves. The laborers in one place often came from many different societies and, in the beginning, would speak with their masters and with each other in some kind of simplified way, using linguistic features of one or more of the languages. Often, most of the vocabulary is drawn from the masters' language.[28] These *pidgin languages* become a new way of communicating. Pidgins are simplified languages and lack many of the building blocks found in the languages of whole societies, building blocks such as prepositions (*to, on,* and so forth) and auxiliary verbs (designating future and other tenses). If a pidgin language is used merely as system of communicating in a limited setting, it may not develop into a fully developed language. However, children may begin to use pidgin as their first language. The pidgin

Applied Anthropology

Can Languages Be Kept from Extinction?

Many peoples and their languages are endangered. In the last few hundred years, and continuing in some places today, Western expansion and colonization have led to the depopulation and extinction of many native societies, mainly as a result of introduced disease and campaigns of extermination. Thus, many languages disappeared with the peoples who spoke them. More than 50 of approximately 200 aboriginal languages in Australia disappeared relatively quickly as a result of massacre and disease.

Today, native languages are endangered more by the fact that they are not being passed on to children. Political and economic dominance by speakers of Western languages undoubtedly play an enormous role in this process. First, schooling is usually conducted in the dominant language. Second, when another culture is dominant, the children may prefer to speak in the language perceived to have higher prestige.

Almost all the languages of aboriginal Australia are now gone. This is a worldwide trend. It is estimated that 50 to 90 percent of the 6,000 to 7,000 of the world's languages will be gone by 2100. What can be done? For a long time, linguists have worked on describing languages that are endangered, often working closely with the few remaining speakers. Although description is essential to language preservation, linguists are increasingly engaging actively in efforts to revitalize endangered languages by participating in community programs and by playing active roles in organizations that are preserving, often in digitized archives, endangered languages and recordings of speech. After all, without speakers or any written records, languages are truly lost. The following are a few examples of "dead" languages being brought back to life. Kaurna, a language of Australia abandoned for over a century, is now used in songs, ritual events, public

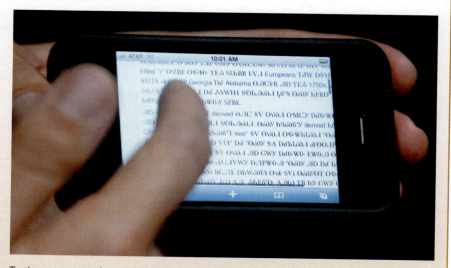
Texting on a smart phone in the Cherokee language at the Cherokee Nation Immersion School.

speeches, and everyday greetings. It has moved from no use to some use. Hebrew is an often-cited example of a "dead" language that was brought back to life because more than 5 million people now speak it. However, Hebrew, like Latin, was never really "dead" in the same sense as Kaurna. Hebrew has been used in religious contexts for over 16 centuries and had extensive written literature. But the Hebrew case indicates that for successful revitalization to occur, a community of people must be strongly motivated to revive it.

Total immersion programs are probably the most likely to work, but they are the most costly and difficult to implement. School programs employing total immersion during the school day beginning with preschool have had considerable success among the Maori of New Zealand, as well as among Hawaiians of the United States and the Mohawk of Canada. Bilingual programs are perhaps the most popular programs, but they use only partial immersion. UNESCO favors a very different approach: to first teach adults, who can then teach their children naturally.

H. Russell Bernard believes that "to keep a language truly alive we must produce authors." With the help

of computer technology, which allows reconfiguring a keyboard to produce special characters for sounds, Bernard has taught native speakers to write their native languages directly on computers. These texts then become the basis for dictionaries. Although these authors may not be using the standardized characters that linguists use, they are producing "written" materials that might otherwise be lost forever. These texts also convey ideas about curing illness, acquiring food, raising children, and settling disputes. On a broader scale, the Web provides a way for far-flung people to access language materials, pick up advice for teaching languages, and even feel more part of a "community" with those whose language is shared.

We are not sure when humans first developed spoken language. But the enormous linguistic diversity on this planet took a long time to develop. Unfortunately, it may take only a short time for that diversity to become a thing of the past.

Sources: Crystal 2000, 4, 142, 154; Holmes 2001, 65–71; Grenoble and Whaley 2006; Kolbert 2005; Shulman 1993; Austin and Sallabank 2011.

language may expand and become more complex grammatically.[29] Many pidgin languages developed into and were replaced by so-called *creole languages*, which incorporate much of the vocabulary of another language (often the masters' language) but also have a grammar that differs from it and from the grammars of the laborers' native languages.[30]

Derek Bickerton argues that there are striking grammatical similarities in creole languages throughout the world.[31] This similarity, he thinks, is consistent with the idea that some grammar is inherited by all humans. Creole languages, therefore, may resemble early human languages. All creoles use intonation instead of a change in word order to ask a question. The creole equivalent of the question "Can you fix this?" would be "You can fix this?" The creole version puts a rising inflection at the end; in contrast, the English version reverses the subject and verb without much inflection at the end. All creoles express the future and the past in the same grammatical way, by the use of particles (such as the English *shall*) between subject and verb, and they all employ double negatives, as in the Guyana English Creole "Nobody no like me."[32]

It is possible that many other things about language are universal, that all languages are similar in many respects, because of the way humans are "wired" or because people in all societies have similar experiences. For example, names for frogs may usually contain *r* sounds because frogs make them.[33]

Children's Acquisition of Language

A child is apparently equipped from birth with the capacity to reproduce all the sounds used by the world's languages and to learn any system of grammar. Research on 6-month-old infants finds that they can distinguish the sounds of approximately 600 consonants and 200 vowels—all the sounds in all the known languages of the world. However, this capability gives way to cultural influences around the time babies turn 1, when they become more adept at recognizing the salient, or prominent, sounds and sound clusters of their parents or caretakers and less adept at distinguishing those of other languages.[34]

Children's acquisition of the structure and meaning of language has been called the most difficult intellectual achievement in life. If that is so, it is pleasing to note that they accomplish it with relative ease and vast enjoyment. All over the world, children begin to learn language at about the same age. By 12 or 13 months of age, children are able to name a few objects and actions, and by 18 to 20 months, they can make one key word stand for a whole sentence: "Out!" for "Take me out for a walk right now"; "Juice!" for "I want some juice now." Evidence suggests that children acquire the concept of a word as a whole and that they especially learn sequences of sounds that are stressed or at the ends of words (e.g., "raffe" for giraffe). These universal ways of acquiring language hold true even for children with hearing impairments who are learning a sign language.[35]

Children the world over tend to progress to two-word sentences at about 18 to 24 months of age. They express themselves in "telegraph" form sentences, using noun-like words and verb-like words but leaving out the seemingly less important words. A two-word sentence, such as "Shoes off," may stand for "Take my shoes off"; "More milk" may stand for "Give me more milk, please."[36] They do not utter their two words in random order, sometimes saying "off" first, other times saying "shoes" first. If children say, "Shoes off," then they will also say, "Clothes off" and "Hat off." They seem to select an order that fits the conventions of adult language, so they are likely to say, "Daddy eat," not "Eat Daddy." In other words, they tend to put the subject first, as adults do. And they tend to say "Mommy coat" rather than "Coat Mommy" to indicate "Mommy's coat."[37] Adults do not utter sentences such as "Daddy eat," so children seem to know a lot

A lot of language instruction occurs by pointing to something and saying what it is called.

Migrants and Immigrants

Why are "Mother Tongues" Retained, and for How Long?

The longer an immigrant group lives in another country, the more they incorporate the culture of their new home. At some point, they no longer even partially understand their original language. Consider the people of Wales, the region west of England in Great Britain. Until about a century ago, they were mostly Welsh speakers. (The Welsh language, along with Irish, Scottish Gaelic, and Breton, belongs to the Celtic subfamily of Indo-European, whereas English belongs to the Germanic subfamily.) When, in 1729, settlers from Wales established the Welsh Society in Philadelphia, the oldest ethnic organization in the United States, many of its members, if not all, spoke Welsh as well as English. But by the 20th century, hardly any of the descendants did.

Although immigrant groups eventually lose their "mother tongues" in many if not most countries, the process does not occur at the same rate in every group. Why is that? Why do some immigrant groups lose their language faster than others? Is it because they do not live in tightly knit ethnic enclaves, or because they marry outside their ethnic group? Or is it because they do not have traditional festivals or celebrations to mark their separate identity? A comparative study by Robert Schrauf revealed some likely reasons.

Schrauf used data on 11 North American ethnic groups drawn from the HRAF Collection of Ethnography. He noted that because these ethnographies were written for more general purposes or for purposes other than linguistic study, they contained a wealth of sociocultural information, allowing him to test several factors for their possible effects on language retention and loss. Based on the data, Schrauf identified three levels of native language retention over time in North America by assessing the degree to which the language was spoken by the third generation (the grandchildren of immigrants):

1. Continued use, which he found among Chicanos, Puerto Ricans, Cubans, and Haitians.

2. Some native language understanding, which he found among Chinese and Koreans.
3. No native language comprehension of the native language except for isolated words, with even the second generation (the children of immigrants) mostly speaking and understood only English, which he found among Italians, Armenians, and Basques.

Schrauf then measured seven social factors that might explain longer versus shorter retention of the mother tongue:

1. Lived in tightly knit communities
2. Maintained religious rituals
3. Had separate schools
4. Held traditional festivals
5. Visited the homeland
6. Did not intermarry with other groups
7. Worked with others of the ethnic group

We might suspect that all of the factors Schrauf measured would lead people to retain their native language (and presumably other native cultural patterns). But not all do, apparently. Only living in tightly knit communities and retaining

religious rituals strongly predict retention of the mother tongue in the home into the third generation. Why? Possibly because life in an ethnic community and religious rituals are experienced early in life, and early socialization might have more lasting effects than such later experiences as schooling, visits to the homeland, marriage, and work. Participation in celebrations and festivals is probably important too, but it does not have quite as strong an effect, perhaps because celebrations and festivals are not everyday experiences.

As always with such studies, the findings raise questions for future research. Would the same effects be found outside of North America? Would the results be the same if we also looked at other immigrant groups in North America? Does frequent travel back to the homeland help language retention? Do some immigrant groups live in close-knit communities because of discrimination or by choice and, if so, is discrimination or choice a factor in language retention? Are some groups more interested in assimilating than others? And, if so, why?

Sources: Caulkins 1997; Schrauf 1999.

about how to put words together with little or no direct teaching from their caretakers. Consider the 5-year-old who, confronted with the unfamiliar "Gloria in Excelsis," sings quite happily, "Gloria eats eggshells." To make the words fit the structure of English grammar is more important than to make the words fit the meaning of the Christmas pageant.

If there is a basic grammar imprinted in the human mind, we would expect that children's early and later speech patterns would be similar in different languages. We might also expect children's later speech to be similar to the structure of creole languages. And it is, according to Derek Bickerton.[38] He says that the "errors" children make in speaking are consistent with the grammar of creoles. For example, English-speaking children 3 to 4 years old tend to ask questions by intonation alone, and they tend to use double negatives, such as "I don't see no dog," even though the adults around them do not speak that way and consider the children's speech "wrong."

But some linguists argue that the evidence for an innate grammar is weak because children the world over do not develop the same grammatical features at similar ages. For example, word order is a more important determinant of meaning in English than in Turkish; the endings of words are more important in Turkish. The word at the beginning of the sentence in English is likely to be the subject. The word with a certain ending in Turkish is the likely subject. Consistent with this difference, English-speaking children learn word order earlier than Turkish children do.[39]

Future research on children's acquisition of language and on the structure of creole languages may bring us closer to an understanding of the origins of human language. But even if much of grammar is universal, we still need to understand how and why the thousands of languages in the world vary, which brings us to the conceptual tools linguists have had to invent to study languages.

Descriptive Linguistics

10.3 Discuss the major components of descriptive linguistics (phonology, morphology, and syntax) and the key findings in each of these areas.

In every society, children do not need to be taught grammar to learn how to speak. They begin to grasp the essential structure of their language at a very early age, without direct instruction. If you show English-speaking children a picture of one "gork" and then a picture of two of these creatures, they will say there are two "gorks." Somehow they know that adding an *s* to a noun means more than one. But they do not know this consciously, and adults may not either. One of the most surprising features of human language is that meaningful sounds and sound sequences are combined according to rules that the speakers often do not consciously know.

These rules should not be equated with the "rules of grammar" you were taught in school so that you would speak "correctly." Rather, when linguists talk about rules, they are referring to the patterns of speaking that are discoverable in actual speech. Needless to say, there is some overlap between the actual rules of speaking and the rules taught in school. But there are rules that children never hear about in school because their teachers are not linguists and are not aware of them. When linguists use the term *grammar*, they are *not* referring to the prescriptive rules that people are supposed to follow in speaking. Rather, *grammar* to the linguist consists of the actual, often unconscious principles that predict how most people talk. As we have noted, young children may speak two-word sentences that conform to a linguistic rule, but their speech is hardly considered "correct."

Discovering the mostly unconscious rules operating in a language is a very difficult task. Linguists have had to invent special concepts and methods of transcription (writing) to permit them to describe these rules that have resulted in three related areas of study:

1. The study of aspects of language that predicts how sounds are made and how they are used is called **phonology**.
2. The study of how sound sequences (and sometimes even individual sounds) convey meaning and how meaningful sound sequences are strung together to form words is called **morphology**.
3. The study of how words are strung together to form phrases and sentences is called **syntax**.

Understanding the language of another people is an essential part of understanding the culture of that people. Although sometimes what people say is contradicted by their observed behavior, there is little doubt that it is hard to understand the beliefs, attitudes,

Phonology The study of the sounds in a language and how they are used.

Morphology The study of how sound sequences convey meaning.

Syntax The ways in which words are arranged to form phrases and sentences.

values, and worldview of a people without understanding their language and the nuances of how that language is used. Even behavior, which theoretically one can observe without understanding language, usually cannot be readily understood without interpretation. Imagine that you see people go by a certain rock and seemingly walk out of their way to avoid it. Suppose they believe that an evil spirit resides there. How could you possibly know that without being able to ask and to understand their answer?

Phonology

Phones A speech sound in a language.

Most of us have had the experience of trying to learn another language and finding that some sounds are exceedingly difficult to make. Although the human vocal tract theoretically can make a very large number of different sounds—**phones**, to linguists—each language uses only some of them. It is not that we cannot make the sounds that are strange to us; we just have not acquired the habit of making those sounds. And until the sounds become habitual for us, they continue to be difficult to make.

Finding it difficult to make certain sounds is only one of the reasons we have trouble learning a "foreign" language. Another problem is that we may not be used to combining certain sounds or making a certain sound in a particular position in a word. Thus, English speakers find it difficult to combine z and d, as Russian speakers often do, whereas Russian speakers may struggle with the *th* at the beginning of many common English words. The position of a sound may also be challenging. English speakers may have trouble pronouncing the *ng* sound at the beginning of some words in Samoan, a South Pacific language, even though the sound is common at the end of English words, such *sing* and *hitting*.

To study the patterning of sounds, linguists who are interested in *phonology* have to write down speech utterances as sequences of sound. This task would be almost impossible if linguists were restricted to using their own alphabet (say, the one they use to write English) because other languages use sounds that are difficult to represent with the English alphabet or because the English alphabet represents a particular sound in different ways. (English writing represents the sound *f* by *f* as in *food*, but also as *gh* in *tough* and *ph* in *phone*.) In addition, in English, different sounds may be represented by the same letter. English has 26 letters and 46 significant sounds (sounds that can change the meaning of a word).[40] To overcome these difficulties in writing sounds with the letters of existing writing systems, linguists have developed systems of transcription with special alphabets in which each symbol represents only one particular sound. Figure 10.1 shows the International Phonetic Alphabet symbols used to represent the phones in English.

Once linguists have identified the sounds or phones used in a language, they try to identify which sounds affect meaning and which sounds do not—that is, they try to determine which sounds just seem like variations in pronunciation to the language speakers and which sounds make an important difference. One way is to start with a simple word like *lake* and change the first sound to *r* to make the word *rake*. A linguist will ask

Phonology of the English Language

Consonants

p - pop, pond
b - bar, bone
t - tale, tune
d - door, dune
k - core, kiss
g - guest, give
f - find, phase
v - vain, vest
θ - thirst, thumb, bath
ð - them, then, clothing
s - same, sip
z - zero, zany
ʃ - shine, shack
ʒ - measure, seizure
h - hot, hug
tʃ - chop, hatch
dʒ - dodge, smudge
m - mane, mumble
n - can, gnat
ŋ - thing, rang
l - lease, fall
r - run, form
w - wake, lower
j - yes, yonder

Short Vowels

ɪ - bill, sick
ɛ - met, thread
æ - hat, mad
ɒ - log, cotton
ʌ - rut, buck
ʊ - put, foot
ə - around, lever

Long Vowels

iː - team, keen
ɜː (or əː) - turn, bird
aː - hard, fall
ɔː - thorn, mourn
uː - boob, glue

Dipthongs

aɪ - nice, tie
ɛɪ - straight, late
ɔɪ - oil, boy
əʊ - moan, tote
aʊ - clown, sound
ɔə - tore, poured
ɪə - fear, bier
ɛə - fair, pear
ʊə - pure, fuel

FIGURE 10.1

The phones in English represented by the International Phonetic Alphabet symbols.

if this new combination of sounds means the same thing. Because an English speaker would say *lake* means something completely different from *rake,* we can say that in the English language the sound *l* at the beginning of a word conveys different meaning from the sound *r* at the beginning of a word. These minimal contrasts enable linguists to identify a **phoneme** in a language—a sound or set of sounds that makes a difference in meaning in that language.[41] So the sound *l* in *lake* is different phonemically from the sound *r* in *rake*. The ways in which sounds are grouped together into phonemes vary from language to language. Each of us is so used to phonemes in our own language that it may be hard to believe that the contrast between *r* and *l* may not make a difference in meaning in some languages. For example, in Samoan, *l* and *r* can be used interchangeably in a word without changing the meaning. Therefore, these two sounds belong to the same phoneme in Samoan. (A Samoan speaker may call an American named Reuben either "Leupena" or "Reupena.")

English speakers may joke about languages that "confuse" *l* and *r,* but they are not usually aware that they do the same thing with other sets of sounds. For example, in English, the beginning of the word spelled *and* may be pronounced like the *a* in *air* or the *a* in *bat* without a change in meaning. If you say *air* and *bat* and focus on how you are forming the vowel sounds, you will realize that your mouth and tongue assume a different position to form the two sounds. Now think about *l* and *r.* Although the two letters of the alphabet are pronounced with very different tongue positions, when you utter them in words (with vowels) you will notice that they are only slightly different with respect to how far the tongue is from the ridge behind the upper front teeth. Languages do tend to consider sounds that are close as belonging to the same phoneme, but why they choose some sounds and not others to group together is not yet fully understood.

Some recent research suggests that infants may learn early to ignore meaningless variations of sound (those that are part of the same phoneme) in the language they hear at home. It turns out that, as early as 6 months of age, infants "ignore" sound shifts within the same phoneme of their own language, but they "hear" a sound shift within the phoneme of another language. Researchers are not sure how babies learn to make the distinction, but they seem to acquire much of the phonology of their language very early indeed.[42]

After discovering which sounds are grouped into phonemes, linguists can begin to discover the sound sequences that are allowed in a language and the usually unconscious rules that predict those sequences. For example, English has a number of *consonant blends,* but they rarely start with three nonvowel sounds. When they do, the first sound or phone is always an *s,* as in *strike* and *scratch*.[43] (Some other words in English may start with three consonants but only two sounds are involved, as in *chrome,* where the *ch* stands for the sound in *k*.)

Linguists' descriptions of the sound patterns (phonology) in different languages may allow them to investigate why languages vary. Why, for example, are two or more consonant sounds strung together in some languages, whereas in other languages vowels are *almost* always put between consonants? The Samoan language now has a word for "Christmas" borrowed from English, but to fit Samoan rules the borrowed word has been changed to *Kerisimasi* (pronounced as if it were spelled Keh-ree-see-mah-see).

What explains why some languages alternate consonants and vowels more or less regularly? Recent cross-cultural research suggests three predictors of this variation. One predictor is a warmer climate. Where people live in warmer climates, the typical syllable is more likely to be a consonant-vowel syllable. Linguists have found that consonant-vowel syllables provide the most contrast in speech. Perhaps when people converse outdoors at a distance, which they are likely to do in a warmer climate, they need more contrast between sounds to be understood. A second predictor of consonant-vowel alternation is literacy. Languages that are written have fewer consonant-vowel syllables. If communication is often in written form, meaning does not have to depend so much on the contrast between adjacent sounds. A third (and indeed strongest) predictor of consonant-vowel alternation is the degree to which babies are held by others. Societies in which babies are held have a greater number of consonant-vowel syllables. Theoretically, babies that are held much of the day come to associate regular rhythm—the caretaker's heartbeat or rhythmic movements—with pleasurable experiences. That experience may generalize to a preference for regular rhythms in adult life, apparently including a regular consonant-vowel alternation in adult speech, as in *Kerisimasi.*[44]

Phoneme A sound or set of sounds that makes a difference in meaning to the speakers of the language.

Morphology

A phoneme in a language usually does not have a meaning by itself. Phonemes are combined with other phonemes to form a meaningful sequence of sounds. *Morphology* is the study of sequences of sounds that have meaning. Often these meaningful sequences of sounds make up what we call *words*, but a word may be composed of a number of smaller meaningful units. We take our words so much for granted that we do not realize how complicated it is to say what words are. People do not usually pause very much between words when they speak; if we did not know our language, a sentence would seem like a continuous stream of sounds. This is how we first hear a foreign language. Only when we understand the language and write down what we say do we separate the sounds (with spaces) into words. But a word is actually an arbitrary sequence of sounds that has a meaning; we would not "hear" words as separate units if we did not understand the spoken language.

Because anthropological linguists traditionally investigated unwritten languages, sometimes without the aid of interpreters, they had to figure out which sequences of sounds conveyed meaning. And because words in many languages can be broken down into smaller meaningful units, linguists had to invent special words to refer to those units. Linguists call the smallest unit of language that has a meaning a **morph**. Just as a phoneme may have one or more phones, one or more morphs with the same meaning may make up a **morpheme**. For example, the prefix *in-*, as in *indefinite*, and the prefix *un-*, as in *unclear*, are morphs that belong to the morpheme meaning *not*. Although some words are single morphs or morphemes (e.g., *for* and *giraffe* in English), many words are a combination of morphs, generally prefixes, roots, and suffixes. Thus *cow* is one word, but the word *cows* contains two meaningful units—a root (*cow*) and a suffix (pronounced like *z*) meaning more than one. The **lexicon** of a language, which a dictionary approximates, consists of words and morphs and their meanings.

It seems likely that the intuitive grasp children have of the structure of their language includes a recognition of morphology. Once they learn that the morph /-z/ added to a noun-type word indicates more than one, they plow ahead with *mans, childs*; once they grasp that the morpheme class pronounced /-t/ or /-d/ or /-ed/ added to the end of a verb indicates that the action took place in the past, they apply that concept generally and invent *runned, drinked*, and *costed*. They see a ball roll near*er* and near*er*, and they transfer that concept to a kite, which goes upp*er* and upp*er*. From their mistakes as well as their successes, we can see that children understand the regular uses of morphemes. By the age of 7, they have mastered many of the irregular forms as well—that is, they learn which morphs of a morpheme are used when.

The child's intuitive grasp of the dependence of some morphemes on others corresponds to the linguist's recognition of free morphemes and bound morphemes. A *free* morpheme has meaning standing alone—that is, it can be a separate word. A *bound* morpheme displays its meaning only when attached to another morpheme. The morph pronounced /-t/ of the bound morpheme meaning *past tense* is attached to the root *walk* to produce *walked*; but the /-t/ cannot stand alone or have meaning by itself.

In English, the meaning of an utterance (containing a subject, verb, object, and so forth) usually depends on the order of the words. "The dog bit the child" is different in meaning from "The child bit the dog." But in many other languages, the grammatical meaning of an utterance does not depend much, if at all, on the order of the words. Rather, meaning may be determined by how the morphs in a word are ordered. For example, in Luo, a language of East Africa, the same bound morpheme may mean the subject or object of an action. If the morpheme is the prefix to a verb, it means the subject; if it is the suffix to a verb, it means the object. Another way that grammatical meaning may be conveyed is by altering or adding a bound morpheme to a word to indicate what part of speech it is. For example, in Russian, when the subject of a sentence, the word for *mail* is pronounced something like *pawchtah*. When *mail* is used as the object of a verb, as in "I gave her the mail," the ending of the word changes to *pawchtoo*. And if I say, "What was in the mail?" the word becomes *pawchtyeh*.

Some languages have so many bound morphemes that they might express as a complex but single word what is considered a sentence in English. For example, the English sentence, "He will give it to you" can be expressed in Wishram, a Chinookan dialect that was spoken along the Columbia River in the Pacific Northwest, as *acimluda* (a-c-i-m-l-ud-a,

Morph The smallest unit of a language that has a meaning.

Morpheme One or more morphs with the same meaning.

Lexicon The words and morphs, and their meanings, of a language; approximated by a dictionary.

literally "will-he-him-thee-to-give-will"). Note that the pronoun *it* in English is gender-neutral; Wishram requires that *it* be given a gender, in this case, "him."[45]

Syntax

Because language is an open system, we can make up meaningful utterances that we have never heard before. We are constantly creating new phrases and sentences. Just as they do for morphology, speakers of a language seem to have an intuitive grasp of *syntax*—the rules that predict how phrases and sentences are generally formed. These "rules" may be partly learned in school, but children know many of them even before they get to school. In adulthood, our understanding of morphology and syntax is so intuitive that we can even understand a nonsense sentence, such as this famous one from Lewis Carroll's *Through the Looking-Glass:*

> *'Twas brillig, and the slithy toves*
> *Did gyre and gimble in the wabe*

Simply from the ordering of the words in the sentence, we can surmise which part of speech a word is, as well as its function in the sentence. *Brillig* is an adjective; *slithy,* an adjective; *toves,* a noun and the subject of the sentence; *gyre* and *gimble,* verbs; and *wabe,* a noun and the object of a prepositional phrase. Of course, an understanding of morphology helps too. The *-y* ending in *slithy* is an indication that the latter is an adjective, and the *-s* ending in *toves* tells us that we most probably have more than one of these creatures. In addition to producing and understanding an infinite variety of sentences, speakers of a language can tell when a sentence is not "correct" without consulting grammar books. For example, an English speaker can tell that "Child the dog the hit" is not an acceptable sentence but "The child hit the dog" is fine. There must, then, be a set of rules underlying how phrases and sentences are constructed in a language.[46] Speakers of a language know these implicit rules of syntax but are not usually consciously aware of them. The linguist's description of the syntax of a language tries to make these rules explicit.

Historical Linguistics

10.4 Describe how historical linguistics establishes historical relationships between languages and language families.

The field of **historical linguistics** focuses on how languages change over time. Written works provide the best data for establishing such changes. For example, the following brief passage from Chaucer's *Canterbury Tales,* written in the English of the 14th century, has recognizable elements but is different enough from modern English to require a translation.

> *A Frere ther was, a wantowne and a merye,*
> *A lymytour, a ful solempne man.*
> *In alle the ordres foure is noon that kan*
> *So muche of daliaunce and fair language.*
> *He hadde maad ful many a mariage*
> *Of yonge wommen at his owene cost.*
> *A Friar there was, wanton and merry,*
> *A limiter [a friar limited to certain districts], a very important man.*
> *In all the orders four there is none that knows*
> *So much of dalliance [flirting] and fair [engaging] language.*
> *He had made [arranged] many a marriage*
> *Of young women at his own cost.*[47]

In this passage, we can recognize several changes. Many words are spelled differently today, and in some cases meaning has changed: *Full,* for example, would be translated today as *very.* What is less evident is that changes in pronunciation have occurred. For example, the *g* in *mariage* (marriage) was pronounced *zh,* as in the French from which it was borrowed, whereas now it is usually pronounced like either *g* in *George.*

Because languages spoken in the past leave no traces unless they were written, and most of the languages known to anthropology were not written by their speakers, you might think that historical linguists can study linguistic change only by studying written languages such as English. But that is not the case. Linguists can reconstruct changes that

Historical linguistics The study of how languages change over time.

have occurred by comparing contemporary languages that are similar. Such languages show phonological, morphological, and syntactical similarities because they usually derive from a common ancestral language. For example, Romanian, Italian, French, Spanish, and Portuguese have many similarities. On the basis of these similarities, linguists can reconstruct what the ancestral language was like and how it changed into what we call the Romance languages. Of course, these reconstructions can easily be tested and confirmed because we know from many surviving writings what the ancestral language, Latin, was like; we also know from documents how Latin diversified as the Roman Empire expanded. Thus, common ancestry is frequently the reason why neighboring, and sometimes even separated, languages show patterns of similarity.

But languages can be similar for other reasons too. Contact between speech communities, often with one group dominant over another, may lead one language to borrow from the other. For example, English borrowed a lot of vocabulary from French after England was conquered by the French-speaking Normans in A.D. 1066. Languages may also show similarities even though they do not derive from a common ancestral language and even though there has been no contact or borrowing between them. Such similarities may reflect common or universal features of human cultures or human brains or both. (As we noted earlier in the chapter, the grammatical similarities exhibited by creole languages may reflect how the human brain is "wired.") Finally, even unrelated and separated languages may show some similarities because of the phenomenon of convergence; similarities can develop because some processes of linguistic change may have only a few possible outcomes.

Language Families and Culture History

Latin is the ancestral language of the Romance languages. We know this from documentary (written) records. But if the ancestral language of a set of similar languages is not known from written records, linguists still can reconstruct many features of that language by comparing the derived languages. (Such a reconstructed language is called a **protolanguage**.) That is, by comparing presumably related languages, linguists can become aware of the features that many of them have in common, features that were probably found in the common ancestral language. The languages that derive from the same protolanguage are called a *language family*. Most languages spoken today can be grouped into fewer than 30 families. The language family that English belongs to is called *Indo-European* because it includes most of the languages of Europe and some of the languages of India. (Persian, spoken in Iran, and Kurdish also belong to this family.) About 50 percent of the world's population (now more than 6 billion people) speak Indo-European languages.[48] (See Figure 10.2 for a simplified diagram of the Indo-European language family.) Another very large language family, now spoken by more than a billion people, is Sino-Tibetan, which includes the languages of northern and southern China as well as those of Tibet and Burma.[49]

The field of historical linguistics got its start in 1786, when a British scholar living in India, Sir William Jones, noticed similarities between Sanskrit, a language spoken and written in ancient India, and classical Greek, Latin, and more recent European languages.[50] In 1822, Jakob Grimm, one of the brothers Grimm of fairy tale fame, formulated rules to describe the sound shifts that had occurred when the various Indo-European languages diverged from each other. So, for example, in English and the other languages in the Germanic branch of the Indo-European family, *d* regularly shifted to *t* (compare the English *two* and *ten* with the Latin *duo* and *decem*), and *p* regularly shifted to *f* (compare the English *father* and *foot*, to Latin's *pater* and *pes*). Scholars generally agree that the Indo-European languages derive from a language spoken 5,000 years to 6,000 years ago.[51] The ancestral Indo-European language, many of whose features have now been reconstructed, is called *proto-Indo-European*, or *PIE* for short.

Where did PIE originate? Some linguists believe that the approximate location of a protolanguage is suggested by the words for plants and animals in the derived languages. More specifically, among these different languages, the words that are cognates—that is, words that are similar in sound and meaning—presumably refer to plants and animals that were present in the original homeland. So, if we know where those animals and plants were located 5,000 years to 6,000 years ago, we can guess where PIE people lived. Among all the cognates for trees in the Indo-European languages, Paul Friedrich has identified 18 that he

Protolanguage A hypothesized ancestral language from which two or more languages seem to have derived.

Cognates Words or morphs that belong to different languages but have similar sounds and meanings.

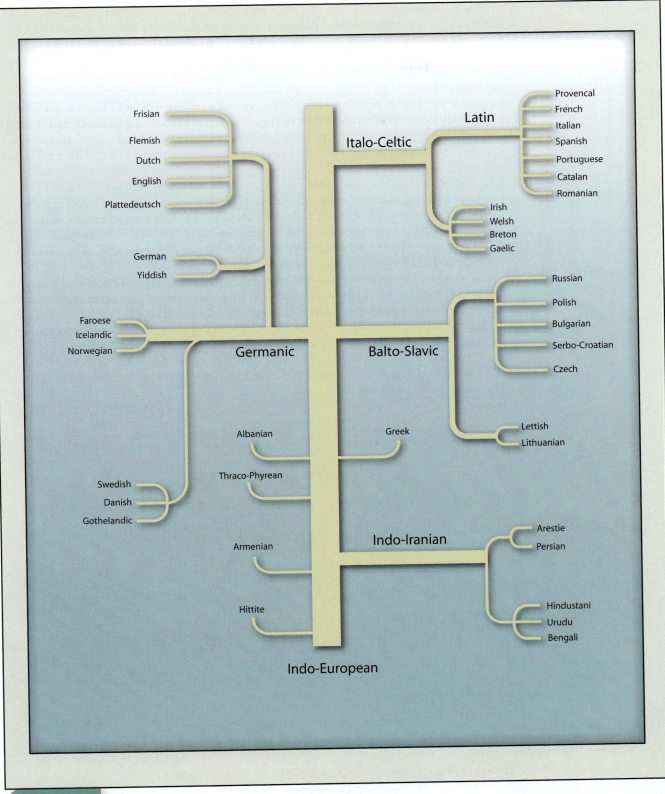

FIGURE 10.2

A simplified version of the Indo-European language family tree. The bottom is the hypothetical proto-Indo-European.

believes were present in the eastern Ukraine in 3000 B.C. On this basis, he suggests that the eastern Ukraine was the PIE homeland.[52] Also consistent with this hypothesis is the fact that the Balto-Slavic subfamily of Indo-European, which includes most of the languages in and around the former Soviet Union, has the most tree names (compared with other subfamilies) that are similar to the reconstructed form in proto-Indo-European.[53]

Marija Gimbutas thinks we can even identify the proto-Indo-Europeans archaeologically. She believes that the PIE people were probably the people associated with what is known as the Kurgan culture (5000 B.C. to 2000 B.C.), which spread out from the Ukraine around 3000 B.C. The Kurgan people were herders, raising horses, cattle, sheep, and pigs. They also relied on hunting and grain cultivation. Burials suggest differences in wealth and special status for men.[54] Why the Kurgan and linguistically similar people were able to expand to many places in Europe and the Near East is not yet clear. Some have suggested that horses and horse-drawn wagons and perhaps horseback riding provided important military advantages.[55] In any case, it is clear that many Kurgan cultural elements were distributed after 3000 B.C. over a wide area of the Old World.

Colin Renfrew disagrees with the notion that the Ukraine was the homeland of PIE. He thinks that PIE is 2,000 years to 3,000 years older than Kurgan culture and that the PIE people lived in a different place. Renfrew locates the PIE homeland in eastern Anatolia (Turkey) in 7000 B.C. to 6000 B.C., and he suggests, on the basis of archaeological evidence, that the spread of Indo-European to Europe and what is now Iran, Afghanistan, and India accompanied the spread of farming to those areas.[56]

Just as some historical linguists and archaeologists have suggested when and where the PIE people may have lived originally and how they may have spread, other linguists and archaeologists have suggested culture histories for other language families. For example, the Bantu languages in Africa (spoken by perhaps 100 million people) form a subfamily of the larger Niger-Congo family of languages. Bantu speakers currently live in a wide band across the center of Africa and down the eastern and western sides of southern Africa. All of the Bantu languages presumably derive from people who spoke proto-Bantu. But where was their homeland?

This 16th century painting by Pieter Bruegel the Elder depicts the well-known story of the Tower of Babel in the biblical Book of Genesis. From an anthropologist's viewpoint, the story of the tower is one of several ancient examples, among them a Mayan and a Sumerian text, that strive to explain the diversity of the world's languages. The idea that humans spoke one language before they dispersed across the world remains a popular theory among anthropological linguists

As in the case of proto-Indo-European, different theories have been proposed. But most historical linguists now agree with Joseph Greenberg's suggestion that the origin of Bantu was in what is now the Middle Benue area of eastern Nigeria.[57] The point of origin is presumably where there is the greatest diversity of related languages and *dialects* (varying forms of a language); it is assumed the place of origin has had the most time for linguistic diversity to develop, compared with an area only recently occupied by a related language. For example, England has more dialect diversity than New Zealand or Australia.

Why were the Bantu able to spread so widely over the last few thousand years? Anthropologists have only begun to guess.[58] Initially, the Bantu probably kept goats and practiced some form of agriculture and thereby were able to spread, displacing hunter-gatherers in the area. As the Bantu speakers expanded, they began to cultivate certain cereal crops and herd sheep and cattle. Around this time, after 1000 B.C., they also began to use and make iron tools, which may have given them significant advantages. In any case, by 1,500 years to 2,000 years ago, Bantu speakers had spread throughout central Africa and into the northern reaches of southern Africa. But speakers of non-Bantu languages still live in eastern, southern, and southwestern Africa.

The Processes of Linguistic Divergence

10.5 Identify the processes by which languages diverge.

Historical or comparative linguists hope to do more than record and date linguistic divergence. Just as physical anthropologists may attempt to develop explanations for human variation, so linguists investigate the possible causes of linguistic variation. Some of the divergence undoubtedly comes about gradually. When groups of people speaking the same language lose communication with one another because they become separated, either physically or socially, they begin to accumulate small changes in phonology, morphology, and syntax (which occur continuously in any language). These variant forms of language are considered **dialects** when the differences in phonology, morphology, and syntax are not great enough to produce unintelligibility. (Dialects should not be confused with accents, which are merely differences in pronunciation.) Eventually, if the separation continues, the former dialects of the same language will become separate languages; that is, they will become mutually unintelligible, as German and English now are. Just as culture change originates from individual changes, language change originates from individual speakers, either from spontaneous innovation or from borrowing. Only when innovative speech patterns are picked up by others does linguistic change occur.[59]

Dialects A variety of a language spoken in a particular area or by a particular social group.

Geographic barriers, such as large bodies of water, deserts, and mountains, may separate speakers of what was once the same language, but distance by itself can also produce divergence. For example, if we compare dialects of English in the British Isles, it is clear that the regions farthest away from each other are the most different linguistically (compare the northeast of Scotland and London).[60] In northern India, hundreds of semi-isolated villages and regions developed hundreds of local dialects. Today, the inhabitants of each village understand the dialects of the surrounding villages and, with a little more difficulty, the dialects of the next circle of villages. But slight dialect shifts accumulate village by village, and it seems as if different languages are being spoken at the opposite ends of the region, which are separated by more than a thousand miles.[61]

Even where there is little geographic separation, there may still be a great deal of dialect differentiation because of social distance. So, for example, the spread of a linguistic feature may be halted by religious, class, or other social differences that inhibit communication.[62] In the village of Khalapur in northern India, John Gumperz found substantial differences in speech between the Untouchables and other groups. Members of the Untouchables have work contacts with members of other groups but no friendships.[63] Without friendships and the easy communication between friends, dialect differentiation can readily develop.

Whereas isolation brings gradual divergence between speech communities, contact results in greater resemblance. This effect is particularly evident when contact between mutually unintelligible languages introduces borrowed words, which usually name some new item borrowed from the other culture—*tomato, canoe, sushi,* and so on. Bilingual groups within a culture may also introduce foreign words, especially when the mainstream language has no real equivalent. Thus, *salsa* has come into English, and *le weekend* into French.

Conquest and colonization often result in extensive and rapid borrowing, if not linguistic replacement. The Norman conquest of England introduced French as the language of the new aristocracy. It was 300 years before the educated classes began to write in English. During this time, the English borrowed words from French and Latin, and the two languages—English and French—became more alike than they would otherwise have been. About 50 percent of the English general vocabulary originated in French. As this example suggests, different social classes may react to language contact differentially. For example, English aristocrats eventually called their meat "pork" and "beef" (derived from the French words), but the people who raised the animals and prepared them for eating continued (at least for a while) to refer to the meat as "pig" and "bull," the original Anglo-Saxon words.

In those 300 years of extensive contact, the grammar of English remained relatively stable. English lost most of its inflections or case endings, but it adopted little of the French grammar. In general, the borrowing of words, particularly free morphemes,[64] is much more common than the borrowing of grammar.[65] As we might expect, borrowing by one language from another can make the borrowing language more different from its *sibling languages* (those derived from a common ancestral language) than it would otherwise be. Partly as a result of the French influence, the English vocabulary looks quite different from the languages to which it is actually most similar in terms of phonology and grammar—German, Dutch, and the Scandinavian languages.

10.6 Discuss the relationship between language and culture.

Relationships Between Language and Culture

Some attempts to explain the diversity of languages have focused on the possible interactions between language and other aspects of culture. On the one hand, if it can be shown that a culture can affect the structure and content of its language, then it would follow that linguistic diversity derives at least in part from cultural diversity. On the other hand, the direction of influence between culture and language might work in reverse: Linguistic features and structures might affect other aspects of the culture.

Cultural Influences on Language

Lexical content
Vocabulary or lexicon.

One way a society's language may reflect its corresponding culture is in **lexical content**, or vocabulary. Which experiences, events, or objects are singled out and given words may be a result of cultural characteristics.

Basic Words for Colors, Plants, and Animals Early in the 20th century, many linguists pointed to the lexical domain (vocabulary) of color words to illustrate the supposed truth that languages vary arbitrarily or without apparent reason. Different languages not only had different numbers of basic color words (from 2 to 12 or so; e.g., the words *red, green,* and *blue* in English), but they also, it was thought, had no consistency in the way they classified or divided the colors of the spectrum. But findings from a comparative (cross-linguistic) study contradicted these traditional presumptions about variation in the number and meaning of basic color words. On the basis of their study of at first 20, then over 100 languages, Brent Berlin and Paul Kay found that languages did not encode color in completely arbitrary ways. Moreover, they suggested that there appears to be a nearly universal sequence by which basic color terms evolve.[66] Paul Kay and his collaborators followed up these earlier studies with a three-decade field study that included 110 additional unwritten languages. Although they added refinements, the later work supports the idea that a culture's basic color words evolve in predictable stages.[67]

Although different languages do have different numbers of basic color words, most speakers of any language are very likely to point to the same color chips as the best representatives of particular colors. Moreover, a culture's set of basic color terms evolves through seven more or less predictable stages of refinement from 2 to 11 colors.[68] If a language has just two basic color words, its speakers will always refer to "black" (or dark) hues and "white" (or light) hues. (Figure 10.3 shows a graphical representation of the proposed evolutionary stages of the development of basic color words.) Speakers of the language will also uniformly associate black with "cold" colors, among which they include blue, green, and purple, while they group red, orange, yellow, and pink, with "warm" white. If a language has three basic color words, the third word will nearly always be "red." (Why red comes third remains unclear.) The next category to appear is either "yellow" or "grue" (green/blue), then different words for green and blue, and so on. To be sure, we usually do not see the process by which basic color words are added to a language. But we can infer the usual sequence because, for example, if a language has a word for "yellow," it will almost always have a word for "red," whereas having a word for "red" does not mean that the language will have a word for "yellow."

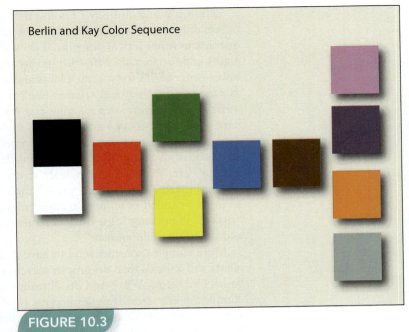

Berlin and Kay Color Sequence

FIGURE 10.3

A graphical representation of the evolution of basic color words.

What exactly is a *basic* color word? All languages, even the ones with only two basic color terms, have many different ways of expressing how color varies. For example, in English, we have words such as *turquoise, blue-green, scarlet, crimson,* and *sky blue.* Linguists do not consider these to be basic color words. In English, the basic color words are *white, black, red, green, yellow, blue, brown, pink, purple, orange,* and *gray.* One feature of a basic color word is that it consists of a single morph; it cannot include two or more units of meaning. This feature eliminates combinations such as *blue-green* and *sky blue.* A second feature of a basic color word is that the color it represents is not generally included in a higher-order color term. For example, scarlet and crimson are usually considered variants of red, turquoise a variant of blue. A third feature is that basic terms tend to be the first-named words when people are asked for color words. Finally, for a word to be considered a basic color word, many individual speakers of the language have to agree on the central meaning (in the color spectrum) of the word.[69]

Why do different societies (languages) vary in number of basic color terms? Berlin and Kay suggest that the number of basic color terms in a language increases with technological specialization as color is used to decorate and distinguish objects.[70] Cross-linguistic variation in the number of basic color terms does not mean that some languages make more color distinctions than others. Every language could make a particular distinction by combining words (e.g., "fresh leaf" for green); a language need not have a separate basic term for that color.

There may also be many basic color terms because of a biological factor.[71] Peoples with darker (more pigmented) eyes seem to have more trouble distinguishing colors at the dark (blue-green) end of the spectrum than do peoples with lighter eyes. It might be expected, then, that peoples who live nearer the equator (who tend to have darker eyes, presumably for protection against damaging ultraviolet radiation) would tend to have fewer basic color terms. And they do.[72] Moreover, it seems that both cultural and biological factors are required to account for cross-linguistic variation in the number of basic color terms. Societies tend to have six or more such terms (with separate terms for blue and green) only when they are relatively far from the equator and only when their cultures are more technologically specialized.[73] As we will see in later chapters, technological specialization tends to go with larger communities, more centralized governments, occupational specialization, and more social inequality. Societies with such traits are often referred to in a shorthand way as more "complex," which should not be taken to mean "better."

Echoing Berlin and Kay's finding that basic color terms seem to be added in a more or less universal sequence, Cecil Brown has found what seem to be developmental sequences in other lexical domains. Two such domains are general, or *life-form,* terms for plants and for animals. Life-form terms are higher-order classifications. All languages have lower-order terms for specific plants and animals. For example, English has words such as *oak, pine, sparrow,* and *salmon.* English speakers make finer distinctions too—*pin oak, white pine, white-throated sparrow,* and *red salmon.* But why, in some languages, do people have a larger number of general terms such as *tree, bird,* and *fish?* It seems that these general terms show a universal developmental sequence too. That is, general terms seem to be added in a somewhat consistent order. After "plant" comes a term for "tree"; then one for "grerb" (small, green, leafy, nonwoody plant); then "bush" (for plants between tree and grerb in size); then "grass"; then "vine."[74] The life-form terms for animals also seem to be added in sequence; after "animal" comes a term for "fish," then "bird," then "snake," then "wug" (for small creatures other than fish, birds, and snakes—e.g., worms and bugs), then "mammal."[75]

More complex societies tend to have a larger number of general, or life-form, terms for plants and animals than do simpler societies, just as they tend to have a larger number of basic color terms. Why? And do all realms or domains of vocabulary increase in size as social complexity increases? If we look at the total vocabulary of a language (as can be counted in a dictionary), more complex societies do have larger vocabularies.[76] But we have to remember that complex societies have many kinds of specialists, and dictionaries will include the terms such specialists use. If we look instead at the nonspecialist, **core vocabulary** of languages, it seems that all languages have a core vocabulary of about the same size.[77] Indeed, although some domains increase in size with social complexity, some remain the same and still others decrease. An example of a smaller vocabulary domain in complex societies is that of specific names for plants. Urban North Americans may know general terms for plants, but they know relatively few names for specific plants. The typical individual in a small-scale society can commonly name 400 to 800 plant species; a typical person in our own and similar societies may be able to name only 40 to 80.[78] The number of life-form terms is larger in societies in which ordinary people know less about particular plants and animals.[79]

The evidence now available strongly supports the idea that the vocabulary of a language reflects the everyday distinctions that are important in the society. Those aspects of environment or culture that are of special importance will receive greater attention in the language.

Grammar Most of the examples we could accumulate would show that a culture influences the names of things visible in its environment. Evidence for cultural influence on the grammatical structure of a language is less extensive. Harry Hoijer draws attention to the verb categories in the language of the Navajo, a traditionally nomadic people. These categories center mainly in the reporting of events, or "eventings," as he calls them. Hoijer notes that, in "the reporting of actions and events, and the framing of substantive concepts, Navajo emphasizes movement and specifies the nature, direction, and status of such movement in considerable detail."[80] For example, Navajo has one category for eventings that are in motion and another for eventings that have ceased moving. Hoijer concludes that the emphasis on events in the process of occurring reflects the Navajo's nomadic experience over the centuries, an experience also reflected in their myths and folklore.

A linguistic emphasis on events may or may not be generally characteristic of nomadic peoples; as yet, no one has investigated the matter cross-culturally or comparatively. But there are indications that systematic comparative research would turn up other grammatical features that are related to cultural characteristics. For example, many languages lack the possessive transitive verb we write as "have," as in "I have." Instead, the language may say something such as "it is to me." A cross-cultural study has suggested that a language may develop the verb "have" after the speakers of that language have developed a system of private property or personal ownership of resources.[81] The concept of private property is far from universal and tends to occur only in complex societies with social inequality. In contrast, many societies have some kind of communal ownership, by kin groups or communities. How people talk about owning seems to reflect how they own; societies that lack a concept of private property also lack the verb "have."

Core vocabulary
Nonspecialist vocabulary.

Linguistic Influences on Culture: The Sapir-Whorf Hypothesis

There is general agreement that culture influences language. But there is less agreement about the opposite possibility—that language influences other aspects of culture. Edward Sapir and Benjamin Lee Whorf suggested that language is a force in its own right, that it affects how individuals in a society perceive and conceive reality. This suggestion is known as the *Sapir-Whorf hypothesis*.[82] In comparing the English language with Hopi, Whorf pointed out that English-language categories convey discreteness with regard to time and space, but Hopi does not. English has a discrete past, present, and future, and things occur at a definite time. Hopi expresses things with more of an idea of ongoing processes without time being apportioned into fixed segments. According to Ronald Wardhaugh, Whorf believed that these language differences lead Hopi and English speakers to see the world differently.[83]

As intriguing as that idea is, the relevant evidence is mixed. Linguists today do not generally accept the view that language coerces thought, but some suspect that particular features of language may facilitate certain patterns of thought.[84] The influences may be clearest in poetry and metaphors, where words and phrases are applied to other than their ordinary subjects, as in "all the world's a stage."[85] One of the serious problems in testing the Sapir-Whorf hypothesis is that researchers need to figure out how to separate the effects of other aspects of culture from the effects of language.

One approach that may reveal the direction of influence between language and culture is to study how children in different cultures (speaking different languages) develop concepts as they grow up. If language influences the formation of a particular concept, we might expect that children will acquire that concept earlier in societies where the languages emphasize that concept. For example, some languages make more of gender differences than others. Do children develop gender identity earlier when their language emphasizes gender? (Very young girls and boys seem to believe they can switch genders by dressing in opposite-sex clothes, suggesting that they have not yet developed a stable sense that they are unchangeably girls or boys.) Alexander Guiora and his colleagues have studied children growing up in Hebrew-speaking homes (Israel), English-speaking homes (the United States), and Finnish-speaking homes (Finland). Hebrew has the most gender emphasis of the three languages; all nouns are either masculine or feminine, and even second-person and plural pronouns are differentiated by gender. English emphasizes gender less, differentiating by gender only in the third-person singular (*she* or *her* or *hers*; *he* or *him* or *his*). Finnish emphasizes gender the least; although some words, such as *man* and *woman*, convey gender, differentiation by gender is otherwise lacking in the language. Consistent with the idea that language may influence thought, Hebrew-speaking children acquire the concept of stable gender identity the earliest on the average, Finnish-speaking children the latest.[86]

Another approach is to predict from language differences how people may be expected to perform in experiments. Comparing the Yucatec Mayan language and English, John Lucy predicted that English speakers might recall the *number* of things presented more than Yucatec Mayan speakers. For most classes of nouns, English requires a linguistic way of indicating whether something is singular or plural. You cannot say "I have dog" (no indication of number), but must say "I have a dog," "I have dogs," or "I have one (two, three, several, many) dogs." Yucatec Maya, like English, can indicate a plural, but it allows the noun to be neutral with regard to number. For example, the translated phrase there-is-dog-over-there (*yàan pèek té'elo'*) can be left ambiguous about whether there is one or more than one dog. In English, the same ambiguity would occur in the sentence "I saw deer over there," but English does not often allow ambiguity for animate or inanimate nouns.[87] In a number of experiments, Yucatec Mayan and American English speakers were equally likely to recall the objects in a picture, but they differed in how often they described the number of a particular object in the picture. Yucatec Mayan speakers did so less often, consistent with their language's lack of insistence on indicating number.[88] So the salience of number in the experiments was probably a consequence of how the languages differ. Of course, it is possible that salience of number is created by some other cultural feature, such as dependence on money in the economy.

10.7 Discuss the relationship between ways of speaking and issues of class, gender, and ethnicity.

The Ethnography of Speaking

Until the early 1960s, linguistic anthropologists concentrated on understanding the structure of the language spoken in a society, particularly those lacking writing. They focused on the linguistic features of the language, such as its phonology, morphology, and syntax. Those interested in historical relationships between languages compared their structures to try to understand linguistic ancestry and divergence. In recent years, many linguists have begun to conduct fieldwork to study what people actually say and how they use language. The focus is on "speech" or "communicative events" to describe the context, who can participate, what topics are discussed, and how people present themselves. The main goal of an *ethnography of speaking* is to find cultural and subcultural patterns of speech variation in different social contexts.[89] We will consider in more detail how speech may vary by social status or gender, but analysis of speech events also helps reveal what is felt important to present or communicate.[90] One sociolinguist might ask, for example, what the cultural functions of story-telling are in a Cree community and then record what occurs during an evening with an elder and his family, an occasion when a story is likely to be told.[91] Another sociolinguist may look at hip-hop language to understand what it reveals not only about a musical movement but also about identity of a subcultural group in the United States.[92]

Social Status and Speech

That a foreign speaker of a language may know little about the small talk of that language is but one example of the sociolinguistic principle that what we say and how we say it are not wholly predictable by the rules of our language. Who we are socially and who we are talking to may greatly affect what we say and how we say it.

In a study interviewing children in a New England town, John Fischer noted that, in formal interviews, children were likely to pronounce the ending in words such as *singing* and *fishing,* but in informal conversations, they said *"singin'"* and *"fishin'."* Moreover, he noted that the phenomenon also appeared to be related to social class; children from higher-status families were less likely to drop the ending than were children from lower-status families. Subsequent studies in English-speaking areas tend to support Fischer's observations with regard to this speech pattern. Other patterns are observed as well. For example, in Norwich, England, lower classes tend to drop the *h* in words such as *hammer,* but in all classes, the pattern of dropping the *h* increases in casual situations.[93] With respect to grammatical differences, in inner-city Detroit, lower-class African Americans are more likely to use double negatives as in "It ain't nobody's business," in contrast to middle-class African Americans who usually say "It isn't anybody's business."[94]

Research has shown that English people from higher-class backgrounds tend to have more *homogeneous* speech, conforming more to what is considered standard English (the type of speech heard on television or radio), whereas people from lower-class backgrounds have very *heterogeneous* speech, varying in their speaking according to the local or dialect area they come from.[95] In some societies, social status differences may be associated with more marked differentiation of words. Clifford Geertz, in his study of Javanese, showed that the vocabularies of the three rather sharply divided groups in Javanese society—peasants, townspeople, and aristocrats—reflect their separate positions. For example, the concept *now* is expressed differently in these three groups. A peasant will use *saiki* (considered the lowest and roughest form of the word); a townsman will use *saniki* (considered somewhat more elegant); and an aristocrat will use *samenika* (the most elegant form).[96]

Status relationships between people can also influence the way they speak to each other. Terms of address are a good example. In English, forms of address are relatively simple. One is called either by a first name or by a title (such as *Doctor, Professor, Ms.,* or *Mister*) followed by a last name. A study by Roger Brown and Marguerite Ford indicates that terms of address in English vary with the nature of the relationship between the speakers.[97] The reciprocal use of first names generally signifies an informal or intimate relationship between two people. A title and last name used reciprocally usually indicates a more formal or businesslike relationship between individuals who are roughly equal in status. Nonreciprocal use of first names and titles in English is reserved for speakers who recognize a marked difference in status between them. This status difference can be a function of age, as when a child refers to her mother's friend as Mrs. Miller and is in turn addressed as Sally, or can be due to occupational hierarchy, as when a person refers to his boss as Ms. Ramirez and is in turn addressed as Joe. In some cases, generally between boys and between men, the use of the last name alone represents a middle ground between the intimate and the formal usages.

Gender Differences in Speech

In many societies, the speech of men differs from the speech of women. The variation can be slight, as in our own society, or more extreme, as with the Carib Indians in the Lesser Antilles of the West Indies, among whom women and men use different words for the same concepts.[98] In Japan, males and females use entirely different words for numerous concepts (e.g., the male word for water is *mizu;* the female version is *ohiya*), and females often add the polite prefix *o-* (females will tend to say *ohasi* for chopsticks; males will tend to say *hasi*).[99] In the United States and other Western societies, there are differences in the speech of females and males, but they are not as dramatic as in the Carib and Japanese cases. For example, earlier we noted the tendency for the *g* to be dropped in words such as *singing* when the situation is informal and when the social class background is lower. But there is also a gender difference. Women are more likely than men to keep the *g* sound and less likely than men to drop the *h* in words such as *happy*. In Montreal, women are less likely than men to drop the *l* in phrases such as *il fait* ("he does") or in the idiom *il y a* ("there is/are").[100] And in Detroit, in each social class, African American women are less likely than men to use double negatives.[101]

Gender differences occur in intonation and in phrasing of sentences as well. Robin Lakoff found that, in English, women tend to answer questions with sentences that have rising inflections at the end instead of a falling intonation associated with a firm answer. Women also tend to add questions to statements, such as "They caught the robber last week, didn't they?"[102]

One explanation for the gender differences, particularly with regard to pronunciation, is that women in many societies may be more concerned than men with being "correct."[103] (This is not in the linguist's sense; it is important to remember that linguists do not consider one form of speech more correct than another, just as they do not consider one dialect superior to another. All are equally capable of expressing a complex variety of thoughts and ideas.) In societies with social classes, what is considered more correct by the average person may be what is associated with the upper class. In other societies, what is older may be considered more correct. For example, in the Native American language of Koasati, which used to be spoken in Louisiana, males and females used different endings in certain verbs. The differences seemed to be disappearing in the 1930s, when the research on Koasati was done. Young girls had begun to use the male forms, and

Strangers shake hands when they meet; friends may touch each other more warmly. How we speak to others also differs according to the degree of friendship.

only older women still used the female forms. Koasati men said that the women's speech was a "better" form of speech.[104] Gender differences in speech may parallel some of the gender differences noted in other social behavior (as we will see in the chapter on sex and gender): Girls are more likely than boys to behave in ways that are acceptable to adults.

There are not enough studies to know just how common it is for women to exhibit more linguistic "correctness." We do know of some instances where it is not the case. For example, in a community in Madagascar where people speak Merina, a dialect of Malagasy, it is considered socially correct to avoid explicit directives. So, instead of directly ordering an action, a Merina speaker will try to say it indirectly. Also, it is polite to avoid negative remarks, such as expressing anger, toward someone. In this community, however, women, not men, often break the rules; women speak more directly and express anger more often.[105] This difference may be related to the fact that women are more involved in buying and selling in the marketplace.

Some researchers have questioned whether it is correctness that is at issue. Rather, we may be dealing in these examples with unequal prestige and power. Women may try to

Perspectives on Gender

Does the English Language Promote Sexist Thinking?

Does English promote sexist thinking, or does the language merely reflect gender inequalities that already exist? For those who wish to promote gender equality, the answers to these questions are important because, if language influences thought (along the lines put forward by Edward Sapir and Benjamin Whorf), then linguistic change will be necessary to bring about change in the culture of gender. If it is the other way around, that is, if language reflects inequality, then social, economic, and political changes have to come before we can expect substantial linguistic change to occur.

Leaving aside for the moment which changes first, how does English represent gender inequity? Consider the following written by Benjamin Lee Whorf: "Speech is the best show man puts on. . . . Language helps man in his thinking." Although *man* in English technically refers to all humans and *his* technically refers to the thinking of a single person of either gender, the frequent use of such words could convey the idea that males are more important. Do the words *chairman* and *policeman* convey that males are supposed to have those jobs? What is conveyed when there are two words for the two genders, as *hero* and *heroine*? Usually the base word is male and the suffix is added for the female form. Does the suffix convey that the

female form is an afterthought or less important?

It is not just the structure of the language that may convey gender inequality. How come in the pairs *sir/madam, master/mistress, wizard/witch*, the female version has acquired negative connotations? Coming back to the original questions, how would we know whether language promotes sexism or sexism influences language? One way to find out is to do experimental studies, such as the one conducted by Fatemeh Khosroshashi. Some individuals were asked to read texts written with *man, he*, and *his* referring to people; others were asked to read texts with more gender-neutral phrasing. Individuals were subsequently asked to draw pictures to go with the texts. The ones who read the texts with more male terminology drew more accompanying pictures of men, strongly suggesting that the use of the terms *man, he*, and *his* conveyed the thought that the people in the text were men, not women, *because* of the vocabulary used.

It would be important to know whether societies with more "male-oriented" language are more male-dominated than other societies. We don't have that kind of comparative research yet. But one study by Robert and Ruth Munroe looked at the *proportion* of female and male nouns in 10 languages (including six

Indo-European languages) in which nouns have gender. The Munroes asked whether those societies with less male bias in social customs (e.g., all children are equally likely to inherit property) had a higher proportion of female nouns than male nouns (more female than male nouns). The answer appears to be yes. Studies like it are important if we want to discover how language differences may be related to other aspects of culture. If male-oriented languages are not related to male dominance, then it is not likely that sexist thinking is a consequence of language.

On the assumption that language may influence thought, many are pushing for changes in the way English is used, if not structured. It is hard to get English speakers to adopt a gender-neutral singular pronoun to replace *he*. Attempts to do so go back to the 18th century and include suggestions of *tey, thon, per*, and *s/he*. Although these efforts have not succeeded, the way English is written and spoken has begun to change. Words or phrases such as *chair* (or *chairperson*) or *police officer* man versions. If Whorf were writing his sentence now, it probably would be written: "Speech is the best show humans put on. . . . Language helps people think."

Sources: Holmes 2001, 305–316; Khosroshashi 1989; Lakoff 1973; Munroe and Munroe 1969; Romaine 1994, 105–116; Wardhaugh 2002, 317.

raise their status by conforming more to standard speech. When they answer a question with a rising inflection, they may be expressing uncertainty and a lack of power. Alternatively, perhaps women want to be more cooperative conversationalists. Speaking in a more "standard" fashion is consistent with being more likely to be understood by others. Answering a question with another question leads to continued conversation.[106]

It is popular wisdom that men and women typically differ in what they do or do not talk about. Deborah Tannen has studied gender differences in speaking patterns and found evidence that supports this belief. For example, when women hear about someone else's troubles, they are likely to express empathy. In contrast, men are likely to offer solutions. Men tend not to ask for directions; women do. Women tend to talk a lot in private settings; men talk more in public settings. These and other differences can cause friction and misunderstanding between the genders. When women express their troubles and men offer solutions, women feel that their feelings are not understood; men are frustrated that the women do not take their solutions seriously. Men may prefer to sit at home quietly and feel put upon to have to engage in conversation; women feel slighted when men avoid extended conversations with them. Why these differences? Tannen suggests that misunderstanding between men and women arises because boys and girls grow up in somewhat different cultures. Girls typically play in small groups, talk frequently, and are intimate with others. Boys more often play in large groups in which jockeying for status and attention is more of a concern. In these groups, they learn that higher-status individuals give rather than seek directions and solutions. Because large play groups resemble public settings, later in life, men feel more comfortable speaking in public, whereas women are typically more comfortable speaking in small, intimate groups.[107]

Multilingualism and Code-Switching

For many people, the ability to speak more than one language is a normal part of life. One language may be spoken at home and another in school, the marketplace, or government. Or more than one language may be spoken at home if family members come from different cultures and still other languages are spoken outside. Some countries explicitly promote multilingualism. Singapore, for example, has four official languages—English, Mandarin (one of the Chinese languages), Tamil, and Malay. English is stressed for trade, Mandarin as the language of communication with most of China, Malay as the language of the general region, and Tamil as the language of an important ethnic group. Moreover, most of the population speaks Hokkien, another Chinese language. Education is likely to be in English and Mandarin.[108]

What happens when people who know two or more languages communicate with each other? Very often you find them **code-switching**, using more than one language in the course of conversing.[109] Switching can occur in the middle of a Spanish-English bilingual sentence, as in "No van a bring it up in the meeting" ("They are not going to bring it up in the meeting").[110] Or switching can occur when the topic or situation changes, such as from social talk to schoolwork. Why do speakers of more than one language sometimes switch? Although speakers switch for a lot of different reasons, what is clear is that the switching is not a haphazard mix that comes from laziness or ignorance. Code-switching involves a great deal of knowledge of two or more languages and an awareness of what is considered appropriate or inappropriate in the community. For example, in the Puerto Rican community in New York City, code-switching within the same sentence seems to be common in speech among friends, but if a stranger who looks like a Spanish speaker approaches, the language will shift entirely to Spanish.[111]

Although each community may have its own rules for code-switching, variations in practice can depend upon the broader political and historical context. Why do German speakers in Transylvania, for example, rarely code-switch to Romanian, the region's national language? Perhaps it is because they historically viewed Romanians as inferior in status. Germans settled in Transylvania as colonists in the 12th and 13th centuries, not long before semi-nomadic Romanians also settled there. However, for centuries afterwards the Germans—or Saxons, as they were called—were given greater privileges by the Hungarian and Austrian rulers of the region. Germans and Hungarians could own land, but the Romanians could not and effectively became the serf class. The

Code-switching Using more than one language in the course of conversing.

Romanian population would see its fortunes rise when the Austro-Hungarian Empire came to an end in World War I and Transylvania was annexed by Romania. When Romania became part of the Soviet bloc after World War II, the German speakers, for their part, would lose their economic privilege. Yet they continued to speak German without code-switching among themselves. In the rare cases that Romanian was used among the German speakers, it tended to be associated with such low-status speech as singing bawdy songs.

An opposite reaction occurred in a Hungarian region of German-speaking Austria. The people of this agricultural region, annexed to Austria in 1921, were fairly poor peasant farmers. After World War II, business expansion began to attract labor from rural areas, and many Hungarians eagerly moved into jobs in industry. Younger generations saw German as a symbol of higher status and upward mobility; not surprisingly, code-switching between Hungarian and German became part of their conversations. Indeed, for the third generation, German has become the language of choice, except when they are speaking to the oldest Hungarians. The Hungarian-Austrian pattern, where the language of the politically dominant group becomes "linguistically dominant," is common in many parts of the world.[112]

Writing and Literacy

10.8 Identify the origins of writing and literacy, and assess the impact of writing and literacy on culture and communication.

Most of us have come to depend on writing for so many things that it is hard to imagine a world without it. Yet humans spent most of their history on earth without written language, and many, if not most, important human achievements predate written language. Parents and other teachers passed on their knowledge by oral instruction and demonstration. Stories, legends, and myths abounded—the stuff we call oral literature—even in the absence of writing. This is not to say that writing is not important. Far more information and far more literature can be preserved for a longer period of time with a writing system. The earliest writing systems are only about 6,000 years old and are associated with early cities and states. Early writing is associated with systematic record-keeping—keeping of ledgers for inventorying goods and transactions. In early times, probably only the elite could read and write—indeed, only recently has universal literacy (the ability to read and write) become the goal of most countries. But in most countries, the goal of universal literacy is far from achieved. Even in countries with universal education, the quality of education and the length of education vary considerably between subcultures and genders. Just as some ways of speaking are considered superior to others, a high degree of literacy is usually considered superior to illiteracy.[113] But literacy in what language or languages? As we discussed in the box on endangered languages, recent efforts to preserve languages have encouraged writing of texts in languages that were only spoken previously. Obviously, there will be few texts in those languages; other languages have vast numbers of written texts. As more accumulated knowledge is written and stored in books, journals, and databases, attainment of literacy in those written languages will be increasingly critical to success. And texts do not only convey practical knowledge—they may also convey attitudes, beliefs, and values that are characteristic of the culture associated with the language in which the texts are written.

The ability to decipher calculations and economic data, or financial literacy, is often stressed today as a way to help people in developing societies. These members of a women's banking group in Dhaka, Bangladesh, are discussing finances.

Summary and Review

Communication

10.1 Define *communication*, and compare and contrast human and nonhuman communication.

- There are many ways in which information is exchanged or imparted, but all systems of communication require a common and shared system of symbols, signs, or behaviors.

- Humans rely heavily on spoken language to communicate, and it is probably the major way culture is transmitted. Any system of language consists of publicly accepted symbols by which individuals try to share private experiences and thoughts, but human language is much more than symbolic communication.

- All human languages are thought to use a large set of symbols that can be combined to produce new meanings (open system), communicate about past and future events, apply linguistic rules for combinations of sounds, and have many kinds of discourse.

- Human communication happens directly through spoken language; indirectly through "body language"; with nonverbal symbolic systems such as writing, algebraic equations, musical scores, and road signs; and through art, music, and dance.

- Some direct nonverbal communication appears to be universal in humans. Humans worldwide seem able to recognize a happy, sad, surprised, angry, disgusted, or afraid face. But many body and hand gestures are not universal.

- Other animal species communicate through sound, chemicals, and body movement. Some animals use symbolic communication; there is general agreement that humans have much more complexity in their systems of communication, but there is debate about how profound the differences are.

> **?** In what ways do human and nonhuman communication differ?

The Origins of Language

10.2 Explain how the study of creole and pidgin languages and of children's acquisition of language might tell us something about the origins of language.

- Unambiguous evidence of human language dates back to 5,000 years ago, but it likely existed 50,000 years ago and may possibly have been used by humans as well Neandertals.

- Actual development of language is neither completely biologically determined nor dependent on a system of writing. Languages of simpler societies are equally as complex as those of developed societies.

- All languages possess the amount of vocabulary their speakers need, and all languages expand in response to cultural changes.

- Pidgin languages combine features of various languages but without basic components such as prepositions or auxiliary verbs. They may or may not develop into full languages.

- Pidgin languages that do develop further (often through children) become creole languages, having grammar different from the source languages. Some argue that creole languages throughout the world have striking grammar similarities and may resemble early human languages.

- A child is apparently equipped from birth with the capacity to reproduce all the sounds used by the world's languages and to learn any system of grammar, an ability that gives way to cultural influences around the age of 1 year.

> **?** What is known or suspected about the origins of language?

Descriptive Linguistics

10.3 Discuss the major components of descriptive linguistics (phonology, morphology, and syntax) and the key findings in each of these areas.

- Grammar to the linguist consists of the actual, often unconscious, principles that predict how most people talk, which linguists study through phonology, morphology, and syntax.

- Even though what people say is sometimes contradicted by their observed behavior, language is important to understanding the beliefs, attitudes, values, and worldview of a people. In many cases, behaviors also cannot be readily understood without verbal interpretation.

- Linguists studying phonology write down speech utterances as sound sequences and then try to identify which sounds affect meaning, which sound sequences are allowed in a language, and what usually unconscious rules predict those sequences.

- Morphology is the study of sequences of sounds that have meaning. The smallest unit of language that has a meaning is called a morph. One or more morphs with the same meaning may make up a morpheme.

- The lexicon of a language consists of words and morphs and their meanings. A free morpheme can be a separate word. A bound morpheme displays its meaning only when attached to another morpheme.

- Syntax reflects the rules that predict how phrases and sentences are generally formed. Speakers of a language follow implicit rules of syntax but are not usually consciously aware of them. The linguist's description of the syntax of a language makes these rules explicit.

 What are the major components of descriptive linguistics (phonology, morphology, and syntax)?

Historical Linguistics

10.4 Describe how historical linguistics establishes historical relationships between languages and language families.

- Historical linguists focus on how languages change over time. Linguists can reconstruct changes that have occurred in a language, written or unwritten, by comparing contemporary languages that are similar.

- Common ancestry, contact between speech communities, and the limited processes of linguistic change may explain why languages show similarities.

- Languages that derive from the same protolanguage are called a language family. Most languages spoken today can be grouped into fewer than 30 families. Linguists still can reconstruct many features of a protolanguage by comparing the derived languages.

- The location of a protolanguage may be suggested by the words for plants and animals in the derived languages. The locations of those animals and plants thousands of years ago may help researchers decipher the origins of the protolanguage.

 How does historical linguistics establish relationships between languages and language families?

The Processes of Linguistic Divergence

10.5 Identify the processes by which languages diverge.

- When groups speaking the same language lose communication with one another through physical or social separation, they accumulate small changes in phonology, morphology, and syntax that lead to dialects and, with continued separation, to separate languages.

- Isolation leads to divergence between speech communities, and contact leads to resemblance. Conquest and colonization often promote extensive and rapid linguistic borrowing or total replacement. Generally, words are borrowed more commonly than grammar.

 How do languages diverge?

Relationships Between Language and Culture

10.6 Discuss the relationship between language and culture.

- A society's language may reflect its corresponding culture in lexical content or vocabulary.

- Both cultural and biological factors influence the number of basic color terms. Societies tend to have six or more color terms only when they are relatively far from the equator and only when their cultures are more technologically specialized.

- Ignoring terms that specialists use within a society, it seems that all languages have a core vocabulary of about the same size.

- Current evidence supports the idea that the vocabulary of a language reflects the everyday distinctions that are important in the society. This finding may also be true of grammar.

- Some evidence supports the Sapir-Whorf hypothesis that language affects how individuals in a society perceive and conceive reality, but more research is needed.

How are language and some other aspects of culture related?

The Ethnography of Speaking

10.7 Discuss the relationship between ways of speaking and issues of class, gender, and ethnicity.

- The main goal of an ethnography of speaking is to find cultural and subcultural patterns of speech variation in different social contexts.

- Social status and whom a person is talking to may greatly affect what a person says and how it is said. Social status may predict variation in speech from "standard" speech, use and differentiation of certain words, and terms of address.

- In many societies, the speech of men and women differs, particularly in terms of word choice, pronunciation, intonation, and phrasing. Some researchers are suggesting that these differences may be related to prestige and power.

- In code-switching, speakers who know two or more languages in common purposefully use words and phrases from both languages in their speech. Each community may have its own rules for code-switching, and variations in practice can depend on political and historical context.

 How do some ways of speaking vary by class, gender, and ethnicity?

Writing and Literacy

10.8 Identify the origins of writing and literacy, and assess the impact of writing and literacy on culture and communication.

- Humans spent most of their history on earth without written language, and many important human achievements predate written language. However, far more information and literature can be preserved for a longer period of time with a writing system.

- The earliest writing systems are only about 6,000 years old and are associated with early cities and states. Early writing is associated with systematic record-keeping—keeping of ledgers for inventories of goods and transactions.

- Universal literacy is far from achieved today. A high degree of literacy is usually considered superior to illiteracy.

- As more accumulated knowledge is written and stored, attainment of literacy in those written languages will be increasingly critical to success. Texts convey not only practical knowledge but also attitudes, beliefs, and values that are characteristic of the related culture.

 What are the origins of writing and literacy? What are some of the impacts of writing and literacy?

Think on it

1. Why might **natural selection** have favored the development of true language in humans but not in apes?

2. Would the world be better off with many different languages spoken or with just one **universal language**? Why do you think so?

3. Discuss some new behavior or way of thinking that led people to adopt or invent new **vocabulary** or some new pattern of speech.

4. How does some aspect of your **speech** differ from your parents or others of the previous generation? Why do you think it has changed?

11 Economics

LEARNING OBJECTIVES

11.1 Describe foraging and complex foraging, and identify the general societal features associated with food collecting.

11.2 Describe three major types of food production and identify the general societal features associated with the different types of food production.

11.3 Identify environmental restraints on food-getting.

11.4 Describe and critically discuss the spread and intensification of food production.

11.5 Compare and contrast the allocation of resources among foragers, horticulturalists, intensive agriculturalists, and pastoralists and how colonialism and the state have affected that allocation.

11.6 Describe variation in different types of economic production, what motivates people to work, how societies divide up the work to be done, and how they organize work.

11.7 Explain the three general types of systems for distributing goods and services (reciprocity, redistribution, and market or commercial exchange).

11.8 Discuss the worldwide trend toward commercialization and its social effects.

When we think of economics, we think of things and activities involving money. We think of the costs of goods and services, such as food, rent, haircuts, and movie tickets. We may also think of factories, farms, and other enterprises that produce the goods and services we need, or think we need. Inevitably, we think about the economy as a system that employs people to produce goods and services in exchange for wages. Workers in industrial societies may stand before a moving belt for eight hours, tightening identical bolts that glide by. In a post-industrial society, workers more likely provide a knowledge-based service, such as computer programming. In either case, people receive money, a symbol of the value placed on a commodity or a service, in exchange for the tasks they perform. The bits of colored paper and coins we call cash— or, as is more often the case today, the value on the checks or plastic cards that stand in for the colored paper—may be exchanged for food, shelter, and other goods and services.

Yet many societies—indeed, most cultures known to anthropology—did not have money or the equivalent of the factory worker until relatively recently. Still, all societies have economic systems, whether or not they involve money. All societies have customs specifying how people gain access to natural resources; customary ways of transforming or converting those resources, through labor, into necessities and other desired goods and services; and customs for distributing and perhaps exchanging goods and services. Many aspects of a culture, including family and kinship groups, the political system, and the presence or absence of inequality based on social class or gender, affect the form its economy takes.

The major factor predicting variation among economic systems is the way in which each society gets its food, which is where we begin this chapter. We first examine traditional food-getting and economic systems and then turn to worldwide shifts toward commercial economies and a world economic system.

The way we get our food has changed dramatically over the course of human history. Today almost half of the world's people live in cities and food is obtained by buying it. Where and when we buy food may be culturally determined; Europeans and Asians, for example, are more likely to prefer going to a market daily to buy fresh food. North Americans have accustomed themselves to going to a supermarket, where they get a stockpile of food for the week. Those of us who buy our food from a supermarket can buy a week's worth of food within an hour, refrigerate it, and move on to other activities. But we do not think of what would happen if the food were not delivered to the supermarket. We wouldn't be able to eat, and without eating for a while, we would die. Despite the old adage "Man [or woman] does not live by bread alone," we could not live at all without bread or the equivalent. Food-getting activities, then, take precedence over other activities important to survival. Reproduction, social control (the maintenance of peace and order within a group), defense against external threat, and the transmission of knowledge and skills to future generations—none could take place without energy derived from food. But it is not merely energy that is required for survival and long-term reproduction. Food-getting strategies need to provide the appropriate combination of nutrients throughout varying seasons and changing environmental conditions. Food-getting activities are also important because the way a society gets its food strongly predicts other aspects of a culture, from community size and permanence of settlement to type of economy and degree of inequality and type of political system, and even art styles and religious beliefs and practices.

Foraging

Foraging or *food collection* may generally be defined as a strategy whereby humans gather, hunt, scavenge, or fish to obtain their food from plants and animals found in the wild. Although foraging was the way humans got their food for most of human history,

Foraging May be generally defined as a food-getting strategy that obtains wild plant and animal resources through gathering, hunting, scavenging, or fishing; also known as food collection.

11.1 Describe foraging and complex foraging, and identify the general societal features associated with food collecting.

Hunter-gatherers
People who collect food from naturally occurring resources, that is, wild plants, animals, and fish. The term *hunter-gatherers* minimizes sometimes heavy dependence on fishing. Also referred to as **foragers** or *food collectors*.

foragers—also commonly referred to as **hunter-gatherers**—are not very numerous in the world today. Most foraging societies currently live in what have been called the *marginal areas* of the earth—deserts, the Arctic, and dense tropical forests—habitats that do not allow easy exploitation by modern agricultural technologies. In the last few hundred years, only about 5 million people have been foragers.[1]

Yet the relatively few foraging societies still available for observation have been the focus of intense anthropological study. Of course, our knowledge of human culture depends on an understanding of all its variations, from foragers to intensive agriculturalists to post-industrial cultures. But why do we focus on hunter-gatherers when there are so few left and foraging as a way of life for the world's humanity is long in the past? The main reason has been a belief in the significance of the hunter-gatherer way of life in the evolution of human culture. Many of the traits we associate with humans may have developed in the long stretch of history in which all humans were hunter-gatherers.

We must nevertheless be cautious in drawing inferences about the past from our observations of recent and contemporary foragers. First, early foragers lived in almost all types of environments, including some bountiful ones. Therefore, what we observe of recent and contemporary foragers, who generally live in deserts, the Arctic, and tropical forests, may not be comparable to what the forager way of life might have been in more favorable past environments.[2] Second, contemporary foragers are not relics of the past. Like all contemporary societies, they have evolved and are still evolving. Indeed, recent research reveals considerable variation in economic behavior, as well as in social structure, among foraging groups that share common ancestry, which suggests that recent foragers have responded to differences in local environmental conditions.[3] Third, recent and contemporary foragers have been interacting with the kinds of societies that did not exist until after 10,000 years ago—agriculturalists, pastoralists, and intrusive, powerful state societies.[4] Evidence from South Asia and Southeast Asia, for example, suggests that trade with agriculturalists was probably an important component of foragers' economic strategies for millennia.[5] In the recent past, foraging people have increasingly depended on not only trade but also agriculture and commercial activities as additional means of subsistence.

The Ngatatjara of Western Australia

Long before the English began to colonize Australia in 1788 (by sending shiploads of convicts to establish settlements), that vast continent was home to several hundred ancient societies that spoke many languages and lived in a variety of environments but had in common the foraging way of life. One of these aboriginal societies, the Ngatatjara, still lived by gathering wild plants and hunting wild animals in the Gibson Desert of western Australia as late as 1967, when Richard Gould's 15-month visit among them was coming to an end. The description of daily life among the Ngatatjara that follows is based on Gould's observations.[6] (Because it is customary in ethnographic writing, we adopt the present tense in the narrative, but readers should remember that we are referring to the society's life in the 1960s.)

The desert environment of the Ngatatjara averages less than 8 inches of rain per year, and the temperature in summer may rise to 118 degrees Fahrenheit. The few permanent water holes are separated by hundreds of square miles of sand, scrub, and rock. Even before Europeans arrived in Australia, the area was sparsely populated, with less than one person per 35 to 40 square miles. Now there are even fewer people, because the aboriginal population was decimated by introduced diseases and colonial mistreatment.

The Ngatatjara, like most Australian aborigines, are traditionally nomadic and move their campsites often in search of food. Each campsite is isolated and inhabited by only a small number of people, or by clusters of groups including as many as 80 people. Camp is never set up right next to a watering spot, which is the natural destination of the game the men hope to capture. If the camp is too close, the noise might frighten away the animals. Ngatatjara are also careful not to encroach on the needs of neighboring bands (some of which may be in-laws) by seeming to take over the scarce watering spots.

On a typical day, the camp begins to stir just before sunrise, while it is still dark. Children are sent to fetch water, and the people breakfast on water and food left over from the night before. In the cool of early morning, the adults talk and make plans for the day. Where should they go for food—to places they have been recently or a new place? Sometimes there are other considerations. One woman, for instance, may want to look for plants that have the kind of bark she uses to make new sandals. The conversation can go on for a while, since the group prefers that everyone is in agreement about what to do.

Once the women decide which plants they want to gather and where they think those plants are most likely to be found, they take up their digging sticks and set out with large wooden bowls of drinking water balanced on their heads. Their children ride on their hips or walk alongside them. Meanwhile, the men may have decided to hunt emus, 6-foot-tall ostrichlike birds that do not fly. The men go to a creek bed where they will wait to ambush any game that may come along. They lie patiently behind a screen of brush they have set up, hoping for a chance to throw a spear at an emu or even a kangaroo. They can throw only once, because the game will run away if they miss.

Like the Ngatatjara, the Aborigine of Australia's Northern Territory are also foragers. This woman is digging for a major source of protein for her family, witchetty grubs, the large moth larvae that are found under the so-called witchetty bush.

By noon, all have returned to camp, the women each with their wooden bowls filled with up to 15 pounds of fruit or other plant foods and perhaps some lizards, the men more often than not with only some small game, such as rabbits. Because the men often return from the hunt empty-handed, the daily cooked meal is likely to be mostly plant food. The women will prepare the meal, and it will be eaten toward evening, after the group has spent an afternoon resting, gossiping, and making or repairing tools.

Life has changed dramatically for Australian aborigines since the late 1960s. Today, many live in small, settled villages. Anthropologist Victoria Burbank describes one such village in the Northern Territory of Australia where she did fieldwork in the 1980s. The once-nomadic aborigines live in a village that Burbank calls "Mangrove." The village, founded around a Protestant mission in the 1950s, is home to a population of 600 who live in houses with stoves, refrigerators, toilets, washing machines, and even television sets. Their children attend school full-time, and there is a health clinic for their medical needs. They still forage occasionally, but most of their food comes from the store. Some earn wages; many more subsist on government welfare checks.[7]

General Features of Foragers

Despite the differences in terrain and climate under which they live and the different food-collecting technologies they use, Australian aborigines, Inuit, and most other recent foragers have certain characteristic cultural patterns (see Table 11.1). Most live in small communities in sparsely populated territories and follow a nomadic lifestyle, forming no permanent settlements. As a rule, they do not recognize individuals' land rights. Their communities generally do not have different classes of people and tend to have no specialized or full-time political officials.[8] Division of labor in foraging societies is based largely on age and gender: Men exclusively hunt large marine and land animals and usually do most of the fishing, and women usually gather wild plant foods.[9] Foragers must decide what plants or animals to target.

Is there a typical pattern of food-getting among foragers? Many anthropologists have assumed that foragers typically get their food more from gathering than from hunting, and that women contribute more than men to subsistence, because women generally do the gathering.[10] Although gathering is the most important food-getting activity for some foragers (e.g., the Ngatatjara aborigines and the !Kung of southern Africa), this is not true for most food-collecting societies known to us. A survey of 180 such societies indicates that there is a lot of variation with regard to which food-getting activity is most important

TABLE 11.1   Variation in Food-Getting and Associated Features

| | FOOD COLLECTORS | | FOOD PRODUCERS | |
	Foragers	Horticulturalists	Pastoralists	Intensive Agriculturalists
Population density	Lowest	Low to moderate	Low	Highest
Maximum community size	Small	Small to moderate	Small	Large (towns and cities)
Nomadism/permanence of settlements	Generally nomadic or seminomadic	More sedentary: communities may move after several years	Generally nomadic or seminomadic	Permanent communities
Food shortages	Infrequent	Infrequent	Frequent	Frequent
Trade	Minimal	Minimal	Very important	Very important
Full-time craft specialists	None	None or few	Some	Many (high degree of craft specialization)
Individual differences in wealth	Generally none	Generally minimal	Moderate	Considerable
Political leadership	Informal	Some part-time political officials	Part- and full-time political officials	Many full-time political officials

to the society. Gathering is the most important activity for 30 percent of the surveyed societies, hunting for 25 percent, and fishing for 38 percent. (That is why we prefer the term *foragers* rather than the often-used *hunter-gatherers;* the term "foragers" allows us to recognize the importance of fishing.) In any case, because men generally do the fishing as well as the hunting, the men usually contribute more to food-getting than do the women among recent foragers.[11]

Because foragers move their camps often and walk great distances, it may seem that the food-collecting way of life is difficult. Although we do not have enough quantitative studies to tell us what is typical of most foragers, studies of two Australian aborigine groups[12] and of one !Kung group[13] indicate that those foragers do not spend many hours getting food. For example, !Kung adults spend an average of about 17 hours per week collecting food. Even when you add the time spent making tools (about 6 hours a week) and doing housework (about 19 hours a week), the !Kung seem to have more leisure time than many agriculturalists, as we discuss later.

Complex Foragers

When we say that foragers tend to have certain traits, this does not mean that all of them have those traits. There is considerable variability among societies that depend on foraging. Foraging societies that depend heavily on fishing (such as on the Pacific Coast of the northwestern United States and Canada or on the south coast of New Guinea) are more likely to have bigger and more permanent communities and more social inequality than foraging societies elsewhere that depend mostly on game and plants.[14] The Pacific Coast and New Guinea coastal people also tend to have higher population densities, food storage,[15] occupational specialization, resource ownership, slavery, and competitiveness.[16] Two foraging groups that have depended heavily on annual salmon runs, the Tlingit of southeastern Alaska and the Nimpkish of British Columbia, have had a three-tiered class system of upper class, commoners, and slaves. The high-status individuals were obliged to stage elaborate, competitive feasts and ritually distribute valuables.[17] The social inequality and competitiveness in these cultures differ greatly from what we find in typical foragers, who generally show little social differentiation. In a worldwide study of foragers, there also tended to be more intercommunity fighting in those societies that were more dependent on fishing. Perhaps conflict arose because some fishing sites were more predictable than others, leading people to fight to defend them.[18]

In New Guinea, about 40 societies depend almost exclusively on foraging. Wild sago provides most of the carbohydrates for these foragers, but the foragers vary considerably on how they obtain animal protein. Paul Roscoe has found that the amount of dependence upon fishing is strongly associated with density of population and settlement size. For example, societies with more than 75 percent dependence upon fishing have average community sizes of about 350 people, as compared with a community size of about 50 for those with less than 25 percent dependence upon fishing. Some villages were much larger. One Asmat village had over 1,400 people and a Waropen village over 1,700.

Food Production

Beginning about 10,000 years ago, certain peoples in widely separated geographic locations made the revolutionary changeover to **food production**. That is, they began to domesticate plants and animals. (Domesticated plants and animals are different from the ancestral wild forms.) With the domestication of these food sources, people acquired control over certain natural processes, such as animal breeding and plant seeding. Today, most peoples in the world depend for their food on some combination of domesticated plants and animals.

Anthropologists generally distinguish three major types of food production systems—horticulture, intensive agriculture, and pastoralism.

Horticulture

The word **horticulture** may conjure up visions of people with "green thumbs" growing orchids and other flowers in greenhouses. But to anthropologists, the word means the growing of crops of all kinds with relatively simple tools and methods, in the absence of permanently cultivated fields. The tools are usually hand tools, such as the digging stick or hoe, not plows or other equipment pulled by animals or tractors. And the methods used do not include fertilization, irrigation, or other ways to restore soil fertility after a growing season.

There are two kinds of horticulture. The more common one involves a dependence on **extensive (shifting) cultivation.** The land is worked for short periods and then left idle for some years. During the years when the land is not cultivated, wild plants and brush grow; when the fields are later cleared by *slash-and-burn techniques,* nutrients are returned to the soil. The other kind of horticulture involves a dependence on long-growing tree crops. The two kinds of horticulture may be practiced in the same society, but in neither case is there permanent cultivation of field crops.

Most horticultural societies do not rely on crops alone for food. Many also hunt or fish; a few are nomadic for part of the year. For example, the Kayapo of the Brazilian Amazon leave their villages for as long as three months at a time to trek through the forest in search of game. The entire village participates in a trek, carrying large quantities of garden produce and moving their camp every day.[19] Other horticulturalists raise domestic animals, but these are usually not large animals, such as cattle and camels.[20] More often than not, horticulturalists raise smaller animals, such as pigs, chickens, goats, and sheep.

Let us look now at one horticultural society, the Yanomamö of the Brazilian-Venezuelan Amazon.

The Yanomamö Dense tropical forest covers most of Yanomamö territory. From the air, the typical village, located in a forest clearing, looks like a single, large, circular lean-to with its inner side open to the central plaza. Each individual family has its own portion of the lean-to under the common roof. Each family's portion of the lean-to has a back wall (part of the closed back wall around the circular village structure), but the portions are open on the sides to each other as well as onto the central plaza of the village. The Yanomamö get most of their calories from garden produce, but according to Raymond Hames, the Yanomamö actually spend most of their time foraging.[21]

11.2 Describe three major types of food production and identify the general societal features associated with the different types of food production.

Food production The form of subsistence technology in which food-getting is dependent on the cultivation and domestication of plants and animals.

Horticulture Plant cultivation carried out with relatively simple tools and methods; nature is allowed to replace nutrients in the soil, in the absence of permanently cultivated fields.

Extensive (shifting) cultivation A type of horticulture in which the land is worked for short periods and then left to regenerate for some years before being used again. Also called **shifting cultivation**.

Slash-and-burn A form of shifting cultivation in which the natural vegetation is cut down and burned off. The cleared ground is used for a short time and then left to regenerate.

Intensive agriculture Food production characterized by the permanent cultivation of fields and made possible by the use of the plow, draft animals or machines, fertilizers, irrigation, water-storage techniques, and other complex agricultural techniques.

Before the people can plant, the forest must be cleared of trees and brush. Like most shifting cultivators, the Yanomamö use a combination of techniques: slashing the undergrowth, felling trees, and using controlled burning to clear a garden spot—in other words, **slash-and-burn** horticulture. Before the 1950s, the Yanomamö had only stone axes, so felling trees was quite difficult. Now they have steel machetes and axes given or traded to them by missionaries.

Because of the work involved in clearing a garden, the Yanomamö prefer to make use of forest patches that have little thorny brush and not too many large trees.[22] After the ground is cleared, the Yanomamö plant plantains, manioc, sweet potatoes, taro, and a variety of plants for medicine, condiments, and craft materials. Men do the heavy clearing work to prepare a garden, and they as well as women plant the crops. Women usually go to the gardens daily to weed and harvest. After two or three years, the yields diminish and the forest starts growing back, making continued cultivation less desirable and more difficult, so they abandon the garden and clear a new one. If they can, they clear adjacent forest, but if gardens are far from the village, they will move the village to a new location. Villages are moved about every five years because of gardening needs and warfare. There is a great deal of intervillage raiding, so villages are often forced to flee to another location.

Extensive cultivation requires a lot of territory because new gardens are not cleared until the forest grows back. What is often misunderstood is why it is so important to shift gardens. Not only is a burned field easier to plant, but the organic matter that is burned provides necessary nutrients for a good yield. If horticulturalists come back too quickly to a spot with little plant cover, a garden made there will not produce a satisfactory yield.

The Yanomamö crops do not provide much protein, so hunting and fishing are important to their diet. Men hunt birds, peccaries, monkeys, and tapir with bows and arrows. Women, men, and children enjoy fishing. They catch fish by hand, with small bows and arrows, and by stream poisoning. Everybody gathers honey, hearts of palm, Brazil nuts, and cashews, although the men usually climb trees to shake down the nuts. Much of the foraging is done from the village base, but the Yanomamö, like the Kayapo, may go on treks to forage from time to time.

General Features of Horticulturalists In most horticultural societies, simple farming techniques have tended to yield more food from a given area than is generally available to foragers. Consequently, horticulture is able to support larger, more densely populated communities. The way of life of horticulturalists is more sedentary than that of foragers, although communities may move after some years to farm a new series of plots. (Some horticulturalists have permanent villages because they depend mostly on food from trees that keep producing for a long time.) In contrast with most recent food-collecting groups, horticultural societies exhibit the beginnings of social differentiation. For example, some individuals may be part-time craftworkers or part-time political officials, and certain members of a kin group may have more status than other individuals in the society.

A Yanomamö woman prepares a cassava meal.

Intensive Agriculture

People engaged in **intensive agriculture** use techniques that enable them to cultivate fields permanently. Essential nutrients may be put back in the soil through the use of fertilizers, which may be organic material (most commonly dung from humans or other animals) or inorganic (chemical) fertilizers. But there are other ways to restore nutrients. The Luo of western Kenya plant beans around corn plants. Bacteria growing around the roots of the bean plant replace lost nitrogen, and the corn plant conveniently provides a pole for the bean plant to wind around as it grows. Some intensive agriculturalists use irrigation from streams and rivers to ensure an adequate supply of waterborne nutrients. Crop rotation and plant stubble that has been plowed under also restore nutrients to the soil.

In general, the technology of intensive agriculturalists is more complex than that of horticulturalists. Plows rather than digging sticks are generally employed. But there is enormous variation in the degree to which intensive agriculturalists rely on mechanization rather than hand labor. In some societies, the most complex machine is an animal-drawn plow; in the corn and wheat belts of the United States, huge tractors till, seed, and fertilize 12 rows at a time.[23]

Let's look at one group of intensive agriculturalists, those of the Mekong Delta in Vietnam.

Rural Vietnam: The Mekong Delta
The village of Khanh Hau, situated along the flat Mekong Delta, comprised about 600 families when Gerald Hickey described it in the late 1950s, before the Vietnam War.[24] The delta area has a tropical climate, with a rainy season that lasts from May to November. As a whole, the area has been made habitable only through extensive drainage.

Wet rice cultivation is the principal agricultural activity of Khanh Hau. It is part of a complex, specialized arrangement that involves three interacting components: (1) a complex system of irrigation and water control; (2) a variety of specialized equipment, including plows, waterwheels, threshing sledges, and winnowing machines; and (3) a clearly defined set of socioeconomic roles—from those of landlord, tenant, and laborer to those of rice miller and rice merchant.

In the dry season, the farmer decides what sort of rice crop to plant, whether of long (120 days) or short (90 days) maturation. The choice depends on the capital at his disposal, the current cost of fertilizer, and the anticipated demand for rice. The seedbeds are prepared as soon as the rains have softened the ground in May. The soil is turned over (plowed) and broken up (harrowed) as many as six separate times, with two-day intervals for "airing" between operations. During this time, the rice seeds are soaked in water for at least two days to stimulate sprouting. Before the seedlings are planted, the paddy is plowed once more and harrowed twice in two directions at right angles.

Planting is a delicate, specialized operation that must be done quickly and is performed most often by hired male laborers. But efficient planting is not enough to guarantee a good crop. Proper fertilization and irrigation are equally important. In the irrigating, steps must be taken to ensure that the water level remains at exactly the proper depth over the entire paddy. Water is distributed by means of scoops, wheels, and mechanical pumps. Successive crops of rice ripen from late September to May; all members of the family may be called upon to help with the harvest. After each crop is harvested, it is threshed, winnowed, and dried. Normally, the rice is sorted into three portions: one is set aside for use by the household in the following year; one is for payment of hired labor and other services (such as loans from agricultural banks); and one is for cash sale on

Vietnamese farmers in the Mekong Delta working in a flooded rice paddy. Much of the delta was originally tropical forest.

the market. Aside from the harvesting, women do little work in the fields, spending most of their time on household chores. In families with little land, however, young daughters help in the fields and older daughters may hire themselves out to other farmers.

The villagers also cultivate vegetables, raise pigs, chickens, and the like, and frequently engage in fishing. The village economy usually supports three or four implement makers and a much larger number of carpenters.

General Features of Intensive Agricultural Societies   Societies with intensive agriculture are more likely than horticulturalists to have towns and cities, a high degree of craft specialization, complex political organization, and large differences in wealth and power. Studies suggest that intensive agriculturalists work longer hours than horticulturalists.[25] For example, men engaged in intensive agriculture average nine hours of work a day, seven days a week; women average almost 11 hours of work per day. Most of the work for women in intensive agricultural societies involves food processing and work in and around the home, but they also spend a lot of time working in the fields.

Intensive agricultural societies are more likely than horticultural societies to face famines and food shortages, even though intensive agriculture is generally more productive than horticulture.[26] Why, if more food can be produced per acre, is there more risk of shortage among intensive agriculturalists? Intensive agriculturalists may be more likely to face food shortages because they are often producing crops for a market. Producing for a market pushes farmers to cultivate plants that give them the highest yield rather than cultivating plants that are drought-resistant or that require fewer nutrients. Farmers producing for a market also tend to concentrate on one crop. Crop diversity is often a protection against total crop failure because fluctuations in weather, plant diseases, or insect pests are not likely to affect all the crops. There are also fluctuations in market demand. If the market demand drops and the price falls for a particular crop, farmers may not have enough cash to buy the other food they need.

The Commercialization and Mechanization of Agriculture   Some intensive agriculturalists produce very little for sale; most of what they produce is for their own use. But there is a worldwide trend for intensive agriculturalists to produce more and more for a market. This trend is called **commercialization,** which may occur in any area of life and which involves increasing dependence on buying and selling, usually with money as the medium of exchange. Some of the push toward commercialization comes from external pressures, from governments that impose taxes that must be paid by money. But some of the shift occurs when subsistence farmers choose to plant a cash crop to earn money for various reasons. For example, the Malayali farmers of India grow a cash crop, tapioca (cassava), as a way of responding to unpredictable rainfall. Tapioca is fairly drought-tolerant, grows in poor soils, and can be planted later in the year when the rainfall has become more predictable.[27]

The increasing commercialization of agriculture is associated with several other trends. One is that farm work is becoming more mechanized as hand labor becomes scarce, because of migration to industrial and service jobs in towns and cities, or because hired hand labor has become too expensive. A second trend is the emergence and spread of *agribusiness,* large corporation-owned farms that may be operated by multinational companies and worked entirely by hired, as opposed to family, labor. For example, consider how cotton farming has changed in the southeastern United States. In the 1930s, tractors replaced mules and horses used in plowing. This change allowed some landowners to evict their sharecroppers and expand their holdings. After World War II, mechanical cotton pickers replaced most of the harvest laborers. But a farmer had to have a good deal of money to acquire those machines, each of which costs many tens of thousands of dollars.[28] So the mechanization of cotton farming sent many rural farm laborers off to the cities of the North in search of employment, and the agricultural sector increasingly became big business. A third trend associated with the commercialization of agriculture, including animal raising, is a reduction in the proportion of the population engaged in food production. In the United States today, for example, less than 2 percent of the total population work on farms.[29] A fourth trend is that much of what people produce for sale nowadays is shipped to or received from markets in other countries. For example, in the summer months, fruits and vegetables are often shipped to markets where consumers have little local fresh

> **Commercialization**   The increasing dependence on buying and selling, with money usually as the medium of exchange.

Migrants and Immigrants

Food on the Move

People in North America get most of their food from stores. Most people do not know where the food comes from originally— where it was first grown or raised. This is partly because relatively few are directly involved in food-getting (less than 2 percent of the workers in the United States). Even when you count all the activities related to food-getting, such as marketing and transportation, only 14 percent of U.S. workers have anything to do with the production and distribution of food. But nowadays, many of the foods we buy in markets—tacos, salsa, bagels, pasta, pizza, sausage, soy sauce, and teriyaki—have become mainstream "North American" food. Where did these foods come from? Originally, they were eaten only by ethnic and immigrant minorities who came to the United States and Canada. Some, but not all, of their foods caught on and became widely consumed. They became, in short, as "American" as apple pie.

The ingredients in many of these food items resulted from previous movements of people even further back in time. Consider the ingredients in pizza, a favorite food now for many of us. The dough is made from wheat flour, which was first grown in the Middle East, perhaps as much as 10,000 years ago. How do anthropologists know that? Archaeologists have discovered wheat kernels that old in Middle Eastern sites, and they have found flat stones and stone rolling pins from that time that we know were used to grind kernels into flour (we can tell from microscopic analysis of the residue on the stone). What about other ingredients that may

Outdoor market in Venice, Italy showing that the potatoes are from America.

be found in pizza? Cheese was first made in the Middle East too, at least 5,000 years ago (we have writings from that time that mention cheese). Tomatoes were first grown in South America, probably several thousand years ago. They got to Italy, the birthplace of the tomato pie (which became transformed into pizza), less than 200 years ago. Just 100 years ago, tomatoes (the key ingredient in pizza for some) were so new in eastern Europe that people were afraid to eat them because their leaves are poisonous to humans and some other animals. Another food we associate with Italian cuisine, spaghetti-type noodles, came to Italy (from China) less than 500 years ago. So the major ingredients of pizza, just like

round-noodle pasta, are all not native to Italy.

The amazing thing about foods is that they so often travel far and wide, generally carried by the people who like to eat them. And some of our foods, when alive, also travel widely. For example, the bluefin tuna (which can weigh more than a 1,000 pounds) swims thousands of miles from feeding to breeding grounds in the North Atlantic, Mediterranean, and Caribbean. This largest of all existing fishes is being hunted into extinction because its meat is so prized for what the Japanese call *sushi*, a kind of food that has spread from Japan throughout the world.

Sources: Diament 2005, A32–34; Revkin 2005, F1, F4.

---

produce. The spread of different kinds of food is not new (see the box "Food on the Move") but is accelerating in today's world.

Pastoralism

Most agriculturalists keep and breed some animals (practice animal husbandry), but a small number of societies depend mostly for their living on domesticated herds of animals that feed on natural pasture.[30] We call such a system **pastoralism**. We might assume that

Pastoralism A form of subsistence technology in which food-getting is based directly or indirectly on the maintenance of domesticated animals.

pastoralists breed animals to eat their meat, but most do not. Pastoralists more often get their animal protein from live animals in the form of milk, and some pastoralists regularly take blood, which is rich in protein, from their animals to mix with other foods. The herds often indirectly provide food because many pastoralists trade animal products for plant foods and other necessities. In fact, a large proportion of their food may actually come from trade with agricultural groups.[31] For example, some pastoral groups in the Middle East derive much of their livelihood from the sale of what we call oriental rugs, which are made from the wool of their sheep on hand looms. We shall examine the Saami (Lapps) of Scandinavia.

The Saami   The Saami practice reindeer herding in northwestern Scandinavia where Finland, Sweden, and Norway share common frontiers. It is a typical Arctic habitat: cold, windswept, with long, dark days for half the year. Considerable change has occurred recently, so we first discuss the food-getting strategy in the 1950s, as described by Ian Whitaker and T. I. Itkonen.[32]

The Saami herd their reindeer either intensively or, more often, extensively. In the *intensive system,* the herd is constantly under observation within a fenced area for the whole year. Intensively herded reindeer and other animals are accustomed to human contact. Hence, the summer corralling of the females for milking and the breaking in of the ox-reindeer for use as work animals are not difficult tasks. The *extensive system* involves allowing the animals to migrate over a large area. It requires little surveillance and encompasses large herds. Under this system, the reindeer are allowed to move through their seasonal feeding cycles watched by only one or two scouts. The other Saami stay with the herd only when it has settled in its summer or winter habitat. But milking, breaking in, and corralling are harder in the extensive than in the intensive system because the animals are less accustomed to humans.

Even under the extensive system, which theoretically permits Saami to engage in subsidiary economic activities such as hunting and fishing, the reindeer herd is the essential, if not the only, source of income. A family might possess as many as 1,000 reindeer, but usually the figure is half that number. Studies show 200 to be the minimum number of reindeer needed to provide for a family of four or five adults. Women may have shared the herding chores in the past under the intensive system, but now, under the extensive system, men do

A Saami reindeer herder feeds two of her animals in the snow.

the herding. Women still do the milking. The Saami eat the meat of the bull reindeer; the female reindeer are kept for breeding purposes. Bulls are slaughtered in the fall, after the mating season. Meat and hides are frequently sold or bartered for other food and necessities.

Reindeer are still herded nowadays, but snowmobiles, all-terrain vehicles, and even helicopters have replaced sleds for herding. Ferries move reindeer to and from different pastures, and the herders communicate by field telephones. With faster transportation, many Saami now live in permanent homes and can still get to their herds in hours. Saami children spend much of their time in school and, consequently, do not learn much of the herding ways. The Norwegian government now regulates pastoralism, licensing pastoralists and trying to limit the number of reindeer they can herd.[33] And many Saami no longer have reindeer.

General Features of Pastoralism In recent times, pastoralism has been practiced mainly in grassland and other semiarid habitats that are not especially suitable for cultivation without some significant technological input such as irrigation. Most pastoralists are nomadic, moving camp fairly frequently to find water and new pasture for their herds. But other pastoralists have somewhat more sedentary lives. They may move from one settlement to another in different seasons, or they may send some people out to travel with the herds in different seasons. Pastoral communities are usually small, consisting of a group of related families.[34] Individuals or families may own their own animals, but the community makes decisions about when and where to move the herds.

As we have noted, there is a great deal of interdependence between pastoral and agricultural groups. That is, trade is usually necessary for pastoral groups to survive. Like agriculturalists, pastoralists are more vulnerable than foragers and horticulturalists to famine and food shortages. Pastoralists usually inhabit drought-prone regions, but recent pastoralists have had their access to grazing lands reduced, and political pressures have pushed them to decrease their movement over large areas. Mobility kept the risk of overgrazing to a minimum, but overgrazing in small territories has increased the risk of desertification.[35]

Environmental Restraints on Food-Getting

11.3 Identify environmental restraints on food-getting.

How much does the physical environment affect food-getting? Anthropologists have concluded that the physical environment by itself has a restraining, rather than a determining, effect on the major types of subsistence. Because they have very short growing seasons, cold regions of the earth are not particularly conducive to growing plants. No society we know of has practiced agriculture in the Arctic; instead, people who live there rely primarily on animals for food. But both foraging (as among the Inuit) and food production (as among the Saami) can be practiced in cold areas. Indeed, cross-cultural evidence indicates that neither foraging nor food production is significantly associated with any particular type of habitat.[36]

We know that foraging has been practiced at one time or another in almost all areas of the earth. The physical environment does seem to have some effect on what kind of foraging is practiced, that is, on the extent to which foragers will depend on plants, animals, or fish. Farther away from the equator, foragers depend much less on plants for food and much more on animals and fish.[37] Lewis Binford argues that fishing becomes increasingly important in cold climates because foragers need nonportable housing in severe winters to protect themselves from the cold. Therefore, they cannot rely on large animals, which usually have to feed themselves by moving over considerable distances in the winter. Fishing is more localized than hunting, and, therefore, foragers who rely on fishing can stay in their nonportable houses in winter.[38]

There is one habitat that may have precluded foraging until recent times. If it were not for the nearness of food producers, particularly agriculturalists, recent foragers such as the Mbuti of central Africa could probably not have supported themselves in the tropical forest habitats where they now live.[39] Tropical forests are lush in plants, but they do not provide much in the way of reachable fruits, seeds, and flowers that humans can eat. Animals are available in tropical forests, but typically they are lean and do not provide humans with sufficient carbohydrates or fat. Like the Mbuti groups who hunt and gather in the forest, many tropical foragers trade for agricultural products; other collectors cultivate some crops in addition to hunting and gathering. It would seem, then, that foragers could not survive in tropical forests were it not for the carbohydrates they obtain from agriculturalists.

When we contrast horticulture and intensive agriculture, the physical environment appears to explain some of the variation. Approximately 80 percent of all societies that practice horticulture or simple agriculture are in the tropics, whereas 75 percent of all societies that practice intensive agriculture are not in tropical forest environments.[40] But today, there are some areas, such as the Mekong Delta in Vietnam, whose tropical forests have been cleared and prevented from growing again by the intensive cultivation of rice in paddies. And, although cultivation is not normally possible in dry lands, because of insufficient natural rainfall to sustain crops, agriculture can be practiced where there are oases—small, naturally watered areas where crops can be grown with a simple technology—or rivers that can be tapped by irrigation, one of the techniques used with intensive agriculture.

11.4 Describe and critically discuss the spread and intensification of food production.

The Origin, Spread, and Intensification of Food Production

We see the first evidence of a changeover to food production—the cultivation and domestication of plants and animals—in the Near East about 8000 B.C. This shift occurred, probably independently, in other areas as well. There is evidence of cultivation around 6000 B.C. in China, Southeast Asia (what is now Malaysia, Thailand, Cambodia, and Vietnam), and Africa. In the New World, there appear to have been several places of original cultivation and domestication. The highlands of Mexico (about 7000 B.C.) and the central Andes around Peru (by about 6000 B.C.) were probably the most important in terms of food plants used today.

There are many theories of why food production developed; most have tried to explain the origin of domestication in the Near East. The possible reasons include the following:

- Population growth in regions of bountiful wild resources pushed people to move to marginal areas, where they tried to reproduce their former abundance.
- Global population growth filled up most of the world's habitable regions and forced people to utilize a broader spectrum of wild resources and to domesticate plants and animals.
- Climatic change—hotter, drier summers and colder winters—favored settling near seasonal stands of wild grain; population growth in such areas would force people to plant crops and raise animals.

Whatever the reasons for the switch to food production, we still need to explain why it supplanted foraging as the primary mode of subsistence. We cannot assume that hunters and gatherers simply adopted production as a superior way of life once they understood the process of domestication. After all, as we have noted, domestication may entail more work and provide less security than the food-collecting way of life.

The spread of agriculture may be linked to the need for territorial expansion. As a sedentary, food-producing population grew, it may have been forced to expand into new territory. Some of this territory may have been vacant, but foragers probably already occupied much of it. Although food production is not necessarily easier than collection, it is generally more productive per unit of land. Greater productivity enables more people to be supported in a given territory. In the competition for land between the faster-expanding food producers and the foragers, the food producers may have had a significant advantage: They had more people in a given area. Thus, the foraging groups may have been more likely to lose out in the competition for land. Some groups may have adopted cultivation, abandoning the foraging way of life to survive. Other groups, continuing as foragers, may have been forced to retreat into areas not desired by the cultivators. Today, as we have seen, the small number of remaining foragers inhabit areas not particularly suitable for cultivation—dry lands, dense tropical forests, and polar regions.

Just as prior population growth might account for the origins of domestication, further population growth and ensuing pressure on resources at later periods might also at least partly explain the transformation of horticultural systems into intensive agricultural systems. Ester Boserup suggested that intensification of agriculture, with a consequent increase in yield per acre, is not likely to develop naturally out of horticulture because intensification requires much more work.[41] She argued that people will be willing to intensify their labor only if they have to. Where emigration is not feasible, the prime mover behind intensification may be prior population growth. The need to pay taxes or tribute to a political authority may also stimulate intensification.

Boserup's argument about intensification is widely accepted. But her assumption that more work is required with intensive agriculture has recently been questioned. Comparing horticultural (swidden or shifting) rice production with rice produced on permanent fields using irrigation, Robert Hunt found that *less,* not more, labor is required with irrigation.[42] Still, population increase may generally provide the impetus to intensify production to increase yields to support the additional people.

Intensive agriculture has not yet spread to every part of the world. Horticulture continues to be practiced in certain tropical regions, and there are still some pastoralists and foragers. Some environments may make it somewhat more difficult to adopt certain subsistence practices. For example, intensive agriculture cannot supplant horticulture in some tropical environments without tremendous investments in chemical fertilizers and pesticides, not to mention the additional labor required.[43] Enormous amounts of water may also be required to make agriculturalists out of foragers and pastoralists who now exploit semiarid environments. But difficulty is not impossibility. Anna Roosevelt points out that, although horticulture was a common food-getting strategy in Amazonia in recent times, archaeological evidence indicates that there were complex societies practicing intensive agriculture on raised, drained fields in the past.[44] The physical environment does not completely control what can be done with it.

The Allocation of Resources

Every society has access to natural resources—land, water, plants, animals, minerals—and every society has cultural rules for determining who has access to particular resources and what can be done with them. In societies like the United States, which have *private property systems,* people buy and sell land and many other things. Land is divided into precisely measurable units, the borders of which may be recorded in a municipal land register. Individuals usually own relatively small plots of land and the resources that exist on them. Generally, large plots of land are collective property. The owner may be a family, a corporation, or a government agency, such as the National Park Service, which owns so-called public land on behalf of the entire population. In the United States, property ownership entails the exclusive right to use land or other resources in whatever *legal* ways the owner wishes, including the right to withhold or prevent use by others. In many societies, including the United States, property owners also have the right to "alienate" property—that is, to sell, give away, bequeath, or destroy the resources owned.

Societies, whether they are small and traditional or large countries, specify what they consider property and the rights and duties associated with that property.[45] Because conceptions of property are social in nature, they may change over time. For example, the French government retroactively made all of the country's beaches public, thereby declaring that the ocean shore is not a resource that an individual can own. As a result, all the hotel owners and individuals who had fenced-off portions of the best beaches for their exclusive use had to remove the barriers. Even in countries like the United States, which has a strong private property system, people cannot do anything they want with their property. Like many other governments around the world, the U.S. government has the right of

11.5 Compare and contrast the allocation of resources among foragers, horticulturalists, intensive agriculturalists, and pastoralists and how colonialism and the state have affected that allocation.

eminent domain: It may take land for use in the construction of a highway or another purpose that serves "the greater public good." The state compensates owners, but individuals cannot prevent confiscation. The notion that the individual property owner has obligations to the greater good of the society is behind other laws. For example, it has long been illegal in the United States to burn down your house or to use it as a brothel or a munitions arsenal. More recently, federal, state, and local governments have adopted legislation that prevents property owners from undertaking activities that pollute the air and the water supply.

Natural Resources: Land

Societies differ in their rules for access to land. Anthropologists have found that the differences relate to a society's food-getting method. Let us now examine how foragers, horticulturalists, pastoralists, and intensive agriculturalists structure rights to land in different ways. We look at traditional patterns first. As we shall see later, state societies that have colonized native societies in the New World, Africa, and Asia have had a considerable impact on traditional rights to land.

Foragers   Individuals in food-collecting societies generally do not own land. Nor do they buy or sell land, probably because what is valued in foraging is the game and wild plant life on the land, not the land itself. The foraging Hadza of Tanzania, for example, believe that they do not have exclusive rights over the land on which they hunt. Members of the group can hunt, gather, or draw water wherever they like.[46] Nor do the Hadza defend the territories they use from outsiders—that is, members of other language groups. But the Hadza are somewhat unusual. Collective ownership by groups of related people (kinship groups) or by territorial groups (bands or villages) is common among foragers. If game migrates away and the supply of plant foods dwindles, the land is of no use to a forager. Where the wild food supply is likely to fluctuate, communal ownership of a large tract of land is more desirable than individually owned small parcels of land.

The Kamayura of the Xingu region of the Amazon practice slash-and-burn horticulture. The rain forest is in the background.

This is not to say that private ownership of land does not exist among foragers. Among foragers heavily dependent on fishing in rivers, individual or family ownership is more common,[47] perhaps because fishing in rivers is more predictable than other kinds of foraging. In some foraging societies, individuals and families have private rights to trees.[48] Although foragers generally do not have private ownership of important land resources, there is considerable variation in the extent of communal ownership. It is more common in food-collecting societies for a group of individuals, usually kin, to "own" land. To be sure, such ownership is not usually exclusive; typically, some degree of access is provided to members of neighboring bands.[49]

Horticulturalists   Like foragers, most horticulturalist individuals and families do not own land. Their lack of interest in laying claim to the land may be explained by the dynamics of subsistence farming. Using simple tools and no fertilizers other than the ash they create when they slash and burn vegetation to clear a field, most horticulturalists must periodically move on to other farmable land because they have depleted the soil in one area of its nutrients. Individuals or families have little incentive to claim permanent access to land that, given the technology available to them, they cannot use permanently. Nevertheless, horticulturalist societies are more likely than foraging societies to assign the use of particular plots of land to individuals or families, perhaps because the land is usable for a number of years. Often horticulture can support somewhat larger communities, even villages.

Among the Mundurucú of Brazil, the village controls the rights to use land. People in the community can hunt and fish where they like, and they have the right to clear a garden plot wherever communal land is not being used. Gardens may be cultivated for only two years before the soil is exhausted; then the land reverts to the community. The Mundurucú distinguish between the land and the produce on the land; the produce belongs to the person who cultivates it. Similarly, the person who kills an animal or catches a fish owns it, no matter where it was obtained, even if he or she will be later expected to share the bounty. Individual rights to land arose among the Mundurucú when they moved beyond subsistence to marketable products: the men began to tap rubber trees and sell the natural latex they harvested. Rights to a particular forest path of tapped trees could be inherited by a son or a son-in-law, but they could not be bought and sold.[50]

Pastoralists The territory of pastoral nomads usually far exceeds that of most horticultural societies. Because their wealth ultimately depends on mobile herds, uncultivated pasture for grazing, and water for drinking, pastoralists often combine the adaptive habits of both foragers and horticulturalists. Like foragers, they generally need to know the potential of a large area of land. The pastoral Basseri of Iran, for example, moved over an area of 15,000 square miles to obtain supplies of grass and water. Like horticulturalists, pastoralists must move on when they have exhausted a resource. In their case, the resource is grass, which must renew itself after extensive grazing.

Because land is only good if there is sufficient pasture and water, there would be considerable risk to individuals or families to own land that did not predictably have grass and water. Therefore, like most foragers and horticulturalists, members of pastoralist communities generally have free access to pasture land.[51] While they tend to hold grazing land communally, pastoralists customarily own their herds individually.[52]

Like hunter-gatherers, pastoralist groups vary in the degree of ownership rights they possess to territories through which they move their animals. The Basseri have rights to pass through certain areas, including agricultural areas and even cities, but they do not own the entire territory upon which they depend. On the other hand, the Baluch, another pastoralist group in the border region between Iran, Pakistan, and Afghanistan, claim a "tribal" territory, which they defend by force, if necessary.[53]

Intensive Agriculturalists Individual ownership of land resources—including the right to use the resources and the right to sell or otherwise dispose of them—is common among intensive agriculturalists. The development of sole ownership is partly the result of the potential to use land season after season, which gives it lasting value. The concept of individual ownership is also partly a political (and social policy) matter. The U.S. Congress, for example, transformed government-owned frontier land west of the Mississippi River into privately owned land shortly before the Civil War, when the South had seceded from the Union. Under the Homestead Act of 1862, if a person cleared a 160-acre piece of land and farmed it for five years, the federal government would consider that person the owner of the land. Aside from being a populist social policy, the Act served other political goals: It preempted the westward spread of the large-scale southern plantation farming that relied on slave labor and created a larger voting population, since only property owners could vote at the time. The Homestead Act is similar to the custom in some societies by which a kin group, a chief, or a community is obligated to assign a parcel of land to anyone who wishes to farm it. Unlike the farmer of such a parcel, once American homesteaders became landowners, the laws of the country gave them the right to dispose of it at will by selling or giving it away. Moreover, property owners could use their economic and, hence, political power to pass laws that favored themselves.

Intensive agriculture is not always associated with private ownership. Nor does it always occur in complex political systems that have differences in wealth and power. Some communist and socialist nations—politically complex systems that seek to diminish differences in wealth and power—undertook intensive agriculture by forming state-run agricultural collectives.

Colonialism, the State, and Land Rights Almost universally around the world, colonial conquerors and settlers have taken land away from the natives or aborigines. Even if the natives were given other land in exchange, as in Brazil and the United States, these so-called reservations were often, if not always, poorer in potential than the original land. (If the reservation land had not been poorer in quality, the settlers might have taken possession of it for themselves.) In addition, the new centralized governments often tried to change how the natives owned the land, almost always in the direction of individual or private ownership. If kin groups or larger social entities owned the land, it would be more difficult for the new settlers to get the natives to give it up, either by sale or threat. Individual owners could be dispossessed more easily.[54]

This is not to say that native peoples in Africa, Asia, and the New World were never guilty of conquering and exploiting others on their continents or elsewhere. They were. The Aztecs in Mexico and Central America, the native kingdoms in West Africa after about 800 years ago, and the Arabs after the rise of Islam were just some of the expanding state societies of the past. Imperialism and colonialism have existed wherever there have been "civilized" (urban) societies.

In much of colonial Africa, governments ceded land to European-owned companies for development. Reserves were established for large native populations, who then were invariably forced to work as laborers on European-owned plantations and in European-owned mines.[55] For example, in the 19th century, the land of the pastoral Masai stretched from the Lake Turkana area of northern Kenya down to northern Tanzania. The British pushed the Masai onto a reserve in the southern part of Kenya, south of the Mombasa-Uganda railway, and gave some of their prime grazing lands and water resources near Nairobi, as well as near the Naivasha and Nakuru lakes, to Europeans for farming and ranching. The Masai grazing land was reduced by about 60 percent, and the Masai were also forbidden to graze in the areas where game parks were established by the British for tourism.[56] Europeans, who constituted less than 1 percent of the population in Kenya, acquired access to or control of 20 percent of the land, mostly in the highlands, where there was the greatest potential for commercial production of tea and coffee.[57]

The taking of land by state authorities does not happen with colonialism and imperialism alone. Indigenous revolutionary movements have collectivized land, as in Russia, or broken up large private landholdings, as in Mexico. Typically, state authorities do not like communal land-use systems, and they particularly view mobile pastoralists unfavorably, because their mobility makes them difficult to control. Governments usually try to settle pastoralists or break up communally held pasture into small units.[58] In Kenya, after independence from the British, the pastoral Masai continued to lose grazing territory. The post-colonial national government, which strongly promotes tourism, not only needed land for the game parks it considered vital, but also undertook the construction of massive greenhouses to grow flowers for the European market. Whereas the flower industry has flourished—flowers are Kenya's major horticultural export today—Lake Naivasha, where many greenhouses are located, has been polluted and overused. The pastoral Masai have also suffered. With the advice of international development agencies, the Kenyan government pushed for privatization of grazing land. But grazing on individually owned plots requires capital to grow or buy food for cattle, pay for medicines, and to get cattle to market.[59]

The Conversion of Resources

11.6 Describe variation in different types of economic production, what motivates people to work, how societies divide up the work to be done, and how they organize work.

All societies transform or convert resources through labor into food, tools, and other goods. This conversion of resources constitutes what economists call *production*. In this section, after briefly reviewing different types of production, we examine what motivates people to work, how societies divide up the work to be done, and how they organize work.

Types of Economic Production

Preindustrial When they were first described, most of the societies known to anthropology had a *domestic*—family or kinship—mode of production. Labor consisted of people getting food and producing shelter and implements for themselves and their kin. Families usually had the right to exploit productive resources and control the products of their labor. Even part-time specialists, such as potters, could support themselves without their craftwork if they needed to.

Industrial At the other extreme, *industrial* societies rely largely on mechanized production, in agriculture, as well as in factories. Because machines and materials are costly, only some individuals (capitalists), corporations, or governments can afford the expenses of production. Therefore, most people in industrial societies labor for others as wage earners. Although wages can buy food, people out of work lose their ability to support themselves, unless they are protected by welfare payments or unemployment insurance.

Tributary Found in nonindustrial societies, a third system is the *tributary* type of production, wherein most people still produce their own food but an elite or aristocracy controls a portion of production, including the products of specialized crafts. As the name implies, people pay a tribute of labor or produce to the elite landowner or ruler who grants them access to land. The feudal societies of medieval Western Europe were examples of tributary production, as was czarist Russia when it practiced serfdom.[60]

Postindustrial It is often suggested that the U.S. economy and other developed economies are now moving from *industrialism* to *postindustrialism*. In many areas of commerce, computers have radically transformed the workplace. Because computers can "drive" machines and robots, much of the manual work required in industry is disappearing. Businesses are now more knowledge- and service-oriented. Information has become so easily accessible through telecommunication that *telecommuting* has entered the English vocabulary to describe how people can now work for wages at home. This economic transformation has important implications for both home life and the workplace. With inexpensive home computers and speedy data transmission by telephone and other means, more people are able to work at home. In addition, when information and knowledge become more important than capital equipment, more people can own and have access to the productive resources of society.[61]

Incentives for Labor

Why do people work? Are the incentives for labor the same in all societies? Anthropologists believe the answer is both yes and no. One reason people work is because they must. But why do people in some societies apparently work *more* than they must?

The Profit Motive and Subsistence Economies We can be fairly certain that a particular and often-cited motive—the profit motive, or the desire to exchange something for more than it costs—is not universal or always the dominant motive. There can be no profit motive among people who produce food and other goods primarily for their own consumption, as do most foragers, most horticulturalists, and

In postindustrial economies, computers and robots rather than people do much of the work in factories.

even some intensive agriculturalists. Such societies have what we call a *subsistence economy*, not a money or commercial economy. Anthropologists have noticed that people in subsistence economies (with a domestic mode of production) often work less than people in commercial economies (with tributary or industrial modes of production). Indeed, foragers appear to have a considerable amount of leisure time, as do many horticulturalists. It has been estimated, for example, that the men of the horticultural Kuikuru tribe in central Brazil spent about three and a half hours a day on subsistence. It appears that the Kuikuru could have produced a substantial surplus of manioc, their staple food, by working 30 minutes more a day.[62]

Social Rewards of Sharing   There appear to be many societies in which some people work harder than they would need to in order to support their own families. What motivates them to work harder? They often share and transfer food and goods well beyond their own households, at times extending their reach to the whole community or even groups of communities. In such societies, social rewards come to those who are generous, who give things away. Thus, people who work harder than they have to for subsistence may be motivated to do so in order to gain respect or esteem.[63] Also, in many societies extra food and goods may be needed at times for special purposes and occasions; goods and services may be needed to arrange and celebrate marriages, to form alliances, and to perform rituals and ceremonies (including what we would call sporting events). Thus, how the culture defines what one works for and what is required may go beyond what is necessary.

Achievement   In commercial economies such as the United States—where food, other goods, and services are sold and bought—people seem to be motivated to keep any extra income for themselves and their families. Extra income is converted into bigger dwellings, more expensive furnishings and food, and other elements of a "higher" standard of living. But the desire to improve one's standard of living is probably not their only motive. Some people may work partly to satisfy a need for achievement,[64] or because they find their work enjoyable. In addition, just as in precommercial societies, some people may work partly to gain respect or influence by giving some of their income away. Not only are philanthropists and movie stars respected for giving to charities, but society encourages such giving by making it an allowable tax deduction. Still, commercial societies emphasize giving less than subsistence economies. People consider charity by the religious or rich appropriate and even admirable, but would find giving away so much as to become poverty-stricken foolish.

Forced and Required Labor

Thus far, we have mostly discussed *voluntary labor*—voluntary in the sense that no formal organization within the society compels people to work and punishes them for not working. Social training and social pressure are powerful enough to persuade an individual to perform some useful task. In both food-collecting and horticultural societies, individuals who can stand being the butt of jokes about laziness will still be fed. At most, the other members of the group will ignore them. There is no reason to punish them and no way to coerce them to do the work expected of them.

Taxation   More complex societies have ways of forcing people to work for the authorities, whether those authorities are kings or presidents. An indirect form of forced labor is taxation. The average tax in the United States (local, state, and federal) is about 33 percent of income, which means that the average person works four months out of the year for the various levels of government. If a person decides not to pay the tax, the money will be taken forcibly or the person may be put in prison.

A child in Bangladesh smashes bricks to earn a little salary.

Corvée Money is the customary form of tax payment in a commercial society. In a politically complex but nonmonetary society, people may pay their taxes in other ways—by performing a certain number of hours of labor or by giving up a certain percentage of what they produce. The **corvée**, a system of required labor, existed in the Inca Empire in the central Andes before the Spanish conquest. Each male commoner was assigned three plots of land to work: a temple plot, a state plot, and his own plot. The enormous stores of food that went into state warehouses were used to supply the nobles, the army, the artisans, and all other state employees. If labor became overabundant, the people were still kept occupied; it is said that one ruler had a hill moved to keep some laborers busy. In addition to subsistence work for the state, Inca commoners were subject to military service, to duty as personal servants for the nobility, and to other "public" service.[65] Elderly villagers in the Chiang Mai area of Thailand describe corvée this way: "Villagers had to work one *rai* [*rai myong* or 0.1 acre] per person for them [the rulers] for nothing. And one had to do it properly. The lord's underlings would take a banana tree trunk and stick it upright in the field after it was plowed. If it fell over, that meant it was well plowed. Otherwise, one would have to keep on plowing until the ground was soft."[66]

Conscription or the draft, or compulsory military service, is also a form of corvée, in that a certain period of service is required, and failure to serve can be punished by a prison term or involuntary exile. Emperors of China had soldiers drafted to defend their territory and to build the Great Wall along the northern borders of the empire. The wall extends over 1,500 miles, and thousands were drafted to work on it.

Slavery Slavery is the most extreme form of forced work, in that slaves have little control over their labor. The practice of enslaving people has existed in almost every part of the world at one time or another, in simpler as well as in more complex societies. Slaves are often obtained from other cultures directly; they are kidnapped, captured in war, or given as tribute. Or they may be obtained indirectly through barter or trade. Slaves have sometimes come from the same culture; people have become slaves to repay a debt, as punishment for a crime, or even because it was an alternative to poverty. The degree to which slaves can gain their freedom varies among slave societies.

Division of Labor

All societies have some division of labor, some customary assignment of different kinds of work to different kinds of people. Universally, males and females and adults and children do not do the same kinds of work. In a sense, then, division of labor by gender and age is a kind of universal specialization of labor. Many societies known to anthropology divide labor only by gender and age; other societies have more complex specialization.

By Gender and Age As we discuss elsewhere, all societies make use of gender differences to some extent in their customary assignment of labor. Age is also a universal basis for division of labor. Clearly, children cannot do work that requires a great deal of strength. But, in many societies, girls and boys contribute much more in labor than do children in our own society. For example, they help in animal tending, weeding, and harvesting and do a variety of domestic chores such as child care, fetching water and firewood, and cooking and cleaning. In agricultural communities in the Ivory Coast, children's tasks mirror the tasks of same-sex adults (see Figure 11.1).

In some societies, a child who is 6 years old is considered old enough to be responsible for a younger sibling for a good part of the day.[67] Animal tending is often important work for children. Children in some societies spend more time at this task than adults.[68]

Why do children do so much work in some societies? If adults, particularly mothers, have heavy workloads, and children are physically and mentally able to do the work, a good part of the work is likely to be assigned to children.[69] As we have seen, food producers probably have more work than foragers, so we would expect that children

Corvée A system of required labor.

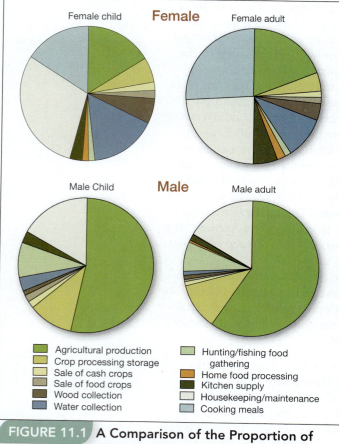

Female child   **Female**   Female adult

Male Child   **Male**   Male adult

Agricultural production
Crop processing storage
Sale of cash crops
Sale of food crops
Wood collection
Water collection

Hunting/fishing food gathering
Home food processing
Kitchen supply
Housekeeping/maintenance
Cooking meals

FIGURE 11.1   A Comparison of the Proportion of Work Tasks Done by Adults and Children in the Cote D'Ivoire

Source: From J. Levine et al. 2002.

would be likely to work more where there is herding and farming. Consistent with this expectation, Patricia Draper and Elizabeth Cashdan found differences in children's work between nomadic and settled !Kung. Even though recently settled !Kung have not switched completely from foraging to food production, children's as well as adults' activities have changed considerably. The children living in nomadic camps had virtually no work at all; adults did all the gathering and hunting. But the settled children were given lots of chores, ranging from helping with animals to helping with the harvest and food processing.[70]

What we have said about the !Kung should not imply that children in foraging societies always do little work. For example, among the Hadza of Tanzania, children between the ages of 5 and 10 are able to get one-third to one-half of their calories as they forage with their mothers. The Hadza also have more children than the !Kung.[71] Is there a relationship between children's work and fertility? When children in a society do a great deal of work, parents may value them more and may consciously want to have more children.[72] This may be one of the reasons why birth rates are especially high in intensive agricultural societies where workloads are very high.[73]

Beyond Gender and Age   In societies with relatively simple technologies, there is little specialization of labor beyond that of gender and age. But as a society's technology becomes more complex and it is able to produce large quantities of food, more of its people are freed from subsistence work to become specialists in some other tasks.

In contrast with foragers, horticultural societies may have some part-time specialists. Some people may devote special effort to perfecting a particular skill or craft—pottery making, weaving, house building, doctoring—and in return for their products or services be given food or other gifts. Among some horticultural groups, the entire village may specialize part-time in making a particular product, which can then be traded to neighboring people.

With the development of intensive agriculture, full-time specialists—potters, weavers, blacksmiths—begin to appear. The trend toward greater specialization reaches its peak in industrialized societies, where workers develop skills in one small area of the economic system. Full-time specialization makes people dependent on the necessity to sell their labor or products to make a living. In societies with full-time occupational specialization, different jobs are usually associated with differences in prestige, wealth, and power, as we shall see in the chapter on social stratification.

11.7   Explain the three general types of systems for distributing goods and services (reciprocity, redistribution, and market or commercial exchange).

The Distribution of Goods and Services

Goods and services are distributed in all societies by systems that, however varied, can be classified under three general types: reciprocity, redistribution, and market or commercial exchange.[74] The three systems often coexist in a society, but one system usually predominates. The predominant system seems to be associated with the society's food-getting technology and, more specifically, its level of economic development.

Reciprocity

Reciprocity consists of giving and taking without the use of money; it mainly takes the form of gift giving or generalized reciprocity. There may also be exchanges of equal value (barter or nonmonetary trade) or balanced reciprocity, without the use of money.[75]

Generalized Reciprocity   When goods or services are given to another, without any apparent expectation of a return gift, we call it **generalized reciprocity.** Generalized reciprocity sustains the family in all societies. Parents give food, clothing, and labor to children because they want to or perhaps feel obliged to, but they do not usually calculate exactly how their children will reciprocate years later. These gifts are one-way transfers. In this sense, all societies have some kind of generalized reciprocity. But some societies depend on it almost entirely to distribute goods and services.

Lorna Marshall recounted how the !Kung divided an eland brought to a site where five bands and several visitors were camping—more than 100 people in all. The owner of the arrow that had first penetrated the eland was, by custom, the owner of the meat. He first distributed the forequarters to the two hunters who had aided him in the kill. After that, the distribution depended on kinship: Each hunter shared with his wives' parents, wives, children, parents, and siblings, and they in turn shared with their kin. Sixty-three gifts of raw meat were recorded, after which further sharing of raw and cooked meat was begun. The !Kung distribution of large game—clearly, generalized reciprocity—is common among foragers.

Parent-child giving may seem easy to understand, but why do some societies rely more on generalized reciprocity than others, particularly beyond the family? Sharing may be most likely when resources are unpredictable. A !Kung band may share its water with other bands because they may have water now but not in the future. A related group in the Kalahari, the G//ana,[76] has been observed to share less than other groups. It turns out that the resources available to the G//ana are more predictable, because the G//ana supplement their hunting and gathering with plant cultivation and goat herding. Cultivated melons (which store water) appear to buffer the G//ana against water shortages, and goats buffer them against shortages of game. Thus, whereas the !Kung distribute the meat right after a kill, the G//ana dry it and then store it in their houses.[77]

The idea that unpredictability favors sharing may also explain why some foods are more often shared than others. Wild game, for example, is usually unpredictable; when hunters go out to hunt, they cannot be sure that they will come back with meat. Wild plants, on the other hand, are more predictable; gatherers can be sure when they go out that they will come back with at least some plant foods. In any case, it does appear that foragers tend to share game much more than wild plant foods.[78] Even among people who depend largely on horticulture, such as the Yanomamö of Venezuela and Brazil, food items that are less predictably obtained (hunted game and fish) are shared more often than the more predictably obtained garden produce.[79] But, although meat is shared more than plant food, horticulturalists often share foraged or cultivated plants. Why? Sharing plant food may be advantageous to horticulturalists who are some distance from their gardens because they may not have to go as often. And sharing may solidify a social relationship so that other families will help in times of need, such as sickness or accident, when it may be hard to work.[80] Does food sharing increase the food supply for an individual? Calculations for the Aché of eastern Paraguay, who get most of their food from hunting when they go on food-collecting trips, suggest that the average individual gets more food when food is shared. Even the males who actually do the hunting get more, although the benefits are greater for the females and children on the trip.[81] Mathematically, the risk that an individual food collector will not find enough food on a particular day will be appreciably reduced if at least six to eight adult collectors share the food they collect. Food-collecting bands may often contain only 25 to 30 people, which is about the size that is needed to ensure that there are six to eight adult collectors.[82]

What happens to a system of generalized reciprocity when resources are scarce because of a drought or other disaster? Does the ethic of giving break down? Evidence

Reciprocity Giving and taking (not politically arranged) without the use of money.

Generalized reciprocity Gift giving without any immediate or planned return.

from a few societies suggests that the degree of sharing may actually *increase* during the period of food shortage.[83] For example, in describing the Netsilik Inuit, Asen Balikci said, "Whenever game was abundant, sharing among non-relatives was avoided, since every family was supposedly capable of obtaining the necessary catch. In situations of scarcity, however, caribou meat was more evenly distributed throughout camp."[84] Sharing may increase during mild scarcity because people can minimize their deprivation, but generalized reciprocity may be strained by extreme scarcity such as famine.[85]

Researchers generally have difficulty explaining sharing because they assume that, other things being equal, individuals would tend to be selfish. But experimental evidence suggests that sharing is likely even with people who do not know each other or who have no expectation of any return in the future from that person. Experimenters set up "games" in which they can control for or eliminate certain responses. For example, in one game, a particular player is given a certain amount of money and the player decides how much of the money to offer to the second player in the game. The second player can accept or reject the offer. If the division is rejected, no one gets any money. If the division is accepted, both players receive the proposed division. If selfishness were normal, one would expect that the proposer of the division would try to give away as little as possible and the second player should always accept whatever is offered because otherwise nothing is gained. Surprisingly, equal divisions are commonly proposed and low offers are commonly rejected because they are viewed as unfair. If a person views the offer as unfair and forfeits any money, that player seems willing to "punish" the greedy individual. Although such experiments were mostly done at first in Western societies, we now have results from over 15 other societies that largely confirm the earlier results.[86] There is now evidence suggesting that cooperation may even evoke pleasure. Researchers studying brain activity in women, who are playing a game allowing either cooperative or greedy strategies, found to their surprise that cooperation made certain areas of the brain light up. These areas are normally associated with pleasure, such as when eating desserts. So cooperation may be more "natural" than some people think.[87]

Balanced reciprocity

Giving with the expectation of a straightforward immediate or limited-time trade.

Balanced Reciprocity   **Balanced reciprocity** is explicit and short term in its expectations of return. In contrast to generalized reciprocity or a one-way transfer, which has no expectation of a return, balanced reciprocity involves either an immediate exchange of goods or services or an agreed-upon exchange over a limited period of time. *Barter* is the term used most often for this type of nonmonetary exchange of goods and services. The !Kung, for instance, trade with the Tswana Bantu: a gemsbok hide for a pile of tobacco, five strings of beads made from ostrich eggshells for a spear, or three small skins for a good-sized knife.[88] In the 1600s, the Iroquois of the North American northeast traded deerskin to Europeans for brass kettles, iron hinges, steel axes, woven textiles, and guns.[89] The !Kung and Iroquois acquired trade goods by balanced reciprocity, but such exchanges were not crucial to their economies.

In contrast, some societies depend much more heavily on balanced reciprocity. For example, the Efe, who hunt and gather in the Ituri forest of central Africa, get most of their calories from manioc, peanuts, rice, and plaintains grown by another group—the agricultural Lese. Efe men and women provide labor to the Lese, and in exchange, receive a portion of the harvest as well as goods such as metal pots and spears.[90] Pastoralists, too, are rarely self-sufficient. They have to trade their pastoral products to agriculturalists to get the grain and other things they need.

Sometimes the line between generalized and balanced reciprocity is not so clear. Consider our gift giving at Christmas. Although such gift giving may appear to be generalized reciprocity, and it often is in the case of gift giving from parents to children, there may be strong expectations of balance. Two friends or relatives may try to exchange presents of fairly equal value, based on calculations of what last year's gift cost. If a person receives a $5 present when he or she gave a $25 present, that person may be hurt and perhaps angry. On the other hand, a person who receives a $500 present when he or she gave a $25 present may well also be dismayed.

Redistribution

Redistribution is the accumulation of goods or labor by a particular person, or in a particular place, for the purpose of subsequent distribution. Although redistribution is found in all societies, it becomes an important mechanism only in societies that have political hierarchies—that is, chiefs or other specialized officials and agencies. In all societies, there is some redistribution, at least within the family. Members of the family pool their labor, products, or income for the common good. But in many societies, there is little or no redistribution beyond the family. It seems that redistribution on a territorial basis emerges when there is a political apparatus to coordinate centralized collection and distribution of goods or to mobilize labor for some public purpose.

Why do redistribution systems develop? Elman Service suggested that they develop in agricultural societies that contain subregions suited to different kinds of crops or natural resources. Foragers can take advantage of environmental variation by moving to different areas. With agriculture, the task is more difficult; it might be easier to move different products across different regions.[91] If the demand for different resources or products becomes too great, reciprocity between individuals might become awkward. So it might be more efficient to have someone—a chief, perhaps—coordinate the exchanges.

Marvin Harris agreed that redistribution becomes more likely with agriculture, but for a somewhat different reason. He argued that competitive feasting, as in New Guinea, is adaptive because it encourages people to work harder to produce somewhat more than they need. Why would this feature be adaptive? Harris argued that, with agriculture, people really have to produce more than they need so that they can protect themselves against crises such as crop failure. The groups that make feasts may be indirectly ensuring themselves against crises by storing up social credit with other villages, who will reciprocate by making feasts for them in the future. On the other hand, inducements to collect more than they need may not be advantageous to food-collecting groups, who might lose in the long run by over collecting.[92]

Zebu meat is divided for villagers as part of a festival in Mananjary, Madagascar

Market or Commercial Exchange

When we think of markets, we usually think of bustling, colorful places where goods are bought and sold. The exchanges usually involve money. In our own society, we have supermarkets and the stock market and other places for buying and selling that we call shops, stores, and malls. In referring to **market** or **commercial exchange,** economists and economic anthropologists are referring to exchanges or transactions in which the "prices" are subject to supply and demand, whether or not the transactions actually occur in a marketplace.[93] Market exchange involves not only the exchange (buying and selling) of goods but also transactions of labor, land, rentals, and credit.

Kinds of Money Although market exchange need not involve money, most commercial transactions, particularly nowadays, do involve what we call money. Some anthropologists define money according to the functions and characteristics of the **general-purpose money** used in our own and other complex societies, for which nearly all goods, resources, and services can be exchanged. According to this definition, money performs the basic functions of serving as an accepted medium of exchange, a standard of value, and a store

Redistribution The accumulation of goods (or labor) by a particular person or in a particular place and their subsequent distribution.

Market (or commercial) exchange Transactions in which the "prices" are subject to supply and demand, whether or not the transactions occur in a marketplace.

General-purpose money A universally accepted medium of exchange.

of wealth. As a medium of exchange, it allows all goods and services to be valued in the same objective way; we say that an object or service is worth so much money. Also, money is nonperishable, and therefore savable or storable, and almost always transportable and divisible, so transactions can involve the buying and selling of goods and services that differ in value.

It is important to realize that money has little or no intrinsic value; rather, it is society that determines its value. In the United States today, paper bills, bank checks, and credit and debit cards are fully accepted as money, and money is increasingly transferred electronically.

In many societies, money is not an all-purpose medium of exchange. Many peoples whose food production per capita is not sufficient to support a large population of non-producers of food have **special-purpose money**. This consists of objects of value for which only some goods and services can be exchanged on the spot or through balanced reciprocity. In some parts of Melanesia, pigs are assigned value in terms of shell money—lengths of shells strung together in units each roughly as long as the distance covered by a man's outstretched arms. According to its size, a pig will be assigned a value in tens of such units up to 100.[94] But shell money cannot be exchanged for all the goods or services a person might need.

Special-purpose money
Objects of value for which only some goods and services can be exchanged.

11.8 ▶ Discuss the worldwide trend toward commercialization and its social effects.

The Worldwide Trend Toward Commercialization

One of the most important changes resulting from the expansion of Western societies and the capitalist system is the increasingly worldwide dependence on commercial exchange. The borrowed customs of buying and selling may at first be supplementary to traditional means of distributing goods in a society. As new commercial customs take hold, however, the economic base of the receiving society alters. Inevitably, social, political, and even biological and psychological changes accompany such a change (see box "Impact of the World System—Deforestation of the Amazon").

Many anthropologists have noted that with the introduction of money, customs of sharing seem to change dramatically. Money, perhaps because it is nonperishable and largely hideable, tends to invoke feelings of not wanting to share. The plight of a man from the central highlands of New Guinea is typical. He agrees that it is not good manners to refuse a request from a relative or village friend; nonetheless, to keep his income from being "eaten," he tries to conceal some of his income. Some of the strategies include opening a savings account into which his pay is deposited, purchasing a semipermanent house, or joining a revolving credit association.[95] A recent series of experiments in the United States, where money has always been fundamental to the economic system, suggests that even the mere reminder of money causes people to behave more independently and to be less helpful to others.[96]

Migratory Labor

One way commercialization can occur is for some members of a community to move to a place that offers the possibility of working for wages. This happened in Tikopia, an island near the Solomon Islands in the South Pacific. In 1929, when Raymond Firth first studied the island, its economy was still essentially noncommercial—simple, self-sufficient, and largely self-contained.[97] Some Western goods were available but, with the exception of iron and steel in limited quantities, not sought after. Their possession and use were associated solely with Europeans. This situation changed dramatically with World War II. During the war, military forces occupied neighboring islands, and people from Tikopia migrated to those islands to find employment. In the period following the war, several large commercial interests extended their activities in the Solomons, thus creating a continued demand for labor. As a result, when Firth revisited Tikopia in 1952,

Applied Anthropology

Impact of the World System—Deforestation of the Amazon

The great rain forest drained by the Amazon River and its tributaries, covers more than a billion acres. The Amazon forest is not only home to many largely self-sufficient indigenous cultures, it also supports about 20 percent of all the earth's plant and animal species.

The vast forests absorb CO_2, which helps to reduce global warming. The forest also puts needed moisture into the atmosphere through evaporation—about 8 trillion tons of water a year. Global warming will lead to reduced rainfall, putting stress on the ability of the forest to grow or the existing trees to survive.

The Amazon forest and other tropical forests have been disappearing at an alarming rate because of the accelerated clearing of forest by humans, primarily for ranching and farming. About 15 percent of the Amazon forests have already been cleared. Some have suggested that the world demand for wood, hamburger, and crops for biofuels, is largely responsible for the diminution of the Amazon forest. Like many tropical forests, the Amazon has large numbers of desirable hardwood trees. Forests in Africa and Asia are already largely depleted, so the demand for wood from the Amazon has grown considerably. In addition, the Amazon Development Agency in Brazil has offered incentives to clear forest for cattle ranching, which can provide hamburger to fast-food restaurants. Clearing land for crops has increased because

of the need for food for cattle and for production of crops suitable for biofuels.

The indigenous people often find themselves in a land squeeze, with loggers, cattle ranchers, and miners trying to encroach on their territory. With less land, food-getting and traditional economic practices are in jeopardy. But it is naive to assume that the indigenous people are interested only in maintaining their traditional economies. They often accept the dilemma of economic development: They might lose some land, but selling rights to loggers and miners brings in money, which they can use to buy things they need and want. And, indigenous people themselves, although they contribute relatively little to the direct deforestation that is occurring, are increasingly involved in the world market economy. Researchers studying the Tsimane' of the Bolivian lowlands, mainly foragers who also farm, have found that those who grow a cash crop are most likely to clear more forest.

Development experts and applied anthropologists are searching for ways to achieve development without destroying or degrading the environment. For example, indigenous groups are encouraged to gather Brazil nuts, a wild but renewable resource, for sale. Others are encouraged to harvest latex (natural rubber) and hearts of palm. Medicinal plants have economic value to multinational

pharmaceutical and biotechnical companies, which have discovered that the conservation of biodiversity may be economically advantageous to themselves as well as to the local people and to scientists who want to study the diversity. The countries with large portions of Amazon forest have played an important role in encouraging development, but have worked to reduce deforestation with international pressure. For example, in Brazil, the annual rate of forest clearing declined between 2005 and 2010, because of the intervention of the Brazilian government. The international community is also working on a plan that would encourage countries to reduce deforestation, perhaps in exchange for monetary credits.

Can development be sustainable? Whether we like it or not, economic development and the desire for it are not going to go away. But we need to do more than applaud or bemoan economic development. In particular, we need more research that reveals what impact particular changes will have on people, other animals, plants, and the environment. Most of all, for the sake of human rights, we need to listen to the people whose lives will be most affected, to understand their needs as well as those of the developers.

Sources: Holloway 1993; Moran 1993; Winterbottom 1995, 60–70; Betts et al. 2008; Nepstad et al. 2008; Vadez et al. 2008; Nolte et al. 2013.

he found the economic situation already significantly altered. More than 100 Tikopians had left the island to work for varying periods. The migrants wanted to earn money because they aspired to standards of living previously regarded as appropriate only to Europeans. Already, living conditions on Tikopia were changing. Western cooking and water-carrying utensils, mosquito nets, kerosene storm lamps, and so forth had come to be regarded as normal items in a Tikopia household. The introduction of money into the economy also affected other areas of life. Compared with the situation in 1929, land was under more intensive cultivation in 1952, with introduced manioc and sweet potatoes supplementing the old principal crop, taro. Pressures on the food supply resulting from improved living standards and an increased population seem to have weakened the

Migrants and Immigrants

Working Abroad to Send Money Home

Throughout recorded history, people have been going to other places to make a living. They do it not only to support themselves, but also to support their families back home. Indeed, the people left behind might suffer terribly, or even starve, without these remittances, the term economists use when referring to the money people send back home. People who went to another country to work generated more than $440 billion in remittances in 2010.

In the 19th century, men from China were recruited to come to North America to build the transcontinental railroads, and Italians were recruited to work on building the railroads in New York State, New Jersey, Connecticut, and Massachusetts. In the years after World War II, when West German businesses were short of labor because so many people had been killed in the war, men from Turkey were recruited to come to Germany to fill the available jobs. Now, 30 to 40 years later, they make up a sizeable proportion of the population. Most if not all of the labor-short countries in western Europe (including England and France, the Netherlands, Sweden, Norway, Italy, and Spain) have attracted considerable numbers of immigrants in recent years. Indeed, much like the United States before them, the countries of western Europe are now becoming quite diverse culturally.

We may think that many if not most immigrants want to stay in the countries they have moved to. But this was not always true in the past, and it is not always true today. Many in the past just wanted to stay a few years. They wanted to earn money to help relatives back home,

Filipino and Chinese domestic workers gather on their day off on a Hong Kong street.

and maybe (if they were lucky) they could earn enough money to return home themselves and buy a farm or other small business. They often didn't become citizens in the new country because they didn't intend to stay. But until recently, most immigrants never went home again, and by the second or third generation, they had lost their native languages. In the last few decades, people who move to other countries to work often go home again—and again and again. They have become "transnationals," fluent in at least two languages, and comfortable living in different countries alternately. They may even retain two (or more) citizenships. Consider how different this is from many past immigrants who were highly motivated to "pass." It is not clear yet what explains why some people are more comfortable now with not passing.

Could it be that some places are less ethnocentric than in the past? If so, why is that?

Not all moves to another country turn out well for the migrants. Consider the poor young women from Sri Lanka who are recruited to work as housemaids in other countries. They may be burned or beaten if their work is deemed unacceptable, and they may return home with no money saved from their work time abroad. One in every 19 citizens of Sri Lanka now works abroad, most of them as housemaids. For a country like Sri Lanka, migration has become a safety valve for the economy. The Sri Lankan economy may be advantaged by the remittances received, but not without suffering for some of the migrants.

Sources: M. Ember et al. 2005; Waldman 2005.

ties of extended kinship. People were no longer as willing to share with members of their extended family, particularly with respect to the money and goods acquired by working in the Solomons.

In many areas of the world, the money sent back home has become a major factor in the economy (see the box "Working Abroad to Send Money Home"). Often remittances are not sent through the formal banking system, but rather through an informal network of brokers. In the Middle East and South Asia, the system is called *hawala* and is based on an honor system. For instance, the Hazara, the third largest ethnic group in Afghanistan, have migrated throughout the 20th century to cities in Afghanistan as well as to Pakistan and Iran. The banks in Afghanistan are not functioning and the Hazara often do not have official identification papers, so they use *hawala* brokers to transfer money back home.[98] The money from remittances often far exceeds the money spent by development efforts.[99] But unlike development efforts, usually supported by wealthier countries, money received by remittances can be channeled where families want. Migration becomes part of a family's economic strategy. Of course, not all families can employ that strategy—the poorest families cannot afford the costs of long-distance migration.[100]

Nonagricultural Commercial Production

Commercialization can also occur when a self-sufficient society comes to depend more and more on trading for its livelihood. Such a change is exemplified by the Mundurucú of the Amazon Basin, who largely abandoned general horticulture for commercial rubber production. A similar change may also be seen in the Montagnais of northeastern Canada, who came to depend increasingly on commercial fur trapping, rather than hunting, for subsistence. Robert Murphy and Julian Steward found that, when modern goods from industrialized areas became available through trade, both the Mundurucú and the Montagnais devoted their energies to producing specialized cash crops or other trade items. They did this to obtain other industrially made objects.[101] The primary socioeconomic change that occurred among the Mundurucú and the Montagnais was a shift from cooperative labor and community autonomy to individualized economic activity and a dependence on an external market.

Among the Mundurucú, for example, before close trading links were established, the native population and the Europeans had been in contact for some 80 years without the Mundurucú way of life being noticeably altered. The men did give up their independent military activities to perform as mercenaries for the Brazilians, but they continued to maintain their horticultural economy. Some trading took place with Brazilians, with the chief acting as agent for the village. Barter was the method of exchange. Traders first distributed their wares, ranging from cheap cottons to iron hatchets, trinkets, and so on; they returned about three months later to collect manioc, India rubber, and beans from the Mundurucú. At this time (1860), however, rubber was only a secondary item of commerce.

The rapidly growing demand for rubber from the 1860s onward increased the importance of Mundurucú-trader relationships. Traders now openly began to appoint agents, called *capitoes,* whose job it was to encourage greater rubber production. *Capitoes* were given economic privileges and hence power, both of which began to undercut the position of the traditional chief. In addition, the process of rubber collection itself began to alter Mundurucú social patterns by moving people away from their jungle-based communities.

The point of no return was reached when significant numbers of Mundurucú abandoned the villages for permanent settlements near their individual territories of trees. These new settlements lacked the unity, the sense of community, of former village life. Nuclear families held and carefully maintained property in the interest of productivity.

With the discovery of gold, many Mundurucú young men have turned to panning for gold in rivers. The required equipment is simple, and gold is easier to transport and trade than rubber. Because gold can be sold for cash, which is then used for purchases, trading relationships are no longer so important. Cash is now used to buy transistor radios, tape recorders, watches, bicycles, and new kinds of clothing, in addition to firearms, metal pots, and tools. With money as a medium of exchange, the traditional emphasis on reciprocity has declined. Even food may now be sold to fellow Mundurucú, a practice that would have been unthinkable in the 1950s.[102]

Supplementary Cash Crops

A third way commercialization occurs is when people cultivating the soil produce a surplus above their subsistence requirements, which is then sold for cash. In many cases, this cash income must be used to pay rent or taxes. Under these circumstances, commercialization may be said to be associated with the formation of a peasantry.

What changes does the development of a peasantry entail? In some respects, there is little disturbance of the cultivator's (now peasant's) former way of life. The peasant still has to produce enough food to meet family needs, to replace what has been consumed, to cover a few ceremonial obligations (e.g., the marriage of a child, village festivals, and funerals). But in other respects, the peasant's situation is radically altered. For, in addition to the traditional obligations—indeed, often in conflict with them—the peasant now has to produce extra crops to meet the requirements of a group of outsiders—landlords or officials of the state. These outsiders expect to be paid rent or taxes in produce or currency, and they are able to enforce their expectations because they control the military and the police.

Introduction of Commercial and Industrial Agriculture

Commercialization can come about through the introduction of commercial agriculture—cultivation for sale rather than personal consumption. The system of agriculture may come to be industrialized. In other words, some of the production processes, such as plowing, weeding, irrigation, and harvesting, can be done by machine. Commercial agriculture is, in fact, often as mechanized as any manufacturing industry. Land is worked for the maximum return it will yield, and labor is hired and fired just as impersonally as in other industries.

The introduction of commercial agriculture brings several important social consequences. Gradually, a class polarization develops. Farmers and landlords become increasingly separated from laborers and tenants, just as the employer in town becomes socially separated from the employees. Gradually, too, manufactured items of all sorts are introduced into rural areas. Laborers migrate to urban centers in search of employment, often meeting even less sympathetic conditions there than exist in the country.

The changeover to commercial agriculture may result in an improved standard of living in the short and long run. But sometimes the switch is followed by a decline in the standard of living if the market price for the commercial crop declines. For example, the changeover of the farmer-herders of the arid *sertão* region of northeastern Brazil after 1940 to the production of sisal (a plant whose fibers can be made into twine and rope) seemed to be a move that could provide a more secure living in their arid environment. But when the world price for sisal dropped and the wages of sisal workers declined, many workers were forced to curtail the caloric intake of their children. The poorer people were obliged to save their now more limited food supplies for the money earners, at the expense of the children.[103]

Commercialization can start in various ways: People can begin to sell and buy because they begin to work near home or away for wages, or because they begin to sell nonagricultural products, surplus food, or cash crops (crops grown deliberately for sale). One type of commercialization does not exclude another; all types can occur in any society. No matter how commercialization begins, it seems to have predictable effects on traditional economics. The ethic of generalized reciprocity declines, particularly with respect to giving away money. (Perhaps because it is nonperishable and hideable, money seems more likely than other goods to be kept for one's immediate family rather than shared with others.) Property rights become individualized rather than collective when people begin to buy and sell. Even in societies that were previously egalitarian, commercialization usually results in more unequal access to resources and hence a greater degree of social stratification.

Summary and Review

Foraging

11.1 Describe foraging and complex foraging, and identify the general societal features associated with food collecting.

- Foraging—hunting, gathering, and fishing—depends on wild plants and animals and is the oldest human food-getting technology.

- Most foraging societies comprise small bands of nomads. Division of labor is along age and gender lines only, personal possessions and land rights are limited, people are usually not differentiated by class, and political leadership is informal.

- Complex foraging societies depend heavily on fishing and likely have bigger and more permanent communities as well as more social inequality. These societies tend to have higher population densities, food storage, occupational specialization, resource ownership, slavery, and competitiveness.

 Explain the difference between foraging and complex foraging.

Food Production

11.2 Describe three major types of food production and identify the general societal features associated with the different types of food production.

- Beginning about 10,000 years ago, certain peoples in widely separated geographic locations began to make the changeover to food production—the cultivation and raising of plants and animals.

- Horticulturalists farm with relatively simple tools and methods and do not cultivate fields permanently. They generally have larger, more densely populated communities than foragers and they tend to be more sedentary, although communities may move after some years to farm a new series of plots.

- Intensive agriculture is characterized by techniques such as fertilization and irrigation that allow fields to be cultivated permanently. In contrast with horticultural societies, intensive agriculturalists are more likely to have towns and cities, a high degree of craft specialization, large differences in wealth and power, and more complex political organization. They are also more likely to face food shortages.

- In the modern world, intensive agriculture is increasingly mechanized and geared to production for a market.

- Pastoralism is a subsistence technology involving principally the raising of large herds of animals. It is generally found in low-rainfall areas. Pastoralists tend to be nomadic, to have small communities consisting of related families, and to depend significantly on trade.

Environmental Restraints on Food-Getting

11.3 Identify environmental restraints on food-getting.

- Cross-cultural evidence indicates that neither foraging nor food production is significantly associated with any particular type of habitat.

- Foragers farther from the equator depend much more on animals and fish, and foragers in tropical forests could not survive without the carbohydrates they obtain from agriculturalists.

- Approximately 80 percent of all societies that practice horticulture or simple agriculture are in the tropics, whereas 75 percent of all societies that practice intensive agriculture are not in tropical forest environments; an exception is tropical rice paddies. Pastoralism is typically practiced in grassland regions.

- The physical environment does not by itself account for the system of food-getting in an area; technological, social, and political factors rather than environmental factors mostly determine food-getting practices in a given environment.

 What are some environmental restraints on food-getting?

The Origin, Spread, and Intensification of Food Production

11.4 Describe and critically discuss the spread and intensification of food production.

- From about 40,000 to about 15,000 years ago, people seem to have gotten most of their food from hunting migratory herds of large animals.

- Beginning about 14,000 years ago, some populations began to depend more on relatively stationary food resources such as fish, shellfish, small game, and wild plants, which may have supported an increasingly settled way of life

- The first evidence of a changeover to food production—the cultivation and domestication of plants and animals—is found in the Near East about 8000 B.C., a shift that occurred, probably independently, also in other areas.

- Theory suggests these factors influencing food production: (a) as growing populations expanded further from bountiful wild resources, they domesticated animals and plants in an effort to reproduce former abundance; (b) global population growth may have filled most of the world's habitable regions, forcing people to domesticate plants and animals; and (c) climate change may have favored settling near seasonal stands of wild grain, and growing populations in such areas may have led to domestication of plants and animals.

> **?** What evidence and theories explain the origin of food production?

The Allocation of Resources

> **11.5** Compare and contrast the allocation of resources among foragers, horticulturalists, intensive agriculturalists, and pastoralists and how colonialism and the state have affected that allocation.

- Every society has access to natural resources—land, water, plants, animals, minerals—and cultural rules for determining who has access to particular resources. Societies differ in their rules for land access, but the differences generally relate to a society's food-getting method.

- Food-collecting societies commonly control land collectively through kinships groups or through bands or villages. Territoriality is stronger when the plants and animals collected are predictably located and abundant.

- Horticulturalist societies also do not own land because their technologies do not enable them to effectively use the same land permanently, but they do assign individuals or families use of a particular plot of land.

- Pastoralists often combine the adaptive habits of both foragers and horticulturalists because they need larger territories for grazing herds. While they tend to hold grazing land communally, pastoralists customarily own their herds individually.

- Individual ownership of land resources is common among intensive agriculturalists. But some communist and socialist nations undertake intensive agriculture by forming state-run agricultural collectives.

- Almost universally, colonial conquerors and settlers from expanding state societies have taken land from the natives or aborigines. Typically, state authorities do not like communal land-use systems and see mobile pastoralists as difficult to control.

> **?** How has the worldwide phenomenon of colonialism and the effects of statehood affected land rights?

The Conversion of Resources

> **11.6** Describe variation in different types of economic production, what motivates people to work, how societies divide up the work to be done, and how they organize work.

- Production is the conversion of resources through labor into food, tools, and other goods.

- In domestic production, the family controls conversion of resources. In industrial production, people labor as wage earners. In tributary production, people pay a tribute of labor/goods to an authority for access to land. In postindustrial production, information/services are the main products.

- People in subsistence economies with a domestic mode of production often work less than people in commercial economies with tributary or industrial modes of production and do not produce more than they need.

- People may be motivated to work harder than they have to for subsistence to gain social respect or esteem or to satisfy a need for achievement, especially in commercial economies.

- Forms of forced labor are found in more complex societies and can be indirect (taxation and corvée) or direct (slavery).

- Many societies divide labor only by gender and age; other societies have more complex specialization. Horticultural societies may have some part-time specialists. Societies with intensive agriculture have some full-time specialists, and industrialized societies have many.

> **?** What are the different types of economic production?

The Distribution of Goods and Services

11.7 Explain the three general types of systems for distributing goods and services (reciprocity, redistribution, and market or commercial exchange).

- Goods and services are distributed in all societies under three general types of systems: reciprocity, redistribution, and market or commercial exchange, each of which is associated with a society's food-getting technology and level of economic development.

- Reciprocity systems do not involve money. Sharing may (a) be likely when resources are unpredictable, (b) create social relationships that ensure help when needed, and (c) equalize distribution of goods between communities.

- In redistribution systems, one person accumulates goods or labor for the purpose of later distribution. Redistribution is found in all societies but is an important mechanism only in societies that have political hierarchies.

- Market or commercial exchange involves the buying/selling of goods and transactions of labor, land, rentals, and credit. General-purpose money provides an objective value for all goods and services. Special-purpose money can be used for only some goods and services.

- Societies may begin to use money when trade and barter increases or when political authorities demand noncommercial fees such as taxes. Social bonds between individuals may become less kinlike in more complex and populated societies, making reciprocity less likely.

What are the major ways of distributing goods and services and how do they relate to a society's food-getting technology?

The Worldwide Trend Toward Commercialization

11.8 Discuss the worldwide trend toward commercialization and its social effects.

- The expansion of Western societies and the capitalist system has led to an increasingly worldwide dependence on commercial exchange. Inevitably, social, political, and even biological and psychological changes accompany such a change.

- Many anthropologists have noted that, with the introduction of money, customs of sharing seem to change dramatically.

- Commercialization can occur when some society members move to places that offer possible work for wages, when a self-sufficient society increasingly depends on trading, and when people cultivating crops produce a surplus to sell it for cash.

- Commercial systems of agriculture may become industrialized. The introduction of commercial agriculture brings several important social consequences, including class polarization.

What are examples of social, political, biological, and psychological changes that might occur as a result of dependence on commercial exchange?

Think on it

1. Why might foragers be less likely than **intensive agriculturalists** to suffer from food shortages?

2. Why do certain **foods** in a society come to be **preferred**?

3. What conditions might enable us to achieve a world of **sustainable resources**?

4. What might be the beneficial consequences of the **worldwide trend** toward commercialization?

12 Social Stratification: Class, Ethnicity, and Racism

LEARNING OBJECTIVES

12.1 Discuss the concepts relating to the variation in degree of social inequality.

12.2 Describe the characteristics of egalitarian societies.

12.3 Describe the characteristics of rank societies.

12.4 Describe the characteristics of class societies.

12.5 Discuss how racism and inequality are related.

12.6 Explain the relationship between ethnicity and inequality.

12.7 Discuss the emergence of stratification.

A long-enduring value in the United States is the belief that "all men are created equal." These famous words from the American Declaration of Independence do not mean that all people are equal in wealth or status but rather that all (including women nowadays) are supposed to be equal before the law. Equality before the law is the ideal. But the ideal is not always the actuality. Some people have advantages in legal treatment, and they generally also have advantages of other kinds, including economic advantages. Without exception, recent and modern industrial and postindustrial societies such as our own are *socially stratified*—that is, they contain social groups such as families, classes, or ethnic groups that have unequal access to important advantages such as economic resources, power, and prestige.

Hasn't such inequality always existed? Anthropologists, based on firsthand observations of recent societies, would say not. To be sure, even the simplest societies (in the technological sense) have some differences in advantages based on age, ability, or gender—adults have higher status than children, the skilled more than the unskilled, men more than women (we discuss this topic in the chapter on sex and gender). But anthropologists would argue that *egalitarian societies* exist where *social groups* (e.g., families) have more or less the same access to rights or advantages, as they tend to in foraging and horticultural societies. Not only do the economic systems of many food collectors and horticulturalists promote equal access to economic resources for all families in the community, but such societies also tend to emphasize the sharing of food and other goods, which tends to equalize any small inequalities in resources between families. Until about 10,000 years ago, all human societies depended on food they hunted, gathered, and/or fished. And so we might expect that egalitarianism characterized most of human history. That is indeed what archaeologists suggest. Substantial inequality generally appears only with permanent communities, centralized political systems, and intensive agriculture, which are cultural features that began to appear in the world only in the last 10,000 years. Before that time, then, most societies were probably egalitarian. In the world today, egalitarian societies have all but disappeared because of two processes—the global spread of commercial or market exchange and the voluntary or involuntary incorporation of many diverse people into large, centralized political systems. In modern societies, some groups have more advantages than others. These groups may include *ethnic* groups. That is, ethnic diversity is almost always associated with differential access to advantages. When ethnic diversity is also associated with differences in physical features such as skin color, the social stratification may involve *racism*, the belief that some "racial" groups are inferior.

Systems of social stratification are strongly linked to the customary ways in which economic resources are allocated, distributed, and converted through labor into goods and services. So we would not expect much inequality if all people had relatively equal access to economic resources. But stratification cannot be understood solely in terms of economic resources; there are other benefits such as prestige and power that may be unequally distributed. We first examine how societies vary in their systems of stratification. Then we turn to possible explanations of why they vary.

Economic resources
Things that have value in a culture, including land, tools and other technology, goods, and money.

Variation in Degree of Social Inequality

Societies vary in the extent to which social groups, as well as individuals, have unequal access to advantages. We are concerned with differential or unequal access to three types of advantages: (1) wealth or economic resources, (2) power, and (3) prestige. **Economic resources** are things that have value in a culture; they include land, tools and other technology, goods, and money. **Power**, a second but related advantage, is the ability to make others do what they do not want to do; power is influence based on the threat of force. When groups in a society have rules or customs that give them unequal access to wealth or resources, they generally also have unequal access to power. So, for example, when we speak of a "company town" in the United States, we are referring to the fact that the

12.1 Discuss the concepts relating to the variation in degree of social inequality.

Power The ability to make others do what they do not want to do or influence based on the threat of force.

TABLE 12.1	Stratification in Three Types of Societies			
	SOME SOCIAL GROUPS HAVE GREATER ACCESS TO			
Type of Society	Economic Resources	Power	Prestige	Examples
Egalitarian	No	No	No	!Kung, Mbuti, Australian aborigines, Inuit, Aché, Yanomamö
Rank	No	No	Yes	Samoans, Tahiti, Trobriand Islands, Ifaluk
Class/caste	Yes	Yes	Yes	United States, Canada, Greece, India, Inca

Prestige Being accorded particular respect or honor.

Egalitarian societies Societies in which all people of a given age-sex category have equal access to economic resources, power, and prestige.

Rank societies Societies that do not have any unequal access to economic resources or power, but with social groups that have unequal access to status positions and prestige.

12.2 Describe the characteristics of egalitarian societies.

Class societies Societies containing social groups that have unequal access to economic resources, power, and prestige.

company that employs most of the residents of the town usually has considerable control over them. Finally, there is the advantage of **prestige**. When we speak of prestige, we mean that someone or some group is accorded particular respect or honor. Even if it is true that there is always unequal access by individuals to prestige (because of differences in age, gender, or ability), some societies in the ethnographic record have no social groups with unequal access to prestige.

Thus, anthropologists conventionally distinguish three types of society in terms of the degree to which different social groups have unequal access to advantages: *egalitarian, rank,* and *class societies* (see Table 12.1). Some societies in the ethnographic record do not fit easily into any of these three types; as with any classification scheme, some cases seem to straddle the line between types.[1] **Egalitarian societies** contain no social groups with greater or lesser access to economic resources, power, or prestige. **Rank societies** do not have very unequal access to economic resources or to power, but they do contain social groups with unequal access to prestige. Rank societies, then, are partly stratified. **Class societies** have unequal access to all three advantages—economic resources, power, and prestige.

Egalitarian Societies

Egalitarian societies can be found not only among foragers such as the !Kung, Mbuti, Australian aborigines, Inuit, and Aché, but also among horticulturalists such as the Yanomamö and pastoralists such as the Lapps. An important point to keep in mind is that egalitarian does not mean that all people within such societies are the same. There will always be differences among

In egalitarian societies, such as among the Mbuti hunter-gatherers, houses tend to look the same.

individuals in age and gender and in such abilities or traits as hunting skill, perception, health, creativity, physical prowess, attractiveness, and intelligence. According to Morton Fried, egalitarian means that, within a given society, "there are as many positions of prestige in any given age/sex grade as there are persons capable of filling them."[2] For instance, if a person can achieve high status by fashioning fine spears, and if many people in the society fashion such spears, then many acquire high status as spear makers. If high status is also acquired by carving bones into artifacts, and if only three people are considered expert carvers of bones, then only those three achieve high status as carvers. But the next generation might produce 8 spear makers and 20 carvers. In an egalitarian society, the number of prestigious positions is adjusted to fit the number of qualified candidates. We would say, therefore, that such a society is not socially stratified.

There are, of course, differences in position and prestige arising out of differences in ability. Even in an egalitarian society, differential prestige exists. But, although some people may be better hunters or more skilled artists than others, there is still *equal access* to status positions for people of the same ability. Any prestige gained by achieving high status as a great hunter, for instance, is neither transferable nor inheritable. Because a man is a great hunter, it is not assumed that his sons are also great hunters. There also may be individuals with more influence, but it cannot be inherited, and there are no groups with appreciably more influence over time. An egalitarian society keeps inequality at a minimal level.

Any differences in prestige that do exist are not related to economic differences. Egalitarian groups depend heavily on *sharing*, which ensures equal access to economic resources despite differences in acquired prestige. For instance, in some egalitarian communities, some members achieve higher status through hunting. But even before the hunt begins, how the animal will be divided and distributed among the members of the band has already been decided according to custom. The culture works to separate the status that members achieve—recognition as great hunters—from actual possession of the wealth, which in this case would be the slain animal.

Just as egalitarian societies do not have social groups with unequal access to economic resources, they also do not have social groups with unequal access to power. As we will see later in the chapter on political life, unequal access to power by social groups seems to occur only in state societies, which have full-time political officials and marked differences in wealth. Egalitarian societies use a number of customs to keep leaders from dominating others. Criticism and ridicule can be very effective. The Mbuti of central Africa shout down an overassertive leader. When a Hadza man (in Tanzania) tried to get people to work for him, other Hadza made fun of him. Disobedience is another strategy. If a leader tries to command, people just ignore the command. In extreme cases, a particularly domineering leader may be killed by community agreement; this behavior was reported among the !Kung and the Hadza. Finally, particularly among more nomadic groups, people may just move away from a leader they don't like. The active attempts to put down upstarts in many egalitarian societies prompts Christopher Boehm to suggest that dominance comes naturally to humans. Egalitarian societies work hard to reverse that tendency.[3] The Mbuti provide an example of a society almost totally equal: "Neither in ritual, hunting, kinship nor band relations do they exhibit any discernible inequalities of rank or advantage."[4] Their hunting bands have no leaders, and recognition of the achievement of one person is not accompanied by privilege of any sort. Economic resources such as food are communally shared, and even tools and weapons are frequently passed from person to person. Only within the family are rights and privileges differentiated.

Foraging societies with extensive sharing of resources are more readily labeled egalitarian as compared with some pastoral societies where households may vary considerably in the number of animals they own. Should we consider a pastoral society with unequal distribution of animals egalitarian? Here there is controversy. One important issue is whether unequal ownership persists through time—that is, inherited. If vagaries of weather, theft, and gifts of livestock to relatives make livestock ownership fluctuate over time, wealth differences may mostly be temporary. A second important issue is whether the inequalities in livestock ownership make any difference in the ease of acquiring other "goods," such as prestige and political power. If wealth in livestock is ephemeral and is not associated with differential access to prestige and power, then some anthropologists would characterize such pastoral societies as egalitarian.[5] While some pastoral societies are egalitarian, most are not; in a worldwide cross-cultural sample only about 20 percent of pastoralist societies lack slavery or social classes.[6] And in a recent comparison of four pastoral societies, explicitly measuring transmission of wealth from parents to children, children were very likely to be in higher wealth categories if their parents were.[7] It is easy to imagine how an egalitarian society with some wealth differences, as opposed to one with no wealth differences, could become a rank or a class society. All you would need is a mechanism for retaining more wealth in some families over time.

12.3 ▶ Describe the characteristics of rank societies.

Rank Societies

Most societies with social *ranking* practice agriculture or herding, but not all agricultural or pastoral societies are ranked. Ranking is characterized by social groups with unequal access to prestige or status but *not* significantly unequal access to economic resources or power. Unequal access to prestige is often reflected in the position of chief, a rank which only some members of a specified group in the society can achieve.

Unusual among rank societies were the 19th-century Native Americans who lived along the northwestern coast of the United States and the southwestern coast of Canada; the Nimpkish, a Kwakiutl group, are an example.[8] These societies were unusual because their economy was based on food collecting. But huge catches of salmon—which were preserved for year-round consumption—enabled them to support fairly large and permanent villages. These societies were similar to food-producing societies in many ways, not just in their development of social ranking. Still, the principal means of proving one's high status was to give away wealth. The tribal chiefs celebrated solemn rites by grand feasts called *potlatches*, at which they gave gifts to every guest.[9]

In rank societies, the position of chief is at least partly hereditary. The criterion of superior rank in some Polynesian societies, for example, was genealogical. Usually the eldest son succeeded to the position of chief, and different kinship groups were differentially ranked according to their genealogical distance from the chiefly line. In rank societies, chiefs are often treated with deference by people of lower rank. For example, among the Trobriand Islanders of Melanesia, people of lower rank must keep their heads lower than a person of higher rank. So, when a chief is standing, commoners must bend low. When commoners have to walk past a chief who happens to be sitting, he may rise and they will bend. If the chief chooses to remain seated, they must crawl.[10]

Although there is no question that chiefs in a rank society enjoy special prestige, there is some controversy over whether they really do not also have material advantages. Chiefs may sometimes look as if they are substantially richer than commoners, for they may receive many gifts and have larger storehouses. In some instances, the chief may even be called the "owner" of the land. However, Marshall Sahlins maintains that the chief's storehouses only house temporary accumulations for feasts or other redistributions. And although the chief may be designated the "owner" of the land, others have the right to use the land. Furthermore, Sahlins suggests that the chief in a rank society lacks power because he usually cannot make people give him gifts or force them to work on communal projects. Often the chief can encourage production only by working furiously on his own cultivation.[11]

This picture of economic equality in rank societies has been questioned. Laura Betzig studied patterns of food sharing and labor on Ifaluk, a small atoll in the Western Carolines.[12] Chiefly status is inherited geneaologically in the female line, although most chiefs are male. (In the chapter on sex and gender, we discuss why political leaders are usually male, even in societies structured around women.) As in other chiefly societies, Ifaluk chiefs are accorded deference. For example, during collective meals prepared by all the island women, chiefs were served first and were bowed to. The Ifaluk chiefs are said to control the fishing areas. Were the catches equitably distributed? Betzig measured the amount of fish each household got. All the commoners received an equal share, but the chiefs got extra fish; their households got twice as much per person as other households. Did the chiefs give away more later?

Theoretically, generosity is supposed to even things out, but Betzig found that the gifts from chiefs to other households did not equal the amount the chiefs received from others. Furthermore, although everyone gave to the chiefs, the chiefs gave mostly to their close relatives. On Ifaluk, the chiefs did not work harder than others; in fact, they worked less. Is this true in other societies conventionally considered to be rank societies? We do not know. However, we need to keep in mind that the chiefs in Ifaluk were not noticeably better off either. If they lived in palaces with servants, had elaborate meals, or were

A Tlingit chief (middle left) in his house with his possessions displayed.

dressed in fine clothes and jewelry, we would not need measures of food received or a special study to see if the chiefs had greater access to economic resources, because their wealth would be obvious. But rank societies may not have had as much economic equality as we used to think.

Class Societies

A social **class** is a category of people who all have about the same opportunity to obtain economic resources, power, and prestige. In class societies, groups of people are *stratified*, or divided into levels, according to their degree of access not only to prestige, as in rank societies, but also to wealth and power. Can an individual in a fully stratified society change his or her class affiliation? It depends on how strictly the society observes its class system. And class societies range in strictness from somewhat open systems, to virtually closed, or *caste*, systems.

Open Class Systems

Class systems are called *open* if there is some possibility of moving from one class to another. Since the 1920s, there have been many studies of classes in towns and cities in the United States. Researchers have produced profiles of these different communities—known variously as Yankee City, Middletown, Jonesville, and Old City—all of which support the premise that the United States has distinguishable, though somewhat open, social classes. Both W. Lloyd Warner and Paul Lunt's Yankee City study[13] and Robert and Helen Lynd's Middletown study[14] concluded that the social status or prestige of a family is generally correlated with the occupation and wealth of the head of the family. Class systems are by no means confined to the United States. They are found in all nations of the modern world.

Although class status is not fully determined at birth in open class societies, there is a high probability that most people will stay close to the class into which they were born and will marry within that class. An important way classes perpetuate themselves is through

12.4 ▶ Describe the characteristics of class societies.

Class A category of people who have about the same opportunity to obtain economic resources, power, and prestige.

inheritance. The transfer of money through bequests accounts for a considerable amount of the wealth of the next generation. As we might expect, the importance of inheritance seems to increase at higher levels of wealth. For example, a majority of individuals on the Forbes list of the 400 wealthiest individuals in America inherited at least $50 million each.[15] But inheritance is much more than money and property that is passed on at death. Children of wealthier parents have better access to health care, higher quality food, better schools, and tutors and see more of the world. They learn the "manners" associated with the upper classes and are introduced to others who may help them later on. Other mechanisms of class perpetuation may be more subtle, but they are still powerful. In the United States, many institutions make it possible for an upper-class person to have little contact with other classes. They may live in remote or isolated houses with long driveways out of view protected by complex security. They socialize in private clubs, private resorts, and exclusive parties. Travel may be on private planes or yachts.[16] Children go to private day and boarding schools that put upper-class children in close contact mostly with others of their class. Attending these schools makes it more likely that they will get into universities with higher prestige. Debutante balls and exclusive private parties ensure that young people meet the "right people." Thus, wealthier children are more likely to marry wealthier people when they grow up. Country clubs, exclusive city clubs, and service in particular charities continue the process of limited association. People of the same class also tend to live in the same neighborhoods. Before 1948, explicit restrictions kept certain groups out of particular neighborhoods, but after the U.S. Supreme Court ruled such discrimination unconstitutional, more subtle methods were developed. For instance, town or neighborhood zoning restrictions may prohibit multiple-family dwellings in a town or neighborhood and lots below a certain acreage.[17] The ability to enact zoning restrictions is just a small part of the way the upper class exerts power. The upper class has more power. Their power comes not just from political contributions, but also from holding important positions in government, in corporations, as lobbyists, and in foundations. Knowing other important people helps maintain that power.[18]

In addition to differences in occupation, wealth, and prestige, social classes vary in many other ways, including religious affiliation, closeness to kin, ideas about childrearing, job satisfaction, leisure-time activities, style of clothes and furniture, and (as noted in the chapter on communication and language) even in styles of speech.[19] People from each class tend to be more comfortable with those from the same class; they talk similarly and are more likely to have similar interests and tastes.

Class boundaries, though vague, have been established by custom and tradition; sometimes they have been reinforced by the enactment of laws. Many of our laws serve to protect property and thus tend to favor the upper and upper-middle classes. The poor, in contrast, seem to be disadvantaged in our legal system. The crimes the poor are most likely to commit are dealt with harshly by the courts, and poor people rarely have the money to secure effective legal counsel.

In open class systems, it is not always clear how many classes there are. In Stanley Barrett's study of "Paradise," Ontario, some people thought that there were only two classes in the past. One person said, "There was the hierarchy, and the rest of us." Another said that there were three classes: "The people with money, the in-between, and the ones who didn't have anything." Many said there were four: "The wealthy businessmen, the middle class, blue collar workers, and the guys that were just existing."[20] A few insisted that there were five classes. With the breakdown of the old rigid class structure, there are more people in the middle.[21]

Degree of Openness   Some class systems are more open than others; that is, it is easier in some societies to move from one class position to another. Social scientists typically compare the class of people with the class of their parent or parents to measure the degree of mobility. Although most people aspire to move up, mobility also includes moving down. Obtaining more education, particularly a university education, is one of the most effective ways to move upward in contemporary societies. For example, in the United States, individuals with a college bachelor's degree working full-time average 67 percent more income than those with only a high school diploma. And individuals with professional degrees earn on average 81 percent more than those with a bachelor's degree.[22] And, individuals with higher degrees are much more likely to be employed full-time.[23] In many countries, educational attainment predicts one's social class better than parents' occupation does.[24]

How do the United States and Canada compare with other countries in degree of class mobility? Canada, Finland, and Sweden have more mobility than the United States and Britain. Mexico and Peru have less mobility than the United States and Brazil, and Colombia considerably less.[25]

Class openness also varies over time. In "Paradise," Ontario, Barrett found that the rigid stratification system of the 1950s opened up considerably as new people moved into the community. No one disputed who belonged to the elite in the past. They were of British background, lived in the largest houses, had new cars, and vacationed in Florida. Moreover, they controlled all the leadership positions in the town. By the 1980s, though, the leaders came mostly from the middle and working classes.[26]

Degree of Inequality Degree of class mobility is related to degree of inequality—more unequal societies generally have less mobility from one class to another.[27] However, the two are not exactly the same. For example, Canada has about as much mobility as Norway, but Canada has much more inequality than Norway.[28] Degree of inequality can vary considerably over time. In the United States, inequality has fluctuated considerably from the 1900s to the present. Two of the highest periods of inequality were just before the 1929 stock market crash and just before the recession of 2007, when the top 10 percent had almost 50 percent of all the income in the country. The least inequality was in the mid-1970s, after the stock market declined by 42 percent. Then the top 10 percent controlled about 33 percent of the income. Except for declines during recessions after the 1970s, inequality has generally increased—the United States now has more inequality than any rich nation on earth.[29]

Homeless children in Recife, Brazil.

Change over time in the degree of inequality sometimes appears to have economic causes; for example, the 1929 crash made the wealthy less wealthy. But some of the change over time is due to shifts in public policy. During the New Deal of the 1930s, tax changes and work programs shifted more income to ordinary people; in the 1980s, tax cuts for the wealthy helped the rich get richer and they have continued to get richer.[30]

One way of measuring inequality is by the Gini coefficient, a number that ranges from a possible 0 score, where everyone has the same income, to 100, where one person has all the income and everyone else has nothing. Although neither 0 nor 100 actually occur, the coefficient gives us a way to compare inequality over time or countries. The spread of Gini coefficients shown in Figure 12.1 for selected countries ranges from a low of 25.8 for Norway and a high of 59.5 for Haiti. The Caribbean and Latin American region has the highest level of inequality than any world region.[31] The United States has more inequality than countries in Europe and even more than Indonesia and India. But we have to keep in mind that inequality is relative. It is possible for a person at the bottom of a country's income level to still be better off than most people from another country. For example, India and the United States do not differ much in terms of income inequality, but the United States is much richer as a country. Most of the poor people in the United States actually have higher purchasing power than 97 percent of the people in India.[32]

Recognition of Class

Societies that have open class systems vary in the degree to which members of the society recognize that there are classes, albeit somewhat open classes. The United States is unusual in that, despite objective evidence of multiple social classes, many people deny their existence. The ideology that hard work and strong character can transform anyone into a success appears to be so powerful that it masks the realities of social inequality.[33] When we were

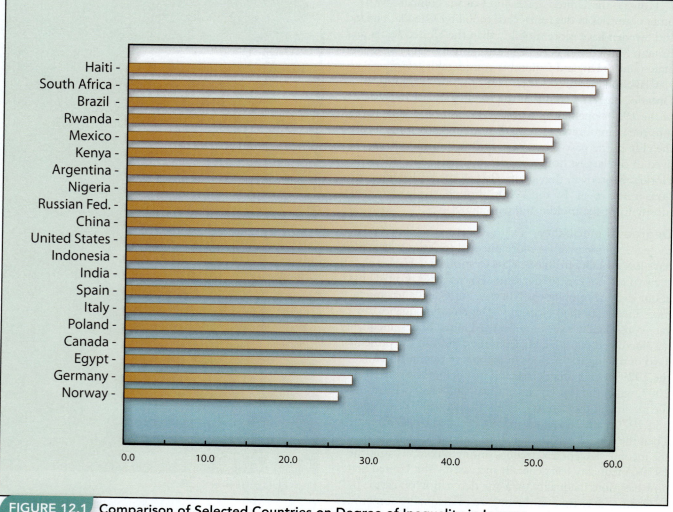

FIGURE 12.1 Comparison of Selected Countries on Degree of Inequality in Income.

The countries are ordered by their Gini coefficients, a widely used measure of degree of income inequality. Hypothetically, a country where everyone has the same income would get a 0 score; a country where all the income goes to one person would get a score of 100.

Source: These data are abstracted from the U.N. Human Development Report 2011. Table 3.

growing up, we were told that "anyone can be President of the United States." As "proof," people pointed to a few individuals who rose from humble beginnings. But consider the odds. How many presidents have come from poor families? How many were not European in background? How many were not Protestant? (And, how many were not male?) As of 2014, almost all of the presidents of the United States have been mainly European in ancestry, all but one have been Protestant, and all have been male. And only a handful came from humble beginnings. The paradox of an open class system is that, to move up in the social ladder, people seem to have to believe that it is possible to do so. However, it is one thing to believe in mobility; it is another thing to deny the existence of classes. Why might people need to deny that classes exist?

Caste Systems

Caste A ranked group, often associated with a certain occupation, in which membership is determined at birth and marriage is restricted to members of one's own caste.

Some societies have classes (called castes) that are virtually closed. A **caste** is a ranked group in which membership is determined at birth, and marriage is restricted to members of one's own caste. The only way you can belong is by being born into the group; and because you cannot marry outside the group, your children cannot acquire another caste status either. In India, for example, there are several thousand hereditary castes. Although the precise ranking of these thousands of groups is not clear, there appear to be four main levels of hierarchy. The castes in India are often thought to be associated with different occupations, but that is not quite true. Most Indians live in rural areas and have agricultural occupations, but their castes vary widely.[34]

Castes may exist in conjunction with a more open class system. Indeed, in India today, members of a low caste who can get wage-paying jobs, chiefly those in urban areas, may improve their social standing in the same ways available to people in other class societies. In general, however, they still cannot marry someone in a higher caste, so the caste system is perpetuated.

Questions basic to all stratified societies, and particularly to a caste society, were posed by John Ruskin, a 19th-century British essayist: "Which of us . . . is to do the hard and dirty work for the rest—and for what pay? Who is to do the pleasant and clean work, and for what pay?"[35] In India, those questions have been answered by the caste system, which mainly dictates how goods and services are exchanged, particularly in rural areas.[36] Who is to do the hard and dirty work for the rest of society is clearly established: A large group of Untouchables forms the bottom of the hierarchy. Among the Untouchables are subcastes such as the Camars, or leatherworkers, and the Bhangis, who traditionally are sweepers. At the top of the hierarchy, performing the pleasant and clean work of priests, are the Brahmans. Between the two extremes are thousands of castes and subcastes.[37] In a typical village, a potter makes clay drinking cups and large water vessels for the entire village population. In return, the principal landowner gives him a house site and supplies him twice yearly with grain. Some other castes owe the potter their services: The barber cuts his hair; the sweeper carries away his rubbish; the washer washes his clothes; the Brahman performs his children's weddings. The barber serves every caste in the village except the Untouchables; he, in turn, is served by half of the others. He has inherited the families he works for, along with his father's occupation. All castes help at harvest and at weddings for additional payment, which sometimes includes a money payment.

This description is, in fact, an idealized picture of the caste system of India. In reality, the system operates to the advantage of the principal landowning caste—sometimes the Brahmans and sometimes other castes. Also, it is not carried on without some resentment; signs of hostility are shown toward the ruling caste by the Untouchables and other lower castes. The resentment does not appear to be against the caste system as such. Instead, the lower castes exhibit bitterness at their own low status and strive for greater equality. For instance, one of the Camars' traditional services is to remove dead cattle; in return, they can have the meat to eat and the hide to tan for their leatherworking. Because handling dead animals and eating beef are regarded as unclean acts, the Camars of one village refused to continue this service. Thus, they lost a source of free hides and food in a vain attempt to escape unclean status.

A Brahman woman in front of her house in Jodhpur, India

Since World War II, the economic basis of the caste system in India has been undermined somewhat by the growing practice of giving cash payment for services. For instance, the son of a barber may be a teacher during the week, earning a cash salary, and confine his haircutting to weekends. But he still remains in the barber caste (Nai) and must marry within that caste.

Perpetuation of the caste system is ensured by the power of those in the upper castes, who derive three main advantages from their position: economic, prestige, and sexual gains. The economic gain is the most immediately apparent. An ample supply of cheap labor and free services is maintained by the threat of sanctions. Lower-caste members may have their use of a house site withdrawn; they may be refused access to the village well or to common grazing land for animals; or they may be expelled from the village. Prestige is also maintained by the threat of sanctions; people in the higher castes expect deference and servility from those in the lower castes. The sexual gain is less apparent but equally real. The high-caste male has access to two groups of females, those of his own caste and those of lower castes. High-caste females are kept free of the "contaminating" touch of low-caste males because low-caste males are allowed access only to low-caste women. Moreover, the constant reminders of ritual uncleanness serve to keep those of the lower castes "in their place." People in higher castes do not accept water from Untouchables, sit next to them, or eat at the same table with them.

Japan also had a caste group within a class society. Now called *burakumin*, this group traditionally had occupations that were considered unclean.[38] They were a hereditary, endogamous (in-marrying) group. Their occupations were traditionally those of farm laborer, leatherworker, and basket weaver; their standard of living was very low. The burakumin are physically indistinguishable from other Japanese.[39] Despite that, the burakumin were considered a separate "race" by some for centuries.[40] The Japanese government officially abolished discrimination against the burakumin in 1871, but the burakumin did not begin organizing to bring about change until the 20th century. Some conditions have changed. As of 1995, 73 percent of burakumin marriages were with non-burakumin and in public opinion polls, two-thirds of burakumin said that they had not encountered discrimination. However, some burakumin still live in segregated neighborhoods, where unemployment, crime, and alcoholism rates are high.[41]

In a considerable number of sub-Saharan African societies, some occupational specialties are only performed by certain castes. The specialties usually involve metalworking, pottery, woodworking, leatherworking, playing musical instruments, and praise-singing. There may be different castes for different specialties or one caste for many specialties. In some cases, the caste consists of people who traditionally hunted and gathered. In almost all cases, the specialists had to marry within their own group and their social position was inherited. These castes usually constituted only a small minority of the society's population and were not the lowest ranking groups in society. Only slaves had a lower rank. Some of the castes took on additional tasks, such as go-betweens for arranging marriages, messengers, and circumcisers. The caste vocational distinctions have weakened in recent times as people have become more educated.[42]

In Rwanda, long before the ethnic division arose between the Hutu and Tutsi (see discussion later in the ethnicity section), the Twa, who comprised less than 1 percent of the population, were subject to serious discrimination. Their bodies were viewed as dangerous and polluting and they were avoided whenever possible. For example, if a Twa were present while others were eating or drinking, separate utensils were reserved only for Twa. The Twa traditional occupations were foraging, making pottery, entertaining, and serving as torturers or executioners for the Rwandan king. Mutton was considered a Twa food and other Rwandans would not eat mutton.[43]

In the United States, African Americans used to have more of a caste-like status determined partly by the inherited characteristic of skin color. Until recently, some states had laws prohibiting an African American from marrying a European American. When interethnic marriage did occur, children of the union were often regarded as having lower status than European American children, even though they may have had blond hair and light skin. In the South, where treatment of African Americans as a caste was most apparent, European Americans refused to eat with African Americans or sit next to them at lunch counters, on buses, and in schools. Separate drinking fountains and toilets reinforced the idea of ritual uncleanness. The economic advantages and gains in prestige that European Americans enjoyed are well documented.[44] In the following sections on slavery, racism, and inequality, we discuss the social status of African Americans in more detail.

Current Research and Issues

Global Inequality

When people support themselves by what they collect and produce themselves, as most people did until a few thousand years ago, there wasn't that much difference in economic wealth. In fact, it is difficult to compare the standards of living of subsistence-level societies because we cannot translate what people have into market or monetary value. Only where people are at least partly involved in the world market economy can we measure the standard of living in monetary terms. Today, this comparison is possible for most of the world. Many people in most societies depend on buying and selling for a living; and the more people who depend on international exchange, the more possible it is to compare them in terms of standard economic indicators. We do not have such indicators for all the different societies in the world, but we do have them for many countries. Since goods and services cost different amounts in different places, economists have had to adjust to one standard (usually the U.S. dollar is used as a standard). So, for example, if a person in China can buy 2½ times the stuff that an American can for the same money equivalent, the per capita gross domestic product for China is adjusted upward by that amount. How do countries compare to each other and how has it changed over time?

Scholars estimate that the wealth gap between countries of the world has grown enormously since the Industrial Revolution. In 1830 Britain and the Netherlands were the richest countries, but they were only three times richer than some of the poorest countries. (India and China were among the poorest countries then.) As of 2010, the ratio between the richest and poorest countries is about 100 to 1. Countries like India and China have improved their economic picture considerably, but overall, the gap between rich and poor countries continues to widen. Branko Milanovic compares the Industrial Revolution to the "Big Bang" of the

These high-rise buildings in Shanghai, China indicate how much China's economy has grown, but in general the gap between developed and developing countries has widened considerably.

universe with the countries getting further apart.

If the world as a whole is seeing improvements in technology and economic development, why is the gap between the rich and poor countries increasing? Most theorists did not expect this to happen. Rather, they expected that with globalization, rich countries would invest in poorer countries, technology could be borrowed, and countries would specialize in what they do best. But although some of this happened in the past, for example between 1870 and 1914, this has not happened recently. In fact, rich nations invest more in rich nations. Money actually flows from poorer countries to the rich as the wealthiest in those countries invest abroad for security. Part of the explanation may be similar to why the rich within a society benefit most from new technology, at least initially. The rich are not only the most likely to be able to afford new technology, they also are the only ones who can afford to take the risks that it involves. The same may be true for nations. Those that already

have capital are more likely to take advantage of improvements in technology. In addition, the poorer countries generally have the highest rates of population growth, so income per capita can fall if population increases faster than the rate of economic development.

If it is true that the disparity between rich and poor countries has increased in recent years, it is also true that the world has seen improvement in some other respects—people are healthier, more educated, live longer, and can buy more goods and services. The United Nations has computed a human development index for many countries, combining measures of life expectancy, literacy, and a measure of per capita purchasing power. According to this index, almost all countries have improved between 1970 and 2010. A quarter of the countries have improved more than 65 percent. Much more will remain to be done if we are to achieve a more equal world.

Sources: United Nations Development Programme 2010; Milanovic 2011.

Slavery

Slavery is difficult to define because slavery systems and the treatment of slaves varied enormously.[45] A definition therefore needs to focus on what is common to slavery systems and to slaves. A common definition of **slaves** is that they are people who do not own their own labor, and as such they represent a class. We may associate slavery with a few well-known examples, such as ancient Egypt, Greece, and Rome or the southern United States, but the practice of enslaving people has existed at some point in time in almost every part of the world at one time or another, in simpler as well as in more complex societies. Slaves are often obtained from other cultures directly; they are kidnapped, captured in war, or given as tribute. Or they may be obtained indirectly through barter or trade. Slaves have sometimes come from the same culture; people have become slaves to repay a debt, as punishment for a crime, or even because it was an alternative to poverty. The degree to which slaves can gain their freedom varies among slave societies.[46] Sometimes slavery has been a closed class, or caste, system; sometimes it has been a relatively open class system. While the legal rights of slaves have also differed, all slave-owning societies have granted them some legal or customary rights.[47]

The slaves in ancient Greece were often conquered enemies. Because city-states were constantly conquering one another or rebelling against former conquerors, anyone could be enslaved. After the Trojan War, the transition of Hecuba from queen to slave was marked by her cry, "Count no one happy, however fortunate, before he dies."[48] Nevertheless, Greek slaves were considered human beings, and they could even acquire some higher-class status along with freedom. Andromache, Hecuba's daughter-in-law, was taken as a slave and concubine by one of the Greek heroes. When his legal wife produced no children, Andromache's slave son became heir to his father's throne. Although slaves had no rights under law, once they were freed, either by the will of their master or by purchase, they and their descendants could become assimilated into the dominant group. In other words, slavery in Greece was not seen as the justified position of inferior people. It was regarded, rather, as an act of fate—"the luck of the draw"—that relegated one to the lowest class in society.

Among the Nupe, a society in central Nigeria, slavery was of quite another type.[49] The methods of obtaining slaves—as part of the booty of warfare and, later, by purchase—were similar to those of Europeans, but the position of the slaves was very different. Mistreatment was rare. Male slaves were given the same opportunities to earn money as other dependent males in the household—younger brothers, sons, or other relatives. A slave might be given a garden plot of his own to cultivate, or he might be given a commission if his master was a craftsman or a tradesman. Slaves could acquire property, wealth, and even slaves of their own. But all of a slave's belongings went to the master at the slave's death.

Manumission—the granting of freedom to slaves—was built into the Nupe system. If a male slave could afford the marriage payment for a free woman, the children of the resulting marriage were free; the man himself, however, remained a slave. Marriage and concubinage were the easiest ways out of bondage for a slave woman. Once she had produced a child by her master, both she and the child had free status. The woman, however, was only figuratively free; if a concubine, she had to remain in that role. As might be expected, the family trees of the nobility and the wealthy were liberally grafted with branches descended from slave concubines.

The most fortunate slaves among the Nupe were the house slaves. They could rise to positions of power in the household as overseers and bailiffs, charged with law enforcement and judicial duties. (Recall the Old Testament story of Joseph, who was sold into slavery by his brothers. Joseph became a household slave of the pharaoh and rose to the position of second in the kingdom because he devised an ingenious system of taxation.) There was even a titled group of Nupe slaves, the Order of Court Slaves, who were trusted officers of the king and members of an elite. Slave status in general, though, placed one at the bottom of the social ladder. In the Nupe system, few slaves, mainly princes from their own societies, ever achieved membership in the titled group. Nupe slavery was abolished at the beginning of the 20th century.

In the United States, slavery originated as a means of obtaining cheap labor, but the slaves soon came to be regarded as deserving of their low status because of their alleged inherent inferiority. Because the slaves were from Africa and were dark-skinned, some European

Slaves A class of people who do not own their own labor or the products thereof.

Manumission The granting of freedom to a slave.

Americans justified slavery and the belief in "black" people's inferiority by quoting scripture out of context ("They shall be hewers of wood and drawers of water."). Slaves could not marry or make any other contracts, nor could they own property. In addition, their children were also slaves, and the master had sexual rights over the female slaves. Because the status of slavery was determined by birth in the United States, slaves constituted a caste. During the days of slavery, therefore, the United States had both a caste and a class system. It is widely assumed that slavery occurred only in the southern United States, but slavery existed in the northern states as well, although not on as large a scale. New Jersey was the last northern state to legally give up slavery, around the time of the U.S. Civil War.[50]

Even after the abolition of slavery, as we have noted, some castelike elements remained. It is important to note that these castelike elements were not limited to the American South, where slavery had been practiced. For example, although Indiana was established as a "free" state in 1816, in its first constitution, "negros" did not have the right to vote, nor could they intermarry with "whites." In the constitution of 1851, Indiana did not allow "negros" to come into the state, nor did it allow the existing African American residents to attend public schools even though they had to pay school taxes.[51] In Muncie, Indiana, in the first half of the 20th century, there was customary segregation in shows, restaurants, and parks. Not until the 1950s was the public swimming pool desegregated.[52]

As for why slavery may have developed in the first place, cross-cultural research is as yet inconclusive. We do know, however, that slavery is not an inevitable stage in economic development, contrary to what some have assumed. In other words, slavery is not found mainly in certain economies, such as those dependent on intensive agriculture. Unlike the United States until the Civil War, many societies with intensive agriculture did not develop any variety of slavery. Also, the hypothesis that slavery develops where available resources are plentiful but labor is scarce is not supported by the cross-cultural evidence. All we can say definitely is that slavery does not occur in developed or industrial economies; either it disappears or it was never present in them.[53]

Racism and Inequality

Racism is the belief that some "races" are inferior to others. In a society composed of people with noticeably different physical features, such as differences in skin color, racism is almost invariably associated with social stratification. Those "races" considered inferior make up a larger proportion of the lower social classes or castes. Even in more open class systems, where individuals from all backgrounds can achieve higher status positions, individuals from groups deemed inferior may be subject to discrimination in housing or may be more likely to be searched or stopped by the police.

In some societies, such as the United States, the idea that humans are divided into "races" is taken so much for granted that people are asked for their "race" on the census. Most Americans probably assume that the classification of people into categories such as "white" or "black" reflects important biological categories. But that is not so. You may have noticed that we put "race" in quotes to reflect the fact that most anthropologists are now persuaded that the biological concept of "race" is not scientifically useful when applied to humans. To understand why, we will briefly discuss how the construct of race is used in biology.

Race as a Construct in Biology

Biological variation is not uniformly distributed in any species. While all members of a species can potentially interbreed with others, most matings take place within smaller groups or breeding populations. Through time, populations inhabiting different geographic regions will come to exhibit some differences in biological traits. When differences within a species become sufficiently noticeable, biologists may classify different populations into different *varieties*, or *races*. If the term **race** is understood to be just a shorthand or classificatory way that biologists describe slight population variants within a species, the concept of race would probably not be controversial as applied to humans. Humans have exhibited so much interbreeding that different populations are not clearly classifiable into

12.5 Discuss how racism and inequality are related.

Racism The belief, without scientific basis, that some "races" are inferior to others.

Race In biology, race refers to a subpopulation or variety of a species that differs somewhat in gene frequencies from other varieties of the species. Many anthropologists do not think that the concept of race is usefully applied to humans because humans do not fall into geographic populations that can be easily distinguished in terms of different sets of biological or physical traits. Thus, race in humans is largely a culturally assigned category.

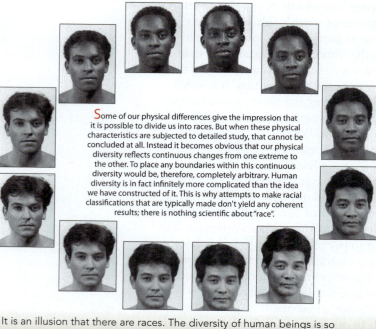

Some of our physical differences give the impression that it is possible to divide us into races. But when these physical characteristics are subjected to detailed study, that cannot be concluded at all. Instead it becomes obvious that our physical diversity reflects continuous changes from one extreme to the other. To place any boundaries within this continuous diversity would be, therefore, completely arbitrary. Human diversity is in fact infinitely more complicated than the idea we have constructed of it. This is why attempts to make racial classifications that are typically made don't yield any coherent results; there is nothing scientific about "race".

It is an illusion that there are races. The diversity of human beings is so great and so complicated that it is impossible to classify the 5.8 billions of individuals into discrete "races."

discrete groups that can be defined in terms of the presence or absence of particular biological traits.[54] The difficulty in employing racial classification is evident by comparing the number of "races" that classifiers come up with. The number of "racial" categories in humans has varied from as few as 3 to more than 37.[55] If different classifiers come up with different "races," there obviously are no clear lines of difference. Perhaps this is because most adaptive biological traits show clines or gradual differences from one region to another.[56] Skin color is a good example of clinal variation. In the area around Egypt, there is a gradient of skin color as one moves from north to south in the Nile Valley. Skin generally becomes darker closer to the equator (south) and lighter closer to the Mediterranean (north). But other adaptive traits may not have north-south clines, because the environmental predictors may be distributed differently. Nose shape varies with humidity, but clines in humidity do not particularly correspond to variation in latitude. So the gradient for skin color would not be the same as the gradient for nose shape. Because adaptive traits tend to be clinally distributed, there is no line you could draw on a world map that would separate "white" from "black" people or "whites" from "Asians."[57]

Racial classification is problematic also because there is sometimes more physical, physiological, and genetic diversity *within* a single geographic group that might be called a "race" (e.g., Africans) than there is *between* supposed "racial" groups. Africans vary more among themselves than they do in comparison with people elsewhere.[58] The genetic diversity within Africa is consistent with the fossil evidence that the African continent is where both early humans and modern humans emerged. This is as you may remember, parallel to linguistic diversity—English developed in England, and there we find the most dialect diversity. Modern humans emerged first in Africa, so it is accurate to say that we are all African, and members of the "human race."

Analyses of all human populations have demonstrated that 93–95% of genetic variation is due to individual differences within populations, while only 3–5% of genetic variation is due to differences between major human population groups.[59]

Race as a Social Category

If physical anthropologists tell us that "race" is not a meaningful construct to apply to humans, how come so many people "see" different races? Jonathan Marks points out that even children can readily sort things into categories, such as putting assorted size blocks into a "large" pile and a "small" pile. When they do this, they will mostly agree with other children about which are largest and which are smallest. But that doesn't mean that there are two types of blocks in the world—large and small. People find it easy to sort by skin color, but that will put people from India, who can be quite dark in skin color, with some people from Africa.[60]

Racial classifications are social categories to which individuals are assigned, by themselves and others, to separate "our" group from others. We have seen that people tend to be *ethnocentric*, to view their culture as better than other cultures. Racial classifications may reflect the same tendency to divide "us" from "them," except that the divisions are supposedly based on biological differences.[61] The "them" are almost always viewed as inferior to "us."

We know that racial classifications have often been, and still are, used by certain groups to justify discrimination, exploitation, or genocide. The "Aryan race" was supposed to be the group of blond-haired, blue-eyed, white-skinned people whom Adolf Hitler wanted to dominate the world, to which end he and others attempted to destroy as many members of the Jewish "race" as they could. (An estimated 6 million Jews and others were murdered in what is now called the Holocaust.[62]) But who were the Aryans? Technically, Aryans are any people, including the German-speaking Jews in Hitler's Germany, who speak one of the Indo-European languages. The Indo-European languages include such disparate modern tongues as Greek, Spanish, Hindi, Polish, French, Icelandic, German, Gaelic, and English. And many Aryans speaking these languages have neither blond hair nor blue eyes. Similarly, all kinds of people may be Jews, whether or not they descend from

Applied Anthropology

Unequal in Death: African Americans Compared with European Americans

Everyone dies of something. Yet, if you consider cardiovascular disease, the leading cause of death in the United States, it turns out that after controlling for the effects of age and gender, African Americans die more often from that disease than European Americans. The same kind of disparity occurs also with almost every other major cause of death—cancer, cirrhosis of the liver, kidney disease, diabetes, injuries, infant mortality, and homicide. Medical anthropologists and health policy researchers want to know why. Without such understanding, it is hard to know how to reduce the disparity.

One reason may be subtle discrimination by the medical profession itself. For example, a European American with chest pain in the United States is more likely than an African American to be given an angiogram, an expensive medical procedure that looks for deficits in blood flow through the coronary arteries that supply blood to the heart. And even if coronary heart disease is detected by an angiogram, an African American is less likely to receive bypass surgery. Thus, the death rate from cardiovascular disease may be higher for African Americans than for European Americans because of unequal medical care. Seeing a patient physically appears to make a difference. When heart specialists reviewed cases to make decisions about subsequent treatment after catheterization, recommendations did not differ by "race" when the doctors did not know the "race" of the patient.

Yet, although some difference in mortality may be due to disparity in

medical treatment, this could only be part of the picture. African Americans may be more prone to cardiovascular disease because they are about twice as likely as European Americans to have high rates of hypertension (high blood pressure). But, why the disparity in hypertension? There is little reason to think that genetic influences are at play. First, there are very large differences in hypertension among populations of African ancestry. In one comparative study of hypertension, African Americans had much higher blood pressure than Africans in Nigeria and Cameroon, even in urban areas. People with African ancestry in the Caribbean were in the middle of the range. Lifestyle differences were also vast—the West Africans had plenty of exercise, were lean, and ate low-fat and low-salt diets. Any possible difference in genes would seem to be insignificant. A theory that has become popular suggests that enslaved individuals who could retain salt would have been most likely to survive the terrible conditions of slavery and slave voyages. If this theory were correct, it might suggest why African Americans have higher blood pressure than other people of African descent. But there is little evidence to support this theory. Critics suggest that salt-depleting diseases were not the leading causes of death in the slave voyages; tuberculosis and violence were more frequent causes of death. Furthermore, the slave ship theory would predict little genetic diversity in African American populations with respect to hypertension, but in fact there is great diversity.

Hypertension could be related also to differences in lifestyle and wealth. As we noted in the section on racism and inequality, African Americans in the United States are disproportionately poorer. Study after study has noted that healthier lifestyle habits are generally correlated with higher positions on the socioeconomic ladder. Moreover, individuals from higher social positions are more likely to have health insurance and access to care in superior hospitals. But even after correcting for factors such as obesity, physical activity, and social class, the health differential persists—African Americans still have a much higher incidence of hypertension than European Americans.

William Dressler suggests that stress is another possible cause of higher rates of hypertension. Despite increased economic mobility in recent years, African Americans are still subject to prejudice and may consequently have more stress even if they have higher income. Stress is related to higher blood pressure. In a color-conscious society, a very dark-skinned individual walking in a wealthy neighborhood may be thought not to live there and may be stopped by the police. If Dressler is correct, darker-skinned African Americans who have objective indicators of higher status should have much higher blood pressure than would be expected from their relative education, age, body mass, or social class alone. And that seems to be true. Racism may affect health.

Sources: Smedley et al. 2003, 3; Geiger 2003; Dressler 1993; Cooper et al. 1999, 56–63; Dressler et al. 2005; Hoberman 2012.

the ancient Near Eastern population that spoke the Hebrew language. There are light-skinned Danish Jews and darker Jewish Arabs. One of the most orthodox Jewish groups in the United States is based in New York City and is composed entirely of African Americans.

The arbitrary and social basis of most racial classifications becomes apparent when you compare how they differ from one place to another. Consider, for example, what used to be thought about the "races" in South Africa. Under apartheid, which was a system of racial segregation and discrimination, someone with mixed "white" and "black" ancestry was considered "colored." However, when important people of African ancestry (from other countries) would visit South Africa, they were often considered "white." Chinese were considered "Asian"; but the Japanese, who were important economically to South Africa, were considered "white."[63] In some parts of the United States, laws against interracial marriage continued in force through the 1960s. You would be considered a "negro" if you had an eighth or more "negro" ancestry (if one or more of your eight grandparents were "negro").[64] In some states, an even smaller proportion made you "negro." Some refer to this concept as the "one-drop" rule—just a tiny bit of "negro" (now called "black") ancestry was sufficient to determine your "racial" classification.[65] So only a small amount of "negro" ancestry made a person "negro." But a small amount of "white" ancestry did not make a person "white." Biologically speaking, this makes no sense, but socially it was another story.[66]

In much of Latin America and the Caribbean, the reverse rule is the case. A small amount of European blood can make you "white." When people from Dominica, Haiti, or Cuba come to the United States, they often find that their "race" has changed. They might have been considered "white" at home, but they are considered "black" in the United States. In contrast to the United States, with a two-part division of "white" and "black," concepts of race in Latin America are on more of a continuum from light to dark, with important middle positions (such as "mestizo"). Wealth makes a difference too—if you are dark-skinned, but wealthy, you will tend to be considered "whiter."[67]

If people of different "races" are viewed as inferior, they are more likely going to end up on the lower rungs of the social ladder in a socially stratified society. Discrimination will keep them out of the better-paying or higher-status jobs and in neighborhoods that are poorer with underperforming schools. One recent study sent résumés for jobs with randomly assigned "white" sounding names or "black" sounding names.[68] The "white" résumé yielded many more callbacks, equivalent to eight more years of experience. As the box "Unequal in Death" shows, people of different "races" also suffer from differential access to health care and have more health problems.

Ethnicity and Inequality

12.6 ▶ Explain the relationship between ethnicity and inequality.

If "race" is not a scientifically useful category because people cannot be clearly divided into different "racial" categories based on sets of physical traits, then racial classifications such as "black" and "white" in the United States might better be described as *ethnic* classifications. How else can we account for the following facts? Groups that are thought of as belonging to the same "race" now in the United States were earlier thought of as belonging to inferior "races." For example, in the latter half of the 19th century, newspapers would often talk about the new immigrants from Ireland as belonging to the Irish "race." At the turn of the century, Italians, with their "swarthy" skin were considered another "race." Before World War II, Jews were thought of as a separate "racial" group, and only became "white" afterward.[69] It is hard to escape the idea that changes in "racial" classification occurred as the Irish, Italians, Jews, and other immigrant groups became more accepted by the majority in the United States.[70]

It is apparent that *ethnic groups* and *ethnic identities* emerge as part of a social and political process. The process of defining **ethnicity** usually involves a group of people emphasizing common origins and language, shared history, and selected cultural differences such as a difference in religion. Those doing the defining can be outside or inside the ethnic group. Outsiders and insiders often perceive ethnic groups differently. In a country with one large core majority group, often the majority group doesn't think of

Ethnicity The process of defining ethnicity usually involves a group of people emphasizing common origins and language, shared history, and selected aspects of cultural difference such as a difference in religion. Because different groups are doing the perceiving, ethnic identities often vary with whether one is inside or outside the group.

itself as an ethnic group. Rather, they consider only the minority groups to have ethnic identities. For example, in the United States, it is not common for the majority to call themselves European Americans, but other groups may be called African Americans, Asian Americans, or Native Americans. The minority groups, on the other hand, may also have different named identities.[71] Asian Americans may identify themselves more specifically as Japanese Americans, Korean Americans, Chinese Americans, or Hmong. The majority population often uses derogatory names to identify people who are different. The majority may also tend to lump people of diverse ethnicities together. Naming a group establishes a boundary between it and other ethnic groups.[72]

Ethnic differences can sometimes arise from class differences. Rwanda is a good case in point. By the end of the 19th century, Rwandans were part of a kingdom with significant class distinctions, but the distinctions between Hutu and Tutsi, so important in recent times, were not very important or clear.[73] Cattle were an important form of wealth and, although many people known as Tutsi were cattle herders and many known as Hutu were agriculturalists, many Tutsi and Hutu were both. If Hutu acquired wealth and intermarried with Tutsi, they could move up in rank. A Tutsi could lose cattle and turn to cultivation.[74] Colonialism did not create differentiation between Tutsi and Hutu, but it did accentuate it. For example, the Belgian administration tried to reinforce the power of the "natural rulers" (the Tutsi), and they issued identity cards in the 1930s to distinguish Tutsi, Hutu, and Twa (the Twa were discussed earlier in the caste section). During the colonial period, the idea developed that the three groups were biologically different from each other. It was commonly thought that the taller Tutsi were different people who originally conquered the others.[75]

When the Hutu united to demand more of the rewards of their labor in 1959, the king and many of the Tutsi ruling elite were driven out of the country. The Hutu then established a republican form of government and declared independence from Belgium in 1962. In 1990, Tutsi rebels invaded from Uganda, and attempts were made to negotiate a multiparty government. However, civil war continued, and in 1994 alone, over a million people, mostly Tutsi, were killed. Almost 2 million refugees, mostly Hutu, fled to Zaire as the Tutsi-led rebels established a new government.[76] In the intervening years, the Rwandan government has made progress in bringing home the refugees, bringing those who committed genocide to trial, and integrating different groups into the government.[77]

Ethnic identity may be manipulated, by insiders and by outsiders, in different situations. A particularly repressive regime that emphasizes nationalism and loyalty to the state may not only suppress the assertiveness of ethnic claims; it may also act to minimize communication among people who might otherwise embrace the same ethnic identity.[78] More democratic regimes may allow more expression of difference and celebrate ethnic difference. However, manipulation of ethnicity does not come just from the top. It may be to the advantage of minority groups to lobby for more equal treatment as a larger entity, such as Asian American, rather than as Japanese, Chinese, Hmong, Filipino, or Korean American. Similarly, even though there are hundreds of Native American groups, originally speaking different languages, there may be political advantages for all if they are treated as Native Americans.

Cuba is a very multiethnic country and has had a lot of intermarriage between diverse groups. A Cuban woman in Havana.

In many multiethnic societies, ethnicity and diversity are things to be proud of and celebrated. Shared ethnic identity often makes people feel comfortable with similar people and gives them a strong sense of belonging. Still, ethnic differences in multiethnic societies are usually associated with inequities in wealth, power, and prestige. In other words, ethnicity is part of the system of *stratification*.

Although some people believe that inequities are deserved, the origins of ethnic stereotypes, prejudice, and discrimination usually follow from historical and political events that give some groups dominance over others. For example, even though there were many early stories of help given by native peoples to the English settlers in the 17th century in the land now known as North America, the English were the invaders, and negative stereotypes about native peoples developed to justify taking their land and their lives. Referring to the negative stereotypes of Native Americans that developed, J. Milton Yinger said, "One would almost think that it had been the Indian who had invaded Europe, driven back the inhabitants, cut their population to one-third of its original size, unilaterally changed treaties, and brought the dubious glories of firewater and firearms."[79]

Similarly, as we noted in the section on slavery, African slaves were initially acquired as cheap labor, but inhumane treatment of slaves was justified by beliefs about their inferiority. Unfortunately, stereotypes can become self-fulfilling prophesies, especially if those discriminated against come to believe the stereotypes. It is easy to see how this can happen. If there is a widespread belief that a group is inferior, and that group is given inferior schools and little chance for improvement or little chance for a good job, the members of that group may acquire few skills and not try hard. The result is often a vicious cycle.[80]

And yet, the picture is not all bleak. Change has occurred. The ethnic identity a minority group forges can help promote political activism, such as the nonviolent civil rights movement in the United States in the 1960s. That activism, helped by some people in the more advantaged groups, helped break down many of the legal barriers and segregationist practices that reinforced inequality.

The traditional barriers in the United States have mostly been lifted in recent years, but the "color line" has not disappeared. African Americans are found in all social classes, but they remain underrepresented in the wealthiest group and overrepresented at the bottom. Discrimination may be lessened, but it is still not gone. Thus, African Americans may have to be better than others to get promoted, or it may be assumed that they got ahead just because they were African American and were hired because of affirmative action programs. European Americans often expect African Americans to be "ambassadors," to be called on mainly for knowledge about how to handle situations involving other African Americans. African Americans may work with others, but they usually go home to African American neighborhoods. Or they may live in mixed neighborhoods and experience considerable isolation. Few African Americans can completely avoid the anguish of racism.[81]

12.7 Discuss the emergence of stratification.

The Emergence of Stratification

Anthropologists are not certain why social stratification developed. Nevertheless, they are reasonably sure that higher levels of stratification emerged relatively recently in human history. Archaeological sites dating before about 8,000 years ago do not show extensive evidence of inequality. Houses do not appear to vary much in size or content, and different communities of the same culture are similar in size and otherwise. Signs of inequality appear first in the Near East, about 2,000 years after agriculture emerged in that region. Inequality in burial suggests inequality in life. Particularly telling are unequal child burials. It is unlikely that children could achieve high status by their own achievements. So, when archaeologists find statues and ornaments only in some children's tombs, as at the 7,500-year-old site of Tell es-Sawwan in Iraq,[82] the grave goods suggest that those children belonged to a higher-ranking family or a higher class.

Another indication that stratification is a relatively recent development in human history is the fact that certain cultural features associated with stratification also developed relatively recently. For example, most societies that depend primarily on agriculture or herding have social classes.[83] Agriculture and herding developed within the past 10,000 years, so we may assume that most food collectors in the distant past lacked social classes. Other recently developed cultural features associated with class stratification include fixed settlements, political integration beyond the community level, the use of money as a medium of exchange, and the presence of at least some full-time specialization.[84]

In 1966, the comparative sociologist Gerhard Lenski suggested that the trend toward increasing inequality since 8,000 years ago was reversing. He argued that inequalities of power and privilege in industrial societies—measured in terms of the concentration of political power and the distribution of income—are less pronounced than inequalities in complex preindustrial societies. Technology in industrialized societies is so complex, he suggested, that those in power are compelled to delegate some authority to subordinates if the system is to work. In addition, a decline in the birth rate in industrialized societies, coupled with the need for skilled labor, has pushed the average wage of workers far above the subsistence level, resulting in greater equality in the distribution of income. Finally, Lenski also suggested that the spread of the democratic ideology, and particularly its acceptance by elites, has significantly broadened the political power of the lower classes.[85] A few studies have tested and supported Lenski's hypothesis that inequality has decreased with industrialization. In general, highly industrialized nations exhibit a lower level of inequality than nations that are only somewhat industrialized.[86] But, as we have seen, even the most industrialized societies may still have an enormous degree of inequality.

Why did social stratification develop in the first place? Some stress the importance of increased productivity resulting in surpluses.[87] Others stress the degree to which wealth can be transmitted across generations.[88] With regard to surpluses, Sahlins suggested that surpluses would result in greater scope and complexity of the distribution system, enhancing the status of chiefs as redistributing agents. Gradually, this would give the chiefs more control over resources and ultimately more power.[89] Lenski, too, argued that production of a surplus is the stimulus in the development of stratification, but he focused primarily on the conflict that arises over control of that surplus. Lenski concluded that the distribution of the surplus will be determined on the basis of power. Thus, inequalities in power promote unequal access to economic resources and simultaneously give rise to inequalities in privilege and prestige.[90] A broader argument is that a surplus may lead to some advantages of one subgroup over another, such as more people to support a stronger military force, or more knowledge that could lead to the development of specialized, productive technology.[91]

The "surplus" theories of Sahlins and Lenski do not really address why people would produce surpluses or why redistributors or leaders will want, or be able, to acquire greater control over resources. Sahlins later amended his theory to suggest the reverse—that leaders may encourage the development of a surplus to enhance their prestige.[92] But even if that were so, prestige enhancement is not the same as wealth enhancement. After all, the redistributors or leaders in many rank societies do not have greater wealth than others, and custom seems to keep things that way. One suggestion is that, as long as followers have mobility, they can vote with their feet by moving away from leaders they do not like. But when people start to make more permanent "investments" in land or technology (e.g., irrigation systems or weirs for fishing), they are more likely to put up with a leader's aggrandizement in exchange for protection.[93] Another suggestion is that access to economic resources becomes unequal only when there is population pressure on resources in rank or chiefdom societies.[94] Such pressure may be what induces redistributors to try to keep more land and other resources for themselves and their families.

Trying to keep resources and ability to keep these resources are two different things. Recently, some scholars have estimated the amount of transmission of resources, including wealth, across generations in 21 societies differing in subsistence. In those societies, horticulturalists and foragers had much less transmission of wealth to the next generation compared to pastoralists and intensive agriculturalists. The researchers noted that the ability to consistently transmit resources to children could be a key to the emergence of inequality—indeed, wealth transmission is a good predictor of inequality.[95] The ability to transmit advantages to offspring generation after generation is essential to stratification. If resources are constantly changing, there is no inherent value of transmitting parcels of land to children. If there aren't enough people to help you defend a valuable parcel, there is no point trying to exclude others. It is only when land begins to have permanent value and a family or kin group can defend it against others that such a group can develop more permanent wealth. Land scarcity and population pressure may also push toward exclusion as people invest in technology to make their land more productive; at the same time, the larger settlements and higher densities of people increase the possibility of having military support.

C. K. Meek offered an example of how population pressure in northern Nigeria may have led to economic stratification. At one time, a tribal member could obtain the right to use land by asking permission of the chief and presenting him with a token gift in recognition of his higher status. But, by 1921, the reduction in the amount of available land had led to a system under which applicants offered the chief large payments for scarce land. As a result of these payments, farms came to be regarded as private property, and differential access to such property became institutionalized.[96]

Future research by archaeologists, sociologists, historians, and anthropologists should provide more understanding of the emergence of social stratification in human societies and how and why it may vary in degree.

Summary and Review

Variation in Degree of Social Inequality

12.1 Discuss the concepts relating to the variation in degree of social inequality.

- Societies vary in the extent to which social groups, as well as individuals, have unequal access to three types of advantages: (1) wealth or economic resources, (2) power, and (3) prestige.

- Economic resources are things that have value in a culture and include land, technology, goods, and money. Power is influence based on the threat of force and is generally related to unequal access to resources. Prestige involves according someone or some group particular respect or honor.

- The three types of society reflect the degree to which different social groups have unequal access to advantages: egalitarian, rank, and class societies.

? How do anthropologists typically distinguish variation in social stratification?

Egalitarian Societies

12.2 Describe the characteristics of egalitarian societies.

- Egalitarian societies contain no social groups with greater or lesser access to economic resources, power,

or prestige; they can be found among forager and horticultural societies.

- In an egalitarian society, some people may be better hunters or more skilled artists than others, but there is still equal access to status positions for people of the same ability, so society is not socially stratified.

- Any prestige gained by one is neither transferable nor inheritable, and there are no groups with appreciably more influence over time. Egalitarian groups depend heavily on sharing, which ensures equal access to economic resources despite differences in acquired prestige.

? How can people in an egalitarian society achieve status?

Rank Societies

12.3 Describe the characteristics of rank societies.

- Rank societies do not have very unequal access to economic resources or to power, but they do contain social groups with unequal access to prestige, often reflected in the position of chief, a rank which only some members of a specified group in the society can achieve.

- Most societies with social ranking practice agriculture or herding, but not all agricultural or pastoral societies are ranked.

- Although chiefs in a rank society enjoy special prestige, there is some controversy over whether they also have material advantages or increased power.

 What are the different anthropological ideas about what advantages chiefs in a rank society actually have?

Class Societies

12.4 ▶ Describe the characteristics of class societies.

- Class systems are found in all countries of the modern world. In class societies, groups of people are stratified according to their degree of access to prestige, economic resources, and power.

- The potential for an individual to change class affiliation varies among class societies. Open class systems allow some possibility of moving from one class to another. Societies with more inequality generally have less mobility from one class to another.

- Classes perpetuate themselves through inheritance, which becomes increasingly important at higher levels of wealth. Other mechanisms of class perpetuation include limited contact between classes and land zoning restrictions.

- Classes vary in terms of religious affiliation, closeness to kin, ideas about childrearing, job satisfaction, leisure-time activities, style of clothes and furniture, and styles of speech.

- Societies that have open class systems vary in the degree to which members of the society recognize that there are classes.

- Some societies have virtually closed classes called castes. A caste is a ranked group into which one is born and in which marriage is restricted to members of one's own caste.

- Slaves are people who do not own their own labor and, as such, represent a class. Practices of enslaving people have existed in almost every part of the world at some point, in simple and in complex societies. All slave-owning societies have granted slaves some type of rights.

 In what ways do slavery systems differ? Why is slavery hard to define?

Racism and Inequality

12.5 ▶ Discuss how racism and inequality are related.

- Racism is the belief that some "races" are inferior to others. Racism is almost invariably associated with social stratification. "Races" make up a larger proportion of lower social classes or castes and can be discriminated against even in open-class systems.

- Biologists use "race" as a shorthand to describe differences within a species that become sufficiently noticeable after populations become separated and develop some distinctive traits. Most anthropologists now agree that the biological concept of "race" is not usefully applied to humans. First, humans have had considerable interbreeding across geographical regions. Second, adaptive traits tend to be clinally distributed, so no clear geographic line separates groups.

- Racial classification is problematic because there can be more physical, physiological, and genetic diversity *within* a single geographic "racial" group than there is *between* supposed "racial" groups.

- Racial classifications are social categories to which individuals are assigned to separate one's own group from others based on biological differences. People tend to be ethnocentric, to view their culture as better than other cultures, and racial classifications operate in similar ways.

 Why do most anthropologists say that "race" is not a useful scientific construct as applied to humans?

Ethnicity and Inequality

12.6 ▶ Explain the relationship between ethnicity and inequality.

- Racial classifications might better be described as ethnic classifications. The process of defining **ethnicity** usually involves a group of people, either outside or inside the ethnic group, emphasizing common origins and language, shared history, and cultural differences.

- In a country with one large core majority group, the majority group often doesn't think of itself as an ethnic group but considers only the minority groups to have ethnic identities.

- The majority population may tend to lump people of diverse ethnicities together whereas those in minority groups may identify themselves more specifically.

- Shared ethnic identity often makes people feel comfortable with similar people and provides a strong sense of belonging. Still, ethnic differences in multiethnic societies are usually associated with inequities in wealth, power, and prestige and are part of the system of stratification.

- The origins of ethnic stereotypes, prejudice, and discrimination usually follow from historical and political events that give some groups dominance over others.

> **?** What does it mean to describe ethnicity as a process?

The Emergence of Stratification

12.7 Discuss the emergence of stratification.

- Substantial inequality generally appears only within permanent communities, centralized political systems, and intensive agriculture, cultural features that began to appear in the world only in the last 10,000 years. Before that time, most societies were probably egalitarian. However, the increase in inequality may have lessened somewhat with industrialization.

- Other cultural features associated with stratification include social classes, fixed settlements, political integration beyond the community level, the use of money as a medium of exchange, and the presence of at least some full-time specialization.

- In the world today, egalitarian societies have all but disappeared because of the global spread of commercial exchange and the voluntary or involuntary incorporation of many diverse people into large, centralized political systems.

- Stratification may be related to the accumulation of surpluses and conflicts over control of those surpluses, the ability of a group to transmit advantages to offspring generation after generation, or to population pressure in rank or chiefdom societies.

> **?** What are some key theories regarding the emergence of stratification?

Think on it

1. What might be some of the **social consequences** of large differences in wealth in a society? Explain your reasoning.

2. Is an industrial or a developed **economy** incompatible with a more egalitarian distribution of resources? Why or why not?

3. In a **multiethnic society**, does strong ethnic identity help or hinder social equality? Explain your answer.

4. We have pointed out that anthropologists believe that **"race"** is scientifically meaningless as applied to humans—if so, why is classification by race present in many multiethnic societies?

Sex and Gender

LEARNING OBJECTIVES

Describe variation in gender concepts.	**13.1**
Identify differences in physique and physiology between males and females.	**13.2**
Explain differences in gender roles.	**13.3**
Analyze relative gender differences in term of contributions to work.	**13.4**
Discuss gender differences in terms of political leadership and warfare cross-culturally.	**13.5**
Analyze relative status among women cross-culturally.	**13.6**
Discuss gender differences in personality.	**13.7**
Explain variability in sexual behavior and attitudes between different cultures.	**13.8**

In North America, it is common for parents and others to remark on how different their little girls or boys are. Even newborn boys and girls are commonly described as having different personalities. And yet trained observers watching infants wrapped in neutral-colored blankets, instead of pink for girls and blue for boys, cannot detect much difference at all. The underlying belief is that boys and girls are born with different natures. This is captured in an old nursery rhyme:

> *What are little boys made of?*
> *"Snips and snails, and puppy dogs' tails*
> *That's what little boys are made of!"*
> *What are little girls made of?*
> *Sugar and spice and all things nice*
> *That's what little girls are made of!"*[1]

Different characterizations are not unique to North American culture; boys and girls are, it appears, perceived differently the world over. Moreover, societies usually have fairly clear ideas about the roles that females and males should have during different life stages. Along with different gender roles at every stage of life comes another mystifying fact: Women nearly everywhere have fewer social advantages than men. Why? Is there a fundamental difference between the sexes, other than the observable physical differences, that explains both gender roles and the relative status of the genders? Or are gender differences created by society to serve the interests of the community—or of men?

It was the beginning of the women's movement in the 1960s that prompted scholars to seriously consider the part society plays in creating gender differences in behavior and the type of roles females and males are assigned. Although it may seem that the debate is about nature *or* nurture, most social scientists recognize that it is nearly impossible to disentangle the two when parents and others do not treat females and males exactly the same way.

One way anthropologists begin to try to understand what might be cultural is to examine similarities and variations in a phenomenon cross-culturally. In the following pages, we will look at how concepts about gender vary across many cultures. We will also review what is known about how and why females and males may differ physically, in gender roles, and in personality. Finally, we will discuss another topic of infinite curiosity: How and why sexual behavior and attitudes about sex vary from culture to culture.

• • •

Humans are born either female or male, with very rare exceptions. And each individual possesses different reproductive organs, a fact of life that humans share with most animal species. But having different organs of reproduction does not explain why males and females may also differ in other physical ways. Unlike some other animal species, such as pigeons, gulls, and chipmunks, in which the two sexes differ little in appearance, human males and females typically also differ physically.[2] In other words, the fact that we are a species with two sexes does not explain why human females and males came to look different, nor does it explain why human males and females should differ in behavior or be treated differently by society. Indeed, as we mentioned earlier, females usually have fewer advantages than males, which is why we were careful in the preceding chapter to say that egalitarian societies have no *social groups* with unequal access to resources, power, and prestige. In fact, within social groups, such as families, even egalitarian societies usually give males greater access to some rewards. Some **gender stratification**, or unequal access by different genders to prestige, authority, power, rights and economic resources, appears to be a cultural universal. However, societies differ in the degree and type of gender stratification.

Because many of the differences between females and males appear to reflect cultural expectations and experiences, researchers now usually prefer to speak of **gender differences**, reserving the term **sex differences** for purely biological differences.[3] Unfortunately, because biological and cultural influences are not always clearly separable, it is sometimes difficult to

Gender stratification The degree of unequal access by the different genders to prestige, authority, power, rights, and economic resources.

Gender differences Differences between females and males that reflect cultural expectations and experiences.

Sex differences The typical differences between females and males that are most likely due to biological differences.

know which term to use. As we discuss differences and similarities between females and males, keep in mind that not all cultures conceive of gender as including just two categories. Sometimes "maleness" and "femaleness" are thought of as opposite ends of a continuum, or there might be three or more categories of gender, such as "female," "male," and "other."[4]

Gender Concepts

13.1 Describe variation in gender concepts.

In the United States and many Western societies, there are only two genders—female and male. Your gender is assigned at birth based on external biological attributes. However, not all individuals feel comfortable with their gender assignment. The term *transgender* is now used to describe people who do not feel that their assigned gender fits them well.

The division into just two genders—male/female—is very common cross-culturally. But a strict dichotomy is far from universal. Some societies, like the Cheyenne Native Americans of the Great Plains, recognized male, female, and a third gender, referred to by the Cheyenne as "two-spirits." (Europeans referred to this third gender type generally as a *berdache*.[5]) "Two-spirit" people were usually biological males. The gender status of "two-spirit" was often recognized after a boy returned from his vision quest, a preadolescent rite of passage of several days that he spent in isolation in the wilderness. The boy's "vision," or epiphany, would lead him to become a two-spirit person. He would wear women's dress and take on many of the activities of women. A two-spirit might even be taken as a second wife by a man, but whether the man and the two-spirit person engaged in sex is not known. The role of a "two-spirit" person was not equivalent to that of a woman. Indeed, two-spirits played unique gender roles at weddings and childbirth. Accounts of "two-spirit" biological females who take on the role of men are less common, but they do occur in a number of native North American societies, such as the Kaska of Yukon Territory, the Klamath of southern Oregon, and the Mohave of the Colorado River area in the southwestern United States. These biological female "two-spirits" could marry women, and such relationships were lesbian relationships.[6]

In Oman, there is a third gender role called *xanith*. Anatomically male, *xaniths* speak of themselves as "women." However, *xaniths* have their own distinctive dress; they wear clothes that are neither male nor female but somewhere in between. Men in Oman typically wear white clothes and women bright patterns, whereas *xaniths* wear unpatterned pastels. Men have short hair, women long, and *xaniths* keep theirs medium-length. Omani women are generally secluded in their houses and can go out only with permission from their husbands, but a *xanith* is free to come and go and to work as a servant and/or a homosexual prostitute. Unlike a "two-spirit," who is likely to maintain a third gender role for life, a *xanith* may change gender role. If a *xanith* decides to marry and is able to have intercourse with his bride, he becomes a "man." An older *xanith* who is no longer attractive may decide to become an "old man."[7]

Physique and Physiology

13.2 Identify differences in physique and physiology between males and females.

As we have noted, males and females cannot readily be distinguished in some animal species. Although they differ in chromosome makeup and in their external and internal organs of reproduction, they do not differ otherwise. In contrast, humans are **sexually dimorphic**—that is, the two sexes of our species are generally different in size and appearance. Females have proportionately wider pelvises. Males typically are taller and have heavier skeletons. Females have a larger proportion of their body weight in fat; males have a larger proportion of body weight in muscle. Males typically have greater grip strength, proportionately larger hearts and lungs, and greater aerobic capacity (greater intake of oxygen during strenuous activity).

North American culture tends to view "taller" and "more muscled" as better, which may reflect a bias toward males. But how did these differences come about? Natural selection may have favored these traits in males but selected against them in females. Females achieve their ultimate height shortly after puberty, but boys continue to grow for years after puberty. Because females bear children, selection may have favored earlier cessation of growth, and therefore less ultimate height so that the nutritional needs of a fetus would

Sexually dimorphic
A marked difference in size and appearance between males and females of a species.

not compete with a growing mother's needs.[8] Similarly, there is some evidence that females are less affected than males by nutritional shortages, presumably because they tend to be shorter and have proportionately more fat.[9] Natural selection may also have favored more proportionate "fatness" in females because it resulted in greater reproductive success.

Athletes can build up their muscle strength and increase their aerobic work capacity through training. Given that fact, cultural factors, such as how much a society expects and allows males and females to engage in muscular activity, could influence the degree to which females and males differ muscularly and in aerobic capacity. Similar training may account for the recent trend toward decreasing differences between females and males in certain athletic events, such as marathons and swim meets, even when we account for the hormonal differences that enable males to develop greater muscle mass. When it comes to female and male physique and physiology, what we see may be the result of both culture and genes.[10]

<table>
<tr><td>13.3</td><td>Explain differences in gender roles.</td></tr>
</table>

Gender Roles

Who Does What Work?

In the chapter on economic systems, we noted that all societies assign or divide labor somewhat differently between females and males. Because role assignments have a clear cultural component, we speak of them as **gender roles**. What is of particular interest about the gender division of labor is not so much that every society has different work for males and females but, rather, that so many societies divide up work in similar ways. The question, then, is: Why are there universal or near-universal patterns in such assignments?

Gender roles Roles that are culturally assigned to genders.

The world of work has changed for much of the world and continues to change. We know a considerable amount about division of labor by gender in societies that make or made their living by collecting or producing their own food. We know less as yet about cross-cultural patterns in industrial and post-industrial societies. Table 13.1 summarizes which activities are performed by which gender in all or almost all societies, which activities are usually performed by one gender, and which activities are commonly assigned to either gender or both. If every culture assigned work arbitrarily to the genders, the table would reveal no patterns. Although many tasks are assigned to both genders (the middle column), clearly some patterns are worldwide. One of the most striking is in primary subsistence activities; males almost always hunt and trap animals, and females usually gather wild plants. Do this and the other distributions of activities in the table suggest why females and males generally do different things? Scholars have suggested four explanations or theories that we label *strength theory, compatibility-with-child-care theory, economy-of-effort theory,* and *expendability theory*.

Strength Theory The idea that males generally possess greater strength and a superior capacity to mobilize their strength in quick bursts of energy (because of greater aerobic work capacity) is called the strength theory. Males may best perform activities that require lifting heavy objects (hunting large animals, butchering, clearing land, or working with stone, metal, or lumber), throwing weapons, and running with great speed (as in hunting). And none of the activities females usually perform, with the possible exception of collecting firewood, seem to require the same degree of physical strength or quick bursts of energy. But the strength theory is not completely convincing, if only because it cannot readily explain all the observed patterns. It is not clear, for example, that the male activities of trapping small animals, collecting wild honey, or making musical instruments require physical strength. Moreover, as we will see shortly, women do hunt in some societies, suggesting that differences in strength cannot play a very important role.

Compatibility-with-Child-Care Theory Males are capable of caring for infants, of course, but for obvious biological reasons, they cannot breast-feed. In most societies, women breast-feed their children, on average, for two years, so the compatibility-with-child-care theory suggests that for much of human history it would have been maladaptive to have women take on roles that interfere with their ability to feed their child regularly or put their child in danger while taking care of them. The tasks women perform may also need to be ones that can be stopped and resumed if an infant needs care.[11]

TABLE 13.1	Worldwide Patterns in the Division of Labor by Gender		
	Primary Subsistence Activities	**Secondary Subsistence and Household Activities**	**Other Activities**
Nearly always males	Hunt and trap animals, large and small		Lumber Make boats Mine and quarry Make musical instruments Make bone, horn, and shell objects Engage in combat
Usually males	Fish Herd large animals Collect wild honey Clear land and prepare soil for planting	Butcher animals	Build houses Make nets and rope Exercise political leadership
Either gender or both	Collect shellfish Care for small animals Plant and tend crops Harvest crops Milk animals	Preserve meat and fish	Prepare skins Make leather products, baskets, mats, clothing, and pottery
Usually females	Gather wild plants	Care for children Cook Prepare vegetable foods, drinks, and dairy products Launder Fetch water Collect fuel Spin yarn	
Nearly always females		Care for infants	

Sources: Murdock and Provost 1973, 203–25; Whyte 1978a, 217 (political leadership and warfare); Weisner and Gallimore 1977, 169–80 (child care).

The compatibility theory may explain why *only* infant care is listed in Table 13.1 as almost always woman's work. Nursing and caring for their infants and other children may have so consumed women's lives that, until recently, there may have been practically no other universal or near-universal women-only activities. This theory may also explain why men usually perform such tasks as hunting, trapping, fishing, collecting honey, lumbering, and mining. Those tasks are dangerous for infants to be around and, in any case, would be difficult to coordinate with infant care. A group may also make fine distinctions in the division of labor that are consistent with the compatibility theory: Among the Aché hunter-gatherers of Paraguay, for example, women collect the type of honey produced by stingless bees, while men collect other honey.[12]

Finally, the compatibility theory may explain why men seem to take over certain crafts in societies that have full-time specialization. Although the distinction is not shown in Table 13.1, crafts such as basket, mat, and pottery making tend to be women's activities in noncommercial societies but men's activities in societies with full-time craft specialists.[13] Similarly, weaving is typically a female activity unless it is produced for trade.[14] Full-time specialization and production for trade may be less compatible with child care. Cooking is a good example in our own society. Many women are excellent cooks and traditionally did most of the cooking at home, but chefs and bakers tend to be men. In order to work as chefs, women would require caretakers for their babies and young children, and shorter hours than chefs and bakers typically work.

The compatibility theory does not explain, however, why men usually prepare soil for planting, make objects out of wood, or work bone, horn, and shell. All of those tasks could probably be stopped to tend to a child, and none of them is any more dangerous to children nearby than is cooking.

Economy-of-Effort Theory Why do males tend to perform tasks such as woodcarving that could be done by women who also tend children? The economy-of-effort theory may help explain task patterns that the strength and compatibility theories do not readily address. For example, it may be advantageous for men to make wooden musical instruments because

Females usually care for young children, but sometimes males do more as this father in Shanghai, China.

they generally lumber.[15] Lumbering may give men more knowledge about the physical properties of various woods and make it more likely that they know how to work with different woods. The economy-of-effort interpretation also suggests that it would be advantageous for one gender to perform tasks that are located near each other. That is, if women have to be near home to nurse and take care of young children, it would be economical for them to perform other chores in or near the home.

Expendability Theory   The idea that men, rather than women, will tend to do the dangerous work in a society because the loss of men is not as great a disadvantage reproductively as the loss of women is called the expendability theory. If some men lose their lives in hunting, deepwater fishing, mining, quarrying, lumbering, and the like, reproduction need not suffer as long as most fertile women have sexual access to men—for example, if the society permits two or more women to be married to the same man.[16] If an activity is dangerous, why would anybody, male or female, be willing to do it? Perhaps it is because societies glorify and reward some such acts.

Theoretical Weaknesses   The productive and domestic tasks that societies everywhere have carried out are a well-established body of knowledge. We also have data on whether men, women, or both perform each task. The theories that we discussed are all, to some extent, based on these data. And singly or in combination, each theory seems to explain much of the division of labor by gender; yet each theory has weaknesses. Critics of the strength theory have pointed out that women in some societies do engage in very heavy labor.[17] They argue that if women in some societies can develop the strength to do such work, then perhaps strength is more a function of training than has been believed.

The compatibility theory's central idea that labor is divided to conform to the requirements of child care is also debatable. In fact, the reverse can be true: Child care can conform to the demands of other work. Women who spend a good deal of time in agricultural work outside the home, for example, often ask others to watch and feed their infants while they are unavailable to nurse.[18] For example, agricultural work in the mountainous areas of Nepal would seem to be especially incompatible with child care. Heavy loads must be carried up and down steep slopes, the fields are far apart, and labor takes up most of the day. Yet women perform this work anyway and leave their infants with others for long stretches of time.[19]

In some societies, women hunt—one of the activities considered most incompatible with child care and generally done only by men. Many Agta women of the Philippines seem able to manage both tasks. They regularly hunt wild pig and deer; and women alone or in groups kill almost 30 percent of the large game in the Agta diet.[20] The compatibility theory, like the other proposed explanations for the division of labor by gender, assumes that women do not perform work that may jeopardize their reproductive ability. Yet Agta women who hunt and even take their nursing babies on hunting trips do not have lower reproductive rates than the women who choose not to hunt. To be fair, the circumstances under which these women hunt may be more compatible with child care: The hunting grounds are only about a half hour from camp; dogs accompany them to assist in the hunting and protect them and their babies; and because they tend to hunt in groups, others can help carry their babies, as well as the carcasses. However, these factors, too, suggest that women can effectively accommodate the differing needs of two competing tasks.

Hunting by women is also fairly common among the Aka, forest foragers in the Central African Republic. Aka women participate in and sometimes lead cooperative net-hunting, in which an area is circled and animals are flushed out and caught in nets. The women spend approximately 18 percent of their time net-hunting, which is more time than Aka men devote to the task.[21] In the Canadian subarctic, teams of Chipewyan women would hunt small animals, such as muskrats or rabbits, and would commonly join their husbands to hunt large animals, such as moose. Some Chipewyan precautions suggest that the compatibility between hunting and child care was a consideration, however. Women would avoid hunting moose after their fourth or fifth month of pregnancy. They usually joined hunting teams as newlyweds and after their childbearing years. Women also did not participate in long-distance hunts.[22]

As these examples of women who hunt and who work in agriculture suggest, we would be in a better position to evaluate the various theories and, perhaps, to propose one if we knew more precisely what each activity humans perform requires. Without a systematic study of how much strength is required for each task, how dangerous each task is, or which tasks can be interrupted for child care and later resumed, theories about the way societies divide up their work can be little more than guesses.

Changing Labor and Gender Roles As fewer societies remain isolated and more adopt technologies to help them perform certain tasks, both the tasks and who performs them are bound to change. As we know from our own and other industrial societies, when machines replace human strength, when women have fewer children, and when child care can be delegated, the division of labor changes, as do the tasks that need to be performed. Yet, remarkably, labor appears to divide by gender even in a post-industrial world.

Relative Contributions to Work: Who Works More?

13.4 Analyze relative gender differences in term of contributions to work.

Most contemporary societies typically equate "work" with earning money. Until relatively recently, "homemaker" did not count as an occupation in the United States, for example. Yet, as we discussed in the chapters on food-getting and economics, we humans lived in subsistence economies for most of our history, and the invention of money is relatively recent. Most societies known to anthropology, whether they were foragers or food producers, focused primarily on the basic necessities.

When anthropologists research the division of labor by gender, they usually focus on **primary subsistence activities**—gathering, hunting, fishing, herding, and farming. As if there were a predisposed bias against household work, less attention has been paid to gender contributions toward **secondary subsistence activities**, such as food preparation for eating or storing. Yet, with a few exceptions, food can never be consumed without some preparation. For example, hunting cannot contribute much to the diet unless the meat is brought home (cut up or carried whole), skinned, cleaned, prepared for cooking, and then cooked. If the animal is large, the meat must be prepared for distribution and/or storage. And as skins and other parts are often used for clothing or tools, someone has to prepare those. As Hetty Jo Brumbach and Robert Jarvenpa point out, the Western model of hunting focuses on the "kill" (perhaps derived from the notion of sport-hunting) and ignores the complexity of processes associated with it. This view may hide women's role in "hunting" and emphasize the male's role as "hunter."[23]

Primary subsistence activities The food-getting activities: gathering, hunting, fishing, herding, and agriculture.

Secondary subsistence activities Activities that involve the preparation and processing of food either to make it edible or to store it.

Overall Work

We can also ask whether males or females generally do more work. We do not yet have that many studies of how females and males spend their time, but studies of horticultural and intensive agricultural societies so far suggest that, if we count all the kinds of economic activities shown in Table 13.1, women typically work more total hours per day than men.[24] We do not know if this is a truly cross-cultural universal. However, we do know that in many societies where women earn wages, they are still responsible for the bulk of the household work as well as the child care at home.

Subsistence Work

Primary subsistence activities are by nature generally located farther from the family's dwelling, and female and male contributions of this kind of work vary across cultures. Because the length of time spent on primary subsistence activities is generally not available, we estimate how much each gender contributes to the diet in terms of caloric intake from primary subsistence activities.

In some societies, women have traditionally contributed more to the economy than men both in terms of time spent and caloric intake. For example, among the Tchambuli of New Guinea in the 1930s, the women did all of the fishing—going out early in the morning by canoe to their fish traps and returning when the sun was hot. Some of the catch was traded for sago (a starch) and sugarcane, and it was the women who went on the long canoe trips to do the trading.[25]

In contrast, men did almost all of the primary subsistence work among the Toda of India. As they were described early in the 20th century, they depended for subsistence almost entirely on the dairy products of their water buffalo, either by using the products directly or by selling them for grain. Only men tended the buffalo and also prepared the dairy products, which women were not permitted to do. Women performed mostly housework, preparing the purchased grain for cooking, cleaning house, and decorating clothing.[26]

A survey of a wide variety of societies has revealed that these extremes are not common. Usually both women and men contribute a good deal toward primary food-getting activities, but men usually contribute more in most societies.[27] Because women are almost always occupied with infant- and child-care responsibilities, it is not surprising that men usually perform most of the primary subsistence work, which generally has to be done away from the home.

Why do women in some societies do as much or more than men in primary subsistence work? Some of the variation is explained by the society's types of food-getting activity. In societies that depend on hunting, fishing, and herding—generally male activities—for most of their calories, men usually contribute more than women.[28] For example, among the Inuit, who traditionally depended mostly on hunting and fishing, as well as among the Toda, who depended mostly on herding, men did most of the primary subsistence work. In societies that depend on gathering, primarily women's work, women tend to do most of the food-getting.[29] The !Kung are an example. But the predominant type of food-getting is not always predictive. For example, among the Tchambuli, who depended mostly on fishing, women did most of the work. Most societies depend upon some

In many farming societies, women can do some agriculture and take care of their young children at the same time, as this mother in Zambia demonstrates.

form of food production rather than foraging. With the exception of clearing land, preparing the soil, and herding large animals, which are usually men's tasks, men, women, or both do the work of planting, crop tending (weeding, irrigating), and harvesting (see Table 13.1). We need some explanation, then, of why women do most of the farming work in some societies but men do it in others. Different patterns predominate in different areas of the world. In Africa, south of the Sahara, women generally do most of the farming. In much of Asia and Europe and the areas around the Mediterranean, men do more.[30]

The type of agriculture may help explain some of the variation. Men's contribution to primary subsistence tends to be much higher than women's in intensive agricultural societies, particularly with plow agriculture. In contrast, women's contribution is relatively high compared with men's and sometimes higher in horticultural societies. According to Ester Boserup, when population increases and there is pressure to make more intensive use of the land, cultivators begin to use the plow and irrigation, and males start to do more.[31] But it is not clear why.

Why should women not contribute a lot to farming just because plows are used? In trying to answer this question, most researchers shift to considering how much time males and females spend in various farming tasks rather than estimating the total caloric contribution of females versus males. The reason for this shift is that gender contribution to farming varies substantially over the various phases of the production sequence, as well as from one crop to another. Thus, the total amount of time females versus males work at farming tasks is easier to estimate than how much each gender contributes to the diet in terms of calories. How would caloric contribution be judged, for example, if men clear the land and plow, women plant and weed, and both harvest the crop?

Plow agriculture could increase male contribution to subsistence because plowing takes longer and minimizes weeding time. Cross-culturally, men usually clear land. (This does not mean that women are not able to plow, for there are examples of women plowing when necessary.[32]) It has been estimated that, in one district in Nigeria, 100 days of work are required to clear one acre of virgin land for plowing by tractor; only 20 days are required to prepare the land for shifting cultivation. Weeding is a task that probably can be combined with child care, and perhaps women may have mostly performed it previously for that reason.[33] But the fact that men do the plowing, which may take a lot of time, does not explain why women do relatively fewer farming tasks, including weeding, in societies that have the plow.[34]

Another explanation for the apparent decrease in women's contribution in intensive agriculture is that they have less time to spend in the fields. Intensive agriculturalists rely heavily on such grain crops as corn, wheat, and oats, which require a great deal of preparation and processing, tasks commonly performed by women. Grains are usually dried before storing. To be edible, dried grains must either be cooked in water for a long time or be preprocessed to cook faster. Cooking requires collecting water and firewood, neither of which is usually close by, and both of which are women's tasks. In addition, there is more cleaning of pots and utensils to be done. Soaking, grinding, or pounding can reduce cooking time for hard grains, but the process that speeds up cooking the most—grinding—is itself very time-consuming unless done by machine.[35] Then there is also child care and the additional housework that children entail.

Household work may also increase substantially with intensive agriculture because women in such societies have *more* children than women in horticultural societies.[36] If we add child care and the housework that children entail to the intensive food processing and cooking the women undertake, it is easy to understand why women cannot contribute more time than men, or as much time as men, to intensive agriculture. Yet women's contribution, though less than men's in the fields, is nonetheless substantial. In addition to working at home, women in such societies may labor outside the home four and a half hours a day, seven days a week, on average.[37]

Unlike intensive agricultural societies, those that subsist on horticulture rely a great deal on women's contributions. Why? Women in horticultural societies may not have as much household work as intensive agricultural women, but neither do the men. Why, then, don't men do relatively more in horticulture also? In fact, men in horticultural societies are often drawn away from cultivation into other types of activities. One of the most common is warfare, in which all able-bodied men are expected to participate.

There is evidence that, if males are engaged in warfare when primary subsistence work has to be done, then the women will do work.[38] Men may also be removed from primary subsistence work if they have to work in distant towns and cities for wages or if they periodically go on long-distance trading trips.[39]

When women contribute a lot to primary food-getting activities, we might expect effects on their childrearing. Several cross-cultural studies suggest that, indeed, this expectation is correct. In contrast to societies with a low female contribution to primary subsistence (in terms of contributing calories), highly contributing females feed their infants solid foods earlier, enabling others besides the mothers to feed them.[40] Also girls in such societies are likely to be trained to be industrious, probably to help their mothers, and female babies are more valued.[41]

Political Leadership and Warfare

13.5 ▶ Discuss gender differences in terms of political leadership and warfare cross-culturally.

In almost every known society, men rather than women tend to lead in the political arena. One cross-cultural survey found that only men were leaders in about 88 percent of the surveyed societies. Among the 10 percent of societies that had women in leadership positions, they were either outnumbered by or less powerful than the male leaders.[42] In the remaining 2 percent, leadership was fairly evenly distributed between men and women. If we look at sovereign nations, not cultures, the mean average of women in national parliaments and legislative bodies is 19 percent.[43]

Whether or not we consider warfare to be part of the political sphere of life, we find an almost universal dominance of males in that arena. In 87 percent of the world's societies in the anthropological record, women never participate actively in war.[44] Among modern nation-states, as of 2013, only 12 countries allow military women in combat.[45] The United States only recently changed its policy to allow such participation. (See the box "Why Do Some Societies Allow Women to Participate in Combat?" for a discussion of women in combat in the remaining 13 percent of societies.)

Even in *matrilineal* societies, in which the descent of a kin group is passed down through the mother and the female ancestors, formal political positions are usually held by men. Among the matrilineal Iroquois of what is now New York State, women controlled the resources and had considerable informal influence on political affairs. They could nominate, elect, and impeach their male representatives. Women could decide between life and death for prisoners of war, forbid the men of their households to go to war, and intervene to bring about peace. Nonetheless, the highest political body among the League of the Iroquois, which comprised five tribal groups, was a council of 50 male chiefs.[46]

Why have men (at least so far) almost always dominated the political sphere of life? Some scholars suggest that men's role in warfare gives them the edge in political leadership, particularly because they control weapons, an important resource.[47] Evidence suggests, however, that force is rarely used to obtain leadership positions;[48] superior strength is not the deciding factor. Rather, warfare may be related to political leadership for another reason. War affects survival, and it occurs regularly in most societies. Therefore, decisions about war may be among the most important kinds of political actions that occur in most societies. It stands to reason that the people who know the most about warfare make these decisions.

Two other factors may be involved in male predominance in politics. One is the generally greater height of men. Why height should be a factor in leadership is unclear, but studies suggest that taller people are more likely to be leaders.[49] Finally, there is the possibility that men dominate politics because they spend more time in the outside world than do women. Men's activities typically take them farther from home, whereas women tend to work more around the home. If societies choose leaders at least in part because of what they know about the larger world, then men will have some advantage. In support of this reasoning, Patricia Draper found that in settled !Kung groups, women no longer engaged in long-distance gathering, and they seemed to have lost much of their former influence in decision-making.[50] Involvement in child care may also detract from influence. In a

Perspectives on Gender

Why Do Some Societies Allow Women to Participate in Combat?

There have been some female warriors throughout history. In the 18th and 19th centuries, women made up one wing of the standing army in the West African Kingdom of Dahomey, for example, and constituted one-third of the armed forces at one point. Yet most societies and most countries have excluded women from combat, and some have excluded women from all military activities or planning.

Why, then, do some societies allow women to be warriors? Psychologist David Adams compared about 70 societies studied by anthropologists to try to answer that question. He found that women are active warriors at least occasionally in 13 percent of the sample societies. In native North America, the Comanche, Crow, Delaware, Fox, Gros Ventre, and Navajo had women warriors. In the Pacific, there were active warrior women among the Maori of New Zealand, on Majuro Atoll in the Marshall Islands, and among the Orokaiva of New Guinea. In none of these societies were the warriors usually women, but women were allowed to engage in combat if they wanted to.

How are societies with women warriors different from those that exclude women from combat? They differ in one of two ways. Either they conduct purely external wars, fighting only against people in other societies, or they marry within their own community in a society. Adams argues that either of these two conditions, which are not particularly common, will preclude conflicts of interest between wives and husbands. In purely external war, couples who come from the same society (though not necessarily the same community) will share the same loyalties. If war occurs internally, between communities and larger groups within a society, there will be no conflict of interest between husband and wife as long as they grew up in the same community. In short, wives who do not have allegiances in the "enemy" camp can, by implication, be trusted to fight alongside their husbands.

In most societies, internal war takes place at least occasionally, but wives also usually come from other communities. If women in such societies engaged in combat, they might have to fight against their fathers, paternal uncles, and brothers. Wouldn't we expect a person in such a situation to have torn loyalties and try to warn her kin of planned attacks against them? The potential for disloyalty would explain why women in such societies are forbidden to make or handle weapons or go near meetings in which war plans are discussed.

Many countries today engage in purely external war. Other things being equal, we might extrapolate from Adams's findings and expect barriers against woman warriors to disappear completely in such societies. In 2011 Australia and in 2013 the United States joined 10 other countries in allowing women in combat. It may be a trend, but most countries disallow such participation, and woman warriors are rare. Even in Adams's study, not all societies with purely external war or intra-community marriage had woman warriors. Other conditions may have to be present before women and men participate equally in combat. We may have to consider the degree to which the society seeks to maximize reproduction (and therefore protect women from danger) and the degree to which the society depends on women for subsistence during wartime.

Inevitably, one inquiry about women and society leads to other compelling questions. Does greater participation in the military increase women's presence in politics? In wartime, do women participate more or less in politics? Does the nature of war change when women play an active role in politics or in the military?

Source: From D. B. Adams 1983; J. S. Goldstein 2001; 2004; Mutrine 2013; Siegel 2011.

---

study of village leadership among the Kayapo of Brazil, Dennis Werner found that women with heavy child-care burdens were less influential than women not as involved in child care; he suggests that they had fewer friends and missed many details of what was going on in the village.[51]

These various explanations suggest why men generally dominate politics, but we still need to explain why women participate in politics more in some societies than in others. Marc Ross investigated this question in a cross-cultural survey of 90 societies.[52] In that sample, the degree of female participation in politics varied considerably. For example, among the Mende of Sierra Leone, women regularly held high office, but among the Azande of Zaire, women took no part in public life. One factor that predicts the exclusion of women from politics is the organization of communities around male kin. As we will see later, when they marry, women usually have to leave their communities and move to their husband's household. If women are outsiders joining a community with many related males, the males will have political advantages because of their inside knowledge of their community's members and its past events.

13.6 Analyze relative status among women cross-culturally.

The Relative Status of Women

In the small Iraqi town of Daghara, women and men live very separate lives.[53] In many respects, women appear to have very little status. Like women in some other parts of the Islamic world, women in Daghara live mostly in seclusion, staying in their houses and interior courtyards. If they must go out, they can do so only with male approval and must shroud their faces and bodies in long black cloaks. These cloaks must be worn in mixed company, even at home. Women are essentially excluded from political activities. Legally, they are considered to be under the authority of their fathers and husbands. Even the sexuality of women is controlled; there is strict emphasis on virginity before marriage. Because women are not permitted even casual conversations with strange men, the possibilities of extramarital or even premarital relationships are very slight. In contrast, hardly any sexual restrictions are imposed on men.

But some societies, such as the Mbuti of Zaire, seem to approach equal status for males and females. Like most food collectors, the Mbuti have no formal political organization to make decisions or to settle disputes. When public disputes occur, both women and men take part in the uproar. Not only do women make their positions known, but their opinions are often heeded. Even in domestic quarrels involving physical violence between husband and wife, others usually intervene to stop them, regardless of who hit whom first.[54] Women control the use of dwellings; they usually have equal say over the disposal of resources they or the men collect, over the upbringing of their children, and about whom their children should marry. One of the few signs of inequality is that women are somewhat more restricted than men with respect to extramarital sex.[55]

But many social scientists have asked why the *status* of women appears to vary from one society to another. There are many theories about why women have relatively high or low status. One of the most common theories is that women's status will be high when they contribute substantially to primary subsistence activities. This theory would predict that women should have very little status when food-getting depends largely on hunting, herding, or intensive agriculture. A second theory suggests that men will be more valued and esteemed than women where warfare is particularly important. A third theory suggests that men will have higher status where there are centralized political hierarchies, since men usually play the dominant role in politics. The fourth theory predicts that women will have higher status where kin groups and couples' places of residence after marriage are organized around women.

One of the problems in evaluating these theories is that decisions have to be made about the meaning of *status*. There are probably as many definitions of status as there are researchers interested in the topic. To some, the relative status of the sexes means how much value society confers on females versus males. To others, it means how much power and authority men and women have relative to each other. To still others, it means what kinds of rights women and men possess to do what they want to do.

Many of the terms, such as value, power, authority, and rights, mean something slightly different. And we have to access what domain we are talking about—for example, with respect to authority, do we mean authority in the home, in the public arena, in the kin group, or in religious life? Do all these aspects of status vary together? Cross-cultural research by Martin Whyte suggests that they do not. For each sample society in his study, Whyte rated 52 items that might be used to define the relative status of the sexes. These items included such things as which sex can inherit property, whose authority is final in disciplining unmarried children, and whether the gods in the society are male, female, or both. The results of the study indicate that very few of these items are related. Therefore, Whyte concluded, we cannot talk about status as a single concept. Rather, it seems more appropriate to talk about the relative status of women in different spheres of life.[56]

Even though Whyte found no necessary connection between one aspect of status and another, he decided to ask whether some of the theories correctly predict why some societies have many, as opposed to few, areas in which the status of women is high. Or, why is there less or more gender stratification? Let us turn first to the ideas *not* supported by the available cross-cultural evidence. Contrary to popular belief, the idea that generally high status stems from a greater caloric contribution to primary subsistence activities is not supported.[57] For example, women seem to have higher status the more a society depends upon hunting, but women do little of the primary subsistence work in hunting societies. And it is commonly thought that warfare should bolster male status, but there is no consistent evidence that a high frequency of warfare generally lowers women's status in different spheres of life.[58]

Perspectives on Gender

Women's Electoral Success on the Northwest Coast

Political life has changed dramatically since first contact with Europeans for most Native American groups, including the Coast Salish of western Washington State and British Columbia. With impetus from the U.S. and Canadian governments, each of the recognized Coast Salish communities now has an elected council. But who is getting elected? Even though women did not have much of a role in traditional politics, now the Coast Salish groups are electing a lot of women. From the 1960s to the 1980s, women held over 40 percent of the council seats in the 12 Washington State groups, and in the 1990s, women held 28 percent of the seats in the 50 British Columbian groups. The proportion of women on the councils varies from 6 percent among the Tulalip to 62 percent among the Stillaguamish. What accounts for the women's electoral success? And why does that success vary from one group to another, even though the groups are closely related culturally?

According to Bruce Miller, who did a comparative study of women's electoral success in Coast Salish communities, women may generally have more of a political role now because new economic opportunities in the service and technical sectors allow them to contribute more to the household economy. But why do women win proportionately more council seats in some communities than in others? Miller found that women win proportionately more seats in communities with less income, the least income derived from fishing, and the smallest populations. Why should lower household income predict more electoral

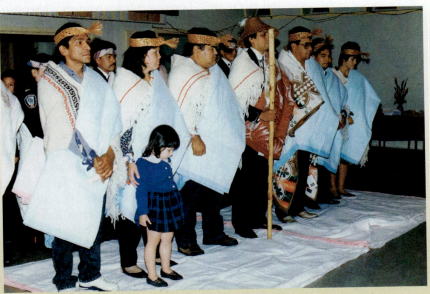

Women as well as men serve on political councils in many Coast Salish communities. Here, we see a swearing-in ceremony for the Special Chiefs' Council in Sardis, British Columbia.

success for women? Miller suggests that it is not so much the amount of income but rather the degree to which women (compared with men) contribute to household income. In groups with economic difficulties, the jobs women are able to get play a vital role in the household. Federally funded programs such as the War on Poverty helped women to acquire technical skills and jobs. Simultaneously, many men in some communities lost their jobs in logging and agriculture.

But a high dependence on fishing income seems to favor men politically. Families that operate vessels with a large drawstring net to catch fish at sea can make hundreds of thousands of dollars a year. Men predominantly do such fishing, and where there is such lucrative fishing, the successful

men dominate the councils. Even though women may have jobs too, their income is not as great as the successful fisherman's.

Why should women be more successful politically in smaller communities? Miller suggests that women have a better chance to be known personally when the community is small, even though working outside the home in technical or service jobs cuts down on the time women can devote to tribal ceremonials and other public events.

Does female income relative to male and community size help explain the relative political success of women elsewhere? We do not know yet, but subsequent research may help us find out.

Source: B. G. Miller 1992, 1994.

What does predict higher status for women in many areas of life? Although the results are not strong, there is some support in Whyte's study for the theory that women have somewhat higher status where kin groups and marital residence are organized around women. (We discuss these features of society more fully in the chapter on marital residence and kinship.) The Iroquois are a good example. Even though Iroquois women could not hold formal political office, they had considerable authority within and beyond the household. Related women lived together in longhouses with husbands who belonged to other kin groups. In the longhouse, the women's authority was clear, and they could ask objectionable men to leave. The women controlled the allocation of the food they produced. Allocation could influence the timing of war parties, because men could not undertake a raid without provisions. Women were involved in the selection of religious leaders, half of whom were women. Even in politics, although women could not speak or serve on the council, they largely controlled the selection of councilmen and could institute impeachment proceedings against those to whom they objected.[59]

In pre-industrial societies, women have generally lower status in societies with more political hierarchy.[60] Lower status for women is also associated with other indicators of cultural complexity—social stratification, plow-and-irrigation agriculture, large settlements, private property, and craft specialization. Only women's informal influence increases with cultural complexity. But informal influence may simply reflect a lack of *real* influence.[61] Why cultural complexity is associated with women having less authority in the home, less control over property, and more restricted sexual lives in pre-industrial societies is not yet understood. However, the relationship between cultural complexity and gender equality appears to be reversed in industrial and post-industrial societies. Judging by a comparative study of gender attitudes in 61 countries, it seems that countries that rely on agriculture, such as Nigeria and Peru, have the least favorable attitudes toward gender equality; industrial societies, such as Russia and Taiwan, have moderately favorable attitudes; and post-industrial societies, such as Sweden and the United States, have the most favorable attitudes toward gender equality.[62] One critical difference that may explain this reversal is the role that formal education plays in industrial and post-industrial societies. Education almost always increases status, and the more girls and young women are educated, the greater the likelihood that their status will increase. Furthermore, although the mechanisms are not well understood, education usually results in lowered fertility, which perhaps frees women to pursue other interests. As we discussed earlier, one study among the Kayapo found that women with more children are considered less influential.[63]

Western colonialism appears to have been generally detrimental to women's status. Although the relative status of men and women may not have been equal before the Europeans arrived, colonial influences seem generally to have undermined the position of women. There are many examples of Europeans restructuring landownership around men and teaching men modern farming techniques, even in places where women were usually the farmers. In addition, men more often than women could earn cash through wage labor or through sales of goods (such as furs) to Europeans.[64] From these historical lessons and from recent developments, we are beginning to understand some of the conditions that enhance or decrease women's status. If we can understand which of these conditions are most important, societies that want to may be able to reduce gender inequality.[65]

Personality Differences

13.7 Discuss gender differences in personality.

Much of the research on gender differences in personality has taken place in the United States and other Western countries where psychology is a major field of study. Although such studies are informative, they do not tell us whether the observed differences hold true in cultures very different from our own. Fortunately, we now have systematic observational studies for various non-Western societies. These studies recorded the minute details of behavior of substantial numbers of males and females. Most of the studies have observed children in different cultural settings. Any conclusions about female-male differences in aggressiveness, for example, are based on actual counts of the number of times a particular individual tried to hurt or injure another person during a given amount of observation time. Almost all of these differences are a matter of degree, not a matter of a behavior being present or absent in females or males.

Applied Anthropology

Economic Development and Women's Status

Based on the writings of Ester Boserup and subsequent scholarship on women in development, the prevailing opinion was that development usually made things worse for women. Development agents commonly targeted men for learning new technology and how to produce crops for sale. Today, women in developing countries are still largely left out and women still face difficulties, but recent research has documented how women often find creative ways to participate in commercial enterprises.

Some of the creative strategies women use in Kenya to get around their structural disadvantages include buying or renting land with their proceeds, "pooling" small pieces of land to meet minimum requirements for commercial growers, joining women's rotating credit associations, and looking to the private sector for training and materials for contract agriculture.

Women's scale of production can range from raising a few extra pigs for sale in southwestern China to more complex activities, such as contract farming for crop exports in Kenya, or market trading in Ghana.

In contrast to men nearly everywhere in developing countries, women use the money from their commercial enterprises to purchase food and household goods and to educate their children. If their incomes or savings grow, they may pay for large appliances, furniture, and farm machinery and vehicles. Most of the recent studies suggest that bringing money into the household translates into lasting

Microfinance programs for small business have helped women in developing countries to build status and independence.

changes in the status of women, including increased educational opportunities, greater say in household decisions, and higher social status in the community.

Some opportunities for women also open up when men move into other domains. For example, among the Ashanti of Ghana, many men moved out of market trading to take advantage of more lucrative cocoa production. Women had long been traders along with men, but with the departure of men, women took over many of men's former market niches and began to engage in longer-distance trade. In Kenya, male migration has increased the number of women who manage the farm and head households.

Such examples of economic empowerment among women in agricultural societies are encouraging, even though farming

keeps them close to home and away from other, more public opportunities. How do women fare in industrial societies, where only a small proportion of people engage in farming? According to a survey of 61 countries, gender equality is more favored in industrializing countries than in agricultural societies. With industrialization, infant and child mortality decline, lessening the pressure on women to reproduce. Perhaps this frees them to pursue education and work outside the home. Post-industrial countries, with even lower fertility rates, are even more accepting of gender equality. As women learn more and get out in the world more, gender inequality appears to decline.

Sources: Anita Spring 2000a; 2000b; 2000c; Bossen 2000; G. Clark 2000; Doyle 2005.

Aggression Which differences in personality are suggested by these systematic studies? The most consistent difference is in the area of aggression. Boys try to hurt others more frequently than girls do. In the Six Cultures project, an extensive comparative study of children's behavior, this difference was statistically significant as early as 3 to 6 years of age.[66] Six different research teams observed children's behavior in Kenya (among the Gusii), Mexico, India, the Philippines, Okinawa, and the United States. A more recent cross-cultural comparison of four other cultures (the Logoli of Kenya, Nepal, Belize, and American Samoa) supports the finding that boys are generally more aggressive.[67] Studies in

Cross-culturally, girls more often play in small, intimate groups, boys in larger groups with more interpersonal distance.

the United States are consistent with the cross-cultural findings as well: In a large number of observational and experimental studies, boys exhibited more aggression than girls.[68]

Other female-male differences have turned up with considerable consistency, but we have to be cautious in accepting them, either because they have not been documented as well or because there are more exceptions. There seems to be a tendency for girls to exhibit more responsible behavior, including nurturance (trying to help others). Girls seem more likely to conform to adult wishes and commands. Boys try more often to exert dominance over others to get their own way. In play, boys and girls show a preference for their own gender. Boys seem to play in large groups, girls in small ones. And boys seem to maintain more personal distance between each other than girls do.[69]

If we assume that these differences are consistent across cultures, how can we explain them? Many writers and researchers believe that because certain female-male differences are so consistent, they are probably rooted in the biological differences between the two sexes. Aggression is one of the traits most often attributed to biology, particularly because gender difference in this behavior appears so early in life.[70] But an alternative argument is that societies bring up boys and girls differently because they almost universally require adult males and females to perform different types of roles. If most societies expect adult males to be warriors or to be prepared to be warriors, shouldn't we expect most societies to encourage or idealize aggression in males? And if females are almost always the caretakers of infants, shouldn't we also expect societies generally to encourage nurturing behaviors in females?

Researchers tend to adopt either the biological or the socialization view, but it is possible that both kinds of causes are important in the development of gender differences. For example, parents might turn a slight biological difference into a large gender difference by maximizing that difference in the way they socialize boys versus girls.

It is difficult for researchers to distinguish the influence of genes and other biological conditions from the influence of socialization. As we discussed in the beginning of this chapter, we have research indicating that parents treat boy and girl infants differently as early as birth.[71] In spite of the fact that objective observers can see no major "personality" differences between girl and boy infants, parents often claim to.[72] But parents may unconsciously want to see differences and may therefore produce them in socialization. Even early differences could be learned, therefore, rather than resulting from biological differences. Remember, too, that researchers cannot do experiments with people; for example, parents' behavior cannot be manipulated to find out what would happen if boys and girls were treated in exactly the same ways.

However, there is considerable experimental research on aggression in nonhuman animals. These experiments suggest that the hormone androgen is partly responsible for higher levels of aggression. For example, in some experiments, females injected with androgen at about the time the sexual organs develop (before or shortly after birth) behave more aggressively when they are older than do females without the hormone.

These results may or may not apply to humans, of course, but some researchers have investigated human females who were "androgenized" in the womb because of drugs given to their mothers to prevent miscarriage. By and large, the results of these studies are similar to the experimental studies—androgenized human females show similar patterns of higher aggression.[73] Some scholars take these results to indicate that biological differences between males and females are responsible for the male-female difference in aggression;[74] others suggest that even these results are not conclusive because females who get more androgen show generally disturbed metabolic systems, and general metabolic disturbance may itself increase aggressiveness. Furthermore, androgen-injected females may look more like males because they develop male-like genitals; therefore, they may be treated like males.[75] Even the degree of aggression in males that can be attributed to androgens—and specifically, testosterone—is variable, it seems. Studies in endocrinology suggest that high testosterone levels in themselves do not cause men to be more aggressive. Rather, it appears that aggression results when testosterone surges in response to a distress signal of a sort sent by the amygdala, which is a part of the brain that communicates with the emotional center of the brain, the hypothalamus. In other words, if a male is otherwise in a mellow mood, a surge of testosterone is not likely to incite him to violence.[76]

Is there any cross-cultural evidence that socialization differences may account for differences in aggression? Although a survey of ethnographers' reports on 101 societies does show that more societies encourage aggression in boys than in girls, most societies show no difference in aggression training.[77] The few societies that do show differences in aggression training can hardly account for the widespread sex differences in actual aggressiveness. But the survey does not necessarily mean that there are no consistent differences in aggression training for boys and girls. All it shows is that there are no *obvious* differences. For all we know, the learning of aggression and other "masculine" traits by boys could be produced by subtle types of socialization.

One possible type of subtle socialization that could create gender differences in behavior is the chores children are assigned. It is possible that little boys and girls learn to behave differently because their parents ask them to do different kinds of work. Beatrice and John Whiting reported from the Six Cultures project that in societies where children were asked to do a great deal of work, they generally showed more responsible and nurturant behavior. Girls, who are almost always asked to do more work than boys, may be more responsible and nurturant for this reason alone.[78] If this reasoning is correct, we should find that boys asked to do girls' work would behave more like girls.

A study of Luo children in Kenya by Carol Ember supports this view.[79] Girls were usually asked to babysit, cook, clean house, and fetch water and firewood. Boys were usually asked to do very little because boys' traditional work was herding cattle, and most families in the community studied had few cattle. But for some reason, more boys than girls had been born, and many mothers without girls at home asked their sons to do girls' chores. Systematic behavior observations showed that much of the behavior of the boys who did girls' work was intermediary between the behavior of other boys and the behavior of girls. The boys who did girls' work were more like girls in that they were less aggressive, less domineering, and more responsible than other boys, even when they

Hadza boy with his first bow and arrow. In most hunting-gathering societies, boys learn hunting skill quite early.

weren't working. So it is possible that task assignment has an important influence on how boys and girls learn to behave.

Research in behavioral biology lends support to another kind of social effect. It seems that social conditioning may be as important as—if not more important than— testosterone in predicting aggression in males. A male who is deprived of testosterone but had been conditioned previously to be aggressive will continue to be so. On the other hand, a formerly nonviolent male who is given extra testosterone is not likely to be more aggressive in the face of frustration.[80]

As we noted, an observed difference in aggression does not mean that males are aggressive and females are not. Perhaps because males are generally more aggressive, female aggression has been studied less often. For that reason, Victoria Burbank focused on female aggression in an Australian aborigine community she calls Mangrove. During her 18 months there, Burbank observed some act of aggression almost every other day. Consistent with the cross-cultural evidence, men initiated aggression more often than women, but women were initiators about 43 percent of the time. The women of Mangrove engaged in almost all the same kinds of aggression as men did, including fighting, except that their aggression tended not to be as lethal as male violence. Men most often used lethal weapons; when women fought with weapons, they mostly used sticks, not spears, guns, or knives. Burbank points out that, in contrast to Western cultures, female aggression is not viewed as unnatural or deviant but, rather, as a natural expression of anger.[81]

Dependence One common mistaken belief is that girls are more dependent than boys. The results obtained by the Six Cultures project cast doubt on this notion.[82] First, girls are no more likely to show "dependent" behavior than boys if we think of dependency as seeking help or emotional reassurance from others. To be sure, the results do indicate that boys and girls have somewhat different styles of dependency. Girls more often seek help and contact, whereas boys more often seek attention and approval.

Sociability and Passivity The Six Cultures results showed no reliable differences in sociability, or seeking and offering friendship, between the sexes. Of course, boys and girls may be sociable in different ways, because boys generally play in larger groups than girls. As for the supposed passivity of girls, the evidence is also not particularly convincing. Girls in the Six Cultures project did not consistently withdraw from aggressive attacks or comply with unreasonable demands. The only thing that emerged as a female-male difference was that older girls were less likely than boys to respond to aggression with aggression. But this finding may not reflect passivity as much as the fact that girls are less aggressive than boys, which we already knew.

Sexuality

13.8 Explain variability in sexual behavior and attitudes between different cultures.

In view of the way the human species reproduces, it is not surprising that sexuality is part of our nature. But no society we know of leaves sexuality to nature; all have at least some rules governing "proper" conduct. There is much variation from one society to another in the degree of sexual activity permitted or encouraged before marriage, outside marriage, and even within marriage. And societies vary markedly in their tolerance of nonheterosexual sexuality.

Cultural Regulations of Sexuality: Permissiveness Versus Restrictiveness

All societies seek to regulate sexual activity to some degree, and there is a lot of variation cross-culturally. Some societies allow premarital sex; others forbid it. The same is true for extramarital sex. In addition, a society's degree of restrictiveness is not always consistent throughout the life span or for all aspects of sex. For example, a number of societies ease sexual restrictions during adolescence but impose more restrictions for adults.[83] Then, too, societies change over time. The United States has traditionally been restrictive, but until recently—before the emergence of the AIDS epidemic—more permissive attitudes had been gaining acceptance.

Premarital Sex The degree to which sex before marriage is approved or disapproved of varies greatly from society to society. The Trobriand Islanders, for example, approved of and encouraged premarital sex, seeing it as an important preparation for marriage. Both girls and boys were given complete instruction in all forms of sexual expression at the onset of puberty and were allowed plenty of premarital opportunity for intimacy. Some societies not only allow premarital sex on a casual basis but specifically encourage trial marriages between adolescents. Among the Ila-speaking peoples of central Africa, at harvest time, girls were given houses of their own and could play at being wife with the boys of their choice.[84]

Premarital sex was discouraged in many other societies. For example, among the Tepoztlan Indians of Mexico, a girl's life became "crabbed, cribbed, confined" from the time of her first menstruation. She was not to speak to or encourage boys in the least way. To do so would be to court disgrace, to show herself to be crazy. The responsibility of guarding the chastity and reputation of one or more daughters of marriageable age was often a burden for the mother. One mother said she wished that her 15-year-old daughter would marry soon because it was inconvenient to "spy" on her all the time.[85] In many Arabic societies, a girl's premarital chastity was tested after her marriage. After the wedding night, blood-stained sheets were displayed as proof of the bride's virginity.

Cultures do not remain the same, however; attitudes and practices can change markedly over time, as they have in the United States and in many European countries. In the past, sex was generally delayed until after marriage in Western societies; in the 1990s, most Americans, like their counterparts in Europe, accepted or even approved of premarital sex.[86]

Sex in Marriage Not surprisingly, there are many common features in the sexual relations of married couples, but there is also considerable cross-cultural variation. In most societies, some form of face-to-face sexual intercourse or coitus is the usual pattern, most preferring the woman on her back and the man on top. Couples in most cultures prefer privacy, which is easier in societies with single-family dwellings or separate rooms. But privacy is difficult to attain in societies that have unpartitioned and multifamily dwellings. The Siriono of Bolivia, for example, slept in hammocks 10 feet apart, and a house could contain as many as 50 hammocks. Not surprisingly, couples in such societies have preferred to have sex outdoors in a secluded location.[87]

Night is often preferred for sex, but some cultures have opted specifically for day. For example, the Chenchu of India believed that a child conceived at night might be born blind. In some societies, couples engage in sex quickly with little or no foreplay; in others, foreplay may take hours.[88] Attitudes toward marital sex and the frequency of it vary widely from culture to culture. In one cross-cultural survey, frequent marital sex is generally viewed as a good thing, but in 9 percent of the societies studied, frequent sex is viewed as undesirable and a cause of weakness, illness, and sometimes death.[89] People in most societies abstain from intercourse during menstruation, during at least part of pregnancy, and for a period after childbirth. Some societies prohibit sexual relations before certain activities, such as hunting, fighting, planting, brewing, and iron smelting. Our own society is among the most lenient regarding restrictions on intercourse within marriage, imposing only rather loose (if any) restraints during mourning, menstruation, and pregnancy.[90]

Extramarital Sex Extramarital sex is not uncommon in many societies. In about 69 percent of the world's societies, men have extramarital sex more than occasionally, as do women in about 57 percent of societies. The frequency of such sexual activity is higher than we might expect, given that only a slight majority of societies admit that they allow extramarital sex for men, and only 11 percent of societies acknowledge allowing it for women.[91]

There is quite a difference, then, between the restrictive code and actual practice of many societies. The Navajo of the 1940s were said to forbid adultery, but young married men under the age of 30 had about a quarter of their heterosexual contacts with women other than their wives.[92] And although people in the United States in the 1970s almost overwhelmingly rejected extramarital sex, 41 percent of married men and about 18 percent of married women had had extramarital sex. In the 1990s, with the onset of the AIDS epidemic, proportionately more men and women reported that they had been faithful to their spouses.[93] Cross-culturally, most societies also have a double standard with regard to men and women, with restrictions on women being considerably greater.[94] A substantial number of societies openly accept extramarital relationships. The Chukchee of Siberia, who often traveled long distances, allowed a married man to engage in sex with his host's wife, with the understanding that he would offer the same hospitality when the host visited him.[95]

Although a society may allow extramarital sex, a recent cross-cultural study of individual reactions to extramarital sex finds that men and women try a variety of strategies to curtail such sex. Men are much more likely than women to resort to physical violence against their wives; women are more likely to distance themselves from their husbands. Gossip may be employed to shame the relationship, and a higher authority may be asked to intervene in more complex societies. Researchers conclude that married women and men universally consider extramarital sex inappropriate, even in societies that occasionally permit it.[96]

Homosexuality When most people, including most researchers, discuss homosexuality, they usually refer to sex between males or sex between females. The biological male-female dichotomy corresponds to the gender male-female dichotomy in Western societies, but as we have seen earlier in this chapter, some other societies do not have the same gender concepts. The meaning of homosexuality, therefore, may differ according to the society. The Navajo of the American Southwest, for example, traditionally recognized four genders. Only relationships between people of the same gender would be considered homosexual, and they considered such relationships inappropriate.[97] Biologically speaking, such cross-gender relationships would be considered homosexual in the Western view, and most of the research to date has adopted this view, labeling sexual relations between biologically males or females as homosexuality.

The range in the world's societies of permissiveness or restrictiveness toward homosexual relations is as great as that for any other kind of sexual activity. Among the Lepcha of the Himalayas, a man was believed to become homosexual if he ate the flesh of an uncastrated pig. At the same time, the Lepcha denied that homosexual behavior existed among them, and they viewed it with disgust.[98] Perhaps because many societies deny that homosexuality exists, little is known about homosexual practices in the restrictive societies. Among the permissive ones, there is variation in the type and pervasiveness of homosexuality. In some societies, homosexuality is accepted but limited to certain times and certain individuals. For example, among the Papago of the southwestern United States, there were "nights of saturnalia" in which homosexual tendencies could be expressed. The Papago also had many male transvestites who wore women's clothing, did women's chores, and, if not married, could be visited by men.[99] A woman did not have the same freedom of expression. She could participate in the saturnalia feasts, but only with her husband's permission, and female transvestites were nonexistent.

Backstage beauty preparations for hijra and gay people in Chennai, India

Homosexuality occurs even more widely in other societies. The Berber-speaking Siwans of North Africa expected all males to engage in homosexual relations. In fact, fathers made arrangements for their unmarried sons to be given to an older man in a homosexual arrangement. Siwan custom limited a man to one boy. Such arrangements were made openly until 1909, when fear of the Egyptian government made them a secret matter. Almost all Siwan men were reported to have engaged in a homosexual relationship as boys; later, when they were between 16 and 20, they married girls.[100] Such prescribed homosexual relationships between people of different ages are a common form of homosexuality.[101] Among the most extremely pro-homosexual societies, the Etoro of New Guinea preferred homosexuality to heterosexuality. Heterosexuality was prohibited as many as 260 days a year and was forbidden in or near the house and gardens. Male homosexuality, on the other hand, was not prohibited at any time and was believed to make crops flourish and boys become strong.[102] Even among the Etoro, however, men were expected to marry women after a certain age.[103]

Only recently have researchers paid much attention to erotic relationships between females. Although early studies found relatively few societies with female-female sexual relationships, Evelyn Blackwood located reports of 95 societies with such practices, suggesting that it is more common than previously thought.[104] As with male homosexuality, some societies institutionalize same-sex sexual relationships—the Kaguru of Tanzania have female homosexual relationships between older and younger women as part of their initiation ceremonies, reminiscent of the male-male "mentor" relationships in ancient Greece.

Cross-culturally, it is extremely unusual to find "gays" or exclusive male or female homosexuals. In most societies, males and females are expected to marry, and homosexuality, if tolerated or approved, either occurs as a phase in one's life or occurs along with heterosexuality.[105]

Reasons for Sexual Restrictiveness

Before we deal with the question of why some societies are more restrictive than others, we must first ask whether all forms of restrictiveness go together. The research to date suggests that societies that are restrictive with regard to one aspect of heterosexual sex tend to be restrictive with regard to other aspects. Thus, societies that frown on sexual expression by young children also punish premarital and extramarital sex.[106] Furthermore, such societies tend to insist on modesty in clothing and are constrained in their talk about sex.[107] But societies that are generally restrictive about heterosexuality are not necessarily restrictive about homosexuality. For instance, societies restrictive about premarital sex are neither more nor less likely to restrict homosexuality. The situation is somewhat different regarding extramarital sex. Societies in which male homosexuality is prevalent tend to disapprove of males having extramarital heterosexual relationships.[108] If we are going to explain restrictiveness, then, it appears we have to consider heterosexual and homosexual restrictiveness separately.

Let us consider homosexual restrictiveness first. One study finds that societies that forbid abortion and infanticide for married women (most societies permit these practices for illegitimate births) are likely to be intolerant of male homosexuality.[109] This and other findings are consistent with the point of view that homosexuality is less tolerated in societies that would like to increase their population. Such societies may be intolerant of all kinds of behaviors that minimize population growth. Homosexuality would have this effect if we assume that a higher frequency of homosexual relations is associated with a lower frequency of heterosexual relations. The less frequently heterosexual relations occur, the lower the number of conceptions there might be. Another indication that intolerance may be related to a desire for population growth is that societies with famines and severe food shortages are more likely to allow homosexuality. Famines and food shortages suggest population pressure on resources; under these conditions, homosexuality and other practices that minimize population growth may be tolerated or even encouraged.[110]

Population pressure may also explain why our own society has become somewhat more tolerant of homosexuality recently. Of course, population pressure does not explain why certain individuals become homosexual or why most individuals in some societies engage in such behavior, but it might explain why some societies view such behavior more or less permissively.

Let us now turn to heterosexual behavior. What kinds of societies are more permissive than others? Although we do not yet understand the reasons, we do know that greater restrictiveness toward premarital sex tends to occur in more complex societies—societies that have hierarchies of political officials, part-time or full-time craft specialists, cities and towns, and class stratification.[111] It may be that, as social inequality increases, parents become more concerned with preventing their children from marrying "beneath them." Permissiveness toward premarital sexual relationships might lead a person to become attached to someone not considered a desirable marriage partner. Even worse, from the family's point of view, an "unsuitable" sexual liaison might result in a pregnancy that could make it impossible for a girl to marry "well." Controlling mating, then, may be a way of trying to control property. Consistent with this view is the finding that virginity is emphasized in rank and stratified societies, in which families are likely to exchange goods and money in the course of arranging marriages.[112]

The biological fact that humans depend on sexual reproduction does not by itself help explain why females and males differ in so many ways across cultures or why societies vary in the way they handle male and female roles. We are only beginning to investigate these questions. When we eventually understand more about how and why females and males differ in gender roles, personality, and sexuality, we may be better able to decide how much we want the biology of sex to shape our lives.

Summary and Review

Gender Concepts

13.1 Describe variation in gender concepts.

- The division into just two genders—male/female—is very common cross-culturally, but a strict dichotomy is far from universal.

- Some cultures have additional gender designations besides male and female.

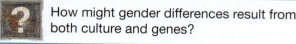 What are some examples of varying gender concepts?

Physique and Physiology

13.2 Identify differences in physique and physiology between males and females.

- Humans are sexually dimorphic: Females have proportionately wider pelvises and a larger proportion of fat; males typically are taller and have heavier skeletons, a larger proportion of muscle, greater grip strength, proportionately larger hearts and lungs, and more aerobic capacity.

- Females achieve their ultimate height shortly after puberty, but boys continue to grow for years after puberty. Natural selection may have favored earlier cessation of female growth so the nutritional needs of a fetus would not compete with a growing mother's needs.

- Gender differences may be the result of both culture and genes.

? How might gender differences result from both culture and genes?

Gender Roles

13.3 Explain differences in gender roles.

- Many societies divide up work in similar ways. Four theories—strength theory, compatibility-with-child-care theory, economy-of-effort theory, and expendability theory—try to explain why females and males generally do different work, but each has theoretical weaknesses.

- Strength theory says that males generally possess greater strength and a superior capacity to mobilize their strength in quick bursts of energy; however, not all male activities require strength, and women do hunt in some societies.

- The compatibility-with-child-care theory suggests that women make child care a priority and fit in other tasks but does not explain why men usually prepare soil for planting and make wood, bone, horn, and shell objects, tasks that can probably be stopped to tend to a child and no more dangerous than cooking.

- The economy-of-effort interpretation suggests that it would be advantageous for one gender to perform tasks that are related in terms of knowledge and training and tasks that are physically located near each other.

- The expendability theory is the idea that men will tend to do the dangerous work in a society because the loss of men is not as great a disadvantage reproductively as the loss of women. However, it does not explain why men would put themselves in danger.

- As societies change, gender roles tend to change but still remain divided in some way.

 What are some of the near-universals and differences in gender roles cross-culturally? Discuss domestic, productive, and political roles.

Relative Contributions to Work: Who Works More?

13.4 Analyze relative gender differences in term of contributions to work.

- Most contemporary societies typically equate "work" with earning money, but that view is relatively recent to human history.

- Anthropologists may skew research about division of labor by focusing more on gathering, hunting, fishing, herding, and farming than on food preparation and storage and, in so doing, distort the importance of each gender's contributions.

- In horticultural and intensive agricultural societies, studies so far suggest that women typically work more total hours per day than men.

- Usually both women and men contribute a good deal toward primary food-getting activities, but men usually contribute more in most societies. The type of agriculture may help explain some of the variation.

- Cross-cultural studies suggest that, when women contribute a lot to primary food-getting activities, infants are fed solid foods earlier, enabling others to feed them; girls are likely to be industrious, probably to help their mothers; and female babies are more valued.

 What might explain why men and women do relatively more work?

Political Leadership and Warfare

13.5 Discuss gender differences in terms of political leadership and warfare cross-culturally.

- In almost every known society, men tend to lead in political arenas, possibly because men's role in warfare may give them the edge in political leadership and because men spend more time in the outside world than do women.

- Males almost universally dominate in warfare, perhaps because warfare requires strength and quick bursts of energy, combat is not compatible with child care, and women's fertility is more important to a population than their usefulness as warriors.

 What theories might support the findings about gender differences in political leadership and warfare?

The Relative Status of Women

13.6 Analyze relative status among women cross-culturally.

- Theories suggest that women will have higher status when: (1) women contribute substantially to primary subsistence activities; (2) where residence is organized around women; (3) where warfare is unimportant; and (4) where political hierarchies are less centralized.

- The idea that generally high status for women stems from greater caloric contribution to primary subsistence activities is not supported by research evidence. Nor is generally higher status for men associated with more warfare.

- The idea of status has multiple dimensions that are not always linked. Thus, research needs to look at women's status in various spheres of life, why some societies have many areas in which women's status is high and others have few, or why there is less or more gender stratification.

- Education almost always increases status, and the more girls and young women are educated, the greater the likelihood that their status will increase.

 How might the relative status of women and men be measured? What are some of the findings on cross-cultural variations in status by gender?

Personality Differences

13.7▸ Discuss gender differences in personality.

- Observed differences between male and female personalities in Western and non-Western countries are a matter of degree, not a matter of a behavior being present or absent.

- Aggression is the most consistent personality difference: Boys try to hurt others more often than girls do. This difference appears early, so it may have biological causes, possibly hormonal. But societies may also raise boys and girls differently from very early ages, so nature and nurture are hard to separate.

- Cross-culturally, girls are no more likely to show "dependent" behavior than boys if dependency is seen as seeking help or emotional reassurance from others; however, studies show that boys and girls have somewhat different styles of dependency.

- Cross-culturally, studies show no reliable differences in levels of sociability between the sexes, although male and female styles of sociability may differ.

- Cross-culturally, studies do not confirm that girls are more passive than boys, but they do show that older girls were less likely than boys to respond to aggression with aggression.

 What are some of the cross-cultural findings about gender differences in personality?

Sexuality

13.8▸ Explain variability in sexual behavior and attitudes between different cultures.

- All societies have rules governing "proper" sexual conduct, but they vary. In addition, a society's degree of restrictiveness is not always consistent throughout the life span or for all aspects of sex. Approval or disapproval of premarital sex varies greatly cross-culturally.

- Sexual attitudes and practices can change markedly over time in societies.

- Attitudes toward marital sex and its frequency and location vary widely cross-culturally. The restrictive codes for extramarital sex in many societies vary greatly from actual practice.

- Cross-culturally, the meaning of homosexuality may differ, and acceptance or limitations vary greatly. In most societies, males and females are expected to marry, and homosexuality, if tolerated or approved, occurs either as a phase in one's life or along with heterosexuality.

- Current research suggests that societies that are restrictive with regard to heterosexual sex may not be restrictive about homosexuality. Homosexuality may be tolerated or encouraged in societies that minimize population growth.

- Greater restrictiveness toward premarital sex tends to occur in more complex societies—societies that have hierarchies of political officials, part-time or full-time craft specialists, cities and towns, and class stratification.

What may explain variability in sexual behavior and attitudes between different cultures?

Think on it

1. Would you expect female-male differences in personality to disappear in a society with complete **gender equality** in the workplace?

2. Under what circumstances would you expect male-female differences in **athletic performance** to disappear?

3. What conditions may make the **election** of a female head of state most likely?

Marriage, Family, and Kinship

LEARNING OBJECTIVES

Define marriage in anthropological terms.	**14.1**
Explain the near-universality of marriage across cultures.	**14.2**
Identify the various ways that marriage is marked in different societies and the economic exchanges that accompany it.	**14.3**
Discuss the types of restrictions on whom one can marry.	**14.4**
Describe the three different forms of marriage and explain social or economic reasons for each.	**14.5**
Describe and explain variation in family form.	**14.6**
Explain why kinship is important.	**14.7**
Identify the various patterns of marital residence.	**14.8**
Discuss the various ways of affiliating with kin and how the systems differ.	**14.9**
Discuss what might explain variation in marital residence patterns.	**14.10**
Discuss what may explain the emergence of unilineal, ambilineal, and bilateral systems.	**14.11**

Marriage is customary in every society known to anthropologists, with only one or two exceptions. When a cultural institution is as common as marriage but apparently not absolutely essential to human survival—people can reproduce and have families without marriage—anthropologists ask *why*. One popular answer today might be that people marry for love.

But mere passion has in much of the world been frowned upon as the basis for as important a social contract as marriage.

We do know that the fundamental concept of marriage is nearly universal, and in this chapter we will look at it in all its forms, for how one marries, whom one marries, and even how many people a person can be married to simultaneously vary from society to society. Indeed, although each marriage usually involves one pair at a time, most societies have allowed a man to be married to more than one woman at a time, and a few have allowed a woman more than one husband. And we will explore the debate over why humans marry.

Families are unequivocally universal, for all societies have parent-child groups. The form and size of the family, however, can also vary from society to society. Extended families with two or more related parent-child groups are the norm in a majority of societies, whereas others have smaller, independent families. Marriage is not necessarily the basis for family life. One-parent families are increasingly common in our own and other societies today. Although marriage has not disappeared in these places—it is still customary to marry—more individuals are choosing to have children without being married. Yet the majority of people continue to think that marriage and family belong together.

As we will see, kin groups that include hundreds of even thousands of related people are found in many societies and have economic, socio-political, and religious functions. In fact, in noncommercial societies, kin groups were probably the most important aspect of social organization.

14.1 Define marriage in anthropological terms.

Marriage

Marriage A socially approved sexual and economic union, usually between a man and a woman, that is presumed, both by the couple and by others, to be more or less permanent, and that subsumes reciprocal rights and obligations between the two spouses and their future children.

Marriage is customary in nearly every known society. The fact that it exists nearly everywhere does not mean that couples everywhere must get marriage certificates or have wedding ceremonies, as in our own society. It does not mean that they even necessarily live together after they are married. Nor does it mean that the marriage will be exclusive, for marriage to more than one spouse at a time is quite common. Rather, **marriage** everywhere is understood to be a socially approved sexual and economic union, usually between a woman and a man. It is presumed, by both the couple and others, to be more or less permanent, and it subsumes reciprocal rights and obligations between the two spouses and between spouses and their future children.[1]

Marriage is a socially approved sexual union in that the couple's sexual relationship is implicitly understood and condoned. A woman might say, "I want you to meet my husband," but she could not say, "I want you to meet my lover" without embarrassment in most societies. Although the union may one day end in divorce, couples in all societies enter into marriage expecting a long-term commitment. Implicit, too, in marriage are reciprocal rights and obligations regarding property, finances, and childrearing. As George Peter Murdock noted, "Sexual relations can occur without economic cooperation, and there can be a division of labor between men and women without sex. But marriage unites the economic and the sexual."[2]

The Na Exception

We say that marriage is customary in almost all societies, but there are some interesting exceptions. The Na of Yunnan in southwest China, with a population of about 40,000, have customarily not married or lived with their sexual partners. Rather, men and women lived their entire lives in residential groups made up of their respective maternal kin (grandmother, great-uncles, brothers, sisters, and their children). The maternal household cooperated economically and raised the children. The Na practice *sese*, the consensual sexual union of an unmarried couple.[3] When a couple agrees to see each other, the man visits the woman discreetly in the evening and returns to his own residence the next morning. No other tie exists between the lovers, nor is there any expectation that the relationship be longstanding or monogamous. The offspring of such relationships normally take the woman's family name and are raised by her family. But the Chinese government has tried off and on since 1959 to impose marriage among the Na and even to fine them for illegitimate births, but without much success. Traditionally, only a few women and men, usually of the aristocratic class, chose to live together. While the government has become more flexible about Na customs, some Na are now choosing to marry, especially when they work in the Chinese government or work away from their community. Young people's attitudes are also changing, largely because of their education in Chinese schools, where they become self-conscious when asked their fathers' names.

Same-Sex Marriages

In addition to male-female marriages, some societies recognize same-sex marriages. Although they are far from common in any known society, same-sex marriages may be socially approved unions and entail reciprocal rights and obligations similar to those between heterosexual women and men. In some cultures, a biological female or male is expected to take on the opposite gender role and become the wife or husband in the union. Cheyenne Indians allowed a married man to take as a second wife a biological man who belonged to the third-gender "two-spirits."[4]

It is not clear that Cheyenne male-male marriages involved homosexual relationships, but temporary homosexual marriages are known to have occurred among the Azande of Africa. Before the British took control over what is now Sudan, Azande warriors who could not afford wives often married "boy-wives." The boy-wives had sexual relations with their husbands and also performed many of the chores traditionally delegated to female wives. As in normal marriages, gifts (although less substantial) were given by the "husband" to the parents of his boy-wife. The husband performed services for the boy's parents and could sue any other lover of the boy in court for adultery.[5]

Female-female marriages are reported to have occurred in many African societies, but there is no evidence of sexual relationships between the partners. It seems, rather, that female-female marriages were a socially approved way for a woman to take on the legal and social roles of father and husband.[6] Such marriages have existed, for example, among the Nandi, a pastoral and agricultural society of Kenya, as a way to resolve the failure to produce a male heir to property through a regular marriage. A woman, even if her husband is still alive, will become "husband" to a younger female and "father" the younger woman's future children. The female husband provides the marriage payments required for obtaining a wife, renounces female work, and takes on the obligations of husband. No sexual relations are permitted between the female husband and the new wife (or between the female husband and her own husband). Rather, the female husband arranges for her new wife to have a male consort in order to have children and subsequently becomes the socially designated father. If asked who their father is, children of such a marriage will name the female husband.[7]

Why Is Marriage Nearly Universal?

14.2 Explain the near-universality of marriage across cultures.

Because virtually all societies practice female-male marriage as we have defined it, we can assume that the custom is adaptive. Several interpretations have traditionally been offered to explain why all human societies have the custom of marriage. Each suggests that marriage solves problems found in all societies—how to share the products of a gender division of labor; how to care for infants, who are dependent for a long time; and how to minimize sexual competition. The comparative study of other animals, some of which have something like marriage, may help us to evaluate these explanations.

Gender Division of Labor

We noted in the preceding chapter that females and males in every society known to anthropology perform different economic activities. This gender division of labor has often been cited as a reason for marriage.[8] As long as there is a division of labor by gender, society has to structure a way for women and men to share the products of their labor. Marriage would be one way to solve that problem. But it seems unlikely that marriage is the only possible solution. The hunter-gatherer rule of sharing could be extended to include all the products brought in by both women and men. Or a small group of men and women, such as brothers and sisters, might be pledged to cooperate economically. Thus, although marriage may solve the problem of sharing the fruits of a division of labor, it clearly is not the only possible solution.

Prolonged Infant Dependency

Humans exhibit the longest period of infant dependency of any primate. The child's prolonged dependence places the greatest burden on the mother, who is the main child caregiver in most societies. The burden of prolonged child care by human females may limit the kinds of work they can do. They may need the help of a man to do certain types of work, such as hunting, that are incompatible with child care. Because of this prolonged dependency, it has been suggested, marriage is necessary.[9] But here the argument becomes essentially the same as the division-of-labor argument, and it has the same logical weakness. It is not clear why a group of women and men, such as a hunter-gatherer band, could not cooperate in providing for dependent children without marriage.

Sexual Competition

Unlike most other female primates, the human female may engage in intercourse at any time throughout the year. Some scholars have suggested that more or less continuous female sexuality may have created a serious problem: considerable sexual competition between males for females. It is argued that society had to prevent such competition to survive, that it had to develop some way of minimizing the rivalry among males for females to reduce the chance of lethal and destructive conflict.[10]

There are several logical problems with this argument. First, why should continuous female sexuality make for more sexual competition in the first place? More availability should make for less competition. When there is only a brief breeding season of a few days, competition should be greater. Second, males of many animal species, even some in which females are frequently sexually receptive (such as many of our close primate relatives), do not show much aggression over females. Third, why couldn't sexual competition, even if it existed, be regulated by cultural rules other than marriage? For instance, society might have adopted a rule whereby men and women circulated among all the opposite-sex members of the group, each person staying a specified length of time with each partner. Such a system presumably would solve the problem of sexual competition. On the other hand, such a system might not work particularly well if individuals came to prefer certain other individuals. Jealousies attending those attachments might give rise to even more competition.

A Look at Other Mammals and Birds

None of the theories we have discussed explain convincingly why marriage is the only or the best solution to a particular problem. In addition, some comparative evidence on mammals and birds casts doubt on those theories.[11] How can evidence from other animals help us evaluate theories about human marriage? If we look at animals that, like humans, exhibit some stable female-male mating, as opposed to those that are completely promiscuous, we can perhaps see what factors may predict male-female bonding in the warm-blooded animal species. Female-male bonding occurs in most species of birds and some mammals, such as wolves and beavers. Among 40 mammal and bird species, neither division of labor, nor prolonged infant dependency, nor greater female sexuality correlates with male-female bonding in the direction predicted by the theories discussed earlier. The birds and mammals studied have nothing comparable to a humanlike division of labor, but they exhibit female-male unions nevertheless. The two other suggested factors—prolonged infant dependency and female sexuality—relate to male-female bonding in the opposite direction to what was expected. Mammal and bird species that have longer infant dependency periods or more female sexuality are less likely to have male-female bonding.

Does any factor predict male-female bonding among other mammals and birds and thereby also help explain human marriage? It appears that animal species in which females are able to simultaneously feed themselves and their babies after birth (*postpartum*) tend not to mate stably. On the other hand, species in which postpartum mothers cannot feed themselves and their babies at the same time do typically form male-female bonds. Among the typical bird species, a mother would have difficulty feeding herself and her babies simultaneously. Because her young cannot fly for some time, the mother risks losing them to predators if she leaves the nest untended to search for food. If a male has bonded with her, as males in most bird species do, he can bring food or take his turn watching the nest. Among animal species that have no postpartum feeding

A black-browed albatross on the Falkland Islands. Most bird species have male-female bonding.

problem, babies are able to travel with the mother almost immediately after birth as she moves about to eat (as do such grazers as horses), or the mother can transport the babies as she moves about to eat (as do baboons and kangaroos). We believe the human female has a postpartum feeding problem. When humans lost most of their body hair, babies could not readily travel with the mother by clinging to her fur. And when humans began to depend on certain kinds of food-getting that could be dangerous, such as hunting, mothers could not engage in such work with their infants along.[12]

Research by Frank Marlowe on the Hadza foragers of Tanzania appears to support this theoretical argument. Hadza women and men both forage for food, with the women providing more berries and other plant foods while the men provide more meat and honey. Generally, it appears that Hadza women could support themselves and their children without a mate. Married women forage more regularly and contribute more food (in terms of calories) to the family diet, *except* when they have a nursing infant. Marlowe found that the father of an infant made up for the mother's lower food contribution while she was nursing. In fact, Hazda fathers with nursing children contributed significantly more food to the household than fathers with older children.[13]

Even if we assume that human mothers have a postpartum feeding problem, we must ask if marriage is the most likely solution to the problem. It may well be, because other conceivable solutions probably would not work as well. If a mother took turns babysitting with another mother, for example, neither might be able to collect enough food for both mothers and the two sets of children dependent on them. A mother and father share the same set of children, making it easier for them to feed themselves and their children adequately. Another possible solution is males and females living in a promiscuous group. We believe that a particular mother in that kind of arrangement would probably not be able to count on any male, if he didn't think he was the father, to watch her baby when she had to go out for food, or to bring her food when she had to watch her baby. The need to solve the postpartum feeding problem by itself may help to explain why some animals, including humans, have relatively stable male-female bonds.[14]

How Does One Marry?

When we say that marriage is a socially approved sexual and economic union, we mean that all societies have some way of marking the onset of a marriage, but the ways of doing so vary considerably. For reasons that we don't fully understand, some cultures mark marriages by elaborate rites and celebrations; others mark marriages in much more informal ways. And most societies have economic transactions before, during, or even after the onset of the marriages.

14.3 Identify the various ways that marriage is marked in different societies and the economic exchanges that accompany it.

Marking the Onset of Marriage

Many societies mark the beginning of a marriage with a ceremony. Others, such as the Taramiut Inuit of the Arctic, the Trobriand Islanders, and the Kwoma of New Guinea, use different social signals to indicate that a marriage has taken place.

Among the Taramiut Inuit, an engaged couple's success at producing offspring marks the onset of marriage. The betrothal, or engagement, is considered extremely important and is arranged between the parents at or before the time their children reach puberty. Later, when the young man is ready, he moves in with his betrothed's family for a trial period. If all goes well—that is, if the young woman gives birth to a baby within a year or so—the couple is considered married and the wife goes with her husband to his camp. If the couple does not conceive, the young man returns to his family without a wife.[15]

The Kwoma practice a trial marriage followed by a ceremony that makes the couple husband and wife. The girl lives for a while in the boy's home. When the boy's mother is satisfied with the match and knows that her son is too, she waits for a day when he is away from the house. Until that time, the girl has been cooking only for herself, and the boy's food has been prepared by his womenfolk. Now the mother has the girl prepare his meal. The young man returns and begins to eat his soup. When the first bowl is nearly finished, his mother tells him that his betrothed cooked the meal, and his eating it means that he is now married. At this news, the boy customarily rushes out of the house, spits out the soup, and shouts, "Faugh! It tastes bad! It is cooked terribly!" A ceremony then makes the marriage official.[16]

Just in the last three decades, "living together" has become more of an option in the United States and other Western countries. For most, living together is a prelude to marriage or kind of a trial marriage. For some, living together has become an alternative to marriage. Statistics in the United States suggest that by 1995 about 56 percent of women had lived with a man without being married for at least some time period.[17]

Economic Aspects of Marriage

"It's not man that marries maid, but field marries field, vineyard marries vineyard, cattle marry cattle," goes a German peasant saying. In its down-to-earth way, the expression states a reality in many societies: Marriage involves economic considerations. In our culture, economic considerations may or may not be explicit. But in about 75 percent of the societies known to anthropology,[18] one or more explicit economic transactions take place before or after the marriage. The economic transaction may include any of several forms: bride price, bride service, exchange of females, gift exchange, dowry, or indirect dowry.

Bride Price A gift of money or goods from the groom or his kin to the bride's kin is known as **bride price** or **bride wealth**. The gift usually grants the groom the right to marry the bride and the right to her children. Of all the forms of economic transaction involved in marriage, bride price is the most common. In one cross-cultural sample, 44 percent of societies that had economic transactions at marriage practiced bride price; in almost all of those societies, the bride price was substantial.[19] Bride price is practiced all over the world, but it is especially common in Africa and Oceania. Payment may be made in different currencies; livestock and food are two of the more common. With the increased importance of commercial exchange, money has increasingly become part of bride price payments.

What kinds of societies are likely to have the custom of bride price? Cross-culturally, societies with bride price are likely to practice horticulture and lack social stratification. Bride price is also likely where women contribute a great deal to primary subsistence activities[20] and where they contribute more than men to all kinds of economic activities.[21] Although these findings might suggest that women are highly valued in such societies, recall that the status of women relative to men is not higher in societies in which women contribute a lot to primary subsistence activities. Indeed, bride price is likely to occur in societies in which men make most of the decisions in the household,[22] and decision making by men is one indicator of lower status for women.

Bride Service The next most common type of economic transaction at marriage—occurring in about 19 percent of the societies with economic transactions—requires the groom to provide **bride service,** or work for the bride's family, sometimes before the

Bride price A substantial gift of goods or money given to the bride's kin by the groom or his kin at or before the marriage. Also called **bride wealth.**

Bride service Work performed by the groom for his bride's family for a variable length of time either before or after the marriage.

marriage begins, sometimes after. Bride service varies in duration. In some societies, it lasts for only a few months; in others, as long as several years. In some societies, bride service sometimes substitutes for bride price. An individual might give bride service to reduce the amount of bride price required. Native North and South American societies were likely to practice bride service, particularly if they were egalitarian food collectors.[23]

Exchange of Females   Of the societies that have economic transactions at marriage, 6 percent have the custom whereby a sister or female relative of the groom is exchanged for the bride. Among the societies that practice exchange of females are the Tiv of West Africa and the Yanomamö of Venezuela and Brazil. These societies tend to be horticultural and egalitarian, and their women make a relatively high contribution to primary subsistence.[24]

Gift Exchange   The exchange of gifts of about equal value by the two kin groups about to be linked by marriage occurs somewhat more often (about 11 percent of those with economic transactions) than the exchange of females.[25] Among the Andaman Islanders, for example, as soon as a boy and girl indicate their intention to marry, their respective sets of parents cease all communication and begin sending gifts of food and other objects to each other through a third party. The gift exchange continues until the marriage is completed and the two kin groups are united.[26]

Dowry   A substantial transfer of goods or money from the bride's family to the bride, the groom, or the couple is known as a **dowry**.[27] Unlike the types of transactions we have discussed so far, the dowry, which is given in about 8 percent of societies with economic transactions, is usually not a transaction between the kin of the bride and the kin of the groom. A family has to have wealth to give a dowry, but because the goods go to the new household, no wealth comes back to the family that gave the dowry. Payment of dowries was common in medieval and Renaissance Europe, where the size of the dowry often determined the desirability of the daughter. The custom is still practiced in parts of eastern Europe and in sections of southern Italy and France, where land is often the major item the bride's family provides. Parts of India also practice dowry.

Dowry   A substantial transfer of goods or money from the bride's family to the bride.

In one Sudanese society the amount of bride price varies by height. A tall girl may bring 150 cows, a short girl just 30.

In contrast to societies with bride price, societies with dowry tend to be those in which women contribute relatively little to primary subsistence activities, there is a high degree of social stratification, and a man is not allowed to be married to more than one woman simultaneously.[28]

Indirect dowry Goods given by the groom's kin to the bride (or her father, who passes most of them to her) at or before her marriage.

Indirect Dowry   The dowry is provided by the bride's family to the bride, the groom, or the couple. But sometimes the payments to the bride originate from the groom's family. Because the goods are sometimes first given to the bride's father, who passes most if not all of them to her, this kind of transaction is called **indirect dowry.**[29] Indirect dowry occurs in about 12 percent of the societies in which marriage involves an economic transaction.

14.4 Discuss the types of restrictions on whom one can marry.

Whom Should One Marry or Not Marry?

Romantic literature and Hollywood notwithstanding, marriage is seldom based solely on mutual love, independently discovered and expressed by the two life-partners-to-be. Nor is it based on sex or wealth alone. Even when love, sex, and economics are contributing factors, regulations specify whom one may or may not marry.

Incest Taboo

Incest taboo Prohibition of sexual intercourse or marriage between mother and son, father and daughter, and brother and sister; often extends to other relatives.

Perhaps the most rigid regulation, found in *all* cultures, is the **incest taboo,** which prohibits sexual intercourse or marriage between some categories of kin.

The most universal aspect of the incest taboo is the prohibition of sexual intercourse or marriage between mother and son, father and daughter, and brother and sister. No society in recent times has permitted either sexual intercourse or marriage between those pairs. A few societies in the past, however, did permit incest, mostly within the royal and aristocratic families, though generally it was forbidden to the rest of the population. For example, the Incan and Hawaiian royal families allowed marriage within the family. Probably the best-known example of allowed incest involved Cleopatra of Egypt.

It seems clear that the Egyptian aristocracy and royalty indulged in father-daughter and brother-sister marriages. Cleopatra was married to two of her younger brothers at different times.[30] The reasons seem to have been partly religious—a member of the family of the pharaoh, who was considered a god, could not marry any "ordinary" human—and partly economic, for marriage within the family kept the royal property undivided. Between 30 B.C. and A.D. 324, incest was allowed in ancient Egypt not only among the royal family but among commoners; an estimated 8 percent of commoner marriages were brother-sister marriages.[31] In spite of such exceptions, no culture we know of today permits or accepts incest within the nuclear family.

Arranged Marriages

Parents invariably play a role in who their offspring marry. In many societies, parents or other family members determine who their sons and daughters will marry, with the respective families or go-betweens handling the negotiations. Sometimes betrothals are completed while the future partners are still children, as was formerly the custom in much of Hindu India, China, Japan, and eastern and southern Europe. Implicit in the arranged marriage is the conviction that the joining together of two different kin groups to form new social and economic ties is too important to be left to free choice and romantic love.

Arranged marriages are becoming less common in many places, and couples are beginning to have more voice in selecting their marriage partners. Marriages were still arranged, for example, on the Pacific island of Rotuma in 1960, and the bride and groom would sometimes not meet until the wedding day. A Rotuma wedding ceremony may be much the same today as it was then, but couples are now allowed to "go out" and have a say about whom they wish to marry.[32]

Exogamy The rule specifying marriage to a person from outside one's own group (kin or community).

Exogamy and Endogamy

A widespread marriage practice is the regulation of whether a partner comes from outside or inside one's own kin group or community. The rule of **exogamy** requires that the

Migrants and Immigrants

Arranging Marriages in the Diaspora

What happens when people move from a place with arranged marriage to a place where marriage is based on free choice and romantic love? Many people around the world or their parents are from places that reject love marriage because it could fizzle out. Love was not considered a sufficient basis for marriage. So parents and other kin, or hired go-betweens, would select your marriage partner, preferably someone from the same socioeconomic background. For example, in many parts of South Asia, one was supposed to marry someone from the same caste and class until recently. Many immigrant parents still insist that their children's marriages be arranged. But this is changing. Consider how some young South Asians in England are "arranging" their own marriages.

Go-betweens are replaced by Web sites, chat rooms, and personal advertisements on the Internet. A couple who "meet" first electronically might arrange a face-to-face meeting, in what's called "South Asian speed dating"; they agree to meet and talk—for just three minutes—at a restaurant or bar, and then they move on. The participants, who are in their 20s and middle class, consider themselves hip. They are quite comfortable blending behaviors from West and East. Is the same true for South Asians in the United States?

Rakhi is a lawyer in New York City. She is the daughter of Sikh

These young South Asian Hindus in Great Britain are "speed dating." They talk with potential spouses for three minutes each. Traditionally, parents arrange marriages.

immigrants from Punjab, India. (The Sikhs are a religious group.) As a young girl, Rakhi had built a shrine to an American movie star in her bedroom. But at the age of 27, she decided to marry someone like herself. Because she was focused on her career and didn't have time to date, her mother enlisted the help of a Sikh matchmaker who had been instructed by the mother of a man named Ranjeet to find a wife for him. Ranjeet also had thought he would marry for love. "But seeing how different cultures treated their families, I realized the importance of making the right match," he said. When the matchmaker organized a party to which she invited Rakhi and Ranjeet (and their mothers), Rakhi's mother whispered: "I think he's the one." After the two young people dated secretly for two months, the matchmaker was once again summoned, this time to negotiate the marital arrangements. Sometime later, Rakhi and Ranjeet were married in a Sikh temple in a New York suburb.

Sources: Alvarez 2003, Section 1, p. 3; Henderson 2002, Section 9, p. 2.

marriage partner come from outside one's own kin group or community. Exogamy can take many forms. It may mean marrying outside a particular group of kin or outside a particular village or group of villages. Often, then, spouses come from a distance. People in exogamous societies with very low population densities often have to travel considerable distances to meet mates. A study of foragers and horticulturalists found a clear relationship between population density and the distance between the communities of the husband and wife—the lower the density, the greater the marriage distance. Because forager societies generally have lower population densities than horticulturalists, they generally have further to go to find mates. Among the !Kung, for instance, the average husband and wife had lived 40 miles (65 kilometers) from each other before they were married.[33]

The opposite rule, **endogamy,** obliges a person to marry within a particular group. The caste groups of India traditionally have been endogamous. The higher castes believed that marriage with lower castes would "pollute" them, and such unions were forbidden. Caste endogamy is also found in some parts of Africa.

Endogamy The rule specifying marriage to a person within one's own group (kin, caste, community).

Cousin Marriages

When referring to their cousins, people in the United States generally do not differentiate between types of cousins. In some other societies, such distinctions can be important, particularly with regard to first cousins. The terms for the different kinds of first cousins may indicate which cousins are suitable marriage partners (sometimes even preferred mates) and which are not. Although most societies prohibit marriage with all types of first cousins,[34] some societies allow and even prefer particular kinds of cousin marriage.

When first-cousin marriage is allowed or preferred, it is usually with some kind of cross-cousin. **Cross-cousins** are children of siblings of the opposite sex; that is, a person's cross-cousins are the father's sisters' children and the mother's brothers' children. The Chippewa Indians used to practice cross-cousin marriage, as well as cross-cousin joking. With his female cross-cousins, a Chippewa man was expected to exchange broad, risqué jokes, but he would not do so with his parallel cousins, with whom severe propriety was the rule.

Parallel cousins are children of siblings of the same sex; a person's parallel cousins, then, are the father's brothers' children and the mother's sisters' children. In general, in any society that allows cross-cousin but not parallel-cousin marriage, a joking relationship exists between a man and his female cross-cousins. In marked contrast, the man will maintain a formal and respectful relationship with female parallel cousins. The joking relationship apparently signifies the possibility of marriage, whereas the respectful relationship extends the incest taboo to parallel cousins.

Parallel-cousin marriage is fairly rare, but some Muslim societies have historically preferred such marriages and allowed other cousin marriages as well. The Kurds, who are mostly Sunni Muslims, preferred that a young man marry his father's brother's daughter (for her part, the young woman would be marrying her father's brother's son). The woman will stay close to home in such a marriage, since her father and his brother usually live near each other. Because the bride and groom are also in the same kin group, marriage in this case also entails kin group endogamy.[35]

There is evidence from cross-cultural research that cousin marriages are most likely to be permitted in relatively large and densely populated societies. Perhaps this is because such marriages, and thus the risks of inbreeding, are less likely in large populations.[36]

Cross-cousins Children of siblings of the opposite sex. One's cross-cousins are the father's sisters' children and mother's brothers' children.

Parallel cousins Children of siblings of the same sex. One's parallel cousins are the father's brothers' children and the mother's sisters' children.

Monogamy Marriage between only one man and only one woman at a time.

Polygamy Plural marriage; one individual is married to more than one spouse simultaneously. **Polygyny** and **polyandry** are types of polygamy.

14.5 Describe the three different forms of marriage and explain social or economic reasons for each.

Polyandry The marriage of one woman to more than one man at a time.

How Many Does One Marry?

Today, in most Western societies, not only is **monogamy,** the form of marriage in which one has only one spouse at a time (usually one man and one woman), customary, but plural marriage is illegal. But cross-culturally, most societies known to anthropology have allowed some form of **polygamy,** or plural spouse marriage. There are two types of polygamy. **Polygyny,** the form of marriage that allows a man to be married to more than one woman at the same time, is very common. The mirror image of polygyny, the marriage of one woman to more than one man at the same time, is called **polyandry.** It is practiced in just a few societies. But societies with polygamy cannot practice it exclusively because few if any societies have twice as many of one gender than the other. So in a polygynous society, for example, most men will be married monogamously at any given time. *Group marriage,* in which more than one man is married to more than one woman at the same time, sometimes occurs but is not customary in any known society.

Polygyny

Although polygyny is now illegal in most Western societies, it was very much a part of Judeo-Christian history and appeared to be a privilege of rulers and elites. The Old Testament includes many references to men with multiple wives. King David and his son, King Solomon, are both said to have had hundreds of wives and concubines, though such extravagant numbers are likely to be exaggerated. In early Medieval Europe, rulers practiced polygyny to ensure that they would have a male heir. And rulers took more than one wife as a way to build alliances with or annex neighboring kingdoms. Polygyny continues to be a mark of great wealth or high status in many societies, but in those societies only the very wealthy are expected to (or can) support more than one wife. Some Muslim societies, especially Arabic-speaking ones, still view polygyny in this light. But a man does not always have to be wealthy to be polygynous; indeed, in some societies in which women are important contributors to the economy, it seems that men try to have more than one wife to become wealthier.

Among the Siwai, a society in the South Pacific, status is achieved through feast giving. Pork is the main dish at these feasts, so the Siwai associate raising pigs with prestige. The great interest in pigs also sparks an interest in wives, because in Siwai society women raise the food needed to feed pigs. Thus, although having many wives does not in itself confer status among the Siwai, the increase in pig herds—and prestige—that can result offers men a strong incentive to be polygynous.[37] Polygynously married Siwai men do seem to have greater prestige, but they also complain that a household with multiple wives is difficult. Sinu, a Siwai, described his plight:

> There is never peace for a long time in a polygynous family. If the husband sleeps in the house of one wife, the other one sulks all the next day. If the man is so stupid as to sleep two consecutive nights in the house of one wife, the other one will refuse to cook for him, saying, So-and-so is your wife; go to her for food. Since I am not good enough for you to sleep with, then my food is not good enough for you to eat.[38]

Sororal and Nonsororal Polygyny Jealousy and conflict between co-wives seem not to be present in a minority of polygynous societies. Margaret Mead reported that married life among the Arapesh of New Guinea, even in polygynous marriages, was "so even and contented that there is nothing to relate of it at all."[39] What might explain such harmony? One possible explanation is that the co-wives are sisters. **Sororal polygyny,** a man's marriage to two or more sisters, seems to work because siblings, having grown up together, are more likely to get along and cooperate than co-wives who practice **nonsororal polygyny**—that is, who are not related. Indeed, a recent cross-cultural study confirms that persistent conflict and resentment were all too common in societies with nonsororal polygyny. The most commonly reported complaint was insufficient access to the husband for sex and emotional support.[40]

Perhaps because conflict is so common among co-wives, particularly with nonsororal polygyny, polygynous societies appear to have invented similar customs to try to lessen conflict and jealousy in co-wives:

1. Whereas sororal co-wives nearly always live under the same roof, co-wives who are not sisters tend to have separate living quarters.
2. Co-wives have clearly defined equal rights in matters of sex, economics, and personal possessions.
3. Senior wives often have special prestige, which may compensate the first wife for her loss of physical attractiveness.[41]

Why Is Polygyny a Common Practice? Although jealousy and conflict are noted as common problems in polygynous marriage, the practice may also offer social benefits. Married females as well as males in Kenya believed that polygyny provided economic and political advantages, according to a study conducted by Philip and Janet Kilbride. Because they tend to be large, polygynous families provide plenty of farm labor and extra food that can be marketed. They also tend to be influential in their communities and are likely to produce individuals who become government officials.[42] And in South Africa, Connie Anderson found that women choose to be married to a man with other wives because the other wives could help with child care and household work, provide companionship, and allow more freedom to come and go. Some women said they chose polygynous marriages because there was a shortage of marriageable males.[43]

How can we account for the fact that polygyny is allowed and often preferred in most of the societies known to anthropology? Ralph Linton suggested that polygyny derives from a general male primate urge to collect females.[44] But if that were so, then why wouldn't all societies allow polygyny? Other explanations of polygyny have been suggested. We restrict our discussion here to those that statistically and strongly predict polygyny in worldwide samples of societies.

Sororal polygyny The marriage of a man to two or more sisters at the same time.

Nonsororal polygyny Marriage of a man to two or more women who are not sisters.

Current Research and Issues

Love, Intimacy, and Sexual Jealousy in Marriage

Americans believe that love should be a basis of marriage. Does this ideal characterize most societies? We know the answer to that question: No. In fact, in many places, romantic love is believed to be a poor basis for marriage and is strongly discouraged. But even though romantic love may not be a basis for marriage everywhere, it does occur almost everywhere. A cross-cultural survey suggests that about 89 percent of the world's societies show signs of romantic love—accounts of personal longing, love songs or love depicted in folklore, elopement because of affection, and passionate love that is described by informants and quoted in ethnographies. If love is nearly universal, then why is it often discouraged as a basis for marriage?

Three conditions appear to predict that society will discourage romantic love in marriage. One is that the husband and wife live in an extended family. In this situation, the family seems more concerned with how the in-marrying person gets along with others, and less concerned with whether the husband and wife love each other. A second condition predicting the discouragement of romantic love as a basis for marriage is that one of the spouses does most of the primary subsistence work or earns most of the couple's income. Third, romantic love is unlikely when men have more sexual freedom than women. In general, then, romantic love is discouraged as a basis for marriage under conditions of inequality—if one of the spouses is highly dependent on the other or the other's kin or the woman has fewer sexual rights than the man.

Intimacy is different from romantic love. It refers to how close the

A nomadic Fulani woman in Ghana grooming her husband.

married couple are to each other—eating together, sleeping in the same bed, spending their leisure time together, as well as having frequent sex. In some societies, couples are together a lot; in others, they spend very little time together. Foraging societies seem on average to have more marital intimacy than more complex herding and agricultural societies, but the reasons are not entirely clear. Also, a high involvement in war seems to detract from intimacy.

When it comes to sexual jealousy, men are far more likely to be violent than women. Infidelity is, incidentally, the most frequently reported reason for a husband to divorce a wife. According to anthropologists with a biological orientation, fathers always have some uncertainty about whether their children are theirs; for that reason alone males are more likely to try to guard against rival males.

But how can we account for the considerable variation in jealousy from one society to another? It does seem that the more a society emphasizes the importance of getting married, the more it limits sex to the marriage relationship, the more it also emphasizes property, the more its males appear to exhibit sexual jealousy.

Does romantic love as a basis for marriage increase or decrease sexual jealousy? Does romantic love predict intimacy, or is romantic love more likely with less frequent contact between the spouses? We are still far from understanding how the different aspects of marriage are related. All we know is that an emphasis on love and intimacy does not preclude marital violence or marital dissolution.

Sources: Hendrix 2009; Betzig 1989; Jankowiak and Fischer 1995; de Munck and Korotayev 1999.

Postpartum sex taboo
Prohibition of sexual intercourse between a couple for a period of time after the birth of their child.

One theory is that polygyny will be permitted in societies that have a long **postpartum sex taboo.**[45] In these societies, a couple must abstain from intercourse until their child is at least a year old. John Whiting suggested that couples abstain from sexual intercourse for a long time after their child is born for health reasons to protect their child from *kwashiorkor.* Common in tropical areas, kwashiorkor is a protein-deficiency disease that occurs particularly in children suffering from intestinal parasites or diarrhea. If a child gets protein from mother's milk during its first few years, the likelihood of contracting kwashiorkor may be greatly reduced. By observing a long postpartum sex taboo, and thereby ensuring that her children are widely spaced, a woman can nurse each child longer. Consistent with Whiting's interpretation, societies whose principal foods are low-protein staples, such as taro, sweet potatoes, bananas, breadfruit, and other root and tree crops, tend to have a long postpartum sex taboo. Societies with long postpartum sex taboos also tend to be polygynous. Perhaps, then, a man's having more than one wife is a cultural adjustment to the taboo.

Even if we agree that men will seek other sexual relationships during the period of a long postpartum sex taboo, it is not clear why polygyny is the only possible solution to the problem. After all, it is conceivable that all of a man's wives might be subject to the postpartum sex taboo at the same time. Furthermore, there may be sexual outlets outside marriage.

Another explanation of polygyny is that it is a response to an excess of women over men. Such an imbalanced sex ratio may occur because of the prevalence of warfare in a society. Because men and not women are generally the warriors, warfare almost always takes a greater toll on men's lives. Given that almost all adults in noncommercial societies are married, polygyny may be a way of providing spouses for surplus women. Indeed, there is evidence that societies with imbalanced sex ratios in favor of women tend to have both polygyny and high male mortality in warfare. Conversely, societies with balanced sex ratios tend to have both monogamy and low male mortality in warfare.[46]

A third explanation is that a society will allow polygyny when men marry at an older age than women. The argument is similar to the sex-ratio interpretation. Delaying the age when men marry would create an artificial, though not an actual, excess of marriageable women. Why marriage for men is delayed is not clear, but the delay does predict polygyny.[47]

Is one of these explanations better than the others, or are all three factors—long postpartum sex taboo, imbalanced sex ratio in favor of women, and delayed age of marriage for men—important in explaining polygyny? One way of trying to decide among alternative explanations is to do what is called a *statistical-control analysis,* which allows us to see if a particular factor still predicts when the effects of other possible factors are removed. In this case, when the possible effect of sex ratio is removed, a long postpartum sex taboo no longer predicts polygyny and hence is probably not a cause of polygyny.[48] But both an actual excess of women and a late age of marriage for men seem to be strong predictors of polygyny. Added together, these two factors predict polygyny even more strongly.[49]

Behavioral ecologists have also suggested ecological reasons why both men and women might prefer polygynous marriages. If there are enough resources, men might prefer polygyny because they can have more children if they have more than one wife. If resources are highly variable and men control resources, women might find it advantageous to marry a man with many resources even if she is a second wife. A recent study of foragers suggests that foraging societies in which men control hunting or fishing territories are more likely to be polygynous. This finding is consistent with the theory, but the authors were surprised that control of gathering sites by men did not predict polygyny.[50] The main problem with the theory of variable resources and their marital consequences is that many societies, particularly in the "modern" world, have great variability in wealth but little polygyny. Behavioral ecologists have had to argue, therefore, that polygyny is lacking because of socially imposed constraints. The sex-ratio interpretation can explain the absence of polygyny in most commercialized modern societies. Very complex societies have standing armies, and in such societies male mortality in warfare is rarely as high *proportionately* as in simpler societies. Also, with commercialization, there are more possibilities for individuals to support themselves in commercialized societies without being married. The degree of disease in the environment may also be a factor.

Bobbi Low has suggested that a high incidence of disease may reduce the prevalence of "healthy" men. In such cases, it may be to a woman's advantage to marry a "healthy" man even if he is already married, and it may be to a man's advantage to marry several unrelated women to maximize genetic variation (and disease resistance) among his children. Indeed, societies with many pathogens are more likely to have polygyny.[51] A recent cross-cultural study compared the degree of disease as an explanation of polygyny with the imbalanced sex-ratio explanation. Both were supported. The number of pathogens predicted particularly well in more densely populated complex societies, where pathogen load is presumably greater. The sex-ratio explanation predicted polygyny particularly well in sparser, nonstate societies.[52] Nigel Barber used data from modern nations to test these ideas. He found that sex-ratio and pathogen stress predicted polygyny in modern nations as well.[53]

Polyandry

Fraternal polyandry
The marriage of a woman to two or more brothers at the same time.

Nonfraternal polyandry
Marriage of a woman to two or more men who are not brothers.

George Peter Murdock's "World Ethnographic Sample" included only four societies (less than 1 percent of the total) in which polyandry, or the marriage of several men to one woman, was practiced.[54] When the husbands are brothers we call it **fraternal polyandry;** if they are not brothers, it is **nonfraternal polyandry.** Some Tibetans, the Toda of India, and the Sinhalese of Sri Lanka have practiced fraternal polyandry. Among some Tibetans who practice fraternal polyandry, biological paternity seems to be of no particular concern; there is no attempt to link children biologically to a particular brother, and all children are treated the same.[55]

One possible explanation for the practice of polyandry is a shortage of women. The Toda practiced female infanticide;[56] the Sinhalese had a shortage of women but denied the practice of female infanticide.[57] A correlation between shortage of women and polyandry would account for why polyandry is so rare in the ethnographic record; an excess of men is rare cross-culturally.

Another possible explanation is that polyandry is an adaptive response to severely limited resources. Melvyn Goldstein studied Tibetans who live in the northwestern corner of Nepal, above 12,000 feet in elevation. Cultivable land is extremely scarce there, with most families having less than an acre. The people say they practice fraternal polyandry to prevent the division of a family's farm and animals. Instead of dividing up their land among them and each taking a wife, brothers preserve the family farm by sharing a wife. Although not recognized by the Tibetans, their practice of polyandry minimizes population growth. There are as many women as men of marriageable age. But about 30 percent of the women do not marry, and, although these women do have some children, they have far fewer than married women. Thus, the practice of polyandry minimizes the number of mouths to feed and therefore maximizes the standard of living of the polyandrous family. In contrast, if the Tibetans practiced monogamy and almost all women married, the birth rate would be much higher and there would be more mouths to feed with the severely limited resources.[58]

14.6 Describe and explain variation in family form.

Family A social and economic unit consisting minimally of a parent and a child.

The Family

Family form varies from one society to another and even within societies, but all societies have families. A **family** is a social and economic unit consisting minimally of one or more parents (or parent substitutes) and their children. Members of a family have certain reciprocal rights and obligations, particularly economic ones. Family members usually live in one household, but common residence is not a defining feature of families. In our society, children may live away while they go to college. Some members of a family may deliberately set up separate households to manage multiple business enterprises while maintaining economic unity.[59] In simpler societies, the family and the household tend to be indistinguishable; only in more complex societies, and in societies that become dependent on commercial exchange may some members of a family live elsewhere.[60]

Adoption

In many societies, the family does not have enough kin in the nuclear or extended family. They need to add new members to perform all of the necessary chores or to inherit access to family property. There may be a shortage of family members because of infertility or deaths (particularly of young children) from introduced diseases or natural disasters, such as hurricanes or because the adults do not get along and cooperate in the traditional ways. Many societies adopt children to deal with one or another of these problems, or families adopt one or more related children to relieve the pressure on resources in the family that adopts the child "out."

The family Melvin Ember lived with at the beginning of his fieldwork in the Pacific islands of American Samoa had six children. The oldest, Tavita, was 11 at the time and in school most of the day, as were three of the other children. Tavita had been adopted informally. His natural mother, who lived in the same village, was a sister of Tavita's adoptive mother. By adopting Tavita "out," his natural family, which already had nine children, was relieved of the responsibility of feeding and caring for him. In addition to depopulation and hurricanes, reducing the number of mouths to feed was a common reason for adoption in Samoan villages then, as it was elsewhere in the far Pacific islands.[61]

Of course adoption occurs in industrial societies as well. As of the 1990s (the latest figures available), there have been more than 100,000 legally recognized adoptions in the United States per year. About 50 percent of the adoptions are of children who are relatives, and usually close relatives; a large number of these adoptions may be solutions to resource problems for the natural mothers. More than 10,000 children from abroad who are not usually relatives are adopted each year. Most of the known adoptions, foreign and domestic, are arranged by middle-class or wealthier people, since a sizeable amount of money may be spent, particularly for foreign adoptions. Most of the adopted children, domestic and foreign, apparently turn out as well adjusted as natural children.[62]

Variation in Family Form

The minimal family has one parent (or parent substitute). Single-parent families, usually headed by the mother, are common in some societies, but most societies typically have larger families. These larger family units usually include at least one **nuclear family** (a married couple and their children), but there is often polygamy, so there may be more than one spouse with more than one set of children. If a single-parent family, nuclear family, polygynous, or polyandrous family lives alone, each is an **independent family**. But the **extended family** is the prevailing form of family in more than half the societies known to anthropology.[63] It may consist of two or more single-parent, monogamous, polygynous, or polyandrous families linked by a blood tie. Most commonly, the extended family consists of a married couple and one or more of the married children, all living in the same house or household. The constituent nuclear families are normally linked through the parent-child tie. An extended family, however, is sometimes composed of families linked through a sibling tie. Such a family might consist of two married brothers, their wives, and their children. Extended families may be very large, containing many relatives and including three or four generations. For a diagram of these different types of family, see Figure 14.1.

Nuclear family A family consisting of a married couple and their young children.

Independent family A family unit consisting of one monogamous (nuclear) family, or one polygynous or one polyandrous family.

Extended family A family consisting of two or more single-parent, monogamous, polygynous, or polyandrous families linked by a blood tie.

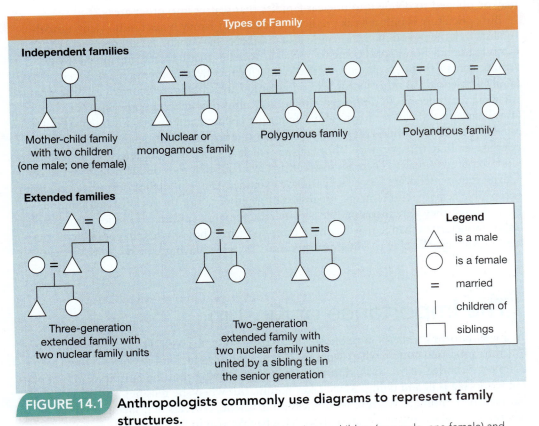

FIGURE 14.1   **Anthropologists commonly use diagrams to represent family structures.**

At the top are four types of independent family assuming only two children (one male, one female) and only two spouses where multiple spouses are allowed. At the bottom are two types of extended family. These diagrams show only small extended families, but extended families can have many constituent family units if there are many children as well as plural marriages.

Extended-Family Households

In a society composed of extended-family households, marriage does not bring as pronounced a change in lifestyle as it does in our culture, where the couple typically moves to a new residence and forms an independent family unit. Newlyweds in extended families are assimilated into an existing family unit. Margaret Mead described such a situation in Samoa:

> . . . the young couple live in the main household, simply receiving a bamboo pillow, a mosquito net and a pile of mats for their bed. The wife works with all the women of the household and waits on all the men. The husband shares the enterprises of the other men and boys. Neither in personal service given or received are the two marked off as a unit.[64]

A young couple in Samoa, as in other societies with extended families, generally has little decision-making power over the governing of the household. Often the responsibility of running the household rests with the senior male. Nor can the new family accumulate its own property and become independent; it is a part of the larger corporate structure.

The extended family is more likely than the independent nuclear family to perpetuate itself as a social unit. In contrast with the independent nuclear family, which by definition disintegrates with the death of its senior members (the parents), the extended family is always adding junior families (monogamous, polygamous, or both), whose members become the senior members when their elders die.

Possible Reasons for Extended-Family Households Why do most societies known to anthropology have extended-family households? Such households usually occur in sedentary, agricultural societies, suggesting that the type of economy could be a determining factor. Agricultural life, as opposed to a hunter-gatherer life, may favor extended families. The extended family may be a social mechanism that prevents the economically ruinous division of family property in societies in which property such as cultivated land is important. Conversely, the need for mobility in hunter-gatherer societies may make it difficult to maintain extended-family households. During certain seasons, the hunter-gatherers may be obliged to divide into nuclear families that scatter into other areas.[65]

But agriculture is only a weak predictor of extended-family households. Many agriculturalists lack them, and many nonagricultural societies have them. A different theory is that extended-family households come to prevail in societies that have incompatible activity requirements—that is, requirements that cannot be met by a mother or a father in a one-family household. In other words, extended-family households are generally favored when the work a mother has to do outside the home (cultivating fields or gathering foods far away) makes it difficult for her to also care for her children and do other household tasks. Similarly, extended families may be favored when the required outside activities of a father (warfare, trading trips, or wage labor far away) make it difficult for him to do the subsistence work required of males. There is cross-cultural evidence that societies with such incompatible activity requirements are more likely to have extended-family households than societies with compatible activity requirements, regardless of whether or not the society is agricultural. Even though they have incompatible activity requirements, however, societies with commercial or monetary exchange may not have extended-family households. In commercial societies, a family may be able to obtain the necessary help by "buying" the required services.[66]

14.7 ▶ Explain why kinship is important.

The Importance of Kinship

In a well-known prose poem published in 1915, Robert Frost tells the story of Mary and Warren, a married couple who own a subsistence farm in the United States. One day the couple's old hired hand, Silas, returns to them after having quit the farm in search of paying work. He is ill and dying. Mary takes him in, but when she tells her husband that Silas has returned "home," Warren, who is less sympathetic, corrects her, saying, "Home is where, when you have to go there, they have to take you in."

"We," he adds, are not Silas's "kin." Mary, who badly wants to help the old man, is quick to appease her husband by agreeing: "I should have called it something you somehow haven't to deserve."[67]

In a few words, Frost captures what all societies known to anthropology believe about kinship: Kin are the people who are obligated to help you (and you they), whether the help is deserved or not. Still, societies differ about what rights and obligations apply to which kin. Also variable is whom a society defines as "kin," which kin are considered important, and whether kin beyond the immediate family matter.

Anthropologists often speak of the web of kinship as providing the main structure of social action in noncommercial societies. Many societies have kin groups that include several or many families and hundreds or even thousands of people, and kinship plays a powerful role in many aspects of an individual's life—from the access an individual has to productive resources to the kinds of political alliances formed between communities and larger territorial groups. In some societies, kinship connections have an important bearing on matters of life and death.

Indeed, at some point kinship is important in all human cultures, regardless of the size of the kin group. We may recall, for example, that during the Recession in the United States between 2007 and 2009, 1.3 million men and women between the ages of 24 and 34 moved in with their parents. Many elderly people moved in with their relatives as well.[68] Kin, it seems, still existed and they still had to "take you in."

In reality though, if you count all your relatives through blood ties, through marriage, and through established social practices such as adoption, there would be an enormously large number of people. All societies through rules and through practice identify which kin are most important. First, there are customs about where you will live as an adult (in most societies an adult will be part of married couple). Second, there will be rules or customary practices about the set of kin you affiliate with; these kin groups have functions, often with spelled out rights and obligations.

Patterns of Marital Residence

In the United States and Canada, young people may be groomed for independence and self-reliance by going to sleep-away summer camps and working in after-school or summer jobs. Young adults of all income levels learn to live away from home most of the year if they join the army or attend an out-of-town college. And often when they form their own families, they move away from their parents. So familiar is this pattern that we tend to assume that all societies must follow the same practice.

On the contrary, of the 565 societies in Murdock's "World Ethnographic Sample," only about 5 percent have had the practice of setting up separate households for newlyweds.[69] In the vast majority of societies, then, a new couple lives within, or very close to, the household of either the groom's or the bride's parents or other close relatives. It stands to reason that when a newly married couple lives near kin, relatives will play important roles in their lives and those of their offspring.

Young people in almost all societies are required to marry outside the nuclear family and, with few exceptions, couples in almost all societies live together after they are married. Therefore, some young people must leave home when they marry. But which married offspring remain at home and which reside elsewhere? We pay particular attention to where these new family units take root and grow, because it can predict *which* relatives and other allied groups are likely to be important in a society. Although societies vary in the way they deal with this question, the prevailing pattern of marital residence is likely to be one of the following:

1. **Patrilocal.** Sons stay and daughters leave, so that a married couple lives with or near the husband's parents (67 percent of all societies).
2. **Matrilocal.** Daughters stay and sons leave, so that a married couple lives with or near the wife's parents (15 percent of all societies).
3. **Bilocal or ambilocal residence.** Either the son or the daughter may leave, so that the married couple lives with or near either the wife's or the husband's parents (7 percent of all societies).
4. **Avunculocal residence.** Both the son and daughter normally leave, but the son and his wife settle with or near his mother's brother (4 percent of all societies).[70]
5. **Neolocal residence.** Both sons and daughters leave; married couples live apart from the relatives of both spouses (5 percent of all societies).

14.8 Identify the various patterns of marital residence.

Patrilocal residence A pattern of residence in which a married couple lives with or near the husband's parents.

Matrilocal residence A pattern of residence in which a married couple lives with or near the wife's parents.

Bilocal residence A pattern of residence in which a married couple lives with or near either the husband's parents or the wife's parents

Avunculocal residence A pattern of residence in which a married couple settles with or near the husband's mother's brother.

Neolocal residence A pattern of residence whereby a married couple lives separately, and usually at some distance, from the kin of both spouses.

In these definitions, we use the phrase "the married couple lives *with or near*" a particular set of in-laws. When couples live with or near the kin of one spouse, the couple may live in the same household with those kin, creating an *extended-family* household, or they may live separately in an *independent-family* household, but nearby. (Also, in contrast to bilocal residence, matrilocal, patrilocal, and avunculocal residences each specify only one pattern and are often called nonoptional or **unilocal residence** patterns.)

How does place of residence affect the social life of the couple? It largely determines which people the couple interacts with and depends upon. The kin group the couple joins is also likely to be more influential in the lives of their offspring. Whether the couple lives in the husband's or the wife's kin group can also be expected to have important consequences for their status. If married couples live patrilocally, as occurs in most societies, the wife may be far from her own kin. The feeling of being an outsider may be particularly strong if the wife has moved into a patrilocal extended-family household. She will be an outsider among a group of male relatives who have grown up together.

Among the Tiv of central Nigeria,[71] the patrilocal extended family consists of the "great father," who is the head of the household, his younger brothers, his sons, and his younger brothers' sons, followed by all the in-marrying wives and all unmarried children. The sisters and daughters of the head of household who have married will have gone to live where their husbands live. Authority is strongly vested in the male line and particularly in the oldest male of the household. The "great father" determines bride price, settles disputes, administers punishment, and plans for new buildings.

Unilocal residence A pattern of residence (patrilocal, matrilocal, or avunculocal) that specifies just one set of relatives that the married couple lives with or near.

Three Iroquois women sing in an Iroquois longhouse in Ontario. The core of a traditional longhouse were matrilineally related women.

If, on the other hand, the husband comes to live with or near his wife's parents, the wife and her kin take on greater importance, and the husband is the outsider. As we shall see, however, matrilocal marital residence does not endow women with the same power that patrilocal residence confers on men. The conditions under which such kin groups exist are often not the same; for example, the husband's kin in matrilocal societies are likely to live nearby. Moreover, even though residence is matrilocal, it is the brothers (or sons of the matriarch), not the sisters (or daughters of the matriarch), who become the kin group's decision-makers. Nevertheless, women in some matrilocal societies do enjoy somewhat greater status.

14.9 Discuss the various ways of affiliating with kin and how the systems differ.

Rules of descent Rules that connect individuals with particular sets of kin because of known or presumed common ancestry.

Unilineal descent Affiliation with a group of kin through descent links of one sex only.

Patrilineal descent The rule of descent that affiliates individuals with kin of both sexes related to them through men only.

Matrilineal descent The rule of descent that affiliates individuals with kin of both sexes related to them through women only.

Types of Affiliation with Kin

Kinship, like a political party (or a private club), derives its meaning and influence from its power to exclude. After all, if every single relative were regarded as equally important, there would be an unmanageably large number of people depending on each other and, perhaps, competing for the group's limited resources. Consequently, most societies in which kinship connections are important have rules that assign each person to a particular and definable set of kin.

Societies observe three main types of affiliation with kin: *unilineal descent, ambilineal descent,* and *bilateral kinship.* The first two types, unilineal and ambilineal descent, are based on **rules of descent,** which are rules that connect individuals with particular sets of kin because of known or presumed common ancestry. By the particular rule of descent operating in their society, individuals can know more or less immediately which set of kin to turn to for support and help. As we shall see, the interconnections of bilateral kinship, which is not based on rules of descent or ancestry, are more ambiguous.

Unilineal Descent

When a person is affiliated with a group of kin through descent links of one sex only—either males only or females only—the kin group is said to follow **unilineal descent.** Unilineal descent can be either patrilineal or matrilineal.

1. **Patrilineal descent** affiliates individuals with kin of both sexes related to them *through men only.* Just as patrilocal residence is much more common than matrilocal residence, patrilineal descent is more common than matrilineal descent. As Figure 14.2 illustrates, children in patrilineal systems in each generation belong to the kin group of their father; their father, in turn, belongs to the group of his father; and so on. Although a man's sons and daughters are all members of the same descent group, affiliation with that group is transmitted only by the sons to their children.
2. **Matrilineal descent** affiliates individuals with kin of both sexes related to them *through women only.* In each generation, then, children belong to the kin group of their mother. As Figure 14.3 illustrates, a woman's sons and daughters are all members of the same descent group, but only her daughters can pass on their descent affiliation to their children.

Unilineal rules of descent affiliate an individual with a line of kin extending back in time and into the future. By virtue of this line of descent, whether it extends through males or females, some very close relatives are excluded. For example, in a patrilineal system, your mother and your mother's parents do not belong to your patrilineal group, but your father and his father (and their sisters) do. In your

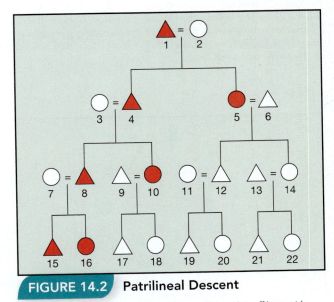

FIGURE 14.2 **Patrilineal Descent**

Individuals 4 and 5, who are the children of 1 and 2, affiliate with their father's patrilineal kin group, represented by the color red. In the next generation, the children of 3 and 4 also belong to the red kin group, because they take their descent from their father, who is a member of that group. However, the children of 5 and 6 do not belong to this patrilineal group, because they take their descent from their father, who is a member of a different group. That is, although the mother of 12 and 14 belongs to the red patrilineal group, she cannot pass on her descent affiliation to her children, and because her husband (6) does not belong to her patrilineage, her children (12 and 14) belong to their father's group. In the fourth generation, only 15 and 16 belong to the red patrilineal group, because their father is the only male member of the preceding generation who belongs to the red patrilineal group. In this diagram, then, 1, 4, 5, 8, 10, 15, and 16 are affiliated by patrilineal descent; all the other individuals belong to other patrilineal groups.

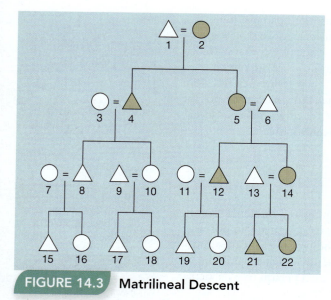

FIGURE 14.3 Matrilineal Descent

Individuals 4 and 5, who are the children of 1 and 2, affiliate with their mother's kin group, represented by the color green. In the next generation, the children of 5 and 6 also belong to the green kin group, because they take their descent from their mother, who is a member of that group. However, the children of 3 and 4 do not belong to this matrilineal group, because they take their descent from their mother, who is a member of a different group; their father, although a member of the green matrilineal group, cannot pass his affiliation on to them under the rule of matrilineal descent. In the fourth generation, only 21 and 22 belong to the green matrilineal group, because their mother is the only female member of the preceding generation who belongs. Thus, individuals 2, 4, 5, 12, 14, 21, and 22 belong to the same matrilineal group.

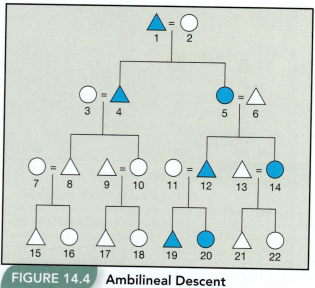

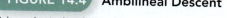

FIGURE 14.4 Ambilineal Descent

A hypothetical ambilineal group of kin is indicated by the color blue. Members 4 and 5 belong to this group because of a male link, their father (1); members 12 and 14 belong because of a female link, their mother (5); and members 19 and 20 belong because of a male link, their father (12). This is a hypothetical example because any combination of lineal links is possible in an ambilineal descent group.

own generation in a matrilineal or patrilineal system, some cousins are excluded, and in your children's generation, some of your nieces and nephews are excluded.

But, although unilineal rules of descent exclude certain relatives from membership in one's kin group, the excluded relatives are not necessarily ignored or forgotten, just as practical considerations restrict the effective size of kinship networks in our own society.

Unilineal rules of descent can form clear-cut, and hence unambiguous, kinship groups. These groups can, and often do, act as separate units even after the death of individual members. Referring again to Figures 14.2 and 14.3, we can see that the individuals in the highlighted color belong to the same patrilineal or matrilineal descent group without ambiguity; individuals in the fourth generation belong to the group just as much as those in the first generation.

Ambilineal Descent

In contrast to unilineal descent, **ambilineal descent** affiliates individuals with kin related to them through men *or* women. In other words, some people in the society affiliate with a group of kin through their fathers; others affiliate through their mothers. Consequently, the descent groups show both female and male genealogical links, as illustrated in Figure 14.4.

The three rules of descent—patrilineal, matrilineal, and ambilineal—are usually, but not always, mutually exclusive. Most societies can be characterized as having only one rule of descent, but two principles are sometimes used to affiliate individuals with different sets of kin for different purposes. Some societies have what is called **double descent or double unilineal descent**, whereby individuals affiliate for some purposes with a group of matrilineal kin and for other purposes with a group of patrilineal kin.

Bilateral Kinship

Many societies, including our own, do not have lineal (matrilineal, patrilineal, or ambilineal) descent groups—sets of kin who believe they descend from a common ancestor. These are societies with **bilateral kinship**. *Bilateral* means "two-sided," and in this case, it refers to the fact that one's relatives on both the mother's and father's sides are equal in importance or, more usually, in unimportance. Kinship reckoning in bilateral societies does not refer to common descent but rather is horizontal, moving outward from close to more distant relatives rather than upward to common ancestors (see Figure 14.5).

The term **kindred** describes a person's bilateral set of relatives who may be called upon for some purpose. Most bilateral societies have kindreds that overlap in membership. In North America, we think of the kindred as including the people we might invite to weddings, funerals, or some other ceremonial occasion; a kindred, however, is not usually a definite group. As anyone who has been involved in creating a wedding invitation list knows, a great deal of time may be spent deciding which relatives ought to be invited and

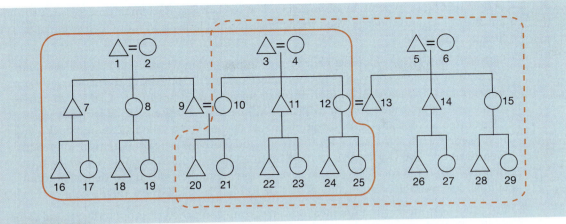

FIGURE 14.5   **Bilateral Kinship**

In a bilateral system, the kindred is ego-centered; hence, it varies with different points of reference (except for brothers and sisters). In any bilateral society, the kindred minimally includes parents, grandparents, aunts, uncles, and first cousins. So, if we look at the close kindred of the brother and sister 20 and 21 (enclosed by the solid line), it would include their parents (9 and 10), their aunts and uncles (7, 8, 11, 12), their grandparents (1, 2, 3, 4), and their first cousins (16–19, 22–25). But the kindred of the brother and sister 24 and 25 (shown by the dashed line) includes only some of the same people (3, 4, 10–12, 20–23); in addition, the kindred of 24 and 25 includes people not in the kindred of 20 and 21 (5, 6, 13–15, 26–29).

which ones can legitimately be excluded. Societies with bilateral kinship differ in precisely how distant relatives have to be before they are lost track of or before they are not included in ceremonial activities. In societies such as our own, in which kinship is relatively unimportant, fewer relatives are included in the kindred. In other bilateral societies, however, where kinship connections are somewhat more important, more would be included.

The distinctive feature of bilateral kinship is that, aside from brothers and sisters, no two people belong to exactly the same kin group. Your kindred contains close relatives spreading out on both your mother's and father's sides, but the members of your kindred are affiliated only by way of their connection to you (**ego,** or the focus). Thus, the kindred is an *ego-centered* group of kin. Because different people (except for brothers and sisters) have different mothers and fathers, your first cousins will have different kindreds, and even your own children will have different kindred from yours. The ego-centered nature of the kindred makes it difficult for it to serve as a permanent or persistent group. The only thing the people in a kindred have in common is the ego or focal person who brings them together. A kindred usually has no name, no common purpose, and only temporary meetings centered around the ego.[72] Furthermore, because everyone belongs to many different and overlapping kindreds, the society is not divided into clear-cut groups.

Although kindreds may not form clear-cut groups as in a unilineal society, this does not mean that the kindred cannot be turned to for help. In a bilateral society, the kindred may provide social insurance against adversity. Among the Chipewyan of subarctic Canada, for example, people would borrow a fishing net from a kindred member, or ask a kindred member to provide child care for a young person whose parent was ill. But recently, with the national and provincial governments providing resources such as housing and medical assistance, and with the increase in opportunities for wage labor, the kindred has ceased to be the main source of help for people in need. Aid from the state is making kinship less useful.[73]

Variation in Unilineal Descent Systems

In a society with unilineal descent, people usually refer to themselves as belonging to a particular unilineal group or set of groups because they believe they share common descent in either the male (patrilineal) or female (matrilineal) line. Anthropologists distinguish several types of unilineal descent groups: lineages, clans, phratries, and moieties.

Lineages   A **lineage** is a set of kin whose members trace descent from a common ancestor through known links. There may be *patrilineages* or *matrilineages*, depending on whether the links are traced through males only or through females only. Lineages are often designated by the name of the common male or female ancestor. In some societies,

Ambilineal descent The rule of descent that affiliates individuals with groups of kin related to them through men or women.

Double descent or double unilineal descent A system that affiliates individuals with a group of matrilineal kin for some purposes and with a group of patrilineal kin for other purposes.

Bilateral kinship The type of kinship system in which individuals affiliate more or less equally with their mother's and father's relatives.

Kindred A bilateral set of close relatives who may be called upon for some purpose.

Ego In the reckoning of kinship, the reference point or focal person.

Lineage A set of kin whose members trace descent from a common ancestor through known links.

Clan A set of kin whose members believe themselves to be descended from a common ancestor or ancestress but cannot specify the links back to that founder; often designated by a totem. Also called a **sib**.

Totem A plant or animal associated with a clan (sib) as a means of group identification; may have other special significance for the group.

Phratry A unilineal descent group composed of a number of supposedly related clans (sibs).

Moiety A unilineal descent group in a society that is divided into two such maximal groups; there may be smaller unilineal descent groups as well.

people belong to a hierarchy of lineages. That is, they first trace their descent back to the ancestor of a minor lineage, then to the ancestor of a larger and more inclusive major lineage, and so on.

Clans   A **clan** (also sometimes called a **sib**) is a set of kin whose members believe themselves to be descended from a common ancestor, but the links back to that ancestor are not specified. In fact, the common ancestor may not even be known. Clans with patrilineal descent are called *patriclans;* clans with matrilineal descent are called *matriclans.* Clans often are designated by an animal name (Bear, Wolf), called a **totem,** which may have some special significance for the group and, at the very least, is a means of group identification. The word *totem* comes from the Ojibwa Indian word *ototeman,* "a relative of mine." In some societies, people have to observe taboos relating to their clan totem animal. For example, clan members may be forbidden to kill or eat their totem.

Phratries   A **phratry** is a unilineal descent group composed of supposedly related clans or sibs. As with clans, the descent links in phratries are unspecified.

Moieties   When a whole society is divided into two unilineal descent groups, we call each group a **moiety.** (The word *moiety* comes from a French word meaning "half.") The people in each moiety believe themselves to be descended from a common ancestor, although they cannot specify how. Societies with moiety systems usually have relatively small populations (fewer than 9,000 people). Societies with phratries and clans tend to be larger.[74]

Combinations   Although we have distinguished several different types of unilineal descent groups, we do not wish to imply that all unilineal societies have only one type of descent group. Many societies have two or more types in various combinations. For example, some societies have lineages and clans; others may have clans and phratries but no lineages; and still others may have clans and moieties but neither phratries nor lineages. Aside from the fact that a society that has phratries must also have clans (because phratries are combinations of clans), all combinations of descent groups are possible. Even if societies have more than one type of unilineal kin group—for example, lineages and clans—there is no ambiguity about membership. Small groups are simply subsets of larger units; the larger units include people who say they are unilineally related further back in time.

Patrilineal Organization

Patrilineal organization is the most frequent type of descent system. The Kapauku Papuans, a people living in the central highlands of western New Guinea, are an example of a patrilineal society with various types of descent groups.[75] All Kapauku belong to a patrilineage, to a patriclan that includes their lineage, and to a patriphratry that includes their clan.

The male members of the lineage live together by virtue of a patrilocal rule of residence and a fairly stable settlement pattern.

The members of the same patrilineage address each other affectionately, and within this group, a headman maintains law and order. Killing within the lineage is considered a serious offense, and any fighting that takes place is done with sticks rather than lethal weapons such as spears.

The Kapauku also belong to larger and more inclusive patrilineal descent groups—clans and phratries. All the people of the same clan believe they are related to each other in the father's line, but they are unable to say how they are related. If a member of the patriclan eats the clan's plant or animal totem, it is believed that the person will become deaf. Kapauku are also forbidden to marry anyone from their clan. In other words, the clan is exogamous.

The most inclusive patrilineal descent group among the Kapauku is the phratry, each of which is composed of two or more clans. The Kapauku believe that the phratry was originally one clan, but that, in a conflict between brothers of the founding family, the younger brother was expelled and he formed a new clan. The two resulting clans are viewed as patrilineally related, because their founders are said to have been brothers. The members of a phratry observe all the totemic taboos of the clans that belong to that phratry. Intermarriage of members of the same clan is forbidden, but members of the same phratry, if they belong to different clans, may marry.

Perspectives on Gender

Variation in Residence and Kinship: What Difference Does It Make to Women?

When we say that residence and kinship have profound effects on people's lives, what exactly do we mean? We may imagine that it is hard for a woman in a patrilocal society to move at marriage into another village where her husband has plenty of relatives and she has few. But do we have evidence of that? Most ethnographies usually do not give details about people's feelings, but some do. For example, Leigh Minturn gives us the text of a letter that one new Rajput bride (who grew up in the village of Khalapur, India) sent to her mother shortly after she married into her husband's village. The letter was written when the bride had been gone six weeks, but she repeatedly asked if her mother, her father, and her aunts had forgotten her. She begged to be called home and said her bags were packed. She described herself as "a parrot in a cage" and complained about her in-laws. The bride's mother was not alarmed; she knew that such complaints were normal, reflections of her daughter's separation anxiety. Seven years later, when Minturn returned to India, the mother reported the daughter to be happy. Still, a few other brides did have more serious symptoms: ghost possession, 24- to 36-hour comas, serious depression, or suicide. What research has not told us is whether these serious symptoms are present more often in patrilocal, patrilineal societies than in other societies, particularly matrilocal, matrilineal societies. Conversely, do men have some symptoms in matrilocal, matrilineal societies that they do not have in patrilocal societies? We do not know.

What about the status of women? Some research suggests that matrilocality and matrilineality enhance some aspects of women's status, but perhaps not as much as we might think. Even in matrilineal societies, men are usually the political leaders. The main effect of matrilocality and matrilineality appears to be that women control

property, but they also tend to have more domestic authority in the home, more equal sexual restrictions, and more value placed on their lives. Alice Schlegel pointed out that women's status is not always relatively high in matrilineal societies, because they can be dominated by the husband or by brothers (because brothers play important roles in their kin groups). Only when neither the husband nor the brother dominates may women have considerable control over their own lives. Matrilocality and matrilineality might not enhance women's status because of the dominance of male matrilineal kin, but patrilocality and patrilineality are very likely to detract from women's status. Residence and descent also predict societal attempts to control reproduction. According to Suzanne Frayser, patrilineal societies are more likely than other societies to prohibit premarital and extramarital sex for women, and they are more likely to make it very difficult for a woman to divorce her husband.

Of course, we have to remember that there is considerable variation within patrilocal/patrilineal societies and matrilocal/matrilineal societies.

In the patrilineal society that Audrey Smedley studied—the Birom of the Jos Plateau in Nigeria—women were formally barred from owning property, from holding political offices, and from major decision making. Yet, her fieldwork revealed that they had considerable autonomy in their personal lives in everyday life, including the legal right to take on lovers. Indeed, they had considerable indirect influence on decision making and were strong supporters of the patrilineal system. Smedley speculates that women support patrilineality in some environmental circumstances because it serves their interests and those of their children too. For example, male crops are highly valued, but such crops are grown on the more dangerous plains where men risked death at the hands of raiders from other groups. Food was scarce, so it may have been adaptive for everyone, including women, to give special status to men for growing crops in dangerous places.

Sources: Minturn 1993, 54–71; M. K. Whyte 1978b, 132–34; Schlegel 2009; N. Diamond 1975; Smedley 2004; Frayser 1985, 338–47.

Matrilineal Organization

Although societies with matrilineal descent seem in many respects like mirror images of their patrilineal counterparts, they differ in one important way. That difference has to do with who exercises authority. In patrilineal systems, descent affiliation is transmitted through males, and it is also the males who exercise authority. Consequently, in the patrilineal system, lines of descent and of authority converge. In a matrilineal system, however, although the line of descent passes through females, females rarely exercise authority in their kin groups. Usually males do. Thus, the lines of authority and descent do not converge.[76] Because males exercise authority in the kin group, an individual's mother's brother becomes an important authority figure, because he is the individual's closest male matrilineal relative in the parental generation. The individual's father does not belong to the individual's own matrilineal kin group and thus has no say in kin group matters.

The divergence of authority and descent in a matrilineal system has some effect on community organization and marriage. Most matrilineal societies practice matrilocal residence. Daughters stay at home after marriage and bring their husbands to live with them; sons leave home to join their wives. But the sons who are required to leave will be the ones who eventually exercise authority in their kin groups. This situation presents a problem. The solution that seems to have been realized in most matrilineal societies is that, although the males move away to live with their wives, they usually do not move too far away; indeed, they often marry women who live in the same village. Thus, matrilineal societies tend not to be locally exogamous—that is, members often marry people from inside the village—whereas patrilineal societies are often locally exogamous.[77]

The matrilineal organization on Chuuk, a group of small islands in the Pacific, illustrates the general pattern of authority in matrilineal systems.[78] The Chuukese have both matrilineages and matriclans. The matrilineage is a property-owning group whose members trace descent from a known common ancestor in the female line. The female lineage members and their husbands occupy a cluster of houses on the matrilineage's land. The property of the lineage group is administered by the oldest brother of the group, who allocates the productive property of his matrilineage and directs the work of the members. He also represents the group in dealings with the district chief and all outsiders, and he must be consulted on any matter that affects the group. There is also a senior woman of the lineage who exercises some authority, but only insofar as the activities of the women are concerned. She may supervise the women's cooperative work (they usually work separately from the men) and manage the household.

Within the nuclear family, the father and mother have the primary responsibility for raising and disciplining their children. When a child reaches puberty, however, the father's right to discipline or exercise authority over the child ceases. The mother continues to exercise her right of discipline, but her brother may interfere. A woman's brother rarely interferes with his sister's child before puberty, but he may exercise some authority after puberty, especially because he is an elder in the child's own matrilineage. On Chuuk, men rarely move far from their birthplace. As Ward Goodenough pointed out, "Since matrilocal residence takes the men away from their home lineages, most of them marry women whose lineage houses are within a few minutes' walk of their own."[79]

Functions of Unilineal Descent Groups

Unilineal descent groups exist in societies at all levels of cultural complexity.[80] Apparently, however, they are most common in noncommercial food-producing, as opposed to food-collecting, societies.[81] Unilineal descent groups often have important functions in the social, economic, political, and religious realms of life.

Regulating Marriage In unilineal societies, individuals are not usually permitted to marry within their own unilineal descent groups. In some, however, marriage may be permitted within more inclusive kin groups but prohibited within smaller kin groups. In a few societies, marriage within the kin group is actually preferred.

Economic Functions Members of a person's lineage or clan are often required to side with that person in any quarrel or lawsuit, to help him or her get established economically, to contribute to a bride price or fine, and to support the person in life crises. Mutual aid often extends to economic cooperation on a regular basis. The unilineal descent group may act as a corporate unit in landownership.

The descent group sometimes views money earned—either by harvesting a cash crop or by leaving the community for a time to work for cash wages—as belonging to all. In recent times, however, young people in some places have shown an unwillingness to part with their money, viewing it as different from other kinds of economic assistance.

Political Functions Headmen or elders may also have the right to settle disputes between two members within a lineage, although they generally lack power to force a settlement. And they may act as intermediaries in disputes between a member of their own clan and a member of an opposing kin group.

Certainly one of the most important political functions of unilineal descent groups is their role in warfare—the attempt to resolve disputes within and outside the society by violent action. In societies without towns or cities, the organization of such fighting is often in the hands of descent groups.

Religious Functions A clan or lineage may have its own religious beliefs and practices, worshiping its own gods or goddesses and ancestral spirits.

Among the Bhil of India, graveyards have ancestral memorials in the fields.

Ambilineal Systems

Societies with ambilineal descent groups are far less numerous than unilineal or even bilateral societies. Ambilineal societies, however, resemble unilineal ones in many ways. For instance, the members of an ambilineal descent group believe that they are descended from a common ancestor, although frequently they cannot specify all the genealogical links. The descent group is commonly named and may have an identifying emblem or even a totem; the descent group may own land and other productive resources; and myths and religious practices are often associated with the group. Marriage is often regulated by group membership, just as in unilineal systems, although kin group exogamy is not nearly as common as in unilineal systems. Moreover, ambilineal societies resemble unilineal ones in having various levels or types of descent groups. They may have lineages and higher orders of descent groups, distinguished (as in unilineal systems) by whether or not all the genealogical links to the supposed common ancestors are specified.[82]

Explaining Variation in Residence

14.10 Discuss what might explain variation in marital residence patterns.

If married couples in most societies live with or near kin, as in patrilocal, matrilocal, bilocal, and avunculocal patterns of residence, then why do couples in some societies, such as our own, typically live apart from kin? And, among the societies in which couples live with or near kin, why do most choose the husband's side (patrilocal residence), but some the wife's side (matrilocal residence)? Why do some non-neolocal societies allow a married couple to go to either the wife's or the husband's kin (bilocal residence), whereas most others do not allow a choice?

Neolocal Residence

Many anthropologists have suggested that neolocal residence is related to the presence of a money or commercial economy. They argue that, when people can sell their labor or their products for money, they can buy what they need to live, without having to depend on kin. Indeed, neolocal residence tends to occur in societies with monetary or commercial exchange, whereas societies without money tend to have patterns of residence that locate a couple near or with kin.[83] The presence of money, then, partially accounts for neolocal residence: Money seems to allow couples to live on their own. Still, this fact does not quite explain why they choose to do so. One reason may be that couples in commercial societies do better on their own because the jobs available require physical or social mobility. Or perhaps couples prefer to live apart from kin because they want to avoid some of the interpersonal tensions and demands that may be generated by living with or near kin. But why couples, when given money, should *prefer* to live on their own is not completely understood.

Matrilocal versus Patrilocal Residence

It is traditionally assumed that, in societies in which married children live near or with kin, the pattern of residence will tend to be patrilocal if males contribute more to the economy and matrilocal if women contribute more. No matter how plausible that assumption may seem, the cross-cultural evidence does not support it. Where men do most of the primary subsistence work, residence is patrilocal no more often than would be expected by chance. Conversely, where women do an equal amount or more of the subsistence work, residence is no more likely to be matrilocal than patrilocal.[84] If we counted all work inside and outside the home, most societies should be matrilocal because women usually do more. But that is not true either; most societies are not matrilocal.

We can predict whether residence will be matrilocal or patrilocal, however, from the type of warfare practiced in the society. In most societies known to anthropology, neighboring communities or districts are enemies. The type of warfare that breaks out periodically between such groups is called *internal,* because the fighting occurs between groups that speak the same language. In other societies, the warfare is never within the same society but only with other language groups. This pattern of warfare is referred to as *purely external.* Cross-cultural evidence suggests that, in societies where warfare is at least sometimes internal, residence is almost always patrilocal rather than matrilocal. In contrast, residence is usually matrilocal when warfare is purely external.[85]

How can we explain this relationship between type of warfare and matrilocal versus patrilocal residence? One theory is that patrilocal residence tends to occur with internal warfare because there may be concern over keeping sons close to home to help with defense. Because women do not usually constitute the fighting force in any society, having sons reside at home after marriage might be favored as a means of maintaining a loyal and quickly mobilized fighting force in case of a surprise attack from nearby. If warfare is purely external, however, people may not be so concerned about keeping their sons at home because families need not fear attack from neighboring communities or districts.

With purely external warfare, then, the pattern of residence may be determined by other considerations, especially economic ones. If the women do most of the primary subsistence work in societies with purely external warfare, families might want their daughters to remain at home after marriage, so the pattern of residence might become matrilocal. If warfare is purely external but men still do more of the primary subsistence work, residence should still be patrilocal. Thus, the need to keep sons at home after marriage when there is internal warfare may take precedence over any considerations based on division of labor. Perhaps only when internal warfare is nonexistent may a female-dominant division of labor give rise to matrilocal residence.[86]

The frequent absence of men because of long-distance trade or wage labor in distant places may also provide an impetus for matrilocal residence even after warfare ceases. For example, among the Miskito of eastern Central America, matrilocality allowed domestic and village life to continue without interruption when men were away from home for long periods of time, working as lumberers, miners, and river transporters. More recently, men have worked away from home as deep-sea divers for lobster, for which there is a lot of demand in the international economy. These jobs were not always available, but when they were, the men went away to work at them to earn money. Even though some men would always be away from home, the Miskito continued to get food in their traditional ways, from farming (done mostly by the women) and from hunting and fishing (which was mostly men's work).[87]

Bilocal Residence

In societies that practice bilocal residence, a married couple goes to live with or near either the husband's or the wife's parents. Although this pattern seems to involve a choice for the married couple, theory and research suggest that bilocal residence may occur out of necessity instead. Elman Service suggested that bilocal residence is likely to occur in societies that have recently suffered a severe and drastic loss of population because of the introduction of new infectious diseases.[88] Over the last 400 years, contact with Europeans in many parts of the world has resulted in severe population losses among non-European societies that lacked resistance to the Europeans' diseases. If couples need to live with some set of kin to make a living in noncommercial societies, it seems likely that couples in depopulated, noncommercial societies might have to live with whichever spouse's parents and other relatives are still alive. This interpretation is supported by the cross-cultural evidence. Recently depopulated societies tend to have bilocal residence or frequent departures from unilocality, whereas societies that are not recently depopulated tend to have one pattern or another of unilocal residence.[89]

In hunter-gatherer societies, a few other circumstances may also favor bilocal residence. Bilocality tends to be found among those hunter-gatherers who have very small bands or unpredictable and low rainfall. Residential "choice" in these cases may be a question of adjusting marital residence to where the couple will have the best chance to survive or to find close relatives with whom to live and work.[90]

Avunculocal Residence

Now that we have learned about matrilineal systems, the avunculocal pattern of residence, whereby married couples live with or near the husband's mother's brother, may become clearer. Although avunculocal residence is relatively rare, just about all avunculocal societies are matrilineal. As we have seen, the mother's brother plays an important role in decision making in most matrilineal societies. Aside from his brothers, who is a boy's closest male matrilineal relative? It is his mother's brother. Going to live with the mother's brother, then, provides a way of localizing male *matrilineal* relatives. But why should some matrilineal societies practice that form of residence? The answer may involve the prevailing type of warfare.

Avunculocal societies, in contrast with matrilocal societies, fight internally. Like patrilocality, avunculocality may be a way of keeping related—in this case, matrilineally related—married men together to mount a quick defense against surprise attacks from nearby. When faced with fighting close to home, societies with strong, functioning matrilineal descent groups may choose to switch initially to avunculocality rather than patrilocality. Such a transition would make sense when the close warfare results in high male mortality, which could make patrilineal descent more difficult to trace in such societies than matrilineal descent.[91]

Explaining the Emergence of Different Systems of Kin Affiliation

14.11 Discuss what may explain the emergence of unilineal, ambilineal and bilateral systems.

Unilineal kin groups play an essential role in the organization of many societies. But not all societies have such groups. In societies that have complex systems of political organization, officials and agencies take over many of the functions that kin groups might perform, such as organizing work and warfare and allocating land. But not all societies that lack complex political organization have unilineal descent systems. Why, then, do some societies have unilineal descent systems, but others do not?

It is generally assumed that unilocal residence, patrilocal or matrilocal, is necessary for the development of unilineal descent. Patrilocal residence, if practiced for some time in a society, will generate a set of patrilineally related males who live in the same territory. Matrilocal residence over time will similarly generate a localized set of matrilineally related females. It is no wonder, then, that matrilocal and patrilocal residence patterns are cross-culturally associated with matrilineal and patrilineal descent, respectively.[92]

Though unilocal residence might be necessary for the formation of unilineal descent groups, it apparently is not the only condition required. For one thing, many societies with unilocal residence lack unilineal descent groups. For another, the fact that related males or related females live together by virtue of a patrilocal or matrilocal rule of residence does not necessarily follow that the related people will actually view themselves as a descent group and function as such. What other conditions are needed, then, to impel the formation of unilineal descent groups?

There is evidence that unilocal societies that engage in warfare are more apt to have unilineal descent groups than those without warfare.[93] The presence of warfare may provide societies that lack complex political organization with an impetus to form an unambiguous, single line of descent. After all, the unity of the group is more certain when no other clan, phratry, or moiety vies for their loyalty.[94] A unilineal descent group can function as a discrete unit—and do so mostly, perhaps, in warfare.

Why do some societies have ambilineal descent groups? Although the evidence is not clear-cut, it may be that societies with unilineal descent groups are transformed into ambilineal ones under special conditions, particularly depopulation. We have noted that depopulation may transform a previously unilocal society into a bilocal society. If a previously unilocal society also had unilineal descent groups, the descent groups may become transformed into ambilineal groups. If a society used to be patrilocal and patrilineal, for example, but some couples began to live matrilocally, their children would be associated through their mother with a previously patrilineal descent group on whose land they may be living. Once this situation happens regularly, the unilineal principle may become transformed into an ambilineal principle.[95] Thus, ambilineal descent systems may be a recent development resulting from depopulation caused by the introduction of European diseases.

The conditions that favor bilateral systems are in large part opposite to those that favor unilineal descent. As we discussed, unilineal descent seems to develop in a nonstate society with unilocal residence that has warfare. If one needs an unambigious set of allies, bilateral systems are unlikely to provide them. Recall that bilateral systems are ego-centered, and every person, other than siblings, has a slightly different set of kin to rely on. Consequently, in bilateral societies, it is often not clear to whom one can turn and which person has responsibility for aiding another. Such ambiguity, however, might not be a liability in societies without warfare. In complex political systems that organize fighting on behalf of large populations, a standing army usually provides the fighting force, and mobilization of kin is not so important. Perhaps because warfare is somewhat less likely in foraging societies,[96] bilateral systems may often develop in foraging societies, just like bilaterality is likely in more complex societies because they don't need to rely on descent groups for war. Neolocal residence, which becomes more common with commercialization and market exchange, also works against unilineal descent, and therefore also makes a bilateral system more likely.

Summary and Review

Marriage

14.1 Define marriage in anthropological terms.

- Marriage is customary in nearly every known society, even though humans can survive and reproduce with marriage.

- Although its form varies, marriage everywhere is understood to be a socially approved sexual and economic union, usually between a woman and a man.

- Marriage is presumed, by both the couple and others, to be more or less permanent, and it subsumes reciprocal rights and obligations between the two spouses and between spouses and their future children.

 What defines the custom of marriage?

Why Is Marriage Nearly Universal?

14.2 Explain the near-universality of marriage across cultures.

- Various explanations for marriage suggest that marriage solves problems found in all societies—how to share the products of a gender division of labor; how to care for infants, who are dependent for a long time; and how to minimize sexual competition.

- Marriage is not the only way to share the products of their labor or to support the prolonged dependency of infants, or minimize sexual competition, so those explanations cannot explain the near-universality of marriage.

- Comparative evidence on female-male bonding in mammals and birds does not support the theories explaining the near-universality of marriage.

- Bird and mammal species in which mothers cannot feed themselves and their babies at the same time *do* typically form male-female bonds, which may be true also for humans and may support a reason for marriage.

 What are four major explanations about why marriage exists? Critically evaluate them.

How Does One Marry?

14.3 Identify the various ways that marriage is marked in different societies and the economic exchanges that accompany it.

- How one marries varies considerably across cultures.

- Marking the onset of marriage seems to be important, whether or not an actual ceremony takes place. Marriage ceremonies may symbolize hostility between the two families or promote harmony between them.

- Marriage involves economic factors, explicit or not, in about 75 percent of the societies known to anthropology. Bride price is the most common form; bride service is second most common. Other forms include exchange of females, gift exchange, and forms of dowry.

 What kinds of economic transactions are associated with marriage?

Whom Should One Marry or Not Marry?

14.4 Discuss the types of restrictions on whom one can marry.

- In addition to the familial incest taboo, societies often have other rules regarding the mate such as whether they maybe cousins, whether they should come from the same community, and even whether the couple has choice in the matter.

- Parents invariably play a role, directly or indirectly, in who their offspring marry, including negotiating arranged marriages, which tend to increase economic benefits. Arranged marriages are becoming less common, and couples have stronger voices in selecting partners.

- Exogamy requires that the marriage partner come from outside one's own kin group or community. Endogamy obliges a person to marry within a particular group. The caste groups of India traditionally have been endogamous.

- When first-cousin marriage is allowed, it is usually between cross-cousins (children of siblings of the opposite sex). Marriage among parallel cousins (children of siblings of the same sex) is rare, but some Muslim societies have historically preferred such marriages.

- Large and densely populated societies may permit cousin marriages more often because such marriages are less likely in large populations. Small societies that have lost many people to epidemics may permit cousin marriage to provide enough mating possibilities.

- Cultural rules that oblige individuals to marry the spouse of a deceased relative are exceedingly common. The levirate custom obliges a man to marry his brother's widow; the sororate custom obliges a woman to marry her deceased sister's husband.

What are some of the ways cultures restrict or express preferences for whom one marries?

How Many Does One Marry?

14.5 Describe the three different forms of marriage and explain social or economic reasons for each.

- Most Western societies allow only monogamy (one spouse at a time) and prohibit polygamy (plural spouse marriage). But most societies known to anthropology have allowed some form of polygamy.

- Polygyny, the form of marriage that allows a man to be married to more than one woman at the same time, has been and is very common, especially among those with high status. In some societies, polygyny provides economic and political advantages.

- The theory that polygyny is permitted in societies that have a long postpartum sex taboo predicts it less strongly than explanations that it is a response to an excess of women over men and that a society will allow polygyny when men marry at an older age than women.

- Polyandry, the marriage of one woman to more than one man at the same time, is practiced in just a few societies. Polyandry appears to be practiced when there is a shortage of women or as an adaptive response to severely limited resources.

- Group marriage, in which more than one man is married to more than one woman at the same time, sometimes occurs but is not customary in any known society.

 How are monogamy, polygyny, and polyandry defined and what may explain why each form is preferred in societies that practice that form?

The Family

14.6 Describe and explain variation in family form.

- All societies have families, but family forms vary considerably. A family is a social and economic unit consisting minimally of one or more parents (or parent substitute) and their children. Family members have reciprocal rights and obligations, particularly economic ones.

- Adoption occurs when a family does not have enough kin to perform chores or to inherit or when one family needs to relieve pressure on resources.

- The extended family is the prevailing form of family in more than half the societies known to anthropology and may consist of two or more single-parent, monogamous, polygynous, or polyandrous families linked by a blood tie.

- In most societies known to anthropology one-parent families are relatively uncommon. But in many Western countries there has been a dramatic increase recently in the percentage of one-parent families, most of which are female-headed.

- Single parenthood occurs more with higher male unemployment and lower ratios of men to women of comparable age and in commercial economies. Evidence does not support the idea that single-parenthood increases because the state supports women to manage independently.

- Marriage in an extended family does not bring as pronounced a change in lifestyle as it does when marriage forms an independent unit. The extended family is more likely than the independent nuclear family to perpetuate itself as a social unit.

What defines the concept of family? How and why does it vary in form?

The Importance of Kinship

14.7 Explain why kinship is important.

- The web of kinship provides the main structure of social action in noncommercial societies. Most societies in which kinship connections are important have rules that assign each person to a particular and definable set of kin.

- Societies differ about what rights and obligations apply to which kin. Also variable is whom a society defines as "kin," which kin are considered important, and whether kin beyond the immediate family matter.

- The more common practice of living with and near kin has meant that the kin group has been the basis of social organization in many cultures.

Why do anthropologists think kinship is so important in noncommercial societies?

Patterns of Marital Residence

14.8 Identify the various patterns of marital residence.

- In many industrial societies, a young man and woman establish neolocal residence when they marry, setting up a new household apart from their parents and other relatives. Worldwide, that practice is much less common.

- Patterns of marital residence include patrilocal, matrilocal, ambilocal, avunculocal, and neolocal. Place of residence largely determines which people the couple and their offspring interact with and depend on and what status a wife or husband has.

 How does patrilocal and matrilocal marital residence affect males and females?

Types of Affiliation with Kin

14.9 Discuss the various ways of affiliating with kin and how the systems differ.

- Societies observe three types of affiliations: unilineal, ambilineal, and bilateral kinship.

- Unilineal and ambilineal rules of descent connect individuals through known or presumed common ancestry.

- Bilateral kinship does not refer to common descent, but is horizontal and moves outward on both sides of the family from close to more distant relatives.

- Various types of unilineal groups can occur—lineages, clans, phratries, moieties (and combinations thereof)

- Unilineal groups often have the following functions: (1) Common for marriage to be prohibited between unilineal relatives; (2) Kin groups may act corporately with respect to land and defense; (3) Kin groups often have their own religious beliefs and practices; often worshipping their own gods and spirits

- Although societies with matrilineal descent seem in many respects like mirror images of their patrilineal counterparts, they differ in one important way. In patrilineal systems, lines of descent and of authority converge. In a matrilineal system, females rarely exercise authority in their kin groups; usually males do.

- Ambilineal descent groups often have similar functions to unilineal kin groups

- In some societies, individuals can affiliate with more than one ambilineal group, but in practice people usually have a primary affiliation.

? How do the forms of affiliation with kin differ?

Explaining Variation in Residence

14.10 Discuss what might explain variation in marital residence patterns.

- Neolocal residence is associated with commercial economies; less commercial societies have residence with or near kin

- Patrilocal residence is associated with internal warfare; matrilocal residence is associated with purely external warfare and women contributing considerably to subsistence

- Bilocal residence is associated with serious depopulation

- Avunculocal residence is associated with matrilineal descent and internal warfare

? What are some theories and evidence that might explain variation in marital residence?

Explaining the Emergence of Different Systems of Kin Affiliation

14.11 Discuss what may explain the emergence of unilineal, ambilineal and bilateral systems.

- Unilineal descent groups are most common in societies in the middle range of cultural complexity

- In nonstate societies unilineal descent is predicted by a unilocal rule of residence in the presence of warfare

- Ambilineal descent is probably associated with depopulation and bilocal residence.

Think on it

1. Will it remain **customary** in our society to marry? Why do you think it will or will not?

2. Do you think **extended-family** households will become more common in our society? Why?

3. What other things about our society would change if we practiced other than **neolocal residence?**

4. Why does **kinship** provide the main structure of social action in noncommercial societies?

15 Political Life: Social Order and Disorder

LEARNING OBJECTIVES

15.1 Discuss the cross-cultural variation in the types of political organization.

15.2 Explain the spread of state societies.

15.3 Describe and explain the variation in political structure in various societies.

15.4 Critically examine the methods used for resolving conflict, including warfare, in different societies.

For people in the United States, the phrase *political life* has many connotations. It may call to mind the various branches of government: the executive branch, from the president on the national level to governors on the state level to mayors on the local level; legislative institutions, from Congress to state legislatures to city councils; and administrative bureaus, from federal government departments to local agencies.

Political life may also evoke thoughts of political parties, interest groups, lobbying, campaigning, and voting. In other words, when people living in the United States think of political life, they may think first of "politics," the activities (not always apparent) that influence who is elected or appointed to political office, what public policies are established, how they get established, and who benefits from those policies.

But in the United States and in many other countries, *political life* involves even more than government and politics. Political life also involves ways of preventing or resolving troubles and disputes both within and outside the society. Internally, a complex society such as ours may employ mediation or arbitration to resolve industrial disputes, a police force to prevent crimes or track down criminals, and courts and a penal system to deal with lawbreakers as well as with social conflict in general. Externally, such a society may establish embassies in other nations and develop and utilize its armed forces both to maintain security and to support domestic and foreign interests.

By means of all these informal and formal political mechanisms, complex societies establish social order and minimize, or at least deal with, social disorder.

Formal governments have become more widespread around the world over the last 100 years, as powerful colonizing countries have imposed political systems upon others or as people less formally organized realized that they needed governmental mechanisms to deal with the larger world. But many societies known to anthropology did not have political officials, political parties, courts, or armies. Indeed, the band or village was the largest autonomous political unit in 50 percent of the societies in the ethnographic record, as of the times they were first described. And those units were only informally organized; that is, they did not have individuals or agencies formally authorized to make and implement policy or resolve disputes. Does this mean they did not have political life? If we mean political life as we know it in our own society, then the answer has to be that they did not. But if we look beyond our formal institutions and mechanisms—if we ask what functions these institutions and mechanisms perform—we find that all societies have had political activities and beliefs to create and maintain social order and cope with social disorder.

Many of the kinds of groups we discussed in the three previous chapters, on families, descent groups, and associations, have political functions. But when anthropologists talk about *political organization* or *political life,* they are particularly focusing on activities and beliefs pertaining to *territorial groups*. Territorial groups, on whose behalf political activities may be organized, range from small communities, such as bands and villages, to large communities, such as towns and cities, to multilocal groups, such as districts or regions, entire nations, or even groups of nations.

As we shall see, the different types of political organizations, as well as how people participate in politics and how they cope with conflict, are often strongly linked to variation in food-getting, economy, and social stratification.

Variation in Types of Political Organization

15.1 Discuss the cross-cultural variation in the types of political organization.

Societies in the ethnographic record vary in *level of political integration*—that is, the largest territorial group on whose behalf political activities are organized—and in the degree to which political authority is centralized or concentrated in the integrated group. When we describe the political integration of particular societies, we focus on their traditional political systems. In many societies known to anthropology, the small community (band or village) was traditionally the largest territorial group on whose behalf political activities were organized. The authority structure in such societies did not involve any centralization; there was no political authority whose jurisdiction included more than one community. In other societies, political activities were traditionally organized sometimes on behalf of a multilocal group, but there was no permanent authority at the top. And in still other societies, political activities were often traditionally organized on behalf of multilocal territorial groups, and there was a centralized or supreme political authority at the top. In the modern world, however, every society has been incorporated into some larger, centralized political system.

Elman Service suggested that most societies can be classified into four principal types of political organization ranging from less to more centralized—bands, tribes, chiefdoms, and states.[1] Although no classification system fits all cases, Service's classification is a useful way to show how societies vary in trying to create and maintain social order.[2] We often use the present tense in our discussion because that is the convention in ethnographic writing, but readers should remember that most societies that used to be organized at the band, tribe, or chiefdom level are now incorporated into larger political entities. With a handful of exceptions, there are no politically autonomous bands or tribes or chiefdoms in the world anymore.

Band Organization

Some societies were composed of fairly small and usually nomadic groups of people. Each of these groups is conventionally called a **band** and is politically autonomous. That is, in **band organization**, the local group (sometimes as small as a family) or community is the largest group that acts as a political unit. Because most recent foragers had band organization, some anthropologists contend that this type of political organization characterized nearly all societies before the development of agriculture, or until about 10,000 years ago. But we have to remember that almost all of the described food-collecting societies are or were located in marginal environments, and almost all were affected by more dominant societies nearby.[3] So it is possible that what we call "band organization" may not have been typical of foragers in the distant or prehistoric past.

Bands are typically small, with less than 100 people usually, often considerably less. Each small band occupies a large territory, so population density is low. Band size often varies by season, with the band breaking up or recombining according to the food resources available at a given time and place. Inuit bands, for example, are smaller in the winter, when food is hard to find, and larger in the summer, when there is sufficient food to feed a larger group.

Political decision making within the band is generally informal. The "modest informal authority"[4] that does exist can be seen in the way decisions affecting the group are made. Because the formal, permanent office of a leader typically does not exist, decisions such as when a camp has to be moved or how a hunt is to be arranged are either agreed upon by the community as a whole or made by the best qualified member. Leadership, when an individual exercises it, is not the consequence of bossing or throwing one's weight about. Each band may have its informal **headman**, or its most proficient hunter, or a person most accomplished in rituals. There may be one person with all these qualities, or several people, but such a person or people will have gained status through the community's recognition of skill, good sense, and humility. Leadership, in other words, stems not from power but from influence, not from office but from admired personal qualities.

In Inuit bands, each settlement may have its headman, who acquires his influence because the other members of the community recognize his good judgment and superior skills. The headman's advice concerning the movement of the band and other community matters is generally heeded, but he possesses no permanent authority and has no power to impose sanctions of any kind. Inuit leaders are male, but men often consult their wives in private, and women who hunt seem to have more influence than those who do not.[5] In any case, leadership exists only in a very restricted sense, as among the Iglulik Inuit, for example:

> *Within each settlement … there is as a rule an older man who enjoys the respect of the others and who decides when a move is to be made to another hunting center, when a hunt is to be started, how the spoils are to be divided, when the dogs are to be fed…. He is called* isumaitoq, *"he who thinks." It is not always the oldest man, but as a rule an elderly man who is a clever hunter or, as head of a large family, exercises great authority. He cannot be called a chief; there is no obligation to follow his counsel, but they do so in most cases, partly because they rely on his experience, partly because it pays to be on good terms with this man.*[6]

Band A fairly small, usually nomadic local group that is politically autonomous.

Band organization The kind of political organization where the local group or band is the largest territorial group in the society that acts as a unit. The local group in band societies is politically autonomous.

Headman A person who holds a powerless but symbolically unifying position in a community within an egalitarian society; may exercise influence but has no power to impose sanctions.

A summary of the general features of band organization can be found in Table 15.1. Note, however, that there are exceptions to these generalizations. For example, not all known foragers are organized at the band level or have all the features of a band type of society. Classic exceptions are the Native American societies of the Northwest Pacific coast, who had enormous resources of salmon and other fish, relatively large and permanent villages, and political organization beyond the level of the typical band societies in the ethnographic record.

Tribal Organization

When local communities mostly act autonomously but there are kinship groups (such as clans or lineages) or associations (such as age-sets) that can potentially integrate several local groups into a larger unit (**tribe**), we say that the society has **tribal organization**. Unfortunately, the term *tribe* is sometimes used to refer to an entire society; that is, an entire language group may be called a tribe. But a tribal type of political system does not usually permit the entire society to act as a unit; all the communities in a tribal society may be linked only occasionally for some political (usually military) purpose. Thus, what distinguishes tribal from band political organization is the presence in the former of some multilocal, but not usually societywide, integration. The multilocal integration, however, is *not permanent,* and it is *informal* in the sense that political officials do not head it. Frequently, the integration is called into play only when an outside threat arises; when the threat disappears, the local groups revert to self-sufficiency.[7] Tribal organization may seem fragile—and, of course, it usually is—but the fact that there are social ways to integrate local groups into larger political entities means that societies with tribal organization are militarily a good deal more formidable than societies with band organization.

Societies with tribal political organization are similar to band societies in their tendency to be egalitarian (see Table 15.1). At the local level, informal leadership is also

A Masai elder blesses a warrior by smearing the fat of a ceremonial ox on his face during an Eunoto ceremony when the warriors become junior elders and thenceforth are permitted to marry.

Tribe A territorial population in which there are kin or nonkin groups with representatives in a number of local groups.

| TABLE 15.1 | Suggested Trends in Political Organization and Other Social Characteristics |

Type of Organization	Highest Level of Political Integration	Specialization of Political Officials	Predominant Mode of Subsistence	Community Size and Population Density	Social Differentiation	Major Form of Distribution
Band	Local group or band	Little or none; informal leadership	Foraging or food collecting	Very small communities; very low density	Egalitarian	Mostly reciprocity
Tribe	Sometimes multilocal group	Little or none; informal leadership	Extensive (shifting) agriculture and/or herding	Small communities; low density	Egalitarian	Mostly reciprocity
Chiefdom	Multilocal group	Some	Extensive or intensive agriculture and/or herding	Large communities; medium density	Rank	Reciprocity and redistribution
State	Multilocal group; often entire language group	Much	Intensive agriculture and herding	Cities and towns; high density	Class and caste	Mostly market exchange

Tribal organization
The kind of political organization in which local communities mostly act autonomously but there are kin groups (such as clans) or associations (such as age-sets) that can temporarily integrate a number of local groups into a larger unit.

Segmentary lineage system A hierarchy of more inclusive lineages; usually functions only in conflict situations.

Complementary opposition The occasional uniting of various segments of a segmentary lineage system in opposition to similar segments.

characteristic. In those tribal societies where kinship provides the basic framework of social organization, the elders of the local kin groups tend to have considerable influence; where age-sets are important, a particular age-set is looked to for leadership. But, in contrast to band societies, societies with tribal organization generally are food producers. And because cultivation and animal husbandry are generally more productive than hunting and gathering, the population density of tribal societies is generally higher, local groups are larger, and the way of life is more sedentary than in hunter-gatherer bands.[8]

Kinship Bonds Frequently communities are linked to each other by virtue of belonging to the same kin group, usually a unilineal group such as a lineage or clan. A **segmentary lineage system** is one type of tribal integration based on kinship. A society with such a system is composed of segments, or parts, each similar to the others in structure and function. Every local segment belongs to a hierarchy of lineages stretching farther and farther back genealogically. The hierarchy of lineages, then, unites the segments into larger and larger genealogical groups. The closer two groups are genealogically, the greater their general closeness. In the event of a dispute among members of different segments, people related more closely to one contestant than to another take the side of their nearest kinsman. The well-known Arab saying "I against my brothers; my brothers and I against our cousins; my brothers and cousins and I against the world" well expresses the contingency of relationships in conflict settings.[9]

The Tiv of Northern Nigeria offer a classic example of a segmentary lineage system, one that happens to link all the Tiv into a single genealogical structure or tribe. The Tiv are a large society, numbering more than 800,000. Figure 15.1 is a representation of the Tiv lineage structure as described by Paul Bohannan. In the figure, there are four levels of lineages. Each of the smallest lineages, symbolized by *a* through *h*, is in turn embedded in more inclusive lineages. So minimal lineages *a* and *b* are together in lineage *1*. Lineages *1* and *2* are embedded in lineage *A*. Territorial organization follows lineage hierarchy. As shown in the bottom of the figure, the most closely related lineages have territories near each other. Minimal lineages *a* and *b* live next to each other; their combined territory is the territory of their higher-order lineage, *1*. Lineage *A* in turn has a territory that is differentiated from lineage *B*. All of Tivland is said to descend from one ancestor, represented by *I*.[10]

Tiv lineage organization is the foundation of Tiv political organization. A look at Figure 15.1 helps to explain how a dispute between lineages (and territories) *a* and *b* remains minor because no more than "brother" segments are involved. But a dispute between *a* and *c* involves lineages *1* and *2* as well, with the requirement that *b* assists *a* and *d* supports *c*. This process of mutual support, called **complementary opposition**, means that segments will unite only in a confrontation with some other group. Groups that will fight with each other in a minor dispute might coalesce at some later time against a larger group.

The segmentary lineage system was presumably very effective in allowing the Tiv to intrude into new territory and take land from other tribal societies with smaller descent groups. Individual Tiv lineage segments could call on support from related lineages when faced with border troubles. Conflicts within the society—that is, between segments—especially in border areas, were often turned outward, "releasing internal pressure in an explosive blast against other peoples."[11]

Segmentary lineage systems may have military advantages even when they do not unite the entire society. A classic example is the Nuer of the Upper Nile region, who had tribal,

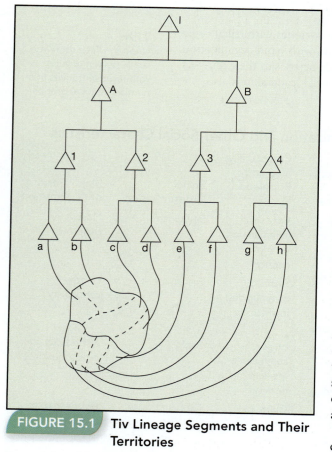

FIGURE 15.1   **Tiv Lineage Segments and Their Territories**

Source: Adapted from P. Bohannan 1954.

but not societywide, organization because of their segmentary lineages. In the early 1800s, the Nuer had a territory of about 8,700 square miles, and the neighboring Dinka had ten times that much. But by 1890, the Nuer had cut a 100-mile swath through Dinka territory, increasing Nuer territory to 35,000 square miles. Even though the Nuer and Dinka were culturally very similar, the segmentary lineage organization of the Nuer seems to have given them a significant military advantage in their incursions into Dinka territory.[12]

A segmentary lineage system may generate a formidable military force, but the combinations of manpower it produces are temporary, forming and dissolving as the occasion demands.[13] Tribal political organization does not make for a political system that more or less permanently integrates a number of communities.

Age-Set Systems Societies with age-sets have a group of people of the same sex and similar age who move through some or all of their life stages together. Usually entry into an age-set begins at or before puberty in a group initiation ceremony held regularly over the years. Often the age-sets encompass a number of communities, so that a sense of solidarity is formed. Age-sets can function as the basis of a tribal type of political organization, as among the Karimojong of northeastern Uganda.[14]

The Karimojong age-set system has an important bearing on day-to-day tribal life. As herders, Karimojong adults are often separated from their usual settlements. Herders will meet, mingle for a while, then go their separate ways, but each may call upon other members of his age-set wherever he goes. The age-set system is important among the Karimojong because it immediately allocates to each individual a place in the system and thereby establishes for him an appropriate pattern of response. A quarrel in camp will be settled by the representatives of the senior age-set who are present, regardless of which section of the tribe they may belong to.

Among the Karimojong, political leaders are not elected from among the elders of a particular age-set, nor are they appointed; they acquire their positions informally. Usually a man's background, and the ability he has demonstrated in public debates over a period of time, will result in his being considered by the men of his neighborhood to be their spokesman. His function is to announce what course of action seems required in a particular situation, to initiate that action, and then to coordinate it after it has begun.

Most political leaders exercise their authority within the local sphere because the pastoral nature of the Karimojong economy, with its dispersed groups and movement from one feeding ground to another, offers no alternative. From time to time, an elder may acquire the status of a prophet and be awarded respect and obedience on a tribal scale. He will be called upon to lead sacrifices (to avert misfortune), to undertake rainmaking (to bring prosperity), and so on. Yet even a prophet's prestige and authority do not warrant him a position of overlord or chief.[15]

In many societies with age-set systems, the authority of the elders has been weakened in recent times. For example, among the Karimojong, the council of elders could mete out punishment to offenders and watch them to make sure they behave. Nowadays, young men are able to get guns during raids, and elders find it risky to punish someone with a gun. Young men can also more readily move away, and social control by the elders becomes more difficult.[16]

Chiefdom Organization

Whereas a tribe has some informal mechanism that can integrate more than one community, a **chiefdom** has some *formal* structure that integrates more than one community into a political unit, such as a district. The formal structure could consist of a council with or without a chief, but most commonly there is a person—the **chief**—who has higher rank or authority than others. Most societies at the chiefdom level of organization contain more than one political unit or chiefdom, each headed by a district chief or a council. There may also be more than one level of chief beyond the community, such as district chiefs and higher-level chiefs. Some chiefdom societies integrate the whole society, with a paramount chief at the top. Others are not as centralized. Compared with tribal societies, societies with chiefdoms are more densely populated

Chiefdom A political unit, with a chief at its head, integrating more than one community but not necessarily the whole society or language group.

Chief A person who exercises authority, usually on behalf of a multicommunity political unit. This role is generally found in rank societies and is usually permanent and often hereditary.

A chief from Moorea in French Polynesia.

and their communities are more permanent, partly as a consequence of their generally greater economic productivity[17] (see Table 15.1).

The position of chief, which is sometimes hereditary and generally permanent, bestows high status on its holder. Most chiefdoms have social ranking and accord the chief and his family greater access to prestige. The chief may redistribute goods, plan and direct the use of public labor, supervise religious ceremonies, and direct military activities on behalf of the chiefdom.[18] In South Pacific chiefdoms, the chiefs carried out most of these duties. In Fijian chiefdoms, for example, the chief was responsible for the redistribution of goods and the coordination of labor:

> [The chief] could summon the community's labor on his own behalf, or on behalf of someone else who requested it, or for general purposes…. Besides his right to summon labor, he accumulated the greater proportion of the first fruits of the yam crop … and he benefited from other forms of food presentation, or by the acquisition of special shares in ordinary village distribution…. Thus, the paramount [chief] would collect a significant part of the surplus production of the community and redistribute it in the general welfare.[19]

In contrast to leaders in tribal societies, who generally have to earn their privileges by their personal qualities, hereditary chiefs are said to have those qualities in their "blood." A high-ranking chief in Polynesia, a huge triangular area of islands in the South Pacific, inherited special religious power called *mana*. *Mana* sanctified his rule and protected him.[20] Chiefs in Polynesia had so much religious power that missionaries could convert people to Christianity only after their chiefs had been converted.[21]

In most chiefdoms, the chiefs did not have the power to compel people to obey them; people would act in accordance with the chief's wishes because the chief was respected and often had religious authority. But in the most complex paramount chiefdoms, such as those of Hawaii and Tahiti, the chiefs seemed to have more compelling sanctions than the "power" of respect or *mana*. Substantial amounts of goods and services collected by the chiefs were used to support subordinates, including specialists such as high priests, political envoys, and warriors who could be sent to quell rebellious factions.[22] When redistributions do not go to everybody—when chiefs are allowed to keep items for their own purposes—and when a chief begins to use armed force, the political system is on the way to becoming what we call a state.

State Organization

A **state**, according to one more or less standard definition, is "an autonomous political unit, encompassing many communities within its territory and having a centralized government with the power to collect taxes, draft men for work or war, and decree and enforce laws."[23] States, then, have a complex, centralized political structure that includes a wide range of permanent institutions with legislative, executive, and judicial functions and a large bureaucracy. Central to this definition is the concept of legitimate force used to implement policies both internally and externally. In states, the government tries to maintain a monopoly on the use of physical force.[24] This monopoly can be seen in the development of formal and specialized instruments of social control: a police force, a militia, or a standing army.

Just as a particular society may contain more than one band, tribe, or chiefdom, so may it contain more than one state. The contiguously distributed population speaking a single language may or may not be politically unified in a single state. Ancient Greece was composed of many city-states; so, too, was Italy until the 1870s. German speakers are also not politically unified; Austria and Germany are separate states, and Germany itself was not politically unified until the 1870s. We say that a society has **state organization** when it is composed of one or more political units that are states.

State An autonomous political unit with centralized decision making over many communities with power to govern by force (e.g., to collect taxes, draft people for work and war, and make and enforce laws). Most states have cities with public buildings; full-time craft and religious specialists; an "official" art style; a hierarchical social structure topped by an elite class; and a governmental monopoly on the legitimate use of force to implement policies.

State organization A society is described as having state organization when it includes one or more states.

A state may include more than one society. Multisociety states are often the result of conquest or colonial control when the dominant political authority, itself a state, imposes a centralized government over a territory with many different societies and cultures, as the British did in Nigeria and Kenya.

Colonialism is a common feature of state societies. But not all colonialisms are alike. Archaeology and history tell us about various kinds of colonialism. The expanding state society may send people to build a new imperial settlement in some other place to trade or protect trade routes, like the British, Spanish, and others did. Or the colonial power may displace and move parts of the original population, as the Inka empire did.[25] Most of the expanding state societies we know about are usually called *empires*. They incorporated other societies and states. The extension of U.S. power in modern times, for example, by persuading other countries to let the United States build military bases, has led some commentators to refer to an American empire, even though the United States did not always establish colonies where they had economic and political control.[26]

Nearly all of the multisociety states that emerged after World War II were the results of successful independence movements against colonial powers.[27] Most have retained their political unity despite the fact that they still contain many different societies. For example, Nigeria remains unified despite a civil war; the eastern section called Biafra (mostly populated by people of Ibo culture) tried unsuccessfully 30 years ago to secede, and subsequently there has been serious conflict among some of the constituent societies.

Migrants and Immigrants

The Growth of Cities

Nearly half of the world's human population now lives in cities, which are usually defined as communities where few are directly involved in food-getting. An even larger proportion of humanity will be urban dwellers in the future.

The explosive growth of cities over the past century is largely the result of migration from rural areas of the country and from rural areas in other countries. Recall the exodus of the Irish to Britain and the United States because of the "potato famine," the massive migrations from the villages of Germany, Italy, and Greece in the 19th and 20th centuries, and the huge migrations particularly in the last 50 years from rural Mexico and China. Poverty is one "push" factor. Flight from persecution is another. Many parts of the world are not safe, particularly for poor people. True, in the modern world, it is possible for some people to go "home" for a visit, even halfway around the world. But, for many migrants now and in the recent past, the move was one way. Because you may have run away from poverty, persecution, and war, you couldn't (or wouldn't) go home again.

Cities everywhere have problems, even in the most developed countries.

Providing water, power, sanitation, and other services to perhaps millions of city dwellers is difficult and expensive. Yet in every country, people are leaving rural areas and going to cities. Some are political refugees, like the Hmong from Laos who now live in St. Paul, Minnesota. Then there are the people from Congo and Sudan, from Kosovo and Northern Ireland, who have fled civil wars. There are other reasons to leave too. Technological improvements may have reduced the need for rural labor, which happened in the U.S. South after the 1930s. Or the rural opportunities cannot support the increased number of mouths to be fed. Usually people do not go to other rural areas but rather to cities, often in other countries, where jobs are available. In the more urbanized countries, the cities have acquired "suburbs," where many of the people in a metropolitan area may actually live. But hardly anyone is left on the farm—only just a few percent of the population in the more developed countries.

In the last half of the 20th century, with the building of suburbs, there seems to have been a turning away from cities in many countries. Cities lost population as people moved

to the suburbs to have more living space, a garden, "better" schools for their children, or to escape from the threat of violence. But recently, the flow has started to reverse in North America and elsewhere. The suburbanites are coming back to the cities, perhaps because people are getting tired of commuting longer distances to jobs and recreation. This is particularly so with wealthier people whose children have grown up and moved away, and with more people living until older ages, many want to move closer to the places where they mostly spend their time. Despite the social inequality and violence, cities have always been the places to go for jobs and other activities. Concerts, theaters, restaurants, museums, amusement parks, hospitals, and professional sports stadiums have always been located in cities or nearby.

The "push" out of the rural areas and the "pull" of the cities are hard to resist, despite the enormous political problems of urban living. As the old song laments, "Howya goin' keep 'em down on the farm after they've seen Paree?"

Source: M. Ember and Ember 2002.

Multisociety or multiethnic states may also form voluntarily, in reaction to external threat. Switzerland comprises cantons, each of which speaks mainly French, German, Italian, or Romansch; the various cantons confederated originally to shake off control by the Holy Roman Empire. But some states have lost their unity recently, including the former Union of Soviet Socialist Republics (USSR) and much of Yugoslavia.

In addition to their strictly political features, intensive agriculture generally supports state-organized societies. The high productivity of the agriculture allows for the emergence of cities, a high degree of economic and other kinds of specialization, and market or commercial exchange. In addition, state societies usually have class stratification (see Table 15.1). Cities have grown tremendously in the last 100 years, largely as a result of migration and immigration. (See the Migrants and Immigrants box on "The Growth of Cities.")

When states come into existence, people's access to scarce resources is radically altered. So, too, is their ability not to listen to leaders: You usually cannot refuse to pay taxes or avoid labor or military conscription and go unpunished. Of course, the rulers of a state do not maintain the social order by force alone. The people must believe, at least to some extent, that those in power have a legitimate right to govern. If the people think otherwise, history suggests that those in power may eventually lose their ability to control. Witness the recent downfall of Communist parties throughout most of eastern Europe and the former Soviet Union.

So force and the threat of force are not enough to explain the legitimacy of power and the inequities that occur commonly in state societies. But then what does? There are various theories. The rulers of early states often claimed divine descent to buttress their legitimacy, but this claim is rare nowadays. Another theory is that, if parents teach their children to accept all authority, such lessons may generalize to the acceptance of political authority. Some analysts think that people accept state authority for no good reason; the rulers are just able to fool them. Finally, some theorists think that states must provide people with real or rational advantages; otherwise, people would not think that the rulers deserve to exercise authority. Legitimacy is not an all-or-none phenomenon; it varies in degree.[28]

A state society can retain its legitimacy, or at least its power, for a long time. For example, the Roman Empire was a complex state society that dominated the Mediterranean and Near East for hundreds of years. It began as a city-state that waged war to acquire additional

Popular demonstrations can have major effects on states. These protests in the Ukraine in 2004 disputed election results and subsequently the courts voided the election.

territory. At its height, the Roman Empire embraced more than 55 million people;[29] the capital city of Rome had a population of well over a million.[30] The empire included parts of what are now Great Britain, France, Spain, Portugal, Germany, Rumania, Turkey, Greece, Armenia, Egypt, Israel, and Syria.

Another example of a state society was the kingdom of Nupe in West Africa, now part of the nation-state of Nigeria. Nupe society was rigidly stratified. At the top of the social system was the king, or *etsu*. Beneath the king, members of the royal family formed the highest aristocratic class. Next in order were two other classes of nobility: the local chiefs and the military leaders. At the bottom were the commoners, who had neither prestige nor power and no share in political authority.

The Nupe king possessed ultimate authority in many judicial matters. Local village councils handled minor disputes and civil cases, but serious criminal cases were the prerogative of the king. Such cases, referred to as "crimes for the king," were brought before the royal court by the king's local representatives. The king and his counselors judged the cases and determined suitable punishments.

The most powerful influence of the state over the Nupe people was in the area of taxation. The king was given the power to impose taxes and collect them from every household. Payment was made either in money (cowrie shells originally and, later, British currency) or certain gifts, such as cloth, mats, and slaves. The king kept much of the revenue collected, and his local representatives and lords shared the remainder. In return for the taxes they paid, the people received security—protection against invasion and domestic disorder.[31]

Although all state societies employ coercion or the threat of it, some states are more autocratic than others. This is not just today, or in the recent past, but also in the distant past. The less autocratic states are characterized by more "collective action." They produce more public goods, such as transportation systems and redistribution systems, in times of need. The rulers do not aggrandize themselves as much or live that luxuriously. And, the rulers must rule within limits and must respond to grievances. They are accountable. The Lozi state of central southern Africa had more collective action than the Nupe state described. The Lozi built an extensive system of drainage canals that also facilitated transportation. In hungry times, royal herds and the "state" gardens were used to feed distressed villages. And rulers were not that much more elevated in standard of living. In contrast, the Nupe state financed very little in the way of public works, had little redistribution, and the rulers lived in elaborate palaces.[32] Collective action is a continuum; states at the higher end of that continuum have not been limited to a few world regions or particular time periods. Collection action theorists suggest that, when the state relies more heavily on resources from taxpayers, the rulers must give the public more in return or else face noncompliance and rebellion. Richard Blanton and Lane Fargher's comparative study of premodern states supports collection action theory.[33]

Nation-State, Nationalism, and Political Identity

States are political entities; people within them do not necessarily share much beyond a bureaucracy, a set of laws, and being subject to similar social controls. People within them may not have a sense of identity with the state they live in. A sense of identity is more likely if a state is composed of a dominant culture or ethnic group, but most states, certainly almost all empires, have commonly been multicultural or multiethnic entities.[34] In order to increase a sense of identity, some states have deliberately tried to incorporate and assimilate other cultural groups by promoting a common language and religion; other states have tolerated and sometimes even promoted multiculturalism. Multiculturalism does not preclude identification with the state as well as one's own ethnicity—after all, toleration of divergent ethnic identities may forge a sense of pride in state government. Scholars often use the term **nation** to refer to the idea that a set of people share a common territory, history, and identity.[35] We may call it a state or a **nation-state** when the concepts of nation and state co-occur; that is when the people in a state share a sense of nationhood. If there is a strong sense of identity with the nation, willingness to fight and die for it, **nationalism** is a term often used as an expression of that loyalty. Arjun Appadurai notes that the concept of nationalism includes "full attachment," which goes well beyond the concept of legitimacy. In his view, full attachment includes strong emotions such as excitement at national parades, tears at hearing the national anthem, and intense anger when a nation is thought

Nation A set of people sharing a common territory, history, and a sense of identity.

Nation-state The co-occurrence of a political state and a nation

Nationalism The strong sense of loyalty, attachment, and devotion to a nation (see nation).

Applied Anthropology

Democracy and Economic Development

As people increasingly produce goods and services for a market and as the pace of economic development quickens, economies are increasingly integrated into the world system. What effect, if any, does economic development have on political participation? Can we speculate about the future on the basis of comparative research?

Most of the comparative research on the relationship between economic development and political participation has been cross-national, comparing data on different countries. Some countries are more democratic than others, with characteristics such as contested elections, an elected head of state, an elected powerful legislature, and the protection of civil liberties. In capitalist countries, more democracy is generally associated with higher levels of economic development, as measured by indicators such as per capita output; in countries that are not very industrialized, there is little democracy at the national level. Why should more democracy be associated with more economic development? The prevailing opinion is that economic development increases the degree of social equality in the country; and the more equality among interest groups, the more they demand participation in the political process, and hence the more democracy.

What about the societies usually studied by anthropologists, the ones in what we call the cross-cultural or ethnographic record? We know that some of the highest levels of political participation occur in foraging societies. Many adults in such societies have a say in decisions, and leadership is informal; leaders can retain their roles only if people voluntarily go along with them. Concentrated power and less political participation are more likely in chiefdoms and states than in band and tribal societies. The more hierarchical chiefdoms and states usually depend on agriculture, particularly intensive agriculture, which can produce more goods and services per capita

Lech Walesa played an important role in the relatively peaceful transition in Poland from communism to democracy.

than foraging economies can. So the relationship between economic development and political participation in the ethnographic record is *opposite* to what we find cross-nationally. That is, the more economic development, the less political participation in the societies studied by anthropologists. Why should this be so? It seems that social equality *decreases* as economic development increases in the ethnographic record (which does not include many industrialized societies). In that record, an economically developed society is likely to have features such as plowing, fertilizers, and irrigation, which make permanent cultivation of the fields and permanent communities possible. Such intensive agricultural activity is more conducive to concentrated wealth than is hunter-gatherer subsistence or shifting cultivation (horticulture). Thus, in the ethnographic record, the more economically developed societies have more social inequality and therefore less democracy.

The two sets of findings, the cross-national and the cross-cultural, are not that hard to reconcile. Social

and economic inequality appears to work against democracy and extensive political participation. Social inequality increases with the switch from foraging to agriculture. But social inequality decreases with the switch from preindustrial agriculture to high (industrial) levels of economic development. Political participation decreases with the first switch and increases with the second, because social inequality first increases and then decreases.

So what does comparative research suggest about the future? If the middle and working classes feel they are not getting a fair return on their labor, their demands should increase. The elite may be willing to satisfy those increased demands; if they do, their power will be reduced. In either case, unless the elite try to retain their power at any cost, there should be more political participation and more democracy, at least in the long run.

Sources: Bollen 1993; Muller 1997; M. Ember, Ember, and Russett 1997; Ross 2009b.

to be insulted.[36] But the concepts of nation and nationalism are not necessarily associated with states. There are groups living within state boundaries that comprise separate nations (some describe French and English Canada as two nations within one) or who strive for separate nationhood for themselves. There are also groups that cross country borders, like the Kurds of Iraq, Iran, Turkey, and Syria who feel a sense of nationhood as Kurds and their homeland "Kurdistan."[37] Nationalism can even transcend big distances. Even when people are widely scattered in other countries, sometimes even are citizens of other countries, they may have a strong sense of nationalism about their ancestral home. They may demonstrate their nationalism by lobbying, demonstrating, setting up Web sites, sending contributions, and even giving their lives for the cause of creating a separate nation.[38]

Factors Associated with Variation in Political Organization

The kinds of political organization we call band, tribal, chiefdom, and state are points on a continuum of levels of political integration or unification, from small-scale local autonomy to large-scale regional unification. There also is variation in political authority, from a few temporary and informal political leaders to large numbers of permanent, specialized political officials, from the absence of coercive political power to the monopoly of public force by a central authority. These aspects of variation in political organization are generally associated with shifts from foraging to more intensive food production, from small to large communities, from low to high population densities, from an emphasis on reciprocity to redistribution to market exchange, and from egalitarian to rank to fully stratified class societies.

The associations just outlined, which seem to be confirmed by the available cross-cultural evidence, are summarized in Table 15.1. With regard to the relation between level of subsistence technology and political complexity, one cross-cultural study employing a small random sample of societies found that the greater the importance of agriculture in a society, the larger the population that is politically unified and the greater the number and types of political officials.[39] A massive cross-cultural survey reported a similar trend: The more intensive the agriculture, the greater the likelihood of state organization; conversely, societies with no more than local political institutions are likely to depend on hunting, gathering, and fishing.[40]

Community size appears to be an especially sensitive predictor of political complexity—larger communities strongly predict not only a wider range of political officials in a society, but also more administrative levels of decision making.[41] In particular, societies with state organization tend to have cities and towns, whereas those with only local political organization are more likely to have communities with an average population of fewer than 200 people.[42] Cross-cultural research also tends to confirm that societies with higher levels of political integration are more likely to exhibit social differentiation, especially in the form of class distinctions.[43]

Does this evidence provide us with an explanation for why political organization varies? Clearly, the data indicate that several factors are associated with political development, but exactly why changes in organization occur is not yet understood. Although economic development may be a necessary condition for political development,[44] that relation does not fully explain why political organization should become more complex just because the economy can support it. Some theorists have suggested that competition among groups may be a more important reason for political consolidation. For example, Elman Service suggested competition as a reason why a society might change from a band level of political organization to a tribal level. Band societies are generally hunter-gatherers. With a changeover to agriculture, population density and competition among groups may increase. Service believed that such competition would foster the development of some informal organization beyond the community—namely, tribal organization—for offense and defense.[45] Indeed, both unilineal kinship groups and age-set systems seem to be associated with warfare.

Among agriculturalists, defensive needs might also be the main reason for switching from informal multivillage political organization to more formal chiefdom organization. Formally organized districts are probably more likely to defeat autonomous villages or even segmentary lineage systems.[46] If warfare were very frequent and intense, it is possible that war leaders, with the help of loyal warriors, could enhance their positions and become more permanent political leaders.[47] In addition, there may be economic reasons for political development. With regard to chiefdoms, Service suggested that chiefdoms will emerge when redistribution among communities becomes important or when large-scale coordinated work groups are required. The more important these activities are, the more important—and hence more "chiefly"—the organizer and his family presumably become.[48] But redistribution is far from a universal activity of chiefs.[49]

Theory and research on the anthropology of political development have focused mostly on the high end of the scale of political complexity, and particularly on the origins of the first state societies. Those earliest states apparently rose independently of one another, after about 3500 B.C., in what are now southern Iraq, Egypt, northwestern India, northern China, and central Mexico. There are several theories of why states arose. The irrigation theory suggests that the administrative needs of maintaining extensive irrigation systems may have been the impetus for state formation.[50] The circumscription theory suggests that states emerge when competition and warfare in physically or socially circumscribed areas lead to the subordination of defeated groups, which are obliged to submit to the control of the most powerful group.[51] Theories involving trade suggest that the organizational requirements of producing exportable items, redistributing imported items, and defending trading parties would foster state formation.[52] The state, by definition, implies the power to organize large populations for collective purposes. But at this point, most anthropologists believe that no one theory is able to explain the formation of every state. Perhaps different organizational requirements in different areas all favored centralized government.[53]

15.2 Explain the spread of state societies.

The Spread of State Societies

The state level of political development has come to dominate the world. Societies with states have larger communities and higher population densities than do band, tribal, and chiefdom societies. They also have armies that are ready to fight at almost any time. State systems that have waged war against chiefdoms and tribes have almost always won, and the result has usually been the political incorporation of the losers. For example, the British and, later, the U.S. colonization of much of North America led to the defeat and incorporation of many Native American societies.

The defeat and incorporation of the Native Americans was at least partly due to the catastrophic depopulations they suffered because of epidemic diseases, such as smallpox and measles, that European colonists introduced. Catastrophic depopulation was commonly the outcome of the first contacts between European Americans and the natives of North and South America, as well as the natives of the far islands in the Pacific. People in the New World and the Pacific had not been exposed, and therefore were not resistant to the diseases the European Americans carried with them when they began to colonize the world. Before the expansion of Europeans, the people of the New World and the Pacific had been separated for a long time from the people and diseases on the geographically continuous landmass we separate into Europe, Africa, and Asia. Smallpox, measles, and the other former scourges of Europe had largely become childhood diseases that most individuals of European ancestry survived.[54]

Whether by depopulation, conquest, or intimidation, the number of independent political units in the world has decreased strikingly in the last 3,000 years, and especially in the last 200 years. Robert Carneiro estimated that in 1000 B.C., there may have been between 100,000 and 1 million separate political units in the world; today, there are fewer than 200.[55] In the ethnographic record, about 50 percent of the 2,000 or so societies described within the last 150 years had only local political integration. That is, the highest level of political integration in one out of two recent societies was the local community.[56] Thus, most of the decrease in the number of independent political units has occurred fairly recently.

But the recent secessions from the former Soviet Union and Yugoslavia and other separatist movements around the world suggest that ethnic rivalries may make for departures from the trend toward larger and larger political units. Ethnic groups that have been dominated by others in multinational states may opt for political autonomy, at least for a while. On the other hand, the separate nations of western Europe are becoming more unified every day, both politically and economically. So the trend toward larger political units may be continuing, even if there are departures from it now and then.

Extrapolating from past history, a number of investigators have suggested that the entire world will eventually come to be politically integrated, perhaps as soon as the 23rd century and no later than A.D. 4850.[57] Only the future will tell if this prediction will come true and if further political integration in the world will occur peacefully—with all parties agreeing—or by force or the threat of force, as has happened so often in the past.

Variation in Political Process

15.3 Describe and explain the variation in political structure in various societies.

Anthropologists are increasingly interested in the politics, or political processes, of the societies they study: who acquires influence or power, how they acquire it, and how political decisions are made. But even though we have descriptive accounts of politics in many societies, there is still little comparative or cross-cultural research on what may explain variation in politics.[58]

Getting to Be a Leader

In those societies that have hereditary leadership, which is common in rank societies and in state societies with monarchies, rules of succession usually establish how leadership is inherited. Such leaders are often identifiable in some obviously visible ways; they may be permanently marked or tattooed, as in chiefdoms in Polynesia, or they may wear elaborate dress and insignia, as in class-stratified societies. But for societies whose leaders are *chosen*, either as informal leaders or as political officials, we need a lot more research to understand why some kinds of people are chosen over others.

A few studies have investigated the personal qualities of leaders in tribal societies. One study, conducted among the Mekranoti-Kayapo of central Brazil, found that leaders, in contrast to followers, tend to be rated by their peers as higher in intelligence, generosity, knowledgeability, ambitiousness, and aggressiveness. Leaders also tend to be older. And despite the egalitarian nature of Mekranoti society (at least with respect to sharing resources), sons of leaders are more likely than others to become leaders.[59] The Mekranoti leaders also tend to be taller, consistent with research in the United States.

Research in another Brazilian society, the Kagwahiv of the Amazon region, suggests another personal quality of leaders: They seem to have positive feelings about their fathers and mothers.[60] In many respects, studies of leaders in the United States show them to be not that different from their counterparts in Brazil. But there is one major difference: Mekranoti and Kagwahiv leaders are not wealthier than others; in fact, they give their wealth away. U.S. leaders are generally wealthier than others.[61]

"Big Men" In some egalitarian tribal societies, the quest for leadership seems quite competitive. In parts of New Guinea and South America, "big men" compete with other ambitious men to attract followers. Men who want to compete must show that they have magical powers, success in gardening, and bravery in war. But, most important, they have to collect enough goods to throw big parties at which the goods are given away. Big men have to work very hard to attract and keep their followings, for dissatisfied followers can always join other aspiring men.[62] The wives of big men are often leaders too. Among the Kagwahiv, for example, a headman's wife is usually the leader of the women in the community; she is responsible for much of the planning for feasts and often distributes the meat at them.[63]

Although the phenomenon of big men leaders is common throughout New Guinea, researchers are beginning to see variation in the type and extent of "bigmanship" in different areas of New Guinea. For example, in the southern Highlands, groups of men (not just big men) may engage in large-scale giveaways, so big men are not so different from ordinary men. In the northwestern Highlands, on the other hand, big men stand out from other men in striking ways. They make policy for groups of people and organize collective events, they have substantial access to pigs or to valuables acquired in exchanges, and they have control over a substantial amount of labor (more than one wife and fellow kin).[64]

We know that some big men are "bigger" than others, but how does a man get to be a big man? Among the Kumdi-Engamoi, a central Highlands group, a man who wants to be considered a *wua nium* (literally, a "great-important-wealthy man") needs to have many wives and daughters, because the amount of land controlled by a man and how much can be produced on that land depend on the number of women in his family. The more wives he has, the more land he is given to cultivate. He must also be a good speaker. Everyone has the right to speak and give speeches, but to get to be known as a big man requires speaking well and forcefully and knowing when to sum up a consensus. It usually takes a man until his thirties or forties to acquire more than one wife and to make his name through exchanges. When a man wants to inaugurate an exchange, he needs to get shells and pigs from his family and relatives. Once he has achieved a reputation as a *wua nium,* he can keep it only if he continues to perform well—that is, if he continues to distribute fairly, make wise decisions, speak well, and conduct exchanges.[65]

"Big Women"   In contrast to most of mainland New Guinea, the islands off the southeastern coast are characterized by matrilineal descent. But, like the rest of New Guinea, the islands also have a shifting system of leadership in which people compete for "big" status. Here, though, the people competing are women as well as men, and so there are "big women" as well as "big men." On the island of Vanatinai, for example, women and men compete with each other to exchange valuables. Women lead canoe expeditions to distant islands to visit male as well as female exchange partners, women mobilize relatives and exchange partners to mount large feasts, and the women get to keep the ceremonial valuables exchanged, at least for a while.[66]

The prominence of women on Vanatinai may be linked to the disappearance of warfare—the colonial powers imposed peace; we call this "pacification." Interisland exchanges became frequent when war became rarer in the early 20th century, giving women and men more freedom to travel. For men, but not women, war provided a path to leadership; champion warriors would acquire great renown and influence. It is not that women did not participate in war; they did, which is unusual cross-culturally, but a woman could not become a war leader. Now, in the absence of war, women have an opportunity through exchanges to become leaders, or "big women."

In one respect, however, women have less of an opportunity to acquire influence now. There are local government councils now, but all the councillors are male. Why? Some women were nominated for the posts, but they withdrew in embarrassment because they could not speak English. Big men or big women do not automatically have a path to these new positions; mostly young males who know English become the councillors. But this situation may change. With the opening of a government primary school in 1984, both girls and boys are learning English, so women in the future may be more likely to achieve leadership by becoming councillors.

Researchers continue to explore other features that may enhance a person's ability to become leaders where leadership is not hereditary. One fascinating new finding is that in the United States, after controlling for age and perceived attractiveness, individuals who are judged prior to the election to be more "competent" from photographs of their faces are more likely to win in congressional elections.[67] What makes a face look more "competent"? Generally, it has fewer "babyish" features—it is less round, has a bigger chin, smaller eyes, and a smaller forehead.[68] However, in wartime, more masculine facial qualities appear to be preferred in a leader; in peacetime, more

In many egalitarian societies, leadership shifts informally from one person to another. In much of New Guinea, there is more competition for achieving "big" status. On Vanatinai, the women compete as well as the men, so there are "big women" as well as "big men." Here a "big woman" paints the face of her cousin's widow for a feast honoring the dead man.

feminine qualities.[69] Whether these facial features also predict leadership cross-culturally is not yet known.

Political Participation

Political scientist Marc Ross conducted cross-cultural research on variation in degree of political participation. Ross phrased the research question: "Why is it that in some polities there are relatively large numbers of persons involved in political life, while in others, political action is the province of very few?"[70]

Political participation in preindustrial societies ranges from widespread to low or nonexistent. In 16 percent of the societies examined, there is widespread participation; decision-making forums are open to all adults. The forums may be formal (councils and other governing bodies) or informal. Next in degree of political participation are societies (37 percent) that have widespread participation by some but not all adults (men but not women, certain classes but not others). Next are societies (29 percent) that have some but not much input by the community. Finally, 18 percent of the societies have low or nonexistent participation, which means that leaders make most decisions, and involvement of the average person is very limited.

Degree of political participation seems to be high in small-scale societies, as well as in modern democratic nation-states, but not in between (feudal states and preindustrial empires). Why? In small-scale societies, leaders do not have the power to force people to act; thus, a high degree of political participation may be the only way to get people to go along with decisions. In modern democracies, which have many powerful groups outside the government—corporations, unions, and other associations are examples—the central authorities may only theoretically have the power to force people to go along; in reality, they rely mostly on voluntary compliance. For example, the U.S. government failed when it tried with force (Prohibition, 1920–1933) to stop the manufacture, transport, and sale of alcoholic beverages.

Another factor may be early family experiences. Some scholars recently have suggested that the type of family people are raised in predicts the degree of political participation in a society. A large extended family with multiple generations tends to be hierarchical, with the older generations having more authority. Children may learn that they have to obey and subordinate their wishes to their elders. Societies with polygyny also seem to have less political participation. The ways of interacting in the family may carry over to the political sphere.[71]

A high degree of political participation seems to have an important consequence. In the modern world, democratically governed states rarely go to war with each other.[72] So, for example, the United States invaded three countries—Grenada, Panama, and Iraq—between 1980 and 1993, but no democracies. Similarly, it appears that more participatory, that is, more "democratic," political units in the ethnographic record fight with each other significantly less often than do less participatory political units, just as seems to be the case among modern nation-states.[73] Does this mean that democracies are more peaceful in general? Here there is more controversy. Judging by the frequency of war, modern democratic states do not look very different from autocratic states in their tendency to go to war. However, if you look at the severity of war as measured by casualty rates, democratic societies do look less warlike.[74] Exactly why more participation or more democracy is likely to lead to peace remains to be established.

Resolution of Conflict

The resolution of conflict may be accomplished peacefully by avoidance, community action, mediation or the negotiation of compromises, apology, appeal to supernatural forces, or adjudication by a third party. As we shall see, the procedures used usually vary with degree of social complexity; decisions by third parties are more likely in hierarchical societies.[75] But peaceful solutions are not always possible, and disputes may erupt into violent conflict. When violence occurs within a political unit in which disputes are usually settled peacefully, we call such violence *crime*, particularly when committed by an individual. When the violence occurs among groups of people from separate political units—groups among which there is no procedure for settling disputes—we usually call such violence

15.4 Critically examine the methods used for resolving conflict, including warfare, in different societies.

warfare. When violence occurs among subunits of a population that had been politically unified, we call it *civil war*. Although we talk about conflict resolution as either peaceful or violent in the sections below, it is important to understand that even when violent resolution methods occur, peace-making efforts often follow, including reconciliation, intervention by third parties, or by avoidance.[76]

Peaceful Resolution of Conflict

Most modern industrialized states have formal institutions and offices, such as police, district attorneys, courts, and penal systems, to deal with minor disputes and more serious conflicts that may arise in society. All these institutions generally operate according to **codified laws**—that is, a set of explicit, usually written rules stipulating what is permissible and what is not. Transgression of the law by individuals gives the state the right to take action against them. The state has a monopoly on the legitimate use of force in the society, for it alone has the right to coerce subjects into agreement with regulations, customs, political edicts, and procedures.

Codified laws Formal principles for resolving disputes in heterogeneous and stratified societies.

Many societies lack such specialized offices and institutions for dealing with conflict. Yet, because all societies have peaceful, regularized ways of handling at least certain disputes, some anthropologists speak of the *universality of law*. E. Adamson Hoebel, for example, stated the principle as follows:

> *Each people has its system of social control. And all but a few of the poorest of them have as a part of the control system a complex of behavior patterns and institutional mechanisms that we may properly treat as law. For, "anthropologically considered, law is merely one aspect of our culture—the aspect that employs the force of organized society to regulate individual and group conduct and to prevent redress or punish deviations from prescribed social norms."*[77]

So how do you know what the laws are in societies without codified law? In Hoebel's view, the laws of a society become evident when you observe authorities threatening or using force when individuals or groups violate the rules. But others suggest that Hoebel's view of law is too narrow because nonviolent mechanisms such as shunning, gossip, and public opinion can be quite effective in the absence of force.[78]

Law, then, whether informal as in simpler societies, or formal as in more complex societies, provides a means of dealing peacefully with whatever conflicts develop. That does not mean that conflicts are always resolved peacefully. But that also does not mean that people cannot learn to resolve their conflicts peacefully. The fact that there are societies with little or no violent conflict means that it may be possible to learn from them; it may be possible to discover how to avoid violent outcomes of conflicts. How come South Africa could move relatively peacefully from a society dominated by people from Europe to one with government and civil rights shared by all groups? On the other hand, Bosnia had very violent conflict among ethnic groups and needed intervention by outside parties to keep the warring sides apart.[79]

Avoidance   Violence can often be avoided if the parties to a dispute voluntarily avoid each other or are separated until emotions cool down. Anthropologists have frequently remarked that foragers are particularly likely to make use of this technique. People may move to other bands or move their dwellings to opposite ends of camp. Shifting horticulturalists may also split up when conflicts get too intense. Avoidance is obviously easier in societies, such as band societies, that are nomadic or seminomadic and in which people have temporary dwellings. And avoidance is more feasible when people live independently and self-sufficiently (e.g., in cities and suburbs).[80] But even if conditions in such societies may make avoidance easier, we still need to know why some societies use avoidance more than confrontation as a way of resolving conflict.

Community Action   Societies have found various ways of resolving disputes peacefully. One such way involves action by a group or the community as a whole; collective action is common in simpler societies that lack powerful authoritarian leaders.[81] Many Inuit societies, for example, frequently resolve disputes through community action. An individual's failure to heed a taboo or to follow the suggestions of a shaman leads to expulsion from the group, because the community cannot accept a risk to its livelihood. People who fail to share goods voluntarily will find them confiscated and distributed to the community, and they may be executed in the process. A single case of murder, as an act of vengeance (usually because of the abduction of a wife or as part of a blood feud), does not concern the community, but repeated murders do. Franz Boas gave a typical example:

> There was a native of Padli by the name Padlu. He had induced the wife of a native of Cumberland Sound to desert her husband and follow him. The deserted husband, meditating revenge ... visited his friends in Padli, but before he could accomplish his intention of killing Padlu, the latter shot him. ... A brother of the murdered man went to Padli to avenge the death ... but he also was killed by Padlu. A third native of Cumberland Sound, who wished to avenge the death of his relatives, was also murdered by him.
>
> On account of these outrages, the natives wanted to get rid of Padlu, but yet they did not dare to attack him. When the pimain (headman) of the Akudmurmuit learned of these events he started southward and asked every man in Padli whether Padlu should be killed. All agreed; so he went with the latter deer hunting ... and ... shot Padlu in the back.[82]

Although mediation is commonly used in relatively egalitarian societies, it is also used in societies with courts and other formal adjudication procedures for minor conflicts. A teacher in the United States tries to mediate a dispute between two boys.

The killing of an individual is the most extreme action a community can take—we call it *capital punishment*. The community as a whole or a political official or a court may decide to administer such punishment, but capital punishment seems to exist in nearly all societies, from the simplest to the most complex.[83] It is often assumed that capital punishment deters crime. If it did, we would expect the abolition of capital punishment to be followed by an increase in homicide rates. But that does not seem to happen. A cross-national study indicates that the abolition of capital punishment tends to be followed by a decrease in homicide rates.[84]

Negotiation and Mediation In many conflicts, the parties to a dispute may come to a settlement themselves by **negotiation**. There aren't necessarily any rules for how they will do so, but any solution is "good" if it restores peace.[85] Sometimes an outside or third party is used to help bring about a settlement among the disputants. We call it **mediation** when the outside party tries to help bring about a settlement, but that third party does not have the formal authority to force a settlement. Both negotiation and mediation are likely when the society is relatively egalitarian and it is important for people to get along.[86]

Among the Nuer of East Africa, a pastoral and horticultural people, disputes within the community can be settled with the help of an informal mediator called the "leopard-skin chief." His position is hereditary and makes its holder responsible for the social well-being of the district. Matters such as cattle stealing rarely come to the attention of the leopard-skin chief. But if, for example, a murder has been committed, the culprit will go at once to the house of the leopard-skin chief. Immediately the chief cuts the culprit's arm so that blood flows; until the cut has been made, the murderer may not eat or drink. If the murderer is afraid of vengeance by the slain man's family, he will remain at the house of the leopard-skin chief, which is considered sanctuary. Then, within the next few months, the chief attempts to mediate among the parties to the crime. He tries to arrange compensation by the slayer's kin to avoid a feud, and he persuades the dead man's kin that they ought to accept the compensation, usually in the form of cattle. The chief then collects the cattle—40 to 50—and takes them to the dead man's home, where he performs various sacrifices of cleansing and atonement.[87] Throughout the process, the chief acts as a go-between. He has no authority to force either party to negotiate, and he has no power to enforce a solution once it has been arrived at. However, he is able to take advantage of the fact that both disputants are anxious to avoid a blood feud.

Negotiation The process by which the parties to a dispute try to resolve it themselves.

Mediation The process by which a third party tries to bring about a settlement in the absence of formal authority to force a settlement.

Ritual Reconciliation—Apology The desire to restore a harmonious relationship may also explain ceremonial apologies. An apology is based on deference—the guilty party shows obeisance and asks for forgiveness. Such ceremonies tend to occur in recent chiefdoms.[88] For example, among the Fijians of the South Pacific, when a person offends someone of higher status, the offended person and other villagers begin to avoid, and gossip about, the offender. If offenders are sensitive to village opinion, they will perform a ceremony of apology called *i soro*. One of the meanings of *soro* is "surrender." In the ceremony, the offender bows the head and remains silent while an intermediary speaks, presents a token gift, and asks the offended person for forgiveness. The apology is rarely rejected.[89]

> **Oath** The act of calling upon a deity to bear witness to the truth of what one says.

Oaths and Ordeals Still another way of peacefully resolving disputes is through oaths and ordeals, both of which involve appeals to supernatural power. An **oath** is the act of calling upon a deity to bear witness to the truth of what one says. An **ordeal** is a means used to determine guilt or innocence by submitting the accused to dangerous or painful tests believed to be under supernatural control.[90]

> **Ordeal** A means of determining guilt or innocence by submitting the accused to dangerous or painful tests believed to be under supernatural control.

A common kind of ordeal, found in almost every part of the world, is scalding. Among the Tanala of Madagascar, the accused person, having first had his hand carefully examined for protective covering, has to reach his hand into a cauldron of boiling water and grasp, from underneath, a rock suspended there. He then plunges his hand into cold water, has it bandaged, and is led off to spend the night under guard. In the morning, his hand is unbandaged and examined. If there are blisters, he is guilty.

How could an innocent person really hope to be vindicated in an ordeal? Lawrence Rosen points out that there may have been a high probability that the person subject to an ordeal was actually guilty since human, not supernatural, judgment would be involved in identifying the suspect in the first place. Especially in small communities, people would have previous knowledge of that person, so there may have been probable cause of guilt.[91]

Oaths and ordeals have also been practiced in Western societies. Both were common in medieval Europe.[92] Even today, in our own society, vestiges of oaths can be found. Children can be heard to say "Cross my heart and hope to die," and witnesses in courts of law are obliged to swear to tell the truth.

Why do some societies use oaths and ordeals? John Roberts suggested that their use tends to be found in fairly complex societies in which political officials lack sufficient power to make and enforce judicial decisions or would make themselves unnecessarily vulnerable were they to attempt to do so. So the officials may use oaths and ordeals to let the gods decide guilt or innocence.[93] In contrast, smaller and less complex societies probably have no need for elaborate mechanisms such as courts, oaths, and ordeals to ascertain guilt. In such societies, everyone is aware of what crimes have been committed and who the guilty parties probably are.

> **adjudication** The process by which a third party acting as judge makes a decision that the parties to a dispute have to accept.

Adjudication, Courts, and Codified Law We call it **adjudication** when a third party acting as judge makes a decision that the disputing parties have to accept. Judgment may be rendered by one person (a judge), a panel of judges, a jury, or a political agent or agency (a chief, a royal personage, a council). Judges and courts may rely on codified law and stipulated punishments, but codified law is not necessary for decisions to be made. Codified laws and courts are not limited to Western societies. From the late 17th century to the early 20th century, for example, the Ashanti of West Africa had a complex political system with elaborate legal arrangements. The Ashanti state was a military-based empire possessing legal codes that resembled those of many ancient civilizations.[94] Ashanti law was based on a concept of natural law, a belief that there is an order of the universe whose principles lawmakers should follow in the decisions they make and in the regulations they design. In Ashanti court procedure, elders examined and cross-examined witnesses as well as parties to the dispute. There were also quasi-professional advocates, and appeals against a verdict could be made directly to a chief. Particularly noteworthy was the emphasis on intent when assessing guilt. Drunkenness constituted a valid defense for all crimes except murder and cursing a chief, and a plea of insanity, if proved, was upheld for all offenses. Ashanti punishments could be severe. Physical mutilation, such as slicing off the nose or an ear—even castration in sexual offenses—was often employed. Fines were more frequent, however, and death sentences could often be commuted to banishment and confiscation of goods.

Perspectives on Gender

New Courts Allow Women to Address Grievances in Papua New Guinea

In most societies in New Guinea, women did not traditionally participate in the resolution of disputes. And they could not bring actions against men. But when village courts were introduced, women began to go to court to redress offenses against them.

In colonial times, the introduced Western-style courts followed Western law, primarily Australian and British common law, not native customary law. After Papua New Guinea became an independent country, those courts remained in place. The lowest of the courts, called local courts, were located in town centers, often far from villages, so villagers rarely brought cases to them. But, in 1973, a new kind of court was created. Called village courts, they were designed to settle local disputes in the villages, using a blend of customary law (relying on compromise) and Western law. In contrast to the local courts, magistrates in the village courts were not outsiders but were selected from the pool of traditional and local leaders who knew the local people.

When Richard Scaglion studied changes in village courts among the Abelam from 1977 to 1987, he noticed a shift toward the increased use of these courts by women. In 1977, most of the complainants were male, but most of them were female by 1987. In a wider study of court cases over many regions of Papua New Guinea, Scaglion and Rose Whittingham found that most of the cases in

Women in a village in the Karawari River area of East Sepik Province.

which women were the plaintiffs were attempts to redress sex-related offenses (sexual jealousy, rape, incest, domestic disputes) committed by males. Most disputes in New Guinea villages are settled informally by self-help or by appeal to a "big man"; the courts are appealed to only as a last resort. Serious sex-related cases are unlikely to be settled informally but, rather, in the village court. Apparently women do not believe that they can get satisfaction informally. So they go to the village court, where they win some sort of punishment for the defendant in about 60 percent of the cases, just about the same rate that men achieve when they bring a case seeking punishment. Even in village courts near big cities, women appear largely successful in breaking their grievances, usually against men.

Culture change introduced from the outside often works against native peoples. But Papuan New Guinea women have benefited from the new village court system, particularly in redressing grievances against males. The traditional system for resolving disputes was largely male-dominated (women could not be plaintiffs), and so the possibility of taking disputes to the new courts has given women some measure of legal equality with men.

Sources: Scaglion 1990; Scaglion and Whittingham 1985. Goddard 2004.

Why do some societies have codified systems and others do not? One explanation, advanced by E. Adamson Hoebel, A. R. Radcliffe-Brown, and others, is that there is little need for formal legal guidelines in small, closely knit communities because competing interests are minimal. Hence, simple societies need little codified law. There are relatively few matters to quarrel about, and the general will of the group is sufficiently well known and demonstrated frequently enough to deter transgressors.

This point of view is echoed in Richard Schwartz's study of two Israeli settlements. In one communal kibbutz, a young man aroused a good deal of community resentment because he had accepted an electric teakettle as a gift. The general opinion was that he had overstepped the code about not having personal possessions, and he was so informed. Accordingly, he gave the kettle to the communal infirmary. Schwartz observed that "no organized enforcement of the decision was threatened, but had he disregarded the expressed will of the community, his life … would have been made intolerable by the antagonism of public opinion."[95]

In this community, where people worked and ate together, not only did everyone know about transgressions, but a wrongdoer could not escape public censure. Thus, public opinion was an effective sanction. In another Israeli community, however, where individuals lived in widely separated houses and worked and ate separately, public opinion did not work as well. Not only were community members less aware of problems, but they had no quick way of making their feelings known. As a result, they established a judicial body to handle trouble cases.

Larger, more heterogeneous and stratified societies are likely to have more frequent disputes, which at the same time are less visible to the public. Individuals in stratified societies are generally not so dependent on community members for their well-being and hence are less likely to know of, or care about, others' opinions. In such societies, codified laws and formal authorities for resolving disputes develop—in order, perhaps, that disputes may be settled impersonally enough so that the parties can accept the decision and social order can be restored.

A good example of how more formal systems of law develop is the experience of towns in the American West during the gold rush period. These communities were literally swamped by total strangers. The townsfolk, having no control (authority) over these intruders because the strangers had no local ties, looked for ways to deal with the trouble cases that were continually flaring up. A first attempt at a solution was to hire gunslingers, who were also strangers, to act as peace officers or sheriffs, but this strategy usually failed. Eventually, towns succeeded in having federal authorities send in marshals backed by federal power.

Is there some evidence to support the theory that codified law is necessary only in larger, more complex societies? Data from a large, worldwide sample of societies suggest that codified law is associated with political integration beyond the local level. Murder cases, for example, are dealt with informally in societies that have only local political organization. In societies with multilocal political units, specialized political authorities tend to judge or adjudicate murder cases.[96] There is also some cross-cultural evidence that violence within a society tends to be less frequent when there are formal authorities (chiefs, courts) who have the power to punish murderers.[97] In general, adjudication or enforced decisions by outside authorities tend to occur in hierarchical societies with social classes and centralized power.[98]

Violent Resolution of Conflict

Controversy exists over whether violence has increased or decreased over the course of human history. Recently studied foragers have appeared to be fairly peaceful, fostering the view that warfare has increased over time. However, many of those foraging societies had considerable fighting in the past, suggesting that it is problematic to extrapolate to prehistory from recent societies.[99] What does prehistoric data tell us? Archaeologists were not always looking for signs of warfare and violence, but recent research suggests much more violence than previously believed. Some scholars have concluded, looking at both archaeological data and data from recent societies, that overall violence has declined markedly over the course of history.[100]

But regardless of the trends over time, the fact remains that there is enormous variation from society to society. In some societies, people often resort to violence when regular, effective alternative means of resolving a conflict are not available. If we can understand that variation, we may be better able to understand the changes over time.

Violence among individuals that is not considered legitimate is generally called **crime**. What is considered legitimate varies considerably from society to society. When socially organized violence occurs among territorial entities such as communities, districts, or nations, we call it **warfare**. The type of warfare varies in scope and complexity from society to society. Sometimes a distinction is made among feuding, raiding, and large-scale confrontations.[101]

Some scholars talk about a cultural pattern of violence. More often than not, societies with one type of violence have others. Societies with more war tend to have warlike sports, malevolent magic, severe punishment for crimes, high murder rates, feuding, and family violence.[102]

There are more peaceful societies. These societies are not conflict-free, but they try more to resolve conflict nonviolently. And like the Semai, they discourage aggression in their children without providing an aggressive model. What explains these more peaceful cultural

Crime Violence not considered legitimate that occurs within a political unit.

Warfare Socially organized violence between political entities such as communities, districts, or nations.

patterns? Cross-cultural evidence supports the view that frequent warfare is the key to understanding all kinds of violence. Not only is war correlated with other kinds of aggression, but societies that are forced to stop fighting by more powerful societies appear to encourage aggression in their children less. It seems that, if war is frequent, the society encourages boys to be aggressive, so that they will grow up to be effective warriors. But socializing for aggression can spill over into other areas of life; high rates of crime and other violence may be inadvertent or unintended consequences of the encouragement of aggressiveness.[103] And societies with a lot of war commonly bestow high status on their warriors. Warriors are generally proud of their accomplishments, considering it an honor to be a brave and fierce warrior.[104]

Individual Violence Although it may seem paradoxical at first, violent behavior itself is often used to try to control behavior. In some societies, it is considered necessary for parents to beat children who misbehave. They don't consider this criminal behavior or child abuse; they consider it punishment. Similar views may attach to interpersonal behavior among adults. If a person trespasses on your property or hurts someone in your family, some societies consider it appropriate or justified to kill or maim the trespasser. Is this social control, or is it just lack of control?

Systems of individual self-help are characteristic of egalitarian societies.[105] How is this different from "community action," which earlier we classified under peaceful resolution of conflict? Because community action is explicitly based on obtaining a consensus, it is likely to lead to the ending of a particular dispute. Individual action, or self-help, particularly if it involves violence, is not.

Feuding Feuding is an example of how individual self-help may not lead to a peaceful resolution of conflict. **Feuding** is a state of recurring hostilities between families or groups of kin, usually motivated by a desire to avenge an offense—whether insult, injury, deprivation, or death—against a member of the group. The most common characteristic of the feud is that all members of the kin group carry the responsibility to avenge. The killing of any member of the offender's group is considered appropriate revenge, because the kin group as a whole is regarded as responsible. Nicholas Gubser told of a feud within a Nunamiut Inuit community, caused by a husband killing his wife's lover, that lasted for decades. The Nunamiut take feuds seriously, as do many societies, especially when murder has been committed. Closely related members of the murdered man recruit as many relatives as they can and try to kill the murderer or one of his close kin. Then the members of the murderer's kindred are brought into the feud. The two kindreds may snipe at each other for years.[106]

Feuds are by no means limited to small-scale societies; they occur as frequently in societies with high levels of political organization.[107]

> **Feuding** A state of recurring hostility between families or groups of kin, usually motivated by a desire to avenge an offense against a member of the group.

Raiding **Raiding** is a short-term use of force, planned and organized, to realize a limited objective. This objective is usually the acquisition of goods, animals, or other forms of wealth belonging to another, often neighboring community.

Raiding is especially prevalent in pastoral societies, in which cattle, horses, camels, or other animals are prized and an individual's own herd can be augmented by theft. Raids are often organized by temporary leaders or coordinators whose authority may not last beyond the planning and execution of the venture. Raiding may also be organized for the purpose of capturing people. Sometimes people are taken to marry—the capture of women to be wives or concubines is fairly common[108]—or to be slaves. Slavery has been practiced in about 33 percent of the world's known societies, and war has been one way of obtaining slaves either to keep or to trade for other goods.[109] Raiding, like feuding, is often self-perpetuating: The victim of a raid today becomes the raider tomorrow.[110]

> **Raiding** A short-term use of force, generally planned and organized, to realize a limited objective.

Large-Scale Confrontations Individual episodes of feuds and raids usually involve relatively small numbers of people and almost always an element of surprise. Because they are generally attacked without warning, the victims are often unable to muster an immediate defense. Large-scale confrontations, in contrast, involve a large number of people and planning of strategies of attack and defense by both sides. Large-scale warfare is usually practiced among societies with intensive agriculture or industrialization. Only these societies possess a technology sufficiently advanced to support specialized armies, military leaders, strategists, and so on. But large-scale confrontations are not limited to state societies; they occur, for example, among the horticultural Dugum Dani of central New Guinea.

Large-scale confrontations occur in societies with armies, but they also occur in nonstate societies. The Masai of Kenya (shown here) battled with Kalenjin (not shown) over a land dispute following the 2008 disputed election.

The military history of the Dani, with its shifting alliances and confederations, is reminiscent of that of Europe, although Dani battles involve far fewer fighters and less sophisticated weaponry. Among the Dani, long periods of ritual warfare are characterized by formal battles announced through a challenge sent by one side to the opposing side. If the challenge is accepted, the protagonists meet at the agreed-upon battle site to set up their lines. Fighting with spears, sticks, and bows and arrows begins at midmorning and continues either until nightfall or until rain intervenes. There may also be a rest period during the midday heat during which the two sides shout insults at each other or talk and rest among themselves.

The front line of battle is composed of about a dozen active warriors and a few leaders. Behind them is a second line, still within arrow range, composed of those who have just left the forward line or are preparing to join it. The third line, outside arrow range, is composed of noncombatants—males too old or too young to participate and those recovering from wounds. This third line merely watches the battle taking place on the grassy plain. On the hillsides far back from the front line, some of the old men help to direct ancestral ghosts to the battle by gouging a line in the ground that points in the direction of the battlefield.[111]

Yet, as total as large-scale confrontations may be, even such warfare has cultural rules. Among the Dani, for instance, no fighting occurs at night, and weapons are limited to simple spears and bows and arrows. Similarly, in state societies, governments will sign "self-denying" pacts restricting the use of poison gas, germ warfare, and so forth. Unofficially, private arrangements are common. One has only to glance through the memoirs of national leaders of the two world wars to become aware of locally arranged truces, visits to one another's front positions, exchanges of prisoners of war, and so on.

Explaining Warfare

Most societies in the anthropological record have had warfare between communities or larger territorial groups. The vast majority of societies had at least occasional wars when they were first described, unless they had been pacified or incorporated by more dominant societies.[112] Yet, relatively little research has been done on the possible causes of war and why it varies in type and frequency. For instance, why have some people fought a great deal, and others only infrequently? Why in some societies does warfare occur internally, within the society or language group?

We have answers, based on cross-cultural studies, to some of those questions. There is evidence that people in preindustrial societies go to war mostly out of fear, particularly a fear of expectable but unpredictable natural disasters that will destroy food resources (e.g., droughts, floods, locust infestations). People may think they can protect themselves against such disasters ahead of time by taking things from defeated enemies. In any case, preindustrial societies with higher frequencies of war are very likely to have had a history of expectable but unpredictable disasters.[113] The fact that chronic (annually recurring and therefore predictable) food shortages do not predict higher frequencies of war suggests that people go to war in an attempt to cushion the impact of the disasters they expect to occur in the future but cannot predict. Consistent with this tentative conclusion is the fact that the victors in war almost always take land or other resources from the defeated. And this is true for simpler as well as more complex preindustrial societies.[114] Might similar motives affect decisions about war and peace in the modern world?

We know that complex or politically centralized societies are likely to have professional armies, hierarchies of military authority, and sophisticated weapons.[115] But surprisingly, the frequency of warfare seems to be not much greater in complex societies than in simple band or tribal societies.[116] We have some evidence that warfare is unlikely to occur internally (within a society or territory) if it is small in population (21,000 or fewer people); in a larger society, there is a high likelihood of warfare within the society, among communities or larger territorial divisions.[117] In fact, complex societies, even if they are politically unified, are not less likely than simpler societies to have internal warfare.[118]

What about the idea that men in band and tribal societies may mostly go to war over women?[119] If this were true, those band and tribal societies with the most frequent wars should have shortages of women, and those with little or no war—less often than once in 10 years—should have more equal numbers of women and men. But the cross-cultural evidence clearly contradicts this theory. Band and tribal societies with more wars do not have fewer women.[120]

What, if anything, do we know about recent warfare among nation-states? Although many people think that military alliances lessen the chance of war, it turns out that nations formally allied with other nations do not necessarily go to war less often than nations lacking formal alliances. Countries that are allies are, of course, less likely to go to war with each other; however, alliances can drag dependent allies into wars they don't want.[121] Countries that are economically interdependent, that trade with each other for necessities, are less likely to go to war with each other.[122] Finally, military equality among nations, particularly when preceded by a rapid military buildup, seems to increase rather than lessen the chance of war among those nations.[123]

Clearly, these findings contradict some traditional beliefs about how to prevent war. Military buildups do not make war less likely, but trade does. What else may? We have already noted that participatory ("democratic") political systems are less likely to go to war with each other than are authoritarian political systems. Although war may be common in the world, it is not inevitable. Societies change over time. The Vikings were extremely militaristic, but Norway today is now a peaceful society. A comparative study of Polynesian societies shows that, although all derive from a common cultural heritage, the size of the islands people settled on strongly influenced their patterns of interpersonal violence and warfare. The smallest islands had the lowest levels of violence and the least warfare. It appears that cooperation and harmony were more likely than violence in small "face-to-face" societies.[124]

Political and Social Change

In addition to commercialization and religious change brought about by the expansion of Western and other countries, political changes have often occurred when a foreign system of government has been imposed. But, as recent events in the former Soviet Union and South Africa indicate, dramatic changes in a political system can also occur more or less voluntarily. Perhaps the most striking type of political change in recent years is the spread of participatory forms of government—"democracy."

To political scientists, democracy is usually defined in terms of voting by a substantial proportion of the citizenry, governments brought to power by periodic contested elections, a chief executive either popularly elected or responsible to an elected legislature, and often also civil liberties such as free speech. Depending on which criteria are used, only 12 to 15 countries qualified as democracies as of the beginning of the 20th century. The number decreased after World War I, as emerging dictatorships in Russia, Italy, Germany, central Europe, Japan, and elsewhere replaced democratic institutions. After World War II, despite all the rhetoric associated with the founding of the United Nations, the picture was not much different. Some members of the new North Atlantic Treaty Organization (NATO) were not democracies, and neither were many members of the wider Western alliance system, in Latin America, the Middle East, and Asia.

Not until the 1970s and 1980s did people, not just political scientists, start noticing that democracy was becoming more common in the world. By the early 1990s, President George H. W. Bush and then-candidate Bill Clinton were talking about the spread of the "democratic peace." As of 1992, about half of the countries in the world had more or less democratic governments, and others were in transition to democracy.[125] Social scientists do not yet understand why this change is happening. But it is possible that the global communication of ideas has a lot to do with it. Authoritarian governments can censor their own newspapers and prevent group meetings, and sophisticated technology can block Internet use and cell phone connections, but ultimately authoritarian governments really cannot stop the movement of ideas. The movement of ideas, of course, does not explain the acceptance of those ideas. Why democracy has recently diffused to more countries than ever before still requires explanation, as does why some countries do not find it appealing.

Summary and Review

Variation in Types of Political Organization

15.1 Discuss the cross-cultural variation in the types of political organization.

- Over the last century, countries have either imposed political systems on others or have developed governmental structures to deal with the larger world. Before colonization, the band or village was the largest autonomous political unit in 50 percent of recorded societies.

- Societies range on a continuum from less to more centralized types of political organization: bands, tribes, chiefdoms, and states.

- Studies support collection action theory: When the state relies more heavily on resources from taxpayers, the rulers must give the public more in return or else face noncompliance and rebellion.

- *Nation* refers to the idea that a people share a common territory, history, and identity. Nations can be associated with states (nation-states), but not necessarily always.

- The more intensive the agriculture, the greater the likelihood of state organization. Larger communities predict a wider range of political officials and more levels of decision making. Societies with higher levels of political integration tend to exhibit social differentiation.

- Anthropologists do not clearly understand why changes in political organization occur, although competition among groups, need for defense, economic and technological variables, and trade may be strong factors.

 What are some factors that may explain change in political organization?

The Spread of State Societies

15.2 Explain the spread of state societies.

- State societies have larger communities and higher population densities than do band, tribal, and chiefdom societies. They also have armies ready to fight. State systems waging war against chiefdoms and tribes have almost always won and politically incorporated the losers.

- Depopulation, conquest, or intimidation has decreased the number of independent political units worldwide, particularly in the last 200 years. It is estimated that, in 1000 B.C., between 100,000 and 1 million separate political units existed in the world; today, fewer than 200.

 How might the spread of state societies be explained?

Variation in Political Process

15.3 Describe and explain the variation in political structure in various societies.

- In some tribal societies where becoming a leader has been studied, leadership appears to depend upon individual characteristics such as intelligence, generosity, and height. In some societies, leadership is more competitive and leaders are described as "big men" or "big women."

- Adult political participation varies considerably in preindustrial societies. Small-scale societies are likely to have high participation, whereas more complex societies less. But with industrialization, the trend reverses somewhat and political participation increases.

- More "democratic," political units in the ethnographic record fight have fought with each other significantly less often or with less severity than have less participatory political units, which also seems to be the case among modern nation-states.

 What are some examples of different political processes? What may explain the differences?

Resolution of Conflict

15.4 Critically examine the methods used for resolving conflict, including warfare, in different societies.

- Resolution of conflict may be accomplished peacefully by avoidance, community action, mediation, apology, appeal to supernatural forces, or adjudication by a third party. The procedures used usually vary according to the degree of social complexity.

- Crime is violence within a political unit that usually settles disputes peacefully. Warfare is socially organized violence among groups of people from different territorial units. Civil war is violence among subunits of a population that had been politically unified.

- Law, whether informal as in simpler societies or formal as in more complex societies, is a means of dealing peacefully with conflict. Data from a large, worldwide sample of societies suggest that codified law is associated with political integration beyond the local level.

- More often than not, societies with one type of violence have other types. Societies with more war tend to have warlike sports, malevolent magic, severe punishment for crimes, high murder rates, feuding, and family violence.

- Systems of individual self-help, characteristic of egalitarian societies, tend toward violence and away from consensus. Systems of community action are explicitly based on obtaining a consensus and likely lead to the ending of particular disputes.

- Societal complexity does not explain warfare frequency, but unpredictable disasters may play a role. Countries that are both democratic are less likely to fight each other. Military buildups do not make war less likely, but trade does.

- Political changes typically occur when a foreign system of government is imposed, but changes in a political system can also occur voluntarily. A striking type of political change in recent years is the spread of participatory forms of government—"democracy."

 What are some of the different types of mechanisms for resolving conflict peacefully and violently? Provide examples.

Think on it

1. When, if ever, do you think the world will be **politically unified**? Why do you think so?

2. Why don't informal methods of **social control** work well in societies like our own? Why don't formal methods work better than they currently do?

3. What does research on **war and violence** suggest about how to reduce their likelihood?

CHAPTER 16

Religion and Magic

LEARNING OBJECTIVES

16.1 Characterize the universality of religion and discuss various explanations for that universality.

16.2 Discuss the range of variability in religious beliefs.

16.3 Describe the variability in religious practices and practitioners cross-culturally.

16.4 Discuss religion in terms of adaptation.

16.5 Explain and give examples of various forms of religious change, such as conversion and revitalization movements.

As far as we know, all societies have possessed beliefs that can be grouped under the term *religion*. These beliefs vary from culture to culture and from time to time. Yet, despite their variety, we shall define **religion** as any set of attitudes, beliefs, and practices pertaining to *supernatural power*, whether that power be forces, gods, spirits, ghosts, or demons.

In our society, we divide phenomena into the natural and the supernatural, but not all languages or cultures make such a neat distinction. Moreover, what is considered **supernatural**—powers believed to be not human or not subject to the laws of nature—varies from society to society. Some of the variation is determined by what a society regards as natural. For example, some illnesses commonly found in our society are believed to result from the natural action of bacteria and viruses. In other societies, and even among some people in our own society, illness is thought to result from supernatural forces, and thus it forms a part of religious belief.

Beliefs about what is, or is not, a supernatural occurrence also vary within a society at a given time or over time. In Judeo-Christian traditions, for example, floods, earthquakes, volcanic eruptions, comets, and epidemics were once considered evidence of supernatural powers intervening in human affairs. It is now generally agreed that they are simply natural occurrences—even though many still believe that supernatural forces may be involved. Thus, the line between the natural and the supernatural varies in a society according to what people believe about the causes of things and events in the observable world. Similarly, what is considered sacred in one society may not be so considered in another.

In many cultures, what we would consider religious is embedded in other aspects of everyday life. That is, it is often difficult to separate the religious, economic, or political from other aspects of the culture. Such cultures have little or no specialization of any kind; there are no full-time priests, no purely religious activities. So the various aspects of culture we distinguish (e.g., in the chapter titles of this book) are not separate and easily recognized in many societies, as they are in complex societies such as our own. However, it is sometimes difficult even for us to agree whether or not a particular custom of ours is religious. After all, the categorizing of beliefs as religious, political, or social is a relatively new custom. The ancient Greeks, for instance, did not have a word for religion, but they did have many concepts concerning the behavior of their gods and their own expected duties to the gods.

When people's duties to their gods are linked with duty to their princes, it is difficult to separate religious from political ideas. As an example of our own difficulty in labeling a particular class of actions or beliefs as religious or social, consider our attitudes about wearing clothes. Is our belief that it is necessary to wear clothing, at least in the company of nonlovers, a religious principle, or is it something else? Recall that in Genesis, the wearing of clothes or fig leaves is distinctly associated with the loss of innocence: Adam and Eve, after eating the apple, covered their nakedness. Accordingly, when Christian missionaries first visited islands in the Pacific in the 19th century, they forced the native women to wear more clothes, particularly to cover their sexual parts. Were the missionaries' ideas about sex religious or social, or perhaps both?

Religion Any set of attitudes, beliefs, and practices pertaining to supernatural power, whether that power rests in forces, gods, spirits, ghosts, or demons.

Supernatural Powers believed to be not human or not subject to the laws of nature.

The Universality of Religion

Religious beliefs and practices are found in all known contemporary societies, and archaeologists think they have found signs of religious belief associated with *Homo sapiens* who lived at least 60,000 years ago. People then deliberately buried their dead, and many graves contain the remains of food, tools, and other objects that were probably thought to be needed in an afterlife. Some of the artistic productions of modern humans after about 30,000 years ago may have been used for religious purposes. For example, sculptures of females with ample secondary sex characteristics may have been fertility charms.

16.1 Characterize the universality of religion and discuss various explanations for that universality.

Animatism A belief in supernatural forces.

Animism A belief in a dual existence for all things—a physical, visible body, and a psychic, invisible soul.

Cave paintings in which the predominant images are animals of the hunt may reflect a belief that the image had some power over events. Perhaps early humans thought that their hunting would be more successful if they drew images depicting good fortune in hunting. The details of religions practiced in the distant past cannot be recovered. Yet evidence of ritual treatment of the dead suggests that early people believed in the existence of supernatural spirits and tried to communicate with, and perhaps influence, them.

We may reasonably assume the existence of prehistoric religion, and we have evidence of the universality of religion in historic times, so we can understand why the subject of religion has been the focus of much speculation, research, and theorizing. As long ago as the 5th century B.C., Herodotus made fairly objective comparisons among the religions of the 50 or so societies he traveled to from his home in Greece. He noted many similarities among their gods and pointed out evidence of diffusion of religious worship. Since Herodotus's time some 2,500 years ago, scholars, theologians, historians, and philosophers have speculated about religion. Some have claimed superiority for their own forms of religion, others have derided the naive simplicity of others' beliefs, and some have expressed skepticism concerning all beliefs.

Speculation about which religion is superior is not an anthropological concern. What is of interest to anthropologists is why religion is found in all societies and how and why it varies from society to society. Many social scientists—particularly anthropologists, sociologists, and psychologists—have offered theories to account for the universality of religion. Most think that religions are created by humans in response to certain universal needs or conditions. We consider five such needs or conditions here: (1) a need for intellectual understanding, (2) reversion to childhood feelings, (3) anxiety and uncertainty, (4) a need for community, and (5) a need for cooperation.

This stone carved pillar from Gobekli Tepe (southeastern Anatolia) in the garden of Sanliurfa Museum, Sanliurfa, Turkey, dates to over 11,000 years ago. Gobekli Tepe is believed to the oldest known place of worship. The mountaintop site had more than 200 stone pillars arranged in circles.

The Need to Understand

One of the earliest social scientists to propose a major theory of the origin of religion was Edward Tylor. In Tylor's view, religion originated in people's speculation about dreams, trances, and death. The dead, the distant, those in the next house, animals—all seem real in dreams and trances. Tylor thought that the lifelike appearances of these imagined people and animals suggest a dual existence for all things—a physical, visible body and a psychic, invisible soul. In sleep, the soul can leave the body and appear to other people; at death, the soul permanently leaves the body. Because the dead appear in dreams, people come to believe that the souls of the dead are still around.[1]

Tylor thought that the belief in souls was the earliest form of religion; **animism** is the term he used to refer to belief in souls.[2] But many scholars criticized Tylor's theory for being too intellectual and not dealing with the emotional component of religion. One of Tylor's students, R. R. Marett, felt that Tylor's animism was too sophisticated an idea to be the origin of religion. Marett suggested that **animatism**—a belief in impersonal supernatural forces (e.g., the power of a rabbit's foot)—preceded the creation of spirits.[3] A similar idea is that when people believe in gods, they are *anthropomorphizing*—attributing human characteristics and motivations to nonhuman, particularly supernatural, events.[4] Anthropomorphizing may be an attempt to understand what is otherwise incomprehensible and disturbing.

Reversion to Childhood Feelings

Sigmund Freud believed that early humans lived in groups, each of which was dominated by a tyrannical man who kept all the women for himself.[5] Freud postulated that, on maturing, the sons were driven out of the group. Later, they joined together to kill and eat the hated father. But then the sons felt enormous guilt and remorse, which they expressed (projected) by prohibiting the killing of a totem animal (the father substitute). Subsequently, on ritual occasions, the cannibalistic scene was repeated in the form of a totem meal. Freud believed that these early practices gradually became transformed into the worship of deities or gods modeled after the father.

Most social scientists today do not accept Freud's interpretation of the origin of religion. But there is widespread agreement with his idea that events in infancy can have long-lasting and powerful effects on beliefs and practices in adult life. Helpless and dependent on parents for many years, infants and children inevitably and unconsciously view their parents as all-knowing and all-powerful. When adults feel out of control or in need, they may unconsciously revert to their infantile and childhood feelings. They may then look to gods or magic to do what they cannot do for themselves, just as they looked to their parents to take care of their needs. As we shall see, there is evidence that feelings about the supernatural world parallel feelings in everyday life.

Anxiety and Uncertainty

Freud thought that humans would turn to religion during times of uncertainty, but he did not view religion positively, believing that humans would eventually outgrow the need for religion. Others viewed religion more positively. Bronislaw Malinowski noted that people in all societies are faced with anxiety and uncertainty. They may have skills and knowledge to take care of many of their needs, but knowledge is not sufficient to prevent illness, accidents, and natural disasters. The most frightening prospect is death itself. Consequently, there is an intense desire for immortality. As Malinowski saw it, religion is born from the universal need to find comfort in inevitable times of stress. Through religious belief, people affirm their convictions that death is neither real nor final, that people are endowed with a personality that persists even after death. In religious ceremony, humans can commemorate and communicate with those who have died and achieve some measure of comfort in these ways.[6]

Theorists such as William James, Carl Jung, Erich Fromm, and Abraham Maslow have viewed religion even more positively: Religion is not just a way of relieving anxiety; it is thought to be therapeutic. James suggested that religion provides a feeling of union with something larger than oneself,[7] and Jung suggested that it helps people resolve their inner conflicts and attain maturity.[8] Fromm proposed that religion gives people a framework of values,[9] and Maslow argued that it provides a transcendental understanding of the world.[10]

A considerable amount of research supports the idea that religion generally relieves stress, anxiety, and uncertainty.[11] Engaging in religious rituals appears to lower individuals' blood pressure; elevated blood pressure is often caused by stress. Regular church-goers have lower incidence of depression than non church-goers. Fisherman who go out on longer deep-sea trips are more likely to believe in magical avoidances. People faced with terrorism close to home are more likely to engage in prayer or psalm recitation.[12] If religion is good for health by reducing anxiety, why has the number of religious believers declined recently in so many countries? A comparison of countries suggests that the number of nonbelievers in a country is related to fewer stresses in the environment. So, greater economic development, less inequality, higher life expectancy, more peacefulness, and lower disease loads are all associated with a higher number of nonbelievers. These relationships support the idea that when uncertainty is lessened, the need for religion is lessened.[13]

The Need for Community

All those theories of religion agree on one thing: Whatever the beliefs or rituals, religion may satisfy psychological needs common to all people. But some social scientists believe that religion springs from society and serves social, rather than psychological, needs. Émile Durkheim, a French sociologist, pointed out that living in society makes humans feel pushed and pulled by powerful forces. These forces direct their behavior, pushing them to resist what is considered wrong, pulling them to do what is considered right. These are the forces of public opinion, custom, and law. Because they are largely invisible and unexplained, people would feel them as mysterious forces and therefore come to

Fishermen working on a boat deck in choppy seas. The more danger involved in fishing, the more taboos fisherman seem to have.

believe in gods and spirits. Durkheim suggested that religion arises out of the experience of living in social groups; religious belief and practice affirm a person's place in society, enhance feelings of community, and give people confidence. He proposed that society is really the object of worship in religion.

Consider how Durkheim explained totemism, so often discussed by early religious theorists. He thought that nothing inherent in a lizard, rat, or frog—animal totems for some Australian aboriginal groups—would be sufficient to make them *sacred*. The totem animal therefore must be a symbol. But a symbol of what? Durkheim noted that there are things that are always unknown about others, particularly their inner states. It is from these unknowns that the mystical aspects of religion arise. But the form religion takes has a lot to do with how societies are structured. Durkheim noted that in societies organized into clans, each clan has its own totem animal; the totem distinguishes one clan from another. So the totem is the focus of the clan's religious rituals and symbolizes both the clan and the clan's spirits. It is the clan that is affirmed in ritual.[14]

Guy Swanson accepted Durkheim's belief that certain aspects or conditions of society generate the responses we call religious, but he thought that Durkheim was too vague about exactly what in society would generate the belief in spirits or gods. So what might? Swanson suggested that the belief in spirits derives from the existence of *sovereign groups* in a society. These are the groups that have independent jurisdiction (decision-making powers) over some sphere of life—the family, the clan, the village, the state. Such groups are not mortal; they persist beyond the lifetimes of their individual members. According to Swanson, then, the spirits or gods that people invent personify or represent the powerful decision-making groups in their society. Just like sovereign groups in a society, the spirits or gods are immortal and have purposes and goals that supersede those of individuals.[15]

Need for Cooperation

While Durkheim stressed the solidarity that religion created in groups, more recently, evolutionary theorists have focused on a specific aspect of solidarity—human cooperation. Evolutionary theorists have to deal with a paradox—human groups are quite cooperative, but how did cooperation arise when helping others has a cost to an individual? If a village needs to be defended, it is advantageous for an individual to run away and let others risk their lives, but if everyone cooperates, the group is more likely to ward off the attackers. What keeps people together and prevents individuals from letting others bear all the costs? Religion, some theorists argue, particularly the kind where supreme beings are concerned with morality, provides a strong mechanism to promote cooperation.[16] First, participating in rituals and ceremonies promotes communal feelings. Second, supernatural beings can "police" better—they cannot only "see all," but they can invoke powerful punishments such as sickness or death.[17] Presumably then people will be more likely watch their behavior. But what if an individual just pretends to participate in religious behavior to gain benefits from others? Here is where another mechanism is suggested. If religions require considerable participation and sacrifices (such as fasting, curtailment of activities, specialized dress), religious participation will be hard to fake for an individual who wants to deceive.

Variation in Religious Beliefs

16.2 ▶ Discuss the range of variability in religious beliefs.

There is no general agreement among scholars as to why people need religion, or how spirits, gods, and other supernatural beings and forces come into existence. (Any or all of the needs we have discussed, psychological or social, may give rise to religious belief and practice.) Yet there is general recognition of the enormous variation in the details of religious beliefs and practices. Societies differ in the kinds of supernatural beings or forces they believe in and the character of those beings. They also differ in the structure or hierarchy of those beings, in what the beings actually do, and in what happens to people after death. Variation exists also in the ways in which the supernatural is believed to interact with humans.

Types of Supernatural Forces and Beings

Supernatural Forces Some supernatural forces have no personlike character. As we discussed earlier, Marett referred to such religious beliefs as animatism. For example, a supernatural, impersonal force called **mana**, after its Malayo-Polynesian name, is thought to inhabit some objects but not others, some people but not others. A farmer in Polynesia places stones around a field; the crops are bountiful; the stones have mana. During a subsequent year, the stones may lose their mana and the crops will be poor. People may also possess mana, as, for example, the chiefs in Polynesia were said to do. However, such power is not necessarily possessed permanently; chiefs who were unsuccessful in war or other activities were said to have lost their mana.

Mana A supernatural, impersonal force that inhabits certain objects or people and is believed to confer success and/or strength.

The word *mana* may be Malayo-Polynesian, but a similar concept is also found in our own society. We can compare mana to the power that golfers may attribute to some, but unhappily not all, of their clubs. A ballplayer might think a certain sweatshirt or pair of pants has supernatural power or force and that more runs or points will be scored when they are worn. A four-leaf clover has mana; a three-leaf clover does not.

Objects, people, or places can be considered **taboo**. Anthony Wallace distinguished mana from taboo by pointing out that things containing mana are to be touched, whereas taboo things are not to be touched, for their power can cause harm.[18] Thus, those who touch them may themselves become taboo. Taboos surround food not to be eaten, places not to be entered, animals not to be killed, people not to be touched sexually, people not to be touched at all, and so on. An Australian aborigine could not normally kill and eat the animal that was his totem; Hebrew tribesmen were forbidden to touch a woman during menstruation or for seven days afterward.

Taboo A prohibition that, if violated, is believed to bring supernatural punishment.

Supernatural Beings Supernatural beings fall within two broad categories: those of nonhuman origin, such as gods and spirits, and those of human origin, such as ghosts and ancestral spirits. Chief among the beings of nonhuman origin, **gods** are named personalities. They are often *anthropomorphic*—that is, conceived in the image of a person—although they are sometimes given the shapes of other animals or of celestial bodies, such as the sun or moon. Essentially, the gods are believed to have created

Gods Supernatural beings of nonhuman origin who are named personalities; often anthropomorphic.

themselves, but some of them then created, or gave birth to, other gods. Although some are seen as creator gods, not all peoples include the creation of the world as one of the acts of gods.

After their efforts at creation, many creator gods retire. Having set the world in motion, they are not interested in its day-to-day operation. Other creator gods remain interested in the ordinary affairs of human beings, especially the affairs of one small, chosen segment of humanity. Whether or not a society has a creator god, the job of running the creation is often left to lesser gods. The Maori of New Zealand, for example, recognize three important gods: a god of the sea, a god of the forest, and a god of agriculture. They call upon each in turn for help and try to get all three to share their knowledge of how the universe runs. The gods of the ancient Romans, on the other hand, specialized to a high degree. There were three gods of the plow, one god to help with the sowing, one for weeding, one for reaping, one for storing grain, one for manuring, and so on.[19]

Beneath the gods in prestige, and often closer to people, are multitudes of unnamed **spirits**. Some may be guardian spirits for people. Some, who become known for particularly efficacious work, may be promoted to the rank of named gods. Some spirits who are known to the people but are never invoked by them are of the hobgoblin type. Hobgoblins delight in mischief and can be blamed for any number of small mishaps; still other spirits take pleasure in deliberately working evil on behalf of people.

Many Native American groups believed in guardian spirits that had to be sought out, usually in childhood. For example, among the Sanpoil of northeastern Washington, boys and sometimes girls would be sent out on overnight vigils to acquire their guardians.

Spirits Unnamed supernatural beings of nonhuman origin who are beneath the gods in prestige and often closer to the people; may be helpful, mischievous, or evil.

On the Day of the Dead, Mexican families adorn their loved ones' tombs and provide offerings of some the deceased's favorite things. It is believed that the spirits of the dead will return for a visit.

Most commonly the spirits were animals, but they could also be uniquely shaped rocks, lakes, mountains, whirlwinds, or clouds. The vigil was not always successful. When it was, the guardian spirit appeared in a vision or dream, and always at first in human form. Conversation with the spirit would reveal its true identity.[20]

Ghosts are supernatural beings who were once human, and **ancestor spirits** are ghosts of dead relatives. The belief that ghosts or their actions can be perceived by the living is almost universal.[21] The near-universality of the belief in ghosts may not be difficult to explain. There are many cues in everyday experience that are associated with a loved one, and even after the death, those cues might arouse the feeling that the dead person is still somehow present. The opening of a door or the smell of tobacco or perfume in a room may evoke the idea that the person is still present, if only for a moment. Then, too, loved ones live on in dreams. Small wonder, then, that most societies believe in ghosts. If the idea of ghosts is generated by these familiar associations, we might expect that ghosts in most societies would be close relatives and friends, not strangers—and they are.[22]

Although the belief in ghosts is nearly universal, the spirits of the dead do not play a very active role in the life of the living in all societies. In his cross-cultural study of 50 societies, Swanson found that people are likely to believe in active ancestral spirits where descent groups are important decision-making units. The descent group is an entity that exists over time, back into the past as well as forward into the future, despite the deaths of individual members.[23] The dead feel concern for the fortunes, the prestige, and the continuity of their descent group as strongly as the living. As a Lugbara elder (in northern Uganda in Africa) put it, "Are our ancestors not people of our lineage? They are our fathers and we are their children whom they have begotten. Those that have died stay near us in our homes and we feed and respect them. Does not a man help his father when he is old?"[24]

> **Ghosts** Supernatural beings who were once human; the souls of dead people.

> **Ancestor spirits** Supernatural beings who are the ghosts of dead relatives.

The Character of Supernatural Beings

Whatever type they may be, the gods or spirits venerated in a given culture tend to have certain personality or character traits. They may be unpredictable or predictable, aloof from or interested in human affairs, helpful or punishing. Why do the gods and spirits in a particular culture exhibit certain character traits rather than others?

We have some evidence from cross-cultural studies that the character of supernatural beings may be related to the nature of child training. Melford Spiro and Roy D'Andrade suggested that the god–human relationship is a projection of the parent–child relationship, in which case child-training practices might well be relived in dealings with the supernatural.[25] For example, if a child was nurtured immediately by her parents when she cried or waved her arms about or kicked, she might grow up expecting to be nurtured by the gods when she attracted their attention by performing a ritual. On the other hand, if her parents often punished her, she would grow up expecting the gods to punish her if she disobeyed them. William Lambert, Leigh Minturn Triandis, and Margery Wolf, in another cross-cultural study, found that societies with hurtful or punitive child-training practices are likely to believe that their gods are aggressive and malevolent; societies with less punitive child training are more likely to believe that the gods are benevolent.[26] These results are consistent with the Freudian notion that the supernatural world should parallel the natural. It is worth noting in this context that some peoples refer to the god as their father and to themselves as his children.

Structure or Hierarchy of Supernatural Beings

The range of social structures in human societies from egalitarian to highly stratified has its counterpart in the supernatural world. Some societies have gods or spirits that are not ranked; one god has about as much power as another. Other societies have gods or spirits that are ranked in prestige and power. For example, on the Pacific islands of Palau, which was a rank society, gods were ranked as people were. Each clan worshiped a god and a goddess that had names or titles similar to clan titles. Although a clan god was generally important only to the members of that clan, the gods of the various clans in a village were believed to be ranked in the same order that the clans were. Thus, the god of the highest-ranking clan was respected by all the clans of the village. Its shrine was given the place of honor in the center of the village and was larger and more elaborately decorated than other shrines.[27]

Although the Palauans did not believe in a high god or supreme being who outranked all the other gods, some societies do. Consider Judaism, Christianity, and Islam, which we call **monotheistic** religions. Although *monotheism* means "one god," most monotheistic religions actually include more than one supernatural being (e.g., demons, angels, the Devil). But the supreme being or high god, as the creator of the universe or the director of events (or both), is believed to be ultimately responsible for all events.[28] A **polytheistic** religion recognizes many important gods, no one of which is supreme.

Why do some societies have a belief in a high god and others do not? Recall Swanson's suggestion that people invent gods who personify the important decision-making groups in their society. He therefore hypothesized that societies with hierarchical political systems should be more likely to believe in a high god. In his cross-cultural study of 50 societies (none of which practiced any of the major world religions), he found that belief in a high god is strongly associated with three or more levels of "sovereign" (decision-making) groups. Of the 20 sample societies that had a hierarchy of three or more sovereign groups—for instance, family, clan, and chiefdom—17 possessed the idea of a high god. Of the 19 societies that had fewer than three levels of decision-making groups, only two had a high god.[29] Consistent with Swanson's findings, societies dependent on food production, particularly plow agriculture, are more likely to have a belief in a high god than are food-collecting societies.[30] These results strongly suggest, then, that the realm of the gods parallels and may reflect the everyday social and political worlds. In the past, many state societies had state religions in which the political officials were also the officials of the temples (e.g., the pharaohs in Egypt). In recent times, most state societies have separated church and state, as in the United States and Canada.

Intervention of the Gods in Human Affairs

According to Clifford Geertz, when people face ignorance, pain, and the unjustness of life, they explain the events by the intervention of the gods.[31] Thus, in Greek religion, the direct intervention of Poseidon as ruler of the seas prevented Odysseus from getting home for 10 years. In the Old Testament, the direct intervention of Yahweh caused the great flood that killed most of the people in the time of Noah. In other societies, people may search their memories for a violated taboo that has brought punishment through supernatural intervention.

In addition to unasked-for divine interference, there are numerous examples of requests for divine intervention, either for good for oneself and friends or for evil for others. Gods are asked to intervene in the weather and to make the crops grow, to send fish to the fisherman and game to the hunter, to find lost things, and to accompany travelers and prevent accidents. They are asked to stop the flow of lava down the side of a volcano, to stop a war, or to cure an illness.

The gods do not intervene in all societies. In some, they intervene in human affairs; in others, they are not the slightest bit interested; and in still others, they interfere only occasionally. We have little research on why gods are believed to interfere in some societies and not in others. We do, however, have some evidence suggesting when the gods will take an interest in the morality or immorality of human behavior. Swanson's study suggests that the gods are likely to punish people for immoral behavior when there are considerable differences in wealth in the society.[32] His interpretation is that supernatural support of moral behavior is particularly useful where inequalities tax the ability of the political system to maintain social order and minimize social disorder. Envy of others' privileges may motivate some people to behave immorally; the belief that the gods will punish such behavior might deter it. More generally, the concern of gods with moral behavior is more likely in large, complex societies (see the box "Religion: A Force for Cooperation and Harmony?").

Monotheistic Believing that there is only one high god and that all other supernatural beings are subordinate to, or are alternative manifestations of, this supreme being.

Polytheistic Recognizing many gods, none of whom is believed to be superordinate.

Applied Anthropology

Religion: A Force for Cooperation and Harmony?

Most social science theories about religion suggest that religious beliefs and rituals promote social cohesion and cooperation within the group that shares them. Some religions, including the major religions in the modern world (Buddhism, Christianity, Islam, Hinduism, Judaism), are more explicit than others in their direct concern with moral behavior. Moralizing religions believe that the gods will reward moral behavior and punish immoral behavior, and are generally found in large and complex societies. Such societies are likely to have towns or cities and neighbors may not know each other well, and although there may be codified law and courts, these mechanisms may not be sufficient to promote social order. Complex societies are likely to have considerable social inequality, increasing the likelihood of property-related crime. The cross-cultural evidence is consistent with the theory that morality-based religions and collective rituals minimize antisocial behavior in groups of unrelated individuals. And within countries, individuals who believe in God or the concepts of heaven or hell are more likely to say that transgressions, such as cheating on taxes or having an affair, are never justified.

Perhaps to promote solidarity, religions in complex societies often extend kin terms to members of the religious communities, calling each other "brothers" and "sisters" or sometimes "God's children." Experimental evidence suggests individuals are more generous toward strangers if their religious feelings have been aroused. Religious communes are also four times as likely to survive compared with secular communes.

These studies raise important questions about exactly why and when moralizing religions came into existence and whether the spread of these religions had to do with their adaptive consequences. But there are also questions raised about mechanisms. For example, religious communes, as compared with secular communes, usually impose more requirements from

The Shaker community in New Lebanon, New York was an example of a strong religious commune. In this 1870s drawing, Shaker members dance and worship.

members, such as food taboos, fasts, constraints on sex and possessions, and so on. A comparative study of communes suggests that the religious elements are more important than the commitments themselves. However, in experimental research, there are some hints that nonreligious conditions could also make people more cooperative. Experimental reminders of secular morality had as much effect as reminders of God. Also, there are examples of modern societies, especially in northern Europe, that are very cooperative but not very religious.

But, even if religious belief and ritual promote greater in-group trust and cooperation, there is a dark side to strongly held religious belief—the potential for greater out-group conflict. History is replete with examples of people hurting others in the name of religion. Christianity and Islam are the two largest religions, possibly because of their zeal to convert others. Some of the biggest conflicts have occurred where the two largest religions meet. The Christian Crusades of the 11th century through 13th century were attempts to "liberate" sites in the Holy Land controlled by Muslims. Osama bin Laden cited the establishment of U.S. bases in Saudi Arabia, which "defiled"

sacred lands in his view, as justification for the September 11, 2001, attacks on the United States. Religions, or, more precisely, religious groups, do not necessarily promote violence. After all, some of the founders of various religions preached nonviolence and harmony. Exactly what persuades a religious group to commit violence is not well understood. There are five warning signs. One is when leaders act as if only they know the truth. A second is a call to blind obedience to a religious leader. A third is when the people believe it is possible to establish an "ideal world." A fourth is acting as if "the end justifies the means." Lastly, and perhaps the clearest, is a call for a "holy war."

In the globalized world today, there is more admixture of all types. Whether the major religions will adapt peacefully to create a new morality for the new global circumstances remains to be seen. We can hope that simply learning more about other individuals and groups—their hopes, dreams, and expectations, how they have adapted to their environments—may enhance tolerance.

Sources: Winkelman and Baker 2010, 259–265, 314–318; Norenzayan and Shariff 2008; Sosis and Bressler 2003; Stark 2001; Roes and Raymond 2003; Atkinson and Bourrat 2011.

Life After Death

In many societies, ideas about an afterlife are vague and seemingly unimportant, but many other peoples have very definite and elaborate ideas of what happens after death. The Lugbara of Uganda see the dead as joining the ancestors of the living and staying near the family homesite. They retain an interest in the behavior of the living, both rewarding and punishing them. The Zuni of the southwestern United States think the dead join the past dead, known as the *katcinas,* in a katcina village at the bottom of a nearby lake. There they lead a life of singing and dancing and bring rain to the living Zuni. Just as they are swift to punish the priest who fails in his duty, they also punish the people in masks who ineffectively impersonate the katcinas during the dance ceremonies.[33]

The Chamulas have merged the ancient Mayan worship of the sun and moon with the Spanish conquerors' Jesus and Mary. Their vision of life after death contains a blending of the two cultures. All souls go to the underworld, where they live a humanlike life except that they are incapable of sexual intercourse. After the sun travels over the world, it travels under the underworld, so that the dead have sunlight. Only murderers and suicides are punished, being burned by the Christ-sun on their journey.[34]

Many Christians believe that the dead are divided into two groups: The unsaved are sent to everlasting punishment and the saved to everlasting reward. Accounts differ, but hell is often associated with torture by fire, heaven with mansions. Several societies see the dead as returning to earth to be reborn. The Hindus use this pattern of reincarnation to justify one's caste in this life and to promise eventual release from the pain of life through the attainment of *nirvana,* or inclusion into the One.

A recent cross-cultural study asks why some societies judge where you will go after death and others do not. Support was found for the idea that judgmental beliefs parallel the society's economic practices. Some societies have considerable delay between labor inputs and return of food. For example, intensive agriculturalists need considerable labor input to plow, fertilize, or create irrigation systems, and many months go by until crops can be harvested. Not planning ahead has dire long-term consequences. In contrast, mistakes by hunter-gatherers are realized more quickly and can be corrected more quickly. Religions that foster the idea that actions in the present will be judged after death reinforce the need for long-term planning. Consistent with this idea, societies with intensive agriculture are the most likely to believe that their actions in life affect where their souls will go after death.[35] This finding is consistent with Swanson's conclusion discussed previously that the gods are generally likely to punish people for immoral behavior when there are considerable differences in wealth in the society. Intensive agricultural societies tend to have considerable differences in wealth.

In many respects, the afterworld in many religions may resemble the everyday world, but we still have only a few comparative studies that show exactly how.

Variation in Religious Practices

Beliefs are not the only elements of religion that vary from society to society. Societies vary in the kinds of religious practitioners they have. There is also variation in how people interact with the supernatural. The manner of approach to the supernatural varies from supplication— requests, prayers, and so on—to manipulation. Many of these interactions are highly *ritualized.* **Rituals** are repetitive sets of behaviors that occur in essentially the same patterns every time they occur. In a certain sense, a good deal of culture is ritualized—from the way we greet people to the way we eat a meal.[36] But usually when we refer to ritual, particularly religious rituals, we mean much more than that. They tend to be elaborated, formal, indicative of something special, and, in the case of religious rituals, involve the supernatural in some way—as audience, as a recipient of a request, as a force to be manipulated, and so on.[37] Religious rituals are generally collective and are thought to strengthen faith.[38]

Rituals Repetitive sets of behaviors that occur in essentially the same patterns every time they occur. Religious rituals involve the supernatural in some way.

Ways to Interact with the Supernatural

How to get in touch with the supernatural has proved to be a universal problem. Wallace identified a number of ways people the world over use—though not necessarily all together—including, but not limited to, prayer (asking for supernatural help), physiological experience (doing things to the body and mind), simulation (manipulating imitations of things), feasts, and sacrifices.[39] Prayer can be spontaneous or memorized, private or public, silent or spoken. The Lugbara do not say the words of a prayer aloud, for doing so would be too powerful; they simply think about the things that are bothering them. The gods know all languages.

Doing things to the body or mind may involve drugs (hallucinogenics such as peyote or opiates) or alcohol; social isolation or sensory deprivation; dancing or running until exhausted; being deprived of food, water, and sleep; and listening to repetitive sounds such as drumming. Such behaviors may induce trances or altered states of consciousness.[40] Erika Bourguignon found that achieving these altered states, which she generally referred to as *trances*, is part of religious practice in 90 percent of the world's societies.[41] In some societies, trances are thought to involve the presence of a spirit or power inside a person that changes or displaces that person's personality or soul. These types are referred to as possession trances. Other types of trances may involve the journey of a person's soul, experiencing visions, or transmitting messages from spirits. Possession trances are especially likely in societies that depend on agriculture and have social stratification, slavery, and more complex political hierarchies. Nonpossession trances are most likely to occur in food-collecting societies. Societies with moderate levels of social complexity have both possession and nonpossession trances.[42]

One puzzle is why there is a preponderance of women thought to be possessed. Alice Kehoe and Dody Giletti suggested that women are more likely than men to suffer from nutritional deficiencies because of pregnancy, lactation, and men's priority in gaining access to food. Calcium deficiency in particular can cause muscular spasms, convulsive seizures, and disorientation, all of which may foster the belief that an individual is possessed.[43] Douglas Raybeck and his colleagues suggest that women's physiology makes them more susceptible to calcium deficiency even with an equivalent diet. In addition, women are subject to more stress because they are usually less able to control their lives. Higher levels of stress, they suggest, lower the body's reserves of calcium.[44] Erika Bourguignon suggests a more psychological explanation of women's preponderance in possession trances. In many societies, women are brought up to be submissive. But when possessed, women are taken over by spirits and are not responsible for what they do or say—therefore, they can unconsciously do what they are not able to do consciously.[45] Although intriguing, these suggestions need to be tested on individuals in field situations.

Voodoo employs simulation, or the imitation of things. Dolls are made in the likeness of an enemy and then are maltreated in hopes that the original enemy will experience pain and even death.

Divination seeks practical answers from the supernatural about anything that is troublesome—decisions to be made, interpersonal problems, or illness. Diviners are believed to have the ability to read the intent of the spirits. Diviners use a variety of methods, including altered states of consciousness and simulation through the use of objects such as Ouija boards or tarot cards.[46]

Divination Getting the supernatural to provide guidance.

Omar Moore suggested that among the Naskapi hunters of Labrador, divination is an adaptive strategy for successful hunting. The Naskapi consult the diviner every three or four days when they have no luck in hunting. The diviner holds a caribou bone over the fire, as if the bone were a map, and the burns and cracks that appear in it indicate where the group should hunt. Moore, unlike the Naskapi, did not believe that the diviner really can find out where the animals will be; the cracks in the bones merely provide a way of randomly choosing where to hunt. Because humans are likely to develop customary patterns of action, they might be likely to look for game according to some plan. But game might learn to avoid hunters who operate according to a plan. Thus, any method of ensuring against patterning or predictable plans—any random strategy—may be advantageous. Divination by "reading" the bones would seem to be a random strategy. It also relieves any individual of the responsibility of deciding where to hunt, a decision that might arouse anger if the hunt failed.[47]

The eating of a sacred meal is found in many religions. For instance, Holy Communion is a simulation of the Last Supper. Australian aborigines, normally forbidden to eat their totem animal, have one totem feast a year at which they eat the totem. Feasts are often part of marriage and funeral ceremonies, as well as a fringe benefit of the sacrifice of food to the gods.

Some societies make sacrifices to a god in order to influence the god's action, either to divert anger or to attract goodwill. Characteristic of all sacrifices is that something of value is given up to the gods, whether it be food, drink, sex, household goods, or the life of an animal or person. Some societies feel that the god is obligated to act on their behalf if they make the appropriate sacrifice. Others use the sacrifice in an attempt to persuade the god, realizing there is no guarantee that the attempt will be successful.

Of all types of sacrifice, we probably think that the taking of human life is the ultimate. Nevertheless, human sacrifice is not rare in the ethnographic and historical records. Why have some societies practiced it? One cross-cultural study found that, among preindustrial societies, those with full-time craft specialists, slavery, and the corvée are most likely to practice human sacrifice. The suggested explanation is that the sacrifice mirrors what is socially important: Societies that depend mainly on human labor for energy (rather than animals or machines) may think of a human life as an appropriate offering to the gods when people want something very important.[48] Later studies found that societies with human sacrifice were at a mid-range level of political complexity, having alliances and confederacies with other polities but only weak political integration. Such societies also seemed to be subject to population pressure and frequently carried out warfare for land and other resources. Human sacrifice, with humans from the outside groups, may have been an attempt to terrorize people from the other polities.[49]

Magic

All these modes of interacting with the supernatural can be categorized in various ways. One dimension of variation is how much people in society rely on pleading, asking, or trying to persuade the supernatural to act on their behalf, as opposed to whether they believe they can compel the supernatural to help by performing certain acts. For example, prayer is asking; performing voodoo is presumably compelling. When people believe their action can compel the supernatural to act in some particular and intended way, anthropologists often refer to the belief and related practice as **magic**.

Magic may involve manipulation of the supernatural for good or for evil. Many societies have magical rituals designed to ensure good crops, the replenishment of game, the fertility of domestic animals, and the avoidance and cure of illness in humans. We tend to associate the belief in magic with societies simpler than our own, but some people in complex societies take magic seriously, and many follow some magical practices.

People who engage in risky activities may try to ensure their safety by carrying or wearing lucky charms. They believe the charms protect them by invoking the help of supernatural beings or forces. We might also believe we can protect ourselves by not doing some things. For example, baseball players on a hitting streak may choose not to change their socks or sweatshirt for the next game (to continue their luck). Why magic appeals to some individuals but not others in our own society may help us explain why magic is an important part of religious behavior in many societies.

As we will see, the witch doctor and the shaman often employ magic to effect a cure. But the use of magic to bring about harm has evoked perhaps the most interest.

Sorcery and Witchcraft   Sorcery and witchcraft are attempts to invoke the spirits to work harm against people. Although the words *sorcery* and *witchcraft* are often used interchangeably, they are also often distinguished. **Sorcery** may include the use of materials, objects, and medicines to invoke supernatural malevolence. **Witchcraft** may be said to accomplish the same ills by means of thought and emotion alone. Evidence of witchcraft can never be found. This lack of visible evidence makes an accusation of witchcraft both harder to prove and harder to disprove.

To the Azande of Zaire, in central Africa, witchcraft was part of everyday living. It was not used to explain events for which the cause was known, such as carelessness or violation of a taboo, but to explain the otherwise unexplainable. A man is gored by an elephant. He must have been bewitched because he had not been gored on other elephant hunts. A man goes to his beer hut at night, lights some straw, and holds it aloft to look at his beer. The thatch catches fire and the hut burns down. The man has been bewitched, for huts did not catch fire on hundreds of other nights when he and others did the same thing. Some of the pots of a skilled potter break; some of the bowls of a skilled carver crack—witchcraft. Other pots and bowls treated exactly the same have not broken.[50]

Magic The performance of certain rituals that are believed to compel the supernatural powers to act in particular ways.

Sorcery The use of certain materials to invoke supernatural powers to harm people.

Witchcraft The practice of attempting to harm people by supernatural means, but through emotions and thought alone, not through the use of tangible objects.

The witch craze in Europe during the 16th and 17th centuries and the witch trials in 1692 in Salem, Massachusetts, remind us that the fear of others, which the belief in witchcraft presumably represents, can increase and decrease in a society within a relatively short period of time. Many scholars have tried to explain these witch hunts. One factor often suggested is political turmoil, which may give rise to widespread distrust and a search for scapegoats. In the case of Europe during the 16th and 17th centuries, small regional political units were being incorporated into national states, and political allegiances were in flux. In addition, as Swanson noted, the commercial revolution and related changes were producing a new social class, the middle class, and "were promoting the growth of Protestantism and other heresies from Roman Catholicism."[51] In the case of Salem, the government of Massachusetts colony was unstable, and there was much internal dissension. In 1692, the year of the witchcraft hysteria, Massachusetts was left without an English governor, and judicial practices broke down. These extraordinary conditions saw the accusation of a single person for witchcraft become the accusation of hundreds and the execution of 20 people. Swanson suggested that the undermining of legitimate political procedures may have generated the widespread fear of witches.[52]

It is also possible that epidemics of witchcraft accusation, like that in Salem as well as other New England and European communities, may be the result of real epidemics—epidemics of disease. The disease implicated in Salem and elsewhere is the fungus disease called ergot, which can grow on rye plants. (The rye flour that went into the bread that the Salem people ate may have been contaminated by ergot.) It is now known that people who eat grain products contaminated by ergot suffer from convulsions, hallucinations, and other symptoms, such as crawling sensations in the skin. We also now know that ergot contains LSD, the drug that produces hallucinations and other delusions that resemble those occurring in severe mental disorders.

The presumed victims of bewitchment in Salem and other places had symptoms similar to those of victims of ergot poisoning today. They suffered from convulsions and the sensations of being pricked, pinched, or bitten. They had visions and felt as if they were flying through the air. We cannot know for sure that ergot poisoning occurred during those times when witchcraft accusations flourished. There is no direct evidence, of course, because the "bewitched" were not medically tested. But we do have some evidence that seems to be consistent with the ergot theory. Ergot is known to flourish on rye plants under certain climatic conditions—particularly a very cold winter followed by a cool, moist spring and summer. Tree-ring growth indicates that the early 1690s were particularly cold in eastern New England, and the outbreaks of witchcraft accusation in Europe seem to have peaked with colder winter temperatures.[53] Interestingly, too, when witchcraft hysteria was greatest in Europe, Europeans were using an ointment containing a skin-penetrating substance that we now know produces hallucinations and a vivid sensation of flying.[54] It may not be cause for wonder, then, that our popular image of witches is of people flying through the air on broomsticks.

But whether or not epidemics of witchcraft hysteria are due to epidemics of ergot poisoning or episodes of political turmoil or both, we still have to understand why so many societies in the ethnographic record believe in witchcraft and sorcery in the first place. Why do so many societies believe that there are ways to invoke the spirits to work harm against people? One possible explanation, suggested by Beatrice Whiting, is that sorcery or witchcraft will be found in societies that lack procedures or judicial authorities to deal with crime and other offenses. Her theory is that all societies need some form of social control—some way of deterring most would-be offenders and of dealing with actual offenders. In the absence of judicial officials who, if present, might deter and deal with antisocial behavior, sorcery may be a very effective mechanism for social control. If you misbehave, the person you mistreated might cause you to become ill or even die. The cross-cultural evidence seems to support this theory. Sorcery is more important in societies that lack judicial authorities than in those that have them.[55]

Types of Practitioners

Individuals may believe that they can directly contact the supernatural, but almost all societies also have part-time or full-time religious or magical practitioners. Research suggests there are four major types of practitioners: shamans, sorcerers or witches, mediums, and priests. As we shall see, the number of types of practitioners in a society seems to vary with degree of cultural complexity.[56]

The Shaman

The word *shaman* may come from a language that was spoken in eastern Siberia. The **shaman** is usually a part-time male specialist who has fairly high status in his community and is often involved in healing.[57] More generally, the shaman deals with the spirits to try to get their help or to keep them from causing harm.[58] Here we focus on the methods shamans use to help others.

The shaman enters into a trance, or some other altered state of consciousness, and then journeys to other worlds to get help from guardians or other spirits. Dreams may be used to provide insight or as a way for shamans to commune with spirits. People may seek help for practical matters, such as where to get food resources or whether to relocate, but solving a health problem is most often the goal of the shaman.[59] Shamans may also bring news from spirits, such as a warning about an impending disaster.[60]

Someone may receive a "call" to the role of shaman in recovering from an illness, through a vision quest, or in a dream. Shamans-in-training may enhance the vividness of their imagery by using hallucinogens, sleep or food deprivation, or engaging in extensive physical activity such as dancing. An important part of the process of being a shaman is learning to control the imagery and the spirit powers. Shamanistic training can take several years under the guidance of a master shaman.[61]

Sorcerers and Witches

In contrast with shamans, who have fairly high status, sorcerers and witches of both sexes tend to have very low social and economic status in their societies.[62] Suspected sorcerers and witches are usually feared because they are thought to know how to invoke the supernatural to cause illness, injury, and death. Because sorcerers use materials for their magic, evidence of sorcery can be found, and suspected sorcerers are often killed for their malevolent activities. Because witchcraft supposedly is accomplished by thought and emotion alone, it may be harder to prove that someone is a witch, but the difficulty of proving witchcraft has not prevented people from accusing and killing others for being witches.

Shaman A religious intermediary, usually part-time, whose primary function is to cure people through sacred songs, pantomime, and other means; sometimes called witch doctor by Westerners.

Shamans are usually male. Here, female shamans in Korea perform a healing ritual.

Mediums **Mediums** tend to be females. These part-time practitioners are asked to heal and divine while in possession trances—that is, when they are thought to be possessed by spirits. Mediums are described as having tremors, convulsions, seizures, and temporary amnesia.[63]

Priests **Priests** are generally full-time male specialists who officiate at public events. They have very high status and are thought to be able to relate to superior or high gods who are beyond the ordinary person's control. In most societies with priests, the people who get to be priests obtain their offices through inheritance or political appointment.[64] Priests are sometimes distinguished from other people by special clothing or a different hairstyle. The training of a priest can be vigorous and long, including fasting, praying, and physical labor, as well as learning the dogma and the ritual of his religion. Priests in the United States complete four years of theological school and sometimes serve first as apprentices under established priests. Priests do not receive a fee for their services but are supported by donations from parishioners or followers. Priests often have some political power as a result of their office— the chief priest is sometimes also the head of state or is a close adviser to the chief of state— and their material well-being is a direct reflection of their position in the priestly hierarchy.

The dependence on memorized ritual both marks and protects the priest. If a shaman repeatedly fails to effect a cure, he will probably lose his following, for he has obviously lost the support of the spirits. But if a priest performs his ritual perfectly and the gods choose not to respond, the priest will usually retain his position and the ritual will preserve its assumed effectiveness. The nonresponse of the gods will be explained in terms of the people's unworthiness of supernatural favor.

Practitioners and Social Complexity More complex societies tend to have more types of religious or magical practitioners. If a society has only one type of practitioner, it is almost always a shaman; such societies tend to be nomadic or seminomadic food collectors. Societies with two types of practitioners (usually shaman healers and priests) have agriculture. Those with three types of practitioners are agriculturalists or pastoralists with political integration beyond the community (the additional practitioner type tends to be either a sorcerer or witch or a medium). Finally, societies with all four types of practitioners have agriculture, political integration beyond the community, and social classes.[65]

Religion and Adaptation

As we have seen in this chapter, many anthropologists take the view that religions are adaptive. Some theorists argue that religion helps individuals reduce anxiety and uncertainty. Others stress societal needs of solidarity and cooperation. These are general needs, and it is easy to imagine why reducing anxiety or increasing cooperation would be important. But some particular customary aspects of religious belief, at least on the surface, do not appear to be adaptive. For example, the Hindu belief in the sacred cow has seemed to many to be the very opposite of a useful or adaptive custom. Their religion does not permit Hindus to slaughter cows. Why do the Hindus retain such a belief? Why do they allow all those cows to wander around freely, defecating all over the place, and not slaughter any of them? The contrast with our own use of cows could hardly be greater.

Marvin Harris suggested that the Hindu use of cows may have beneficial consequences that some other use of cows would not have. Harris pointed out that there may be a sound economic reason for not slaughtering cattle in India. The cows, and the males they produce, provide resources that could not easily be gotten otherwise. At the same time, their wandering around to forage is no strain on the food-producing economy.

The resources provided by the cows are varied. First, a team of oxen and a plow are essential for the many small farms in India. The Indians could produce oxen with fewer cows, but to do so they would have to devote some of their food production to feeding those cows. In the present system, they do not feed the cows, and even though poor nutrition makes the cows relatively infertile, males, which are castrated to make oxen, are still produced at no cost to the economy. Second, cow dung is essential as a cooking fuel and fertilizer. The National Council of Applied Economic Research estimated that an amount of dung equivalent to 45 million tons of coal is burned annually. Moreover, it is delivered practically to the door each day at no cost. Alternative sources of fuel, such as wood, are scarce or costly. In

Mediums Part-time religious practitioners who are asked to heal and divine while in a trance.

Priests Generally full-time specialists, with very high status, who are thought to be able to relate to superior or high gods beyond the ordinary person's access or control.

16.4 Discuss religion in terms of adaptation.

addition, about 340 million tons of dung are used as manure—essential in a country obliged to derive three harvests a year from its intensively cultivated land. Third, although Hindus do not eat beef, cattle that die naturally or are butchered by non-Hindus are eaten by the lower castes, who, without the upper-caste taboo against eating beef, might not get this needed protein. Fourth, the hides and horns of the cattle that die are used in India's enormous leather industry. Therefore, because the cows do not themselves consume resources needed by people and it would be impossible to provide traction, fuel, and fertilizer as cheaply by other means, the taboo against slaughtering cattle may be very adaptive.[66]

Religious Change

16.5 Explain and give examples of various forms of religious change, such as conversion and revitalization movements.

In any society, religious beliefs and practices change over time, but some types of change are quite dramatic. Perhaps the most dramatic is religious conversion, particularly when large numbers of people switch to a completely new religion presented by missionaries or other proselytizers. Changing religion so drastically is perplexing to many scholars of religion who believe that religious beliefs are deeply connected to one's sense of identity, one's family, one's community, and ideas about the world.[67] Within the last few centuries, conversion has sometimes followed Western expansion and exploration. Contact with Westerners and other outsiders has also produced religious change in more indirect ways. In some native societies, contact has led to a breakdown of social structure and the growth of feelings of helplessness and spiritual demoralization. *Revitalization movements* have arisen as apparent attempts to restore such societies to their former confidence and prosperity. In recent times, religious *fundamentalist* movements have flourished. Some scholars have argued that such movements are also responses to the stress of rapid social change.

As we will see, religious change, particularly of the dramatic kind, usually does not occur in a vacuum but is often associated with other dramatic changes—economic, political, and demographic.

Religious Conversion

The two world religions with the greatest interest now in obtaining converts have been Christianity and Islam. Christian missionaries, supported by their churches back home, have been some of the earliest Western settlers in interior regions and out-of-the-way places. Traders have been the main proselytizers of Islam. Conversion to one of the world religions has often been associated with colonization and the expansion of state societies (see the box "Colonialism and Religious Affiliation"). The presence of people from other religions does not necessarily mean that people convert to the new religion. For example, missionaries have not met with equal success in all parts of the world. In some places, large portions of the native population have converted to the new religion with great zeal. In others, missionaries have been ignored, forced to flee, or even killed. We do not fully understand why missionaries have been successful in some societies and not in others.

We now examine the process of conversion on the island of Tikopia as an example of religious change brought about by direct contact with missionaries.

Christianity on Tikopia Tikopia was one of the few Polynesian societies to retain its traditional religious system into the first decades of the 20th century. An Anglican mission was first established on the island in 1911. With it came a deacon and the founding of two schools for about 200 pupils. By 1929, approximately half the population had converted, and in the early 1960s, almost all of Tikopia gave at least nominal allegiance to Christianity.[68]

Traditional Tikopian belief embraced a great number of gods and spirits of various ranks who inhabited the sky, the water, and the land. One god in particular—the original creator and shaper of the culture—was given a place of special importance, but he was in no way comparable to the all-powerful God of Christianity. Unlike Christianity, Tikopian religion made no claim to universality. The Tikopian gods did not rule over all creation, only over Tikopia. It was thought that if one left Tikopia, one left the gods behind.

The people of Tikopia interacted with their gods and spirits primarily through religious leaders who were also the heads of descent groups. Clan chiefs presided over rituals associated with the everyday aspects of island life, such as house construction, fishing, planting,

Migrants and Immigrants

Colonialism and Religious Affiliation

Many of us might like to think that we belong to a particular religious group because we prefer its beliefs and practices. And that may be true for people who have chosen to switch their religious affiliation. But many religious people affiliate with the religion they grew up with, or one very much like it.

Clearly, religious affiliation is a complex issue. But one thing stands out. You are not likely to choose an affiliation you have never been exposed to. This goes for people who believe in religion and also for people who don't. Most North Americans say they are Christians. But how come?

Would so many in North America be Christians if Europeans (mostly Christian) hadn't established colonies here and elsewhere in the last 500 years? Would there be Muslims in Indonesia, the Philippines, and North Africa if Arab kingdoms hadn't established colonies in those places after the 7th century? Would there have been Hindus in Sumatra if South Asians hadn't migrated and established the Srivijayan kingdom in Sumatra before the time of Christ? Would there have been Jews in Yemen (until their emigration to Israel 50 years ago) if King Solomon's state had not colonized in the land of the Queen of Sheba more than 2,000 years ago? An expanding state society can directly or indirectly force a change in people's religious affiliation. It is not coincidental that the new religious affiliation usually matches the dominant society's.

Religion in some form may be a cultural universal. People may worship the supernatural, pray to it for help and guidance, and even try to control it (with "lucky charms" and other

Church on Rangiroa, French Polynesia.

magic). But religion is not the same everywhere, as is evident in this chapter. Why people convert to a major religion carried by an expanding state society is still not completely understood. Sometimes the people do not convert, or do not convert right away. Anthropologist Elizabeth Brusco has written that one primary motivation for conversion, long recognized by scholars, is the desire to maximize advantages. In recent times, missionaries have offered new beliefs and practices that may be appealing, but they have also offered what Brusco calls "protection, access to food and other desirable goods, medical care, literacy, technology, status, and, at times, political power." Was the same true, at least somewhat, in the past? Was adopting the new religion the best way to survive colonialism and its consequences?

Even if people adopt a religion, they often change important parts of it. For example, the Lahu of southwest China became Buddhist, but the Buddha became a male-female couple rather than just a male. The Lahu were a stateless society (prior to the expansion of the Han Chinese) with a strong emphasis on gender equality. By identifying Buddha with their indigenous god, Xeul Sha, the image of the Buddha was changed. According to Lahu origin myths, Xeul Sha is a male-female pair of twins. They marry and propagate humanity. The identification of Xeul Sha with Buddha means that Buddha is considered a pair of male-female gods by most Lahu Buddhist villagers.

Sources: Brusco 1996; Stevens 1996; Du 2003.

and harvesting. The chief was expected to intercede with the gods on the people's behalf, to persuade them to bring happiness and prosperity to the group. Indeed, when conditions were good, it was assumed that the chief was doing his job well. When disaster struck, the prestige of the chief often fell in proportion. Why did the Tikopia convert to Christianity? Firth suggested several contributing factors.

First, the mission offered the people the prospect of acquiring new tools and consumer goods. Although conversion alone did not provide such benefits, attachment to the mission made them more attainable. Later, it became apparent that education, particularly in reading and writing English, was helpful in getting ahead in the outside world. Mission schooling became valued and provided a further incentive for adopting Christianity.

Second, conversion may have been facilitated by the ability of chiefs, as religious and political leaders, to bring over entire descent groups to Christianity. Should a chief decide to transfer his allegiance to Christianity, the members of his kin group usually followed him. In 1923, when Tafua, chief of the Faea district of Tikopia, converted to the new religion, he brought with him his entire group—nearly half the population of the island. The ability of the chiefs to influence their kin groups, however, was both an asset and a hindrance to missionary efforts because some chiefs steadfastly resisted conversion.

A final blow to traditional Tikopian religion came in 1955, when a severe epidemic killed at least 200 people in a population of about 1,700. According to Firth, "the epidemic was largely interpreted as a sign of divine discrimination" because three of the outstanding non-Christian religious leaders died.[69] Subsequently, the remaining non-Christian chiefs voluntarily converted to Christianity, and so did their followers. By 1966, all Tikopia, with the exception of one old woman, had converted to the new faith.

Although many Tikopians feel their conversion to Christianity has been a unifying, revitalizing force, the changeover from one religion to another has not been without problems. Christian missionaries on Tikopia have succeeded in eliminating the traditional Tikopian population-control devices of abortion, infanticide, and male celibacy. It is very possible that the absence of these controls will continue to intensify population pressure. The island, with its limited capacity to support life, can ill afford this outcome. Firth summed up the situation Tikopian society faced:

> In the history of Tikopia complete conversion of the people to Christianity was formerly regarded as a solution to their problems; it is now coming to be realized that the adoption and practice of Christianity itself represents another set of problems. As the Tikopia themselves are beginning to see, to be Christian Polynesians in the modern technologically and industrially dominated world, even in the Solomon Islands, poses as many questions as it supplies answers.[70]

Unfortunately, not all native peoples have made the transition to Christianity as painlessly as the Tikopia. In fact, the record is dismal in most cases. All too frequently, missionary activity tends to destroy a society's culture and self-respect. It offers nothing in return but an alien, repressive system of values ill suited to the people's real needs and aspirations. Phillip Mason, a critic of European evangelists in Africa, pointed out some of the psychological damage inflicted by missionary activity.[71] The missionaries repeatedly stressed sin and guilt; they used the color black to represent evil and the color white to signify good; and they showed hostility toward pagan culture. Most damaging of all was their promise that Africans, provided they adopted the European's ways, would gain access both to the Europeans' heaven and to European society. But no matter how diligently Africans attempted to follow missionary precepts or climb the socioeconomic ladder, they were soon blocked from entry into European homes, clubs, and even churches and seminaries.

Explaining Conversion Anthropologists have just begun to try to understand religious conversion. As the box on colonialism and religious affiliation and the Tikopia case suggest, some of the motivation for switching to a new religion may have to do with economic and political advantages associated with converting to the new religion. With regard to the recent spread of Islam in Africa, Jean Ensminger suggests that Islam provided opportunities for those who wanted to engage in trade— "Islam brought a common language of trade (Arabic), a monetary system, an accounting system, and a legal code to adjudicate financial contracts and disputes."[72] These institutions were shared across ethnic groups, making it possible to engage in long-distance trade. But what increased the attractiveness of Islamic trade? Ensminger's study of the Orma, a pastoralist group in Kenya, is instructive, for despite the presence of Islam for 300 years, it did not appear to be of interest to them. The Orma chiefs did trade, but the Orma were mostly self-sufficient, and the need for trade appeared to be relatively low. However, the Orma were in serious trouble after successful attacks by the Masai and Somali in the late 1800s, which almost decimated them and depleted their cattle. After 1920, as they began to recover their population somewhat and their cattle began to be replenished, there was rapid conversion to Islam, mostly led by the young, who perhaps were attracted by the economic opportunities.[73]

Loss of population and the demoralization that it brings may also have played a significant role in conversion. Daniel Reff, comparing widespread conversion to Christianity in the Roman Empire after A.D. 150 and in northern Mexico after A.D. 1593, notes the parallels in both. In both situations, there were ravaging epidemics along with the presence of Christian personnel ready to help heal the sick. In Europe, about 8 percent of the population died before smallpox epidemics subsided in A.D. 190, and population continued to decline into the Middle Ages, perhaps to half of what it was. Population losses might have been more extreme in Mexico. In northern Mexico, an estimated 75 percent of the native populations died from disease. In Europe, Christians provided charity, food, and shelter for the ill, without regard to their status. The Jesuit missions in Mexico did not have that many personnel, but they did what they could to provide food, water, and "medicine."[74] Do epidemics play a role in other places? An exploratory cross-cultural study suggests that rapid population loss, usually from introduced diseases, predicts religious conversion, particularly when people believe that their traditional gods could help them.[75] If gods could have helped but didn't and people are dying in unusual numbers, people may think that the "gods have failed." In such circumstances, it is not surprising that people would be receptive to a new religion, particularly if it is preached by missionaries who are not dying.

Revitalization

The long history of religion includes periods of strong resistance to change as well as periods of radical change. Anthropologists have been especially interested in the founding of new religions or sects. The appearance of new religions is one of the things that may happen when cultures are disrupted by contact with dominant societies. Various terms have been suggested for these religious movements—cargo cults, nativistic movements, messianic movements, millenarian cults. Wallace suggested that they are all examples of **revitalization movements**, efforts to save a culture by infusing it with a new purpose and new life.[76] We turn to examples of such movements from North America and Melanesia.

Revitalization movements New religious movements intended to save a culture by infusing it with a new purpose and life.

A revitalization movement that became known as the Ghost Dance spread eastward from the Northwest from the 1870s to the 1890s. It was generally believed that, if people did the dance correctly, ghosts would come to life with sufficient resources to allow the people to return to their old ways, and, as a result of some cataclysm, the whites would disappear.

Source: Ogallala Sioux performing the Ghost Dance at the Pine Ridge Indian Agency, South Dakota. Illustration by Frederic Remington, 1890.

The Seneca and the Religion of Handsome Lake The Seneca reservation of the Iroquois on the Allegheny River in New York State was a place of "poverty and humiliation" by 1799.[77] Demoralized by whiskey and dispossessed from their traditional lands, unable to compete with the new technology because of illiteracy and lack of training, the Seneca were at an impasse. In this setting, Handsome Lake, the 50-year-old brother of a chief, had the first of a number of visions. In them, he met with emissaries of the Creator who showed him heaven and hell and commissioned him to revitalize Seneca religion and society. This he set out to do for the next decade and a half. As his principal text, he used the *Gaiwiio,* or "Good Word," a gospel that contains statements about the nature of religion and eternity and a code of conduct for the righteous. The *Gaiwiio* is interesting both for the influence of Quaker Christianity it clearly reveals[78] and for the way the new material was merged with traditional Iroquois religious concepts.

The first part of the "Good Word" has three main themes, one of which is the concept of an apocalypse. Handsome Lake offered many signs by which the faithful could recognize impending cosmic doom. Great drops of fire would rain from the skies and a veil would be cast over the earth. False prophets would appear, witch women would openly cast spells, and poisonous creatures from the underworld would seize and kill those who had rejected the *Gaiwiio.* Second, the *Gaiwiio* emphasized sin. The great sins were disbelief in the "good way," drunkenness, witchcraft, and abortion. Sins had to be confessed and repented. Finally, the *Gaiwiio* offered salvation. Salvation could be won by following a code of conduct, attending certain important traditional rites, and performing public confession.

The second part of the *Gaiwiio* sets out the code of conduct. This code seems to orient the Seneca toward advantageous European American practices without separating them from their culture. The code has five main sections:

1. *Temperance.* All Seneca leaders were fully aware of the social disorders arising out of abuse of liquor. Handsome Lake went to great lengths to illustrate and explain the harmfulness of alcohol.
2. *Peace and social unity.* Seneca leaders were to cease their futile bickering, and all were to be united in their approach to the larger society.
3. *Preservation of tribal lands.* Handsome Lake, fearing the piecemeal alienation of Seneca lands, was far ahead of his contemporaries in demanding a halt in land sales to non-Seneca.
4. *Proacculturation (favoring external culture traits).* Though individual property and trading for profit were prohibited, the acquisition of literacy in English was encouraged so that people would be able to read and understand treaties and to avoid being cheated.
5. *Domestic morality.* Sons were to obey their fathers, mothers should avoid interfering with daughters' marriages, and husbands and wives should respect the sanctity of their marriage vows.

Handsome Lake's teaching seems to have led to a renaissance among the Seneca. Temperance was widely accepted, as were schooling and new farming methods. By 1801, corn yields had been increased tenfold, new crops (oats, potatoes, flax) had been introduced, and public health and hygiene had improved considerably. Handsome Lake himself acquired great power among his people. He spent the remainder of his life fulfilling administrative duties, acting as a representative of the Iroquois in Washington, and preaching his gospel to neighboring tribes. By the time of Handsome Lake's death in 1815, the Seneca clearly had undergone a dramatic rebirth, attributable at least in part to the new religion. Later in the century, some of Handsome Lake's disciples founded a church in his name that, despite occasional setbacks and political disputes, survives to this day.

Although many scholars believe cultural stress gives rise to these new religious movements, it is still important to understand exactly what the stresses are and how strong they have to become before a new movement emerges. Do different kinds of stresses produce different kinds of movements? And does the nature of the movement depend on the cultural elements already present? Let us consider some theory and research on the causes of the millenarian cargo cults that began to appear in Melanesia from about 1885 on.

Cargo Cults The *cargo cults* can be thought of as religious movements "in which there is an expectation of, and preparation for, the coming of a period of supernatural bliss."[79] Thus, an explicit belief of the cargo cults was the notion that some liberating power would bring all the Western goods (cargo in pidgin English) the people might want. For example, around 1932, on Buka in the Solomon Islands, the leaders of a cult prophesied that a tidal wave would sweep away the villages and a ship would arrive with iron, axes, food, tobacco, cars, and arms. Work in the gardens ceased, and wharves and docks were built for the expected cargo.[80]

What may explain such cults? Peter Worsley suggested that an important factor in the rise of cargo cults and millenarian movements in general is the existence of oppression—in the case of Melanesia, colonial oppression. He suggested that the reactions in Melanesia took religious rather than political forms because they were a way of pulling together people who previously had no political unity and who lived in small, isolated social groups.[81] Other scholars, such as David Aberle, suggested that *relative deprivation* is more important than oppression in explaining the origins of cults; when people feel that they could have more, and they have less than what they used to have or less than others, they may be attracted to new cults.[82] Consistent with Aberle's general interpretation, Bruce Knauft's comparative study of cargo cults found that such cults were more important in Melanesian societies that had had decreasing cultural contact with the West, and presumably *decreasing* contact with valued goods, within the year prior to the cult's emergence.[83]

Fundamentalism For some scholars, one of the main attributes of fundamentalism is the literal interpretation of a sacred scripture. But recent scholars have suggested that fundamentalist movements need to be understood more broadly as religious or political movements that appear in response to the rapidly changing environment of the modern world. In this broader view, fundamentalism occurs in many religions, including those of Christians, Jews, Islamics, Sikhs, Buddhists, and Hindus. Although each movement is different in content, Richard Antoun suggests that fundamentalist movements have the following elements in common: the selective use of scripture to inspire and assert proof of particular certainties; the quest for purity and traditional values in what is viewed as an impure world; active opposition to what is viewed as a permissive secular society and a nation-state that separates religion from the state; and an incorporation of selected modern elements such as television to promote the movements' aims.[84]

Fundamentalist religious movements do appear to be linked to the anxieties and uncertainties associated with culture change in general and globalization in particular. Many people in many countries are repelled by new behaviors and attitudes, and react in a way that celebrates the old. As Judith Nagata puts it, fundamentalism is a "quest for certainty in an uncertain world."[85] Protestant fundamentalism flourished at the end of the 19th century in the United States as immigrant groups came into the country in great numbers and the country became industrialized and increasingly urbanized. The fundamentalists denounced foreign influences, the decline of the Bible as a guide to moral behavior, and the teaching of evolution, and they succeeded in getting the country to prohibit the sale of alcoholic beverages. Recent Islamic fundamentalist movements seem to be responses to a different kind of challenge to the social order—increasing Westernization. Westernization may have first arrived in conjunction with colonial rule. Later, it may have been promoted by Western-educated native elites.[86] Antoun suggests that fundamentalist movements deliberately push certain practices because the leaders know they will outrage the secular opposition. Examples in recent Islamic fundamentalist movements are the extreme punishment of cutting off a hand for theft and requiring women to be covered by veils or head-to-toe covering in public.[87] Unfortunately, in present-day discourse, fundamentalism tends to be equated by Westerners with Islam itself. But, in historical perspective, all major religions have had fundamentalist movements in times of rapid culture change.

Few of us realize that nearly all of the major churches or religions in the world began as minority sects or cults. Indeed, some of the most established and prestigious Protestant churches were considered radical social movements at first. For example, what we now know as the United Church of Christ, which includes the Congregational Church, was founded by radicals in England who wanted church governance to be in the hands of the local congregation. Many of these radicals became the people we call Pilgrims, who had to flee to the New World. But they were very fundamentalist in their beliefs; for example, as late as the 1820s, Congregationalist-dominated towns in Connecticut prohibited celebrations of Christmas outside of church because such celebrations were not mentioned in the Bible. Nowadays, Congregationalists are among the most liberal Protestants.[88]

We should not be surprised to learn that most of the various Protestant churches today, including some considered very conservative, began as militant sects that set out to achieve a better world. After all, that's why we call them "Protestant." At first, the rebellion was against Rome and the Catholic Church. Later, sects developed in opposition to church and government hierarchies. And remember that Christianity itself began as a radical group in the hinterland of the Roman Empire. So new sects or cults were probably always political and social, as well as religious, movements. Recall that the word *millennium,* as used in discussions of religious movements, refers to a wished-for or expected future time when human life and society will be perfect and free of troubles; the world will then be prosperous, happy, and peaceful. Nowadays, the wish for a better world may or may not be religiously inspired. Some people who seek a more perfect world believe that humans alone must achieve it.

Ideas about the millennium, and the origins of new cults and religions, might best be viewed then as human hopes: Which ones do people have? Do they vary from culture to culture, and why? Are some hopes universal? And how might they be achieved?

If the recent as well as distant past is any guide, we expect religious belief and practice to be revitalized periodically, particularly during times of stress. And even though the spread of world religions minimizes some variation, globalization has also increased the worldwide interest in shamanism and other features of religion that are different from the dominant religions. Thus, we can expect the world to continue to have religious variation.

Summary and Review

The Universality of Religion

16.1 Characterize the universality of religion and discuss various explanations for that universality.

- Religion is any set of attitudes, beliefs, and practices pertaining to supernatural power, whether that power be forces, gods, spirits, ghosts, or demons.

- Religious beliefs and practices are found in all known contemporary societies, and archaeologists think they have found signs of religious belief associated with *Homo sapiens* who lived at least 60,000 years ago.

- Theories about the universality of religion suggest that humans create religions in response to universal needs or conditions, including a need for intellectual understanding, reversion to childhood feelings, anxiety and uncertainty, and a need for community and/ or cooperation.

 How might the universality of religion be explained? Critically discuss various theories.

Variation in Religious Beliefs

16.2 Discuss the range of variability in religious beliefs.

- Although scholars generally do not agree as to why people need religion or how supernatural beings and forces come into existence, they recognize the enormous variation in the details of religious beliefs.

- Variation in religious belief are reflected in the kinds and characters of supernatural beings or forces, the structure or hierarchy of those beings, what the beings actually do, and what happens to people after death.

- Across all cultures, objects, people, or places can embody good forces or harmful forces, and supernatural beings can have either nonhuman or human origins as well as varying character traits; specifics vary from culture to culture.

- Religious belief can promote in-group trust/cooperation or out-group conflict. Warning signs of conflict are leaders claiming only they know the truth, a call to blindly obey, a belief that no ideal world is possible, actions using the end to justify the means, and calls for a holy war.

- Among societies, concepts of life after death can include heaven, hell, and reincarnation. Support was found for the idea that judgmental beliefs parallel the society's economic practices.

 What are some important variations in beliefs about a supernatural beings or forces across societies?

Variation in Religious Practices

16.3 Describe the variability in religious practices and practitioners cross-culturally.

- Religious practices can vary in terms of kinds of religious practitioners and how people interact with the supernatural. Many practices involve rituals, repeated behaviors and patterns, which are generally collective and thought to strengthen faith.

- People's interactions with the supernatural vary widely and include prayer, divination, physiological experience, simulation, feasts, and sacrifices. Achieving altered states, referred to as trances, is part of religious practice in 90 percent of the world's societies.

- Interacting with the supernatural can be categorized as pleading, asking, or persuading the supernatural to act a certain way or as compelling the supernatural through magic, which can be used for good or harm. Sorcery is important in societies that lack judicial authorities.

- Almost all societies have part-time or full-time religious or magical practitioners that can fall into four major types: shamans, sorcerers or witches, mediums, and priests. The number of types of practitioners in a society seems to increase with degree of cultural complexity.

 What are some of the important variations in religious practices? What different types of religious practitioners are found across cultures?

Religion and Adaptation

16.4 Discuss religion in terms of adaptation.

- Some theorists argue that religion is adaptive because it helps individuals reduce anxiety and uncertainty as well as develop solidarity and cooperation.

- Some particular customary aspects of religious belief such as the Hindu taboo against slaughtering cows may not appear to be adaptive but probably are.

 What is an example of an adaptive religious belief?

Religious Change

16.5 Explain and give examples of various forms of religious change, such as conversion and revitalization movements.

- Perhaps the most dramatic is religious conversion, particularly when large numbers of people switch to a completely new religion presented by missionaries or other proselytizers.

- Religious change also happens in more indirect ways, including revitalization and fundamentalist movements, which appear to be responses to the stress of rapid social change. All major religions have had fundamentalist movements in times of rapid culture change.

- Dramatic economic, political, and demographic change is associated with religious change, particularly of the dramatic kind.

- Nearly all of the major churches or religions in the world began as minority sects or cults, which were probably always political and social, as well as religious, movements.

 What are examples of various types of religious change?

Think on it

1. How does your conception of **God** compare with beliefs about supernatural beings in other religious systems?

2. What do you think is the future of **religion**? Explain your answer.

3. Could any of the religious practices you know about be classified as **magic**? Are they associated with anxiety-arousing situations?

LEARNING OBJECTIVES

17.1 Analyze the purposes of body decoration and adornment.

17.2 Explain variation in the arts in relationship to other societal features.

17.3 Identify ethnocentric attitudes and practices toward non-Western art by Westerners.

17.4 Assess the relationship of culture contact and artistic change.

Most societies do not have a word for art.[1] Perhaps that is because art, particularly in societies with relatively little specialization, is often an integral part of religious, social, and political life. Indeed, most of the aspects of culture we have already discussed—economics, kinship, politics, religion—are not easily separated from the rest of social life.[2]

The oldest art found so far comes from caves in South Africa. Pieces of red ochre were engraved there more than 77,000 years ago. In Australia, people painted on walls of rock shelters and on cliff faces between 70,000 and 60,000 years ago. And in southern Africa, Spain, and France, people painted slabs of rock 28,000 years ago (see the box "Rock Art: Preserving a Window into the Past"). Art is clearly an old feature of human cultures. We say that those earliest paintings are art, but what do we mean by "art"? A stone spear point and a bone fishhook obviously require skill and creativity to make. But we do not call them art. Why do we feel that some things are art and others are not?

Some definitions of art emphasize its evocative quality. From the viewpoint of the person who creates it, art expresses feelings and ideas; from the viewpoint of the observer or participant, it evokes feelings and ideas. The feelings and ideas on each side may or may not be exactly the same. And they may be expressed in a variety of ways—drawing, painting, carving, weaving, body decoration, music, dance, or story. An artistic work or performance is intended to excite the senses, to stir the emotions of the beholder or participant. It may produce feelings of pleasure, awe, repulsion, or fear, but usually not indifference.[3]

But emphasizing the evocative quality of art may make it difficult to compare the art of different cultures because what is evocative in one culture may not be evocative in another. For example, a humorous story in one culture may not be funny in another. Thus, most anthropologists agree that art is more than an attempt by an individual to express or communicate feelings and ideas. There is also some cultural patterning or meaning; societies vary in their characteristic kinds and styles of art.[4] The anthropological study of art places particular emphasis on the cultural context in which art is produced.[5]

Artistic activities are always cultural in part, involving shared and learned patterns of behavior, belief, and feeling. What are some of the ideas about art in our own culture? We tend to think that anything useful is not art.[6] If a basket has a design that is not necessary to its function, we may possibly consider it art, especially if we keep it on a shelf; but the basket with bread on the table would probably not be considered art. The fact that such a distinction is not made in other societies strongly suggests that our ideas about art are cultural. Among Native Americans in the Pacific Northwest, elaborately carved totem poles not only displayed the crests of the lineages of their occupants, they also supported the house.[7] The fact that artistic activities are partly cultural is evident when we compare how people in different societies treat the outsides of their houses. Most North Americans share the value of decorating the interiors of their homes with pictures—paintings, prints, or photographs hung on the walls. But they do not share the value of painting pictures on the outside walls of their houses, as Native Americans did in the Pacific Northwest.

In our society, we also insist that a work must be unique to be considered art. This aspect is clearly consistent with our emphasis on the individual. However, even though we require that artists be unique and innovative, the art they produce must still fall within some range of acceptable variation. Artists must communicate to us in a way we can relate to, or at least learn to relate to. Often, they must follow certain current styles of expression that other artists or critics have set if they hope to have the public accept their art. The idea that an artist should be original is a cultural idea; in some societies, the ability to replicate a traditional pattern is more valued than originality.

So art seems to have several qualities: It expresses as well as communicates. It stimulates the senses, affects emotions, and evokes ideas. It is produced in culturally patterned ways and styles. It has cultural meaning. In addition, some people are thought to be better at it than others.[8] Art does not require some people to be full-time artistic specialists; many societies in the ethnographic record had no full-time specialists of any kind. But although everyone in some societies may participate in some arts (dancing, singing, body decoration), it is usually thought that certain individuals have superior artistic skill.[9]

To illustrate the cross-cultural variation that exists in artistic expression, we will consider first the art of body decoration and adornment.

17.1 Analyze the purposes of body decoration and adornment.

Body Decoration and Adornment

In all societies, people decorate or adorn their bodies. The decorations may be permanent—scars, tattoos, or changes in the shape of a body part. Or they may be temporary, in the form of paint or objects such as feathers, jewelry, skins, and clothing that are not strictly utilitarian. Much of this decoration seems to be motivated by aesthetic considerations, which, of course, vary from culture to culture. The actual form of the decoration depends on cultural traditions. Body ornamentation includes the pierced noses of some women in India, the elongated necks of the Mangebetu of central Africa, the tattooing of North American males and females, the body painting of the Caduveo of South America, and the variety of ornaments found in almost every culture.

Applied Anthropology

Rock Art: Preserving a Window into the Past

If the art of an ancient or earlier culture reflects the preoccupations and ideas of the culture, and if we are interested in understanding what the creators of the art thought, the art of the past and its surroundings must be preserved as much as possible. One type of ancient art frequently found is what anthropologists call "rock art," drawings and paintings on cliff faces and the walls of caves. Some of the most famous are the cave paintings of Europe, dating from about 30,000 years ago, but a large number of other rock art sites are in danger and in need of preserving.

Unlike a painting or a decorated object, rock art is part of its environment, and the environmental area as well as the rock art needs to be preserved. Excavation of the area may provide information that not only allows us to date the drawings and paintings, it may also tell us what the people did to produce the art and why they produced it. For example, in one French cave, analysis of charcoal indicates that the artists made fires to produce the charcoal they would use in their drawings. In another cave in Montana, pollen found below the paintings came from a number of plants. Many of the plants have known medicinal properties, and the pollens may indicate what shamans had in their medicine bags. Talking to the descendants of the creators of the rock art is also essential. Sometimes anthropologists learn things that surprise them. For instance, near Alice Springs, Australia, some branches were knocking against some rock art and the preservers considered cutting some of the branches. The aboriginal elders were horrified at the idea because the trees were believed to harbor the souls of the deceased, and it would have been a crime to cut them.

Although there are natural threats to rock art, the greatest threats come from humans. Religious change with European contact often lessened the interest of indigenous populations in their earlier sacred sites, making for less protest when development projects are proposed. Tours to previously isolated sites often lead to more destruction from graffiti or unauthorized attempts to reproduce or photograph the art. Ironically, though, making the rock art the center of a park helps protect it.

Raising awareness of rock art is one of the most important ways of protecting it in its environment. Although nothing beats seeing rock art in its natural setting, modern methods (holograms, laser recording, 3D imagery) and computer-assisted enhancement have made it possible to have life-size replicas, allowing the public to see more than they can in some mostly inaccessible caves. These replicas and images also give anthropologists and other scientists materials for appreciation and study. The greater the number of displays in public facilities (museums, parks) that expose tourists to rock art, the more valuable it may become. Anthropologists or not, we all seem to be fascinated by the ancient graphics. We try to imagine what motivated the original artists. If we could reconstruct those motives, they might suggest why we choose subjects and techniques in our own art, as well as in our graffiti.

The archaeological context of rock art can help us understand the rock art. Teaching people how to preserve rock art is applied anthropology that will help to preserve a priceless heritage and a source of knowledge about humans in the past.

Source: Clottes 2008.

However, in addition to satisfying aesthetic needs, body decoration or adornment may be used to delineate social position, rank, sex, occupation, local and ethnic identity, or religion within a society. Along with social stratification come visual means of declaring status. The symbolic halo (the crown) on the king's head, the scarlet hunting jacket of the English gentleman, the eagle feathers of the Native American chief's bonnet, the gold-embroidered jacket of the Indian rajah—each mark of high status is recognized in its own society. Jewelry in the shape of a cross or the Star of David indicates Christian or Jewish inclinations. Clothes may set apart the priest, nun, or member of a sect such as the Amish.

The erotic significance of some body decoration is also apparent. Women draw attention to erogenous zones of the body by painting, as on the lips, and by attaching some object—an earring, a flower behind the ear, a necklace, bracelet, brooch, anklet, or belt. Men draw attention, too, by beards, tattoos, and penis sheaths (in some otherwise naked societies) that point upward. We have only to follow the fashion trends for women of Europe and North America during the past 300 years, with their history of pinched waists, ballooned hips, bustled rumps, exaggerated breasts, painted faces, and exposed bosoms, to realize the significance of body adornment for sexual provocation. Why some societies emphasize the erotic adornment of women and others emphasize it in men is not yet understood.

Type of body adornment may reflect politics. Polynesians decorate their bodies with tattoos, which are permanent. In Samoa, for example, tattoos distinguished the chiefly class from commoners. Bands and stripes were restricted to people of high status; low-status people could have tattoos only of solid black and only from waist to knees. Within the ruling class, the number of tattooed triangles down a man's leg indicated his relative rank. Because tattooing is permanent, it is a form of body decoration well suited to a society with inherited social stratification. On the other hand, in Melanesia, as is typical with the "big men" type of leadership that is somewhat fluid, Melanesians paint their bodies, and the painting is ephemeral. It disappears within a short time or after the first wash.[10]

A need to decorate the human body seems universal. We have noted some of the various methods people have used to adorn themselves in different societies. We are also aware of body-decoration practices that raise questions to which we have no ready answers. What explains adornment of the body by permanent marking such as scarification, bound feet, elongated ears and necks, shaped heads, pierced ears and septums, and filed teeth? Why do different societies adorn, paint, or otherwise decorate different parts of the body for sexual or other reasons? And what leads some members of our society to transfer body decoration to their animals? Why the shaped hair of the poodle, the braided manes of some horses, and the diamond collars, painted toenails, coats, hats, and even boots for some pets?

A Wodaabe Fulani man from Niger attending a ceremony.

Explaining Variation in the Arts

17.2 Explain variation in the arts in relationship to other societal features.

In our society, we stress the freedom of the artist, so it may seem to us that art is completely free to vary. But our emphasis on uniqueness obscures the fact that different cultures not only use or emphasize different materials and have different ideas of beauty, but they also may have characteristic styles and themes. It is easy to see styles when we look at art that is different from our own; it is harder to see similarity when we look at the art of our own culture. If we look at dance styles, for example, we may think that the dance style of the 1940s is completely different from the dance style of today. It might take an outsider to notice that, in our culture, we still generally see couples dancing as a pair rather than in a group line or circle, as in dances we call "folk dances." And, in our culture, females and males dance together rather than separately. Furthermore, our popular music still has a beat or combination of beats and is made by many of the same kinds of instruments as in the past.

But where do these similarities in form and style come from? Much of the recent research on variation in the arts supports the idea that form and style in visual art, music, dance, and folklore are very much influenced by other aspects of culture. Some psychological anthropologists would go even further, suggesting that art, like religion, expresses the typical feelings, anxieties, and experiences of people in a culture. And the typical feelings and anxieties in turn are influenced by basic institutions such as childrearing, economy, social organization, and politics.

Consider how the physical form of art a society prefers may reflect its way of life. For example, Richard Anderson pointed out that the art of traditionally nomadic people such as the !Kung, Inuit, and Australian aborigines is mostly carryable.[11] Song, dance, and oral literature are very important in those societies and are as portable as they can be. Those societies decorate useful objects that they carry with them—harpoons for the Inuit, boomerangs for the Australian aborigines, ostrich egg "canteens" for the !Kung. But they don't have bulky things such as sculpture or elaborate costumes. And what about the presence of artists or art critics? Although some people in small-scale societies are more artistic than others, specialized artists, as well as critics or theoreticians of art, tend to be found only in societies with a complex, specialized division of labor.

Visual Art

Perhaps the most obvious way artistic creations reflect how we live is by mirroring the environment—the materials and technologies available to a culture. Stone, wood, bones, tree bark, clay, sand, charcoal, berries for staining, and a few mineral-derived ochres are generally available materials. In addition, depending on the locality, other resources are accessible: shells, horns, tusks, gold, copper, and silver. The different uses to which societies put these materials are of interest to anthropologists, who may ask, for example, why a people chooses to use clay and not copper when both items are available. Although we have no conclusive answers as yet, such questions have important ramifications. The way in which a society views its environment is sometimes apparent in its choice and use of artistic materials. Certain metals, for example, may be reserved for ceremonial objects of special importance. Or the belief in the supernatural powers of a stone or tree may cause a sculptor to be sensitive to that particular material.[12]

The traditional political systems of Africa ranged from centralized kingdoms (on the complex end of the continuum) to village-based or segmentary lineage systems in which leadership was ephemeral or secret (tied to secret societies). Masks that conceal identity are often used in the uncentralized systems; crowns or other headdresses indicating high status are frequent in the kingdoms. Among the uncentralized Ibo of eastern Nigeria, masks are often worn by the young men of a village when they criticize the behavior of the village elders. In the kingdom of Ngoyo, in western Zaire, the king's status is indicated by his special cap as well as by his special three-legged stool.

What is particularly meaningful to anthropologists is the realization that although the materials available to a society may to some extent limit or influence what it can do artistically, the materials by no means determine what is done. Why does the artist in Japanese society rake sand into patterns, the artist in Navajo society paint sand, and the artist in Roman society melt sand to form glass? Moreover, even when the same material is used in the same way in different societies, the form or style of the work varies enormously from culture to culture.

A society may choose to represent objects or phenomena that are especially important to the people or elite. An examination of the art of the Middle Ages tells us something about the medieval preoccupation with theological doctrine. In addition to revealing the primary concerns of a society, the content of that society's art may also reflect the culture's social stratification. Authority figures may be represented in obvious ways. In the art of ancient Sumerian society, the sovereign was portrayed

The same materials may be used artistically in different ways. In Japan (on the left), sand is raked into patterns. In the Northern Territory of Australia (on the right), the Yuendumu paint the sand.

as being much larger than his followers, and the most prestigious gods were given oversized eyes. Also, differences in clothing and jewelry styles within a society usually reflect social stratification.

Art historians have always recognized certain possible relationships between the art of a society and other aspects of its culture. Much of this attention has been concentrated on the content of art because European art has been representational for such a long time. But the style of the art may reflect other aspects of culture. John Fischer, for example, examined the stylistic features of art with the aim of discovering "some sort of regular connection between some artistic feature and some social situation."[13] He argued that the artist expresses a form of social fantasy. In other words, in a stable society, artists will respond to those conditions in the society that bring security or pleasure to them and the society.

Assuming that "pictorial elements in design are, on one psychological level, abstract, mainly unconscious representations of persons in the society,"[14] Fischer reasoned that egalitarian societies would tend to have different stylistic elements in their art as compared with stratified societies. Egalitarian societies are generally composed of small, self-sufficient communities that are structurally similar and have little differentiation between people. Stratified societies, on the other hand, generally have larger, more interdependent, and more dissimilar communities and great differences among people in prestige, power, and access to economic resources. Fischer hypothesized, and found in a cross-cultural study, that certain elements of design were strongly related to the presence of social hierarchy. His findings are summarized in Table 17.1.

Repetition of a simple element, for example, tends to be found in the art of egalitarian societies, which have little political organization and few authority positions. If each element unconsciously represents individuals within the society, the relative sameness of people seems to be reflected in the repetitiveness of design elements. Conversely, the combinations of different design elements in complex patterns that tend to be found in the art of stratified societies seem to reflect the high degree of social differentiation that exists in such societies.[15]

According to Fischer, the egalitarian society's empty space in a design represents the society's relative isolation. Because egalitarian societies are usually small and self-sufficient, they tend to shy away from outsiders, preferring to find security within their own group. In contrast, the art of stratified societies is generally crowded. The hierarchical society does not seek to isolate individuals or communities within the group because they must be interdependent, each social level ideally furnishing services for those above it and help for those beneath it. As Fischer suggested, we can, in general, discern a lack of empty space in the designs of societies in which security is not sought by avoiding strangers but rather "security is produced

TABLE 17.1	Stylistic Differences by Type of Society	
Stratified Society		**Egalitarian Society**
Integrated unlike elements		Repetition of simple motifs
Little empty space		Ample unused or empty space
Asymmetrical design		Symmetrical design
Framed figures		Unframed figures

Source: Based on Fischer 1961.

by incorporating strangers into the hierarchy, through dominance or submission as the relative power indicates."[16]

Symmetry, the third stylistic feature related to type of society, is similar to the first. Symmetry may suggest likeness or an egalitarian society; asymmetry suggests difference and perhaps stratification. The fourth feature of interest here, the presence or absence of enclosures or boundaries—"frames" in our art—may indicate the presence or absence of hierarchically imposed rules circumscribing individual behavior. An unenclosed design may reflect free access to most property; in egalitarian societies, the fencing off of a piece of property for the use of only one person is unknown. In the art of stratified societies, boundaries or enclosures may reflect the idea of private property. Or they may symbolically represent the real differences in dress, occupation, type of food allowed, and manners that separate the different classes of people.

Studies such as Fischer's offer anthropologists new tools with which to evaluate ancient societies that are known only by a few pieces of pottery or a few tools or paintings. If art reflects certain aspects of a culture, then the study of whatever art of a people has been preserved may provide a means of testing the accuracy of the guesses we make about their culture on the basis of more ordinary archaeological materials. For example, even if we did not know from classical Greek writings that Athens became much more socially stratified between 750 B.C. and 600 B.C., we might guess that such a transformation had occurred because of the changes we can see over time

Changes in Greek vases show how increasing stratification is associated with integration of unlike elements as well as more crowded design. The one on the left dates from around 1000 B.C. when there was less stratification. The vase on the right dates from the time period between 750 B.C. and 600 B.C., when stratification was at its maximum.

in the way the Athenians decorated vases. Consistent with Fischer's cross-cultural findings, as Athens became more stratified, its vase painting became more complex, more crowded, and more enclosed.[17]

Music

When we hear the music of another culture, we often don't know what to make of it. We may say it does not "mean" anything to us, not realizing that the "meaning" of music has been programmed into us by our culture. In music as well as in art, our culture largely determines what we consider acceptable variation, what we say has "meaning" to us. Even

Migrants and Immigrants

The Spread of Popular Music

Music is a very visceral art. You feel it in your gut. Hearing a piece of music can make your belly vibrate and give you goosebumps. You don't forget that experience. The ideas expressed in a song can get to you, but you're mostly moved by the sound. You feel it. Music can lift you up or make you sad.

In the past, we wouldn't have known about lots of music if not for migration. Would there be "country music" radio stations in the United States if lots of people hadn't moved out of the South in the 20th century? Country music itself was an amalgam of Appalachian folk music heavily influenced by music from the British Isles and also by African music. The banjo, adapted by country musicians, was created by African Americans who modeled it on the African stringed musical instrument called a banjar. Though the fiddle, an important instrument in country music, was European in origin, many of the fiddlers in the South were African American, and country music incorporated African rhythmic styles and improvisation. There were other influences also—the guitar came from Spain, and yodeling from the Swiss. African American music also influenced much of popular American music—ragtime, the blues, jazz, rhythm and blues, rock and roll, disco, and rap, to name just a few. African influences also came to the United States via the Caribbean and South America where people from different cultures created a creolized music. Would we have liked "salsa" dancing, a form of Afro-Cuban music, or reggae and hip-hop from

Korean rapper Psy performs in Rockefeller Plaza in New York City.

Jamaica, if there were no immigration? The answer is probably not.

Of course, now there are other ways of hearing music besides migration. Satellite television and Internet sites like YouTube now make popular culture from other places internationally accessible. Such accessibility can help create fusion of different cultural styles such as the music and dance of the South Korean pop star Psy.

The movement of popular music is not guaranteed. For example, although there are many immigrants and migrants of Chinese or South Asian descent in the United States and Canada, Chinese or South Asian music has not become popular. Why the music of some immigrants and migrants is adopted or incorporated whereas other music is not is not yet understood.

Some technologies like cell phones are perceived as very useful and spread widely as people earn more and can afford to buy them. Music is not something that is or is not useful—the ideas and feelings communicated answer our needs. Although young people, the most frequent consumers of popular music, are often looking for something "new," the latest style is probably not that different in some respects from the last style. Cultures have musical preferences, and musical styles that are very different are not readily accepted. However, with all the migration, immigration, and communication in the modern world, it is likely that the market demand for new popular music will continue to expand.

Sources: Nicholls 1998; D. R. Hill 2005, 363–73.

a trained musicologist, listening for the first time to music of a different culture, will not be able to hear the subtleties of tone and rhythm that members of the culture hear with ease. This predicament is similar to that of the linguist who, exposed to a foreign language, cannot at first distinguish phonemes, morphemes, and other regular patterns of speech.

Not only do instruments vary, but music itself varies widely in style from society to society. For example, in some societies, people prefer music with a regularly recurring beat; in others, they prefer changes in rhythm. There are also variations in singing styles. In some places, it is customary to have different vocal lines for different people; in other places, people all sing together in the same way.

Is variation in music, as in the other arts, related to other aspects of culture? On the basis of a cross-cultural study of more than 3,500 folk songs from a sample of the world's societies, Alan Lomax and his co-researchers found that song style seems to vary with cultural complexity. Now many of these folk songs are available as part of an online Global Jukebox.[18] As we will see, these findings about variation in song style are similar to Fischer's findings about variation in art.

Lomax and his co-researchers found some features of song style to be correlated with cultural complexity. (The societies classified as more complex tend to have higher levels of food-production technology, social stratification, and higher levels of political integration.) For example, wordiness and clearness of enunciation were found to be associated with cultural complexity. The association is a reasonable one: The more a society depends on verbal information, as in giving complex instructions for a job or explaining different points of law, the more strongly will clear enunciation in transmitting information be a mark of its culture. Thus, hunter-gatherer bands, in which people know their productive role and perform it without ever being given complex directions, are more likely than we are to base much of their singing on lines of nonwords, such as our refrain line "tra-la-la-la-la." Their songs are characterized by lack of explicit information, by sounds that give pleasure in themselves, by much repetition, and by relaxed, slurred enunciation.[19]

Examples of the progression from repetition or nonwords to wordy information are found within our society. The most obvious, and universal, example of a song made entirely of repetition is the relaxed lullaby of a mother repeating a comforting syllable to her baby while improvising her own tune. But this type of song is not characteristic of our society. Although our songs sometimes have single lines of nonwords, it is rare for an entire song to be made of them. Usually, the nonwords act as respites from information:

Deck the halls with boughs of holly,
Fa la la la la,
La la la la.[20]

In associating variation in music with cultural complexity, Lomax found that elaboration of song parts also corresponds to the complexity of a society. Societies in which leadership is informal and temporary seem to symbolize their social equality by an *interlocked* style of singing. Each person sings independently but within the group, and no one singer is differentiated from the others. Rank societies, in which there is a leader with prestige but no real power, are characterized by a song style in which one "leader" may begin the song but the others soon drown out his or her voice. In stratified societies, where leaders have the power of force, choral singing is generally marked by a clear-cut role for the leader and a secondary "answering" role for the others. Societies marked by elaborate stratification show singing parts that are differentiated and in which the soloist is deferred to by the other singers.

Polyphony Two or more melodies sung simultaneously.

Lomax also found a relationship between **polyphony**, where two or more melodies are sung simultaneously, and a high degree of female participation in food-getting. In societies in which women's work is responsible for at least half of the food, songs are likely to contain more than one simultaneous melody, with the higher tunes usually sung by women. Moreover:

Counterpoint was once believed to be the invention of European high culture. In our sample it turns out to be most frequent among simple producers, especially gatherers, where women supply the bulk of the food. Counterpoint and perhaps even polyphony may then be very old feminine inventions. . . . Subsistence complementarity is at its maximum among gatherers, early gardeners, and horticulturalists. It is in such societies that we find the highest occurrence of polyphonic singing.[21]

In societies in which women do not contribute much to food production, the songs are more likely to have a single melody and to be sung by males.[22]

In some societies, survival and social welfare are based on a unified group effort; in those cultures, singing tends to be marked by cohesiveness. That is, cohesive work parties, teams of gatherers or harvesters, and kin groups, who work voluntarily for the good of the family or community, seem to express their interconnectedness in song by blending both tone and rhythm.

Some variations in music may be explained as a consequence of variation in childrearing practices. For example, researchers are beginning to explore childrearing as a way to explain why some societies respond to, and produce, regular rhythm in their music, whereas others enjoy free rhythm that has no regular beat. One hypothesis is that a regular beat in music is a simulation of the regular beat of the heart. For nine months in the womb, the fetus feels the mother's regular 80 or so heartbeats a minute. Moreover, mothers generally employ rhythmic tactics in quieting crying infants—patting their backs or rocking them. But the fact that children respond positively to an even tempo does not mean that the regular heartbeat is completely responsible for their sensitivity to rhythm. In fact, if the months in the womb were sufficient to establish a preference for rhythm, then every child would be affected in exactly the same manner by a regular beat, and all societies would have the same rhythm in their music.

Barbara Ayres suggested that the importance of regular rhythm in the music of a culture is related to the rhythm's *acquired reward value*—that is, its associations with feelings of security or relaxation. In a cross-cultural study of this possibility, Ayres found a strong correlation between a society's method of carrying infants and the type of musical rhythm the society produced. In some societies, the mother or an older sister carries the child, sometimes for two or three years, in a sling, pouch, or shawl, so that the child is in bodily contact with her for much of the day and experiences the motion of her rhythmic walking. Ayres discovered that such societies tend to have a regularly recurring beat in their songs. Societies in which the child is put into a cradle or is strapped to a cradleboard tend to have music based either on irregular rhythm or on free rhythm.[23]

The question of why some societies have great tonal ranges in music whereas others do not was also studied by Ayres, who suggested that this difference might also be explained by certain childrearing practices. Ayres theorized that painful stimulation of infants before weaning might result in bolder, more exploratory behavior in adulthood, which would be apparent in the musical patterns of the culture. This hypothesis was suggested to her by laboratory experiments with animals. Contrary to expectations, those animals given electric shocks or handled before weaning showed greater-than-usual physical growth and more exploratory behavior when placed in new situations as adults. Ayres equated the range of musical notes (from low to high) with the exploratory range of animals and forcefulness of accent in music with boldness in animals.

The kinds of stress Ayres looked for in ethnographic reports were those that would be applied to all children or to all of one sex—for example, scarification; piercing of the nose, lips, or ears; binding, shaping, or stretching of feet, head, ears, or any limb; inoculation; circumcision; or cauterization. The results showed that in societies in which infants are stressed before the age of 2, music is marked by a wider tonal range than in societies in which children are not stressed or are stressed only at a later age. Also, a firm accent or beat is characteristic of music more often in societies that subject children to stress than in societies that do not.[24]

Cultural emphasis on obedience or independence in children is another variable that may explain some aspects of musical performance. In societies in which children are generally trained for compliance, cohesive singing predominates; where children are encouraged to be assertive, singing is mostly individualized. Moreover, assertive training of children is associated with a raspy voice or harsh singing. A raspy voice seems to be an indication of assertiveness and is most often a male voice quality. Interestingly enough, in societies in which women's work predominates in subsistence production, the women sing with harsher voices.

Current Research and Issues

Do Masks Show Emotion in Universal Ways?

Face masks are commonly used in rituals and performances. They not only hide the real face of the mask wearer but often evoke powerful emotions in the audience—anger, fear, sadness, joy. You might think, because so many things vary cross-culturally, that the ways in which emotion is displayed and recognized in masks vary too. But apparently they do not vary that much.

Research on the universality of emotion evoked by masks builds on work done by Paul Ekman and Carroll Izard. Ekman and Izard showed photographs to members of different cultural groups and asked them to identify the emotions displayed in the photographs. A particular emotion was identified correctly by most viewers, whatever the viewer's native culture. Coding schemes were developed to enable researchers to compare the detailed facial positions of individual portions of the face (eyebrows, mouth, etc.) for different emotions. What exactly do we do when we scowl? We contract the eyebrows and lower the corners of the mouth; in geometric terms, we make angles and diagonals on our faces. When we smile, we raise the corners of the mouth; we make it curved.

Psychologist Joel Aronoff and his colleagues compared two types of wooden face masks from many different societies—masks described as threatening (e.g., designed to frighten off evil spirits) versus masks associated with nonthreatening functions (a courtship dance). As

Maori wood carving in the Auckland War Memorial Museum, Auckland, New Zealand.

suspected, the two sets of masks had significantly different proportions of certain facial elements. The threatening masks had eyebrows and eyes facing inward and downward and a downward-facing mouth. The threatening masks also were more likely to have pointed heads, chins, beards, and ears, as well as projections from the face such as horns. In more abstract or geometrical terms, threatening features generally tend to be angular or diagonal, and nonthreatening features tend to be curved or rounded.

But is it the facial features themselves that convey threat, or is it the design elements of angularity and diagonality that convey threat? To help answer this question, students in the United States were asked to associate adjectives with drawings of abstract pairs of design features (e.g., a V shape and a U shape). Even with abstract shapes, the angular patterns were thought of as less "good," more "powerful," and "stronger" than the curved shapes. In subsequent studies, students recognized the V shape more quickly than other shapes, and this shape triggered more response in the brain in areas associated with threat.

We should not be surprised to discover that humans all over the world use their faces, and masks, to show emotions in the same ways. Aren't we all members of the same species? That's why a movie made in Hollywood or Beijing may evoke the same feelings wherever people see it. The universality of human emotion as expressed in the face becomes obvious only when we see faces (and masks) from elsewhere, showing emotions in ways that are unmistakable to us.

Thus, we become aware of universality (in masks as well as other cultural things) in the same way we become aware of variation—by exposure through reading and direct experience with the ways cultures do and do not vary.

Sources: Aronoff et al. 1988; Aronoff et al. 1992; Larson et al. 2007; Larson et al. 2009.

Other voice characteristics may also be associated with elements of culture. For example, sexual restrictions in a society seem to be associated with voice restrictions, especially with a nasalized or narrow, squeezed tone. These voice qualities are associated with anxiety and are especially noticeable in sounds of pain, deprivation, or sorrow. Restrictive sexual practices may be a source of pain and anxiety, and the nasal tone in song may reflect such emotions.[25]

The cross-cultural results about music should be able to explain change over time as well as variation within a society. Future research in a variety of societies may help test the theories of Lomax and Ayres.[26]

Folklore

Folklore Includes all the myths, legends, folktales, ballads, riddles, proverbs, and superstitions of a cultural group. Generally, folklore is transmitted orally, but it may also be written.

Folklore is a broad category comprising all the myths, legends, folktales, ballads, riddles, proverbs, and superstitions of a cultural group.[27] In general, folklore is transmitted orally, but it may also be written. Games are also sometimes considered folklore, although they may be learned by imitation as well as transmitted orally. All societies have a repertoire of stories that they tell to entertain each other and teach children. Examples of our folklore include fairy

Just as in art and song, dance style seems to reflect societal complexity. In less complex societies, everyone participates in dances in much the same way, as among the Huli of New Guinea.

tales and the legends we tell about our folk heroes, such as George Washington's confessing that he chopped down the cherry tree. Folklore is not always clearly separable from the other arts, particularly music and dance; stories often are conveyed in those contexts.

Although some folklore scholars emphasize the traditional aspects of folklore and the continuity between the present and the past, more recently attention has been paid to the innovative and emergent aspects of folklore. In this view, folklore is constantly created by any social group that has shared experiences. So, for example, computer programmers may have their jokes and their own proverbs (e.g., "Garbage in, garbage out!").[28] Jan Brunvand compiled a set of *urban legends*. One such legend is "The Hook." The story, which has many versions, is basically about a young couple parked on Lover's Lane with the radio on. There is an announcement that a killer with an artificial hand is loose, so the girl suggests that they leave. The boy starts the car and drives her home. When he walks around the car to open her door, he finds a bloody hook attached to the door handle.[29] There are even legends on college campuses. What is the answer to the question of how long students should wait for a tardy professor? Students have an answer, ranging from 10 to 20 minutes. Is this a rule, or only a legend? Brunvand reported that he never found a regulation about how long to wait for the professor on any campus that tells this story![30]

Some folklore scholars are interested in universal or recurrent themes. Clyde Kluckhohn suggested that five themes occur in the myths and folktales of all societies: catastrophe, generally through flood; the slaying of monsters; incest; sibling rivalry, generally between brothers; and castration, sometimes actual but more commonly symbolic.[31] Edward Tylor, who proposed that religion is born from the human need to explain dreams and death, suggested that hero myths follow a similar pattern the world over—the central character is exposed at birth, is subsequently saved by others (humans or animals), and grows up to become a hero.[32] Joseph Campbell argued that hero myths resemble initiations—the hero is separated from the ordinary world, ventures forth into a new world (in this case, the supernatural world) to triumph over powerful forces, and then returns to the ordinary world with special powers to help others.[33]

In more complex societies, such as Japan, there tend to be leading roles and minor roles as in a Geisha show.

Myths may indeed have universal themes, but few scholars have looked at a representative sample of the world's societies, and therefore we cannot be sure that current conclusions about universality are correct. Indeed, most folklore researchers have not been interested in universal themes but in the particular folktales told in specific societies or regions. For example, some scholars have focused on the "Star Husband Tale," a common Native American story. Stith Thompson presented 84 versions of this tale; his goal was to reconstruct the original version and pinpoint its place of origin. By identifying the most common elements, Thompson suggested that the basic story (and probably the original) is the following:

> *Two girls sleeping out of doors wish that stars would be their husbands. In their sleep the girls are taken to the sky where they find themselves married to stars, one of which is a young man and the other an old man. The women are warned not to dig, but they disregard the warning and accidentally open up a hole in the sky. Unaided they descend on a rope and arrive home safely.*[34]

The tale, Thompson suggested, probably originated in the Plains and then spread to other regions of North America.

Alan Dundes has concentrated on the structure of folktales; he thinks that Native American folktales, including the "Star Husband Tale," have characteristic structures. One is a movement away from disequilibrium. Equilibrium is the desirable state; having too much or too little of anything is a condition that should be rectified as soon as possible. Disequilibrium, which Dundes calls *lack*, is indicated by the girls in the "Star Husband Tale" who do not have husbands. The lack is then corrected, in this case by marriage with the stars. This tale has another common Native American structure, says Dundes—a sequence of prohibition, interdiction, violation, and consequence. The women are warned not to dig, but they do—and as a consequence, they escape for home.[35] It should be noted that the consequences in folktales are not always good. Recall the Garden of Eden tale. The couple are warned not to eat the fruit of a tree; they eat the fruit; they are cast out of their paradise. Similarly, Icarus in the Greek tale is warned not to fly too high or low. He flies too high; the sun melts the wax that holds his feathered wings, and he falls and drowns.

As useful as it might be to identify where certain tales originated, or what their common structures might be, many questions remain. What do the tales mean? Why did they arise in the first place? Why are certain structures common in Native American tales? We are still a long way from answering many of these questions, and trying to answer them is difficult. How does one try to understand the meaning of a tale?

It is easy for people to read different meanings into the same myth. For example, consider the myth the Hebrews told of a paradise in which only a man was present until Eve, the first woman, arrived and ate the forbidden fruit of knowledge. One might conclude that men in that society had some grudge against women. If the interpreter were a psychoanalyst, he, or especially she, might assume that the myth reflected the male's deeply hidden fears of female sexuality. A historian might believe that the myth reflected actual historical events and that men were living in blissful ignorance until women invented agriculture—the effect of Eve's "knowledge" led to a life of digging rather than gathering.

It is clearly not enough to suggest an interpretation. Why should we believe it? We should give it serious consideration only if some systematic test seems to support it. For example, Michael Carroll suggested a Freudian interpretation of the "Star Husband Tale"—that the story represents repressed sentiments in the society. Specifically, he suggested that incestuous intercourse is the underlying concern of this myth, particularly the desire of a daughter to have intercourse with her father. He assumed that the stars symbolize fathers. Fathers, like stars, are high above, in children's eyes. Carroll predicted that, if the "Star Husband Tale" originated on the Plains, and if it symbolizes intercourse, then the Plains groups should be more likely than other societies to have intercourse imagery in their versions of the tale. That seems to be the case. Analyzing 84 versions of the tale, Carroll found that Plains societies are the Native American groups most likely to have imagery suggesting intercourse, including the lowering of a rope or ladder—symbolizing the penis—through a sky hole—symbolizing the vagina.[36]

Few studies have investigated why there is cross-cultural variation in the frequency of certain features in folktales. One feature of folktale variation that has been investigated cross-culturally is aggression. George Wright found that variation in childrearing patterns predicted some aspects of how aggression is exhibited in folktales. Where children are severely punished for aggression, more intense aggression appears in the folktales. And in such societies, strangers are more likely than the hero or friends of the hero to be the aggressors in the folktales. It seems that where children may be afraid to exhibit aggression toward their parents or those close to them because of fear of punishment, the hero or close friends in folktales are also not likely to be aggressive.[37]

Other kinds of fears may be reflected in folktales. A cross-cultural study by Alex Cohen found that unprovoked aggression is likely in folktales of societies that are subject to unpredictable food shortages. Why? One possibility is that the folktales reflect reality; after all, a serious drought may seem capricious, not possibly provoked by any human activity, brought on by the gods or nature "out of the blue." Curiously, however, societies with a history of unpredictable food shortages hardly mention natural disasters in their folktales, perhaps because disasters are too frightening. In any case, the capriciousness of unpredictable disasters seems to be transformed into the capricious aggression of characters in the folktales.[38]

Folklore, just like other aspects of art, may at least partly reflect the feelings, needs, and conflicts that people acquire as a result of growing up in their culture.

Viewing the Art of Other Cultures

17.3 Identify ethnocentric attitudes and practices toward non-Western art by Westerners.

Sally Price raised some critical questions about how Western museums and art critics look at the visual art of less complex cultures. Why is it that when artworks from Western or Oriental civilizations are displayed in a museum here, they carry the artist's name? In contrast, art from less complex cultures, often labeled "primitive art," tends to be displayed without the name of the artist; instead, it is often accompanied by a description of where it came from, how it was constructed, and what it may be used for. More words of explanation seem to accompany displays of unfamiliar art. Price suggested that the art pieces that we consider the most worthy require the least labeling, subtly conveying that the viewer needs no help to judge a real work of art.[39] In addition, art acquired from less complex cultures tends to be labeled by the name of the Westerner who acquired it. It is almost as if the fame of the collector, not the art itself, sets the value of such art.[40]

Just as the art from less complex cultures tends to be nameless, it also tends to be treated as timeless. We recognize that Western art and the art from classical civilizations change over time, which is why it must be dated, but the art from other places seems to be viewed as representing a timeless cultural tradition.[41] Do we know that the art of peoples with simpler technology changes less, or is this assumption a kind of ethnocentrism? Price, who has studied the art of the Saramakas of Suriname, points out that although Westerners think of Saramakan art as still representing its African ancestry, Saramakans themselves can identify shifts in their art styles over time. For example, they describe how calabashes used to be decorated on the outside, then the style changed to decorating the inside. With respect to textile arts, Saramakans articulate four transitions beginning from free-form embroidery to elaborate cross-stitch embroidery. They can also recognize the artist who made particular carved calabashes as well as identify those who were innovators of designs and techniques.[42]

Although it seems that individual artists can usually be recognized in any community, some societies do appear to be more "communal" than others in their art style. For example, let us compare the Puebloan peoples of the Southwest with native peoples of the Great Plains. Traditionally, women Puebloan potters did not sign their pots, and they largely followed their pueblo's characteristic style. In contrast, each Plains warrior stressed his individual accomplishments by painting representations of those accomplishments on animal hides. Either the warrior would do it himself or he would ask someone else to do it for him. These hides were worn by the warrior or displayed outside his tipi.[43]

17.4 Assess the relationship of culture contact and artistic change.

Artistic Change, Culture Contact, and Global Trade

It is unquestionably true that contact with the West did alter some aspects of the art of other cultures, but that does not imply that their art was changeless before. What kinds of things changed with contact? In some places, artists began to represent European contact itself. For example, in Australia, numerous rock paintings by aborigines portray sailing ships, men on horseback carrying pistols, and even cattle brands. With encouragement from Europeans, indigenous artists also began drawing on tree bark, canvas, and fiberboard to sell to Europeans. Interestingly, the art for sale mostly emphasizes themes displayed before contact and does not include representations of ships and guns.[44] As aboriginal populations were decimated by European contact, a lot of their traditional art forms disappeared, particularly legends and rock paintings that were associated with the sacred sites of each clan. The legends described the creation of the sacred places, and art motifs with painted human or animal heroes marked the sites.[45]

In North America, contact between native groups produced changes in art even before the Europeans came. Copper, sharks' teeth, and marine shells were traded extensively in precontact times and were used in the artwork of people who did not have access to those materials locally. Ceremonies were borrowed among groups, and with the new ceremonies came changes in artistic traditions. Borrowing from other native groups continued after European contact. The Navajo, who are well known today for their rug weaving, were not weavers in the 17th century. They probably obtained their weaving technology from the Hopi and then began to weave wool and herd sheep. European contact also produced material changes in art; new materials, including beads, wool cloth, and silver, were introduced. Metal tools such as needles and scissors could now be used to make more tailored and more decorated skin clothing. In the Northwest, the greater availability of metal tools made it possible to make larger totem poles and house posts.[46]

"Tourist" Art and "Fine" Art

When Westerners do notice changes over time in the art of less complex societies, it seems to be because they are concerned about whether the art represents traditional, "authentic" forms or is "tourist art." As we have seen, the concept of "traditional" art is problematic because it suggests that the art of less complex societies does not change. Tourist art is often evaluated negatively, perhaps because of its association with just being produced for money. But famous Western artists often also worked for fees or were supported by elite patrons, and yet the fact that they were paid does not seem to interfere with our evaluation of their art.[47]

After they were placed on reservations, virtually all Native Americans had to change their ways of making a living. Selling arts and crafts earned some of them supplementary income. Most of these crafts used traditional techniques and traditional designs, altered somewhat to suit European expectations. Outsiders played important roles in encouraging changes in arts and crafts. Some storekeepers became patrons to particular artists who were then able to devote themselves full time to their craft. Traders would often encourage changes, such as new objects—for example, ashtrays and cups made of pottery. Scholars have played a role too. Some have helped artisans learn about styles of the past that had disappeared. For example, with the encouragement of anthropologists and others in the Santa Fe area, Maria and Julian Martinez of San Ildefonso Pueblo brought back a polished black-on-black pottery style originally produced by nearby ancient peoples.[48]

Modern Navajo weavings at the Hubbell Trading Post National Historic Site, Arizona. Navajo weaving generally became more complex over time.

Until about 50 years ago the Pintupi of the western Australian desert were foragers. They were not involved in commercial activities until they were settled on reserves by the government. The Pintupi still maintain a rich ceremonial life reenacting the mystery of events that gives the world its shape and social meaning. These rituals involve song, myths, body decoration, and the production of objects. In 1971, after encouragement from an "outsider," some Pintupi began to turn their designs into acrylic paintings on canvas or wood and put them up for sale. Are these designs "authentic" or just made up for others, such as tourists and art dealers? Painters insist that the designs are not "made up" but rather represent the Dreaming, or stories of the ancestral beings. These paintings are now sold in major Australian cities and have made their way to cities all over the world. Some are now considered "fine art" and are accompanied by documentation of stories of the ancestral beings' travel across the landscape. Thus, the acrylic paintings acquire value in the outside world by invoking tradition.[49]

One characteristic of what is labeled "fine art" appears to be its exclusivity.[50] If it is prepared for tourists, the presumption is that it is turned out in quantity and is therefore lacking in the innovativeness and skill of "fine art." The presumption is that is bought by people, not very knowledgeable, as souvenirs rather than art. However, the fuzzy line between the two is illustrated by the creation of the New Guinea Sculpture Garden at Stanford University.[51] A group of Iatmul and Kwoma men from the Sepik River region of New Guinea called "master-carvers" were brought to Stanford to create sculptures in a forest-like space on the campus meant to "evoke" the Sepik River environment. They were treated as "artists" and they had titles for their art and their name indicated on the work, but despite being encouraged to avoid traditional forms and to express their individual artistry and innovation in this new space, they created variations of their work back home. Yet back home, where supposedly art was just for money and tourists, carvers actually strived for creating unique objects. They also procured new materials and experimented with new aesthetic styles, as we believe artists do. So, were the carvers brought to Stanford doing more "fine art" because they were more creative, or were the carvers back home labeled doing "tourist art" more creative?

Some of the artistic changes that have occurred after contact with the West are partly predictable from the results of cross-cultural research on artistic variation. Remember that Fischer found that egalitarian societies typically had less complex designs and more symmetry than did stratified societies. With the loss of traditional ways of making a living and with the increase in wage labor and commercial enterprises, many Native American groups have become more socially stratified. Extrapolating from Fischer's results, we would predict that designs on visual art should become more complex and asymmetrical as social stratification increases. Indeed, if early reservation art (1870–1901) among the Shoshone-Bannock of southeastern Idaho is compared with their recent art (1973–1983), it is clear that the art has become more complex as social stratification has increased.[52] It could also be true that the art changed because the artists came to realize that more asymmetry and complexity would sell better to people who collect art.

Summary and Review

Body Decoration and Adornment

17.1 Analyze the purposes of body decoration and adornment.

- People in all societies decorate or adorn their bodies for aesthetic considerations; to delineate social position, rank, sex, occupation, local and ethnic identity, or religion within a society; and for sexual provocation.

- The level of permanence of body decoration and adornment can reflect important characteristics of a culture.

 Body decoration is universal; what are some of the ways it varies among cultures?

Explaining Variation in the Arts

17.2 Explain variation in the arts in relationship to other societal features.

- Societies vary in terms of an emphasis on uniqueness, materials, ideas of beauty, and characteristic styles and themes. Form and style in visual art, music, dance, and folklore are very much influenced by other aspects of culture.

- Art may express the typical feelings, anxieties, and experiences of people in a culture. The form of art a society prefers may reflect its way of life; choice and use of artistic materials often reflects how a society views its environment.

- Repetition of elements, use of space, symmetry, and presence or absence of enclosed figures are stylistic features that vary strongly depending on the degree of stratification.

- Making sense of another culture's music is similar to making sense of a foreign language. Cultural differences in music reflect widely varying rhythms, singing styles, and tonal ranges. Some features of song style can be correlated with cultural complexity.

- Folklore is not always clearly separable from the other arts, particularly music and dance.

 How do some aspects of art (visual art and music) vary with differences in social and political systems?

Viewing the Art of Other Cultures

17.3 Identify ethnocentric attitudes and practices toward non-Western art by Westerners.

- Westerners tend to classify art from less complex societies as "primitive art" and display it differently from Western and Oriental art.

- To Westerners, non-Western art is considered unchanging in style, but studies indicate that members of the non-Western cultures are aware of nuanced changes in their art.

- Although it seems that individual artists can usually be recognized in any community, some societies do appear to be more communal than others in their art style.

 What are some of the specific differences in how Westerners view their own art and art of non-Western societies?

Artistic Change, Culture Contact, and Global Trade

17.4 Assess the relationship of culture contact and artistic change.

- As cultures come into contact, the art within those cultures tends to change, partly to reflect the contact itself and partly because new materials and techniques are introduced.

- As societies change and become more complex after cultural contact and global trade, changes such as social stratification may well affect the art of those societies.

 What are some examples of changes in art?

Think on it

1. How **innovative** or original can a successful artist be? Explain your answer.

2. What kind of **art** do you prefer, and why?

3. Do you think art made for **tourists** is inferior? Whatever you think, why do you think so?

LEARNING OBJECTIVES

18.1 Explain how cultural, economic, and social factors can cause or exacerbate natural events and cause disasters and famine.

18.2 Describe the factors that lead to inadequate housing and homelessness.

18.3 Discuss the magnitude, causes, and consequences of family violence.

18.4 Explain how cultural and societal features relate to crime, especially in regard to homicide.

18.5 Discuss warfare in terms of cultural, social, and ecological factors, and describe the reasons societies go to war.

18.6 Describe the difficulty of defining terrorism and discuss what is known about the factors associated with it.

18.7 Discuss some lessons learned from anthropology that could make the world a better place.

Almost every day, the news makes us aware that terrible social problems threaten people around the world. War, crime, family violence, natural disasters, poverty, famine—all these and more are the lot of millions of people in many places. And now there is an increasing threat of terrorism. Can anthropological and other research help us solve these global social problems? Many anthropologists and other social scientists think so.

High-tech communications have increased our awareness of problems all over the world, and we seem to be increasingly more aware of, and bothered by, problems in our own society. For these two reasons, and perhaps also because we know much more than we used to about human behavior, we may be more motivated now to try to solve those problems. We call them "social problems" not just because a lot of people worry about them but also because they have social causes and consequences, and treating or solving them requires changes in social behavior.

The idea that we can solve social problems, even the enormous ones such as war and family violence, is based on two assumptions. First, we have to assume that it is possible to discover the causes of a problem. And second, we have to assume that we may be able to do something about the causes, once they are discovered, and thereby eliminate or reduce the problem. Not everyone would agree with these assumptions. Some would say that our understanding of a social problem cannot ever be sufficient to suggest a solution guaranteed to work. To be sure, no understanding in science is perfect or certain; there is always some probability that even a well-supported explanation is wrong or incomplete. But the uncertainty of knowledge does not rule out the possibility of application. With regard to social problems, the possible payoff from even incomplete understanding could be a better and safer world. This possibility is what motivates many researchers who investigate social problems. After all, the history of the various sciences strongly supports the belief that scientific understanding can often allow humans to control nature, not just predict and explain it. Why should human behavior be any different?

So what do we know about some of the global social problems, and what policies or solutions are suggested by what we know?

Natural Events, Disasters, and Famine

18.1 ▶ Explain how cultural, economic, and social factors can cause or exacerbate natural events and cause disasters and famine.

Natural events such as floods, droughts, earthquakes, and insect infestations are usually but not always beyond human control, but their effects are not.[1] We call such events accidents or emergencies when only a few people are affected, but we call them disasters when large numbers of people or large areas are affected. The harm caused is not just a function of the magnitude of the natural event. Between 1980 and 2002, the United States had slightly more earthquakes than India. Yet over 32,000 people died in those earthquakes compared to about 140 people in the United States. More broadly, richer countries have lower death tolls even though there is no significant differences in exposure to natural shocks or their magnitude between rich and poor countries.[2] The vast majority of deaths occurred in lower income countries.[3] These comparative figures demonstrate that climatic and other events in the physical environment become worse disasters because of events or conditions in the social environment.

If people live in houses that are designed to withstand earthquakes—if governing bodies require such construction and the economy is developed enough so that people can afford such construction—the effects of an earthquake will be minimized. If poor people are forced to live in deforested floodplains to be able to find land to farm (as in coastal Bangladesh), if the poor are forced to live in shanties built on precarious hillsides (like those of Rio de Janeiro), the floods and landslides that follow severe hurricanes and rainstorms can kill thousands and even hundreds of thousands.

Thus, because natural events can have greater or lesser effects on human life, depending on social conditions, they are also social problems, problems that have social causes and possible social solutions. Legislating safe construction of a house is a social solution. The 1976 earthquake in Tangsham, China, killed 250,000 people, mostly because they lived in top-heavy adobe houses that could not withstand severe shaking, whereas the 1989 Loma Prieta earthquake in California, which was of comparable intensity, killed 65 people.

A family in Sichuan gathers for a meal outside their home after a 2013 earthquake. Tens of thousands of homeless survivors of China's devastating quake are living in makeshift tents or on the streets, facing shortages of food and supplies as well as an uncertain future.

One might think that floods, of all disasters, are the least influenced by social factors. After all, without a huge runoff from heavy rains or snow melt, there cannot be a flood. But consider why so many people have died from Hwang River floods in China. (One such flood, in 1931, killed nearly 4 million people, making it the deadliest single disaster in history.) The floods in the Hwang River basin have occurred mostly because the clearing of nearby forests for fuel and farmland has allowed enormous quantities of silt to wash into the river, raising the riverbed and increasing the risk of floods that burst the dams that normally would contain them. The risk of disastrous flooding would be greatly reduced if different social conditions prevailed—if people were not so dependent on firewood for fuel, if they did not have to farm close to the river, or if the dams were higher and more numerous.

Famines, episodes of severe starvation and resultant death, often appear to be triggered by physical events such as a severe drought or a hurricane that kills or knocks down food trees and plants. But famines do not inevitably follow such an event. Social conditions can prevent a famine or increase the likelihood of one. Consider what is likely to happen in Samoa after a hurricane.[4] Whole villages that have lost their coconut and breadfruit trees, as well as their taro patches, pick up and move for a period of time to other villages where they have relatives and friends. The visitors stay and are fed until some of their cultivated trees and plants start to bear food again, at which point they return home. This kind of intervillage reciprocity probably could occur only in a society that has relatively little inequality in wealth. Nowadays, the central government or international agencies may also help out by providing food and other supplies.

Researchers point out that famine rarely results from just one bad food production season. During one bad season, people can usually cope by getting help from relatives, friends, and neighbors or by switching to less desirable foods. The 1974 famine in the African Sahel occurred after eight years of bad weather; a combination of drought, floods, and a civil war in 1983 to 1984 contributed to the subsequent famine in the Sahel, Ethiopia, and Sudan.[5] Famine almost always has some social causes. Who has rights to the available food, and do those who have more food distribute it to those who have less? Cross-cultural research suggests that societies with individual property rights rather than shared rights are more likely to suffer famine.[6] Nonetheless, government assistance can lessen the risk of famine in societies with individual property.

Relief provided by government may not always get to those who need it the most. In fact, famine can occur in countries that have adequate food but that fail to distribute it to populations with severe food stress.[7] Or, if food is distributed, it may not be equitable. In India, for example, the central government provides help in time of drought to minimize the risk of famine. But the food and other supplies provided to a village may end up being unequally distributed, following the rules of social and gender stratification. Members of the local elite arrange to function as distributors and find ways to manipulate the relief efforts to their advantage. Lower-class and lower-caste families still suffer the most. Within the family, biases against females, particularly young girls and elderly women, translate into their getting less food. It is no wonder, then, that in times of food shortage and famine, the poor and other socially disadvantaged people are especially likely to die.[8]

Considerable progress has been made in eliminating famine. There have been no famines in Europe since the 1940s and none in Asia since the 1970s. Contemporary famines are now confined to sub-Saharan Africa. Why do they persist? Since a majority of Africans produce their own food, failures of production are partially to blame. But for a famine to occur, there also must be exchange failures (inability to barter or purchase food). In addition, a famine will only result if social support networks, governments, or the international community provide inadequate help. The famine of 1999–2000 in Ethiopia in the pastoral Somali region followed a multi-year drought in 1997 and 1998. Both drought and disease killed many livestock. The Somali relied heavily on sales of livestock to the Middle East, and the loss of cash meant that they could not buy sufficient food. Ethiopia had an "early warning system" in place, but it focused on the highland areas, not the lowlands where the pastoralists lived. Some NGOs sounded warnings, but they were ignored until the BBC started broadcasting information. By the time information got out, the response by the international community could not avert much of the loss of life.[9]

Thus, the people of a society may not all be equally at risk in case of disaster. In socially stratified societies, the poor particularly suffer. They are likely to be forced to overcultivate, overgraze, and deforest their land, making it more susceptible to degradation. A society most helps those it values the most.

People in the past, and even recently in some places, viewed extreme natural events as divine retribution for human immorality. For example, the great flood described in the Old Testament was understood to be God's doing. But scientific research increasingly allows us to understand the natural causes of disasters, and particularly the social conditions that magnify or minimize their effects. To reduce the impact of disasters, then, we need to reduce the social conditions that magnify the effects of disasters. If humans are responsible for those social conditions, humans can change them. If earthquakes destroy houses that are too flimsy, we can build stronger houses. If floods caused by overcultivation and overgrazing kill people directly (or indirectly by stripping their soils), we can grow new forest cover and provide new job opportunities to flood-plain farmers. If prolonged climate-related disasters or wars threaten famine, social distribution systems can lessen the risk. In short, we may not be able to do much about the weather or other physical causes of disasters, but we can do a lot—if we want to—about the social factors that make disasters disastrous. The challenge is—how do you make people want to?

Inadequate Housing and Homelessness

18.2 Describe the factors that lead to inadequate housing and homelessness.

The world's urban population, particularly in developing countries, is growing rapidly. In 2010, a slight majority of the people in the world lived in urban areas, and it is projected to be about 70 percent by 2050.[10] But rapid growth is occurring in places with inadequate ability to provide decent infrastructure. And so, in most nations, those who are poor typically live in inadequate housing, in areas we call *slums*. In many of the developing nations, where cities are growing very rapidly, squatter settlements emerge as people build dwellings (often makeshift) that are typically declared illegal, either because the land is illegally occupied or because the dwellings violate building codes. Squatter settlements are often located in degraded environments that are subject to flooding and mudslides or have inadequate or polluted water.[11] The magnitude of the problem is made clear in some statistics. As of 2012, it was estimated that 1 billion people or about 33 percent of urban dwellers lived in slums. In some world regions, the slum problem is much worse. In Africa,

62 percent of urban dwellers live in slums.[12] Four in ten of the nonpermanent houses in slums were in high-risk environments such as flood zones or landslide-prone areas.[13]

But contrary to what some people have assumed, not all dwellers in illegal settlements are poor; all but the upper-income elite may be found in such settlements.[14] Moreover, although squatter settlements have problems, they are not chaotic and unorganized places that are full of crime. Most of the dwellers are employed, aspire to get ahead, live in intact nuclear families, and help each other.[15] People live in such settlements because they cannot find affordable housing, and they house themselves as best they can. Many researchers think that such self-help tendencies should be assisted to improve housing because governments in developing countries can seldom afford costly public housing projects. But they could invest somewhat in infrastructure—sewers, water supplies, roads—and provide construction materials to those who are willing to do the work required to improve their dwellings.[16] In some countries, the urban slum and shack dwellers have organized into more formal local collective action groups that have even joined into international alliances with the support of some NGOs. Local federations have pushed for co-production, which means that the local collective action group becomes actively engaged in design, implementation, and management of improvements to their communities.[17] Thailand is one of the countries that supports these collective efforts to upgrade slums by offering subsidies and soft loans. But the communities must first form community savings groups before they can get government assistance. They then need to negotiate for land to lease or buy collectively. The cooperative can then make plans and loans to individuals. The importance of collective ownership is not only that it fosters working together for a collective good, but it also prevents individuals from selling out as soon as their house is upgraded.[18]

Housing in slum areas or shantytowns does provide shelter, minimal though it may be. But many people in many areas of the world have no homes at all. Even in countries such as the United States, which is affluent by world standards, large numbers of people are homeless. They sleep in parks, over steam vents, in doorways, subways, and cardboard boxes. Homelessness is difficult to measure. In 1987, more than 1 million people were estimated to be homeless in the United States.[19] About 3.5 million people experienced homelessness in 2000, almost 40 percent of them children. Most researchers agree that homelessness has increased in the last few decades; the United States Conference of Mayors reported increases after the recession in 2007.[20]

Who are the homeless, and how did they get to be homeless? We have relatively little research on these questions, but what we do have suggests differences in the causes of homelessness in different parts of the world. In the United States, unemployment and the shortage of decent low-cost housing appear to be at least partly responsible for the large number of homeless people.[21] But there is also another factor: the deliberate policy to reduce the number of people hospitalized for mental illness and other disabilities. For example, from the mid-1960s to the mid-1990s, New York State released thousands of patients from mental hospitals. Many of these ex-patients had to live in cheap hotels or poorly monitored facilities with virtually no support network. With very little income, they found it especially hard to cope with their circumstances. Ellen Baxter and Kim Hopper, who studied the homeless in New York City, suggest that one event is rarely sufficient to render a person homeless. Rather, poverty and disability (mental or physical) seem to lead to one calamity after another and, finally, homelessness.[22]

Many people cannot understand why homeless individuals do not want to go to municipal shelters, but observations and interviews with the homeless individuals suggest that violence pervades the municipal shelters, particularly the men's shelters. Many feel safer on the streets. Some private charities provide safe shelters and a caring environment. These shelters are filled, but the number of homeless people they can accommodate is small.[23] Even single-room-occupancy hotels are hardly better. Many of them are infested with vermin, the common bathrooms are filthy, and they, like the shelters, are often dangerous.[24]

Some poor individuals may be socially isolated, with few or no friends and relatives and little or no social contact. But a society with many such individuals does not necessarily have much homelessness. Socially isolated individuals, even mentally ill individuals, could still have housing, or so the experience of Melbourne, Australia, suggests. Universal health insurance there pays for health care as well as medical practitioners' visits to isolated and ill individuals, wherever they live. Disabled individuals receive a pension or sickness benefits sufficient to allow them to live in a room or apartment. And there is still a considerable supply of cheap

Applied Anthropology

Climate Change: What Can Anthropologists Contribute to Research and Policy?

Climate change is a global concern. Scientists are about 90 percent certain that human activities, such as the burning of coal and fossil fuels, over the past 250 years have led to the world heating up. And they are worried about the worsening consequences. There is already increased melting of polar ice and the more the temperature rises, the more the higher sea level will flood low-lying coastal areas, including many world cities. Storms, floods, and droughts will continue to intensify. The weather will become even more erratic. Places at high latitudes are likely to see increased rainfall and snow; places at low latitudes are likely to have less rainfall and more drought. The earth normally traps heat in the atmosphere by gases such as carbon dioxide, water vapor, and methane. These are called "greenhouse gases." And while some warmth is essential for life, the amounts of these gases have dramatically increased. Scientists have told us that the need to reduce greenhouse gases and prepare for more extreme conditions is *now*. But bringing about change is not easy.

Many environmental anthropologists use ethnographic methods to study how communities perceive changes in the weather and landscapes around them as well as the measures they take to try to adapt. So, for example, Sakka horse and cattle breeders living in Siberia live in land with extreme temperature fluctuations from −76 degrees to 104 degrees Fahrenheit. Their cattle are in barns for nine months a year and live on hay gathered in the summer. But almost everyone notes that the climate has changed; winter and spring both come later, the weather is erratic, and there is so much rain in the summer that hay doesn't grow well and doesn't dry out. But the Sakka do not frame climate change the way we do. Some attribute the changes to the building of hydroelectric dams, others to rockets "mixing up" the sky. The Sakka adapted before around the year 1200 when they moved from more southerly climates to Siberia. But it is not clear that they can adapt now. The melting permafrost may turn their land into swampland unfit for animal husbandry.

Susan Crate points out that "global climate change—its causes, effects, and amelioration—is intimately and ultimately about culture (p. 570)," but it is the industrialized and post-industrial world that has largely caused global warming—therefore dramatic change will be needed in the cultural behavior of that world. Therefore, many argue that cultural anthropologists need to broaden their horizons and become more engaged in understanding how policy is formulated by climate scientists and governments, and they need to work with interdisciplinary teams. They also need to show how the effects of climate change are related to the broader social, political, and economic context of the people they study, and finally, they need to engage more—both by making the situation known of the people they study and engaging in projects that plan and pursue how to cope with climate change.

Understanding how societies have responded to climate change in the past is an important component. Archaeologists have studied livelihoods, the interaction of groups, and changes in local environments in the past. In some places, decades-long or century-long droughts have led to extreme changes—abandonment of sites, regional collapses, and movements to other places; smaller environmental changes, such as the Little Ice Age in Europe; and decreased agricultural productivity.

Sources: Oerlemans 2005; Baer and Singer 2009; IPPC 2007; Crate 2008; Roncoli, Crane and Orlove 2009.

housing in Melbourne. Research in Melbourne suggests that a severe mental disorder often precedes living in marginal accommodations—city shelters, commercial shelters, and cheap single rooms. About 50 percent of the people living in such places were diagnosed as previously having some form of mental illness; this percentage is similar to what seems to be the case for homeless people and people living in marginal accommodations in the United States.

The contrast between the United States and Australia makes it clear that social and political policies cause homelessness. Individuals with similar characteristics live in both Australia and the United States, but a larger percentage of them are homeless in the United States.[25] As Kim Hopper noted, perhaps the important question is not what makes some people homeless but rather why the rest of the people in a society tolerate homelessness.[26]

Because homelessness cannot occur if everybody can afford housing, some people would say that homelessness can happen only in a society with great extremes in income. Statistics on income distribution in the United States clearly show that, since the 1970s, the rich have gotten much richer and the poor have gotten much poorer.[27] The United States now has more income inequality than any country in Western Europe and more than most high-income countries. In fact, the profile of inequality in the United States more closely resembles that of developing countries, such as Cambodia and Morocco[28] (see the discussion in the chapter on social stratification).

In the United States and many other countries, most homeless people are adults. Whereas adults are "allowed" to be homeless, public sensibilities in the United States appear to be outraged by the sight of children living in the streets; when authorities discover homeless children, they try to find shelters or foster homes for them. But many countries have "street children." In the late 1980s, 80 million of the world's children lived in the streets: 40 million in Latin America, 20 million in Asia, 10 million in Africa and the Middle East, and 10 million elsewhere.[29] In the 2000s, the estimated number grew to about 150 million worldwide.[30]

Lewis Aptekar, who studied street children in Cali, Colombia, reported some surprises.[31] Whereas many of the homeless in the United States and Australia are mentally disabled, the street children in Cali, ranging in age from 7 to 16, are mostly free of mental problems; by and large, they also test normally on intelligence tests. In addition, even though many street children come from abusive homes or never had homes, they usually seem happy and enjoy the support and friendship of other street children. They cleverly and creatively look for ways to get money, frequently through entertaining passersby.

Although observers might think that the street children must have been abandoned by their families, most of them in actuality have at least one parent they keep in touch with. Street life begins slowly, not abruptly; children usually do not stay on the streets full time until they are about 13 years old. Though street children in Cali seem to be in better physical and mental shape than their siblings who stay at home, they often are viewed as a "plague." The street children come from poor families and cope with their lives as best they can, so why are they not viewed with pity and compassion? Aptekar suggests that well-off families see the street children as a threat because a life independent of family may appeal to children, even those from well-off families, who wish to be free of parental constraint and authority.

Whether people become homeless and whether they have shantytowns seem to depend on a society's willingness to share wealth and help those in need. The street children of Cali may remind us that children as well as adults need companionship and care. Addressing physical needs without responding to emotional needs may get people off the streets, but it won't get them a "home."

A homeless boy in Calcutta, India with his belongings.

Migrants and Immigrants

Refugees Are a Global Social Problem

The continuing turmoil in many countries throughout the world has created a flow of refugees that is much larger than ever before in world history. An estimated 140 million people became refugees in the 20th century. In 2012 alone, over 45 million people were displaced; the highest number since 1994. More than half of the refugees in 2012 came from five countries—Afghanistan, Somalia, Iraq, Syria, and Sudan. In the past, thousands of people might have had to flee persecution and war. Now that refugees number in the many millions per year, the problems of how to minimize suffering and find long-term solutions are more complex. Refugees flee to other parts of the country (internally displaced persons), to neighboring countries, and some to countries on the other side of the world. The refugees from the civil wars in Somalia are not unusual; 10 percent of the Somali population is now living outside of Somalia, perhaps a million people altogether. Much of the burden of sheltering refugees falls to nearby countries. For example, over 640,000 have sought refuge from the Syrian conflict in Iraq, Turkey, Lebanon, Jordan, and Egypt. Often people are channeled into refugee camps where the United Nations and other international agencies try to find "durable" solutions. Voluntary repatriation is considered the ideal solution, but it requires that the conflict be over and that the home country is willing to protect and reintegrate those who have fled. The process, however, can be a long one, especially if conflict is protracted. Resettlement in other countries is another option, but not that many countries are willing to take a large number of people. For example, in 2012, half a million refugees were repatriated,

Kachin women gather as children play at a camp for internally displaced people in northern Kachin state, Myanmar.

but only about 89,000 people were resettled in other countries (the United States received about 66,000 people).

What is often not realized about refugees is that often families strategize about who stays and who goes. Persecution is real, but it takes resources to flee. That is, those who are better off in the first place have the best chance to flee the furthest. Those family members who do get out may be able to channel money to other family members back home to help them leave as well.

Almost all people seeking refuge are fleeing conflict. Therefore the ultimate answer to the problem of refugees has to be to prevent those conflicts in the first place or to minimize their escalation.

Some researchers are predicting that a whole new type of refugee problem will soon emerge—"climate change refugees." With changes in climate, millions of people will be forced to leave their homes because of flooding or worsening drought. The crisis is likely to be worse in developing countries that haven't been able to commit resources to adapt to climate changes. Migration may be the only choice for some nations like Tuvalu, which consists of low-lying islands in the Pacific. One estimate is that by 2050 there will be over 200 million climate refugees. The world has not only been slow to acknowledge climate change, but little has been done to plan for it. If there will be so many climate refugees, there will need to be some analogous mechanisms for coping with and resettling these refugees, just like some have developed for refugees fleeing persecution.

Sources: Van Hear 2004, 2006; UNHCR 2013; Biermann and Boas 2010.

Family Violence and Abuse

18.3 Discuss the magnitude, causes, and consequences of family violence.

In U.S. society, we hear regularly about the abuse of spouses and children, which makes us think that such abuse is increasing—but is it? This seems to be a simple question, but it is not so simple to answer. We have to decide what we mean by *abuse*.

Is physical punishment of a child who does something wrong child abuse? Not so long ago, teachers in public schools in the United States were allowed to discipline children by hitting them with rulers or paddles, and many parents used switches or belts. Many would consider these practices to be child abuse, but were they abusive when they were generally accepted? Some would argue that abuse is going beyond what a culture considers appropriate behavior. Others would disagree and would focus on the violence and severity of parents' or teachers' behavior, not the cultural judgment of appropriateness. And abuse need not involve physical violence. It could be argued that verbal aggression and neglect may be just as harmful as physical aggression. Neglect presents its own problems of definition. People from other cultures might argue that we act abusively when we put an infant or child alone in a room to sleep.[32] Few would disagree about severe injuries that kill a child or spouse or require medical treatment, but other disciplinary behaviors are more difficult to judge.

To avoid having to decide what is or is not abuse, many researchers focus their studies on variation in the frequencies of specific behaviors. For example, one can ask which societies have physical punishment of children without calling physical punishment abusive.

According to four national interview surveys of married or cohabiting couples in the United States conducted from 1975 onwards, physical violence against older children appears to have decreased in frequency over time, as did serious assaults by husbands against wives. But serious assaults by wives on husbands did not decrease.[33] In fact, to many people's surprise, in over 200 studies of partner violence carried out mostly in the United States, husbands and wives commit about an equal number of attacks on their partners.[34] Perhaps the perception that males commit more violence toward their wives stems from the fact that wives are more often injured. The United States remains a society with a lot of physical violence in families. By far the most violence is directed to children by parents. Ninety-four percent of parents report hitting a 3- to 5-year-old child during the year. (Parents often do not consider slapping or spanking violence.) Next most violent group are siblings to other siblings, then toddlers hitting parents. While parents being violent to each other is the rarest type of family violence in the family, it is far from rare. About 16 percent of men and women report experiencing violence from a partner.[35] If we focus on crimes reported to the police, family violence accounted for 33 percent of all crimes, and nearly a quarter of murders were against a family member. And in terms of crime, females are more likely than males to be victims of family violence crimes, but males are more likely to experience violent crime from strangers and acquaintances.[36] Just as women face more risk from those close to them, so do children. When a child is the target of violence, it usually comes from the birth mother.[37]

Cross-culturally, if one form of family violence occurs, others are also likely. So, for example, wife beating, husband beating, child punishment, and fighting among siblings are all significantly associated with each other. But the relationships among these types of family violence are not that strong, which means that they cannot be considered as different facets of the same phenomenon. Indeed, somewhat different factors seem to explain different forms of family violence.[38] We focus here on two forms of violence that are most prevalent cross-culturally: violence against children and violence against wives.

Violence Against Children

Cross-culturally, many societies practice and allow infanticide. Frequent reasons for infanticide include illegitimacy, deformity of the infant, twins, too many children, or that the infant is unwanted. Infanticide is usually performed by the mother, but this does not mean that she is uncaring; it may mean that she cannot adequately feed or care for the infant or that it has a poor chance to survive. The reasons for infanticide are similar to those given for abortion. Therefore, it seems that infanticide may be performed when abortion does not work or when unexpected qualities of the infant (e.g., deformity) force the mother to reevaluate her ability to raise the child.[39]

Much of the violence directed at children is believed to be morally correct—a necessary way of teaching children to behave. The old proverb warns: "Spare the rod and spoil the child." In recent years in the United States and elsewhere, there has been some turning away from corporal or bodily punishment, and more people in this country and elsewhere would like parents to stop spanking their children. They point to evidence that spanking and other corporal punishment is associated with a child later hitting others in kindergarten or elsewhere. Later in life, children who are corporally punished are more likely to physically assault their dating partners or spouses, be convicted of a crime, and have bouts of depression.[40] So it is possible that corporal punishment is a cradle of violence.

So if we want to reduce family violence, one thing we could do is reduce the conditions that predict corporal punishment of children. The frequency of corporal punishment does not vary that much from one country to another, and most approve of the practice. There is more variation in the cross-cultural record, and we can use that record to predict the variation.

Physical punishment of children occurs at least sometimes in over 70 percent of the world's societies.[41] And physical punishment is frequent or typical in 40 percent of the world's societies.

The main predictors of corporal punishment in the ethnographic or cross-cultural record are two conditions that are practically universal in the nation-states of the world, namely, a money economy and a stratified social system. If parents want children to do well when they grow up in a world with power inequality, might parents practice corporal punishment to convey that some people (particularly employers) are much more powerful than others? To a child, parents are clearly powerful. Not only are they taller and physically stronger, they also control and dispense important resources (food, love). So, perhaps, parents may consciously or unconsciously think that, if children fear those who are more powerful, they may be less likely to get into trouble and more likely to be able to get and keep a job.[42] Research in the United States is consistent with the cross-cultural finding: Those at the bottom of the socioeconomic hierarchy are more likely than those at the top to practice corporal punishment of children.[43] Unfortunately, parents probably do not realize that physical punishment may produce more violent behavior in their children, an outcome they probably do not want or intend. Donna Goldstein poignantly describes the plight of a woman in a shantytown near Rio de Janeiro who supports more than 10 children in a one-room shack. Her discipline is harsh, but she is trying, as Goldstein points out, to ensure that the kids "have the skills, as well as the attitudes of obedience, humility, and subservience, necessary for a poor black person to survive in urban Brazil."[44]

Do these results suggest how corporal punishment of children could decrease? At one level, it is difficult to see how. Societies that use money and have social classes are not likely to become egalitarian. But societies could move in the direction of de-emphasizing economic and power inequality. When parents hit their children, it is generally not because they want their children to be violent; they want them to behave properly. If they understood the connection between parental violence and child violence, they might begin to change their practices.

Some countries already have not-so-high rates of corporal punishment. These are the more democratic countries—with contested elections that allow people to replace leaders peacefully, and laws that protect civil rights such as the right to express dissent. (The agreement to disagree, and protecting civil rights, means that you don't have to worry so much about losing your job if you disagree with your employer's beliefs.) Sweden and the other Scandinavian countries have lower rates of approval of corporal punishment. Is this because Scandinavia is more democratic, allowing people (even workers in factories) to participate more in decision making in the workplace and not just in elections? We think so. But only time will tell if increasing democracy, and less need for workers to act subservient, will translate into less violent ways of socializing children.

Violence Against Wives

Cross-culturally, wife beating is a common form of family violence; it occurs at least occasionally in about 85 percent of the world's societies. In about half the societies, wife beating is sometimes serious enough to cause permanent injury or death.[45] It is often assumed that wife beating is common in societies in which males control economic and political resources. In a cross-cultural test of this assumption, David Levinson found that not all indicators of male dominance predict wife beating, but many do. Specifically, wife beating is most common when men control the products of family labor, when men have the final say in decision making in the home, when divorce is difficult for women, when remarriage for a widow is controlled by the husband's kin, or when women do not have any female work groups.[46] Similarly, in the United States, the more one spouse in the family makes the decisions and has the power, the more physical violence occurs in the family. Wife beating is even more likely when the husband controls the household and is out of work.[47]

When we compare countries, although wife beating is widespread, there is very wide variability in prevalence. For example, in Japan, 13 percent of women report ever experiencing violence from their male partner, but it is reported as high as 61 percent in rural Peru.[48]

In some places, such as the United States and other Western countries, women are about as equally likely to be violent toward their husbands as their husbands are to them. So wife beating seems unlikely to be caused by gender inequality. As it turns out, degree of gender empowerment, or the relative emancipation of women, does predict the variability among nations. The United States and many other Western countries do not have gender equality, but they have more equality than countries like India, Korea, and Jordan. And it is in the countries with more equality that male and female partners are about equal in their propensity to hit each other; it is in the more male-dominated countries that males are much more likely to hit their spouses than the other way around. It is also the case that in such countries, wife beating tends to be approved of.[49]

Wife beating appears to be related to broader patterns of violence. Societies that have violent methods of conflict resolution within communities, physical punishment of criminals, high frequency of warfare, and cruelty toward enemies generally have more wife beating.[50]

Reducing the Risk

What can be done to minimize family violence? First, we have to recognize that probably nothing can be done as long as people in a society do not acknowledge that a problem exists. If severe child punishment and wife beating are perfectly acceptable to almost everyone in a society, they are unlikely to be considered social problems that need solutions. In our own society, many programs are designed to take abused children or wives out of the family situation or to punish the abuser. (Of course, in these situations, the violence has already occurred and was serious enough to have been noticed.) Cross-culturally, at least with respect to wife beating, intervention by others seems to be successful only if the intervention occurs before violence gets serious. As one would expect, however, those societies most prone to a high rate of wife beating are the least likely to practice immediate intervention. More helpful perhaps, but admittedly harder to arrange, is the promotion of conditions of life that are associated with low family violence. Research so far suggests that promoting the equality of men and women and the sharing of childrearing responsibilities may go a long way toward lessening incidents of family violence.[51] And reducing the risk of corporal punishment of children may reduce the risk of violence when they have families.

18.4 Explain how cultural and societal features relate to crime, especially in regard to homicide.

Crime

What is a crime in one society is not necessarily a crime in another. Just as it is difficult to decide what constitutes abuse, it is difficult to define *crime*. In one society, it may be a crime to walk over someone's land without permission; in another, there might not be any concept of personal ownership and therefore no concept of trespassing. In seeking to understand variation in crime, many researchers have not surprisingly preferred to compare those behaviors that are more or less universally considered crimes and that are reliably reported. For example, in a large-scale comparison of crime in 110 nations over a span of 70 years, Dane Archer and Rosemary Gartner concentrated on homicide rates. They argued that homicide is harder for the public to hide and for officials to ignore than other crimes. A comparison of interviews about crime with police records suggests that homicide is the most reliably reported crime in official records.[52]

Nations not only have very different crime rates when we compare them at a given point in time, the rates also vary over time within a nation. In the last 600 years, homicide rates have generally declined in Western societies. In England, where homicide rates have been well documented for centuries, the chance of murder during the 13th and 14th centuries was 10 times higher than in England today. Around 2010, some of the lowest homicide rates were found in Norway, Austria, Hong Kong, Japan, Bahrain, and Oman. Some of the highest homicide rates were in Jamaica, El Salvador, and Venezuela. The United States has a higher homicide rate than almost any of the countries in Europe.[53]

One of the clearest findings to emerge from comparative studies of crime is that war is associated with higher rates of homicide. Archer and Gartner compared changes in homicide rates of nations before and after major wars. Whether a nation is defeated or victorious, homicide rates tend to increase after a war. This result is consistent with the idea that a society or nation legitimizes violence during wartime. That is, during wartime, societies approve of killing the enemy; afterward, homicide rates may go up because inhibitions against killing have been relaxed.[54] Ted Gurr suggested that the long-term downtrend in crime in Western societies seems to be consistent with an increasing emphasis on humanistic values and nonviolent achievement of goals. But such goals may be temporarily suspended during wartime. In the United States, for example, surges in violent crime rates occurred during the 1860s and 1870s (during and after the Civil War), after World War I, after World War II, and during the Vietnam War.[55] But recently the homicide rate in the United States has declined.[56]

In the types of societies that anthropologists have typically studied, homicide statistics are not often available. However, where statistics are available the variation appears to be much greater than among modern nations. Nations vary from about .5 homicides per 100,000 people to about 52 per 100,000. Using statistics calculated by anthropologists, the range is from about 1 to 683.[57] Thus, some of the highest homicide rates described are more than 10 times the rate of any known country today. Cross-cultural studies of homicide usually measure homicide rates by comparing and rank-ordering ethnographers' statements about the frequency of homicide. For example, the statement that murder is "practically unheard of" is taken to mean that the murder rate is lower than where it is reported that "homicide is not uncommon." Despite the fact that the data on cultural homicide rates are not quantitative, the cross-cultural results are consistent with the cross-national results; more war is usually associated with more homicide and assault, as well as with socially approved aggressive behaviors (as in aggressive games) and severe physical punishment for wrongdoing.[58] A cross-cultural study suggests that the more war a society has, the more the society socializes or trains boys in aggression, and such socialization strongly predicts higher rates of homicide and assault.[59]

Capital punishment—execution of criminals—is severe physical punishment for wrongdoing. It is commonly thought that the prospect of capital punishment deters would-be murderers. Yet, cross-national research suggests otherwise. More countries show murder rates going down rather than up after capital punishment was abolished.[60] Capital punishment may legitimize violence rather than deter it.

Research conducted in the United States suggests that juvenile delinquents (usually boys) are likely to come from broken homes, with the father absent for much of the time the boy is growing up. The conclusion often drawn is that father absence somehow increases the likelihood of delinquency and adult forms of physical violence. But other conditions that may cause delinquency are also associated with broken homes, conditions such as the stigma of not having a "regular" family and the generally low standard of living of such families. It is therefore important to conduct research in other societies, in which father absence does not occur in concert with these other factors, to see if father absence by itself is related to physical violence.

For example, in many polygynous societies, children grow up in a mother-child household; the father lives separately and is seldom around the child. Does the father absence explanation of delinquency and violence fit such societies? The answer is apparently yes: Societies in which children are reared in mother-child households, where fathers sleep at a distance, or the father spends little time caring for the child tend to have more physical violence by males than do societies in which fathers spend time with children.[61] The rate of violent crime is also more frequent in nations that have more women than men, which is consistent with the theory that father absence increases violence.[62]

More research is needed to discover exactly what accounts for these relationships. It is possible, as some suggest, that boys growing up without fathers are apt to act "supermasculine" to show how "male" they are. But it is also possible that mothers who rear children alone have more frustration and more anger, and therefore are likely to provide an aggressive role model for the child. In addition, high male mortality in war and an excess of women predicts polygyny; therefore, boys in polygynous societies are likely to be exposed to a warrior tradition.[63]

Trying to act supermasculine, however, may be likely to involve violence only if aggression is an important component of the male gender role in society. If men were expected by society to be sensitive, caring, and nonviolent, boys who grew up without fathers might try to be supersensitive and supercaring. So society's expectations for males probably shape how growing up in a mother-child household affects behavior in adolescence and later.[64] The media may also influence the expectations for males. Numerous studies in the United States show that, even controlling for other factors like parental neglect, family income, and mental illness, more television watching in childhood and adolescence predicts

Evidence indicates that violence on TV encourages violence in real life.

more overt aggression later. Estimates show that an hour of prime-time television depicts 3–5 violent acts, and an hour of children's television depicts 20–25 violent acts.[65]

One widely held idea is that poor economic conditions increase the likelihood of crime, but the relationship does not appear to be strong. Also, the findings are somewhat different for different types of crime. For example, hundreds of studies in this and other countries do not show a clear relationship between changes in economic well-being as measured by unemployment rates and changes in violent crime as measured by homicide. The rate of homicide does not appear to increase in bad times. Property crimes, however, do increase with increases in unemployment. There are some stressful conditions though that do predict more homicide. A high disease load is one such condition.[66] Homicide is usually highest in nations or societies with high poverty and income inequality.[67] Why income inequality predicts homicide but downturns in the economy do not is something of a puzzle.[68]

The fact that property crime is linked to unemployment is consistent with the cross-cultural finding that theft (but not violent crime) tends to occur less often in egalitarian societies than in stratified ones. Societies with equal access to resources usually have distribution mechanisms that offset any differences in wealth. Hence, theft should be less of a temptation and therefore less likely in an egalitarian society. Theft rates are higher in socially stratified societies despite the fact that they are more likely than egalitarian societies to have police and courts to punish crime. Societies may try to deter property and other crimes when the rates of such are high, but we do not know that these efforts actually reduce the rates.

So what does the available research suggest about how we might be able to reduce crime? The results so far indicate that homicide rates are highest in societies that socialize their boys for aggression. Such socialization is linked to war and other forms of socially approved violence—capital punishment, television and movie violence by heroes, violence in sports. The statistical evidence suggests that war encourages socialization for aggression, which in turn results unintentionally in high rates of violence. The policy implication of these results is that, if we can reduce socialization for aggression by reducing the risk of war and therefore the necessity to produce effective warriors, and if we can reduce other forms of socially approved violence, we may thereby reduce the rates of violent crime. The reduction of inequalities in wealth may also help to reduce crime, particularly theft. And although it is not yet clear why, it appears that raising boys with a male role model around may reduce the likelihood of male violence in adulthood.

War

18.5 Discuss warfare in terms of cultural, social, and ecological factors, and describe the reasons societies go to war.

There are two important points to note about war. First, war is an unfortunate fact of life in most societies known to anthropology. Almost every society had at least occasional wars when it was first described, unless it had been pacified (usually by Western colonial powers).[69] However, this does not imply that war is inevitable or "natural" since some societies were peaceful. Second, it is now fairly clear that warfare has declined over the long stretch of history.[70] That being so, the presumption is that if warfare has already declined, it can continue to decline further.

Since the Civil War, the United States has not had any wars within its territory, but it is unusual in that respect. Before pacification, most societies in the ethnographic record had frequent armed combat among communities or larger units that spoke the same language. That is, most warfare was internal to the society or language group. Even some wars in modern times involved speakers of the same language; recall the wars among Italian states before the unification of Italy and many of the "civil" wars of the last two centuries. Although people in some societies might fight against people in other societies, such "external" wars were usually not organized on behalf of the entire society or even a major section of it.[71] That is, warfare in the ethnographic record did not usually involve politically unified societies. The absolute numbers of people killed may have been small, but this does not mean that warfare in nonindustrial societies was a trivial matter. Indeed, it appears that nonindustrial warfare may have been even more lethal *proportionately* than modern warfare, judging by the fact that wars killed from 25 percent to 30 percent of the males in some nonindustrial societies.[72]

In nonindustrial societies, warfare appears to be more likely when there are unpredictable climate-related disasters (droughts, floods, hurricanes, among others) that destroy food supplies.[73] Since warfare is not predicted by chronic food shortages, it seems that people may be motivated to fight mostly by fear of future loss. If so, we would expect them to take resources when they win. And they do. The victors in war almost always take resources (land, animals, other things) from the defeated, even when the victors have no current resource problems.[74] The relationship between climate change and war has been analyzed over centuries in both China and Korea. Armed conflict appears to be greater in periods of worsening climate and more frequent disasters.[75] Another factor apparently making for more war is teaching children to mistrust others. People who grow up to be mistrustful of others may be more likely to go to war than to negotiate or seek conciliation with "enemies." Mistrust or fear of others seems to be partly caused by threat or fear of disasters.[76]

Is warfare in and between modern state societies explainable in much the same way that nonindustrial warfare seems to be explainable? Here the evidence is less clear. First, the relationship between natural disasters and war seems to be opposite in state societies. Perhaps because states usually have standing armies that need to be supplied, states appear less likely to fight when there are food-related disasters. Second, the realities of industrialized societies probably require an expanded conception of disasters. In the modern world, with its complex economic and political dependencies among nations, possible curtailments of other resources, such as oil, may be more important factors. However, interstate wars today are uncommon, and it is internal wars and civil wars that constitute most of the present armed conflict. While disasters might not clearly be related to war in state societies, recent research suggests that civil wars are predicted by the per capita income of the country—all of the wars today are in poorer regions. Conversely, in rich nations, prosperity appears to make war unattractive.[77]

Threat of disasters and poverty both indicate that people face risks to their livelihoods. War is one way to try to obtain resources, but the costs are enormous. But we may be coming to realize (since the end of the Cold War) that war is not the only way to ensure access to resources. There may be a better way in the modern world, a way that is more cost-effective as well as more preserving of human life. The international community, governments and NGOs, has already shown commitment to intervening in the face of disasters. Assurance of disaster relief worldwide might reduce the fear of disasters. But far more important than responding to disasters that have already occurred is to reduce the vulnerability of populations to disasters in the first place by reducing poverty. With respect to poverty, the United Nations has declared a commitment to reducing world poverty by half by 2015 in its Millenium Development Goals statement. If poverty is also a condition making civil war more likely, reduction in such wars should also be more likely. The certainty of international cooperation could compensate for the uncertainty of resources.

Consider how Germany and Japan have fared in the years since their "unconditional surrender" in World War II. They were forbidden to participate in the international arms race and could rely on others, particularly the United States, to protect them. Without a huge burden

Current Research and Issues

Ethnic Conflicts: Ancient Hatreds or Not?

In the period after World War II, ethnic conflicts appeared to rise dramatically and reached a peak in the early 1990s. Violent conflicts erupted between ethnic groups in the former Yugoslavia, Russia, and Spain (in Europe), in Rwanda, Sierra Leone, and the Sudan (in Africa), and in Sri Lanka and Indonesia (in Asia)—to name just a few of the many instances. Such conflicts are often thought to be intractable and inevitable because they are supposedly based on ancient hatreds. But is that true?

Social scientists are a long way from understanding the conditions that predict ethnic conflicts, but they do know that ethnic conflicts are not necessarily ancient or inevitable. For example, anthropologists who did fieldwork in the former Yugoslavia in the 1980s described villages where different ethnic groups had lived side by side for a long time without apparent difficulty. The differences between them were hardly emphasized. Mary Kay Gilliland worked in a midsize town (Slavonski Brod) in the Slavonian region of Croatia, which was part of Yugoslavia. The people in the town identified themselves as from Slavonia rather than as Croats, Serbs, Hungarians, Czechs, Muslims (from Bosnia or from Albania), or Roma (Gypsies). Mixed marriages were not uncommon, and people discussed differences in background without anger. But in 1991, when Gilliland returned to Croatia, people complained about Serb domination of the Yugoslav government and there was talk of Croatia seceding. Symbols of Croat nationalism had appeared—new place names, a new flag—and Croats were now said to speak Croatian rather than the language they shared with the Serbs (Serbo-Croatian or Croato-Serbian). Later in 1991, violence broke out between Serbs and Croats, and atrocities were committed on both sides. Ethnicity became

An Iraqi policeman of Kurdish descent walks between coffins draped with Kurdish flags. More than 700 Kurds were honored in a ceremony in northern Iraq in 2012. Estimates are that up to 180,000 people were killed when Saddam Hussein's troops began a military campaign against Iraq's minority Kurds in 1988.

a matter of life or death, and Croatia seceded from Yugoslavia. At the same time, Tone Bringa, a Norwegian anthropologist who worked in Bosnia (which was then still a region of Yugoslavia), reported that the people there also paid little attention to ethnicity. A few years later, however, ethnic violence erupted among Bosnian Serbs, Muslims, and Croats, and only the intervention of the United Nations established a precarious peace.

Ethnic differences do not always lead to violence. Most of the time, even when ethnic groups have faced discrimination, people of different ethnic backgrounds live in peace with each other. So the basic question is why do some places with ethnic differences erupt in violence, but not all? Why do different ethnic groups get along in some places?

We need more research to answer this question. With all of the forced and voluntary immigration in the world, many countries are becoming

more multiethnic or multicultural. The possibility of ethnic violence has become a global social problem. Gilliland suggests, among other things, that discontent over economic and political power (inequitable access to resources and opportunities) drove the Croatians to violence and secession. Does this predict ethnic violence more generally? Some cross-national studies have tested this and other theories, but so far there are no clear answers. A lot more is known about what doesn't predict ethnic violence than what does. For example, the degree of political repression does not predict ethnic conflict generally, nor does degree of intergroup hatred, income inequality, or colonial history. If we knew which factors generally give rise to ethnic violence, we might be able to think of ways to reduce or eliminate the causal conditions.

Sources: Gilliland 1995; Bringa 1995; M. H. Ross 2009a; J. Goldstein 2011.

of armaments, Germany and Japan thrived. But countries that competed militarily, particularly the United States and the Soviet Union at the height of the Cold War, experienced economic difficulties. Doesn't that scenario at least suggest the wisdom of international cooperation, particularly the need for international agreements to ensure worldwide disaster relief? Compared with going to war and its enormous costs, going to peace would be a bargain!

Recent research in political science and anthropology suggests an additional way to reduce the risk of war. Among the societies known to anthropology, studies indicate that people in more participatory—that is, more "democratic"—political systems rarely go to war with each other.[78] Thus, if authoritarian governments were to disappear from the world because the powerful nations of the world stopped supporting them militarily and otherwise, the world could be more peaceful for this reason too.

Although democratically governed states rarely go to war with each other, it used to be thought that they are not necessarily more peaceful in general, that they are as likely to go to war as are other kinds of political systems, but not so much with each other. For example, the United States has gone to war with Grenada, Panama, and Iraq—all authoritarian states—but not with democratic Canada, with which the United States has also had disputes. But now a consensus is emerging among political scientists that democracies are not only unlikely to go to war with each other, they are also less warlike in general.[79] The theory suggested by the cross-national and cross-cultural results is that democratic conflict resolution within a political system generalizes to democratic conflict resolution between political systems, particularly if the systems are both democratic. If our participatory institutions and perceptions allow us to resolve our disputes peacefully, internally and externally, we may think that similarly governed people would also be disposed to settle things peacefully. Therefore, disputes between participatory political systems should be unlikely to result in war.

The understanding that participatory systems rarely fight each other, and knowing why they do not, would have important consequences for policy in the contemporary world. The kinds of military preparations believed necessary and the costs people would be willing to pay for them might be affected. On the one hand, understanding the relationship between democracy and peace might encourage war making against authoritarian regimes to overturn them—with enormous costs in human life and otherwise. On the other hand, understanding the consequences of democracy might encourage us to assist the emergence and consolidation of more participatory systems of government in the countries of Eastern Europe, the former Soviet Union, and elsewhere. In any case, the relationship between democracy and peace strongly suggests that it is counterproductive to support any undemocratic regimes, even if they happen to be enemies of our enemies, if we want to minimize the risk of war in the world. The latest cross-national evidence suggests that extending democracy around the world will in the long run minimize the risk of war. However, change in political systems is not easy or simple. In fact, societies transitioning to democracy are more prone to ethnic conflict and civil war. It is between stable or mature democracies that you find the lowest likelihood of war.[80] Encouraging nations to be more interdependent economically, and encouraging the spread of international nongovernmental organizations (like professional societies and trade associations) to provide informal ways to resolve conflicts, would also minimize the risk of war, judging by results of recent research by political scientists.[81]

Terrorism

18.6 Describe the difficulty of defining terrorism and discuss what is known about the factors associated with it.

Ever since September 11, 2001, when terrorists crashed airliners into the World Trade Center towers in New York City and into the Pentagon in Arlington, Virginia, people all over the world realize that terrorism has become a social problem globally. It is now painfully clear that organized groups of terrorists can train their people to kill themselves and thousands of others half a world away, not only by hijacking airliners and flying them into skyscrapers but also by using easily transported explosives and biological weapons. Social scientists are now actively trying to understand terrorism, in the hope that research may lead to ways to minimize the likelihood of future attacks. But there are lots of questions to answer. What is *terrorism*, and how shall it be defined? How long has terrorist activity been around? What are the causes of terrorism? What kinds of people are likely to become terrorists? And what are the consequences of terrorism?

Answering these questions is not so simple. Most people can point to instances that hardly anyone would have trouble calling terrorism—spraying nerve gas in a Japanese subway, Palestinian suicide bombers targeting Israeli civilians, Ku Klux Klan members lynching African Americans.[82] It is harder to identify the boundaries among terrorism, crime, political repression, and warfare.[83] Most researchers agree that terrorism involves the threat or use of violence against civilians. Terrorism is usually also politically or socially organized, in contrast to most crimes, which are usually perpetrated by individuals acting on their own. (To be sure, crime can be socially organized too, as, for example, in what we call "organized crime.") One marker of the difference between most crime and terrorism is that criminals rarely take public credit for their activities because they want to avoid being caught. In terrorism, the perpetrators usually proclaim their responsibility. In terrorism also, the violence is directed mostly at unarmed people, including women and children. It is intended to frighten the "enemy," to *terrorize* them, to scare them into doing something that the terrorists want to see happen. Generally, then, **terrorism** may be defined as the use or threat of violence to create terror in others, usually for political purposes.[84] Some define terrorism as perpetrated by groups that are not formal political entities. However, this criterion presents some difficulty. What are we to call it when governments support death squads and genocide against their own civilians? Some scholars call this "state terror."[85] And what are we to call the activities of some governments that support secret operations against other countries (often referred to as "state-sponsored terrorism")? Finally, although some nations conducting war explicitly try to avoid civilian casualties and focus primarily on combatants (armed soldiers), their weapons, and resources or "assets" such as factories, air strips, and fuel depots, many attacks in wartime throughout history have purposefully targeted civilians (e.g., the United States dropped atomic bombs on Hiroshima and Nagasaki to persuade the Japanese to end World War II).

Terrorism The use or threat of violence to create terror in others, usually for political purposes.

One thing is certain about terrorism: It is not a new development. Some of the words we use for terrorists—for example, "zealots" and "assassins"—derive from terrorist movements in the past. The Zealots, Jewish nationalists who revolted against the Romans occupying Judea in the first century, would hide in crowds and stab officials and priests as well as soldiers. In the 11th and 12th centuries in southwest Asia, the Fedayeen (a group of Muslim Isma'ili Shi'ites) undertook to assassinate Sunni rulers despite the almost certainty of their own capture or death. The rulers said that the Fedayeen were under the influence of hashish and called them "Hashshashin," which is the root of the later term *assassin*.[86] In the late 18th and early 19th centuries, the "reign of terror" occurred during and after the French Revolution.

A woman cries during a candlelight interfaith service at Arlington Street Church April 16, 2013 in Boston, Massachusetts, in the aftermath of two explosions that struck near the finish line of the Boston Marathon April 15.

In the early and middle 20th century, the dictator Joseph Stalin ordered the execution of many millions of people who were considered enemies of the Soviet state. Six million Jews and millions of other innocents were exterminated by the German Third Reich in the 1930s and 1940s.[87] And many Latin American regimes, such as that in Argentina, terrorized and killed dissidents in the 1970s and 1980s.[88] Now there is a heightened fear of terrorists who may have access to weapons of mass destruction. In a world made smaller by global transportation, cell phones, and the Internet, terrorism is a greater threat than ever before.

We still lack much systematic research that explains why terrorism occurs and why people are motivated to become terrorists. But there is a good deal of research about state terrorism. Political scientist R. J. Rummel estimates that governments have killed nearly 262 million people in the 20th century (he calls this kind of terrorism "democide"). State terrorism has been responsible for four times more deaths than all the wars, civil and international, that occurred in the 20th century. Regimes in the Soviet Union (1917–1987), China (1923–1987), and Germany (1933–1945) were responsible for killing more than a total of 190 million civilians. Proportionately, the Khmer Rouge regime in Cambodia topped them all, killing over 30 percent of its population from 1975 to 1978.[89] What predicts state terrorism against one's own people? Rummel finds one clear predictor—totalitarian governments. By far, they have the highest frequencies of domestic state terrorism, controlling for factors such as economic wealth, type of religion, and population size. As Rummel puts it, "power kills; absolute power kills absolutely."[90] Democratic countries are less likely to practice state terrorism, but when they do, it occurs during or after a rebellion or a war.[91] If state terrorism is more likely to occur in totalitarian regimes, terrorists and terrorist groups may be more likely to occur in such societies. If so, the spread of democracy may be our best hope of minimizing the risk of terrorism in the world, just as the spread of democracy seems to minimize the likelihood of war between countries.

We know relatively little so far about what predicts who will become a terrorist. We do know that terrorists often come from higher social statuses and generally have more education than the average person.[92] But while terrorists are not commonly poor, it is important to ask whether the societies in which terrorism thrives are deprived in some way. A suggestive piece of evidence is that if we focus on the most deadly terrorist organizations, they do tend to occur in countries that are lower in measures of human development, that have poor records of political rights and civil liberties, and that have higher concentrations of young people.[93]

Making the World Better

18.7 ▶ Discuss some lessons learned from anthropology that could make the world a better place.

Many social problems afflict our world, not just the ones discussed in this chapter and elsewhere in this book.[94] But we have tried in this chapter to encourage positive thinking about global social problems; we have suggested how the results of past and future scientific research could be applied to solving some of those problems.

We may know enough now that we can do something about our problems, and we will discover more through future research. Social problems are mostly of human making and are, therefore, susceptible to human unmaking. There may be obstacles on the road to solutions, but we can overcome them if we want to. So let's go for it!

Summary and Review

Natural Disasters and Famine

18.1 ▶ Explain how cultural, economic, and social factors can cause or exacerbate natural events and cause disasters and famine.

- Climatic and other events in the physical environment become worse disasters because of events or conditions in the social environment. Therefore, disasters are also social problems, which have social causes and possible social solutions.

- Famine almost always has some social causes and is determined by who has rights to the available food and whether those who have more food distribute it to those who have less.

- Cross-cultural research suggests that societies with individual rather than shared property rights are more likely to suffer famine.

 What are some examples of how cultural, economic, and social factors cause or exacerbate natural disasters? What might be some solutions?

Inadequate Housing and Homelessness

18.2 Describe the factors that lead to inadequate housing and homelessness.

- In 2010, half of the people in the world lived in urban areas, and it is projected to be about 70 percent by 2050.

- As of 2012, approximately 1 billion people or about 33 percent of urban dwellers lived in slums. Four in ten of nonpermanent houses in slums were in high-risk areas such as flood zones or areas prone to landslides.

- All but the upper-income elite may be found in illegal settlements. Squatter settlements are not chaotic, unorganized, or full of crime. Most dwellers cannot find affordable housing, but they are employed, aspire to get ahead, live in intact nuclear families, and help each other.

- Research suggests differences in the causes of homelessness in different parts of the world. Social and political policies cause homelessness.

- Many countries have "street children." In the late 1980s, 80 million of the world's children lived in the streets. In the 2000s, the estimated number grew to about 150 million worldwide.

 What factors lead to inadequate housing and homelessness and what may help minimize these conditions?

Family Violence and Abuse

18.3 Discuss the magnitude, causes, and consequences of family violence.

- To avoid having to decide what is or is not abuse, many researchers focus their studies on variation in the frequencies of specific behaviors, for example, which societies have physical punishment of children.

- Much of the violence directed at children is believed to be morally correct by the people practicing it.

- Children who are corporally punished are more likely to later physically assault their dating partners or spouses, be convicted of a crime, and have depression. Corporal punishment is possibly a cradle of violence.

- Two main predictors of corporal punishment in the cross-cultural record that are practically universal in the nation-states of the world are a money economy and a stratified social system.

- Wife beating occurs in 85 percent of the world's societies; it is most common when men control family labor and have the final say in the home, when divorce is difficult for women, when a husband's kin control remarriage for a widow, or when women have no female work groups.

 What are some of the causes and consequences of family violence? What might be done to minimize it?

Crime

18.4 Explain how cultural and societal features relate to crime, especially in regard to homicide.

- What is a crime in one society is not necessarily a crime in another. Researchers tend to look at homicide rates to assess variability among societies in terms of crime.

- Whether a nation is defeated or victorious, homicide rates tend to increase after a war.

- More countries show murder rates going down rather than up after capital punishment was abolished.

- Homicide is usually highest in nations or societies with high poverty and income inequality.

 What are some of the conditions that increase the likelihood of crime? What might decrease it?

War

18.5 Discuss warfare in terms of cultural, social, and ecological factors, and describe the reasons societies go to war.

- Armed conflict appears to be greater in periods of worsening climate and more frequent climate-related natural events associated with disasters.

- Teaching children to mistrust others may be another factor predicting war. People who grow up to be mistrustful may be more likely to go to war than to negotiate or seek conciliation. Mistrust or fear of others seems to be partly caused by threat or fear of disasters.

- Interstate wars today are uncommon; internal wars and civil wars constitute most of the present armed conflict. Recent research suggests that civil wars are predicted by the per capita income of the country—all of the wars today are in poorer regions.

 What are some of the predictors of more warfare? What might minimize warfare?

Terrorism

18.6 Describe the difficulty of defining terrorism and discuss what is known about the factors associated with it.

- One marker of the difference between most crime and terrorism is that criminals rarely take public credit for their activities because they do not want to be caught. Terrorist perpetrators usually proclaim their responsibility.

- Terrorist violence is directed mostly at unarmed people, including women and children. It is intended to frighten the "enemy," to scare them into doing something that the terrorists want to see happen.

- Terrorism is not a new development and goes back to at least the first century. Today, there is a heightened fear of terrorists who may have access to weapons of mass destruction.

- More research has been done on state terrorism than on terrorism. State terrorism has resulted in four

times more deaths than all the wars, civil and international, that occurred in the 20th century. A clear predictor of state terrorism is the presence of a totalitarian government.

- Terrorists generally come from higher statuses and have higher levels of education. Terrorist organizations tend to arise in countries that have lower measures of human development, poor records of political rights and civil liberties, and higher concentrations of young people.

 What are the difficulties in defining terrorism? What may explain state terrorism?

Making the World Better

18.7 Discuss some lessons learned from anthropology that could make the world a better place.

- Social problems such as disasters, famine, inadequate housing, homelessness, family violence, crime, war, and terrorism can be studied, and the research findings can be applied to improve or resolve those problems.

- Factors that create social problems are not always obvious, so it is important to look carefully at beliefs and practices within and among cultures to better understand the dynamics of these problems.

 For each of the global problems discussed, what may lessen the problems?

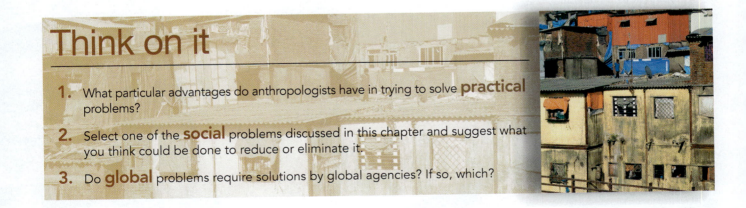

Think on it

1. What particular advantages do anthropologists have in trying to solve **practical** problems?

2. Select one of the **social** problems discussed in this chapter and suggest what you think could be done to reduce or eliminate it.

3. Do **global** problems require solutions by global agencies? If so, which?

CHAPTER 19

Practicing and Applying Anthropology

LEARNING OBJECTIVES

19.1 Discuss the applied anthropology code of ethics and discuss some ethical issues faced by practicing anthropologists.

19.2 Discuss the need to evaluate the effects of planned change.

19.3 Identify and give examples of some difficulties in implementing planned change.

19.4 Describe the field of environmental anthropology.

19.5 Describe the field of business and organizational anthropology.

19.6 Describe the field of cultural resource management.

19.7 Describe the field of museum anthropology.

19.8 Describe the field of forensic anthropology.

19.9 Discuss the goals of medical anthropology.

19.10 Discuss cultural understandings of health and illness.

19.11 Describe political and economic influences on health.

19.12 Discuss a sampling of health conditions and diseases studied by medical anthropologists.

CHINESE RESEARCH CENTRE

Anthropology is no longer a merely academic subject. A large number of anthropologists in the United States are practicing and applied anthropologists, employed outside of colleges and universities.[1] The fact that so many organizations hire anthropologists suggests an increasing realization that anthropology, what it has discovered and can discover about humans, is useful. Anthropologists who call themselves practicing or applied anthropologists work for a large variety of organizations, government agencies, international development agencies, private consulting firms, public health organizations, medical schools, public interest law firms, community development agencies, charitable foundations, and profit-seeking corporations.

Practicing or applied anthropology as a profession is explicitly concerned with making anthropological knowledge useful. Applied or practicing anthropologists may be involved in one or more phases of a project: assembling relevant knowledge and collecting data, developing plans and policies, assessing the likely social and environmental impacts, implementing the project, and evaluating the project and its effects.[2] Anthropologists are most often involved in gathering information rather than constructing policy or initiating action.[3] The organizations that hire the applied anthropologists usually set policy and have staff to execute projects. But anthropologists are increasingly finding themselves involved in policy making and action. The field of applied or practicing anthropology is very diverse. In this chapter, we first focus on issues affecting applied anthropology generally: ethics; evaluating the effects of planned change; and the difficulties of implementing change. In these first sections, we mainly use examples from *development anthropology*, one of the oldest applied fields. **Development anthropology** is one of the main subfields of applied or practicing anthropology, aimed at improving people's lives, particularly decreasing poverty and hunger.[4] We then turn to some other applied specialties such as *environmental anthropology, business or organizational anthropology, museum anthropology, cultural resource management, and forensic anthropology*. Medical anthropology, which has both basic and applied aspects, is also discussed in this chapter. These fields by no means exhaust the wide-ranging applications in which anthropologists participate.

> **Practicing or applied anthropology** The branch of anthropology that concerns itself with applying anthropological knowledge to achieve practical goals, usually in the service of an agency outside the traditional academic setting.

> **Development anthropology** One of the main subfields of applied or practicing anthropology, aimed at improving people's lives, particularly decreasing poverty and hunger.

Ethics of Applied Anthropology

> **19.1** Discuss the applied anthropology code of ethics and discuss some ethical issues faced by practicing anthropologists.

Anthropologists have usually studied people who are disadvantaged—by imperialism, colonialism, and other forms of exploitation—and so it is no wonder that we care about the people's lives we have shared. But caring is not enough to improve others' lives. We may need basic research that allows us to understand how a condition might be successfully treated. A particular proposed "improvement" might actually not be an improvement; well-meaning efforts have sometimes produced harmful consequences. Even if we know that a change would be an improvement, there is still the problem of how to make that change happen. The people to be affected may not want to change. Is it ethical to try to persuade them? And, conversely, is it ethical *not* to try? Applied anthropologists must take all of these matters into consideration in determining whether and how to act in response to a perceived need.

Anthropology as a profession has adopted certain principles of responsibility. Above all, an anthropologist's first responsibility is to those who are being studied; everything should be done to ensure that their welfare and dignity will be protected. Anthropologists also have a responsibility to those who will read about their research; research findings should be reported openly and truthfully.[5] But because applied anthropology often deals with planning and implementing changes in some population, ethical responsibilities can become complicated. Perhaps the most important ethical question is: Will the change truly benefit the potentially affected population?

In May 1946, the Society for Applied Anthropology established a committee to draw up a specific code of ethics for professional applied anthropologists. After many meetings and revisions, a statement on ethical responsibilities was finally adopted in 1948 and revised subsequently.[6] According to the code, the targeted community should be included as much as possible in the formulation of policy, so that people in the community may know in advance how the program will affect them. Perhaps the most important aspect of the code is the pledge not to recommend or take any action that is harmful to the interests of the community. The National Association for the Practice of Anthropology goes further: If the work the employer expects of the employee violates the ethical principles of the profession, the practicing anthropologist has the obligation to try to change those practices or, if change cannot be brought about, to withdraw from the work.[7]

Ethical issues are often complicated. Thayer Scudder described the situation of Gwembe Tonga villagers who were relocated after a large dam was built in the Zambezi Valley of central Africa. Economic conditions improved during the 1960s and early 1970s as the people increasingly produced goods and services for sale. But then conditions deteriorated. By 1980, the villagers were in a miserable state; rates of mortality, alcoholism, theft, assault, and murder were up. Why? One reason was that they had cut back on producing their own food in favor of producing for the world market. Such a strategy works well when world market prices are high; however, when prices fall, so does the standard of living.[8] The situation described by Scudder illustrates the ethical dilemma for many applied anthropologists. As he said, "So how is it that I can still justify working for the agencies that fund such projects?" He points out that large-scale projects are almost impossible to stop. The anthropologist can choose to stand on the sidelines and complain or try to influence the project to benefit the affected population as much as possible.[9] Along these lines, Michael Cernea has modeled eight risks of displacement due to water projects, which include landlessness, joblessness, homelessness, marginalization, food insecurity, increased morbidity, loss of access to common property resources, and community disarticulation.[10] He asserts that all these risks make it important to avoid resettlement, but if it is undertaken there needs to be serious political commitment by governments to provide adequate resources and legal protections.

Some of the problems result from the fact that anthropologists are not often involved until after a decision is made to go ahead with a change program. This situation has begun to change as applied anthropologists are increasingly asked to participate in earlier stages of the planning process. Anthropologists are also increasingly asked to help in projects initiated by the affected party. Such requests may range from help in solving problems in corporate organizations to helping Native Americans with land claims. Because the project is consistent with the wishes of the affected population, the results are not likely to put the anthropologist into an ethical dilemma.

Evaluating the Effects of Planned Change

19.2 Discuss the need to evaluate the effects of planned change.

The decision as to whether a proposed change would benefit the affected population is not always easy to make. In certain cases, as when improved medical care is involved, the benefits offered to the target group would seem to be unquestionable—we all feel sure that health is better than illness. But what about the long-term effects? Consider a public health innovation such as inoculation against disease. Once the inoculation program was begun, the number of children surviving would probably increase. But will there be enough food for the additional population? Given the level of technology, capital, and land resources possessed by the population, there might not be enough resources to feed more people. Thus, the death rate, because of starvation, might rise to its previous level and perhaps even exceed it. Without additional changes to increase the food supply, the inoculation program in the long term might merely change the causes of death. This example shows that even if a program of planned change has beneficial consequences in the short run, a great deal of thought and investigation has to be given to its long-term effects.

Applied Anthropology

Getting Development Programs to Include Women Farmers

When Anita Spring first did fieldwork in Zambia in the 1970s, she was not particularly interested in agriculture. Rather, medical anthropology was her interest. Her work focused on customary healing practices, particularly involving women and children. She was surprised at the end of the year when a delegation of women came to tell her that she did not understand what it meant to be a woman. "To be a woman is to be a farmer," they said. She admits that it took her a while to pay attention to women as farmers, but then she began to participate in efforts to provide technical assistance to them. Spring realized that all too often development agents downplay women's contributions to agriculture.

How does one bring about change in male-centered attitudes and practices? One way is to document how much women actually contribute to agriculture. Beginning with the influential writing of Ester Boserup in *Woman's Role in Economic Development* (1970), scholars began to report that in Africa south of the Sahara, in the Caribbean, and in parts of Southeast Asia, women were the principal farmers or agricultural laborers. Moreover, as agriculture became more complex, it required more work time in the fields, so the women's contribution to agriculture increased. In addition, because men increasingly went away to work, women had to do much of what used to be men's work on the farms.

In the 1980s, Spring designed and directed the Women in Agricultural Development Project in Malawi, funded by the Office of Women in the U.S. Agency for International Development. Rather than focusing just on women, the project aimed to collect data on both female and male agriculturalists and how development agents treated them. The project did more than collect information; miniprojects were set up and evaluated, and successful training techniques were shared with development agents in other regions. Spring points out that the success of the program was due not just to the design of the project, but to the Malawi's willingness to change. It also helped that the United Nations and other donor organizations increasingly focused attention on women. It takes the efforts of many to bring about change. Increasingly, applied anthropologists like Anita Spring are involved in these efforts from beginning to end, from the design stage to implementation and evaluation.

Source: Spring 1995; 2000b.

Debra Picchi raised questions about the long-term effects on the Bakairí Indians of a program by the Brazilian National Indian Foundation (FUNAI) to produce rice with machine technology.[11] The Bakairí of the Mato Grosso region largely practice slash-and-burn horticulture in gallery forests along rivers, with supplementary cattle raising, fishing, and hunting. In the early part of the 20th century, their population had declined to 150 people and they were given a relatively small reserve, much of it parched and infertile (*cerrado*). When the Bakairí population began to increase, FUNAI introduced a scheme to plant rice on formerly unused *cerrado* land using machinery, insecticides, and fertilizer. FUNAI paid the costs for the first year and expected that the scheme would be self-supporting by the third year. The project did not go so well because FUNAI did not deliver all the equipment needed and did not provide adequate advice. Only half the expected rice was produced. Still, it was more food than the Bakairí had previously, so the program should have been beneficial to them.

But there were unanticipated negative side effects. Using *cerrado* land for agriculture reduced the area on which cattle could be grazed; cattle are an important source of high-quality protein. Mechanization also makes the Bakairí more dependent on cash for fuel, insecticides, fertilizer, and repairs. But cash is hard to come by. Only some individuals can be hired—usually men with outside experience who have the required knowledge of machinery. So the cash earned in the now-mechanized agriculture goes mainly to a relatively small number of people, creating new inequalities of income.

The benefits of programs or applied efforts are sometimes obvious. For example, Haiti has experienced serious deforestation. The process began in colonial times when the Spanish exported wood and the French cleared forests to grow sugarcane, coffee, and indigo. After Haiti's independence, foreign lumber companies continued to cut and sell hardwood. Wood is needed by the local population for fuel and for construction, but rapid population increases have increased the demand for fuel and wood, and the trees were rapidly diminishing. The loss of tree cover also speeds up erosion of topsoil. Forestry experts, environmentalists, and anthropologists all agree about the need to stop this trend. How to bring about the appropriate change is not so easy. The poorer people become, the more likely they are to cut down trees to sell.[12]

These failures were not the fault of anthropologists—indeed, most instances of planned change by governments and other agencies usually have begun without the input of anthropologists at all. Applied anthropologists have played an important role in pointing out the problems with programs like these that fail to evaluate long-term consequences. Such evaluations are an important part of convincing governments and other agencies to ask for anthropological help in the first place. Ironically, failure experiences are learning experiences: Applied anthropologists who study previous examples of planned change can often learn a great deal about what is likely or not likely to be beneficial in the long run.

Difficulties in Instituting Planned Change

19.3 Identify and give examples of some difficulties in implementing planned change.

After numerous reforestation projects failed in Haiti, an anthropologist, Gerald Murray, was asked to help design a program that would work.[13] Understanding why previous projects failed was the first step in helping Murray design an effective project. One problem seems to have been that previous projects were run through the government's Ministry of Agriculture. The seedling trees that were given away were referred to as "the state's trees." So, when project workers told farmers not to cut the new trees down so as to protect the environment, farmers took this statement to mean that the land on which the trees were planted might be considered government land, which the farmers could not care less about. In the project proposed by Murray, private voluntary organizations rather than the Haitian government were used to distribute trees and the farmers were told that they were the tree owners. Ownership included the right to cut the trees and sell the wood, just as they could sell crops. In previous projects, farmers were given heavy, hard-to-transport seedlings that took a long time to mature. They were told to plant in a large communal woodlot, an idea inconsistent with the more individualistic Haitian land tenure arrangements. In the new plan, the tree seedlings given away were fast-growing species that matured in as little as four years. In addition, the new seedlings were very small and could be planted quickly. Perhaps most important of all, the new trees could be planted in borders or interspersed with other crops, interfering little with traditional crop patterns. To Murray's great surprise, by the end of two years, 2,500 Haitian households had planted 3 million seedlings. Over 20 years, the estimate is that over a 100 million trees were planted and over 350,000 farm families were involved in the project, more than 40 percent of rural households.[14] Also, farmers were not rushing to cut down trees. Because growing trees do not spoil, farmers were postponing their cutting and sale until they needed cash. So even though farmers were told that it was all right to cut down trees, a statement contrary to the message of previous reforestation projects, the landscape was filling up with trees.

Whether a program of planned change can be successfully implemented depends largely on whether the people want the proposed change and like the proposed program. Before an attempt can be made at cultural innovation, the innovators must determine whether the population is aware of the benefits of the proposed change. Lack of awareness can be a temporary barrier to solving the problem at hand. For example, health workers have often had difficulty convincing people that they were becoming ill because something was wrong with their water supply. Many people do not believe that disease can be transmitted by water. At other times, the population is perfectly aware of the problem. A case in point involved Taiwanese women who were introduced to family-planning methods beginning in the 1960s. The women knew they were having more children than they wanted or could easily afford, and they wanted to control their birth rate. They offered no resistance—they merely had to be given the proper devices and instructions, and the birth rate quickly fell to a more desirable, and more manageable, level.[15]

Anthropologists as Advocates and Collaborators

Development anthropologists have played an important role researching and documenting the mostly negative effects on populations that have been relocated. Occasionally, a few projects have had better outcomes and researchers try to understand what factors appear to ameliorate the situation. Two factors critical to success appear to be collecting good data in affected communities prior to the project and consulting with the community.

In the past, anthropologists mostly played a role in researching change projects. There were some notable exceptions however. For example, in the 1950s, Sol Tax advocated "action anthropology, which emphasized the role of the anthropologist in helping communities make choices and decide how they want to change."[16] One famous action-oriented project (the Vicos Project) led by Cornell anthropologists actually took over a hacienda in Peru with the aim of transforming the serf-like system into one where the indigenous population controlled the resources and ran the community.[17] For a long time those projects were exceptions. But in the 1990s, anthropologists have increasingly become advocates for affected communities, working with NGOs to resist resettlement or to lobby for better conditions. Advocates see themselves as providing a voice that is not otherwise heard. Critics are concerned that the advocate is only representing one point of view.

Even if the programs are well intentioned and even if the appropriate evaluations are made to ensure that the population will not be seriously harmed, the population targeted for the change is usually not involved in the decision making. Some anthropologists think that collaborative research is more ethical because it involves the people affected in all phases of the project, from participating in the research design to execution and publishing.[18] Wayne Warry decided to be more collaborative when he was asked by a Native Canadian elder whether he (Warry) would tolerate his own methods and interpretations if he were the native.[19] This question prompted him to involve himself in a project with Native Canadian collaborators, directed by the Mamaweswen Tribal Council. The project assesses health care needs and develops plans to improve local community health care. Funding is provided by the Canadian government as part of a program to transfer health care to the First Nations. Native researchers are conducting the surveys and workshops to keep the community informed about the project. The tribal council also reviews any publications and shares in any profits resulting from those publications.

Applied anthropologists are also increasingly asked to work on behalf of indigenous grassroots organizations, which have proliferated recently in the developing world. In some cases, these small groups and networks of such groups are starting to hire their own technical assistance.[20] When such organizations do the hiring, they control the decision making. There is increasing evidence that grassroots organizations are the key to effective

Native South Americans from different groups gather to show their unity as they protest against the construction of the Belo Monte Dam. They are demanding that the Brazilian government hold prior consultations with indigenous peoples before building dams that affect their lands and livelihoods.

development. For example, Kenyan farmers who belong to grassroots organizations produce higher farm yields than those farmers who do not belong, even though the latter group is exposed to more agricultural extension agents.[21] Grassroots organizations can succeed where government or outside projects fail. We have plenty of instances of people effectively resisting projects. Their willingness to change, and their participation in crucial decision making, may be mostly responsible for the success of a change project.

Large development projects planned by powerful governments or agencies rarely are stoppable, but even they can be resisted successfully. The Kayapo of the Xingu River region of Brazil were able to cancel a plan by the Brazilian government to build dams along the river for hydroelectric power. The Kayapo gained international attention when some of their leaders appeared on North American and European television and then successfully organized a protest in 1989 by members of several tribal groups. Their success seemed to come in part from their ability to present themselves to the international community as guardians of the rain forest—an image that resonated with international environmental organizations that supported their cause. Although to outsiders it might seem that the Kayapo want their way of life to remain as it was, the Kayapo are not opposed to all change. In fact, they want greater access to medical care, other government services, and manufactured goods from outside.[22]

There is another kind of collaboration that is becoming increasingly important. Many projects require team efforts, working with people from other disciplines. Anthropologists increasingly have to be conversant with the theory and methods in other fields to understand and negotiate with other members of their team. Earlier anthropologists might have been more likely to work alone. Now that is less likely.[23]

19.4 ▶ Describe the field of environmental anthropology.

Environmental anthropology Focuses on issues relating to the interaction of humans with their environments, at the local, regional, and global levels, particularly on how to understand and alleviate the degradation of the environment.

Environmental Anthropology

Given the looming environmental challenges that humans face, it is not surprising that *environmental anthropology* has become a rapidly growing field. The field of **environmental anthropology** focuses on issues relating to the interaction of humans with their environments, at the local, regional and global levels, particularly on how to understand and alleviate the degradation of the environment.[24] Researchers ask questions such as: How do local people view the environment? What are the effects of those views? How can needed resources be sustained? Does participation by communities in change programs lead to better outcomes? What kinds of programs can help to improve the lives of those living in the worst environments?

There is increasing recognition that imposition of environmental policies from the top down does not work very well and that efforts are more likely to succeed if the affected communities participate in the planning of programs. Erin Dean describes a pilot program in Tanzania to manage forest resources that attempts to be participatory.[25] Tanzania has about 2 million hectares of land under some participatory management program. There are two kinds of forestry management programs. In one, the government retains ownership of the forestland and trees, but responsibilities and benefits are shared with communities. In the second one, communities register for full ownership of the forestland and trees as well as full responsibility. The Meru-Usa plantation, on the upper slopes of Mount Meru, has its roots in colonial times when the Germans seized land for European settlement and at the same time created a forest reserve. Because of land seizures, the agricultural Masai living in this area had to intensify their agriculture. But this did not solve the Masai's need for timber because agricultural intensification deprived the Masai of timber that would formerly grow in fields that lay fallow. Consequently, the forest reserve became contested. And, to make matters worse, the trees that were planted in the reserve used more water than native trees. To deal with the increased tension, the manager of the Meru-Usa plantation decided to try to get village cooperation and the Tanzanian government decided to make it a pilot program. Masai farmers help weed in areas where young trees are growing and in exchange are allowed to collect fallen limbs and plant some crops until the trees grow tall enough and make too much shade. The pilot project also included school environmental programs and lessons in some revenue generating projects, such as beekeeping. While progress has occurred, Dean reports that comanagement was a goal, but not yet achieved.

Much of the work that environmental anthropologists do is at the local level where they can employ detailed ethnographic methods. But when the environmental issue involves a large region, this strategy does not work well because a single community or even a few communities will not provide representative information. Researchers make use of methods such as remote sensing from satellites combined with geographic information systems (GIS) for a large region. Satellite data, which can be geo-referenced using GIS, can be analyzed for changes in vegetation.[26] But these technological advances alone are not sufficient, for without research on the ground, scientists cannot be sure how the land is used now and in the past. For instance, they would want to know whether land was previously burned, or when the land was last logged, what species of tree have been cut, how many people live in a household or how households allocate labor. Working with interdisciplinary teams, smaller units of land can be sampled, and anthropological fieldworkers can talk to people in those areas to find out how land was actually used and who lives on the land.

The example just given indicates how anthropologists need to interface with other methods and people from other disciplines to tackle more than local problems. But that doesn't mean that local knowledge is irrelevant. Climate change is a worldwide phenomenon, yet environmental anthropologists believe that understanding the resilience of local communities and their resourcefulness is necessary. As described by Jennifer Hirsch and colleagues, the Field Museum in Chicago is undertaking research in 10 Chicago neighborhoods designed to facilitate the involvement of different communities in reducing carbon emissions.[27] If successful, community leaders will participate in long-term planning for their communities and the larger area. The research team consists of anthropologists, Chicago Department of Environment staff, and community leaders. The anthropologists employed mixed methods, including about four months of ethnographic research in each community to assess concerns about climate change and steps people were taking to conserve energy. They found awareness, but the anthropologists also identified some barriers. For example, in one middle-class neighborhood some people objected to putting clothes out to dry as it was seen as a marker of low status. In a lower income neighborhood, people were afraid that building "green" housing would ultimately lead to increase in housing prices and ultimately force them to move. Also, there was significant distrust of the city, including distrust of the climate action plan. The researchers suggested that the city build on existing concerns of the communities (such as interest in weatherization and retrofitting houses to make them more energy efficient). They also suggested that local organizations could become role models and demonstration sites. The good news is that the city government has implemented some of the suggestions.

Business and Organizational Anthropology

19.5 Describe the field of business and organizational anthropology.

More and more businesses and organizations have come to realize that anthropologists have useful knowledge to contribute. Anthropologists holistically look at the larger culture in which organizations are situated, the culture and subcultures of the organization, and the perspectives of different groups. And anthropologists understand the need to observe and listen first in an unstructured way. Doing ethnographic research is not just for understanding the businesses themselves and their *organizational cultures* but also to enable businesses to assess the needs of potential customers and users. Understanding cultures becomes even more important as trade becomes more global, international investments and joint ventures increase, and the multinational corporations spread their reach.

Business anthropologists often do not have the luxury of a year or more of study. Often they may only have a few days or weeks and have to make a "rapid assessment." To address this problem, teams of researchers often work together using observation, videos, interviewing, analyses of social networks and documents (such as emails) to see if different types of data collected by different people lead to the same conclusion.[28]

Differences between people from different cultures can have profound effects on how people work together. Anthropologists know that communication is much more than the formal understanding of another language. People in some countries, such as the United States, expect explicit, straightforward verbal messages, but people in other countries are more indirect in their verbal messages.[29] In Japan and China, for example, negative messages are less likely than messages expressing politeness and harmony. Many Eastern cultures have ways of saying no without saying the word. People in the United States emphasize the future, youth, informality, and competitiveness, but the emphases in other societies are often the opposite. In any business arrangement, perhaps no difference is as salient as the value a culture places on time. As we say, "Time is money."[30] If a meeting is arranged and the other person is late, say, by 45 minutes, people from the United States consider it rude; but such a delay is well within the range of acceptable behavior in many South American countries. (For a long-term project design to change a business culture see box "General Motors: Creating a Better Business Culture.")

Businesses usually will ask for help in understanding their organizational culture when they perceive a problem. The culture of a business may interfere with the acceptance of new kinds of workers, mergers with other companies, or changing to meet new business needs. If the culture needs to be changed, it is first necessary to understand that culture and how and why it developed the way it did. Even something as seemingly minor as observing a parking lot and surrounding grounds is revealing. If there are many reserved spaces for executives and few amenities for workers, this may suggest a rigid hierarchy and less concern for employees.[31] Of course an anthropologist would need to verify this inference with information from other sources.

Anthropologist Jill Kleinberg's research provides a case study on the challenges of having people from very different cultures work together successfully. Kleinberg studied six Japanese-owned firms in the United States.[32] All six firms employed both Japanese and Americans, although the Japanese dominated the managerial positions. The main goal of the study was to discover why there was considerable tension in the six firms. Kleinberg's first order of business was to interview people about their views of work and their jobs. She found clear differences between the Japanese and the American employees that seemed to reflect broader cultural differences. Americans wanted a clear definition of the job and its attached responsibilities, and they also wanted their job titles, authority, rights, and pay to match closely. The Japanese, on the other hand, emphasized the need to be flexible in their responsibilities as well as their tasks. They also felt that part of their responsibility was to help their co-workers. Americans were uncomfortable because the Japanese managers did not indicate exactly what the workers were supposed to do; even if there was a job description, the manager did not appear to pay attention to it. Americans were given little information, were left out of decision making, and were frustrated by the lack of opportunity to advance. The Japanese thought that the Americans were too hard to manage, too concerned with money and authority, and too concerned with their own interests.

Kleinberg recommended giving all employees more information about the company as well as conducting training sessions about cross-cultural differences in business cultures.

Applied Anthropology

General Motors: Creating a Better Business Culture

After World War II, General Motors (GM) was the largest corporation in the United States. But beginning in the 1960s, imported cars from Germany and Japan began to seriously challenge GM's dominance. In addition, tastes were changing as consumers began opting for better fuel economy, cleaner emissions, and greater safety.

GM realized that it needed to change and in the 1980s began to explore new partnerships. They also hired an anthropologist, Elizabeth Briody, to conduct organizational research. In the mid-2000s, Briody led an expanded research team of six. In both time periods, the aim was the same. The researchers realized that in order to change, you first have to "see" what is going on. So, using ethnographic methods, the researchers undertook to understand the culture of the organization, including how work was organized, how people related to each other, and how people thought about their work and work conditions. They also asked people of all statuses at GM how they wanted it to be—in other words, their ideal workplace culture.

Briody's observations of the mid-1980s suggested that the GM culture emphasized efficiency and meeting quotas. The emphasis was on the productivity of an individual and rewards and blame were assigned to individuals. Departments tried to optimize their own productivity. Leadership was authoritarian. In short, there was little cooperation or collaboration and there was more emphasis on quantity rather than quality.

Applied anthropologists Elizabeth Briody and Robert Trotter, part of the research team studying the culture at GM.

Interviews though revealed that almost everyone, from top management on down, wanted a culture of collaboration, where everyone could contribute ideas, where teams took responsibility for solving problems, and where people were respectful of each other. Although most of the people interviewed wanted a different culture, the research team knew that culture change in organizations, just as in the broader society, is not easy to accomplish. So the researchers set out to design 10 "tools" designed to help individuals appreciate and learn collaboration techniques. Many of the exercises required small group discussion, itself a collaborative enterprise. They even invented a video game to learn about the impact of different types of decision making

to solve a problem (one that actually occurred).

Did GM change? By many objective measures, GM improved substantially since the 1980s. Measures of quality increased, injuries and illnesses are down, and even productivity is 54 percent higher. The manufacturing culture has shifted to more sharing and team responsibilities. Jobs are now rotated so work injuries decline and people have more understanding of the wider process. With more responsibilities, workers are more empowered. All cultures change, but the process of change is aided by the will to do so and the willingness to undertake steps to learn how to make the process easier.

Source: Briody, Trotter, and Meerwarth 2010.

She also recommended making the Japanese philosophy of management more explicit during the hiring process so that the company would be able to find Americans who were comfortable with their philosophy. But she also suggested that the managerial structure be somewhat "Americanized" so that American employees could feel at ease. Finally, she recommended that Americans be given more managerial positions and contact with their Japanese counterparts overseas. These suggestions might not eliminate all problems, but they would increase mutual understanding and trust.

Businesses and organizations also need help in developing and marketing products that people may want. And many have found that anthropologists are quite good at finding out because they go out and watch and ask questions. For example, Susan Squires watched families with young kids at breakfast to help a breakfast food company develop products. Parents tried to get kids to eat nutritious breakfasts, but kids typically didn't want to eat at 6:30 or 7 or only wanted a heavily sugared cereal. Some kids skipped breakfast and got hungry later in the morning and ended up eating their lunch early. Squires's observations led the company to develop a portable yoghurt in a tube called Go-Gurt.[33]

Cultural Resource Management

19.6 Describe the field of cultural resource management.

Cultural resource management (CRM) The branch of applied anthropology that seeks to recover and preserve the archaeological record before programs of planned change disturb or destroy it.

Large-scale programs of planned change like those discussed earlier in this chapter have an impact not only on living people but can also have an impact on the archaeological record left by the ancestors of living people. Recovering and preserving the archaeological record before programs of planned change disturb or destroy it is called **cultural resource management (CRM)**. CRM work is carried out by archaeologists who are often called "contract archaeologists" because they typically work under contract to a government agency, a private developer, or a native group.

What kinds of impact can programs of planned change have on the archaeological record? In the 1960s, a large number of hydroelectric dam projects were initiated to provide flood control and to bring a stable source of electrical power to developing nations. In Egypt, a dam was built on the Nile River at a site called Aswan. Archaeologists realized that once the dam was in place a huge lake would form behind it, submerging thousands of archaeological sites, including the massive temple of Rameses II. Something needed to be done; the archaeological record had to be salvaged or protected. In the language of CRM, there needed to be a *mitigation plan* put into action. And there was. As the Aswan dam was being built, archaeologists went to work excavating sites that would be flooded. Archaeologists and engineers designed a way to take apart the temple of Rameses II and rebuild it, piece by piece, on higher ground where it would not be flooded. By the time the dam was completed in 1965, hundreds of sites had been investigated and two entire temple complexes moved.

Large-scale development projects are not the only projects that involve CRM archaeologists. In many nations, including the United States and Canada, historic preservation laws require any project receiving federal funds to ensure that archaeological resources are protected or their damage mitigated. Highway construction projects in the United States are common places to find CRM archaeologists at work. Virtually all highway projects rely on federal funding, and before a highway can be built, a complete archaeological survey of the proposed right-of-way has to be made. If archaeological sites are found, potential damage to them must be mitigated. A CRM archaeologist will work with the construction company, the state archaeologist, and perhaps a federal archaeologist to decide on the best course of action. In some cases, the archaeological site will be excavated. In others, the right-of-way may be moved. In still others, the decision is to allow the archaeological site to be destroyed, because it would be too costly to excavate or the site may not be significant enough to warrant excavation. Regardless of the decision, the CRM archaeologist plays a crucial role in assessing and protecting the archaeological record.

CRM archaeologists do not work only for state or federal agencies. In many nations today, CRM archaeologists are also working with native peoples to protect, preserve, and manage archaeological materials for them. Indeed, archaeologist John Ravesloot recently stated that "the future of American archaeology is with Indian communities functioning as active, not passive, participants in the interpretation, management, and preservation of their rich cultural heritage."[34] One example of such a working relationship is the Zuni Heritage and Historic Preservation Office. During the 1970s, the

Pueblo of Zuni decided it needed to train tribal members in archaeology to ensure that Zuni cultural resources and properties were managed properly. It hired three professional archaeologists and, with additional assistance from the National Park Service and the Arizona State Museum, initiated a program to train and employ tribal members in cultural resource management. Working with these non-Zuni archaeologists, the Pueblo of Zuni were able to establish their own historic preservation office that today manages and coordinates all historic preservation on the Zuni reservation, a task that the federal government managed until 1992. The Pueblo also established the Zuni Cultural Resource Enterprise, a Zuni-owned CRM business that employs both Zuni and non-Zuni archaeologists and carries out contract archaeology projects both on and off the Zuni reservation.[35]

In addition to working with native peoples, CRM archaeologists are also working with the public through what has come to be known as public archaeology. One of the basic ideas behind public archaeology is that because most CRM archaeology is done with public money, it is important for the public to benefit from the results of archaeological research. Unfortunately, that is not always the case, and today popular media is far more likely to discuss archaeology in the context of ancient alien contact or Biblical fundamentalism than the context of mainstream anthropology. Working directly with the public, for example, by having "open houses" at archaeological sites or hosting artifact identification days, is one way that CRM archaeologists can help to overcome popular misconceptions of the past, as well as learn more about the past.[36]

Equally important is for archaeologists to undertake work that is meaningful to local communities, and this too is part of public archaeology. For example, CRM archaeologists in Hawaii are starting to work directly with Native Hawaiian communities to provide information on ancestral practices, and in turn, Native Hawaiian communities are helping CRM archaeologists to identify and preserve important archaeological sites. As explained by Hawaiian archaeologists Sean Nāleimaile and Lokelani Brant, by incorporating Native Hawaiian "cultural practices and resource management systems into existing frameworks of CRM, we will reestablish successful strategies to maintain our resources. More importantly, these foundations work to reestablish these cultural practices in the now."[37] Public archaeologists believe that engaging the interests and needs of local communities, as is happening in Hawaii, serves to improve both the CRM work and the local community.

Cultural resource management accounts for the majority of archaeology jobs in the United States.[38] As development and construction projects continue to affect the archaeological record, the need for well-trained CRM archaeologists is likely to persist.

Museum Anthropology

19.7 Describe the field of museum anthropology.

Museums have been an important part of anthropology since the very beginnings of the field. As early anthropologists returned from archaeological excavations and ethnographic explorations they brought with them artifacts from the peoples and cultures they encountered. These materials were collected in museums—often natural history museums since, at the time (the mid to late 19th century), non-Western artifacts were not considered art, nor were the cultures of non-Western peoples considered part of history. Thus the objects non-Western peoples produced and the information about their cultures were deposited with similar items from other forms of animal life. Today we recognize this as an ethnocentric, perhaps even racist, view of non-Western people, but many anthropological and archaeological collections are still deposited and maintained in natural history museums. Many other museums exist today as well, from cultural museums to historic site museums to museums showcasing traditional works of art, and anthropologists work in all of these.

Anthropologists typically hold one of three positions in museums: curators, collection managers, or educators. Curators are responsible for the overall content and use of collections. They oversee the museum collections with an eye to their value for research and their importance to the history of their field. In some cases curators acquire (or accession) materials in order to fill areas that are inadequately represented in their collections; in other cases they have to make difficult decisions about discarding (or de-accessioning) materials that are no longer of use. Curators also lead teams that evaluate and develop the museum's exhibits. Collection managers work to ensure that the museum's collections are preserved. They make sure that storage facilities and records are properly maintained, and they regularly check the collections to make sure they are not deteriorating. When deterioration is found, collections managers work with conservators to repair damage and determine ways to keep further damage from occurring. Finally, museum educators work with the public to teach them about the peoples and cultures represented in the museum's collections.[39]

Regardless of their position, public education is a central role for all museum anthropologists. A good example can be seen in recent work involving a traditional native New Zealand Maori meeting house, or *marae,* on display at the Field Museum in Chicago. A *marae* is used in Maori culture as a place where individuals are allowed to air grievances and settle disputes in an atmosphere of respect and open-mindedness. Field Museum curator of Pacific anthropology John Terrell wished that Chicago had such a space, and then realized that the *marae* itself might be used as one; in other words, that the Maori *marae* might become a Chicago *marae.* Terrell worked with a group of Maori and a group of teachers from Chicago public schools to explore this idea, and today the *marae* is used by groups seeking to discuss difficult issues in a context of mutual respect.[40] In this way Terrell was able to not only display an important cultural object, but also, with the assistance of the collections manager and museum education staff, develop a way for the object to be used by the Chicago community in a manner similar to its use within Maori culture.

A Maori meeting house in New Zealand.

Forensic Anthropology

Many of us are fascinated by detective stories. We are interested in crimes and why they occur, and we like to read about them, fictional or not. **Forensic anthropology** is the specialty in anthropology that is devoted to helping solve crimes and identifying human remains, usually by applying knowledge of physical anthropology.[41] It is attracting increasing attention by the public, and an increasing number of practitioners. One forensic anthropologist says she is called "the bone lady" by law enforcement personnel.[42] Like others in her line of work, she is asked to dig up or examine human bones to help solve crimes. Narrowing down identification is one of the first priorities, but it is not as simple as on television shows. Are these the bones of a man or woman? How old was the person? How well the forensic anthropologist can answer these seemingly simple questions depends upon whether the remains include most bones of the skeleton. Identification of an adult's sex from remains is easier if the pelvis is present, but establishing sex in nonadult remains is not reliable from skeletal remains.[43] With regard to estimating age, only a wide age range can be estimated for adults, but a much narrower range can be estimated for nonadult remains. Forensic anthropologists are often asked for "race" as well. As we discussed in earlier chapters, "race" is not a useful biological category when applied to humans, but it is a significant social category. Forensic anthropologists can estimate with fairly high accuracy whether a person's ancestors came from Asia, Europe, or Africa, but they cannot detect skin color.[44] The police files may suggest that an adult male with Asian ancestry disappeared five years ago. The forensic anthropologist could say with a high probability that the remains were of an Asian male adult. Dental, surgical, or hospital records from that individual might lead to unique features that could be matched for more precise identification. Sometimes the forensic anthropologist can suggest the cause of death when the law enforcement people are stumped.

Another important piece of evidence that is often provided by forensic anthropologists is the time of death. Establishing when a victim died can be essential to solving a crime. Forensic anthropologists use changes in the body as it decays to estimate how long an individual has been dead. In the short term, one to three days after death, the body decays primarily through the action of digestive enzymes and bacteria already in the body. Forensic anthropologists use indicators such as body temperature (which decreases about one degree an hour after death), skin discoloration, or the build-up of lactic acid in the muscles (which causes them to progressively stiffen over the 12 hours after death) to determine time of death. Over the longer term, three days to a month after death, the action of factors outside the body contribute significantly to decay. The most important of these factors is the activity of insects. Blow flies, for example, deposit eggs on dead tissue during specific periods after death. The eggs then hatch into maggots, again during a specific period of time, and the maggots slowly grow into adults. By carefully examining the presence and maturity of the eggs and maggots of various species of flies, the forensic anthropologist can provide a good estimate of the time of death.[45]

Some cultural anthropologists have also done forensic work, often in connection with legal cases involving Native Americans. For example, in 1978, Barbara Joans was asked to advise the defense in a trial of six older Bannock-Shoshoni women from the Fort Hall reservation who were accused of fraud. They had received "supplemental security income (SSI)," which the social service agency claimed they had no right to receive because they had not reported receiving rent money on land that they owned. Joans presented evidence that the women, although they spoke some English, did not have enough proficiency to understand the nuances of what the SSI people told them. The judge agreed with the defense and ruled that the SSI would have to use a Bannock-Shoshoni interpreter in the future when they went to the reservation to describe the requirements of the program.[46]

19.8 Describe the field of forensic anthropology.

Forensic anthropology The application of anthropology, usually physical anthropology, to help identify human remains and assist in solving crimes.

A forensic anthropologist digs out a body, apparently a victim of state-sponsored violence in Argentina between 1976 and 1983.

In recent years, Clyde Snow and other forensic anthropologists have been called on to confirm horrendous abuses of human rights. Governments have been responsible for the systematic killing of their citizens, and forensic anthropologists have helped to bring the perpetrators to justice. For example, Snow and other forensic anthropologists helped to confirm that the military dictatorship in Argentina in the 1980s was responsible for the deaths of many Argentine civilians who had "disappeared." The forensic anthropologists were also able to determine the location of mass graves and the identity of victims of state-organized brutality in Guatemala. In addition to bringing the perpetrators to justice, confirming the massacres and identifying the victims help the families of the "disappeared" put their anguish behind them. A special session (called "Uncovering the 'Disappeared': Clyde Snow and Forensic Anthropologists Work for Justice"[47]) at the annual meeting of the American Anthropological Association in November 2000 honored Snow and other forensic anthropologists.

Medical Anthropology

19.9 Discuss the goals of medical anthropology.

Illness and death are significant events for people everywhere. No one is spared. So it should not be surprising that how people understand the causes of illness and death, how they behave, and what resources they marshal to cope with these events are extremely important parts of culture. Some argue that we will never completely understand how to treat illness effectively until we understand the cultural behaviors, attitudes, values, and larger social and political milieu in which people live. Others argue that society and culture have little to do with the outcome of illness—the reason that people die needlessly is that they do not get the appropriate medical treatment.

medical anthropology The anthropological study of health and illness and associated beliefs and practices.

But anthropologists, particularly those in **medical anthropology,** who are actively engaged in studying health and illness and associated beliefs and practices, are increasingly realizing that biological *and* social factors need to be considered if we are to reduce human suffering. For instance, some populations have an appalling incidence of infant deaths due to diarrhea. The origin of this situation is mostly biological in the sense that the deaths are caused by bacterial infection. But why are so many infants exposed to those bacteria? Usually, the main reason is social. The affected infants are likely to be poor. Because they are poor, they are likely to live with infected drinking water. Similarly, malnutrition may be the biological result of a diet poor in protein, but such a diet is usually also a cultural phenomenon, reflecting a society with classes of people with very unequal access to the necessities of life. In many ways, therefore, medical anthropology, and anthropology in general, is developing in the direction of a "biocultural synthesis."[48]

Cultural Understandings of Health and Illness

19.10 Discuss cultural understandings of health and illness.

Medical researchers and medical practitioners in the United States and other Western societies do not exist in a social vacuum. Many of their ideas and practices are influenced by the culture in which they live. We may think of medicine as purely based on "fact," but it is clear on reflection that many ideas stem from the culture in which the researchers reside. Consider the recent shift in attitudes toward birth. Not so long ago in the United States, fathers were excluded from the birth, hospitals whisked the baby away from the mother and only brought the baby to her infrequently, and visitors (but not attending nurses and doctors) had to wear masks when holding the baby. Rationalizations were given for those practices, but looking back at them, they do not appear to be based on scientific evidence. Many medical anthropologists now argue that the *biomedical paradigm* (the system in which physicians are trained) itself needs to be understood as part of the culture.[49]

ethnomedicine The health-related beliefs, knowledge, and practices of a cultural group.

Discovering the health-related beliefs, knowledge, and practices of a cultural group—its **ethnomedicine**—is one of the goals of medical anthropology. How do cultures view health and illness? What are their theories about the causes of illness? Do those theories impact how illnesses are treated? What is the therapeutic process? Are there specialized medical practitioners, and how do they heal? Are there special medicines, and how are they administered? These are just some of the questions asked by the anthropological study of ethnomedicine.

Concepts of Balance or Equilibrium

Many cultures have the view that the body should be kept in equilibrium or balance. The balance may be between hot and cold, or wet and dry, as in many cultures of Latin America and the Caribbean.[50] The notion of balance is not limited to opposites. For example, the ancient Greek system of medicine, stemming from Hippocrates, assumed that there were four "humors"—blood, phlegm, yellow bile, and black bile—that must be kept in balance. These humors have hot and cold as well as wet and dry properties. The Greek medical system was widely diffused in Europe and spread to parts of the Islamic world. In Europe, the humoral medical system was dominant until the germ theory replaced it in the 1900s.[51] In the Ayurvedic system, whose practice dates back 4,000 years in North India, Pakistan, Bangladesh, Sri Lanka, and in the Arab world, there are three humors (phlegm, bile, and flatulence), and a balance between hot and cold is also important.[52] The Chinese medical system, which dates back about 3,500 years, initially stressed the balance between the contrasting forces of *yin* and *yang* and later added the concept of humors, which were six in number in Chinese medicine.[53]

The concepts of hot and cold and *yin* and *yang* are illustrated in Emily Ahern's ethnographic description of the medical system of the Taiwanese Hokkien.[54] The body requires both hot and cold substances; when the body is out of balance, a lack of one substance can be restored by eating or drinking the missing substance. So, for example, when Ahern was faint with heat, she was told to drink some bamboo shoot soup because it was "cold." In the winter, you need more hot substances; in the summer, you want fewer. Some people can tolerate more imbalance than others; people who are older, for instance, can tolerate less imbalance than those who are young. A loss of blood means a loss of heat. So, for a month after childbirth, women eat mostly a soup made of chicken, wine, and sesame oil—all "hot" ingredients. Hot things to eat are generally oily, sticky, or come from animals; cold things tend to be soupy, watery, or made from plants.

Morning tai chi exercise in Shanghai, China.

Supernatural Forces

The Taiwanese Hokkien believe that most illnesses have natural or physiological causes, but around the world, it is more common to believe that illnesses are caused by supernatural forces. In fact, in a cross-cultural study of 139 societies, George P. Murdock found that only two societies did not have the belief that gods or spirits could cause illness, making such a belief a near universal. And 56 percent of those sample societies thought that gods or spirits were the major causes of illness.[55] As we discussed in the chapter on religion and magic, sorcery and witchcraft are common in the world's societies. Although humans practice both sorcery and witchcraft for good or evil, making people ill is one of their major uses. Illness can also be thought of as caused by the loss of one's soul, fate, retribution for violation of a taboo, or contact with a polluting or taboo substance or object. Sorcery is believed to be a cause of illness by most societies on all continents; retribution because of violation of a taboo is also very frequent in all but one region of the world. The belief that soul loss can cause illness is absent in the area around the Mediterranean, uncommon in Africa, infrequent in the New World and the Pacific, and has its highest frequency in Eurasia.[56]

On Chuuk (Truk), an atoll in the central Pacific, serious illnesses and death are mainly believed to be the work of spirits. Occasionally, the spirits of relatives are to blame, although they usually do not cause serious damage. More often, illness is caused by the spirit of a particular locality or a ghost on a path at night.[57] Nowadays, one of two therapeutic options or their combination is often chosen—hospital medicine or Chuuk medicine. Chuuk medical treatment requires a careful evaluation of symptoms by the patient and the patient's relatives, because different spirits inflict different symptoms. If the symptom match is clear, the patient may choose an appropriate Chuuk medical formula to cure the illness. The patient may also ask whether he or she has done something wrong, and if so, what might point to the appropriate spirit and countervailing formula. For example, there is a taboo on having sexual relations before going to sea. If a person who violated this prohibition becomes ill, the reef spirits will be suspected. The Chuuk medical formula is supposed to cure illness quickly and dramatically. For this reason, Chuuk patients ask for a discharge from a hospital if their condition does not improve quickly. If treatment fails, the Chuukese believe that they need to reevaluate the diagnosis, sometimes with the aid of a diviner.[58] In contrasting their theories of illness to the American germ theory, the people of Chuuk point out that, although they have seen ghosts, they have never seen the germs that Americans talk about. Using both methods, some people recover and some do not, so the ultimate cause is a matter of faith.[59]

The Biomedical Paradigm

In most societies, people simply think that their ideas about health and illness are true. Often people are not aware that there may be another way of viewing things until they confront another medical system. Western medical practice has spread widely. People with other medical systems have had to recognize that Western practitioners may consider their ideas about health and illness to be deficient, so they often need to decide which course (Western or non-Western) to follow in dealing with illness. Change, however, is not entirely one-way. For example, for a long time, the Western medical profession disparaged the Chinese practice of acupuncture, but now more medical practitioners are recognizing that acupuncture may provide effective treatment of certain conditions.

Biomedicine The dominant medical paradigm in Western societies today.

Most medical anthropologists use the term **biomedicine** to refer to the dominant medical paradigm in Western cultures today, with the *bio* part of the word emphasizing the biological emphasis of this medical system. Biomedicine appears to focus on specific diseases and cures for those diseases. Health is not the focus, as it is thought to be the *absence* of disease. Diseases are considered to be largely from physical (e.g. trauma, accidents) or biological (e.g., bacteria, viruses, infection) causes, and there is relatively little interest in psychological factors affecting the person or the larger social and cultural systems in which they are embedded. Metaphorically, the body seems to be viewed as a "machine," and it is believed that technological advances can transcend our biological limitations. Doctors generally do not treat the whole body but tend to specialize, with the human body partitioned into zones that belong to different specialties. Death is seen as a failure, and biomedical practitioners do everything they can to prolong life, regardless of the circumstances under which the patient would live life.[60]

Treatment of Illness

Anthropologists who study diseases in this and other cultures can be roughly classified into two camps. First, there are those (the more relativistic) who think that the culture so influences disease symptoms, incidence, and treatment that there are few if any cultural universals about any illness. If each culture is unique, we should expect its conception and treatment of an illness to be unique too, not like beliefs and practices in other cultures. Second, there are those (the more universalistic) who see cross-cultural similarities in the conception and treatment of illness, despite the unique qualities (particularly in the belief system) of each culture. For example, native remedies may contain chemicals that are the same as, or similar in effect to, chemicals used in remedies by Western biomedicine.[61] Readers should note that our classification here of medical anthropologists is a crude one; many medical anthropologists do not fall unambiguously into one or the other group. And the reality might be that a given culture is very much like other cultures in some respects but unique in other respects.

In their extensive research on Maya ethnomedicine, Elois Ann Berlin and Brent Berlin make a strong case that, although studies of the Maya have emphasized beliefs about illness that are based on supernatural causes, a good deal of Maya ethnomedicine is about natural conditions, their signs and symptoms, and the remedies used to deal with those conditions. In regard to gastrointestinal diseases, the Berlins found that the Maya have a wide-ranging and accurate understanding of anatomy, physiology, and symptoms. Furthermore, the remedies they use, including recommendations for food, drink, and herbal medicines, have properties that are not that different from those of the bio-medical profession.[62]

Carole Browner also suggests that the emphasis on "hot-cold" theories of illness in Latin America has been overemphasized to the neglect of other factors that influence choices about reproductive health and female health problems. In a study of the medical system in a highland Oaxacan community, Browner finds that certain plants are used to expel substances from the uterus—to facilitate labor at full term, to produce an abortion, or to induce menstrual flow. Other plants are used to retain things in the uterus—to prevent excess blood loss during menstruation, to help healing after delivery, and to prevent miscarriage. Most of these plant remedies appear to work.[63]

Dayak woman handling a medicinal plant in Sarawak, Malaysia.

The biomedical establishment has become increasingly aware of the value of studying the "traditional" medicinal remedies discovered or invented by people around the world. In studying the indigenous medicines of the Hausa of Nigeria, Nina Etkin and Paul Ross asked individuals to describe the physical attributes of more than 600 plants and their possible medicinal uses, more than 800 diseases and symptoms, and more than 5,000 prepared medicines. Although many medicines were used for treating sorcery, spirit aggression, or witchcraft, most medicines were used for illnesses regarded by the Hausa as having natural causes. Malaria is a serious endemic medical problem in the Hausa region, as in many areas of Africa. The Hausa use approximately 72 plant remedies for conditions connected with malaria—among them anemia, intermittent fever, and jaundice. Experimental treatment of malaria in laboratory animals supports the efficacy of many of the Hausa remedies. But perhaps the most important part of the Etkin and Ross findings is the role of diet. Although most medical research does not consider the possible medical efficacy of the *foods* that people eat in combating illness, food is, of course, consumed in much larger quantities and more often than medicine. It is noteworthy, therefore, that the Hausa eat many plants with antimalarial properties; in fact, dietary consumption of these plants appears to be greatest during the time of year when the risk of malarial infection is at its highest. Recent research has also discovered that foods and spices like garlic, onions, cinnamon, ginger, and pepper have antiviral or antibacterial properties.[64]

Medical Practitioners   In our society, we may be so used to consulting a full-time medical specialist (if we do not feel better quickly) that we tend to assume that biomedical treatment is the only effective medical treatment. If we are given a medicine, we expect it to have the appropriate medical effect and make us feel better. So, many in the biomedical system, practitioners and patients alike, are perplexed by the seeming effectiveness of other medical systems that are based in part on symbolic or ritual healing. As we noted earlier, many native plants have been shown to be medically effective, but their use is often accompanied by singing, dancing, noise making, or rituals. Our difficulty in understanding the healing in such practices probably stems from the assumption in biomedicine that the mind is fundamentally different from the body. Yet, there is increasing evidence that the *form* of treatment may be just as important as the *content* of treatment.[65]

The practitioners who deal with more than the body are sometimes referred to as *personalistic* practitioners. In a personalistic view, illness may be viewed as being due to something in one's social life being out of order. The cause could be retribution by gods or spirits for one's own bad behavior or thoughts, or the work of an angry individual practicing sorcery or witchcraft. A bad social situation or a bad relationship may be thought of as provoking physical symptoms because of anxiety or stress. In societies with occupational specialization, priests, who are formally trained full-time religious practitioners, may be asked to convey messages or requests for healing to higher powers.[66] Societies with beliefs in sorcery and witchcraft as causes of illness typically have practitioners who are believed to be able to use magic in reverse—that is, to undo the harm invoked by sorcerers and witches. Sometimes sorcerers or witches themselves may be asked to reverse illnesses caused by others. But they may not be sought out because they are often feared and have relatively low status.[67]

The Shaman   Shamans are charismatic leaders who perform many functions in societies lacking political hierarchies, but perhaps one of their most important functions is their role as medical practitioner.[68] Shamans, mediums, sorcerers, and priests are usually acting as personalistic healers. A more naturalistic view of illness, common to most physicians as well as chemists and herbalists, is that certain substances or treatments will fix the problem.[69]

A Mongolian shaman kisses niece during healing.

After working with shamans in Africa, E. Fuller Torrey, a psychiatrist and anthropologist, concluded that they use the same mechanisms and techniques to cure patients as psychiatrists and achieve about the same results. He isolated four categories used by healers the world over:

1. **The naming process.** If a disease has a name—"neurasthenia" or "phobia" or "possession by an ancestral spirit" will do—then it is curable; the patient realizes that the doctor understands his case.
2. **The personality of the doctor.** Those who demonstrate some empathy, nonpossessive warmth, and genuine interest in the patient get results.
3. **The patient's expectations.** One way of raising the patient's expectations of being cured is the trip to the doctor; the longer the trip—to the Mayo Clinic, Menninger Clinic, Delphi, or Lourdes—the easier the cure. An impressive setting (the medical center) and impressive paraphernalia (the stethoscope, the couch, attendants in uniform, the rattle, the whistle, the drum, the mask) also raise the patient's expectations. The healer's training is important. And high fees also help to raise a patient's expectations. (The Paiute doctors always collect their fees before starting a cure; if they don't, it is believed that they will fall ill.)
4. **Curing techniques.** Drugs, shock treatment, conditioning techniques, and so on have long been used in many different parts of the world.[70]

Biomedical research is not unaware of the effect of the mind on healing. In fact, considerable evidence has accumulated that psychological factors can be very important in illness. Patients who believe that medicine will help them often recover quickly even if the medicine is only a sugar pill or a medicine not particularly relevant to their condition. Such effects are called *placebo* effects.[71] Placebos do not just have psychological effects. Although the mechanisms are not well understood, they may also alter body chemistry and bolster the immune system.[72]

Shamans may coexist with medical doctors. Don Antonio, a respected Otomi Indian shaman in central Mexico, has many patients, perhaps not as many as before modern medicine, but still plenty. In his view, when he was born, God gave him his powers to cure, but his powers are reserved for removing "evil" illnesses (those caused by sorcerers). "Good" illnesses can be cured by herbs and medicine, and he refers patients with those illnesses to medical doctors; he believes that doctors are more effective than he could be in those cases. The doctors, however, do not seem to refer any patients to Don Antonio or other shamans.[73]

Physicians   The most important full-time medical practitioner in the biomedical system is the physician, and the patient-physician relationship is central. In the ideal scheme of things, the physician is viewed as having the ability, with some limits, of being able to treat illness, alleviate suffering, and prolong the life of the patient, as well as offering promises of patient confidentiality and privacy. The patient relies on the physician's knowledge, skill, and ethics. Consistent with the biomedical paradigm, doctors tend to treat patients as having "conditions" rather than as complete people. Physicians presumably rely on science for authoritative knowledge, but they place a good deal of importance on the value of their own clinical experience. Often, physicians consider their own observations of the patient to be more valuable than the reports by the patient. Because patients commonly go to physicians to solve a particular condition or sickness, physicians tend to try to do something about it even in the face of uncertainty. Physicians tend to rely on technology for diagnoses and treatment and place relatively low value on talking with patients. In fact, physicians tend to give patients relatively little information, and they may not listen very well.[74]

Despite the importance of physicians in biomedicine, patients do not always seek physician care. In fact, one-third of the population of the United States regularly consults with alternative practitioners, such as acupuncturists or chiropractors, often unbeknownst to the physician. Somewhat surprisingly, individuals with more education are more likely to seek alternative care.[75]

Political and Economic Influences on Health

People with more social, economic, and political power in a society are generally healthier.[76] Inequality in health in socially stratified societies is not surprising. The poor usually have more exposure to disease because they live in more crowded conditions and are more likely to lack the resources to get quality care. For many diseases, health problems, and death rates, incidence or relative frequency varies directly with social class. In the United Kingdom, for example, people in the higher social classes are less likely to have headaches, bronchitis, pneumonia, heart disease, arthritis, injuries, and mental disorders, to name just a few of the differences.[77] Ethnic differences also predict health inequities. In the United States recently, the differences between African Americans and European Americans in health have narrowed somewhat in some respects, but those favoring European Americans are still substantial. As of 1987, the difference in life expectancy was seven years. As of 2009, the difference in life expectancy was about four years. Infant mortality has not shown improvement. In 1987, African American infant mortality was about twice the rate for European American infants; in 2007, the ratio was 2.4.[78] Robert Hahn has estimated that poverty accounted for about 19 percent of the overall mortality in the United States.[79]

Inequities, because of class and ethnicity, are not limited to within-society differences. Power and economic differentials *between* societies also have profound health consequences. Over the course of European exploration and expansion, indigenous peoples died in enormous numbers from introduced diseases, wars, and conquests; they had their lands expropriated and diminished in size and quality. When incorporated into colonial territories or into countries, indigenous people usually become minorities and they are almost always very poor. These conditions of life not only affect the incidence of disease; they also tend to lead to greater substance abuse, violence, depression, and other mental pathologies.[80]

Health Conditions and Diseases

Medical anthropologists have studied an enormous variety of conditions. What follows is only a small sampling.

AIDS

AIDS (acquired immune deficiency syndrome) A disease caused by the HIV virus.

The current state of medical science and technology may lull us into thinking that epidemics are a thing of the past. But the sudden emergence of the disease we call **AIDS (acquired immune deficiency syndrome)** reminds us that new diseases, or new varieties of old diseases, can appear at any time. Like all other organisms, disease-causing organisms also evolve. The human immunodeficiency virus (HIV) that causes AIDS emerged only relatively recently. Viruses and bacteria are always mutating, and new strains emerge that are initially a plague on our genetic resistance and on medical efforts to contain them.

Millions of people around the world now have the symptoms of AIDS, and millions more are infected with HIV but do not know they are infected. As of 2011, 34 million adults and children in the world were living with HIV/AIDS.[81] There are a few signs of improvement since the beginning of the epidemic. The percentage of people newly infected globally is now stable. Some countries and regions have improved in countering AIDS deaths with prevention efforts—notable examples are in the Caribbean, where deaths declined 48 percent from 2005 to 2011, and in sub-Saharan Africa, where deaths declined by nearly 33 percent in the same period. In addition, the number of new cases worldwide each year has gone down and also fewer people are dying from AIDS. But some regions of the world such as Eastern Europe, Central Asia, the Middle East, and North Africa have gotten worse. And despite improvements in sub-Saharan Africa, the region still has the majority of HIV cases in the world.

AIDS is a frightening epidemic not only because of its death toll, but also because it takes a long time (on average four years) after exposure for symptoms to appear. This means that many people who have been infected by HIV but do not know they are infected may continue, unknowingly, to transmit the virus to others.[82]

Transmission occurs mostly via sexual encounters, through semen and blood. Drug users may also transmit HIV by way of contaminated needles. Transmission by blood transfusion has been virtually eliminated in this and other societies by medical screening of blood supplies. In some countries, however, there is still no routine screening of blood prior to transfusions. HIV may be passed from a pregnant woman to her offspring through the placenta and after birth through her breast milk. The rate of transmission between a mother and her baby is from 20 percent to 40 percent. Children are also at great risk because they are likely to be orphaned by a parent's death from AIDS. At the turn of the 21st century, approximately 14 million children were parentless because of AIDS.[83]

Millions of children in sub-Saharan Africa are orphaned because of AIDS. These orphaned children in Uganda look on during a visit by Britain's Queen Elizabeth to their center.

Many people think of AIDS as only a medical problem that requires only a medical solution, without realizing that behavioral, cultural, and political issues need to be addressed as well. It is true that developing a vaccine or a drug to prevent people from getting AIDS and finding a permanent cure for those who have it will ultimately solve the problem. But, for a variety of reasons, we can expect that the medical solution alone will not be sufficient, at least not for a while. First, to be effective worldwide, or even within a country, a vaccine has to be inexpensive and relatively easy to produce in large quantities; the same is true of any medical treatment. Second, governments around the world have to be willing and able to spend the money and hire the personnel necessary to manage an effective program.[84] Third, future vaccination and treatment will require the people at risk to be willing to get vaccinated and treated, which is not always the case. Witness the fact that a considerable number of parents in the United States refuse to have their children vaccinated against some childhood diseases. Researchers who have studied the reasons for parental refusal find that the refusers are likely to believe that vaccines are not necessary to protect their child or that vaccines are not safe. Although it may seem counterintuitive, vaccine refusers are more likely to be of higher status and education.[85]

A significant barrier to HIV/AIDS treatment has been the expense of the needed drugs. Fortunately, the Clinton Health Access Initiative negotiated a much-reduced cost for 70 poorer countries.[86] The reduced cost of less than $200 per year is still not cheap for people with little money, but the lower cost makes it possible for aid organizations to foot the bills.

In the meantime, the risk of HIV infection can be reduced only by changes in social, particularly sexual, behavior. But to persuade people to change their sexual behavior, it is necessary to find out exactly what they do sexually, why they do what they do, and to evaluate the efficacy of intervention programs.

Research so far suggests that different sexual patterns are responsible for HIV transmission in different parts of the world. In the United States, England, northern Europe, Australia, and Latin America, the recipients of anal intercourse, particularly men, are the most likely individuals to acquire HIV infection; vaginal intercourse can also transmit the infection, usually from the man to the woman. Needle sharing can transmit the infection, too. In Africa, the most common mode of transmission is vaginal intercourse, and so women get infected more commonly in Africa than elsewhere.[87] In fact, in Africa there are slightly more cases of HIV in women as compared with men.[88]

It is important to recognize these differences because prevention outcomes that work for some epidemics may not work for others. HIV epidemics can be divided into those that are concentrated in some populations such as sex workers, drug-users, and men having sex with other men or more generalized. Promotion of condom use has been effective in some cases in some specialized epidemics, such as in Thailand and Cambodia where condom use became required in brothels. But generalized epidemics of AIDS such as those in Africa occur among the majority populations, most of whom are heterosexual married people.[89] Prevention programs have largely stressed condom use, testing for HIV, and treatment for sexually transmitted infections. In some places such programs have been successful. Perhaps for this reason, such programs have been the predominant form of intervention. But some recent critics have argued that the predominant programs are not effective where the epidemic is generalized, and it is time to try new methods.[90] Some research even shows negative effects. For example, while people testing positive are more likely to use condoms, there is some evidence that people who test negative (the majority of those tested) are more likely to engage in risky behavior. Edward Green points out that AIDS-prevention community has failed to consider the importance of trying to change sexual behavior, either because they believe it won't work or because they do not believe in curtailing sexual freedom. But the main successes have come from countries that have employed low-cost education programs stressing abstinence and avoidance of multiple sexual partners. Uganda showed remarkable change. In just 10 years from 1992 to 2002, prevalence of HIV declined from 18 percent to 6 percent. This corresponded with a dramatic reduction in premarital sex and a decline in extramarital sex.[91] There is also increasing recognition that prevention groups need to work with local leaders, including traditional healers to figure out the best ways to proceed.

As of now, there are only two known ways to reduce the likelihood of sexual HIV transmission. One way is to abstain from sexual intercourse; the other is to use condoms. Male circumcision now appears to decrease the risk of HIV infection, but studies have not yet evaluated long-term effects.[92] Educational programs that teach how AIDS spreads and what one can do about it may reduce the spread somewhat, but such programs may fail where people have incompatible beliefs and attitudes about sexuality. For example, people in some central African societies believe that deposits of semen after conception are necessary for a successful pregnancy and generally enhance a woman's health and ability to reproduce. It might be expected then that people who have these beliefs about semen would choose not to use condoms; after all, condoms in their view are a threat to public health.[93] Educational programs may also emphasize the wrong message. Promiscuity may increase the risk of HIV transmission, so hardly anyone would question the wisdom of advertising to reduce the number of sexual partners. And, at least in the homosexual community in the United States, individuals report fewer sexual partners than in the past. What was not anticipated, however, was that individuals in monogamous relationships, who may feel safe, are less likely to use condoms or to avoid the riskiest sexual practices. Needless to say, sex with a regular partner who is infected is not safe.[94] In what may seem like something of a paradox, the United Nations observed that, for most women in the world today, the major risk factor for being infected with HIV is being married.[95] It is not marriage *per se* that heightens the risk of HIV infection; rather, the proximate cause may be the lower likelihood of condom use or less abstinence by a married couple.

To solve the problem of AIDS, we may hope that medical science will develop an effective and inexpensive vaccination or treatment that all can afford. There is a vaccine that seems to reduce HIV infection in monkeys to hardly detectable levels.[96] Perhaps soon there will be a similar vaccine for humans.

Mental and Emotional Disorders

Diagnosing mental or emotional disorders in one culture is difficult enough; diagnosing them in others poses much greater difficulty. Many researchers start with Western categories of mental illness and try to apply them elsewhere without first trying to understand native conceptions of mental disorder. In addition, "mental" and "physical" disorders are rarely separate. For example, a host of illnesses can produce a loss of energy that some may see as depression, and fear or anger can produce physical symptoms such as a heart attack.[97]

When Western anthropologists first started describing mental illness in non-Western societies, there seemed to be unique illnesses in different cultures. These are referred to as *culture-bound syndromes*. For example, a mental disorder called *pibloktoq* occurred among some Eskimo adults of Greenland, usually women, who became oblivious to their surroundings and acted in agitated, eccentric ways. They might strip themselves naked

Applied Anthropology

Eating Disorders, Biology, and the Cultural Construction of Beauty

Cultures differ about what they consider beautiful. In many cultures, fat people are considered more beautiful than thin people. Melvin Ember did fieldwork years ago on the islands of American Samoa. When he returned to the main island after three months on a distant island, a prominent chief said: "You look good. You gained weight." In reality, he had lost 30 pounds! The chief clearly thought that fat was better than thin and was trying to say something nice. Among the Azawagh Arabs of Niger, fatness was not merely valued and considered beautiful; great care was taken to ensure that young girls became fat by insisting and sometimes forcing them to drink large quantities of milk-based porridge.

Around the world, fatness is generally considered more desirable than thinness not only because it is considered more beautiful but also because it is thought to be a marker of health and fertility. This view is in strong contrast to the ideal in the United States and many other Western societies, where fatness is thought to be unattractive and to reflect poor health. Thinness, particularly in the upper classes, is considered beautiful. How can we explain these differences in what is considered beautiful?

A common assumption is that fatness will be valued in societies subject to food scarcity. But cross-cultural research suggests that the picture is more complicated. It appears that many societies with unpredictable resources actually value thinness, particularly in societies that have little or no technological means of storing food. At first glance, this seems puzzling. Shouldn't an individual who stores calories on the body be better off than an individual who is thin when

Cultures vary in their ideals of beauty, and ideals change over time. In the United States in the 1950s, "somewhat plump" was idealized. Beginning in the 1960s, thinness became idealized.

facing starvation? Perhaps. But 10 thin individuals will generally consume less than 10 heavier people, so perhaps there is a group advantage to being thin. Indeed, many societies with frequent episodes of famine encourage fasting or eating very light meals, as among the Gurage of Ethiopia. The strongest cross-cultural predictor of valuing fatness in women is what is often referred to as "machismo." Societies with a strong emphasis on male aggression and sexuality are the most likely to value fatness in women; those with little machismo value thinness. Why? One theory is that machismo actually reflects male insecurity and fear of women. Such men may not be looking for closeness or intimacy with their wives, but they may want to show how potent they are by having lots

of children. If fatness suggests fertility, men may look for wives who are fatter. Consistent with this idea, the ideal of thinness in women became more common in North America with the rise of women's movements in the 1920s and late 1960s. Consider that Marilyn Monroe epitomized beauty in the 1950s; she was well-rounded, not thin. Thin became more popular only when women began to question early marriage and having many children. Behaviors associated with machismo became less acceptable at those times.

Cultural beliefs about what is considered a beautiful body impose enormous pressures on females to achieve the ideal body type—whether it be fat or thin. In the United States and other Western countries, the effort to be thin can be carried to an extreme, resulting in the eating disorders anorexia and bulimia. The irony of "thinness" being idealized in the United States and other Western countries is that obesity is becoming more common in those societies. As of 2010, the incidence of obesity in adults increased in the United States to 36 percent, and medical researchers worried about the increase in heart disease and diabetes resulting from obesity. Whether or not obesity is a result of an eating disorder (in the psychological sense) is more debatable. Researchers are finding biological causes of obesity, such as resistance to the hormone leptin, which regulates appetite, suggesting that much of the obesity "epidemic" has biological causes. Still, fast food, increasing sedentariness, and extremely large portion sizes are probably contributing factors also.

Sources: P. J. Brown and Sweeney 2009; Loustaunau and Sobo 1997, 85; N. Wolf 1991; R. Popenoe 2004; C. R. Ember et al. 2005; J. M. Friedman 2003; Ogden et al. 2012.

and wander across the ice and over hills until they collapsed of exhaustion. Another disorder, *amok*, occurred in Malaya, Indonesia, and New Guinea, usually among males. John Honigmann characterized it as a "destructive maddened excitement … beginning with depression and followed by a period of brooding and withdrawal [culminating in] the final mobilization of tremendous energy during which the 'wild man' runs destructively berserk."[98] *Anorexia nervosa*, the disorder involving aversion to food, may be unique to the relatively few societies that idealize slimness.[99] (See the box "Eating Disorders, Biology, and the Cultural Construction of Beauty.")

Some scholars think that each society's views of personality and concepts of mental illness have to be understood in their own terms. Western understandings and concepts cannot be applied to other cultures. For example, Catherine Lutz suggested that the Western concept of depression cannot be applied to the Pacific island of Ifaluk. The people there have many words for thinking or feeling about "loss and helplessness," but all their words are related to a specific need for someone, such as when someone dies or leaves the island. Such thoughts and feelings of loss are considered perfectly normal, and there is no word in their language for general hopelessness or "depression."[100] Therefore, Lutz questioned the applicability of the Western concept of depression as well as other Western psychiatric categories.

Other researchers are not so quick to dismiss the possible universality of psychiatric categories. Some think they have found a considerable degree of cross-cultural uniformity in conceptions of mental illness. Jane Murphy studied descriptions by the Inuit and the Yoruba, in Nigeria, of severely disturbed people. She found that their descriptions not only were similar to each other but also corresponded to North American descriptions of schizophrenia. The Inuit word for "crazy" is *nuthkavihak.* They use this word when something inside a person seems to be out of order. *Nuthkavihak* people are described as talking to themselves, believing themselves to be animals, making strange faces, becoming violent, and so on. The Yoruba have a word, *were,* for people who are "insane." People described as *were* sometimes hear voices, laugh when there is nothing to laugh at, and take up weapons and suddenly hit people.[101] More recently, a careful study of symptoms of schizophrenia in the Republic of Palau, which has one of the highest incidences of schizophrenia in the world, finds that principal symptoms and their relationships are comparable to patterns found in New York.[102]

Some mental illnesses, such as schizophrenia and depression, seem so widespread that many researchers think they are probably universal. Consistent with this idea is the fact that schizophrenic individuals in different cultures seem to share the same patterns of distinctive eye movements.[103] Still, cultural factors may influence the risk of developing such diseases, the specific symptoms that are expressed, and the effectiveness of different kinds of treatment.[104] There may be some truly culture-bound (nearly unique) syndromes, but others thought at one time to be unique may be culturally varying expressions of conditions that occur widely. *Pibloktoq,* for example, may be a kind of hysteria.[105]

Biological, but not necessarily genetic, factors may be very important in the etiology of some of the widespread disorders such as schizophrenia.[106] With regard to hysteria, Anthony Wallace theorized that nutritional factors such as calcium deficiency may cause hysteria and that dietary improvement may account for the decline of this illness in the Western world since the 19th century.[107] By the early 20th century, the discovery of the value of good nutrition, coupled with changes in social conditions, had led many people to drink milk, eat vitamin-rich foods, and spend time in the sun (although spending a lot of time in the sun is no longer recommended because of the risk of skin cancer). These changes in diet and activity increased the intake of vitamin D and helped people to maintain a proper calcium level. Consequently, the number of cases of hysteria declined.

Regarding *pibloktoq,* Wallace suggested that a complex set of related variables may cause the disease. The Inuit live in an environment that supplies only a minimum amount of calcium. A diet low in calcium could result in two different conditions. One condition, rickets, would produce physical deformities potentially fatal in the Inuit hunting economy. People whose genetic makeup made them prone to rickets would be eliminated from the population through natural selection. A low level of calcium in the blood could also cause muscular spasms known as tetany. Tetany, in turn, may cause emotional and mental disorientation similar to the symptoms of *pibloktoq.* Such attacks last for only a relatively short time and are not fatal, so people who developed *pibloktoq* would have a far greater chance of surviving in the Arctic environment with a calcium-deficient diet than would people who had rickets.

Depression It is estimated that hundreds of millions of people suffer from depression. Depressive symptoms include feelings of hopelessness and sadness, often with thoughts of death. There are often other symptoms as well—weight loss, fatigue, and disrupted sleep.[108] Cultures appear to vary in how depression is expressed; in many societies the somatic symptoms are more often presenting symptoms.[109] One of the most important stressors may be economic deprivation. Many studies have found that the lower classes in socially stratified societies have much higher proportions of all kinds of mental illness. Acute stressors like death of a loved one, divorce, loss of a job, or a natural disaster predict higher rates of mental illness for all social classes; however, these events take more of a toll in lower-class families.[110]

In a study designed to evaluate the effect of these and other stressors on the prevalence of depression in an African American community in a southern city, William Dressler combined fieldwork methods and hypothesis testing to try to better understand depression.[111] Although many studies rely on treatment or hospitalization rates, Dressler decided that such rates drastically underestimate the incidence of depression, inasmuch as many people do not seek treatment. He decided to rely on a symptom checklist, which asked such questions as how often in the last week a person felt like crying, felt lonely, or felt hopeless about the future. Although such checklists do not provide clear divisions for characterizing someone as mildly depressed or seriously depressed, they do allow researchers to compare people along a continuum.

Dressler measured a variety of different possible stressors, including life crises, economic worries, perceived racial inequality, and problems in social roles, and found that some of the objective stressors, like life crises and unemployment, predict depression in the expected direction only in the lower classes. That is, for lower-class African Americans, unemployment and other life crises predicted more depression, but that result was not found among middle- and upper-class individuals. These results are consistent with previous findings that many stressors take more of a toll among poorer individuals. On the other hand, more subjective economic stressors, such as feeling you are not making enough money, predict depression across all class lines. So does "social role" stress, such as thinking you are missing promotions because you are African American or thinking that your spouse expects too much.[112]

Undernutrition

What people eat is intrinsically connected to their survival and the ability of a population to reproduce itself, so we would expect that the ways people obtain, distribute, and consume food have been generally adaptive.[113] For example, the human body cannot synthesize eight amino acids. Meat can provide all of these amino acids, and combinations of particular plants can also provide them for a complete complement of protein. The combination of maize and beans in many traditional Native American diets, or *tortillas* and *frijoles* in Mexico, can provide all the needed amino acids. In places where wheat (often made into bread) is the staple, dairy products combined with wheat also provide complete protein.[114] Even the way that people have prepared for scarcity, such as breaking up into mobile bands, cultivating crops that can better withstand drought, and preserving food in case of famine, are probably adaptive practices in unpredictable environments. Geneticists have proposed that populations in famine-prone areas may have had genetic selection for "thrifty genes"—genes that allow individuals to need a minimum of food and store the extra in fatty tissue to get them past serious scarcity.[115] Customary diets and genetic changes may have been selected over a long stretch of time, but many serious nutritional problems observed today are due to rapid culture change. For instance, although "thrifty genes" may be adaptive during famine, they may become maladaptive when food is readily available. The high prevalence of diabetes and obesity in many populations today may be linked to such genes.

Often the switch to commercial or cash crops has harmful effects in another direction—creating undernutrition. For example, when the farmer-herders of the arid region in northeastern Brazil started growing sisal, a drought-resistant plant used for making twine and rope, many of them abandoned subsistence agriculture. The small landholders used most of their land for sisal growing and, when the price of sisal fell, they had to work as laborers for others to try to make ends meet. Food then had to be mostly bought, but if a laborer or sisal grower didn't earn enough, there was not enough food for the whole family.

Analysis of allocation of food in some households by Daniel Gross and Barbara Underwood suggests that the laborer and his wife received adequate nutrition, but the children often received much less than required. Lack of adequate nutrition usually results in retarded weight and height in children. As is commonly the case when there is substantial social inequality, the children from lower-income groups weigh substantially less than those from higher-income groups. But even though there were some economic differences before sisal production, the effects on nutrition appeared negligible before, judging from the fact that there was little or no difference in weight among adults from higher and lower socioeconomic positions who grew up prior to sisal production. But after sisal production, 45 percent of the children from lower economic groups were undernourished as compared with 23 percent of those children from the higher economic groups.[116]

People who now depend on buying food for their subsistence are subject to global economic changes as well. In 2008, not only was there a global economic recession, but there were serious increases in the cost of food. There were riots and demonstrations in over 50 countries, and it was estimated that 40 million more people became undernourished in 2008 on top of the already existing 923 million people.[117] As of 2010–2012, there was slight improvement, but 12 percent of the world's population was estimated to be undernourished.[118]

This is not to say that commercialization is always deleterious to adequate nutrition. For example, in the Highlands of New Guinea, there is evidence that the nutrition of children improved when families started growing coffee for sale. But in this case, the families still had land to grow some crops for consumption. The extra money earned from coffee enabled them to buy canned fish and rice, which provided children with higher amounts of protein than the usual staple of sweet potatoes.[119]

Nutritional imbalances for females have a far-reaching impact on reproduction and the health of the infants they bear. In some cultures, the lower status of women has a direct bearing on their access to food. Although the custom of feeding males first is well known, it is less often realized that females end up with less nutrient-dense food such as meat. Deprivation of food sometimes starts in infancy where girl babies, as in India, are weaned earlier than boy babies.[120] Parents may be unaware that their differential weaning practice has the effect of reducing the amount of high-quality protein that girl infants receive. Indeed, in Ecuador, Lauris McKee found that parents thought that earlier weaning of girls was helpful to them. They believed that mothers' milk transmitted sexuality and aggression, both ideal male traits, to their infants and so it was important that girl babies be weaned early. Mothers weaned their girls at about 11 months and their boys at about 20 months, a 9-month difference. McKee found that girl infants had a significantly higher mortality than boy infants in their second year of life, suggesting that the earlier weaning time for girls and their probable undernutrition may have been responsible.[121]

Often minimized in the discussion of undernutrition is the powerful relationship between conflict and hunger. Not only does hunger sometimes lead to unrest and conflict, but food deprivation is often used as "weapon" during war. Examples are stealing or destroying food resources, destroying economic infrastructure, and diversion of food aid to the military. Indirectly, food production is hurt by terrorizing the population, disrupting migration routes and health care services, recruiting people for military service, or outright killing.[122]

Summary and Review

Ethics of Applied Anthropology

19.1 Discuss the applied anthropology code of ethics and discuss some ethical issues faced by practicing anthropologists.

- Basic and applied research may be needed to understand how a condition might be successfully treated; well-meaning efforts have sometimes produced harmful consequences. There is still the problem of how to make that change happen. The people to be affected may not want to change. Applied anthropologists must take all of these matters into consideration in determining whether and how to act in response to a perceived need.

- Anthropology as a profession has adopted ethical codes of responsibility: above all, a responsibility to ensure the welfare and dignity of those who are being studied and a responsibility to report openly and truthfully to those who will read about their research.

- Even with a code of ethics, ethical issues are usually complicated, especially since anthropologists are not always involved in planning or initiation of projects.

 What are some important ethical issues and dilemmas facing those practicing applied anthropology?

Evaluating the Effects of Planned Change

19.2 Discuss the need to evaluate the effects of planned change.

- Even if a program of planned change has beneficial consequences in the short run, a great deal of thought and investigation has to be given to its long-term effects, which could eventually produce negative results.

- Applied anthropologists have played an important role in pointing out the problems with development programs that fail to evaluate long-term consequences. Governments and other agencies are beginning to ask for anthropological help in the planning stages of projects.

 What factors may be important in bringing about successful change?

Difficulties in Instituting Planned Change

19.3 Identify and give examples of some difficulties in implementing planned change.

- Whether a program of planned change can be successfully implemented depends largely on whether the people want the proposed change and like the proposed program. Lack of awareness can be a temporary barrier to solving the problem at hand.

- A growing trend is for anthropologists to become advocates for affected communities, involving the people affected in all phases of the project, from participating in the research design to execution and publishing.

- Applied anthropologists are increasingly asked to work on behalf of indigenous grassroots organizations. Grassroots organizations can succeed with development projects where government or outside projects fail.

- Anthropologists are also collaborating more with people from other disciplines.

 In what way are anthropologists mediators between affected communities and those initiating change? Give an example.

Environmental Anthropology

19.4 Describe the field of environmental anthropology.

- Environmental anthropology focuses on issues relating to the interaction of humans with their environments at the local, regional and global levels, particularly focusing on how to understand and alleviate the degradation of the environment.

- There is increasing recognition that imposing environmental policies from the top down does not work very well and that efforts are more likely to succeed if the affected communities participate in the planning of programs.

 What kinds of questions do environmental anthropologists ask?

Business and Organizational Anthropology

19.5 Describe the field of business and organizational anthropology.

- Anthropologists can help businesses understand other cultures, which is becoming even more important as trade becomes more global, international investments and joint ventures increase, and the multinational corporations spread their reach.

- Within a business, anthropologists can help business members understand their own organizational culture, especially when it may interfere with the acceptance of new kinds of workers, mergers with other companies, or changing to meet new business needs.

- Businesses and organizations also need help in developing and marketing products that people may want, and anthropologists are quite good at finding out because they observe and ask questions.

 What issues related to globalization affect the work of business and organizational anthropologists?

Cultural Resource Management

19.6 Describe the field of cultural resource management.

- Cultural resource management involves recovering and preserving the archaeological record before programs of planned change disturb or destroy it.

- Another focus of cultural resource management is public archaeology, educating the public about the past.

 Why is it important for cultural resource management anthropologists to educate the public?

Museum Anthropology

19.7 Describe the field of museum anthropology.

- An early practice, which still occurs, was to archive artifacts from non-Western societies in museums of natural history. More and more today, other types

of museums are providing less biased views of non-Western cultures.

- Public education is a central role for all museum anthropologists.

 How have practices in museum anthropology changed in the past several decades? Give an example.

Forensic Anthropology

19.8 Describe the field of forensic anthropology.

- Forensic anthropology is devoted to helping solve crimes and identifying human remains, usually by applying knowledge of physical anthropology.

- A relatively new area of forensic anthropology is work to confirm abuses of human rights, especially in terms of systematic killings of citizens.

 What kinds of challenges do forensic anthropologists face? Give examples.

Medical Anthropology

19.9 Discuss the goals of medical anthropology.

- Medical anthropologists are actively engaged in studying health and illness and associated beliefs and practices.

- They need to understand the the broader context—that is, the cultural behaviors, attitudes, values, and larger social and political milieu in which people live.

- Biological *and* social factors need to be considered if we are to reduce human suffering.

Cultural Understandings of Health and Illness

19.10 Discuss cultural understandings of health and illness.

- Western medical researchers and medical practitioners may think of medicine as purely based on "fact," but it is clear on reflection that many ideas stem from the culture in which the researchers reside.

- Many cultures have the view that the body should be kept in equilibrium or balance, although the balance may entail varying elements and varying means to maintain equilibrium.

- Research shows that a majority of cultures believe that gods or spirits could cause illness to some degree. Illness can also be thought of as caused by the loss of one's soul, fate, retribution for violation of a taboo, or contact with a polluting or taboo substance or object.

- In most societies, people simply think that their ideas about health and illness are true. Often people are not aware that there may be another way of viewing things until they confront another medical system.

- Biomedicine is the dominant Western medical paradigm today, focusing on diseases and cures. Health is seen as the *absence* of disease; death, as failure. Medical interest tends not to consider psychological factors, social/cultural influences, or links within the human body.

 When medical anthropologists are looking to understand ethnomedical systems, what kinds of questions do they ask?

Political and Economic Influences on Health

19.11 Describe political and economic influences on health.

- The incidence or relative frequency for many diseases, health problems, and death rates varies directly with social class and ethnicity.

- Power and economic differentials *between* societies also have profound health consequences.

 In what ways do political and economic forces affect health?

Health Conditions and Diseases

19.12 Discuss a sampling of health conditions and diseases studied by medical anthropologists.

- Medical anthropologists have studied an enormous variety of conditions, including epidemics of infectious disease such as AIDS as well as conditions related to mental and emotional disorders and undernutrition.

- Epidemics of infectious disease, including AIDS, have killed millions of people within short periods of time throughout recorded history. Epidemics like AIDS are more than a medical problem and need to be addressed through behavioral, cultural, and political measures.

- Although researchers disagree about the comparability of mental illnesses among cultures, most agree that effective treatment requires understanding a culture's ideas about a mental illness.

- Biological but not necessarily genetic factors may be very important in the etiology of some of the widespread mental disorders. Nutritional factors may play a large role.

- The ways people obtain, distribute, and consume food have been generally adaptive; many serious nutritional problems observed today are due to rapid culture change.

 What are some of the approaches medical anthropologists have used to research the AIDS epidemic?

Think on it

1. What particular **advantages** do anthropologists have in trying to solve practical problems?

2. What disadvantages do anthropologists have in trying to solve **practical problems**?

3. Drawing on your own experiences with the **health system** (biomedical or another system), explain what ideas about medicine may be cultural.

4. Why do **native remedies** often contain chemicals that are the same as, or similar in effect to, chemicals used in Western biomedicine remedies?

Glossary

Absolute dating A method of dating fossils in which the actual age of a deposit or specimen is measured. Also known as **chronometric dating**.

Accent Differences in pronunciation characteristic of a group.

Acclimatization Impermanent physiological changes that people make when they encounter a new environment.

Acculturation The process of extensive borrowing of aspects of culture in the context of superordinate–subordinate relations between societies; usually occurs as the result of external pressure.

Acheulian A stone toolmaking tradition dating from 1.5 million years ago. Compared with the Oldowan tradition, Acheulian assemblages have more large tools created according to standardized designs or shapes. One of the most characteristic and prevalent tools in the Acheulian tool kit is the so-called hand axe, which is a teardrop-shaped bifacially flaked tool with a thinned sharp tip. Other large tools might have been cleavers and picks.

Achieved qualities Those qualities people acquire during their lifetime.

Adapid A type of prosimian with many lemurlike features; appeared in the Early Eocene.

Adaptation Refers to genetic changes that allow an organism to survive and reproduce in a specific environment.

Adaptive customs Cultural traits that enhance survival and reproductive success in a particular environment.

Adjudication The process by which a third party acting as judge makes a decision that the parties to a dispute have to accept.

Aegyptopithecus An Oligocene anthropoid and probably the best-known propliopithecid.

Affinal kin One's relatives by marriage.

Age-grade A category of people who happen to fall within a particular, culturally distinguished age range.

Age-set A group of people of similar age and the same sex who move together through some or all of life's stages.

Agriculture The practice of raising domesticated crops.

AIDS (Acquired Immune Deficiency Syndrome) A disease caused by the HIV virus.

Allele One member of a pair of genes.

Allen's rule The rule that protruding body parts (particularly arms and legs) are relatively shorter in the cooler areas of a species' range than in the warmer areas.

Ambilineal descent The rule of descent that affiliates individuals with groups of kin related to them through men or women.

Ancestor spirits Supernatural beings who are the ghosts of dead relatives.

Animatism A belief in supernatural forces.

Animism A belief in a dual existence for all things—a physical, visible body, and a psychic, invisible soul.

Anthropoids One of the two suborders of primates; includes monkeys, apes, and humans.

Anthropological linguistics The anthropological study of languages.

Anthropology A discipline that studies humans, focusing on the study of differences and similarities, both biological and cultural, in human populations. Anthropology is concerned with typical biological and cultural characteristics of human populations in all periods and in all parts of the world.

Applied (practicing) anthropology The branch of anthropology that concerns itself with applying anthropological knowledge to achieve practical goals.

^{40}Ar–^{39}Ar dating Used in conjunction with potassium-argon dating, this method gets around the problem of needing different rock samples to estimate potassium and argon. A nuclear reactor is used to convert the ^{39}Ar to ^{39}K, on the basis of which the amount of ^{40}K can be estimated. In this way, both argon and potassium can be estimated from the same rock sample.

Arboreal Adapted to living in trees.

Archaeology The branch of anthropology that seeks to reconstruct the daily life and customs of peoples who lived in the past and to trace and explain cultural changes. Often lacking written records for study, archaeologists must try to reconstruct history from the material remains of human cultures. See also **Historical archaeology.**

Archaic Time period in the New World during which food production first developed.

Ardipithecus ramidus Perhaps the first hominin, dating to about 4.5 million years ago. Its dentition combines apelike and australopithecine-like features, and its skeleton suggests it was bipedal.

Artifact Any object made by a human.

Ascribed qualities Those qualities that are determined for people at birth.

Association An organized group not based exclusively on kinship or territory.

Atlatl A spear propelled off a grooved board; named for the Aztec word for "spear-thrower."

Australopithecines Members of the genus *Australopithecus*

Australopithecus Genus of Pliocene and Pleistocene hominins.

Australopithecus afarensis A species of *Australopithecus* that lived 4 million to 3 million years ago in East Africa and was definitely bipedal.

Australopithecus africanus A species of *Australopithecus* that lived between about 3 million and 2 million years ago.

Australopithecus anamensis A species of *Australopithecus* that lived perhaps 4.2 million years ago.

Australopithecus bahrelghazali An early australopithecine, dating to about 3 million years ago, and currently represented by only a single jaw. It is an interesting species because it is found in western Chad, distant from the East African Rift Valley where all other early australopithecines have been found.

Australopithecus garhi An australopithecine, dating to about 2.5 million years ago.

Australopithecus sediba An australopithecine from South Africa that dates to around 2 million years ago and has some *Homo*-like features.

Avunculocal residence A pattern of residence in which a married couple settles with or near the husband's mother's brother.

Balanced reciprocity Giving with the expectation of a straightforward immediate or limited-time trade.

Balancing selection A type of selection that occurs when a heterozygous combination of alleles is positively favored even though a homozygous combination is disfavored.

Band A fairly small, usually nomadic local group that is politically autonomous.

Band organization The kind of political organization where the local group or band is the largest territorial group in the society that acts as a unit. The local group in band societies is politically autonomous.

Behavioral ecology Typically tries to understand contemporary human behavior using evolutionary principles. In addition to the principle of individual selection, behavioral ecologists point to the importance of analyzing economic tradeoffs because individuals have limited time and resources.

Bergmann's rule The rule that smaller-sized subpopulations of a species inhabit the warmer parts of its geographic range and larger-sized subpopulations the cooler areas.

Bifacial tool A tool worked or flaked on two sides.

Bilateral kinship The type of kinship system in which individuals affiliate more or less equally with their mother's and father's relatives.

Bilocal residence A pattern of residence in which a married couple lives with or near either the husband's parents or the wife's parents.

Bilophodont Having four cusps on the molars that form two parallel ridges. This is the common molar pattern of Old World monkeys.

Biological (physical) anthropology The study of humans as biological organisms, dealing with the emergence and evolution of humans and with contemporary biological variations among human populations.

Biomedicine The dominant medical paradigm in Western societies today.

Bipedalism Locomotion in which an animal walks on its two hind legs.

Blade A thin flake whose length is usually more than twice its width. In the blade technique of toolmaking, a core is prepared by shaping a piece of flint with hammerstones into a pyramidal or cylindrical form. Blades are then struck off until the core is used up.

Brachiators Animals that move through the trees by swinging hand over hand from branch to branch. They usually have long arms and fingers.

Bride price A substantial gift of goods or money given to the bride's kin by the groom or his kin at or before the marriage. Also called **bride wealth**.

Bride service Work performed by the groom for his bride's family for a variable length of time either before or after the marriage.

Burin A chisel-like stone tool used for carving and for making such artifacts as bone and antler needles, awls, and projectile points.

Canines The cone-shaped teeth immediately behind the incisors; used by most primates to seize food and in fighting and display.

Carpolestes A mouse-sized arboreal creature living about 56 million years ago; a strong candidate for the common primate ancestor.

Cash crop A cultivated commodity raised for sale rather than for personal consumption by the cultivator.

Caste A ranked group, often associated with a certain occupation, in which membership is determined at birth and marriage is restricted to members of one's own caste.

Catarrhines The group of anthropoids with narrow noses and nostrils that face downward. Catarrhines include monkeys of the Old World (Africa, Asia, and Europe), as well as apes and humans.

Cercopithecoids Old World monkeys.

Cerebral cortex The "gray matter" of the brain; the center of speech and other higher mental activities.

Chief A person who exercises authority, usually on behalf of a multicommunity political unit. This role is generally found in rank societies and is usually permanent and often hereditary.

Chiefdom A political unit, with a chief at its head, integrating more than one community but not necessarily the whole society or language group.

Chromosomes Paired rod-shaped structures within a cell nucleus containing the genes that transmit traits from one generation to the next.

Chronometric dating See **Absolute dating.**

Civilization Urban society, from the Latin word for "city-state."

Clan A set of kin whose members believe themselves to be descended from a common ancestor but cannot specify the links back to that founder; often designated by a totem. Also called a **sib**.

Class A category of people who have about the same opportunity to obtain economic resources, power, and prestige.

Classificatory terms Kinship terms that merge or equate relatives who are genealogically distinct from one another; the same term is used for a number of different kin.

Class societies Societies containing social groups that have unequal access to economic resources, power, and prestige.

Cline The gradually increasing (or decreasing) frequency of a gene from one end of a region to another.

Code-switching Using more than one language in the course of conversing.

Codified laws Formal principles for resolving disputes in heterogeneous and stratified societies.

Cognates Words or morphs that belong to different languages but have similar sounds and meanings.

Commercial exchange See **Market (or commercial) exchange.**

Commercialization The increasing dependence on buying and selling, with money usually as the medium of exchange.

Complementary opposition The occasional uniting of various segments of a segmentary lineage system in opposition to similar segments.

483

Consanguineal kin   One's biological relatives; relatives by birth.

Context   The relationships between and among artifacts, ecofacts, fossils, and features.

Continental drift   The movement of the continents over the past 135 million years. In the early Cretaceous (circa 135 million years ago), there were two "supercontinents": *Laurasia,* which included North America and Eurasia; and *Gondwanaland,* which included Africa, South America, India, Australia, and Antarctica. By the beginning of the Paleocene (circa 65 million years ago), Gondwanaland had broken apart, with South America drifting west away from Africa, India drifting east, and Australia and Antarctica drifting south.

Core vocabulary   Nonspecialist vocabulary.

Corvée   A system of required labor.

Cretaceous   Geological epoch 135 million to 65 million years ago, during which dinosaurs and other reptiles ceased to be the dominant land vertebrates, and mammals and birds began to become important.

Crime   Violence not considered legitimate that occurs within a political unit.

Cro-Magnons   Humans who lived in western Europe about 35,000 years ago; they were once thought to be the earliest specimens of modern-looking humans, or *Homo sapiens.* But it is now known that modern-looking humans appeared earlier outside of Europe; the earliest so far found lived in Africa.

Cross-cousins   Children of siblings of the opposite sex. One's cross-cousins are the father's sisters' children and mother's brothers' children.

Cross-cultural researcher   An ethnologist who uses ethnographic data about many societies to test possible explanations of cultural variation to discover general patterns about cultural traits—what is universal, what is variable, why traits vary, and what the consequences of the variability might be.

Crossing-over   Exchanges of sections of chromosomes from one chromosome to another.

Cultural anthropology   The study of cultural variation and universals in the past and present.

Cultural ecology   The analysis of the relationship between a culture and its environment.

Cultural relativism   The attitude that a society's customs and ideas should be viewed within the context of that society's problems and opportunities.

Cultural resource management (CRM)   The branch of applied anthropology that seeks to recover and preserve the archaeological record before programs of planned change disturb or destroy it.

Culture   The set of learned behaviors, beliefs, attitudes, values, and ideals that are characteristic of a particular society or other social group.

Culture history   A history of the cultures that lived in a given area over time. Until the 1950s, building such culture histories was a primary goal of archaeological research.

Cuneiform   Wedge-shaped writing invented by the Sumerians around 3000 B.C.

Descriptive term   A unique term used for a distinct relative.

Descriptive (structural) linguistics   The study of how languages are constructed.

Development anthropology   One of the main subfields of applied or practicing anthropology, aimed at improving people's lives, particularly decreasing poverty and hunger.

Dialect   A variety of a language spoken in a particular area or by a particular social group.

Diastema   A gap between the canine and first premolar found in apes.

Diffusion   The borrowing by one society of a cultural trait belonging to another society as the result of contact between the two societies.

Directional selection   A type of natural selection that increases the frequency of a trait (the trait is said to be positively favored, or adaptive).

Diurnal   Active during the day.

Divination   Getting the supernatural to provide guidance.

DNA   Deoxyribonucleic acid; a long, two-stranded molecule in the genes that directs the makeup of an organism according to the instructions in its genetic code.

Domestication   Modification or adaptation of plants and animals for use by humans. When people plant crops, we refer to the process as cultivation. It is only when the crops cultivated and the animals raised have been modified—are different from wild varieties—that we speak of plant and animal domestication.

Dominant   The allele of a gene pair that is always phenotypically expressed in the heterozygous form.

Double descent or double unilineal descent   A system that affiliates individuals with a group of matrilineal kin for some purposes and with a group of patrilineal kin for other purposes.

Dowry   A substantial transfer of goods or money from the bride's family to the bride.

Dryopithecus   Genus of ape from the later Miocene found primarily in Europe. It had thin tooth enamel and pointed molar cusps very similar to those of the fruit-eating chimpanzees of today.

Dual-inheritance theory   In contrast to other evolutionary ecological perspectives, this theory gives much more importance to culture as part of the evolutionary process. Dual inheritance refers to both genes and culture playing different, but nonetheless important and interactive roles in transmitting traits to future generations.

Ecofacts   Natural items that humans have used; things such as the remains of animals eaten by humans or plant pollens found on archaeological sites are examples of ecofacts.

Economic resources   Things that have value in a culture, including land, tools and other technology, goods, and money.

Egalitarian societies   Societies in which all people of a given age-sex category have equal access to economic resources, power, and prestige.

Ego   In the reckoning of kinship, the reference point or focal person.

Enculturation   See **Socialization.**

Endogamy   The rule specifying marriage to a person within one's own group (kin, caste, community).

Environmental anthropology   Focuses on issues relating to the interaction of humans with their environments, at the local, regional, and global levels, particularly focusing on how to understand and alleviate the degradation of the environment.

Eocene   A geological epoch 55 million to 34 million years ago during which the first definite primates appeared.

Epipaleolithic   Time period during which food production first developed in the Near East.

Ethnicity   The process of defining ethnicity usually involves a group of people emphasizing common origins and language, shared history, and selected aspects of cultural difference such as a difference in religion. Because different groups are doing the perceiving, ethnic identities often vary with whether one is inside or outside the group.

Ethnocentric   Refers to judgment of other cultures solely in terms of one's own culture.

Ethnocentrism   The attitude that other societies' customs and ideas can be judged in the context of one's own culture.

Ethnogenesis   Creation of a new culture.

Ethnographer   A person who spends some time living with, interviewing, and observing a group of people to describe their customs.

Ethnographic analogy   Method of comparative cultural study that extrapolates to the past from recent or current societies.

Ethnography   A description of a society's customary behaviors and ideas.

Ethnohistorian   An ethnologist who uses historical documents to study how a particular culture has changed over time.

Ethnology   The study of how and why recent cultures differ and are similar.

Ethnomedicine   The health-related beliefs, knowledge, and practices of a cultural group.

Evolutionary psychology   A type of evolutionary ecological approach that is particularly interested in universal human psychology. It is argued that human psychology was primarily adapted to the environment that characterized most of human history—the hunting-gathering way of life.

Excavation   The careful removal of archaeological deposits; the recovery of artifacts, ecofacts, fossils, and features from the soil in which those deposits have been buried.

Exogamy   The rule specifying marriage to a person from outside one's own group (kin or community).

Explanation   An answer to a *why* question. In science, there are two kinds of explanation that researchers try to achieve: associations and theories.

Extended family   A family consisting of two or more single-parent, monogamous, polygynous, or polyandrous families linked by a blood tie.

Extensive cultivation   A type of horticulture in which the land is worked for short periods and then left to regenerate for some years before being used again. Also called **shifting cultivation.**

Falsification   Showing that a theory seems to be wrong by finding that implications or predictions derivable from it are not consistent with objectively collected data.

Family   A social and economic unit consisting minimally of a parent and a child.

Features   Artifacts of human manufacture that cannot be removed from an archaeological site. Hearths, storage pits, and buildings are examples of features.

Feuding   A state of recurring hostility between families or groups of kin, usually motivated by a desire to avenge an offense against a member of the group.

Fieldwork   Firsthand experience with the people being studied and the usual means by which anthropological information is obtained. Regardless of other methods that anthropologists may use (e.g., censuses, surveys), fieldwork usually involves participant-observation for an extended period of time, often a year or more. See **Participant-observation.**

Folklore   Includes all the myths, legends, folktales, ballads, riddles, proverbs, and superstitions of a cultural group. Generally, folklore is transmitted orally, but it may also be written.

Food production   The form of subsistence technology in which food-getting is dependent on the cultivation and domestication of plants and animals

Foragers   People who subsist on the collection of naturally occurring plants and animals. Also referred to as **hunter-gatherers** or *food collectors.*

Foraging   May be generally defined as a food-getting strategy that obtains wild plant and animal resources through gathering, hunting, scavenging, or fishing; also known as food collection.

Foramen magnum   Opening in the base of the skull through which the spinal cord passes en route to the brain.

Forensic anthropology   The application of anthropology, usually physical anthropology, to help identify human remains and assist in solving crimes.

Fossils   The hardened remains or impressions of plants and animals that lived in the past.

Fraternal polyandry   The marriage of a woman to two or more brothers at the same time.

Gender differences   Differences between females and males that reflect cultural expectations and experiences.

Gender roles   Roles that are culturally assigned to genders.

Gender stratification   The degree of unequal access by the different genders to prestige, authority, power, rights, and economic resources.

Gene   Chemical unit of heredity.

Gene flow   The process by which genes pass from the gene pool of one population to that of another through mating and reproduction.

Generalized reciprocity   Gift giving without any immediate or planned return.

General-purpose money   A universally accepted medium of exchange.

Genetic drift   The various random processes that affect gene frequencies in small, relatively isolated populations.

Genotype   The total complement of inherited traits or genes of an organism.

Genus   A group of related species; pl., genera.

Ghosts   Supernatural beings who were once human; the souls of dead people.

Globalization   The ongoing spread of goods, people, information, and capital around the world.

Gloger's rule   The rule that populations of birds and mammals living in warm, humid climates have more melanin (and therefore darker skin, fur, or feathers) than populations of the same species living in cooler, drier areas.

Gods   Supernatural beings of nonhuman origin who are named personalities; often anthropomorphic.

Group marriage   Marriage in which more than one man is married to more than one woman at the same time; not customary in any known human society.

Half-life   The time it takes for half of the atoms of a radioactive substance to decay into atoms of a different substance.

Hand axe   A teardrop-shaped stone tool characteristic of Acheulian assemblages.

Hard hammer   A technique of stone tool manufacture where one stone is used to knock flakes from another stone. Flakes produced through hard hammer percussion are usually large and crude.

Headman   A person who holds a powerless but symbolically unifying position in a community within an egalitarian society; may exercise influence but has no power to impose sanctions.

Hermeneutics   The study of meaning.

Heterozygous   Possessing differing genes or alleles in corresponding locations on a pair of chromosomes.

Hieroglyphics   "Picture writing," as in ancient Egypt and in Mayan sites in Mesoamerica (Mexico and Central America).

Historical archaeology   A specialty within archaeology that studies the material remains of recent peoples who left written records.

Historical linguistics   The study of how languages change over time.

Holistic   Refers to an approach that studies many aspects of a multifaceted system.

Hominins   The group of hominoids consisting of humans and their direct ancestors.

Hominoids   The group of catarrhines that includes both apes and humans.

Homo   Genus to which modern humans and their ancestors belong.

Homo antecessor   Refers to a group of hominin fossils found in the Atapuerca region of Spain that appear to be transitional between Neandertals and modern humans. They are closely related to *Homo heidelbergensis*, and many scholars believe they are the same species.

Homo erectus   The first hominin species to be widely distributed in the Old World. The earliest finds are possibly 1.8 million years old. The brain (averaging 895–1,040 cc) was larger than that found in any of the australopithecines or *H. habilis* but smaller than the average brain of a modern human.

Homo ergaster   A species closely related to *Homo erectus* but found only in East Africa. Some scholars do not see enough difference between *Homo erectus* and *Homo ergaster* to count them as different species.

Homo floresiensis   A dwarf species of hominin that lived on the Indonesian island of Flores until about 12,000 years ago and probably descended from an isolated *Homo erectus* population.

Homo habilis   Dating from about 2 million years ago, an early species belonging to our genus, *Homo*, with cranial capacities averaging about 630–640 cc, about 50 percent of the brain capacity of modern humans.

Homo heidelbergensis   A transitional species between *Homo erectus* and *Homo sapiens*.

Homo neandertalensis   The technical name for the Neandertals, a group of robust and otherwise anatomically distinct hominins that are close relatives of modern humans—so close that some believe they should be classified as *Homo sapiens neandertalensis*.

Homo rudolfensis   Early species belonging to our genus, *Homo*. Similar enough to *Homo habilis* that some paleoanthropologists make no distinction between the two.

Homo sapiens   All living people belong to one biological species, *Homo sapiens*, which means that all human populations on earth can successfully interbreed. The first *Homo sapiens* may have emerged about 200,000 years ago.

Homozygous   Possessing two identical genes or alleles in corresponding locations on a pair of chromosomes.

Horticulture   Plant cultivation carried out with relatively simple tools and methods; nature is allowed to replace nutrients in the soil, in the absence of permanently cultivated fields.

Human paleontology   The study of the emergence of humans and their later physical evolution. Also called **paleoanthropology.**

Human variation   The study of how and why contemporary human populations vary biologically.

Hunter-gatherers   People who collect food from naturally occurring resources, that is, wild plants, animals, and fish. The term *hunter-gatherers* minimizes sometimes heavy dependence on fishing. Also referred to as **foragers** or *food collectors*.

Hybridization   The creation of a viable offspring from the mating of two different species.

Hylobates   The family of hominoids that includes gibbons and siamangs; often referred to as the lesser apes (as compared with the great apes such as gorillas and chimpanzees).

Hypotheses   Predictions, which may be derived from theories, about how variables are related.

Hypoxia   A condition of oxygen deficiency that often occurs at high altitudes. The percentage of oxygen in the air is the same as at lower altitudes, but because the barometric pressure is lower, less oxygen is taken in with each breath. Often, breathing becomes more rapid, the heart beats faster, and activity is more difficult.

Incest taboo   Prohibition of sexual intercourse or marriage between mother and son, father and daughter, and brother and sister; often extends to other relatives.

Independent family   A family unit consisting of one monogamous (nuclear) family, or one polygynous or one polyandrous family.

Indirect dowry   Goods given by the groom's kin to the bride (or her father, who passes most of them to her) at or before her marriage.

Indicator artifacts and ecofacts   Items that changed relatively rapidly and which, thus, can be used to indicate the relative age of associated items.

Indirect percussion   A toolmaking technique common in the Upper Paleolithic. After shaping a core into a pyramidal or cylindrical form, the toolmaker can put a punch of antler or wood or another hard material into position and strike it with a hammer. Using a hammer-struck punch enabled toolmakers to strike off consistently shaped blades.

Insectivore   The order or major grouping of mammals, including modern shrews and moles, that is adapted to feeding on insects.

Intensive agriculture   Food production characterized by the permanent cultivation of fields and made possible by the use of the plow, draft animals or machines, fertilizers, irrigation, water-storage techniques, and other complex agricultural techniques.

Kenyanthropus platyops   A nearly complete 3.5 million year old skull found in western Kenya. It is thought by some scholars to be a species of australopithecine (and hence should not be regarded as a separate genus).

Kenyapithecus   An apelike primate from the Middle Miocene found in East Africa. It had very thickly enameled teeth and robust jaws, suggesting a diet of hard, tough foods. Probably somewhat terrestrial.

Kindred   A bilateral set of close relatives who may be called upon for some purpose.

Kinesics   The study of communication by nonvocal means, including posture, mannerisms, body movement, facial expressions, and signs and gestures.

Knuckle walking   A locomotor pattern of primates such as the chimpanzee and gorilla in which the weight of the upper part of the body is supported on the thickly padded knuckles of the hands.

Laws (scientific)   Associations or relationships that almost all scientists accept.

Levalloisian method   A method that allowed flake tools of a predetermined size to be produced from a shaped core. The toolmakers first shaped the core and prepared a "striking platform" at one end. Flakes of predetermined and standard sizes could then be knocked off. Although some Levallois flakes date from as far back as 400,000 years ago, they are found more frequently in Mousterian tool kits.

Levirate   A custom whereby a man is obliged to marry his deceased brother's wife.

Lexical content   Vocabulary or lexicon.

Lexicon   The words and morphs, and their meanings, of a language; approximated by a dictionary.

Lineage   A set of kin whose members trace descent from a common ancestor through known links.

Lithics   The technical name for tools made from stone.

Lower Paleolithic   The period of the Oldowan and Acheulian stone tool traditions.

Magic   The performance of certain rituals that are believed to compel the supernatural powers to act in particular ways.

Maladaptive customs   Cultural traits that diminish the chances of survival and reproduction in a particular environment.

Mana   A supernatural, impersonal force that inhabits certain objects or people and is believed to confer success and/or strength.

Manumission   The granting of freedom to a slave.

Market (or commercial) exchange   Transactions in which the "prices" are subject to supply and demand, whether or not the transactions occur in a marketplace.

Marriage   A socially approved sexual and economic union, usually between a man and a woman, that is presumed, both by the couple and by others, to be more or less permanent, and that subsumes reciprocal rights and obligations between the two spouses and their future children.

Matrilineal descent   The rule of descent that affiliates individuals with kin of both sexes related to them through women only.

Matrilocal residence   A pattern of residence in which a married couple lives with or near the wife's parents.

Measure   To describe how something compares with other things on some scale of variation.

Mediation   The process by which a third party tries to bring about a settlement in the absence of formal authority to force a settlement.

Medical anthropology   The anthropological study of health and illness and associated beliefs and practices.

Mediums   Part-time religious practitioners who are asked to heal and divine while in a trance.

Meiosis   The process by which reproductive cells are formed. In this process of division, the number of chromosomes in the newly formed cells is reduced by half, so that when fertilization occurs the resulting organism has the normal number of chromosomes appropriate to its species, rather than double that number.

Mesolithic   The archaeological period in the Old World beginning about 12,000 B.C. Humans were starting to settle down in semipermanent camps and villages, as people began to depend less on big game (which they used to have to follow over long distances) and more on relatively stationary food resources such as fish, shellfish, small game, and wild plants rich in carbohydrates, proteins, and oils.

Messenger RNA   A type of ribonucleic acid that is used in the cell to copy the DNA code for use in protein synthesis.

Microlith   A small, razorlike blade fragment that was probably attached in a series to a wooden or bone handle to form a cutting edge.

Middle Paleolithic   The time period of the Mousterian stone tool tradition.

Miocene   The geological epoch from 24 million to 5.2 million years ago.

Mitosis   Cellular reproduction or growth involving the duplication of chromosome pairs.

Moiety   A unilineal descent group in a society that is divided into two such maximal groups; there may be smaller unilineal descent groups as well.

Molars   The large teeth behind the premolars at the back of the jaw; used for chewing and grinding food.

Monogamy   Marriage between only one man and only one woman at a time.

Monotheistic   Believing that there is only one high god and that all other supernatural beings are subordinate to, or are alternative manifestations of, this supreme being.

Morph   The smallest unit of a language that has a meaning.

Morpheme   One or more morphs with the same meaning.

Morphology   The study of how sound sequences convey meaning.

Mousterian tool assemblage   Named after the tool assemblage found in a rock shelter at Le Moustier in the Dordogne region of southwestern France. Compared with an Acheulian assemblage, the Middle Paleolithic (40,000–300,000 years ago) Mousterian has a smaller proportion of large core tools such as hand axes and cleavers and a bigger proportion of small flake tools such as scrapers. Flakes were often altered or "retouched" by striking small flakes or chips from one or more edges.

Mutation   A change in the DNA sequence, producing an altered gene.

Nation   A set of people sharing a common territory, history, and a sense of identity.

Nation-state   The co-occurrence of a political state and a nation.

Nationalism   The strong sense of loyalty, attachment, and devotion to a nation (see nation).

Natural selection   The outcome of processes that affect the frequencies of traits in a particular environment. Traits that enhance survival and reproductive success increase in frequency over time.

Neandertal   The common name for the species *Homo neandertalensis*.

Negotiation   The process by which the parties to a dispute try to resolve it themselves.

Neolithic   Originally meaning "the new stone age," now meaning the presence of domesticated plants and animals. The earliest evidence of domestication comes from the Near East about 8000 B.C.

Neolocal residence A pattern of residence whereby a married couple lives separately, and usually at some distance, from the kin of both spouses.
Nocturnal Active during the night.
Nonfraternal polyandry Marriage of a woman to two or more men who are not brothers.
Nonsororal polygyny Marriage of a man to two or more women who are not sisters.
Normalizing selection The type of natural selection that removes harmful genes that arose by mutation.
Norms Standards or rules about what is acceptable behavior.
Nuclear family A family consisting of a married couple and their young children.
Oath The act of calling upon a deity to bear witness to the truth of what one says.
Obsidian A volcanic glass that can be used to make mirrors or sharp-edged tools.
Occipital torus A ridge of bone running horizontally across the back of the skull in apes and some hominins.
Oldowan The earliest stone toolmaking tradition, named after the tools found in Bed I at Olduvai Gorge, Tanzania, from about 2.5 million years ago. The stone artifacts include core tools and sharp-edged flakes made by striking one stone against another. Flake tools predominate. Among the core tools, so-called choppers are common.
Oligocene The geological epoch 34 million to 24 million years ago during which definite anthropoids emerged.
Omnivorous Eating both meat and vegetation.
Omomyid A type of prosimian with many tarsierlike features that appeared in the early Eocene.
Operational definition A description of the procedure that is followed in measuring a variable.
Opposable thumb A thumb that can touch the tips of all the other fingers.
Optimal foraging theory The theory that individuals seek to maximize the returns (in calories and nutrients) on their labor in deciding which animals and plants they will go after.
Ordeal A means of determining guilt or innocence by submitting the accused to dangerous or painful tests believed to be under supernatural control.
Orrorin tugenensis An apparently bipedal primate dating to between 5.8 and 6 million years, making it possibly the earliest known hominin.
Paleoanthropology See **Human paleontology.**
Paleocene The geological epoch 65 million to 55 million years ago.
Paralanguage Refers to all the optional vocal features or silences apart from the language itself that communicate meaning.
Parallel cousins Children of siblings of the same sex. One's parallel cousins are the father's brothers' children and the mother's sisters' children.
Paranthropoid Members of the genus *Paranthropus.*
Paranthropus A genus of early hominins that had very large teeth and jaws. Once thought to be part of the *Australopithecus* genus, but now considered a separate genus.
Paranthropus aethiopicus An early paranthropoid.
Paranthropus boisei An East African paranthropoid species dating from 2.2 million to 1.3 million years ago with somewhat larger cranial capacity than *A. africanus.* No longer thought to be larger than australopithecines, it is robust primarily in the skull and jaw, most strikingly in the teeth. Compared with *P. robustus, P. boisei* has even more features that reflect a huge chewing apparatus.
Paranthropus robustus A paranthropoid species found in South African caves dating from about 1.8 million to 1 million years ago. Not as large in the teeth and jaws as *P. boisei.*
Parapithecids Small monkeylike Oligocene primates found in the Fayum area of Egypt.
Participant-observation Living among the people being studied—observing, questioning, and (when possible) taking part in the important events of the group. Writing or otherwise recording notes on observations, questions asked and answered, and things to check out later are parts of participant-observation.
Pastoralism A form of subsistence technology in which food-getting is based directly or indirectly on the maintenance of domesticated animals.
Patrilineal descent The rule of descent that affiliates individuals with kin of both sexes related to them through men only.
Patrilocal residence A pattern of residence in which a married couple lives with or near the husband's parents.
Peasants Rural people who produce food for their own subsistence but who must also contribute or sell their surpluses to others (in towns and cities) who do not produce their own food.
Percussion flaking A toolmaking technique in which one stone is struck with another to remove a flake.
Personality integration of culture The theory that personality or psychological processes may account for connections between certain aspects of culture.
Pierolapithecus A Middle Miocene ape that has wrists and vertebrae that would have made it capable of brachiation, but also has relatively short fingers like modern monkeys.
Phenotype The observable physical appearance of an organism, which may or may not reflect its genotype or total genetic constitution.
Phone A speech sound in a language.
Phoneme A sound or set of sounds that makes a difference in meaning to the speakers of the language.
Phonology The study of the sounds in a language and how they are used.
Phratry A unilineal descent group composed of a number of supposedly related clans (sibs).
Physical (biological) anthropology See **Biological (physical) anthropology.**
Platyrrhines The group of anthropoids that have broad, flat-bridged noses, with nostrils facing outward; these monkeys are currently found only in the New World (Central and South America).
Pleistocene A geological epoch that started 1.6 million years ago and, according to some, continues into the present. During this period, glaciers have often covered much of the earth's surface and humans became the dominant life form.
Plesiadipis The most well known of the plesiadipiforms, possibly an archaic primate.
Pliocene The geological epoch 5.2 million to 1.6 million years ago during which the earliest definite hominins appeared.
Political economy The study of how external forces, particularly powerful state societies, explain the way a society changes and adapts.
Polyandry The marriage of one woman to more than one man at a time.
Polygamy Plural marriage; one individual is married to more than one spouse simultaneously. **Polygyny** and **polyandry** are types of polygamy.
Polygyny The marriage of one man to more than one woman at a time.
Polyphony Two or more melodies sung simultaneously.
Polytheistic Recognizing many gods, none of whom is believed to be superordinate.
Pongids Hominoids whose members include both the living and extinct apes.
Potassium-argon (K-Ar) dating A chronometric dating method that uses the rate of decay of a radioactive form of potassium (^{40}K) into argon (^{40}Ar) to date samples from 5,000 years to 3 billion years old. The K-Ar method dates the minerals and rocks in a deposit, not the fossils themselves.
Postpartum sex taboo Prohibition of sexual intercourse between a couple for a period of time after the birth of their child.
Potlatch A feast among Pacific Northwest Native Americans at which great quantities of food and goods are given to the guests in order to gain prestige for the host(s).
Power The ability to make others do what they do not want to do or influence based on the threat of force.
Practicing anthropology The branch of anthropology that concerns itself with applying anthropological knowledge to achieve practical goals, usually in the service of an agency outside the traditional academic setting.
Prairie Grassland with a high grass cover.
Prehensile Adapted for grasping objects.
Prehistory The time before written records.
Pressure flaking Toolmaking technique whereby small flakes are struck off by pressing against the core with a bone, antler, or wooden tool.
Prestige Being accorded particular respect or honor.
Priests Generally full-time specialists, with very high status, who are thought to be able to relate to superior or high gods beyond the ordinary person's access or control.
Primary subsistence activities The food-getting activities: gathering, hunting, fishing, herding, and agriculture.
Primate A member of the mammalian order Primates, divided into the two suborders of prosimians and anthropoids.
Primatologists People who study primates.
Probability value (p-value) The likelihood that an observed result could have occurred by chance.
Proconsul The best-known genus of proto-apes from the Early Miocene.
Prognathic A physical feature that is sticking out or pushed forward, such as the faces in apes and some hominid species.
Propliopithecids Apelike anthropoids dating from the Early Oligocene, found in the Fayum area of Egypt.
Prosimians Literally "pre-monkeys," one of the two suborders of primates; includes lemurs, lorises, and tarsiers.
Protolanguage A hypothesized ancestral language from which two or more languages seem to have derived.
Quadrupeds Animals that walk on all fours.
Race In biology, race refers to a subpopulation or variety of a species that differs somewhat in gene frequencies from other varieties of the species. Many anthropologists do not think that the concept of race is usefully applied to humans because humans do not fall into geographic populations that can be easily distinguished in terms of different sets of biological or physical traits. Thus, "race" in humans is largely a culturally assigned category.
Rachis The seed-bearing part of a plant. In the wild variety of grain, the rachis shatters easily, releasing the seeds. Domesticated grains have a tough rachis, which does not shatter easily.
Racism The belief, without scientific basis, that some "races" are inferior to others.
Radiocarbon (or carbon-14, 14C) dating A dating method that uses the decay of carbon-14 to date organic remains. It is reliable for dating once-living matter up to 50,000 years old.
Raiding A short-term use of force, generally planned and organized, to realize a limited objective.
Random sample A sample in which all cases selected have had an equal chance to be included.
Rank societies Societies that do not have any unequal access to economic resources or power, but with social groups that have unequal access to status positions and prestige.
Recessive An allele phenotypically suppressed in the heterozygous form and expressed only in the homozygous form.
Reciprocity Giving and taking (not politically arranged) without the use of money.
Redistribution The accumulation of goods (or labor) by a particular person or in a particular place and their subsequent distribution.
Relative dating A method of dating fossils that determines the age of a specimen or deposit relative to a known specimen or deposit.
Religion Any set of attitudes, beliefs, and practices pertaining to supernatural power, whether that power rests in forces, gods, spirits, ghosts, or demons.
Revitalization movements New religious movements intended to save a culture by infusing it with a new purpose and life.
Revolution A usually violent replacement of a society's rulers.
Ribosome A structure in the cell used in making proteins.
Rituals Repetitive sets of behaviors that occur in essentially the same patterns every time they occur. Religious rituals involve the supernatural in some way.
Rules of descent Rules that connect individuals with particular sets of kin because of known or presumed common ancestry.
Sagittal crest A ridge of bone running along the top of the skull in apes and early hominins.
Sagittal keel An inverted V-shaped ridge running along the top of the skull in *Homo erectus.*
Sahelanthropus tchadensis A hominoid found in Chad dating to around 7 million years ago.
Sampling universe The list of cases to be sampled from.
Savanna Tropical grassland.
Secondary institutions Aspects of culture, such as religion, music, art, folklore, and games, which presumably reflect or are projections of the basic, or typical, personality in a society.

Secondary subsistence activities   Activities that involve the preparation and processing of food either to make it edible or to store it.

Sedentarism   Settled life.

Segmentary lineage system   A hierarchy of more inclusive lineages; usually functions only in conflict situations.

Segregation   The random sorting of chromosomes in meiosis.

Sex differences   The typical differences between females and males that are most likely due to biological differences.

Sexually dimorphic   A marked difference in size and appearance between males and females of a species.

Sexual dimorphism   See **Sexually dimorphic.**

Shaman   A religious intermediary, usually part-time, whose primary function is to cure people through sacred songs, pantomime, and other means; sometimes called witch doctor by Westerners.

Shifting cultivation   See **Extensive cultivation.**

Sib   See **Clan.**

Siblings   A person's brothers and sisters.

Sickle-cell anemia (sicklemia)   A condition in which red blood cells assume a crescent (sickle) shape when deprived of oxygen, instead of the normal (disk) shape. The sickle-shaped red blood cells do not move through the body as readily as normal cells, and thus cause damage to the heart, lungs, brain, and other vital organs.

Sites   Locations where the material remains of human activity have been preserved in a way that archaeologists or paleoanthropologists can recover them.

Sivapithecus   A genus of ape from the later Miocene known for its thickly enameled teeth, suggesting a diet of hard, tough, or gritty items. Found primarily in western and southern Asia and now thought to be ancestral to orangutans.

Slash-and-burn   A form of shifting cultivation in which the natural vegetation is cut down and burned off. The cleared ground is used for a short time and then left to regenerate.

Slaves   A class of people who do not own their own labor or the products thereof.

Socialization   A term anthropologists and psychologists use to describe the development, through the direct and indirect influence of parents and others, of children's patterns of behavior (and attitudes and values) that conform to cultural expectations. Also called **enculturation.**

Society   A group of people who occupy a particular territory and speak a common language not generally understood by neighboring peoples. By this definition, societies do not necessarily correspond to nations.

Sociobiology   Systematic study of the biological causes of human behavior. Compare with **behavioral ecology, evolutionary psychology,** and **dual-inheritance theory.**

Sociolinguistics   The study of cultural and subcultural patterns of speaking in different social contexts.

Soft hammer   A technique of stone tool manufacture in which a bone or wood hammer is used to strike flakes from a stone.

Sorcery   The use of certain materials to invoke supernatural powers to harm people.

Sororal polygyny   The marriage of a man to two or more sisters at the same time.

Sororate   A custom whereby a woman is obliged to marry her deceased sister's husband.

Special-purpose money   Objects of value for which only some goods and services can be exchanged.

Speciation   The development of a new species.

Species   A population that consists of organisms able to interbreed and produce viable and fertile offspring.

Spirits   Unnamed supernatural beings of nonhuman origin who are beneath the gods in prestige and often closer to the people; may be helpful, mischievous, or evil.

State   An autonomous political unit with centralized decision making over many communities with power to govern by force (e.g., to collect taxes, draft people for work and war, and make and enforce laws). Most states have cities with public buildings; full-time craft and religious specialists; an "official" art style; a hierarchical social structure topped by an elite class; and a governmental monopoly on the legitimate use of force to implement policies.

State organization   A society is described as having state organization when it includes one or more states.

Statistical association   A relationship or correlation between two or more variables that is unlikely to be due to chance.

Statistically significant   Refers to a result that would occur very rarely by chance. The result (and stronger ones) would occur fewer than 5 times out of 100 by chance.

Steppe   Grassland with a dry, low grass cover.

Stratified   An archaeological deposit that contains successive layers or strata.

Stratigraphy   The study of how different rock formations and fossils are laid down in successive layers or strata. Older layers are generally deeper or lower than more recent layers.

Structural linguistics   See **Descriptive (structural) linguistics.**

Subculture   The shared customs of a subgroup within a society.

Subsistence economies   Economies in which almost all able-bodied adults are largely engaged in getting food for themselves and their families.

Supernatural   Believed to be not human or not subject to the laws of nature.

Symbolic communication   An arbitrary (not obviously meaningful) gesture, call, word, or sentence that has meaning even when its *referent* is not present.

Syntax   The ways in which words are arranged to form phrases and sentences.

Taboo   A prohibition that, if violated, is believed to bring supernatural punishment.

Taurodontism   Having teeth with an enlarged pulp cavity.

Terrestrial   Adapted to living on the ground.

Terrorism   The use or threat of violence to create terror in others, usually for political purposes.

Theoretical construct   Something that cannot be observed or verified directly.

Theoretical orientation   A general attitude about how phenomena are to be explained.

Theories   Explanations of associations or laws.

Totem   A plant or animal associated with a clan (sib) as a means of group identification; may have other special significance for the group.

Tribal organization   The kind of political organization in which local communities mostly act autonomously but there are kin groups (such as clans) or associations (such as age-sets) that can temporarily integrate a number of local groups into a larger unit.

Tribe   A territorial population in which there are kin or nonkin groups with representatives in a number of local groups. There is no formal integration of the local groups.

Unifacial tool   A tool worked or flaked on one side only.

Unilineal descent   Affiliation with a group of kin through descent links of one sex only.

Unilocal residence   A pattern of residence (patrilocal, matrilocal, or avunculocal) that specifies just one set of relatives that the married couple lives with or near.

Unisex association   An association that restricts its membership to one sex, usually male.

Universally ascribed qualities   Those ascribed qualities (age, sex) that are found in all societies.

Upper Paleolithic   The time period associated with the emergence of modern humans and their spread around the world.

Variable   A thing or quantity that varies.

Variably ascribed qualities   Those ascribed qualities (such as ethnic, religious, or social class differences) that are found only in some societies.

Vertical clinging and leaping   A locomotor pattern characteristic of several primates, including tarsiers and galagos. The animal normally rests by clinging to a branch in a vertical position and uses its hind limbs alone to push off from one vertical position to another.

Warfare   Socially organized violence between political entities such as communities, districts, or nations.

Witchcraft   The practice of attempting to harm people by supernatural means, but through emotions and thought alone, not through the use of tangible objects

Notes

Chapter 1

1. Harrison 1975; Durham 1991, 228–37; Ingram et al. 2009.
2. Chimpanzee Sequencing and Analysis Consortium 2005.
3. Nolan 2003, 2.
4. Van Willigen 2002, 7.
5. Kedia and van Willigen 2005; Miracle 2009.
6. Hill and Baba 2006.
7. White 1968.
8. Baba and Hill 2006; Moran and Harris 2007, 64, 84–87.

Chapter 2

1. Salzman 2001, 135.
2. J. Whiting 1964.
3. Nagel 1961, 88–89.
4. Ibid., 83–90.
5. Ibid., 85. See also McCain and Segal 1988, 75–79.
6. McCain and Segal 1988, 62–64.
7. Tylor 1971/1958.
8. Ceci and Williams 2009.
9. Langness 1974, 50.
10. Steward 1955a, 30–42.
11. Vayda and Rappaport 1968, 493.
12. Irons 1979, 10–12.
13. Low 2009.
14. Boyd and Richerson 2005, 103–04.
15. Clifford 1986, 3.
16. Geertz 1973c, 3–30, 412–53; see also Marcus and Fischer 1986, 26–29.
17. Caws 1969, 1378.
18. McCain and Segal 1988, 114.
19. Ibid., 56–57, 131–32.
20. Whiting 1964, 519–20.
21. McCain and Segal 1988, 67–69.
22. For examples, see Murdock 1967 and Murdock and White 1969, 329–69.
23. See the HRAF Web site: www.yale.edu/hraf.
24. Ogburn 1922, 200–80.
25. Bernard 2011, 257–58.
26. Peacock 1986, 54.
27. Bernard 2011, 278–80.
28. Romney et al. 1986; Bernard 2011, 371–78.
29. Bernard 2011, 151–52.
30. See Murdock and White 1969 for a description of the SCCS sample; *eHRAF World Cultures* is described at www.yale.edu/hraf; for a description of many different cross-cultural samples, see C. R. Ember and M. Ember 2009.
31. C. R. Ember 2007.
32. Helms 2009.
33. Trigger 1989.
34. Martin 1990, 42.
35. Etienne 1992.
36. Isaac 1997.
37. Leakey 1965, 73–78.
38. R. E. Taylor 1998.
39. R. C. Walter 1998.
40. F. H. Brown 2000, 225.
41. American Anthropological Association (http://www.aaanet.org/coe/Code_of_Ethics.pdf).
42. Szklut and Reed 1991.
43. Lambert et al. 2000, 405.
44. Hill and Hurtado 2004.
45. Waldbaum 2005.

Chapter 3

1. Sagan 1975.
2. Lovejoy 1964, 58–63.
3. Ibid., 63.
4. Mayr 1982, 339–60; Bowler 2009.
5. Wallace 1858/1970.
6. Mayr 1982, 423; Bowler 2009.
7. Darwin had a still longer title. It continued, *Or the Preservation of the Favoured Races in the Struggle for Life*. Darwin's notion of "struggle for life" is often misinterpreted to refer to a war of all against all. Although animals may fight with each other at times over access to resources, Darwin was referring mainly to their metaphorical "struggle" with the environment, particularly to obtain food.
8. Darwin 1970/1859.
9. Futuyma 1995 provides an overview of this long controversy.
10. Huxley 1970.
11. Bowler 2009, 325–46.
12. G. Williams 1992, 7.
13. J. M. Smith 1989, 42–45.
14. Hooper 2002.
15. Grant 2002.
16. Devillers and Chaline 1993, 22–23.
17. Beadle and Beadle 1966, 216.
18. Golden et al. 2000; Hayden 2000; Marshall 2000; Pennisi 2000; Travis 2000.
19. Daiger 2005.
20. Olsen 2002.
21. Dobzhansky 1962, 138–40.
22. Relethford 1990, 94.
23. G. A. Harrison et al. 1988, 198–200.
24. Brace 1996.
25. Grant and Grant 2002.
26. Rennie 2002, 83.
27. Chatterjee 1997.
28. Paley 1810.
29. Center for Renewal of Science and Culture, "The Wedge Strategy," cited in Forrest 2001, 16.
30. McMullin 2001, 174.
31. Rennie 2002.
32. Barash 1977.
33. Krebs and Davies 1984; 1987.
34. Badcock 2000.
35. Boyd and Richerson 2005.
36. Schaller 1972.
37. Hare et al. 2002.
38. E. O. Wilson 1975.
39. B. Low 2009.
40. D. Campbell 1965.
41. Nissen 1958.
42. Boyd and Richerson 1985/1996, 2005.
43. Durham 1991.

Chapter 4

1. Devillers and Chaline 1993.
2. See Stone and Lurquin 2007 and Boyd and Richerson 2008 for extensive discussions of the relationship between genes and culture.
3. Stewart 1950.
4. *Genesis* 17: 9–15.
5. Leonard and Katzmarzyk 2010.
6. D. F. Roberts 1953; Leonard and Katzmarzyk 2010.
7. Ibid.
8. Leonard and Katzmarzyk 2010.
9. Riesenfeld 1973, 427–59.
10. Ibid., 452–53.
11. J. S. Weiner 1954, 615–18; Steegman 1975. See also Larsen 2009.
12. Jablonski 2010.
13. Polednak 1974, 49–57. See also Branda and Eaton 1978.
14. Loomis 1967.
15. Post, Daniels, and Binford 1975, 65–80.
16. Holden 2000; Jablonski and Chaplin 2000.
17. Brutsaert 2010.
18. Ibid.
19. Greksa and Beall 1989, 223.
20. Ibid., 226.
21. Frisancho and Greksa 1989, 204.
22. Eveleth and Tanner 1990, 176–79.
23. Ibid., 205–06.
24. Bogin 1988, 105–06.
25. G. A. Harrison et al. 1988, 300.
26. Ibid., 198.
27. Huss-Ashmore and Johnston 1985, 482–83.
28. G. A. Harrison et al. 1988, 385–86.
29. Martorell 1980, 81–106.
30. Martorell et al. 1991.
31. Landauer and Whiting 1964; 1981; Gunders and Whiting 1968; Gray and Wolfe 1980.
32. Landauer and Whiting 1964; 1981; Gunders and Whiting 1968.
33. Gray and Wolfe 2009.
34. Landauer and Whiting 1981.
35. Eveleth and Tanner 1990, 205.
36. Landauer 1973.
37. Motulsky 1971, 223.
38. Ibid., 226.
39. Ibid., 229.
40. Ibid., 230.
41. Ibid., 233.
42. Ibid.
43. Black 1992.
44. An examination of the epidemic diseases spread by Europeans can be found in Chapter 11 of J. Diamond 1997a.
45. Neel et al. 1970; Patrick Tierney in his *Darkness in El Dorado* (New York: Norton, 2000) accused the Neel research team of fueling a measles outbreak among the Yanomamö by administering a harmful measles vaccine. However, the scientific evidence indicates that Tierney is wrong. The vaccine Neel and associates used was widely pretested, and there was no way that the vaccine could have caused the epidemic. Measles was already spreading in the Amazon, which was why the vaccination program was initiated. See Gregor and Gross 2004.
46. Merbs 1992; see also Armelagos and Harper 2005, 115 for more recent findings.
47. Stone and Lurquin 2007, 96–98.
48. Ibid., 104–05.
49. G. A. Harrison et al. 1988, 231.
50. For a review of the early research, see Durham 1991, 123–27. The particular form of malaria that is discussed is caused by the species *Plasmodium falciparum*.
51. See Madigral 1989 for a report of her own research and a review of earlier studies.
52. Pennisi 2001a.
53. Durham 1991, 124–45; Stone and Lurquin 2007, 104–05.
54. Motulsky 1971, 238.
55. J. Diamond 1993.
56. Molnar 1998, 158; Pennisi 2001b.
57. Durham 1991, 230.
58. Brodey 1971.
59. Stone and Lurquin 2007, 102.
60. McCracken 1971; see also references to the work of F. J. Simoons as referred to in Durham 1991, 240–41.
61. Ibid., Huang 2002.
62. Durham 1991, 263–69.
63. Marks 1994; Tattersall and DeSalle 2011, 130–42.
64. Molnar 1998, 19.
65. Brace et al. 1993.
66. Brooks et al. 1993.
67. Dupré 2008, 50–52.
68. Brooks et al. 1993.
69. M. King and Motulsky 2002.
70. Ebrey 2010, 22–37.
71. Coe 2011.
72. Phillipson 2005, 275–83.
73. McNeill 1998; Crosby 2004.
74. Motulsky 1971, 232; Crosby 2004, 195–216.
75. Ibid.
76. MacArthur and Wilson 1967.
77. Johanson and Edey 1981; Langdon 2005, 273–75.
78. Peregrine et al. 2000; 2003.
79. Lieberman 1999.
80. Klineberg 1935; 1944.
81. Jensen 1969.
82. Herrnstein and Murray 1994.
83. Kamin 1995; Marks 2008, 31–33.
84. Grubb 1987.
85. M. W. Smith 1974; Montagu 1997, 161–64.
86. Dobzhansky 1973, 11; Brace 2005, 254–55.
87. Ibid., 14–15.
88. Research by Sandra Scarr and others reported in Boyd and Richerson 1985, 56; see also Montagu 1997.
89. Nisbett 2009.
90. Dobzhansky 1962, 243.
91. Haldane 1963.
92. Simpson 1971, 297–308; Tattersall and DeSalle 2011, 196–99.

Chapter 5

1. The classic description of common primate traits is from Napier and Napier 1967. For primate social organization, see Smuts et al. 1987.
2. Bearder 1987, 14; Ankel-Simons 2007, 224–27.
3. Richard 1985, 22ff; Ankel-Simons 2007, 199–206.
4. Doyle and Martin 1979; Tattersall 1982; Fleagle 1999, 62–72.
5. Richard 1987, 32.
6. Bearder 1987, 13; Fleagle 1999, 110–16.
7. MacKinnon and MacKinnon 1980.
8. Fleagle 1999, 118–22; Cartmill 2010, 22; Ankel-Simons 2007, 31–32.
9. Napier and Napier 1967, 32–33; Fleagle 1999, 133–36.
10. Richard 1985, 164–65; Fleagle 1999, 136–70.
11. Cartmill 1992a, 29; Goldizen 1987, 34; see also Eisenberg 1977; Fleagle 1999, 168–74; Sussman and Kinzey 1984.
12. Eisenberg 1977, 15–17; Ankel-Simons 2007, 526–27.
13. Crockett and Eisenberg 1987; Robinson and Janson 1987; Robinson, Wright, and Kinzey 1987.
14. Hrdy 1977, 18.
15. Napier 1970, 80–82; Fleagle 1999, 187–97.

16. Fedigan 1982, 11; Ankel-Simons 2007, 98–99.
17. Fleagle 1999, 302.
18. LeGros Clark 1964, 184; Ankel-Simons 2007, 276–80.
19. Pennisi 2007.
20. Preuschoft et al. 1984; Fleagle 1999, 242.
21. Carpenter 1940; Chivers 1974, 1980.
22. Rijksen 1978, 22; Ankel-Simons 2007, 150–52.
23. Fossey 1983, xvi.
24. Tuttle 1986, 99–114.
25. Schaller 1963; 1964; Ankel-Simons 2007, 155–57.
26. Fossey 1983, 47.
27. Harcourt 1979, 187–92; Ankel-Simons 2007, 156.
28. Susman 1984; F. J. White 1996; Ankel-Simons 2007, 153–54.
29. Goodall 1963; van Lawick-Goodall 1971.
30. Teleki 1973.
31. Stanford 2009.
32. Ibid.
33. Falk 1987.
34. Female bonobos, or pygmy chimpanzees, engage in sexual intercourse nearly as often as human females—see Thompson-Handler et al. 1984.
35. By male–female bonding, we mean that at least one of the sexes is "faithful," that is, typically has intercourse with just one opposite-sex partner throughout at least one estrus or menstrual cycle or breeding season. Note that the bonding may not be monogamous; an individual may be bonded to more than one individual of the opposite sex. See M. Ember and C. R. Ember 1979.
36. C. R. Ember and M. Ember 1984, 207.
37. Ibid., 208–09.
38. de Waal and Lanting 1997.
39. Rumbaugh 1970, 52–58.
40. Boesche et al. 1994.
41. Observation by others cited by A. Jolly 1985, 53.
42. Hannah and McGrew 1987.
43. Seyfarth, Cheney, and Marler 1980.
44. Gardner and Gardner 1969.
45. Gardner and Gardner 1980.
46. Greenfield and Savage-Rumbaugh 1990.
47. Gingerich 1986; Szalay 1972; Szalay, Tattersall, and Decker 1975.
48. Cartmill 2009; Ciochon and Etler 1994, 41; Fleagle 1994.
49. Block and Boyer 2002.
50. Conroy 1990, 49–53.
51. Ibid., 53.
52. Habicht 1979.
53. Sussman 1991.
54. Cartmill 1974; Richard 1985, 31.
55. Szalay 1968.
56. Cartmill 1974; for more recent statements, see Cartmill 1992b; 2009.
57. Sussman and Raven 1978.
58. Fleagle 1994, 22–23.
59. Conroy 1990, 119; Gunnell and Rose 2002, 47–50.
60. Radinsky 1967.
61. Conroy 1990, 105; Fleagle 1994, 21; Gebo 2002.
62. Alexander 1992; Conroy 1990, 111; Gebo 2002, 37–39.
63. Kay, Ross, and Williams 1997; Dagosto 2002.
64. Conroy 1990, 46; Martin 1990, 46; Phillips and Walker 2002, 91–94.
65. Fleagle and Kay 1985, 25; Kay, Ross, and Williams 1997; Beard 2002, 146–48.

66. Jaeger et al. 1999; Beard 2002, 135.
67. Simons 1995; Simons and Rassmussen 1996.
68. Kay 2000b, 441.
69. Conroy 1990, 156; Kay 2000b, 441–42.
70. Fleagle 1999, 404–09.
71. Rosenberger 1979.
72. Fleagle and Kay 1987.
73. Aiello 1993; Hartwig 1994.
74. Andrews 2000b, 486.
75. Conroy 1990, 160–61; Fleagle and Kay 1985, 25, 30; Rasmussen 2002.
76. Fleagle 1999, 413–15; Fleagle and Kay 1983, 205; Rasmussen 2002.
77. Begun 2002.
78. Conroy 1990, 206–11; Harrison 2002.
79. Begun 2002; Harrison 2002.
80. Andrews 2000a, 485; Harrison 2002.
81. Begun 2002.
82. Ward et al. 1999; Zimmer 1999.
83. Begun 2002; Kelley 1992, 225; Ward and Duren 2002, 394–95.
84. Moyà-Solà et al. 2004.
85. T. Harrison 1986; T. Harrison and Rook 1997; Begun 2002b, 356–60.
86. Ward 1997; Kelley 2002.
87. Begun 2002; 2002b.
88. Ibid.
89. Fleagle 1999, 480–83.
90. Bilsborough 1992, 65.
91. Simons 1992, 207.

Chapter 6

1. Thorpe, Holder, and Crompton 2007.
2. Rose 1984; Langdon 2005, 116–117, 126–128.
3. Bilsborough 1992, 64–65; Klein 2009, 54–63.
4. Oakley 1964.
5. Kingston, Marino, and Hill 1994.
6. Hewes 1961.
7. Lovejoy 1981.
8. C. Jolly 1970.
9. Washburn 1960.
10. Pilbeam 1972, 153.
11. Wolpoff 1971.
12. Savage-Rumbaugh 1994.
13. Wolpoff 1983.
14. Zimmer 2004.
15. Zihlman 1992.
16. Wheeler 1984; 1991.
17. Falk 1988.
18. Zihlman 1992, 414.
19. Lovejoy 1988; Langdon 2005, 116–121.
20. Aiello and Dean 2002, 268–74.
21. Ibid., 507–08.
22. Gibbons 2002.
23. Brunet et al. 2002; Wong 2003.
24. Aiello and Collard 2001; Pickford et al. 2002; Wong 2003.
25. Richmond and Jungers 2008.
26. White et al. 1995.
27. White et al. 2009; White et al. 1994.
28. Ibid.; Hailie-Selassie 2001.
29. Susman et al. 1985; Rose 1984.
30. Culotta 1995.
31. Leakey et al. 1995.
32. Tattersall and Schwartz 2000, 93.
33. Simpson 2009; White et al. 1981; Johanson and White 1979.
34. Johanson and Edey 1981, 17–18.
35. Johanson and White 1979.
36. Lewin 1983b.
37. Conroy 1990, 291–92; Simpson 2009.
38. Fleagle 1999, 515–18; Klein 2009, 194–98, 206–18.
39. Ibid., 515, 520; Klein 2009, 207–11.

40. Ungar and Sponheimer 2011.
41. Kimbel et al. 1984.
42. Jungers 1988a; Clarke and Tobias 1995.
43. Lovejoy 1988.
44. Tattersall and Schwartz 2000, 88–89; Clarke and Tobias 1995.
45. Conroy 1990, 280–82; Klein 2009, 271–73.
46. Pilbeam 1972, 107.
47. Holloway 1974.
48. Szalay and Delson 1979, 504.
49. Asfaw et al. 1999.
50. Brunet et al. 1995.
51. Berger et al. 2010.
52. Carlson et al. 2011; Pickering et al. 2011
53. Brunet et al. 1995.
54. Leakey et al. 2001.
55. Fleagle 1999, 511–15.
56. Wood 1992; Klein 2009, 244–48.
57. McHenry 2009; Tobias 1994.
58. Simpson 2009.
59. Susman 1994; Klein 2009, 249–51, 260–61.
60. Ibid.
61. Holden 1997.
62. Leakey 1960.
63. Clark 1970, 68; Schick and Toth 1993, 97–99; Klein 2009, 253–59.
64. Schick and Toth 1993, 153–70.
65. Ibid., 129; Klein 2009, 257–58.
66. Schick and Toth 1993, 157–59.
67. Isaac 1984.
68. Schick and Toth 1993, 175–76.
69. Speth 2009.
70. Shipman 1986. For the idea that scavenging may have been an important food-getting strategy even for protohominins, see Szalay 1975.
71. M. Leakey 1971.
72. Potts 1988, 253–58.
73. Potts 1984; Klein 2009, 261.
74. Potts 1988, 278–81.
75. Boyd and Silk 2000, 249–50.
76. Dobzhansky 1962, 196.
77. Bromage and Dean 1985; B. H. Smith 1986; Gibbons 2008.
78. Chapais 2008.
79. Gowlett 2008; Lovejoy 2009.
80. McHenry 1982; Langdon 2005, 152–55.
81. McHenry 1982; Langdon 2005, 154–55.
82. Dunbar and Shultz 2007; Fuentes, Wyczalkowski, and MacKinnon 2010; Herrmann et al. 2007; Silk 2007.
83. Simpson et al. 2008.
84. Pilbeam and Gould 1974; cf. Klein 2009, 262–70.
85. Leonard 2002; Wrangham 2009.
86. Stedman et al. 2004.
87. Rightmire 2000.
88. Swisher et al. 1994.
89. Balter and Gibbons 2000; Gabunia et al. 2000.
90. Vekua et al. 2002; Gore 2002.
91. Wolpoff and Nkini 1988. See also Rightmire 2000; Balter 2001.
92. Fleagle 1999, 534–35; Day 1986, 409–12; Kramer 2009.
93. Rightmire 2000; Tobias 1994.
94. Franciscus and Trinkaus 1988.
95. Feibel and Brown 1993.
96. Ruff and Walker 1993.
97. Morwood et al. 2004; Brown et al. 2004.
98. Falk et al. 2005
99. Diamond 2004.
100. Tocheri et al. 2007.
101. Jungers et al. 2009.
102. Wong 2005; Weston and Lister 2009.
103. Fleagle 1999, 306; Langdon 2005, 260–68.
104. M. Ember and C. R. Ember 1979; cf. Lovejoy 1981.
105. Clayman 1989, 857–58.

106. Bordes 1968, 51–97.
107. Phillipson 1993, 57; Klein 2009, 377, 391.
108. Schick and Toth 1993, 227, 233.
109. Ibid., 231–33; Whittaker 1994, 27.
110. Bordes 1968, 24–25; Whittaker 1994, 27.
111. Schick and Toth 1993, 258–60; Whittaker 1994, 27.
112. Lawrence Keeley's analysis reported in Schick and Toth 1993, 260; see that page for their analysis of tool use.
113. Calvin 1983.
114. Yamei et al. 2000.
115. Ciochon et al. 1990, 178–83; Pope 1989.
116. Howell 1966.
117. Klein 1987; Binford 1987.
118. L. G. Freeman 1994; Klein 2009, 401.
119. A good example of this problem is the ongoing debate about fire use at Zhoukoudian cave, as reported by Weiner et al. 1998.
120. Beaumont 2011; Brain and Sillen 1988; Isaac 1984, 35–36. Other evidence for deliberate use of fire comes from the Swartkrans cave in South Africa and is dated 1 million to 1.5 million years ago and from Kenya and is dated to about 1.4 million years ago.
121. Alperson-Afil et. al. 2009; Goren-Inbar et al. 2004.
122. Binford and Ho 1985.
123. Wrangham 2009; Leonard 2002.
124. Clark 1970, 94–95; cf. Klein 2009, 397–401.
125. Clark 1970, 96–97; Klein 2009, 398–99.
126. de Lumley 1969.

Chapter 7

1. Stringer 1985.
2. Ibid.
3. Rightmire 1997.
4. Ibid.; Fleagle 1999, 535–37; Klein 2009, 330–43.
5. Spencer 1984.
6. Trinkaus 1985.
7. Stringer 2000.
8. Trinkaus and Shipman 1993a; 1993b; Klein 2009, 456, 585.
9. Krings et al. 1997.
10. Ibid.
11. Ovchinnikov et al. 2000; Green et al. 2010.
12. Green et. al. 2010.
13. Krause et al. 2007.
14. Lalueza-Fox et al. 2007.
15. Burbano et al. 2010.
16. Serre et al. 2004; Hodgson and Driscoll 2008.
17. Tattersall 1999, 115–16; Gibbons 2001.
18. Mellars 1996, 405–19.
19. Mellars 1998.
20. Strauss 1989.
21. Schick and Toth 1993, 288–92; Klein 2009, 481–91.
22. Klein 2009, 491–95.
23. Schick and Toth 1993, 288–92; Whittaker 1994, 30–31.
24. Klein 2009, 487–88.
25. Binford and Binford 1969.
26. Fish 1981, 377.
27. Butzer 1982, 42.
28. Phillipson 1993, 63; also see Klein 2009, 516–24.
29. For the controversy about whether the inhabitants of the Dordogne Valley lived in their homesites year-round, see Binford 1973.
30. Balter 2009.
31. Klein 1977; 2009, 540.
32. Klein 1974.
33. Bordes 1961.
34. T. Patterson 1981.

35. Phillipson 1993, 64; Klein 2009, 555–64.
36. Klein 1983, 38–39; Klein 2009, 564–68.
37. Binford 1984, 195–97. To explain the lack of complete skeletons of large animals, Klein (1983) suggests that the hunters may have butchered the large animals elsewhere because they could carry home only small cuts.
38. Wilford 1997.
39. Chase and Dibble 1987; Klein 2009, 572–73.
40. Gibbons 2012.
41. Krause et al. 2010
42. Reich et al. 2010
43. Stringer et al. 1984, 107.
44. Singer and Wymer 1982, 149.
45. Gibbons 2003.
46. Bräuer 1984, 387–89, 394; Rightmire 1984, 320.
47. Valladas et al. 1988.
48. Stringer et al. 1984, 121.
49. For arguments supporting the single-origin theory, see the chapters by Günter Bräuer, F. Clark Howell, and C. B. Stringer et al., in F. Smith and Spencer 1984. For arguments supporting the multiregional theory, see the chapters by C. L. Brace et al., David W. Frayer, Fred H. Smith, and Milford H. Wolpoff et al. in the same volume.
50. Smith 2010.
51. Cann et al. 1987.
52. Gibbons 2011.
53. Hammer and Zegura 1996.
54. Hammer and Zegura 2002.
55. Cavalli-Sforza and Feldman 2003.
56. Stringer 2003.
57. Wolpoff 1999, 501–504, 727–31; Frayer et al. 1993.
58. Wolpoff 1999, 735–43; Frayer et al. 1993.
59. D. Lieberman 1995.
60. Eswaran 2002.
61. Abi-Rached et al. 2011
62. Bahn 1998; Balter 2010.
63. Tattersall 1999, 198–203.
64. Trinkaus 1986; see also Trinkaus and Howells 1979.
65. Culotta 2005.
66. Klein 2003.
67. Mellars and French 2011.
68. Strauss 1982; Klein 2009, 656–58.
69. Dawson 1992, 24–71.
70. COHMAP 1988.
71. Martin and Wright 1967.
72. Mellars 1994; Klein 2009, 683.
73. Klein 2009, 674.
74. Klima 1962.
75. Whittaker 1994, 33; Schick and Toth 1993, 293–99.
76. Whittaker 1994, 31; Klein 2009, 658.
77. Bordaz 1970, 68.
78. Whittaker 1994, 33.
79. Phillipson 1993, 60; Klein 2009, 672.
80. Bordaz 1970, 68.
81. We thank Robert L. Kelly (personal communication) for bringing this possibility to our attention. See also J. D. Clark 1977, 136.
82. Ascher 1961.
83. Semenov 1970, 103. For a more recent discussion of research following this strategy, see Keeley 1980.
84. Klein 1994, 508; 2009, 668.
85. Soffer 1993, 38–40.
86. Phillipson 1993, 74.
87. Morell 1995.
88. Henshilwood et al. 2002.
89. Ucko and Rosenfeld 1967.
90. Rice and Paterson 1985; 1986.
91. Rice and Paterson 1985, 98.
92. Hawkins and Kleindienst 2001.

93. Peregrine 2001a.
94. Jayaswal 2002.
95. O'Connor, Ono, and Clarkson 2011; Summerhayes et al. 2010.
96. Waters et al. 2011.
97. McDonald 1998.
98. Goebel et al. 2008.
99. Dillehay 2000.
100. Gilbert et al. 2008.
101. Hoffecker et al. 1993.
102. Pringle 2011.
103. Wheat 1967.
104. Waguespack 2012.
105. Waters and Stafford 2007.
106. Anderson 2012.
107. Judge and Dawson 1972.
108. Wheat 1967.
109. Morgan and Bettinger 2012 .
110. Wheat 1967.
111. Ibid.
112. Anderson 2012.
113. Erlandson and Braje 2012.
114. McElrath and Emerson 2012.
115. Collins 1976, 88–125.
116. Chard 1969, 171.
117. G. Clark 1975, 101–61.
118. Petersen 1973, 94–96.
119. Daniel 2001; McElrath and Emerson 2012.
120. Sassaman 1996, 58–83.
121. Ibid.
122. J. Brown 1983, 5–10.

Chapter 8

1. N. Miller 1992; Scarre 2009.
2. Crawford 1992; Phillipson 2005, 165; MacNeish 1991, 256, 268; Bellwood 2005.
3. Flannery 1986, 6–8; Pearsall 1992; B. Smith 1992a; Browman, Fritz, and Watson 2009.
4. Hole 1992.
5. Binford 1971; Scarre 2012.
6. Flannery 1973a; Scarre 2012.
7. Simcha et al. 2000.
8. Harlan 1967.
9. Flannery 1971.
10. Henry 1989, 214–15; Watkins 2009.
11. Brown and Price 1985; Bellwood 2005, 49–54.
12. Henry 1989, 38–39, 209–10; 1991. See Olszewski 1991 for some questions about the degree of social complexity in Natufian sites.
13. Martin and Wright 1967.
14. A recent analysis of these changes can be found in Kuehn 1998; see also J. Brown 1985.
15. Marcus and Flannery 1996, 49–50.
16. Ibid., 50–53.
17. Balter 2007; Jones and Liu 2009.
18. Gorman 1970; Higham 2009.
19. Chang 1970; Gorman 1970; Bellwood 2005, 128–45; Higham 2009.
20. J. Clark 1970, 171–72; Connah 2009.
21. Phillipson 2005, 147–55.
22. Gill et al. 2009.
23. Alroy 2001.
24. Martin 1973.
25. Grayson 1977; 1984. See also L. G. Marshall 1984; Guthrie 1984; Barnosky et al. 2004.
26. Holdaway and Jacomb 2000.
27. Cohen 1977b, 12; 85.
28. Cohen 1989, 112–13.
29. Ibid., 113–15.
30. Flannery 1973b.
31. Patterson 1971.
32. G. Johnson 1977; D. Harris 1977.
33. Sussman 1972; Lee 1972.
34. For some examples of societies that have practiced infanticide, D. Harris 1977.
35. Howell 1979; Lee 1979.
36. Frisch 1980; Howell 1979.
37. Zohary 1969.

38. Flannery 1965.
39. Zeder 2011.
40. Chessa et al. 2009; Zeder 2011.
41. Hole et al. 1969.
42. Flannery 1986, 3–5; Pringle 1998.
43. Marcus and Flannery 1996, 64–66.
44. Flannery 1986, 6–8.
45. Fedoroff 2003.
46. Flannery 1986, 8–9; Marcus and Flannery 1996, 66–67.
47. Ibid., 66–68.
48. Piperno and Stothert 2003.
49. MacNeish 1991, 37, 47; Hole 1992.
50. B. Smith 1992b, 163, 287.
51. Asch and Asch 1978.
52. Clutton-Brock 1992; Browman, Fritz, and Watson 2009, 343–44.
53. Müller-Haye 1984, Browman, Fritz, and Watson 2009, 343–44.
54. Wenke and Olszewski 2007, 262.
55. Cohen 2011.
56. MacNeish 1991, 267–68.
57. Neumann 2003; Denham et al. 2003.
58. Hole 1992.
59. Connah 2009, 360–65.
60. Hanotte et al. 2002; Clutton-Brock 1992.
61. Childe 1956.
62. Braidwood 1960.
63. Wright 1971.
64. Flannery 1986, 10–11.
65. Cohen 1977a; 1977b, 279.
66. Byrne 1987, referred to in Blumler and Byrne 1991; see also Henry 1989, 30–38; McCorriston and Hole 1991.
67. Henry 1989, 41.
68. McCorriston and Hole 1991.
69. Henry 1989, 54.
70. Speth and Spielmann 1983.
71. B. White 1973; see also Kasarda 1971.
72. C. R. Ember 1983.
73. Konner and Worthman 1980.
74. Roosevelt 1984; see also M. N. Cohen and Armelagos 1984b, 585–602; Cohen 1987; 2009. For evidence suggesting that the transition to food production was not generally associated with declining health, see Wood et al. 1992; Starling and Stock 2007.
75. Roosevelt 1984
76. Renfrew 1969.
77. Service 1975; Wenke and Olszewski 2007, 289–90.
78. Flannery 1972; also Wenke and Olszewski 2007, 292–98.
79. Flannery 1972; Redman 1978, 215–16.
80. Wright and Johnson 1975.
81. The discussion in the remainder of this section draws from Wright and Johnson 1975; see also G. Johnson 1987.
82. Wright and Johnson 1975.
83. Flannery 1972; Matthews 2009, 432–33.
84. Service 1975, 207; Matthews 2009, 436–37.
85. Service 1975; Flannery 1972.
86. This description of Sumerian civilization is based on Kramer 1963; also see Crawford 2004.
87. Diamond 1989.
88. Helms 1975, 34–36, 54–55; Sanders et al. 1979.
89. Millon 1967; Wenke and Olszewski 2007, 496–500.
90. Millon 1976.
91. Millon 1967.
92. Helms 1975, 61–63; Weaver 1993.
93. Bard 2008, 121–28.
94. Connah 1987, 67; 2009, 382.
95. Ibid., 216–17; 2009, 383–86.
96. Vogel 2009.

97. Wenke and Olszewski 2007, 412–24.
98. Ebrey 1996, 22–30; Wenke and Olszewski 2007, 445–49.
99. Solis et al. 2001; Haas et al. 2004.
100. For an overview, see Lumbreras 1974.
101. M. Fowler 1975.
102. For a more complete review of the available theories, see various chapters in Cohen and Service 1978; also Wenke and Olszewski 2007, 298–16.
103. Wittfogel 1957.
104. Adams 1960; H. T. Wright 1986.
105. Wheatley 1971, 291.
106. Adams 1960.
107. Adams 1981, 244.
108. Adams 1981, 243; Service 1975, 274–75.
109. Carneiro 1970; Sanders and Price 1968, 230–32.
110. M. Harris 1979, 101–02.
111. T. C. Young 1972.
112. Sanders and Price 1968, 141.
113. Blanton et al. 1981, 224. For the apparent absence of population pressure in the Teotihuacàn Valley, see Brumfiel 1976. For the Oaxaca Valley, see Feinman et al. 1985.
114. Wright and Johnson 1975. Carneiro (1988), however, argued the opposite, that the population grew just before the states emerged in southwestern Iran. Whether or not population declined, Frank Hole (1994) has suggested that climate change around that time may have forced local populations to relocate, some to centers that became cities.
115. Polanyi et al. 1957, 257–62; Sanders 1968.
116. Wright and Johnson 1975.
117. Rathje 1971.
118. Chang 1986, 234–94.
119. For a discussion of how political dynamics may play an important role in state formation, see Brumfiel 1983.
120. Johnson and Earle 1987, 324–26.
121. Childe 1950.
122. Service 1975, 12–15, 89–90.
123. J. Diamond 1997a, 205–07.
124. Dirks 1993.
125. Johnson and Earle 1987, 243–48, 304–306.
126. Ferguson and Whitehead 1992.
127. Weiss et al. 1993.
128. Kerr 1998; Grossman 2002.
129. Haug et al. 2003.
130. DeMenocal 2001; Haug et al. 2003; Hodell et al. 2001.
131. Holden 1996.

Chapter 9

1. Linton 1945, 30.
2. Sapir 1938, cited by Pelto and Pelto 1975, 1.
3. Pelto and Pelto 1975, 14–15.
4. Castle 2013.
5. Bland 2013.
6. Simoons 1994, 65–71, 101, 109–11, 261–65.
7. de Waal 2001, 269.
8. DeMunck 2000, 22.
9. Ibid., 2000, 8.
10. Durkheim 1938/1895.
11. O'Gorman, Wilson, and Miller 2008.
12. Durkheim 1938/1895, 3.
13. Asch 1956.
14. Bond and Smith 1996.
15. Berns et al. 2005.
16. M. F. Brown 2008, 372.
17. Hewlett 2004.
18. Miner 1956, 504–505, reproduced by permission of the American Anthropological Association.
19. Lee 1972.

20. M. F. Brown 2008, 364.
21. Hatch 1997.
22. M. F. Brown. 2008, 363.
23. Zechenter 1997.
24. Rosenblatt 2004.
25. E. T. Hall and Hall 1990, 11–12.
26. Hall 1966, 159–60.
27. R. Brown 1965, 549–609.
28. Wagley 1974.
29. Chibnik 1981, 256–68.
30. Linton 1936, 306.
31. Ibid., 310–11.
32. Silver 1981.
33. Greenfield et al. 2000.
34. Rogers 1983, 263–69.
35. Cancian 1980.
36. Efferson et al. 2008.
37. Hewlett and Cavalli-Sforza 1986; Cavalli-Sforza and Feldman 1981.
38. Valente 1995, 21.
39. W. Cohen 1995.
40. Linton 1936, 326–27.
41. *Britannica Online* 1998; *Academic American Encyclopedia* 1980.
42. Linton 1936, 338–39.
43. G. M. Foster 1962, 26.
44. Bodley 1990, 7.
45. Pelto and Müller-Wille 1987, 207–43.
46. Aporta and Higgs 2005.
47. Bodley 1990, 38–41.
48. T. Kroeber 1967, 45–47.
49. Roth 2001.
50. Boyd and Richerson 1996/1985, 106.
51. Ibid., 135.
52. D. T. Campbell 1965. See also Boyd and Richerson 1996/1985 and Durham 1991.
53. Bentley et al. 2007; Mesoudi and Lycett 2009.
54. The historical information we refer to comes from a book by Nevins 1927. For how radical the American Revolution was, see G. Wood 1992.
55. Brinton 1938.
56. Paige 1975.
57. Tanter and Midlarsky 1967
58. Blight, Pulham, and Torpey 2012
59. Howard, Duffy, and Freelon et al. 2011
60. Bestor 2001, 76.
61. Trouillot 2001, 128.
62. Durrenberger 2001a; see also Hannerz 1996.
63. McNeill 1967, 283–87; Guest and Jones 2005, 4.
64. Guest and Jones 2005, 4.
65. Traphagan and Brown 2002.
66. Bradsher 2002, 3.
67. Guest and Jones 2005.
68. Yergin 2002, A29.
69. G. Thompson 2002, A3.
70. Sengupta 2002, A3.
71. Conklin 2002.
72. J. D. Hill 1996, 1.
73. Bilby 1996, 127–28, referring to Hoogbergen 1990, 23.
74. Bilby 1996, 128–37.
75. Sattler 1996, 42.
76. Ibid., 50–51.
77. Ibid., 54.
78. Ibid., 58–59.
79. Kottak 1996, 136; 153.
80. Roosens 1989, 9.
81. Cashdan 2001.
82. C. R. Ember and Levinson 1991.

Chapter 10

1. Keller 1974/1902, 34.
2. Poyatos 2002, 103–05, 114–18.
3. Wilden 1987, 124, referred to in Christensen et al. 2001.
4. Ekman and Kelmer 1997.
5. Larson, Aronoff, and Stearns 2007.
6. Wierzbicka 2005, 279; Russell 1994, 115–18; Ekman 1994, 269.
7. Ekman and Keltner 1997.
8. R. T. Moran, Harris and Moran 2007.

9. Chaplin et al. 2000.
10. Chen, Katdare, and Lucas 2006.
11. Schmid et al. 2011.
12. Poyatos 2002, 103–105, 114–18
13. von Frisch 1962.
14. King 1999a; Gibson and Jessee 1999, 189–90.
15. Seyfarth and Cheney 1982, 242, 246.
16. Hockett and Ascher 1964.
17. Eliot 1963.
18. Snowdon 1999, 81.
19. Pepperberg 1999.
20. Mukerjee 1996, 28.
21. Savage-Rumbaugh 1992, 138–41.
22. J. H. Hill 1978, 94; J. H. Hill 2009.
23. Ibid.
24. Trinkaus 2007.
25. Senner 1989.
26. Hauser, Chomsky, and Fitch 2002.
27. Southworth and Daswani 1974, 312. See also Boas 1911/1964, 121–23.
28. Akmajian et al. 2001, 296.
29. Ibid., 298.
30. Bickerton 1983.
31. For a critique of Bickerton's thesis, see J. Siegel 2009.
32. Ibid., 122.
33. B. Berlin 1992; Hays 1994.
34. G. Miller 2004.
35. Gleitman and Wanner 1982; Blount 1981.
36. R. Brown 1980, 93–94.
37. de Villiers and de Villiers 1979, 48; see also Wanner and Gleitman 1982.
38. Bickerton 1983, 122.
39. E. Bates and Marchman 1988 as referred to by Snowdon 1999, 88–91.
40. Crystal 1971, 168.
41. Ibid., 100–101.
42. Barinaga 1992, 535.
43. Akmajian et al. 1984, 136.
44. R. L. Munroe et al. 1996; M. Ember and C. R. Ember 1999. The theory about the effect of baby-holding on consonant-vowel alternation is an extension of the theory that regular baby-holding encourages a preference for regular rhythm in music; see Ayres 1973.
45. Sapir and Swadesh 1964, 103.
46. Akmajian et al. 2001, 149–54.
47. Chaucer 1926, 8. Our modern English translation is based on the glossary in this book.
48. Katzner 2002, 10.
49. Akmajian et al. 2001, 334.
50. Baldi 1983, 3.
51. Ibid., 12.
52. Friedrich 1970, 168.
53. Ibid., 166.
54. Gimbutas 1974, 293–95. See Skomal and Polomé 1987.
55. Anthony et al. 1991.
56. Renfrew 1987.
57. Greenberg 1972; see also Phillipson 1976, 71.
58. Phillipson 1976, 79.
59. Holmes 2001, 194–95.
60. Trudgill 1983, 34.
61. Gumperz 1961, 976–88.
62. Trudgill 1983, 35.
63. Gumperz 1971, 45.
64. Weinreich 1968, 31.
65. But see Thomason and Kaufman 1988 for a discussion of how grammatical changes due to contact may be more extensive than was previously assumed.
66. Berlin and Kay 1969.
67. Kay 1996.
68. Berlin and Kay 1969; Kay et al. 2009.
69. Ibid., 5–6.
70. Ibid., 104; Witkowski and Brown 1978.

71. Bornstein 1973, 41–101.
72. M. Ember 1978, 364–67.
73. Ibid.
74. C. H. Brown 1977.
75. C. H. Brown 1979.
76. Witkowski and Burris 1981.
77. Ibid.
78. C. H. Brown and Witkowski 1980, 379.
79. C. H. Brown 1984, 106.
80. Hoijer 1964, 146.
81. Webb 1977, 42–49; see also Rudmin 1988.
82. Sapir 1931, 578; see also J. B. Carroll 1956.
83. Wardhaugh 2002, 222.
84. Denny 1979, 97.
85. Friedrich 1986.
86. Guiora et al. 1982.
87. Lucy 1992, 46.
88. Ibid., 85–148.
89. Hymes 1974, 83–117.
90. Gumperz and Cook-Gumperz 2008.
91. Darnell 1989.
92. Alim et al. 2009.
93. Fischer 1958; Wardhaugh 2002, 160–88.
94. Chambers 2002, 352; citing research by Shuy.
95. Trudgill 1983, 41–42.
96. Geertz 1960, 248–60; see also Errington 1985.
97. R. Brown and Ford 1961.
98. Wardhaugh 2002, 315.
99. Shibamoto 1987, 28.
100. Holmes 2001, 153.
101. Chambers 2002, 352, citing research by Shuy.
102. Lakoff 1973; Lakoff 1990.
103. Wardhaugh 2002, 328; Holmes 2001, 158–59; Trudgill 1983, 87–88.
104. M. R. Haas 1944, 142–49.
105. Keenan 1989.
106. Holmes 2001, 289.
107. Tannen 1990, 49–83.
108. Wardhaugh 2002, 100.
109. Heller 1988, 1.
110. Pfaff 1979.
111. Wardhaugh 2002, 108.
112. Gal 1988, 249–55.
113. Collins and Blot 2003, 1–3.

Chapter 11

1. Hitchcock and Beisele 2000, 5.
2. C. R. Ember 1978b.
3. Kent 1996.
4. Schrire 1984a; Myers 1988.
5. Morrison and Junker 2002.
6. The discussion of the Australian aborigines is based on R. A. Gould 1969.
7. Burbank 1994, 23; Burbank 2009b.
8. Data from Textor 1967; and Service 1979.
9. Murdock and Provost 1973, 207.
10. R. B. Lee 1968; DeVore and Konner 1974.
11. C. R. Ember 1978b.
12. McCarthy and McArthur 1960.
13. R. B. Lee 1979, 256–58, 278–80.
14. Palsson 1988; Roscoe 2002.
15. Keeley 1991.
16. R. L. Kelly 1995, 293–315.
17. Mitchell 2009; Tollefson 2009.
18. C. Ember 1975.
19. D. Werner 1978.
20. Textor 1967.
21. This section is largely based on Hames 2009.
22. Chagnon 1987, 60.
23. S. S. King 1979.
24. Hickey 1964, 135–65.
25. C. R. Ember 1983, 289.
26. Textor 1967; Dirks 2009; Messer 1996, 244.
27. Finnis 2006.
28. Barlett 1989, 253–91.

29. U.S. Census Bureau 1993.
30. Salzman 1996.
31. Lees and Bates 1974; A. L. Johnson 2002.
32. Whitaker 1955; Itkonen 1951.
33. Paine 1994.
34. Textor 1967.
35. Dirks 2009.
36. Data from Textor 1967.
37. L. R. Binford 1990; see also Low 1990a, 242–43.
38. The few foragers in cold areas relying primarily on hunting have animals (dogs, horses, reindeer) that can carry transportable housing; see L. R. Binford 1990.
39. Bailey et al. 1989.
40. Data from Textor 1967.
41. Boserup 1993/1965.
42. R. C. Hunt 2000.
43. Janzen 1973.
44. Roosevelt 1992.
45. Hoebel 1968/1954, 46–63.
46. Woodburn 1968.
47. Pryor 2005, 36.
48. Ibid.
49. Leacock and Lee 1982, 8; Pryor 2005, 36.
50. R. Murphy 1960, 69, 142–43.
51. Salzman 1996.
52. Not all pastoralists have individual ownership. For example, the Tungus of northern Siberia have kin group ownership of reindeer. See Dowling 1975, 422.
53. Salzman 2002.
54. Bodley 1990, 77–93; Wilmsen 1989, 1–14.
55. Ibid., 106–8.
56. Fratkin 2008.
57. Ibid., 86–9.
58. Salzman 1996, 904–05.
59. Salzman 2002. Lawrence 2011.
60. Plattner 1989b, 379–96.
61. Hage and Powers 1992.
62. Carneiro 1968, cited in Sahlins 1972, 68.
63. Sahlins 1972, 101–48.
64. McClelland 1961.
65. Steward and Faron 1959, 122–25.
66. Bowie 2006, 251.
67. B. B. Whiting and Edwards 1988, 164.
68. Nag et al. 1978, 295–96.
69. B. B. Whiting and Edwards 1988, 97–107.
70. Draper and Cashdan 1988, 348.
71. N. B. Jones et al. 1996, 166–69.
72. Nag et al. 1978, 293; see also Bradley 1984–1985, 160–64.
73. C. R. Ember 1983, 291–97.
74. Polanyi 1957.
75. Sahlins 1972, 188–96.
76. The "//" sign in the name for the G//ana people symbolizes a click sound not unlike the sound we make when we want a horse to move faster.
77. Cashdan 1980, 116–20.
78. H. Kaplan and Hill 1985; H. Kaplan et al. 1990; Gurven et al. 2002, 114.
79. Hames 1990.
80. Gurven et al. 2002, 114.
81. H. Kaplan et al. 1990.
82. Winterhalder 1990.
83. Mooney 1978.
84. Balikci 1970 quoted in Mooney 1978, 392.
85. Mooney 1978, 392.
86. Fehr and Fischbacher 2003; Ensminger 2002; Henrich et al. 2004, as cited by Ensminger 2002.
87. Angier 2002, F1, F8.
88. Marshall 1961, 242.
89. Abler 2009.
90. N. Peacock and Bailey 2004.
91. Service 1962, 145–46.
92. M. Harris 1975, 118–21.
93. Plattner 1985, viii.
94. Thurnwald 1934, 122.

95. Pollier 2000.
96. Vohs et al. 2006.
97. The description of Tikopia is based on Firth 1959, Chapters 5, 6, 7, and 9, passim.
98. Monsutti 2004.
99. Monsutti 2004; Eversole 2005.
100. Eversole 2005.
101. Most of this discussion is based on R. F. Murphy and Steward 1956.
102. Burkhalter and Murphy 1989.
103. Gross and Underwood 1971.

Chapter 12

1. In an analysis of many native societies in the New World, Gary Feinman and Jill Neitzel argue that egalitarian and rank societies ("tribes" and "chiefdoms," respectively) are not systematically distinguishable. See Feinman and Neitzel (1984, 57).
2. Fried 1967, 33.
3. Boehm 1993, 230–31; Boehm 1999.
4. M. G. Smith 1966, 152.
5. Salzman 1999.
6. Borgerhoff Mulder et al. 2010.
7. Ibid.
8. D. Mitchell 2009.
9. Drucker 1965, 56–64.
10. Service 1978, 249.
11. Sahlins 1958, 80–81.
12. Betzig 1988.
13. W. L. Warner and Lunt 1941.
14. Lynd and Lynd 1929; and Lynd and Lynd 1937.
15. McNamee and Miller 2009: 61–62.
16. Ibid., 62–71.
17. Higley 1995, 1–47.
18. McNamee and Miller 2009: 73–74.
19. Argyle 1994.
20. S. R. Barrett 1994, 17–19, 34–35.
21. Ibid., 155.
22. Julian and Kominski 2011.
23. Ibid.
24. Treiman and Ganzeboom 1990, 117; Featherman and Hauser 1978, 4, 481.
25. Solon 2002; Behrman et al. 2001.
26. S. R. Barrett 1994, 17, 41.
27. Smeeding et al. 2011, 4–8.
28. DeParle 2012.
29. Smeeding et al. 2011, 3.
30. K. Phillips 1990; U.S. Census Bureau 1993; *New York Times* 1997, A26; Johnston 1999, 16.
31. Huber et al. 2006.
32. Milanovic 2011: 118.
33. Durrenberger 2001b, who refers to Goldschmidt 1999 and Newman 1988; 1993.Klass 2009.
34. Ruskin 1963, 296–314.
35. O. Lewis 1958.
36. Ibid.
37. Kristof 1995, A18.
38. For more information about caste in Japan, see Berreman 1973 and 1972, 403–14.
39. Takezawa 2006.
40. Kristof 1995; 1997.
41. Tamari 1991; 2005.
42. Taylor 2005.
43. Berreman 1960, 120–27.
44. Kopytoff 1996.
45. O. Patterson 1982, vii–xiii, 105.
46. Pryor 1977, 219.
47. Euripides 1937, 52.
48. Nadel 1942.
49. Harper 2003.
50. Lassiter et al. 2004, 49–50.
51. Ibid., 59–67.
52. Pryor 1977, 217–47.
53. Marks 1994; Shanklin 1993: 15–17.
54. Molnar 1998: 19.
55. Brace et al. 1993.
56. Brooks et al. 1993.
57. Ibid.

58. King and Motulsky 2002.
59. Rothman 2011, 62, referring to Marks.
60. M. D. Williams 2009.
61. S. S. Friedman 1980, 206.
62. M. H. Ross 2009a.
63. Marks 1994, 32.
64. Fluehr-Lobban 2006, 12.
65. Marks 1994, 32.
66. Fluehr-Lobban 2006, 12.
67. Bertrand and Mullainathan 2011.
68. Armelagos and Goodman 1998, 365; Foner 2011, 194.
69. O. Patterson 2000.
70. M. Nash 1989, 2.
71. Ibid., 10.
72. Newbury 1988.
73. C. Taylor 2005.
74. Newbury 1998.
75. Britannica Online 1995.
76. See "Rwanda" in later Books of the Year from Britannica Online http://search.eb.com/search?query=rwanda&x=0&y=0&ct=.
77. Barth 1994, 27.
78. Yinger 1994, 169.
79. Ibid., 169–71.
80. Benjamin 1991; see also M. D. Williams 2009.
81. Flannery 1972.
82. Data from Textor 1967.
83. Ibid.
84. Lenski 1984/1966, 308–18; Nielsen 2004.
85. Treiman and Ganzeboom 1990, 117; Cutright 1967, 564.
86. Sahlins 1958; Lenski 1984/1966.
87. Bowles et al. 2010; Smith et al. 2010.
88. Sahlins 1958: 4.
89. Lenski 1984/1966.
90. Heinrich and Boyd 2008.
91. Sahlins 1972.
92. Gilman 1990.
93. Fried 1967, 201ff; and Harner 1975.
94. Smith et al. 2010; Bowles et al. 2010.
95. Meek 1940, 149–50.

Chapter 13

1. Attributed to English poet Robert Southey (1774–1843) in Opie and Opie, 100–01.
2. Leibowitz 1978, 43–44.
3. Schlegel 1989, 266; Epstein 1988, 5–6; Chafetz 1990, 28.
4. Jacobs and Roberts 1989.
5. Segal 2004; Segal also cites the work of W. Williams 1992.
6. Lang 1999, 93–94; Blackwood 1984b.
7. Wikan 1982, 168–86.
8. Stini 1971.
9. Frayer and Wolpoff 1985, 431–32.
10. For reviews of theories and research on sexual dimorphism and possible genetic and cultural determinants of variation in degree of dimorphism over time and place, see Frayer and Wolpoff 1985 and Gray 1985, 201–209, 217–25.
11. J. K. Brown 1970, 1074.
12. See Hurtado et al. 1985, 23.
13. Murdock and Provost 1973, 213; Byrne 1994.
14. R. O'Brian 1999.
15. D. R. White et al. 1977, 1–24.
16. Mukhopadhyay and Higgins 1988, 473.
17. J. K. Brown 1970b, 1073–78; and D. R. White et al. 1977.
18. Nerlove 1974.
19. N. E. Levine 1988.
20. M. J. Goodman et al. 1985.
21. Noss and Hewlett 2001.
22. Brumbach and Jarvenpa 2006a; Jarvenpa and Brumbach 2006.
23. Brumbach and Jarvenpa 2006b.
24. C. R. Ember 1983, 288–89.

25. Mead 1950 [originally published 1935], 180–84.
26. Rivers 1967 [originally published 1906], 567.
27. M. Ember and Ember 1971, 573, table 1.
28. Schlegel and Barry 1986.
29. Wood and Eagly 2002, 706, drawing on data from H. Kaplan et al. 2000.
30. Boserup 1970, 22–25; see also Schlegel and Barry 1986, 144–45.
31. Boserup 1970, 22–25.
32. Bossen 2000.
33. Ibid., 31–34.
34. C. R. Ember 1983, 286–87; data from Murdock and Provost 1973, 212; Bradley 1995.
35. C. R. Ember 1983.
36. Ibid.
37. Ibid., 287–93.
38. M. Ember and Ember 1971, 579–80.
39. Ibid., 581; see also Sanday 1973, 1684.
40. Nerlove 1974.
41. Schlegel and Barry 1986.
42. Whyte 1978a, 217.
43. World Bank 2011, 386–87.
44. Whyte 1978a; D. B. Adams 1983.
45. Mutrine 2013.
46. J. K. Brown 1970a.
47. Sanday 1974; Divale and Harris 1976.
48. Quinn 1977, 189–90.
49. D. Werner 1982; Stogdill 1974, cited in ibid.; see also Handwerker and Crosbie 1982.
50. Draper 1975, 103.
51. D. Werner 1984.
52. M. H. Ross 1986.
53. This description is based on the fieldwork of Elizabeth and Robert Fearnea (1956–1958), as reported in M. K. Martin and Voorhies 1975, 304–31.
54. Begler 1978.
55. Ibid. See also Whyte 1978a, 229–32.
56. Whyte 1978b, 95–120; see also Quinn 1977.
57. Whyte 1978b, 124–29, 145; see also Sanday 1973.
58. Whyte 1978b, 129–30.
59. J. K. Brown 1970a.
60. Whyte 1978b, 135–36.
61. Ibid., 135.
62. Doyle 2005.
63. D. Werner 1984.
64. Quinn 1977, 85; see also Etienne and Leacock 1980, 19–20.
65. Chafetz 1990, 11–19.
66. B. B. Whiting and Edwards 1973.
67. R. L. Munroe et al. 2000, 8–9.
68. Maccoby and Jacklin 1974.
69. For a more extensive discussion of behavior differences and possible explanations of them, see C. R. Ember 1981.
70. B. B. Whiting and Edwards 1973.
71. For references to this research, see C. R. Ember 1981, 559.
72. Rubin et al. 1974.
73. For a discussion of this evidence, see Ellis 1986, 525–27; C. R. Ember 1981.
74. For example, Ellis (1986) considers the evidence for the biological view of aggression "beyond reasonable dispute."
75. For a discussion of other possibilities, see C. R. Ember 1981.
76. R. M. Sapolsky 1997, 23–26.
77. Rohner 1976.
78. B. B. Whiting and Whiting 1975; see also B. B. Whiting and Edwards 1988, 273.
79. C. R. Ember 1973, 424–39.
80. R. M. Sapolsky 1997, 25–26.
81. Burbank 1994.

82. B. B. Whiting and Edwards 1973, 175–79; see also Maccoby and Jacklin 1974.
83. Heise 1967.
84. C. S. Ford and Beach 1951, 191.
85. O. Lewis 1951, 397.
86. Farley 1996, 60.
87. C. S. Ford and Beach 1951, 23–25, 68–71.
88. Ibid., 40–41, 73.
89. Broude 2009.
90. C. S. Ford and Beach 1951, 82–83.
91. Broude and Greene 1976.
92. Kluckhohn 1948, 101.
93. M. Hunt 1974, 254–57; Lewin 1994.
94. Broude 1980, 184.
95. C. S. Ford and Beach 1951, 114.
96. Jankowiak et al. 2002.
97. Lang 1999, 97, citing Thomas 1993.
98. J. Morris 1938, 191.
99. Underhill 1938, 117, 186.
100. 'Abd Allah 1917, 7, 20.
101. Cardoso and Werner 2004.
102. R. C. Kelly 1974.
103. Cardoso and Werner 2004.
104. Blackwood and Wieringa 1999, 49; Blackwood 1984a.
105. Cardoso and Werner 2004, 207.
106. Data from Textor 1967.
107. W. N. Stephens 1972, 1–28.
108. Broude 1976, 243.
109. D. Werner 1979; D. Werner 1975.
110. D. Werner 1979, 345–62; see also D. Werner 1975, 36.
111. Data from Textor 1967.
112. Schlegel 1991.

Chapter 14

1. W. N. Stephens 1963, 5.
2. Murdock 1949, 8.
3. Hua 2001.
4. Hoebel 1960, 77.
5. Evans-Pritchard 1970, 1428–34.
6. D. O'Brien 1977; Oboler 1980.
7. Oboler 2009.
8. Murdock 1949, 7–8.
9. Ibid., 9–10.
10. See, for example, Linton 1936, 135–36.
11. M. Ember and C. R. Ember 1979.
12. Ibid.
13. Marlowe 2003, 221–23.
14. M. Ember and C. R. Ember 1979.
15. Graburn 1969, 188–200.
16. J. W. M. Whiting 1941, 125.
17. Bumpass and Lu 2000.
18. Schlegel and Eloul 1987. Huber, Danaher and Breedlove (2011) point out that most societies have more than one type of transaction.
19. Schlegel and Eloul 1988, 295, Table 1. We used the data to calculate the frequency of various types of economic transaction in a worldwide sample of 186 societies.
20. Schlegel and Eloul 1988, 298–99.
21. Pryor 1977, 363–64.
22. Ibid.
23. Schlegel and Eloul 1988, 296–97.
24. Ibid.
25. Ibid.
26. Radcliffe-Brown 1922, 73.
27. Murdock 1967; Goody 1973, 17–21.
28. Pryor 1977, 363–65; Schlegel and Eloul 1988, 296–99.
29. Schlegel and Eloul 1988, following Goody 1973, 20.
30. Middleton 1962, 606.
31. Durham 1991, 293–94, citing research by Hopkins 1980.
32. A. Howard and Rensel 2004.
33. MacDonald and Hewlett 1999, 504–06.
34. M. Ember 1975, 262, Table 3.
35. Busby 2009.
36. M. Ember 1975, 260–69; see also Durham 1991, 341–57.

37. Oliver 1955, 352–53.
38. Ibid., 223–24, quoted in W. Stephens 1963, 58.
39. Mead 1950, 101.
40. Jankowiak et al. 2005.
41. The discussion of these customs is based on W. Stephens 1963, 63–67.
42. Kilbride and Kilbride 1990, 202–06.
43. C. Anderson 2000, 102–03.
44. Linton 1936, 183.
45. J. W. M. Whiting 1964.
46. M. Ember 1974b.
47. M. Ember 1984–1985. The statistical relationship between late age of marriage for men and polygyny was first reported by Witkowski 1975.
48. M. Ember 1974b, 202–205.
49. M. Ember 1984–1985. For other predictors of polygyny, see D. R. White and Burton 1988.
50. Sellen and Hruschka 2004.
51. Low 1990b.
52. M. Ember et al. 2007.
53. Barber 2008.
54. Coult and Habenstein 1965; Murdock 1957.
55. M. C. Goldstein 1987, 39.
56. Stephens 1963, 45.
57. Hiatt 1980.
58. M. Goldstein 1987. Formerly, in feudal Tibet, a class of serfs who owned small parcels of land also practiced polyandry. Goldstein suggests that a shortage of land would explain their polyandry too. See M. C. Goldstein 1971.
59. For example, see M. L. Cohen 1976.
60. Pasternak 1976, 96.
61. Silk 1980; Damas 1983.
62. K. Gibson 2009.
63. Coult and Habenstein 1965.
64. Mead 1961/1928, quoted in Stephens 1963, 134–35.
65. Nimkoff and Middleton 1960.
66. Pasternak et al. 1976, 109–23.
67. R. Frost 1915.
68. Taylor et al. 2010, p. 7.
69. Coult and Habenstein 1965; Murdock 1957.
70. Percentages calculated from Coult and Habenstein 1965.
71. L. Bohannan and P. Bohannan 1953.
72. J. D. Freeman 1961.
73. Jarvenpa 2004.
74. C. R. Ember et al. 1974, 84–89.
75. Pospisil 1963.
76. Schneider 1961a.
77. M. Ember and Ember 1971, 581.
78. Schneider 1961b.
79. Goodenough 1951, 145.
80. Coult and Habenstein 1965.
81. Data from Textor 1967.
82. Davenport 1959.
83. M. Ember 1967.
84. M. Ember and C. R. Ember 1971. See also Divale 1974.
85. Ibid., 583–85; Divale 1974.
86. M. Ember and Ember 1971. For a different theory—that matrilocal residence precedes, rather than follows, the development of purely external warfare—see Divale 1974.
87. Helms 2009; Herlihy 2007; see also M. Ember and Ember 1971.
88. Service 1962, 137.
89. C. R. Ember and M. Ember 1972.
90. C. R. Ember 1975.
91. M. Ember 1974a.
92. Data from Textor 1967.
93. C. R. Ember et al. 1974.
94. The importance of warfare and competition as factors in the formation of unilineal descent groups is also suggested by Service 1962 and Sahlins 1961, 332–45.
95. C. R. Ember and Ember 1972.
96. C. R. Ember and Ember 1997.

Chapter 15

1. Service 1962; Lewellen 2003, 17–18.
2. See A. Johnson and Earle 2000 for a different classification scheme.
3. Schrire 1984b; see also Leacock and Lee 1982, 8.
4. Service 1962, 109.
5. Briggs 1974.
6. Mathiassen 1928, 213.
7. Service 1962, 114–15; Lewellen 2003: 26–27.
8. Lewellen 2003, 27.
9. Salzman 2008, 68.
10. Bohannan 1954, 3.
11. Sahlins 1961, 342.
12. R. C. Kelly 1985, 1.
13. Sahlins 1961, 345.
14. N. Dyson-Hudson 1966, Chapters 5 and 6.
15. Ibid.
16. Chapman and Kagaha 2009; see also Skoggard and Abate 2010.
17. Lewellen 2003, 31.
18. Ibid., 31–34.
19. Sahlins 1962, 293–94.
20. Sahlins 1963, 295.
21. Sahlins 1983, 519.
22. Sahlins 1963, 297.
23. Carneiro 1970, 733.
24. Weber 1947, 154.
25. Lightfoot 2005.
26. Ferguson 2004.
27. Wiberg 1983.
28. For an extensive review of the various theories about legitimacy, see R. Cohen 1988, 1–3.
29. Finley 1983.
30. Carcopino 1940, 18–20.
31. Our discussion of Nupe is based on S. F. Nadel 1935, 257–303.
32. Blanton and Fargher 2008.
33. Ibid.
34. Goldmann, Hannerz, and Westin 2000; Appadurai 2000.
35. Glick-Schiller 2004.
36. Appadurai 2000, 130.
37. Hassanpour and Mojab 2004.
38. Glick Schiller 2004,
39. M. Ember 1963.
40. Textor 1967.
41. M. Ember 1963; Feinman 2011.
42. Textor 1967.
43. Naroll 1961. See also Ross 1981.
44. M. Ember 1963, 244–46.
45. Service 1962; see also Braun and Plog 1982; Haas 1990.
46. A. Johnson and Earle 1987, 158; Carneiro 1990.
47. Carneiro 2012, 17–18.
48. Service 1962, 112, 145.
49. Feinman and Nietzel 1984.
50. Wittfogel 1957; see also discussion in Carneiro 2012, 8–9.
51. Carneiro 1970; Carneiro 2012.
52. Polanyi et al. 1957, 257–62; Sanders 1968; Wright and Johnson 1975; Chang 1986, 234–94.
53. For a more detailed description and evaluation of the available theories, see Chapter 11 in C. Ember et al. 2014.
54. McNeill 1976.
55. Carneiro 1978, 215.
56. Textor 1967.
57. Carneiro 1978; Hart 1948; Naroll 1967; Marano 1973, 35–40 (cf. Peregrine, Ember, and Ember 2004 and other articles in Graber 2004).
58. For a review of the descriptive literature until the late 1970s, see Vincent 1978.
59. D. Werner 1982.
60. Kracke 1979, 232.
61. D. Werner 1982.
62. Sahlins 1963.
63. Kracke 1979, 41.
64. Lederman 1990.
65. Brandewie 1991.
66. Lepowsky 1990.
67. Todorov et al. 2005.
68. Zebrowitz and Montepare 2005.
69. A. C. Little et al. 2007; Todorov et al. 2005.
70. Ross 1988, 73. The discussion in this section draws mostly from Zebrowitz and Montepare 2005, 73–89, and from Ross 2009b.
71. Bondarenko and Korotayev 2000; Korotayev and Bondarenko 2000.
72. For studies of international relations that support these conclusions, see footnotes 2 and 3 in C. R. Ember, Ember, and Russett 1992; see also Chapter 3 in Russett and Oneal 2001.
73. C. R. Ember, Ember, and Russett 1992.
74. Rummel 2002b.
75. Scaglion 2009b.
76. Boehm 2012.
77. Hoebel 1968/1954, 4, quoting S. P. Simpson and Field 1946, 858.
78. Donovan and Anderson 2003, 10–13; Rosen 2006, 16–17.
79. Fry and Björkqvist 1997.
80. D. Black 1993, 79–83.
81. Ross 1988.
82. Boas 1888, 668.
83. Otterbein 1986, 107.
84. Archer and Gartner 1984, 118–39.
85. Scaglion 2009b; D. Black 1993, 83–86.
86. Ibid.
87. Evans-Pritchard 1940, 291. The discussion of the Nuer follows this source.
88. Hickson 1986.
89. Ibid.; and Koch et al. 1977, 279.
90. J. M. Roberts 1967, 169.
91. Rosen 2006, 72.
92. Rosen 2006, 72–77.
93. Ibid., 192.
94. Hoebel 1968/1954, Chapter 9.
95. Schwartz 1954, 475; see also discussion in Rosen 2006, 16
96. Textor 1967.
97. Masumura 1977, 388–99.
98. Scaglion 2009b; Black 1993; Newman 1983, 131.
99. C. R. Ember and Ember 1997.
100. Keeley 1996; Gat 2006; Pinker 2011; J. Goldstein 2011.
101. Otterbein and Otterbein 1965 and Fry 2006, 88 do not consider feuding to be warfare.
102. C. R. Ember and Ember 2005; see also Fry 2006.
103. C. R. Ember and Ember 1994.
104. Chacon and Mendoza 2007.
105. Newman 1983, 131; Ericksen and Horton 1992.
106. Gubser 1965, 151.
107. Otterbein and Otterbein 1965, 1476; Otterbein 1994, 131
108. D. R. White 1988.
109. Patterson 1982, 345–52.
110. Gat 1999, 373, as referred to in Wadley 2003.
111. Heider 1970, 105–11; Heider 1979, 88–99.
112. M. Ember and Ember 1992, 188–89; M. Ember and Ember 2004.
113. Burtsev and Korotayev 2004, 35; see also Korotayev 2008, reanalyzing the Embers' (1992a, 1992b) data suggest that the relationship between resource unpredictability (with regard to food) and warfare is reversed in state societies.
114. C. R. Ember and Ember 1992; M. Ember 1982; C. R. Ember et al. 2013. For a discussion of how Dani warfare seems to be motivated mainly by economic considerations, see Shankman 1991. B. W. Kang (2000, 878–79) finds a strong correlation between environmental stress and warfare frequency in Korean history.
115. Otterbein 1970.
116. C. R. Ember and Ember 1992; see also Otterbein 1970 and Loftin 1971.
117. C. R. Ember 1974.
118. Otterbein 1968, 283; Ross 1985.
119. Divale and Harris 1976, 521–38; see also Gibbons 1993.
120. C. R. Ember and Ember 1992, 251–52.
121. Singer 1980.
122. Russett and Oneal 2001, 89.
123. Ibid., 145–48.
124. Younger 2008.
125. Russett 1993, 10–11, 14, 138.

Chapter 16

1. Tylor 2010 [1873].
2. Tylor 1979.
3. Marett 1909.
4. Guthrie 1993.
5. Freud 2010 [1950]; Badcock 1988, 126–27, 133–36.
6. Malinowski 1939, 959; Malinowski 1954, 50–51.
7. W. James 1902.
8. Jung 1938.
9. Fromm 1950.
10. Maslow 1964.
11. Barber 2011.
12. Sosis 2007.
13. Barber 2011.
14. Durkheim 1961/1912; see also S. Davis 2008.
15. Swanson 1969, 1–31.
16. Sosis and Alcorta 2003 and references therein.
17. Henrich 2009.
18. A. Wallace 1966, 60–61.
19. Malefijt 1968, 153.
20. Ray 1954, 172–89.
21. Rosenblatt et al. 1976, 51.
22. Ibid., 55.
23. Swanson 1969, 97–108; see also Sheils 1975; Steadman, Palmer, and Tilley 2010 [1996] suggest that ancestor worship is universal.
24. Middleton 1971, 488.
25. Spiro and D'Andrade 1958.
26. Lambert et al. 1959; Rohner 1975, 108.
27. H. G. Barnett 1960, 79–85.
28. Swanson 1969, 56.
29. Ibid., 55–81; see also W. D. Davis 1971. Peregrine (1996, 84–112) replicated Swanson's finding for North American societies.
30. Textor 1967; R. Underhill 1975; Sanderson and Roberts 2008.
31. Geertz 1966.
32. Swanson 1969, 153–74. In a more recent test, D. Johnson found the presence of money to be related to a high god's concern with morality.
33. Bunzel 1971.
34. Gossen 1979.
35. Dickson et al. 2005.
36. Eller 2007, 111.
37. Ibid., 128.
38. Stark and Finke 2000, 107–08.
39. A. Wallace 1966, 52–67.
40. Winkelman 1986b, 178–83.
41. Bourguignon 1973.
42. Bourguignon and Evascu 1977; Winkelman 1986b, 196–98.
43. Kehoe and Giletti 1981.
44. Raybeck 1998, referring to Raybeck et al. 1989.
45. Bourguignon 2004, 572.
46. Winkleman and Peck 2004; Eller 2007, 75.
47. O. K. Moore 1957.
48. Sheils 1980.
49. Winkelman and Baker 2010, 293–96 and references therein.
50. Evans-Pritchard 1979, 362–66.
51. Swanson 1969, 150; see also H. R. Trevor-Roper 1971, 444–49.

52. Swanson 1969, 150–51.
53. Caporael 1976; Matossian 1982; and Matossian 1989, 70–80. For possible reasons to dismiss the ergot theory, see Spanos 1983.
54. Harner 1972.
55. B. B. Whiting 1950, 36–37; see also Swanson 1969, 137–52, 240–41.
56. Winkelman 2010, 50–58.
57. Ibid.
58. Knecht 2003, 11.
59. Harner and Doore 1987, 3, 8–9; Noll 1987, 49; Krippner 1987, 128.
60. De Laguna 1972, 701C.
61. Noll 1987, 49–50; Krippner 2000.
62. Winkelman 1986a, 27–28; Winkelman 2010, 50–58.
63. Ibid.
64. Ibid.
65. Ibid.
66. M. Harris 1966.
67. Buckser and Glazier 2003; Rambo 2003.
68. Discussion is based on Firth 1970.
69. Ibid., 387.
70. Ibid., 418.
71. Mason 1962.
72. Ensminger 1997, 7.
73. Ibid.
74. Reff 2005; see also McNeill 1998 and Stark 1996.
75. C. R. Ember 1982.
76. A. Wallace 1966, 30.
77. A. Wallace 1970, 239.
78. The Quakers, long-time neighbors and trusted advisers of the Seneca, took pains not to interfere with Seneca religion, principles, and attitudes.
79. Worsley 1957, 12.
80. Ibid., 11, 115.
81. Ibid., 122.
82. Aberle 1971.
83. Knauft 1978.
84. Antoun 2001, 2008.
85. Nagata 2001.
86. Antoun 2008, 18–19.
87. Ibid., 46–47.
88. Stark 1985; Trompf 1990.

Chapter 17

1. Maquet 1986, 9; Perkins 2006.
2. R. L. Anderson 1989, 21.
3. R. P. Armstrong 1981, 11.
4. R. L. Anderson 1990, 278; R. L. Anderson 1992.
5. Morphy and Perkins 2006, 15.
6. Davies 2000, 201.
7. Malin 1986, 27.
8. R. L. Anderson 1989, 11.
9. Dutton 2000, 234.
10. Steiner 1990.
11. R. L. Anderson 1990, 225–26.
12. Sweeney 1952, 335.
13. Fischer 1961, 80.
14. Ibid., 81.
15. Peregrine 2007b also finds that the ceramics of complex societies tend toward nonrepetition and complex designs.
16. Ibid., 83.
17. Dressler and Robbins 1975, 427–34.
18. Rohter 2012.
19. Lomax 1968, 117–28; Global Jukebox 2013.
20. Words from "Deck the Halls," printed in the *Franklin Square Song Collection*, 1881.
21. Lomax 1968, 166–67.
22. Ibid., 167–69.
23. Ayres 1973.
24. Ayres 1968.
25. E. Erickson 1968.
26. For a study of variation in music within India that does not support some of Lomax's findings, see E. O. Henry 1976.

27. Dundes 1989, 2005, xxv.
28. Bauman 1992.
29. Brunvand 1993, 14.
30. Ibid., 296.
31. Kluckhohn 1965.
32. As discussed in Robert A. Segal 1987, 1–2.
33. J. Campbell 1949, 30, as quoted in Segal 1987, 4.
34. S. Thompson 1965, 449.
35. Dundes 1965, reported in F. W. Young 1970.
36. Carroll 1979.
37. G. O. Wright 1954.
38. A. Cohen 1990.
39. S. Price 1989 [2001], 82–85.
40. Ibid., 102–103.
41. S. Price 1989, 56–67; S. Price 2006, 168–169.
42. S. Price 1989, 112; S. Price 2006, 169–170.
43. J. A. Warner 1986, 172–75.
44. Layton 1992, 93–94.
45. Ibid., 31, 109.
46. J. C. H. King 1986.
47. S. Price 1989, 77–81.
48. J. A. Warner 1986, 178–86.
49. Myers 2002, 1–3, 17–18; Myers 2006, 182–183, 193.
50. Svašek 2007, 154.
51. Silverman 2006.
52. Merrill 1987.

Chapter 18

1. The discussion in this section draws extensively from Aptekar 1994.
2. Kahn 2005.
3. Gaiha et al. 2013.
4. Information collected during Melvin Ember's fieldwork in American Samoa, 1955–1956.
5. Mellor and Gavian 1987.
6. Dirks 1993.
7. Sen 1981; Devereux 2009.
8. Torry 1986.
9. Devereux 2009.
10. UN-HABITAT 2012.
11. Hardoy and Satterthwaite 1987.
12. UN-HABITAT 2012.
13. UN-HABITAT 2009.
14. Rodwin and Sanyal 1987.
15. Mangin 1967.
16. Rodwin and Sanyal 1987; for a critique of self-help programs, see Ward 1982.
17. Satterthwaite 2008.
18. Boonyabancha 2009.
19. A. Cohen and Koegel 2009.
20. National Coalition for the Homeless 2009.
21. A. Cohen and Koegel 2009.
22. Baxter and Hopper 1981, 30–33, 50–74; Hopper 2003.
23. Ibid.
24. A. Cohen and Koegel 2009.
25. Herrman 1990.
26. Hopper 2003, 214.
27. Congressional Budget Office 2011.
28. World Bank 2004.
29. Aptekar 1991, 326.
30. UN Works n.d.
31. Aptekar 1991, 326–49; Aptekar 1988.
32. Korbin 1981, 4.
33. Straus 2001, 195–96.
34. Straus 2010.
35. Straus 2001 based on surveys in 1999.
36. U.S. Department of Justice 2005.
37. Office on Child Abuse and Neglect 2006.
38. Levinson 1989, 11–12, 44.
39. Minturn and Stashak 1982. Using a sociobiological orientation, a study by Daly and Wilson (1988, 43–59) also suggests that infanticide is largely due to the difficulty of raising the infant successfully.
40. Straus 2001.

41. Levinson 1989, 26–28.
42. C. R. Ember and Melvin Ember 2005.
43. Lareau 2003, 230.
44. D. Goldstein 1998.
45. Levinson 1989, 31.
46. Ibid., 71.
47. Gelles and Straus 1988, 78–88.
48. WHO 2005.
49. Archer 2006; WHO 2005.
50. Erchak 2009; Levinson 1989, 44–45.
51. Levinson 1989, 104–107.
52. Archer and Gartner 1984, 35.
53. UNODC 2012.
54. Archer and Gartner 1984, 63–97; see other references in J. Warner et al. 2007.
55. Gurr 1989a, 47–48.
56. U.S. Department of Justice n.d.
57. Nivette 2011.
58. Russell 1972; Eckhardt 1975; Sipes 1973.
59. C. R. Ember and Ember 1994.
60. Archer and Gartner 1984, 118–39.
61. Bacon et al. 1963; B. B. Whiting 1965; C. Ember and M. Ember 2001; Barry 2007.
62. Barber 2000, 2007.
63. C. R. Ember and Ember 1994, 625.
64. C. R. Ember and Ember 1993, 227; C. Ember and M. Ember 2001.
65. C. A. Anderson and Bushman 2002, 2377; J. G. Johnson et al. 2002.
66. Thornhill and Fincher 2011.
67. McCall, Parker, and MacDonald 2007; Bond 2004.
68. In preindustrial societies, homicide and assault are similarly predicted by the presence of indigenous money, almost always associated with wealth concentration—see Barry 2007.
69. Loftin et al. 1989; Krahn et al. 1986, as referred to in Daly and Wilson 1988, 287–88; Gartner 2009.
70. C. R. Ember and Ember 1997.
71. J. S. Goldstein 2011; Pinker 2011.
72. M. Ember and Ember 1992, 204–206.
73. Meggitt 1977, 201; Gat 1999, 563–83.
74. C. R. Ember and Ember 1992a. Data from Korea is consistent with this explanation of war: More environmental stress strongly predicts higher frequencies of warfare in Korea between the 1st century B.C. and the 8th century A.D. See B. W. Kang 2000, 878.
75. C. R. Ember and Ember 1992a.
76. Zhang et al. 2007; B. W. Kang 2000.
77. For the cross-cultural results suggesting the theory of war described here, see C. R. Ember and M. Ember 1992a
78. J. S. Goldstein, 292; see research referred to therein.
79. For the results on political participation and peace in the ethnographic record, see C. R. Ember, Ember, and Russett 1992. For the results on political participation and peace in the modern world, see the references in that essay.
80. Russett and Oneal 2001, 49.
81. Mansfield and Snyder 2007.
82. Ibid., 125ff.
83. Some of these examples are from Henderson 2001.
84. See the discussions in Ibid., 3–9, and S. K. Anderson and Sloan 2002, 1–5.
85. S. K. Anderson and Sloan 2002, 465.
86. This definition is adapted from Chomsky, who is quoted in Henderson 2001, 5.

87. Pinker 2011, 347; S. K. Anderson and Sloan 2002, 6–7.
88. S. K. Anderson and Sloan 2002, 6–8.
89. Suárez-Orozco 1992.
90. R. J. Rummel 2002a.
91. R. J. Rummel 2002c.
92. R. J. Rummel 2002d.
93. S. K. Anderson and Sloan 2002, 422; E. Newman 2006.
94. E. Newman 2006.
95. Crossroads for Planet Earth 2005.

Chapter 19

1. Nolan 2003, 2.
2. Kushner 1991.
3. Van Willigen 2002, 10.
4. Nolan 2002, 32.
5. American Anthropological Association. Statement on Ethics: Principles of Professional Responsibility 2012. www.aaanet.org/profdev/ethics.
6. Society for Applied Anthropology. Ethical and professional responsibilities. http://www.sfaa.net/sfaaethic.html Accessed May 11, 2013.
7. NAPA Ethical Guidelines for Practitioners. http://practicinganthropology.org/about/ethical-guidelines/ Accessed May 11, 2013.
8. Scudder 1978.
9. Ibid., 204ff.
10. Cernea 2000, 20.
11. Picchi 1991, 26–38; for a more general description of the Bakairí, see Picchi 2009.
12. Murray 1997, 131.
13. Wulff and Fiste 1987; Murray and Bannister 2004.
14. Ibid.
15. Niehoff 1966, 255–67.
16. Tax 1975; Rylko Bauer, Singer, and van Willigen 2006.
17. Rylko-Bauer, Singer, and van Willigen. 2006.
18. Fluehr-Lobban 2008; Lassiter 2008.
19. Warry 1990, 61–62.
20. J. Fisher 1996, 57.
21. Ibid., 91; data from Kenya referred to in Oxby 1983.
22. W. H. Fisher 1994.
23. Kedia 2008.
24. Shoreman-Ouimet and Kopnina 2011; McGuire 2005.
25. E. Dean 2011.
26. E. Moran 2011.
27. J. Hirsch et al. 2011.
28. A. Jordan 2013, 41; Sunderland and Denny 2007, 33–37.
29. Ferraro 2002, 57.
30. Ibid., 115.
31. A. Jordan 2013, 25.
32. Kleinberg 1994.
33. Squires 2000 as referred to in A. Jordan 2013, 91–92.
34. Ravesloot 1997, 174.
35. Anyon and Ferguson 1995.
36. Anderson, Card, and Feder 2013.
37. Nāleimaile, Sean and Lokelani Brandt 2013.
38. Society for American Archaeology 2009.
39. Schattler 2008, Edson and Dean 1994.
40. Terrell 2011.
41. Komar and Buikstra 2008, 11–12.
42. Manhein 1999.
43. Komar and Buikstra 2008, 126–45.
44. Brace 1995.
45. Komar and Buikstra 2008, 189–200.
46. Joans 1997.
47. "Association Business: Clyde Snow … " 2000.
48. A. H. Goodman and Leatherman 1998; Kleinman et al. 1997.

49. Gaines and Davis-Floyd 2004.
50. Rubel and Haas 1996, 120; Loustaunau and Sobo 1997, 80–81.
51. Loustaunau and Sobo 1997, 82–83, referring to Magner 1992, 93.
52. Loustaunau and Sobo 1997, referring to Gesler 1991, 16.
53. Loustaunau and Sobo 1997, referring to C. Leslie 1976, 4; and G. Foster 1994, 11.
54. Ahern 1975, 92–97, as seen in eHRAF World Cultures, 2000.
55. Murdock 1980, 20.
56. C. C. Moore 1988.
57. T. Gladwin and Sarason 1953, 64–66.
58. Mahony 1971, 34–38, as seen in eHRAF World Cultures, 2000.
59. Gladwin and Sarason 1953, 65.
60. Hahn 1995, 133–39; Gaines and Davis-Floyd 2004; Winkelman 2009, 38–50.
61. For an exhaustively documented presentation of the more universalistic approach, see E. A. Berlin and Berlin 1996; see also Browner 1985, 13–32; and Rubel et al. 1984.

62. E. A. Berlin 1996.
63. Browner 1985; Ortiz de Montellano and Browner 1985.
64. Etkin and Ross 1997.
65. Moerman 1997, 240–41.
66. Loustaunau and Sobo 1997, 98–101.
67. Winkelman 1986a.
68. Winkleman 2009, 390.
69. M. Singer 2007, 105.
70. Torrey 1972.
71. Womack 2010, 88–89. Winkelman 2009, 340–41.
72. Loustaunau and Sobo 1997, 102.
73. Dow 1986, 6–9, 125.
74. Hahn 1995, 131–72.
75. Winkelman 2009, 181.
76. For a discussion of some of the relevant research, see M. Singer 2007, 152–80.
77. Mascie-Taylor 1990, 118–21.
78. Hahn 1995, 82–87; CDC. Black or African American Populations; MacDorman and Mathews 2011
79. See references in Hahn 1995, 82–87.
80. A. Cohen 1999.
81. UN AIDS 2007/2012. Global fact sheet, 1. http://www.unaids .org. Accessed May 18, 2013.

82. E. C. Green 2011, 131.
83. Reported in Carey et al. 2004, 462.
84. Bolton 1989.
85. P. J. Smith et al. 2011.
86. D. McNeill 2011.
87. Carrier and Bolton 1991; Schoepf 1988, 625, cited in Carrier and Bolton 1991.
88. Simmons et al. 1996, 64.
89. E. C. Green 2011, 111.
90. Ibid., 136–54.
91. E. C. Green and Ruark 2011, 169.
92. L. K. Altman 2008.
93. Schoepf 1988, 637–38.
94. Bolton 1992.
95. Farmer 1997, 414. Married men in Thailand are gradually turning away from commercial sex and having affairs with married women who are believed to be safe; see Lyttleton 2000, 299.
96. Shen and Siliciano 2000.
97. A. Cohen 2004.
98. Honigmann 1967, 406.
99. Kleinman 1988, 3.
100. Lutz 1985, 63–100.

101. J. Murphy 1981, 813.
102. R. Sullivan et al. 2007.
103. J. S. Allen et al. 1996; R. Sullivan et al. 2007.
104. Kleinman 1988, 34–52; Berry et al. 1992, 357–64.
105. Honigmann 1967, 401.
106. Kleinman 1988, 19.
107. A. Wallace 1972.
108. A. Cohen 2004.
109. Kleinman 2004.
110. Dressler 1991, 11–16.
111. Ibid., 66–94.
112. Ibid., 165–208.
113. Quandt 1996, 272–89.
114. McElroy and Townsend 2002.
115. See discussion in Leslie Lieberman 2004.
116. Gross and Underwood 1971.
117. Himmelgreen and Romero-Diaz 2009.
118. FAO. Hunger.
119. McElroy and Townsend 2002, 187, referring to Harvey and Heywood 1983, 27–35.
120. Quandt 1996, 277.
121. McKee 2009.
122. Messer 2009.

Bibliography

'Abd Allah, Mahmud M. 1917. Siwan customs. *Harvard African Studies* 1:1–28.

Abel, Thomas and John Richard Stepp. 2003. A new ecosystems ecology for anthropology. *Conservation Ecology* 7, no. 3:12.

Aberle, David. 1971. A note on relative deprivation theory as applied to millenarian and other cult movements. In *Reader in comparative religion*, 3rd ed., eds. W. A. Lessa and E. Z. Vogt. New York: Harper & Row.

Abi-Rached, L., et al. 2011. The shaping of modern human immune systems by multiregional admixture with archaic humans. *Science* 334 (October 7):89–94.

Abler, Thomas S. 2009. Iroquois: The tree of peace and the war kettle. In MyAnthroLibrary, eds. C. R. Ember, M. Ember, and P. N. Peregrine. MyAnthroLibrary.com. Pearson.

Academic American encyclopedia. 1980. Princeton, NJ: Areté.

Acheson, James M. 2006. Lobster and groundfish management in the Gulf of Maine: A rational choice perspective. *Human Organization* 65:240–52.

Adams, David B. 1983. Why there are so few women warriors. *Behavior Science Research* 18:196–212.

Adams, Robert McCormick. 1960. The origin of cities. *Scientific American* (September):153–68.

Adams, Robert McCormick. 1981. *Heartland of cities: Surveys of ancient settlement and land use on the central floodplain of the Euphrates*. Chicago: University of Chicago Press.

Ahern, Emily M. 1975. Sacred and secular medicine in a Taiwan village: A study of cosmological disorders. In *Medicine in Chinese cultures: Comparative studies of health care in Chinese and other societies*, eds. A. Kleinman, P. Kunstadter, E. R. Alexander and J. L. Gale. Washington, DC: U.S. Department of Health, Education, and Welfare, National Institutes of Health.

Aiello, Leslie C. 1992. Body size and energy requirements. In *The Cambridge encyclopedia of human evolution*, eds. S. Jones, R. Martin, and D. Pilbeam. New York: Cambridge University Press.

Aiello, Leslie C. 1993. The origin of the New World monkeys. In *The Africa-South America connection*, ed. W. George and R. Lavocat, 100–118. Oxford: Clarendon Press.

Aiello, Leslie C., and Mark Collard. 2001. Our newest oldest ancestor? *Nature* 410 (November 29):526–27.

Aiello, Leslie C., and Christopher Dean. 1990. *An introduction to human evolutionary anatomy*. London: Academic Press.

Akmajian, Adrian, Richard A. Demers, Ann K. Farmer, and Robert M. Harnish. 2001. *Linguistics: An introduction to language and communication*. Cambridge, MA: The MIT Press.

Akmajian, Adrian, Richard A. Demers, and Robert M. Harnish. 1984. *Linguistics: An introduction to language and communication*. 2nd ed. Cambridge, MA: MIT Press.

Albert, Steven M., and Maria G. Cattell. 1994. *Old age in global perspective: Cross-cultural and cross-national views*. New York: G. K. Hall/Macmillan.

Alberts, Bruce, president of the National Academy of Sciences. 2000. Setting the record straight regarding *Darkness in El Dorado*, November 9. http://www4.nationalacademies.org/nas/nashome.nsf.

Alexander, John P. 1992. Alas, poor *Notharctus. Natural History* (August):55–59.

Algaze, Guillermo. 1993. *The Uruk world system: The dynamics of expansion of early Mesopotamian civilization*. Chicago: University of Chicago Press.

Allen, John S., and Susan M. Cheer. 1996. The non-thrifty genotype. *Current Anthropology* 37:831–42.

Allen, John S., A. J. Lambert, F. Y. Attah Johnson, K. Schmidt, and K. L. Nero. 1996. Antisaccadic eye movements and attentional asymmetry in schizophrenia in three Pacific populations. *Acta Psychiatrica Scandinavia* 94:258–65.

Alperson-Afil, N., et al. 2009. Spatial organization of hominin activities at Gesher Benot Ya'aqov, Israel. *Science* 326 (December 18):1677–83.

Alroy, John. 2001. A multispecies overkill simulation of the End-Pleistocene megafaunal mass extinction. *Science* 292 (June 8):1893–96.

Altman, Lawrence K. 2008. Protective effects of circumcision are shown to continue after trials' end. *New York Times*, August 12. http://www.nytimes.com.

Alvarez, Lizette. 2003. Arranged marriages get a little rearranging. *New York Times*, June 22, p. 1.3.

Ambient Corporation. 2000. Energy: Investing for a new century. *New York Times*, October 30, pp. EN1–EN8. A special advertisement produced by energy companies.

American Anthropological Association. 1991. Revised principles of professional responsibility, 1990. In *Ethics and the profession of anthropology: Dialogue for a new era*, ed. Carolyn Fluehr-Lobban, 274–79. Philadelphia: University of Pennsylvania Press. http://www.aaanet.org/coe/Code_of_Ethics.pdf.

American Anthropological Association. 2012. Statement on ethics: Principles of professional responsibility 2012. http://www.aaanet.org/coe/Code_of_Ethics.pdf (accessed May 5, 2013).

Anbarci, Nejat, Monica Escaleras, and Charles A. Register. 2005. Earthquake fatalities: The interaction of nature and political economy. *Journal of Public Economics* 89, no.9:1907–33.

Anderson, Connie M. 2000. The persistence of polygyny as an adaptive response to poverty and oppression in apartheid South Africa. *Cross-Cultural Research* 34:99–112.

Anderson, Craig A., and Brad J. Bushman. 2002. The effects of media violence on society. *Science* 295 (March 29):2377–79.

Anderson, David C. 2012. Pleistocene settlement in the East. In *Oxford handbook of North American archaeology*, ed. T. Pauketat. Oxford: Oxford University Press.

Anderson, David G., Jeb J. Card, and Kenneth Feder. 2013. Speaking up and speaking out: Collective efforts in the fight to reclaim the public perception of archaeology. *SAA Archaeological Record* 13, no.2:24–27.

Anderson, J. L., C. B. Crawford, J. Nadeau, and T. Lindberg. 1992. Was the Duchess of Windsor right? A cross-cultural review of the socioecology of ideal female body shape. *Ethnology and Sociobiology* 13:197–227.

Anderson, Richard L. 1989. *Art in small-scale societies*. 2nd ed. Englewood Cliffs, NJ: Prentice Hall.

Anderson, Richard L. 1990. *Calliope's sisters: A comparative study of philosophies of art*. Upper Saddle River, NJ: Prentice Hall.

Anderson, Richard L. 1992. Do other cultures have "art"? *American Anthropologist* 94:926–29.

Anderson, Sean K., and Stephen Sloan. 2002. *Historical dictionary of terrorism*. 2nd ed. Lanham, MD: Scarecrow Press.

Andrefsky, William. 1998. *Lithics: Macroscopic approaches to analysis*. New York: Cambridge University Press.

Andrews, Elizabeth. 1994. Territoriality and land use among the Akulmiut of Western Alaska. In *Key issues in hunter-gatherer research*, eds. E. S. Burch Jr., and L. J. Ellanna. Oxford: Berg.

Andrews, Peter. 2000a. Propliopithecidae. In *Encyclopedia of human evolution and prehistory*, eds. I. Tattersall, E. Delson, and J. van Couvering. New York: Garland.

Andrews, Peter. 2000b. Proconsul. In *Encyclopedia of human evolution and prehistory*, eds. I. Tattersall, E. Delson, and J. van Couvering. New York: Garland.

Angier, Natalie. 2002. Why we're so nice: We're wired to cooperate. *New York Times*, Science Times, July 23, pp. F1, F8.

Ankel-Simons, Friederun. 2007. *Primate anatomy*, 3rd ed. San Diego: Academic Press.

Anthony, David, Dimitri Y. Telegin, and Dorcas Brown. 1991. The origin of horseback riding. *Scientific American* (December):94–100.

Antoun, Richard T. 2001. *Understanding fundamentalism: Christian, Islamic, and Jewish movements*. Walnut Creek, CA: AltaMira Press.

Antoun, Richard T. 2008. *Understanding fundamentalism*. 2nd ed. Lanham, MD: Rowman & Littlefield.

Anyon, Roger, and T. J. Ferguson. 1995. Cultural resources management at the Pueblo of Zuni, New Mexico, USA. *Antiquity* 69:913–30.

Aporta, Claudio, and Eric Higgs. 2005. Satellite culture: Global positioning systems, Inuit wayfinding, and the need for a new account of technology. *Current Anthropology* 46:729–46.

Apostolou, Menelaos. 2010. Parental choice: What parents want in a son-in-law and a daughter-in-law across 67 pre-industrial societies. *British Journal of Psychology* 101:695–704.

Appadurai, Arjun. 2000. The grounds of the nation-state: Identity, violence and territory. In *Nationalism and internationalism in the post-cold war era*, eds. U. H. Goldman and C. Westin. London: Routledge.

Appendix A: Report of the Committee on Ethics, Society for Applied Anthropology. 2002. In *Ethics and the profession of anthropology*, ed. C. Fluehr-Lobban. Philadelphia: University of Pennsylvania Press.

Appendix C: Statements on Ethics: Principles of Professional Responsibility, Adopted by the Council of the American Anthropological Association, May 1971. 1991. In *Ethics and the profession of anthropology*, ed. C. Fluehr-Lobban. Philadelphia: University of Pennsylvania Press.

Appendix F: Professional and Ethical Responsibilities, SfAA. 2002. In *Ethics and the profession of anthropology*, ed. C. Fluehr-Lobban. Philadelphia: University of Pennsylvania Press.

Appendix H: National Association of Practicing Anthropologists' Ethical Guidelines for Practitioners, 1988. 1991. In *Ethics and the profession of anthropology*, ed. C. Fluehr-Lobban. Philadelphia: University of Pennsylvania Press.

Appendix I: Revised Principles of Professional Responsibility, 1990. 1991. In *Ethics and the profession of anthropology*, ed. C. Fluehr-Lobban. Philadelphia: University of Pennsylvania Press.

Aptekar, Lewis. 1988. *Street children of Cali*. Durham, NC: Duke University Press.

Aptekar, Lewis. 1991. Are Colombian street children neglected? The contributions of ethnographic and ethnohistorical approaches to the study of children. *Anthropology and Education Quarterly* 22:326–49.

Aptekar, Lewis. 1994. *Environmental disasters in global perspective*. New York: G. K. Hall/Macmillan.

Archer, Dane, and Rosemary Gartner. 1984. *Violence and crime in cross-national perspective*. New Haven, CT: Yale University Press.

Archer, John. 2006. Cross-cultural differences in physical aggression between partners: A social-role analysis. *Personality and Social Psychology Review* 10:133–53.

Ardener, Shirley. 1995a/1964. The comparative study of rotating credit associations. In *Money-go-rounds*, eds. S. Ardener and S. Burman. Oxford: Berg.

Ardener, Shirley. 1995b/1964. Women making money go round: ROSCAs revisited. In *Money-go-rounds*, eds. S. Ardener and S. Burman. Oxford: Berg.

Ardener, Shirley, and Sandra Burman, eds. 1995/1964. *Money-go-rounds: The importance of rotating savings and credit associations for women*. Oxford: Berg.

Argyle, Michael. 1994. *The psychology of social class*. New York: Routledge.

Armelagos, George J., and Alan H. Goodman. 1998. Race, racism, and anthropology. In *Building a new biocultural synthesis: Political-economic perspectives on human biology*, eds. A. H. Goodman and T. L. Leatherman. Ann Arbor: University of Michigan Press.

Armelagos, George J., and Kirstin H. Harper. 2005. Genomics at the origins of agriculture, Part Two. *Evolutionary Anthropology* 14:109–21.

Armstrong, Robert P. 1981. *The powers of presence*. Philadelphia: University of Pennsylvania Press.

Aronoff, Joel, Andrew M. Barclay, and Linda A. Stevenson. 1988. The recognition of threatening facial stimuli. *Journal of Personality and Social Psychology* 54:647–55.

Aronoff, Joel, Barbara A. Woike, and Lester M. Hyman. 1992. Which are the stimuli in facial displays of anger and happiness? Configurational bases of emotion recognition. *Journal of Personality and Social Psychology* 62:1050–66.

Aronson, Joshua. 2002. Stereotype threat: Contending and coping with unnerving expectations. In *Improving academic performance*, ed. J. Aronson. San Francisco: Academic Press.

Aronson, Joshua, Carrie B. Fried, and Catherine Good. 2002. Reducing the effects of stereotype threat on African American college students by shaping theories of intelligence. *Journal of Experimental Social Psychology* 38:113–25.

Asch, Nancy B., and David L. Asch. 1978. The economic potential of *Iva annua* and its prehistoric importance in the Lower Illinois Valley. In *The nature and status of ethnobotany*, ed. R. Ford. Anthropological Papers No 67, Museum of Anthropology. Ann Arbor: University of Michigan.

Asch, Solomon. 1956. Studies of independence and conformity: A minority of one against a unanimous majority. *Psychological Monographs* 70:1–70.

Ascher, Robert. 1961. Analogy in archaeological interpretation. *Southwestern Journal of Anthropology* 17:317–25.

Asfaw, Berhane, Tim White, Owen Lovejoy, Bruce Latimer, Scott Simpson, and Glen Suwa. 1999. *Australopithecus garhi*: A new species of early hominid from Ethiopia. *Science* 284 (April 23):629–36.

Association business: Clyde Snow, forensic anthropologist, works for justice. 2000. *Anthropology News* (October):12.

Association for Cultural Equity. 2013. Global jukebox. http://www.culturalequity.org/rc/ce_rc_psr_global_jukebox.php (accessed April 28, 2013).

Atkinshon, Quentin D., and Patrick Bourrat. 2011. Beliefs about god, the afterlife and morality support the role of supernatural policing in human cooperation. *Evolution and Human Behavior* 32:41–49.

Austin, Peter K., and Julia Sallabank. 2011. Introduction. In *Cambridge handbook of endangered languages*, eds. Peter K. Austin and Julia Sallabank. Cambridge University Press.

Ayala, Francisco J. 1995. The myth of Eve: Molecular biology and human origins. *Science* 270 (December 22):1930–36.

Ayala, Francisco J. 1996. Communication. *Science* 274 (November 29):1354.

Ayres, Barbara C. 1968. Effects of infantile stimulation on musical behavior. In *Folk song style and culture*, ed. A. Lomax. Washington, DC: Transaction Publishers.

Ayres, Barbara C. 1973. Effects of infant carrying practices on rhythm in music. *Ethos* 1:387–404.

Baba, Marietta L., and Carole E. Hill. 2006. What's in the name "Applied Anthropology"? An encounter with global practice. *NAPA Bulletin* 25:176–207. Washington, DC: American Anthropological Association.

Bachnik, Jane M. 1992. The two "faces" of self and society in Japan. *Ethos* 20:3–32.

Bacon, Margaret, Irvin L. Child, and Herbert Barry, III. 1963. A cross-cultural study of correlates of crime. *Journal of Abnormal and Social Psychology* 66:291–300.

Badcock, Christopher. 1988. *Essential Freud*. Oxford: Blackwell.

Badcock, Christopher. 2000. *Evolutionary psychology: A critical introduction*. Cambridge: Blackwell.

Baer, Hans A., and Merrill Singer. 2009. *Global warming and the political ecology of health: Emerging crises and systemic solutions*. Walnut Creek, CA: Left Coast Press.

Baer, Hans A., Merrill Singer, and Ida Susser. 1997. *Medical anthropology and the world system: A critical perspective*. Westport, CT: Bergin & Garvey.

Bahn, Paul. 1998. Neanderthals emancipated. *Nature* 394 (August 20):719–20.

Bailey, Robert C., Genevieve Head, Mark Jenike, Bruce Owen, Robert Rectman, and Elzbieta Zechenter. 1989. Hunting and gathering in tropical rain forest: Is it possible? *American Anthropologist* 91:59–82.

Baldi, Philip. 1983. *An introduction to the Indo-European languages*. Carbondale: Southern Illinois University Press.

Balikci, Asen. 1970. *The Netsilik Eskimo*. Garden City, NY: Natural History Press.

Balter, Michael. 2001. In search of the first Europeans. *Science* 291 (March 2):1722–25.

Balter, Michael. 2007. Seeking agriculture's ancient roots. *Science* 316 (June 29):1830–35.

Balter, Michael. 2009. Better homes and hearths, Neandertal-style. *Science* 326 (November 20):1056–57.

Balter, Michael. 2010. Neandertal jewelry shows their symbolic smarts. *Science* 327 (January 15):255–56.

Balter, Michael, and Ann Gibbons. 2000. A glimpse of humans' first journey out of Africa. *Science* 288 (May 12):948–50.

Bandy, Michael. 2005. Energetic efficiency and political expediency in Titicaca Basin raised field agriculture. *Journal of Anthropological Archaeology* 24, no. 3:271–296.

Barak, Gregg. 1991. *Gimme shelter: A social history of homelessness in contemporary America*. New York: Praeger.

Barash, David P. 1977. *Sociobiology and behavior*. New York: Elsevier.

Barber, Nigel. 2000. The sex ratio as a predictor of cross-national variation in violent crime. *Cross-Cultural Research* 34:264–82.

Barber, Nigel. 2003. Paternal investment prospects and cross-national differences in single parenthood. *Cross-Cultural Research* 37:163–77.

Barber, Nigel. 2007. Evolutionary explanations for societal differences and historical change in violent crime and single parenthood. *Cross-Cultural Research* 41:123–48.

Barber, Nigel. 2008. Explaining cross-national differences in polygyny intensity: Resource-defense, sex-ratio, and infectious diseases. *Cross-Cultural Research* 42:103–17.

Barber, Nigel. 2011. A cross-national test of the uncertainty hypothesis of religious belief. *Cross-Cultural Research* 45:318–33.

Bard, Kathryn A. 2008. *An introduction to the archaeology of ancient Egypt*. Malden, MA: Blackwell.

Barinaga, Maria. 1992. Priming the brain's language pump. *Science* 255 (January 31):535.

Barlett, Peggy F. 1989. Industrial agriculture. In *Economic Anthropology*, ed. S. Plattner. Stanford, CA: Stanford University Press.

Barnes, Jessica, et al. 2013. Contribution of anthropology to the study of climate change. *Nature Climate Change* 3:541–4.

Barnett, H. G. 1960. *Being a Palauan*. New York: Holt, Rinehart & Winston.

Barnosky, Anthony, Paul Koch, Robert Feranec, Scott Wing, and Alan Shabel. 2004. Assessing the causes of Late Pleistocene extinctions on the continents. *Science* 306 (October 1):70–75.

Barrett, D. E. 1984. Malnutrition and child behavior: Conceptualization, assessment and an empirical study of social-emotional functioning. In *Malnutrition and behavior: Critical assessment of key issues*, eds. J. Brozek and B. Schürch. Lausanne, Switzerland: Nestlé Foundation.

Barrett, Stanley R. 1994. *Paradise: Class, commuters, and ethnicity in rural Ontario*. Toronto: University of Toronto Press.

Barry, Herbert, III. 2007. Wealth concentration associated with frequent violent crime in diverse communities. *Social Evolution & History* 6:29–38.

Barry, Herbert, III, Irvin L. Child, and Margaret K. Bacon. 1959. Relation of child training to subsistence economy. *American Anthropologist* 61:51–63.

Barth, Fredrik. 1965. *Nomads of South Persia*. New York: Humanities Press.

Barth, Fredrik. 1994. Enduring and emerging issues in the analysis of ethnicity. In *The anthropology of ethnicity*, eds. H. Vermeulen and C. Govers. Amsterdam: Het Spinhuis.

Bates, Daniel G., and Susan H. Lees, eds. 1996. *Case studies in human ecology*. New York: Plenum Press.

Bates, E., and V. A. Marchman. 1988. What is and is not universal in language acquisition. In *Language, communication, and the brain*, ed. F. Plum. New York: Raven Press.

Bauman, Richard. 1992. Folklore. In *Folklore, cultural performances, and popular entertainments*, ed. R. Bauman. New York: Oxford University Press.

Baxter, Ellen, and Kim Hopper. 1981. *Private lives/public spaces: Homeless adults on the streets of New York City*. New York: Community Service Society of New York.

Beadle, George, and Muriel Beadle. 1966. *The language of life*. Garden City, NY: Doubleday.

Beard, K. Christopher. 2002. Basal anthropoids. In *The primate fossil record*, ed. W. C. Hartwig. Cambridge: Cambridge University Press.

Bearder, Simon K. 1987. Lorises, bushbabies, and tarsiers: Diverse societies in solitary foragers. In *Primate societies*, eds. Barbara B. Smuts, Dorothy L. Cheney, Robert M. Seyfarth, and Richard W. Wrangham. Chicago: University of Chicago Press.

Beattie, John. 1960. *Bunyoro: An African kingdom*. New York: Holt, Rinehart & Winston.

Beaumont, P. B. 2011. The edge: More on fire-making by about 1.7 million years ago at Wonderwerk Cave in South Africa. *Current Anthropology* 52:585–95.

Begler, Elsie B. 1978. Sex, status, and authority in egalitarian society. *American Anthropologist* 80:571–88.

Begun, David. 2002a. European hominoids. In *The primate fossil record*, ed. W. C. Hartwig. Cambridge: Cambridge University Press.

Begun, David. 2002b. Miocene apes. In *Physical anthropology: Original readings in method and practice*, eds. P. N. Peregrine, C. R. Ember, and M. Ember. Upper Saddle River, NJ: Prentice Hall.

Behar, Ruth, and Deborah Gordon, eds. 1995. *Women writing culture*. Berkeley: University of California Press.

Behrman, Jere R., Alejandro Gaviria, and Miguel Székely. 2001. Intergenerational mobility in Latin America. Inter-American Development Bank, Working Paper #45. http://www.iadb.org/res/publications/pubfiles/pubWP-452.pdf (accessed June 2009).

Bellman, Beryl L. 1984. *The language of secrecy: Symbols and metaphors in Poro ritual*. New Brunswick, NJ: Rutgers University Press.

Bellwood, Peter. 2005. *First farmers*. Malden, MA: Blackwell.

Benjamin, Lois. 1991. *The Black elite: Facing the color line in the twilight of the twentieth century*. Chicago: Nelson-Hall.

Bentley, R. Alexander, Carl P. Lipo, Harold A. Herzog, and Matthew W. Hahn. 2007. Regular rates of popular culture change reflect random copying. *Evolution and Human Behavior* 28:151–58.

Berger, L. R., et al. 2010. *Australopithecus sediba*: A new species of *Homo*-like australopith from South Africa. *Science* 328 (April 9):195–204.

Berggren, William A., Dennis V. Kent, John D. Obradovich, and Carl C. Swisher, III. 1992. Toward a revised paleogene geochronology. In *Eocene-Oliocene climatic and biotic evolution*, eds. D. R. Prothero and W. A. Berggren. Princeton, NJ: Princeton University Press.

Berlin, Brent. 1992. *Ethnobiological classification: Principles of categorization of plants and animals in traditional societies*. Princeton, NJ: Princeton University Press.

Berlin, Brent, and Paul Kay. 1969. *Basic color terms: Their universality and evolution*. Berkeley: University of California Press.

Berlin, Elois Ann. 1996. General overview of Maya ethnomedicine. In *Medical ethnobiology of the highland Maya of Chiapas, Mexico*, eds. E. A. Berlin and B. Berlin. Princeton, NJ: Princeton University Press.

Berlin, Elois Ann, and Brent Berlin. 1996. *Medical ethnobiology of the highland Maya of Chiapas, Mexico: The gastrointestinal diseases*. Princeton, NJ: Princeton University Press.

Bernard, H. Russell. 2001. *Research methods in cultural anthropology: Qualitative and quantitative approaches*. 3rd ed. Walnut Creek, CA: AltaMira Press.

Bernard, H. Russell. 2011. *Research methods in anthropology*, 5th ed. Lanham, MD: AltaMira.

Bernardi, B. 1952. The age-system of the Nilo-Hamitic peoples. *Africa* 22:316–332.

Berns, G., J. Chappelow, C. Zink, G. Pagnoni, M. Martin-Skurski, and J. Richards. 2005. Neurobiological correlates of social conformity and independence during mental rotation. *Biological Psychiatry* 58:245–253.

Berreman, Gerald D. 1960. Caste in India and the United States. *American Journal of Sociology* 66:120–27.

Berreman, Gerald D. 1972. Race, caste and other invidious distinctions in social stratification. *Race* 13:403–14.

Berreman, Gerald D. 1973. *Caste in the modern world*. Morristown, NJ: General Learning Press.

Berry, John W. 1971. Ecological and cultural factors in spatial perceptual development. *Canadian Journal of Behavioural Science* 3:324–36.

Berry, John W. 1976. *Human ecology and cognitive style*. New York: Wiley.

Berry, John W., and J. Bennett. 1989. Syllabic literacy and cognitive performance among the Cree. *International Journal of Psychology* 24:429–50.

Berry, John W., Ype H. Poortinga, Marshall H. Segall, and Pierre R. Dasen. 1992. *Cross-cultural psychology: Research and applications.* New York: Cambridge University Press.

Bertrand, Marianne, and Sendhil Mullainathan. 2011. Are Emily and Greg more employable than Lakisha and Jamal? In *Race in an era of change: A reader*, eds. H. Dalmage and B. Katz Rothman. New York: Oxford University Press.

Bestor, Theodore C. 2001. Supply-side sushi: Commodity, market, and the global city. *American Anthropologist* 103:76–95.

Betts, Richard A., Yadvinder Malhi, and J. Timmons Roberts. 2008. The future of the Amazon: New perspectives from climate, ecosystem, and social sciences. *Philosophical Transactions of the Royal Society B* 363:1729–35.

Betzig, Laura. 1988. Redistribution: Equity or exploitation? In *Human reproductive behavior*, eds. L. Betzig, M. B. Mulder, and P. Turke. Cambridge: Cambridge University Press.

Betzig, Laura. 1989. Causes of conjugal dissolution: A cross-cultural study. *Current Anthropology* 30:654–76.

Bickerton, Derek. 1983. Creole languages. *Scientific American* (July):116–22.

Biermann, Frank, and Ingrid Boas. 2010. Preparing for a warmer world: Towards a global governance system to protect climate refugees. *Global Environmental Politics* 10:60–88.

Bilby, Kenneth. 1996. Ethnogenesis in the Guianas and Jamaica: Two Maroon cases. In *Ethnogenesis in the Americas*, ed. J. D. Hill. Iowa City: University of Iowa Press.

Bilsborough, Alan. 1992. *Human evolution.* New York: Blackie Academic & Professional.

Bindon, James R., and Douglas E. Crews. 1993. Changes in some health status characteristics of American Samoan men: Preliminary observations from a 12-year follow-up study. *American Journal of Human Biology* 5:31–37.

Bindon, James R., Amy Knight, William W. Dressler, and Douglas E. Crews. 1997. Social context and psychosocial influences on blood pressure among American Samoans. *American Journal of Physical Anthropology* 103:7–18.

Binford, Lewis R. 1971. Post-Pleistocene adaptations. In *Prehistoric agriculture*, ed. S. Struever. Garden City, NY: Natural History Press.

Binford, Lewis R. 1973. Interassemblage variability: The Mousterian and the "functional" argument. In *The explanation of culture change*, ed. C. Renfrew. Pittsburgh: University of Pittsburgh Press.

Binford, Lewis R. 1984. *Faunal remains from Klasies River mouth.* Orlando, FL: Academic Press.

Binford, Lewis R. 1987. Were there elephant hunters at Torralba? In *The evolution of human hunting*, eds. M. Nitecki and D. Nitecki. New York: Plenum.

Binford, Lewis R. 1990. Mobility, housing, and environment: A comparative study. *Journal of Anthropological Research* 46:119–52.

Binford, Lewis R., and Chuan Kun Ho. 1985. Taphonomy at a distance: Zhoukoudian, 'The cave home of Beijing Man'? *Current Anthropology* 26:413–42.

Binford, Sally R., and Lewis R. Binford. 1969. Stone tools and human behavior. *Scientific American* (April):70–84.

Bishop, Ryan. 1996. Postmodernism. In *Encyclopedia of cultural anthropology*, vol. 3, eds. D. Levinson and M. Ember. New York: Henry Holt.

Black, Donald. 1993. *The social structure of right and wrong.* San Diego: Academic Press.

Black, Francis L. 1992. Why did they die? *Science* 258 (December 11):1739–40.

Blackwood, Evelyn. 1984a. *Cross-cultural dimensions of lesbian relations.* Master's Thesis. San Francisco State University. As referred to in Blackwood and Wieringa 1999.

Blackwood, Evelyn. 1984b. Sexuality and gender in certain Native American tribes: The case of cross-gender females. *Signs* 10:27–42.

Blackwood, Evelyn, and Saskia E. Wieringa. 1999. Sapphic shadows: Challenging the silence in the study of sexuality. In *Female desires: Same-sex relations and transgender practices across cultures*, eds. E. Blackwood and S. E. Weiringa. New York: Columbia University Press.

Blalock, Hubert M. 1972. *Social statistics.* 2nd ed. New York: McGraw-Hill.

Bland, Alastair. 2013. From pets to plates: Why more people are eating guinea pigs. *The Salt: What's on Your Plate.* npr.org, April 2.

Blanton, Richard E. 1976. The origins of Monte Albán. In *Cultural continuity and change*, ed. C. E. Cleland. New York: Academic Press.

Blanton, Richard E. 1978. *Monte Albán: Settlement patterns at the ancient Zapotec capital.* New York: Academic Press.

Blanton, Richard E. 1981. The rise of cities. In *Supplement to the handbook of Middle American Indians*, vol. 1, ed. J. Sabloff. Austin: University of Texas Press.

Blanton, Richard E. 2009. Variation in economy. In MyAnthroLibrary, eds. C. R. Ember, M. Ember, and P. N. Peregrine. MyAnthroLibrary.com. Pearson.

Blanton, Richard E., and Lane Fargher. 2008. *Collective action in the formation of pre-modern states.* New York: Springer.

Blanton, Richard E., Stephen A. Kowalewski, Gary Feinman, and Jill Appel. 1981. *Ancient Mesoamerica: A comparison of change in three regions.* New York: Cambridge University Press.

Bledsoe, Caroline H. 1980. *Women and marriage in Kpelle society.* Stanford, CA: Stanford University Press.

Blight, Garry, Sheila Pulham, and Paul Torpey. 2012. Arab spring: An interactive timeline of the Middle East protests. *The Guardian.* www.guardian.co.uk.

Block, Jean L. 1983. Help! They've all moved back home! *Woman's Day* (April 26):72–76.

Block, Jonathan I., and Doug M. Boyer. 2002. Grasping primate origins. *Science* 298 (November 22):1606–10.

Blount, Ben G. 1981. The development of language in children. In *Handbook of cross-cultural human development*, eds. R. H. Munroe, R. L. Munroe, and B. B. Whiting. New York: Garland.

Bluebond-Langner, Myra. 2007. Challenges and opportunities in the anthropology of childhoods: An introduction to "children, childhoods, and childhood studies." *American Anthropologist* 109:241–46.

Blumenschine, Robert J., et al. 2003. Late Pliocene *Homo* and hominid land use from Western Olduvai Gorge, Tanzania. *Science* 299 (February 21):1217–21.

Blumler, Mark A., and Roger Byrne. 1991. The ecological genetics of domestication and the origins of agriculture. *Current Anthropology* 32:23–35.

Boas, Franz. 1888. *Central Eskimos.* Bureau of American Ethnology Annual Report No. 6. Washington, DC: Smithsonian Institution.

Boas, Franz. 1930. *The religion of the Kwakiutl.* Columbia University Contributions to Anthropology, pt. 2. vol. 10. New York: Columbia University.

Boas, Franz. 1940. *Race, language, and culture.* New York: Macmillan.

Boas, Franz. 1964/1911. On grammatical categories. In *Language in culture and society*, ed. D. Hymes. New York: Harper & Row.

Boaz, Noel T., and Alan J. Almquist. 1997. *Biological anthropology: A synthetic approach to human evolution.* Upper Saddle River, NJ: Prentice Hall.

Boaz, Noel T., and Alan J. Almquist. 1999. *Essentials of biological anthropology.* Upper Saddle River, NJ: Prentice Hall.

Boaz, Noel T., and Alan J. Almquist. 2002. *Biological anthropology: A synthetic approach to human evolution.* 2nd ed. Upper Saddle River, NJ: Prentice Hall.

Bock, Philip K. 1980. *Continuities in psychological anthropology: A historical introduction.* San Francisco: W. H. Freeman and Company.

Bock, Philip K. 1996. Psychological anthropology. In *Encyclopedia of cultural anthropology*, vol. 3, eds. D. Levinson and M. Ember. New York: Henry Holt.

Bodley, John H. 2008. *Victims of progress.* 5th ed. Lanham, MD: AltaMira Press.

Boehm, Christopher. 1993. Egalitarian behavior and reverse dominance hierarchy. *Current Anthropology* 34:230–31.

Boehm, Christopher. 1999. *Hierarchy in the forest: The evolution of egalitarian behavior.* Cambridge, MA: Harvard University Press.

Boehm, Christopher. 2008. Purposive social selection and the evolution of human altruism. *Cross-Cultural Research* 42, no.4:319–52.

Boehm, Christopher. 2012. Ancestral hierarchy and conflict. *Science* 336 (May 18): 844–7.

Boesche, Christophe, P. Marchesi, N. Marchesi, B. Fruth, and F. Joulian. 1994. Is nut cracking in wild chimpanzees a cultural behavior? *Journal of Human Evolution* 26:325–38.

Bogin, Barry. 1988. *Patterns of human growth.* Cambridge: Cambridge University Press.

Bogin, Barry. 1997. Evolutionary hypotheses for human childhood. *Yearbook of Physical Anthropology* 40:63–89.

Bogoras, Waldemar. 1909. The Chukchee. Part 3. *Memoirs of the American Museum of Natural History*, 2.

Bohannan, Laura, and Paul Bohannan. 1953. *The Tiv of central Nigeria.* London: International African Institute.

Bohannan, Paul. 1954. The migration and expansion of the Tiv. *Africa* 24:2–16.

Bollen, Kenneth A. 1993. Liberal democracy: Validity and method factors in cross-national measures. *American Journal of Political Science* 37:1207–30.

Bolton, Ralph. 1973. Aggression and hypoglycemia among the Qolla: A study in psychobiological anthropology. *Ethnology* 12:227–57.

Bolton, Ralph. 1989. Introduction: The AIDS pandemic, a global emergency. *Medical Anthropology* 10:93–104.

Bolton, Ralph. 1992. AIDS and promiscuity: Muddled in the models of HIV prevention. *Medical Anthropology* 14:145–223.

Bond, Michael Harris. 2004. Culture and aggression—From context to coercion. *Personality and Social Psychology Review* 8, no.1:62–78.

Bond, Rod, and Peter B. Smith. 1996. Culture and conformity: A meta-analysis of studies using Asch's (1952b, 1956) line judgment task. *Psychological Bulletin* 11:111–37.

Bondarenko, Dmitri, and Andrey Korotayev. 2000. Family size and community organization: A cross-cultural comparison. *Cross-Cultural Research* 34:152–89.

Boonyabancha, Somsook. 2009. Land for housing the poor—by the poor: Experiences from the Baan Mankong Nationwide Slum Upgrading Programme in Thailand. *Environment and Urbanization* 21:309–29.

Bordaz, Jacques. 1970. *Tools of the Old and New Stone Age.* Garden City, NY: Natural History Press.

Bordes, François. 1961. Mousterian cultures in France. *Science* 134 (September 22): 803–10.

Bordes, François. 1968. *The Old Stone Age.* New York: McGraw-Hill.

Borgerhoff Mulder, Monique, Margaret George-Cramer, Jason Eshleman, and Alessia Ortolani. 2001. A study of East African kinship and marriage using a phylogenetically based comparative method. *American Anthropologist* 103:1059–82.

Borgerhoff Mulder, Monique, et al. 2010. Pastoralism and wealth inequality: Revisiting an old question. *Current Anthropology* 51:35–48.

Bornstein, Marc H. 1973. The psychophysiological component of cultural difference in color naming and illusion susceptibility. *Behavior Science Notes* 8:41–101.

Bortei-Doku, Ellen, and Ernest Aryeetey. 1995/1964. Mobilizing cash for business: Women in rotating *Susu* clubs in Ghana. In *Money-go-rounds*, eds. S. Ardener and S. Burman. Oxford: Berg.

Boserup, Ester. 1970. *Woman's role in economic development.* New York: St. Martin's Press.

Boserup, Ester. 1993/1965. *The conditions of agricultural growth: The economics of agrarian change under population pressure.* Toronto: Earthscan Publishers.

Bossen, Laurel. 2000. Women farmers, small plots, and changing markets in China. In *Women farmers and commercial ventures: Increasing food security in developing countries*, ed. A. Spring. Boulder, CO: Lynne Rienner Press.

Bourguignon, Erika. 1973. Introduction: A framework for the comparative study of altered states of consciousness. In *Religion, altered states of consciousness, and social change*, ed. E. Bourguignon. Columbus: Ohio State University Press.

Bourguignon, Erika. 2004. Suffering and healing, subordination and power: Women and possession trance. *Ethos* 32:557–74.

Bourguignon, Erika, and Thomas L. Evascu. 1977. Altered states of consciousness within a general evolutionary perspective: A holocultural analysis. *Behavior Science Research* 12:197–216.

Bowen, Gabriel J., et al. 2002. Mammalian dispersal at the Paleocene/Eocene boundary. *Science* 295 (March 15):2062–64.

Bowie, Katherine A. 2006. Of corvée and slavery: Historical intricacies of the division of labor and state power in Northern Thailand. In *Labor in cross-cultural perspective*, eds. E. Paul Durrenberger and Judith E. Martí. Lanham: Roman & Littlefield.

Bowler, Peter J. 2009. *Evolution: The history of an idea.* Berkeley: University of California Press.

Bowles, Samuel, H. Gintis, and M. Osborne. 2001. The determinants of earnings: A behavioral approach. *Journal of Economic Literature* 39:1137–76, as referred to in Godoy et al. 2004.

Bowles, Samuel, Eric Alden Smith, and Monique Borgerhoff Mulder. 2010. The emergence and persistence of inequality in premodern societies: Introduction to the special section. *Current Anthropology* 51:7–17.

Boyd, Robert, and Peter J. Richerson. 1996/1985. *Culture and the evolutionary process.* Chicago: University of Chicago Press.

Boyd, Robert, and Peter J. Richerson. 2005. *The origin and evolution of cultures.* New York: Oxford University Press.

Boyd, Robert, and Joan Silk. 2000. *How humans evolved.* 2nd ed. New York: Norton.

Brace, C. Loring. 1995. Region does not mean 'race'—Reality versus convention in forensic anthropology. *Journal of Forensic Sciences* 40:171–75.

Brace, C. Loring. 1996. A four-letter word called race. In *Race and other misadventures: Essays in honor of Ashley Montague in his ninetieth year*, eds. L. T. Reynolds and L. Leiberman. New York: General Hall.

Brace, C. Loring. 2005. *"Race" is a four-letter word.* New York: Oxford University Press.

Brace, C. Loring, David P. Tracer, Lucia Allen Yaroch, John Robb, Kari Brandt, and A. Russell Nelson. 1993. Clines and clusters versus 'race': A test in ancient Egypt and the case of a death on the Nile. *Yearbook of Physical Anthropology* 36:1–31.

Bradley, Candice. 1984–1985. The sexual division of labor and the value of children. *Behavior Science Research* 19:159–85.

Bradley, Candice. 1995. Keeping the soil in good heart: Weeding, women and ecofeminism. In *Ecofeminism*, ed. K. Warren. Bloomington: Indiana University Press.

Bradsher, Keith. 2002. Pakistanis fume as clothing sales to U.S. tumble. *New York Times*, June 23, p. 3.

Braidwood, Robert J. 1960. The agricultural revolution. *Scientific American* (September):130–48.

Braidwood, Robert J., and Gordon R. Willey. 1962. Conclusions and afterthoughts. In *Courses toward urban life*, eds. R. Braidwood and G. Willey. Chicago: Aldine.

Brain, C. K., and A. Sillen. 1988. Evidence from the Swartkrans Cave for the earliest use of fire. *Nature* 336 (December 1):464–66.

Branda, Richard F., and John W. Eaton. 1978. Skin color and nutrient photolysis: An evolutionary hypothesis. *Science* 201 (August 18):625–26.

Brandewie, Ernest. 1991. The place of the big man in traditional Hagen society in the central highlands of New Guinea. In *Anthropological approaches to political behavior*, eds. F. McGlynn and A. Tuden. Pittsburgh, PA: University of Pittsburgh Press.

Brandon, Robert N. 1990. *Adaptation and environment.* Princeton, NJ: Princeton University Press.

Bräuer, Günter. 1984. A craniological approach to the origin of anatomically modern *Homo sapiens* in Africa and implications for the appearance of modern Europeans. In *The origins of modern humans*, eds. F. Smith and F. Spencer. New York: Alan R. Liss.

Braun, David P., and Stephen Plog. 1982. Evolution of "tribal" social networks: Theory and prehistoric North American evidence. *American Antiquity* 47:504–25.

Brettell, Caroline B. 1996. Migration. In *Encyclopedia of cultural anthropology*, vol. 3, 4 vols., eds. D. Levinson and M. Ember. New York: Henry Holt.

Brettell, Caroline B., and Robert V. Kemper. 2002. Migration and cities. In *Encyclopedia of urban cultures: Cities and cultures around the world*, vol. 1, 4 vols., eds. M. Ember and C. R. Ember. Danbury, CT: Grolier/Scholastic.

Briggs, Jean L. 1974. Eskimo women: Makers of men. In *Many sisters: Women in cross-cultural perspective*, ed. C. J. Matthiasson. New York: Free Press.

Bringa, Tone. 1995. *Being Muslim the Bosnian way: Identity and community in a central Bosnian village.* Princeton, NJ: Princeton University Press, as seen in eHRAF World Cultures. ehrafworldcultures.yale.edu. Accessed May 2000.

Brinton, Crane. 1938. *The anatomy of revolution.* Upper Saddle River, NJ: Prentice Hall.

Briody, Elizabeth K., Robert T. Trotter, II, and Tracy L. Meerwarth. 2010. *Transforming culture: Creating and sustaining a better manufacturing organization.* New York: Palgrave Macmillan.

Britannica Online. 1995. Book of the year (1995): World affairs: Rwanda; and Book of the year (1995): Race and ethnic relations: Rwanda's complex ethnic history. *Britannica Online*, December.

Britannica Online. 1998. Printing, typography, and photoengraving; History of prints: Origins in China: Transmission of paper to Europe (12th century). *Britannica Online*, February.

Brittain, John A. 1978. *Inheritance and the inequality of material wealth.* Washington, DC: Brookings Institution.

Brodey, Jane E. 1971. Effects of milk on Blacks noted. *New York Times*, October 15, p. 15.

Brodwin, Paul E. 1996. Disease and culture. In *Encyclopedia of cultural anthropology*, vol. 1, eds. D. Levinson and M. Ember. New York: Henry Holt.

Bromage, Timothy G. 2002. Paleoanthropology and life history, and life history of a paleoanthropologist. In MyAnthroLibrary, eds. Carol R Ember, Melvin Ember, and Peter N. Peregrine. MyAnthroLibrary.com. Pearson.

Bromage, Timothy G., and M. Christopher Dean. 1985. Reevaluation of the age at death of immature fossil hominids. *Nature* 317 (October 10):525–27.

Brooks, Alison S., Fatimah Linda Collier Jackson, and R. Richard Grinker. 1993. Race and ethnicity in America. *Anthro Notes (National Museum of Natural History Bulletin for Teachers)* 15, no. 3(Fall):1–3, 11–15.

Broom, Robert. 1950. *Finding the missing link.* London: Watts.

Broude, Gwen J. 1976. Cross-cultural patterning of some sexual attitudes and practices. *Behavior Science Research* 11:227–62.

Broude, Gwen J. 1980. Extramarital sex norms in cross-cultural perspective. *Behavior Science Research* 15:181–218.

Broude, Gwen J. 2004. Sexual attitudes and practices. In *Encyclopedia of sex and gender: Men and women in the world's cultures*, vol. 1, eds. C. Ember and M. Ember. New York: Kluwer Academic/Plenum Publishers.

Broude, Gwen J. 2009. Variations in sexual attitudes, norms, and practices. In MyAnthroLibrary, eds. C. R. Ember, M. Ember, and P. N. Peregrine. MyAnthroLibrary.com. Pearson.

Broude, Gwen J., and Sarah J. Greene. 1976. Cross-cultural codes on twenty sexual attitudes and practices. *Ethnology* 15:409–29.

Browman, David, Gayle Fritz, and Patty Jo Watson. 2009. Origins of food-producing economies in the Americas. In *The human past*, ed. C. Scarre. New York: Thames and Hudson.

Brown, Cecil H. 1977. Folk botanical life-forms: Their universality and growth. *American Anthropologist* 79:317–42.

Brown, Cecil H. 1979. Folk zoological life-forms: Their universality and growth. *American Anthropologist* 81:791–817.

Brown, Cecil H. 1984. World view and lexical uniformities. *Reviews in Anthropology* 11:99–112.

Brown, Cecil H., and Stanley R. Witkowski. 1980. Language universals. In *Toward explaining human culture*, eds. D. Levinson and M. J. Malone. New Haven, CT: HRAF Press.

Brown, Donald E. 1991. *Human universals.* Philadelphia: Temple University Press.

Brown, Donald E. 2000. Human universals and their implications. In *Being humans: Anthropological universality and particularity in transdisciplinary perspectives*, ed. N. Roughley. Berlin: Walter de Gruyter.

Brown, Frank H. 1992. Methods of dating. In *The Cambridge encyclopedia of human evolution*, eds. S. Jones, R. Martin, and D. Pilbeam. New York: Cambridge University Press.

Brown, Frank H. 2000. Geochronometry. In *Encyclopedia of human evolution and prehistory*, eds. I. Tattersall, G. Delson, and J. van Couvering. New York: Garland.

Brown, James A. 1983. Summary. In *Archaic hunters and gatherers in the American Midwest*, eds. J. L. Phillips and J. A. Brown. New York: Academic Press.

Brown, James A. 1985. Long-term trends to sedentism and the emergence of complexity in the American Midwest. In *Prehistoric hunter-gatherers*, eds. T. Price and J. Brown. Orlando, FL: Academic Press.

Brown, James A., and T. Douglas Price. 1985. Complex hunter-gatherers: Retrospect and prospect. In *Prehistoric hunter-gatherers*, eds. T. Price and J. Brown. Orlando, FL: Academic Press.

Brown, Judith K. 1970a. Economic organization and the position of women among the Iroquois. *Ethnohistory* 17:151–67.

Brown, Judith K. 1970b. A note on the division of labor by sex. *American Anthropologist* 72:1073–78.

Brown, Michael F. 2008. Cultural relativism 2.0. *Current Anthropology* 49:363–83.

Brown, Peter J. 1997. Culture and the evolution of obesity. In *Applying cultural anthropology*, eds. A. Podolefsky and P. J. Brown. Mountain View, CA: Mayfield.

Brown, Peter J., and Jennifer Sweeney. 2009. The anthropology of overweight, obesity, and the body. *AnthroNotes* 30, no.1:6–12.

Brown, Roger. 1965. *Social psychology.* New York: Free Press.

Brown, Roger. 1980. The first sentence of child and chimpanzee. In *Speaking of apes*, eds. T. A. Sebeok and J. Umiker-Sebeok. New York: Plenum Press.

Brown, Roger, and Marguerite Ford. 1961. Address in American English. *Journal of Abnormal and Social Psychology* 62:375–85.

Browner, C. H. 1985. Criteria for selecting herbal remedies. *Ethnology* 24:13–32.

Brues, Alice. 1992. Forensic diagnosis of race—General race versus specific populations. *Social Science and Medicine* 34:125–28.

Brumbach, Hetty Jo, and Robert Jarvenpa. 2006a. Chipewyan society and gender relations. In *Circumpolar lives and livelihood: A comparative ethnoarchaeology of gender and subsistence*, eds. R. Jarvenpa and H. J. Brumbach. Lincoln, Nebraska: University of Nebraska Press.

Brumbach, Hetty Jo, and Robert Jarvenpa. 2006b. Conclusion: Toward a comparative ethnoarchaeology of gender. In *Circumpolar lives and livelihood: A comparative ethnoarchaeology of gender and subsistence*, eds. R. Jarvenpa and H. J. Brumbach. Lincoln, Nebraska: University of Nebraska Press.

Brumfiel, Elizabeth M. 1976. Regional growth in the eastern Valley of Mexico: A test of the "population pressure" hypothesis. In *The early Mesoamerican village*, ed. K. Flannery. New York: Academic Press.

Brumfiel, Elizabeth M. 1983. Aztec state making: Ecology, structure, and the origin of the state. *American Anthropologist* 85:261–84.

Brumfiel, Elizabeth M. 1992. Distinguished lecture in archeology: Breaking and entering the ecosystem—Gender, class, and faction steal the show. *American Anthropologist* 94:551–67.

Brumfiel, Elizabeth M. 2009. Origins of social inequality. In MyAnthroLibrary, eds. C. R. Ember, M. Ember, and P. N. Peregrine. MyAnthroLibrary.com. Pearson.

Brunet, Michel, Alain Beauvilain, Yves Coppens, Elile Heintz, Aladji H. E. Moutaye, and David Pilbeam. 1995. The first australopithecine 2,500 kilometers west of the Rift Valley (Chad). *Nature* 378:273–75.

Brunet, Michel, et al. 2002. A new hominid from the upper Miocene of Chad, Central Africa. *Nature* 418 (July 11):145–51.

Brunvand, Jan Harold. 1993. *The baby train: And other lusty urban legends.* New York: Norton.

Brusco, Elizabeth E. 1996. Religious conversion. In *Encyclopedia of cultural anthropology*, vol. 3, eds. D. Levinson and M. Ember. New York: Henry Holt.

Brutsaert, Tom. 2010. Human adaptation to high altitude. In *Human evolutionary biology*, ed. M. Muehlenbein. Cambridge: Cambridge University Press.

Bryant, Carol A., and Doraine F. C. Bailey. 1990. The use of focus group research in program development. *NAPA Bulletin* 10:24–39.

Buckser, Andrew, and Stephen D. Glazier, eds. 2003. Preface. In *The anthropology of religious conversion*, eds. A. Buckser and S. D. Glazier. Lanham, MD: Roman & Littlefield.

Budiansky, Stephen. 1992. *The covenant of the wild: Why animals chose domestication.* New York: Morrow.

Buettner-Janusch, John. 1973. *Physical anthropology: A perspective.* New York: Wiley.

Bumpass, Larry, and Hsien-Hen Lu. 2000. Trends in cohabitation and implications for children's family contexts in the united states. *Population Studies* 54, no.1:29–41.

Bunzel, Ruth. 1971. The nature of Katcinas. In *Reader in comparative religion*, 3rd ed., eds. W. A. Lessa and E. Z. Vogt. New York: Harper & Row.

Burbank, Victoria K. 1994. *Fighting women: Anger and aggression in aboriginal Australia*. Berkeley: University of California Press.

Burbank, Victoria K. 2009a. Adolescent socialization and initiation ceremonies. In MyAnthroLibrary, eds. C. R. Ember, M. Ember, and P. N. Peregrine. MyAnthroLibrary. com. Pearson.

Burbank, Victoria K. 2009b. Australian Aborigines: An adolescent mother and her family. In MyAnthroLibrary, eds. C. R. Ember, M. Ember, and P. N. Peregrine. MyAnthroLibrary.com. Pearson.

Burbano, H., et al. 2010. Targeted investigation of the Neandertal genome by array-based sequence capture. *Science* 328 (May 7):723–26.

Burch, Ernest S., Jr. 1988. *The Eskimos*. Norman: University of Oklahoma Press.

Burch, Ernest S., Jr. 2009. North Alaskan Eskimos: A changing way of life. In MyAnthroLibrary, eds. C. R. Ember, M. Ember, and P. N. Peregrine. MyAnthroLibrary.com. Pearson.

Burkhalter, S. Brian, and Robert F. Murphy. 1989. Tappers and sappers: Rubber, gold and money among the Mundurucú. *American Ethnologist* 16:100–16.

Burns, Alisa, and Cath Scott. 1994. *Mother-headed families and why they have increased*. Hillsdale, NJ: Lawrence Erlbaum Associates.

Burton, Roger V., and John W. M. Whiting. 1961. The absent father and cross-sex identity. *Merrill-Palmer Quarterly of Behavior and Development* 7, no. 2:85–95.

Burtsev, Mikhail S., and A. Korotayev. 2004. An evolutionary agent-based model of pre-state warfare patterns: Cross-cultural tests. *World Cultures* 15, no. 1:28–36.

Busby, Annette. 2009. Kurds: A culture straddling national borders. In MyAnthroLibrary, eds. C. R. Ember, M. Ember, and P. N. Peregrine. MyAnthroLibrary.com. Pearson.

Butzer, Karl W. 1982. Geomorphology and sediment stratigraphy. In *The Middle Stone Age at Klasies River mouth in South Africa*, eds. R. Singer and J. Wymer. Chicago: University of Chicago Press.

Byrne, Bryan. 1994. Access to subsistence resources and the sexual division of labor among potters. *Cross-Cultural Research* 28:225–50.

Byrne, Roger. 1987. Climatic change and the origins of agriculture. In *Studies in the Neolithic and urban revolutions*, ed. L. Manzanilla. Oxford: British Archaeological Reports, International Series 349.

Calvin, William H. 1983. *The throwing Madonna: Essays on the brain*. New York: McGraw-Hill.

Campbell, Donald T. 1965. Variation and selective retention in socio-cultural evolution. In *Social change in developing areas*, eds. H. Barringer, G. Blankstein, and R. Mack. Cambridge, MA: Schenkman.

Campbell, Joseph. 1949. *The hero with a thousand faces*. New York: Pantheon.

Cancian, Frank. 1980. Risk and uncertainty in agricultural decision making. In *Agricultural decision making*, ed. P. F. Barlett. New York: Academic Press.

Cann, Rebecca, M. 1988. DNA and human origins. *Annual Review of Anthropology* 17:127–43.

Cann, Rebecca, M. Stoneking, and A. C. Wilson. 1987. Mitochondrial DNA and human evolution. *Nature* 325 (January 1):31–36.

Caporael, Linnda R. 1976. Ergotism: The Satan loosed in Salem? *Science* (April 2):21–26.

Carbonell, Eudald, et al. 2008. The first hominin of Europe. *Nature* 452 (March 27):465–69.

Carcopino, Jerome. 1940. *Daily life in ancient Rome: The people and the city at the height of the empire*. Edited with bibliography and notes by Henry T. Rowell. Translated from the French by E. O. Lorimer. New Haven, CT: Yale University Press.

Cardoso, Fernando Luis, and Dennis Werner. 2004. Homosexuality. In *Encyclopedia of sex and gender: Men and women in the world's cultures*, vol. 1, eds. C. Ember and M. Ember. New York: Kluwer Academic/Plenum Publishers.

Carey, James W., Erin Picone-DeCaro, Mary Spink Neumann, Devorah Schwartz, Delia Easton, and Daphne Cobb St. John. 2004. HIV/AIDS research and prevention. In *Encyclopedia of medical anthropology: Health and illness in the world's cultures*, vol. 1, eds. C. R. Ember and M. Ember. New York: Kluwer Academic/Plenum.

Carlson, K. J., et al. 2011. The endocast of MH1, *Australopithecus sediba*. *Science* 333 (September 9):1402–1407.

Carneiro, Robert L. 1968. Slash-and-burn cultivation among the Kuikuru and its implications for settlement patterns. In *Man in adaptation*, ed. Y. Cohen. Chicago, Aldine.

Carneiro, Robert L. 1970. A theory of the origin of the state. *Science* 169 (August 21):733–38.

Carneiro, Robert L. 1978. Political expansion as an expression of the principle of competitive exclusion. In *Origins of the state*, eds. R. Cohen and E. R. Service. Philadelphia: Institute for the Study of Human Issues.

Carneiro, Robert L. 1988. The circumscription theory: Challenge and response. *American Behavioral Scientist* 31:497–511.

Carneiro, Robert L. 1990. Chiefdom-level warfare as exemplified in Fiji and the Cauca Valley. In *The anthropology of war*, ed. J. Haas. New York: Cambridge University Press.

Carneiro, Robert L. 2000. Process vs. Stages: A false dichotomy in tracing the rise of the state. In *Alternatives of social evolution*, eds. N. N. Kradin, A. V. Korotayev, D. M. Bondarenko, V. De Munck, and P. K. Wason. Vladivostok: FEB RAS.

Carneiro, Robert L. 2012. The circumscription theory: A clarification, amplification, and reformulation. *Social Evolution & History* 11, no. 2: 5–30.

Carpenter, C. R. 1940. A field study in Siam of the behavior and social relations of the gibbon (*Hylobates lar*). *Comparative Psychology Monographs* 16, no. 5:1–212.

Carpenter, Sandra. 2000. Effects of cultural tightness and collectivism on self-concept and causal attributions. *Cross-Cultural Research* 34:38–56.

Carrasco, Pedro. 1961. The civil-religious hierarchy in Mesoamerican communities: Pre-Spanish background and colonial development. *American Anthropologist* 63:483–97.

Carrier, Joseph, and Ralph Bolton. 1991. Anthropological perspectives on sexuality and HIV prevention. *Annual Review of Sex Research* 2:49–75.

Carroll, John B., ed. 1956. *Language, thought, and reality: Selected writings of Benjamin Lee Whorf*. New York: Wiley.

Carroll, Michael. 1979. A new look at Freud on myth. *Ethos* 7:189–205.

Cartmill, Matt. 1974. Rethinking primate origins. *Science* (April 26):436–37.

Cartmill, Matt. 1992a. New views on primate origins. *Evolutionary Anthropology* 1:105–11.

Cartmill, Matt. 1992b. Non-human primates. In *The Cambridge encyclopedia of human evolution*, eds. S. Jones, R. Martin, and D. Pilbeam. New York: Cambridge University Press.

Cartmill, Matt. 2009. Explaining primate origins. In MyAnthroLibrary, eds. C. R. Ember, M. Ember, and P. N. Peregrine. MyAnthroLibrary.com. Pearson.

Cartmill, Matt. 2010. Primate classification and diversity. In *Primate neuroethology*, eds. M. Platt and A. Ghazanfar. Oxford: Oxford University Press.

Cashdan, Elizabeth A. 1980. Egalitarianism among hunters and gatherers. *American Anthropologist* 82:116–20.

Cashdan, Elizabeth A. 2001. Ethnic diversity and its environmental determinants: Effects of climate, pathogens, and habitat diversity. *American Anthropologist* 103:968–91.

Castle, Stephen. 2013. Horse meat in food stirs a furor in the British Isles. *New York Times*, February 8. www.nytimes.com.

Caulkins, D. Douglas. 1997. Welsh. In *American immigrant cultures: Builders of a nation*, vol. 2, eds. D. Levinson and M. Ember. New York: Macmillan Reference.

Caulkins, D. Douglas. 2009. Norwegians: Cooperative individualists. In MyAnthroLibrary, eds. C. R. Ember, M. Ember, and P. N. Peregrine. MyAnthroLibrary. com. Pearson.

Cavalli-Sforza, L. Luca, and Marcus W. Feldman. 1981. *Cultural transmission and evolution: A quantitative approach*. Princeton, NJ: Princeton University Press.

Cavalli-Sforza, L. Luca, and Marcus W. Feldman. 2003. The application of molecular genetic approaches to the study of human evolution. *Nature Genetics Supplement* 33:266–75.

Caws, Peter. 1969. The structure of discovery. *Science* 166 (December 12):1375–80.

CDC. n.d. Black or African American populations. http://www.cdc.gov/minorityhealth/populations/REMP/black.html (accessed May 18, 2013).

Ceci, Stephen, and Wendy M. Williams. 2009. YES: The scientific truth must be pursued. *Nature* 457 (February 12):788–789.

Center for Renewal of Science and Culture. 2001. The wedge strategy, cited in Barbara Forrest, "The wedge at work." In *Intelligent design creationism and its critics*, ed. R. Pennock, 16. Boston: IT Press.

Cernea, Michael M., ed. 1991. *Putting people first: Sociological variables in development*, 2nd ed. New York: Oxford University Press.

Cernea, Michael M. 2000. *Risk, safeguards, and reconstruction: A model for population displacement and resettlement*, eds. M. M. Cernea and C. McDowell. Washington, DC: World Bank.

Chacon, Richard J., and Rubén G. Mendoza. 2007. Ethical considerations and conclusions regarding indigenous warfare and ritual violence in Latin America. In *Latin American indigenous warfare and ritual violence*, eds. R. J. Chacon and R. G. Mendoza. Tucson: University of Arizona Press.

Chafetz, Janet Saltzman. 1990. *Gender equity: An integrated theory of stability and change*. Sage Library of Social Research No. 176. Newbury Park, CA: Sage.

Chagnon, Napoleon. 1983. *Yanomamö: The fierce people*. 3rd ed. New York: Holt, Rinehardt, and Winston.

Chambers, J. K. 2002. Patterns of variation including change. In *The handbook of language variation and change*, eds. J. K. Chambers, Peter Trudgill, and Natalie Schilling-Estes. Malden, MA: Blackwell Publishers.

Chang, Kwang-Chih. 1968. *The archaeology of ancient China*. New Haven, CT: Yale University Press.

Chang, Kwang-Chih. 1970. The beginnings of agriculture in the Far East. *Antiquity* 44:175–85.

Chang, Kwang-Chih. 1981. In search of China's beginnings: New light on an old civilization. *American Scientist* 69:148–60.

Chang, Kwang-Chih. 1986. *Archaeology of ancient China*, 4th ed. New Haven, CT: Yale University Press.

Chapais, Bernard. 2008. *Primeval kinship: How pair-bonding gave birth to human society*. Cambridge, MA: Harvard University Press.

Chaplin, William F., J. B. Phillips, J. D. Brown, N. R. Clanton, and J. L. Stein. 2000. Handshaking, gender, personality, and first impressions. *Journal of Personality and Social Psychology* 79, no.1:110–17.

Chapman, Chris, and Alexander Kagaha. 2009. *Resolving conflicts using traditional mechanisms in the Karamoja and Teso regions of Uganda*. London, UK: Minority Rights Group International. http://www.unhcr.org/refworld/pdfid/4a97dc232.pdf (accessed April 13, 2013).

Charanis, Peter. 1953. Economic factors in the decline of the Roman Empire. *Journal of Economic History* 13:412–24.

Chard, Chester S. 1969. *Man in prehistory*. New York: McGraw-Hill.

Charles-Dominique, Pierre. 1977. *Ecology and behaviour of nocturnal primates* trans. R. D. Martin. New York: Columbia University Press.

Chase, Philip, and Harold Dibble. 1987. Middle Paleolithic symbolism: A review of current evidence and interpretations. *Journal of Anthropological Archaeology* 6:263–69.

Chatterjee, Sankar. 1997. *The rise of birds: 225 million years of evolution*. Baltimore: Johns Hopkins.

Chatty, Dawn. 1996. *Mobile pastoralists: Development planning and social change in Oman*. New York: Columbia University Press.

Chatty, Dawn. 2006. Adapting to biodiversity conservation: The mobile pastoralist Harasiis tribe of Oman. In *Modern pastoralism and conservation: Old problems, new challenges*, eds. D. Chatty and T. Sternberg. Beijing: Intellectual Property Publishing House.

Chaucer, Geoffrey. 1926. *The prologue to the Canterbury Tales, the Knights Tale, the Nonnes Prestes Tale*, ed. M. H. Liddell. New York: Macmillan.

Chayanov, Alexander V. 1966. *The theory of peasant economy*, eds. D. Thorner, B. Kerblay, and R. E. F. Smith. Homewood, IL: Richard D. Irwin.

Chen, Denise, Ammeta Katdare, and Nadia Lucas. 2006. Chemosignals of fear enhance cognitive performance in humans. *Chemical Senses* 31:415–23.

Cheney, Dorothy, L., and Richard W. Wrangham. 1987. Predation. In *Primate societies*, eds. B. B. Smuts, D. L. Cheney, R. M. Seyfarth, and R. W. Wrangham. Chicago: University of Chicago Press.

Chessa, Bernardo, et al 2009. Revealing the history of sheep domestication using retrovirus integrations. *Science* 324 (April 24):532–36.

Chibnik, Michael. 1980. The statistical behavior approach: The choice between wage labor and cash cropping in rural Belize. In *Agricultural decision making*, ed. P. F. Barlett. New York: Academic Press.

Chibnik, Michael. 1981. The evolution of cultural rules. *Journal of Anthropological Research* 37:256–68.

Chibnik, Michael. 1987. The economic effects of household demography: A cross-cultural assessment of Chayanov's theory. In *Household economies and their transformations*, ed. M. D. MacLachlan. Monographs in Economic Anthropology, No 3. Lanham, MD: University Press of America.

Chick, Garry. 1998. Games in culture revisited: A replication and extension of Roberts, Arth, and Bush [1959]. *Cross-Cultural Research* 32:185–206.

Childe, Vere Gordon. 1950. The urban revolution. *Town Planning Review* 21:3–17.

Childe, Vere Gordon. 1956. *Man makes himself*. London: Watts.

Chimpanzee Sequencing and Analysis Consortium. 2005. Initial sequence of the chimpanzee genome and comparison with the human genome. *Nature* 437 (September 1):69–87.

Chivers, David J. 1974. *The siamang in Malaya*. Basel, Switzerland: Karger.

Chomsky, Noam. 1975. *Reflections on language*. New York: Pantheon.

Christensen, Pia, Jenny Hockey, and Allison James. 2001. Talk, silence and the material world: Patterns of indirect communication among agricultural farmers in Northern England. In *An anthropology of indirect communication*, eds. J. Hendry and C. W. Watson. London: Routledge.

Ciochon, Russell L., and Dennis A. Etler. 1994. Reinterpreting past primate diversity. In *Integrative paths to the past*, eds. R. Corruccini and R. Ciochon. Upper Saddle River, NJ: Prentice Hall.

Ciochon, Russell L., and John G. Fleagle, eds. 1993. *The human evolution source book*. Upper Saddle River, NJ: Prentice Hall.

Ciochon, Russell L., John Olsen, and Jamie James. 1990. *Other origins: The search for the giant ape in human prehistory*. New York: Bantam.

Claassen, Cheryl. 1991. Gender, shellfishing, and the Sell Mound Archaic. In *Engendering archaeology*, eds. J. Gero and M. Conkey. Oxford: Blackwell.

Claassen, Cheryl. 2009. Gender and archaeology. In MyAnthroLibrary, eds. C. R. Ember, M. Ember, and P. N. Peregrine. MyAnthroLibrary.com. Pearson.

Clark, J. Desmond. 1970. *The prehistory of Africa*. New York: Praeger.

Clark, J. Desmond. 1977. Interpretations of prehistoric technology from ancient Egyptian and other sources. Part II: Prehistoric arrow forms in Africa as shown by surviving examples of the traditional arrows of the San Bushmen. *Paleorient* 3:127–50.

Clark, Gracia. 2000. Small-scale traders' key role in stabilizing and diversifying Ghana's rural communities and livelihoods. In *Women farmers and commercial ventures: Increasing food security in developing countries*, ed. A. Spring. Boulder, CO: Lynne Rienner Publishers, Inc.

Clark, Grahame. 1975. *The earlier Stone Age settlement of Scandinavia*. Cambridge: Cambridge University Press.

Clark, Grahame, and Stuart Piggott. 1965. *Prehistoric societies*. New York: Knopf.

Clark, W. E. Le Gros. 1964. *The fossil evidence for human evolution*, 184. Chicago: University of Chicago Press.

Clarke, Ronald J., and P. V. Tobias. 1995. Sterkfontein member 2 foot bones of the oldest South African hominid. *Science* 269 (July 28):521–24.

Clayman, Charles B. 1989. *American Medical Association encyclopedia of medicine*, 857–58. New York: Random house.

Clifford, James. 1986. Introduction: Partial truths. In *Writing culture: The poetics and politics of ethnography*, eds. J. Clifford and G. E. Marcus. Berkeley: University of California Press.

Clottes, Jean. 2008. Rock art: An endangered heritage worldwide. *Journal of Anthropological Research* 64:1–18.

Clutton-Brock, Juliet. 1984. Dog. In *Evolution of domesticated animals*, ed. I. Mason. New York: Longman.

Clutton-Brock, Juliet. 1992. Domestication of animals. In *The Cambridge encyclopedia of human evolution*, eds. S. Jones, R. Martin, and D. Pilbeam. New York: Cambridge University Press.

Clutton-Brock, T. H., and Paul H. Harvey. 1977. Primate ecology and social organization. *Journal of Zoology* 183:1–39.

Clutton-Brock, T. H., and Paul H. Harvey. 1980. Primates, brains and ecology. *Journal of Zoology* 190:309–23.

Coale, Ansley J. 1974. The history of the human population. *Scientific American* (September):41–51.

Coe, Michael D. 1966. *The Maya*. New York: Praeger.

Coe, Michael D. 2011. *The Maya*, 8th ed. New York: Thames and Hudson.

Cohen, Alex. 1990. A cross-cultural study of the effects of environmental unpredictability on aggression in folktales. *American Anthropologist* 92:474–79.

Cohen, Alex. 1999. *The mental health of indigenous peoples: An international overview*. Geneva: Department of Mental Health, World Health Organization.

Cohen, Alex. 2004. Mental disorders. In *Encyclopedia of medical anthropology: Health and illness in the world's cultures*, vol. 1, eds. C. R. Ember and M. Ember. New York: Kluwer Academic/Plenum.

Cohen, Alex, and Paul Koegel. 2009. Homelessness. In MyAnthroLibrary, eds. C. R. Ember, M. Ember, and P. N. Peregrine. MyAnthroLibrary.com. Pearson.

Cohen, Joel D. 2011. The beginnings of agriculture in China. *Current Anthropology* 52, Supplement 4:S273–93.

Cohen, Mark Nathan. 1977a. *The food crisis in prehistory: Overpopulation and the origins of agriculture*. New Haven, CT: Yale University Press.

Cohen, Mark Nathan. 1977b. Population pressure and the origins of agriculture. In *Origins of agriculture*, ed. C. A. Reed. The Hague: Monton.

Cohen, Mark Nathan. 1987. The significance of long-term changes in human diet and food economy. In *Food and evolution*, eds. M. Harris and E. Ross. Philadelphia: Temple University Press.

Cohen, Mark Nathan. 1989. *Health and the rise of civilization*. New Haven, CT: Yale University Press.

Cohen, Mark Nathan. 2009. Were early agriculturalists less healthy than food-collectors? In MyAnthroLibrary, eds. C. R. Ember, M. Ember, and P. N. Peregrine. MyAnthroLibrary.com. Pearson.

Cohen, Mark Nathan, and George J. Armelagos. 1984. Paleopathology at the origins of agriculture: Editors' summation. In *Paleopathology at the origins of agriculture*, eds. M. N. Cohen and G. J. Armelagos. Orlando, FL: Academic Press.

Cohen, Myron L. 1976. *House united, house divided: The Chinese family in Taiwan*. New York: Columbia University Press.

Cohen, Ronald. 1988. Introduction. In *State formation and political legitimacy, Vol. 6: Political anthropology*, eds. R. Cohen and J. D. Toland. New Brunswick, NJ: Transaction Books.

Cohen, Ronald, and Elman R. Service, eds. 1978. *Origins of the state: The anthropology of political evolution*. Philadelphia: Institute for the Study of Human Issues.

Cohen, Wesley. 1995. Empirical studies of innovative activity. In *Handbook of the economics of innovation and technological change*, ed. P. Stoneman. Oxford: Blackwell.

COHMAP (Cooperative Holocene Mapping Project) Personnel. 1988. Climatic changes of the last 18,000 years. *Science* 241 (August 26):1043–52.

Colby, Benjamin N. 1996. Cognitive anthropology. In *Encyclopedia of cultural anthropology*, vol. 1, eds. David Levinson and Melvin Ember. New York: Henry Holt.

Collier, Stephen, and J. Peter White. 1976. Get them young? Age and sex inferences on animal domestication in archaeology. *American Antiquity* 41:96–102.

Collins, Desmond. 1976. Later hunters in Europe. In *The origins of Europe*, ed. D. Collins. New York: Thomas Y. Crowell.

Collins, James, and Richard Blot. 2003. *Literacy and literacies*. Cambridge: Cambridge University Press.

Congressional Budget Office. 2011. Trends in the distribution of household income. http://www.cbo.gov/publication/42729 (accessed June 1, 2013).

Conklin, Beth A. 2002. Shamans versus pirates in the Amazonian treasure chest. *American Anthropologist* 104:1050–61.

Connah, Graham. 1987. *African civilizations: Precolonial cities and states in tropical Africa*. Cambridge: Cambridge University Press.

Connah, Graham. 2009. Holocene Africa. In *The human past*, ed. C. Scarre. New York: Thames and Hudson.

Conroy, Glenn C. 1990. *Primate evolution*. New York: Norton.

Coontz, Stephanie. 2005. *Marriage, a history: How love conquered marriage*. New York: Penguin Group.

Cooper, Richard S., Charles N. Rotimi, and Ryk Ward. 1999. The puzzle of hypertension in African Americans. *Scientific American* (February):56–63.

Cordain, Loren, Janette Brand Miller, S. Boyd Eaton, Neil Mann, Susanne H. A. Holt, and John D. Speth. 2000. Plant-animal subsistence ratios and macronutrient energy estimations in worldwide hunter-gatherer diets. *The American Journal of Clinical Nutrition* 71, no.3:682–92.

Coreil, Jeannine. 1989. Lessons from a community study of oral rehydration therapy in Haiti. In *Making our research useful*, eds. J. Van Willigen, B. Rylko-Bauer, and A. McElroy. Boulder, CO: Westview.

Coreil, Jeannine. 2004. Malaria and other major insect vector diseases. In *Encyclopedia of medical anthropology: Health and illness in the world's cultures*, vol. 1, eds. C. R. Ember and M. Ember. New York: Kluwer Academic/Plenum.

Costin, Cathy Lynne. 2009. Cloth production and gender relations in the Inka Empire. In MyAnthroLibrary, eds. C. R. Ember, M. Ember, and P. N. Peregrine. MyAnthroLibrary.com. Pearson.

Coult, Allan D., and Robert W. Habenstein. 1965. *Cross tabulations of Murdock's "World Ethnographic Sample."* Columbia: University of Missouri Press.

Crate, Susan A. 2008. Gone the bull of winter? Grappling with the cultural implications of and anthropology's role(s) in global climate change. *Current Anthropology* 49:569–95.

Crate, Susan A., and Mark Nuttall. 2009. Introduction: Anthropology and climate change. In *Anthropology and climate change: From encounters to actions*, eds. S. A. Crate and M. Nuttall. Walnut Creek, CA: Left Coast Press.

Crawford, Gary W. 1992. Prehistoric plant domestication in East Asia. In *The origins of agriculture*, eds. C. Cowan and P. Watson. Washington, DC: Smithsonian Institution Press.

Crawford, Harriet. 2004. *Sumer and the Sumerians*. Cambridge: Cambridge University Press.

Crawford, R. D. 1984. Turkey. In *Evolution of domesticated animals*, ed. I. Mason. New York: Longman.

Creed, Gerald W. 2009. Bulgaria: Anthropological corrections to Cold War stereotypes. In MyAnthroLibrary, eds. C. R. Ember, M. Ember, and P. N. Peregrine. MyAnthroLibrary.com. Pearson.

Crittenden, Alyssa. 2013. Juvenile foraging among the Hadza: Implications for human life history. *Evolution & Human Behavior* 34:299–304.

Crockett, Carolyn, and John F. Eisenberg. 1987. Howlers: Variations in group size and demography. In *Primate societies*, eds. B. B. Smuts, D. L. Cheney, R. M. Seyfarth, and R. W. Wrangham. Chicago: University of Chicago Press.

Crossroads for Planet Earth. 2005. *Scientific American*, Special issue, September.

Crystal, David. 1971. *Linguistics*. Middlesex, UK: Penguin.

Crystal, David. 2000. *Language death*. Cambridge: Cambridge University Press.

Culotta, Elizabeth. 1995. New hominid crowds the field. *Science* 269 (August 18):918.

Culotta, Elizabeth. 2005. Calorie count reveals Neandertals out-ate hardiest modern humans. *Science* 307 (February 11):840.

Curtin, Philip D. 1984. *Cross-cultural trade in world history*. Cambridge: Cambridge University Press.

Cutright, Phillips. 1967. Inequality: A cross-national analysis. *American Sociological Review* 32:562–78.

Dagosto, Marian. 2002. The origin and diversification of anthropoid primates: Introduction. In *The primate fossil record*, ed. W. C. Hartwig. Cambridge: Cambridge University Press.

Daiger, Stephen. 2005. Was the human genome project worth the effort? *Science* 308 (April 15):362–64.

Daly, Martin, and Margo Wilson. 1988. *Homicide*. New York: Aldine.

Damas, David. 1983. Demography and kinship as variables of adoption in the Carolines. *American Ethnologist* 10:328–44.

Daniel, I. Randolph. 2001. Early Eastern Archaic. In *Encyclopedia of prehistory, Vol. 6: North America*, eds. P. N. Peregrine and M. Ember. Kluwer: Academic/Plenum.

Darnell, Regna. 1989. Correlates of Cree narrative performance. In *Explorations in the ethnography of speaking*, eds. R. Bauman and Joel Sherzer. New York: Cambridge University Press.

Dart, Raymond. 1925. *Australopithecus africanus*: The man-ape of South Africa. *Nature* 115:195.

Darwin, Charles. 1970/1859. The origin of species. In *Evolution of man*, eds. L. B. Young. New York: Oxford University Press.

Dasen, Pierre R., and Alastair Heron. 1981. Cross-cultural tests of Piaget's theory. In *Handbook of cross-cultural psychology, Vol. 4: Developmental psychology*, eds. H. C. Triandis and A. Heron. Boston: Allyn & Bacon.

Dasen, Pierre R., John W. Berry, and N. Sartorius, eds. 1988. *Health and cross-cultural psychology: Toward applications*. Newbury Park, CA: Sage.

Davenport, William. 1959. Nonunilinear descent and descent groups. *American Anthropologist* 61:557–72.

Davies, Stephen. 2000. Non-Western art and art's definition. In *Theories of art today*, ed. N. Carroll. Madison: University of Wisconsin Press.

Davis, Deborah, and Stevan Harrell, eds. 1993. *Chinese families in the post-Mao era*. Berkeley: University of California Press.

Davis, Sarah Henning. 2008. What's not to know? A Durkheimian critique of Boyer's theory of religion. *Ethos* 36:268–81.

Davis, Susan Schaefer. 1993. Rebellious teens? A Moroccan instance. Paper presented at the annual meeting of the Middle East Studies Association, Tucson, AZ, November.

Davis, Susan Schaefer. 2009. Morocco: Adolescents in a small town. In MyAnthroLibrary, eds. C. R. Ember, M. Ember, and P. N. Peregrine. MyAnthroLibrary.com. Pearson.

Davis, William D. 1971. Societal complexity and the nature of primitive man's conception of the supernatural. Ph.D. dissertation. University of North Carolina, Chapel Hill.

Dawson, Alistair. 1992. *Ice age earth*. London: Routledge.

Dawson, J. L. M. 1967. Cultural and physiological influences upon spatial-perceptual processes in West Africa. *International Journal of Psychology* 2:115–28, 171–85.

Day, Michael. 1986. *Guide to fossil man*. 4th ed. Chicago: University of Chicago Press.

DeGreef, S., and G. Willems. 2005. Three-dimensional cranio-facial reconstruction in forensic identification: Latest progress and new tendencies in the 21st century. *Journal of Forensic Sciences* 50:12–17.

De la Puente, Manuel, et al. 2013. *Social security programs throughout the world*. Washington, DC: Social Security Administration.

De Laguna, Frederica. 1972. *Under Mount Saint Elias: The history and culture of the Yakutat Tlingit*. Washington, DC: Smithsonian Institution Press, as seen in eHRAF World Cultures. ehrafworldcultures.yale.edu. Accessed May 2000.

De Lumley, Henry. 1969. A Paleolithic camp at Nice. *Scientific American* (May):42–50.

de Menocal, Peter B. 2001. Cultural responses to climate change during the late Holocene. *Science* 292 (April 27):667–73.

de Menocal, Peter B. 2011. Climate and human evolution. *Science* 331 (February 4):540–42.

de Munck, Victor C. 2000. *Culture, self, and meaning*. Prospect Heights, IL: Waveland Press.

de Munck, Victor C., and Andrey Korotayev. 1999. Sexual equality and romantic love: A reanalysis of Rosenblatt's study on the function of romantic love. *Cross-Cultural Research* 33:265–273.

DeParle, Jason. 2012. Harder for Americans to rise from economy's lower rungs. *New York Times National*, January 5, p. A17.

De Villiers, Peter A., and Jill G. De Villiers. 1979. *Early language*. Cambridge, MA: Harvard University Press.

DeVore, Irven, and Melvin J. Konner. 1974. Infancy in hunter-gatherer life: An ethological perspective. In *Ethology and psychiatry*, ed. N. F. White. Toronto: Ontario Mental Health Foundation and University of Toronto Press.

De Waal, Frans. 2001. *The ape and the sushi master: Cultural reflections of a primatologist*. New York: Basic Books.

De Waal, Frans, and Frans Lanting. 1997. *Bonobo: The forgotten ape*. Berkeley: University of California Press.

Deacon, Terrence. 1992. Primate brains and senses. In *The Cambridge encyclopedia of human evolution*, eds. S. Jones, R. Martin, and D. Pilbeam. New York: Cambridge University Press.

Dean, Erin. 2011. Birds of one tree: Participatory forestry and land claims in Tanzania. *Human Organization* 70:300–309.

Denham, T. P., et al. 2003. Origins of agriculture at Kuk Swamp in the highlands of New Guinea. *Science* 301 (July 11):189–93.

Denny, J. Peter. 1979. The "extendedness" variable in classifier semantics: Universal features and cultural variation. In *Ethnolinguistics*, ed. M. Mathiot. The Hague: Mouton.

Dentan, Robert K. 1968. *The Semai: A nonviolent people of Malaya*. New York: Holt, Rinehart & Winston.

Devereux, Stephen. 2009. Why does famine persist in Africa? *Food security* 1:25–35.

Devillers, Charles, and Jean Chaline. 1993. *Evolution: An evolving theory*. New York: Springer Verlag.

Diament, Michelle. 2005. Diversifying their crops: Agriculture schools, focusing on job prospects, reach out to potential students from cities and suburbs. *The Chronicle of Higher Education*, May 6, pp. A32–34.

Diamond, Jared. 1989. The accidental conqueror. *Discover* (December):71–76.

Diamond, Jared. 1991. The saltshaker's curse—Physiological adaptations that helped American Blacks survive slavery may now be predisposing their descendants to hypertension. *Natural History* (October):20–27.

Diamond, Jared. 1993. Who are the Jews? *Natural History* (November):12–19.

Diamond, Jared. 1997a. *Guns, germs, and steel*, 205–207. New York: Norton.

Diamond, Jared. 1997b. Location, location, location: The first farmers. *Science* 278 (November 14):1243–44.

Diamond, Jared. 2004. The astonishing micropygmies. *Science* 306 (December 17):2047–48.

Diamond, Norma. 1975. Collectivization, kinship, and the status of women in rural China. In *Toward an anthropology of women*, ed. R. R. Reiter. New York: Monthly Review Press.

Diamond, Stanley. 1974. *In search of the primitive: A critique of civilization*. New Brunswick, NJ: Transaction Books.

Dickson, D. Bruce. 1990. *The dawn of belief*. Tucson: University of Arizona Press.

Dickson, D. Bruce, Jeffrey Olsen, P. Fred Dahm, and Mitchell S. Wachtel. 2005. Where do you come when you die? A cross-cultural test of the hypothesis that infrastructure predicts individual eschatology. *Journal of Anthropological Research* 1:53–79.

Dillehay, Thomas. 2000. *The settlement of the Americas*. New York: Basic Books.

Dincauze, Dina. 2000. *Environmental archaeology: Principles and practice*. Cambridge: Cambridge University Press.

Dirks, Robert. 1993. Starvation and famine. *Cross-Cultural Research* 27:28–69.

Dirks, Robert. 2009. Hunger and famine. In MyAnthroLibrary, eds. C. R. Ember, M. Ember, and P. N. Peregrine. MyAnthroLibrary.com. Pearson.

Divale, William T. 1974. Migration, external warfare, and matrilocal residence. *Behavior Science Research* 9:75–133.

Divale, William T. 1977. Living floor area and marital residence: A replication. *Behavior Science Research* 2:109–15.

Divale, William T., and Marvin Harris. 1976. Population, warfare, and the male supremacist complex. *American Anthropologist* 78:521–38.

Dobres, Marcia-Anne. 1998. Venus figurines. In *Oxford companion to archaeology*, ed. B. Fagan. Oxford: Oxford University Press.

Dobzhansky, Theodosius. 1962. *Mankind evolving: The evolution of the human species*. New Haven, CT: Yale University Press.

Dobzhansky, Theodosius. 1973. *Genetic diversity and human equality*. New York: Basic Books.

Donovan, James M., and H. Edwin Anderson, III. 2003. *Anthropology and law*. New York: Berghahn Books.

Dohlinow, Phyllis Jay, and Naomi Bishop. 1972. The development of motor skills and social relationships among primates through play. In *Primate patterns*, ed. Phyllis Jay Dohlinow. New York: Holt, Rinehart & Winston.

Douglas, Mary. 1975. *Implicit meanings: Essays in anthropology*. London: Routledge and Kegan Paul.

Dow, James. 1986. *The shaman's touch: Otomi Indian symbolic healing*. Salt Lake City: University of Utah Press.

Dowling, John H. 1975. Property relations and productive strategies in pastoral societies. *American Ethnologist* 2:419–26.

Doyle, G. A., and R. D. Martin, eds. 1979. *The study of prosimian behavior*. New York: Academic Press.

Doyle, Rodger. 2004. Living together: In the U.S. cohabitation is here to stay. *Scientific American* (January):28.

Doyle, Rodger. 2005. Leveling the playing field: Economic development helps women pull even with men. *Scientific American* (June):32.

Draper, Patricia. 1975. !Kung women: Contrasts in sexual egalitarianism in foraging and sedentary contexts. In *Toward an anthropology of women*, ed. R. R. Reiter. New York: Monthly Review Press.

Draper, Patricia, and Elizabeth Cashdan. 1988. Technological change and child behavior among the !Kung. *Ethnology* 27:339–65.

Dressler, William W. 1991. *Stress and adaptation in the context of culture*. Albany: State University of New York Press.

Dressler, William W. 1993. Health in the African American community: Accounting for health inequalities. *Medical Anthropology Quarterly* 7:325–45.

Dressler, William W., and Michael C. Robbins. 1975. Art styles, social stratification, and cognition: An analysis of Greek vase painting. *American Ethnologist* 2:427–34.

Dressler, William W., Kathryn S. Oths, and Clarence C. Gravlee. 2005. Race and ethnicity in public health research: models to explain health disparities. *Annual Review of Anthropology* 34:231–52.

Driscoll, Carlos A., Juliet Clutton-Brock, Andrew Kitchener, and Stephen O'Brien. 2009. The taming of the cat. *Scientific American* (June):68–75.

Driscoll, Carlos A., et al. 2007. The Near Eastern origin of cat domestication. *Science* (July 27):519–23.

Drucker, Philip. 1965. *Cultures of the north Pacific coast*. San Francisco: Chandler.

Drucker, Philip. 1967. The potlatch. In *Tribal and peasant economies*, ed. G. Dalton. Garden City, NY: Natural History Press.

Du, Shanshan. 2003. Is Buddha a couple: Gender-unitary perspectives from the Lahu of Southwest China. *Ethnology* 42:253–71.

Duane, Daniel. 2003. Turning garbage into oil. *New York Times Magazine*, December 14, p. 100.

Duarte, Cidalia, et al. 1999. The early Upper Paleolithic human skeleton from the Abrigo do Lagar Velho (Portugal) and modern human emergence in Iberia. *Proceedings of the National Academy of Sciences of the United States* 96:7604–7609.

Duhard, Jean-Pierre. 1993. Upper Paleolithic figures as a reflection of human morphology and social organization. *Antiquity* 67:83–91.

Dunbar, Robin, and Susanne Shultz. 2007. Evolution of the social brain. *Science* 317(September 7): 1344–47.

Dundes, Alan. 1965. Structural typology in North American Indian folktales. In *The study of folklore*, ed. A. Dundes. Upper Saddle River, NJ: Prentice Hall.

Dundes, Alan. 1989. *Folklore matters*. Knoxville: University of Tennessee Press.

Dundes, Alan. 2005. *Folklore: Critical concepts in literary and cultural studies*, vol. 1. London: Routledge.

Dupré, John. 2008. What genes are and why there are no genes for race. In *Revisiting race in a genomic age*, eds. B. A. Koening, S. S. J. Lee, and S. S. Richardson. New Brunswick, NJ: Rutgers University Press.

Durham, William H. 1991. *Coevolution: Genes, culture and human diversity*. Stanford, CA: Stanford University Press.

Durkheim, Émile. 1938/1895. *The rules of sociological method*. 8th ed. Trans. Sarah A. Soloway and John H. Mueller. Ed. G. E. Catlin. New York: Free Press.

Durkheim, Émile. 1961/1912. *The elementary forms of the religious life.* Trans. Joseph W. Swain. New York: Collier Books.

Durrenberger, E. Paul. 1980. Chayanov's economic analysis in anthropology. *Journal of Anthropological Research* 36:133–48.

Durrenberger, E. Paul. 2001a. Anthropology and globalization. *American Anthropologist* 103:531–35.

Durrenberger, E. Paul. 2001b. Explorations of class and consciousness in the U.S. *Journal of Anthropological Research* 57:41–60.

Durrenberger, E. Paul, and Nicola Tannenbaum. 2002. Chayanov and theory in economic anthropology. In *Theory in economic anthropology*, ed. J. Ensminger. Walnut Creek, CA: AltaMira Press.

Dutton, Denis. 2000. "But they don't have our concept of art." In *Theories of art today*, ed. N. Carroll. Madison: University of Wisconsin Press.

Dyson-Hudson, Neville. 1966. *Karimojong politics.* Oxford: Clarendon Press.

Dyson-Hudson, Rada, and Eric Alden Smith. 1978. Human territoriality: An ecological reassessment. *American Anthropologist* 80:21–41.

Ebrey, Patricia B. 2010. *The Cambridge illustrated history of China.* Cambridge: Cambridge University Press.

Eckhardt, William. 1975. Primitive militarism. *Journal of Peace Research* 12:55–62.

Eddy, Elizabeth M., and William L. Partridge, eds. 1987. *Applied anthropology in America*, 2nd ed. New York: Columbia University Press.

Edgerton, Robert B. 1966. Conceptions of psychosis in four East African societies. *American Anthropologist* 68:408–25.

Edgerton, Robert B. 1971. *The individual in cultural adaptation: A study of four East African peoples.* Berkeley: University of California Press.

Edgerton, Robert B. 1992. *Sick societies: Challenging the myth of primitive harmony.* New York: Free Press.

Edson, Gary, and David Dean. 1994. *The handbook for museums.* New York: Routledge.

Eiseley, Loren C. 1958. The dawn of evolutionary theory. In *Darwin's century: Evolution and the men who discovered it*, ed. L. C. Eiseley. Garden City, NY: Doubleday.

Eisenberg, John F. 1977. Comparative ecology and reproduction of new world monkeys. In *The biology and conservation of the Callitrichidae*, ed. Devra Kleinman. Washington, DC: Smithsonian Institution.

Eisenstadt, S. N. 1954. African age groups. *Africa* 24:100–111.

Eisner, Manuel. 2012. What causes large-scale variation in homicide rates? In *Aggression in humans and other primates: Biology, psychology, sociology*, eds. Hans-Henning Kortüm and Jürgen Heinze. Berlin; New York: Walter de Guyter.

Ekman, Paul. 1994. Strong evidence for universals in facial expressions: A reply to Russell's mistaken critique. *Psychological Bulletin* 115, no.2:268–87.

Ekman, Paul, and Dachner Keltner. 1997. Universal facial expressions of emotion: An old controversy and new findings. In *Nonverbal communication: Where nature meets culture*, eds. U. Segerstrale and P. Molnar. Mahwah, NJ: Lawrence Erlbaum.

Eldredge, Niles, and Ian Tattersall. 1982. *The myths of human evolution.* New York: Columbia University Press.

Eliot, T. S. 1963. The love song of J. Alfred Prufrock. In *Collected poems, 1909–1962.* New York: Harcourt, Brace & World.

Eller, Jack David. 2007. *Introducing anthropology of religion: Culture to the ultimate.* New York: Routledge.

Ellis, Lee. 1986. Evidence of neuroandrogenic etiology of sex roles from a combined analysis of human, nonhuman primate and nonprimate mammalian studies. *Personality and Individual Differences* 7:519–52.

Ember, Carol R. 1973. Feminine task assignment and the social behavior of boys. *Ethos* 1:424–39.

Ember, Carol R. 1974. An evaluation of alternative theories of matrilocal versus patrilocal residence. *Behavior Science Research* 9:135–49.

Ember, Carol R. 1975. Residential variation among hunter-gatherers. *Behavior Science Research* 9:135–49.

Ember, Carol R. 1977. Cross-cultural cognitive studies. *Annual Review of Anthropology* 6:33–56.

Ember, Carol R. 1978a. Men's fear of sex with women: A cross-cultural study. *Sex Roles* 4:657–78.

Ember, Carol R. 1978b. Myths about Hunter-Gatherers. *Ethnology* 17:439–48.

Ember, Carol R. 1981. A cross-cultural perspective on sex differences. In *Handbook of cross-cultural human development*, eds. R. H. Munroe, R. L. Munroe, and B. B. Whiting. New York: Garland.

Ember, Carol R. 1982. The conditions favoring religious conversion. Paper presented at the annual meeting of the Society for Cross-Cultural Research. Minneapolis, Minnesota, February.

Ember, Carol R. 1983. The relative decline in women's contribution to agriculture with intensification. *American Anthropologist* 85:285–304.

Ember, Carol R. 2007. Using the HRAF Collection of Ethnography in Conjunction with the Standard Cross-cultural Sample and the Ethnographic Atlas. *Cross-Cultural Research* 41, no. 4:396–427.

Ember, Carol R. 2009. Universal and variable patterns of gender difference. In MyAnthroLibrary, eds. C. R. Ember, M. Ember, and P. N. Peregrine. MyAnthroLibrary.com. Pearson.

Ember, Carol R., and Melvin Ember. 1972. The conditions favoring multilocal residence. *Southwestern Journal of Anthropology* 28:382–400.

Ember, Carol R., and Melvin Ember. 1984. The evolution of human female sexuality: A cross-species perspective. *Journal of Anthropological Research* 40:202–10.

Ember, Carol R., and Melvin Ember. 1992a. Resource unpredictability, mistrust, and war: A cross-cultural study. *Journal of Conflict Resolution* 36:242–62.

Ember, Carol R., and Melvin Ember. 1992b. Warfare, aggression, and resource problems: Cross-cultural codes. *Cross-Cultural Research* 26, no. 1–4: 169–226.

Ember, Carol R., and Melvin Ember. 1993. Issues in cross-cultural studies of interpersonal violence. *Violence and Victims* 8:217–33.

Ember, Carol R., and Melvin Ember. 1994. War, socialization, and interpersonal violence: A cross-cultural study. *Journal of Conflict Resolution* 38:620–46.

Ember, Carol R., and Melvin Ember. 1997. Violence in the ethnographic record: Results of cross-cultural research on war and aggression. In *Troubled times*, eds. D. Martin and D. Frayer. Langhorn, PA: Gordon and Breach.

Ember, Carol R., and Melvin Ember. 2001. Father absence and male aggression: A re-examination of the comparative evidence. *Ethos* 29:296–314.

Ember, Carol R., and Melvin Ember. 2005. Explaining corporal punishment of children: A cross-cultural study. *American Anthropologist* 107:609–19.

Ember, Carol R., and Melvin Ember. 2009. *Cross-cultural research methods.* 2nd ed. Lanham, AltaMira Press.

Ember, Carol R., and Melvin Ember. 2010. Explaining male initiation ceremonies: New cross-cultural tests and a catalytic model. *Journal of Cross-Cultural Psychology* 41:605–16.

Ember, Carol R., and David Levinson. 1991. The substantive contributions of worldwide cross-cultural studies using secondary data. *Behavior Science Research* (Special issue, Cross-cultural and comparative research: Theory and method), 25:79–140.

Ember, Carol R., Teferi Abate Adem, and Ian Skoggard. 2013. Risk, uncertainty, and violence in eastern Africa: A cross-regional comparison. *Human Nature* 24:33–58.

Ember, Carol R., Melvin Ember, and Burton Pasternak. 1974. On the development of unilineal descent. *Journal of Anthropological Research* 30:69–94.

Ember, Carol R., Melvin Ember, and Bruce Russett. 1992. Peace between participatory polities: A cross-cultural test of the "democracies rarely fight each other" hypothesis. *World Politics* 44:573–99.

Ember, Carol R., Melvin Ember, Andrey Korotayev, and Victor de Munck. 2005. Valuing thinness or fatness in women: Reevaluating the effect of resource scarcity. *Evolution and Human Behavior* 26:257–70.

Ember, Carol R., Teferi Abate Adem, and Ian Skoggard. 2013. Risk, uncertainty, and violence in Eastern Africa: A regional comparison. *Human Nature* 24:33–58.

Ember, Melvin. 1959. The nonunilinear descent groups of Samoa. *American Anthropologist* 61:573–77.

Ember, Melvin. 1963. The relationship between economic and political development in nonindustrialized societies. *Ethnology* 2:228–48.

Ember, Melvin. 1967. The emergence of neolocal residence. *Transactions of the New York Academy of Sciences* 30:291–302.

Ember, Melvin. 1970. Taxonomy in comparative studies. In *A handbook of method in cultural anthropology*, eds. R. Naroll and R. Cohen. Garden City, NY: Natural History Press.

Ember, Melvin. 1973. An archaelogical indicator of matrilocal versus patrilocal residence. *American Antiquity* 38:177–82.

Ember, Melvin. 1974a. The conditions that may favor avunculocal residence. *Behavior Science Research* 9:203–209.

Ember, Melvin. 1974b. Warfare, sex ratio, and polygyny. *Ethnology* 13:197–206.

Ember, Melvin. 1975. On the origin and extension of the incest taboo. *Behavior Science Research* 10:249–81.

Ember, Melvin. 1978. Size of color lexicon: Interaction of cultural and biological factors. *American Anthropologist* 80:364–67.

Ember, Melvin. 1982. Statistical evidence for an ecological explanation of warfare. *American Anthropologist* 84:645–49.

Ember, Melvin. 1983. The emergence of neolocal residence. In *Marriage, family, and kinship: Comparative studies of social organization*, eds. Melvin Ember and Carol R. Ember. New Haven, CT: HRAF Press.

Ember, Melvin. 1984–1985. Alternative predictors of polygyny. *Behavior Science Research* 19:1–23.

Ember, Melvin. 1985. Evidence and science in ethnography: Reflections on the Freeman-Mead controversy. *American Anthropologist* 87:906–909.

Ember, Melvin, and Carol R. Ember. 1971. The conditions favoring matrilocal versus patrilocal residence. *American Anthropologist* 73:571–94.

Ember, Melvin, and Carol R. Ember. 1979. Male-female bonding: A cross-species study of mammals and birds. *Behavior Science Research* 14:37–56.

Ember, Melvin, and Carol R. Ember. 1983. *Marriage, family, and kinship: Comparative studies of social organization.* New Haven, CT: HRAF Press.

Ember, Melvin, and Carol R. Ember. 1992. Cross-cultural studies of war and peace: Recent achievements and future possibilities. In *Studying war*, eds. S. P. Reyna and R. E. Downs. New York: Gordon and Breach.

Ember, Melvin, and Carol R. Ember. 1999. Cross-language predictors of consonant-vowel syllables. *American Anthropologist* 101:730–42.

Ember, Melvin, and Carol R. Ember, eds. 2002. *Encyclopedia of urban cultures: Cities and cultures around the world*, 4 vols. Danbury, CT: Grolier/Scholastic.

Ember, Melvin, and Carol R. Ember. 2004. Toward the evolution of a more civil world. *Social Evolution & History* 3:137–61.

Ember, Melvin, Carol R. Ember, and Bobbi S. Low. 2007. Comparing explanations of polygyny. *Cross-Cultural Research* 41:428–40.

Ember, Melvin, Carol R. Ember, and Bruce Russett. 1997. Inequality and democracy in the anthropological record. In *Inequality, democracy, and economic development*, ed. M. I. Midlarsky. Cambridge: Cambridge University Press.

Ember, Melvin, Carol R. Ember, and Ian Skoggard, eds. 2005. In *Encyclopedia of diasporas: Immigrant and refugee cultures around the world*, 2 vols. New York: Kluwer Academic/Plenum.

Ensminger, Jean. 1997. Transaction costs and Islam: Explaining conversion in Africa. *Journal of Institutional and Theoretical Economics* 153:4–29.

Ensminger, Jean. 2002. Experimental economics: A powerful new method for theory testing in anthropology. In *Theory in economic anthropology*, ed. J. Ensminger. Walnut Creek, CA: Altamira Press.

Ensor, Bradley E. 2003. Kinship and marriage among the Omaha, 1886–1902. *Ethnology* 42:1–14.

Epple, Suzanne. 2006. Women's life in a society with age organizations: The Bashad of Southern Ethiopia. In *Proceedings of the XVth International Conference on Ethiopian Studies*, 66–74. Wiesbaden: Otto Harrassowitz Verlag.

Epstein, Cynthia Fuchs. 1988. *Deceptive distinctions: Sex, gender, and the social order.* New York: Russell Sage Foundation.

Erchak, Gerald M. 2009. Family violence. In MyAnthroLibrary, eds. C. R. Ember, M. Ember, and P. N. Peregrine. MyAnthroLibrary.com. Pearson.

Ericksen, Karen Paige. 1989. Male and female age organizations and secret societies in Africa. *Behavior Science Research* 23:234–64.

Ericksen, Karen Paige, and Heather Horton. 1992. "Blood feuds": Cross-cultural variations in kin group vengeance. *Behavior Science Research* 26:57–85.

Erickson, Clark. 1988. Raised field agriculture in the Lake Titicaca basin. *Expedition* 30, no. 1:8–16.

Erickson, Clark. 1989. Raised fields and sustainable agriculture in the Lake Titicaca basin of Peru. In *Fragile lands of Latin America*, ed. J. Browder. Boulder: Westview.

Erickson, Clark. 1998. Applied archaeology and rural development. In *Crossing currents: Continuity and change in Latin America*, eds. M. Whiteford and S. Whiteford. Upper Saddle River, NJ: Prentice Hall.

Erickson, Edwin. 1968. Self-assertion, sex role, and vocal rasp. In *Folk song style and culture*, ed. A. Lomax. Washington, DC: Transaction Publishers.

Erlandson, Jon and Todd Braje. 2012. Foundations for the Far West: Paleoindian cultures on the western fringe of North America. In *Oxford handbook of North American archaeology*, ed. T. Pauketat. Oxford: Oxford University Press.

Errington, J. Joseph. 1985. On the nature of the sociolinguistic sign: Describing the Javanese speech levels. In *Semiotic mediation*, eds. E. Mertz and R. J. Parmentier. Orlando, FL: Academic Press.

Ervin, Alexander M. 1987. Styles and strategies of leadership during the Alaskan Native land claims movement: 1959–71. *Anthropologica* 29:21–38.

Eswaran, Vinayak. 2002. A diffusion wave out of Africa. *Current Anthropology* 43:749–74.

Etienne, Mona, and Eleanor Leacock, eds. 1980. *Women and colonization: Anthropological perspectives*. New York: Praeger.

Etienne, Robert. 1992. *Pompeii: The day a city died*. New York: Abrams.

Etkin, Nina L., and Paul J. Ross. 1997. Malaria, medicine, and meals: A biobehavioral perspective. In *The anthropology of medicine*, eds. L. Romanucci-Ross, D. E. Moerman, and L. R. Tancredi. Westport, CT: Bergin & Garvey.

Euripides. 1937. The Trojan women. In *Three Greek plays*, Trans. E. Hamilton, 52. New York: Norton.

Evans-Pritchard, E. E. 1940. The Nuer of the southern Sudan. In *African political systems*, eds. M. Fortes and E. E. Evans-Pritchard. New York: Oxford University Press.

Evans-Pritchard, E. E. 1970. Sexual inversion among the Azande. *American Anthropologist* 72:1428–34.

Evans-Pritchard, E. E. 1979. Witchcraft explains unfortunate events. In *Reader in comparative religion*, 3rd ed., eds. W. A. Lessa and E. Z. Vogt. New York: Harper & Row.

Eveleth, Phyllis B., and James M. Tanner. 1990. *Worldwide variation in human growth*. 2nd ed. Cambridge: Cambridge University Press.

Everett, Margaret. 2007. The "I" in gene: Divided property, fragmented personhood, and the making of a genetic privacy law. *American Ethnologist* 34, no. 2:375–86.

Eversole, Robyn. 2005. "Direct to the poor" revisited: Migrant remittances and development assistance. In *Migration and economy: Global and local dynamics*, ed. L. Trager. Walnut Creek, CA: Altamira Press.

Fagan, Brian M. 1972. *In the beginning*. Boston: Little, Brown.

Fagan, Brian M. 1989. *People of the earth: An introduction to world prehistory*. 6th ed. Glenview, IL: Scott, Foresman.

Fagan, Brian M. 1991. *Ancient North America: The archaeology of a continent*. London: Thames and Hudson.

Falk, Dean. 1987. Hominid paleoneurology. *Annual Review of Anthropology* 16:13–30.

Falk, Dean. 1988. Enlarged occipital/marginal sinuses and emissary foramina: Their significance in hominid evolution. In *Evolutionary history of the "robust" australopithecines*, ed. F. E. Grine. New York: Aldine.

Falk, Dean, et al. 2005. The brain of LBI, *Homo floresiensis*. *Science* 308 (April 8):242–45.

FAO. n.d. Hunger. http://www.fao.org (accessed May 20, 2013).

Farley, Reynolds. 1996. *The new American reality: Who we are, how we got here, where we are going*. New York: Russell Sage Foundation.

Farmer, Paul. 1997. Ethnography, social analysis, and the prevention of sexually transmitted HIV infection among poor women in Haiti. In *The anthropology of infectious disease*, eds. M. C. Inhorn and P. J. Brown. Amsterdam: Gordon and Breach.

Farmer, Paul, Margaret Connors, and Janie Simmons. 2011. *Women, poverty and AIDS: Sex, drugs and structural violence*. 2nded. Monroe, ME: Common Courage Press.

Featherman, David L., and Robert M. Hauser. 1978. *Opportunity and change*. New York: Academic Press.

Feder, Kenneth. 2000. *Past in perspective*. 2nd ed. Mountain View, CA: Mayfield Publishing Company.

Fedigan, Linda Marie. 1982. *Primate paradigms: Sex roles and social bonds*. Montreal: Eden Press.

Fedoroff, Nina. 2003. Prehistoric GM corn. *Science* 302 (November 14):1158–59.

Fehr, Ernst, and Urs Fischbacher. 2003. The nature of human altruism. *Nature* (October 23):785–91.

Feibel, Craig S., and Francis H. Brown. 1993. Microstratigraphy and paleoenvironments. In *The Nariokotome* Homo erectus *skeleton*, eds. A. Walker and R. Leakey. Cambridge, MA: Harvard University Press.

Feinman, Gary M. 2011. Size, complexity, and organizational variation: A comparative approach. *Cross-Cultural Research* 45:37–58. (Special issue in honor of Melvin Ember. Part I, ed. Peter N. Peregrine).

Feinman, Gary M., and Jill Neitzel. 1984. Too many types: An overview of sedentary prestate societies in the Americas. In *Advances in archaeological method and theory*, vol. 7, ed. M. B. Schiffer. Orlando, FL: Academic Press.

Feinman, Gary M., Stephen A. Kowalewski, Laura Finsten, Richard E. Blanton, and Linda Nicholas. 1985. Long-term demographic change: A perspective from the Valley of Oaxaca, Mexico. *Journal of Field Archaeology* 12:333–62.

Feldman, Douglas A., and Thomas M. Johnson. 1986. Introduction. In *The social dimensions of AIDS*, eds. D. A. Feldman and T. M. Johnson. New York: Praeger.

Ferguson, R. Brian, and Neil L. Whitehead. 1992. Violent edge of empire. In *War in the tribal zone*, eds. R. B. Ferguson and N. Whitehead. Santa Fe, NM: School of American Research Press.

Ferguson, Niall. 2004. *Colossus: The price of America's empire*. New York: Penguin Press.

Fernea, Elizabeth, and Robert Fernea, as reported in M. Kay Martin and Barbara Voorhies, 1975. *Female of the species*. New York: Columbia University Press.

Ferraro, Gary P. 2002. *The cultural dimension of international business*. 4th ed. Upper Saddle River, NJ: Prentice Hall.

Fessler, Daniel M. T. 2002. Windfall and socially distributed willpower: The psychocultural dynamics of rotating savings and credit associations in a Bengkulu village. *Ethos* 30:25–48.

Finley, M. I. 1983. *Politics in the ancient world*. Cambridge: Cambridge University Press.

Finnis, Elizabeth. 2006. Why grow cash crops? Subsistence farming and crop commercialization in the Kolli Hills, South India. *American Anthropologist* 108:363–69.

Firth, Raymond. 1957. *We, the Tikopia*. Boston: Beacon Press.

Firth, Raymond. 1959. *Social change in Tikopia*. New York: Macmillan.

Firth, Raymond. 1970. *Rank and religion in Tikopia*. Boston: Beacon Press.

Fischer, John L. 1958. Social influences on the choice of a linguistic variant. *Word* 14:47–56.

Fischer, John L. 1961. Art styles as cultural cognitive maps. *American Anthropologist* 63:80–83.

Fish, Paul R. 1981. Beyond tools: Middle Paleolithic debitage analysis and cultural inference. *Journal of Anthropological Research* 37:374–86.

Fisher, Julie. 1996. Grassroots organizations and grassroots support organizations: Patterns of interaction. In *Transforming societies, transforming anthropology*, ed. E. F. Moran. Ann Arbor: University of Michigan Press.

Fisher, William F. 1997. Doing good? The politics and antipolitics of NGO practices. *Annual Review of Anthropology* 26:439–64.

Fisher, William H. 1994. Megadevelopment, environmentalism, and resistance: The institutional context of Kayapo indigenous politics in central Brazil. *Human Organization* 53:220–32.

Flannery, Kent V. 1965. The ecology of early food production in Mesopotamia. *Science* 147 (March 12):1247–56.

Flannery, Kent V. 1971. The origins and ecological effects of early domestication in Iran and the Near East. In *Prehistoric agriculture*, ed. S. Struever. Garden City, NY: Natural History Press.

Flannery, Kent V. 1972. The cultural evolution of civilizations. *Annual Review of Ecology and Systematics* 3:399–426.

Flannery, Kent V. 1973a. The origins of agriculture. *Annual Review of Anthropology* 2:271–310.

Flannery, Kent V. 1973b. The origins of the village as a settlement type in Mesoamerica and the Near East: A comparative study. In *Territoriality and proxemics*, ed. R. Tringham. Andover, MA: Warner.

Flannery, Kent V., ed. 1986. *Guila Naquitz: Archaic foraging and early agriculture in Oaxaca, Mexico*. Orlando, FL: Academic Press.

Fleagle, John G. 1994. Anthropoid origins. In *Integrative paths to the past*, eds. R. Corruccini and R. Ciochon. Upper Saddle River, NJ: Prentice Hall.

Fleagle, John G. 1999. *Primate adaptation and evolution*. 2nd ed. San Diego: Academic Press.

Fleagle, John G., and Richard F. Kay. 1983. New interpretations of the phyletic position of Oligocene hominoids. In *New interpretations of ape and human ancestry*, eds. R. Ciochon and R. Corruccini. New York: Plenum.

Fleagle, John G., and Richard F. Kay. 1985. The paleobiology of catarrhines. In *Ancestors*, ed. E. Delson. New York: Alan R. Liss.

Fleagle, John G., and Richard F. Kay. 1987. The phyletic position of the *Parapithecidae*. *Journal of Human Evolution* 16:483–531.

Fluehr-Lobban, Carolyn. 2006. *Race and racism: An introduction*. Lanham: AltaMira Press.

Fluehr-Lobban, Carolyn. 2008. Collaborative anthropology as twenty-first century ethical anthropology. *Collaborative Anthropologies* 1:175–82.

Foner, Nancy. 2011. The social construction of race in two immigrant eras. In *Race in an era of change: A reader*, eds. H. Dalmage and B. Katz Rothman. New York: Oxford University Press.

Ford, Clellan S. 1941. *Smoke from their fires*. New Haven, CT: Yale University Press.

Ford, Clellan S., and Frank A. Beach. 1951. *Patterns of sexual behavior*. New York: Harper.

Forrest, Barbara. 2001. The wedge at work. In *Intelligent design creationism and its critics*, ed. R. Pennock. Boston: MIT Press.

Fortes, Meyer. 1949. *The web of kinship among the Tallensi*. New York: Oxford University Press.

Fossey, Dian. 1983. *Gorillas in the mist*. Boston: Houghton Mifflin.

Foster, Brian L. 1974. Ethnicity and commerce. *American Ethnologist* 1:437–47.

Foster, George M. 1962. *Traditional cultures and the impact of technological change*. New York: Harper & Row.

Foster, George M. 1969. *Applied anthropology*. Boston: Little, Brown.

Foster, George M. 1994. *Hippocrates' Latin American legacy: Humoral medicine in the New World*. Amsterdam: Gordon and Breach.

Foucault, Michel. 1970. *The order of things: An archaeology of the human sciences*. New York: Random House.

Fowler, Melvin L. 1975. A pre-Columbian urban center on the Mississippi. *Scientific American* (August):92–101.

Frake, Charles O. 1960. The Eastern Subanun of Mindanao. In *Social structure in Southeast Asia*, ed. G. P. Murdock. Chicago: Quadrangle.

Franciscus, Robert G., and Erik Trinkaus. 1988. Nasal morphology and the emergence of *Homo erectus*. *American Journal of Physical Anthropology* 75:517–27.

Frank, André Gunder. 1967. *Capitalism and underdevelopment in Latin America: Historical studies of Chile and Brazil*. New York: Monthly Review Press.

Fratkin, Elliot. 2008. Pastures lost: The decline of mobile pastoralism among Maasai and Rendille in Kenya, East Africa. In *Economies and the transformation of landscape*, eds. Lisa Cliggett and Christopher A. Pool. Lanham: Altamira Press.

Frayer, David W. 1981. Body size, weapon use, and natural selection in the European Upper Paleolithic and Mesolithic. *American Anthropologist* 83:57–73.

Frayer, David W., and Milford H. Wolpoff. 1985. Sexual dimorphism. *Annual Review of Anthropology* 14:429–73.

Frayer, David W., M. Wolpoff, A. Thorne, F. Smith, and G. Pope. 1993. Theories of modern human origins: The paleontological test. *American Anthropologist* 95:24–27.

Frayser, Suzanne G. 1985. *Varieties of sexual experience.* New Haven, CT: HRAF Press.

Freedman, Daniel G. 1979. Ethnic differences in babies. *Human Nature* (January):36–43.

Freeman, Derek. 1983. *Margaret Mead and Samoa: The making and unmaking of an anthropological myth.* Cambridge, MA: Harvard University Press.

Freeman, J. D. 1961. On the concept of the kindred. *Journal of the Royal Anthropological Institute* 91:192–220.

Freeman, Leslie G. 1994. Torralba and Ambrona: A review of discoveries. In *Integrative paths to the past*, eds. R. Corruccini and R. Ciochon. Upper Saddle River, NJ: Prentice Hall.

Freud, Sigmund. 1943/1917. *A general introduction to psychoanalysis.* Garden City, NY: Garden City Publishing. (Originally published in German)

Freud, Sigmund. 1967/1939. *Moses and monotheism.* Trans. Katherine Jones. New York: Vintage Books.

Freud, Sigmund. 2007/1950. The return of totemism in childhood. In *Ritual and belief: Readings in the anthropology of religion*, 3rd ed., ed. David Hicks, 7–12. Lanham, MD: AltaMira Press.

Freyman, R. 1987. The first technology. *Scientific American* (April):112.

Fried, Morton H. 1967. *The evolution of political society: An essay in political anthropology.* New York: Random House.

Friedl, Ernestine. 1962. *Vasilika: A village in modern Greece.* New York: Holt, Rinehart & Winston.

Friedman, Jeffrey M. 2003. A war on obesity, not the obese. *Science* 299 (February 7):856–58.

Friedman, Saul S. 1980. Holocaust. In *Academic American [now Grolier] encyclopedia*, vol. 10. Princeton, NJ: Areté.

Friedrich, Paul. 1970. *Proto-Indo-European trees: The arboreal system of a prehistoric people.* Chicago: University of Chicago Press.

Friedrich, Paul. 1986. *The language parallax.* Austin: University of Texas Press.

Frisancho, A. Roberto, and Lawrence P. Greksa. 1989. Development responses in the acquisition of functional adaptation to high altitude. In *Human population biology*, eds. M. Little and J. Haas. New York: Oxford University Press.

Frisch, Rose E. 1980. Fatness, puberty, and fertility. *Natural History* (October):16–27.

Fromm, Erich. 1950. *Psychoanalysis and religion.* New Haven, CT: Yale University Press.

Frost, Robert. 1915. The death of the hired hand. In *North of Boston.* New York: Henry Holt.

Fry, Douglas P. 2006. *The human potential for peace: An anthropological challenge to assumptions about war and violence.* New York: Oxford University Press.

Fry, Douglas P., and Kaj Björkqvist, eds. 1997. *Cultural variation in conflict resolution: Alternatives to violence.* Mahwah, NJ: Lawrence Erlbaum Associates.

Fuentes, A., M. A. Wyczalkowski, and K. MacKinnon. 2010. Nich construction through cooperation: A nonlinear dynamics contribution to modeling facets of the evolutionary history of the genus *Homo. Current Anthropology* 51:435–44.

Futuyma, Douglas. 1982. *Science on trial.* New York: Pantheon.

Gabunia, Leo, et al. 2000. Earliest Pleistocene hominid cranial remains from Dmanisi, Republic of Georgia: Taxonomy, geological setting, and age. *Science* 288 (May 12):1019–25.

Gaiha, Raghav, Kenneth Hill, Ganesh Thapa, and Varsha Kulkarni. 2013. Have natural disasters become deadlier? Brooks World Poverty Institute Working Paper No. 181. Available through the Social Science Research Network: http://ssrn.com/abstract=2209714 or http://dx.doi.org/10.2139/ssrn.2209714(accessed May 31, 2013).

Gaines, Atwood D., and Robbie David-Floyd. 2004. Biomedicine. In *Encyclopedia of medical anthropology: Health and illness in the world's cultures*, eds. Carol R. Ember and Melvin Ember. New York: Kluwer Academic/Plenum Publishers.

Gal, Susan. 1988. The political economy of code choice. In *Codeswitching*, ed. M. Heller. Berlin: Mouton de Gruyter.

Galdikas, Biruté M. F. 1979. Orangutan adaptation at Tanjung Puting Reserve: Mating and ecology. In *The great apes*, eds. D. Hamburg and E. McCown. Menlo Park, CA: Benjamin/Cummings.

Gardner, Beatrice T., and R. Allen Gardner. 1980. Two comparative psychologists look at language acquisition. In *Children's language*, vol. 2, ed. K. Nelson. New York: Halsted Press.

Gardner, R. Allen, and Beatrice T. Gardner. 1969. Teaching sign language to a chimpanzee. *Science* 165 (August 15):664–72.

Garn, Stanley M. 1971. *Human races.* 3rd ed. Springfield, IL: Charles C Thomas.

Gartner, Rosemary. 2009. Crime: Variations across cultures and nations. In MyAnthroLibrary, eds. C. R. Ember, M. Ember, and P. N. Peregrine. MyAnthroLibrary.com. Pearson.

Gat, Azar. 1999. The pattern of fighting in simple, small-scale, prestate societies. *Journal of Anthropological Research* 55:563–83.

Gat, Azar. 2006. *War in human civilization.* Oxford: Oxford University Press.

Gaulin, Steven J. C., and James S. Boster. 1990. Dowry as female competition. *American Anthropologist* 92:994–1005.

Gay, Kathlyn. 1986. *Ergonomics: Making products and places fit people.* Hillside, New Jersey: Enslow.

Gebo, Daniel. 2002. Apidiformes: Phylogeny and adaptation. In *The primate fossil record*, ed. W. C. Hartwig, 21–44. Cambridge: Cambridge University Press.

Geertz, Clifford. 1960. *The religion of Java.* New York: Free Press.

Geertz, Clifford. 1966. Religion as a cultural system. In *Anthropological approaches to the study of religion*, ed. M. Banton. New York: Praeger.

Geertz, Clifford. 1973a. Deep play: Notes on the Balinese cockfight. In *The interpretation of cultures*, ed. C. Geertz. New York: Basic Books.

Geertz, Clifford. 1973b. Thick description: Toward an interpretative theory of culture. In *The interpretation of cultures*, ed. C. Geertz. New York: Basic Books.

Geertz, Clifford. 1984. "From the native's point of view": On the nature of anthropological understanding. In *Culture theory*, eds. R. A. Shweder and R. A. LeVine. New York: Cambridge University Press.

Geiger, H. Jack. 2003. Racial and ethnic disparities in diagnosis and treatment: A review of the evidence and a consideration of causes. In *Unequal treatment: Confronting racial and ethnic disparities in health care*, eds. B. D. Smedley, A. Y. Stith, and A. R. Nelson. Washington, DC: National Academy Press.

Gelfand, Michele J., et al. 2011. Differences between tight and loose cultures: A 33-nation study. *Science* 123 (May 27):1100–1104.

Gelles, Richard J., and Murray A. Straus. 1988. *Intimate violence.* New York: Simon & Schuster.

Gentner, W., and H. J. Lippolt. 1963. The potassium-argon dating of upper tertiary and Pleistocene deposits. In *Science in archaeology*, eds. D. Brothwell and E. Higgs. New York: Basic Books.

Gero, Joan M., and Margaret W. Conkey, eds. 1991. *Engendering archaeology: An introduction to women and prehistory.* Oxford: Blackwell.

Gesler, W. 1991. *The cultural geography of health care.* Pittsburgh, PA: University of Pittsburgh Press.

Gibbons, Ann. 1993. Warring over women. *Science* 261 (August 20):987–88.

Gibbons, Ann. 1995. First Americans: Not mammoth hunters, but forest dwellers? *Science* 268 (April 19):346–47.

Gibbons, Ann. 2001. The riddle of co-existence. *Science* 291 (March 2):1725–29.

Gibbons, Ann. 2002. One scientist's quest for the origin of our species. *Science* 298 (November 29):1708–11.

Gibbons, Ann. 2003. Oldest members of *Homo sapiens* discovered in Africa. *Science* 300 (June 13):1641.

Gibbons, Ann. 2008. The birth of childhood. *Science* 322 (November 14):1040–43.

Gibbons, Ann. 2011. A new view of the birth of *Homo sapiens. Science* 311 (January 28):392–94.

Gibbons, Ann. 2012. A crystal-clear view of an extinct girl's genome. *Science* 337 (August 31):1028–29.

Gibbs, James L., Jr. 1965. The Kpelle of Liberia. In *Peoples of Africa*, ed. J. L. Gibbs, Jr. New York: Holt, Rinehart & Winston.

Gibson, Kathleen R., and Stephen Jessee. 1999. Language evolution and expansions of multiple neurological processing areas. In *The origins of language*, ed. B. J. King, 189–227. Santa Fe, NM: School of American Research Press.

Gibson, Kyle. 2009. Differential parental investment in families with both adopted and genetic children. *Evolution and Human Behavior* 30:184–89.

Gilbert, M. Thomas P., et al. 2008. DNA from pre-Clovis human coprolites in Oregon, North America. *Science* 320 (May 9):786–89.

Gill, J. L., J. W. Williams, S. T. Jackson, K. B. Lininger, and G. S. Swanson. 2009. Pleistocene megafaunal collapse, novel plant communities, and enhanced fire regimes in North America. *Science* 326 (November 20): 1100–1103.

Gilligan, Carol. 1982. *In a different voice: Psychological theory and women's development.* Cambridge, MA: Harvard University Press.

Gilligan, Carol, and Jane Attanucci. 1988. Two moral orientations. In *Mapping the moral domain*, eds. C. Gilligan, J. V. Ward, and J. M. Taylor. Cambridge, MA: Harvard University Press.

Gilliland, Mary Kay. 1995. Nationalism and ethnogenesis in the former Yugoslavia. In *Ethnic identity: Creation, conflict, and accommodation*, 3rd ed., eds. L. Romanucci-Ross and G. A. De Vos. Walnut Creek, CA: Alta Mira Press.

Gilman, Antonio. 1990. The development of social stratification in Bronze Age Europe. *Current Anthropology* 22:1–23.

Gimbutas, Marija. 1974. An archaeologist's view of PIE* in 1975. *Journal of Indo-European Studies* 2:289–307.

Gingerich, P. D. 1986. *Pleisiadipis* and the delineation of the order primates. In *Major topics in primate evolution*, eds. B. Wood, L. Martin, and P. Andrews. Cambridge: Cambridge University Press.

Gladwin, Christina H. 1980. A theory of real-life choice: Applications to agricultural decisions. In *Agricultural decision making*, ed. P. F. Barlett. New York: Academic Press.

Gladwin, Thomas, and Seymour B. Sarason. 1953. *Truk: Man in paradise.* New York: Wenner-Gren Foundation for Anthropological Research.

Gleitman, Lila R., and Eric Wanner. 1982. Language acquisition: The state of the state of the art. In *Language acquisition*, eds. E. Wanner and L. R. Gleitman. Cambridge: Cambridge University Press.

Glick Schiller, Nina. 2004. Long-distance nationalism. In *Encyclopedia of diasporas: Immigrant and refugee cultures around the world*, vol. 1, eds. M. Ember, C. R. Ember, and I. Skoggard. New York: Springer.

Goddard, Michael B. 2004. Women in Papua New Guinea village courts. State, society and governance discussion paper. Research School of Pacific and Asian Studies, Australian National University, Acton, Australia.

Godoy, Ricardo, et al. 2004. Patience in a foraging-horticultural society: A test of competing hypotheses. *Journal of Anthropological Research* 60:179–202.

Goebel, Ted, Michael Waters, and Dennis O'Rourke. 2008. The Late Pleistocene dispersal of modern humans in the Americas. *Science* 319 (March 14):1479–1502.

Golden, Frederic, Michael Lemonick, and Dick Thompson. 2000. The race is over. *Time* (July 3):18–23.

Goldizen, Anne Wilson. 1987. Tamarins and marmosets: Communal care of offspring. In *Primate societies*, eds. B. B. Smuts, D. L. Cheney, R. M. Seyfarth, and Richard W. Wrangham. Chicago: University of Chicago Press.

Goldmann, Kjell, Ulf Hannerz, and Charles Westin. 2000. Introduction: Nationalism and internationalism in the post-cold war era. In *Nationalism and internationalism in the post-cold war era*, eds. G. U. Hannerz and C. Westin. London: Routledge.

Goldschmidt, Walter. 1999. Dynamics and status in America. *Anthropology Newsletter* 40, no. 5:62, 64.

Goldstein, Donna. 1998. Nothing bad intended: Child discipline, punishment, and survival in a shantytown in Rio de Janeiro. In *Small wars: The cultural politics of childhood*, eds. N. Scheper-Hughes and C. Sargeant. Berkeley: University of California-Berkeley Press.

Goldstein, Joshua S. 2001. *War and gender: How gender shapes the war system and vice versa.* New York: Cambridge University Press.

Goldstein, Joshua S. 2004. War and gender. In *Encyclopedia of sex and gender: Men and women in the world's cultures*, vol. 1, eds. C. R. Ember and M. Ember. New York: Kluwer Academic/Plenum Publishers.

Goldstein, Joshua S. 2011. *Winning the war on war: The decline of armed conflict worldwide*. New York: Dutton.

Goldstein, Melvyn C. 1971. Stratification, polyandry, and family structure in central Tibet. *Southwestern Journal of Anthropology* 27:65–74.

Goldstein, Melvyn C. 1987. When brothers share a wife. *Natural History* (March): 39–48.

Goodall, Jane. 1963. My life among wild chimpanzees. *National Geographic* (August):272–308.

Goode, William J. 1970. *World revolution and family patterns*. New York: Free Press.

Goode, William J. 1982. *The family*. 2nd ed. Upper Saddle River, NJ: Prentice Hall.

Goodenough, Ward H. 1951. *Property, kin, and community on Truk*. New Haven, CT: Yale University Press.

Goodman, Alan H., and George J. Armelagos. 1985. Disease and death at Dr. Dickson's Mounds. *Natural History* (September):12–19.

Goodman, Alan H., and Thomas L. Leatherman, eds. 1998. *Building a new biocultural synthesis: Political-economic perspectives on human biology*. Ann Arbor: University of Michigan Press.

Goodman, Alan H., John Lallo, George J. Armelagos, and Jerome C. Rose. 1984. Health changes at Dickson Mounds, Illinois (A.D. 950–1300). In *Paleopathology at the origins of agriculture*, eds. M. N. Cohen and G. J. Armelagos. Orlando, FL: Academic Press.

Goodman, Madeleine J., P. Bion Griffin, Agnes A. Estioko-Griffin, and John S. Grove. 1985. The compatibility of hunting and mothering among the Agta hunter-gatherers of the Philippines. *Sex Roles* 12:1199–209.

Goodman, Morris. 1992. Reconstructing human evolution from proteins. In *The Cambridge encyclopedia of human evolution*, eds. S. Jones, R. Martin, and D. Pilbeam. New York: Cambridge University Press.

Goodrich, L. Carrington. 1959. *A short history of the Chinese people*. 3rd ed. New York: Harper & Row.

Goody, Jack. 1970. Cousin terms. *Southwestern Journal of Anthropology* 26:125–42.

Goody, Jack. 1973. Bridewealth and dowry in Africa and Eurasia. In *Bridewealth and dowry*, eds. J. Goody and S. H. Tambiah. Cambridge: Cambridge University Press.

Gordon, C. G., and K. E. Friedl. 1994. Anthropometry in the U.S. armed forces. In *Anthropometry: The individual and the population*, eds. S. J. Ulijaszek and C. G. N. Mascie-Taylor. Cambridge: Cambridge University Press.

Gore, Rick. 2002. The first pioneer? *National Geographic* 202 (August).

Goren-Inbar, Naama, et al. 2004. Evidence of hominid control of fire at Gesher Benot Ya'aqov, Israel. *Science* 304 (April 30):725–27.

Gorman, Chester. 1970. The Hoabinhian and after: Subsistence patterns in Southeast Asia during the Late Pleistocene and early recent periods. *World Archaeology* 2:315–19.

Gossen, Gary H. 1979. Temporal and spatial equivalents in Chamula ritual symbolism. In *Reader in comparative religion*, 4th ed., eds. W. A. Lessa and E. Z. Vogt. New York: Harper & Row.

Gough, Kathleen. 1959. The Nayars and the definition of marriage. *Journal of the Royal Anthropological Institute* 89:23–34.

Gould, Richard A. 1969. *Yiwara: Foragers of the Australian desert*. New York: Scribner's.

Gowlett, John A. J. 2008. Deep roots of kin: Developing the evolutionary perspective from prehistory. In *Early human kinship: From sex to social reproduction*, eds. N. Allen, H. Callan, R. Dunbar, and W. James. Oxford: Blackwell.

Graber, Robert, eds. 2004. Special issue. The future state of the world: An anthropological symposium. *Cross-Cultural Research* 38:95–207.

Graburn, Nelson H. 1969. *Eskimos without igloos*. Boston: Little, Brown.

Graham, Susan Brandt. 1979. Biology and human social behavior: A response to van den Berghe and Barash. *American Anthropologist* 81:357–60.

Grant, Bruce S. 2002. Sour grapes of wrath. *Science* 297 (August 9):940–41.

Grant, Peter R. 1991. Natural selection and Darwin's finches. *Scientific American* (October):82–87.

Grant, Peter R., and Rosemary Grant. 2002. Unpredictable evolution in a 30-year study of Darwin's finches. *Science* 296 (April 26):707–11.

Gravlee, Clarence C., H. R. Bernard, and W. R. Leonard. 2003. Heredity, environment, and cranial form: A reanalysis of Boas's immigrant data. *American Anthropologist* 105:125–38.

Gray, J. Patrick. 1985. *Primate sociobiology*. New Haven, CT: HRAF Press.

Gray, J. Patrick. 1996. Sociobiology. In *Encyclopedia of cultural anthropology*, vol. 4, eds. D. Levinson and M. Ember. New York: Henry Holt.

Gray, J. Patrick, and Linda D. Wolfe. 1980. Height and sexual dimorphism of stature among human societies. *American Journal of Physical Anthropology* 53:446–52.

Gray, J. Patrick, and Linda D. Wolfe. 2009. What accounts for population variation in height? In MyAnthroLibrary, eds. C. R. Ember, M. Ember, and P. N. Peregrine. MyAnthroLibrary.com. Pearson.

Grayson, Donald K. 1977. Pleistocene avifaunas and the overkill hypothesis. *Science* 195 (February 18):691–92.

Grayson, Donald K. 1984. Explaining Pleistocene extinctions: Thoughts on the structure of a debate. In *Quaternary extinctions*, eds. P. S. Martin and R. Klein. Tucson: University of Arizona Press.

Green, Edward C., and Allison Herling Ruark. 2011. *Aids, behavior, and culture: Understanding evidence-based prevention*. Walnut Creek, CA: Left Coast Press.

Green, Richard E., et al. 2008. A complete Neandertal mitochondrial genome sequence determined by high-throughput sequencing. *Cell* 134:416–26.

Green, Richard E., et al. 2010. A draft sequence of the Neandertal genome. *Science* 328 (May 7):710–22.

Greenberg, Joseph H. 1972. Linguistic evidence regarding Bantu origins. *Journal of African History* 13:189–216.

Greenberg, Joseph H., and Merritt Ruhlen. 1992. Linguistic origins of Native Americans. *Scientific American* (November):94–99.

Greenfield, Patricia Marks, and E. Sue Savage-Rumbaugh. 1990. Grammatical combination in *Pan paniscus*: Processes of learning and invention in the evolution and development of language. In *"Language" and intelligence in monkeys and apes*, eds. S. Parker and K. Gibson. New York: Cambridge University Press.

Greenfield, Patricia Marks, Ashley E. Maynard, and Carla P. Childs. 2000. History, culture, learning, and development. *Cross-Cultural Research* 34:351–74.

Gregor, Thomas A., and Daniel R. Gross. 2004. Guilt by association: The culture of accusation and the American Anthropological Association' investigation of *Darkness in El Dorado*. *American Anthropologist* 106:687–98.

Gregory, C. A. 1982. *Gifts and commodities*. New York: Academic Press.

Greksa, Lawrence P., and Cynthia M. Beall. 1989. Development of chest size and lung function at high altitude. In *Human population biology*, eds. M. Little and J. Haas. New York: Oxford University Press.

Grenoble, Lenore A., and Lindsay J. Whaley. 2006. *Saving languages: An introduction to language revitalization*. Cambridge: Cambridge University Press.

Grine, Frederick E. 1988a. Evolutionary history of the "robust" australopithecines: A summary and historical perspective. In *Evolutionary history of the "robust" australopithecines*, ed. F. E. Grine. New York: Aldine.

Grine, Frederick E., eds. 1988b. *Evolutionary history of the "robust" australopithecines*. New York: Aldine.

Grine, Frederick E. 1993. Australopithecine taxonomy and phylogeny: Historical background and recent interpretation. In *The human evolution source book*, eds. R. Ciochon and J. Fleagle. Upper Saddle River, NJ: Prentice Hall.

Gröger, B. Lisa. 1981. Of men and machines: Cooperation among French family farmers. *Ethnology* 20:163–75.

Gross, Daniel R., and Barbara A. Underwood. 1971. Technological change and caloric costs: Sisal agriculture in northeastern Brazil. *American Anthropologist* 73:725–40.

Gross, Daniel R., George Eiten, Nancy M. Flowers, Francisca M. Leoi, Madeline Lattman Ritter, and Dennis W. Werner. 1979. Ecology and acculturation among native peoples of central Brazil. *Science* 206 (November 30):1043–50.

Grossman, Daniel. 2002. Parched turf battle. *Scientific American* (December): 32–33.

Grubb, Henry J. 1987. Intelligence at the low end of the curve: Where are the racial differences? *Journal of Black Psychology* 14:25–34.

Gubser, Nicholas J. 1965. *The Nunamiut Eskimos: Hunters of caribou*. New Haven, CT: Yale University Press.

Guest, Greg, and Eric C. Jones. 2005. Globalization, health, and the environment: An introduction. In *Globalization, health, and the environment: An integrated perspective*, ed. G. Guest. Lanham, MD: Roman & Littlefield.

Guiora, Alexander Z., Benjamin Beit-Hallahmi, Risto Fried, and Cecelia Yoder. 1982. Language environment and gender identity attainment. *Language Learning* 32:289–304.

Gumperz, John J. 1961. Speech variation and the study of Indian civilization. *American Anthropologist* 63:976–88.

Gumperz, John J. 1971. Dialect differences and social stratification in a North Indian village. In *Language in social groups: Essays by John J. Gumperz*, selected and introduced by Anwar S. Dil. Stanford, CA: Stanford University Press.

Gumperz, John J., and Jenny Cook Gumperz. 2008. Studying language, culture, and society: Sociolinguistics or linguistic anthropology? *Journal of Sociolinguistics* 12, no.4:532–45.

Gunders, S., and J. W. M. Whiting. 1968. Mother-infant separation and physical growth. *Ethnology* 7:196–206.

Gunnell, Gregg F., and Kenneth D. Rose. 2002. *Tarsiiformes*: Evolutionary history and adaptation. In *The primate fossil record*, ed. W. C. Hartwig. Cambridge: Cambridge University Press.

Gurr, Ted Robert. 1989a. Historical trends in violent crime: Europe and the United States. In *Violence in America, Vol. 1: The history of crime*, ed. T. R. Gurr. Newbury Park, CA: Sage.

Gurr, Ted Robert. 1989b. The history of violent crime in America: An overview. In *Violence in America, Vol. 1: The history of crime*, ed. T. R. Gurr. Newbury Park, CA: Sage.

Gurven, Michael, Kim Hill, and Hillard Kaplan. 2002. From forest to reservation: Transitions in food-sharing behavior among the Ache of Paraguay. *Journal of Anthropological Research* 58:93–120.

Guthrie, Dale R. 1984. Mosaics, allelochemics, and nutrients: An ecological theory of Late Pleistocene megafaunal extinctions. In *Quaternary extinctions*, eds. P. S. Martin and R. Klein. Tucson: University of Arizona Press.

Guthrie, Stewart Elliott. 1993. *Faces in the clouds: A new theory of religion*. New York: Oxford University Press.

Guttman-Bond, Erica. 2010. Sustainability out of the past: How archaeology can save the planet. *World Archaeology* 42:355–366.

Haas, Jonathan. 1990. Warfare and the evolution of tribal polities in the prehistoric Southwest. In *The anthropology of war*, ed. J. Haas. New York: Cambridge University Press.

Haas, Jonathan. 2007. Warfare and the evolution of culture. In *Archaeology at the millennium: A sourcebook*, eds. G. M. Feinman and T. D. Price, 329–50. New York: Springer.

Haas, Jonathan, Winifred Creamer, and Alvaro Ruiz. 2004. Dating the Late Archaic occupation of the Norte Chico region in Peru. *Nature* 432 (December 23):1020–23.

Haas, Mary R. 1944. Men's and women's speech in Koasati. *Language* 20:142–49.

Habicht, J. K. A. 1979. *Paleoclimate, paleomagnetism, and continental drift*. Tulsa, OK: American Association of Petroleum Geologists.

Haddix, Kimber A. 2001. Leaving your wife and your brothers: When polyandrous marriages fall apart. *Evolution and Human Behavior* 22:47–60.

Hage, Jerald, and Charles H. Powers. 1992. *Post-industrial lives: Roles and relationships in the 21st century*. Newbury Park, CA: Sage.

Hahn, Robert A. 1995. *Sickness and healing: An anthropological perspective*. New Haven, CT: Yale University Press.

Hailie-Selassie, Yohannes. 2001. Late Miocene hominids from the Middle Awash, Ethiopia. *Nature* 412 (July 12):178–81.

Haldane, J. B. S. 1963. Human evolution: Past and future. In *Genetics, paleontology, and evolution*, eds. G. Jepsen, E. Mayr, and G. Simpson. New York: Atheneum.

Hall, Edward T. 1966. *The hidden dimension*. Garden City, NY: Doubleday.

Hall, Edward T., and Mildred Reed Hall. 1990. *Understanding cultural differences.* Nicholas Brealey Publishing.

Hallowell, A. Irving. 1976. Ojibwa world view and disease. In *Contributions to anthropology: Selected papers of A. Irving Hallowell*, 410–13. Chicago: University of Chicago Press.

Halpern, Diane F. 2000. *Sex differences in cognitive abilities.* 3rd ed. Mahwah, NJ: Lawrence Erlbaum Associates.

Hames, Raymond B. 1990. Sharing among the Yanomamö. Part I. The effects of risk. In *Risk and uncertainty in tribal and peasant economies*, ed. E. Cashdan. Boulder, CO: Westview.

Hames, Raymond B. 2009. Yanomamö: Varying adaptations of foraging horticulturalists. In MyAnthroLibrary, eds. C. R. Ember, M. Ember, and P. N. Peregrine. MyAnthroLibrary.com. Pearson.

Hammer, Michael F., and Stephen L. Zegura. 1996. The role of the Y chromosome in human evolutionary studies. *Evolutionary Anthropology* 5:116–34.

Hammer, Michael F., and Stephen L. Zegura. 2002. The human Y chromosome haplogroup tree. *Annual Review of Anthropology* 31:303–21.

Handler, Richard. 2005. Vigorous male and aspiring female: Poetry, personality and culture in Edward Sapir and Ruth Benedict. In *Critics against culture: Anthropological observers of mass society*, 96–122. Madison: University of Wisconsin Press.

Handwerker, W. Penn, and Paul V. Crosbie. 1982. Sex and dominance. *American Anthropologist* 84:97–104.

Hanna, Joel M., Michael A. Little, and Donald M. Austin. 1989. Climatic physiology. In *Human population biology*, eds. M. Little and J. Haas. New York: Oxford University Press.

Hannah, Alison C., and W. C. McGrew. 1987. Chimpanzees using stones to crack open oil palm nuts in Liberia. *Primates* 28:31–46.

Hannerz, Ulf. 1996. *Transnational connections: Culture, people, places.* London: Routledge.

Hanotte, Olivier, D. G. Bradley, J. W. Ochieng, Y. Verjee, E. W. Hill, and J. E. Rege. 2002. African pastoralism: Genetic imprints of origins and migrations. *Science* 296 (April 12):336–43.

Hanson, Jeffery R. 1988. Age-set theory and Plains Indian age-grading: A critical review and revision. *American Ethnologist* 15:349–64.

Harcourt, A. H. 1979. The social relations and group structure of wild mountain gorillas. In *The great apes*, eds. D. Hamburg and E. McCown. Menlo Park, CA: Benjamin/Cummings.

Hardin, Garrett. 1968. The tragedy of the commons. *Science* 162 (December 13):1243–48.

Hardoy, Jorge, and David Satterthwaite. 1987. The legal and the illegal city. In *Shelter, settlement, and development*, ed. L. Rodwin. Boston: Allen & Unwin.

Hare, Brian, Michelle Brown, Christina Williamson, and Michael Tomasello. 2002. The domestication of social cognition in dogs. *Science* 298 (November 22):1634–36.

Harkness, Sara, and Charles M. Super. 1997. "An infant's three Rs." A box in M. Small, "Our babies, ourselves." *Natural History* (October):45.

Harkness, Sara, and Charles M. Super. 2006. Themes and variations: Parental ethnotheories in Western cultures. In *Parenting beliefs, behaviors, and parent-child relations: A cross-cultural perspective*, eds. Kenneth H. Rubin and Ock Boon Chung. New York: Psychology Press.

Harkness, Sara, and C. Jason Throop. 2008. Bruner's search for meaning: A conversation between psychology and anthropology. *Ethos* 36:5.

Harlan, Jack R. 1967. A wild wheat harvest in Turkey. *Archaeology* 20:197–201.

Harlow, Harry F., M. K. Harlow, R. O. Dodsworth, and G. L. Arling 1966. Maternal behavior of rhesus monkeys deprived of mothering and peer association in infancy. *Proceedings of the American Philosophical Society* 110:58–66.

Harner, Michael J. 1972. The role of hallucinogenic plants in European witchcraft. In *Hallucinogens and shamanism.* New York: Oxford University Press.

Harner, Michael J. 1975. Scarcity, the factors of production, and social evolution. In *Population, ecology, and social evolution*, ed. S. Polgar. The Hague: Mouton.

Harner, Michael J., and Gary Doore. 1987. The ancient wisdom in shamanic cultures. In *Shamanism*, ed. S. Nicholson. Wheaton, IL: Theosophical Publishing House.

Harper, Douglas. 2003. Slavery in the North. http://www.slavenorth.com/ (accessed June, 2009).

Harrell-Bond, Barbara. 1996. Refugees. In *Encyclopedia of cultural anthropology*, vol. 3, eds. D. Levinson and M. Ember. New York: Henry Holt.

Harris, David R. 1977. Settling down: An evolutionary model for the transformation of mobile bands into sedentary communities. In *The evolution of social systems*, eds. J. Friedman and M. Rowlands. London: Duckworth.

Harris, Eugene. 2008. Searching the genome for our adaptations. *Evolutionary Anthropology* 17:146–157.

Harris, Marvin. 1964. *Patterns of race in the Americas.* New York: Walker.

Harris, Marvin. 1966. The cultural ecology of India's sacred cattle. *Current Anthropology* 7:51–63.

Harris, Marvin. 1968. *The rise of anthropological theory: A history of theories of culture.* New York: Thomas Y. Crowell.

Harris, Marvin. 1975. *Cows, pigs, wars and witches: The riddles of culture.* New York: Random House, Vintage.

Harris, Marvin. 1979. *Cultural materialism: The struggle for a science of culture.* New York: Random House.

Harrison, G. A., James M. Tanner, David R. Pilbeam, and P. T. Baker. 1988. *Human biology: An introduction to human evolution, variation, growth, and adaptability.* 3rd ed. Oxford: Oxford University Press.

Harrison, Gail G. 1975. Primary adult lactase deficiency: A problem in anthropological genetics. *American Anthropologist* 77:812–35.

Harrison, Peter D., and B. L. Turner, II, eds. 1978. *Pre-Hispanic Maya agriculture.* Albuquerque: University of New Mexico Press.

Harrison, Terry 1986. A reassessment of the phylogenetic relationships of *Oreopithecus bamboli*. *Journal of Human Evolution* 15:541–84.

Harrison, Terry. 2002. Late Oligocene to Middle Miocene catarrhines from Afro-Arabia. In *The primate fossil record*, ed. W. C. Hartwig. Cambridge: Cambridge University Press.

Harrison, T., and L. Rook. 1997. Enigmatic anthropoid or misunderstood ape? The phylogenetic status of *Oreopithecus bamboli* reconsidered. In *Function, phylogeny and fossils: Miocene hominoid evolution and adaptation*, eds. D. R. Begun, C. V. Ward, and M. D. Rose. New York: Plenum.

Hart, Hornell. 1948. The logistic growth of political areas. *Social Forces* 26:396–408.

Hartwig, W. C. 1994. Pattern, puzzles and perspectives on platyrrhine origins. In *Integrative paths to the past*, eds. R. Corruccini and R. Ciochon. Upper Saddle River, NJ: Prentice Hall.

Harvey, Philip W., and Peter F. Heywood. 1983. Twenty-five years of dietary change in Simbu Province, Papua New Guinea. *Ecology of Food and Nutrition* 13:27–35.

Hassan, Fekri A. 1981. *Demographic archaeology.* New York: Academic Press.

Hassanpour, Amir, and Shahrzad Mojab. 2004. Kurdish diaspora. In *Encyclopedia of diasporas: Immigrant and refugee cultures around the world*, vol. 1, eds. M. Ember, C. R. Ember, and I. Skoggard. New York: Springer.

Hatch, Elvin. 1997. The good side of relativism. *Journal of Anthropological Research* 53:371–81.

Haug, Gerald, Detlef Günther, Larry C. Peterson, Daniel M. Sigman, Konrad A. Hughen, and Beat Aeschlimann. 2003. Climate and the collapse of Maya civilization. *Science* 299 (March 14):1731–35.

Hauser, Marc D., Noam Chomsky, and W. Tecumseh Fitch. 2002. The faculty of language: What is it, who has it, and how did it evolve? *Science* 298 (November 22):1569–79.

Hausfater, Glenn, Jeanne Altmann, and Stuart Altmann. 1982. Long-term consistency of dominance relations among female baboons. *Science* 217 (August 20):752–54.

Hawkins, Alicia, and M. Kleindienst. 2001. Aterian. In *Encyclopedia of prehistory, Vol. 1: Africa*, eds. P. N. Peregrine and M. Ember. New York: Kluwer Academic/Plenum.

Hayashi, Akiko, and Joseph Tobin. 2011. The Japanese preschool's pedagogy of peripheral participation. *Ethos* 39:139–64.

Hayden, Thomas. 2000. A genome milestone. *Newsweek* (July 3):51–52.

Haynes, Vance. 1973. The Calico site: Artifacts or geofacts? *Science* 181 (July 27):305–10.

Hays, Terence E. 1994. Sound symbolism, onomatopoeia, and New Guinea frog names. *Journal of Linguistic Anthropology* 4:153–74.

Hays, Terence E. 2009. From ethnographer to comparativist and back again. In MyAnthroLibrary, eds. C. R. Ember, M. Ember, and P. N. Peregrine. MyAnthroLibrary.com. Pearson.

Heider, Karl. 1970. *The Dugum Dani.* Chicago: Aldine.

Heider, Karl. 1979. *Grand Valley Dani: Peaceful warriors.* New York: Holt, Rinehart & Winston.

Heinrich, Joseph, and Robert Boyd. 2008. Division of labor, economic specialization, and the evolution of social stratification. *Current Anthropology* 49, no.4:715–24.

Heise, David R. 1967. Cultural patterning of sexual socialization. *American Sociological Review* 32:726–39.

Higham, Charles. 2009. East Asian agriculture and its impact. In *The human past*, ed. C. Scarre. New York: Thames and Hudson.

Heller, Monica, eds. 1988. *Codeswitching: Anthropological and sociolinguistic perspectives.* Berlin: Mouton de Gruyter.

Helms, Mary W. 1975. *Middle America.* Upper Saddle River, NJ: Prentice Hall.

Helms, Mary W. 2009. Miskito: Adaptations to colonial empires, past and present. In MyAnthroLibrary, eds. C. R. Ember, M. Ember, and P. N. Peregrine. MyAnthroLibrary.com. Pearson.

Henderson, Harry. 2001. *Global terrorism: The complete reference guide.* New York: Checkmark Books.

Henderson, Stephen. 2002. Weddings: Vows; Rakhi Dhanoa and Ranjeet Purewal. *New York Times*, August 18, p. 9.2.

Hendrix, Lewellyn. 1985. Economy and child training reexamined. *Ethos* 13:246–61.

Hendrix, Lewellyn. 2009. Varieties of marital relationships. In MyAnthroLibrary, eds. C. R. Ember, M. Ember, and P. N. Peregrine. MyAnthroLibrary.com. Pearson.

Henrich, Joseph. 2009. The evolution of costly displays, cooperation and religion: Credibility enhancing displays and their implications for cultural evolution. *Evolution and Human Behavior* 30:244–60.

Henrich, Joseph, Robert Boyd, Samuel Bowles, Colin Camerer, Ernst Fehr, and Herbert Gintis, eds. 2004. *Foundations of human sociality: Economic experiments and ethnographic evidence from fifteen small-scale societies.* Oxford: Oxford University Press.

Henrich, Joseph, et al. 2005. "Economic man" in cross-cultural perspective: Behavioral experiments in 15 small-scale societies. *Behavioral and Brain Sciences* 28:795–814.

Henry, Donald O. 1989. *From foraging to agriculture: The Levant at the end of the Ice Age.* Philadelphia: University of Pennsylvania Press.

Henry, Donald O. 1991. Foraging, sedentism, and adaptive vigor in the Natufian: Rethinking the linkages. In *Perspectives on the past*, eds. G. A. Clark. Philadelphia: University of Pennsylvania Press.

Henry, Edward O. 1976. The variety of music in a North Indian village: Reassessing cantometrics. *Ethnomusicology* 20:49–66.

Henshilwood, Christopher, et al. 2002. Emergence of modern human behavior: Middle Stone Age engravings from South Africa. *Science* 295 (February 15):1278–80.

Herlihy, Laura Hobson. 2007. Matrifocality and women's power on the Miskito Coast. *Ethnology* 46:133–49.

Herrman, Helen. 1990. A survey of homeless mentally ill people in Melbourne, Australia. *Hospital and Community Psychiatry* 41:1291–92.

Herrmann, Esther, Joseph Call, Maria Victoria Herandez-Lloreda, Brain Hare, and Michael Tomasello. 2007. Humans have evolved specialized skills in social cognition: The cultural intelligence hypothesis. *Science* 317 (September 7):1360–65.

Herrnstein, Richard J., and Charles Murray. 1994. *The bell curve: Intelligence and class structure in American life.* New York: Free Press.

Hewes, Gordon W. 1961. Food transport and the origin of hominid bipedalism. *American Anthropologist* 63:687–710.

Hewlett, Barry S. 2004. Diverse contexts of human infancy. In MyAnthroLibrary, eds. C. R. Ember, M. Ember, and P. N. Peregrine. MyAnthroLibrary.com. Pearson.

Hewlett, Barry S., and L. L. Cavalli-Sforza. 1986. Cultural transmission among Aka Pygmies. *American Anthropologist* 88:922–34.

Hiatt, L. R. 1980. Polyandry in Sri Lanka: A test case for parental investment theory. *Man* 15:583–98.

Hickey, Gerald Cannon. 1964. *Village in Vietnam.* New Haven, CT: Yale University Press.

Hickson, Letitia. 1986. The social contexts of apology in dispute settlement: A cross-cultural study. *Ethnology* 25:283–94.

Higley, Stephen Richard. 1995. *Privilege, power, and place: The geography of the American upper class.* Lanham, MD: Rowman & Littlefield.

Hill, Carole. 2000. Strategic issues for rebuilding a theory and practice synthesis. *NAPA Bulletin* 18:1–16.

Hill, Carole E., and Marietta L. Baba. 2006. Global connections and practicing anthropology in the 21st century. *NAPA Bulletin* 25, no.1:1–13.

Hill, Donald R. 2005. Music of the African diaspora in the Americas. In *Encyclopedia of diasporas: Immigrant and refugee cultures around the world*, eds. M. Ember, C. R. Ember, and I. Skoggard. New York: Kluwer Academic/Plenum.

Hill, James N. 1970. *Broken K Pueblo: Prehistoric social organization in the American Southwest.* Anthropological Papers of the University of Arizona, Number 18. Tucson: University of Arizona Press.

Hill, Jane H. 1978. Apes and language. *Annual Review of Anthropology*7:89–112.

Hill, Jane H. 2009. Do apes have language? In MyAnthroLibrary, eds. C. R. Ember, M. Ember, and P. N. Peregrine. MyAnthroLibrary.com. Pearson.

Hill, Jonathan D. 1996. Introduction: Ethnogenesis in the Americas. 1492-1992. In *Ethnogenesis in the Americas*, ed. J. D. Hill, 1–19. Iowa City: University of Iowa Press.

Hill, Kim, and A. Magdalena Hurtado. 2004. The ethics of anthropological research with remote tribal populations. In *Lost paradises and the ethics of research and publication*, eds. F. M. Salzano and A. M. Hurtado. Oxford: Oxford University Press.

Hill, Kim, Hillard Kaplan, Kristen Hawkes, and A. Magdalena Hurtado. 1987. Foraging decisions among Aché hunter-gatherers: New data and implications for optimal foraging models. *Ethology and Sociobiology* 8:1–36.

Hill, Susan T. 2001. *Science and engineering doctorate awards: 2000*, NSF 02-305. National Science Foundation, Division of Science Resources Statistics. VA: Arlington.

Hillel, Daniel. 2000. *Salinity management for sustainable irrigation: Integrating science, environment, and economics.* Washington, DC: The World Bank.

Himmelgreen, David A., and Deborah L. Crooks. 2005. Nutritional anthropology and its application to nutritional issues and problems. In *Applied anthropology: Domains of application*, eds. S. Kedia and J. van Willigen, 149–88. Westport, CT: Praeger.

Himmelgreen, David, and Nancy Romero-Daza. 2009. Anthropological approaches to the global food crisis: Understanding and addressing the "silent tsunami." *NAPA Bulletin* 32:1–11.

Hinkes, Madeleine. 1993. Race, ethnicity, and forensic anthropology. *NAPA Bulletin* 13:48–54.

Hirsch, Jennifer, Sarah Van Deusen Phillips, Edward Labenski, Christine Dunford, and Troy Peters. 2011. Linking climate action to local knowledge and practice. In *Environmental anthropology today*, eds. H. Kopnina and E. Shoreman-Ouimet. New York: Routledge.

Hitchcock, Robert K., and Megan Beisele. 2000. Introduction. In *Hunters and gatherers in the modern world: Conflict, resistance, and self-determinations*, eds. P. P. Schweitzer, M. Biesele, and R. K. Hitchcock. New York: Berghahn Books.

Hoberman, John. 2012. *Black and blue: The origins and consequences of medical racism.* Berkeley: University of California Press.

Hobsbawm, E. J. 1970. *Age of revolution.* New York: Praeger.

Hockett, C. F., and R. Ascher. 1964. The human revolution. *Current Anthropology* 5:135–68.

Hodgson, Jason, and Todd Driscoll. 2008. No evidence of a Neandertal contribution to modern human diversity. *Genome Biology* 9:206.1–206.7.

Hoebel, E. Adamson. 1960. *The Cheyennes: Indians of the Great Plains.* New York: Holt, Rinehart & Winston.

Hoebel, E. Adamson. 1968/1954. *The law of primitive man.* New York: Atheneum.

Hoffecker, John F., W. Roger Powers, and Ted Goebel. 1993. The colonization of Beringia and the peopling of the New World. *Science* 259 (January 1):46–53.

Hoffman, Lois Wladis. 1988. Cross-cultural differences in child-rearing goals. In *Parental behavior in diverse societies*, eds. R. A. LeVine, P. M. Miller, and M. M. West. San Francisco: Jossey-Bass.

Hoijer, Harry. 1964. Cultural implications of some Navaho linguistic categories. In *Language in culture and society*, ed. D. Hymes. New York: Harper & Row.

Holdaway, R. N., and C. Jacomb. 2000. Rapid extinction of the Moas (*Aves: Dinornithiformes*): Model, test, and implications. *Science* 287 (March 24):2250–57.

Holden, Constance. 2000. Selective power of UV. *Science* 289 (September 1):1461.

Hole, Frank. 1992. Origins of agriculture. In *The Cambridge encyclopedia of human evolution*, eds. S. Jones, R. Martin, and D. Pilbeam. New York: Cambridge University Press.

Hole, Frank. 1994. Environmental shock and urban origins. In *Chiefdoms and early states in the Near East*, eds. G. Stein and M. Rothman. Madison, WI: Prehistory Press.

Hole, Frank, Kent V. Flannery, and James A. Neely. 1969. *Prehistory and human ecology of the Deh Luran Plain.* Memoirs of the Museum of Anthropology, No. 1. Ann Arbor: University of Michigan.

Hollan, Douglas. 1992. Cross-cultural differences in the self. *Journal of Anthropological Research* 48:289–90.

Holloway, Marguerite. 1993. Sustaining the Amazon. *Scientific American* (July):91–99.

Holloway, Ralph L. 1974. The casts of fossil hominid brains. *Scientific American* (July):106–15.

Holmes, Janet. 2001. *An introduction to sociolinguistics.* 2nd ed. London: Longman.

Honigmann, John J. 1967. *Personality in culture.* New York: Harper & Row.

Hoogbergen, Wim. 1990. *The Boni Maroon Wars in Suriname.* Leiden: E. J. Brill.

Hooper, Judith. 2002. *Of moths and men: The untold story of science and the peppered moth.* New York: W. W. Norton.

Hopkins, K. 1980. Brother-sister marriage in Roman Egypt. *Comparative Studies in Society & History* 22:303–54.

Hopper, Kim. 2003. *Reckoning with homelessness.* Ithaca, NY: Cornell University Press.

Houston, Stephen D. 1988. The phonetic decipherment of Mayan Glyphs. *Antiquity* 62:126–35.

Howard, Alan, and Jan Rensel. 2009. Rotuma: Interpreting a Wedding. In MyAnthroLibrary, eds. C. R. Ember, M. Ember, and P. N. Peregrine. MyAnthroLibrary.com. Pearson.

Howard, Philip N., Aiden Duffy, Deen Freelon, M. Hussain, W. Mari, and M. Mazaid. 2011. Opening closed regimes: what was the role of social media during the Arab spring? Project on Information Technology & Political Islam. Working paper.

Howell, F. Clark. 1966. Observations on the earlier phases of the European Lower Paleolithic. In *Recent studies in paleoanthropology. American Anthropologist.* Special publication, eds. J. Desmond Clark and F. Clark Howell. April.

Howell, Nancy. 1979. *Demography of the Dobe !Kung.* New York: Academic Press.

Howrigan, Gail A. 1988. Fertility, infant feeding, and change in Yucatan. *New directions for child development* 40:37–50.

Hrdy, Sarah Blaffer. 1977. *The Langurs of Abu: Female and male strategies of reproduction.* Cambridge, MA: Harvard University Press.

Hua, Cai. 2001. *A society without fathers or husbands: The Na of China.* Trans. Asti Hustvedt. New York: Zone Books.

Huang, H. T. 2002. Hypolactasia and the Chinese diet. *Current Anthropology* 43:809–19.

Huber, Evelyne, François Nielsen, Jenny Pribble, and John D. Stephens. 2006. Politics and inequality in Latin America and the Caribbean. *American Sociological Review* 71:943–63.

Human Development Report 1993. 1993. Published for the United Nations Development Programme. New York: Oxford University Press.

Human Development Report 2001. 2001. Published for the United Nations Development Programme. New York: Oxford University Press.

Humphrey, Caroline, and Stephen Hugh-Jones. 1992. Introduction: Barter, exchange and value. In *Barter, exchange and value*, eds. C. Humphrey and S. Hugh-Jones. New York: Cambridge University Press.

Hunt, Morton. 1974. *Sexual behavior in the 1970s.* Chicago: Playboy Press.

Hunt, Robert C. 2000. Labor productivity and agricultural development: Boserup revisited. *Human Ecology* 28:251–77.

Hurtado, Ana M., Kristen Hawkes, Kim Hill, and Hillard Kaplan. 1985. Female subsistence strategies among the Aché hunter-gatherers of eastern Paraguay. *Human Ecology* 13:1–28.

Huss-Ashmore, Rebecca, and Francis E. Johnston. 1985. Bioanthropological research in developing countries. *Annual Review of Anthropology* 14:475–527.

Huxley, Thomas H. 1970. Man's place in nature. In *Evolution of man*, ed. L. Young. New York: Oxford University Press.

Hymes, Dell. 1974. *Foundations in sociolinguistics: An ethnographic approach.* Philadelphia: University of Pennsylvania Press.

Ingram, Catherine J. E., Charlotte A. Mulcare, Yuval Itan, Mark G. Thomas, and Dallas M. Swallow. 2009. Lactose digestion and the evolutionary genetics of lactase persistence. *Human Genetics* 124, no. 6:579–91.

IPPC. 2007. Climate change 2007: Synthesis report. http://www.ipcc.ch/pdf/assessment-report/ar4/syr/ar4_syr_spm.pdf.

Irons, William. 1979. Natural selection, adaptation, and human social behavior. In *Evolutionary biology and human social behavior*, eds. N. Chagnon and W. Irons. North Scituate, MA: Duxbury.

Irwin, Marc H., Gary N. Schafer, and Cynthia P. Feiden. 1974. Emic and unfamiliar category sorting of Mano farmers and U.S. undergraduates. *Journal of Cross-Cultural Psychology* 5:407–23.

Isaac, Glynn. 1971. The diet of early man: Aspects of archaeological evidence from Lower and Middle Pleistocene sites in Africa. *World Archaeology* 2:277–99.

Isaac, Glynn. 1984. The archaeology of human origins: Studies of the Lower Pleistocene in East Africa, 1971-1981. In *Advances in world archaeology*, eds. F. Wendorf and A. Close. Orlando, FL: Academic Press.

Isaac, Glynn, ed., assisted by Barbara Isaac. 1997. *Plio-Pleistocene archaeology.* Oxford: Clarendon Press.

Itkonen, T. I. 1951. The Lapps of Finland. *Southwestern Journal of Anthropology* 7:32–68.

Jablonski, Nina G. 2010. Skin coloration. In *Human evolutionary biology*, ed. M. Muehlenbein. Cambridge: Cambridge University Press.

Jablonski, Nina G., and George Chaplin. 2000. The evolution of human skin color. *Journal of Human Evolution* 39:57–106.

Jacobs, Sue-Ellen, and Christine Roberts. 1989. Sex, sexuality, gender and gender variance. In *Gender and anthropology*, ed. S. Morgen. Washington, DC: American Anthropological Association.

Jaeger, J., et al. 1999. A new primate from the Middle Eocene of Myanmar and the Asian early origins of anthropoids. *Science* 286 (October 15):528–30.

James, Allison. 2007. Giving voice to children's voices: Practices and problems, pitfalls and potentials. *American Anthropologist* 109:261–72.

James, William. 1902. *The varieties of religious experience: A study in human nature.* New York: Modern Library.

Jankowiak, William R. 2009. Urban Mongols: Ethnicity in communist China. In MyAnthroLibrary, eds. C. R. Ember, M. Ember, and P. N. Peregrine. MyAnthroLibrary.com. Pearson.

Jankowiak, William R., and Edward F. Fischer. 1992. A cross-cultural perspective on romantic love. *Ethnology* 31:149–55.

Jankowiak, William, M. Diane Nell, and Ann Buckmaster. 2002. Managing infidelity: A cross-cultural perspective. *Ethnology* 41:85–101.

Jankowiak, William, Monica Sudakov, and Benjamin C. Wilreker. 2005. Co-wife conflict and co-operation. *Ethnology* 44:81–98.

Janzen, Daniel H. 1973. Tropical agroecosystems. *Science* 182 (December 21):1212–19.

Jarvenpa, Robert. 2004. *Silot'ine*: An insurance perspective on Northern Dene kinship networks in recent history. *Journal of Anthropological Research* 60:153–78.

Jarvenpa, Robert, and Hetty Jo Brumbach. 2006. Chipewyan hunters: A task differentiation analysis. In *Circumpolar lives and livelihood: A comparative ethnoarchaeology of gender and subsistence*, eds. R. Jarvenpa and H. J. Brumbach. Lincoln, Nebraska: University of Nebraska Press.

Jayaswal, Vidula. 2002. South Asian Upper Paleolithic. In *Encyclopedia of prehistory, Vol. 8: South and Southwest*

Asia, eds. P. N. Peregrine and M. Ember. New York: Kluwer Academic/Plenum.

Jenkins, D. L., et al. 2012. Clovis age western stemmed projectile points and human coprolites at the Paisley Caves. *Science* 337 (July 13):223–28.

Jelliffe, Derrick B., and E. F. Patrice Jelliffe. 1975. Human milk, nutrition, and the world resource crisis. *Science* 188 (May 9):557–61.

Jennings, J. D. 1968. *Prehistory of North America*. New York: McGraw-Hill.

Jensen, Arthur. 1969. How much can we boost IQ and scholastic achievement? *Harvard Educational Review* 29:1–123.

Joans, Barbara. 1997. Problems in Pocatello: A study in linguistic misunderstanding. In *Applying cultural anthropology: An introductory reader*, 3rd ed., eds. A. Podolefsky and P. J. Brown. Mountain View, CA: Mayfield.

Jobling, Mark A., Matthew E. Hurles, and Chris Tylor-Smith. 2004. *Human evolutionary genetics*. New York: Garland.

Johannes, R. E. 1981. *Words of the lagoon: Fishing and marine lore in the Palau District of Micronesia*. Berkeley: University of California Press.

Johanson, Donald C., and Maitland Edey. 1981. *Lucy: The beginnings of humankind*. New York: Simon & Schuster.

Johanson, Donald C., and Tim D. White. 1979. A systematic assessment of early African hominids. *Science* 203 (January 26):321–30.

Johnson, Allen W., and Timothy Earle. 1987. *The evolution of human societies: From foraging group to agrarian state*. Stanford, CA: Stanford University Press.

Johnson, Allen W., and Timothy Earle. 2000. *The evolution of human societies: From foraging group to agrarian state*. 2nd ed. Stanford, CA: Stanford University Press.

Johnson, Amber Lynn. 2002. Cross-cultural analysis of pastoral adaptations and organizational states: A preliminary study. *Cross-Cultural Research* 36:151–80.

Johnson, Dominic D. P. 2005. God's punishment and public goods: A test of the supernatural punishment hypothesis in 186 world cultures. *Human Nature* 16:410–46.

Johnson, Eric Michael. 2011. I've got your back. *Scientific American* 305 (October):22.

Johnson, Gregory A. 1977. Aspects of regional analysis in archaeology. *Annual Review of Anthropology* 6:479–508.

Johnson, Gregory A. 1987. The changing organization of Uruk administration on the Susiana plain. In *Archaeology of western Iran*, ed. F. Hole. Washington, DC: Smithsonian Institution Press.

Johnson, Jeffrey G., Cohen Patricia, Elizabeth M. Smailies, Stephanie Kasen, and Judith S. Brook. 2002. Television viewing and aggressive behavior during adolescence and adulthood. *Science* 295 (March 29):2468–70.

Johnson-Hanks, Jennifer. 2006. *Uncertain honor: Modern motherhood in an African crisis*. Chicago: University of Chicago Press.

Johnston, David Cay. 1999. Gap between rich and poor found substantially wider. *New York Times*, National, September 5, p. 16

Jolly, Alison. 1985. *The evolution of primate behavior*. 2nd ed. New York: Macmillan.

Jolly, Clifford. 1970. The seed-eaters: A new model of hominid differentiation based on a baboon analogy. *Man* 5:5–28.

Jones, Martin, and Xinyi Liu. 2009. Origins of agriculture in East Asia. *Science* 324 (May 8):730–31.

Jones, Nicholas Blurton, Kristen Hawkes, and James F. O'Connell. 1996. The global process and local ecology: How should we explain differences between the Hadza and the !Kung? In *Cultural diversity among twentieth-century foragers*, ed. S. Kent. Cambridge: Cambridge University Press.

Jones, Steve, Robert Martin, and David Pilbeam, eds. 1992. *The Cambridge encyclopedia of human evolution*. New York: Cambridge University Press.

Jordan, Ann. 2013. *Business anthropology*. 2nd ed. Long Grove, IL: Waveland Press.

Judge, W. James, and Jerry Dawson. 1972. Paleo-Indian settlement technology in New Mexico. *Science* 176 (June 16):1210–16.

Julian, Tiffany A., and Robert A. Kominski. 2011. *Education and synthetic work-life earnings estimates*. American Community Survey Reports, ACS-14. Washington, DC: U.S. Census Bureau.

Jung, Carl G. 1938. *Psychology and religion*. New Haven, CT: Yale University Press.

Jungers, William L. 1988a. New estimates of body size in australopithecines. In *Evolutionary history of the "robust" australopithecines*, ed. F. Grine. New York: Aldine.

Jungers, William L. 1988b. Relative joint size and hominoid locomotor adaptations with implications for the evolution of hominid bipedalism. *Journal of Human Evolution* 17:247–65.

Jungers, William L., et al. 2009. The foot of *Homo floresiensis*. *Nature* 459 (May 7):81–84.

Kahn, Matthew E. 2005. The death toll from natural disasters: The role of income, geography, and institutions. *The Review of Economics and Statistics* 87:271–84.

Kamin, Leon J. 1995. Behind the curve. *Scientific American* (February):99–103.

Kang, Bong W. 2000. A reconsideration of population pressure and warfare: A protohistoric Korean case. *Current Anthropology* 41:873–81.

Kang, Gay Elizabeth. 1979. Exogamy and peace relations of social units: A cross-cultural test. *Ethnology* 18:85–99.

Kaplan, Hillard, and Kim Hill. 1985. Food sharing among Achéforagers: Tests of explanatory hypotheses. *Current Anthropology* 26:223–46.

Kaplan, Hillard, Kim Hill, and A. Magdalena Hurtado. 1990. Risk, foraging and food sharing among the Aché. In *Risk and uncertainty in tribal and peasant economies*, ed. E. Cashdan. Boulder, CO: Westview.

Kaplan, Hillard, Kim Hill, Jane Lancaster, and A. Magdalena Hurtado. 2000. A theory of human life history evolution, diet, intelligence, and longevity. *Evolutionary Anthropology* 9:156–84.

Kardiner, Abram, with Ralph Linton. 1946/1939. *The individual and his society*. New York: Golden Press.

Kasarda, John D. 1971. Economic structure and fertility: A comparative analysis. *Demography* 8, no.3:307–18.

Katzner, Kenneth. 2002. *Languages of the world*. London: Routledge.

Kay, Paul, Brent Berlin, Luisa Maffi, William R. Merrifield, and Richard Cook. 2009. *The world color survey*. Stanford, California: Center for the Study of Languages and Information.

Kay, Richard F. 2000a. *Parapithecidae*. In *Encyclopedia of human evolution and prehistory*, eds. I. Tattersall, E. Delson, and J. Van Couvering. New York: Garland.

Kay, Richard F. 2000b. Teeth. In *Encyclopedia of human evolution and prehistory*, eds. I. Tattersall, E. Delson, and J. Van Couvering. New York: Garland.

Kay, Richard F., C. Ross, and B. A. Williams. 1997. Anthropoid origins. *Science* 275 (February 7):797–804.

Kedia, Satish. 2008. Recent changes and trends in the practice of anthropology. *NAPA Bulletin* 29:14–28.

Kedia, Satish, and John van Willigen. 2005. Applied anthropology: Context for domains of application. In *Applied anthropology: Domains of application*, eds. S. Kedia and J. van Willigen. Westport, CT: Praeger.

Keeley, Lawrence H. 1980. *Experimental determination of stone tool uses: A microwear analysis*. Chicago: University of Chicago Press.

Keeley, Lawrence H. 1991. Ethnographic models for late glacial hunter-gatherers. In *The late glacial in North-West Europe: Human adaptation and environmental change at the end of the Pleistocene*, eds. N. Barton, A. J. Roberts, and D. A. Roe. London: Council for British Archaeology (CBA Research Report 77).

Keeley, Lawrence H. 1996. *War before civilization: The myth of the peaceful savage*. Oxford: Oxford University Press.

Keenan, Elinor. 1989. Norm-makers, norm-breakers: Uses of speech by men and women in a Malagasy community. In *Explorations in the ethnography of speaking*, 2nd ed., eds. R. Bauman and J. Sherzer. New York: Cambridge University Press.

Kehoe, Alice B., and Dody H. Giletti. 1981. Women's preponderance in possession cults: The calcium-deficiency hypothesis extended. *American Anthropologist* 83:549–61.

Keller, Helen. 1974/1902. *The story of my life*. New York: Dell.

Kelley, J. 1992. The evolution of apes. In *The Cambridge encyclopedia of human evolution*, eds. S. Jones, R. Martin, and D. Pilbeam. New York: Cambridge University Press.

Kelley, Jay. 2002. The hominoid radiation in Asia. In *The primate fossil record*, ed. W. C. Hartwig. Cambridge: Cambridge University Press.

Kelly, Raymond C. 1974. Witchcraft and sexual relations: An exploration in the social and semantic implications of the structure of belief. Paper presented at the annual meeting of the American Anthropological Association, Mexico City.

Kelly, Raymond C. 1985. *The Nuer conquest: The structure and development of an expansionist system*. Ann Arbor: University of Michigan Press.

Kelly, Robert L. 1995. *The foraging spectrum: Diversity in hunter-gatherer lifeways*. Washington, DC: Smithsonian Institution Press.

Kent, Susan, ed. 1996. *Cultural diversity among twentieth-century foragers: An African perspective*. Cambridge: Cambridge University Press.

Kerr, Richard A. 1998. Sea-floor dust shows drought felled Akkadian empire. *Science* 299 (January 16):325–26.

Khosroshashi, Fatemeh. 1989. Penguins don't care, but women do: A social identity analysis of a Whorfian problem. *Language in Society* 18:505–25.

Kilbride, Philip L., and Janet C. Kilbride. 1990. Polygyny: A modern contradiction? In *Changing family life in East Africa: Women and children at risk*, eds. P. L. Kilbride and J. C. Kilbride. University Park: Pennsylvania State University Press.

Kimbel, William H., T. D. White, and D. C. Johansen. 1984. Cranial morphology of *Australopithecus afarensis*: A comparative study based on composite reconstruction of the adult skull. *American Journal of Physical Anthropology* 64:337–88.

King, Barbara J. 1999a. Introduction. In *The origins of language*, ed. B. J. King. Santa Fe, NM: School of American Research Press.

King, Barbara J. 1999b. *The origins of language: What nonhuman primates can tell us*. Santa Fe: School of American Research Press.

King, J. C. H. 1986. Tradition in Native American art. In *The arts of the North American Indian*, ed. E. L. Wade. New York: Hudson Hills Press.

King, Marie-Claire, and Arno Motulsky. 2002. Mapping human history. *Science* 298 (December 20):2, 342–43.

King, Seth S. 1979. Some farm machinery seems less than human. *New York Times*, April 8, p. E9.

Kingston, John D., Bruno D. Marino, and Andrew Hill. 1994. Isotopic evidence for Neogene hominid paleoenvironments in the Kenya Rift Valley. *Science* 264 (May 13):955–59.

Kitchen, Andrew, Michael Miyamoto, and Connie Mulligan. 2008. A three-stage colonization model for the peopling of the Americas. *PLoS ONE* 3, no. 2:e1596.

Klass, Morton. 2009. Is there "caste" outside of India? In *MyAnthroLibrary*, eds. C. R. Ember, M. Ember, and P. N. Peregrine. MyAnthroLibrary.com. Pearson.

Klein, Richard G. 1974. Ice-age hunters of the Ukraine. *Scientific American* (June):96–105.

Klein, Richard G. 1977. The ecology of early man in Southern Africa. *Science* 197 (July 8):115–26.

Klein, Richard G. 1983. The Stone Age prehistory of Southern Africa. *Annual Review of Anthropology* 12:25–48.

Klein, Richard G. 1987. Reconstructing how early people exploited animals: Problems and prospects. In *The evolution of human hunting*, eds. M. Nitecki and D. Nitecki. New York: Plenum.

Klein, Richard G. 1989. *The human career: Human biological and cultural origins*. Chicago: University of Chicago Press.

Klein, Richard G. 1994. Southern Africa before the Ice Age. In *Integrative paths to the past*, eds. R. Corruccini and R. Ciochon. Upper Saddle River, NJ: Prentice Hall.

Klein, Richard G. 2003. Whither the Neanderthals? *Science* 299 (March 7):1525–28.

Klein, Richard G. 2009. *The human career: Human biological and cultural origins*, 3rd ed. Chicago: University of Chicago Press.

Klein, Richard G., and Blake Edgar. 2002. *The dawn of human culture*. New York: John Wiley and Sons.

Kleinberg, Jill. 1994. Practical implications of organizational culture where Americans and Japanese work together. In *Practicing anthropology in corporate America*, ed. A. T. Jordan. Arlington, VA: American Anthropological Association.

Kleinman, Arthur. 1988. *Rethinking psychiatry: From cultural category to personal experience*. New York: Macmillan.

Kleinman, Arthur. 2004. Culture and depression. *New England Journal of Medicine* 351:951–2.

Kleinman, Arthur, Veena Das, and Margaret Lock, eds. 1997. *Social suffering*. Berkeley: University of California Press.

Klima, Bohuslav. 1962. The first ground-plan of an Upper Paleolithic loess settlement in Middle Europe and its meaning. In *Courses toward urban life*, eds. R. Braidwood and G. Willey. Chicago: Aldine.

Klineberg, Otto. 1935. *Negro intelligence and selective migration*. New York: Columbia University Press.

Klineberg, Otto, ed. 1944. *Characteristics of the American Negro*. New York: Harper & Brothers.

Klineberg, Otto. 1979. Foreword. In *Cross-cultural psychology*, ed. M. H. Segall. Monterey, CA: Brooks/Cole.

Kluckhohn, Clyde. 1948. As an anthropologist views it. In *Sex habits of American men*, ed. A. Deutsch. Upper Saddle River, NJ: Prentice Hall.

Kluckhohn, Clyde. 1965. Recurrent themes in myths and mythmaking. In *The study of folklore*, ed. A. Dundes. Upper Saddle River, NJ: Prentice Hall.

Knauft, Bruce M. 1978. Cargo cults and relational separation. *Behavior Science Research* 13:185–240.

Knecht, Peter. 2003. Aspects of shamanism: An introduction. In *Shamans in Asia*, eds. C. Chilson and P. Knecht. London: Routledge Curzon.

Knight, Chris and Camilla Power. 2006. Words are not costly displays: Shortcomings of a testosterone-fuelled model of language evolution. *Behavioral and Brain Sciences* 29:290–291.

Koch, Klaus-Friedrich, Soraya Altorki, Andrew Arno, and Letitia Hickson. 1977. Ritual reconciliation and the obviation of grievances: A comparative study in the ethnography of law. *Ethnology* 16:269–84.

Kolbert, Elizabeth. 2005. Last words. *The New Yorker*, June 6, 46–59.

Komar, Debra A., and Jane E. Buikstra. 2008. *Forensic anthropology: Contemporary theory and practice*. New York: Oxford University Press.

Konner, Melvin. 2010. *The evolution of childhood: Relationships, emotion, mind*. Cambridge, MA: Belknap Press.

Konner, Melvin, and Carol Worthman. 1980. Nursing frequency, gonadal function, and birth spacing among !Kung hunter-gatherers. *Science* 267 (February 15):788–91.

Kopytoff, Igor. 1996. Slavery. In *Encyclopedia of cultural anthropology*, vol. 4, eds. D. Levinson and M. Ember. New York: Henry Holt.

Korbin, Jill E. 1981. Introduction. In *Child abuse and neglect*, ed. J. E. Korbin. Berkeley: University of California Press.

Korotayev, Andrey. 2008. Trade and warfare in cross-cultural perspective. *Social Evolution and History* 7:40–55.

Korotayev, Andrey, and Dmitri Bondarenko. 2000. Polygyny and democracy: A cross-cultural comparison. *Cross-Cultural Research* 34:190–208.

Kottak, Conrad Phillip. 1996. The media, development, and social change. In *Transforming societies, transforming anthropology*, ed. E. F. Moran. Ann Arbor: University of Michigan Press.

Kottak, Conrad Phillip. 1999. The new ecological anthropology. *Current Anthropology* 101:23–35.

Kracke, Waud H. 1979. *Force and persuasion: Leadership in an Amazonian society*. Chicago: University of Chicago Press.

Krahn, H., T. F. Hartnagel, and J. W. Gartrell. 1986. Income inequality and homicide rates: Cross-national data and criminological theories. *Criminology* 24:269–95.

Kramer, Andrew. 2009. The natural history and evolutionary fate of *Homo erectus*. In MyAnthroLibrary, eds. C. R. Ember, M. Ember, and P. N. Peregrine. MyAnthroLibrary.com. Pearson.

Kramer, Samuel Noel. 1963. *The Sumerians: Their history, culture, and character*. Chicago: University of Chicago Press.

Krause, Johannes, et al. 2007. The derived FOXP2 variant of modern humans was shared with Neandertals. *Current Biology* 17, no.21:1908–12.

Krause, Johannes, et al. 2010. The complete mitochondrial DNA genome of an unknown hominin from southern Siberia. *Nature* 464 (April 8):894–97.

Krebs, J. R., and N. B. Davies, eds. 1984. *Behavioural ecology: An evolutionary approach*. 2nd ed. Sunderland, MA: Sinauer.

Krebs, J. R., and N. B. Davies. 1987. *An introduction to behavioural ecology*. 2nd ed. Sunderland, MA: Sinauer.

Kremer-Sadlik, Tamar, Marilena Fatigante, and Alessandra Fasulo. 2008. Discourses on family time: The cultural interpretation of family togetherness in Los Angeles and Rome. *Ethos* 36:283–309.

Krings, Matthias, A. Stone, R. W. Schmitz, H. Krainitzki, M. Stoneking, and S. Paabo. 1997. Neandertal DNA sequences and the origin of modern humans. *Cell* 90:19–30.

Krippner, Stanley. 1987. Dreams and shamanism. In *Shamanism*, comp. S. Nicholson, 125–32. Wheaton, IL: Theosophical Publishing House.

Krippner, Stanley. 2000. The epistemology and technologies of shamanic states of consciousness. *Journal of Consciousness Studies* 7:11–12.

Kristof, Nicholas D. 1995. Japan's invisible minority: Better off than in past, but still outcasts. *New York Times*, International, November 30, p. A18.

Kristof, Nicholas D. 1997. Japan's invisible minority: Burakumin. *Britannica Online*, December.

Kroeber, Theodora. 1967. *Ishi in two worlds*. Berkeley: University of California Press.

Kuehn, Steven. 1998. New evidence for Late Paleoindian—Early Archaic subsistence behavior in the western Great Lakes. *American Antiquity* 63:457–76.

Kulick, Don. 1992. *Language shift and cultural reproduction*. Cambridge: Cambridge University Press.

Kushner, Gilbert. 1991. Applied anthropology. In *Career explorations in human services*, eds. W. G. Emener and M. Darrow. Springfield, IL: Charles C Thomas.

Lacruz, Rodrigo S., Fernando Ramirez Rozzi, and Timothy G. Bromage. 2005. Dental enamel hypoplasia, age at death, and weaning in the Taung child. *South African Journal of Science* 101:567–69.

Lacruz, Rodrigo S., Fernando Ramirez Rozzi, and Timothy G. Bromage. 2006. Variation in enamel development of South African fossil hominids. *Journal of Human Evolution* 51, no. 6:580–90.

Lakoff, Robin. 1973. Language and woman's place. *Language in Society* 2:45–80.

Lakoff, Robin. 1990. Why can't a woman be less like a man? In *Talking power*, ed. R. Lakoff. New York: Basic Books.

Lalueza-Fox, Carles, et al. 2007. A melanocortin 1 receptor allele suggests varying pigmentation among Neanderthals. *Science* 318 (November 30):1453–55.

Lambert, Helen. 2001. Not talking about sex in India: Indirection and the communication of bodily intention. In *An anthropology of indirect communication*, eds. J. Hendry and C. W. Watson. London: Routledge.

Lambert, Patricia M., Banks L. Leonard, Brian R. Billman, Richard A. Marlar, Margaret E. Newman, and Karl J. Reinhard. 2000. Response to critique of the claim of cannibalism at Cowboy Wash. *American Antiquity* 65, no.2:397–406.

Lambert, William W., Leigh Minturn Triandis, and Margery Wolf. 1959. Some correlates of beliefs in the malevolence and benevolence of supernatural beings: A cross-societal study. *Journal of Abnormal and Social Psychology* 58:162–69.

Lamphere, Louise. 2006. Foreward: Taking stock—The transformation of feminist theorizing in anthropology. In *Feminist anthropology: Past, present, and future*, eds. P. L. Geller and M. K. Stockett, ix–xvi. Philadelphia: University of Pennsylvania Press.

Lancy, David F. 2007. Accounting for variability in mother-child play. *American Anthropologist* 109:273–84.

Lancy, David F. 2008. *The anthropology of childhood: Cherubs, chattel, changelings*. Cambridge: Cambridge University Press.

Landauer, Thomas K. 1973. Infantile vaccination and the secular trend in stature. *Ethos* 1:499–503.

Landauer, Thomas K., and John W. M. Whiting. 1964. Infantile stimulation and adult stature of human males. *American Anthropologist* 66:1007–28.

Landauer, Thomas K., and John W. M. Whiting. 1981. Correlates and consequences of stress in infancy. In *Handbook of cross-cultural human development*, eds. R. H. Munroe, R. Munroe, and B. Whiting. New York: Garland.

Landecker, Hannah. 2000. Immortality, in vitro: A history of the HeLa cell line. In *Biotechnology and culture:*

Bodies, anxieties, ethics, ed. P. Brodwin. Bloomington: Indiana University Press.

Lang, Sabine. 1999. Lesbians, men-women and two-spirits: Homosexuality and gender in Native American cultures. In *Female desires: Same-sex relations and transgender practices across cultures*, eds. E. Blackwood and S. E. Weiringa. New York: Columbia University Press.

Langdon, John. 2005. *The human strategy*. New York: Oxford University Press.

Langness, Lewis L. 1974. *The study of culture*. San Francisco: Chandler and Sharp.

Lareau, Annette. 2003. *Unequal childhoods: Class, race, and family life*. Berkeley, CA: University of California Press.

Larsen, Clark Spencer. 1997. *Bioarchaeology: Interpreting behavior from the human skeleton*. Cambridge: Cambridge University Press.

Larsen, Clark Spencer. 2009. Bare bones anthropology: The bioarchaeology of human remains. In MyAnthroLibrary, eds. C. R. Ember, M. Ember, and P. N. Peregrine. MyAnthroLibrary.com. Pearson.

Larson, Christine L., J. Aronoff, I. C. Sarinopoulos, and D. C. Zhu. 2009. Recognizing threat: A simple geometric shape activates neural circuitry for threat detection. *Journal of Cognitive Neuroscience* 21:1523–35.

Larson, Christine L., J. Aronoff, and J. Stearns. 2007. The shape of threat: Simple geometric forms evoke rapid and sustained capture of attention. *Emotion* 7:526–34.

Larson, Christine L., Joel Aronoff, Issidoros C. Sarinopoulos, and David C. Zhu. 2009. Recognizing threat: A simple geometric shape activates neural circuitry for threat detection. *Journal of Cognitive Neuroscience* 21:1523–35.

Lassiter, Luke Eric. 2008. Moving past public anthropology and doing collaborative research. *NAPA Bulletin* 29:70–86.

Lassiter, Luke Eric, Hurley Goodall, Elizabeth Campbell, and Michelle Natasya Johnson, eds. 2004. *The other side of Middletown: Exploring Muncie's African American community*. Walnut Creek, CA: AltaMira Press.

Lawless, Robert, Vinson H. Sutlive, Jr., and Mario D. Zamora, eds. 1983. *Fieldwork: The human experience*. New York: Gordon and Breach.

Lawrence, Felicity. 2011. Kenya's flower industry shows budding improvement. *The Guardian*, April 1.

Layton, Robert. 1992. *Australian rock art: A new synthesis*. Cambridge: Cambridge University Press.

Le, Huynh-Nhu. 2000. Never leave your little one alone: Raising an Ifaluk child. In *A world of babies: Imagined child care guides for seven societies*, eds. J. DeLoache and A. Gottlieb. Cambridge: Cambridge University Press.

Leach, Jerry W. 1983. Introduction. In *The Kula*, eds. J. W. Leach and E. Leach. Cambridge: Cambridge University Press.

Leacock, Eleanor. 1954. The Montagnais 'hunting territory' and the fur trade. *American Anthropological Association Memoir* 78:1–59.

Leacock, Eleanor, and Richard Lee. 1982. Introduction. In *Politics and history in band societies*, eds. E. Leacock and R. Lee. Cambridge: Cambridge University Press.

Leakey, Louis S. B. 1960. Finding the world's earliest man. *National Geographic* (September): 420–35.

Leakey, Louis S. B. 1965. *Olduvai Gorge, 1951–1961, Vol. I: A preliminary report on the geology and fauna*. Cambridge: Cambridge University Press.

Leakey, Maeve, C. S. Feibel, I. McDougall, and A. Walker. 1995. New four-million-year-old hominid species from Kanapoi and Allia Bay, Kenya. *Nature* 376 (August 17): 565–71.

Leakey, Maeve, et al. 2001. New hominin genus from eastern Africa shows diverse Middle Pliocene lineages. *Nature* 410 (March 22):433–51.

Leakey, Mary. 1971. *Olduvai Gorge: Excavations in Beds I and II*. Cambridge: Cambridge University Press.

Leakey, Mary. 1979. *Olduvai Gorge: My search for early man*. London: Collins.

Lederman, Rena. 1990. Big men, large and small? Towards a comparative perspective. *Ethnology* 29:3–15.

Lee, Kristen Schultz. 2010. Gender, care work, and the complexity of family membership in Japan. *Gender & Society* 24, no. 5:647–71.

Lee, Phyllis C. 1983. Home range, territory and intergroup encounters. In *Primate social relationship: An integrated approach*, ed. R. A. Hinde. Sunderland, MA: Sinauer.

Lee, Richard B. 1968. What hunters do for a living, or, how to make out on scarce resources. In *Man the hunter*, eds. R. B. Lee and I. DeVore. Chicago: Aldine.

Lee, Richard B. 1972. Population growth and the beginnings of sedentary life among the !Kung bushmen. In *Population growth*, ed. B. Spooner. Cambridge, MA: MIT Press.

Lee, Richard B. 1979. *The !Kung San: Men, women, and work in a foraging society*. Cambridge: Cambridge University Press.

Lees, Susan H., and Daniel G. Bates. 1974. The origins of specialized nomadic pastoralism: A systemic model. *American Antiquity* 39:187–93.

Leibowitz, Lila. 1978. *Females, males, families: A biosocial approach*. North Scituate, MA: Duxbury.

Leis, Nancy B. 1974. Women in groups: Ijaw women's associations. In *Woman, culture, and society*, eds. M. Z. Rosaldo and L. Lamphere. Stanford, CA: Stanford University Press.

Lenski, Gerhard. 1984/1966. *Power and privilege: A theory of social stratification*. Chapel Hill: University of North Carolina Press.

Leonard, William R. 2002. Food for thought: Dietary change was a driving force in human evolution. *Scientific American* (December):108–15.

Leonard, William R., and Peter T. Katzmarzyk. 2010. Body size and shape: Climatic and nutritional influences on human body morphology. In *Human evolutionary biology*, ed. M. Muehlenbein. Cambridge: Cambridge University Press.

Leonhardt, David, and Geraldine Fabrikant. 2009. Rise of the super-rich hits a sobering wall. *New York Times*, New York, August 20, p. A1.

Lepowsky, Maria. 1990. Big men, big women and cultural autonomy. *Ethnology* 29:35–50.

Leslie, C. 1976. Introduction. In *Asian medical systems: A comparative study*, ed. C. Leslie. Los Angeles: University of California Press.

Lev-Yadun, Simcha, Avi Gopher, and Shahal Abbo, 2000. The cradle of agriculture. *Science* 288 (June 2):1602–1603.

Levine, James A., Robert Weisell, Simon Chevassus, Claudio D. Martinez, and Barbara Burlingame. 2002. The distribution of work tasks for male and female children and adults separated by gender. *Science* 296 (May 10):1025.

Levine, Nancy E. 1988. Women's work and infant feeding: A case from rural Nepal. *Ethnology* 27:231–51.

LeVine, Robert A. 1966. *Dreams and deeds: Achievement motivation in Nigeria*. Chicago: University of Chicago Press.

LeVine, Robert A. 1988. Human parental care: Universal goals, cultural strategies, individual behavior. In *Parental behavior in diverse societies*, eds. R. A. LeVine, P. M. Miller, and M. M. West. San Francisco: Jossey-Bass.

LeVine, Robert A. 2007. Ethnographic studies of childhood: A historical overview. *American Anthropologist* 109:247–60.

LeVine, Robert A. 2011. Traditions in transition: Adolescents remaking culture. *Ethos* 39:426–31.

LeVine, Robert A., and Barbara B. LeVine. 1963. Nyansongo: A Gusii Community in Kenya. In *Six cultures*, ed. B. B. Whiting. New York: Wiley.

LeVine, Robert A., and Karin Norman. 2001. The infant's acquisition of culture: Early attachment reexamined in anthropological perspective. In *The psychology of cultural experience*, eds. H. F. Mathews and C. C. Moore. Cambridge: Cambridge University Press.

Levinson, David. 1989. *Family violence in cross-cultural perspective*. Newbury Park, CA: Sage.

Levinson, David, and Melvin Ember, eds. 1997. *American immigrant cultures: Builders of a nation*, 2 vols. New York: Macmillan Reference.

Lévi-Strauss, Claude. 1963a. The sorcerer and his magic. In *Structural anthropology*, ed. C. Lévi-Strauss. New York: Basic Books.

Lévi-Strauss, Claude. 1963b. *Structural anthropology*. Trans. Claire Jacobson and Brooke Grundfest Schoepf. New York: Basic Books.

Lévi-Strauss, Claude. 1966. *The savage mind*. Trans. George Weidenfeld and Nicolson, Ltd. Chicago: University of Chicago Press.

Lévi-Strauss, Claude. 1969a. *The elementary structures of kinship*, rev. ed. Trans. James H. Bell and J. R. Von Sturmer. Boston: Beacon Press.

Lévi-Strauss, Claude. 1969b. *The raw and the cooked*. Trans. John Weightman and Doreen Weightman. New York: Harper & Row.

Levy, Jerrold E. 1994. Hopi shamanism: A reappraisal. In *North American Indian anthropology: Essays on society and culture*, eds. R. J. DeMallie and A. Ortiz. Norman: University of Oklahoma Press.

Lewellen, Ted C. 2003. *Political anthropology: An introduction*. 3rd ed. Westport, CT: Praeger.

Lewin, Roger. 1983a. Fossil Lucy grows younger, again. *Science* 219 (January 7):43–44.

Lewin, Roger. 1983b. Is the orangutan a living fossil? *Science* 222 (December 16):1222–23.

Lewin, Tamar. 1994. Sex in America: Faithfulness in marriage is overwhelming. *New York Times*, National, October 7, pp. A1, A18.

Lewis, Oscar. 1951. *Life in a Mexican village: Tepoztlan revisited*. Urbana: University of Illinois Press.

Lewis, Oscar (with the assistance of Victor Barnouw). 1958. *Village life in Northern India*. Urbana: University of Illinois Press.

Lewontin, Richard. 1972. The apportionment of human diversity. *Evolutionary Biology* 6, no. 1:381–98.

Lichter, Daniel T., Diane K. McLaughlin, George Kephart, and David J. Landry. 1992. Race and the retreat from marriage: A shortage of marriageable men? *American Sociological Review* 57:781–99.

Lieberman, Daniel E. 1995. Testing hypotheses about recent human evolution from skulls: integrating morphology, function, development, and phylogeny. *Current Anthropology* 36:159–97.

Lieberman, Leonard. 1999. Scientific insignificance. *Anthropology Newsletter* 40:11–12.

Lieberman, Leonard, Rodney Kirk, and Alice Littlefield. 2003. Perishing paradigm: Race 1931–99. *American Anthropologist* 105:110–13.

Lieberman, Leslie Sue. 2004. Diabetes mellitus and medical anthropology. In *Encyclopedia of medical anthropology: Health and illness in the world's cultures*, vol. I, eds. C. R. Ember and M. Ember. New York: Kluwer Academic Press/Plenum Publishers.

Light, Ivan, and Zhong Deng. 1995/1964. Gender differences in ROSCA participation within Korean business households in Los Angeles. In *Money-go-rounds: The importance of rotating savings and credit associations for women*, eds. S. Ardener and S. Burman. Oxford: Berg.

Lightfoot, Kent G. 2005. The archaeology of colonialism: California in cross-cultural perspective. In *The archaeology of colonial encounters: Comparative perspectives*, ed. G. J. Stein. Santa Fe, NM: School of American Research.

Lingenfelter, Sherwood G. 2009. Yap: Changing roles of men and women. In *MyAnthroLibrary*, eds. C. R. Ember, M. Ember, and P. N. Peregrine. MyAnthroLibrary.com. Pearson.

Linton, Ralph. 1936. *The study of man*. New York: Appleton-Century-Crofts.

Linton, Ralph. 1945. *The cultural background of personality*. New York: Appleton-Century-Crofts.

Little, A. C., Robert P. Burriss, Benedict C. Jones, and S. Craig Roberts. 2007. Facial appearance affects voting decisions. *Evolution and Human Behavior* 28:18–27.

Little, Kenneth. 1957. The role of voluntary associations in West African urbanization. *American Anthropologist* 59:582–93.

Little, Kenneth. 1965. *West African urbanization*. New York: Cambridge University Press.

Little, Kenneth. 1965/1966. The political function of the *Poro*. *Africa* 35:349–65; 36: 62–71.

Lock, Margaret. 2009. Japan: Glimpses of everyday life. In *MyAnthroLibrary*, eds. C. R. Ember, M. Ember, and P. N. Peregrine. MyAnthroLibrary.com. Pearson.

Lockett, Hattie Green. 1933. *The unwritten literature of the Hopi*. Social Science Bulletin No. 2, 6, 9–12. Tucson, Arizona: University of Arizona Press.

Loftin, Colin K. 1971. Warfare and societal complexity: A cross-cultural study of organized fighting in preindustrial societies. PhD dissertation, University of North Carolina at Chapel Hill.

Loftin, Colin K., David McDowall, and James Boudouris. 1989. Economic change and homicide in Detroit, 1926-1979. In *Violence in America, Vol. 1: The history of crime*, ed. T. R. Gurr. Newbury Park, CA: Sage.

Lomax, Alan, ed. 1968. *Folk song style and culture*. American Association for the Advancement of Science Publication No. 88. Washington, DC.

Long, Susan Orpett. 2000. Introduction. In *Caring for the elderly in Japan and the U.S.*, ed. S. Orpett Long. London: Routledge.

Long, Susan Orpett, Ruth Campbell, and Chie Nishimura. 2009. Does it matter who cares? A comparison of daughters versus daughters-in-law in Japanese elder care. *Social Science Japan Journal* 12, no. 1:1–21.

Longacre, William. 1970. *Archaeology as anthropology: A case study*. Anthropological papers of the University of Arizona, Number 17. Tucson: University of Arizona Press.

Loomis, W. Farnsworth. 1967. Skin-pigment regulation of vitamin-D biosynthesis in man. *Science* 157 (August 4):501–506.

Los Angeles Times. 1994. Plundering earth is nothing new. Reported in the *New Haven Register*, June 12, pp. A18–A19.

Loustaunau, Martha O., and Elisa J. Sobo. 1997. *The cultural context of health, illness, and medicine*. Westport, CT: Bergin & Garvey.

Lovejoy, Arthur O. 1964. *The great chain of being: A study of the history of an idea*. Cambridge, MA: Harvard University Press.

Lovejoy, C. Owen. 1981. The origin of man. *Science* 211 (January 23):341–50.

Lovejoy, C. Owen. 1988. Evolution of human walking. *Scientific American* (November):118–25.

Lovejoy, C. Owen. 2009. Reexamining human origins in light of *Ardipithecus ramidus*. *Science* 326 (October 2):74, 74e1–74e8.

Low, Bobbi. 1990a. Human responses to environmental extremeness and uncertainty. In *Risk and uncertainty in tribal and peasant economies*, ed. E. Cashdan. Boulder, CO: Westview.

Low, Bobbi. 1990b. Marriage systems and pathogen stress in human societies. *American Zoologist* 30:325–39.

Low, Bobbi S. 2009. Behavioral ecology, "sociobiology," and human behavior. In *MyAnthroLibrary*, eds. C. R. Ember, M. Ember, and P. N. Peregrine. MyAnthroLibrary.com. Pearson.

Lowe, Edward D. 2002. A widow, a child, and two lineages: Exploring kinship and attachment in Chuuk. *American Anthropologist* 104:123–37.

Lucy, John A. 1992. *Grammatical categories and cognition: A case study of the linguistic relativity hypothesis*. Cambridge: Cambridge University Press.

Lumbreras, Luis. 1974. *The peoples and cultures of ancient Peru*. Washington, DC: Smithsonian Institution Press.

Luria, A. R. 1976. *Cognitive development: Its cultural and social foundations*. Cambridge, MA: Harvard University Press.

Lutz, Catherine. 1985. Depression and the translations of emotional worlds. In *Culture and depression*, eds. A. Kleinman and B. Good. Berkeley: University of California Press.

Lynd, Robert S., and Helen Merrell Lynd. 1929. *Middletown*. New York: Harcourt, Brace.

Lynd, Robert S., and Helen Merrell Lynd. 1937. *Middletown in transition*. New York: Harcourt, Brace.

Lyons, Nona Plessner. 1988. Two perspectives: On self, relationships, and morality. In *Mapping the moral domain*, eds. C. Gilligan, J. V. Ward, and J. M. Taylor. Cambridge, MA: Harvard University Press.

Lyttleton, Chris. 2000. *Endangered relations: Negotiating sex and AIDS in Thailand*. Bangkok: White Lotus Press.

MacArthur, R. H., and E. O. Wilson. 1967. *Theory of island biogeography*. Princeton, NJ: Princeton University Press.

Maccoby, Eleanor E., and Carol N. Jacklin. 1974. *The psychology of sex differences*. Stanford, CA: Stanford University Press.

Macdonald, Douglas H., and Barry S. Hewlett. 1999. Reproductive interests and forager mobility. *Current Anthropology* 40:501–23.

MacDorman, Marian F., and T. J. Mathews. 2011. *Understanding racial and ethnic disparities in U.S. infant mortality rates*. NCHS Data Brief. No. 74. Hyattsville, MD: National Center for Health Statistics.

MacKinnon, John, and Kathy MacKinnon. 1980. The behavior of wild spectral tarsiers. *International Journal of Primatology* 1:361–79.

MacNeish, Richard S. 1991. *The origins of agriculture and settled life*. Norman: University of Oklahoma Press.

Madrigal, Lorena. 1989. Hemoglobin genotype, fertility, and the malaria hypothesis. *Human Biology* 61:311–25.

Magner, L. 1992. *A history of medicine*. New York: Marcel Dekker.

Mahony, Frank Joseph. 1971. *A Trukese theory of medicine*. Ann Arbor, MI: University Microfilms.

Malefijt, Annemarie De Waal. 1968. *Religion and culture: An introduction to anthropology of religion*. New York: Macmillan.

Malin, Edward. 1986. *Totem poles of the Pacific Northwest Coast*. Portland, OR: Timber Press.

Malinowski, Bronislaw. 1920. Kula: The circulating exchange of valuables in the archipelagoes of eastern New Guinea. *Man* 51, no. 2:97–105.

Malinowski, Bronislaw. 1927. *Sex and repression in savage society*. London: Kegan Paul, Trench, Trubner.

Malinowski, Bronislaw. 1932. *The sexual life of savages in northwestern Melanesia*. New York: Halcyon House.

Malinowski, Bronislaw. 1939. The group and the individual in functional analysis. *American Journal of Sociology* 44:938–64.

Malinowski, Bronislaw. 1954. Magic, science, and religion. In *Magic, science, and religion and other essays*, ed. B. Malinowski. Garden City, NY: Doubleday.

Mangin, William P. 1965. The role of regional associations in the adaptation of rural migrants to cities in Peru. In *Contemporary cultures and societies of Latin America*, eds. D. B. Heath and R. N. Adams. New York: Random House.

Mangin, William P. 1967. Latin American squatter settlements: A problem and a solution. *Latin American Research Review* 2:65–98.

Manhein, Mary H. 1999. *The bone lady: Life as a forensic anthropologist*. Baton Rouge: Louisiana State University Press.

Mansfield, Edward D., and Jack Snyder. 2007. *Electing to fight: Why emerging democracies go to war*. Cambridge, MA: MIT Press.

Maquet, Jacques. 1986. *The aesthetic experience: An anthropologist looks at the visual arts*. New Haven, CT: Yale University Press.

Marano, Louis A. 1973. A macrohistoric trend toward world government. *Behavior Science Notes* 8:35–40.

Marcus, George E., and Michael M. J. Fischer. 1986. *Anthropology as cultural critique: An experimental moment in the human sciences*. Chicago: University of Chicago Press.

Marcus, Joyce. 1983. On the nature of the Mesoamerican city. In *Prehistoric settlement patterns*, eds. E. Vogt and R. Leventhal. Albuquerque: University of New Mexico Press.

Marcus, Joyce. 2009. Maya hieroglyphs: History or propaganda? In MyAnthroLibrary, eds. C. R. Ember, M. Ember, and P. N. Peregrine. MyAnthroLibrary.com. Pearson.

Marcus, Joyce, and Kent V. Flannery. 1996. *Zapotec civilization*. London: Thames and Hudson.

Marett, R. R. 1909. *The thresholds of religion*. London: Methuen.

Marks, Jonathan. 1994. Black, white, other: Racial categories are cultural constructs masquerading as biology. *Natural History* (December):32–35.

Marks, Jonathan. 2002. Genes, bodies, and species. In *Physical anthropology: Original readings in method and practice*, eds. P. N. Peregrine, C. R. Ember, and M. Ember. Upper Saddle River, NJ: Prentice Hall.

Marks, Jonathan. 2008. Race: Past, present, future. In *Revisiting race in a genomic age*, eds. B. A. Koening, S. S. J. Lee, and S. S. Richardson. New Brunswick, NJ: Rutgers University Press.

Marks, Jonathan. 2009. Genes, bodies, and species. In MyAnthroLibrary, eds. C. R. Ember, M. Ember, and P. N. Peregrine. MyAnthroLibrary.com. Pearson.

Marlowe, Frank W. 2003. A critical period for provisioning by Hadza men: Implications for pair bonding. *Evolution and Human Behavior* 24:217–29.

Marshack, Alexander. 1972. *The roots of civilization*. New York: McGraw-Hill.

Marshall, Eliot. 2000. Rival genome sequencers celebrate a milestone together. *Science* 288 (June 30):2294–95.

Marshall, Larry G. 1984. Who killed Cock Robin? An investigation of the extinction controversy. In *Quaternary extinctions*, eds. P. Martin and R. Klein. Tucson: University of Arizona Press.

Marshall, Lorna. 1961. Sharing, talking and giving: Relief of social tensions among !Kung Bushmen. *Africa* 31:239–42.

Martin, M. Kay, and Barbara Voorhies. 1975. *Female of the species*. New York: Columbia University Press.

Martin, Paul S. 1973. The discovery of America. *Science* 179 (March 9):969–74.

Martin, Paul S., and H. E. Wright, eds. 1967. *Pleistocene extinctions: The search for a cause*. New Haven, CT: Yale University Press.

Martin, Robert D. 1975. Strategies of reproduction. *Natural History* (November):48–57.

Martin, Robert D. 1990. *Primate origins and evolution: A phylogenetic reconstruction*. Princeton, NJ: Princeton University Press.

Martin, Robert D. 1992. Classification and evolutionary relationships. In *The Cambridge encyclopedia of human evolution*, eds. S. Jones, R. Martin, and D. Pilbeam. New York: Cambridge University Press.

Martin, Robert D., and K. Bearder Simon. 1979. Radio bush baby. *Natural History* (October):77–81.

Martorell, Reynaldo. 1980. Interrelationships between diet, infectious disease and nutritional status. In *Social and biological predictors of nutritional status, physical growth and neurological development*, eds. L. Greene and F. Johnston. New York: Academic Press.

Martorell, Reynaldo, Juan Rivera, Haley Kaplowitz, and Ernesto Pollitt. 1991. Long-term consequences of growth retardation during early childhood. Paper presented at the Sixth International Congress of Auxology, Madrid, September 15–19.

Marx, David M., Sei Jin Ki, and Ray A. Friedman. 2009. The "Obama effect": How a salient role model reduces race-based performance differences. *Journal of Experimental Social Psychology* 45:953–56.

Mascie-Taylor, C. G. Nicholas. 1990. The biology of social class. In *Biosocial aspects of social class*, ed. C. G. N. Mascie-Taylor. Oxford: Oxford University Press.

Maslow, Abraham H. 1964. *Religions, values, and peak-experiences*. Columbus: Ohio State University Press.

Mason, Philip. 1962. *Prospero's magic*. London: Oxford University Press.

Masumura, Wilfred T. 1977. Law and violence: A cross-cultural study. *Journal of Anthropological Research* 33:388–99.

Mathiassen, Therkel. 1928. *Material culture of Iglulik Ekimos*. Copenhagen: Glydendalske.

Matossian, Mary K. 1982. Ergot and the Salem witchcraft affair. *American Scientist* 70:355–57.

Matossian, Mary K. 1989. *Poisons of the past: Molds, epidemics, and history*. New Haven, CT: Yale University Press.

Matt, Siegel. 2011. Australia says it will open combat roles to women. *New York Times*, September 27.

Matthews, Roger. 2009. Peoples and complex societies of Southwest Asia. In *The human past*, ed. C. Scarre. New York: Thames and Hudson.

Mattingly, Cheryl, Nancy C. Lukehaus, and C. Jason Throop. 2008. Bruner's search for meaning: A conversation between psychology and anthropology. *Ethos* 36:1–28.

Maybury-Lewis, David. 1967. *Akwe-Shavante society*. Oxford: Clarendon Press.

Mayer, Philip, and Iona Mayer. 1970. Socialization by peers: The youth organization of the Red Xhosa. In *Socialization: The approach from social anthropology*, ed. P. Mayer. London: Tavistock.

Mayr, Ernst. 1982. *The growth of biological thought: Diversity, evolution, and inheritance*. Cambridge, MA: Belknap Press of Harvard University Press.

Mazess, Richard B. 1975. Human adaptation to high altitude. In *Physiological anthropology*, ed. A. Damon. New York: Oxford University Press.

McCain, Garvin, and Erwin M. Segal. 1988. *The game of science*. 5th ed. Monterey, CA: Brooks/Cole.

McCall, Patricia L., Karen F. Parker, and John M. MacDonald. 2008. The dynamic relationship between homicide rates and social, economic, and political factors from 1970 to 2000. *Social Science Research* 37:721–35.

McCarthy, Frederick D., and Margaret McArthur. 1960. The food quest and the time factor in Aboriginal economic life. In *Records of the Australian-American scientific expedition to Arnhem Land, Vol. 2: Anthropology and nutrition*, ed. C. P. Mountford. Melbourne: Melbourne University Press.

McCaskey, J. P. 1881. *Franklin Square song collection*. Vol. 1. New York Harper& Brothers.

McClelland, David C. 1961. *The achieving society*. New York: Van Nostrand.

McCorriston, Joy, and Frank Hole. 1991. The ecology of seasonal stress and the origins of agriculture in the Near East. *American Anthropologist* 93:46–69.

McCracken, Robert D. 1971. Lactase deficiency: An example of dietary evolution. *Current Anthropology* 12:479–500.

McDermott, LeRoy. 1996. Self-representation in female figurines. *Current Anthropology* 37:227–75.

McDonald, Kim A. 1998. New evidence challenges traditional model of how the New World was settled. *Chronicle of Higher Education*, March 13, p. A22.

McElrath, Dale and Thomas Emerson. 2012. Reenvisioning Eastern Woodlands archaic origins. In *Oxford handbook of North American archaeology*, ed. T. Pauketat. Oxford: Oxford University Press.

McElreath, Richard, and Pontus Strimling. 2008. When natural selection favors imitation of parents. *Current Anthropology* 49:307–16.

McElroy, Ann, and Patricia Townsend. 2002. *Medical anthropology in ecological perspective*. 3rd ed. Boulder, CO: Westview.

McGuire, Thomas R. 2005. The domain of the environment. In *Applied anthropology: Domains of application*, eds. S. Kedia and J. van Willigen. Westport, CT: Praeger.

McHenry, Henry M. 1982. The pattern of human evolution: Studies on bipedalism, mastication, and encephalization. *Annual Review of Anthropology* 11:151–73.

McHenry, Henry M. 1988. New estimates of body weight in early hominids and their significance to encephalization and megadontia in "robust" australopithecines. In *Evolutionary history of the "robust" australopithecines*, ed. F. E. Grine. New York: Aldine.

McHenry, Henry M. 2009. "Robust" australopithecines, our family tree, and homoplasy. In MyAnthroLibrary, eds. C. R. Ember, M. Ember, and P. N. Peregrine. MyAnthroLibrary.com. Pearson.

McKee, Lauris. 1984. Sex differentials in survivorship and the customary treatment of infants and children. *Medical Anthropology* 8:91–108.

McKee, Lauris. 2009. Andean Mestizos: Growing up female and male. In *MyAnthroLibrary*, eds. C. R. Ember, M. Ember, and P. N. Peregrine. MyAnthroLibrary.com. Pearson

McKeown, Adam. 2005. Chinese diaspora. In *Encyclopedia of diasporas: Immigrant and refugee cultures around the world*, vol. 1, eds. M. Ember, C. R. Ember, and I. Skoggard. New York: Kluwer Academic/Plenum.

McMullin, Ernan. 2001. Plantinga's defense of special creation. In *Intelligent design creationism and its critics*, ed. R. Pennock. Boston: MIT Press.

McNamee, Stephen, and Robert K. Miller. 2009. *The meritocracy myth*. 2nd ed. Lanham: Roman & Littlefield.

McNeil, Donald G., Jr. 2011. AIDS: A price break for antiretroviral drugs in 70 of the world's poorest countries. *New York Times*, May 23. http://www.nytimes.com/2011/05/24/health/24global.html (accessed May 19, 2013).

McNeill, William H. 1967. *A world history*. New York: Oxford University Press.

McNeill, William H. 1976. *Plagues and peoples*. Garden City, NY: Doubleday/Anchor.

McNeill, William H. 1998. *Plagues and peoples*. New York: Anchor Books/Doubleday.

Mead, Margaret. 1931. *Growing up in New Guinea*. London: Routledge & Kegan Paul.

Mead, Margaret. 1950/1935. *Sex and temperament in three primitive societies*. New York: Mentor.

Mead, Margaret. 1961/1928. *Coming of age in Samoa*. 3rd ed. New York: Morrow.

Meek, C. K. 1940. *Land law and custom in the colonies*. London: Oxford University Press.

Meggitt, Mervyn J. 1964. Male-female relationships in the highlands of Australian New Guinea. *American Anthropologist* 66:204–24.

Meggitt, Mervyn J. 1977. *Blood is their argument: Warfare among the Mae Enga tribesmen of the New Guinea highlands*. Palo Alto, CA: Mayfield.

Mehu, Marc, Karl Grammer, and Robin I. M. Dunbar. 2007. Smiles when sharing. *Evolution and Human Behavior* 28, no. 6:415–22.

Meillassoux, Claude. 1968. *Urbanization of an African community*. Seattle: University of Washington Press.

Mellaart, James. 1961. Roots in the soil. In *The dawn of civilization*, ed. S. Piggott. London: Thomas & Hudson.

Mellaart, James. 1964. A Neolithic city in Turkey. *Scientific American* (April):94–104.

Mellars, Paul. 1994. The Upper Paleolithic revolution. In *The Oxford illustrated prehistory of Europe*, ed. B. Cunliffe. Oxford: Oxford University Press.

Mellars, Paul. 1996. *The Neanderthal legacy,* 405–19. Princeton, NJ: Princeton University Press.

Mellars, Paul. 1998. The fate of the Neaderthals. *Nature* 395 (October 8):539–40.

Mellars, Paul, and J. French. 2011. Tenfold population increase in Western Europe at the Neadertal-to-modern human transition. *Science* 333 (July 29):623–27.

Mellor, John W., and Sarah Gavian. 1987. Famine: Causes, prevention, and relief. *Science* 235 (January 30):539–44.

Meltzer, David J. 1993. Pleistocene peopling of the Americas. *Evolutionary Anthropology* 1, no. 1:157–69.

Meltzer, David J. 2009. *First peoples in a new world: Colonizing Ice Age America*. Berkeley: University of California Press.

Mendoza-Denton, Norma. 2008. *Homegirls: Language and cultural practice among Latina youth gangs.* Oxford: Blackwell Publishing.

Merbs, Charles F. 1992. A new world of infectious disease. *Yearbook of Physical Anthropology* 35:3–42.

Merrill, Elizabeth Bryant. 1987. Art styles as reflections of sociopolitical complexity. *Ethnology* 26:221–30.

Mesoudi, Alex, and Stephen J. Lycett. 2009. Random copying, frequency-dependent copying and culture change. *Evolution and Human Behavior* 30:41–48.

Messer, Ellen. 1996. Hunger vulnerability from an anthropologist's food system perspective. In *Transforming societies, transforming anthropology*, ed. E. F. Moran. Ann Arbor: University of Michigan Press.

Messer, Ellen. 2009. Rising food prices, social mobilizations, and violence: Conceptual issues in understanding and responding to the connections linking hunger and conflict. *NAPA Bulletin* 32:12–22.

Middleton, John. 1971. The cult of the dead: Ancestors and ghosts. In *Reader in comparative religion*, 3rd ed., eds. W. A. Lessa and E. Z. Vogt. New York: Harper & Row.

Middleton, Russell. 1962. Brother-sister and father-daughter marriage in ancient Egypt. *American Sociological Review* 27:603–11.

Milanovic, Branko. 2005. *World's apart: Measuring international and global inequality.* Princeton: Princeton University Press.

Milanovic, Branko. 2011. *The haves and the have-nots: A brief and idiosyncratic history of global inequality.* New York: Basic Books.

Miller, Bruce G. 1992. Women and politics: Comparative evidence from the Northwest Coast. *Ethnology* 31:367–82.

Miller, Greg. 2004. Listen, baby. *Science* 306 (November 12):1127.

Miller, Joan G. 1994. Cultural diversity in the morality of caring: Individually oriented versus duty-based interpersonal moral codes. *Cross-Cultural Research* 28:3–39.

Millon, René. 1967. Teotihuacán. *Scientific American* (June):38–48.

Millon, René. 1976. Social relations in ancient Teotihuacán. In *The Valley of Mexico*, ed. E. Wolf. Albuquerque: University of New Mexico Press.

Milner, George. 1998. *The Cahokia chiefdom: The archaeology of a Mississippian society.* Washington, DC: Smithsonian Institution Press.

Milton, Katharine. 1981. Distribution patterns of tropical plant foods as an evolutionary stimulus to primate mental development. *American Anthropologist* 83:534–48.

Milton, Katharine. 1988. Foraging behaviour and the evolution of primate intelligence. In *Machiavellian intelligence: Social expertise and the evolution of intellect in monkeys, apes, and humans*, eds. R. W. Bryne and A. Whiten. Oxford: Clarendon Press.

Milton, Katharine. 2009. The evolution of a biological anthropologist. In MyAnthroLibrary, eds. C. R. Ember, M. Ember, and P. N. Peregrine. MyAnthroLibrary.com. Pearson.

Miner, Horace. 1956. Body rituals among the Nacirema. *American Anthropologist* 58:504–505.

Minturn, Leigh. 1993. *Sita's daughters: Coming out of Purdah: The Rajput women of Khalapur revisited.* New York: Oxford University Press.

Minturn, Leigh, and Jerry Stashak. 1982. Infanticide as a terminal abortion procedure. *Behavior Science Research* 17:70–85.

Mintz, Sidney W. 1956. Canamelar: The subculture of a rural sugar plantation proletariat. In *The people of Puerto Rico*, eds. J. H. Steward, R. A. Manners, E. R. Wolf, E. Padilla Seda, S. W. Mintz, and R. L. Scheele. Urbana: University of Illinois Press.

Minugh-Purvis, Nancy. 2009. Neandertal growth: Examining developmental adaptations in earlier *Homo sapiens*. In MyAnthroLibrary, eds. C. R. Ember, M. Ember, and P. N. Peregrine. MyAnthroLibrary.com. Pearson.

Miracle, Andrew W. 2009. A shaman to organizations. In MyAnthroLibrary, eds. C. R. Ember, M. Ember, and P. N. Peregrine. MyAnthroLibrary.com. Pearson.

Mitchell, Donald. 2009. Nimpkish: Complex foragers on the Northwest Coast of North America. In MyAnthroLibrary, eds. C. R. Ember, M. Ember, and P. N. Peregrine. MyAnthroLibrary.com. Pearson.

Mittermeier, Russell A., and Eleanor J. Sterling. 1992. Conservation of primates. In *The Cambridge encyclopedia of human evolution*, eds. S. Jones, R. Martin, and D. Pilbeam. New York: Cambridge University Press.

Mittermeier, Russell A., et al. 2009. Primates in Peril: The World's 25 Most Endangered Primates, 2008-2010. *Primate Conservation* 24:1–57.

Moerman, Daniel E. 1997. Physiology and symbols: The anthropological implications of the placebo effect. In *The anthropology of medicine*, 3rd ed., eds. L. Romanucci-Ross, D. E. Moerman, and L. R. Tancredi. Westport, CT: Bergin & Garvey.

Molnar, Stephen. 1998. *Human variation: Races, types, and ethnic groups.* 4th ed. Upper Saddle River, NJ: Prentice Hall.

Monot, Marc, et al. 2005. On the origin of leprosy. *Science* 308 (May 13):1040–42.

Monsutti, Alessandro. 2004. Cooperation, remittances, and kinship among the Hazaras. *Iranian Studies* 37:219–40.

Montagu, Ashley. 1997. *Man's most dangerous myth.* Walnut Creek, CA: AltaMira.

Mooney, Kathleen A. 1978. The effects of rank and wealth on exchange among the coast Salish. *Ethnology* 17:391–406.

Moore, Carmella C. 1988. An optimal scaling of Murdock's theories of illness data—An approach to the problem of interdependence. *Behavior Science Research* 22:161–79.

Moore, Carmella C. 1997. Is love always love? *Anthropology Newsletter* (November):8–9.

Moore, Carmella C., A. Kimball Romney, Ti-Lien Hsia, and Craig D. Rusch. 1999. The universality of the semantic structure of emotion terms: Methods for the study of inter- and intra-cultural variability. *American Anthropologist* 101:529–46.

Moore, John H., and Janis E. Campbell. 2002. Confirming unilocal residence in Native North America. *Ethnology* 41:175–88.

Moore, Omar Khayyam. 1957. Divination: A new perspective. *American Anthropologist* 59:69–74.

Moran, Emilio F. 1993. *Through Amazon eyes: The human ecology of Amazonian populations.* Iowa City: University of Iowa Press.

Moran, Emilio F., ed. 1996. *Transforming societies, transforming anthropology.* Ann Arbor: University of Michigan Press.

Moran, Emilio F. 2000. *Human adaptability: An introduction to ecological anthropology.* 2nd ed. Boulder, CO: Westview.

Moran, Emilio. 2011. Environmental anthropology as one of the spatial sciences. In *Environmental anthropology today*, eds. H. Kopnina and E. Shoreman-Ouimet. New York: Routledge.

Moran, Robert T., Philip R. Harris, and Sarah V. Moran. 2007. *Managing cultural differences: Global leadership strategies for the 21st century.* Burlington, MA: Butterworth Heinemann.

Morell, Virginia. 1995. The earliest art becomes older—And more common. *Science* 267 (March 31):1908–1909.

Morgan, Christopher and Robert Bettinger. 2012. Great Basin foraging strategies. In *Oxford handbook of North American archaeology*, ed. Timothy Pauketat, 185–98. Oxford: Oxford University Press.

Morgan, Lewis H. 1964/1877. *Ancient society.* Cambridge, MA: Harvard University Press.

Morphy, Howard, and Morgan Perkins. 2006. The anthropology of art: A reflection on its history and contemporary practice. In *The anthropology of art: A reader*, eds. H. Morphy and M. Perkins. Malden, MA: Blackwell.

Morris, Arthur. 2004. *Raised field technology: The raised field projects around Lake Titicaca.* Burlington, VT: Ashgate.

Morris, John. 1938. *Living with Lepchas: A book about the Sikkim Himalayas.* London: Heinemann.

Morrison, Kathleen D., and Laura L. Junker. 2002. *Forager-traders in South and Southeast Asia: Long-term histories.* Cambridge: Cambridge University Press.

Morwood, M. J., et al. 2004. Archaeology and age of a new hominin from Flores in Eastern Indonesia. *Nature* 431 (October 28):1087–91.

Moser, Stephanie. 1998. *Ancestral images: The iconography of human origins.* Ithaca, NY: Cornell University Press.

Motulsky, Arno. 1971. Metabolic polymorphisms and the role of infectious diseases in human evolution. In *Human populations, genetic variation, and evolution*, ed. L. N. Morris. San Francisco: Chandler.

Moyá-solá, Salvador, Meike Köhler, David M. Alba, Isaac Casanovas-Vilar, and Jordi Galindo. 2004. *Pierolapithecus catalaunicus.* A new Middle Miocene great ape from Spain. *Science* 306 (November 19):1339–44.

Mukerjee, Madhusree. 1996. Field notes: Interview with a parrot. *Scientific American* (April):28.

Mukherjee, Joia. 2007. Preface to the second edition. In *Women, poverty, and AIDS: Sex, drugs, and structural violence*, 2nd ed., eds. P. Farmer, M. Connors, and J. Simmons. Monroe, Maine: Common Courage Press.

Mukhopadhyay, Carol C., and Patricia J. Higgins. 1988. Anthropological studies of women's status revisited: 1977–1987. *Annual Review of Anthropology* 17:461–95.

Muller, Edward N. 1997. Economic determinants of democracy. In *Inequality, democracy, and economic development*, ed. M. Midlarsky. Cambridge: Cambridge University Press.

Müller-Haye, B. 1984. Guinea pig or cuy. In *Evolution of domesticated animals*, ed. I. Mason. New York: Longman.

Munroe, Robert L., Robert Hulefeld, James M. Rodgers, Damon L. Tomeo, and Steven K. Yamazaki. 2000. Aggression among children in four cultures. *Cross-Cultural Research* 34:3–25.

Munroe, Robert L., and Ruth H. Munroe. 1969. A cross-cultural study of sex, gender, and social structure. *Ethnology* 8:206–11.

Munroe, Robert L., Ruth H. Munroe, and John W. M. Whiting. 1981. Male sex-role resolutions. In *Handbook of cross-cultural human development*, eds. R. H. Munroe, R. L. Munroe, and B. B. Whiting. New York: Garland.

Munroe, Robert L., Ruth H. Munroe, and Stephen Winters. 1996. Cross-cultural correlates of the consonant-vowel (cv) syllable. *Cross-Cultural Research* 30:60–83.

Munroe, Ruth H., and Robert L. Munroe. 1980. Infant experience and childhood affect among the Logoli: A longitudinal study. *Ethos* 8:295–315.

Munroe, Ruth H., Robert L. Munroe, and Harold S. Shimmin. 1984. Children's work in four cultures: Determinants and consequences. *American Anthropologist* 86:369–79.

Murdock, George P. 1949. *Social structure.* New York: Macmillan.

Murdock, George P. 1957. World ethnographic sample. *American Anthropologist* 59:664–87.

Murdock, George P. 1967. Ethnographic atlas: A summary. *Ethnology* 6:109–236.

Murdock, George P. 1980. *Theories of illness: A world survey.* Pittsburgh: University of Pittsburgh Press.

Murdock, George P., and Caterina Provost. 1973. Factors in the division of labor by sex: A cross-cultural analysis. *Ethnology* 12:203–25.

Murdock, George P., and Douglas R. White. 1969. Standard cross-cultural sample. *Ethnology* 8:329–69.

Murphy, Jane. 1981. Abnormal behavior in traditional societies: Labels, explanations, and social reactions. In *Handbook of cross-cultural human development*, eds. R. H. Munroe, R. L. Munroe, and B. B. Whiting. New York: Garland.

Murphy, Robert F. 1960. *Headhunter's heritage: Social and economic change among the Mundurucú.* Berkeley: University of California Press.

Murphy, Robert F., and Julian H. Steward. 1956. Tappers and trappers: Parallel process in acculturation. *Economic development and cultural change* 4 (July):335–55.

Murray, G. F. 1997. The domestication of wood in Haiti: A case study in applied evolution. In *Applying* cultural anthropology: An introductory reader, eds. A. Podolefsky and P. J. Brown. Mountain View, CA: Mayfield.

Murray, G. F., and M. E. Bannister. 2004. Peasants, agroforesters, and anthropologists: A 20-year venture in income-generating trees and hedgerows in Haiti. Agroforestry Systems 61:383–97.

Musgrave, Jonathan H., R. A. H. Neave, and A. J. N. W. Prag. 1984. The skull from Tomb II at Vergina: King Philip II of Macedon. Journal of Hellenistic Studies 104:60–78.

Mutrine, Ann. 2013. Eight other nations that send women to combat. National Geographic News. http://news.nationalgeographic.com/news/2013/13/130125-women-combat-world-Australia-Israel-Canada-Norway/ (accessed June 21, 2013).

Myers, Fred R. 1988. Critical trends in the study of hunter-gatherers. Annual Review of Anthropology 17:261–82.

Myers, Fred R. 2002. Painting culture. Durham, North Carolina: Duke University Press.

Myers, Fred R. 2006. The unsettled business of tradition, indigenous being, and acrylic painting. In Exploring world art, eds. E. Venbrux, P. S. Rosi, and R. L. Welsch. Los Angeles: J. Paul Getty Museum.

Nadel, S. F. 1935. Nupe state and community. Africa 8:257–303.

Nadel, S. F. 1942. A black Byzantium: The kingdom of Nupe in Nigeria. London: Oxford University Press.

Nag, Moni, Benjamin N. F. White, and R. Creighton Peet. 1978. An anthropological approach to the study of the economic value of children in Java and Nepal. Current Anthropology 19:293–301.

Nagata, Judith. 2001. Beyond theology: Toward an anthropology of "fundamentalism." American Anthropologist 103:481–98.

Nagel, Ernest. 1961. The structure of science: Problems in the logic of scientific explanation. New York: Harcourt, Brace & World.

Nāleimaile, Sean, and Lokelani Brandt. 2013. Is Hawaiian archaeology really Hawaiian? A Native Hawaiian perspective. SAA Archaeological Record 13, no. 1:31–32.

Napier, J. R. 1970. Paleoecology and catarrhine evolution. In Old World monkeys: Evolution, systematics, and behavior, eds. J. R. Napier and P. H. Napier. New York: Academic Press.

Napier, J. R., and P. H. Napier. 1967. A handbook of living primates. New York: Academic Press.

Naroll, Raoul. 1961. Two solutions for Galton's problem. In Readings in cross-cultural methodology, ed. F. Moore. New Haven, CT: HRAF Press.

Naroll, Raoul. 1967. Imperial cycles and world order. Peace Research Society: Papers 7:83–101.

Naroll, Raoul. 1983. The moral order: An introduction to the human situation. Beverly Hills, CA: Sage.

Nash, Manning. 1989. The cauldron of ethnicity in the modern world. Chicago: University of Chicago Press.

National Association for the Practice of Anthropology. 1988. NAPA ethical guidelines for practitioners. http://practicinganthropology.org/about/ethical-guidelines/ (accessed May 11, 2013).

National Coalition for the Homeless. 2008. How many people experience homelessness? NCH Fact Sheet #2, June. http://www.nationalhomeless.org/factsheets/How_Many.html (accessed September 3, 2009).

National Coalition for the Homeless. 2009. How many people experience homelessness? http://www.nationalhomeless.org/factsheets/How_Many.html (accessed June 1, 2013).

National Science Foundation, Division of Science Resources Statistics. 2008. Science and engineering doctorate awards: 2006. Detailed Statistical Tables NSF 09-311. Arlington, VA: National Science Foundation. http://www.nsf.gov/statistics/nsf09311/ (accessed August 14, 2009).

Neel, James V., Willard R. Centerwall, Napoleon A. Chagnon, and Helen L. Casey. 1970. Notes on the effect of measles and measles vaccine in a virgin-soil population of South American Indians. American Journal of Epidemiology 91:418–29.

Neihardt, John G. 1951. When the tree flowered, 772–83. New York: Macmillan.

Nelson, Nici. 1995/1964. The Kiambu group: A successful women's ROSCA in Mathare Valley, Nairobi (1971 to 1990). In Money-go-rounds: The importance of rotating savings and credit associations for women, eds. S. Ardener and S. Burman. Oxford: Berg.

Nepstad, Daniel C., Claudia M. Stickler, Britaldo Soares-Filho, and Frank Merry. 2008. Interactions among Amazon land use, forests, and climate: Prospects for a near-term forest tipping point. Philosophical Transactions of the Royal Society B, 363:1737–46.

Nerlove, Sara B. 1974. Women's workload and infant feeding practices: A relationship with demographic implications. Ethnology 13:207–14.

Neumann, Katharina. 2003. New Guinea: A cradle of agriculture. Science 301 (July 11):180–81.

Nevins, Allan. 1927. The American states during and after the revolution. New York: Macmillan.

Newbury, Catherine. 1988. The cohesion of oppression: Clientship and ethnicity in Rwanda, 1860–1960. New York: Columbia University.

Newman, Edward. 2006. Exploring the "root causes" of terrorism. Studies in Conflict and Terrorism 29:749–72.

Newman, K. S. 1983. Law and economic organization: A Comparative study of preindustrial societies. Cambridge, MA: Cambridge University Press.

Newman, K. S. 1988. Falling from grace: The experience of downward mobility in the American middle class. New York: The Free Press.

Newman, K. S. 1993. Declining fortunes: The withering of the American dream. New York: Basic Books.

Newsweek. 1973. The first dentist, March 5, p. 73.

Nicholls, David, ed. 1998. The Cambridge history of American music. Cambridge. Cambridge University Press.

Nicolson, Nancy A. 1987. Infants, mothers, and other females. In Primate societies, eds. B. B. Smuts, D. L. Cheney, R. M. Seyfarth, and R. W. Wrangham. Chicago: University of Chicago Press.

Niehoff, Arthur H. 1966. A casebook of social change. Chicago: Aldine.

Nielsen, François. 2004. The ecological-evolutionary typology of human societies and the evolution of social inequality. Sociological Theory 22:292–314.

Nimkoff, M. F., and Russell Middleton. 1960. Types of family and types of economy. American Journal of Sociology 66:215–25.

Nisbett, Richard E. 2009. Education is all in your mind. New York Times, Sunday Opinion, February 8, p. 12.

Nishida, Toshisada. 1992. Introduction to the conservation symposium. In Topics in primatology, vol. 2, eds. N. Itoigawa, Y. Sugiyama, G. P. Sackett, and R. K. R. Thompson. Tokyo: University of Tokyo Press.

Nissen, Henry W. 1958. Axes of behavioral comparison. In Behavior and evolution, eds. A. Roe and G. G. Simpson. New Haven, CT: Yale University Press.

Nivette, Amy E. 2011. Violence in non-state societies. British Journal of Criminology 51:578–98.

Nolan, Riall W. 2002. Development anthropology: Encounters in the real world. Boulder, CO: Westview Press.

Nolan, Riall W. 2003. Anthropology in practice: Building a career outside the academy. Boulder, CA: Lynne Rienner Publishers.

Nolan, Riall W. 2013. A handbook for practicing anthropology, 2. Malden, MA: Blackwell Publishing.

Noll, Richard. 1987. The presence of spirits in magic and madness. In Shamanism, comp. S. Nicholson, 47–61. Wheaton, IL: Theosophical Publishing House.

Nolte, Christoph, Arun Agrawal, Kirsten M. Silvius, and Britaldo S. Soares-Filho. 2013. Governance regime and location influence avoided deforestation success of protected areas in the Brazilian Amazon. Proceedings of the National Academy of Sciences 110, no. 3: 4956–61.

Norenzayan, Ara, and Azim F. Shariff. 2008. The origin and evolution of religious prosociality. Science 322 (October 3):58–62.

Normile, Dennis. 1998. Habitat seen playing larger role in shaping behavior. Science 279 (March 6):1454–55.

Noss, Andrew J., and Barry S. Hewlett. 2001. The contexts of female hunting in central Africa. American Anthropologist 103:1024–40.

Nussbaum, Martha C. 1995. Introduction. In Women, culture, and development: A study of human capabilities, eds. M. C. Nussbaum and J. Glover. Oxford: Clarendon Press.

Oakley, Kenneth. 1964. On man's use of fire, with comments on tool-making and hunting. In Social life of early man, ed. S. L. Washburn. Chicago: Aldine.

Oboler, Regina Smith. 1980. Is the female husband a man? Woman/woman marriage among the Nandi of Kenya. Ethnology 19:69–88.

Oboler, Regina Smith. 2009. Nandi: From cattle-keepers to cash-crop farmers. In MyAnthroLibrary, eds. C. R. Ember, M. Ember, and P. N. Peregrine. MyAnthroLibrary.com. Pearson.

O'Brian, Robin. 1999. Who weaves and why? Weaving, loom complexity, and trade. Cross-Cultural Research 33:30–42.

O'Brien, Denise. 1977. Female husbands in southern Bantu societies. In Sexual stratification, ed. A. Schlegel. New York: Columbia University Press.

O'Brien, Patricia. 1989. Cahokia: The political capital of the "Ramey" state? North American Archaeologist 10, no. 4:275–92.

O'Connor, S., R. Ono, and C. Clarkson. 2011. Pelagic fishing at 42,000 years before the present and the maritime skills of modern humans. Science 334 (November 25):1117–21.

Oerlemans, J. 2005. Extracting a climate signal from 169 glacial records. Science 38 (April 28):675–77.

Office on Child Abuse and Neglect, U.S. Children's Bureau, Jeffrey Rosenberg, and Bradley W. Wilcox. 2006. The importance of fathers in the healthy development of children. https://www.childwelfare.gov/pubs/usermanuals/fatherhood/chapterthree.cfm.

Ogburn, William F. 1922. Social change. New York: Huebsch.

Ogden, Cynthia, Margaret D. Carroll, Brian K. Kit, and Katherine M. Flegal. 2012. Prevalence of obesity in the United States 2009-2010. NCHS Data Brief, no. 82 (January). Hyattsville, MD: National Center for Health Statistics.

O'Gorman, Rick, David Sloan Wilson, and Ralph R. Miller. 2008. An evolved cognitive bias for social norms. Evolution and Human Behavior 29:71–78.

Okamura, Jonathan Y. 1983. Filipino hometown associations in Hawaii. Ethnology 22:341–53.

Oliver, Douglas L. 1955. A Solomon Island society. Cambridge, MA: Harvard University Press.

Oliver, Douglas L. 1974. Ancient Tahitian society: Ethnography, vol. 1. Honolulu: University of Hawaii Press.

Oliver-Smith, Anthony. 2005. Applied anthropology and development-induced displacement and resettlement. In Applied anthropology: Domains of application, eds. S. Kedia and J. van Willigen. Westport, CT: Praeger.

Olsen, Steve. 2002. Seeking the signs of selection. Science 298 (November 15):1324–25.

Olszewski, Deborah I. 1991. Social complexity in the Natufian? Assessing the relationship of ideas and data. In Perspectives on the past, ed. G. Clark. Philadelphia: University of Pennsylvania Press.

Orlove, Benjamin, and Stephen Brush. 1996. Anthropology and the conservation of biodiversity. Annual Review of Anthropology 25:329–52.

Ortiz de Montellano, B. R., and C. H. Browner. 1985. Chemical bases for medicinal plant use in Oaxaca, Mexico. Journal of Ethnopharmacology 13:57–88.

Ortner, Sherry B. 1984. Theory in anthropology since the sixties. Comparative Studies in Society & History 26:126–66.

Osti, Roberto. 1994. The eloquent bones of Abu Hureyra. Scientific American (August):1.

Otterbein, Keith. 1968. Internal war: A cross-cultural study. American Anthropologist 70:277–89.

Otterbein, Keith. 1970. The evolution of war. New Haven, CT: HRAF Press.

Otterbein, Keith. 1986. The ultimate coercive sanction: A cross-cultural study of capital punishment. New Haven, CT: HRAF Press.

Otterbein, Keith. 1994. Feuding and warfare: Selected works of Keith F. Otterbein. Langhorne, PA: Gordon and Breach.

Otterbein, Keith, and Charlotte Swanson Otterbein. 1965. An eye for an eye, a tooth for a tooth: A cross-cultural study of feuding. American Anthropologist 67:1470–82.

Ovchinnikov, Igor V., Anders Götherström, Galina P. Romanova, Vitaliy M. Kharitonov, Kerstin Lidén, and William Goodwin. 2000. Molecular analysis of Neanderthal DNA from the northern Caucasus. Nature 404 (March 30):490–94.

Oxby, Clare. 1983. Farmer groups in rural areas of the third world. Community Development Journal 18:50–59.

Paige, Jeffery M. 1975. *Agrarian revolution: Social movements and export agriculture in the underdeveloped world*. New York: Free Press.

Paine, Robert. 1994. *Herds of the tundra*. Washington, DC: Smithsonian Institution Press.

Paley, William. 1810. *Natural theology*. Boston: Joshua Belcher.

Palsson, Gisli. 1988. Hunters and gatherers of the sea. In *Hunters and gatherers. Vol. 1. History, evolution and social change*, eds. T. Ingold, D. Riches, and J. Woodburn. New York: St. Martin's Press.

Paradise, Ruth, and Barbara Rogoff. 2009. Side by side: Learning by observing and pitching in. *Ethos* 37:102–38.

Parfit, Michael. 2000. Who were the first Americans? *National Geographic* (December):41–67.

Parker, Hilda, and Seymour Parker. 1986. Father-daughter sexual abuse: An emerging perspective. *American Journal of Orthopsychiatry* 56:531–49.

Parker, Seymour. 1976. The precultural basis of the incest taboo: Toward a biosocial theory. *American Anthropologist* 78:285–305.

Parker, Seymour. 1984. Cultural rules, rituals, and behavior regulation. *American Anthropologist* 86:584–600.

Parker, Sue Taylor. 1990. Why big brains are so rare. In *"Language" and intelligence in monkeys and apes*, eds. S. Parker and K. Gibson. New York: Cambridge University Press.

Pasternak, Burton. 1976. *Introduction to kinship and social organization*. Upper Saddle River, NJ: Prentice Hall.

Pasternak, Burton. 2009. Han: Pastoralists and farmers on a Chinese frontier. In MyAnthroLibrary, eds. C. R. Ember, M. Ember, and P. N. Peregrine. MyAnthroLibrary.com. Pearson.

Pasternak, Burton, Carol R. Ember, and Melvin Ember. 1976. On the conditions favoring extended family households. *Journal of Anthropological Research* 32:109–23.

Patterson, Leland. 1983. Criteria for determining the attributes of man-made lithics. *Journal of Field Archaeology* 10:297–307.

Patterson, Orlando. 1982. *Slavery and social death: A comparative study*. Cambridge, MA: Harvard University Press.

Patterson, Orlando. 2000. Review of *One drop of blood: The American misadventure of race*, by Scott L. Malcomson. *New York Times Book Review*, October 22, pp. 15–16.

Patterson, Thomas C. 1971. Central Peru: Its population and economy. *Archaeology* 24:316–21.

Patterson, Thomas C. 1981. *The evolution of ancient societies: A world archaeology*. Upper Saddle River, NJ: Prentice Hall.

Pauketat, Timothy. 2004. *Ancient Cahokia and the Mississippians*. Cambridge: Cambridge University Press.

Peacock, James L. 1986. *The anthropological lens: Harsh light, soft focus*. Cambridge: Cambridge University Press.

Peacock, Nadine R., and Robert C. Bailey. 2009. Efe: Investigating food and fertility in the Ituri Forest. In MyAnthroLibrary, eds. C. R. Ember, M. Ember, and P. N. Peregrine. MyAnthroLibrary.com. Pearson.

Peak, Lois. 1991. *Learning to go to school in Japan: The transition from home to preschool*. Berkeley: University of California Press.

Pearsall, Deborah. 1992. The origins of plant cultivation in South America. In *The origins of agriculture*, eds. C. Cowan and P. Watson. Washington, DC: Smithsonian Institution Press.

Pelto, Gretel H., Alan H. Goodman, and Darna L. Dufour. 2000. The biocultural perspective in nutritional anthropology. In *Nutritional anthropology: Biocultural perspectives on food and nutrition*, eds. Alan H. Goodman, Darna L. Dufour, and Gretel H. Pelto. Mountain View, CA: Mayfield Publishing.

Pelto, Pertti J. 1968. The difference between "tight" and "loose" societies. *Transaction* 5:37–40.

Pelto, Pertti J., and Ludger Müller-Wille. 1987. Snowmobiles: Technological revolution in the Arctic. In *Technology and social change*, 2nd ed., eds. H. R. Bernard and P. J. Pelto. Prospect Heights, IL: Waveland Press.

Pelto, Pertti J., and Gretel H. Pelto. 1975. Intra-cultural diversity: Some theoretical issues. *American Ethnologist* 2:1–18.

Pennisi, Elizabeth. 2000. Finally, the book of life and instructions for navigating it. *Science* 288 (June 30):2304–07.

Pennisi, Elizabeth. 2001a. Malaria's beginnings: On the heels of hoes? *Science* 293 (July 20):416–17.

Pennisi, Elizabeth. 2001b. Genetic change wards off malaria. *Science* 294 (November 16):1439.

Pennisi, Elizabeth. 2007. Genomicists tackle the primate tree. *Science* 316 (April 13):218–21.

Pennisi, Elizabeth. 2009. Tales of a prehistoric human genome. *Science* 323 (February 13):866–71.

Pepperberg, Irene Maxine. 1999. *The Alex studies: Cognitive and communicative abilities of grey parrots*. Cambridge, MA: Harvard University Press.

Peregrine, Peter N. 1996. The birth of the gods revisited: A partial replication of Guy Swanson's (1960) cross-cultural study of religion. *Cross-Cultural Research* 30:84–112.

Peregrine, Peter N. 2001a. Cross-cultural approaches in archaeology. *Annual Review of Anthropology* 30:1–18.

Peregrine, Peter N. 2001b. Southern and Eastern Africa Later Stone Age. In *Encyclopedia of prehistory Africa*, vol. 1, eds. P. N. Peregrine and M. Ember. New York: Kluwer Academic/Plenum.

Peregrine, Peter N. 2007a. Cultural correlates of ceramic styles. *Cross-Cultural Research* 41:223–35.

Peregrine, Peter N. 2007b. Racial hierarchy: I. Overview. In *Encyclopedia of race and racism*, ed. John H. Moore, 461–62. New York: Macmillan.

Peregrine, Peter N., and Peter Bellwood. 2001. Southeast Asia Upper Paleolithic. In *Encyclopedia of prehistory: East Asia and Oceania*, eds. P. N. Peregrine and M. Ember, vol. 3. New York: Kluwer Academic/ Plenum.

Peregrine, Peter N., Carol R. Ember, and Melvin Ember. 2000. Teaching critical evaluation of Rushton. *Anthropology Newsletter* 41 (February):29–30.

Peregrine, Peter N., Carol R. Ember, and Melvin Ember. 2003. Cross-cultural evaluation of predicted associations between race and behavior. *Evolution and Human Behavior* 24:357–64.

Peregrine, Peter N., Melvin Ember, and Carol R. Ember. 2004. Predicting the future state of the world using archaeological data: An exercise in archaeomancy. *Cross-Cultural Research* 38:133–46.

Perkins, Morgan. 2006. "Do we still have no word for art?" A contemporary Mohawk question. In *Exploring world art*, eds. E. Venbrux, P. S. Rosi, and R. L. Welsch. Los Angeles: J. Paul Getty Museum.

Perry, Donna L. 2005. Wolof women, economic liberalization, and the crisis of masculinity in rural Senegal. *Ethnology* 44:207–26.

Petersen, Erik B. 1973. A survey of the Late Paleolithic and the Mesolithic of Denmark. In *The Mesolithic in Europe*, ed. S. K. Kozlowski. Warsaw: Warsaw University Press.

Petersen, L. R., G. R. Lee, and G. J. Ellis. 1982. Social structure, socialization values, and disciplinary techniques: A cross-cultural analysis. *Journal of Marriage and the Family* 44:131–42.

Pfaff, C. 1979. Constraints on language mixing. *Language* 55:291–318, as cited in *An introduction to sociolinguistics*, 2nd ed., ed. R. Wardhaugh. Oxford: Blackwell.

Pfeiffer, John E. 1978. *The emergence of man*. 3rd ed. New York: Harper & Row.

Phillips, Erica M., and Alan Walker. 2002. Fossil lorisoids. In *The primate fossil record*, ed. W. C. Hartwig. Cambridge: Cambridge University Press.

Phillips, Kevin. 1990. *The politics of rich and poor: Wealth and the American electorate in the Reagan aftermath*. New York: Random House.

Phillipson, David W. 1976. Archaeology and Bantu linguistics. *World Archaeology* 8:65–82.

Phillipson, David W. 1993. *African archaeology*. 2nd ed. New York: Cambridge University Press.

Phillipson, David W. 2005. *African archaeology*, 3rd ed. Cambridge: Cambridge University Press.

Piaget, Jean. 1970. Piaget's theory. In *Carmichael's manual of child psychology*, vol. 1, 3rd ed., ed. P. Mussen. New York: Wiley.

Piaget, Jean, and Bärbel Inhelder. 2000. *The psychology of the child*. New York: Basic Books.

Picchi, Debra. 1991. The impact of an industrial agricultural project on the Bakairí Indians of central Brazil. *Human Organization* 50:26–38.

Picchi, Debra. 2009. Bakairí: The death of an Indian. In MyAnthroLibrary, eds. C. R. Ember, M. Ember, and P. N. Peregrine. MyAnthroLibrary.com. Pearson.

Pickering, R., et al. 2011. *Australopithecus sediba* at 1.977 Ma and Implications for the origins of the genus homo. *Science* 333 (September 9):1421–23.

Pickford, Martin, Brigette Senut, Dominique Gommercy, and Jacques Treil. 2002. Bipedalism in *Orrorin tugenensis* revealed by its femora. *Comptes Rendu de l'Académie des Science des Paris*, Palevol 1, 1–13.

Pilbeam, David. 1972. *The ascent of man*. New York: Macmillan.

Pilbeam, David, and Stephen Jay Gould. 1974. Size and scaling in human evolution. *Science* 186 (December 6):892–900.

Pinker, Steven. 2011. *The better angels of our nature: Why violence has declined*. New York: Viking.

Piperno, Dolores, and Karen Stothert. 2003. Phytolith evidence for early Holocene cucurbita domestication in southwest Ecuador. *Science* 299 (February 14):1054–57.

Plattner, Stuart, ed. 1985. *Markets and marketing*. Monographs in economic anthropology, No. 4. Lanham, MD: University Press of America.

Plattner, Stuart. 1989. Marxism. In *Economic anthropology*, ed. S. Plattner. Stanford, CA: Stanford University Press.

Poggie, John J., Jr., and Richard B. Pollnac. 1988. Danger and rituals of avoidance among New England fishermen. *MAST: Maritime Anthropological Studies* 1:66–78.

Poggie, John J., Jr., Richard B. Pollnac, and Carl Gersuny. 1976. Risk as a basis for taboos among fishermen in Southern New England. *Journal for the Scientific Study of Religion* 15:257–62.

Polanyi, Karl. 1957. The economy as instituted process. In *Trade and market in the early empires*, eds. K. Polanyi, C. M. Arensberg, and H. W. Pearson. New York: Free Press.

Polanyi, Karl, Conrad M. Arensberg, and Harry W. Pearson, eds. 1957. *Trade and market in the early empires*. New York: Free Press.

Polednak, Anthony P. 1974. Connective tissue responses in Negroes in relation to disease. *American Journal of Physical Anthropology* 41:49–57.

Pollier, Nicole. 2000. Commoditization, cash, and kinship in postcolonial Papua New Guinea. In *Commodities and globalization: Anthropological perspectives*, eds. A. Haugerud, M. P. Stone, and P. D. Little. Lanham, MD: Rowman & Littlefield.

Pope, Geoffrey G. 1989. Bamboo and human evolution. *Natural History* (October):49–57.

Popenoe, Rebecca. 2004. *Feeding desire: Fatness, beauty, and sexuality among a Saharan people*. London: Routledge.

Pospisil, Leopold. 1963. *The Kapauku Papuans of West New Guinea*. New York: Holt, Rinehart & Winston.

Post, Peter W., Farrington Daniels, Jr., and Robert T. Binford, Jr. 1975. Cold injury and the evolution of "white" skin. *Human Biology* 47:65–80.

Potts, Richard. 1984. Home bases and early hominids. *American Scientist* 72:338–47.

Potts, Richard. 1988. *Early hominid activities at Olduvai*. New York: Aldine.

Powell, Joseph. 2005. *The first Americans*. New York: Cambridge University Press.

Powers, William K., and Marla N. Powers. 2009. Lakota: A study in cultural continuity. In MyAnthroLibrary, eds. C. R. Ember, M. Ember, and P. N. Peregrine. MyAnthroLibrary.com. Pearson.

Poyatos, Fernando. 2002. *Nonverbal communication across disciplines*, vol. 1. Philadelphia: John Benjamins Publishing Company.

Prag, A. J. N. W. 1990. Reconstructing Phillip II of Macedon: The "nice" version. *American Journal of Archaeology* 94:237–47.

Prag, John, and Richard Neave. 1997. *Making faces: Using forensic and archaeological evidence*. College Station: Texas A&M University Press.

Preuschoft, Holger, David J. Chivers, Warren Y. Brockelman, and Norman Creel, eds. 1984. *The lesser apes: Evolutionary and behavioural biology*. Edinburgh: Edinburgh University Press.

Price, Sally. 1989. *Primitive art in civilized places*. Chicago: University of Chicago Press.

Price, Sally. 2001. *Primitive art in civilized places*. 2nd ed. Chicago: University of Chicago Press.

Price, Sally. 2006. A case in point and afterwords to *Primitive art in civilized places*. In *The anthropology* of art: A reader, eds. H. Morphy and M. Perkins. Malden, MA: Blackwell.

Price-Williams, Douglass. 1961. A study concerning concepts of conservation of quantities among primitive children. Acta Psychologica 18:297–305.

Pringle, Heather. 1998. The slow birth of agriculture. Science 282 (November 20):1446–50.

Pringle, Heather. 2011. The First Americans. Scientific American 305 (November):36–42.

Pryor, Frederic L. 1977. The origins of the economy: A comparative study of distribution in primitive and peasant economies. New York: Academic Press.

Pryor, Frederic L. 2005. Economic systems of foraging, agricultural, and industrial societies. Cambridge: Cambridge University Press.

Public Law 101-601 25 U.S.C. 3001–3013.

Putnam, Robert D. 1995. Bowling alone: America's declining social capital. Journal of Democracy (January):65–78.

Quandt, Sara A. 1996. Nutrition in anthropology. In Handbook of medical anthropology, Rev. ed., eds. C. F. Sargent and T. M. Johnson. Westport, CT: Greenwood Press.

Quinn, Naomi. 1977. Anthropological studies on women's status. Annual Review of Anthropology 6:181–225.

Radcliffe-Brown, A. R. 1922. The Andaman Islanders: A study in social anthropology. Cambridge: Cambridge University Press.

Radcliffe-Brown, A. R. 1952. Structure and function in primitive society. London: Cohen & West.

Radin, Paul. 1923. The Winnebago tribe, 138. Washington, DC: Smithsonian institute.

Radinsky, Leonard. 1967. The oldest primate endocast. American Journal of Physical Anthropology 27:358–88.

Rambo, Lewis R. 2003. Anthropology and the study of conversion. In The anthropology of religious conversion, eds. A. Buckser and S. D. Glazier. Lanham, MD: Roman & Littlefield.

Rapp, George and Christopher Hill. 2006. Geoarchaeology: The earth-science approach to archaeological interpretation. New Haven, CT: Yale University Press.

Rappaport, Roy A. 1967. Ritual regulation of environmental relations among a New Guinea people. Ethnology 6:17–30.

Rasmussen, David Tab. 1990. Primate origins: Lessons from a neotropical marsupial. American Journal of Primatology 22:263–77.

Rasmussen, David Tab. 2002. Early catarrhines of the African Eocene and Oligocene. In The primate fossil record, ed. W. C. Hartwig. Cambridge: Cambridge University Press.

Rathje, William L. 1971. The origin and development of Lowland Classic Maya civilization. American Antiquity 36:275–85.

Ravesloot, John. 1997. Changing Native American perceptions of archaeology and archaeologists. In Native Americans and archaeologists, eds. N. Swidler, K. Dongoske, R. Anyon, and A. Downer. Walnut Creek, CA: AltaMira Press.

Ray, Verne F. 1954. The Sanpoil and Nespelem: Salishan peoples of northeastern Washington. New Haven, CT: Human Relations Area Files.

Raybeck, Douglas. 1998. Toward more holistic explanations: Cross-cultural research and cross-level analysis. Cross-Cultural Research 32:123–42.

Raybeck, Douglas, J. Shoobe, and J. Grauberger. 1989. Women, stress and participation in possession cults: A reexamination of the calcium deficiency hypothesis. Medical Anthropology Quarterly 3:139–61.

Redman, Charles L. 1978. The rise of civilization: From early farmers to urban society in the ancient Near East. San Francisco: W. H. Freeman.

Redman, Charles L. 1999. Human impact on ancient environments. Tucson: University of Arizona Press.

Reed, David, V. Smith, S. Hammond, A. Rogers, and D. Clayton. 2004. Genetic analysis of lice supports direct contact between modern and archaic humans. PLoS Biology 2 (November):1972–83.

Reff, Daniel T. 2005. Plagues, priests, and demons: Sacred narratives and the rise of Christianity in the Old World and the New. Cambridge: Cambridge University Press.

Reich, D, et al. 2010. Genetic history of an archaic hominin group from Denisova Cave in Siberia. Nature 468 (December 23/30):1053–60.

Reich, David, et al. 2012. Reconstructing native American population history. Nature 488 (July 11):370–4.

Reisner, Marc. 1993. Cadillac desert: The American West and its disappearing water. Rev. ed. New York: Penguin.

Reitz, Elizabeth and Myra Shackley. 2012. Environmental archaeology. New York: Springer.

Relethford, John. 1990. The human species: An introduction to biological anthropology. Mountain View, CA: Mayfield.

Renfrew, Colin. 1969. Trade and culture process in European history. Current Anthropology 10:156–69.

Renfrew, Colin. 1987. Archaeology and language: The puzzle of Indo-European origins. London: Jonathan Cape.

Rennie, John. 2002. Fifteen answers to creationist nonsense. Scientific American (July):78–85.

Revkin, Andrew C. 2005. Tracking the imperiled blue-fin from ocean to sushi platter. New York Times, May 3, pp. F1, F4.

Rhine, Stanley. 1993. Skeletal criteria for racial attribution. NAPA Bulletin 13:54–67.

Rice, Patricia C. 1981. Prehistoric Venuses: Symbols of motherhood or womanhood? Journal of Anthropological Research 37:402–14.

Rice, Patricia C., and Ann L. Paterson. 1985. Cave art and bones: Exploring the interrelationships. American Anthropologist 87:94–100.

Rice, Patricia C., and Ann L. Paterson. 1986. Validating the cave art—Archeofaunal relationship in Cantabrian Spain. American Anthropologist 88:658–67.

Richard, Alison F. 1985. Primates in nature. New York: W. H. Freeman.

Richard, Alison F. 1987. Malagasy prosimians: Female dominance. In Primate societies, eds. B. B. Smuts, D. L. Cheney, R. M. Seyfarth, and R. W. Wrangham. Chicago: University of Chicago Press.

Richardson, Curtis J., Peter Reiss, Najah A. Hussain, Azzam J. Alwash, and Douglas J. Pool. 2005. The restoration potential of the Mesopotamian marshes of Iraq. Science 307 (February 25):1307–11.

Richerson, Peter J., and Robert Boyd. 2005. Not by genes alone: How culture transformed human evolution. Chicago: University of Chicago Press.

Richmond, Brian G., and William L. Jungers. 2008. Orrorin tugenensis femoral morphology and the evolution of human bipedalism. Science 319 (March 21):1662–65.

Riesenfeld, Alphonse. 1973. The effect of extreme temperatures and starvation on the body proportions of the rat. American Journal of Physical Anthropology 39:427–59.

Rightmire, G. Philip. 1984. Homo sapiens in sub-Saharan Africa. In The origins of modern humans, eds. F. H. Smith and F. Spencer. New York: Alan R. Liss.

Rightmire, G. Philip. 1990. The evolution of Homo erectus: Comparative anatomical studies of an extinct human species. Cambridge: Cambridge University Press.

Rightmire, G. Philip. 1997. Human evolution in the Middle Pleistocene: The role of Homo heidelbergensis. Evolutionary Anthropology 6:218–27.

Rightmire, G. Philip. 2000. Homo erectus. In Encyclopedia of human evolution and prehistory, eds. I. Tattersall, E. Delson, and J. van Couvering. New York: Garland.

Rijksen, H. D. 1978. A field study on Sumatran Orang utans (Pongo pygmaeus abelii Lesson 1827): Ecology, behaviour and conservation. Wageningen, Netherlands: H. Veenman and Zonen.

Ritter, Madeline Lattman. 1980. The conditions favoring age-set organization. Journal of Anthropological Research 36:87–104.

Rivers, W. H. R. 1967/1906. The Todas. Oosterhout, Netherlands: Anthropological Publications.

Roberts, D. F. 1953. Body weight, race, and climate. American Journal of Physical Anthropology 11:533–58.

Roberts, D. F. 1978. Climate and human variability. 2nd ed. Menlo Park, CA: Cummings.

Roberts, John M. 1967. Oaths, autonomic ordeals, and power. In Cross-cultural approaches, ed. C. S. Ford. New Haven, CT: HRAF Press.

Roberts, John M., and Brian Sutton-Smith. 1962. Child training and game involvement. Ethnology 1:166–85.

Roberts, John M., Malcolm J. Arth, and Robert R. Bush. 1959. Games in culture. American Anthropologist 61:597–605.

Robins, Ashley H. 1991. Biological perspectives on human pigmentation. New York: Cambridge University Press.

Robinson, John G., and Charles H. Janson. 1987. Capuchins, squirrel monkeys, and atelines: Socioecological convergence with Old World primates. In Primate societies, eds. B. B. Smuts, D. L. Cheney, R. M. Seyfarth, and R. W. Wrangham. Chicago: University of Chicago Press.

Robinson, John G., Patricia C. Wright, and Warren G. Kinzey. 1987. Monogamous cebids and their relatives: Intergroup calls and spacing. In Primate societies, eds. Barbara B. Smuts, Dorothy L. Cheney, Robert M. Seyfarth, and Richard W. Wrangham. Chicago: University of Chicago Press.

Robinson, Roy. 1984. Cat. In Evolution of domesticated animals, ed. I. Mason. New York: Longman.

Rodwin, Lloyd, and Bishwapriya Sanyal. 1987. Shelter, settlement, and development: An overview. In Shelter, settlement, and development, ed. L. Rodwin. Boston: Allen & Unwin.

Roes, Frans L., and Michel Raymond. 2003. Belief in moralizing gods. Evolution and Human Behavior 24:126–35.

Rogers, Alan, D. Iltis, and S. Wooding. 2004. Genetic variation at the MC1R locus and the time since loss of human body hair. Current Anthropology 45:105–08.

Rogers, Everett M. 1983. Diffusion of innovations. 3rd ed. New York: Free Press.

Rogoff, Barbara. 1981. Schooling and the development of cognitive skills. In Handbook of cross-cultural psychology: Developmental psychology, vol. 4, eds. H. C. Triandis and A. Heron. Boston: Allyn & Bacon.

Rogoff, Barbara. 1990. Apprenticeship in thinking: Cognitive development in social context. New York: Oxford University Press.

Rogoff, Barbara. 2003. The cultural nature of human development. New York: Oxford University Press.

Rohner, Ronald P. 1975. They love me, they love me not: A worldwide study of the effects of parental acceptance and rejection. New Haven, CT: HRAF Press.

Rohner, Ronald P. 1976. Sex differences in aggression: Phylogenetic and enculturation perspectives. Ethos 4:57–72.

Rohner, Ronald P., and Preston A. Britner. 2002. Worldwide mental health correlates of parental acceptance-rejection: Review of cross-cultural research and intracultural evidence. Cross-Cultural Research 36:16–47.

Rohter, Larry. 2012. Folklorist's global jukebox goes digital. New York Time, January 30. http://www.nytimes.com.

Romaine, Suzanne. 1994. Language in society: An introduction to sociolinguistics. Oxford: Oxford University Press.

Romanucci-Ross, Lola, and George A. De Vos, eds. 1995. Ethnic identity: Creation, conflict, and accommodation. 3rd ed. Walnut Creek, CA: AltaMira Press.

Romanucci-Ross, Lola, Daniel E. Moerman, and Laurence R. Tancredi, eds. 1997. The anthropology of medicine: From culture to method. 3rd ed. Westport, CT: Bergin & Garvey.

Romney, A. Kimball, Carmella C. Moore, and Craig D. Rusch. 1997. Cultural universals: Measuring the semantic structure of emotion terms in English and Japanese. Proceedings of the National Academy of Sciences, U.S.A., 94:5489–94.

Romney, A. Kimball, Susan C. Weller, and William H. Batchelder. 1986. Culture as consensus: A theory of culture and informant accuracy. American Anthropologist 88:313–38.

Roncoli, Carla, Todd Crane, and Ben Orlove. 2009. Fielding climate change in cultural anthropology. In Anthropology and climate change: From encounters to actions, eds. S. A. Crate and M. Nuttall. Walnut Creek, CA: Left Coast Press.

Roosens, Eugeen E. 1989. Creating ethnicity: The process of ethnogenesis. Newbury Park, CA: Sage Publications.

Roosevelt, Anna Curtenius. 1984. Population, health, and the evolution of subsistence: Conclusions from the conference. In Paleopathology at the origins of agriculture, eds. M. Cohen and G. Armelagos. Orlando, FL: Academic Press.

Roosevelt, Anna Curtenius. 1992. Secrets of the forest. The Sciences (November/December):22–28.

Roosevelt, Anna Curtenius, et al. 1996. Paleoindian cave dwellers in the Amazon: The peopling of the Americas. Science 272 (April 19):373–84.

Roscoe, Paul. 2002. The hunters and gatherers of New Guinea. *Current Anthropology* 43:153–62.

Rose, M. D. 1984. Food acquisition and the evolution of positional behaviour: The case of bipedalism. In *Food acquisition and processing in primates*, eds. D. Chivers, B. Wood, and A. Bilsborough. New York: Plenum.

Roseberry, William. 1988. Political economy. *Annual Review of Anthropology* 17:161–259.

Rosen, Lawrence. 2006. *Law as culture: An invitation*. Princeton: Princeton University Press.

Rosenberger, A. L. 1979. Cranial anatomy and implications of *Dolichocebus*, a Late Oligocene ceboid primate. *Nature* 279 (May 31):416–18.

Rosenblatt, Paul C. 2009. Human rights violations. In MyAnthroLibrary, eds. C. R. Ember, M. Ember, and P. N. Peregrine. MyAnthroLibrary.com. Pearson.

Rosenblatt, Paul C., R. Patricia Walsh, and Douglas A. Jackson. 1976. *Grief and mourning in cross-cultural perspective*. New Haven, CT: HRAF Press.

Ross, Marc Howard. 1981. Socioeconomic complexity, socialization, and political differentiation: A cross-cultural study. *Ethos* 9:217–47.

Ross, Marc Howard. 1985. Internal and external conflict and violence. *Journal of Conflict Resolution* 29:547–79.

Ross, Marc Howard. 1986. Female political participation: A cross-cultural explanation. *American Anthropologist* 88:843–58.

Ross, Marc Howard. 1988. Political organization and political participation: Exit, voice, and loyalty in preindustrial societies. *Comparative Politics* 21:73–89.

Ross, Marc Howard. 2009a. Ethnocentrism and ethnic conflict. In MyAnthroLibrary, eds. C. R. Ember, M. Ember, and P. N. Peregrine. MyAnthroLibrary.com. Pearson.

Ross, Marc Howard. 2009b. Political participation. In MyAnthroLibrary, eds. C. R. Ember, M. Ember, and P. N. Peregrine. MyAnthroLibrary.com. Pearson.

Roth, Eric Abella. 2001. Demise of the *sepaade* tradition: Cultural and biological explanations. *American Anthropologist* 103:1014–23.

Rothman, Barbara Katz. 2011. From the book of life: A personal guide to race, normality, and the implications of the genome project. In *Race in an era of change: A reader*, eds. H. Dalmage and B. Katz Rothman. New York: Oxford University Press.

Rubel, Arthur J., and Michael R. Hass. 1996. Ethnomedicine. In *Medical anthropology*, Rev. ed., eds. C. F. Sargent and T. M. Johnson. Westport, CT: Praeger.

Rubel, Arthur J., Carl O'Nell, and Rolando Collado-Ardón (with the assistance of John Krejci and Jean Krejci). 1984. *Susto: A folk illness*. Berkeley: University of California Press.

Rubel, Paula, and Abraham Rosman. 1996. Structuralism and poststructuralism. In *Encyclopedia of cultural anthropology*, eds. D. Levinson and M. Ember, vol. 4. New York: Henry Holt.

Rubin, J. Z., F. J. Provenzano, and R. F. Haskett. 1974. The eye of the beholder: Parents' views on the sex of new borns. *American Journal of Orthopsychiatry* 44:512–19.

Rudan, Igor, and Harry Campbell. 2004. Five reasons why inbreeding may have considerable effect on postreproductive human health. *Collegium Antropologicum* 28:943–50.

Rudmin, Floyd Webster. 1988. Dominance, social control, and ownership: A history and a cross-cultural study of motivations for private property. *Behavior Science Research* 22:130–60.

Ruff, Christopher B., and Alan Walker. 1993. Body size and body shape. In *The Nariokotome Homo erectus skeleton*, eds. A. Walker and R. Leakey. Cambridge, MA: Harvard University Press.

Rumbaugh, Duane M. 1970. Learning skills of anthropoids. In *Primate behavior*, vol. 1, ed. L. Rosenblum. New York: Academic Press.

Rummel, R. J. 2002a. Death by Government, Chapter 1. http://www.hawaii.edu/powerkills/DBG.CHAP1.HTM.

Rummel, R. J. 2002b. Democracies are less warlike than other regimes. http://www.hawaii.edu/powerkills/DP95.htm.

Rummel, R. J. 2002c. Statistics of democide, Chapter 17. http://www.hawaii.edu/powerkills/SOD.CHAP17.HTM.

Rummel, R. J. 2002d. Statistics of democide, Chapter 21. http://www.hawaii.edu/powerkills/SOD.CHAP21.HTM.

Rummel, R. J. 2009. 20th century democide. http://www.hawaii.edu/powerkills/20th.htm (accessed September 5, 2009).

Ruskin, John. 1963. Of king's treasures. In *The genius of John Ruskin*, ed. J. D. Rosenberg. New York: Braziller.

Russell, Elbert W. 1972. Factors of human aggression. *Behavior Science Notes* 7:275–312.

Russell, James A. 1994. Is there universal recognition of emotion from facial expressions? A review of the cross-cultural studies. *Psychological Bulletin* 115, no. 1:102–41.

Russett, Bruce (with the collaboration of William Antholis, Carol R. Ember, Melvin Ember, and Zeev Maoz). 1993. *Grasping the democratic peace: Principles for a post–cold war world*. Princeton, NJ: Princeton University Press.

Russett, Bruce, and John R. Oneal. 2001. *Triangulating peace: Democracy, interdependence, and international organizations*. New York: Norton.

Russon, Anne E. 1990. The development of peer social interaction in infant chimpanzees: Comparative social, Piagetian, and brain perspectives. In *"Language" and intelligence in monkeys and apes*, eds. S. Parker and K. Gibson. New York: Cambridge University Press.

Ruvolo, Maryellen. 1997. Genetic diversity in hominoid primates. *Annual Review of Anthropology* 26:515–40.

Rylko-Bauer, Barbara, Merrill Singer, and John van Willigen. 2006. Reclaiming applied anthropology: Its past, present, and future. *American Anthropologist* 108:178–90.

Sade, D. S. 1965. Some aspects of parent-offspring and sibling relationships in a group of rhesus monkeys, with a discussion of grooming. *American Journal of Physical Anthropology* 23:1–17.

Saez, Emmanuel. 2012. Striking it richer: The evolution of top incomes in the United States (Updated with 2009 and 2010 Estimates). http://saez-UStopincomes-2010-1.pdf.

Sagan, Carl. 1975. A cosmic calendar. *Natural History* (December):70–73.

Sahlins, Marshall D. 1958. *Social stratification in Polynesia*. Seattle: University of Washington Press.

Sahlins, Marshall D. 1961. The segmentary lineage: An organization of predatory expansion. *American Anthropologist* 63:332–45.

Sahlins, Marshall D. 1962. *Moala: Culture and nature on a Fijian island*. Ann Arbor: University of Michigan Press.

Sahlins, Marshall D. 1963. Poor man, rich man, big-man, chief: Political types in Melanesia and Polynesia. *Comparative Studies in Society and History* 5:285–303.

Sahlins, Marshall D. 1972. *Stone Age economics*. Chicago: Aldine.

Sahlins, Marshall D. 1983. Other times, other customs: The anthropology of history. *American Anthropologist* 85:517–44.

Sahlins, Marshall D., and Elman Service. 1960. *Evolution and culture*. Ann Arbor: University of Michigan Press.

Saito, Osamu. 1998. Two kinds of stem family system? Traditional Japan and Europe compared. *Continuity and Change* 13, no. 1:17–45.

Salzman, Philip Carl. 1996. Pastoralism. In *Encyclopedia of cultural anthropology*, vol. 3, eds. D. Levinson and M. Ember. New York: Henry Holt.

Salzman, Philip Carl. 1999. Is inequality universal? *Current Anthropology* 40:31–61.

Salzman, Philip Carl. 2001. *Understanding culture: An introduction to anthropological theory*. Long Grove, IL: Waveland, 135.

Salzman, Philip Carl. 2002. Pastoral nomads: Some general observations based on research in Iran. *Journal of Anthropological Research* 58:245–64.

Salzman, Philip Carl. 2008. *Culture and conflict in the Middle East*. Amherst, NY: Humanity Books.

Samy, Alim, H., Ibrahim Awad, and Alastair Pennycook, eds. 2009. *Global linguistic flows: Hip Hop cultures, youth identities, and the politics of language*. New York: Routledge.

Sanday, Peggy R. 1973. Toward a theory of the status of women. *American Anthropologist* 75:1682–700.

Sanday, Peggy R. 1974. Female status in the public domain. In *Woman, culture, and society*, eds. M. Z. Rosaldo and L. Lamphere. Stanford, CA: Stanford University Press.

Sanders, William T. 1968. Hydraulic agriculture, economic symbiosis, and the evolution of states in central Mexico. In *Anthropological archaeology in the Americas*, ed. B. Meggers. Washington, DC: Anthropological Society of Washington.

Sanders, William T., and Barbara J. Price. 1968. *Mesoamerica*. New York: Random House.

Sanders, William T., Jeffrey R. Parsons, and Robert S. Santley. 1979. *The Basin of Mexico: Ecological processes in the evolution of a civilization*. New York: Academic Press.

Sanderson, Stephen K. 1995. Expanding world commercialization: The link between world-systems and civilizations. In *Civilizations and world systems: Studying world-historical change*, ed. S. K. Sanderson. Walnut Creek, CA: AltaMira Press.

Sanderson, Stephen K., and Wesley W. Roberts. 2008. The evolutionary forms of the religious life: A cross-cultural, quantitative analysis. *American Anthropologist* 110, no. 4: 454–66.

Sapir, Edward. 1931. Conceptual categories in primitive languages. Paper presented at the autumn meeting of the National Academy of Sciences, New Haven, CT. Published in *Science* 74.

Sapir, Edward. 1938. Why cultural anthropology needs the psychiatrist. *Psychiatry* 1:7–12.

Sapir, Edward, and M. Swadesh. 1964. American Indian grammatical categories. In *Language in culture and society*, ed. D. Hymes. New York: Harper & Row.

Sapolsky, Robert M. 1997. Testosterone rules. *Discover* (March 1997). Reprinted in *The gendered society reader*, eds. M. Kimmel and A. Aronson. New York: Oxford University Press.

Sarich, Vincent M. 1968. The origin of hominids: An immunological approach. In *Perspectives on human evolution*, vol. 1, eds. S. L. Washburn and P. C. Jay. New York: Holt, Rinehart & Winston.

Sarich, Vincent M., and Allan C. Wilson. 1966. Quantitative immunochemistry and the evolution of primate albumins: Micro-component fixations. *Science* 154 (December 23):1563–66.

Sassaman, Kenneth. 1996. Early Archaic settlement in the South Carolina coastal plain. In *The Paleoindian and Early Archaic Southeast*, eds. D. G. Anderson and K. E. Sassaman. Tuscaloosa: University of Alabama Press.

Satterthwaite, David. 2008. Editorial: The social and political basis for citizen action on urban poverty reduction. *Environment and Urbanization* 20:307–18.

Sattler, Richard A. 1996. Remnants, renegades, and runaways: Seminole ethnogenesis reconsidered. In *Ethnogenesis in the Americas*, ed. J. D. Hill. Iowa City: University of Iowa Press.

Savage-Rumbaugh, E. S. 1992. Language training of apes. In *The Cambridge encyclopedia of human evolution*, eds. S. Jones, R. Martin, and D. Pilbeam. New York: Cambridge University Press.

Savage-Rumbaugh, E. S. 1994. Hominid evolution: Looking to modern apes for clues. In *Hominid culture in primate perspective*, eds. D. Quiatt and J. Itani. Niwot: University Press of Colorado.

Savolainen, Peter, J. Luo, J. Lunderberg, and T. Leitner. 2002. Genetic evidence for an East Asian origin of domestic dogs. *Science* 296 (November 22):1610–14.

Scaglion, Richard. 1990. Legal adaptation in a Papua New Guinea village court. *Ethnology* 29:17–33.

Scaglion, Richard. 2009a. Abelam: Giant yams and cycles of sex, warfare, and ritual. In MyAnthroLibrary, eds. C. R. Ember, M. Ember, and P. N. Peregrine. MyAnthroLibrary.com. Pearson.

Scaglion, Richard. 2009b. Law and society. In MyAnthroLibrary, eds. C. R. Ember, M. Ember, and P. N. Peregrine. MyAnthroLibrary.com. Pearson.

Scaglion, Richard, and Rose Whittingham. 1985. Female plaintiffs and sex-related disputes in rural Papua New Guinea. In *Domestic violence in Papua New Guinea*, ed. S. Toft. New Guinea: Law Reform Commission.

Scarr, Sandra, and Kathleen McCartney. 1983. How people make their own environments: A theory of genotype–environment effects. *Child Development*, 54:424–35.

Scarre, Christopher. 2009. The world transformed: From foragers and farmers to states and empires. In *The human past*, ed. C. Scarre. New York: Thames and Hudson.

Schaller, George. 1963. *The mountain gorilla: Ecology and behavior*. Chicago: University of Chicago Press.

Schaller, George. 1964. *The year of the gorilla*. Chicago: University of Chicago Press.

Schaller, George. 1972. *The Serengeti lion: A study of predator-prey relations.* Chicago: University of Chicago Press.

Schick, Kathy D., and Nicholas Toth. 1993. *Making silent stones speak.* New York: Simon & Schuster.

Schlatter, N. Elizabeth. 2008. *Museum careers: A practical guide for students and novices.* Walnut Creek, CA: Left Coast Press.

Schlegel, Alice. 1989. Gender issues and cross-cultural research. *Behavior Science Research* 23:265–80.

Schlegel, Alice. 1991. Status, property, and the value on virginity. *American Ethnologist* 18:719–34.

Schlegel, Alice. 2009. The status of women. In MyAnthroLibrary, eds. C. R. Ember, M. Ember, and P. N. Peregrine. MyAnthroLibrary.com. Pearson.

Schlegel, Alice, and Herbert Barry, III. 1986. The cultural consequences of female contribution to subsistence. *American Anthropologist* 88:142–50.

Schlegel, Alice, and Herbert Barry, III. 1991. *Adolescence: An anthropological inquiry.* New York: Free Press.

Schlegel, Alice, and Rohn Eloul. 1987. A new coding of marriage transactions. *Behavior Science Research* 21:118–40.

Schlegel, Alice, and Rohn Eloul. 1988. Marriage transactions: Labor, property, and status. *American Anthropologist* 90:291–309.

Schmid, Petra, Marianne Schmid Mast, Dario Bombari, and Fred Mast. 2011. Gender effects in information processing on a nonverbal decoding task. *Sex Roles* 65:102–7.

Schneider, David M. 1961a. Introduction: The distinctive features of matrilineal descent groups. In *Matrilineal kinship*, eds. D. M. Schneider and K. Gough. Berkeley: University of California Press.

Schneider, David M. 1961b. Truk. In *Matrilineal kinship*, eds. D. M. Schneider and K. Gough. Berkeley: University of California Press.

Schoepf, B. 1988. Women, AIDS and economic crisis in central Africa. *Canadian Journal of African Studies* 22:625–44.

Schrauf, Robert W. 1999. Mother tongue maintenance among North American ethnic groups. *Cross-Cultural Research* 33:175–92.

Schrire, Carmel, ed. 1984a. *Past and present in hunter-gatherer studies.* Orlando, FL: Academic Press.

Schrire, Carmel. 1984b. Wild surmises on savage thoughts. In *Past and present in hunter-gatherer studies*, ed. C. Schrire. Orlando, FL: Academic Press.

Scheper-Hughes, Nancy. 2008. A talent for life: Reflections on human vulnerability and resilence. *Ethnos* 73:25–56.

Scheper-Hughes, Nancy. 2013. No more angel babies on the Alto do Cruzeiro. *Natural History* (June):28–38.

Schwartz, Richard D. 1954. Social factors in the development of legal control: A case study of two Israeli settlements. *Yale Law Journal* 63 (February):471–91.

Scott, Janny, and David Leonhardt. 2005. Class in America: Shadowy lines that still divide. *New York Times*, National, May 15, pp. 1, 26.

Scribner, Sylvia, and Michael Cole. 1981. *The psychology of literacy.* Cambridge, MA: Harvard University Press.

Scudder, Thayer. 1978. Opportunities, issues and achievements in development anthropology since the mid-1960s: A personal view. In *Applied anthropology in America*, 2nd ed., eds. E. M. Eddy and W. L. Partridge. New York: Columbia University Press.

Seemanová, Eva. 1971. A study of children of incestuous matings. *Human Heredity* 21:108–28.

Segal, Edwin S. 2004. Cultural constructions of gender. In *Encyclopedia of sex and gender: Men and women in the world's cultures*, vol. 1, eds. C. Ember and M. Ember. New York: Kluwer Academic/Plenum Publishers.

Segal, Robert A. 1987. *Joseph Campbell: An introduction.* New York: Garland.

Segall, Marshall H. 1979. *Cross-cultural psychology: Human behavior in global perspective.* Monterey, CA: Brooks/Cole.

Segall, Marshall H., Pierre R. Dasen, John W. Berry, and Ype H. Poortinga. 1990. *Human behavior in global perspective: An introduction to cross-cultural psychology.* New York: Pergamon.

Sellen, Daniel W., and Daniel J. Hruschka. 2004. Extracted-food resource-defense polygyny in Native Western North American societies at contact. *Current Anthropology* 45:707–14.

Semenov, S. A. 1970. *Prehistoric technology.* Trans. M. W. Thompson. Bath, England: Adams & Dart.

Sen, Amartya. 1981. Ingredients of famine analysis: Availability and entitlements. *The Quarterly Journal of Economics* 96, no. 3:433–64.

Sengupta, Somini. 2002. Money from kin abroad helps Bengalis get by. *New York Times*, June 24, p. A3.

Senner, Wayne M. 1989. Theories and myths on the origins of writing: A historical overview. In *The origins of writing*, ed. W. M. Senner. Lincoln: University of Nebraska Press.

Serre, David, et al. 2004. No evidence of Neandertal mtDNA contribution to early modern humans. *PLoS Biology* 2:313–17.

Service, Elman R. 1962. *Primitive social organization: An evolutionary perspective.* New York: Random House.

Service, Elman R. 1975. *Origins of the state and civilization: The process of cultural evolution.* New York: Norton.

Service, Elman R. 1978. *Profiles in ethnology.* 3rd ed. New York: Harper & Row.

Service, Elman R. 1979. *The hunters.* 2nd ed. Upper Saddle River, NJ: Prentice Hall.

Seyfarth, Robert M., and Dorothy L. Cheney. 1982. How monkeys see the world: A review of recent research on East African vervet monkeys. In *Primate communication*, eds. C. T. Snowdon, C. H. Brown, and M. R. Petersen. New York: Cambridge University Press.

Seyfarth, Robert M., Dorothy L. Cheney, and Peter Marler. 1980. Monkey response to three different alarm calls: Evidence of predator classification and semantic communication. *Science* 210 (November 14):801–803.

Shanklin, Eugenia. 1993. *Anthropology and race.* Belmont, CA: Wadsworth.

Shankman, Paul. 1991. Culture contact, cultural ecology, and Dani warfare. *Man* 26:299–321.

Shankman, Paul. 2009a. Sex, lies, and anthropologists: Margaret Mead, Derek Freeman, and Samoa. In MyAnthroLibrary, eds. C. R. Ember, M. Ember, and P. N. Peregrine. MyAnthroLibrary.com. Pearson.

Shankman, Paul. 2009b. *The trashing of Margaret Mead: Anatomy of an anthropological controversy.* Madison: University of Wisconsin Press.

Sheils, Dean. 1975. Toward a unified theory of ancestor worship: A cross-cultural study. *Social Forces* 54:427–40.

Sheils, Dean. 1980. A comparative study of human sacrifice. *Behavior Science Research* 15:245–62.

Shen, Xuefei, and Robert F. Siliciano. 2000. Preventing AIDS but not HIV-1 infection with a DNA vaccine. *Science* 290 (October 20):463–65.

Shibamoto, Janet S. 1987. The womanly woman: Japanese female speech. In *Language, gender, and sex in comparative perspective*, eds. S. U. Philips, S. Steele, and C. Tanz. Cambridge: Cambridge University Press.

Shipman, Pat. 1986. Scavenging or hunting in early hominids: Theoretical framework and tests. *American Anthropologist* 88:27–43.

Shoreman-Ouimet, Eleanor, and Helen Kopnina. 2011. Introduction: Environmental anthropology of yesterday and today. In *Environmental anthropology today*, eds. H. Kopnina and E. Shoreman-Ouimet. New York: Routledge.

Shulman, Seth. 1993. Nurturing native tongues. *Technology Review* (May/June):16.

Shuy, Roger. 1960. Sociolinguistic research at the Center for Applied Linguistics: The correlation of language and sex. *Giornata Internazionale di Sociolinguistica*, Rome: Palazzo Baldassini: 849–57.

Siegel, Jeff. 2009. Pidgins/creoles and second language acquisition. In *The handbook of pidgin and creole studies*, eds. S. Kouwenberg and J. V. Singler. Wiley-Blackwell.

Sih, Andrew, and Katharine A. Milton. 1985. Optimal diet theory: Should the !Kung eat mongongos? *American Anthropologist* 87:395–401.

Silk, Joan. 1980. Adoption and kinship in Oceania. *American Anthropologist* 82:799–820.

Silk, Joan. 2007. Social components of fitness in primate groups. *Science* 317 (September 7):1347–51.

Silver, Harry R. 1981. Calculating risks: The socioeconomic foundations of aesthetic innovation in an Ashanti carving community. *Ethnology* 20:101–14.

Silverman, Eric K. 2006. High art as tourist art, tourist art as high art: Comparing the New Guinea sculpture garden at Stanford University and Sepik River tourist art. In *Exploring world art*, eds. E. Venbrux, P. S. Rosi, and R. L. Welsch. Los Angeles: J. Paul Getty Museum.

Simmons, Alan H., Ilse Köhler-Rollefson, Gary O. Rollefson, Rolfe Mandel, and Zeidan Kafafi. 1988. Ain Ghazal: A major Neolithic settlement in central Jordan. *Science* 240 (April 1):35–39.

Simmons, Janie, Paul Farmer, and Brooke G. Schoepf. 1996. A global perspective. In *Women, poverty, and AIDS: Sex, drugs, and structural violence*, eds. P. Farmer, M. Connors, and J. Simmons. Monroe, ME: Common Courage Press.

Simons, Elwyn L. 1992. The primate fossil record. In *The Cambridge encyclopedia of human evolution*, eds. S. Jones, R. Martin, and D. Pilbeam. New York: Cambridge University Press.

Simons, Elwyn L. 1995. Skulls and anterior teeth of *Catopithecus* (Primates: Anthropoidea) from the Eocene shed light on anthropoidean origins. *Science* 268 (June 30):1885–88.

Simons, Elwyn L., and D. T. Rassmussen. 1996. Skull of *Catopithecus browni*, an Early Tertiary catarrhine. *American Journal of Physical* Anthropology 100:261–92.

Simoons, Frederick J. 1994. *Eat not this flesh: Food avoidances from prehistory to the present*, 65–71, 101, 109–111, 261–265. Madison: University of Wisconsin Press.

Simpson, George Gaylord. 1971. *The meaning of evolution.* New York: Bantam.

Simpson, S. P., and Ruth Field. 1946. Law and the social sciences. *Virginia Law Review* 32:858.

Simpson, Scott W. 2009. *Australopithecus afarensis* and human evolution. In MyAnthroLibrary, eds. C. R. Ember, M. Ember, and P. N. Peregrine. MyAnthroLibrary.com. Pearson.

Simpson, Scott W., et al. 2008. A female *Homo erectus* pelvis from Gona, Ethiopia. *Science* 322 (November 14):1089–91.

Singer, J. David. 1980. Accounting for international war: The state of the discipline. *Annual Review of Sociology* 6:349–67.

Singer, Merrill. 2007. *Introducing medical anthropology: A discipline in action.* Lanham, MD: AltaMira.

Singer, Ronald, and John Wymer. 1982. *The Middle Stone Age at Klasies River Mouth in South Africa.* Chicago: University of Chicago Press.

Sipes, Richard G. 1973. War, sports, and aggression: An empirical test of two rival theories. *American Anthropologist* 75:64–86.

Skoggard, Ian, and Teferi Abate Adem. 2010. From raiders to rustlers: The filial disaffection of a Turkana age-set. *Ethnology* 49:249–62.

Skomal, Susan N., and Edgar C. Polomé, eds. 1987. *Proto-Indo-European: The archaeology of a linguistic problem.* Washington, DC: Washington Institute for the Study of Man.

Slayman, Andrew. 1997. A battle over old bones. *Archaeology* 50:16–23.

Slocum, Sally. 1975. Woman the gatherer: Male bias in anthropology. In *Toward an anthropology of women*, ed. R. Reiter. New York: Monthly Review Press.

Small, Meredith. 1997. Our babies, ourselves. *Natural History* (October):42–51.

Smay, Diana, and George Armelagos. 2000. Galileo wept: A critical assessment of the use of race in forensic anthropology. *Transforming Anthropology* 9:19–29.

Smedley, Audrey. 2004. *Women creating patrilyny.* Walnut Creek, CA: AltaMira.

Smedley, Brian D., Adrienne Y. Stith, and Alan R. Nelson, eds. 2003. *Unequal treatment: Confronting racial and ethnic disparities in health care.* Washington, DC: National Academy Press.

Smeeding, Timothy M., Robert Erikson, and Marcus Jäntti. 2011. Introduction. In *Persistence, privilege, and parenting*, eds. T. M. Smeeding, R. Erikson, and M. Jätti. New York: Russell Sage Foundation.

Smith, B. Holly. 1986. Dental development in *Australopithecus* and early *Homo. Nature* 323 (September 25):327–30.

Smith, Bruce D. 1992a. Prehistoric plant husbandry in eastern North America. In *The origins of agriculture*, eds. C. Cowan and P. Watson. Washington, DC: Smithsonian Institution Press.

Smith, Bruce D. 1992b. *Rivers of change.* Washington, DC: Smithsonian Institution Press.

Smith, Eric Alden. 1983. Anthropological applications of optimal foraging theory: A critical review. *Current Anthropology* 24:625–40.

Smith, Eric Alden, Monique Borgerhoff Mulder, Samuel Bowles, Michael Gurven, Tom Hertz, and Mary K. Shenk. 2010. Production systems, inheritance, and inequality in premodern societies: Conclusions. *Current Anthropology* 51:85–94.

Smith, Fred H. 1984. Fossil hominids from the Upper Pleistocene of central Europe and the origin of modern humans. In *The origins of modern humans*, eds. F. H. Smith and F. Spencer. New York: Alan R. Liss.

Smith, Fred H. 2010. Species, populations and assimilation in later human evolution. In *A companion to biological anthropology*, ed. C. S. Larsen. Hoboken, NJ: Wiley-Blackwell.

Smith, Fred H., and Frank Spencer, eds. 1984. *The origins of modern humans: A world survey of the fossil evidence*. New York: Alan R. Liss.

Smith, John Maynard. 1989. *Evolutionary genetics*. New York: Oxford University Press.

Smith, Michael G. 1966. Preindustrial stratification systems. In *Social structure and mobility in economic development*, eds. N. J. Smelser and S. M. Lipset. Chicago: Aldine.

Smith, M. W. 1974. Alfred Binet's remarkable questions: A cross-national and cross-temporal analysis of the cultural biases built into the Stanford-Binet Intelligence Scale and other Binet tests. *Genetic Psychology Monographs* 89:307–34.

Smith, Philip J., et al. 2011. Parental delay or refusal of vaccine doses, childhood vaccination coverage at 24 months of age, and the health belief model. *Public Health Reports* 126, Supplement 2:135–46.

Smith, Waldemar R. 1977. *The fiesta system and economic change*. New York: Columbia University Press.

Smuts, Barbara B., Dorothy L. Cheney, Robert M. Seyfarth, Richard W. Wrangham, and Thomas T. Struhsaker, eds. 1987. *Primate societies*. Chicago: University of Chicago Press.

Snowdon, Charles T. 1999. An empiricist view of language evolution and development. In *The origins of language*, ed. B. J. King. Santa Fe, NM: School of American Research Press.

Society for American Archaeology. 2009. FAQs for students. http://www.saa.org/ForthePublic/FAQs/ForStudents/tabid/101/Default.aspx (accessed August 26, 2009).

Society for Applied Anthropology. Ethical and professional responsibilities. http://www.sfaa.net/about/ethics/ (accessed May 11, 2013).

Soffer, Olga. 1993. Upper Paleolithic adaptations in central and eastern Europe and man-mammoth interactions. In *From Kostenki to Clovis*, eds. O. Soffer and N. D. Praslov. New York: Plenum.

Soffer, Olga, J. M. Adovasio, and D. C. Hyland. 2000. The "Venus" figurines: Textiles, basketry, gender, and status in the Upper Paleolithic. *Current Anthropology* 41:511–37.

Solis, Ruth Shady, Jonathan Haas, and Winifred Creamer. 2001. Dating Caral, a preceramic site in the Supe Valley on the central coast of Peru. *Science* 292 (April 27):723–26.

Solon, Gary. 2002. Cross-country differences in intergenerational earnings mobility. *Journal of Economic Perspectives* 16:59–66.

Sosis, Richard. 2002. Patch choice decisions among Ifaluk fishers. *American Anthropologist* 104:583–98.

Sosis, Richard. 2007. Psalms for safety: Magico-religious responses to threats of terror. *Current Anthropology* 48:903–11.

Sosis, Richard, and Candace Alcorta. 2003. Signaling, solidarity, and the sacred: The evolution of religious behavior. *Evolutionary Anthropology* 12:264–74.

Sosis, Richard, and Eric R. Bressler. 2003. Cooperation and commune longevity: A test of the costly signaling theory of religion. *Cross-Cultural Research* 37:211–39.

Southworth, Franklin C., and Chandler J. Daswani. 1974. *Foundations of linguistics*. New York: Free Press.

Spanos, Nicholas P. 1983. Ergotism and the Salem witch panic: A critical analysis and an alternative conceptualization. *Journal of the History of the Behavioral Sciences* 19:358–69.

Sparks, Corey, and R. L. Jantz. 2003. Changing times, changing faces: Franz Boas's immigrant study in modern perspective. *American Anthropologist* 105:333–37.

Spencer, Frank. 1984. The Neandertals and their evolutionary significance: A brief historical survey. In *The origins of modern humans*, eds. F. H. Smith and F. Spencer. New York: Alan R. Liss.

Spencer, Robert F. 1968. Spouse-exchange among the North Alaskan Eskimo. In *Marriage, family and residence*, eds. P. Bohannan and J. Middleton. Garden City, NY: Natural History Press.

Sperber, Dan. 1985. *On anthropological knowledge: Three essays*. Cambridge: Cambridge University Press.

Speth, John D. 2009. Were our ancestors hunters or scavengers? In MyAnthroLibrary, eds. C. R. Ember, M. Ember, and P. N. Peregrine. MyAnthroLibrary.com. Pearson.

Speth, John D., and Dave D. Davis. 1976. Seasonal variability in early hominid predation. *Science* 192 (April 30):441–45.

Speth, John D., and Katherine A. Spielmann. 1983. Energy source, protein metabolism, and hunter-gatherer subsistence strategies. *Journal of Anthropological Archaeology* 2:1–31.

Spiro, Melford E. 1982. *Oedipus in the Trobriands*. Chicago: University of Chicago Press.

Spiro, Melford E. 1993. Is the Western conception of the self "peculiar" within the context of the world cultures? *Ethos* 21:107–53.

Spiro, Melford E., and Roy G. D'Andrade. 1958. A cross-cultural study of some supernatural beliefs. *American Anthropologist* 60:456–66.

Spring, Anita. 1995. *Agricultural development and gender issues in Malawi*. Lanham, MD: University Press of America.

Spring, Anita. 2000a. Agricultural commercialization and women farmers in Kenya. In *Women farmers and commercial ventures: Increasing food security in developing countries*, ed. A. Spring. Boulder, CO: Lynne Rienner Publishers.

Spring, Anita. 2000b. Commercialization and women farmers: Old paradigms and new themes. In *Women farmers and commercial ventures: Increasing food security in developing countries*, ed. A. Spring. Boulder, CO: Lynne Rienner Publishers.

Spring, Anita, ed. 2000c. *Women farmers and commercial ventures: Increasing food security in developing countries*. Boulder, CO: Lynne Rienner Publishers.

Squires, Susan. 2002. Doing the work: Customer research in the product development and design industry. In *Creating breakthrough ideas: The collaboration of anthropologists and designers in the product development industry*, eds., S. Squires and B. Byrne. Westport, CT: Greenwood Press.

Stairs, Arlene. 1992. Self-image, world-image: Speculations on identity from experiences with Inuit. *Ethos* 20:116–26.

Stanford, Craig B. 2009. Chimpanzee hunting behavior and human evolution. In MyAnthroLibrary, eds. C. R. Ember, M. Ember, and P. N. Peregrine. MyAnthroLibrary.com. Pearson.

Stark, Rodney. 1985. *The future of religion: Secularization, revival and cult formation*. Berkeley: University of California Press.

Stark, Rodney. 1996. *The rise of Christianity: A sociologist reconsiders history*. Princeton, NJ: Princeton University Press.

Stark, Rodney. 2001. Gods, rituals and the moral order. *Journal for the Scientific Study of Religion* 40:619–36.

Stark, Rodney, and Roger Finke. 2000. *Acts of faith: Explaining the human side of religion*. Berkeley: University of California Press.

Starling, Anne, and Jay Stock. 2007. Dental indicators of health and stress in early Egyptian and Nubian agriculturalists: A difficult transition and gradual recovery. *American Journal of Physical Anthropology* 134:520–28.

Steadman, Lyle B., Craig T. Palmer, and Christopher F. Tilley. 2010 [orig. 1996]. In *Ritual and belief: Readings in the anthropology of religion*, 3rd ed., ed. D. Hicks. Lanham, MD: AltaMira Press.

Stedman, Hansell, et al. 2004. Myosin gene mutation correlates with anatomical changes in the human lineage. *Nature* 428 (March 25):415–18.

Steegman, A. T., Jr. 1975. Human adaptation to cold. In *Physiological anthropology*, ed. A. Damon. New York: Oxford University Press.

Stein, P., and B. Rowe. 2000. *Physical anthropology*. 7th ed. Boston: McGraw-Hill.

Steiner, Christopher B. 1990. Body personal and body politic: Adornment and leadership in cross-cultural perspective. *Anthropos* 85:431–45.

Stephens, William N. 1963. *The family in cross-cultural perspective*. New York: Holt, Rinehart & Winston.

Stephens, William N. 1972. A cross-cultural study of modesty. *Behavior Science Research* 7:1–28.

Stern, Curt. 1973. *Principles of human genetics*. 3rd ed. San Francisco: W. H. Freeman.

Stevens, Phillips, Jr. 1996. Religion. In *Encyclopedia of cultural anthropology*, vol. 3, eds. D. Levinson and M. Ember. New York: Henry Holt.

Steward, Julian H. 1955a. The concept and method of cultural ecology. In *Theory of culture change*, eds. J. H. Steward. Urbana: University of Illinois Press.

Steward, Julian H. 1955b. *Theory of culture change*. Urbana: University of Illinois Press.

Steward, Julian H., and Louis C. Faron. 1959. *Native peoples of South America*. New York: McGraw-Hill.

Stewart, T. D. 1950. Deformity, trephanating, and mutilation in South American Indian skeletal remains. In *Handbook of South American Indians, Vol. 6: Physical anthropology, linguistics, and cultural geography*, ed. J. A. Steward. Washington, DC: Smithsonian Institution Bureau of American Ethnology Bulletin 143.

Stimpson, David, Larry Jensen, and Wayne Neff. 1992. Cross-cultural gender differences in preference for a caring morality. *Journal of Social Psychology* 132:317–22.

Stini, William A. 1971. Evolutionary implications of changing nutritional patterns in human populations. *American Anthropologist* 73:1019–30.

Stini, William A. 1975. *Ecology and human adaptation*. Dubuque, IA: Wm. C. Brown.

Stockett, Miranda K., and Pamela L. Geller. 2006. Introduction. In *Feminist anthropology: Past, present, and future*, eds. P. L. Geller and M. K. Stockett. Philadelphia: University of Pennsylvania Press.

Stodder, James. 1995. The evolution of complexity in primitive exchange. *Journal of Comparative Economics* 20:205.

Stogdill, Ralph M. 1974. *Handbook of leadership: A survey of theory and research*. New York: Macmillan.

Stokstad, Erik. 2008. Privatization prevents collapse of fish stocks, global analysis shows. *Science* 321:1619.

Stone, Linda and Paul E. Lurquin. 2007. *Genes, culture, and human evolution*. Malden, MA: Blackwell.

Stoneking, Mark. 1997. Recent African origin of human mitochondrial DNA. In *Progress in population genetics and human evolution*, eds. P. Donnelly and S. Tavaré. New York: Springer.

Strachan, Laura. 2011. Political ecology and identity: A study of the Harasiis of Oman. *Totem: The University of Western Ontario Journal of Anthropology* 11, no. 1:101–13.

Straus, Murray A. 1991. Physical violence in American families: Incidence rates, causes, and trends. In *Abused and battered*, eds. D. D. Knudsen and J. L. Miller. New York: Aldine.

Straus, Murray A. 1995. Trends in cultural norms and rates of partner violence: An update to 1992. In *Understanding partner violence: Prevalence, causes, consequences, and solutions*, eds. S. M. Stith and M. A. Straus. Minneapolis, MN: National Council on Family Relations. http://pubpages.unh.edu/~mas2/v56.pdf/ (accessed August 2002).

Straus, Murray A. 2001. Physical aggression in the family: Prevalence rates, links to non-family violence, and implications for primary prevention of societal violence. In *Prevention and control of aggression and the impact on its victims*, ed. M. Martinez. New York: Kluwer Academic/Plenum.

Straus, Murray A. 2009. Prevalence and social causes of corporal punishment by parents in world perspective. Paper presented at the annual meeting of the Society for Cross-Cultural Research, Las Vegas, Nevada, February 20, 2009.

Straus, Murray. 2010. Thirty years of denying the evidence on gender symmetry in partner violence: Implications for prevention and treatment. *Partner Abuse* 1:332–63.

Straus, Murray A., and Glenda Kaufman Kantor. 1994. Change in Spouse assault rates from 1975 to 1992: A comparison of three national surveys in the United States. Paper presented at the 13th World Congress of Sociology, Bielefeld, Germany, July. http://pubpages.unh.edu/~mas2/v55.pdf/ (accessed August 2002).

Straus, Murray A., and Glenda Kaufman Kantor. 1995. Trends in physical abuse by parents from 1975 to 1992: A comparison of three national surveys. Paper presented at the annual meeting of the American Society of Criminology, Boston, MA, November 18. http://pubpages.unh.edu/~mas2/V57.pdf/ (accessed August 2002).

Straus, Murray A., and Carrie L. Yodanis. 1996. Corporal punishment in adolescence and physical assaults on spouses in later life: What accounts for the link? *Journal of Marriage and the Family* 58:825–41.

Strauss, Lawrence Guy. 1982. Comment on White. *Current Anthropology* 23:185–86.

Strauss, Lawrence Guy. 1989. On early hominid use of fire. *Current Anthropology* 30:488–91.

Stringer, Christopher B. 1985. Evolution of a species. *Geographical Magazine* 57:601–607.

Stringer, Christopher B. 2000. Neandertals. In *Encyclopedia of human evolution and prehistory*, eds. I. Tattersall, E. Delson, and J. van Couvering. New York: Garland.

Stringer, Christopher B. 2003. Out of Ethiopia. *Nature* 423 (June 12):692–95.

Stringer, Christopher B., and Clive Gamble. 1993. *In search of the Neanderthals*. New York: Thames and Hudson.

Stringer, Christopher B., J. J. Hublin, and B. Vandermeersch. 1984. The origin of anatomically modern humans in western Europe. In *The origins of modern humans*, eds. F. H. Smith and F. Spencer. New York: Alan R. Liss.

Suárez-Orozco, Marcelo. 1992. A grammar of terror: Psychocultural responses to state terrorism in dirty war and post-dirty war Argentina. In *The paths to domination, resistance, and terror*, eds. C. Nordstrom and J. Martin. Berkeley, CA: University of California Press.

Sullivan, Roger J., John S. Allen, and Karen L. Nero. 2007. Schizophrenia in Palau: A biocultural analysis. *Current Anthropology* 48:189–213.

Summerhayes, G. R., et al. 2010. Human adaptation and plant use in highland New Guinea 49,000 to 44,000 years ago. *Science* 330 (October 1):78–81.

Sunderland, Patricia L., and Rita M. Denny. 2007. *Doing anthropology in consumer research*. Walnut Creek, CA: Left Coast Press.

Super, Charles M., and Sara Harkness. 1997. The cultural structuring of child development. In *Handbook of cross-cultural psychology*, vol. 2, 2nd ed., eds. J. W. Berry, P. R. Dasen, and T. S. Saraswathi. Boston: Allyn & Bacon.

Susman, Randall L., ed. 1984. *The Pygmy Chimpanzee: Evolutionary biology and behavior*. New York: Plenum.

Susman, Randall L. 1994. Fossil evidence for early hominid tool use. *Science* 265 (September 9):1570–73.

Susman, Randall L., Jack T. Stern, Jr., and William L. Jungers. 1985. Locomotor adaptations in the Hadar hominids. In *Ancestors: The hard evidence*, ed. E. Delson. New York: Alan R. Liss.

Sussman, Robert W. 1972. Child transport, family size, and the increase in human population size during the Neolithic. *Current Anthropology* 13:258–67.

Sussman, Robert W. 1991. Primate origins and the evolution of angiosperms. *American Journal of Primatology* 23:209–23.

Sussman, Robert W., and W. G. Kinzey. 1984. The ecological role of the *Callitrichidae*: A review. *American Journal of Physical Anthropology* 64:419–49.

Sussman, Robert W., and Peter H. Raven. 1978. Pollination by lemurs and marsupials: An archaic coevolutionary system. *Science* 200 (May 19):734–35.

Svašek, Maruška. 2007. *Anthropology, art and cultural production*. London: Pluto Press.

Swanson, Guy E. 1969. *The birth of the gods: The origin of primitive beliefs*. Ann Arbor: University of Michigan Press.

Sweeney, James J. 1952. African Negro culture. In *African folktales and sculpture*, ed. P. Radin. New York: Pantheon.

Swisher, C. C., III, G. H. Curtis, T. Jacob, A. G. Getty, A. Suprijo, and Widiasmoro. 1994. Age of the earliest known hominids in Java, Indonesia. *Science* 263 (February 25):1118–21.

Szalay, Frederick S. 1968. The beginnings of primates. *Evolution* 22:32–33.

Szalay, Frederick S. 1972. Paleobiology of the earliest primates. In *The functional and evolutionary biology of the primates*, ed. R. Tuttle. Chicago: University of Chicago Press.

Szalay, Frederick S. 1975. Hunting-scavenging protohominids: A model for hominid origins. *Man* 10:420–29.

Szalay, Frederick S., and Eric Delson. 1979. *Evolutionary history of the primates*. New York: Academic Press.

Szalay, Frederick S., I. Tattersall, and R. Decker. 1975. Phylogenetic relationships of "*Plesiadipis*"—Postcranial evidence. *Contributions to Primatology* 5:136–66.

Szklut, Jay, and Robert Roy Reed. 1991. Community anonymity in anthropological research: A reassessment. In *Ethics and the profession of anthropology: Dialogue for a new era*, ed. C. Fluehr-Lobban. Philadelphia: University of Pennsylvania Press.

Tainter, Joseph. 1988. *The collapse of complex societies*. Cambridge: Cambridge University Press, 128–52.

Takahata, Naoyuki, and Yoko Satta. 1997. Evolution of the primate lineage leading to modern humans: Phylogenetic and demographic inferences from DNA sequences. *Publications of the National Academy of Sciences* 94 (April 29):4811–15.

Takezawa, Yasuko. 2006. Race should be discussed and understood across the globe. *Anthropology News* (February/March):6–7.

Talmon, Yonina. 1964. Mate selection in collective settlements. *American Sociological Review* 29:491–508.

Tamari, Tal. 1991. The development of caste systems in West Africa. *Journal of African History* 32:221–50.

Tamari, Tal. 2005. Kingship and caste in Africa: History, diffusion and evolution. In *The character of kingship*, ed. D. Quigley. Oxford: Berg Publishers.

Tannen, Deborah. 1990. *You just don't understand: Women and men in conversation*. New York: William Morrow and Company.

Tannenbaum, Nicola. 1984. The misuse of Chayanov: "Chayanov's Rule" and empiricist bias in anthropology. *American Anthropologist* 86:927–42.

Tanter, Raymond, and Manus Midlarsky. 1967. A theory of revolution. *Journal of Conflict Resolution* 11:3, 266.

Tattersall, Ian. 1982. *The primates of Madagascar*. New York: Columbia University Press.

Tattersall, Ian. 1997. Out of Africa again…and again? *Scientific American* 276 (April):60–68.

Tattersall, Ian. 1999. *The last Neanderthal*. Boulder, CO: Westview, 115–16.

Tattersall, Ian. 2002. Paleoanthropology and evolutionary theory. In *Physical anthropology: Original readings in method and practice*, eds. P. N. Peregrine, C. R. Ember, and M. Ember. Upper Saddle River, NJ: Prentice Hall.

Tattersall, Ian. 2009. Paleoanthropology and evolutionary theory. In MyAnthroLibrary, eds. C. R. Ember, M. Ember, and P. N. Peregrine. MyAnthroLibrary. com. Pearson.

Tattersall, Ian, and Jeffrey Schwartz. 2000. *Extinct humans*. Boulder, CO: Westview.

Tattersall, Ian, Eric Delson, and John Van Couvering, eds. 2000. *Encyclopedia of human evolution and prehistory*. New York: Garland.

Tattersall, Ian and Rob DeSalle. 2011. *Race? Debunking a scientific myth*. College Station, TX: Texas A&M University Press.

Tax, Sol. 1975. Action anthropology. *Current Anthropology* 16:514–7.

Taylor, Christopher C. 2005. Mutton, mud, and runny noses: A hierarchy of distaste in early Rwanda. *Social Analysis* 49:213–30.

Taylor, Paul, et al. 2010. *The return of the multigenerational family household*. Pew Research Center Report. Washington, DC: Pew Research Center.

Taylor, R. E. 1998. Radiocarbon dating. In *Chronometric dating in archaeology*, eds. R. E. Taylor and M. J. Aiken. New York: Plenum.

Taylor, R. E., and M. J. Aitken, eds. 1997. *Chronometric dating in archaeology*. New York: Plenum.

Teleki, Geza. 1973. The omnivorous chimpanzee. *Scientific American* (January):32–42.

Templeton, Alan R. 1993. The "Eve" hypotheses: A genetic critique and reanalysis. *American Anthropologist* 95:51–72.

Templeton, Alan R. 1996. Gene lineages and human evolution. *Science* 272 (May 31):1363.

Terborgh, John. 1983. *Five New World primates: A study in comparative ecology*. Princeton, NJ: Princeton University Press.

Terrell, John. 2011. *Building new bridges, not new walls: A handbook for hosting Marae encounters*. Chicago: Field Museum.

Textor, Robert B., comp. 1967. *A cross-cultural summary*. New Haven, CT: HRAF Press.

Thomas, David Hurst. 1986. *Refiguring anthropology: First principles of probability and statistics*. Prospect Heights, IL: Waveland.

Thomas, David Hurst. 2000. *Skull wars*. New York: Basic Books.

Thomas, Elizabeth Marshall. 1959. *The harmless people*. New York: Knopf.

Thomas, Richard. 2013. Personal communication, May.

Thomas, Wesley. 1993. A traditional Navajo's perspectives on the cultural construction of gender in the

Navajo world. Paper presented at the University of Frankfurt, Germany. As referred to in Lang 1999.

Thomason, Sarah Grey, and Terrence Kaufman. 1988. *Language contact, creolization, and genetic linguistics*. Berkeley: University of California Press.

Thompson, Elizabeth Bartlett. 1966. *Africa, past and present*. Boston: Houghton Mifflin.

Thompson, Ginger. 2002. Mexico is attracting a better class of factory in its south. *New York Times*, June 29, p. A3.

Thompson, Richard H. 1996. Assimilation. In *Encyclopedia of cultural anthropology*, vol. 1, 4 vols., eds. D. Levinson and M. Ember. New York: Henry Holt.

Thompson, Richard H. 2009. Chinatowns: Immigrant communities in transition. In MyAnthroLibrary, eds. C. R. Ember, M. Ember, and P. N. Peregrine. MyAnthroLibrary.com. Pearson.

Thompson, Stith. 1965. Star Husband Tale. In *The study of folklore*, ed. A. Dundes. Upper Saddle River, NJ: Prentice Hall.

Thompson-Handler, Nancy, Richard K. Malenky, and Noel Badrian. 1984. Sexual behavior of *Pan paniscus* under natural conditions in the Lomako Forest, Equateur, Zaire. In *The Pygmy Chimpanzee*, ed. R. Susman. New York: Plenum.

Thornhill, Randy, and Corey L. Fincher. 2011. Parasite stress promotes homicide and child maltreatment. *Philosophical Transactions of the Royal Society B* 366:3466–77.

Thorpe, S. K. S., R. L. Holder, and R. H. Compton. 2007. Origin of human bipedalism as an adaptation for locomotion on flexible branches. *Science* 316 (June):1328–31.

Thurnwald, R. C. 1934. Pigs and currency in Buin: Observations about primitive standards of value and economics. *Oceania* 5:119–41.

Tierney, Patrick. 2000. *Darkness in El Dorado*. New York: Norton.

Tishkoff, Sarah A., et al. 2009. The genetic structure and history of Africans and African Americans. *Science Express* 22 324, no. 5930 (May):1035–44.

Tobias, Philip V. 1994. The craniocerebral interface in early hominids: Cerebral impressions, cranial thickening, paleoneurobiology, and a new hypothesis on encephalization. In *Integrative paths to the past*, eds. R. Corruccini and R. Ciochon. Upper Saddle River, NJ: Prentice Hall.

Tobin, Joseph J., David Y. H. Wu, and Dana H. Davidson. 1989. *Preschool in three cultures: Japan, China, and the United States*. New Haven, CT: Yale University Press.

Tocheri, Matthew, et al. 2007. The primitive wrist of *Homo floresiensis* and its implications for hominin evolution. *Science* 317 (September 21):1743–44.

Todorov, Alexander, Anesu N. Mandisodza, Amir Goren, and Crystal C. Hall. 2005. Inference of competence from faces predict election outcomes. *Science* 308 (June 10):1623–26.

Tollefson, Kenneth. 2009. Tlingit: Chiefs past and present. In MyAnthroLibrary, eds. C. R. Ember, M. Ember, and P. N. Peregrine. MyAnthroLibrary.com. Pearson.

Tomasello, Michael. 1990. Cultural transmission in the tool use and communicatory signaling of chimpanzees. In *"Language" and intelligence in monkeys and apes*, eds. S. Parker and K. Gibson. New York: Cambridge University Press.

Torrey, E. Fuller. 1972. *The mind game: Witchdoctors and psychiatrists*. New York: Emerson Hall.

Torry, William I. 1986. Morality and harm: Hindu peasant adjustments to famines. *Social Science Information* 25:125–60.

Traphagan, John W. 2006. Power, family, and filial responsibility related to elder care in rural Japan. *Case Management Journals* 7, no. 4:205–12.

Traphagan, John W. 2009. The oddness of things: Morality games and interpretations of social change among elders in rural Japan. *The Asia Pacific Journal of Anthropology* 10, no. 4:329–47.

Traphagan, John W., and L. Keith Brown. 2002. Fast food and intergenerational commensality in Japan: New styles and old patterns. *Ethnology* 41:119–34.

Travis, John. 2000. Human genome work reaches milestone. *Science News* (July 1):4–5.

Treiman, Donald J., and Harry B. G. Ganzeboom. 1990. Cross-national comparative status-attainment research. *Research in Social Stratification and Mobility* 9:117.

Trevor-Roper, H. R. 1971. The European witch-craze of the sixteenth and seventeenth centuries. In *Reader in comparative religion*, 3rd ed., eds. W. A. Lessa and E. Z. Vogt. New York: Harper & Row.

Triandis, Harry C. 1995. *Individualism and collectivism.* Boulder, CO: Westview.

Trigger, Bruce G. 1989. *A history of archaeological thought.* Cambridge: Cambridge University Press.

Trinkaus, Erik. 1984. Western Asia. In *The origins of modern humans*, eds. F. H. Smith and F. Spencer. New York: Alan R. Liss.

Trinkaus, Erik. 1985. Pathology and the posture of the La Chapelle-aux-Saints Neandertal. *American Journal of Physical Anthropology* 67:19–41.

Trinkaus, Erik. 1986. The Neandertals and modern human origins. *Annual Review of Anthropology* 15:193–218.

Trinkaus, Erik. 1987a. Bodies, brawn, brains and noses: Human ancestors and human predation. In *The evolution of human hunting*, eds. M. Nitecki and D. Nitecki. New York: Plenum.

Trinkaus, Erik. 1987b. The Neandertal face: Evolutionary and functional perspectives on a recent hominid face. *Journal of Human Evolution* 16:429–43.

Trinkaus, Erik. 2007. Human evolution: Neandertal gene speaks out. *Current Biology* 17, no. 21:R917–R919.

Trinkaus, Erik, and William W. Howells. 1979. The Neanderthals. *Scientific American* (December):118–33.

Trinkaus, Erik, and Pat Shipman. 1993a. *The Neandertals: Changing the image of mankind.* New York: Knopf.

Trinkaus, Erik, and Pat Shipman. 1993b. Neandertals: Images of ourselves. *Evolutionary Anthropology* 1:194–201.

Trompf, G. W., ed. 1990. *Cargo cults and millenarian movements: Transoceanic comparisons of new religious movements.* Berlin: Mouton de Gruyter.

Trouillot, Michel-Rolph. 2001. The anthropology of the state in the age of globalization: Close encounters of the deceptive kind. *Current Anthropology* 42:125–38.

Trudgill, Peter. 1983. *Sociolinguistics: An introduction to language and society.* Rev. ed. New York: Penguin.

Turner, B. L. 1970. Population density in the Classic Maya lowlands: New evidence for old approaches. *Geographical Review* 66 (January):72–82.

Turner, Christy G. 1987. Telltale teeth. *Natural History* (January):6–9.

Turner, Christy G. 1989. Teeth and prehistory in Asia. *Scientific American* (February):88–95.

Turner, Christy G. 2005. A synoptic history of physical anthropological studies on the peopling of Alaska and the Americas. *Alaska Journal of Anthropology* 3:157–70.

Turner, Terence. 1993. The role of indigenous peoples in the environmental crisis: The example of the Kayapo of the Brazilian Amazon. *Perspectives in Biology and Medicine* 36:526–45.

Turner, Terence. 1995. An indigenous people's struggle for socially equitable and ecologically sustainable production: The Kayapo revolt against extractivism. *Journal of Latin American Anthropology* 1:98–121.

Tuttle, Russell H. 1986. *Apes of the world: Their social behavior, communication, mentality, and ecology.* Park Ridge, NJ: Noyes.

Tylor, Edward B. 1971/1958. *Primitive culture.* New York: Harper Torchbooks.

Tylor, Edward B. 2010 [orig. 1873]. Animism. In *Ritual and belief: Readings in the anthropology of religion*, 3rd ed., ed. D. Hicks. Lanham, MD: AltaMira Press.

Uberoi, J. P. Singh. 1962. *The politics of the Kula Ring: An analysis of the findings of Bronislaw Malinowski.* Manchester, UK: University of Manchester Press.

Ucko, Peter J., and Andrée Rosenfeld. 1967. *Paleolithic cave art.* New York: McGraw-Hill.

Udy, Stanley H., Jr. 1970. *Work in traditional and modern society.* Upper Saddle River, NJ: Prentice Hall.

UNAIDS. 2007. AIDS epidemic update, December. http://data.unaids.org/pub/EPISlides/2007/2007_epiupdate_en.pdf.

UNAIDS. 2012. Global fact sheet. http://www.unaids.org (accessed May 18 2013).

UN-HABITAT. 2009. Planning sustainable cities: Global report on human settlements 2009. http://www.unhabitat.org/content.asp?typeid=19&catid=555&cid=5607 (accessed May 31, 2013).

UN-HABITAT. 2012. State of the world's cities 2012/2013. http://sustainabledevelopment.un.org/content/documents/745habitat.pdf.

UNHCR. 2013. Displacement: The new 21st century challenge. http://www.unhcr.org/51bacb0f9.html.

U.N. Human Development Report. 2011. http://hdr.undp.org/en/media/HDR_2011_EN_Table3.pdf (accessed September 7, 2012).

UN News Centre. 2005. Norway at top, Niger at bottom of UN's 2005 human development index. http://www.un.org/apps/news/story.asp?NewsID=15707&Cr=human&Cr1=development (accessed June 20, 2009).

UNODC. 2012. Homicide statistics. http://www.unodc.org/unodc/en/data-and-analysis/homicide.html.

UN Works. n.d. United Nations, Homeless Kids in Mongolia, with National Standards linked lesson plans http://www.un.org/works/goingon/mongolia/lessonplan_homelessness.html.

Underhill, Ralph. 1975. Economic and political antecedents of monotheism: A cross-cultural study. *American Journal of Sociology* 80:841–61.

Underhill, Ruth M. 1938. *Social organization of the Papago Indians.* New York: Columbia University Press.

Ungar, P. S., and M. Sponheimer. 2011. The diets of early hominins. *Science* 334 (October 14):190–93.

Union of International Associations. 2013. www.uia.be.

United Nations. n.d. We can end poverty. 2015 Millenium Development Goals. http://www.un.org/millenniumgoals/environ.shtml.

United Nations Development Programme (UNDP). 2007. Human development report 2007/2008: Fighting climate change: Human solidarity in a divided world. http://hdr.undp.org/en/media/HDR_20072008_EN_Complete.pdf (accessed June 20, 2009).

United Nations Development Programme (UNDP). 2010. The real wealth of nations: Pathways to human development. In Summary: Human Development Report 2010. http://hdr.undp.org/en/media/HDR10%20EN%20summary_without%20table.pdf.

United Nations Human Settlements Programme. 2003. The challenge of slums: global report on human settlements. http://www.unhabitat.org/pmss/listItemDetails.aspx?publicationID=1156 (accessed January 17, 2014).

Unnithan, N. Prabha. 2009. Nayars: Tradition and change in marriage and family. In MyAnthroLibrary, eds. C. R. Ember, M. Ember, and P. N. Peregrine. MyAnthroLibrary.com. Pearson.

U.S. Census Bureau. 2002. The big payoff: Educational entertainment and synthetic estimates of work-life earnings. In *Statistical abstract of the United States: 1993*, 113th ed. Washington, DC: U.S. Government Printing Office.

U.S. Department of Justice. 1988. *Prevalence, incidence, and consequences of violence against women: Findings from the National Violence against Women Survey*, November. Washington, DC: Bureau of Justice Statistics.

U.S. Department of Justice. 1994. *Violent crime.* NCJ-147486, April. Washington, DC: Bureau of Justice Statistics.

U.S. Department of Justice. 2000. *Children as victims. Juvenile Justice Bulletin 1999.* National Report Series. Washington, DC: Bureau of Justice Statistics.

U.S. Department of Justice. 2005. *Family violence statistics: including statistics on strangers and acquaintances.* Washington, DC: Bureau of Justice Statistics.

U.S. Department of Justice. n.d. Bureau of Justice statistics homicide trends in the U.S: Long-term trends and patterns. http://www.ojp.gov/bjs/homicide/hmrt.htm (accessed September5, 2009).

U. S. Department of State. 2013. Fact sheet: Non-Governmental Organizations (NGOs) in the United States. www.humanrights.gov.

U.S. Environmental Protection Agency. 2009. http://www.epa.gov/oecaagct/ag101/demographics.html (accessed February 2, 2014).

Vadez, Vincent, Victoria Reyes-Garcia, Tomás Huanca, and William R. Leonard. 2008. Cash cropping, farm technologies, and deforestation: What are the connections? A model with empirical data from the Bolivian Amazon. *Human Organization* 67:384–96.

Valente, Thomas W. 1995. *Network models of the diffusion of innovations.* Cresskill, NJ: Hampton Press.

Valla, Jeffrey M., Stephen J. Ceci, and Wendy M. Williams. 2011. The accuracy of inferences about criminality based on facial appearance. *Journal of Social, Evolutionary, and Cultural Psychology* 5, no. 1:66–91.

Valladas, H., J. L. Joron, G. Valladas, O. Bar-Yosef, and B. Vandermeersch. 1988. Thermoluminescence dating of Mousterian "Proto-Cro-Magnon" remains from Israel and the origin of modern man. *Nature* 337 (February 18):614–16.

Van der Leeuw, Sander. 1999. *The Archaeomedes Project: Understanding the natural and anthropogenic causes of desertification and land degradation.* Luxembourg: European Union.

Van der Leeuw, Sander, François Favory, and Jean Jacques Girardot. 2002. The archaeological study of environmental degradation: An example from south-eastern France. In *The archaeology of global change*, eds. C. Redman, S. R. James, P. Fish, and J. D. Rogers. Washington, DC: Smithsonian.

Van der Merwe, N. J. 1992. Reconstructing prehistoric diet. In *The Cambridge encyclopedia of human evolution*, eds. S. Jones, R. Martin, and D. Pilbeam. New York: Cambridge University Press.

Van Hear, Nicholas. 2004. Refugee diasporas or refugees in diaspora. In *Encyclopedia of diasporas: Immigrant and refugee cultures around the world*, vol. 1, eds. M. Ember, C. R. Ember, and I. Skoggard. New York: Kluwer Academic/Plenum.

Van Hear, Nicholas. 2006. Refugees in diaspora: From durable solutions to transnational relations. *Refuge: Canada's Journal on Refugees* 23:9–14.

Van Hemert, Dianne A., Ype H. Poortinga, and Fons J. R. van de Vijver. 2007. Emotion and culture: A meta-analysis. *Cognition & Emotion* 21:913–43.

Van Hemert, Dianne A., Fons J. R. Van de Vijver, and Ad J. J. M. Vingerhoets. 2011. Culture and crying: Prevalences and gender differences. *Cross-Cultural Research* 45:399–431.

Van Ijzendoorn, Marinus H., Marian J. Bakermans-Kranenburg, and Abraham Sagi-Schwartz. 2006. Attachment across diverse sociocultural contexts: The limits of universality. In *Parenting beliefs, behaviors, and parent-child relations: A cross-cultural perspective*, eds. K. H. Rubin and O. B. Chung. New York: Psychology Press.

Van Lawick-Goodall, Jane. 1971. *In the shadow of man.* Boston: Houghton Mifflin.

Van Schaik, C. P. M. Ancrenaz, et al. 2003. Orangutan cultures and the evolution of material culture. *Science* 299 (January 3):102–05.

Van Willigen, John. 2002. *Applied anthropology: An introduction.* 3rd ed. Westport, CT: Bergin and Garvey.

Vayda, Andrew P., and Roy A. Rappaport. 1968. Ecology: Cultural and noncultural. In *Introduction to cultural anthropology*, ed. J. H. Clifton. Boston: Houghton Mifflin.

Vayda, Andrew P., Anthony Leeds, and David B. Smith. 1962. The place of pigs in Melanesian subsistence. In *Symposium* on patterns of land utilization, ed. V. E. Garfield. Seattle: University of Washington Press.

Vekua, Abesalom, et al. 2002. A new skull of early *Homo* from Dmanisi, Georgia. *Science* 297 (July 5):85–89.

Vigil, James Diego. 1988. Group processes and street identity: Adolescent Chicano gang members. *Ethos* 16:421–45.

Vigil, James Diego. 2009. Mexican Americans: Growing up on the streets of Los Angeles. In MyAnthroLibrary, eds. C. R. Ember, M. Ember, and P. N. Peregrine. MyAnthroLibrary.com. Pearson.

Vigilant, Linda, Mark Stoneking, Henry Harpending, Kristen Hawkes, and Allan C. Wilson. 1991. African populations and the evolution of human mitochrondrial DNA. *Science* 253 (September 27):1503–1507.

Vincent, Joan. 1978. Political anthropology: Manipulative strategies. *Annual Review of Anthropology* 7:175–94.

Visaberghi, Elisabetta, and Dorothy Munkenbeck Fragaszy. 1990. Do monkeys ape? In *"Language" and intelligence in monkeys and apes*, eds. S. Parker and K. Gibson. New York: Cambridge University Press.

Vogel, Joseph O. 2009. De-mystifying the past: The Great Zimbabwe, King Solomon's mines, and other tales of Old Africa. In MyAnthroLibrary, eds. C. R. Ember, M. Ember, and P. N. Peregrine. MyAnthroLibrary.com. Pearson.

Vohs, Kathleen D., Nicole L. Mead, and Miranda R. Goode. 2006. The psychological consequences of money. *Science* 314 (November 17):154–56.

von Frisch, Karl. 1962. Dialects in the language of the bees. *Scientific American* (August):78–87.

Vrba, Elizabeth S. 1995. On the connection between paleoclimate and evolution. In *Paleoclimate and evolution*, eds. E. S. Vrba, G. H. Denton, T. C. Partridge, and L. H. Burckle. New Haven, CT: Yale University Press.

Vrba, Elizabeth S. 1996. Climate, heterochrony, and human evolution. *Journal of Anthropological Research* 52, no. 1:1–28.

Wadley, Reed L. 2003. Lethal treachery and the imbalance of power in warfare and feuding. *Journal of Anthropological Research* 59:531–54.

Wagley, Charles. 1974. Cultural influences on population: A comparison of two Tupi tribes. In *Native South Americans*, ed. P. J. Lyon. Boston: Little, Brown.

Waguespack, Nicole. 2012. Early Paleoindians from colonization to Folsom. In *Oxford handbook of North American archaeology*, ed. T. Pauketat. Oxford: Oxford University Press.

Wald, Matthew L. 2000. Hybrid cars show up in M.I.T.'s crystal ball. *New York Times*, November 3, p. Fl.

Waldbaum, Jane C. 2005. Helping hand for China. *Archaeology* 58:6.

Waldman, Amy. 2005. Sri Lankan maids' high price for foreign jobs. *New York Times*, May 8, pp. 1, 20.

Walker, Alan, and R. Leakey. 1988. The evolution of *Australopithecus boisei*. In *Evolutionary history of the "robust" australopithecines*, ed. F. Grine. New York: Aldine.

Wallace, Alfred Russell. 1970/1858. On the tendency of varieties to depart indefinitely from the original type. In *Evolution of man*, ed. L. B. Young. New York: Oxford University Press. (Originally published in 1858.)

Wallace, Anthony. 1966. *Religion: An anthropological view*. New York: Random House.

Wallace, Anthony. 1970. *The death and rebirth of the Seneca*. New York: Knopf.

Wallace, Anthony. 1972. Mental illness, biology and culture. In *Psychological anthropology*, 2nd ed., ed. F. L. K. Hsu. Cambridge, MA: Schenkman.

Wallerstein, Immanuel. 1974. *The modern world-system*. New York: Academic Press.

Walter, R. C. 1998. Potassium-argon/argon-argon dating methods. In *Chronometric dating in archaeology*, eds. R. E. Taylor and M. J. Aiken. New York: Plenum.

Wanner, Eric, and Lila R. Gleitman, eds. 1982. *Language acquisition: The state of the art*. Cambridge: Cambridge University Press.

Ward, Peter M. 1982. Introduction and purpose. In *Self-help housing*, ed. P. M. Ward. London: Mansell.

Ward, Steve. 1997. The taxonomy and phylogenetic relationships of *Sivapithecus* revisited. In *Function, phylogeny and fossils: Miocene hominoid evolution and adaptation*, eds. D. R. Begun, C. V. Ward, and M. D. Rose. New York: Plenum.

Ward, Steve, B. Brown, A. Hill, J. Kelley, and W. Downs. 1999. *Equatorius*: A new hominoid genus from the Middle Miocene of Kenya. *Science* 285 (August 27):1382–86.

Ward, Steven C., and Dana L. Duren. 2002. Middle and Late Miocene African hominoids. In *The primate fossil record*, ed. W. C. Hartwig. Cambridge: Cambridge University Press.

Wardhaugh, Ronald. 2002. *An introduction to sociolinguistics*. 4th ed. Oxford: Blackwell.

Warneken, Felix, and Michael Tomasello. 2009. The roots of human altruism. *British Journal of Psychology* 100:355–471.

Warner, Jessica, Gerhard Gmel, Kathryn Graham, and Bonnie Erickson. 2007. A time-series analysis of war and levels of interpersonal violence in an English military town 1700–1781. *Social Science History* 31, no. 4:575.

Warner, John Anson. 1986. The individual in Native American art: A sociological view. In *The arts of the North American Indian*, ed. E. L. Wade. New York: Hudson Hills Press.

Warner, W. Lloyd, and Paul S. Lunt. 1941. *The social life of a modern community*. New Haven, CT: Yale University Press.

Warren, Dennis M. 1989. Utilizing indigenous healers in national health delivery systems: The Ghanaian experiment. In *Making our research useful*, eds. J. van Willigen, B. Rylko-Bauer, and A. McElroy. Boulder, CO: Westview.

Warry, Wayne. 1986. Kafaina: Female wealth and power in Chuave, Papua New Guinea. *Oceania* 57:4–21.

Warry, Wayne. 1990. Doing unto others: Applied anthropology, collaborative research and native self-determination. *Culture* 10:61–62.

Washburn, Sherwood. 1960. Tools and human evolution. *Scientific American* (September):62–75.

Waters, M. R., et al. 2011. Pre-Clovis mastodon hunting 13,800 years ago at the Manis site, Washington. *Science* 334 (October 21):351–53.

Watkins, Trevor. 2009. From foragers to complex societies in Southwest Asia. In *The human past*, ed. C. Scarre, 200–33. New York: Thames and Hudson.

Watson, James L. 2004. Presidential address: Virtual kinship, real estate, and diaspora formation—The man lineage revisited. *Journal of Asian Studies* 63:893–910.

Weaver, Muriel Porter. 1993. *The Aztecs, Maya, and their predecessors*. 3rd ed. San Diego: Academic Press.

Webb, Karen E. 1977. An evolutionary aspect of social structure and a verb "have." *American Anthropologist* 79:42–49.

Weber, Max. 1947. *The theory of social and economic organization*, Trans. A. M. Henderson and Talcott Parsons. New York: Oxford University Press.

Weiner, Annette B. 1976. *Women of value, men of renown: New perspectives in Trobriand exchange*. Austin: University of Texas Press.

Weiner, Annette B. 1987. *The Trobrianders of Papua New Guinea*. New York: Holt, Rinehart and Winston.

Weiner, J. S. 1954. Nose shape and climate. *Journal of Physical Anthropology* 4:615–18.

Weiner, Jonathan. 1994. *Beak of the finch*. New York: Vintage.

Weiner, Steve, Q. Xi, P. Goldberg, J. Liu, and O. Bar-Yousef. 1998. Evidence for the use of fire at Zhoukoudian, China. *Science* 281 (July 10):251–53.

Weingarten, Carol Popp, and James S. Chisholm. 2009. Attachment and cooperation in religious groups: An example of a mechanism for cultural group selection. *Current Anthropology* 50:759–85.

Weinreich, Uriel. 1968. *Languages in contact*. The Hague, The Netherlands: Mouton.

Weisner, Thomas S. 2004. The American dependency conflict. *Ethos* 29:271–95.

Weisner, Thomas S., and Ronald Gallimore. 1977. My brother's keeper: Child and sibling caretaking. *Current Anthropology* 18:169–90.

Weisner, Thomas S., Mary Bausano, and Madeleine Kornfein. 1983. Putting family ideals into practice: Pronaturalism in conventional and nonconventional California families. *Ethos* 11:278–304.

Weiss, Harvey, and Raymond S. Bradley. 2001. What drives societal collapse? *Science* 291 (January 26):609–10.

Weiss, Harvey, et al. 1993. The genesis and collapse of third millennium north Mesopotamian civilization. *Science* 261 (August 20):995–1004.

Weller, Susan C. 2009. The research process. In MyAnthroLibrary, eds. C. R. Ember, M. Ember, and P. N. Peregrine. MyAnthroLibrary.com. Pearson.

Weller, Susan C., Roberta D. Baer, Javier Garcia de Alba Garcia, and Ana L. Salcedo Rocha. 2008. Susto and nervios: Expressions for stress and depression. *Culture, Medicine, and Psychiatry* 32, no. 3: 406–20.

Wells, Jonathan C. K. and Jay T. Stock. 2007. The biology of the colonizing ape. *Yearbook of Physical Anthropology* 50:191–222.

Wenke, Robert J. 1984. *Patterns in prehistory: Humankind's first three million years*. 2nd ed. New York: Oxford University Press.

Wenke, Robert J. 1990. *Patterns in prehistory: Humankind's first three million years*. 3rd ed. New York: Oxford University Press.

Wenke, Robert J., and Deborah Olszewski. 2007. *Patterns in prehistory*, 5th ed. New York: Oxford.

Werner, Dennis. 1975. On the societal acceptance or rejection of male homosexuality. Master's thesis, Hunter College of the City University of New York.

Werner, Dennis. 1978. Trekking in the Amazon forest. *Natural History* (November):42–54.

Werner, Dennis. 1979. A cross-cultural perspective on theory and research on male homosexuality. *Journal of Homosexuality* 4:345–62.

Werner, Dennis. 1982. Chiefs and presidents: A comparison of leadership traits in the United States and among the Mekranoti-Kayapo of central Brazil. *Ethos* 10:136–48.

Werner, Dennis. 1984. Child care and influence among the Mekranoti of central Brazil. *Sex Roles* 10:395–404.

Westermarck, Edward. 1894. *The history of human marriage*. London: Macmillan.

Weston, Eleanor, and Adrian Lister. 2009. Insular dwarfism in hippos and a model for brain size reduction in *Homo floresiensis*. *Nature* 459 (May 7):85–88.

Wheat, Joe B. 1967. A Paleo-Indian bison kill. *Scientific American* (January):44–52.

Wheatley, Paul. 1971. *The pivot of the four quarters*. Chicago: Aldine.

Wheeler, Peter. 1984. The evolution of bipedality and loss of functional body hair in hominids. *Journal of Human Evolution* 13:91–98.

Wheeler, Peter. 1991. The influence of bipedalism in the energy and water budgets of early hominids. *Journal of Human Evolution* 23:379–88.

Whitaker, Ian. 1955. *Social relations in a nomadic Lappish community*. Oslo: Utgitt av Norsk Folkemuseum.

White, Benjamin. 1973. Demand for labor and population growth in colonial Java. *Human Ecology* 1, no. 3 (March):217–36.

White, Douglas R. 1988. Rethinking polygyny: Co-wives, codes, and cultural systems. *Current Anthropology* 29:529–88.

White, Douglas R., and Michael L. Burton. 1988. Causes of polygyny: Ecology, economy, kinship, and warfare. *American Anthropologist* 90:871–87.

White, Douglas R., Michael L. Burton, and Lilyan A. Brudner. 1977. Entailment theory and method: A cross-cultural analysis of the sexual division of labor. *Behavior Science Research* 12:1–24.

White, Frances J. 1996. *Pan paniscus* 1973 to 1996: Twenty-three years of field research. *Evolutionary Anthropology* 5:11–17.

White, Leslie A. 1939. A problem in kinship terminology. *American Anthropologist* 41:569–70.

White, Leslie A. 1949. *The science of culture: A study of man and civilization*. New York: Farrar, Straus & Cudahy.

White, Leslie A. 1968. The expansion of the scope of science. In *Readings in anthropology*, vol. 1, 2nd ed., ed. M. H. Fried. New York: Thomas Y. Crowell.

White, Randall. 1982. Rethinking the Middle/Upper Paleolithic transition. *Current Anthropology* 23:169–75.

White, Tim D. 2003. Early hominids—Diversity or distortion? *Science* 299 (March 28):1994–97.

White, Tim D., and Pieter Arend Folkens. 2000. *Human osteology*. 2nd ed. San Diego: Academic Press.

White, Tim D., Donald C. Johanson, and William H. Kimbel. 1981. *Australopithecus africanus*: Its phyletic position reconsidered. *South African Journal of Science* 77:445–70.

White, Tim D., et al. 2009. *Ardipithecus ramidus* and the paleobiology of early hominids. *Science* 326 (October 2):75–86.

White, Timothy D., G. Suwa, and B. Asfaw. 1994. *Australopithecus ramidus*, a new species of early hominid from Aramis, Ethiopia. *Nature* 371 (September 22):306–33.

White, Timothy D., G. Suwa, and B. Asfaw. 1995. Corrigendum: *Australopithecus ramidus*, a new species of early hominid from Aramis, Ethiopia. *Nature* 375 (May 4):88.

Whitehead, Barbara Defoe, and David Popenoe. 2005. *The state of our unions: Marriage and family: What does the Scandinavian experience tell us?* National Marriage Project. Charlottesville: University of Virginia.

Whiten, A., et al. 1999. Cultures in chimpanzees. *Nature* 399 (June 17):682–85.

Whiting, Beatrice B. 1950. *Paiute sorcery*. Viking Fund Publications in Anthropology No. 15. New York: Wenner-Gren Foundation.

Whiting, Beatrice B. 1965. Sex identity conflict and physical violence. *American Anthropologist* 67:123–40.

Whiting, Beatrice B., and Carolyn Pope Edwards. 1973. A cross-cultural analysis of sex differences in the behavior of children aged three through eleven. *Journal of Social Psychology* 91:171–88.

Whiting, Beatrice B., and Carolyn Pope Edwards (in collaboration with Carol R. Ember, Gerald M. Erchak, Sara Harkness, Robert L. Munroe, Ruth H. Munroe, Sara B. Nerlove, Susan Seymour, Charles M. Super, Thomas S. Weisner, and Martha Wenger). 1988. *Children of different worlds: The formation of social behavior*. Cambridge, MA: Harvard University Press.

Whiting, Beatrice B., and John W. M. Whiting (in collaboration with Richard Longabaugh). 1975. *Children of six cultures: A psycho-cultural analysis*. Cambridge, MA: Harvard University Press.

Whiting, John W. M. 1941. *Becoming a Kwoma*. New Haven, CT: Yale University Press.

Whiting, John W. M. 1964. Effects of climate on certain cultural practices. In *Explorations in cultural anthropology*, ed. W. Goodenough. New York: McGraw-Hill.

Whiting, John W. M., and Irvin L. Child. 1953. *Child training and personality: A cross-cultural study.* New Haven, CT: Yale University Press.

Whiting, John W. M., Richard Kluckhohn, and A. Anthony. 1958. The function of male initiation ceremonies at puberty. In *Readings in social psychology*, eds. E. E. Maccoby, T. M. Newcomb, and E. L. Hartley. New York: Holt Rinehardt and Winston.

Whittaker, John C. 1994. *Flintknapping: Making and understanding stone tools.* Austin: University of Texas Press.

WHO. 2005. *WHO multi-country study on women's health and domestic violence against women: Summary report of initial results on prevalence, health outcomes and women's responses.* Geneva: World Health Organization.

Whyte, Martin K. 1978a. Cross-cultural codes dealing with the relative status of women. *Ethnology* 17:211–37.

Whyte, Martin K. 1978b. *The status of women in preindustrial societies.* Princeton, NJ: Princeton University Press.

Wiberg, Hakan. 1983. Self-determination as an international issue. In *Nationalism and self-determination in the Horn of Africa*, ed. I. M. Lewis. London: Ithaca Press.

Wierzbicka, Anna. 2005. Empirical universals of language as a basis for the study of other human universals and as a tool for exploring cross-cultural differences. *Ethos* 33, no. 2:256–91.

Wikan, Unni. 1982. *Beyond the veil in Arabia.* Baltimore: The Johns Hopkins University Press.

Wilden, Anthony. 1987. *The rules are no game: The strategy of communication.* London: Routledge and Kegan Paul.

Wilford, John Noble. 1995. The transforming leap, from 4 legs to 2. *New York Times*, September 5, p. C1ff.

Wilford, John Noble. 1997. Ancient German spears tell of mighty hunters of Stone Age. *New York Times*, March 4, p. C6.

Wilkinson, Robert L. 1995. Yellow fever: Ecology, epidemiology, and role in the collapse of the Classic Lowland Maya civilization. *Medical Anthropology* 16:269–94.

Williams, George C. 1992. *Natural selection: Domains, levels, and challenges.* New York: Oxford University Press.

Williams, Melvin D. 2009. Racism: The production, reproduction, and obsolescence of social inferiority. In *MyAnthroLibrary*, eds. C. R. Ember, M. Ember, and P. N. Peregrine. MyAnthroLibrary.com. Pearson.

Williams, Walter L. 1992. *The spirit and the flesh.* Boston: Beacon Press.

Wilmsen, Edwin N., ed. 1989. *We are here: Politics of aboriginal land tenure.* Berkeley: University of California Press.

Wilson, Christopher G. 2008. Male genital mutilation: An adaptation to sexual conflict. *Evolution and Human Behavior* 29:149–64.

Wilson, Edward O. 1975. *Sociobiology: The new synthesis.* Cambridge, MA: Belknap Press of Harvard University Press.

Wilson, Monica. 1963/1951. *Good company: A study of Nyakyusa age villages.* Boston: Beacon Press.

Winkelman, Michael. 1986a. Magico-religious practitioner types and socioeconomic conditions. *Behavior Science Research* 20:17–46.

Winkelman, Michael. 1986b. Trance states: A theoretical model and cross-cultural analysis. *Ethos* 14:174–203.

Winkelman, Michael. 2009. *Culture and health: Applying medical anthropology.* San Francisco: Wiley and Sons.

Winkelman, Michael. 2010. *Shamanism: A biopsychosocial paradigm of consciousness and healing.* 2nd ed. Santa Barbara, CA: Praeger/ABC-CLIO.

Winkelman, Michael, and John R. Baker. 2010. *Supernatural as natural: A biocultural approach to religion.* Upper Saddle River, NJ: Pearson Prentice Hall.

Winkleman, Michael, and Philip M. Peck, eds. 2004. *Divination and healing: Potent vision.* Tucson: University of Arizona Press.

Winterbottom, Robert. 1995. The tropical forestry plan: Is it working? *NAPA Bulletin* 15:60–70.

Winterhalder, Bruce. 1990. Open field, common pot: Harvest variability and risk avoidance in agricultural and foraging societies. In *Risk and uncertainty in tribal and peasant economies*, ed. E. Cashdan. Boulder, CO: Westview.

Witkin, Herman A. 1967. A cognitive style approach to cross-cultural research. *International Journal of Psychology* 2:233–50.

Witkowski, Stanley R. 1975. Polygyny, age of marriage, and female status. Paper presented at the annual meeting of the American Anthropological Association, San Francisco.

Witkowski, Stanley R., and Cecil H. Brown. 1978. Lexical universals. *Annual Review of Anthropology* 7:427–51.

Witkowski, Stanley R., and Harold W. Burris. 1981. Societal complexity and lexical growth. *Behavior Science Research* 16:143–59.

Wittfogel, Karl. 1957. *Oriental despotism: A comparative study of total power.* New Haven, CT: Yale University Press.

Wolf, Arthur. 1968. Adopt a daughter-in-law, marry a sister: A Chinese solution to the problem of the incest taboo. *American Anthropologist* 70:864–74.

Wolf, Arthur P., and Chieh-Shan Huang. 1980. *Marriage and adoption in China, 1845–1945.* Stanford, CA: Stanford University Press.

Wolf, Eric R. 1955. Types of Latin American peasantry: A preliminary discussion. *American Anthropologist* 57:452–71.

Wolf, Eric R. 1956. San José: Subcultures of a "traditional" coffee municipality. In *The people of Puerto Rico*, eds. J. H. Steward, R. A. Manners, E. R. Wolf, E. Padilla Seda, S. W. Mintz, and R. L. Scheele. Urbana: University of Illinois Press.

Wolf, Eric R. 1966. *Peasants.* Upper Saddle River, NJ: Prentice Hall.

Wolf, Eric R. 1984. Culture: Panacea or problem. *American Antiquity* 49:393–400.

Wolf, Naomi. 1991. *The beauty myth: How images of beauty are used against women.* New York: Morrow.

Wolff, Ronald G. 1991. *Functional chordate anatomy.* Lexington, MA: D. C. Heath.

Wolpoff, Milford H. 1971. Competitive exclusion among Lower Pleistocene hominids: The single species hypothesis. *Man* 6:601–13.

Wolpoff, Milford H. 1983. *Ramapithecus* and human origins: An anthropologist's perspective of changing interpretations. In *New interpretations of ape and human ancestry*, eds. R. Ciochon and R. Corruccini. New York: Plenum.

Wolpoff, Milford H. 1999. *Paleoanthropology*, 2nd ed. Boston: McGraw-Hill.

Wolpoff, Milford H., and Abel Nkini. 1985. Early and Early Middle Pleistocene hominids from Asia and Africa. In *Ancestors*, ed. E. Delson. New York: Alan R. Liss.

Wolpoff, Milford H., A. G. Thorne, J. Jelinek, and Zhang Yinyun. 1993. The case for sinking *Homo erectus*: 100 years of *Pithecanthropus* is enough! In *100 years of Pithecanthropus: The* Homo erectus *problem*, ed. J. L. Franzen.

Courier Forschungsinstitut Senckenberg 171:341–61.

Womack, Mari. 2010. *The anthropology of health and healing.* Lanham, MD: AltaMira.

Women in Science '93: Gender and the culture of science. 1993. *Science* 260 (April 16):383–430.

Wong, Kate. 2003. An ancestor to call our own. *Scientific American* (January):54–63.

Wong, Kate. 2005. The littlest human. *Scientific American* (February):56–65.

Wood, Bernard A. 1992. Evolution of australopithecines. In *The Cambridge encyclopedia of human evolution*, eds. S. Jones, R. Martin, and D. Pilbeam. New York: Cambridge University Press.

Wood, Bernard A. 1994. Hominid paleobiology: Recent achievements and challenges. In *Integrative paths to the past*, eds. R. Corruccini and R. Ciochon. Upper Saddle River, NJ: Prentice Hall.

Wood, Gordon S. 1992. *The radicalism of the American Revolution.* New York: Knopf.

Wood, James W., George R. Milner, Henry C. Harpending, and Kenneth M. Weiss. 1992. The osteological paradox: Problems of inferring prehistoric health from skeletal samples. *Current Anthropology* 33:343–70.

Wood, Wendy, and Alice H. Eagly. 2002. A cross-cultural analysis of the behavior of women and men: Implications for the origins of sex differences. *Psychological Bulletin* 128:699–727.

Woodburn, James. 1968. An introduction to Hadza ecology. In *Man the hunter*, eds. R. B. Lee and I. DeVore. Chicago: Aldine.

World Bank. 2004. *World development indicators 2004.* Washington, DC: World Bank Publications.

World Bank. 2011. *World bank development report 2012: Gender equality and development.* Washington, DC: World Bank.

Worsley, Peter. 1957. *The trumpet shall sound: A study of "cargo" cults in Melanesia.* London: MacGibbon & Kee.

Wrangham, Richard W. 1980. An ecological model of female-bonded primate groups. *Behaviour* 75:262–300.

Wrangham, Richard W. 2009. *Catching fire: How cooking made us human.* New York: Basic Books.

Wright, Gary A. 1971. Origins of food production in Southwestern Asia: A survey of ideas. *Current Anthropology* 12:447–78.

Wright, George O. 1954. Projection and displacement: A cross-cultural study of folktale aggression. *Journal of Abnormal and Social Psychology* 49:523–28.

Wright, Henry T. 1986. The evolution of civilizations. In *American archaeology past and future*, eds. D. Meltzer, D. Fowler, and J. Sabloff. Washington, DC: Smithsonian Institution Press.

Wright, Henry T., and Gregory A. Johnson. 1975. Population, exchange, and early state formation in southwestern Iran. *American Anthropologist* 77:267–77.

Wulff, Robert, and Shirley Fiste. 1987. The domestication of wood in Haiti. In *Anthropological praxis*, eds. R. M. Wulff and S. J. Fiste. Boulder, CO: Westview.

Yamei, Hou, et al. 2000. Mid-Pleistocene Acheulean-like stone technology of the Bose Basin, South China. *Science* 287 (March 3):622–26.

Yan, Yunxiang. 2006. Girl power: Young women and the waning of patriarchy in rural North China. *Ethnology* 45:105–23.

Yergin, Daniel. 2002. Giving aid to world trade. *New York Times*, June 27, p. A29.

Yinger, J. Milton. 1994. *Ethnicity: Source of strength? Source of conflict?* Albany: State University Press.

Young, Frank W. 1970. A fifth analysis of the Star Husband Tale. *Ethnology* 9:389–413.

Young, T. Cuyler, Jr. 1972. Population densities and early Mesopotamian urbanism. In *Man, settlement and urbanism*, eds. P. J. Ucko, R. Tringham, and G. W. Dimbleby. Cambridge, MA: Scherkmn.

Younger, Stephen M. 2008. Conditions and mechanisms for peace in precontact Polynesia. *Current Anthropology* 49:927–34.

Zebrowitz, Leslie A., and Joann M. Montepare. 2005. Appearance does matter. *Science* 308 (June 10):1565–66.

Zechenter, Elizabeth M. 1997. In the name of culture: Cultural relativism and the abuse of the individual. *Journal of Anthropological Research* 53:319–47.

Zeder, Melinda A. 1991. *Feeding cities: Specialized animal economy in the ancient Near East.* Washington, DC: Smithsonian Institution Press.

Zeder, Melinda A. 1994. After the revolution: Post-Neolithic subsistence in northern Mesopotamia. *American Anthropologist* 96:97–126.

Zeder, Melinda A. 2011. The origins of agriculture in the Near East. *Current Anthropology* 52, Supplement 4:S221–235.

Zhang, David D., Jane Zhang, Harry F. Lee, and Yuan-qing He. 2007. Climate change and war frequency in Eastern China over the last millennium. *Human Ecology* 35:403–14.

Zihlman, Adrienne L. 1992. The emergence of human locomotion: The evolutionary background and environmental context. In *Topics in primatology*, vol. 1, eds. T. Nishida, William McGrew, Peter Marler, Martin Pickford, and Frans de Waal. Tokyo: University of Tokyo.

Zimmer, Carl. 1999. Kenyan skeleton shakes ape family tree. *Science* 285 (August 27):1335–37.

Zimmer, Carl. 2004. Faster than a hyena? Running may make humans special. *Science* 306 (November 19):1283.

Zohary, Daniel. 1969. The progenitors of wheat and barley in relation to domestication and agriculture dispersal in the Old World. In *The domestication and exploitation of plants and animals*, eds. P. J. Ucko and G. W. Dimbleby. Chicago: Aldine.

Credits

Text Credits

Chapter 1. Page 6: Crittenden, Alyssa. 2013. Juvenile Foraging among the Hadza: Implications for Human Life History. *Evolution & Human Behavior* 34: 299–304.

Chapter 2. Page 18: Salzman, Philip Carl. 2001. *Understanding culture: An introduction to anthropological theory,* 135. Long Grove, IL: Waveland; Page 21: Vayda, Andrew P., and Roy A. Rappaport. 1968. Ecology: Cultural and noncultural. In *Introduction to cultural anthropology,* ed. J. H. Clifton. Boston: Houghton Mifflin; Page 23: Caws, Peter. 1969. *The structure of discovery.* Science 166 (December 12): 1375–80; Page 38: Leakey, Louis S. B. 1965. *Olduvai Gorge, 1951–1961, Vol. I: A Preliminary Report on the Geology and Fauna.* Copyright ©1965 Cambridge University Press. Reprinted with the permission of Cambridge University Press; Page 39: ©Pearson Education, Upper Saddle River, New Jersey.

Chapter 3. Page 45: Lovejoy, Arthur O. 1964. *The great chain of being: A study of the history of an idea.* Cambridge, MA: Harvard University Press; Page 46: Darwin, Charles. 1970/1859. The origin of species. *In Evolution of man,* ed. L. B. Young. New York: Oxford University Press; Page 47: Huxley, Thomas H. 1970. Man's place in nature. In *Evolution of man,* ed. L. Young. New York: Oxford University Press; Page 52: Beadle, George, and Muriel Beadle. 1966. *The language of life.* Garden City, NY: Doubleday; Page 55: Boaz, Noel T., and Alan J. Almquist. 1997. *Biological anthropology: A synthetic approach to human evolution.* Upper Saddle River, NJ: Prentice Hall; Page 56: Dobzhansky, Theodosius. 1962. *Mankind evolving: The evolution of the human species.* New Haven, CT: Yale University Press; Page 58: Paley, William. 1810. *Natural theology.* Boston: Joshua Belcher; Page 59: McMullin, Ernan. 2001. Plantinga's defense of special creation. In *Intelligent design creationism and its critics,* ed. R. Pennock, 174. Boston: MIT Press; Page 61: Nissen, Henry W. 1958. Axes of behavioral comparison. In *Behavior and evolution,* eds. A. Roe and G. G. Simpson. New Haven, CT: Yale University Press.

Chapter 4. Page 67: Based on Roberts, D. F. 1953. Body weight, race, and climate. *American Journal of Physical Anthropology,* 533–58; Page 69: Robins, Ashley H. 1991. *Biological perspectives on human pigmentation.* New York: Copyright ©1991 Cambridge University Press. Reprinted with the permission of Cambridge University Press; Page 72: Motulsky, Arno. 1971. Metabolic polymorphisms and the role of infectious diseases in human evolution. In *Human populations, genetic variation, and evolution,* ed. L. N. Morris. San Francisco: Chandler.

Chapter 5. Page 86: With permission by the estate of Ronald G. Wolff. 1991. *Functional chordate anatomy.* Lexington, MA: D.C. Heath; Page 86: Deacon, Terrence. 1992. Primate Brains and Senses. In *The Cambridge Encyclopedia of Human Evolution,* eds. S. Jones, R. Martin, and D. Pilbeam. New York: Copyright ©1992 Cambridge University Press. Reprinted with the Permission of Cambridge University Press; Page 86: Cartmill, Matt. 1992. Non-human primates. In *The Cambridge encyclopedia of human evolution,* eds. S. Jones, R. Martin, and D. Pilbeam. New York: Copyright ©1992 Cambridge University Press. Reprinted with the permission of Cambridge University Press; Page 90: Boaz, Noel T., and Alan J. Almquist. 1999. *Essentials of biological anthropology.* Upper Saddle River, NJ: Prentice Hall; Page 91: Boaz, Noel T., and Alan J. Almquist. 1999. *Essentials of biological anthropology.* Upper Saddle River, NJ: Prentice Hall; Page 97: Based on Martin, Robert D. 1990. *Primate origins and evolution: A phylogenetic reconstruction.* Princeton, NJ: Princeton University Press.. The dates for the Paleocene, Eocene, Oligocene, and the beginning of the Miocene are from Berggren et al. 1992, 29–45. The dates for the end of the Miocene, Pliocene, and Pleistocene are from Jones et al. 1992; Page 98: Boaz, Noel T., and Alan J. Almquist.1999. *Essentials of biological anthropology.* Upper Saddle River, NJ: Prentice Hall.

Chapter 6. Page 110: Savage-Rumbaugh, E. S. 1994. Hominid evolution: Looking to modern apes for clues. In *Hominid culture in primate perspective,* eds. D. Quiatt and J. Itani. Niwot: University Press of Colorado; Page 111: Jones, Steve, Robert Martin, and David Pilbeam, eds. 1992. *The Cambridge encyclopedia of human evolution.* New York: Copyright ©1992 Cambridge University Press. Reprinted with the permission of Cambridge University Press; Page 114: Russell Ciochon and John Fleagle. 2006. *The human evolution source book,* Second Edition. PH; Page 116: Based on Wilford, J.N., "The Transforming Leap," New York Times, September 5, 1995: C1, C9; Page 118: Dart, Raymond. 1925. Australopithecus africanus: The man-ape of South Africa. *Nature* 115:195. Page 121: Based on Wilford, J. N., The Transforming Leap, *New York Times,* September 5, 1995: C1, C9; Page 122: Based on Encyclopedia of Human Evolution and Prehistory; Estimated cranial capacities from Tattersall et al. 2000. The Taylor & Francis Group; Page 129: Courtesy of Executor of the Estate of Eric Mose: Illustrations by Eric O Mose. Ciochon, Russell L., and John G. Fleagle, eds. 1993. The human evolution source book.

Chapter 7. Page 137: Krings, Matthias, A. Stone, R. W. Schmitz, H. Krainitzki, M. Stoneking, and S. Paabo. 1997. Neandertal DNA sequences and the origin of modern humans. Cell 90:19–30; Page 150: Meltzer, David J. 1993. Pleistocene peopling of the Americas. *Evolutionary Anthropology* 1(1):157–69.

Chapter 8. Page 159: Based on Clutton-Brock, Juliet. 1992. Domestication of animals. In The Cambridge encyclopedia of human evolution, eds. S. Jones, R. Martin, and D. Pilbeam. New York: Cambridge University Press; Page 160: Based on D.Q. fuller, "An Emerging Paradigm Shift in the Origins of Agriculture," General Anthropology 17 (2):1–12; Page 172: Coale, Ansley J. 1974. The history of the human population. *Scientific American* (September):41–51.

Chapter 9. Page 192: Durkheim, Émile. 1938/1895. *The rules of sociological method.* 8th ed. Trans. Sarah A. Soloway and John H. Mueller. Ed. George E. Catlin. New York: Free Press; Page 193: Horace Miner's Body Rituals Among the Nacirema as published in the *American Anthropologist* 58, Issue 3, pages 503–507, June 1956; Page 198: Based on Rosenblatt, Paul C. 2009. Human rights violations. In MyAnthroLibrary, eds. C. R. Ember, M. Ember, and P. N. Peregrine. MyAnthroLibrary.com. Pearson; Page 198: Courtesy of Carol Ember; Page 213: Data extracted from http://www.socialsecurity.gov/OACT/babynames/decades/index.html; Courtesy of the United States Social Security Administration.

Chapter 10. Page 224: Christensen, Pia, Jenny Hockey, and Allison James. 2001. Talk, silence and the material world: Patterns of indirect communication among agricultural farmers in northern England. In *An anthropology of indirect communication,* eds. J. Hendry and C. W. Watson, 68–82. London: Routledge; Page 224: Keller, Helen. 1974/1902. *The story of my life.* New York: Dell; Page 234: Based on ©Copyright: Andrew Moore, 2001. http://www.universalteacher.org.uk/lang/phonology.pd; Page 237: Carroll, Lewis. 1875. *Through the looking-glass: And what Alice found there.* New York: MacMillan; Page 237: Chaucer, Geoffrey. 1478. *Canterbury Tales.* William Caxton; Page 239: Courtesy of the author; Page 243: Based on Berlin, Brent, and Paul Kay. 1969. *Basic color terms: Their universality and evolution.* Berkeley: University of California Press; and Kay, Paul, Brent Berlin, Luisa Maffi, William R. Merrifield, and Richard Cook. 2009. *The World Color Survey.* Stanford, California: Center for the Study of Languages and Information; Page 244: Hoijer, Harry. 1964. *Cultural implications of some Navaho linguistic categories.* In *Language in culture and society,* ed. D. Hymes. New York: Harper & Row.

Chapter 11. Page 273: Bowie, Katherine A. 2006. Of corvée and slavery: Historical intricacies of the division of labor and state power in northern Thailand. In Labor in cross-cultural perspective, eds. E. Paul Durrenberger and Judith E. Martí, 245–64. Lanham: Roman & Littlefield; Page 274: Levine, James A., Robert Weisell, Simon Chevassus, Claudio D. Martinez, and Barbara Burlingame. 2002. The distribution of work tasks for male and female children and adults separated by gender. In Science 296 (May 10):1025; Page 276: Mooney, Kathleen A. 1978. The effects of rank and wealth on exchange among the coast Salish. Ethnology 17:391–406.

Chapter 12. Page 289: Fried, Morton H. 1967. *The evolution of political society: An essay in political anthropology.* New York: Random House; Page 292: Barrett, Stanley R.1994. *Paradise: Class, commuters, and ethnicity in rural Ontario.* Toronto: University of Toronto Press; Page 294: These data are abstracted from the U.N. Human Development Report 2011. Table 3; Page 304: Yinger, J. Milton. 1994. *Ethnicity: Source of strength? Source of conflict?* Albany: State University Press.

Chapter 13. Page 310: I. Opie and P. Opie, *The Oxford Dictionary of Nursery Rhymes* (Oxford: Oxford University Press, 1951, 2nd edn., 1997), pp. 100–1; Page 313: Based on Murdock, George P., and Caterina Provost. 1973. Factors in the division of labor by sex: A cross-cultural analysis. *Ethnology* 12: 203–25; Whyte, Martin K. 1978a. Cross-cultural codes dealing with the relative status of women. *Ethnology* 17: 211–37; Weisner, Thomas S., and Ronald Gallimore. 1977. My brother's keeper: Child and sibling caretaking. *Current Anthropology* 18:169–90.

Chapter 14. Page 334: Murdock, George P. 1949. Social structure. New York: Macmillan.

Chapter 15. Page 368: Salzman, Philip Carl. 2008. Culture and Conflict in the Middle East. *Humanities Press;* Page 493: Adapted from Bohannan, Laura, and Paul Bohannan. 1953. *The Tiv of central Nigeria.* London: International African Institute; Page 370: Carneiro, Robert L. 1970. A theory of the origin of the state. *Science* 169 (August 21): 733–38; Page 370: Sahlins, Marshall D. 1962. *Moala: Culture and nature on a Fijian island.* Ann Arbor: University of Michigan Press; Page 379: Ross, Marc Howard. 1988. Political organization and political participation: Exit, voice, and loyalty in preindustrial societies. *Comparative Politics* 21: 73–89; Page 380: Hoebel, E. Adamson. 1968/1954. *The law of primitive man.* New York: Atheneum; Page 381: Boas, Franz. 1888. Central Eskimos. *Bureau of American Ethnology Annual Report No. 6.* Washington, DC; Pages 383 and 384: Schwartz, Richard D. 1954. Social factors in the development of legal control: A case study of two Israeli settlements. *Yale Law Journal* 63 (February): 471–91.

Chapter 16. Page 397: Middleton, John. 1971. The cult of the dead: Ancestors and ghosts. In *Reader in comparative religion,* 3rd ed., eds. W. A. Lessa and E. Z. Vogt. New York: Harper & Row.

Chapter 17. Pages 422 and 423: Lomax, Alan, ed. 1968. Folk song style and culture. *American Association for the Advancement of Science Publication* No. 88. Washington, DC; Page 426: Thompson, Stith. 1965. Star Husband Tale. In *The study of folklore,* ed. A. Dundes. Upper Saddle River, NJ: Prentice Hall.

Chapter 18. Page 441: Goldstein, Donna. 1998. Nothing bad intended: Child discipline, punishment, and survival in a shantytown in Rio de Janeiro. In *Small wars: The cultural politics of childhood,* eds. Nancy Scheper-Hughes and Carolyn Sargeant, 389–415. Berkeley: University of California-Berkeley Press.

Chapter 19. Page 457: Tax, Sol. 1975. Action anthropology. Current Anthropology 16: 514–517; Rylko-Bauer, Barbara, Merrill Singer, and John van Willigen. 2006. Reclaiming applied anthropology: Its past, present, and future. American Anthropologist 108: 178–190; Page 462: Ravesloot, John. 1997. Changing Native American perceptions of archaeology and archaeologists. In Native Americans and archaeologists, eds. N. Swidler et al. Walnut Creek, CA: Alta Mira Press; Page 463: Naleimaile, Sean and Lokelani Brandt. 2013. Is Hawaiian Archaeology Really Hawaiian? A Native Hawaiian Perspective. SAA Archaeological Record 13(1):31–32; Page 475: Honigmann, John J. 1967. Personality in culture. New York: Harper & Row.

Photo Credits

Chapter 1. Page 1: Bruno Morandi/Robert Harding World Imagery; Page 5: Spooner/Redmond-Callow/Zuma Press; Page 6: Firestick Productions - UNLV; Page 7: Darla Hallmark/Fotolia; Page 8: Mireille Vautier/Alamy; Page 10: Timothy G. Bromage, New York University College of Dentistry, and Friedemann Schrenk, Senckenberg Research Institute, at their camp discussing the jaw fragment, UR 501, the oldest fossil representative of the genus *Homo*, which they recovered from Late Pliocene sediments in northern Malawi. Photo by Thomas Ernsting.; Page 12: Mark Peterson/Corbis Saba/Corbis News/Corbis; Page 16: Bruno Morandi/Robert Harding World Imagery.

Chapter 2. Page 17: National Geographic Image Collection/Alamy; Page 18: Ron Hilton/Shutterstock; Page 22: Richard Scaglion/University of Pittsburgh; Page 24: Ariana Cubillos/AP Images; Page 25: Doc White/Nature Picture Library; Page 28: Irven DeVore/Anthro-Photo; Page 31: The Trustees of the British Museum/Art Resource, NY; Page 34: Richard Vogel/AP Images; Page 36: World History Archive /AGE Fotostock; Page 40: Lincoln Journal Star/AP Images; Page 43: National Geographic Image Collection/Alamy.

Chapter 3. Page 44: Michael Willmer Forbes Tweedie/Science Source; Page 46: English School/Natural History Museum, London, UK/The Bridgeman Art Library; Page 50: Biophoto Associates/Science Source; Page 50: Biophoto Associates/Science Source; Page 53: t.w./Shutterstock; Page 56: Eye of Science/Science Source; Page 57: BMJ/Shutterstock; Page 60: Nikita G. Sidorov/Shutterstock; Page 61: Lightpoet/Shutterstock; Page 63: Michael Willmer Forbes Tweedie/Science Source.

Chapter 4. Page 64: John Birdsall/The Image Works; Page 66: Charles Lenars /Corbis; Page 68: Ton Koene/AGE Fotostock; Page 68: David Hiser/Getty Images; Page 70: Hans Neleman/Getty Images; Page 72: James Robert Fuller/Corbis; Page 76: vita khorzhevska/Shutterstock; Page 77: Ton Koene/AGE Fotostock; Page 78: Lipowski Milan/Shutterstock; Page 79: Werner Forman/Art Resource, NY; Page 80: Peter Dennis/DK Images; Page 82: Don Hamerman; Page 84: John Birdsall/The Image Works.

Chapter 5. Page 85: rubiks80/Shutterstock; Page 88: Jordan Tan/Shutterstock; Page 89: Kevin Schafer/Getty Images; Page 90: Anna Kucherova/Shutterstock; Page 91: Stephane Bidouze/Shutterstock; Page 92: Micha Klootwijk/Shutterstock; Page 92: Kennan Ward/Corbis; Page 93: Anup Shah/Nature Picture Library; Page 95: Karl & Kay Amman/AGE Fotostock; Page 101: Pearson Dorothy Norton; Page 102: Harry Taylor/DK Images; Page 103: Harry Taylor/DK Images; Page 106: rubiks80 /Shutterstock.

Chapter 6. Page 107: Hess. Landesmuseum/Akg-Images; Page 111: Nature-M.P.F.T. /Getty Images; Page 113: John Reader/Science Source; Page 114: Christophe Boisvieux/Corbis; Page 115: Shaen Adey/Corbis; Page 117: Marion Kaplan/Alamy; Page 128: Publiphoto/Science Source; Page 129: Copyright © 1969 by Eric Mose.; Page 132: Hess. Landesmuseum/Akg-Images.

Chapter 7. Page 133: Mikhail Zahranichny/Shutterstock; Page 136: Hess. Landesmuseum/Akg-mages; Page 141: M&G Therin-Weise/AGE Fotostock; Page 145: Gianni Dagli Orti/Corbis; Page 147: Alain Bonhoure/Roger-Viollet /The Image Works; Page 148: Fine Art Images/AGE Fotostock; Page 151: Dmytro Pylypenko/Shutterstock; Page 154: Carver Mostardi/Alamy; Page 157: Mikhail Zahranichny/Shutterstock.

Chapter 8. Page 158: Peter Giovannini/AGE Fotostock; Page 161: PhotoStock-Israel /AGE Fotostock; Page 164: lumen-digital/Fotolia; Page 169: Blanscape/Shutterstock; Page 170: Hady Khandani/vario images GmbH & Co.KG/Alamy; Page 174: Nigel Hicks/Museo Tumbas Reales de Sipan/DK Images; Page 176: Gianni Dagli Orti /Fine Art/Corbis; Page 176: Brian Brake/Science Source; Page 177: CatchaSnap /Shutterstock; Page 178: Chris Sloan, Courtesy J.M. Kenoyer/Harappa; Page 179: Werner Forman/UIG/Universal Images Group/AGE Fotostock; Page 182: Paul Harris/Getty Images; Page 183: bumihills/Shutterstock; Page 187: Peter Giovannini /AGE Fotostock.

Chapter 9. Page 188: Scott Stulberg/Corbis; Page 193: Skjold Photographs/The Image Works; Page 193: Bubbles Photolibrary/Alamy; Page 196: Blend Images /John Lund/Getty Images; Page 198: Jeremy Horner/Corbis; Page 198: Jonathan Blair/Corbis; Page 202: Reza/Webistan; Page 206: Joseph Van Os/Stone/Getty Images; Page 208: HG/Magnum Photos; Page 211: Abdeljalil Bounhar/AP Images;

Page 214: Robert Huberman/SuperStock/Alamy; Page 216: Smithsonian American Art Museum, Washington, DC/Art Resource, NY; Page 217: Marco Baroncini /Corbis; Page 222: Scott Stulberg/Corbis.

Chapter 10. Page 223: Anthony Bannister/Gallo Images/Corbis; Page 226: Susan Kuklin/Science Source; Page 227: Pop! Studio Photography/www.alamy.com/Corbis; Page 230: Sue Ogrocki/AP Images; Page 231: Scott Hortop/E+/Getty Images; Page 232: Cindy Charles/PhotoEdit; Page 240: The Print Collector/Alamy; Page 247: Stockbroker/MBI/Alamy; Page 247: Laurence Mouton/PhotoAlto sas/Alamy; Page 250: Richard Lord/PhotoEdit; Page 253: Anthony Bannister/Gallo Images/Corbis.

Chapter 11. Page 254: Alan Copson/Jon Arnold Images Ltd/Alamy; Page 257: Claire Leimbach/Robert Harding World Imagery; Page 260: Stringer/Reuters/Corbis; Page 261: Bill Bachmann/PhotoEdit; Page 263: Steven Lunetta/PhotoEdit; Page 264: Tiziana and Gianni Baldizzone/Corbis; Page 268: Aurora Photos/Robert Harding World Imagery; Page 271: Benelux Press BV/Science Source; Page 272: Still Pictures /Robert Harding World Imagery; Page 277: Chris Hellier/Alamy; Page 280: Radharc Images/Alamy; Page 285: Alan Copson/Jon Arnold Images Ltd/Alamy.

Chapter 12. Page 286: David Mdzinarishvili/Reuters/Corbis; Page 288: Wendy Stone/Corbis; Page 291: University of Washington Libraries, Special Collections, PH Coll 130/10.52, NA 3728; Page 293: Mike Goldwater/Alamy; Page 295: AGE Fotostock/Robert Harding World Imagery; Page 297: View Stock/Alamy; Page 300: Syracuse University; Page 303: Michael Runkel/Robert Harding World Imagery; Page 308: David Mdzinarishvili/Reuters/Corbis.

Chapter 13. Page 309: Athit Perawongmetha/Reuters/Landov; Page 314: Tina Manley/Alamy; Page 316: Still Pictures/Robert Harding World Imagery; Page 321: Bruce G. Miller; Page 323: Jake Lyell/Alamy; Page 324: Kevin Cozad/O'Brien Productions/Corbis; Page 324: John Neubauer/PhotoEdit; Page 325: EmmePi Stock Images/Alamy; Page 328: Maciej Dakowicz/Alamy; Page 332: Athit Perawongmetha/Reuters/Landov.

Chapter 14. Page 333: Stock Connection USA/Newscom; Page 337: John Shaw/ Science Source; Page 339: Susan Meiselas/Magnum Photos; Page 341: Jonathan Player/The New York Times/Redux; Page 344: Michele Burgess/Alamy; Page 350: Stock Montage/Getty Images; Page 355: Tom Allwood/Alamy; Page 357: Shrikrishna Paranjpe/ephotocorp/Alamy; Page 363: Stock Connection USA/Newscom.

Chapter 15. Page 364: David McNew/Getty Images; Page 367: John Warburton-Lee Photography/Alamy; Page 370: Danita Delimont/Alamy; Page 372: Peter Andrews /Reuters/Corbis; Page 374: Bettmann/Corbis; Page 378: Maria Lepowsky; Page 381: Bill Aron/PhotoEdit; Page 383: jackie ellis/Alamy; Page 386: Yasuyoshi Chiba/AFP/Getty Images; Page 389: David McNew/Getty Images.

Chaper 16. Page 390: Images and Stories/Alamy; Page 392: Michele Burgess/ Alamy; Page 394: Joshua Roper/Alamy; Page 396: Aurora Photos/Robert Harding World Imagery; Page 399: North Wind Picture Archives/Alamy; Page 404: Catherine Karnow/Terra/Corbis; Page 407: Carles Zamorano Cabello/Alamy; Page 409: The Granger Collection, NYC; Page 413: Images and Stories/Alamy.

Chapter 17. Page 414: Ueslei Marcelino/Reuters/Landov; Page 417: Hemis/Alamy; Page 419: B.S.P.I./Corbis; Page 419: Paul Chesley/National Geographic Image Collection/Alamy; Page 420: The Trustees of the British Museum/Art Resource, NY; Page 420: The Trustees of the British Museum/Art Resource, NY; Page 421: Debby Wong/Shutterstock; Page 424: Travelscape Images/Alamy; Page 425: Wendy Stone /Corbis; Page 426: Susan McCartney/Science Source; Page 429: George H.H. Huey/Alamy; Page 431: Ueslei Marcelino/Reuters/Landov.

Chapter 18. Page 432: Stuart Kelly/Alamy; Page 434: STR/AFP/Getty Images; Page 438: Sucheta Das/Reuters/Corbis Wire/Corbis; Page 439: Gemunu Amarasinghe /AP Images; Page 444: BSIP/UIG/Getty Images; Page 446: Iraq/Reuters/Corbis; Page 448: Honda/AFP/Getty Images; Page 451: Stuart Kelly/Alamy.

Chapter 19. Page 452: UniversalImagesGroup/Getty Images; Page 455: Paul Jeffrey /Kairos Photos; Page 458: Ricardo Moraes/Reuters; Page 461: Robert T. Trotter, II; Page 464: Bob Elam/Alamy; Page 465: Horacio Villalobos/Corbis; Page 467: Jochen Schlenker/Robert Harding World Imagery; Page 469: Still Pictures/Robert Harding; Page 470: epa european pressphoto agency b.v./Alamy; Page 473: Jon Hursa/Pool /epa/Corbis; Page 475: Tony Anderson/Corbis; Page 481: UniversalImagesGroup /Getty Images.

Index